MW01252344

GAYEL

INFORMING THE LGBTQI+ and ALLIES COMMUNITY SINCE 1973
Edition #42 2020-2021
This is the FINAL PRINT EDITION
Please see free monthly online edition at gayellowpages.com/online.htm

Women's Section page 3

Entries for the Women's Section comprise any that have selected the ♀ or ♀ symbol; any that have chosen to pay for additional placement in this section; any others that have what the editor in her infinite wisdom considers appropriate but not exclusive female appeal. *All entries in the Women's Section also appear in the main section and, when appropriate, in the Ethnic/Multicultural section.*

7

Ethnic/Multicultural Section page 43

A work in progress. Corrections, additions and constructive criticism very welcome. *All entries in the Ethnic/Multicultural Section also appear in the main section and, when appropriate, in the Women's section.*

USA listings begin page 57

To locate any city or subject please see the index page 349

This is the FINAL PRINT EDITION
Please see free monthly online edition at gayellowpages.com/online.htm

FINAL PRINT EDITION #42 2020-2021
Please see our free monthly online edition at
gayellowpages.com/online.htm

Editor & Publisher
Typesetting & Data Processing
You Name It
FRANCES GREEN
email gypages@gmail.com

Gayellow Pages is published by Renaissance House, PO Box 533 Village Station, New York, NY 10014-0533

Phone and fax 646-213-0263 Email gypages@gmail.com

Web page http://gayellowpages.com

No business or organization listed in Gayellow Pages is necessarily owned by LGBTQIA+, or specifically welcomes their participation or patronage, unless so indicated by the appropriate symbols.

★ A not-for-profit enterprise (regardless of tax status) primarily operated by lesbian/gay/bisexual/transgender/queer people.

☆ A not-for-profit enterprise (regardless of tax status) not primarily operated by lesbian/gay/bisexual/transgender/queer people.

● A business, wishing to be listed as wholly or partly lesbian/ gay/bisexual/transgender/queer owned.

○ A gay-friendly business, not wishing to be listed as wholly or partly lesbian/gay/bisexual/transgender/queer owned.

☎ CALL FOR LOCAL INFORMATION

⚣ GLBTQI ⚢ Gay/nongay ⚥ bisexual

⚲ LBTQI women ♀ all women ⚢ bisexual women

⚣ GBTQI men ♂ all men ⚤ bisexual men

T specifically transsexual/transgender/transvestite

♉ ✕ Bar and Restaurant ✕ Restaurant ☕ Cafe
🏨 Entertainment/Cabaret/Showbar

D Dancing **V** Video bar **K** Karaoke **S** Sports bar

C Country **L** Leather/Levi **W** Western

P Private Club (ask about visitor memberships)

H Assistance available for the deaf and hearing-impaired

HD devices **HS** sign **HDS** devices and sign

H? Check for assistance available for the deaf and hearing-impaired

⊗⊗ smoke-free property ⊗smoke-free indoors

(⊗) indoor smoking areas

🐾 Pets welcome (🐾?) Ask about pets

✈ High speed internet available to visitors

Wheelchair Accessibility of premises or meeting place:

♿♿ Accessible premises and lavatory

(♿♿) Accessible premises with help; accessible lavatory

♿ Accessible premises; lavatory not known to be accessible

(♿) Accessible premises with help

(?♿) Call ahead for details: places of meetings or activities vary, or special arrangements available.

◇ Asian ✚ Latin/Hispanic

✢ African-descent/Black

❖ People of Color ✳ Two-Spirit ✪ Diverse

Paid advertisers' entries appear in bold type. Bold type may also be purchased without display advertising, and, at the publisher's discretion, may be used by way of thanks to information contributors. Comments are made by the entrant: they are not editorial evaluations.

If your business or organization is not yet listed in GAYELLOW PAGES, email us at gypages@gmail.com.

WOMEN
USA: National Resources
WOMEN **3** WOMEN
GAYELLOW PAGES #42 2020-2021
WOMEN
National Resources : USA

WOMEN
National Resources

Crisis, Anti-violence, & Helplines

⚥ ★ National Coalition of Anti-Violence Programs, 116 Nassau St Flr 3, New York, NY 212-714-1184 avp.org/ncavp/

♀ ☆ National Sexual Assault Hotline, Rape, Abuse, & Incest National Network (RAINN), 1220 L St NW #505, Washington, DC 800-656-4673 www.rainn.org

♀ ☆ Womenslaw.org, For victims of domestic violence www.womenslaw.org

Information, Media & Publications

♀ ☆ Bitch Media, POB 11929, Portland, OR 97211 503-282-5699 www.bitchmedia.org general@b-word.org

⚥ • **Damron Guides, 415-255-0404 fax 415-703-9049 Annual pocket-sized guide to USA, Canada, Mexico, Europe & Asia. Also Women's Traveller. www.damron.com**

♀ • FEMSPEC, Batya Weinbaum, 1610 Rydalmount Rd, Cleveland Heights, OH 44118-1352 540-695-3043 www.femspec.org

⚥ • **Gayellow Pages, POB 533 Village Stn, New York, NY 10014-0533 646-213-0263 v/f Classified directory of services, businesses, resources, etc in USA & Canada. Mailing lists available. www.gayellowpages.com gypages@gmail.com**

⚥ ★ **Lesbian Connection Magazine, Ambitious Amazons, POB 811, East Lansing, MI 48826-0811 517-371-5257 fax 517-371-5200 A free, worldwide magazine for, by & about Lesbians. www.lconline.org LC@LConline.org**

⚥ ★ (♿) **Sinister Wisdom, 2333 McIntosh Rd, Dover, FL 33527-5980 www.sinisterwisdom.org sinisterwisdom@gmail.com**
◆ *Advertisement page 42*

Adoption, Surrogacy, Assisted Fertility Support, see also Reproductive

♂ ○ **Surrogate Mothers, Inc, mail to SMI, 6010 Deerwood Dr, Greenwood, IN 46143 317-996-2000 888-SURROGATE World's most reputable surrogacy program for over 30 years www.surrogatemothers.com**

Archives/Libraries/Museums/History Projects

⚥ ★ June Mazer Lesbian Archives, POB 691866, West Hollywood, CA 90069 310-659-2478 www.mazerlesbianarchives.org

⚥ ★ Legacy Project Outdoor Museum Walk (Chicago), 312-608-1198 www.legacyprojectchicago.org ✪

⚥ Lesbian Avengers Documentary Project, www.lesbianavengers.com

⚥ ★ ♿ **Lesbian Herstory Archives/Lesbian Herstory Educational Foundation, Inc, 484 14th St, Brooklyn, NY 718-768-3953 Lesbian history and cultural resource center. Please check on line for info on how to contact or visit. www.lesbianherstoryarchives.org**

♂ ☆ ♿ National Museum of Women in the Arts, 1250 New York Ave NW, Washington, DC 202-783-5000 nmwa.org

⚥ ★ ♿ Ohio Lesbian Archives, PO Box 20075, Cincinnati, OH 45220-0075 513-256-7695 tinyurl.com/97r3dbf OLArchives@gmail.com

⚥ ★ ♿ ONE Archives at the USC Libraries, 909 W Adams Blvd, Los Angeles, CA 90007-2406 213-821-2771 one.usc.edu askONE@usc.edu

⚥ ★ ♿ ONE Archives Foundation, 7655 W Sunset Blvd, Los Angeles, CA 323-419-2159 www.onearchives.org

Astrology/Numerology/Tarot/Psychic Readings

⚥ • Madam Lichtenstein, LLC, POB 1726 Old Chelsea Stn, New York, NY 10011 thestarryeye.typepad.com Astroweek@aol.com

Bookstores

⚥ ★ (♿) Sources of Hope Gifts & Books, 5910 Cedar Springs Rd, Dallas, TX 800-501-4673

⚥ GLBTQI ♀ Gay/nongay ⚦ bisexual
⚥ LBTQI women ♀ all women ⚦ bisexual women
⚥ GBTQI men ♂ all men ♂ bisexual men
T specifically transsexual/transgender/transvestite

♀ ✕ Bar and Restaurant ✕ Restaurant ☞ Cafe
🏛Entertainment/Cabaret/Showbar
D Dancing **V** Video bar **K** Karaoke **S** Sports bar
C Country **L** Leather/Levi **W** Western
P Private Club (ask about visitor memberships)

❤ Wedding-related services or marriage equality
H Assistance available for the deaf and hearing-impaired
HD devices **HS** sign **HDS** devices and sign
H? Check for assistance available for the deaf and. hearing-impaired
🚭 🚭 smoke-free property 🚭smoke-free indoors
(🚭) indoor smoking areas
🐾 Pets welcome (🐾?) Ask about pets
✎ High speed internet available to visitors
Wheelchair Accessibility of premises or meeting place:
♿ Accessible premises and lavatory
(♿) Accessible premises with help; accessible lavatory
♿ Accessible premises; lavatory not known to be accessible
(♿) Accessible premises with help
(♿) Call ahead for details: places of meetings or activities vary, or special arrangements available.
◇ Asian ◆ Latin/Hispanic
❖ African-descent/Black
✦ People of Color ✷ Two-Spirit ✪ Diverse

WOMEN
USA: National Resources

WOMEN **4** WOMEN
GAYELLOW PAGES #42 2020-2021

WOMEN
National Resources : USA

Broadcast Media

♀ ★ The Lesbian Lounge Podcast, 44 7703658039 www.MyLesbianRadio.com

Conferences/Events/Festivals/Workshops

♀ ☆ ♿ National Women's Music Festival / Women in the Arts, POB 1427, Indianapolis, IN 46206 317-395-3809 www.wiaonline.org

♀ ★ (♿) WomenFest Northwest Festivals, Jacqueline Harrington (Owner) 7554 N Burlington Ave, Portland, OR 97203 954-296-5674 www.womenfest.com womenfest@yahoo.com

Counseling/Psychotherapy/Mental Health

♀ ● Jill Denton, Sex Therapist, 805-534-1101 www.accesspt.com www.jillsextherapist.com

♂ ○ Johnson, Pia, LMSW, Online counseling services 347-867-6152 freshpathny.com pia@freshpathny.com

Funding: Endowment, Fundraising

♀ ★ ♿ ASTRAEA Lesbian Foundation for Justice, 116 E 16th St 7th flr, New York, NY 212-529-8021 www.astraeafoundation.org ♣

♀ ☆ National Network of Abortion Funds, POB 170280, Boston, MA 02117 www.fundabortionnow.org

Gifts, Cards, Pride, etc.

♀ ● For the Little Ones Inside.., POB 725, Ojai, CA 93024-0725 805-646-4518 tinyurl.com/2knbhj rposin@hotmail.com

♀ ● ♿ ZEBRAZ.com, 1608 N Main Ave, San Antonio, TX 78212-4311 210-472-2800 800-788-4729 orders only www.zebraz.com zebraz@zebraz.com

Health Care: Physical (see also Counseling/Mental Health)

♀ ★ Lesbian Health Fund, GLMA Health Professionals Advancing LGBT Health, 1133 19th St NW, Washington, DC 202-600-8037 www.glma.org/lhf

Leather Resources & Groups

♂ ☆ (♿) International Ms. Leather, IMsL Productions, LLC, 1271 Washington Ave # 121, San Leandro, CA 94577 imsl.org

Mortgages/Home Ownership (see also Banks, Real Estate)

♂ ○ ♿ Wilt, Tammy L., NMLS #195702, Movement Mortgage, 3510 Remson Cr Ste 301, Charlottesville, VA 434-242-0046 movement.com/lo/tammy-wilt/

Organizations/Resources: Business & Professional Associations, Labor Advocacy

♂ ☆ Association of Nurses in AIDS Care, 11230 Cleveland Ave NW #986, Uniontown, OH 800-260-6780 www.nursesinaidscare.org

♀ ☆ Tradeswomen Inc, 337 17th St Ste 207, Oakland, CA 510-891-1243 www.tradeswomen.org

Organizations/Resources: Cultural, Dance, Performance

♂ ☆ GroundSpark, 4104 24th St Ste 2013, San Francisco, CA 415-641-4616 groundspark.org

♀ ★ Ladyslipper Music, POB 14, Cedar Grove, NC 27231 919-245-3737 ladyslipper.org

♀ ☆ POWER UP, 419 N Larchmont Blvd #283, Los Angeles, CA 323-463-3154 www.powerupfilms.org

Organizations/Resources: Ethnic, Multicultural

♀ ★ Mamaroots: Ajama-Jebi Sistahood, POB 21066, Long Beach, CA 90801 562-498-3318 An AfraGoddess(tm) Tradition ♣

Organizations/Resources: Family and Supporters

♀ ★ U.S. National Longitudinal Lesbian Family Study, www.nllfs.org

Organizations/Resources: Political/Legislative/Advocacy

♀ Equal Rights Advocates, 1170 Market St Ste 700, San Francisco, CA 415-621-0672 www.equalrights.org

♂ ★ ♿ National Center for Lesbian Rights, 870 Market St Ste 370, San Francisco, CA 415-392-6257 www.nclrights.org

♀ ☆ Radical Women National Office, 5018 Rainier Ave S, Seattle, WA 98118 206-722-6057 radicalwomen.org radicalwomenus@gmail.com

♀ ★ Zuna Institute, 2701 Del Paso Rd Ste 130358, Sacramento, CA 916-207-1037 www.zunainstitute.org ♣

Organizations/Resources: Senior Resources

♀ ★ Old Lesbians Organizing for Change (OLOC), PO Box 834, Woodstock, NY 12498 888-706-7506 www.oloc.org info@oloc.org

Organizations/Resources: Social, Recreation, Support

♀ Kappa Xi Omega, www.kappaxiomega.org

Performance: Entertainment, Music, Theater, Space

♀ ● Music By Sandy Rapp, 66 Hildreth Place, East Hampton, NY 11937 631-329-5193 www.SandyRapp.com sandyrapp@aol.com

Public Relations/Advertising/Marketing

♀ ● Michele Karlsberg Marketing & Management, 917-359-2803 michelekarlsberg.com michelekarlsberg@me.com

Publishers/Publishing-related Services

♀ ★ Golden Crown Literary Society, POB 720154, Dallas, TX 75372 www.goldencrown.org

Religious / Spiritual Resources

♀ ★ BALM Ministries, Marsha Stevens, POB 609, Nolensville, TN 37135 714-206-8004 www.balmministries.net

♀ ★ Jewish Lesbian Daughters of Holocaust Survivors, 608-256-8883 tinyurl.com/ztewxec ⚥

Reproductive Legal Services

♂ ○ Worldwide Surrogacy Specialists, 2150 Post Rd #401, Fairfield, CT 06825 203-255-9877 www.worldwidesurrogacy.org info@worldwidesurrogacy.org

Reproductive Medicine & Fertility Services

♂ ● ♿ Circle Surrogacy, LLC, 200 High St Ste 600, Boston, MA 617-439-9900 www.circlesurrogacy.com

♂ ○ RESOLVE: the National Infertility Association, #300 7918 Jones Branch Dr Ste 300, McLean, VA 703-556-7172 www.resolve.org

WOMEN
Alabama: Huntsville

WOMEN 5 WOMEN
GAYELLOW PAGES #42 2020-2021

WOMEN
Sedona Area: Arizona

Sports & Outdoor

♀ ☆ Flag Football - International Women's Flag Football Association, 305-293-9315 www.iwffa.com

♀ ★ Sisters of Scota Womens Motorcycle Club, 530-635-7797 www.sistersofscotawmc.org soswmc@gmail.com

♀ ☆ Women Outdoors, POB 158, Northampton, MA 01061 www.womenoutdoors.org

Travel & Tourist Services (see also Accommodation)

♀ ○ Adventure Associates of WA, Inc, POB 16304, Seattle, WA 98116-0304 206-932-8352 www.adventureassociates.net info@adventureassociates.net

Alabama
Huntsville

Sports & Outdoor

♀ ☆ Dixie Derby Girls, POB 18514; 35804 www.dixiederbygirls.com

Alaska
Anchorage

Counseling/Psychotherapy/Mental Health

♂ ○ ♿ Strisik, Suzanne, PhD, 1500 W 33rd Ave Ste 210 907-868-7843 www.strisik.com

Real Estate (see also Mortgages)

♂ ○ ♿ Florio, Rona, Homes Unlimited, Downtown, 1343 G St Ste 104; 99501 907-748-4500 rona@ak.net

Juneau

Organizations/Resources: Cultural, Dance, Performance

♀ ★ ♿ PFLAG Juneau Pride Chorus, PO Box 32245; 99803 H? juneaupridechorus.com

Mat-Su Valley

Accommodation: Hotels, Inns, Guesthouses, B&B, Resorts
Palmer

♂ ● ♿ Alaska Garden Gate B&B, 950 S Trunk Rd, Palmer; 907-746-2333 www.gardengatebnb.com (♿?) ✔

Sitka

Counseling/Psychotherapy/Mental Health

♂ ● ♿ Westergaard, Cindy, Neurobehavioral Consultants, 300 Harbor Dr; 99835 907-747-3743 nbc.sitka@live.com

Sterling

Accommodation Rental: Furnished / Vacation (& AirBNB)

♂ ● Alaska Red Fish Lodge, POB 650; 99672 907-262-7080 www.alaskaredfishlodge.com ✔

Arizona
Bisbee/Sierra Vista Area

Real Estate (see also Mortgages)

♂ ● Linda Grale Realty, POB 1552, Bisbee; 85603 602-430-7071 www.lindagrale.com linda@lindagrale.com

Phoenix Area

Information, Media & Publications

♀ ★ ♿ Lesbian Social Network, Phoenix Pride LGBT Center, 801 N 2nd Ave, Phx; 480-946-5570 tinyurl.com/6glabgq ✔

Bars, Cafes, Clubs, Restaurants
Phoenix

♀ Boycott, 4301 N 7th Ave, Phx; 602-515-3667 www.boycottbar.com **DK** ▦

Counseling/Psychotherapy/Mental Health

♂ ○ House, Sabra, ACSW., The Lighthouse Center, 9929 N 95th Street Ste 101, Scottsdale; 480-451-0819 www.sabrahouse.com

Legal Services

♀ ● (♿) Gummere, Kathie, 1215 W Woodland Ave, Phx; 85007 602-952-0293 Estate planning & document preparation: protect your family & your choices. www.kathiegummere.com kathie@kathiegummere.com

Organizations/Resources: Cultural, Dance, Performance

♀ ★ Phoenix Women's Chorus, POB 34464, Phx 85067 602-487-1940 www.phoenixwomenschorus.org

Organizations/Resources: Student, Academic, Education

♀ ★ Gamma Rho Lambda Alpha Chapter, Arizona State University, POB 871301, Tempe; 85287 tinyurl.com/y8v67z76

Sedona Area

Real Estate (see also Mortgages)

♂ ● ♿ Stadelman, Audra & Prelle, Carolyn, Coldwell Banker-Mabery Real Estate, 1075 S State Rt 260, Cottonwood 86326 928-649-4634 fax 888-711-4024 www.cottonwoodhometeam.com hometeam2@cwbanker.com

WOMEN
Arizona: Tucson

WOMEN **6** WOMEN
GAYELLOW PAGES #42 2020-2021

WOMEN
East Bay Area: California

Tucson

Bookstores

♀ ● ♿ **Antigone Books, 411 N 4th Ave; 85705-8444 520-792-3715 www.antigonebooks.com ⚲ info@ antigonebooks.com**

Organizations/Resources: Student, Academic, Education

♀ ☆ ♿ University of Arizona Women's Resource Center, AZ Student Union, #404, 1303 E University Ave; 520-621-4498 www.rc.arizona.edu

Real Estate (see also Mortgages)

♂ ○ Segal, Sharon, Long Realty, 4051 E Sunrise Dr Ste 101; 520-907-6683 www.sharonsegal.com

Arkansas
Little Rock

Gifts, Cards, Pride, etc.

♂ ○ Domestic Domestic, 5501 Kavanaugh Blvd #C; 72207 501-661-1776 www.domesticdomestic.com hello@domestic domestic.com

California
State/County Resources

Sperm Banks

♂ ● ♿ The Sperm Bank of California, 2115 Milvia St, Ste 201, Berkeley, CA 94704-1157 510-841-1858 fax 510-841-0332 www.thespermbankofca.org

Bakersfield

Counseling/Psychotherapy/Mental Health

♂ ○ ♿ Ritter, Kathleen M, PhD, MFT, 2212 F St; 661-327-7010

Central Coast

Crisis, Anti-violence, & Helplines
Paso Robles

♂ ☆ ♿ RISE, 1030 Vine St Paso Robles 855-886-7473 805-226-5400 www.RISEslo.org contact@RISEslo.org
San Luis Obispo

♂ ☆ ♿ RISE, 51 Zaca Ln Ste 100, San Luis Obispo 855-886-7473 805-226-5400 www.RISEslo.org contact@RISEslo.org

Accommodation Rental: Furnished / Vacation (& AirBNB)
Cambria

♂ ○ **Maisons de Cambria Vacation Rentals, 800-240-2277 805-927-0306 Beautiful Oceanfront or Oceanview Vacation Rentals in Cambria, CA. www.maisonsdecambria.com ⚲ ☺ vacation@maisons decambria.com**

Health Care: Physical (see also Counseling/Mental Health)

♂ ● ♿ Gwen Pillow Chiropractic, Inc., DC, 1502 Spring St Ste B, Paso Robles; 93446 805-237-2654 www.GwenPillowDC.com ⚲ GwenPillowDC@gmail.com

Veterinarians

♂ ○ ♿ Cat & Bird Clinic, 101 W Mission St, Santa Barbara; 93101 805-569-2287 www.catandbirds.com

Chico

Crisis, Anti-violence, & Helplines

♂ ☆ (?♿) Catalyst Domestic Violence Services, POB 4184; 95927 800-895-8476 530-343-7711; Oroville Drop-in 530-532-6427 **H?** www.catalystdvservices.org ⚲ catalyst@catalystdvservices.org

Davis

Organizations/Resources: Student, Academic, Education

♀ ☆ Women's Resource Center, UC Davis, 113 North Hall 180 E; 530-752-3372 wrrc.ucdavis.edu

East Bay Area

Crisis, Anti-violence, & Helplines

♂ ☆ Contra Costa Crisis Center, POB 3364, Walnut Creek; 94598 925-939-1916 www.crisis-center.org

♀ ☆ A Safe Place, POB 23006, Oakland; 94623-0006 510-536-7233 www.asafeplacedvs.org

Counseling/Psychotherapy/Mental Health

♂ ○ (?♿) Bowman, Melissa K, MA, MS, LMFT #78865, 2329 Santa Clara Ave #202, Alameda; 94501 510-263-8476 **H?** (I make house-calls) www.mkbowmanlmft.com melissa@ mkbowmanlmft.com

♀ ● Deaner, Cheryl, LMFT, 1148 Stanford Ave, Oakland; 94608 / 3896 24th St, San Francisco 415-828-2200 www.cheryldeaner.com cdd.mft@gmail.com

♀ ● Felder, Elena, LMFT, MFC 37248, 4281 Piedmont Ave, Oakland; 94611 / 414 Gough St, San Francisco 510-982-1949 www.elenafeldermft.com elenafelder42@gmail.com

♀ ○ (?♿) Marcus, Lynn Ellen, LMFT, POB 27206, Oakland; 94602 510-632-2244 www.lynnellen.com

♀ ● Watson, Courtney, LMFT, CST, Doorway Therapeutic Services, 298 Grand Ave Ste 100, Oakland; 94610 510-463-4471 **H?** www.doorwaytherapeutics.com ❖ Doorwaytherapeutics@ gmail.com

Health Care: Physical (see also Counseling/Mental Health)

♀ ☆ ♿ Charlotte Maxwell Clinic Integrative Cancer Care, 411 30th St Ste 508, Oakland; 94609 510-601-7660 www.charlottemaxwell.org mail@charlottemaxwell.org

♂ ● (?♿) Island Acupuncture, Zollinger, Tracy, L.Ac, 2424 Blanding Ave Ste 102, Alameda; 94501 510-299-0057 tinyurl.com/omdo39z ⚲ tracyzollingerlac@gmail.com

♀ ☆ ♿ Women's Cancer Resource Center, 2908 Ellsworth St, Berkeley; 510-420-7900 www.wcrc.org

WOMEN
California: East Bay Area

WOMEN **7** WOMEN
GAYELLOW PAGES #42 2020-2021

WOMEN
Los Angeles Area: California

Organizations/Resources: Cultural, Dance, Performance

⚲ Voices Lesbian A Cappella For Justice, POB 11054, Oakland; 94611 510-545-3726 voiceslafj.wordpress.com

Organizations/Resources: Ethnic, Multicultural

⚲ ★ Asian Pacific Islander Queer Women & Transgender Community (APIQWTC), 708-274-7982 Lesbian, Queer, Transgender www.apiqwtc.org ⬦ info@apiqwtc.org

Organizations/Resources: Senior Resources

⚲ Aging Lesbians, Pacific Center, 2712 Telegraph Ave, Berkeley; 510-548-8283 tinyurl.com/y3xs6euo

⚲ ★ Women Over Fifty & Friends (WOFF), bj_patbond@yahoo.com

Organizations/Resources: Student, Academic, Education

⚲ ★ Gamma Rho Lambda, Lambda Chapter, tinyurl.com/3s8nxpg

Travel & Tourist Services (see also Accommodation)

♀ ● French Escapade, 2389 Blackpool Pl, San Leandro; 94577-6005 510-483-5713 Sightseeing, painting and cooking tours for small groups to Europe. www.frenchescapade.com ⚹ contact@frenchescapade.com

Eureka/Humboldt County

Information, Media & Publications

⚲ ★ The L-Word, POB 272, Bayside; 95524-0272 www.lword.mamajudy.com

Organizations/Resources: Social, Recreation, Support

⚲ ★ Lesbian Single Mingle, 707-822-6470

Gold Country/Sierra Foothills/Yosemite

Crisis, Anti-violence, & Helplines

♂ Center for Violence Free Relationships, 344 Placerville Dr Ste 11, Placerville; 530-626-1131 www.thecenternow.org

Inland Empire

Counseling/Psychotherapy/Mental Health

♂ ● ♿ Hayman, Yisraela, MA. LMFT, 5033 Carriage Rd, Rancho Cucamonga; 91737 310-388-7779 www.yisraelahayman.com ⚹ yisraelahayman@gmail.com

Lake Tahoe (CA/NV) Area

Crisis, Anti-violence, & Helplines

♂ ☆ Live Violence Free, 2941 Lake Tahoe Blvd, S Lake Tahoe; 530-544-2118 www.liveviolencefree.org

Accommodation Rental: Furnished / Vacation (& AirBNB)
South Lake Tahoe

♂ ● (🐾) Holly's Place, 1201 Rufus Allen Blvd, S Lake Tahoe; 800-745-7040 www.hollysplace.com ⚹

Long Beach

Bars, Cafes, Clubs, Restaurants

♀ ● ♿ The Suite, 3428 E Pacific Coast Hwy; 562-597-3884 **H?** www.thesuitelb.com **DKLV** 🏨 ⚹

Counseling/Psychotherapy/Mental Health

♂ ○ Pudewa, Pam, 5848 Naples Plaza Dr #204; 90803 562-391-6116 www.pampudewatherapy.com pampudewatherapy@gmail.com

♂ ○ Tessina, Tina B., LMFT, PhD, 562-438-8077 www.tinatessina.com tina@tinatessina.com

Gifts, Cards, Pride, etc.

♀ ● ♿ Hot Stuff, 2121 E Broadway 90803-5704 562-433-0692 hotstufflongbeach.com

Los Angeles Area

Crisis, Anti-violence, & Helplines

♀ East Los Angeles Women's Center, 1431 S Atlantic Blvd, LA; 323-526-5819 www.elawc.org

Accounting, Bookkeeping, Tax Services

♂ ● ♿ Wilson, Cathy E, CPA, 11965 Venice Blvd #404, LA; 90066 310-566-7980 fax 310-566-7981 www.cathywilsoncpa.com cathy@cathywilsoncpa.com

Archives/Libraries/Museums/History Projects

⚲ ★ June Mazer Lesbian Archives, POB 691866, W Hwd; 90069 310-659-2478 www.mazerlesbianarchives.org ⚹

Bars, Cafes, Clubs, Restaurants
Los Angeles

⚲ Booby Trap, check schedule fb.com/BoobyTrapFanClub/

♂ ○ Border Grill Downtown LA, 445 S Figueroa St, LA; 213-486-5171 www.bordergrill.com ⚥ ✗

North Hollywood

♂ ● ♿ The Other Door, 10437 Burbank Blvd, N Hwd; 818-508-7008 www.theotherdoorbar.com **DK** 🏨 ⚹

Studio City

⚲ Club Shine at Serra's, 12449 Ventura Blvd, Studio City; / unverified, check ahead 818-997-9666 **D**

West Hollywood

⚲ Girl Bar, check website www.girlbar.com **D** 🏨

Coaching: Career, Life, Relationship etc

♂ ● Bander, Ricki, PhD (CA Psychologist Lic. PSY7652 Board Certified Coach), offices: Los Angeles & Palm Desert 310-470-1435 www.rbanderphd.com

Counseling/Psychotherapy/Mental Health

♂ ● ♿ Cooper, Chris D, PhD, 95 N Marengo Ave Ste 100, Pasadena; 626-744-9472 www.chriscooperphd.com ⚹ @ixx=

♂ ● ♿ Hayman, Yisraela, MA. LMFT, 1827 Virginai Rd, LA; 90019 310-388-7779 www.yisraelahayman.com ⚹ yisraelahayman@gmail.com

WOMEN
California: Los Angeles Area

WOMEN 8 WOMEN
GAYELLOW PAGES #42 2020-2021

WOMEN
Sacramento Valley Area: California

♀ ● ♿ Jordan, Terry, LCSW, DCSW, 2001 S Barrington Ave #202, LA; 90025 310-895-4848 psychotherapyinla.com

♀ ○ ♿ Leviton, Susan J, MA, LMFT, 16055 Ventura Blvd Ste 1110, Encino; 91436 818-788-7101 (experienced with trans people) www.susanlevitonmft.com

♀ ○ Quinn, Susan, MA, MFT, 12011 San Vicente Blvd # 402, LA; 310-600-3458 www.susanquinn.net

♀ ○ Wright, April, MA. LMFT, 4500 Via Marina, Marina Del Rey; 90292 310-502-4944 aprilwrighttherapy.com april@aprilwright therapy.com

Health Care: Physical (see also Counseling/Mental Health)

♀ ● Seaton, Jessica, DC, 4212 Overland Ave, Culver City; 424-603-4088 www.drjessicaseaton.com

Legal Services

♀ ○ Goodman, Diane, 17043 Ventura Blvd, Encino 91316 818-386-2889 www.goodmanmediation.com info@goodmanmediation.com

Organizations/Resources: Cultural, Dance, Performance

♀ ☆ POWER UP, 419 N Larchmont Blvd #283, LA 323-463-3154 www.powerupfilms.org

♀ ☆ Vox Femina, 3341 Caroline Ave, Culver City 310-922-0025 www.voxfemina.org

Organizations/Resources: Social, Recreation, Support

● ★ Women on a Roll, POB 4353, Culver City 90231 310-398-1628 womenonaroll.com

Organizations/Resources: Student, Academic, Education

♀ ☆ Gamma Rho Lambda Zeta Chapter, Student Activities Center, 220 Westwood Plaza B36, LA fb.com/zeta.uclagrl/

Organizations/Resources: Transgender/Gender Non-Conforming/Diverse

T ○ Milrod, Christine, PhD, LMFT, ACS, Southern California Transgender Counseling, 519 N La Cienega Blvd #209, W Hwd 90048-2007 310-281-9658 tinyurl.com/2mys8h info@transgender counseling.com

Recovery

♀ ☆ ♿ Alcoholism Center for Women, 1147 S Alvarado St, LA; 90006-4100 213-381-8500 tinyurl.com/2qtp79 ♣

Mendocino Area

Accommodation Rental: Furnished / Vacation (& AirBNB)
Mendocino

♀ ● Sallie & Eileen's Place, POB 409, Mendocino; 95460 707 937-2028 www.seplace.com ☆ ✔ ⊗

Bars, Cafes, Clubs, Restaurants
Elk

♂ ● Queenies Roadhouse Cafe, 6061 S Hwy 1, Elk 707-877-3285 queeniesroadhousecafe.com ☞

Real Estate (see also Mortgages)

♂ ● ♿ Priceman, Ann Beth, A.B., Realtor, Garden Ranch Real Estate, 124 E Pine St, Fort Bragg 707-357-1801 **HS** www.absea.com ✔ absea@comcast.net

Palm Springs Area

Legal Services

♀ ○ Baker, Elizabeth, 155 W Hermosa Place, Palm Sp 760-320-3556

♂ ● Barrett, Barbara, 555 S Sunrise Way #211, Palm Sp; 92264-7869 760-323-2622 www.barbarabarrettlaw.com bbarrett92262@ aol.com

Organizations/Resources: Senior Resources

♥ ★ Old Lesbians Organizing for Change (OLOC) - Coachella Valley/Palm Springs, 760-318-6794 www.oloc.org

Real Estate (see also Mortgages)

♂ ● ♿ Lundgren, Melissa, Realtor, Better Homes and Gardens Real Estate Leaskou Partners, 200 N Sunrise Way Ste B, Palm Sp; 92262 760 668-2544 www.melissalundgren.com ✔ melissa@ melissalundgren.com

Russian River/Sonoma

Bars, Cafes, Clubs, Restaurants
Petaluma

♂ ○ Brixx Pizzeria, 16 Kentucky St, Petaluma 707-766-8162 www.brixxpetaluma.com ☖ ✗

Gifts, Cards, Pride, etc.

♂ ● ♿ Milk & Honey, 123 N Main St, Sebastopol; 95472-3448 707-824-1155 www.milk-and-honey.com ☞ ✔

Sports & Outdoor

♀ ☆ ♿ Resurrection Roller Girls, Cal Skate, 6100 Commerce Blvd, Rohnert Park 707-585-0500 fb.com/rrderby/ ✔

Travel & Tourist Services (see also Accommodation)

♂ ● Sharp Tongued Consulting, 9596 Orion Dr, Windsor; 95492-8822 707-481-7692 tinyurl.com/23f5xf sharptongued@mac.com

Sacramento Valley Area

Bars, Cafes, Clubs, Restaurants
Sacramento

♥ ♿ The Hush at Depot Video Bar, n/a, Sacto; / check schedule 916-441-6823 fb.com/HushLadiesNight **V**

Legal Services

♂ ● ♿ Pearce, M Jane, 455 University Ave Ste 370, Sacto; 916-452-3883

Organizations/Resources: Cultural, Dance, Performance

♀ ☆ ♂ Sacramento Women's Chorus, PO Box 661705, Sacto; 95866 tinyurl.com/ny93bo

Organizations/Resources: Student, Academic, Education

♀ ☆ Women's Resource Center CSU, University Union, 6000 J St, Sacto; 916-278-7388 www.csus.edu/wrc/

Organizations/Resources: Transgender/Gender Non-Conforming/Diverse

♀ ☆ River City Gems, POB 601203, Sacto; 95860 Trans women social group rivercitygems.org info@rivercitygems.org

Sports & Outdoor

⚥ ★ Sisters of Scota Womens Motorcycle Club, 530-635-7797 www.sistersofscotawmc.org soswmc@gmail.com

San Diego Area

Crisis, Anti-violence, & Helplines

♂ Center for Community Solutions, 4508 Mission Bay Dr, San Diego; 888-385-4657 www.ccssd.org

Accommodation: Hotels, Inns, Guesthouses, B&B, Resorts
San Diego

♂ ○ **Beach Hut Bed and Breakfast, 3761 Riviera Dr, San Diego; 92109-6643 858-272-6131 Amazing and unique private experience in beautiful Mission Bay Park.** beachhutbb.com ⚲ ⊛ beachhutbb@gmail.com

♂ ○ Carole's B&B Inn, 3227 Grim Ave, San Diego 92104-4656 619-280-5258 www.carolesbnb.com ⚲ ⊛

AIDS/HIV Services, Education & Support

♀ ☆ Christie's Place, 2440 3rd Ave, San Diego 619-702-4186 www.christiesplace.org

Bars, Cafes, Clubs, Restaurants

⚥ Queer Girl Events, www.queergirlevents.com
San Diego

⚥ ● ♿ Gossip Grill, 1220 University Ave, San Diego; 619-260-8023 gossipgrill.com **D** ? ✕ ⚲

Counseling/Psychotherapy/Mental Health

♂ ○ (?♿) Vernazza, Trish E, MFT, ATR, 2774 Jefferson Street, Carlsbad 760-439-8874 www.trishv.com

♂ ○ Vernazza, Trish, MA, MFT, 2774 Jefferson St, Carlsbad; 92008 760-439-8874 www.trishv.com info@trishv.com

♂ ● Weissman, Abigail, PsyD, Waves, a Psychological Corporation, 2055 Third Ave #B, San Diego; 92101 619-403-5578 www.wavespsych.com/doctorabi office@wavespsych.com

Legal Services

♂ ○ The Ahrens Law, APC, 1901 1st Ave 2nd Flr, San Diego; 92101 619-230-0300 fax 619-230-0610 www.ahrenslawoffice.com ka@ahrenslawoffice.com

Metaphysical, Occult, Alternative Healing

♂ ● Minerva Wisdom Arts, 541-349-0595 www.minervawisdomarts.com ⚲ info@minervawisdomarts.com

Organizations/Resources: Cultural, Dance, Performance

♀ ★ ♿ San Diego Women's Chorus, POB 632794, San Diego; 92163-2794 619-291-3366 **H?** www.sdwc.org info@sdwc.org

Organizations/Resources: Social, Recreation, Support

⚥ ★ Butch Voices, POB 635333, San Diego 92163 www.butchvoices.com

Real Estate (see also Mortgages)

♂ ○ Hefni-Pyle, Suzanne, Orange & San Diego Counties 760-451-1500 tinyurl.com/yaokufux

♂ ● ♿ Z (Zyhylij), Tamara, Ascent Real Estate, 410 Kalmia St, San Diego; 92101 619-865-1389 **H?** www.TamaraZhomes.com ⚲ Tamara@TamaraZhomes.com

San Francisco Bay/Peninsula

Crisis, Anti-violence, & Helplines

⚥ ★ ♿ Community United Against Violence, 427 S Van Ness Ave, SF; 415-777-5500 www.cuav.org

♀ ☆ W.O.M.A.N., Inc., 26 Boardman Place, SF 877-384-3578 www.womaninc.org

Community Centers and/or Pride Organizations

⚥ ★ ♿ San Francisco Dyke March, 3543 18th St #2, SF; **HS** www.thedykemarch.org

Bars, Cafes, Clubs, Restaurants
San Francisco: Mission District

⚥ ● (?♿) El Rio, 3158 Mission St, SF 415-282-3325 www.elriosf.com **DK** ✦⚲
San Francisco: South of Market

⚥ UHAUL SF Friday at Oasis, 298 11th St, SF 415-595-3725 fb.com/uhaul.SanFrancis/ **D** 🏳
San Francisco

⚥ ● Mecca 2,00, check schedule fb.com/groups/mecca2.0

Body Art

♂ ● ♿ Black & Blue Tattoo, 381 Guerrero, SF; 94103 415-626-0770 www.blackandbluetattoo.com ⚲

Counseling/Psychotherapy/Mental Health

♂ ○ Croner, Barbara, MFT, MFC24761, 1947 Divisadero #1, SF; 94115-2532 415-346-8678

Health Care: Physical (see also Counseling/Mental Health)

♂ ☆ ♿ Lyon Martin Women's Service, 1735 Mission St, SF; 415-565-7667 All women and transgender people www.lyon-martin.org

♀ ☆ ♿ Women's Community Clinic, 1735 Mission St, SF; 415-379-7800 tinyurl.com/2kz7wm ⚲

Leather Resources & Groups

♀ ★ ♿ The Exiles, POB 14338, SF 94114-0338 415-938-7376 **HS** (women and non males) www.theexiles.org info@theexiles.org

♀ San Francisco Girls of Leather, fb.com/SFgoL

WOMEN
California: San Francisco Bay/Peninsula

WOMEN **10** WOMEN
GAYELLOW PAGES #42 2020-2021

WOMEN
Boulder Area : Colorado

Legal Services

♂ ● ⚥ Kinney, Deb L, Johnston, Kinney & Zulaica LLP, 101 Montgomery St Ste 1600, SF; 94104 415-693-0550 www.jkzllp.com ✎ office@jkzllp.com

Organizations/Resources: Cultural, Dance, Performance

♀ ☆ Brava! for Women in the Arts, 2781 24th St, SF; 94110 415-641-7657 www.brava.org info@brava.org

♀ ☆ Purple Moon Dance Project, 1385 Mission St Ste 340, SF; 415-552-1105 www.purplemoondance.org ✪

● ★ ⚥ Queer Women of Color Film Festival, 1014 Torney Ave Ste 111, SF; 94129 415-752-0868 **H** June 14-16, 2019 www.qwocmap.org ✤ ✎ festival@qwocmap.org

● ★ (♿) Queer Women of Color Media Arts Project (QWOCMAP), 1014 Torney Ave Ste 111, SF; 94129 415-752-0868 **H?** Film festival & workshops www.qwocmap.org ✎ festival@qwocmap.org

Organizations/Resources: Senior Resources

● ★ Old Lesbians Organizing for Change (OLOC) - San Francisco Bay Area, patcull70@gmail.com

Organizations/Resources: Social, Recreation, Support

● ★ (♿) adyke (Ain't Dead Yet Kick-Azz Events), For lesbians over 40 www.adyke.org WeAre@adyke.org

♀ ☆ ⚥ WTF Night at the Bike Kitchen, 650H Florida, SF; 415-506-7433 **H?** tinyurl.com/ms5mqg9

Organizations/Resources: Transgender/Gender Non-Conforming/Diverse

T ○ ⚥ Bowers, Marci L, MD, POB 1044, Trinidad, CO 81082 / 345 Lorton Ave Ste 101, Burlingame, CA 94010 650-570-2270 www.marcibowers.com ✎

Reproductive Medicine & Fertility Services

♂ ☆ LGBTQ Perinatal Wellness Center, 3207 Lakeshore Ave, Oakland, CA 94610 tinyurl.com/y4nwa5bw lgbtqperinatalwellnesscenter@gmail.com

Sports & Outdoor

● ★ San Francisco Dykes on Bikes, POB 401166, San Francisco, CA 94140 www.dykesonbikes.org

Travel & Tourist Services (see also Accommodation)

●' ● ♿ Cruisin' the Castro LGBTQ Walking Tours, 415-550-8110 www.cruisinthecastro.com kathy@cruisinthecastro.com

Women's Centers

♀ ☆ Women's Building, 3543 18th St, SF 415-431-1180 womensbuilding.org ✪

San Jose & South Bay Area

Counseling/Psychotherapy/Mental Health

♂ ☆ (♿) Community Solutions, 9015 Murray #100, Gilroy; 408-842-7138 Also serve survivors of domestic violence, sexual assault and human trafficking. www.communitysolutions.org

Health Care: Physical (see also Counseling/Mental Health)

♀ ○ Kamiak, Sandra, MD, 14583 Big Basin Way Ste 3B, Saratoga; 95070-6072 408-741-1332 www.sandrakamiakmd.com skamiak@aol.com

Organizations/Resources: Cultural, Dance, Performance

♂ ★ (♿) Rainbow Women's Chorus, 14938 Camden Ave Ste 61, San Jose; 95124 408-603-9367 **H?** www.rainbowwomen.org ✎ contact@rainbowwomen.org

Organizations/Resources: Social, Recreation, Support

● ★ Peninsula - Sappho, www.lavenderevents.com/women

● ★ South Bay Sappho, tinyurl.com/j3mbwd3

● ★ Women Over Fifty South Bay, tinyurl.com/dy226x

Sports & Outdoor

♀ ☆ San Jose Women's Softball League, POB 6112, San Jose; 95150 408-800-2425 www.sjwsoftball.com

Santa Cruz Area

Legal Services

♂ ○ Law Offices of Moira Leigh, 621 Seabright Ave, Santa Cruz; 831-454-0226 santacruzattorney.com

Women's Centers

♀ ☆ ⚥ Walnut Avenue Family & Women's Center, 303 Walnut Ave, Santa Cruz; 95060 831-426-3062 www.wafwc.org

Colorado
State/County Resources

Health Care: Physical (see also Counseling/Mental Health)

♂ ● Colorado Mountain Doulas, 719-581-9041 **H?** coloradomountaindoulas.com comtndoulas@gmail.com

Organizations/Resources: Senior Resources

● ★ Old Lesbians Organizing for Change (OLOC) - Colorado, OLOCinColorado@comcast.net

Boulder Area

Health Care: Physical (see also Counseling/Mental Health)

♂ ☆ Boulder Valley Women's Health Center, 2855 Valmont Rd, Boulder; 80301 303-442-5160 www.boulderwomenshealth.org info@bvwhc.org

♂ ○ ⚥ Lefthand Community Acupuncture, 424 E Simpson St, Lafayette; 80026 720-378-6090 www.lefthandacu.com info@lefthandacu.com

Legal Services

♂ ● ⚥ Lisa A. Polansky, Founding Partner, Polansky Law Firm, 4999 Pearl E Circle Ste 201, Boulder; 80301 303-415-2583 Criminal defense www.polanskylawfirm.com Lisa@polanskylawfirm.com

WOMEN
Colorado: Boulder Area

WOMEN 11 WOMEN
GAYELLOW PAGES #42 2020-2021

WOMEN
Mystic Area: Connecticut

Organizations/Resources: Cultural, Dance, Performance

♀ ☆ Resonance Women's Chorus of Boulder, 2525 Arapahoe Ave #E4-186, Boulder; 80302 303-473-8337 www.resonancechorus.org resonancechorus@gmail.com

♀ ☆ Sound Circle, 2525 Arapahoe Ave E4-186, Boulder; 80302 303-473-8337 www.soundcirclesings.org soundcircle@ecentral.com

Colorado Springs Area

Legal Services

♂ ○ ♿ Wolfe, Julie, 10 Boulder Crescent St #201, Colorado Springs; 80903 719-633-7101

Denver Area

Bars, Cafes, Clubs, Restaurants
Denver

♀ ● Babes Around Denver, check schedule 303-475-4620 www.babesaroundenver.com

♂ Blush & Blu, 1526 E Colfax Ave, Denver 303-484-8548 www.blushblubar.com

♀ Hip Chicks Out, www.hipchicksout.com

Counseling/Psychotherapy/Mental Health

♂ ● ♿ Hsieh, Linda, MA, LPC, Open Forest Counseling, 950 S Cherry St #220, Denver; 80246 720-429-3047 lindahsieh.com

Insurance (see also Financial Planning)

♂ ● ♿ Boynton, Susan, State Farm, 9200 W Cross Dr Ste 122, Littleton; 80123 303-948-2905 www.susanboynton.com sue@sueboynton.com

Organizations/Resources: Cultural, Dance, Performance

♀ ★ (?♐) Denver Women's Chorus, Rocky Mountain Arts Association, 700 Colorado Blvd #325, Denver; 303-325-3959 www.rmarts.org

Real Estate (see also Mortgages)

♂ ● ♿ Mathis, Dawn, Realtor, ABR, GRI, SRES, Coldwell Banker, 141 Union Blvd Ste 200, Lakewood; 80228 970-481-5263 realestatebydawn.com ✔ Dawn@RealEstateByDawn.com

Estes Park

Accommodation Rental: Furnished / Vacation (& AirBNB)

♂ ● River Spruce Cabins, 2334 Tunnel Rd 970-586-4543 www.riverspruce.com

Fort Collins/Loveland Area

Crisis, Anti-violence, & Helplines

♂ ☆ ♿ Crossroads Safehouse, POB 993, Fort Collins; 80522 970-482-3502 www.crossroadssafehouse.org

Counseling/Psychotherapy/Mental Health

♂ ● Blue Spruce Counseling, Judy Underwood, PhD & Pam Gaynor, PhD, 515 S Sherwood St, Fort Collins; 80521-2842 970-221-0581 www.bluesprucecounseling.com judy@bluespruce counseling.com

Legal Services

♂ ○ ♿ Kling, Celeste Holder, Wallace & Kling, P.C. 425 W Mulberry St Ste 107, Fort Collins; 80521 970-221-5602 www.wallace-kling.com wkpc@frii.com

Organizations/Resources: Social, Recreation, Support

♀ ★ Back Country Bettys, POB 273337, Fort Collins; 80527 970-568-6116 tinyurl.com/lofng9x

Greeley

Insurance (see also Financial Planning)

♂ ● Lozano, Oralia, Farmers, 2122 9th St Ste 3 80631 970-518-7239 www.farmersagent.com/olozano

San Juan National Forest Area

Organizations/Resources: Social, Recreation, Support

♀ ★ Four Corners Lesbian Network, fb.com/groups/fourcornersln/

Connecticut
State/County Resources

Legal Services

♀ ☆ ♿ Connecticut Women's Education & Legal Fund, 75 Charter Oak Ave Ste 1-300, Hartford, CT 860-247-6090 www.cwealf.org

Organizations/Resources: Cultural, Dance, Performance

♀ ☆ (?♐) Another Octave: Connecticut Women's Chorus, POB 185234, Hamden, CT 06518 203-672-1919 www.anotheroctave.org

Bridgeport

Bookstores

♂ ● ♿ Bloodroot Vegetarian Restaurant & Bookstore, 85 Ferris St; 203-576-9168 www.bloodroot.com ✗ ✔

Hartford Area

Counseling/Psychotherapy/Mental Health

♀ ● Osadchey, Sherry L, MA, LMFT, SEP, 780 Farmington Ave, Farmington; 06032 860-677-5300 www.sherryosadchey.com Sherry@sherryosadchey.com

♂ ● Women's Center for Psychotherapy, 784 Farmington Ave, W Hartford; 860-523-4450 www.womens-center.com

Mystic Area

Accommodation: Hotels, Inns, Guesthouses, B&B, Resorts
Ledyard

♂ ● Mare's Inn B&B, 333 Col Ledyard Hwy, Ledyard 860-572-7556 www.almostinmystic.com (♐?) ⊛

Mystic

♂ ● Mermaid Inn of Mystic, 2 Broadway Av, Mystic 860-536-6223 mermaidinnofmystic.com ✔ ⊛

Counseling/Psychotherapy/Mental Health

♂ ● ♿ Korman, Nicki, LMFT, EdD, 2514 Boston Post Rd #8C, Guilford; 06437 203-458-0900

♀♂ ○ Ziskind, Katie, LMFT, RYT500, 8 W Main St Ste 3-15, Niantic; 06335 860-451-9364KatieZis. fax 860-294-8428 Video and phone sessions available www.WisdomWithinCt.com KatieZiskindMFT@gmail.com

New Haven Area

Bars, Cafes, Clubs, Restaurants
New Haven

♂ ○ ♂♿ Claire's Corner Copia, 1000 Chapel St, New Haven; 203-562-3888 www.clairescornercopia.com ✕ ✔ info@clairescorner copia.com

Counseling/Psychotherapy/Mental Health

♂ ○ ♂♿ Altbrandt, Robina, LCSW, MPH, 441 Orange St, New Haven; 203-640-6564 www.robinaaltbrandt.com

Organizations/Resources: Student, Academic, Education

♀ ☆ ♿ Yale Women's Center, 198 Elm St, New Haven; 06520 www.yale.edu/wc/ wcboard@mailman.yale.edu

Norwalk

Bars, Cafes, Clubs, Restaurants

♀ ● ♂♿ SIREN Party at Troupe429, 3 Wall St, Norwalk; / Every 2nd Sat Troupe429 is Connecticut's best gay bar for the LGBTQ+ community! www.troupe429.com D ▦ ✔

Storrs

Women's Centers

♂ ☆ ♂♿ Women's Center, SU Room 421, 2110 Hillside Rd Unit 3118, Storrs; 860-486-4738 **H?** www.womenscenter.uconn.edu ✔

Westport

Art & Photography (see also Graphic Design)

♀ ● Sheridan Photography, 277A North Ave 203-222-1441 www.suzannesheridan.com

Delaware
Rehoboth Area

Accommodation: Hotels, Inns, Guesthouses, B&B, Resorts
Lewes

♂ ● Lazy L Bed & Breakfast Resort, 16061 Willow Creek Rd, Lewes; 302-644-7220 www.LazyL.net ❖ ✔ ⊗

Rehoboth Beach

♂ ● (?♂) Homestead at Rehoboth B&B, 35060 Warrington Rd, Rehoboth Bch; 302-226-7625 www.homesteadatrehoboth.com ❖⊗

Bars, Cafes, Clubs, Restaurants
Rehoboth Beach

♂ ○ Lori's Oy-vey Cafe, 39 Baltimore Ave, Rehoboth Bch; 302-226-3066 www.lorisoyveycafe.com ☞

♂ ● The Pond Bar & Grill, 3 S 1st St, Rehoboth Bch 302-227-2234 www.thepondrehoboth.com ▦

Real Estate (see also Mortgages)

♂ ● ♂♿ Giove, Susan, Mann & Sons, 414 Rehoboth Ave, Rehoboth Bch; 19971 302-227-9477 tinyurl.com/y6v6vyhv ✔ sngiove0806@gmail.com

♀ ○ Kalvinsky, Shirley, Jack Lingo Realtor, 246 Rehoboth Ave, Rehoboth Bch; 19971 302-236-4254 www.homesofrehoboth.com Shirley@jacklingo.com

Wilmington

Counseling/Psychotherapy/Mental Health

♂ ○ ♿ Alliance Counseling, 3411 Silverside Rd Weldin Building Ste 100; 19810 302-477-0708 fax 302-477-0136 www.getmeaningfulresults.com

District of Columbia
DC Washington Area

Information, Media & Publications

♀ PhatGirlChic.com, www.phatgirlchic.com ✪

♀ ● Tagg Magazine, 1638 R St NW Ste 210, DC 20009 703-567-7643 www.taggmagazine.com info@taggmagazine.com

♀ Where the Girls Go, fb.com/wherethegirlsgo

Archives/Libraries/Museums/History Projects

♂ ☆ ♂♿ National Museum of Women in the Arts, 1250 New York Ave NW, DC; 202-783-5000 **H?** nmwa.org ✔

Bars, Cafes, Clubs, Restaurants
Washington

♂ ○ Hamilton's Bar & Grill, 233 2nd St NW, DC 202-347-6555 www.hamiltonsdc.com **S** ♈ ✕

♂ A League Of Her Own, 2319 18th St NW, DC 202-733-2568 fb.com/alohodc/ **S**

♀ Lure DC, at Cobalt, 1639 R St NW, DC; / 3rd Sat, check schedule 202-232-4416 fb.com/lurewdc **D**

♀ XX+ Crostino, 1926 9th St NW, DC 202-797-0523 www.xxcrostino.com

Counseling/Psychotherapy/Mental Health

♂ ● (?♂) LGBT Counseling, 3000 Connecticut Ave NW Ste 400A; 202-319-8541 www.lgbtc.com information@lgbtc.com

♂ ○ ♂♿ Riddell, Grace C, LICSW, LCSW-C, MEd, 3000 Connecticut Ave NW Ste 137, DC; 20008-2500 301-942-3237 www.Grace-Riddell.com

♀ ● **Zeiger, Robyn S., PhD, LCPC, 10300 Sweetbriar Parkway, Silver Spring, MD 20903-1523 301-445-7333 Licensed Clinical Professional Counselor and Certified Imago Relationship Therapist www.drrobynzeiger.com drrobynzeiger@aol.com**

Financial Planning, Investment (see also Insurance)

♂ ● ♂♿ Third Eye Associates, Ltd, 1717 K St NW, Ste 900 202-667-2266 www.thirdeyeassociates.com ✔

Organizations/Resources: Cultural, Dance, Performance

♂ ☆ ♿ Fortissima: DC's Feminist Singers, 728 Fairmont, DC; 20002 202-684-6353 www.fortissima.org goddess@fortissima.org

Organizations/Resources: Social, Recreation, Support

♀ ★ Nice Jewish Girls DC, fb.com/NJGDC ✡

Organizations/Resources: Student, Academic, Education

♀ ★ Association of Queer Women and Allies (AQWA), fb.com/AQWAatGWU/

Sports & Outdoor

♀ ☆ Washington Women Outdoors, POB 9568, Washington, DC 20018 240-720-7819 tinyurl.com/7nwhow9

Weddings and Ceremonies

♂ ● (♿) The DC Marriage Knot, 4722 Morning Glory Trail, Bowie, MD 202-253-3629 www.thedcmarriageknot.com ♥

Florida
State/County Resources

Mortgages/Home Ownership (see also Banks, Real Estate)

♂ ● Frey, Carolyn, OH & FL & PA 305-735-2524 www.carolyn-frey.com cafrey@mortgagelendingsolutions.com

Weddings and Ceremonies

♂ ○ Reverend Lyn Daniels, 386-503-6885 www.revlynsweddings.com ♥

Fort Lauderdale/Wilton Manors Area

Information, Media & Publications

♀ ● GIR(L) Magazine, POB 468, Lake Worth, FL 33460 954-829-1982 www.girlmag.us editor@girlmagazine.us

Bars, Cafes, Clubs, Restaurants
Dania Beach

♀ Beach Bettys, 625 E Dania Beach Blvd, Dania Beach; 954-921-9893 tinyurl.com/lgob3hq **KS**

Davie

♂ ○ ♿ Cloud 9 Lounge, 7126 Stirling Rd, Davie; 954-499-3525 fb.com/cloudninenight/ **CDK** ⚥ ✕ 📶

Fort Lauderdale

♀ ● J's Bar, 2780 Davie Blvd, Ft Laud 954-581-8400 tinyurl.com/hy8pnnq **D**

Counseling/Psychotherapy/Mental Health

♂ ○ Fischetto, Julia, MS, LMHC, 218 Commercial Blvd Ste 232, Lauderdale By The Sea; 33308-4457 954-491-9040 fax 954-492-0334 jfpsych218@aol.com

Organizations/Resources: Business & Professional Associations, Labor Advocacy

♀ ★ ♿ Women In Network, POB 9744, Ft Laud; 33310 www.womeninnetwork.com

---

Real Estate (see also Mortgages)

♂ ○ Wish, Vickie, GRI, Realtor, Coldwell Banker Residential Real Estate, 5810 Coral Ridge Drive Ste 100, Coral Springs; 33076 954-242-8200 954-688-5406 www.vickiewish.com vickie@vickiewish.com

Jacksonville

Crisis, Anti-violence, & Helplines

♂ ☆ ♿ Women's Center of Jacksonville, 5644 Colcord Ave; 904-722-3000 **H?** (Also serve male rape victims) www.womenscenterofjax.org ✂

Bars, Cafes, Clubs, Restaurants

♀ ● ♿ InCahoots Nightclub, 711 Edison Ave; 904-353-6316 www.incahootsnightclub.com **DKLV** ☯ ✂

♀ ● The Sappho, Upstairs at Metro, 859 Willow Branch Ave; 904-388-8719 www.metrojax.com **DKLCW** 📶 ☯ ✂

Keys & Key West

Health Care: Physical (see also Counseling/Mental Health)

♂ ☆ Womankind, 1511 Truman Ave, Key West; 33040 305-294-4004 www.womankindkeywest.org info@womankindkeywest.org

Miami Area

Bars, Cafes, Clubs, Restaurants
Miami Beach

♀ ● Pandora Events for Women, Check for current venues 305-975-6933 tinyurl.com/6m3ygku

Funding: Endowment, Fundraising

♀ ☆ Aqua Foundation for Women, 1951 NW 7 Ave, Mi 33136 305-576-2782 www.aquafoundation.org info@aquafoundation.org

Legal Services

♂ ○ Angie Angelis Law, 13554 SW 47th Lane Ste 100, Mi; 33175 305-598-2540 fax 305-330-9248 fb.com/AngieAngelisLaw angie@angieangelislaw.com

♂ ○ Law Offices of Barbara Buxton, P.A., 20801 Biscayne Blvd Ste 400, Aventura; 305-932-2293 Elder Law www.buxtonlaw.com

Organizations/Resources: Social, Recreation, Support

♀ Rainbow Ladies - Our Space, Inc., fb.com/RainbowLadies ☯

Orlando Area

Accounting, Bookkeeping, Tax Services

♀ ● James, Leah, CPA, MSTax, Gecko CPA Firm, POB 5277, Orl; 32793 407-478-4513 www.geckocpa.com

Bars, Cafes, Clubs, Restaurants
Orlando

♀ ○ ♿ Nora's Sugar Shack, 636 Virginia Dr, Orl; 407-447-5885 bar package store lounge noraswinecigars.com

Legal Services

♀ ○ Law Office of Blaine McChesney, P.A., 390 N Orange Ave Ste 2300, Orl; 32801 407-246-1112 Criminal Defense www.BlaineMcChesneyLaw.com Blaine@Blaine McChesneyLaw.com

Pensacola Area

Counseling/Psychotherapy/Mental Health

♀ ○ Bright, Regina, MS, LMHC, BCST, Stepping Stones Professional Counseling, 151 Mary Esther Blvd Ste 310 A, Mary Esther 850-226-6430 tinyurl.com/yco28o6b

Sarasota/Bradenton/Venice Area

Counseling/Psychotherapy/Mental Health

♀ ● ♿ Eslien, Heather D, MA, LHMC, 330 South Pineapple Ave Ste 101, Sarasota; 34236 941-840-0878 www.swfltranssptgp.org heather.d.eslien@gmail.com

♀ ○ Twitchell, Carol, Psy.D., 3205 Southgate Circle Ste 12, Sarasota; 34239 941-954-1506 www.caroltwitchell.com caroltwitchell@comcast.net

Legal Services

♀ ● ♿ Petruff, Patricia, Dye Harrison, 1206 Manatee Ave W, Bradenton; 34205 941-748-4411 dyeharrison.com ✎

Tampa Bay Area

Information, Media & Publications

♀ ★ ProSuzy: Your LGBT Connection, POB 530544, Gulfport; 33747 727-289-9365 www.prosuzy.com

Bars, Cafes, Clubs, Restaurants

♀ ● Honey Pot, 1507 E 7th Ave, Tampa 813-247-4663 tinyurl.com/mjxjszx ▦

Tampa

♀ ● Twirl Girl Events & Promotions, fb.com/TwirlGirlPromotions

Counseling/Psychotherapy/Mental Health

♀ ○ Maguire, Jane, MA, LMHC, MCAP, Integrity Counseling, 1101 Belcher Rd S Ste J, Largo; 727-531-7988 www.janemaguire.com ✎

Weddings and Ceremonies

♀ ● (♿) Ceremonies By Nan, 3402-G S Dale Mabry Hwy, Tampa; 33629 813-839-5564 fax 813-832-8303 www.ceremoniesbynan.com ♥ ceremoniesbynan@aol.com

Georgia
State/County Resources

Organizations/Resources: Social, Recreation, Support

♀ ★ ♿ Fourth Tuesday of Georgia, 404-688-2524 fb.com/FourthTuesdayAtlanta/ ✎

Atlanta Area

Crisis, Anti-violence, & Helplines

♀ ☆ Women's Resource Center To End Domestic Violence, POB 171, Decatur; 30031 404-688-9436 404-370-7670 www.wrcdv.org info@wrcdv.org

Bars, Cafes, Clubs, Restaurants
Atlanta

♀ ● My Sisters' Room, 66 12th St NE, Atl 678-705-4585 www.mysistersroom.com **S** ⚥ ✕

♀ ● Traxx Girls, check schedule 888-935-8729 www.traxxgirls.com **D** ▦ ✤

Decatur

♀ ○ Eddie's Attic, 515-B N McDonough St, Decatur 404-377-4976 eddiesattic.com ⚥ ✕ ▦

Stone Mountain

♀ Phaze One, 4933 Memorial Dr, Stone Mountain; 404-296-4895 tinyurl.com/opz6ojq ✤

Bookstores

♀ ● ♿ **Charis Books & More, 184 S Candler St, Decatur; 30030 404-524-0304 Best Lesbian Fiction/Erotica/Mystery, LGBTQ Studies, Weekly Author/Social/Political Program Events www.charisbooksandmore.com** ✎ **info@charisbooksandmore.com**

Health Care: Physical (see also Counseling/Mental Health)

♀ ☆ ♿ Feminist Women's Health Center, 1924 Cliff Valley Way NE Flr 2, Atl; 404-728-7900 www.feministcenter.org

Immigration, Citizenship, Political Asylum, Refugees

♀ ○ ♿ **McGrath, Kerry E, 1100 Spring St NW Ste 760, Atl; 30309 404-377-6600 Immigration & Nationality Law www.kerrylaw.com** ✎ **info@kerrylaw.com**

Legal Services

♀ ○ ♿ DiSalvo, Loraine M, Morgan & DiSalvo, PC, 5755 N Point Parkway Ste 17, Alpharetta; 30022 678-720-0750 www.morgandisalvo.com ✎ info@morgandisalvo.com

♀ ● ♿ Katz, Barbara, 3136 Clairmont Road NE; 30329 404-298-5050 www.bekatzlaw.com

♀ ○ ♿ **McGrath, Kerry E, 1100 Spring St NW Ste 760, Atl; 30309 404-377-6600 Immigration & Nationality Law www.kerrylaw.com** ✎ **info@kerrylaw.com**

♀ ● Womack, Kathleen, PC, 750 Hammond Dr Bldg 9 Ste 300, Atl; 404-303-0130 www.kwomacklaw.com

WOMEN
Georgia: Atlanta Area

WOMEN **15** WOMEN
GAYELLOW PAGES #42 2020-2021

WOMEN
Coeur d'Alene : Idaho

Organizations/Resources: Political/Legislative/Advocacy

♀ ☆ 9to5 Atlanta, 501 Pulliam St SW #344, Atl 404-222-0001 9to5.org/chapters/georgia/ ✕

Publishers/Publishing-related Services

♂ ● (?⛓) McWit Creative Works, 770-385-0007 **H?** www.mcwit.net ♥ info@mcwit.net

Real Estate (see also Mortgages)

♂ ● ♿ Carroll, Chris, Atlanta Intown Real Estate Servicesm 181 10th St NE, Atl; 30309 404-388-0023 404-881-1810 www.AtlantaEcoBroker.com ✕

Sports & Outdoor

♀ ☆ Atlanta Rollergirls, POB 8629, Atl; 31106 www.atlantarollergirls.com

♀ ☆ Women's Outdoor Network, www.wonatlanta.com

Cherry Log

Campgrounds and RV Parks

♀ ● Fox Mountain Camp & Artist Retreat, 350 Black Ankle Way; 30522 404-502-3538 Women's campground, men welcome as guests of women www.foxmtncamp.com ♣ foxmountaincamp@gmail.com

Lavonia

Health Care: Physical (see also Counseling/Mental Health)

♂ ● (?⛓) Payne, Patty, Reiki Master, PO Box 280; 30553 678-696-1787 706-356-1776 www.georgiahealing.com

Ringgold

Pets & Pet Services & Supplies

♂ ○ Classie Dawg Grooming, 6709 Hwy 41; 30736 706-937-2121 classiedawggrooming.com classiedawggrooming@gmail.com

Religious / Spiritual Resources

♂ ☆ Kingdom Seekers, 6735 Hwy 41; 30736 706-618-4732 tinyurl.com/ycw6exgb

Hawaii
Statewide/County Resources

Crisis, Anti-violence, & Helplines

♀ Sexual Assault Services, YWCA, 145 Ululani St, Hilo, HI 808-935-0677 tinyurl.com/l2qqxut

Hawaii (Big Island) before eruption

Accommodation: Hotels, Inns, Guesthouses, B&B, Resorts
Kalapana

♀ ● Sapphire Moon's Mermaid Palace, 12-7825 Kalapana Kapoho Beach Rd 808-965-1733 Sacred Space for Spiritual Women and Ho'omana Initiations www.greenfireproductions.com ✕ ⊗ ⊗ ♥

Volcano

♀ ● Kulana Goddess Sanctuary, POB 783, Volcano 96785 creative/spiritual retreat; mostly women but check ahead tinyurl.com/jojo573 ❂ (✿?) ✕ ⊗ ⊗ discoverkulana@yahoo.com

Organizations/Resources: Student, Academic, Education

♀ ☆ University of Hawaii Women's Center, 2600 Campus Rd. QLCSS #211, Hilo; 808-956-8059 **WC** tinyurl.com/yc88o7hn ✕

Maui

Health Care: Physical (see also Counseling/Mental Health)

♂ ● (?⛓) Maya, Lucia, Reiki Master, 808-866-8246 www.luminousadventures.com lucia@luminousadventures.com

Real Estate (see also Mortgages)

♂ ● Burton, Sylvia, 808-446-0256 MauiPropertiesBySylvia.com ✕

Oahu

Liquor & Wine Stores

♂ ● Speakeasy Productions, 1154 Fort St Mall Ste 206, Honolulu; 96813 808-721-1688 Bar Catering and Gifts tinyurl.com/y2c4s4lu

Sports & Outdoor

♀ ● Rainbow Sailing Charters, Kewalo Basin, 1125 Ala Moana Blvd, Honolulu; 96814 808-347-0235 tinyurl.com/32eblj

Weddings and Ceremonies

♂ ● A Rainbow in Paradise Weddings/Gay Wedding Planner, POB 64, Kailua; 96734-0064 808-372-0343 www.arainbowinparadise.com ♥ info@arainbowinparadise.com

Idaho
State/County Resources

Crisis, Anti-violence, & Helplines

♂ ☆ Idaho Coalition Against Sexual & Domestic Violence, 1402 W Grove St, Boise, ID 208-384-0419 idvsa.org

Boise

Counseling/Psychotherapy/Mental Health

♂ ○ ♿ Stewart, Jill, MA, LCPC, NCC, 1674 Hill Rd #12; 83702 208-890-8366 **H?** tinyurl.com/y8lnt4qw ✕

Health Care: Physical (see also Counseling/Mental Health)

♀ ○ ♿ Weyhrich, Darin, MD, 222 N 2nd St Ste 206; 208-342-2516 weyhrichobgyn.com

Coeur d'Alene

Counseling/Psychotherapy/Mental Health

♂ ○ ♿ Asbell, Laura, 17080 W Laura Ln, Post Falls 509-534-1731 www.asbellhealth.com ✕ ahs@asbellhealth.com

WOMEN
Idaho: Moscow

WOMEN **16** WOMEN
GAYELLOW PAGES #42 2020-2021

WOMEN
Indianapolis Area: Indiana

Moscow

Organizations/Resources: Student, Academic, Education

♀ ★ ♿ University of Idaho LGBTQA Office, 875 Perimeter Dr MS 2431, Moscow; 208-885-6583 www.uidaho.edu/lgbtqa ✎

♂ ☆ ♿ Women's Center, University of Idaho, MS 1064, 875 Perimeter Dr, Moscow; 208-885-2777 www.uidaho.edu/womenscenter ✎

Illinois
State/County Resources

Crisis, Anti-violence, & Helplines

♂ ☆ Illinois Coalition Against Sexual Assault, 100 N 16th St, Springfield, IL 217-753-4117 www.icasa.org

Champaign/Urbana Area

Organizations/Resources: Cultural, Dance, Performance

♀ ★ Amasong, c/o McKinley Foundation, 809 S 5th St, Champaign; 61820 www.amasong.org office@amasong.org

Chicago Area

Crisis, Anti-violence, & Helplines

♂ ☆ ♿ Anti-Violence Project, Center on Halsted, 3656 N Halsted, Chi; 773-472-6469 tinyurl.com/hlcejq2 ✎

♂ ☆ ♿ South Suburban Family Shelter, PO Box 937, Homewood; 60430 708-335-3028 (hotline) www.ssfs1.org

Accommodation: Hotels, Inns, Guesthouses, B&B, Resorts
Chicago

♀ ★ Athena's House: a women's residence, Chicago Urban Art Retreat Center, 1957 S Spaulding Ave, Chi; 60623-2616 773-542-9126 www.urbanartretreat.com ✎ ⊗ contact@urbanart retreat.com

AIDS/HIV Services, Education & Support

♀ ☆ ♿ Chicago Women's AIDS Project, 1815 E 71st St, Chi; 773-329-3941 cwapchicago.org

♀ ★ ♿ Howard Brown Health, 4025 N Sheridan Rd, Chi; 773-388-1600 howardbrown.org

Archives/Libraries/Museums/History Projects

♀ ★ Legacy Project Outdoor Museum Walk (Chicago), 312-608-1198 **H?** www.legacyprojectchicago.org ✪

Bars, Cafes, Clubs, Restaurants
Chicago

♂ ○ Joie de Vine, 1744 W Balmoral Ave, Chi 773-989-6846 tinyurl.com/y8x3oyte

Bookstores

♀ ● ♿ Women & Children First, 5233 N Clark St, Chi; 773-769-9299 tinyurl.com/2rmskv

Counseling/Psychotherapy/Mental Health

♂ ● Ritzman, Elizabeth, LCPC, 6832 W North Ave, Chi; 60707 312-815-9607 www.elizabethritzman.com elizabeth@elizabeth ritzman.com

♀ ● Sholl, Starla R, LCSW, PC, 5349 N Winthrop Ave #2, Chi; 60640-2309 773-878-5809 www.starlasholl.com

Health Care: Physical (see also Counseling/Mental Health)

♀ ☆ ♿ Chicago Women's Health Center, 1025 W Sunnyside Ave, Chi; 773-935-6126 Transgender welcome tinyurl.com/yufmrd

Legal Services

♀ ● (♿) Metz + Jones LLC, 5443 N Broadway #2-North, Chi; 60640-1703 773-878-4480 www.metzandjoneslaw.com ✎

♂ ● (♿) Yearwood & Associates, 636 S River Rd Ste 104, Des Plaines; 60016 847-824-0358 www.ellenyearwoodlaw.com

Organizations/Resources: Business & Professional Associations, Labor Advocacy

♀ ☆ Chicago Women In Trades, 2444 W 16th St Ste 3E, Chi; 312-942-1444 www.chicagowomenintrades.org

Organizations/Resources: Cultural, Dance, Performance

♀ ★ (♿) Artemis Singers, POB 578296, Chi; 60657-8296 773-764-4465 **H?** www.artemissingers.org info@artemissingers.org

Organizations/Resources: Ethnic, Multicultural

♀ ★ (♿) Affinity, 2850 S Wabash Ste 108, Chi; 773-324-0377 **H?** www.affinity95.org ♣

Organizations/Resources: Social, Recreation, Support

♀ Suburban Adventures, tinyurl.com/yax4hxa

Weddings and Ceremonies

♀ ○ Pine Manor, 401 S Pine St, Chi; 60602 847-873-7463 773-307-2128 samesexweddingvenue.com ✎ ♥ info@gaywedding chicagosite.com

Peoria

Counseling/Psychotherapy/Mental Health

♂ ○ ♿ Joy Miller & Associates, 7617 N Villa Wood Lane; 61614-1588 309-693-8200 www.joymiller.com ✎

Indiana
State/County Resources

Organizations/Resources: Social, Recreation, Support

♀ ★ (♿) Sappho's Network, sandlisa@sbcglobal.net

Indianapolis Area

Counseling/Psychotherapy/Mental Health

♂ ● ♿ O'Mara, Michele, LCSW, 2680 E Main St #121, Plainfield; 46168 317-517-0065 www.micheleomara.com ✎

WOMEN
Indiana: Indianapolis Area

WOMEN **17** WOMEN
GAYELLOW PAGES #42 2020-2021

WOMEN
Louisville : Kentucky

Legal Services

⚥ ● ⚢ Baird, Barbara J, 445 N Pennsylvania #401, Indpls; 317-637-2345 www.bjbairdlaw.com

♂ ● ⚢ Duvall, Lesa, Duvall & Fall, PC, 4911 E 56th St, Indpls; 46220 317-634-9100 www.duvallfall.com. ✗ lduvall@duvallfall.com

Organizations/Resources: Cultural, Dance, Performance

♀ ★ ⚢ Indianapolis Women's Chorus, 4550 Central Ave, Indpls; 46205 317-682-4946 indianapoliswomenschorus.org info@indianapoliswomenschorus.org

Iowa
State/County Resources

Organizations/Resources: Political/Legislative/Advocacy

♂ ☆ Iowa NOW, 3635 E 43rd Crt, Des Moines, IA 515-265-3193 www.iowanow.org

Ames

Organizations/Resources: Student, Academic, Education

♂ ☆ Margaret Sloss Center for Women and Gender Equity, Iowa State University, 203 Sloss House, 501 Farm House Lane 515-294-1020 sloss.dso.iastate.edu

Des Moines

Bars, Cafes, Clubs, Restaurants

♂ ● ⚢ Ritual Cafe, 1301 Locust St Ste D; 515-288-4872 www.ritualcafedsmiowa.net ✗

Counseling/Psychotherapy/Mental Health

♂ ○ (?⚥) Stewart-Sandusky, Shelly, 4725 Merle Hay Rd #205; 50322 515-528-8135 **H?** tinyurl.com/yxdwyl99 sandusky@sstherapyandconsulting.com

Organizations/Resources: Social, Recreation, Support

♀ ☆ (?⚥) Women's Cultural Collective, www.iowawcc.com iowawcc@gmail.com

Women's Centers

♀ ☆ Young Women's Resource Center, 818 5th Ave 515-244-4901 www.ywrc.org

Iowa City/Cedar Rapids/Marion Area

Women's Centers

♀ ☆ ⚢ Women's Resource & Action Center, 230 N Clinton St, Iowa City; 319-335-1486 wrac.uiowa.edu

Kansas
State/County Resources

Crisis, Anti-violence, & Helplines

⚥ ★ Kansas City Anti-Violence Project, 4050 Pennsylvania Ave Ste 135, Kansas City, MO 816-561-0550 www.kcavp.org

Lawrence

Crisis, Anti-violence, & Helplines

♀ ☆ ⚢ Sexual Trauma & Abuse Care Center, 708 W 9th St Ste 105; 785-843-8985 **H?** www.stacarecenter.org ✗

♀ ☆ The Willow Domestic Violence Center, POB 633 66044 800-770-3030 **H** www.willowdvcenter.org

Manhattan/Flint Hills

Organizations/Resources: Student, Academic, Education

♀ ☆ ⚢ Kansas State University Center for Advocacy, Response and Education (CARE), 207A/B Holton Hall, Manhattan 785-532-6444 www.k-state.edu/care/ ✗

Wichita

Crisis, Anti-violence, & Helplines

♀ Wichita Area Sexual Assault Center, 355 N Waco #100; 316-263-3002 www.wichitasac.com

♀ Wichita Family Crisis Center, 1111 N St Francis; 316-263-7501 tinyurl.com/y6usdt3q

Art & Photography (see also Graphic Design)

♂ ○ Images by Kelsy Gossett, 316-263-8500 www.imagesbykelsy.com kelsy@imagesbykelsy.com

Bars, Cafes, Clubs, Restaurants

⚥ Kirby's Beer Store, 3210 E Osie St 316-683-9781 kirbysbeerstore.com

Kentucky
Bowling Green

Counseling/Psychotherapy/Mental Health

♂ ○ Jones, Jessica, M.Ed. LPCC-S, NCC, Mapletree Mental Wellness, 1183 Kentucky St; 42101 270-282-2202 tinyurl.com/ryl6lhh jessicaj@mapletreemw.com

Lexington

Organizations/Resources: Social, Recreation, Support

♀ Lexington Lesbian Coffee House, fb.com/groups/LexLCH

Real Estate (see also Mortgages)

♂ ○ Combs, Teresa, ABR, GRI, QSC, 859-489-1150 859-276-4811 teresacombs.rhr.com teresasellsky@gmail.com

Louisville

Counseling/Psychotherapy/Mental Health

♂ ○ Heitzman, Judy C, PhD, LCSW, 1711 Bardstown Rd #102; 40205 502-608-2472 www.drjudyheitzman.com drjudyheitzman@gmail.com

Legal Services

♂ ● (?⚥) Diane Haag Law, 2241 State St Ste A PMB 240, New Albany, IN 47150 812-301-2155 fax 812-610-8259 **H?** Small business law dianehaaglaw.com admin@dianehaaglaw.com

WOMEN
Louisiana: Baton Rouge

WOMEN 18 WOMEN
GAYELLOW PAGES #42 2020-2021

WOMEN
Baltimore Area: Maryland

Louisiana
Baton Rouge

Grooming, Personal Care, Spa Services

♂ ● ⚥ Shear Illusions Hair Salon, 7942 Picardy Ave Ste A; 70809 225-757-9118 tinyurl.com/292ghc ✂ shear illusions_salon@yahoo.com

New Orleans Area

Information, Media & Publications

♀ Dykeadence, fb.com/dykeadence/

Accommodation: Communities, Intentional

♀ ☆ ⚥ Hagar's House, First Grace Community Alliance, 3401 Canal St, NO; 504-210-5064 Trans-inclusive www.HagarsHouseNOLA.org ✂

Archives/Libraries/Museums/History Projects

⚢ Last Call: New Orleans Dyke Bar History Project, 504-358-8654 www.lastcallnola.org

Organizations/Resources: Social, Recreation, Support

⚢ Girl Crush, www.xxcrush.com

Sports & Outdoor

♀ ☆ Big Easy Rollergirls, www.bigeasyrollergirls.com

Maine
Augusta

Legal Services

♀ ● (?⚥) Farnsworth, Susan, Esq, Farnsworth Law Office, 2 Beech St, Hallowell; / 100 2nd St 207-626-3312 www.susanfarnsworth.com

Bangor

Health Care: Physical (see also Counseling/Mental Health)

♀ ☆ Mabel Wadsworth Women's Health Center, 700 Mount Hope Ave #420; 800-948-5337 www.mabelwadsworth.org

Ogunquit Area

Accommodation: Hotels, Inns, Guesthouses, B&B, Resorts
Ogunquit

♀ ● Beauport Inn, POB 811, Ogunquit; 03907 / 339 Clay Hill/Agamenticus Rd 207-361-2400 www.beauportinn.com ✂ ☺ ☹ info@beauportinn.com

Bars, Cafes, Clubs, Restaurants
Ogunquit

♂ ○ Backyard Coffeehouse & Eatery, Rte 1, Ogunquit 207-251-4554 www.backyardogunquit.com ✕

⚢ ● ⚥ Women's T Dance at Maine Street, check schedule 207-646-5101 tinyurl.com/h62b8mp **DV**

Portland Area

Crisis, Anti-violence, & Helplines

♀ ☆ ⚥ Family Crisis Services, POB 704, Portland; 04104 800-537-6066 **H** www.familycrisis.org

♀ ☆ Sexual Assault Response Services of Southern Maine, POB 1371, Portland; 04104 800-871-7741 www.sarssm.org

Legal Services

♀ ○ Buchanan, Brenda M., 57 Exchange St #201, Portland; 04101-5000 207-772-1262 fax 207-772-1279 www.wacubu.com

Organizations/Resources: Cultural, Dance, Performance

♀ ☆ Women In Harmony, POB 8042, Portland; 04104 www.wihmaine.org

Stockton Springs

Accommodation Rental: Furnished / Vacation (& AirBNB)

♀ ● (?⚥) Cabin on the Ocean Cove, 2 W Eagle Way; 04981 330-414-0695 **H?** www.cabinontheoceancove.com ✂ ☺ ☹ cabinontheoceancove@gmail.com

Maryland
State/County Resources

Crisis, Anti-violence, & Helplines

♀ ☆ ⚥ House of Ruth Maryland, 2201 Argonne Dr, Baltimore, MD 410-889-RUTH (7884) **H?** www.hruth.org

Baltimore Area

Crisis, Anti-violence, & Helplines

♀ ☆ ⚥ Turnaround, 8503 LaSalle Rd flr 2, Towson; 21286 410-377-8111 443-279-0379 (helpline 24/7) **H?** Domestic violence, sexual assault and sex trafficking www.turnaroundinc.org info@turnaroundinc.org

Body Art

♀ ● Jacki Randall's Charm City Tattoo, 300 S Monroe St, Balt; 21223 410-566-7528 charmcitytattoo.com ta2jac@verizon.net

Counseling/Psychotherapy/Mental Health

⚢ ● Barb Elgin, LGBTQIA affirmative therapy and life coaching., 410-967-3848 www.barbelgin.com

♀ ● (?⚥) Brinkerhoff, Sara, MA, LCPC, LCDP, MAC, 4 North Ave, Ste 303B, Bel Air; 21014 410-457-7767 Substance abuse

♀ ○ ⚥ Broadbent, Janan, PhD, 2 Hamill Rd Ste 120, Balt; 21210 410-825-5577 **H?** drjanan.com drjanan@hush.com

♀ ☆ ⚥ Women's Growth Center, 5209 York Rd #B12, Balt; 410-532-2476 womensgrowthcenter.com

Organizations/Resources: Cultural, Dance, Performance

⚢ Charm City Kitty Club, Baltimore Theater Project, 45 W Preston St, Balt; 443-468-0102 charmcitykittyclub.com

WOMEN
Maryland: Baltimore Area

WOMEN **19** WOMEN
GAYELLOW PAGES #42 2020-2021

WOMEN
North Shore Area: Massachusetts

Organizations/Resources: Ethnic, Multicultural

⚲ Sistahs of Pride, GLCCB, 2530 N Charles St Flr 3, Balt; 410-777-8145 tinyurl.com/zqx35qp

Organizations/Resources: Student, Academic, Education

♂ ☆ University of Maryland Baltimore County Women's Center, The Commons, Room 004, 1000 Hilltop Circle, Balt; 410-455-2714 womenscenter.umbc.edu/

Sports & Outdoor

♀ Charm City Roller Girls, LLC, POB 19939, Balt; 21211 443-475-0088 www.charmcityrollergirls.com

Bethesda/Rockville Area

Accounting, Bookkeeping, Tax Services

♂ ● 👪 **CPA Connie, LLC, 15811 Crabbs Branch Way, Rockville; 20855 301-987-0048 www.cpaconnie.com** ✍ connie@cpaconnie.com

Frederick Area

Crisis, Anti-violence, & Helplines

♂ ☆ Heartly House, POB 857, Frederick; 21705 301-662-8800 www.heartlyhouse.org

Silver Spring

Counseling/Psychotherapy/Mental Health

♂ ○ (?👪) Riley, E. Anne, PhD, 3144 Gracefield Rd Apt T-19, Silver Spring; 301-273-2424 thetherapist.homestead.com

⚲ ● **Zeiger, Robyn S., PhD, LCPC, 10300 Sweetbriar Parkway, Silver Spring; 20903-1523 301-445-7333 Licensed Clinical Professional Counselor and Certified Imago Relationship Therapist www.drrobynzeiger.com** drrobynzeiger@aol.com

Legal Services

♂ ● 👪 Zavos Juncker Law Group PLLC, 8455 Colesville Rd Ste 1500, Silver Spring; 301-562-8220 **H?** www.zavosjunckerlawgroup.com ✍

Massachusetts
Boston Area

Crisis, Anti-violence, & Helplines

♂ ☆ 👪 Boston Area Rape Crisis Center, 99 Bishop Allen Dr, Cambridge; 800-841-8371 **H** www.barcc.org ✍

Bars, Cafes, Clubs, Restaurants
Boston

⚲ ● (?👪) Dyke Night, check event schedule www.kristenporterpresents.com **D** ✪

Counseling/Psychotherapy/Mental Health

♂ ○ Zoldan, Judi, 67 Leonard St #3, Belmont; 02478 617-484-5522 judizoldan@gmail.com

Health Care: Physical (see also Counseling/Mental Health)

♂ ○ 👪 Turnock, Elizabeth, MD, North End Waterfront Health, 332 Hanover St, Boston; 617-643-8000 northendwaterfronthealth.org

Legal Services

♂ ● (?👪) Kauffman, Joyce, Kauffman Law & Mediation, 4238 Washington St Ste 313, Roslindale; 02131 617-577-1505 fax 617-469-8440 www.kauffmanlaw.net ✍ joyce@kauffmanlaw.net

♂ ● Koffman & Dreyer, 324 Common St, Belmont 617-965-9525 **H?** www.koffmandreyer.com ✍

♂ ○ **Macy, Barbara J, 65A Atlantic Ave, Boston 02110 617-720-4005 Thoughtfully serving the GLBTQ community since 1985 www.barbarajmacy.com** bjm@macwein.com

Organizations/Resources: Bisexual Focus

⚲ ★ Boston Bisexual Women's Network, POB 301727, Jamaica Plain; 02130 www.biwomenboston.org biwomeneditor@gmail.com

Organizations/Resources: Cultural, Dance, Performance

♀ ☆ 👪 Voices Rising, POB 300476, Jamaica Plain; 02130 617-396-7086 www.voicesrising.org

Sports & Outdoor

♀ Boston Women's Flag Football League, www.bwffl.com

♀ ☆ Moving Violations Motorcycle Club, 16 Cummins Highway #14, Roslindale; 02131 www.movingviolationsmc.com info@movingviolationsmc.com

Women's Centers

♀ ★ (?👪) Women's Center, 46 Pleasant St, Cambridge; 617-354-8807 tinyurl.com/2jdbw5 ✍

Cape Cod & Islands

Weddings and Ceremonies

♂ ○ Weddings By Design, 142 Brier Lane, Brewster 02631 508-896-8121 www.weddingsbydesign.info ♥ brwstr@verizon.net

Merrimack Valley

Counseling/Psychotherapy/Mental Health

♂ ● 👪 Counts, Holly, PsyD, Life Transformations, LLC, POB 15, Newburyport; 01950 / 21 Pleasant St Ste 235 802-359-9139 tinyurl.com/y3zotwn4 ✍

North Shore Area

Organizations/Resources: Student, Academic, Education

♀ ☆ Salem State College Florence Luscomb Women's Center, Women Center Office, ECC211, 352 Lafayette St, Salem; 978-542-6555 tinyurl.com/y82zyhmr

Sports & Outdoor

♀ ☆ Boston Roller Derby, www.bostonrollerderby.com

WOMEN
Massachusetts: Provincetown Area

WOMEN **20** WOMEN
GAYELLOW PAGES #42 2020-2021

WOMEN
Flint : Michigan

Provincetown Area

Accommodation: Hotels, Inns, Guesthouses, B&B, Resorts
Provincetown

● Admiral's Landing, 158 Bradford St, Provincetown; 508-487-9665 www.admiralslanding.com ✓ ⊛

♂ ● Eben House, 90 Bradford St, Provincetown 508-487-0386 www.ebenhouse.com ✓ ⊛

♀ ● (♿) The Provincetown Hotel at Gabriel's, 102 Bradford St, Provincetown; 508-487-3232 www.provincetownhotel.com ✿ ✓ ⊛

♂ ● ♿ Rose & Crown Guest House, 158 Commercial st, Provincetown; 508-487-3332 www.roseandcrownptown.com ✿⊛

♀ ● Rose Acre, 5 Center St, Provincetown 508-487-2347 www.RoseAcreGuests.com ✓ ⊛

♀ ● Women Innkeepers of Provincetown, POB 573, Provincetown; 02657 www.womeninnkeepers.com

Accommodation Rental: Furnished / Vacation (& AirBNB)
Provincetown

● Bayshore, 493 Commercial St, Provincetown 508-487-9133 www.bayshorechandler.com

Bars, Cafes, Clubs, Restaurants
Provincetown

● ● Girl Power Events, www.provincetownforwomen.com ◎

Health Care: Physical (see also Counseling/Mental Health)

♀ ☆ Helping Our Women, 34 Conwell St, Provincetown; 508-487-4357 All women living with chronic, life threatening, or disabling illness on outer Cape Cod www.helpingourwomen.org ✓

Western MA/Berkshires

Crisis, Anti-violence, & Helplines

● ☆ ♿ Elizabeth Freeman Center LGBQT Services, 43 Francis Ave, Pittsfield; 01201 866-401-2425 413-499-2425 **H** tinyurl.com/o39bcsz info@elizabethfreemancenter.org

♂ ☆ ♿ Safe Passage,. Carlon Drive, Northampton; 888-345-5282 **H?** www.safepass.org ✓

Accommodation: Hotels, Inns, Guesthouses, B&B, Resorts
Adams

♂ ● ♿ Topia Inn, 10 Pleasant St, Adams; 413-743-9600 **H?** www.topiainn.com ✓ ⊛ ⊛

Shelburne Falls

♂ ○ Bird's Nest Bed & Breakfast, 2 Charlemont Rd, Buckland; 413-625-9523 Winner of the TripAdvisor Certificate of Excellence 2013-2018. All are welcome! www.birdsnestbnb.com ✓ ⊛

Women's Centers

♂ ☆ (♿) Center for Women & Community, New Africa House, 180 Infirmary Way, Amherst; 01003-9315 413-545-0883 www.umass.edu/cwc/ ◎ cwc@umass.edu

Michigan
State/County Resources

Information, Media & Publications

● ★ What Helen Heard, Ambitious Amazons, POB 811, East Lansing, MI 48826-0811 517-351-5257 fax 517-371-5200 What's Happening For Michigan Lesbians www.lconline.org LC@LConline.org

Ann Arbor/Ypsilanti Area

Bookstores

● ● ♿ Common Language Bookstore, 317 Braun Court, Ann Arbor; 734-663-0036 fax 734-994-1396 www.glbtbooks.com

♂ ○ (♿) Crazy Wisdom Bookstore & Tea Room, 114 S Main St, Ann Arbor; 734-665-2757 www.crazywisdom.net ☞

Counseling/Psychotherapy/Mental Health

♂ ○ Greene, Marge, LMSW LMFT, 2311 Shelby Ave Ste 106, Ann Arbor; 48103 734-668-8667

♂ ○ ♿ Samuel, Michelle, LLP, LCSW, ACSW, 1817 W Stadium BLVD Ste G, Ann Arbor; 734-926-9169 tinyurl.com/4ggk7to ✓

Legal Services

♂ ● ♿ Bassett, Jane, Bassett & Associates, PLLC, 2045 Hogback Rd, Ann Arbor; 734-930-9200 www.bassettlaw.com

Real Estate (see also Mortgages)

♂ ● ♿ Lombardini, Linda, Trillium Real Estate, 323 Braun Court, Ann Arbor; 48104 734-216-6415 **H** www.LindaLom.com Linda@TrilliumRealtors.com

Detroit Area

Counseling/Psychotherapy/Mental Health

♂ ● ♿ Caretto, Antonia, PhD, PLLC, 25882 Orchard Lake Rd Ste 201, Farmington Hills; 48336 248-553-9053 www.betreatedwell.com drcaretto@aol.com

Sports & Outdoor

♀ ☆ ♿ Detroit Derby Girls, Masonic Temple, 500 Temple St, Detroit www.detroitderbygirls.com

Empire

Accommodation: Hotels, Inns, Guesthouses, B&B, Resorts

♂ ● (♿) Duneswood, 7194 S Dune Hwy 231-668-6789 www.duneswood.com (✿?) ✓ ⊛

Flint

Counseling/Psychotherapy/Mental Health

♂ ● ♿ Wedda, Sue, MSW, LMSW, BCD, DCSW, 3549 S Dort Highway Ste 114; 810-742-7052

WOMEN
Michigan: Grand Rapids

WOMEN **21** WOMEN
GAYELLOW PAGES #42 2020-2021

WOMEN
State/County Resources : Mississippi

Grand Rapids

Organizations/Resources: Cultural, Dance, Performance

♀ ☆ Grand Rapids Women's Chorus, POB 68486 49516 grwc.org info@grwc.org

Sports & Outdoor

♀ Grand Raggidy Roller Girls, 616-752-8475 grandraggidy.com

Honor

Accommodation Rental: Furnished / Vacation (& AirBNB)

♀ ● ♿ Labrys Wilderness Resort, 231-882-5994 www.labryswoods.com (♣?) ⊗

Lansing Area

Organizations/Resources: Cultural, Dance, Performance

♀ ☆ Sistrum, POB 4191, E Lansing; 48826 www.sistrum.org

Macomb

Health Care: Physical (see also Counseling/Mental Health)

♀ ● ♿ Partridge Creek Obstetrics and Gynecology, 19991 Hall Rd Ste 105; 586-247-8609 www.partridgecreekobgyn.com

Marquette

Accommodation: Hotels, Inns, Guesthouses, B&B, Resorts

♂ ● Birchmont Motel, 2090 US 41 South; 877-458-7805 www.Birchmontmotel.com ♣ ♯ ⊗

Minnesota
Duluth/Superior Area

Bars, Cafes, Clubs, Restaurants
Duluth

♂ ● ♿ At Sara's Table: Chester Creek Cafe, 1902 E 8th St, Duluth; 218-724-6811 www.astccc.net ⅄ ✕ ⃠ ♯

Mankato

Crisis, Anti-violence, & Helplines

♂ ☆ ♿ Committee Against Domestic Abuse (CADA), POB 466; 56002 800-477-0466 507-625-8688 www.cadamn.org

Organizations/Resources: Student, Academic, Education

♀ ★ ♿ Women's Center at Minnesota State University, Mankato, 218 Centennial Student Union; 507-389-6146 www.mnsu.edu/wcenter/

Minneapolis/St Paul Area

Crisis, Anti-violence & Helplines

♂ ● ♿ Sexual Violence Center, 2021 E Hennepin Ave Ste 418, Mpls; 55413 612-871-5111 **H?** www.sexualviolencecenter.org ♯ info@sexualviolencecenter.org

Accounting, Bookkeeping, Tax Services

♂ ○ ♿ Palm, Karen R, CPA, CFP, CMA, 940 E Hennepin Ave, Mpls; 612-379-1393 www.palmkcpa.com ♯

Bars, Cafes, Clubs, Restaurants
Minneapolis

♂ ○ ♿ Barbette, 1600 W Lake St, Mpls 612-827-5710 www.barbette.com ⅄ ✕ ⃠ ♯

Bookstores

♂ ○ (?♿) Birchbark Books & Native Arts, 2115 W 21st St, Mpls; 612-374-4023 www.birchbarkbooks.com ♯

Counseling/Psychotherapy/Mental Health

♂ ● ♿ Ulbee, Maureen, MS, MSW, LICSW, 2446 University Ave W Ste 108, Mpls; 55414 651-209-2767 moulbee@hotmail.com

Health Care: Physical (see also Counseling/Mental Health)

♀ ○ ♿ Thorp, Deborah, MD, OB/GYN Care, Women's Center, 6500 Excelsior Blvd, Flr 5 HVC, St Louis Park; 55426 952-993-3282 **H?** www.parknicollet.com ♯

Legal Services

♂ ● Gaborsky, Kelli A, Gaborsky Law Office, LLC, 10 S 5th St Ste 1005, Mpls; 612-275-0169 Criminal defense www.gaborskylaw.com

Organizations/Resources: Cultural, Dance, Performance

♀ ★ Calliope Women's Chorus, POB 4474, St Paul 55104 www.Calliopewomenschorus.org

Organizations/Resources: Social, Recreation, Support

⚢ ★ Out To Brunch, POB 582682, Mpls 55458-2682 763-391-3449 www.outtobrunch.org outtobrunch1@gmail.com

Real Estate (see also Mortgages)

♂ ○ (?♿) RE/MAX Results, Shannon Lindstrom, REALTOR(R), AHWD, CRS, GREEN 748 Grand Ave, St Paul; 55105 612-616-9714 **H?** ShannonLindstromRealtor.com ♯ Shannon@ShannonLindstromRealtor.com

Women's Centers

♀ ☆ ♿ Harriet Tubman Center, 3111 1st Ave S, Mpls; 612-825-0000 www.tubman.org

Pine City / East Central Minnesota

Organizations/Resources: Social, Recreation, Support

⚢ East Central Purple Circle, ecpurplecircle.blogspot.com

Mississippi
State/County Resources

Reproductive Medicine & Fertility Services

♂ ○ Planned Parenthood of Tennessee and North Mississippi (PPTNM), 2430 Poplar Ave #100, Memphis, TN 38112 866-711-1717 tinyurl.com/y3qaqgf5 info@pptnm.org

WOMEN
Mississippi: Jackson

WOMEN 22 WOMEN
GAYELLOW PAGES #42 2020-2021

WOMEN
Missoula : Montana

Jackson

Bars, Cafes, Clubs, Restaurants

⚨ Metro 2001, 4670 Hwy 80 West; / Fri (ladies night) & Sat 601-259-0661 fb.com/MetroFridayNights/ **D** 🏠

Counseling/Psychotherapy/Mental Health

♀ ○ ♿ Weems, Julia L, LCSW, 200 Park Circle Dr, Flowood; 39232 601-933-1136 juliakweemslcsw@gmail.com

Erotica / Adult Stores / Safe Sex Supplies

♂ ○ Romantic Adventures, 175 Hwy 80 E, Pearl; 39208 601-932-2811 www.romanticadventures.com

Ocean Springs

Legal Services

♂ ○ Silin Law Firm PLLC, 1016 Robinson St; 39564 228-244-9987 www.silinlaw.com ✗ rita@silinlaw.com

Missouri
State/County Resources

Crisis, Anti-violence, & Helplines

⚨ ★ Kansas City Anti-Violence Project, 4050 Pennsylvania Ave Ste 135, Kansas City, MO 816-561-0550 www.kcavp.org

Columbia

Organizations/Resources: Student, Academic, Education

♀ ☆ University of Missouri Women's Center, G108 MU Student Center; 573-882-6621 womenscenter.missouri.edu

Kansas City Metro Area (MO & KS)

Crisis, Anti-violence, & Helplines

⚨ ★ Kansas City Anti-Violence Project, 4050 Pennsylvania Ave Ste 135, KC; 816-561-0550 www.kcavp.org

♂ ☆ Safe Home, 913-262-2868 www.safehome-ks.org

Counseling/Psychotherapy/Mental Health

⚨ ● ♿ Monroe, Megan, MSW, LSCSW, Country Club Plaza area 816-435-2829 www.meganmonroemsw.com mmonroemsw@gmail.com

Legal Services

♂ ○ Foley, Rachel Lynn, 4016 S Lynn Court #B, Independence; 64055 816-472-4357 www.kcbankruptcy.com clients@kcbankruptcy.com

Sports & Outdoor

♀ ☆ Kansas City Roller Warriors, POB 901383, KC; 64190 816-809-8496 www.kcrollerwarriors.com

St Louis Area (MO & IL)

Crisis, Anti-violence, & Helplines

♂ ☆ ALIVE (Alternatives To Living In Violent Environments), POB 28733, St Louis; 63146 800-941-9144 **H?** www.alivestl.org

♀ ☆ Safe Connections, 2165 Hampton Ave, St Louis 63139 314-531-2003 314-646-7500 www.safeconnections.org info@safeconnections.org

Bars, Cafes, Clubs, Restaurants
St Louis

⚨ Attitudes Nightclub, 4100 Manchester Ave, St Louis; 314-534-0044 fb.com/AttitudesNightclubSTL

Bookstores

♂ ● ♿ Left Bank Books, 399 N Euclid Ave, St Louis; 314-367-6731 www.left-bank.com ✗

Counseling/Psychotherapy/Mental Health

⚨ ● Betz, Cindy, MSW, LCSW, LGBT Counseling STL, 3115 Hampton Ave, St Louis; 63139 314-602-5534 www.lgbtcounsel-ingstl.com cbetzcounseling@gmail.com

♀ ○ Marshall, Michele, MSW., 1606 S Big Bend Blvd, St Louis; 314-645-1075

⚨ ● (?♿) Murrell, Pat, NA, MSW, St Louis metro area 314-973-1890 618-462-4051 tinyurl.com/2kv7pg ✗ mothersource@gmail.com

♂ ○ ♿ Pevnick, Linda, MSW, LCSW, 655 Craig Rd Ste 320, Creve Coeur; 314-567-5360 www.lindapevnickmsw.com

Legal Services

♀ ● (?♿) Wysack-Rood, Kathryn J., 3203A S Grand Blvd Ste A, St Louis; 63118 314-771-4494 618-791-8091 www.kathywysack.com kathy@kathywysack.com

♂ ● (?♿) Zarembka, Arlene, 9378 Olive Blvd #206, St Louis; 63132 / Missouri clients only 314-567-6355 Probate www.zarem-bkalaw.justia.net arlenezarembkalaw@sbcglobal.net

Organizations/Resources: Cultural, Dance, Performance

♀ ☆ CHARIS: St Louis Women's Chorus, POB 21624, St Louis; 63104 314-664-9340 www.charischorus.org

Montana
Bozeman

Organizations/Resources: Student, Academic, Education

♀ ● ♿ Montana State University Women's Center, 372 Strand Union Building; 59717 406-994-3836 www.mon-tana.edu/wwwwomen

Missoula

Organizations/Resources: Student, Academic, Education

♀ ☆ Women's Resource Center, University Of Montana, UC 210; 406-243-4153 tinyurl.com/y4v8fdq8

Real Estate (see also Mortgages)

♂ ○ ♿ Portico Real Estate, K D, 445 W Alder; 59802 406-240-5227 www.porticorealestate.com ✗ kd@porticorealestate.com

Nebraska
Lincoln

Crisis, Anti-violence, & Helplines

♀ ☆ Friendship Home, POB 85358; 68501 402-437-9302 www.friendshiphome.org

♀ ☆ Voices of Hope, 2545 N St; 402-475-7273 www.voicesofhope-lincoln.org

Counseling/Psychotherapy/Mental Health

♂ ○ ♿ Furr, Gina, PhD, 1919 S 40th St Ste 111; 402-617-7237 www.drginafurr.com

♀ ○ Wellman, Carrie Ann, 1701 S 17th St Ste #1C 402-560-4683

Counseling/Psychiatry

♂ ○ ♿ Dohrman, Heather, MA, LIMHP, 3701 Union Dr Ste 100; 68516 402-875-9270 www.cheneypsych.com hdohrman@cheneypsych.com

Legal Services

♂ ○ ♂ Mary Kay Hansen Law and Mediation, PC LLO, 1101 Cornhusker Hwy Ste 201; 68521 402-477-0230 **H?** mkhansenlaw.com ✗ marykay@mkhansenlaw.com

Real Estate (see also Mortgages)

♂ ○ Keck, Victoria, Realtor, Team Victory at Nebraska Realty, 6301 S 58th St; 68516 402-730-4878 victoriamkeck@gmail.com

Nevada
State/County Resources

Organizations/Resources: Political/Legislative/Advocacy

♀ ☆ Nevada Women's Lobby, POB 5565, Reno, NV 89513 www.nevadawomenslobby.org

Las Vegas Area

Crisis, Anti-violence, & Helplines

♂ ☆ Rape Crisis Center, 801 S Rancho Ste B-2, LV 888-366-1640 www.rcclv.org

Information, Media & Publications

♀ Lesbians in Vegas, fb.com/lezinvegas/

Accounting, Bookkeeping, Tax Services

♂ ● ♿ Stout, Brenda, CPA, 5836 S Pecos Rd Ste 104, LV; 89120 702-736-0992 Tax debt resolution, IRS Nonprofit compliance www.brendastoutcpa.com ✗ brenda@brendastoutcpa.com

Bars, Cafes, Clubs, Restaurants
Las Vegas

♂ ● ♿ Freezone, 610 E Naples Dr, LV; 702-794-2300 www.freezonelv.com **D** Ⴤ ✗ ▦

Bookstores

♂ ● ♂ Get Booked, 4640 Paradise Rd #15, LV; 702-737-7780 getbooked.com

Health Care: Physical (see also Counseling/Mental Health)

♂ ○ (?♿) AAA Wuxin Healing Arts, Fiona Kelley, OMD 2920 N Green Valley Pkwy Ste 723, Henderson; 89014 702-369-3406 www.acupuncturelasvegas.com ✗ drkelley@acupuncture lasvegas.com

♂ ○ (?♿) Kelley, Fiona, OMD, 2920 N Green Valley Parkway Ste 723, Henderson; 89014 702-369-3406 www.acupuncturelasvegas.com drkelley@acupuncturelasvegas.com

Organizations/Resources: Social, Recreation, Support

♀ ★ Betty's Outrageous Adventures, 702-636-8552 www.bettysout.com

Organizations/Resources: Student, Academic, Education

♀ ☆ University of Nevada Jean Nidetch Women's Center, Box 452025, 4505 Maryland Parkway, LV; 702-895-4475 tinyurl.com/oqd237r

Real Estate (see also Mortgages)

♂ ○ **Liz Thompson, Desert Realty, 3160 W Sahara Ave #A22; 89102 702-876-0098 Email: liz@realtysales.estate For all your residential & commercial needs. Your family Realtor, since 1985. www.desert-realty.com liz@realtysales.estate**

♂ ● ♿ Margolin, Sandy, Urban Nest Realty, 10220 W Charleston Blvd #3, LV; 89135 702-683-3362 **HS** SandyMargolin.com Realtrchik@gmail.com

Travel & Tourist Services (see also Accommodation)

♂ ○ (?♿) Adventure Photo Tours, 3111 S Valley View Blvd #X-106, LV; 89102 702-889-8687 888-363-8687 www.adventurephototours.com

Reno

Counseling/Psychotherapy/Mental Health

♂ ○ Jackson, Karen, LCSW, 1325 Airmotive Way Ste 175; 89502 775-786-1179 www.karenjacksontherapy.com karen@karenjacksontherapy.com

New Hampshire
State/County Resources

Weddings and Ceremonies

♂ ○ Siebert, Carol, JP, 603-494-7586 ♥ jotp2008@yahoo.com

Concord

Counseling/Psychotherapy/Mental Health

♂ ★ (?♿) Womankind Counseling Center, 21 Green St; 603-225-2985 womankindcounseling.webs.com

Health Care: Physical (see also Counseling/Mental Health)

♂ ☆ (?♿) Equality Health Center, 38 S Main St; 603-225-2739 equalityhc.org

WOMEN
New Hampshire: Lebanon

WOMEN **24** WOMEN
GAYELLOW PAGES #42 2020-2021

WOMEN
Morristown Area : New Jersey

Lebanon

Crisis, Anti-violence, & Helplines

♀ ☆ ☺☺ Women's Information Service (WISE), 38 Bank St; 03766 866-348-9473 **H** www.wiseuv.org

Portsmouth

Health Care: Physical (see also Counseling/Mental Health)

♀ ☆ (♋) The Joan G Lovering Health Center, POB 456, Greenland; 03840 / 559 Portsmouth Ave 603-436-7588 **H?** www.jglhc.org

Organizations/Resources: Cultural, Dance, Performance

☺ ☺☺ Women Singing Out!, POB 1553; 03802 tinyurl.com/t69cqoc

White Mountains Area

Accommodation: Hotels, Inns, Guesthouses, B&B, Resorts
Bethlehem

☺ ● (♋) The Highlands Inn, POB 118GP, Bethlehem; 03574 603-869-3978 www.highlandsinn-nh.com (♣?) ✗ ⊛ ♥

New Jersey
State/County Resources

Crisis, Anti-violence, & Helplines

♂ ☆ (♋) 180 Turning Lives Around Inc., 1 Bethany Rd Bldg 3 #42, Hazlet, NJ 888-843-4262 **HD** 180nj.org

♀ New Jersey Coalition to End Domestic Violence, 1670 Whitehorse-Hamilton Square Rd, Trenton, NJ 800-572-7233 www.njcedv.org

Insurance (see also Financial Planning)

♀ ● Shrem, Eileen, RHU, CLTC, LUTCF, 215 McCabe Ave #C1, Bradley Beach, NJ 732-988-7256 fax 732-988-3009 tinyurl.com/y83w7w78

Security & Investigation Services

♂ ● Martinez Security & Investigations, LLC, POB 2286, Trenton, NJ 08629 609-424-7949

Berlin

Legal Services

♀ ● (♋) Law Offices of Kristine W. Holt, 339 Rte 73 N; 08009 856-599-5555 Bankruptcy; transgender issues www.HoltEsq.com

Eatontown

Legal Services

♀ ○ ☺☺ Posnock, Leslie B, Schwartz and Posnock, 99 Corbett Way Ste 203, Eatontown; 07724 / offices Livingston, East Brunswick and Linden 732-544-1460 www.schwartzposnock.com ✗

Hazlet

Legal Services

♀ ● ☺☺ Wernik & Salvatore, Robin T, Esq., 34 Village Ct; 07730-1534 732-888-3338 For caring, committed and comprehensive guidance on any family law matter. www.robinwernik.com

Jersey City

Counseling/Psychotherapy/Mental Health

☺ ● ☺☺ Institute for Personal Growth, Offices in Highland Park, Freehold and Jersey City 800-379-9220 **H?** Providing psychotherapy, relationship counseling and sex therapy to our community. www.ipgcounseling.com

Jersey Shore

Counseling/Psychotherapy/Mental Health

☺ ● ☺☺ Institute for Personal Growth, Offices in Highland Park, Freehold and Jersey City 800-379-9220 **H?** Providing psychotherapy, relationship counseling and sex therapy to our community. www.ipgcounseling.com

Mahwah

Organizations/Resources: Student, Academic, Education

♀ ☆ Ramapo College of New Jersey Women's Center, 505 Ramapo Valley Rd #C-Wing 220; 201-684-7468 www.ramapo.edu/womenscenter/

Metuchen

Websites: Design & Maintenance Services (see also Internet)

♂ ● Pressing Issues, Inc., POB 224; 08840-0224 732-549-9054 www.pressingissues.com info@pressingissues.com

Milltown

Legal Services

♂ ● Lozito Law LLC, 187-189 N Main St; 08850 848-202-1650 lozitolaw.com ✗ lozito@lozitolaw.com

Morristown Area

Counseling/Psychotherapy/Mental Health

♀ ○ ☺☺ Vlazny, Maggie, MSW, LCSW, GAT. LLC, 973-236-0020 www.florhamparkcounsleing.com maggievlazny@gmail.com

WOMEN
New Jersey: Mount Holly

WOMEN **25** WOMEN
GAYELLOW PAGES #42 2020-2021

WOMEN
Albuquerque : New Mexico

Mount Holly

Legal Services

♂ • (?⚥) Shreter, Stephanie, 105 High St #1; 08060 609-265-9600 Bankruptcy thebankruptcycounselor.com sshreter@comcast.net

New Brunswick Area

Counseling/Psychotherapy/Mental Health

⚥ • ⚤ Institute for Personal Growth, Offices in Highland Park, Freehold and Jersey City 800-379-9220 **H?** Providing psychotherapy, relationship counseling and sex therapy to our community. www.ipgcounseling.com

Newark/Montclair Area

Counseling/Psychotherapy/Mental Health

♂ • (?⚥) Boyer, Carol A, MA, LPC, NCC, 50 Church St Ste L3, Montclair; 07042 973-493-8006 www.carolboyerlpc.com carolboyerlpc@gmail.com

⚥ • ⚤ Koempel, Stephanie, MA, LPC, LCADC, 2115 Millburn Ave 908-581-5681 tinyurl.com/yd8vnmgu

⚥ • Maplewood Counseling Services, 973-902-8700 MaplewoodCounseling.com

Oceanport

Counseling/Psychotherapy/Mental Health

♂ • ⚤ Bradley, Carolyn A, PhD, LCSW, LCADC, 108 Main St Ste 5; 07757 732-768-5781

Piscataway

Legal Services

♂ ○ ⚤ Law Office of Jennifer Marshall. LLC, 200 Centennial Ave Ste 101; 732-412-3737 www.jlmarshallesq.com @ixx=

Princeton Area

Women's Centers

♀ Princeton University Women's Center, 33 Frist Campus Center Room 243, Princeton; 609-258-5565 www.princeton.edu/~womenctr/

Somerville

Legal Services

♂ ○ (?⚥) **Gargano, Francine A., Esq, 34 E Main St; 08876 908-753-2079 fax 908-755-3586 A General Practice for the Gay, Lesbian and Transgender Community and Their Families.** garganof@msn.com

Southern Shore of NJ

Accommodation Rental: Furnished / Vacation (& AirBNB)
Cape May

♂ • Antoinette's Apartments & Suites, 717 Washington St, Cape May; 08204-2330 609-898-0502 www.antoinettescapemay.com ⚲ ⊛

New Mexico
Albuquerque

Crisis, Anti-violence, & Helplines

♂ ☆ Rape Crisis Center of Central New Mexico, 9741 Candelaria NE; 505-266-7711 www.rapecrisiscnm.org

Counseling/Psychotherapy/Mental Health

♂ ○ (?⚥) Johnson, Lisa, PhD, LMFT, 505-288-2162 lisa-johnsonlmft.com

Erotica / Adult Stores / Safe Sex Supplies

♂ • Self Serve Toys, 112 Morningside Dr NE; 87108 505-265-5815 www.selfservetoys.com ⚲ info@selfservetoys.com

Organizations/Resources: Cultural, Dance, Performance

♀ ☆ New Mexico Women's Chorus, 215 Locust St NE 505-750-3038 www.nmwomenschorus.org

Organizations/Resources: Student, Academic, Education

♂ ☆ ⚤ UNM Women's Resource Center, MSC06 3910, #1 UNM; / Mesa Vista Hall Room 1160 505-277-3716 **H?** women.unm.edu ⚲

Public Relations/Advertising/Marketing

♂ • ⚤ Graphicbliss Branding Agency, 4200 Silver Ave SE Ste C; 87108 505-299-0713 Branding agenyc www.gblissdesigns.com ⚲ graphicblissgd@gmail.com

Real Estate (see also Mortgages)

♂ • Talia Freedman and Co, 4116 Lomas Blvd NE 505-263-7892 **H?** www.abq-realty.com

WOMEN
New Mexico: Ramah

WOMEN **26** WOMEN
GAYELLOW PAGES #42 2020-2021

WOMEN
Hudson Valley & Catskills Area : New York

Ramah

Campgrounds and RV Parks

⚥ ● (♿) El Morro RV Park & Cabins, Sharron, HC 61 Box 44; 87321-9603 505-783-4612 www.elmorro-nm.com ✿ ✘ ⊗ elmorrorv@gmail.com

Santa Fe/Pecos/Tesuque Area

Crisis, Anti-violence, & Helplines

⚥ ☆ ♿ Solace Crisis Treatment Center, 6601 Valentine Way, SFe; 505-988-1951 **H?** www.findsolace.org

Accommodation: Hotels, Inns, Guesthouses, B&B, Resorts
Serafina

♀ ● (♿) New Mexico Women's Guest House Retreat & Healing Center, POB 130, Serafina; 87569 575-421-2533 www.NMWomensRetreat.org ✘ ⊗

Real Estate (see also Mortgages)

⚥ ● ♿ Orth, Susan, Realtor, City Different Realty 518 Old Santa Fe Trail #190, SFe; 87505 505-216-6688 www.susaninsantafe.com ✘ SantaFe@SusanOrth.com

Taos

Crisis, Anti-violence, & Helplines

⚥ ☆ Community Against Violence, POB 169; 87571 575-758-8082 www.taoscav.org

New York
Albany & Capital Area

Accommodation: Hotels, Inns, Guesthouses, B&B, Resorts
Saratoga Springs

⚥ ● Saratoga Farmstead B&B, 41 Locust Grove Rd, Saratoga Springs; 12866-9108 518-587-2074 www.saratogafarmstead.com ✘ ⊗ saratogafarmstead@gmail.com

Legal Services

⚥ ○ ♿ Copps DiPaola, Kathleen ("Casey"), Copps DiPaola Silverman, PLLC, 126 State St, Albany; 518-436-4170 **H?** www.thecdslawfirm.com ✘

Binghamton

Crisis, Anti-violence, & Helplines

⚥ ☆ ♿ A New Hope Center, 20 Church Street, Owego; 800-696-7600 **H?** www.anewhopecenter.org ✘

Buffalo/Niagara Falls Area

Counseling/Psychotherapy/Mental Health

⚥ ○ Urdang, Nicole, MS, NCC, DHM, 650 Lafayette Ave, Buffalo; 14222-1436 716-882-0848 tinyurl.com/9gyu84y info@nicoleurdang.com

Sports & Outdoor

♀ ☆ Queen City Roller Girls, POB 225, Buffalo 14205 888-740-7274 www.qcrg.net

Hudson Valley & Catskills Area

Crisis, Anti-violence, & Helplines

⚥ My Sisters' Place, 1 Water St 3rd Flr, White Plains; 800-298-7233 www.mspny.org

⚥ ☆ Putnam/Northern Westchester Women's Resource Center, 935 South Lake Blvd Ste 2, Mahopac; 845-628-2166 Northern Westchester, Putnam & lower Dutchess counties www.pnwwrc.org

⚥ Women's Justice Center, Pace Law School, 27 Crane Ave, White Plains; 914-287-0739 www.law.pace.edu/wjc

Art & Craft Galleries/Services, Supplies

⚥ ○ Knitting Nation, 30 N Broadway, Nyack 845-348-0100 www.knittingnation.com

Counseling/Psychotherapy/Mental Health

⚥ ● Greenman, Janet, LCSW-R POB 602, Hopewell Junction; 12533 845-227-0161 jvgreenman@aol.com

⚥ ○ Shuman, Randee, LCSWR, 55 Old Turnpike Rd Ste 206, Nanuet; 10954 845-708-0143 www.randeeshuman.com rlynne345@aol.com

Counseling/Psychiatry

⚥ ○ Lovrin, Mellen, DNP, Psychiatric Nurse Practitioner, 50 Piermont Ave, Nyack; 845-353-6780

Financial Planning, Investment (see also Insurance)

⚥ ● Third Eye Associates, Ltd, 38 Spring Lake Rd, Red Hook; 12571 845-752-2216 www.thirdeyeassociates.com bjones@thirdeyeassociates.com

Gifts, Cards, Pride, etc.

⚥ ○ ♿ Dreaming Goddess, 44 Raymond Ave, Poughkeepsie; 12603 845-473-2206 **H?** DreamingGoddess.com ✘ info@DreamingGoddess.com

Insurance (see also Financial Planning)

⚥ ○ ♿ McGuinness, Debbie, State Farm Insurance, 75 Lake Rd Ste C & D, Congers; 10920-2323 845-267-2900 www.debbiemcguinness.com ✘ debbie@debbiemcguinness.com

Legal Services

⚥ ○ (♿) Law & Mediation Offices of Carolyn M. Laredo, PLLC, 28 New Hempstead Rd Ste A, New City; 10956 845-639-1836 **H?** Divorce services www.lawmediationny.com ✘

Organizations/Resources: Senior Resources

⚨ ★ Old Lesbians Organizing for Change (OLOC-HV) - Hudson Valley, meets at Hudson Valley LGBTQ Community Center 845-679-7586 www.oloc.org

Organizations/Resources: Social, Recreation, Support

⚨ ★ (♿) The Link, POB 505, Nyack 10960 / Hudson Valley & Northern NJ linkmembers@gmail.com

Real Estate (see also Mortgages)

⚥ ● Mordica, Kristi, Gay Broker, Welch Realty, PO Box 833, Kerhonkson; 12446 661-607-6559 welchrealtyny.com

WOMEN
New York: Hudson Valley & Catskills Area

WOMEN **27** WOMEN
GAYELLOW PAGES #42 2020-2021

WOMEN
New York City & Long Island Area: New York

♂ ○ ♿ Silverberg, Diane B., Lic Assoc RE Broker, CRS, ABR, Westwood Metes & Bounds Realty, Main St. (Rte 209) 845-750-0744 845-687-0232 x109 www.buyfromdi.com ✗ dsilverberg@bhhshudsonvalley.com

Ithaca

Organizations/Resources: Student, Academic, Education

♀ ☆ Cornell University Women's Resource Center, 209 Willard Straight Hall Mailbox 71; 607-255-0015 tinyurl.com/ybxxbpx8

New York City & Long Island Area

Crisis, Anti-violence, & Helplines

♂ ☆ The Center for Anti-Violence Education, 327 7th St Flr 2, Bklyn; 718-788-1775 All women, girls, trans-adults and trans-youth www.caeny.org

♀ Connect, 127 W 127th St Ste 431; 212-683-0015 www.connect-nyc.org

♀ Joyful Heart Foundation, 212-475-2026 tinyurl.com/d7qmpu

♀ ● ♿ New York City Anti-Violence Project, 116 Nassau St 3rd Flr; 212-714-1141 www.avp.org

♀ ☆ Safe Horizon, Victim Services Agency, 2 Lafayette St 3rd Flr; 800-621-4673 www.safehorizon.org

♀ ☆ Sanctuary for Families, POB 1406 Wall St Stn; 10268 212-349-6009 www.sanctuaryforfamilies.org

Community Centers and/or Pride Organizations
Manhattan

♀ ★ New York City Dyke March, www.nycdykemarch.com

Information, Media & Publications

♀ ● Gayellow Pages, POB 533 Village Stn 10014-0533 646-213-0263 v/f Classified directory of services, businesses, resources, etc in USA & Canada. Mailing lists available. www.gayellowpages.com gypages@gmail.com

Accommodation Rental: Furnished / Vacation (& AirBNB)
Manhattan

♂ ○ A Garden In Chelsea, 439 W 22nd St; 10011-2512 212-243-8621 www.agardeninchelsea.com ✗ ⊘

Accounting, Bookkeeping, Tax Services
Queens

♂ ● BGS Services, Inc., 718-459-3690 www.bgsservices.com

AIDS/HIV Services, Education & Support
Manhattan & Citywide

♀ ☆ SMART/Smart University, East Harlem Neighborhood Health Action Center, 158 E 115th St; 10029 212-289-3900 www.smartuniversity.org info@smartuniversity.org

Archives/Libraries/Museums/History Projects

♀ ★ ♿ Lesbian Herstory Archives/Lesbian Herstory Educational Foundation, Inc, 484 14th St, Bklyn 718-768-3953 Lesbian history and cultural resource center. Please check on line for info on how to contact or visit. www.lesbianherstoryarchives.org ✗

Bars, Cafes, Clubs, Restaurants
Brooklyn: DUMBO

♂ ○ Superfine, 126 Front St, Bklyn; 718-243-9005 www.superfine.nyc ♈ ✗ iheartsuperfine@gmail.com

Brooklyn: Park Slope

♀ ● Ginger's Bar, 363 5th Ave, Bklyn 718-788-0924 fb.com/Gingersbar/ **DK** ✗

Manhattan & Citywide

♀ A Different Kind of Ladies' Night, tinyurl.com/j58dhs9

♀ ● girlNATIONnyc, check for details www.girlnation-nyc.com ♈ ✗ girlnationnyc1@aol.com

♀ ● Lovergirl, Sat, check details 212-252-3397 www.lovergirlnyc.com **D** ✪

Manhattan: West Village

♂ ● Cubby Hole, 281 W 12th St (at 4th St) 212-243-9041 www.cubbyholebar.com

♀ ● ♿ Henrietta Hudson, 438 Hudson St; (Morton St) 212-924-3347 www.henriettahudson.com ✗

♀ ● Pure Silk Productions, 516-474-1707 tinyurl.com/yybnvdk2 puresilkproductions@gmail.com

Bookstores
Manhattan

♂ ● ♿ Bluestockings Bookstore & Activist Center, 172 Allen St; (Rivington & Stanton St) 212-777-6028 bluestockings.com ☞

♀ ● ♿ **Bureau of General Services-Queer Division, LGBT Community Center, 208 W 13th St Rm 210 10011-7702 646-457-0859 H?** Tue-Sun 1-7pm **www.bgsqd.com contact@bgsqd.com**

♂ ○ Three Lives & Company, 154 W 10th St 212-741-2069 www.threelives.com

Queens

♂ ● ♿ Astoria Bookshop, 31-29 31st Street, Astoria; 718-278-2665 www.astoriabookshop.com

Counseling/Psychotherapy/Mental Health
Brooklyn

♀ ● Geier, Patti, LCSW, Park Slope 347-262-0905 www.pattigeier.com

T ○ Juran, Shelley, PhD, 163 Clinton St, Brooklyn Heights 718-625-6526 Specialist in sexual orientation & gender-identity. Non-sexist. Gay & transgender individuals & couples welcome. www.brooklyntherapist.org

♂ ● Goldstein, Nancy R, LCSW, 12 Deering St, E Setauket; 11733 631-941-4704 www.nancygoldstein.net ✗ nancygoldstein1@gmail.com

Long Island

♂ ● Dyer, Theresa M, LCSW-R, 137 Bay Ave, Patchogue; 11772 631 553-5212 tmdlcsw@gmail.com

♀ ● ♿ Heart & Soul Counseling, 17 Fordham Rd, W Babylon; 11704-5803 / 1400 Wantagh Ave Wantagh NY 631-321-7011 fax 631-669-8532 www.heartandsoulcenter.com heartsoul@att.net

♂ ○ &. Kranenberg, Laura Ann, LCSW, 2175 Wantagh Ave, Wantagh; 11793 516-319-7896 Laurakranenberglcsw.com laura@laurakranenberglcsw.com

♀ ○ Shapiro, Joan E, LCSW, BCD, 177 Main St #207, Huntington; / 153 Main St, Roslyn 631-271-4037 www.talkpsychotherapy.com

Manhattan

♂ ● &. Cipriani, Maria, LCSW, 19 W 34th St, PH and in Kings Park, LI 212-594-4659 www.mariacipriani.com maria.cipriani@gmail.com

♂ ● (?&.) Davies, Ann C., LCSW, 740 West End Ave Ste 1 (96 & WEA) 917-923-2257

♂ ○ Frank, Michele, LCSW-R, 19 W 34th St #PH; 10001 212-947-7111 x255 www.MicheleFrank.com helper50@gmail.com

♀ ○ Frankel, Susan, LCSW, BCD, CGP, 365 West End Ave 11J; 10024 212-866-5756 tinyurl.com/ydmzkav susanif@verizon.net

♂ ● (?&.) **Gringorten, Judith, LCSW, ACSW, CGP, Psychotherapy and Training Collective of New York, 853 Broadway Ste 1608 10003 845-709-1939 Individual, Couples, Family, Group (short & long-term) www.psychotherapistsnyc.com judithgringorten@gmail.com**

♀ ● The IHI Therapy Center, 322 8th Ave Ste 802 212-243-2830 www.ihitherapy.org

♂ ● &. Kaplan, Ami B, LCSW, 113 University Place Ste #1008; 10003 212-358-1884 www.amikaplan.net info@amikaplan.net

♀ ● Manhattan Psychotherapy, Upper West Side 212-724-8767 call 10am-noon tinyurl.com/y5sydack

Counseling/Psychiatry
Long Island

♂ ● &. Rubinstein, Joan, MD, 60 N Country Rd Ste 104, Port Jefferson; 11777-2188 631-331-0974 joan.rubinstein27@gmail.com

Dentists
Manhattan

♂ ○ Cauntiz, Beth, DDS, 30 E 40th St Ste 406; 10016 212-206-9002 www.bethcaunitzdds.com caunitzdds@gmail.com

Financial Planning, Investment (see also Insurance)

♂ ● Third Eye Associates, Ltd, 745 Fifth Ave Ste 500; 10151 212-787-4292 www.thirdeyeassociates.com

Funding: Endowment, Fundraising

♀ ★ &. ASTRAEA Lesbian Foundation for Justice, 116 E 16th St 7th flr; 212-529-8021 www.astraeafoundation.org ✛

♀ ★ & Bee's Fund, Stonewall Community Foundation, 1270 Broadway Ste 501; 212-457-1341 **H?** Small grants for LBT women discarded by their families. tinyurl.com/yxcnccom ✗

♀ ★ **North Fork Women For Women Fund, Inc., POB 804, Greenport; 11944-0924 631-477-8464 Helping lesbians on the North Fork for over 25 years. www.nfwfwf.org**

Health Care: Physical (see also Counseling/Mental Health)
Brooklyn

♀ Caribbean Women's Health Association, 3512 Church Ave, Bklyn; 718-826-2942 www.cwha.org ✛

Manhattan

♂ ● Greenberg, Elizabeth, DC, 89 5th Ave #604; 10003 212-627-2660

♂ ○ Physical Exam NYC, 1550 York Ave; 212-960-8643 www.physicalexamnyc.com

♀ ● Repetto, Vittoria, DC, 230 W 13th St; 10011 212-431-3724 www.drvittoriarepetto.com DrVittoriaRepett@aol.com

Organizations/Resources: Cultural, Dance, Performance

♀ ★ (?&.) WOW Cafe Theatre, 59 E 4th St #4W; 917-725-1482 **H?** www.wowcafe.org ✗

Organizations/Resources: Ethnic, Multicultural

♀ ★ (?&.) African Ancestral Lesbians United for Societal Change, Inc., LGBT Community Center, 208 W 13th St 475-422-5872 **H?** fb.com/AALUSC1974 ✛ ✗

♀ ★ Q-Wave, POB 1896; 10013 fb.com/groups/qwave/ ✧

Organizations/Resources: Sexual Focus / Safe Sex
Manhattan & Citywide

♀ ★ (?&.) Lesbian Sex Mafia, LGBT Community Center, 208 W 13th St; 10011 646-450-0576 **H?** www.lesbiansexmafia.org ✗ lesbiansexmafia@gmail.com

Organizations/Resources: Social, Recreation, Support
Manhattan & Citywide

♀ ★ &. Butch/Femme Society, POB 750652, Forest Hills; 11375 347-709-0561 tinyurl.com/24r7pb

Manhattan

♀ Lezervations New York, - - lezervations.com

Organizations/Resources: Student, Academic, Education
Brooklyn

♀ ☆ CUNY Brooklyn College Women's Center, 227 New Ingersoll Hall, 2900 Bedford Ave, Bklyn; 718-951-5777 tinyurl.com/tnzvrqk

Organizations/Resources: Transgender/Gender Non-Conforming/Diverse
Manhattan & Citywide

T ● Kaufman, Randi, PsyD, 113 University Pl; 10003 212-979-1110 tinyurl.com/ycyft8tt randi.kaufman2@verizon.net

Organizers & Life Management

♂ ● U Name It Organizers, Eleni O, 629 E 11 St Ste 4C; 917-880-8031 www.masterorganizers.com ♥

Performance: Entertainment, Music, Theater, Space

♀ ● Music By Sandy Rapp, 66 Hildreth Place, E Hampton; 11937 631-329-5193 www.SandyRapp.com sandyrapp@aol.com

Real Estate (see also Mortgages)
Long Island: Fire Island: Cherry Grove

♂ ● **A Summer Place Realty, POB 4062, Cherry Grove; 11782-0997 / Bay & Main Walks 631-597-6140 summer; 212-752-8074 winter The most exclusives in Cherry Grove - Fire Island Rentals & Sales www.asummerplacerealty.com asprcg@aol.com**

WOMEN
New York: New York City & Long Island Area

WOMEN 29 WOMEN
GAYELLOW PAGES #42 2020-2021

WOMEN
Asheville/Smoky Mtns Area: North Carolina

Recovery
Manhattan

♀ ☆ Win (Women in Need), 115 W 31st St Fl 7 212-695-4758 www.winnyc.org

Religious / Spiritual Resources
Manhattan & Citywide

♀ ★ ᕦᕤ Catholic Lesbians, Church of St. Francis Xavier, 55 W 15th St; 10011 929) 333-5011 www.sfxavier.org SFXWomen@aol.com

Spiritual Counseling
Manhattan

♂ • Dr Chaplain Eléni, 629 E 11 St Ste 4C 917-880-8031 www.masterorganizers.com ♥

Sports & Outdoor

♀ ★ Pride Basketball League NYC Women's+ Division (PBLNYC), POB 1244; 10163-1244 www.pblnyc.org women@pride basketballnyc.org

♀ ★ (?ᕤ) Sirens Women's Motorcycle Club, LGBT Community Center, 208 W 13th St; 10011-7702 212-620-7310 **H?** www.sirensnyc.com ✔

Weddings and Ceremonies

♂ • Dr Chaplain Eléni, 629 E 11 St Ste 4C 917-880-8031 www.masterorganizers.com ♥

Rochester & Finger Lakes Area

Accommodation: Hotels, Inns, Guesthouses, B&B, Resorts
Canandaigua

♀ • The Chalet of Canandaigua, 3770 State Route 21, Canandaigua; 14424 585-394-9080 chaletbandb.com ✔ ⊗ staychalet@chaletbandb.com

Counseling/Psychotherapy/Mental Health

♀ ○ ᕦᕤ Russow, Tara, PhD, 120 Allens Creek Rd, Roch; 14618 585-442-4447 www.RussowConsulting.com

Organizations/Resources: Cultural, Dance, Performance

♀ ☆ ᕦᕤ Rochester Women's Community Chorus, Inc, 121 N Fitzhugh St Ste 314, Roch; 14614 585-376-7464 www.therwcc.org therwcc@gmail.com

Syracuse

Counseling/Psychotherapy/Mental Health

♀ • Stein, Linda J., LCSW, PC, 132 Albany St, Cazenovia; 13035 315-655-0699 www.lindajsteintherapy.com

Health Care: Physical (see also Counseling/Mental Health)

♀ • ᕤ Harrington, Laura E, DC, Liverpool Chiropractic & Wellness, PLLC, 403 Tulip St, Liverpool; 13088-4966 315-461-4510 tinyurl.com/494t4d

Utica Area

Organizations/Resources: Student, Academic, Education

♀ ☆ Hamilton College Womyn's Center, Days-Massolo Center 2nd Flr, 198 College Hill Rd, Clinton; 315-859-4398 fb.com/HCWomxnsCenter

North Carolina
State/County Resources

Crisis, Anti-violence, & Helplines

♀ ☆ North Carolina Coalition Against Domestic Violence, NCCADV, 3710 University Dr Ste 140, Durham, NC 27707 888-232-9124 nccadv.org

Asheville/Smoky Mtns Area

Crisis, Anti-violence, & Helplines

♀ ☆ ᕦᕤ Helpmate, POB 2263, Asheville; 28802 828-254-0516 **H?** www.helpmateonline.org

Information, Media & Publications

♀ ★ Sheville of Western Carolina, 23 A Trillium Court, Asheville; 828-215-2915 www.sheville.org

Accommodation: Hotels, Inns, Guesthouses, B&B, Resorts
Asheville

♀ • 27 Blake St, 27 Blake St, Asheville; 28801-2203 828-252-7390 www.sheville.org/27blake ✔ ⊗ 27blake@charter.net

Leicester

♀ • (?ᕤ) Compassionate Expressions Mountain Inn & Healing Sanctuary, 828-683-6633 tinyurl.com/lo453 ⊗

Accommodation Rental: Furnished / Vacation (& AirBNB)
Asheville

♀ • **Asheville's Downtown Loft, 828-713-0141 828-337-3362 (Sarah Nie) Live in the heart of downtown Asheville. Free parking. Walk to all galleries, bookstores, restaurants. www.vrbo.com/218070** ✔ ⊗ **ashevillesdowntownloft@gmail.com**

♀ • Wolf Branch Cabin, Near Asheville, NC 828-231-2152 www.wolfbranchcabin.com ✿ ⊗

Astrology/Numerology/Tarot/Psychic Readings

♀ ○ ᕦᕤ Gunther, Christy, MA, 3 Woodfin Ave, Asheville; 28804 828-258-3229 astrocounseling.byregion.net ✔

Bars, Cafes, Clubs, Restaurants
Asheville

♀ ○ Tupelo Honey Cafe, 12 College St, Asheville 828-255-4863 tupelohoneycafe.com ☲ ✕

Bookstores

♀ ★ ᕦᕤ Firestorm Books & Coffee, 610 Haywood Rd, Asheville; 28801 828-255-8115 www.firestorm.coop ☐ ✔ info@firestorm.coop

♀ ○ ᕦᕤ Malaprop's Bookstore/Cafe, 55 Haywood St, Asheville; 828-254-6734 www.malaprops.com ☐ ✔

Legal Services

♂ ○ ♿ The Law Office of Leah Broker, P.A., One Oak Plaza Ste 201, Asheville; 28801 828-253-0336 Social Security disability, workers' compensation www.leahbrokerlaw.com ✓

♀ ● (♺) Rockey, Arlaine, POB 656, Marshall; 28753 828-279-6735 **H?** www.arlainerockey.com ✓ AttorneyRockey@gmail.com

Metaphysical, Occult, Alternative Healing

♀ ● ♿ Crystal Visions, 5426 Asheville Hwy, Hendersonville 828-687-1193 crystalvisionsbooks.com

Organizations/Resources: Cultural, Dance, Performance

♀ Womansong Asheville, POB 61, Asheville 28802 www.womansong.org

Weddings and Ceremonies

♀ ○ Marlan, Susan, Interfaith Officiant, Asheville & Western North Carolina 828-891-6323 828-505-5220 www.belovedceremony.com ♥

Charlotte Area

Bookstores

♀ ● ○ White Rabbit, 920 Central Ave, Charlotte; 704-377-4067 www.WhiteRabbitBooks.com

Hickory

Counseling/Psychotherapy/Mental Health

♂ ● Brand New Day Counseling, POB 242, Conover 28613 828-310-2959 tinyurl.com/yewgw3e ✓ brandnewdaycounseling@gmail.com

Triad Area

Legal Services

♂ ○ ♿ David, Cheryl K, 528 College Rd, Greensboro; 27410 336-547-9999 Estate & Elder Law www.cheryldavid.com ✓

Organizations/Resources: Cultural, Dance, Performance

♀ ★ Triad Pride Women's Chorus, 200 N Davie St Box 20, Greensboro; 336-589-6267 triadprideperformingarts.org

Triangle Area

Crisis, Anti-violence, & Helplines

♂ ☆ Orange County Rape Crisis Center, POB 4722, Chapel Hill; 27514 866-935-4783 www.ocrcc.org

Accommodation: Hotels, Inns, Guesthouses, B&B, Resorts
Durham

♀ ● TheLRoom, 919-638-0050 www.thelroombnb.com ✓ ⊗ ⊗ TheLRoomNC@gmail.com

Counseling/Psychotherapy/Mental Health
Cary

♂ ● ♿ Powell, Judith C, PhD, 1135 Kildaire Farm Rd Ste 200, Cary; 27511 / 301 W Weaver St, Carrboro 919-467-4782 fax 919-420-0199 tinyurl.com/2wqcenr

Durham

♂ ○ Grigsby, Mary K, 6208 Fayetteville Rd Ste 106, Durham; 27713 919-286-9659 www.counselingdurhamnc.com mkgrigsby03@gmail.com

Fuquay Varina

♂ ○ Maltbie, Alice, RN, MS, LMHC, 206 Raleigh St, Fuquay Varina; 27526 518-463-6582 www.alicemaltbie.com alicemaltbie@gmail.com

Raleigh

♂ ○ (♺) Luper, Suzanne W., Triangle Pastoral Counseling, Inc., 312 W Millbrook Rd #109, Raleigh; 27609 919-845-9977 x206 tpccounseling.org SWLuper59@gmail.com

Dentists
Durham

♂ ● ♿ Conner, Deb, DDS, MS, Endodontist, 922 Broad St Ste B, Durham; 27705 919-416-4200 Practice limited to endodontics www.debconnerdds.com ✓

Legal Services
Durham

♂ ● (♺) The Law Office of Cheri Patrick, 3500 Westgate Dr Ste 701, Durham; 919-956-7171 **H?** cheripatricklaw.com ✓

♂ ● ♿ Thompson, Sharon, 113 Broadway St, Durham; 919-688-9646 **H** www.nicholsonpham.com ✓

♂ ○ ♿ Whisnant, Judy, 123 W Main St Ste 612, Durham; 919-688-6860 www.judywhisnantlaw.com

Raleigh

♂ ● (♺) Haas, Angela L, Haas Tharrington, PA, 5100 Oak Park Rd Ste 200, Raleigh; 27612 919-783-9669 **H?** www.carolinafamilylaw.com ✓

Organizations/Resources: Cultural, Dance, Performance

♀ ☆ Common Woman Chorus, POB 51631, Durham 27717 www.commonwomanchorus.net

Organizations/Resources: Student, Academic, Education
Durham

♀ ☆ (♺) Duke University Women's Center, POB 90920, Durham; 27708 / 001 Crowell Building 919-684-3897 tinyurl.com/y8lno9j ✓

Real Estate (see also Mortgages)
Chapel Hill

♂ ○ Tanson, Wendy, Realtor, RE/MAX United, 1526 E Franklin St Ste 101, Chapel Hill; 27514 919-971-7180 www.wendytanson.com wendy@tanson.com

Women's Centers
Chapel Hill

♀ ☆ (♺) The Compass Center for Women and Families, POB 1057, Chapel Hill; 27514 / 210 Henderson St 919-968-4610 compassctr.org

Raleigh

♀ Women's Center of Wake County, 112 Cox Ave, Raleigh; 919-829-3711 www.wcwc.org

WOMEN
North Carolina: Wilmington

WOMEN **31** WOMEN
GAYELLOW PAGES #42 2020-2021

WOMEN
Dayton/Springfield Area: Ohio

Wilmington

Crisis, Anti-violence, & Helplines

♀ Domestic Violence Shelter, POB 1555; 28402 910-343-0703 tinyurl.com/7zns9sl

Ohio
State/County Resources

Archives/Libraries/Museums/History Projects

♀ ★ ♿ Ohio Lesbian Archives, POB 20075, Cincinnati, OH 45220-0075 513-256-7695 tinyurl.com/97r3dbf ⚥ OLArchives@gmail.com

Mortgages/Home Ownership (see also Banks, Real Estate)

♂ • Frey, Carolyn, OH & FL & PA 614-891-9625 www.carolyn-frey.com cafrey@mortgagelendingsolutions.com

Athens

Accommodation: Communities, Intentional

♂ ★ SuBAMUH, POB 5853; 45701 740-448-6424 Susan B. Anthony Memorial Unrest Home Womyn's Land Trust. All women, LGBTQ people, and allies welcome. www.subamuh.com SuBAMUH@gmail.com

Bowling Green

Organizations/Resources: Social, Recreation, Support

♀ ★ ♿ Bowling Green Lavender Women, fb.com/BGLavender-Women/

Organizations/Resources: Student, Academic, Education

♂ ☆ ♿ Center for Women and Gender Equity, BGSU, 280 Hayes Hall; 43403 419-372-7227 tinyurl.com/zxosz8t cwge@bgsu.edu

Cincinnati Area

Bars, Cafes, Clubs, Restaurants
Cincinnati

♂ • ♿ Home Base Tavern, 2401 Vine St, Cinci; 513-721-1212 tinyurl.com/wktusfs **DK** 💳⚥

Covington

♂ ○ Rosie's Tavern, 643 Bakewell St, Covington, KY 859-291-9707 www.rosiestavernnky.com rosiestav@aol.com

Legal Services

♂ • (♿) Cook, Cathy R, 114 E 8th St, Cinci; 45202-2102 513-241-4029 www.cathycooklaw.com info@cathycooklaw.com

Organizations/Resources: Cultural, Dance, Performance

♀ ☆ ♿ MUSE, Cincinnati's Women's Choir, POB 23292, Cinci; 45223 513-221-1118 **HS** www.musechoir.org

Organizations/Resources: Student, Academic, Education

♀ ☆ ♿ University of Cincinnati Women's Center, POB 210179, Cinci; 45221 513-556-4401 www.uc.edu/ucwc/

Real Estate (see also Mortgages)

♂ • Fletcher Realty, Inc, 1624 Bruce Ave, Cinci 45223-2002 513-542-5877 fax 513-542-3877 www.fletcherrealtyinc.com

Cleveland Area

Crisis, Anti-violence, & Helplines

♀ Domestic Violence & Child Advocacy Center, PO Box 5466, Cleveland; 44101 216-391-4357 www.dvcac.org

Organizations/Resources: Cultural, Dance, Performance

♀ Windsong, Cleveland's Feminist Chorus, POB 771212, Lakewood; 44107 216-521-5434 www.windsongcleveland.org

Recovery

♀ Women's Recovery Center, 6209 Storer Ave, Cleveland; 216-651-1450 www.womensctr.org

Columbus Area

Crisis, Anti-violence, & Helplines

♀ ★ ♿ Buckeye Region Anti-Violence Organization, POB 82068, Col; 43202 614-294-7867 (STOP) www.bravo-ohio.org

♀ Center for New Beginnings, POB 786, Newark 43058 800-686-2760 tinyurl.com/y9pzmwaj

Automobile Services

♂ • ♿ Alternative Auto Care, 136 W 5th St, Col; 43201-3221 614-294-0580 www.alternativeautocare.com chris@alternative autocare.com

Legal Services

♂ • ♿ Ball, Karen, POB 2815, Col 43216 614-743-2315 KBLawOhio@gMail.com

♂ ○ ♿ Pamela N Maggied Co, LPA, 85 E Gay St Ste 600, Col; 43215 614-464-2236 **H?** Bankruptcy www.pamelamaggied.com maggiedlaw@pamelamaggied.com

Organizations/Resources: Business & Professional Associations, Labor Advocacy

♀ Dames Bond, 1188 N High St, Col; 614-209-3556 www.dames-bond.com

Organizations/Resources: Cultural, Dance, Performance

♀ ☆ (♿) Columbus Women's Chorus, POB 141542, Col; 43214-1542 614-636-3541 www.colswomenschorus.org info@colswomenschorus.org

Recovery

♀ ☆ Amethyst, 455 E Mound St, Col; 614-242-1284 www.amethyst-inc.org

Dayton/Springfield Area

Information, Media & Publications

♀ Lesbian Dayton, tinyurl.com/ycnj8pyf

WOMEN
Ohio: Oberlin

WOMEN **32** WOMEN
GAYELLOW PAGES #42 2020-2021

WOMEN
Eugene/Springfield Area: Oregon

Oberlin

Counseling/Psychotherapy/Mental Health

♂ ○ Miller, Jane, LISW, CDBC, 5 S Main St #205, Oberlin; 44074 800-457-0345 www.healing-companions.org jmiller@oberlin.net

Oxford

Organizations/Resources: Student, Academic, Education

♀ ☆ Miami University Women's and LGBTQ Center, Armstrong Student Center 3012; 513-529-1510 tinyurl.com/249dyun

Toledo

Legal Services

♂ ● 🦽 Kirby, Cindy M., Atty at Law, Kirby & Kirby, Ltd. 316 N Michigan St Ste 818; 43604 419-693-4433 KirbyFamilyLaw.com Cindy@KirbyFamilyLaw.com

Youngstown Area

Travel & Tourist Services (see also Accommodation)

♂ ○ (♿) Burger Travel Service, 2324 Coronado Ave, Ytn; 330-744-5035 www.burgertravel.com

Oklahoma
Oklahoma City Area

Crisis, Anti-violence, & Helplines

♀ ☆ 🦽 Women's Resource Center, Inc., PO Box 5089, Norman; 73070 405-701-5540 **H** WRCNormanOK.org

Bars, Cafes, Clubs, Restaurants
Oklahoma City

♂ Alibis Club, 1200 N Pennsylvania Ave, OKC 405-604-3684 fb.com/alibisclubokc

♂ ● 🦽 Partners, 2805 NW 36th St, OKC; 405-942-2199 www.partnersokc.com **DK** ▥

Organizations/Resources: Social, Recreation, Support

♀ ★ 🦽 Herland Sisters, 2312 NW 39th St, OKC; Feminist bookstore & women's resource center; of various events, concerts, retreats, etc. www.herlandsisters.org ⚢ ✗

Tulsa

Bars, Cafes, Clubs, Restaurants

♂ Yellow Brick Road Pub, 2630 E 15th St 918-293-0304 fb.com/YBRTulsa

Health Care: Physical (see also Counseling/Mental Health)

♂ ○ Acupuncture Associates of NE OK, 302 N McKinley Ave, Sand Springs; 918-261-1126

Legal Services

♀ ○ (♿) Wilkins, Karen Keith, 1515 S Denver Ave; 74119 918-599-8118 www.wilkinslawtulsa.com Karen@WilkinsLawTulsa.com

Oregon
State/County Resources

Campgrounds and RV Parks

♀ ● (♿) Oregon Women's Land Trust-OWL Farm, 541-844-5038 Welcomes women-born-women visitors to our forests & meadows. tinyurl.com/z52cohd ♣ ⊘

Organizations/Resources: Social, Recreation, Support

♀ ★ Lavender Womyn, Lesbian, bi, & trans women tinyurl.com/lb2c38

Ashland/Medford/Rogue River Valley

Crisis, Anti-violence, & Helplines

♀ ☆ 🦽 Community Works, 2594 E Barnett Rd - Ste C, Medford; 541-779-2393 **H?** www.community-works.org

♀ ☆ Women's Crisis Support Team, 560 NE F St #A430, Grants Pass; 800-750-9278 www.wcstjoco.org

Erotica / Adult Stores / Safe Sex Supplies

♂ ● ♿ As You Like It - A Love Revolution, 383 E Main St, Ashland; 97520 541-201-2060 Awareness - Love - Pleasure. Serving all people with love & care since 2011. www.asyoulikeitshop.com

Corvallis/Albany

Organizations/Resources: Student, Academic, Education

♀ ☆ 🦽 OSU Women's Center, Benton Annex, 1700 SW Pioneer Place, Corvallis; 541-737-3186 dce.oregonstate.edu/wc

Eugene/Springfield Area

Crisis, Anti-violence, & Helplines

♂ ☆ Womenspace, POB 50127, Eugene; 97405 / 1577 Pearl St #200 800-281-2800 (crisis) www.womenspaceinc.org

Counseling/Psychotherapy/Mental Health

♂ ○ 🦽 Fletcher, Grace, MA, ATR, LPC, 390 Lincoln St #240, Eugene; 97401 541-954-6494 tinyurl.com/yams99tw ✗ grace@artwithgracecounseling.com

♂ ● Norberg, Patricia L, MS, NCC, 541-345-9409

Insurance (see also Financial Planning)

♂ ● 🦽 Dambach, Christine, Farmers' Insurance, 313 E 8th Ave, Eugene; 97401 541-743-4388 fax 800-346-1853 tinyurl.com/y5lw5uhr cdambach@farmersagent.com

Legal Services

♂ ○ 🦽 Livermore, Megan, Hutchinson Cox, POB 10886, Eugene; 97440 541-686-9160 **H?** www.eugenelaw.com ✗ mlivermore@eugenelaw.com

Organizations/Resources: Cultural, Dance, Performance

♀ ★ (♿) Soromundi Lesbian Chorus, POB 40934, Eugene; 97404-0169 541-520-0753 www.soromundi.org

WOMEN
Oregon: Eugene/Springfield Area

WOMEN **33** WOMEN
GAYELLOW PAGES #42 2020-2021

WOMEN
Salem : Oregon

Organizations/Resources: Student, Academic, Education

♀ ☆ UO Women's Center, 1228 Emu University Ste 3, Eugene; 541-346-4095 blogs.uoregon.edu/women/ ✚

Real Estate (see also Mortgages)

♂ ○ ㅎㅎ Swing, Rebecca, Windermere Real Estate/Lane County, 1600 Oak St, Eugene; 97401 541-465-8177 **H?** www.swingonhome.com ✚ swingonhome@windermere.com

Portland/Vancouver Area

Crisis, Anti-violence, & Helplines

♂ ☆ ㅎㅎ Bradley Angle, 5432 N Albina Ave, Portland; 503-232-1528 www.bradleyangle.org ✚

♂ ☆ Call to Safety, POB 42610, Portland; 97242 503-235-5333 calltosafety.org

♀ ☆ ㅎㅎ Clackamas Women's Services, 256 Warner Milne Rd, Oregon City; 97045 503-654-2288 888-654-2288 **H?** www.cwsor.org ✚ info@cwsor.org

♂ ☆ Domestic Violence Resource Center, 735 SW 158th Ave Ste 100, Beaverton; 97006 503-640-5352 www.dvrc-or.org dvrc@dvrc-or.org

Accounting, Bookkeeping, Tax Services

♀ ○ ㅎㅎ Kennedy, Amy, CPA, LTC, Clarity Tax Service, 1730 SW Skyline Blvd Ste 201, Portland; 97221 503-236-1040 (WA #31861/OR #28250) www.claritytax.net ✚

Bars, Cafes, Clubs, Restaurants
Portland

♀ ● ㅎㅎ Hot Flash Women's Dances, www.hotflashdances.com
P

Counseling/Psychotherapy/Mental Health

♂ ○ Hort, Barbara, PhD, Jungian Consultant, 3485 NW Thurman St, Portland; 97210 503-285-4212 ✚

♂ ● ㅎㅎ Kibel, Laney, LCSW, 1020 SW Taylor #820, Portland; 97205 503-781-3900 www.laneykibel.com ✚ laneykibel@hotmail.com

♀ ● O'Dell, Susan, PhD, LCSW, 1732 SE Ash St, Portland; 97214 503-232-5640 susan@susanodellphd.com

♂ ○ Steinbrecher, Diane, LCSW, A Safe Place for Growth and Healing, 2700 SE 26th Ave #C, Portland; 97202-1288 503-235-2005 archetypalassociates.com

Erotica / Adult Stores / Safe Sex Supplies

♀ ○ ㅎ She Bop, 3213 SE Division St, Portland; 97202 503-688-1196 **HS** www.sheboptheshop.com

♀ ○ ㅎ She Bop, 909 N Beech St, Portland; 97227 503-473-8018 **HS** www.sheboptheshop.com

Immigration, Citizenship, Political Asylum, Refugees

♂ ○ ㅎㅎ Riggs Immigration Law, 405 W 13th St, Vancouver, WA 98660 360-553-7210 www.riggsimmigrationlaw.com mercedes@riggsimmigrationlaw.com

Legal Services

♀ ● ㅎㅎ Findling, Marlene E, Findling Law Office, PC 2105 NE Cesar Chavez Blvd Ste 250, Portland; 97212 503-288-3133 www.findlinglawoffice.com marlene@findlinglawoffice.com

♂ ● ㅎㅎ Paulson, Jane, Paulson Coletti Trial Attorneys PC, 1022 NW Marshall #450, Portland; 97209 503-433-3524 Www.paulsoncoletti.com ✚ jane@paulsoncoletti.com

♀ ● ㅎㅎ Wolfsong Law PC, 9900 SW Wilshire St Ste 100, Portland; 97225 503-616-8880 www.wolfsonglaw.com

Organizations/Resources: Cultural, Dance, Performance

♀ ★ (ㅎㅎ) Portland Lesbian Choir, POB 12693, Portland; 97212 www.plchoir.org

Organizations/Resources: Sexual Focus / Safe Sex

♀ ★ Bad Girls, POB 14113, Portland; 97293 www.pdxbadgirls.net

Organizations/Resources: Social, Recreation, Support

♀ Dykes on Bikes - Portland Oregon Chapter, - - www.dykesonbikespdx.org

Real Estate (see also Mortgages)

♂ ● Betron, Deborah, Principal Broker, Bridgetown Realty, 3300 NW 185th #232, Portland; 97229 503-679-9741 www.bridgetownrealty.com ✚ deborah@bridgetownrealty.com

♂ ○ Casteel, Shelly, Oregon Realty Co, 8552 SW Apple Way, Portland; 97225 503-957-7705 503-297-2523 oregonrealty.com/shellyc

Religious / Spiritual Resources

♀ ☆ ㅎㅎ SisterSpirit, POB 9246, Portland; 97207-9246 503-736-3297 tinyurl.com/y93w9nl6 ✚ sisterspirit.portland@gmail.com

Sports & Outdoor

♀ Amazon Dragons Paddling Club, POB 13111, Portland; 97213 www.amazondragons.org

♀ Portland Shockwave, Women's Full Contact Football tinyurl.com/ybb5dy2g

♀ Rose City Rollers, POB 86885, Portland 97286 www.rosecityrollers.com

Salem

Crisis, Anti-violence, & Helplines

♀ ☆ The Center for Hope & Safety, 605 Center St NE 97301 503-399-7722 hopeandsafety.org ✪

Legal Services

♂ ● ㅎㅎ Pacheco, Monica D, Douglas, Conroyd, Gibb & Pacheco, P.C., POB 469; 97308 503-364-7000 Planning dcm-law.com monica@dcm-law.com

Organizations/Resources: Social, Recreation, Support

♀ ★ Salem Lavender Womyn, tinyurl.com/oxq2tx5

Pennsylvania
State/County Resources

Mortgages/Home Ownership (see also Banks, Real Estate)

♂ • Frey, Carolyn, OH & FL & PA 614-891-9625 www.carolyn-frey.com cafrey@mortgagelendingsolutions.com

Erie

Crisis, Anti-violence, & Helplines

♂ ☆ ♿ Crime Victim Center of Erie County, 125 W 18th St; 814-455-9414 www.cvcerie.org

♂ ☆ ♿ SafeNet, POB 1436; 16512 814-454-8161 www.safeneterie.org ✔

Organizations/Resources: Social, Recreation, Support

♀ ★ LBT Women of Erie, 814-490-3994 Fb.Com/Lbtwomenoferie

Harrisburg Area

Organizations/Resources: Cultural, Dance, Performance

♀ ☆ ♿ Central Pennsylvania Womyn's Chorus, POB 60426, Harrisburg; 17106-0426 717-564-0112 www.cpwchorus.org cpwc@lucytv.net

Johnstown

Bars, Cafes, Clubs, Restaurants

♂ • (♿) Lucy's Place, 520 Washington St, Johnstown; 814-539-4448 fb.com/lucillesjohnstown **DK** ▥ ✪

Lehigh Valley Area

Crisis, Anti-violence, & Helplines

♂ ☆ ♿ Turning Point of Lehigh Valley, (Administrative Office) 444 E Susquehanna St, Allentown; 18103 610-437-3369 (24/7 helpline) **H?** www.turningpointlv.org ✔

Bars, Cafes, Clubs, Restaurants
Catasauqua

♂ ○ ♿ Cathy's Creative Catering & Cafe, 752 Front St, Catasauqua; 610-443-0670 tinyurl.com/y3msrfu8 ▷

Food Specialties (see also Catering)

♂ ○ Sweet Girlz Bakery, 40 N Third St, Easton 610-829-1030 www.sweetgirlzpa.com

New Hope PA/Lambertville NJ Area

Grooming, Personal Care, Spa Services
New Hope

♂ ○ Bangz Salon, 3 Market Pl, New Hope; 18938 215-862-9877 www.bangznewhope.com bangznewhope@gmail.com

Philadelphia Area

Crisis, Anti-violence, & Helplines

♀ ☆ (♿) Women In Transition, 718 Arch St Ste 401N, Phila; 19106 215-751-1111 www.helpwomen.org witinfo@helpwomen.org

♂ ☆ (♿) Women Organized Against Rape, 1617 JFK Blvd #1100, Phila; 215-985-3333 www.woar.org

Bars, Cafes, Clubs, Restaurants
Philadelphia

♀ Stimulus, Check monthly party fb.com/TheStimulus ✪

♀ Toasted Walnut Bar & Kitchen, 1316 Walnut St, Phila; 215-546-8888 www.toastedwalnut.com

Bookstores

♂ • Big Blue Marble Bookstore, 551 Carpenter Lane, Phila; 215-844-1870 www.bigbluemarblebooks.com ▷ ✔

♀ • (♿) **Philly AIDS Thrift at Giovanni's Room, 345 S 12th St, Phila; 215-923-2960 www.queerbooks.com** ✔

Counseling/Psychotherapy/Mental Health

♂ ○ Alternative Choices, 319 Vine St #110, Phila 19106 215-592-1333 www.alternativechoices.com cariel@alternativechoices.com

♂ ○ (♿) Carter, Bonnie Frank, PhD, 640 Crestwood Rd, Wayne; 19087-2315 610-213-6695 www.bfcnetworks.net bonnie.frank.carter@bfcnetworks.net

♂ • Jeanette, Doris, PsyD, Center for New Psychology, 503 S 21st St, Phila; 215-732-6197 www.drjeanette.com

♀ • **Lavender Visions, 215-242-6334 Counseling, phone consultation, workshops: for lesbian, bisexual & questioning women. www.lavendervisions.com**

♀ ☆ ♿ Therapy Center of Philadelphia, 1315 Walnut St Ste 1004, Phila; 215-567-1111 Women & Transgender Communities www.therapycenterofphila.org ✔

Erotica / Adult Stores / Safe Sex Supplies

♂ ○ Pleasure Chest, 2039 Walnut St, Phila; 19103 215-561-7480 pleasurechestphilly.com papleasurechest@verizon.net

Health Care: Physical (see also Counseling/Mental Health)

♂ ○ ♿ Myers, Allison, MD, MPH, Penn Family Care, 3737 Market St Flr 9, Phila; 19104 215-662-8777 tinyurl.com/jxdtagw

♀ ☆ Rainbow Circle of the Linda Creed Breast Cancer Org, 614 S 8th St #277, Phila; 19147 877-992-7333 215-564-3700 www.lindacreed.org contact@lindacreed.org

Immigration, Citizenship, Political Asylum, Refugees

♂ ○ Hykel Law, 1500 JFK Blvd #1040, Phila; 19102 215-246-9400 www.hykellaw.com info@hykellaw.com

Legal Services

♂ ○ Giampolo Law Group, 319 S 12th St #1F, Phila 215-645-2415 Business, family, estate, LGBT law www.giampololaw.com

♂ (♿) Law Offices of Kristine W. Holt, 525 S 4th St Ste240A, Phila; 215-545-7789 Bankruptcy; transgender issues www.HoltEsq.com ✔

♂ • Steerman, Amy F, 1900 Spruce St, Phila; 19103 215-735-1006 www.amysteerman.com ✔

Organizations/Resources: Cultural, Dance, Performance

♂ ☆ (?♿) Anna Crusis Women's Choir, POB 42277, Phila; 19101-2277 267-825-7464 **H** www.annacrusis.org info@annacrusis.org

Organizations/Resources: Social, Recreation, Support

♀ ★ (?♿) Ladies 2000, POB 1, Oaklyn, NJ 08107 856-869-0193 www.ladies2000.com

♀ ★ Sisterspace of the Delaware Valley, POB 22476, Phila; 19110 888-294-1110 www.sisterspace.org

Sports & Outdoor

♀ Fairmont Park Women's Softball League, 267-225-4848 www.fpwsl.com

♀ LezRun Philadelphia, fb.com/LezRun

♀ ☆ Philadelphia Flames Soccer Club, 107 Alison Road #F-24, Horsham; 19044 267-784-5663 www.flamessc.us

Weddings and Ceremonies

♂ ○ Journeys of The Heart, 215-633-8980 www.journeysoftheheart.org ♥

Pittsburgh Area

Accounting, Bookkeeping, Tax Services

♂ ● Schneider, Kathleen, Atty/CPA, 1227 S Braddock Ave, Pgh; 15218-1239 412-371-8831 **Tax preparation & planning: individuals. estates, businesses. Convenient location, free parking.** www.kdschneiderlawoffice.com office@kdschneider.law

Bars, Cafes, Clubs, Restaurants
Pittsburgh

♂ ● Cattivo, 146 44th St, Pgh; 412-687-2157 www.cattivopgh.com ⚲ ✕ ▥

Bookstores

♂ The Big Idea Bookstore, 4812 Liberty Ave, Pgh 412-687-4323 thebigideapgh.org ⟲ ●

Counseling/Psychotherapy/Mental Health

♂ ○ ♿ Bertini, Michele, PhD, MEd, NCC, 5850 Ellsworth Ave, Pgh; 412-365-2020 www.michelebertini.com

Legal Services

♂ ● Schneider, Kathleen, Atty/CPA, 1227 S Braddock Ave, Pgh; 15218-1239 412-371-8831 **Tax preparation & planning: individuals. estates, businesses. Convenient location, free parking.** www.kdschneiderlawoffice.com office@kdschneider.law

State College

Crisis, Anti-violence, & Helplines

♂ ☆ ♿ Centre Safe, 140 W Nittany Ave 814-234-5050 **H** ccwrc.org

Puerto Rico
San Juan Area

Bars, Cafes, Clubs, Restaurants
San Juan

♀ Mujer-es Bar, 151 Calle O'Neill, San Juan; / Fri/Sat

Rhode Island
State/County Resources

Organizations/Resources: Social, Recreation, Support

♀ ★ RIWA (RI Women's Association), POB 3586, Cranston, RI 02910-0586 www.riwa.net

Newport

Women's Centers

♀ ☆ ♿ Women's Resource Center, 114 Touro St; 02840 401-846-5263 **H?** www.wrcnbc.org ✗ info@wrcnbc.org

Pawtucket

Counseling/Psychotherapy/Mental Health

♀ ● Johnson, Ros, LICSW, 100 Lafayette St 02860-6008 401-727-4749 www.mindingtherapy.com

Providence Area

Organizations/Resources: Student, Academic, Education

♀ ☆ (?♿) Sarah Doyle Center for Women and Gender, POB 1829, Providence; 02912-1829 401-863-2189 **H?** tinyurl.com/cn37cx ✗ sdwc@brown.edu

Sports & Outdoor

♀ ☆ ♿ Providence Roller Derby, POB 2516, Providence; 02096 tinyurl.com/44oeoq

South Carolina
Charleston Area

Organizations/Resources: Social, Recreation, Support

♀ ★ Charleston Social Club, www.charlestonsocialclub.com

Columbia

Crisis, Anti-violence, & Helplines

♀ ☆ Sistercare, Inc., POB 1029; 29202 803-765-9428 www.sistercare.org

Pets & Pet Services & Supplies

♂ ● Watchful Owl PetSitters, 803-606-0403 fb.com/TheWatchfulOwls WatchfulOwl@aol.com

Greenville Area

Legal Services

♂ ○ Chamberlain, Margaret A., Chamberlain Law Firm, LLC 600 Pettigru St, Greenville; 29601 864-250-0505 www.chamberlainlawfirmllc.com info@chamberlainlawfirmllc.com

South Dakota
Rapid City

Counseling/Psychotherapy/Mental Health

♂ ○ && Summers Temple, Irene, PhD LLC, 2218 Jackson Blvd Ste 13; 57702 605-519-8744 www.irenestphd.com ∕ irene@irenestphd.com

Tennessee
State/County Resources

Organizations/Resources: Political/Legislative/Advocacy

♀ ☆ National Organization For Women, POB 120523, Nashville, TN 37212 615-269-7141 tinyurl.com/ycdvbl9u

Reproductive Medicine & Fertility Services

♂ ○ Planned Parenthood of Tennessee and North Mississippi (PPTNM), 2430 Poplar Ave #100, Memphis, TN 38112 866-711-1717 tinyurl.com/y3qaqgf5 info@pptnm.org

Knoxville

Counseling/Psychotherapy/Mental Health

♂ ● (?&) Mott, Nancy, MS, Ed.S, 3117 E 5th Ave; 37914-4427 865-637-8801 Licensed in Psychology fb.com/nancymottcounseling ∕ nancymott16@gmail.com

Organizations/Resources: Social, Recreation, Support

♀ ★ && Lesbian Social Group (LSG), www.lesbiansocialgroup.com

Memphis

Health Care: Physical (see also Counseling/Mental Health)

♂ ★ && CHOICES: Memphis Center for Reproductive Health, 1726 Poplar Ave; 901-274-3550 **H?** tinyurl.com/y2cfk4mq ∕

Legal Services

♂ ○ & Mackenzie, Susan, 2157 Madison Ave Ste 104; 901-272-2729 www.susanmackenzielaw.com

♂ ○ && Wurzburg, Jocelyn D., JD, 5159 Wheelis Ste 101; 38117-4519 901-684-1332 Mediation services. www.wurzburgmediation.com ∕ wurzburg@mediate.com

Nashville Area

Bars, Cafes, Clubs, Restaurants
Nashville

♂ ● && The Lipstick Lounge, 1400 Woodland St, Nashville; 615-226-6343 www.thelipsticklounge.com **DK** Y ✕ ▥ ∕

Counseling/Psychotherapy/Mental Health

♂ ○ && Ingram, Jeannie, LPC, 4525 Harding Pike Ste 200, Nashville; 37205 404-444-1058 www.jeannieingram.com Ingram.jeannie@gmail.com

♂ ○ && Sanders, Barbara, LCSW, 1710 Stokes Lane, Nashville; 37215 615-414-2553 dignitytherapynashville.com Barbara SandersLCSW@gmail.com

Legal Services

♀ ● Rubenfeld, Abby R, Rubenfeld Law Office, PC 202 S 11th St, Nashville; 615-386-9077 www.rubenfeldlaw.com

Real Estate (see also Mortgages)

♀ ○ Sheila D Barnard, Realtor, 3 Yrs FAV GLBTQ Realtor 615-424-6924 tinyurl.com/yxadrjyv Barnard@realtracs.com

Texas
Austin Area

Crisis, Anti-violence, & Helplines

♀ ☆ && The SAFE Alliance, POB 19454, Austin; 78760 512-267-7233 **H** www.safeaustin.org ∕

Accommodation: Hotels, Inns, Guesthouses, B&B, Resorts
Austin

♀ ● Park Lane Guest House, 221 Park Lane, Austin 512-447-7460 parklaneguesthouse.com (❀?) ∕ ⊗ ⊗

Kingsbury

● ● River Barn Suites, Fentress Area 512-488-2175 www.riverbarnsuites.com ⊗ ⊗

Bookstores

♀ ● && **BookWoman, 5501 N Lamar Blvd # A-105, Austin; 78751 512-472-2785 Support your feminist bookstore, she supports you! www.ebookwoman.com** ∕ **bookwomanaustin@gmail.com**

Erotica / Adult Stores / Safe Sex Supplies

♀ ● && Dreamers - 3401, 3401 N I-35, Austin; 512-469-0539 **H?** dreamerstexas.com

♀ ○ && Dreamers North Austin, 11218 N Lamar Blvd, Austin; 512-837-5534 **H?** dreamerstexas.com

● ● & Forbidden Fruit, 108 E North Loop Blvd, Austin; 78751-1227 512-453-8090 **HS** www.forbiddenfruit.com **L** info@forbiddenfruit.com

Gardening/Landscaping Services & Supplies

♂ ● Red Sun Landscape Design, POB 2575, Austin 78630-2575 512-844-6493 redsunlandscapedesign.com michelle.austen07@gmail.com

Legal Services

♂ ○ & Andresen, Christine Henry, 4103 Manchaca Rd 512-394-4230 www.chalaw.com/lgbt ∕ @ixx=

♂ ● 占占 The Shefman Law Group, 4131 Spicewood Springs Rd Ste A-6, Austin; 78759 512-975-1005 Personal Injury www.shefmanlawgroup.com

Organizations/Resources: Social, Recreation, Support

⚲ Austin Lesbian CoffeehouseAustin, tinyurl.com/btj858v

Real Estate (see also Mortgages)

⚲ ● Hunter, Janie, Broker/Owner, Austin Homes Realty, 512-507-8252 www.austinhomesrealty.com janie@austinhomesrealty.com

Sports & Outdoor

♀ ☆ Austin Valkyries (Rugby), www.austinvalkyries.com

Travel & Tourist Services (see also Accommodation)

♂ ● 占占 Century Travel, 2714 Bee Cave Rd #101, Austin; 512-327-8760 www.centurytravelaustin.com ✓

Corpus Christi

Accommodation: Hotels, Inns, Guesthouses, B&B, Resorts
Rockport

♂ ● (?占) Anthony's By The Sea, 732 S Pearl St, Rockport; 78382-2420 361-729-6100 800-460-2557 www.anthonysbythesea.com (♣?) ✓ ⊛ anthonysbandb@att.net

Dallas/Fort Worth Area

Bars, Cafes, Clubs, Restaurants
Dallas

⚲ Marty's Live, 4207 Maple Ave, Dallas; / Tue Lesbian night 214-599-2151 tinyurl.com/q8vysae **D** 🎵 ✦

⚲ Sue Ellen's, 3014 Throckmorton St, Dallas 214-559-0707 sueellensdallas.com **D**

Bookstores

⚲ ★ (占占) Sources of Hope Gifts & Books, 5910 Cedar Springs Rd, Dallas; 800-501-4673 ✓

Counseling/Psychotherapy/Mental Health

♂ ○ Inclusive Counseling, 2121 W Spring Creek Pkwy Ste 110, Plano; 75023 214-504-4420 www.inclusivecounseling.com therapy@inclusivecounseling.com

♂ ● 占占 New Perspective Counseling Services, 9555 Lebanon Rd Ste 602, Frisco; 75035 469-362-8004 www.npcs.com info@npcs.com

Erotica / Adult Stores / Safe Sex Supplies

♂ ○ 占占 Dreamers Hillsboro, 2705 N. IH 35 Exit 364A, Hillsboro; 254-582-9305 **H?** dreamerstexas.com

Immigration, Citizenship, Political Asylum, Refugees

♂ ○ 占占 Kinser, Kimberly J, 2425 N Central Expressway Ste 200, Richardson; 75080 972-491-1145 www.kinserlaw.com ✓

Legal Services

♂ ○ 占占 Law Office of Jodi McShan, PLLC, 4144 N Central Expy Ste 1000, Dallas; 75204 214-800-2091 www.jodimcshanlaw.com ✓ jodi@jodimcshanlaw.com

Organizations/Resources: Cultural, Dance, Performance

♀ ☆ Women's Chorus of Dallas, 3630 Harry Hines Blvd #210, Dallas; 75219-3201 214-520-7828 www.twcd.org TWCDoffice@twcd.org

Organizations/Resources: Social, Recreation, Support

⚲ ★ 占占 Women with Pride, 2701 Reagan St, Dallas; 214-528-0144 tinyurl.com/y8tabqov

♀ Words of Women, POB 180777, Dallas; 75218 347-933-1256 www.wordsofwomen.org

Organizations/Resources: Student, Academic, Education

⚲ ★ Texas Women's University LGBTQIA Resources, Jones Hall Ste 200, Denton; 940-898-3679 tinyurl.com/y7m99bju

Reproductive Medicine & Fertility Services

♂ ○ Berkson, Mindy, Newborn Advantage, 3131 McKinney Ave Ste 600, Dallas; 75204 847-989-8628 www.NewbornAdvantage.com mindy@NewbornAdvantage.com

El Paso

Bars, Cafes, Clubs, Restaurants

⚲ Epic, 510 N Stanton St; 915-525-0984 tinyurl.com/pxckw32 **D** 🎵

Forest Hill

Erotica / Adult Stores / Safe Sex Supplies

♂ ● 占占 Dreamers North Austin, 6616 Oak Crest Dr; 817-516-7708 **H?** dreamerstexas.com

Houston Area

Crisis, Anti-violence, & Helplines

♂ ☆ 占占 Houston Area Women's Center, 1010 Waugh Dr, Houston; 800-256-0551 www.hawc.org

Bars, Cafes, Clubs, Restaurants
Houston

♀ ● 占 Beaver's, 6025 Westheimer Rd, Houston; 713-714-4111 www.beavershtx.com ✗ ✓

♥ Pearl, 4216 Washington Ave, Houston 832-740-4933 www.pearlhouston.com **D** ⚥ ✗ ▦

Counseling/Psychotherapy/Mental Health

♂ ● 占占 Gray, Enod, LCSW, CSAT-S, CGP, Trueself Transitions, 3100 Edloe #290, Houston; 281-788-9436 www.trueselftransitions.com @ixx=

Health Care: Physical (see also Counseling/Mental Health)

♥ ★ 占占 AssistHers, 401 Branard St 2nd Flr, Houston; 713-521-4628 **H?** Disabled or chronically ill Lesbian Women www.assisthers.org ✗

Legal Services

♂ ○ 占占 Kalish Law Texas, 3 Grogan's Park Dr Ste 200, The Woodlands; 77380 281-363-3700 fax 281-367-7340 www.kalishlawtexas.com laura@kalishlawtexas.com

Organizations/Resources: Cultural, Dance, Performance

♀ ★ 占占 Bayou City Women's Chorus, Bayou City Performing Arts, POB 541004, Houston; 77254 832-835-1643 www.bcpahouston.org/

Organizations/Resources: Education

♥ ★ 占占 Lesbian Health Initiative of Houston, Inc (LHI), 401 Branard St, Houston; 77006 713-426-3356 www.lhihouston.org info@lhihouston.org

Organizations/Resources: Student, Academic, Education

♀ ☆ Center for the Study of Women, Gender, & Sexuality, POB 1892, Houston; 77251 713-348-5784 cswgs.rice.edu

Sports & Outdoor

♀ ★ Monday Night Women, 2517 Julian, Houston 77009 281-437-6218 Bowling www.houstoninvite.com wiccado@sbcglobal.net

San Antonio Area

Crisis, Anti-violence, & Helplines

♂ Rape Crisis Center, 4606 Centerview Ste 200, San Antonio; 210-349-7273 rapecrisis.com

Accommodation Rental: Furnished / Vacation (& AirBNB)
Bandera

♀ ● (?占) Desert Hearts Cowgirl Club, 10101 Hwy 173 N, Bandera; 830-796-7001 tinyurl.com/huv4tws (☻?) ⊗

Erotica / Adult Stores / Safe Sex Supplies

♂ ● 占 Dreamers San Antonio, 2376 Austin Hwy, San Antonio; 210-653-3538 **H?** dreamerstexas.com

Gifts, Cards, Pride, etc.

♥ ● 占 ZEBRAZ.com, 1608 N Main Ave, San Antonio; 78212-4311 210-472-2800 800-788-4729 orders only www.zebraz.com zebraz@zebraz.com

Pets & Pet Services & Supplies

♂ ● Four Paws Pet Sitting, 210-446-7387 4pawspetsittingsa.com

San Marcos

Crisis, Anti-violence, & Helplines

♂ ☆ (?占) Hays-Caldwell Women's Center, PO Box 234, San Marcos; 78667 800-700-4292 **H** www.hcwc.org

Terrel

Erotica / Adult Stores / Safe Sex Supplies

♂ ● 占 Dreamers, 6086 W Us Highway 80 972-524-1449 **H?** dreamerstexas.com

Wimberley

Accommodation Rental: Furnished / Vacation (& AirBNB)

♂ ● (?占) Abundance: A Hill Country River Retreat, 330 Mill Race Lane, Wimberley, TX 713-819-9339 www.abundanceretreat.com ⊙ ☻✗ ⊗

Utah
Ogden

Organizations/Resources: Family and Supporters

♂ Mama Dragons, Support for mothers of LGBTQIA children. mamadragons.org

Salt Lake City Area

Crisis, Anti-violence, & Helplines

♂ ☆ 占占 Rape Recovery Center, 2035 S 1300 E, Salt Lake City; 84105 801-467-7273 801-467-7282 www.raperecoverycenter.org ✗

Counseling/Psychotherapy/Mental Health

♂ ○ McQuade, Shannon, LCSW, LMT, 2290 E 4500 S #210, Holladay; 84117 801-712-6140 www.realcaring.org shannon@realcaring.org

Organizations/Resources: Student, Academic, Education

♀ ☆ 占占 U of U Women's Resource Center, 200 S Central Campus Dr Rm 411, Salt Lake City; 84112 801-581-8030 **H?** womenscenter.utah.edu ✗ wrc@sa.utah.edu

Zion & Bryce Canyon National Parks Area

Accommodation: Hotels, Inns, Guesthouses, B&B, Resorts
Rockville

♂ ● (?占) 2 Cranes Inn Zion, 125 E Main St (Hwy 9), Rockville; 84763 435-216-7700 2craneszion.com (☻?) ✗ ⊗ ⊗

Vermont
State/County Resources

Crisis, Anti-violence, & Helplines

♂ ☆ 占占 Vermont Network Against Domestic & Sexual Violence, POB 405, Montpelier, VT 05601 802-223-1302 **H?** www.vtnetwork.org ✗ vtnetwork@vtnetwork.org

Financial Planning, Investment (see also Insurance)

♂ ● Lescoe, Donna, Choice Financial Services, POB 42, Starksboro, VT 05487 802-453-6677 www.donnalescoe.com

Sports & Outdoor

♀ ☆ (?♿) Vermont Outdoors Woman, POB 10, North Ferrisburg, VT 05473 800-425-8747 www.voga.org

Barre

Crisis, Anti-violence, & Helplines

♂ ☆ ♿ Circle, POB 652; 05641 877-543-9498 **H** Services to abused women & men, but only women in our shelter. www.circlevt.org

Brattleboro

Crisis, Anti-violence, & Helplines

♀ Women's Freedom Center, POB 933; 05302 802-257-7364 www.womensfreedomcenter.net

Bookstores

♀ ○ ♿ Everyone's Books, 25 Elliot St 05301-3376 802-254-8160 **H?** www.everyonesbks.com ✗ everyonesbks@gmail.com

Burlington/Lake Champlain Area

Crisis, Anti-violence, & Helplines

♂ ☆ ♿ HOPE Works, POB 92, Burlington; 05402 802-864-0555 Rape Crisis www.hopeworksvt.org ✗

♂ ★ ♿ SafeSpace Anti-Violence Program, Pride Center of Vermont, 255 S Champlain St Ste 12, Burlington; 05401 802-863-0003 866-869-7341 **H?** www.pridecentervt.org ✗

♂ ☆ ♿ Steps to End Domestic Violence, POB 1535, Burlington; 05402 802-658-1996 www.stepsvt.org

Bookstores

♂ ● The Flying Pig Bookstore, 5247 Shelburne Rd, Shelburne; 802-985-3999 www.flyingpigbooks.com

Counseling/Psychotherapy/Mental Health

♂ ● ♿ Barnett, Autumn, MSW, 270 Battery St, Burlington; 05401 802-622-1131 www.autumnbarnett.net autumn@autumnbarnett.net

Health Care: Physical (see also Counseling/Mental Health)

♀ ● ♿ Boyman, Kym, MD, FACOG, Vermont Gynecology, 1775 Williston Rd #110, S Burlington; 05403 802-735-1252 877-698-8496 (transmen & transwomen welcome) www.vtgyn.com ✗ kboyman@vtgyn.com

Legal Services

♂ ● ♿ Lashman, Deborah, PC, 47 Maple St Ste 318, Burlington; 05401 802-861-7800 **H?** dlashman@lashmanlaw.com

Green Mountains Area

Accommodation: Hotels, Inns, Guesthouses, B&B, Resorts
Marshfield

♂ ● (?♿) Marshfield Inn & Motel, 5630 US Rte 2, Marshfield; 05658 802-426-3383 www.marshfieldinn.com (✿?) ✗ ⊛

Huntington

Accommodation: Communities, Intentional

♀ ☆ (?♿) Huntington Open Women's Land (HOWL), POB 53; 05462 802-434-3953 www.howlvt.org ✗ howlvt@gmail.com

Middlebury

Crisis, Anti-violence, & Helplines

♀ ☆ (?♿) WomenSafe, Inc, POB 67; 05753 802-388-4205 www.womensafe.net ✗

Norwich

Financial Planning, Investment (see also Insurance)

♂ ○ (?♿) Clean Yield Asset Management, Elizabeth Glenshaw, POB 874; 05055 802-526-2525 800-809-6439 www.cleanyield.com elizabeth@cleanyield.com

St Johnsbury

Crisis, Anti-violence, & Helplines

♂ ☆ ♿ Umbrella, 1216 Railroad St Ste C 802-748-1992 **H?** www.umbrellanek.org

Virginia
State/County Resources

Mortgages/Home Ownership (see also Banks, Real Estate)

♂ ○ ♿ Wilt, Tammy L., NMLS #195702, Movement Mortgage, 3510 Remson Cr Ste 301, Charlottesville, VA 434-242-0046 movement.com/lo/tammy-wilt/

Charlottesville Area

Campgrounds and RV Parks

♀ ● (?♿) CampOut, 9505 Minna Dr, Henrico, VA 804-301-3553 www.campoutva.com **P** (✿?) ⊛

Legal Services

♂ ○ Tiller, Jessica A, Estate Planning of Charlottesville, PLLC, POB 6094, Charlottesville; 22906 434-219-9896 tinyurl.com/zvyjulj

Organizations/Resources: Student, Academic, Education

♀ ☆ University of Virginia Women's Center, 1400 University Ave, Charlottesville; 434-982-2361 tinyurl.com/y9dvope

Fairfax

Legal Services

♂ ● ♿ Abrams, Sheri R., 10467 White Granite Dr Ste 306, Oakton; 22124 571-328-5795 www.sheriabrams.com sheri@sheriabrams.com

WOMEN
Virginia: Hampton Roads Area

WOMEN **40** WOMEN
GAYELLOW PAGES #42 2020-2021

WOMEN
Seattle & Tacoma Area : Washington

Hampton Roads Area

Counseling/Psychotherapy/Mental Health

♂ ○ Hansen, Cynthia A, LCSW, 1878 E Ocean View Ave, Norfolk; 23503-2564 757-583-1878 lcswhansen@cox.net

♂ ● よよ Hooper, Kathleen, LCSW, Associates At York, Inc 909 Glenrock Rd Ste A, Norfolk; 23502 757-828-4893 **H?** www.therapistnorfolkva.com

Real Estate (see also Mortgages)

♂ ○ よよ Judy Boone Realty, 809 E Ocean View Ave, Norfolk; 23503 757-587-2800 www.judyboonerealty.com ✗ jbr@judyboonerealty.com

♂ ○ Kovach, Colleen, Howard Hanna/WEW, 2204 Hampton Blvd, Norfolk; 23517 757-575-9005 757-625-2580 tinyurl.com/yamxdz88 ColleenKovach@howardhanna.com

Sports & Outdoor

♀ ☆ Womens United Softball Association, www.norfolkwusa.com

Richmond Area

Bars, Cafes, Clubs, Restaurants
Richmond

⚥ ● Babe's of Carytown, 3166 W Cary St, Richmond; 804-355-9330 fb.com/babesofcarytown ⚲ ✗

Counseling/Psychotherapy/Mental Health

♂ ● Jean, Paula J., PhD, 907 Westwood Ave, Richmond; 23222-2533 804-329-3940 fax 804-329-3945 tinyurl.com/oqer5eg drpjjean3@gmail.com

Legal Services

♂ ○ よよ North, Pia J, 5913 Harbour Park Dr, Midlothian; 23112 804-739-3700 Bankruptcy www.pianorth.com ✗ help@pianorth.com

Real Estate (see also Mortgages)

♂ ● (♿) Fears, Wanda, ABR GRI CRS Realtor, Treehouse Realty VA, 1100 Jefferson Green Cir, Midlothian; 804-909-2777 **H?** www.bestRVAhomes.com ✗

Shenandoah Valley

Real Estate (see also Mortgages)

♂ ○ Aguilar, Betty, Nest Realty, 105 Baldwin St, Staunton; 24401 434-996-9699 tinyurl.com/ycxtyar4 Betty.aguilar@NestRealty.com

Washington
State/County Resources

Travel & Tourist Services (see also Accommodation)

♀ ○ Adventure Associates of WA, Inc, POB 16304, Seattle, WA 98116-0304 206-932-8352 www.adventureassociates.net info@adventureassociates.net

Bellingham

Organizations/Resources: Student, Academic, Education

♀ ☆ よよ Western Washington University Womxn's Identity Resource Center, Viking Union #514; 360-650-6114 as.wwu.edu/womxn/

Everett

Health Care: Physical (see also Counseling/Mental Health)

♀ ☆ Citrine Health, 2940 W Marine View Dr 425-259-9899 www.citrinehealth.org

Olympia Area

Crisis, Anti-violence, & Helplines

♂ ☆ Human Response Network, POB 337, Chehalis 98532 800-244-7414 www.hrnlc.org

♂ ☆ よよ SafePlace, 360-754-6300 **H?** www.safeplaceolympia.org ✗ safeplace@safeplaceolympia.org

Pullman

Organizations/Resources: Student, Academic, Education

♂ ☆ よよ Washington State University Women's Center, POB 644005; 99164 509-335-6849 **H?** www.women.wsu.edu ✗

Seattle & Tacoma Area

Crisis, Anti-violence, & Helplines

♀ New Beginnings, POB 75125, Seattle; 98175 206-522-9472 www.newbegin.org

Community Centers and/or Pride Organizations

⚧ ★ Seattle Dyke March, www.seattledykemarch.com

Information, Media & Publications

⚧ ● The Seattle Lesbian, 206-714-2277 www.theseattlelesbian.com info@theseattlelesbian.com

Adoption, Surrogacy, Assisted Fertility Support, see also Reproductive

♂ ☆ よよ Open Adoption & Family Services, 2815 Eastlake Ave E Ste 160, Seattle; 206-782-0442 www.openadopt.org

AIDS/HIV Services, Education & Support

♀ ☆ Babes Network, 1118 5th Ave, Seattle; 98101 888-292-1912 206-720-5566 www.babesnetwork.org the_staff@babesnetwork.org

Bars, Cafes, Clubs, Restaurants
Seattle

⚧ ● よよ Hot Flash Women's Dances, www.hotflashdances.com **P**

⚧ ● (よよ) WildRose, 1021 E Pike St, Seattle; 206-324-9210 www.thewildrosebar.com **DK** ⚲ ✗ ▦

WOMEN
Washington: Seattle & Tacoma Area

WOMEN **41** WOMEN
GAYELLOW PAGES #42 2020-2021

WOMEN
Charleston : West Virginia

Coaching: Career, Life, Relationship etc

♀ ● ♿ SharonSanborn.com, 206-283-9767 www.SharonSanborn.com ✂ Sharon@SharonSanborn.com

Counseling/Psychotherapy/Mental Health

♀ ● ♿ MacQuivey, Karen, LICSW, 6527 21 Ave NE #4, Seattle; 98115-6947 206-285-9168

♀ ● ♿ Mending Connections, PllC, 4141 6th Ave STE C, Tacoma; 98406 253-303-2074 www.annemauro.com ✂ contact@mendingmyconnections.com

♀ ● ♿ Salewske, Cassie, LMHC, Healing Tree Counseling & Wellness, LLC, 1812 E Madison St Ste 106, Seattle; 98122 206-595-8621 www.healingtreeseattle.com ✂ cassie.salewske@gmail.com

♀ ● ♿ Scherer, Taen M, MA, LMFT, Abanian Counseling, 19550 International Blvd Ste 105, SeaTac; 98188 / and 4218 S Chicago St 206-303-7584 www.abaniancounseling.com

♀ ● ♿ SharonSanborn.com, 18 W Mercer St Ste 360, Seattle; 98119 206-283-9767 www.SharonSanborn.com ✂ Sharon@SharonSanborn.com

Legal Services

♀ ○ ♿ A. Alene Anderson Law Offices, 1455 NW Leary Way Ste 400, Seattle; 206-781-2570 www.aleneandersonlaw.com @ixx=

♀ ● ♿ Buhr, Cynthia F, Law Offices of Cynthia F. Buhr PLLC, 1700 7th Ave Ste 2100, Seattle; 98101 206-357-8565 fax 206-357-8565 www.cbuhrlaw.com cynthia@cbuhrlaw.com

♀ Legal Voice, 907 Pine St #500, Seattle 206-682-9552 www.legalvoice.org

♀ ○ (♿) Longley, Sara D, Ivy Law Group PLLC, 1734 NW Market St, Seattle; 98107 206-706-2909 www.ivylawgroup.com sara@ivylawgroup.com

Organizations/Resources: Cultural, Dance, Performance

♀ ★ ♿ Seattle Women's Chorus, 319 12th Ave, Seattle; 206-323-0750 www.seattlechoruses.org

Organizations/Resources: Political/Legislative/Advocacy

♀ ☆ ♿ Radical Women, 5018 Rainier Ave S, Seattle; 206-722-6057 **H?** www.radicalwomen.org ✂

Organizations/Resources: Senior Resources

● ★ Puget Sound Old Lesbians Organizing for Change (PS OLOC), 253-777-3357 www.psoloc.org

Organizations/Resources: Social, Recreation, Support

● ★ (♿) Tacoma Lesbian Connection, PO Box 64487, Tacoma; 98464 253-777-3357 www.tacomalesbianconcern.org tacomalesbianconcern@gmail.com

Real Estate (see also Mortgages)

♀ ○ Grassley, Teresa J, Windermere Real Estate, 4526 California Ave SW, Burien; 98166 206-650-3141 tinyurl.com/bfqlzln realestate@teresagrassley.com

315 W Gorham St
Madison, WI 53703
Tel: 608-257-7888
Fax: 608-257-7457
room@chorus.net

A Room of One's Own Feminist Bookstore

www.roomofonesown.com

Religious / Spiritual Resources

● ★ Lotus Sister LBQT Women's Insight Meditation Sangha, 206-329-5908 www.lotussisters.org @ixx=

Sports & Outdoor

♀ ☆ Emerald City Mudhens, Rugby mudhenrugby.com

♀ Tilted Thunder Rail Birds, www.tiltedthunder.com

Skagit Valley Area

Travel & Tourist Services (see also Accommodation)

♀ ○ ♿ Plumeria Breezes Travel, 810 Metcalf St, Sedro-Woolley; 98284 360-391-6001 Destination Wedding Planning tinyurl.com/zkaolka ♥ monique@plumeriabreezestravel.com

Spokane

Legal Services

♀ ○ ♿ **Sayre, Sayre & Fossum, PS, 201 W North River Dr Ste 460; 99201-2262 509-325-7330 H? Employment law; estate, disability & long term care planning for special needs of G/L Partners & their families. www.sayrelaw.com** ✂ **info@sayrelaw.com**

West Virginia
State/County Resources

Crisis, Anti-violence, & Helplines

♀ ☆ West Virginia Coalition Against Domestic Violence, 5004 Elk River Rd S, Elkview, WV 304-965-3552 www.wvcadv.org

Charleston

Bars, Cafes, Clubs, Restaurants

♀ ○ Ellen's Homemade Ice Cream, 225 Capitol St 304-343-6488 www.ellensicecream.com ☞ ellensicecream@gmail.com

WOMEN
Wisconsin: Chippewa Valley Area

WOMEN **42** WOMEN
GAYELLOW PAGES #42 2020-2021

WOMEN
Laramie : Wyoming

Sinister Wisdom

A Multicultural Lesbian Literary & Art Journal

http://www.SinisterWisdom.org

Wisconsin
Chippewa Valley Area

Health Care: Physical (see also Counseling/Mental Health)

♀ ○ ♿ Radiant Health Chiropractic, 115 9th Ave, Eau Claire; 54703 715-838-9432 www.radianthealthchiro.com

Madison Area

Crisis, Anti-violence, & Helplines

♂ ☆ ♿ Rape Crisis Center, 2801 Coho St #301, Madison; 53713 608-251-7273 608-251-5126 **H?** www.thercc.org info@thercc.org

Bookstores

♂ ● ♿ **A Room of One's Own Books & Gifts, 315 W Gorham St, Madison; 53703 608-257-7888 H?** Feminist/LGBT/Used Books www.roomofonesown.com room.bookstore@gmail.com

Erotica / Adult Stores / Safe Sex Supplies

♂ ● ♿ A Woman's Touch Sexuality Resource Center, 302 S Livingston St, Madison; 53703 608-250-1928 888-621-8880 **H?** www.a-womans-touch.com

Organizations/Resources: Student, Academic, Education

♂ ☆ ♿ Campus Women's Center, 333 East Campus Mall Room 4416, Madison; 608-262-8093 www.campuswomenscenter.org

Religious / Spiritual Resources

♀ ☆ Re-formed Congregation of the Goddess, POB 6677, Madison; 53716 608-226-9998 www.rcgi.org

Milwaukee Area

Crisis, Anti-violence, & Helplines

♀ Milwaukee Women's Center, 728 N James Lovell St, Milwaukee; 414-449-4777 tinyurl.com/cvlt5gd

Bars, Cafes, Clubs, Restaurants
Milwaukee

♀ ● Walker's Pint, 828 S 2nd St, Milwaukee 414-643-7468 www.walkerspint.com **D** ⚥

Bookstores

♀ ● ♿ Outwords Books, Gifts & Coffee, 2710 N Murray Ave, Milwaukee; 53211-3645 414-963-9089 www.outwordsbooks.com ▯ ⚥ outwordsbooks@msn.com

Funding: Endowment, Fundraising

♀ Lesbian Fund, c/o Women's Fund Greater Milwaukee, 316 N Milwaukee St #215, Milwaukee; 414-290-7350 tinyurl.com/ctlk5lj

Legal Services

♀ ● ♿ Lewison, Brenda, Law Offices of Arthur Heitzer, 633 W Wisconsin Ave #1410, Milwaukee; 53203 414-273-1040 **H?** www.equalrightswi.com ⚥ lewisonlaw@yahoo.com

Organizations/Resources: Cultural, Dance, Performance

♀ ★ ♿ Miltown Kings, **H?** fb.com/miltownkings/

♀ ☆ Women's Voices Milwaukee, fb.com/womensvoicesmilwaukee/

Organizations/Resources: Social, Recreation, Support

♀ ★ Lesbian Alliance Metro Milwaukee, 315 W Court St, Milwaukee; 414-272-9442 fb.com/groups/16093277822

Organizations/Resources: Transgender/Gender Non-Conforming/Diverse

T ☆ SHEBA (Sisters Helping Each Other Battle AIDS), Diverse and Resilient, 2439 N Holton St, Milwaukee; 414-390-0444 African American MTF tinyurl.com/bpmndzf

Norwalk

Campgrounds and RV Parks

♀ ● (?♿) Daughters of the Earth, 18134 Index Ave; 54648-7028 608-269-5301 Bio female born, and still bio female women only (♣?) ⚥ ⊗ doejo777@yahoo.com

Wascott

Campgrounds and RV Parks

♀ ● (?♿) Wilderness Way Resort/Campground, 16139 S Chipmunk Hollow Rd, Gordon; 715-466-2635 tinyurl.com/j39tn5v (♣?) ⊗

Wyoming
Cheyenne

Accounting, Bookkeeping, Tax Services

♂ ○ ♿ Richey, Mary, CPA, MER Tax, Accounting, and Consulting, 4104 Laramie St; 82001 307-632-0841 www.mer-tax.com merichey@mer-tax.com

Laramie

Accommodation: Hotels, Inns, Guesthouses, B&B, Resorts

♂ ● Cowgirls Horse Hotel, 6822 Black Elk Trail 307-745-8794 www.cowgirlshorsehotel.com ♣ ⚥ ⊗

Ethnic & Multicultural Resources

USA: National Resources

Information, Media & Publications

♂ • FlavaMen, Flava Works, Inc POB 2495, Chicago, IL 60690 305-438-9450 www.flavamen.com ❖ sales@flavaworks.com

AIDS/HIV Services, Education & Support

♀ ☆ ظ The Black AIDS Institute, 1833 W 8th St Ste 200, Los Angeles, CA 90057-4920 213-353-3610 www.blackaids.org ❖

♀ ☆ ظ National AIDS Education/Services for Minorities, 2140 MLK Jr Dr #602, Atlanta, GA 404-691-8880 www.naesm.org ❖

♀ ☆ National Native American AIDS Prevention Center, 1031 33rd St, Denver, CO 720-382-2244 www.nnaapc.net ✳

Archives/Libraries/Museums/History Projects

♀ ☆ ظ Black Gay & Lesbian Archive, Schomburg Center for Research in Black Culture, New York Public Library, 515 Malcolm X Blvd, New York, NY 212-491-2200 www.nypl.org/archives/4117 ❖

♀ ★ Latino GLBT History Project, 2000 14th St NW Ste 105, Washington, DC 202-670-5547 www.latinoglbthistory.org ✦

♀ ★ Legacy Project Outdoor Museum Walk (Chicago), 312-608-1198 www.legacyprojectchicago.org ✪

Graphic Design/Printing/Type

♂ • BLK Media Services, POB 83912, Los Angeles, CA 90083-0912 213-410-0808 fax 213-410-9250 www.blkmedia.com ❖

Organizations/Resources: Education

♀ • Diversity Builder, Inc., 2821 Lebanon Rd Ste 201, Nashville, TN 615-823-1717 www.diversitybuilder.com ✪

♂ ☆ LGBTQQ Workshops / Bully Ban, c/o Creative Response, 145 College Rd, Rm 4300, Suffern, NY 10901 845-574-4225 tinyurl.com/ouy9v3e ✪ inquiries@crc-global.org

Organizations/Resources: Ethnic, Multicultural

♀ ★ Center for Black Equity, POB 77313, Washington, DC 20019 202-641-8527 centerforblackequity.org ❖ cbe@centerfor blackequity.org

♀ ★ Mamaroots: Ajama-Jebi Sistahood, POB 21066, Long Beach, CA 90801 562-498-3318 An AfraGoddess(tm) Tradition ❖

♂ ★ (?ظ) National Association of Black & White Men Together, POB 589, Hollywood, CA 90078 800-624-2968 www.nabwmt.org ✪

♀ ★ National Black Justice Coalition, POB 71395, Washington, DC 20024 202-319-1552 fax 202-319-7365 www.nbjc.org ❖

♀ ★ National Youth Pride Services, 180 N Michigan Ste 1200, Chicago, IL 60601 773-977-8051 fb.com/YouthPrideServices ❖ youthpridecenter@gmail.com

♀ ★ NativeOUT, fb.com/nativeout/

♀ ★ Trikone: GLBT South Asians, 60 29th St #614, San Francisco, CA 908-367-3374 www.trikone.org ◇

♀ ★ Two Spirit National Cultural Exchange, Inc, POB 280805, Lakewood, CO 80228 720-261-1854 tinyurl.com/jd6vydo

Organizations/Resources: Political/Legislative/Advocacy

♀ ★ Zuna Institute, 2701 Del Paso Rd Ste 130358, Sacramento, CA 916-207-1037 www.zunainstitute.org ❖

Organizations/Resources: Transgender/Gender Non-Conforming/Diverse

T ☆ Black Trans Advocacy, 3530 Forest Lane Ste 290, Dallas, TX 855-255-8636 www.blacktrans.org ❖

T ☆ Black Transmen, 3530 Forest Lane Ste 290, Dallas, TX 855-255-8636 www.blacktransmen.org ❖

T ☆ Black Transwomen, 3530 Forest Lane Ste 290, Dallas, TX 855-255-8636 BlackTranswomen.org ❖

Publishers/Publishing-related Services

♀ • Redbone Press, POB 15815, New Orleans, LA 70175 Lisa C. Moore www.redbonepress.com ❖ info@redbonepress.com

---

♂ GLBTQI ♂ Gay/nongay ⚥ bisexual
♀ LBTQI women ♀ all women ⚥ bisexual women
♂ GBTQI men ♂ all men ♂ bisexual men
T specifically transsexual/transgender/transvestite

Ⴛ ✕ Bar and Restaurant ✕ Restaurant ▷ Cafe
▥ Entertainment/Cabaret/Showbar
D Dancing V Video bar K Karaoke S Sports bar
C Country L Leather/Levi W Western
P Private Club (ask about visitor memberships)

♥ Wedding-related services or marriage equality
H Assistance available for the deaf and hearing-impaired
HD devices HS sign HDS devices and sign
H? Check for assistance available for the deaf and. hearing-impaired
⊗ ⊛ smoke-free property ⊛ smoke-free indoors
(⊛) indoor smoking areas
✿ Pets welcome (✿?) Ask about pets
✐ High speed internet available to visitors
Wheelchair Accessibility of premises or meeting place:
ظ Accessible premises and lavatory
(ظ) Accessible premises with help; accessible lavatory
ظ Accessible premises; lavatory not known to be accessible
(ظ) Accessible premises with help
(?ظ) Call ahead for details: places of meetings or activities vary, or special arrangements available.
◇ Asian ✦ Latin/Hispanic
❖ African-descent/Black
❖ People of Color ✳ Two-Spirit ✪ Diverse

Religious / Spiritual Resources

⚥ ★ Eshel, c/o Makom Hadash, 125 Maiden Lane Ste 8B, New York, NY 724-374-3501 www.eshelonline.org ✡

⚥ ★ Gay & Lesbian Vaishnava Association, www.galva108.org ✧

⚥ ★ International Association of Lesbian & Gay Children of Holocaust Survivors, 261 Broadway #8C, New York, NY 212-233-7867 www.infotrue.com/gay.html ✡

♀ ★ Jewish Lesbian Daughters of Holocaust Survivors, 608-256-8883 tinyurl.com/ztewxec ✡

⚥ ★ Keshet, 284 Amory St, Boston, MA 617-524-9227 www.keshetonline.org ✡

⚥ ♿ Latinx Roundtable, Center for LGBTQ and Gender Studies in Religion (CLGS), Pacific School of Religion, 1798 Scenic Ave, Berkeley, CA 510-849-8206 www.clgs.org ✚

⚥ Resources for Gay and Lesbian Orthodox Jews, www.orthogays.org ✡

⚥ ★ (♫) World Congress of GLBT Jews, Keshet Ga'avah, POB 23379, Washington, DC 20026 www.glbtjews.org ✡

Arizona
Navajo Nation

Organizations/Resources: Ethnic, Multicultural

♀ Diné Equality, 505-236-4116 www.EqualityNavajo.org

Phoenix Area

Bars, Cafes, Clubs, Restaurants
Phoenix

♂ Karamba, 1724 E McDowell Rd, Phx; 602-254-0231 www.karambanightclub.com **DK** ✚

Organizations/Resources: Ethnic, Multicultural

⚥ Native Out, fb.com/pg/nativeout/

Tucson

Religious / Spiritual Resources

⚥ ★ JFSA Pride, 3800 E River Rd; 520-299-3000 x168 www.jewishtucson.org/lgbt/ ✡

California
Central Coast

Bars, Cafes, Clubs, Restaurants
Castroville

⚥ ● Francos Norma Jean's Nightclub, 10639 Merritt St, Castroville; / Sat 10pm 831-633-2090 Sat only fb.com/Francos831 **D** ▥ ✚

Davis

Organizations/Resources: Student, Academic, Education

⚥ ★ Asian Pacific Islander Queers at UC Davis, c/o LGBT Resource Center, 1 Shields Ave; 916-370-0555 ✧

East Bay Area

Community Centers and/or Pride Organizations

♂ ☆ La Peña Cultural Center, 3105 Shattuck Ave, Berkeley; 510-849-2568 www.lapena.org ☉

Information, Media & Publications

⚥ Queer in Oakland, www.queerinoakland.com ☉

AIDS/HIV Services, Education & Support

♂ ☆ ♿ Asian Health Services, 416 8th St, Oakland; 94607 510-972-4483 HIV care, Hormone Replacement Treatment, ADAP, Medi-Cal and Covered California enrollment, PrEP, PEP, Education & Support www.hch510.org ✧ testing@ahschc.org

Bars, Cafes, Clubs, Restaurants
Oakland

⚥ Club 21, 2111 Franklin St, Oakland 510-268-9425 www.club21oakland.com **D** ✚

Counseling/Psychotherapy/Mental Health

♂ ● Watson, Courtney, LMFT, CST, Doorway Therapeutic Services, 298 Grand Ave Ste 100, Oakland; 94610 510-463-4471 **H?** www.doorwaytherapeutics.com ❖ Doorwaytherapeutics@gmail.com

Health Care: Physical (see also Counseling/Mental Health)

♀ La Clínica de La Raza Inc, POB 22210, Oakland; 94623 510-535-4000 www.laclinica.org ✚

Organizations/Resources: Ethnic, Multicultural

⚥ ★ Asian & Pacific Islander Family Pride, PO Box 473, Fremont; 94537 510-818-0887 apifamilypride.org ✧

♀ ★ Asian Pacific Islander Queer Women & Transgender Community (APIQWTC), 708-274-7982 Lesbian, Queer, Transgender www.apiqwtc.org ✧ info@apiqwtc.org

♀ DeQH - Desi lgbtQ Helpline for South Asians, 908-367-3374 www.deqh.org ✧

Religious / Spiritual Resources

⚥ ♿ Latinx Roundtable, Center for LGBTQ and Gender Studies in Religion (CLGS), Pacific School of Religion, 1798 Scenic Ave, Berkeley; 510-849-8206 www.clgs.org ✚

♂ ☆ ♿ Temple Israel of Alameda, 3183 Mecartney Rd, Alameda; 94502-6912 510-522-9355 templeisraelalameda.org ✡

Inland Empire

AIDS/HIV Services, Education & Support

♂ Bienestar Human Services Pomona Center, 180 E Mission Blvd, Pomona; 909-397-7660 www.bienestar.org ✚

Long Beach

AIDS/HIV Services, Education & Support

♂ ☆ Bienestar Long Beach, Long Beach Center, 1464 Cherry Ave; 562-438-5800 www.bienestar.org ✚

Organizations/Resources: Ethnic, Multicultural

♀ ★ Black & White Men Together of Southern CA (BWMTSC), 562-366-4573 www.bwmtsc.org ⊙ info@bwmtsc.org

Los Angeles Area

AIDS/HIV Services, Education & Support

♂ APAIT Asian Pacific AIDS Intervention Team, 3055 Wilshire Blvd Flr 3, LA; 213-375-3830 www.apaitonline.org ◇

♀ Bienestar Human Services, 3131 Santa Anita Ave Ste 109, El Monte; 626-444-9453 www.bienestar.org ✦

♂ Bienestar Human Services, 5326 E Beverly Blvd, LA; 866-590-6411 www.bienestar.org ✦

♂ Bienestar Human Services Hollywood Center, 4955 Sunset Blvd, LA; 323-660-9680 tinyurl.com/mnawke6 ✦

♀ ★ Bienestar Human Services San Fernando Valley, 8134 Van Nuys Blvd #200, Panorama City; 818-908-3820 www.bienestar.org ✦

♂ ★ Bienestar Human Services South Los Angeles Center, 130 W Manchester Ave, LA; 323-752-3100 www.bienestar.org ✦

♀ ★ ♿ Red Circle Project, 2741 S La Brea Ave, LA; 323-329-9905 **H?** Native American HIV/AIDS Prevention & Education Program. redcircleproject.org ✳

♂ ☆ The Wall Las Memorias Project, 5619 Monte Vista St, LA; 323-257-1056 www.thewalllasmemorias.org ✦

Bars, Cafes, Clubs, Restaurants
Hollywood

♂ ○ Avalon, 1735 Vine St, Hwd; 323-462-8900 www.avalonhollywood.com **D** ✦

♂ Tempo, 5520 Santa Monica Blvd, Hwd 323-466-1094 ✦

♂ ○ TigerHeat, at Avalon, 1735 Vine St, Hwd; / Thu check ahead 323-467-4571 www.clubtigerheat.com **D** ✦

Los Angeles

♂ The New Jalisco Bar, 245 S Main St, LA 213-613-1802 tinyurl.com/msn44o3 ▥ ✦

Montebello

♂ Chico, 2915 W Beverly Blvd, Montebello 323-721-3403 www.clubchico.com **D** ✦

North Hollywood

♂ ● ♿ Cobra, 10937 Burbank Blvd, N Hwd; 818-760-9798 www.clubcobrala.com **DCLW** ▥ ✦

Reseda

♂ Coco Bongo Reseda, 19655 Sherman Way, Reseda; 818-998-8464 fb.com/cocobongoreseda **D** ✦

West Hollywood

♂ ● Club Papi, at Micky's 8857 Santa Monica Blvd, W Hwd; / check schedule 323-692-9573 www.clubpapi.com ✦ clubpapi@aol.com

♂ Mother Lode, 8944 Santa Monica Blvd, W Hwd 310-659-9700 tinyurl.com/6mhx5jr **D** ✦

♀ Plaza, 739 N La Brea, W Hwd; 323-939-0703 tinyurl.com/y4e78aka **D** ▥ ✦

Graphic Design/Printing/Type

♂ ● BLK Media Services, POB 83912, LA 90083-0912 213-410-0808 fax 213-410-9250 www.blkmedia.com ✤ ⟋

Organizations/Resources: Ethnic, Multicultural

♀ ★ Asian/Pacific Gays & Friends, 1049 Havenhurst Dr Box 443, W Hwd; 90046 www.apgf.org ◇ info@apgf.org

♂ Color in Common, LA Gay and Lesbian Center, 1125 N McCadden Place, LA; 323-860-5833 tinyurl.com/y2ymb3o6 ✤

♀ ★ Gay & Lesbian Armenian Society of Los Angeles, 8721 Santa Monica Blvd Box 654, W Hwd; 310-203-1587

♂ In the Meantime Men's Group, 2146 W Adams Blvd, LA; 323-733-4868 inthemeantimemen.org ✤

♀ ★ Long Yang Club of Los Angeles (LYCLA), fb.com/groups/293252197243 ◇

♀ ★ SATRANG, 3055 Wilshire Blvd Ste #300, LA 888-370-5569 www.satrang.org ◇

Organizations/Resources: Family and Supporters

♀ ☆ PFLAG San Gabriel Valley Asian Pacific Islander, tinyurl.com/avp7d98 ◇

Organizations/Resources: Transgender/Gender Non-Conforming/Diverse

T Center for Transyouth Health and Development, Children's Hospital Los Angeles, 5000 Sunset Blvd Flr 4, LA; 323-361-5372 tinyurl.com/y2wy4n8j ⊙

T ☆ Gender Justice LA, 3055 Wilshire Blvd Flr 3, LA; 323-300-8599 www.gjla.org ⊙

Organizations/Resources: Youth (see also Family)

♀ Reach LA, 1400 E Olympic Blvd #240, LA 213-622-1650 www.reachla.org ✤

Recovery

♀ ☆ ♿ Alcoholism Center for Women, 1147 S Alvarado St, LA; 90006-4100 213-381-8500 tinyurl.com/2qtp79 ✤

Religious / Spiritual Resources

♂ ★ ♿ Beth Chayim Chadashim, 6090 W Pico Blvd, LA; 323-931-7023 www.bcc-la.org ⚨

♀ ☆ ♿ Congregation Kol Ami, 1200 N LaBrea Ave, W Hwd; 90038-1024 323-606-0996 **H?** www.kol-ami.org ⚨ ⟋ reception@kol-ami.org

♀ ★ Gay & Lesbian Vaishnava Association, www.galva108.org ◇

Orange County

AIDS/HIV Services, Education & Support

♂ Asian Pacific AIDS Intervention Team/Turntable, 12900 Garden Grove Blvd #220, Gdn Grv; 714-636-1349 www.apaitonline.org ◇

Bars, Cafes, Clubs, Restaurants
Anaheim

♂ ○ Bravo Night Club, 1490 S Anaheim Blvd, Anaheim 714-533-2291 tinyurl.com/j4srxho **D** ♀ ✂ ▥ ✦

Garden Grove

♀ • Frat House, 8112 Garden Grove Blvd, Gdn Grv; 714-373-3728 fb.com/frathouseoc/ **D** 🖩 ✚ ✗

Sacramento Valley Area

AIDS/HIV Services, Education & Support

♂ ☆ Golden Rule Services, 4433 Florin Rd #820, Sacto; 916-426-4653 tinyurl.com/y2nkkm9p ❖

San Diego Area

Organizations/Resources: Ethnic, Multicultural

♂ ★ Long Yang Club San Diego, POB 34102, San Diego; 92163 fb.com/groups/lycsd ◇

San Francisco Bay/Peninsula

AIDS/HIV Services, Education & Support

♂ ☆ Asian & Pacific Islander Wellness Center, 730 Polk St, SF; 415-292-3400 www.apiwellness.org ◇

♂ ☆ 👥 Rafiki Coalition for Health & Wellness, 601 Cesar Chavez St, SF; 415-615-9945 **H?** rafikicoalition.org ✚ ✗

Bars, Cafes, Clubs, Restaurants
San Francisco: Mission District

♀ • (?👥) El Rio, 3158 Mission St, SF 415-282-3325 www.elriosf.com **DK** ✚ ✗

San Francisco: South of Market

♂ • 👥 Club Papi San Francisco, at Roccapulco Nightclub, 3140 Mission St www.clubpapi.com **D** ✚

♂ O 👥 The Endup, 401 6th St, SF 415-896-1075 theendupsf.com **D** ✪

♂ O Mezzanine, 444 Jessie St, SF; 415-625-8880 mezzaninesf.com **D** 🖩 ✪

♂ ★ 👥 Sundance Saloon, Sun & Thu at Space 550, 550 Barneveld Ave (check ahead) 415-820-1403 **H?** www.sundance-saloon.org **DCW** ✪ ✗ info@sundancesaloon.org

Health Care: Physical (see also Counseling/Mental Health)

♂ Clinica Martin-Baro, 3013 24th St, SF 415-933-1198 clinicamb.blogspot.com ✚

♂ ★ 👥 Magnet, 470 Castro St, SF 415-581-1600 www.magnetsf.org ✪

♂ 👥 Strut, 470 Castro St, SF 415-437-3400 strutsf.org ✪

Organizations/Resources: Cultural, Dance, Performance

♂ Gay Asian Pacific Men's Chorus (GAPA Chorus), fb.com/GA-PAchorus/ ◇

♀ ☆ Purple Moon Dance Project, 1385 Mission St Ste 340, SF; 415-552-1105 www.purplemoondance.org ✪

♀ ★ 👥 Queer Women of Color Film Festival, 1014 Torney Ave Ste 111, SF; 94129 415-752-0868 **H** June 14-16, 2019 www.qwocmap.org ❖ ✗ festival@qwocmap.org

♂ ★ Sundance Association for Country Western Dancing, 2261 Market St PMB 225, SF; 94114-1600 415-820-1403 www.sundance-saloon.org ✪ info@sundancesaloon.org

Organizations/Resources: Ethnic, Multicultural

♂ ★ Aguilas, 2261 Market St Box 496, SF; / 1800 Market St. 3rd Floor Rm. Q32 415-558-8403 www.sfaguilas.org ✚

♂ ★ Bay Area American Indian Two-Spirits, 77 Van Ness Ave Ste 101-1043, SF; 415-865-5616 www.baaits.org ✳

♂ Bay Area American Indian Two-Spirits (BAAITS), 77 Van Ness Ave #101-1043, SF; 415-865-5616 www.baaits.org

♂ ★ Gay Asian Pacific Alliance, POB 880672, SF 94188 www.gapa.org ◇

♂ ★ United Territories of Polynesian Islanders Alliance (UTOPIA), utopiasf.org ◇

Organizations/Resources: Transgender/Gender Non-Conforming/Diverse

T El/la Para TransLatinas, 2940 16th St Room 319, SF; 415-864-7278 tinyurl.com/twj5m74 ✚

T ☆ 👥 Trans Day of Remembrance (TDOR), **HS** Spanish Interpretation provided www.TDoRSF.org ✪ info@TDoRSF.org

Religious / Spiritual Resources

♂ ☆ Congregation B'nai Emunah, 3595 Taraval St, SF 94116 415-664-7373 www.bnaiemunahsf.org ⚳ office@bnaiemunahsf.org

♂ ★ 👥 Congregation Sha'ar Zahav, 290 Dolores St, SF; 415-861-6932 www.shaarzahav.org ⚳ ✗

♂ LGBT Alliance of the Jewish Community Federation, 121 Steuart St, SF; 415-777-0411 tinyurl.com/oejbonm ⚳

San Francisco

♂ Keshet SF Bay Office, 2 Embarcadero Center Flr 8, SF; www.keshetonline.org ⚳

Women's Centers

♀ ☆ Women's Building, 3543 18th St, SF 415-431-1180 womensbuilding.org ✪

San Jose & South Bay Area

Organizations/Resources: Ethnic, Multicultural

♂ ★ South Bay Queer & Asian, 938 The Alameda, San Jose; 408-293-2429 www.sbqa.com ◇

Organizations/Resources: Student, Academic, Education

♀ ★ 👥 Queer & Asian (Q&A SJSU), Mailbox #53, c/o Student Involvement, 1 Washington Square, 1411 Student Union Building, San Jose; 408-924-5950 **H?** qnasjsu.tumblr.com ◇ ✗

Santa Cruz Area

Religious / Spiritual Resources

♂ ★ 👥 Out in Our Faith/Twice Blessed, Temple Beth El, 3055 Porter Gulch Rd, Aptos; 95003 831-479-3444 tinyurl.com/y4mn47gp ⚳ ✗ info@tbeaptos.org

Colorado
Denver Area

Bars, Cafes, Clubs, Restaurants
Denver

⚥ El Potrero, 4501 E Virginia Ave, Denver 303-388-8889
fb.com/elpotreroclub **D** ⚥ ✕▦ ✦

♀ ⚲ Tracks, 3500 Walnut St, Denver; 303-863-7326
www.tracksdenver.com **D** ▦ ✪

Organizations/Resources: Family and Supporters

♀ ★ (?⚥) PFLAG Denver, POB 18901, Denver; 80218 303-573-5861 www.pflagdenver.org ✦

Connecticut
Hartford Area

AIDS/HIV Services, Education & Support

♀ Latino Community Services, 184 Wethersfield Ave, Hartford; 860-296-6400 lcs-ct.org ✦

District of Columbia
DC Washington Area

Information, Media & Publications

♀ PhatGirlChic.com, www.phatgirlchic.com ✪

AIDS/HIV Services, Education & Support

⚥ ☆ ⚥ Us Helping Us, Inc, 3636 Georgia Ave NW, DC; 202-446-1100 www.uhupil.org ✚

Archives/Libraries/Museums/History Projects

♀ ★ Latino GLBT History Project, 2000 14th St NW Ste 105, DC; 202-670-5547 www.latinoglbthistory.org ✦

Bars, Cafes, Clubs, Restaurants
Washington

⚥ ● ⚥ The Fireplace, 2161 P St NW, DC 202-293-1293 fb.com/thefireplacedc **V** ✪

Health Care: Physical (see also Counseling/Mental Health)

♀ ☆ La Clinica Del Pueblo, 2831 15th St NW, DC 202-462-4788 www.lcdp.org ✦

Organizations/Resources: Ethnic, Multicultural

♀ ★ AQUA (Asian/Pacific Islander Queers United for Action), www.aquadc.us ✧

⚥ ★ Asians & Friends, POB 18974, DC; 20036 fb.com/groups/AFWashington ✧

♀ ★ DC Black Pride, POB 77313, DC; 20013 202-641-8527 centerforblackequity.org ✚ dcbp@centerforblackequity.org

♀ ★ KhushDC, 571-210-5474 fb.com/khushdc/ ✧

♀ LULAC Lambda DC, z 1204 5th St NW, DC 202-374-9227 lulaclambda.org ✦

⚥ ★ Men of All Colors Together of Washington DC, PO Box 77472, DC; 20013 tinyurl.com/y83444dt ✪

Organizations/Resources: Social, Recreation, Support

♀ ★ ⚥ GLOE - Kurlander Program for GLBT Outreach & Engagement at the DCJCC, Washington DCJCC, 1529 16th St NW, DC; 202-777-3253 **H?** Jewish LGBT and our friends washingtondcjcc.org/gloe ✡ ✔

⚥ Nice Jewish Boys DC, fb.com/NJB.DC ✡

♀ ★ Nice Jewish Girls DC, fb.com/NJGDC ✡

Religious / Spiritual Resources

♀ ★ (?⚥) Bet Mishpachah, POB 1410, DC; 20013-1410 **H?** www.betmish.org ✡ office@betmish.org

Sports & Outdoor

⚥ ★ Washington Renegades Rugby Football Club, Inc., POB 2067, DC; 20013 www.dcrugby.com ✪

Florida
Fort Lauderdale/Wilton Manors Area

Bars, Cafes, Clubs, Restaurants
Wilton Manors

⚥ Johnsons Fort Lauderdale, 2340 Wilton Dr, Wilton Manors; 954-908-1272 johnsonsfl.com ▦ ✪ ✔

Religious / Spiritual Resources

♀ ★ (?⚥) Congregation Etz Chaim, 2038 N Dixie Hwy, Wilton Manors; 954-564-9232 www.EtzChaimFlorida.org ✡

Jacksonville

Bars, Cafes, Clubs, Restaurants

♀ ● ⚥ InCahoots Nightclub, 711 Edison Ave; 904-353-6316 www.incahootsnightclub.com **DKLV** ✪ ✔

♀ ● ⚥ Park Place Lounge, 931 King St; 904-389-6616 tinyurl.com/ycu4kk2r **D** ✪

♀ ● The Sappho, Upstairs at Metro, 859 Willow Branch Ave; 904-388-8719 www.metrojax.com **DKLCW** ▦ ✪ ✔

Miami Area

Bars, Cafes, Clubs, Restaurants
Miami Beach

⚥ Club Boi, 1216 Washington Ave, Miami Beach; / Sat 10pm 786-617-4746 www.clubboi.com **D** ✚

Miami

♀ Azucar, 2301 SW 32nd Ave, Mi; 786-444-0736 www.Azucar-Miami.net ▦ ✦

Organizations/Resources: Ethnic, Multicultural

⚥ Miami Beach Bruthaz, 1850 Collins Ave, Miami Beach; / annual event 866-981-5009 www.miamibeachbruthaz.com ✪

♀ Unity Coalition/Coalicion Unida, 777 Brickell Ave, Mi; 786-271-6982 www.unitycoalition.org ✦

Organizations/Resources: Social, Recreation, Support

⚲ Rainbow Ladies - Our Space, Inc., fb.com/RainbowLadies ✪

Orlando Area

Organizations/Resources: Family and Supporters

♀ ☆ PFLAG Lady Lake, 352-693-2173 www.pflagladylake.org ✦

Tampa Bay Area

Community Centers and/or Pride Organizations

♀ ☆ ♿ Metro Wellness & Community Centers, 3251 3rd Ave N
Ste #125, St Pete; 727-321-3854 **H?** www.metrotampabay.org ✪

Organizations/Resources: Youth (see also Family)

♀ Metro Youth Group, 3251 3rd Ave N #125, St Pete; 727-321-
3854 x233 www.metrotampabay.org ✪

Georgia
Atlanta Area

Bars, Cafes, Clubs, Restaurants
Atlanta

♂ ● Bulldogs, 893 Peachtree St, Atl; 404-872-3025 fb.com/bull-
dogsbaratlanta/ ❖ bulldogsbaratl@gmail.com

♀ ● Traxx Atlanta, check schedule 404-740-5122 fb.com/TraxxAt-
lanta D ▦ ❖

♀ ● Traxx Girls, check schedule 888-935-8729
www.traxxgirls.com D ▦ ❖

Stone Mountain

♂ Phaze One, 4933 Memorial Dr, Stone Mountain; 404-296-4895
tinyurl.com/opz6ojq ❖

Leather Resources & Groups

♂ ★ ONYX Southeast, www.onyxsoutheast.com ❖

Men's & Sex Clubs (not primarily Health Clubs)

♂ ● ♿ The Den, 2135 Liddell Dr, Atl 404-292-7746 thedenat-
lanta.com P ❖

Organizations/Resources: Ethnic, Multicultural

♂ In The Life Atlanta, 1530 Dekalb Ave NE, Atl; 678-964-4852
www.inthelifeatlanta.org ❖

♂ ★ People of All Colors Together Atlanta, PO Box 14858, Atl;
30324 www.bwmtatlanta.org ✪

Organizations/Resources: Political/Legislative/Advocacy

♂ ★ ♿ Southerners on New Ground (SONG), 561 W Whitehall
St, Atl; 404-549-8628 tinyurl.com/6nqa9p ✪ ✗

Religious / Spiritual Resources

♂ ★ ♿ Congregation Bet Haverim, PO Box 29548, Atl; 30359
404-315-6446 tinyurl.com/36q9m8 ✡

Hawaii
Hawaii (Big Island) before eruption

Accommodation: Hotels, Inns, Guesthouses, B&B, Resorts
Volcano

♀ ● Kulana Goddess Sanctuary, POB 783, Volcano 96785 crea-
tive/spiritual retreat; mostly women but check ahead
tinyurl.com/jojo573 ✪ (♣?) ✗ ✆ ✆ discoverkulana@yahoo.com

Illinois
Chicago Area

AIDS/HIV Services, Education & Support

♀ ☆ Project Vida, 2659 S Kedvale Ave, Chi 773-277-2291
www.projectvida.org ✪

Archives/Libraries/Museums/History Projects

♂ ★ Legacy Project Outdoor Museum Walk (Chicago), 312-608-
1198 **H?** www.legacyprojectchicago.org ✪

Bars, Cafes, Clubs, Restaurants
Chicago

♂ Club Escape, 1530 E 75th St, Chi 773-599-9372
tinyurl.com/y82uloyp D ▦ ❖

♀ ● Jeffery Pub, 7041 S Jeffery Blvd, Chi 773-363-8555
fb.com/thejefferypub/ DS ▦ ❖

♂ ● Urbano, at Fantasy Nightclub, 3641 N Halsted St, Chi; / check
schedule 773-957-4021 www.facebook.com/SXChicagoNet ✪

Leather Resources & Groups

♂ ★ ONYX/Midwest, 3712 N Broadway PMB #271, Chi
www.onyxmidwest.com ❖

Organizations/Resources: Ethnic, Multicultural

♀ ★ (♂♀) Affinity, 2850 S Wabash Ste 108, Chi; 773-324-0377
H? www.affinity95.org ❖

♂ ★ Asians & Friends Chicago, POB A3916, Chi 60690 312-409-
1573 www.afchicago.org ✧

♂ ★ (♂♀) **Association of Latino Men for Action, 3656 N
Halsted St, Chi; 773-234-5591 ALMA is an educational,
social, advocacy, and support group. www.almachi-
cago.org ✦ ♥**

♂ ★ ⚥ Chicago Black Gay Men's Caucus, Public Health Institute
of Metropolitan Chicago, 180 N Michigan Ave #1200, Chi 312-629-
2988 x12 www.chiblackgaycaucus.org ❖

♂ ★ (♂♀) I2I: Invisible to Invincible, **H?** www.invisible2invinci-
ble.org ✧

Organizations/Resources: Naturist/Nudist

♂ ★ Chicago Area Naturist Sons (C.A.N.S), www.cansguys.org **N**
✪

Religious / Spiritual Resources

♂ ★ ♿ Congregation Or Chadash, Temple Sholom of Chicago, 3480 N Lake Shore Dr, Chi; 773-271-2148 fb.com/orchadashchicago/ ⚧

Indiana
Indianapolis Area

AIDS/HIV Services, Education & Support

♂ ★ Brothers United, 3737 N Meridian St Ste 401, Indpls; 317-931-0292 www.brothersunitedinc.org ✤

Iowa
Cedar Rapids

Bars, Cafes, Clubs, Restaurants
Cedar Rapids

♂ ● Belle's Basix, 3916 1st Ave NE, Cedar Rapids; 319-363-3194 fb.com/bellesbasix **D** 📖 ✪

Des Moines

Religious / Spiritual Resources

♀ ☆ (♺) Trinity Las Americas United Methodist Church., POB 41005; 50311 515-288-4056 trinitylasamericas.org ✦ ⚲ Office@TrinityLasAmericas.org

Iowa City/Cedar Rapids/Marion Area

Bars, Cafes, Clubs, Restaurants
Iowa City

♂ ● ♿ Studio 13, 13 S Linn St, Iowa City; (alley) 267-713-2697 www.sthirteen.com **D** ✪

Kansas
Wichita

Health Care: Physical (see also Counseling/Mental Health)

♀ ☆ ♿ Hunter Health Clinic, 2318 E Central Ave; 316-262-2415 www.hunterhealthclinic.org ✴

Kentucky
Lexington

Community Centers and/or Pride Organizations

♀ Kentucky Black Pride Inc, 859-285-3091 tinyurl.com/r7stdhl ✤

Maine
Portland Area

Religious / Spiritual Resources

♀ ☆ ♿ Congregation Bet Ha'am, 81 Westbrook St, S Portland; 04106-5232 207-879-0028 **H?** www.bethaam.org ⚧⚲ karen@bethaam.org

Maryland
Baltimore Area

Bars, Cafes, Clubs, Restaurants
Baltimore

♀ Gallery Bar & Restaurant, 1735 Maryland Ave, Balt; 410-539-6965 **DL** ♈ ✕ ✪

Organizations/Resources: Ethnic, Multicultural

♀ ★ The Center for Black Equity-Baltimore, 2530 N Charles St 3rd Flr, Balt; 443-218-2478 www.cbebaltimore.org ✤ ⚲

♀ Sistahs of Pride, GLCCB, 2530 N Charles St Flr 3, Balt; 410-777-8145 tinyurl.com/zqx35qp

Columbia

Religious / Spiritual Resources

♀ ☆ ♿ St John United Church, Wilde Lake Interfaith Center, 10431 Twin Rivers Rd; 21044-2331 410-730-9137 www.sjunited.org ✪ ⚲ SJUColumbia@gmail.com

Massachusetts

Crisis, Anti-violence, & Helplines

♀ ★ ♿ The Network/La Red, POB 6011, Boston, MA 02114 617-742-4911 **H** www.tnlr.org ✪

AIDS/HIV Services, Education & Support

♀ ☆ ♿ Multicultural AIDS Coalition, Inc, 566 Columbus Ave, Boston, MA 617-442-1622 www.mac-boston.org ✪ ⚲

Boston Area

Community Centers and/or Pride Organizations

♀ Latino Pride, 398 Columbus Ave #285, Boston; 617-262-9405 tinyurl.com/oxbn5jo ✦

Bars, Cafes, Clubs, Restaurants
Boston

♀ ● (♺) Dyke Night, check event schedule www.kristenporterpresents.com **D** ✪

Jamaica Plain

♀ ○ ♿ Bella Luna Restaurant & Milky Way Lounge, 284 Amory St, Jamaica Plain; 617-524-3740 www.milkywayjp.com **D** ♈ ✕ 📖 ✪

Organizations/Resources: Ethnic, Multicultural

♀ ★ Boston MASALA - Massachusetts Area South Asian Lambda Association, South Asian tinyurl.com/y95hn5qa ✧

♀ ★ Queer Asian Pacific Alliance, **H?** www.qapa.org ✧

♀ Somos Latinos LGBT Coalition/ Latino Pride of New England, 398 Columbus Ave #285, Boston; 617-262-9405 tinyurl.com/oxbn5jo ✦

Organizations/Resources: Youth (see also Family)

♀ ★ ♿ Boston Alliance of GLBT Youth (BAGLY, Inc), POB 960814, Boston; 02196 617-227-4313 **H** www.bagly.org ☯

♂ ★ ♿ Boston GLASS Community Center, 75 Amory St Garden Level, Boston; 857-399-1920 tinyurl.com/moy7mxj ❖

♀ ★ ♿ Boston GLASS Community Center for GLBTQ Youth & Young Adults, 75 Amory St, Roxbury; 857-399-1920 Ages 13-25 tinyurl.com/moy7mxj ❖

Religious / Spiritual Resources

♀ ★ ♿ Congregation Am Tikva, POB 990441, Boston; 02199 617-383-9539 www.amtikva.org ⚧

♀ ★ Keshet, 284 Amory St, Boston; 617-524-9227 www.kesheton-line.org ⚧

Provincetown Area

Bars, Cafes, Clubs, Restaurants
Provincetown

♀ ● Girl Power Events, www.provincetownforwomen.com ☯

Western MA/Berkshires

AIDS/HIV Services, Education & Support

♀ ☆ ♿ A Positive Place, POB 1299, Northampton; 01061 413-586-8288 **H** Bilingual/bicultural staff in Spanish and interpretation available for other languages tinyurl.com/ybgdth27 ☯ ⚕

Women's Centers

♀ ☆ (♋) Center for Women & Community, New Africa House, 180 Infirmary Way, Amherst; 01003-9315 413-545-0883 www.umass.edu/cwc/ ☯ cwc@umass.edu

Worcester

Immigration, Citizenship, Political Asylum, Refugees

♀ ★ ♿ LGBT Asylum Task Force, Hadwen Park Congregational Church, 6 Clover St; www.lgbtasylum.org ☯

Michigan
Detroit Area

Bars, Cafes, Clubs, Restaurants
Detroit

♂ Woodward Bar & Grill, 6426 Woodward, Det 313-872-0166 tinyurl.com/otxnln9 **DV** ⚥ ✗▦ ❖

Organizations/Resources: Ethnic, Multicultural

♂ ★ Al Gamea, POB 471, Hazel Park; 48030 313-427-3771 LGBT Middle Eastern www.algamea.org

Grand Rapids

AIDS/HIV Services, Education & Support

♀ ☆ ♿ The Grand Rapids Red Project, 401 Hall St SE; 616-456-9063 redprojectgr.org ❖

Minnesota
Minneapolis/St Paul Area

AIDS/HIV Services, Education & Support

♀ ★ ♿ Indigenous People's Task Force, 1335 E 23rd St, Mpls; 612-870-1723 indigenouspeoplestf.org ✳

Organizations/Resources: Social, Recreation, Support

♀ ☆ (♋) The Twin Cities Men's Center, 3249 Hennepin Ave S #55, Mpls; 612-822-5892 www.tcmc.org ☯

Missouri
St Louis Area (MO & IL)

Religious / Spiritual Resources

♂ ★ ♿ MCC of Greater St Louis, 7423 Michigan Ave, St Louis; 63111 314-361-3221 www.mccgsl.org ☯ info@mccgsl.org

Nevada
Reno

Religious / Spiritual Resources

♀ ☆ ♿ Temple Sinai, 3405 Gulling Rd 89503-2043 775-747-5508 **HD** www.sinaireno.org ⚧ ⚕ admin@sinaireno.org

New Jersey
State/County Resources

AIDS/HIV Services, Education & Support

♂ North Jersey Community Research Initiative, 393 Central Ave FL 3, Newark, NJ 973-483-3444 www.njcri.org ☯

Organizations/Resources: Ethnic, Multicultural

♀ ★ Long Yang Club New Jersey, 85 Raritan Ave Ste 100, New Brunswick, NJ 732-247-0515 Ray or Bob www.lycnj.com ⟡

Organizations/Resources: Youth (see also Family)

♂ Project WOW, NJCRI, 393 Central Ave FL 3, Newark, NJ 866-448-5812 tinyurl.com/c5bw263 ☯

Morristown Area

AIDS/HIV Services, Education & Support

♀ ☆ ♿ Morristown Medical Center, 200 South St 3rd flr, Morristown; 973-889-6810 tinyurl.com/yyldxv2h ✚ ⚕

Newark/Montclair Area

Community Centers and/or Pride Organizations

♀ ★ Newark LGBTQ Community Center, POB 200434, Newark; 07102 973-424-9555 www.newarklgbtcenter.org ☯ ⚕

AIDS/HIV Services, Education & Support

♂ ★ African American Office of Gay Concerns, 877 Broad St Ste 211, Newark; 973-639-0700 www.aaogc.org ❖

♂ Broadway House for Continuing Care, 298 Broadway, Newark; 973-268-9797 www.broadwayhouse.org ✪

Counseling/Psychotherapy/Mental Health

♂ ○ Chan, Joseph A, MSW, LCSW, 94 Valley Rd, Montclair; 07042 973-202-1421 ✪

Religious / Spiritual Resources

♀ ☆ UFC NewArk, POB 9891, Newark; 07104 973-565-9340 www.ufcnewark.org ✪ info@ufcnewark.org

Ridgewood

Religious / Spiritual Resources

♀ ☆ ♂♂ Reconstructionist Congregation Beth Israel, c/o Temple Israel & JCC, 475 Grove St; 07450 201-444-9320 www.synagogue.org ⚥ ✒ rcbi@synagogue.org

New York
State/County Resources

AIDS/HIV Services, Education & Support

♀ ☆ ♂♂ ACR Health, 627 W Genessee St, Syracuse, NY 315-475-2430 GRADS (Guys Responding and Demanding Safety) www.acrhealth.org ✪ ✒

Albany & Capital Area

Organizations/Resources: Ethnic, Multicultural

♀ ★ In Our Own Voices, Inc, 245 Lark St Ste 1, Albany; 518-432-4188 www.inourownvoices.org ❖

Buffalo/Niagara Falls Area

Health Care: Physical (see also Counseling/Mental Health)

♀ ★ MOCHA Center, 1092 Main St, Buffalo 716-852-1142 www.mochacenter.org ❖

Hudson Valley & Catskills Area

Organizations/Resources: Family and Supporters

♂ ☆ PFLAG Westchester, c/o The Loft, 252 Bryant Ave, White Plains; 10605 914-468-4636 www.pflagwestchester.org ✦ info@pflagwestchester.org

Morrisville

Organizations/Resources: Student, Academic, Education

♀ ★ SUNY Morrisville State College Mo'Pride, PO Box 901; 13408 315-684-6554 tinyurl.com/hnlmwhf ✪

New York City & Long Island Area

Community Centers and/or Pride Organizations
Bronx

♀ Latino Pride Center, 975 Kelly St #402, Bronx; 718-328-4188 www.latinopridecenter.org ✦

Brooklyn

♀ ★ (♫) Audre Lorde Project, 147 W 24th St 3rd Flr; 212-463-0342 alp.org ❖

♀ ★ (♫) Audre Lorde Project, 85 S Oxford St Flr 3, Bklyn; 718-596-0342 alp.org ❖

Manhattan

♀ ★ Harlem Pride, 42 Macombs Place 347-846-0362 www.harlempride.org ✪

♀ ★ The Harlem SGL/LGBTQ Center, 42 Macombs Place; 212-634-7895 fb.com/HarlemCenterNYC/ ✪

AIDS/HIV Services, Education & Support
Manhattan & Citywide

♂ ☆ The Alliance for Positive Change, 64 W 35th St 3rd Flr; 212-645-0875 alliance.nyc ✪

♂ ☆ Chinese-American Planning Council, Community Health Services - HIV/AIDS Services, 150 Elizabeth St; 212-941-0920 www.cpc-nyc.org ✧

♀ ☆ (♫) FACES, 123 W 115th St; 10026 212-283-9180 fax 212-283-9195 www.facesny.org ✪

♂ ☆ ♂♂ Harlem United Community AIDS Center, Inc., 306 Malcolm X Blvd 3rd Fl; 10027 212-803-2850 www.harlemunited.org ✪ intake@harlemunited.org

♀ Hispanic AIDS Forum, 1767 Park Ave 5th Flr 212-563-4500 ✦

♀ Latino Commission on AIDS, 24 W 25th St Fl 9 212-675-3288 www.latinoaids.org ✦

Archives/Libraries/Museums/History Projects

♀ ☆ ♂♂ Black Gay & Lesbian Archive, Schomburg Center for Research in Black Culture, New York Public Library, 515 Malcolm X Blvd; 212-491-2200 www.nypl.org/archives/4117 ❖ ✒

Bars, Cafes, Clubs, Restaurants
Brooklyn: Sunset Park

♂ Xstasy, 758 5th Ave, Bklyn; 718-499-2348 fb.com/clubxstasybk/ D ▥ ✦

Manhattan & Citywide

♂ ● Habibi, Monthly party for gay Middle Eastern Men 646-431-5369 www.habibinyc.com ✎

♀ ● Lovergirl, Sat, check details 212-252-3397 www.lovergirlnyc.com D ✪

♀ Sholay Productions, 212-713-5111 www.sholayevents.com ✎
Manhattan: Harlem

♂ ● Alibi, 2376 Adam Clayton Powell 917-472-7789 fb.com/alibi-harlem ❖

Manhattan: Hell's Kitchen

♀ ● ♂♂ Lucky Cheng's, 605 W 48th St 212-995-5500 Drag cabaret Shows www.luckychengs.com D ⚥ ✖▥ ✧ ✒ info@luckychengs.com

Queens: Elmhurst

♀ Music Box, 4008 74th St, Elmhurst (Broadway) 718-424-8612 ▥ ◆

Queens: Jackson Heights

♂ ● Friends Tavern, 7811 Roosevelt Ave, Jackson Hts; (78th St) 718-397-7256 fb.com/friendstavern ▥ ◆

♀ True Colors, 79-15 Roosevelt Ave, Jackson Hts; 718-672-7505 fb.com/truecolorsbarNY/ **DK** ▥ ◆

Broadcast Media

♀ ★ Out FM Collective, c/o WBAI 99.5 FM, 388 Atlantic Ave 3th Flr, Bklyn; 917-653-7267 www.outfm.org ◓

Health Care: Physical (see also Counseling/Mental Health)
Brooklyn

♀ Caribbean Women's Health Association, 3512 Church Ave, Bklyn; 718-826-2942 www.cwha.org ✤

Manhattan

♀ ★ APICHA Community Health Center, 400 Broadway; 866-274-2429 www.apicha.org ✧

Queens

♀ ★ APICHA Community Health Center, 400 Broadway; 866-274-2429 www.apicha.org ✧

Organizations/Resources: Cultural, Dance, Performance

♀ ★ && Lavender Light Gospel Choir, 70-A Greenwich Ave #315; 212-714-7072 www.lavenderlight.com ◓

Organizations/Resources: Ethnic, Multicultural

♀ ★ (?&) African Ancestral Lesbians United for Societal Change, Inc., LGBT Community Center, 208 W 13th St 475-422-5872 **H?** fb.com/AALUSC1974 ✤ ✁

♂ ★ (?&) Armenian Gay & Lesbian Association, **H?** www.aglany.org ✁

♂ ★ && The Barbershop, c/o GMHC, 307 W 38th St; 10018-9502 212-367-1388 **H?** tinyurl.com/wdg6tly ✤ ✁ durellk@gmhc.org

♀ ★ Black & Latino LGBTQ Coalition, 55 W 116th St Ste 236; 10026 212-457-8954 bllgbtqc.org info@bllgbtqc.org

♀ ★ Caribbean American PRIDE, fb.com/caribameripride ✤

♀ Caribbean Equality Project, 347-709-3179 tinyurl.com/ya4y42ka ✤

♀ ★ Chutney Pride (Caribbean), 347-869-2601 fb.com/chutneypridelgbt ✤

♂ ★ && Gay Asian/Pacific Islander Men of NY (GAPIMNY), POB 1608; 10113 www.gapimny.org ✧

♀ ★ && Gay Men of African Descent, Inc., 540 Atlantic Ave - Lower Level, Bklyn; 718-222-5555 www.gmad.org ✤

♀ (?&) Irish Queers, 212-289-1101 **H?** irishqueers.blogspot.com ✁

♂ ★ (?&) Italian Conversation Group, LGBT Community Center, 208 W 13th St; 10011-7702 212-772-3511 **H?** ✁

♂ ★ **Jacks of Color, 212-222-9794 NYC's Pre-Eminent Safer Sex Club for Gay Men Of Color 'And Their Friends'. www.JacksOfColor.com** ✤

♀ ★ Puerto Rican Initiative to Develop Empowerment (PRIDE), 24 W 25th St Flr 9; 212-675-3288 x469 www.prideny.org ◆

♀ ★ Q-Wave, POB 1896; 10013 fb.com/groups/qwave/ ✧

♀ ★ (?&) South Asian Lesbian & Gay Association, LGBT Community Center, 208 W 13th St; 212-358-5132 **H?** Serving the Desi Queer Community of New York www.salganyc.org ✧ ✁

♀ Tarab NYC, Arab, Middle Eastern, and/or North African www.tarabnyc.org

Organizations/Resources: Family and Supporters

♀ Desi Rainbow Parents and Allies, PFLAG NYC, 130 E 25th St #M1; 646-397-4032 www.pflagnyc.org/support/api ✧

Organizations/Resources: Senior Resources
Brooklyn

♀ ★ && GRIOT Circle, Inc, 25 Flatbush Ave. F5, Bklyn; 718-246-2775 www.griotcircle.org ✤

Manhattan & Citywide

♀ ★ SAGE Center Harlem, 220 W 143rd St; 10027 646-660-8951 tinyurl.com/y3zcamhj ◓ sageharlem@sageusa.org

Organizations/Resources: Social, Recreation, Support
Manhattan & Citywide

♀ ★ Out at the J, Jewish Community Center in Manhattan, 334 Amsterdam Ave; 646-505-5472 x727 tinyurl.com/y848u6uy ✿

Manhattan

♀ HEBRO, www.myhebro.com ✿

Organizations/Resources: Youth (see also Family)
Manhattan & Citywide

♀♂ ★ && The Door, 555 Broome St 212-941-9090 www.door.org ◓

♀ ★ FIERCE!, 2427 Morris Ave, Bronx; 10468 929-246-5273 www.fiercenyc.org ✤ info@fiercenyc.org

♀ ★ (?&) Project Speak Out Loud, Grand St. Settlement, 80 Pitt St; 10002 646-201-4255 www.grandsettlement.org ✤ ✁ psol@grandsettlement.org

Religious / Spiritual Resources
Long Island

♀ ★ Gay & Lesbian Inclusion Committee (GLIC), Temple Beth-El of Great Neck, 5 Old Mill Rd, Great Neck; 516-487-0900 tinyurl.com/l6ldx34 ✿

Manhattan & Citywide

♂ ☆ && B'nai Jeshurun, 270 W 89th St 10024 Community House & offices / Synagogue at 257 W 88th St 212-787-7600 **HD** www.bj.org ✿ ✁

♀ ★ ♂ Congregation Beit Simchat Torah, 130 W 30th St; 212-929-9498 **H?** www.cbst.org ✿ ✁

♀ ★ Eshel, c/o Makom Hadash, 125 Maiden Lane Ste 8B; 724-374-3501 www.eshelonline.org ✿

♀ ★ && Gay & Lesbian Yeshiva Day School Alumni Association, 212-780-4656 orthogays.org/glydsa.html ✿

♀ Jewish Queer Youth, 551-579-4673 www.jqyouth.org ✿

Manhattan

♀ JQYouth, 1460 Broadway; 551-579-4673 Social support group for Orthodox Jewish youth. www.jqyouth.org ✿

♀ Keshet NY Office, 60 1 W 26th St Ste 325 www.keshetonline.org
✡

Rochester & Finger Lakes Area

Religious / Spiritual Resources

♂ ★ ⚥ Ray of Hope Church of Our Lord Jesus Christ, 380 W 1st St, Elmira; 14901 607-280-0374 www.rayofhopechurch.com ✪ ✗

Syracuse

AIDS/HIV Services, Education & Support

♀ ✰ AIDS Community Resources, 627 W Genesee St 800-475-2430 www.acrhealth.org ✪

Bars, Cafes, Clubs, Restaurants

♂ Rain Lounge, 103 N Geddes St; 315-218-5951 fb.com/Rain-LoungeSyracuse/ 🏳️ ✪

North Carolina
Charlotte Area

Leather Resources & Groups

♂ ★ ⚥ Tradesmen Levi/Leather Club, PO Box 31654, Charlotte; 28231 **H?** www.charlottetradesmen.org **LW** ✪ ✗

Organizations/Resources: Ethnic, Multicultural

♂ ★ Charlotte Black Pride, 5009 Beatties Ford Rd Ste 107-347, Charlotte; charlotteblackpride.org ❖

Religious / Spiritual Resources

♀ ✰ (?⚥) Havurat Tikvah, POB 12684, Charlotte; 28220 980-225-5330 www.HavuratTikvah.org ✡ havurattikvah@gmail.com

♀ ✰ Temple Beth El Keshet Committee, 5101 Providence Rd, Charlotte; 704-366-1948 Welcoming, pro-LGBT rights Reform Jewish community. tinyurl.com/yac43grn ✡

Ohio
Akron/Canton/Kent Area

Organizations/Resources: Student, Academic, Education

♂ ★ ⚥ PRIDE! Kent, Box 17, Office of Campus Life, Kent; fb.com/pridekent/ ✪

Cleveland Area

Men's & Sex Clubs (not primarily Health Clubs)

♂ ● Flex Cleveland, 2600 Hamilton Ave, Cleveland 216-812-3304 www.flexspas.com/cleveland ✪

Organizations/Resources: Ethnic, Multicultural

♂ ★ (?⚥) Asians & Friends Cleveland, POB 25095, Cleveland; 44125 www.afcleveland.org ✦

Religious / Spiritual Resources

♂ ★ ⚤ Chevrei Tikva Chavurah, Anshe Chesed Fairmount Temple, 23737 Fairmount Blvd, Beachwood; 44122-2296 216-464-1330 x126 tinyurl.com/ohjkou4 ✡ mail@fairmounttemple.org

Columbus Area

AIDS/HIV Services, Education & Support

♂ ✰ Greater Columbus Mpowerment Center, Equitas Health, 889 E Long St, Col; 614-359-2033 **H?** Gay/bi men of color, ages 13-29 www.columbusmpowerment.org ❖ ✗

Religious / Spiritual Resources

♂ ★ ⚥ B'nai Keshet at OSU, OSU Hillel, Wexner Jewish Student Center, 46 E 16th St, Col; 614-294-4797 **H?** www.osuhillel.org ✡ ✗

Oregon
Portland/Vancouver Area

Organizations/Resources: Ethnic, Multicultural

♂ ★ ⚥ Portland Black Pride, POB 6743, Portland; 97228 503-232-7676 fb.com/PortlandBlackPride ❖

♂ Portland Two Spirit Society, 971-231-4999 fb.com/Portland2Spirits/

♂ ★ ⚥ Sankofa Collective Northwest, 4115 N Mississippi Ave, Portland; 503-234-7837 **H?** (previously PFLAG Portland Black Chapter) sankofanw.org ❖ ✗

Religious / Spiritual Resources

♀ ✰ Congregation Neveh Shalom, 2900 SW Peaceful Lane, Portland; 97239 503-246-8831 www.nevehshalom.org ✡

Salem

Crisis, Anti-violence, & Helplines

♀ ✰ The Center for Hope & Safety, 605 Center St NE 97301 503-399-7722 hopeandsafety.org ✪

Pennsylvania
Erie

Religious / Spiritual Resources

♀ ✰ Temple Anshe Hesed, 5401 Old Zuck Rd; 16508 814-454-2426 www.anshehesederie.org ✡ office@taherie.org

Johnstown

Bars, Cafes, Clubs, Restaurants

♀ ● (⚥) Lucy's Place, 520 Washington St, Johnstown; 814-539-4448 fb.com/lucillesjohnstown **DK** 🏳️ ✪

Philadelphia Area

AIDS/HIV Services, Education & Support

⚥ ★ GALAEI: Gay & Lesbian Latino AIDS Education Initiative, 149 W Susquehanna Ave, Phila; 267-457-3912 www.galaei.org ✦

Bars, Cafes, Clubs, Restaurants
Philadelphia

♀ Stimulus, Check monthly party fb.com/TheStimulus ○

Organizations/Resources: Ethnic, Multicultural

⚥ ★ The COLOURS Organization, Inc, 1211 Chestnut St Ste 910, Phila; 215-832-0100 coloursorganization.org ✣ ✗

⚥ ★ (♿) Men of All Colors Together/MACT Philadelphia, POB 42257, Phila; 19101 215-397-3669 tinyurl.com/p8e4l7f ○

⚥ ★ Philadelphia Black Pride, POB 22515, Phila; 19110 www.philly-blackpride.org ✣

Organizations/Resources: Family and Supporters

♀ ★ Philadelphia Family Pride, POB 31848, Phila 19104 215-888-0722 www.phillyfamilypride.org ○

Pittsburgh Area

Bookstores

♀ The Big Idea Bookstore, 4812 Liberty Ave, Pgh 412-687-4323 thebigideapgh.org ☞ ○

Religious / Spiritual Resources

⚥ ★ ♿ Bet Tikvah, POB 10140, Pgh; 15232-0140 412-256-8317 www.bettikvah.org ⚧ ✗ info@bettikvah.org

Puerto Rico
State/County Resources

Information, Media & Publications

⚥ ★ Orgullo Boricua LGBT, fb.com/groups/19481998232 ✦

San Juan Area

Community Centers and/or Pride Organizations

⚥ ★ Centro Comunitario LGBTT de Puerto Rico, PO Box 9501, San Juan; 00908 / Calle Mayaguez #37, Urb Perez Morris, San Juan 00917 787-294-9850 www.centrolgbttpr.org ✦ centrolgbttpr@gmail.com

Bars, Cafes, Clubs, Restaurants
San Juan

♂ VIP Bar, 613 Calle Condado, San Juan (Santurce) 787-722-5509 L 🏳 ○

Santurce

♂ SX, 1204 Ponce de Leon, Santurce fb.com/Sxtheclub/ 🏳 ✦

Broadcast Media

⚥ ★ Saliendo del Closet, POB 9501 Santurce Stn, San Juan; 00908 787-607-3939 fb.com/SaliendoDelCloset/ ✦

South Carolina
State/County Resources

Organizations/Resources: Ethnic, Multicultural

⚥ ★ South Carolina Black Pride, POB 8191, Columbia, SC 29202 410-207-3822 scblackpride.weebly.com ✣

Tennessee
Memphis

AIDS/HIV Services, Education & Support

⚥ ☆ ♿ Friends For Life HIV Resources, 43 N Cleveland; 901-272-0855 www.fflmemphis.org ○

Nashville Area

AIDS/HIV Services, Education & Support

⚥ ☆ Metropolitan Interdenominational Church First Response Center, LLC, 1219 9th Ave N, Nashville; 37208 615-321-9791 metropolitanfrc.com ✣

Organizations/Resources: Ethnic, Multicultural

⚥ ★ ♿ Brothers United, Nashville Cares, POB 68335, Nashville; 37206 615-921-0340 fb.com/BrothersUnitedTN ✣

⚥ ★ Nashville Black Pride, POB 68335, Nashville; 37206 615-974-2832 www.nashvilleblackpride.org ✣

Organizations/Resources: Youth (see also Family)

⚥ ☆ ♿ Young Brothers United, Nashville Cares, 442 Metroplex Dr Bldg D STE 100, Nashville; 615-974-2832 tinyurl.com/ya8nmldu ✣

Texas
State/County Resources

Organizations/Resources: Ethnic, Multicultural

⚥ ★ ♿ ALLGO, 701 Tillery St Box 4, Austin, TX 512-472-2001 www.allgo.org ✣

⚥ ★ Texas Two Spirit Society, POB 141361, Dallas, TX 75214 www.texastwospirits.org

Austin Area

Bookstores

♀ ○ Red Salmon Arts (casa de Resistencia Books), 4926 E Cesar Chavez St Unit C1, Austin; / check schedule 512-389-9881 www.resistenciabooks.com ○

Dallas/Fort Worth Area

AIDS/HIV Services, Education & Support

♀ ☆ ♿ Access and Information Network (AIN), 2600 N Stemmons Fwy Ste 151, Dallas; 214-943-4444 H? www.AINDallas.org ✦ @ixx=

Bars, Cafes, Clubs, Restaurants
Dallas

Club Los Rieles, 4930 Military Pkwy, Dallas 214-546-1109 fb.com/clublosrielesdallas/ **D** ✦

Havana Bar & Grill, 4006 Cedar Springs Rd, Dallas; 214-886-6804 fb.com/HavanaDallas/ **D** ✦

• Kaliente, 4350 Maple Ave, Dallas 469-556-1395 fb.com/kalienteclub ✦

Marty's Live, 4207 Maple Ave, Dallas; / Tue Lesbian night 214-599-2151 tinyurl.com/q8vysae **D** ✦

Legal Services

♂ • Herrera, Roger, 1005 W Jefferson Blvd Ste 403 214-943-6062 tinyurl.com/ksjgz5 ✦ law_rogelioherrera@sbcglobal.net

Organizations/Resources: Ethnic, Multicultural

★ Dallas Southern Pride, 1075 W Griffin St Ste 204, Dallas; 214-405-5475 www.dallassouthernpride.com ❖

♀ ☆ LULAC 4871 - Dallas Rainbow Council, POB 192336, Dallas; 75219 www.lulac4871.org ✦ LULAC4871@gmail.com

Organizations/Resources: Transgender/Gender Non-Conforming/Diverse

T ☆ Black Trans Advocacy, 3530 Forest Lane Ste 290, Dallas; 855-255-8636 www.blacktrans.org ❖

T ☆ Black Transmen, 3530 Forest Lane Ste 290, Dallas; 855-255-8636 www.blacktransmen.org ❖

T ☆ Black Transwomen, 3530 Forest Lane Ste 290, Dallas; 855-255-8636 BlackTranswomen.org ❖

Religious / Spiritual Resources

★ ᕫᕫ Congregation Beth El Binah, 11211 Preston Road www.bethelbinah.org ✡

Sports & Outdoor

★ Different Strokes Golf Association, www.dsgadallas.org ☉

El Paso

AIDS/HIV Services, Education & Support

♀ ☆ La Fe Care Center, 1314 E Yandell Dr 915-209-2667 www.lafe-ep.org ✦

Bars, Cafes, Clubs, Restaurants

• Chiquitas Bar, 310 E Missouri Ave 915-351-0095 tinyurl.com/yc874cww ✦

Houston Area

Bars, Cafes, Clubs, Restaurants
Houston

Crystal, 6680 Southwest Freeway, Houston 713-532-2582 fb.com/LatinClub/ **D** ✦

Viviana's, 4624 Dacoma St, Houston 713-681-4101 fb.com/7132690493vnc/ **D** ✦

Organizations/Resources: Ethnic, Multicultural

★ (?ᕫ) Asians & Friends Houston, PO Box 667100, Houston; 77266 tinyurl.com/yo3od7 ✧

Houston Splash, 6017 Ardmore St, Houston www.houstonsplash.com ❖

Religious / Spiritual Resources

★ Keshet Houston, POB 920552, Houston 77292-0552 832-429-5392 www.keshethouston.org ✡ info@keshethouston.org

San Antonio Area

Bars, Cafes, Clubs, Restaurants
San Antonio

• Silver Dollar Saloon, 1812 N Main Ave, San Antonio; 210-227-2623 www.facebook.com/tejanotalk/ **DW** ✦

Organizations/Resources: Family and Supporters

♂ ☆ ᕫᕫ PFLAG, POB 761475, San Antonio; 78245 210-848-7407 pflagsanantonio.org ✦

RFD
🌑 A COUNTRY JOURNAL 🌑
FOR GAY MEN EVERYWHERE
SPRING. SUMMER. FALL. WINTER

P.O. Box 302 Hadley MA 01035-0302
http://www.rfdmag.org

Organizations/Resources: Political/Legislative/Advocacy

♀ ☆ &&. Esperanza Peace & Justice Center, 922 San Pedro Ave, San Antonio; 78212-4642 210-228-0201 Also cultural arts center. www.esperanzacenter.org ✦ esperanza@esperanzacenter.org

Tyler/Longview Area

Religious / Spiritual Resources

♂ ☆ Congregation Beth El, 1010 Charleston Dr, Tyler; 75703 903-581-3764 www.jewishtyler.com ✡

Wimberley

Accommodation Rental: Furnished / Vacation (& AirBNB)

♂ • (🐾) Abundance: A Hill Country River Retreat, 330 Mill Race Lane, Wimberley, TX 713-819-9339 www.abundanceretreat.com
✪ ♣ ✗ ⊛

Virginia
Richmond Area

Bars, Cafes, Clubs, Restaurants
Richmond

♂ • Club Colours, After 7 Lounge, 5737 Hull Street Rd, Richmond; / check schedule 804-353-9776 tinyurl.com/3pm35gn **D** ✤

Religious / Spiritual Resources

♂ ☆ Beth Ahabah, 1121 W Franklin St, Richmond 23220-3700 804-358-6757 www.bethahabah.org ✡

Washington
Seattle & Tacoma Area

AIDS/HIV Services, Education & Support

♂ ★ &&. People of Color Against AIDS Network, 4437 Rainier Ave S, Seattle; 206-322-7061 www.pocaan.org ✤

Bars, Cafes, Clubs, Restaurants
Seattle

♂ • &&. AzuQar! Queer latinx Dance Night, Re-bar, 1114 Howell St, Seattle; 206-233-9873 Theater and Nightclub fb.com/azuqar.dance/ **D** ✪ ✗

Organizations/Resources: Ethnic, Multicultural

♀ ★ Entre Hermanos, 1105 23rd Ave, Seattle 206-322-7700 www.entrehermanos.org ✦

♀ ★ Trikone Northwest, 1122 E Pike St #1174, Seattle; LGBT South Asians www.trikonenw.org ✧

♀ UTOPIA - United Territories of Pacific Islanders Alliance - Seattle, POB 68206, Seattle; 98168 253-478-3941 www.utopiaseattle.org ✧

Religious / Spiritual Resources

♀ ★ (🐾) Congregation Tikvah Chadashah, 1122 E Pike St PMB 734, Seattle; 206-355-1414 www.tikvahchadashah.org ✡

Wisconsin
Elkhorn

Accommodation: Hotels, Inns, Guesthouses, B&B, Resorts

♂ ○ Ye Olde Manor House B&B, N7622 US 12; 53121 262-742-2450 fax 262-742-2425 www.yeoldemanorhouse.com ✤ ✗ ⊛⊛ innkeeper@yeoldemanorhouse.com

Milwaukee Area

Organizations/Resources: Student, Academic, Education

♂ ☆ Alliance School of Milwaukee, 850 W Walnut, Milwaukee; 414-267-5400 www.allianceschool.net ✪

Religious / Spiritual Resources

♀ ☆ &&. Congregation Shir Hadash, POB 170632, Milwaukee; 53217 414-297-9159 shirmke.org ✡ ✗ info@shirmke.org

USA National Resources

USA: National Resources

Crisis, Anti-violence, & Helplines

♂ ★ **GLBT National Hotline, 888-843-4564 fax 415-552-5498 www.GLBThotline.org**
◆ *Advertisement page 2*

♂ ★ National Coalition of Anti-Violence Programs, 116 Nassau St Flr 3, New York, NY 212-714-1184 avp.org/ncavp/

♀ ☆ National Sexual Assault Hotline, Rape, Abuse, & Incest National Network (RAINN), 1220 L St NW #505, Washington, DC 800-656-4673 www.rainn.org

♂ ☆ Womenslaw.org, For victims of domestic violence www.womenslaw.org

Community Centers and/or Pride Organizations

♂ ★ ♿ CenterLink: the Community of LGBT Centers, POB 24490, Fort Lauderdale, FL 33307 954-765-6024 www.lgbtcenters.org

♂ ★ InterPride, International Association of Lesbian, Gay, Bisexual & Transgender Pride Coordinators www.interpride.org

Information, Media & Publications

♀ ☆ Bitch Media, POB 11929, Portland, OR 97211 503-282-5699 www.bitchmedia.org general@b-word.org

♂ ● Connextions Magazine, POB 242, Calverton, NY 11933 www.connextionsmagazine.com

♂ ● **Damron Guides, 415-255-0404 fax 415-703-9049 Annual pocket-sized guide to USA, Canada, Mexico, Europe & Asia. Also Women's Traveller. www.damron.com**

♂ ● FEMSPEC, Batya Weinbaum, 1610 Rydalmount Rd, Cleveland Heights, OH 44118-1352 540-695-3043 www.femspec.org

♂ ● FlavaMen, Flava Works, Inc POB 2495, Chicago, IL 60690 305-438-9450 www.flavamen.com ❖ sales@flavaworks.com

♂ ★ Fusion Magazine, Kent State University, Kent State University, 205 Franklin Hall, Kent, OH 330-672-2586 www.ohiofusion.com

♂ ● The Gay & Lesbian Review, POB 180300, Boston, MA 02118-9719 617-421-0082 www.glreview.org

♂ ● **Gay Parent Magazine, POB 750852, Forest Hills, NY 11375-0852 718-380-1780 Resources for building and nurturing your family, since 1998. www.gayparentmag.com gayparentmag@gmail.com**

♂ ● **Gayellow Pages, POB 533 Village Stn, New York, NY 10014-0533 646-213-0263 v/f Classified directory of services, businesses, resources, etc in USA & Canada. Mailing lists available. www.gayellowpages.com gypages@gmail.com**

♂ GLBTQI ♀ Gay/nongay ♂ bisexual
♀ LBTQI women ♀ all women ♀ bisexual women
♂ GBTQI men ♂ all men ♂ bisexual men
T specifically transsexual/transgender/transvestite

Ϋ ✕ Bar and Restaurant ✕ Restaurant ⊽ Cafe
▦ Entertainment/Cabaret/Showbar
D Dancing **V** Video bar **K** Karaoke **S** Sports bar
C Country **L** Leather/Levi **W** Western
P Private Club (ask about visitor memberships)

♥ Wedding-related services or marriage equality
H Assistance available for the deaf and hearing-impaired
HD devices **HS** sign **HDS** devices and sign
H? Check for assistance available for the deaf and. hearing-impaired
🚭 🚭 smoke-free property 🚭 smoke-free indoors
(🚬) indoor smoking areas
🐾 Pets welcome (🐾?) Ask about pets
⟋ High speed internet available to visitors
Wheelchair Accessibility of premises or meeting place:
♿ Accessible premises and lavatory
(♿) Accessible premises with help; accessible lavatory
♿ Accessible premises; lavatory not known to be accessible
Accessible premises with help
(♿) Call ahead for details: places of meetings or activities vary, or special arrangements available.
◇ Asian ✦ Latin/Hispanic
✤ African-descent/Black
❖ People of Color ✳ Two-Spirit ✪ Diverse

♀ ★ Gertrude Press, POB 28281, Portland, OR 97228 www.gertrudepress.org

♀ ● The GLBT Guide, POB 34965, Phoenix, AZ 85067 888-396-1666 www.glbtguide.com

♀ ★ **GLBT National Help Center, 2261 Market St PMB #296, San Francisco, CA 415-355-0003 fax 415-552-5498 www.GLBThotline.org**
◆ *Advertisement page 2*

♂ ● Instigator Magazine, IXAmedia, 8419 Santa Monica Blvd #280, West Hollywood, CA 90046 213-629-2936 fax 213-596-0840 instigator.co info@instigator.co

♀ ● **Lesbian Connection Magazine, Ambitious Amazons, POB 811, East Lansing, MI 48826-0811 517-371-5257 fax 517-371-5200 A free, worldwide magazine for, by & about Lesbians. www.lconline.org LC@LConline.org**

♀ ● (♿) Metrosource, 213 W 35th St 12W, New York, NY 212-315-0800 www.metrosource.com

♀ ★ OutWrite Newsmagazine - UCLA, 149B Kerckhoff Hall 308 Westwood Plz, Los Angeles, CA 310-825-8500 www.outwritenews-mag.org

♀ ★ Posture Magazine, www.posturemag.com

♀ ● ♿ Pride & Equality, 4200 Silver Ave SE Ste C, Albuquerque, NM 87108 505-450-4706 Annual, May www.myprideonline.com NMEntertains@gmail.com

♀ ● proudout.com, International LGBTQ+ directory. Events, travel and more International listing of LGBT social events www.proudout.com hello@proudout.com

♂ ● (♿) **RFD, POB 302, Hadley, MA 01035 413-334-9973 A Reader Created Journal Celebrating Queer Diversity Since 1974 www.rfdmag.org**

♀ ★ (♿) **Sinister Wisdom, 2333 McIntosh Rd, Dover, FL 33527-5980 www.sinisterwisdom.org sinisterwisdom@gmail.com**
◆ *Advertisement page 42*

Accommodation: Residential/Sharing/Roommates

♀ ● RoomieMatch.com, www.roomiematch.com RoomieMatch@RoomieMatch.com

---

Adoption, Surrogacy, Assisted Fertility Support, see also Reproductive

♂ ○ **Surrogate Mothers, Inc, mail to SMI, 6010 Deerwood Dr, Greenwood, IN 46143 317-996-2000 888-SURROGATE World's most reputable surrogacy program for over 30 years www.surrogatemothers.com**

AIDS/HIV Services, Education & Support

♂ Actors Fund of America AIDS Volunteer Program, 729 7th Ave 10th Flr, New York, NY 800-221-7303 actorsfund.org

♂ AIDS Community Research Initiative of America, 230 W 38th St 17th Flr, New York, NY 212-924-3934 www.acria.org

♂ AIDS Healthcare Foundation, 6255 W Sunset Blvd 21st flr, Hollywood, CA 323-860-5200 www.aidshealth.org

♂ ☆ ♿ The AIDS Institute, 1705 DeSales St NW Ste 700, Washington, DC / 17 Davis Blvd Ste 403, Tampa, FL 33606-3438 202-835-8373 www.theaidsinstitute.org

♂ ☆ AIDS United, 1101 14th St NW, Suite 300z, Washington, DC 202-408-4848 www.aidsunited.org

♂ ☆ AIDSpirit USA, POB 30734, Billings, MT 59107 406-696-1164 www.aidspirit.org

♂ American Foundation for AIDS Research, 1100 Vermont Ave NW Ste 600, Washington, DC 00-342-2437 www.amfar.org

♂ amFAR - American Foundation for AIDS Research, 120 Wall St Fl 13, New York, NY 212-806-1600 www.amfar.org

♂ ☆ ♿ The Black AIDS Institute, 1833 W 8th St Ste 200, Los Angeles, CA 90057-4920 213-353-3610 www.blackaids.org ♣

♂ ☆ The Body, 212-541-8500 www.thebody.com

♂ ☆ DAB the AIDS BEAR Project, 4615 Philips Highway, Jacksonville, FL / 299 E Screech Owl Drive, Kuna, ID 83634 904-894-1054 tinyurl.com/mmtqf8

♂ Forum for Collaborative HIV Research, 1608 Rhode Island Ave NW #212, Washington, DC 202-833-4617 www.hivforum.org

♂ ☆ Foundation for Integrative AIDS Research (FIAR), 62 Sterling Place Ste 2, Brooklyn, NY 11217 718-622-0212 www.fiar.us

♂ ★ ♿ Gay Men's Health Crisis, 307 W 38th St, New York, NY 212-367-1000 www.gmhc.org

♂ Names Project Foundation AIDS Memorial Quilt, 117 Luckie St, Atlanta, GA 404-688-5500 www.aidsquilt.org

♂ ☆ National AIDS & STD Hotline CDC Info, 1600 Clifton Rd, Atlanta, GA 800-232-4636 www.cdc.gov/hiv

♂ ☆ ♿ National AIDS Education/Services for Minorities, 2140 MLK Jr Dr #602, Atlanta, GA 404-691-8880 www.naesm.org ♣

♂ ☆ ♿ National AIDS Memorial Grove, PO Box 2270, San Francisco, CA 94126 415-765-0446 www.aidsmemorial.org

♂ ☆ ♿ National Minority AIDS Council, 1000 Vermont Ave NW Ste 200, Washington, DC 202-870-0918 www.nmac.org

♂ ☆ National Native American AIDS Prevention Center, 1031 33rd St, Denver, CO 720-382-2244 www.nnaapc.net ✳

♂ Rural AIDS Action Network, 300 E St Germain St Ste 220, St Cloud, MN 800-966-9735 www.raan.org

♂ ☆ Search for a Cure, 17 Worcester St B, Cambridge, MA 617-945-5350 www.searchforacure.org

♂ ☆ ♿ TPAN, 5537 N Broadway, Chicago, IL 773-989-9400 www.tpan.com

♂ ☆ Treatment Action Group (TAG), 90 Broad St #2503, New York, NY 212-253-7922 www.treatmentactiongroup.org

♂ ☆ World AIDS Marathon, Richard M. Brodsky Foundation, 1247 Mara Court, Atlantic Beach, NY 11509-1635 516-770-7724 www.worldaidsmarathon.com RichardM.Brodsky@gmail.com

---

Archives/Libraries/Museums/History Projects

♂ AIDS History Project, University of California, 530 Parnassus Ave, San Francisco, CA 415-476-8112 tinyurl.com/nqfctpg

♂ ☆ ♿ Black Gay & Lesbian Archive, Schomburg Center for Research in Black Culture, New York Public Library, 515 Malcolm X Blvd, New York, NY 212-491-2200 www.nypl.org/archives/4117 ♣

♂ Carter/Johnson Leather Library, POB 1211, Newburgh, IN 47630 812-297-0431 carterjohnsonlibrary.com

⚢ ★ Committee on LGBT History (CLGBTH), 614 Zulauf Hall, Northern IL University, DeKalb, IL www.clgbthistory.org

♀ ★ Diverse Sexuality and Gender Section, Society of American Archivists, 17 N State St #1425, Chicago, IL 60602-3315 312-606-0722 tinyurl.com/y67np67f

⚢ ★ ♋ Gay & Lesbian Archives of the Pacific Northwest, POB 3646, Portland, OR 97208-3646 www.glapn.org info@glapn.org

⚢ Gay Erotic Archives, www.gayeroticarchives.com

⚢ ★ ᕔᕔ Gerber/Hart Library and Archives, 6500 N Clark St, Chicago, IL 60626 773-381-8030 www.gerberhart.org info@gerberhart.org

⚢ ★ ♋ GLBT Historical Society Archives, 989 Market St Lower Level, San Francisco, CA 415-777-5455 www.glbthistory.org

⚢ ★ ᕔᕔ Gulf Coast Archive & Museum of GLBT History, Inc., 822 W 14th St, Houston, TX 77008 832-722-5785 www.gcam.org info@gcam.org

⚢ ★ The History Project, 29 Stanhope St, Boston, MA 617-266-7733 www.historyproject.org

♂ ☆ **Homosexual Information Center, Tangent Group, 8721 Santa Monica Blvd #37, West Hollywood, CA 818-527-5442 www.tangentgroup.org**

⚢ ★ ᕔᕔ John J. Wilcox Jr. Archives of Philadelphia, William Way LGBT Community Center, 1315 Spruce St, Philadelphia, PA 215-732-2220 www.waygay.org/archives

⚢ ★ June Mazer Lesbian Archives, POB 691866, West Hollywood, CA 90069 310-659-2478 www.mazerlesbianarchives.org

♂ ☆ ᕔᕔ The Kinsey Institute, Indiana University, 150 S Woodlawn Ave - Lindley Hall 428, Bloomington, IN 47405 812-855-7686 kinsey-institute.org kinsey@indiana.edu

⚢ ★ ᕔᕔ Lambda Archives of San Diego, 4545 Park Blvd Ste 104, San Diego, CA 92116 619-260-1522 www.lambdaarchives.org info@lambdaarchives.org

⚢ ★ Latino GLBT History Project, 2000 14th St NW Ste 105, Washington, DC 202-670-5547 www.latinoglbthistory.org ◆

⚢ ★ ᕔᕔ Lavender Library, Archives & Cultural Exchange of Sacramento, 1414 21st St, Sacramento, CA 916-492-0558 www.lavender-library.com

⚢ ★ Leather Archives & Museum, 6418 N Greenview Ave, Chicago, IL 773-761-9200 www.LeatherArchives.org

⚢ ★ Legacy Project Outdoor Museum Walk (Chicago), 312-608-1198 www.legacyprojectchicago.org ✪

⚢ Lesbian Avengers Documentary Project, www.lesbianavengers.com

⚢ ★ ᕔᕔ **Lesbian Herstory Archives/Lesbian Herstory Educational Foundation, Inc, 484 14th St, Brooklyn, NY 718-768-3953 Lesbian history and cultural resource center. Please check on line for info on how to contact or visit. www.lesbianherstoryarchives.org**

⚢ ★ ᕔᕔ LGBT Community Center National History Archive, 208 W 13th St, New York, NY 10011-7702 212-620-7310 x205 tinyurl.com/9eeye4 ◆ archive@gaycenter.org

⚢ ★ LGBT Religious Archives Network, c/0 Center for LGBTQ and Gender Studies in Religion (CLGS), 1798 Scenic Ave, Berkeley, CA 773-316-8892 fsnamestran.org

⚢ ★ LGBTQIA Archives, Terry, c/o James Hormel LGBTQIA Ctr SF Library, 100 Larkin St 3rd Flr, San Francisco, CA 415-557-4400 tinyurl.com/26jyhnz

♂ ★ Lombardi-Nash, Michael (Urania Manuscripts), 6858 Arthur Court, Jacksonville, FL 904-401-0222 tinyurl.com/vpeux @ixx=

♀ ☆ ᕔᕔ National Museum of Women in the Arts, 1250 New York Ave NW, Washington, DC 202-783-5000 nmwa.org

⚢ ★ ♂ Ohio Lesbian Archives, PO Box 20075, Cincinnati, OH 45220-0075 513-256-7695 tinyurl.com/97r3dbf OLArchives@gmail.com

⚢ ★ ᕔᕔ ONE Archives at the USC Libraries, 909 W Adams Blvd, Los Angeles, CA 90007-2406 213-821-2771 one.usc.edu askONE@usc.edu

⚢ ★ ᕔᕔ ONE Archives Foundation, 7655 W Sunset Blvd, Los Angeles, CA 323-419-2159 www.onearchives.org

⚢ ★ ᕔᕔ OutHistory, Center for Lesbian & Gay Studies, 365 5th Ave #7115, New York, NY 212-817-1955 www.outhistory.org

⚢ ★ ᕔᕔ Quatrefoil Library, 1220 E Lake St, Minneapolis, MN 55407-2787 612-729-2543 www.qlibrary.org info@qlibrary.org

⚢ ★ Queery Librarians, www.queeryparty.org

⚢ ★ Rainbow History Project, POB 73176, Washington, DC 20056-3176 202-810-5068 www.rainbowhistory.org

⚢ ★ ♋ Sexual Minorities Archives, POB 6579, Holyoke, MA 01041 413-538-4750 tinyurl.com/luo5zja sexualminorities.archives@yahoo.com

⚢ ★ ♂ Stonewall National Museum & Archives Library, Library, Archives, and Business Office, 1300 E Sunrise Blvd, Fort Lauderdale, FL 33304 / Stonewall National Museum - Wilton Manors Gallery, 2157 Wilton Dr 954-763-8565 www.stonewall-museum.org info@stonewall-museum.com

⚢ ★ ᕔᕔ Terry Mangan Memorial Library, The Center, 1301 E Colfax Ave, Denver, CO 303-951-5209 tinyurl.com/gq9jakf

♀ ★ Tom of Finland Foundation, POB 26658, Los Angeles, CA 90026 213-250-1685 tinyurl.com/2ptz5r

⚢ ★ ᕔᕔ **Tretter Collection in GLBT Studies, 111 Elmer L Andersen Library, U of Minnesota, 222 21st Ave S, Minneapolis, MN 55455-4400 612-624-7526 The Collection is dedicated to preserving GLBT history and culture. tinyurl.com/m9mr9lk**

♀ ★ University of Wisconsin-Milwaukee Archives, PO Box 604, Milwaukee, WI 53201 414-229-5402 tinyurl.com/yzmxdrs

⚢ ★ ♋ Williams-Nichols Collection, Archives and Special Collections, Ekstrom LL 17, University of Louisville, 2301 S 3rd St, Louisville, KY 40292 502-852-6752 tinyurl.com/r6h376c

Art & Photography (see also Graphic Design)

♀ ● Cruse, Howard, 413-664-0735 Freelance cartoonist, creator of "Wendel" www.howardcruse.com

♀ ● Nikos Diaman Limited Editions, 2950 Van Ness Ave #4, San Francisco, CA 94109-1036 415-775-6143 www.nikosdiaman.com

♀ ● Photo Captures by Jeffery, 615-579-4471 photocapturesbyjeffery.com Jeffery.Johnson@photocapturesbyjeffery.com

Astrology/Numerology/Tarot/Psychic Readings

⚢ ● Madam Lichtenstein, LLC, POB 1726 Old Chelsea Stn, New York, NY 10011 thestarryeye.typepad.com Astroweek@aol.com

Bars, Cafes, Clubs, Restaurants

⚢ ● GayBarMaps, www.GayBarMaps.com

Bookstores

⚥ ★ (♂♀) Sources of Hope Gifts & Books, 5910 Cedar Springs Rd, Dallas, TX 800-501-4673

Broadcast Media

⚥ ★ The Lesbian Lounge Podcast, 44 7703658039 www.MyLesbianRadio.com

⚥ This Way Out, KUCR 88.3FM Radio, University of California, Riverside, CA 951-827-3737 tinyurl.com/ocwojp9

♀ ★ This Way Out, POB 1065, Los Angeles, CA 90078 818-986-4106 www.thiswayout.org tworadio@aol.com

Campgrounds and RV Parks

⚥ ● 'Camp' Camp, 347-453-5257 www.campcamp.com info@campcamp.com

Caregivers: Child, Elder, Special Needs

♀ ○ ♂♀ Au Pair in America, Live-In Cultural Child Care 800-929-7247 203-399-5161 aupair.info@aifs.com

Clothes (see also Erotica, Leather)

♂ ○ Over Easy Down Under Online Store, 87-149 Helelua St #1, Waianae, HI 808-926-4994 www.overeasydownunder.com

Coaching: Career, Life, Relationship etc

♀ ● True Azimuth, LLC, 265 Franklin St #1702, Boston, MA 02110 617-475-0081 TrueAzimuth.biz

Conferences/Events/Festivals/Workshops

♀ ☆ ♂♀ National Women's Music Festival / Women in the Arts, POB 1427, Indianapolis, IN 46206 317-395-3809 www.wiaonline.org

⚥ ● (♀♂) WomenFest Northwest Festivals, Jacqueline Harrington (Owner) 7554 N Burlington Ave, Portland, OR 97203 954-296-5674 www.womenfest.com womenfest@yahoo.com

Counseling/Psychotherapy/Mental Health

♀ ☆ Gender Spectrum Education & Training, 510-788-4412 tinyurl.com/ygck97ky

⚥ The Healthcare Guild, 9233 Ward Parkway Ste 305, Kansas City, MO www.healthcareguild.com

⚥ ● Jill Denton, Sex Therapist, 805-534-1101 www.accesspt.com www.jillsextherapist.com

♀ ○ Johnson, Pia, LMSW, Online counseling services 347-867-6152 freshpathny.com pia@freshpathny.com

♀ ● Yost, Merle James, LMFT, CA# MFC32346, Personal consultations (phone only) 510-627-0090 Personal consultations (phone only), Five Day Intensives, Workshops www.merleyost.com

Editing/Writing/Proofreading Services

♂ ○ (♀♂) EditAmerica, Paula Plantier, 115 Jacobs Creek Rd, Ewing, NJ 08628-1014 609-882-5852 fax 609-882-5851 www.editamerica.com paula@editamerica.com

Erotica / Adult Stores / Safe Sex Supplies

♂ ● The Back Room store, POB 608652, Orlando, FL 32860-8652 www.TheBackRoomOrlando.com info@TheBackRoomOrlando.com

⚥ ● Cybersocket, 8581 Santa Monica Blvd #331, West Hollywood, CA 323-650-9906 www.cybersocket.com

♀ ○ Pacific Media, 8201 Canoga Ave Ste 9489, Canoga Park, CA 91309 805-418-7552 Erotica info@pac-media.com

⚥ ● Prerogatives, 415-551-1016 www.pridecatalog.com

Film (see also Video)

⚥ ● Ariztical Entertainment Inc, 12400 Ventura Blvd #686, Studio City, CA 91604-2406 818-760-3740 www.ariztical.com info@ariztical.com

Financial Planning, Investment (see also Insurance)

♀ ● **LGBT Financial, 801-613-7119 Your premier LGBTQIA+ partner for insurance, investments, and financial planning. www.lgbtfinancial.org ryan@lgbtfinancial.org**

♀ ● ♂♀ Next Generation Trust Company, c/o Next Generation Services, 75 Livingston Ave Ste 304, Roseland, NJ 07068 888-857-8058 www.nextgenerationtrust.com NewAccounts@NextGenerationTrust.com

Funding: Endowment, Fundraising

♀ ☆ Arcus Foundation, 44 W 28th St 17th Flr, New York, NY 212-488-3000 www.arcusfoundation.org

⚥ ★ ♂♀ ASTRAEA Lesbian Foundation for Justice, 116 E 16th St 7th flr, New York, NY 212-529-8021 www.astraeafoundation.org ✤

⚥ The David Bohnett Foundation, 245 S Beverly Dr, Beverly Hills, CA 310-276-0001 www.bohnettfoundation.org

♀ ☆ DIFFA (Design Industries Foundation Fighting AIDS), 16 W 32nd St Ste 402, New York, NY 212-727-3100 www.diffa.org

♀ Elton John AIDS Foundation, 584 Broadway Ste 906, New York, NY www.ejaf.org

⚥ ★ Free2Luv, 4701 SW Admiral Way #378, Seattle, WA 98116 www.free2luv.org info@free2luv.org

⚥ ★ ♂♀ Funders For LGBTQ Issues, 45 W 36th St 8th Flr, New York, NY 212-475-2930 www.lgbtfunders.org

⚥ ★ Gamma Mu Foundation, POB 23520, Fort Lauderdale, FL 33307-3520 866-463-6007 www.gammamufoundation.org

⚥ ★ Gill Foundation, 1550 Wewatta St Ste 720, Denver, CO 80202 303-292-4455 www.gillfoundation.org info@gillfoundation.org

♂ Matthew Shepard Foundation, 800 18th St Ste 101, Denver, CO 303-830-7400 www.MatthewShepard.org

♀ ☆ National Network of Abortion Funds, POB 170280, Boston, MA 02117 www.fundabortionnow.org

⚥ ● ♂♀ Point Foundation Los Angeles, 5055 Wilshire Blvd, Ste 501, Los Angeles, CA 323-933-1234 National LGBTQ Scholarship Fund pointfoundation.org

⚥ ★ Point Foundation New York, 357 Broadway Ste 401, Los Angeles, CA 323-933-1234 www.pointfoundation.org

⚥ ● ♂♀ Pride Foundation, 2014 E Madison St Ste 300, Seattle, WA 800-735-7287 www.pridefoundation.org

♀ ★ ♂♀ Provincetown Harbor Swim for Life & Paddler Flotilla, POB 819, Provincetown, MA 02657-0819 508-487-1930 www.swim4life.org thecompact@comcast.net

♀ ★ Rainbow World Fund, 4111 18th St #5, San Francisco, CA 415-431-1485 rainbowfund.org

♀ • Southern Equality Fund, POB 364, Asheville, NC 28802 828-242-1559 southernequality.org

Gardening/Landscaping Services & Supplies

♀ • Gardens by Robert, 134 W 95th St Apt #1, New York, NY 10025-6600 917-499-2413 gardensby.roberturban.com themusenyc@aol.com

Gifts, Cards, Pride, etc.

♀ • For the Little Ones Inside.., POB 725, Ojai, CA 93024-0725 805-646-4518 tinyurl.com/2knbhj rposin@hotmail.com

♀ • Milestone Candles, 714-928-6398 milestonecandles.com jamie@milestonecandles.com

♀ • Pergamo Paper Goods, 201-673-1179 www.pergamopapergoods.com

♀ • Rainbowdepot.com, 866-828-5314 951-226-0347 fax 949-716-1882 www.rainbowdepot.com

♀ • ♿ ZEBRAZ.com, 1608 N Main Ave, San Antonio, TX 78212-4311 210-472-2800 800-788-4729 orders only www.zebraz.com zebraz@zebraz.com

Graphic Design/Printing/Type

♂ • BLK Media Services, POB 83912, Los Angeles, CA 90083-0912 213-410-0808 fax 213-410-9250 www.blkmedia.com ✚

Health Care: Physical (see also Counseling/Mental Health)

♀ ★ GLMA: Health Professionals Advancing LGBTQ Equality, 1133 19th St NW #302, Washington, DC 202-600-8037 www.glma.org

♀ ★ Lesbian Health Fund, GLMA Health Professionals Advancing LGBT Health, 1133 19th St NW, Washington, DC 202-600-8037 www.glma.org/lhf

♀ ★ ♿ LGBT HealthLink, POB 24490, Fort Lauderdale, FL 33307 954-765-6024 www.mylgbthealthlink.org

♀ ★ National LGBT Cancer Network, 136 W 16th St #1E, New York, NY 212-675-2633 www.cancer-network.org

Immigration, Citizenship, Political Asylum, Refugees

♂ ☆ ♿ Immigration Equality, Inc, 40 Exchange Place #1300, New York, NY 212-714-2904 www.immigrationequality.org

♀ Queer Detainee Empowerment Project, 505 8th Ave #1212, New York, NY 347-645-9339

♀ Rainbow Railroad USA, 601 W 26th St #325-41, New York, NY www.rainbowrailroad.org

♀ Rainbow Welcome Initiative, Heartland Alliance International, 208 S laSalle St #1818, Chicago, IL www.rainbowwelcome.org

Leather Resources & Groups

♂ ○ ♿ Adam & Gillian's Sensual Whips & Toys, 40 Grant Ave, Copiague, NY 11726-3817 631-842-1711 www.aswgt.com siradam@ix.netcom.com

♀ ★ (⚥) Defenders USA, c/o Dignity USA, POB 376, Medford, MA 02155 tinyurl.com/2pz996

♂ ★ International Mr Leather, 5015 N Clark St, Chicago, IL 773-907-9700 www.imrl.com

♂ ☆ (⚥) International Ms. Leather, IMsL Productions, LLC, 1271 Washington Ave # 121, San Leandro, CA 94577 imsl.org

T ☆ La Fraternitie Du Loup-Garou, www.lagarou.org

♀ • The Leather Journal, POB 3596, Hollywood, CA 90078 323-469-5922 **L** www.theleatherjournal.com tljandcuir@aol.com

♂ National Leather Association International, PO Box 470395, Aurora, CO 80047 780-454-1992 www.nla-international.com

♂ ☆ (⚥) Southeast Conference of Clubs, Inc., 2300 Bethelview Rd #110-242, Cumming, GA **L** www.secclubs.org

Legal Services

♂ Center for Consitutional Rights, 666 Broadway Flr 7, New York, NY 212-614-6464 www.ccrjustice.org

♀ ★ ♿ GLBTQ Legal Advocates & Defenders - GLAD, 18 Tremont St Ste 950, Boston, MA 02108 617-426-1350 800-455-GLAD hotline (New England) fax 617-426-3594 www.glad.org gladlaw@glad.org

♀ ★ ♿ Lambda Legal Defense & Education Fund (LLDEF), Inc, 120 Wall St #1500, New York, NY 212-809-8585 www.lambdalegal.org

♀ ★ LegalOut, www.legalout.com

♀ ★ National Lawyers Guild Queer Caucus, 132 Nassau St #922, New York, NY 212-679-5100 www.nlg.org/committee

♀ ★ National LGBT Bar Association, 1200 18th St NW Ste 700, Washington, DC 202-637-7661 lgbtbar.org

Mailing Lists

♀ • **Gayellow Pages Mailing Lists, POB 533 Village Stn, New York, NY 10014-0533 646-213-0263 v/f Contents of Gayellow Pages on mailing lists, constantly updated. (NOT a list of individual buyers!) gayellowpages.com/mailing.htm♥ gypages@gmail.com**

Mortgages/Home Ownership (see also Banks, Real Estate)

♀ ○ ♿ Wilt, Tammy L., NMLS #195702, Movement Mortgage, 3510 Remson Cr Ste 301, Charlottesville, VA 434-242-0046 movement.com/lo/tammy-wilt/

Moving/Transportation/Storage

♂ • Custom Movers Select, 131 Sycamore St, Bay Saint Louis, MS 39520 225-937-0700 FHWA Lic #MC370752B Interstate moving broker www.custommovers.net

Organizations/Resources: Bisexual Focus

♂ ☆ **Bi MEN Network, POB 1811, Asheville, NC 28802 760-464-6489 www.bimen.org**

♂ ★ (⚥) BiNet USA, 4201 Wilson Blvd #110-311, Arlington, VA 800-585-9368 www.BiNetUSA.org

♂ ☆ Bisexual Organizing Project, 310 E 38th St Ste 209, Minneapolis, MN tinyurl.com/yhho2mw

Organizations/Resources: Blind

♀ ★ Blind-LGBT Pride International,,. 786-547-5465 blindlgbtpride.org

Organizations/Resources: Business & Professional Associations, Labor Advocacy

♀ ★ Aetna Network of LGBT Employees, 113 Polo Rd, Glenwood Springs, CO 970-945-3060 www.aetna.com

♀ • American Association of Museums LGBTQ Alliance, 2451 Crystal Dr Ste 1005, Arlington, VA 202-289-1818 tinyurl.com/y7lgszjk

♀ ★ American Folklore Society LGBTQA Section, c/o Center for Trad. Music & Dance, 32 Broadway #1314, New York, NY 212-571-1555 x35 www.afsnet.org

♀ ★ ♿ American Psychological Association, Office on Sexual Orientation and Gender Diversity, Public Interest Directorate, 750 1st St NE, Washington, DC 20002-4241 202-336-6041 fax 202-336-6040 tinyurl.com/7r4d5vj

♀ Association for LGBT Issues in Counseling, www.algbtic.org

♀ ★ Association of Gay & Lesbian Psychiatrists (AGLP), 4514 Chester Ave, Philadelphia, PA 215-222-2800 www.aglp.org

♂ ☆ Association of Nurses in AIDS Care, 11230 Cleveland Ave NW #986, Uniontown, OH 800-260-6780 www.nursesinaidscare.org

♀ Chubb & Son, Inc. Gay & Lesbian Employee Network, 15 Mountain View Rd, Warren, NJ 908-903-2000 tinyurl.com/y2letotu

♂ ☆ Coalition for Sexuality and Gender Identities (CSGI), American College Personnel Association, 1 Dupont Circle NW Ste 300, Washington, DC 202-835-2272 www.myacpa.org/csgi

♀ ★ EAGLE at IBM, tinyurl.com/cnq9m

♀ ★ EQUAL!, Nokia www.equal.org

♀ ★ Federal Aviation Authority GLOBE, 808-782-9880 fb.com/groups/15270953171

♀ ★ (⬆) FireFLAG/EMS, LGBT Community Center, 208 W 13th St, New York, NY 917-885-0127 fb.com/fireflag.ems

♀ Gay Officers Action League of New England, POB 171587, Boston, MA 02117 781-983-5816 fb.com/NewEnglandGOAL/

♀ Gayglers, Google LGBT Employee Affinity Group, 1600 Amphitheatre Parkway, Mountain View, CA 650-263-0000 tinyurl.com/qa2tsh2

♀ Intel LGBT Employees (IGLOBE), 2200 Mission College Boulevard, Santa Clara, CA 408-765-8080

♀ ★ International Association of LGBTQ+ Judges, POB 122724, San Diego, CA 92112 ialgbtj.org

♂ ★ ♿ International Association of Providers of AIDS Care, 2200 Pennsylvania Ave NW 4th Flr E, Washington, DC 202-507-5899 www.iapac.org

♀ ★ (⬆) International Gay & Lesbian Travel Association (IGLTA), 1201 NE 26th St Ste 103, Fort Lauderdale, FL 954-630-1637 www.iglta.org

♀ ★ (⬆) Johnson & Johnson Open&Out, 1 Johnson & Johnson Plaza, New Brunswick, NJ 508-977-3906 tinyurl.com/o9o89d2

♀ ★ LGBT Caucus of Public Health Professionals, www.aphlagbt.org

♀ ★ LGBT Returned Peace Corps Volunteers, PO Box 14332, San Francisco, CA 94114 lgbrpcv.org

♀ ★ Microsoft GLEAM, One Microsoft Way, Redmond, WA tinyurl.com/lmf3op8

♀ National Association of Social Workers LGBT, 750 1st St NE #700, Washington, DC 202-408-8600 tinyurl.com/l3z842x

♀ ★ National Gay & Lesbian Chamber of Commerce (NGLCC), 1331 F St Ste 900, Washington, DC 202-234-9181 www.nglcc.org

♀ ★ National Gay Pilots Association, 4931 W 35th St Ste 200, Saint Louis Park, MN 866-800-NGPA www.ngpa.org

♀ ★ National Lesbian & Gay Journalists Association, 2120 L St NW Ste 850, Washington, DC 20037 202-588-9888 www.nlgja.org info@nlgja.org

♀ ★ National Organization of Gay & Lesbian Scientists & Technical Professionals (NOGLSTP), POB 91803, Pasadena, CA 91109-1803 626-791-7689 www.noglstp.org

♀ ★ ♿ Out & Equal Workplace Advocates, 155 Sansome St Ste 450, San Francisco, CA 415-694-6500 www.outandequal.org

♀ ★ Pride At Work National Office, AFL-CIO, 815 16th St NW, Washington, DC 202-637-5014 www.prideatwork.org

♀ ★ Pride VMC LGBTQ+ Veterinary Medical Community, 584 Castro St #492, San Francisco, CA pridevmc.org

♀ ★ Publishing Triangle, 511 Ave of the Americas #D36, New York, NY 10011 www.publishingtriangle.org

♂ ★ Rainbow Round Table (RRT), American Library Association, 50 E Huron St, Chicago, IL 60611-2788 800-545-2433 www.ala.org/rt/glbtrt/ ala@ala.org

♂ Sodexo Pride, 9801 Washington Blvd, Gaithersburg, MD 301-987-4000 tinyurl.com/h3tw7xf

♀ Starbucks Pride Alliance Network, 2401 Utah Ave S, Seattle, WA fb.com/StarbucksPride

♀ ★ StartOut, 555 Mission St Ste 2414, San Francisco, CA 415-275-2446 startout.org

♀ ★ Target LGBT Business Council, 1000 Nicollet Mall, Minneapolis, MN

♀ ☆ Tradeswomen Inc, 337 17th St Ste 207, Oakland, CA 510-891-1243 www.tradeswomen.org

♂ Travelers LGBT & Allies Diversity Network, One Tower Square, Hartford, CT 860-954-8422 tinyurl.com/wmz8pdw

♀ Unite Here!, 275 7th Ave, New York, NY 212-265-7000 www.unitehere.org

♀ ★ United, NCR Corporation, 864 Spring St, Atlanta, GA 30308 678-379-9364 united.ncr@ncr.com

♀ Verizon GLOBE, 212-321-8394

Organizations/Resources: Cultural, Dance, Performance

♀ ★ All Join Hands Foundation, POB 9942, Phoenix, AZ 85068 602-703-2298 www.alljoinhands.org

♀ ★ (⬆) Frameline, 145 9th St Ste 300, San Francisco, CA 415-703-8650 www.frameline.org

♀ ★ ♿ Gay & Lesbian Association of Choruses, POB 99998, Pittsburgh, PA 15233 412-418-7709 www.galachoruses.org

♀ ★ Gay Callers Association, 505-507-7320 www.gaycallers.org

♂ ☆ GroundSpark, 4104 24th St Ste 2013, San Francisco, CA 415-641-4616 groundspark.org

♀ ★ (⬆) International Association of Gay/Lesbian Country Western Dance Clubs, 5380 W 34th St #207, Houston, TX iaglcwdc.org

♀ ★ International Association of Gay Square Dance Clubs, POB 9176, Denver, CO 80209 **D** www.iagsdc.com

♀ ★ Ladyslipper Music, POB 14, Cedar Grove, NC 27231 919-245-3737 ladyslipper.org

♀ ★ ♿ Lavender Country & Folk Dancers, 617-876-5461 **D** www.lcfd.org

♀ ★ Lesbian & Gay Bands Association, 1030 15th St NW Ste 500, Washington, DC 202-656-5422 www.lgba.org

♀ ★ (⬆) North American Same-Sex Partner Dance Association (NASSPDA), www.nasspda.org

♀ ★ OUTmedia, 646 Argyle Rd #18E, Brooklyn, NY 718-789-1776 www.outmedia.org

♀ ☆ POWER UP, 419 N Larchmont Blvd #283, Los Angeles, CA 323-463-3154 www.powerupfilms.org

♂ ★ Purple Circuit, 921 N Naomi St, Burbank, CA 91505 818-953-5096 buddybuddy.com/pc.html purplecir@aol.com

♀ ● Robert Urban/Urban Productions, 134 W 95th St Apt #1, New York, NY 10025-6600 917-499-2413 www.roberturban.com themusenyc@aol.com

♀ ★ Square Dancer Directory, Bradley Bell, 2811 W Pollack St, Phoenix, AZ 85041 602-703-2298 www.bradleybell.org

Organizations/Resources: Deaf

♀ Deaf Queer Resource Center, POB 14431, San Francisco, CA 94114 www.deafqueer.org

♀ ★ Rainbow Alliance of the Deaf, POB 1616, Langley, WA 98260 www.deafrad.org RADDPR@radeaf.org

Organizations/Resources: Education

♀ ★ AdRespect Advertising Education Program, www.adrespect.org

♀ ● Diversity Builder, Inc., 2821 Lebanon Rd Ste 201, Nashville, TN 615-823-1717 www.diversitybuilder.com ✪

♀ ★ Equality Forum, 1420 Locust St Ste 300, Philadelphia, PA 215-732-3378 equalityforum.com

♂ ★ Gay Men of Wisdom, 72 Summit St, Hudson, NY 12534 914-479-7645 www.gaymenofwisdom.org ray@gaymenofwisdom.org

♀ ★ (♻) GLAAD, 5455 Wilshire Blvd Ste 1500, Los Angeles, CA 323-933-2240 www.glaad.org

♀ ★ ♿ GLAAD, 104 W 29th St 4th Flr, New York, NY 800-429-6334 www.glaad.org

♀ ★ Global Village School, POB 480, Ojai, CA 93024-0480 805-646-9792 (homeschooling program) www.globalvillageschool.org info@globalvillageschool.org

♀ ☆ LGBTQQ Workshops / Bully Ban, c/o Creative Response, 145 College Rd, Rm 4300, Suffern, NY 10901 845-574-4225 tinyurl.com/ouy9v3e ✪ inquiries@crc-global.org

♂ MERGE for Equality, POB 590512, Newton Centre, MA 02159 413-586-3743 www.mergeforequality.org

♂ ☆ National Organization for Men Against Sexism (NOMAS), 3500 E 17th Ave, Denver, CO 303-997-9581 www.nomas.org

♀ ★ Partners Task Force for Gay & Lesbian Couples, Dr Demian, director, 206-935-1206 www.buddybuddy.com demian@buddybuddy.com

♀ ☆ ♿ SIECUS: Sexuality Information & Education Council of the US, 1012 14th St NW Ste 1108, Washington, DC 202-265-2405 National education/advocacy organization www.siecus.org

♀ ★ (♻) Unmarried Equality, 347-987-1068 www.unmarried.org ue@unmarried.org

Organizations/Resources: Ethnic, Multicultural

♀ ★ Center for Black Equity, POB 77313, Washington, DC 20019 202-641-8527 centerforblackequity.org ✤ cbe@centerforblackequity.org

♀ ● Mamaroots: Ajama-Jebi Sistahood, POB 21066, Long Beach, CA 90801 562-498-3318 An AfraGoddess(tm) Tradition ✤

♀ ★ (♻) National Association of Black & White Men Together, POB 589, Hollywood, CA 90078 800-624-2968 www.nabwmt.org ✪

♀ ★ National Black Justice Coalition, POB 71395, Washington, DC 20024 202-319-1552 fax 202-319-7365 www.nbjc.org ✤

♀ ★ National Youth Pride Services, 180 N Michigan Ste 1200, Chicago, IL 60601 773-977-8051 fb.com/YouthPrideServices ✤ youthpridecenter@gmail.com

♀ ★ NativeOUT, fb.com/nativeout/

♀ ★ Trikone: GLBT South Asians, 60 29th St #614, San Francisco, CA 908-367-3374 www.trikone.org ✧

♀ ★ Two Spirit National Cultural Exchange, Inc, POB 280805, Lakewood, CO 80228 720-261-1854 tinyurl.com/jd6vydo

Organizations/Resources: Family and Supporters

♀ ☆ AFFIRM Network, c/o Marvin Goldfried, Psychology Department, SUNY at Stony Brook, Stony Brook, NY www.sunysb.edu/affirm

♀ ☆ Family Acceptance Project, 3004 16th St #203, San Francisco, CA 94103 917-757-6123 familyproject.sfsu.edu fap@sfsu.edu

♀ ☆ Family Diversity Projects Inc., POB 1246, Amherst, MA 01004 413-256-1611 www.familydiv.org

♀ ★ (♻) Family Equality Council, 475 Park Ave S Ste 2100, New York, NY 646-880-3005 www.familyequality.org

♀ ☆ Free Mom Hugs, POB 12731, Oklahoma City, OK 73157 www.freemomhugs.org info@freemomhugs.org

♀ ☆ (♻) PFLAG, 1828 L St NW Ste 600, Washington, DC 202-467-8180 www.pflag.org

♀ ☆ (♻) Straight Spouse Network, POB 4985, Chicago, IL 60680 773-413-8213 www.straightspouse.org

♀ ★ U.S. National Longitudinal Lesbian Family Study, www.nllfs.org

Organizations/Resources: Military/Veterans

♀ ★ American Veterans for Equal Rights, 15127 Main Street E, Ste 104 PMB 416, Sumner, WA 718-849-5665 www.aver.us

♀ ♿ American Veterans for Equal Rights, PMB 416 15127 Main St E Ste 104, Sumner, WA 718-849-5665 aver.us

♂ ★ Modern Military Association of America, 1725 I St NW Ste 300, Washington, DC 202-328-3244 modernmilitary.org

♀ ☆ Palm Center, 310-825-1432 www.palmcenter.org

♂ ☆ Sparta - A Transgender Military Advocacy Organization, spartapride.org inquiries@spartapride.org

♂ ☆ Transgender American Veterans Association (TAVA), POB 4513, Akron, OH 44310 516-828-2911 transveteran.org media@transveteran.org

Organizations/Resources: Media (see also Publications)

♀ ★ Pink Banana Media, 8391 Beverly Blvd #318, Los Angeles, CA 90048 323-963-3653 www.pinkbananamedia.com

Organizations/Resources: Naturist/Nudist

♂ ★ Gay Naturists International (GNI), mail to GNI 5175 W Ajo Hwy #A-14, Tucson, AZ 954-567-2700 N www.gaynaturists.org

♂ ★ (♻) IMEN, POB 578, Rising Sun, MD 21911 N www.imen4allmen.org

Organizations/Resources: Political/Legislative/Advocacy

♀ ☆ ♿ American Civil Liberties Union, 125 Broad St, 18th fl, New York, NY 212-549-2600 www.aclu.org

♀ Equal Rights Advocates, 1170 Market St Ste 700, San Francisco, CA 415-621-0672 www.equalrights.org

♂ ★ Equality Federation, 818 SW 3rd Ave #141, Portland, OR 929-373-3370 www.equalityfederation.org

♂ Fight OUT Loud, www.fightoutloud.org

♂ ★ ♿ Gay & Lesbian Victory Fund, 1225 I St NW #525, Washington, DC 202-842-8679 www.victoryfund.org

♂ Gays Against Guns, www.gaysagainstguns.net

♂ ★ Human Rights Campaign, 1640 Rhode Island Ave NW, Washington, DC 202-628-4160 www.hrc.org

♂ ★ Lavender Green Caucus, Green Party of the US, POB 75075, Washington, DC 20013 202-319-7191 www.lavendergreens.net

♂ ☆ Liberty Education Forum, 1090 Vermont Ave NW Ste 825, Washington, DC 202-420-7873 tinyurl.com/y9ob5hn

♂ ★ ♿ Log Cabin Republicans, 1090 Vermont Ave NW Ste 850, Washington, DC 202-420-7873 www.dclogcabin.org

♂ ★ Movement Advancement Project (MAP), 1905 15th St #1097, Boulder, CO 303-578-4600 www.lgbtmap.org

♂ ★ ᏜᏜ National Center for Lesbian Rights, 870 Market St Ste 370, San Francisco, CA 415-392-6257 www.nclrights.org

♂ ☆ National Coalition for Sexual Freedom, 822 Guilford Ave Box 127, Baltimore, MD 21202 410-539-4824 www.ncsfreedom.org ncsfreedom@ncsfreedom.org

♂ ★ ᏜᏜ National LGBTQ Task Force, 1325 Massachusetts Ave NW Ste 600, Washington, DC 20005-4171 202-393-5177 www.thetaskforce.org

♂ ★ OutRight Action International, 80 Maiden Lane Ste 1505, New York, NY 212-430-6054 tinyurl.com/nnbk9ns

♂ ★ Outright Libertarians, 8050 N 19th Ave #259, Phoenix, AZ 415-738-7544 www.outrightusa.org

♂ People for the American Way, 1101 15th St NW Ste 600, Washington, DC 800-326-7329 www.pfaw.org

♂ ★ (?♿) Pro-Life Alliance of Gays & Lesbians, POB 3005, York, PA 17402 202-223-6697 www.plagal.org

♀ ☆ Radical Women National Office, 5018 Rainier Ave S, Seattle, WA 98118 206-722-6057 radicalwomen.org radicalwomenus@gmail.com

♂ ★ Soulforce Inc., POB 2499, Abilene, TX 79604 800-810-9143 www.soulforce.org

♂ Southern Poverty Law Center LGBT Rights, 400 Washington Ave, Montgomery, AL 334-956-8200 tinyurl.com/y6lrq8z7

♂ Stonewall Democrats US, POB 514 Old Chelsea Stn, New York, NY 10113 www.stonewalldemocrats.us

♂ ★ ᏜᏜ STONEWALL Rebellion Veterans' Association, Willson Henderson, Founder, 70-A Greenwich Ave #120, New York, NY 10011-8300 212-627-1969 fax 718-294-1969 S.V.A. meets monthly the last Saturday at NYC Gay Center at 3:15 p.m.until 6 p.m. www.STONEWALLvets.org SVA@STONEWALLvets.org

♂ ☆ Woodhull Freedom Foundation, 3302 Gleneagles Dr, Silver Spring, MD 888-960-3332 www.woodhullfoundation.org

♂ ★ Zuna Institute, 2701 Del Paso Rd Ste 130358, Sacramento, CA 916-207-1037 www.zunainstitute.org ♣

Organizations/Resources: Prisoner Resources

♀ ★ ᏜᏜ The Midwest Pages to Prisoners Project, 408 E 6th St, Bloomington, IN 812-339-8710 www.boxcarbooks.org

Organizations/Resources: Senior Resources

♂ ★ ᏜᏜ Gay & Lesbian Association of Retiring Persons Inc. (GLARP), 10940 Wilshire Blvd #1600, Los Angeles, CA 310-722-1806 www.gaylesbianretiring.org

♂ lgbtSr, www.lgbtsr.org

♂ ★ National Resource Center on LGBT Aging, c/o SAGE, 305 7th Ave, New York, NY 212-741-2247 www.lgbtagingcenter.org

♀ ★ Old Lesbians Organizing for Change (OLOC), PO Box 834, Woodstock, NY 12498 888-706-7506 www.oloc.org info@oloc.org

♂ ★ (?♿) **SAGE (Services & Advocacy for GLBT Elders), 305 7th Ave Fl 15, New York, NY 212-741-2247 www.sageusa.org**

♂ ★ Stonewall Seniors, www.stonewallseniors.com

Organizations/Resources: Sexual Focus / Safe Sex

♂ ★ The Fraternity, 5247 Wilson Mills Rd #132, Cleveland, OH 44143 216-440-1065 www.footfraternity.com DugGaines@AOL.com

♂ ● (?♿) Tantra4GayMen, www.tantra4gaymen.com info@tantra4gaymen.com

Organizations/Resources: Social, Recreation, Support

♂ ★ Gay for Good, 6444 E Spring St Ste 321, Long Beach, CA 90815 562-684-8210 Volunteer organization. www.gayforgood.org info@gayforgood.org

♂ ★ GayCowboyCentral.com, www.gaycowboycentral.com

♂ Kappa Xi Omega, www.kappaxiomega.org

♂ ★ Lambda Car Club International (LCCI), PO Box 45140, Phoenix, AZ 85064 602-371-8532 www.lccimembers.com

♀ ★ NoLose, POB 580113, Elk Grove, CA 95758 Creating vibrant fat queer culture www.nolose.org feedback@nolose.org

♂ ★ Prime Timers Worldwide, 469-660-4668 www.primetimersww.org info@primetimersww.com

♂ Rainbow Amateur Radio Association, POB 18541, Rochester, NY 14618 954-502-6969 www.rara.org

♂ ★ Yankee Lambda Car Club, POB 3296, Wakefield, MA 01880 / New England Area New England Area www.yankeelcc.com

Organizations/Resources: Student, Academic, Education

♂ ★ (?♿) AMS LGBTQ Study Group, 20 Cooper Square, Room 225, New York, NY 10003-7112 212-992-6340 tinyurl.com/y57etu2e ams@amsmusicology.org

♂ ★ BJUnity, 4768 Broadway #911, New York, NY 864-735-7598 Bob Jones University Students & Alumni bjunity.org

♂ ★ Brown University TBGALA (Alumni), Brown Alumni Association, POB 1859, Providence, RI 02912 fb.com/BrownTBGALA

♂ ★ The Citadel Gay & Lesbian Alliance, www.citadelvmigala.org citadelgala@yahoo.com

♂ ★ Columbia University Pride, 622 W 113th St, New York, NY 212-851-7484 tinyurl.com/27t8ad8

♂ ★ Consortium of Higher Education LGBT Resource Professionals, www.lgbtcampus.org

♂ ★ Delta Lambda Phi Social Fraternity, 2020 Pennsylvania Ave NW PMB 355, Washington, DC 202-558-2801 www.dlp.org

♂ ★ Gay-Straight Alliance Network, 1714 Franklin St #100-418, Oakland, CA 415-552-4229 gsanetwork.org

♀ ★ (♌) GLSEN, 110 William St, New York, NY 212-727-0135 www.glsen.org

♂ ★ (♌) Harvard Gender and Sexuality Caucus, POB 381809, Cambridge, MA 02238 hgsc.sigs.harvard.edu

♂ ★ Heartstrong, 478 E Altamonte Dr Ste 108, Altamonte Springs, FL 206-388-3894 GLBT students from religious educational institutions www.heartstrong.org

♂ ★ Indiana University GLBT Alumni, Virgil T. DeVault Alumni Center, 1000 E 17th St, Bloomington, IN 812-855-4822 alumni.indiana.edu/glbtaa/

♂ ★ Knights Out - LGBT West Point Alumni and Allies, 360-957-5468 www.knightsout.org

♂ ★ Miami University 1809 LGBT Alumni, 725 E Chestnut, Oxford, OH 513-529-3587

♂ ★ Mount Holyoke Lyon's Pride, www.mhlp.org

♂ ★ Northwestern University Pride Alumni Club (NUPAC), Northwestern Alumni Associatio, 1201 Davis St, Evanston, IL 60208 847-491-7200 tinyurl.com/tcsqtzw nupac@alum.northwestern.edu

♂ ★ NYU LGBTQ Alumni Council, 25 W 4th St Rm 404A, New York, NY 212-992-6892 tinyurl.com/ybczcnxb

♂ ★ oSTEM, 2885 Sanford Ave SW #34480, Grandville, MI 49418 www.ostem.org info@ostem.org

♂ ★ Rice Alumni Pride (RAP), POB 1892, Houston, TX 77251 713-348-4057 alumni.rice.edu/rap

♂ ★ (♌) Safe Schools Coalition, c/o Equal Rights Washington, POB 2388, Seattle, WA 98111 206-451-7233 www.safeschoolscoalition.org

♂ ★ Scarlet & Gay OSU LGBTQ Alumni Society, PO Box 2012, Columbus, OH 43216-2012 614-292-5130 scarletandgay.alumni.osu.edu

♂ ★ Stanford Pride, POB 19312, Stanford, CA 94309-9312 www.stanfordpride.org

♂ ★ UCLA Anderson GLBA, Box 951481 110 Westwood Plaza Ste F301, Los Angeles, CA 90095-0001 323-739-4522 fb.com/pg/GLBAAlumni/

♂ ★ UCLA Lambda Alumni Association, Epstein Family Alumni Center, 3607 Trousdale Parkway, TCC 305, Los Angeles, CA 213-740-0845 alumni.usc.edu/lambda/

♂ ★ US Naval Academy Alumni Out, POB 3571, Annapolis, MD 21403 www.usnaout.org

♂ ★ USC Lambda LGBT Alumni Association, 3607 Trousdale Parkway, TCC 305, Los Angeles, CA 213-740-1606 alumni.usc.edu/lambda/

♂ ★ USF LGBTQ + Alumni, Gibbons Alumni Center, 4202 E Fowler Ave ALC100, Tampa, FL 727-873-4561 fb.com/USFALUMLGBTQ

♂ ★ UW-Madison GLBT Alumni Council, 650 N Lake St, Madison, WI 608-262-2551 tinyurl.com/qalpnm2

♂ ★ 👫 Yale GALA (Alumnae/i), PO Box 207118, New Haven, CT 06520-7118 www.yalegala.org natasha@yalegalaevents.org

Organizations/Resources: Transgender/Gender Non-Conforming/Diverse

♀ Accord Alliance (Intersex), 531 Route 22 East #244, Whitehouse Station, NJ 908-349-0534 www.accordalliance.org

T ☆ Black Trans Advocacy, 3530 Forest Lane Ste 290, Dallas, TX 855-255-8636 www.blacktrans.org ♣

T ☆ Black Transmen, 3530 Forest Lane Ste 290, Dallas, TX 855-255-8636 www.blacktransmen.org ♣

T ☆ Black Transwomen, 3530 Forest Lane Ste 290, Dallas, TX 855-255-8636 BlackTranswomen.org ♣

T ★ CDI-NYC's CrossGender Community, 212-564-4847 (Wed 6-9pm EST) www.cdinyc.org

♀ ○ DressTech, 844-623-7467 www.ProCrossDresser.com

T ● En Femme, 888-485-9142 EnFemmeStyle.com support@enfemmestyle.com

T ☆ Gender Diversity, 6523 California Ave SW #360, Seattle, WA 98136 855-443-6337 www.genderdiversity.org info@genderdiversity.org

T ☆ Gender Education Center, POB 1861, Maple Grove, MN 55311 763-424-5445 www.debradavis.org

♪ ☆ 👫 Gender Odyssey Conference, 6523 California Ave SW #360, Seattle, WA 855-443-6337 www.genderodyssey.org

♀ ☆ InterACT - Intersex, 365 Boston Post Rd Ste 163, Sudbury, MA 707-793-1190 www.interactadvocates.org

♂ ○ Le Dame Footwear, 805 Tamarack Way, Verona, WI 877-365-6147 www.ledame.com

T ○ (♌) Michael Salem Cross Dressing Boutique, POB 1781, New York, NY 10150 212-697-0644 www.michaelsalem.com michsalem3@gmail.com

T ☆ The National Center for Transgender Equality, 1133 19th St NW Ste 302, Washington, DC 202-642-4542 www.transequality.org

T ○ Point 5cc - Apparel, POB 70505, Springfield, OR 97475 point5cc.com @ixx=

T ☆ Point 5cc Annual Transgender Surgery Fund, PO Box 70505, Springfield, OR 97475 tinyurl.com/yc7sz8cm

T Refuge Restrooms, Bathrooms for everyone Gender free, inclusive bathrooms www.refugerestrooms.org

♂ ★ TQ Nation, www.transqueernation.org

T ☆ Trans Lifeline, 101 Broadway Ste 311, Oakland, CA 94607 877-565-8860; 877-330-6366 Canada 510-771-1417 www.translifeline.org contact@translifeline.org

T Trans Student Educational Resources, 1050 N Mills Ave #295, Claremont, CA www.transstudent.org

T Trans-Parent USA, 520 W 103rd St Ste 252, Kansas City, MO 800-513-1715 www.trans-parenting.com

T ☆ TransActive Gender Project, Center for Community Engagement, Lewis & Clark Graduate School of Education and Counseling, 0615 SW Palatine Hill Rd MSC, Portland, OR 97219 503-768-6024 tinyurl.com/y3xmpzz3 transactive@lclark.edu

T Transathlete, www.transathlete.com

T ☆ Transgender Foundation of America, 604 Pacific St, Houston, TX 713-520-8586 tfahouston.com

T Transguys, www.transguys.com

T TransPulse, POB 44272, Boise, ID 83711 www.transgenderpulse.com

T World Professional Association For Transgender Health, 1300 S 2nd St Ste 180, Minneapolis, MN www.wpath.org

Organizations/Resources: Youth (see also Family)

⚥ ☆ (♿) Camp Highlight, POB 5173, Astoria, NY 11105 646-535-2267 www.camphighlight.com info@camphighlight.com

⚥ ★ Camp Ten Trees, 1122 E Pike St #1488, Seattle, WA 98122-3916 206-288-9568 www.camptentrees.org

⚥ ★ **GLBT National Youth Talkline, 800-246-PRIDE 415-355-0003 fax 415-552-5498 www.youthtalkline.org**

◆ *Advertisement page 2*

⚥ ★ It Gets Better Project, 110 S Fairfax Ave Ste A11-71, Los Angeles, CA 323-782-4934 itgetsbetter.org

⚥ ★ Live Out Loud, 25 Broadway 12th Flr, New York, NY 212-378-4095 www.liveoutloud.info

⚥ ☆ National Runaway Safeline, 800-786-2929 24/7 nationwide crisis intervention services for runaway, homeless, and at-risk youth and their families. Live chat, crisis emails or forum postings. www.1800runaway.org

⚥ ★ Safe & Supportive Schools Project, American Psychological Association, 750 1st St NE, Washington, DC 202-336-6055 tinyurl.com/ylzt6ge

⚥ ★ (♿) Supporting and Mentoring Youth Advocates and Leaders (SMYAL), 410 7th St SE, Washington, DC 202.546.5940 Ages 13-21 www.smyal.org

T ☆ TransYouth Family Allies, Inc, POB 1471, Holland, MI 49422 888-462-8932 www.imatyfa.org

⚥ ★ **The Trevor Project / Lifeline, POB 69232, West Hollywood, CA 90069 866-488-7386 (Lifeline); 310-271-8845 www.thetrevorproject.org**

Performance: Entertainment, Music, Theater, Space

⚥ ● **Aboveground Records: Tom Wilson Weinberg, 215-732-7494 Distributes Tom Wilson Weinberg's recordings, via tomwilsonweinberg.com or Giovanni's Room (queerbooks.com); licenses Tom's revues and musicals: Ten Percent Revue, Get Used to It!, Sixty Years with Bruhs and Gean, Eleanor & Hick and Oscar Visits Walt. www.tomwilsonweinberg.com**

⚥ ● Music By Sandy Rapp, 66 Hildreth Place, East Hampton, NY 11937 631-329-5193 www.SandyRapp.com sandyrapp@aol.com

Printing/Mailing & Promotional Items

⚥ ● Page Marketing Solutions LLC, 540-743-7746 866-893-1490 fax 866-676-4425 tinyurl.com/yanycadm

Public Relations/Advertising/Marketing

⚥ ● Michele Karlsberg Marketing & Management, 917-359-2803 michelekarlsberg.com michelekarlsberg@me.com

♂ ● Rivendell Media Company, 1248 Route 22 W, Mountainside, NJ 07092 908-232-2021 Media Rep. Firm www.rivendellmedia.com info@rivendellmedia.com

Publishers/Publishing-related Services

⚥ ● **Amazing Dreams Publishing, POB 1811, Asheville, NC 28802 Featuring coming out guide, Online Support for Lesbians Coming Out Group, lesbian movie reviews & over 1,000 free Lesbian Ecards. www.amazingdreamspublishing.com**

⚥ ● Chelsea Station Editions, 917-407-9276 tinyurl.com/d8p7bs4 info@chelseastationeditions.com

♀ ☆ (♿) The Feminist Press at the City University of New York, 365 5th Ave Ste 5406, New York, NY 212-817-7915 www.feministpress.org

⚥ ★ Golden Crown Literary Society, POB 720154, Dallas, TX 75372 www.goldencrown.org

⚥ ● Ignite! Entertainment, 41718 Ambervalley Ave Unit 1, Murrieta, CA 92562 310-806-0325 www.ignite-ent.com orders@ignite-ent.com

⚥ ● JMS Books LLC, POB 2478, Petersburg, VA 23804 www.jms-books.com admin@jms-books.com

⚥ ● Lambda Literary Foundation, 811 W 7th St 12th Flr, Los Angeles, CA 213-277-5755 www.lambdaliterary.org

⚥ ● Pagan Press, c/o John Lauritsen, 11 Elton St, Dorchester, MA 02125-1412 www.paganpressbooks.com info@paganpressbooks.com

⚥ ● Persona Press, 2950 Van Ness Ave #4, San Francisco, CA 94109-1036 415-775-6143 www.nikosdiaman.com personapress@att.net

⚥ Prism Comics, Ted Abenheim, President 3624 Westwood Blvd #202, Los Angeles, CA www.prismcomics.org

⚥ ● Redbone Press, POB 15815, New Orleans, LA 70175 Lisa C. Moore www.redbonepress.com ✤ info@redbonepress.com

♀ ○ Sibling Rivalry Press, POB 26147, Little Rock, AR 72221 870-723-6008 www.siblingrivalrypress.com info@siblingrivalrypress.com

Real Estate (see also Mortgages)

⚥ ● Gay Realty Network, 916-594-9100 fax 916-376-7498 www.gayrealtynetwork.com info@gayrealtynetwork.com

Recovery

♀ ☆ (♿) Al-Anon Family Groups, 1600 Corporate Landing Pkwy, Virginia Beach, VA 757-563-1600 www.al-anon.org

♀ ☆ Crystal Meth Anonymous, 4470 W Sunset Blvd #107 PMB 555, Los Angeles, CA 855-638-4383 crystalmeth.org

♀ ☆ Recovery Connection, 1900 Corporate Square Blvd., Jacksonville, FL 866-812-8231 www.recoveryconnection.org

♀ ☆ Sex Addicts Anonymous, POB 70949, Houston, TX 77270 800-477-8191 www.saa-recovery.org

♀ ☆ Sexual Compulsives Anonymous, 70A Greenwich Ave #337, New York, NY 10113 917-722-6912 www.scany.org info@scany.org

Religious / Spiritual Resources

⚥ ★ Affirmation: Gay & Lesbian Mormons, 912 E 32nd St, Minneapolis, MN affirmation.org

⚥ ★ Affirmation: United Methodists for LGBTQ Concerns, POB 1021, Evanston, IL 60204-1021 www.umaffirm.org affirmation lgbtq@gmail.com

⚥ ★ Association of Welcoming & Affirming Baptists, POB 7834, Louisville, KY 40257 888-906-2922 www.awab.org

⚥ ★ BALM Ministries, Marsha Stevens, POB 609, Nolensville, TN 37135 714-206-8004 www.balmministries.net

♀ ☆ (♿) Believe Out Loud, Intersections International, 145 W 28th St 11th Flr, New York, NY 10001 212-951-7006 www.believeoutloud.com contact@believeoutloud.com

♀ ★ ♿ Center for LGBTQ and Gender Studies in Religion (CLGS), Pacific School of Religion, 1798 Scenic Ave, Berkeley, CA 510-849-8206 www.clgs.org

♀ ★ ♫ DignityUSA, POB 376, Medford, MA 02155 202-861-0017 www.dignityusa.org

♀ ★ The Disciples LGBTQ+ Alliance, POB 44400, Indianapolis, IN 46244-0400 317-721-5230 www.disciplesallianceq.org alliance@disciplesallianceq.org

♀ ★ Emergence International, c/o Robert McCullough, 444 Third Ave #4, New York, NY 480-648-8502 tinyurl.com/2qj2qh

♀ ★ Eshel, c/o Makom Hadash, 125 Maiden Lane Ste 8B, New York, NY 724-374-3501 www.eshelonline.org ⚥

♀ ★ The Evangelical Network (TEN), POB 324, Savannah, GA 31420 812-298-6593 www.ten.lgbt

♀ ★ Evangelicals Concerned, 311 E 72nd St #1G, New York, NY 212-517-3171 www.ecinc.org

♀ ★ GALIP Foundation, www.gaychurch.org

♀ ★ Gay & Lesbian Vaishnava Association, www.galva108.org ✧

♀ ★ The Harmony, POB 16973, Kansas City, MO 64133 816-368-5773 www.harmony.lgbt

♀ ★ Integrity USA, POB 390170, Cambridge, MA 02139 713-392-7725 LGBT Episcopalians www.integrityusa.org

♀ ★ International Association of Lesbian & Gay Children of Holocaust Survivors, 261 Broadway #8C, New York, NY 212-233-7867 www.infotrue.com/gay.html ⚥

♀ ★ Jewish Lesbian Daughters of Holocaust Survivors, 608-256-8883 tinyurl.com/ztewxec ⚥

♀ ★ Keshet, 284 Amory St, Boston, MA 617-524-9227 www.keshetonline.org ⚥

♀ ♿ Latinx Roundtable, Center for LGBTQ and Gender Studies in Religion (CLGS), Pacific School of Religion, 1798 Scenic Ave, Berkeley, CA 510-849-8206 www.clgs.org ✛

♀ ★ Metropolitan Community Churches, POB 50488, Sarasota, FL 34232 310-360-8640. www.mccchurch.org

♀ ★ More Light Presbyterians, PMB 246 4737 County Rd 101, Minnetonka, MN www.mlp.org

♀ ☆ Mormons Building Bridges, 978-394-4947 mormonsbuildingbridges.org info@mormonsbuildingbridges.org

♀ ★ New Ways Ministry (Catholic), 4012 29th St, Mount Rainier, MD 301-277-5674 www.newwaysministry.org

♀ ★ Open and Affirming Coalition, United Church of Christ, 700 Prospect Ave, Cleveland, OH 44115 216-736-3228 www.openandaffirming.org office@openandaffirming.org

♀ ★ Q Christian Fellowship, POB 25947, Federal Way, WA 98093 800-268-3688 qchristian.org

♀ ★ Rainbow Sash Movement, 1340 N Dearborn Parkway #16B, Chicago, IL 312-266-0182 tinyurl.com/y8g4uzu5

♀ ★ ♿ Reconciling Ministries Network, 123 W Madison St Ste 1450, Chicago, IL 773-736-5526 www.rmnetwork.org

♀ Reconciling Works, POB 8070, Saint Paul, MN 55108 651-665-0861 www.reconcilingworks.org

♀ Resources for Gay and Lesbian Orthodox Jews, www.orthogays.org ⚥

♀ ☆ Rising Sun Christian Community, POB 10203, Albuquerque, NM 87184 505-898-0908 rsccabq.com info@rsccabq.com

♀ ★ Seventh-day Adventist Kinship International, POB 244, Orinda, CA 94563 www.sdakinship.org

♀ ☆ The Trinitarian Catholic Church, Franciscans of Divine Providence, 17 Shawnee Rd, East Hartford, CT 06118-2554

♂ ☆ Unitarian Universalist Association office of LGBTQ Ministries, 24 Farnsworth St, Boston, MA 02108 617-742-2100 www.uua.org/lgbtq lgbtq@uua.org

♀ ★ ♫ World Congress of GLBT Jews, Keshet Ga'avah, POB 23379, Washington, DC 20026 www.glbtjews.org ⚥

Reproductive Legal Services

♂ ○ Worldwide Surrogacy Specialists, 2150 Post Rd #401, Fairfield, CT 06825 203-255-9877 www.worldwidesurrogacy.org info@worldwidesurrogacy.org

Reproductive Medicine & Fertility Services

♂ ● ♂ Circle Surrogacy, LLC, 200 High St Ste 600, Boston, MA 617-439-9900 www.circlesurrogacy.com

♂ ○ Donor Sibling Registry (DSR), POB 1571, Nederland, CO 80466 303-258-0902 www.donorsiblingregistry.com wendy@donorsiblingregistry.com

♂ ○ RESOLVE: the National Infertility Association, #300 7918 Jones Branch Dr Ste 300, McLean, VA 703-556-7172 www.resolve.org

Research & Genealogy Services

♂ ● Grimard, Andre R, M.Ed, Freelance Researcher, tinyurl.com/cav6o9v andre_grimard@yahoo.com

Social Networks (Online)

♀ ● Gay Villager, Connecting the GLBTQ Community gayvillager.com

Sports & Outdoor

♂ ★ Atlantic Motorcycle Coordinating Council, PO Box 206, Washington, DC 20044 www.amcc76.org

♀ ★ ♫ Diving for Life, check web for details www.divingforlife.org

♀ ★ The Federation of Gay Games, 584 Castro St #343, San Francisco, CA 94114-2512 866-459-1261 www.gaygames.org contact@gaygames.com

♀ ☆ Flag Football - International Women's Flag Football Association, 305-293-9315 www.iwffa.org

♀ ★ Gay & Lesbian Rowing Federation, 10153 Riverside Dr #698, Toluca Lake, CA 323-774-1903 www.glrf.info

♀ ★ Gay & Lesbian Tennis Association, www.glta.net

♂ ★ Gay Outdoors, www.gayoutdoors.org

♀ ★ Gay Polo League, 323-712-3514 www.gaypolo.com

♀ ★ Homo Climbtastic, www.homoclimbtastic.com

♀ ★ International Gay & Lesbian Football Association, www.iglfa.org

♀ International Gay Bowling Organization, PO Box 30722, Charlotte, NC 28230 www.igbo.org

♂ ★ ♫ International Gay Rodeo Association, POB 460504, Aurora, CO 80046 www.igra.com

♀ ★ National Gay Basketball Association, 888-642-2871 www.ngba.org

♀ ★ North American Gay Amateur Athletic Alliance, www.nagaaa-softball.org

♀ ★ Outsports, 850 Tularosa Dr Apt D, Los Angeles, CA 323-841-8293 www.outsports.com

⚲ Rainbow RV, 951-830-5997 www.rainbowrv.com

⚲ ★ Sisters of Scota Womens Motorcycle Club, 530-635-7797 www.sistersofscotawmc.org soswmc@gmail.com

⚲ ★ US LGBT Soccer, 612-927-2257 www.uslgbtsoccer.org

♀ ☆ Women Outdoors, POB 158, Northampton, MA 01061 www.womenoutdoors.org

⚲ ★ You Can Play, Inc., POB 7460, Denver, CO 80207 720-565-5236 www.youcanplayproject.org

RFD

🌸 A COUNTRY JOURNAL 🌸
FOR GAY MEN EVERYWHERE
SPRING. SUMMER. FALL. WINTER

P.O. Box 302 Hadley MA 01035-0302
http://www.rfdmag.org

⚲ You Can Play, Inc., POB 7460, Denver, CO 80207 www.youcanplayproject.org

Travel & Tourist Services (see also Accommodation)

♀ ○ Adventure Associates of WA, Inc, POB 16304, Seattle, WA 98116-0304 206-932-8352 www.adventureassociates.net info@adventureassociates.net

⚥ ○ **Adventure Bound Expeditions, 711 Walnut St, Boulder, CO 80302-5362 303-449-0990 877-440-0990 fax 303-449-9038 Adventure travel for gay men to destinations throughout the world. www.adventureboundmen.com**

⚲ ★ Decadent Duck Events, LLC, 802-445-5303 www.decadentducks.com

⚲ ● Gay Travel Information.Com, 800-842-4753 fax 401-821-1151 www.gaytravelinformation.com info@gaytravelinformation.com

⚲ ● (♿) Oscar Wilde Tours, 31 Barnard Ave, Watertown, MA 02472 646-560-3205 www.oscarwildetours.com info@oscarwildetours.com

⚲ ● **Purple Roofs GLBT Travel Directory, 916-933-8514 fax 916-933-8516 GLBT Travel directory listing accommodations, real estate agents, travel agents and tour operators worldwide www.purpleroofs.com WhereTo Stay@purpleroofs.com**

⚲ ● Rainbow Destinations, 800-387-2462 www.rainbowdest.com rainbowdest@yahoo.com

⚲ ● Spirit Journeys, 428 Riverview Dr, Asheville, NC 28806 828-475-2581 www.spiritjourneys.com info@spiritjourneys.com

⚲ ● (♿) Toto Tours, 1326 W Albion #3-W, Chicago, IL 773-274-8686 www.tototours.com

Video Sales & Rentals

♂ ● TLA Video, POB 898, Wexford, PA 15090 888-852-3837 www.tlavideo.com

Websites: Design & Maintenance Services (see also Internet)

♂ ● Spilled Ink Publishing, 641-278-6972

Weddings and Ceremonies

♂ ○ (♿) Beautiful Calligraphy by Lianda, www.beautifulcalligraphy.com ❤

Alabama
State/County Resources

AIDS/HIV Services, Education & Support

♂ ☆ AIDS Alabama, POB 55703, Birmingham, AL 35222 205-324-9822 www.aidsalabama.org

♀ ☆ ♿ Health Services Center, Inc., PO Box 1347, Anniston, AL 36202 256-832-0100 www.hscal.org ✎

♀ (?♿) Medical Advocacy and Outreach, 2900 McGehee Rd, Montgomery, AL 334-280-3349 maoi.org

Organizations/Resources: Business & Professional Associations, Labor Advocacy

♂ Association for LGBT Issues in Counseling, www.algbtical.org

Organizations/Resources: Political/Legislative/Advocacy

♀ Southern Poverty Law Center LGBT Rights, 400 Washington Ave, Montgomery, AL 334-956-8200 tinyurl.com/y6lrq8z7

Anniston

Accommodation: Hotels, Inns, Guesthouses, B&B, Resorts

♂ ○ ♿ Springwood Inn, 1301 Booger Hollow Rd; 36207 843-384-2618 www.springwoodinn.com (❀?) ✎ ⊛

Organizations/Resources: Family and Supporters

♀ ☆ ♿ PFLAG Anniston, 256-393-9119 fb.com/pflagaIniston/

Auburn/Opelika Area

Community Centers and/or Pride Organizations

♂ Pride on the Plains, 334-329-4824 www.prideontheplains.com

Organizations/Resources: Family and Supporters

♀ PFLAG Auburn & Surrounding Areas, POB 2846, Auburn; 36831 auburnpflag.com

Birmingham

Community Centers and/or Pride Organizations

♂ ★ Central Alabama Pride, 205 32nd St S 256-813-4227 www.centralalabamapride.org

AIDS/HIV Services, Education & Support

♂ ☆ (?♿) Birmingham AIDS Outreach, 205 32nd St S; 205-322-4197 **H?** tinyurl.com/yy78nfgj ✎

Bars, Cafes, Clubs, Restaurants

♂ ● Al's on Seventh, 2627 7th Ave S 205-321-2812 fb.com/alson-seventh/ **DP** ▦ alson7thave@gmail.com

♂ The Chapel Bar & Nightclub, 620 27th St S 205-703-9778 TheChapelBarBham.com **DL** ▦

♀ ○ Chez Lulu, 1909 Cahaba Rd; 205-870-5584 www.chezlulu.us ✖

♀ ○ Paper Doll, 2320 1st Ave N; 205-283-6391 www.paperdoll-bar.com info@paperdollbar.com

♀ ● Quest Club, 416 24th St S; 205-251-4313 www.the-quest-club.com **DP**

♂ ○ ♿ Rojo, 2921 Highland Ave S 205-328-4733 www.rojobirm-ingham.com ⧓ ✖ ✎

♂ ○ The Wine Loft, 2200 1st Ave N; 205-323-8228 www.wineloftbham.com

Broadcast Media

♂ ★ Rainbow World Radio / OutVoice, StoneWall Society Network, POB 1438, Alabaster; 35007 205-358-7672 www.rainbowworldra-dio.com

Health Care: Physical (see also Counseling/Mental Health)

♀ LGBT Vet Care, Birmingham VA Medical Center, 700 S 19th St; 205-933-8101 tinyurl.com/y6zl9omd

♀ ★ ♿ Magic City Wellness Center, 2500 4th Ave S; 205-877-8677 LGBTQ primary care facility. A program of Birmingham AIDS Outreach. tinyurl.com/guora7r ✎

Organizations/Resources: Cultural, Dance, Performance

♂ Steel City Men's Chorus, POB 2212; 35201 205-861-0636 steel-citymenschorus.org

♀ Terrific New Theatre, 2821 2nd Ave S 205-328-0868 www.terrific-newtheatre.com

---

♀ GLBTQI ♀ Gay/nongay ♂ bisexual
♀ LBTQI women ♀ all women ♀ bisexual women
♂ GBTQI men ♂ all men ♂ bisexual man
T specifically transsexual/transgender/transvestite
⧓ ✖ Bar and Restaurant ✖ Restaurant ⊃ Cafe
▦ Entertainment/Cabaret/Showbar
D Dancing **V** Video bar **K** Karaoke **S** Sports bar
C Country **L** Leather/Levi **W** Western
P Private Club (ask about visitor memberships)

♥ Wedding-related services or marriage equality
H Assistance available for the deaf and hearing-impaired
HD devices **HS** sign **HDS** devices and sign
H? Check for assistance available for the deaf and. hearing-impaired
⊛ ⊛ smoke-free property ⊛ smoke-free indoors
(⊛) indoor smoking areas
❀ Pets welcome (❀?) Ask about pets
✎ High speed internet available to visitors
Wheelchair Accessibility of premises or meeting place:
♿ Accessible premises and lavatory
(♿) Accessible premises with help; accessible lavatory
♿ Accessible premises; lavatory not known to be accessible
Accessible premises with help
(?♿) Call ahead for details: places of meetings or activities vary, or spe-cial arrangements available.
◇ Asian ✦ Latin/Hispanic
⬤ African-descent/Black
✦ People of Color ✳ Two-Spirit ✪ Diverse

Organizations/Resources: Family and Supporters

♂ ☆ PFLAG Birmingham, 4300 Hampton Hts Dr 205-591-0528 pflagbham.org

Organizations/Resources: Social, Recreation, Support

♂ Mystic Krewe of Apollo Birmingham, www.mkabirmingham.com

♀ ★ StoneWall Society Network, POB 1438, Alabaster; 35007-1438 205-358-7672 www.stonewallsociety.net sysop@stonewall society.net

Organizations/Resources: Student, Academic, Education

♀ ★ Birmingham Southern College Spexctrum, Box 549014, 900 Arkadelphia Rd; 205-226-4733 fb.com/groups/171263442934241

♀ ★ University of Alabama Gender and Sexuality Union, HUC Box 44, 1530 3rd Ave S; 205-934-9679 tinyurl.com/y3ztzxjq

Organizations/Resources: Youth (see also Family)

♀ ★ ♿ Magic City Acceptance Center, 2500 4th Ave S; 205-774-1173 tinyurl.com/gmf6bhm ✗

Religious / Spiritual Resources

♀ ★ ♿ Covenant Community Church UCC, 2205 3rd St NE; 205-599-3363 covenantbirmingham.org ✗

Sports & Outdoor

♀ ★ New South Softball League, 205 32nd St S www.newsouth-softball.net

Dothan

Organizations/Resources: Family and Supporters

♂ PFLAG of Dothan and the Wiregrass, 1721 Choctaw 334-794-4066 tinyurl.com/lrllucs

Florence

Community Centers and/or Pride Organizations

♀ ★ ♿ Shoals Diversity Center, 220 Tennessee St Ste 205; 36530 256-284-2708 shoalsdiversitycenter.org ✗ shoalsdiversity center@gmail.com

Organizations/Resources: Family and Supporters

♂ ☆ PFLAG Florence/Shoals, 220 W Tennessee St Ste 205; 256-248-7177 fb.com/pflagsupportgroup/

Organizations/Resources: Political/Legislative/Advocacy

♀ Equality Shoals, POB 674; 35632 256-762-9436 fb.com/equality-shoals

Organizations/Resources: Student, Academic, Education

♀ ★ University of North Alabama Student Alliance for Equality, Office of Student Life, Guillot University Center 202 256-765-4210 fb.com/groups/unagsa/

Huntsville

Community Centers and/or Pride Organizations

♀ ★ Rocket City Pride, fb.com/RocketCityPrideAL/ info@ tnvalleyrcp.org

Bars, Cafes, Clubs, Restaurants

♂ Convergent, 2616 N Memorial Pkwy 256-859-9112 fb.com/Club-Convergent/ **D** 📖

♂ Deja Vieux Night Club, 1204 Posey St 256-715-0436 tinyurl.com/y6h8zjol **D** 📖

Health Care: Physical (see also Counseling/Mental Health)

♀ ☆ ♿ Thrive Alabama, 600 St Clair Ave Bldg 3; 256-536-4700 PrEP services thrivealabama.org

Organizations/Resources: Family and Supporters

♂ ☆ PFLAG Huntsville, POB 485, Meridianville 35759 256-415-5670 fb.com/PflagHuntsville pflag.huntsville@gmail.com

Organizations/Resources: Social, Recreation, Support

♂ ★ Rocket City Bears, 256-258-9663 fb.com/RocketCityBears/

Religious / Spiritual Resources

♀ ☆ (♿) Unitarian Universalist Church of Huntsville, 3921 Broad-mor Rd; 35810 256-534-0508 www.uuch.org uuch@uuch.org

Sports & Outdoor

♀ ☆ Dixie Derby Girls, POB 18514; 35804 www.dixiederbygirls.com
» Meridianville: see Huntsville

Mobile

Community Centers and/or Pride Organizations

♀ ★ Mobile Alabama Pride, Inc., POB 227 36601 www.mob-pride.org

AIDS/HIV Services, Education & Support

♀ ☆ ♿ AIDS Alabama South, 4321 Downtowner Loop N; 36609 / 2054 Dauphin St 251-471-5277 **H?** www.aidsalabamasouth.org

Bars, Cafes, Clubs, Restaurants

♀ ● ♿ B-Bob's Downtown, 213 Conti St; 251-433-2262 b-bobs.com **DKLV** 📖 ✗ bbobsmob@gmail.com

♀ ● ♿ Flip Side Bar & Patio, 54 S Conception St; 251-431-8869 flipsidebarpatio.com **DV** ✗

♀ ● (♿) Gabriel's Downtown, 55 S. Joachim St; 36602 251-432-4900 www.gabrielsdowntown.com **KVP** ✗

♀ ● The Midtown Pub, 153 S Florida St 251-450-1555 www.themidtownpub.com **DK** 📖 ✗

Organizations/Resources: Social, Recreation, Support

♀ ★ ♿ Gulf Coast Bears, c/o B-Bob's, 213 Conti St; 251-433-2262 www.GulfCoastBears.com

♀ Order of Osiris, POB 1991; 36633 orderofosiris.com

Religious / Spiritual Resources

♀ ★ ♿ Cornerstone MCC, 1007 Government St; 36604 251-438-7080 www.cornerstonemccchurch.com cmcc1@bellsouth.net

Montevallo

Organizations/Resources: Family and Supporters

⚥ ☆ PFLAG Montevallo, 820 Vine St; 35115 fb.com/PFLAGMontevallo/ pflagmontevallo@gmail.com

Organizations/Resources: Student, Academic, Education

⚥ ☆ University of Montevallo Spectrum, Student Union - COMER 205; fb.com/SpectrumUMGSA

Montgomery

Community Centers and/or Pride Organizations

⚥ Montgomery Pride United, 635 Madison Ave 334-356-2464 tinyurl.com/y3uaheat

Accommodation: Hotels, Inns, Guesthouses, B&B, Resorts

⚥ ● The Lattice Inn, 1414 S Hull St; 36104 / near Governor's Mansion, & intersection of I-65 and I-85 334-263-1414 Award-winning B&B in heart of Montgomery's Garden District, in a tastefully updated 1906-era cottage. www.thelatticeinn.com ⚲ ⊗ info@ thelatticeinn.com

Counseling/Psychotherapy/Mental Health

♂ ○ &⅘ Riser, Susan, PhD, LPC, NCC, A Better Way Counseling and Psychotherapy, 5510 Wares Ferry Rd #U3; 36117 334-387-2317 **H?** www.montgomerytherapist.com seriser@bellsouth.net

Organizations/Resources: Family and Supporters

♀ ☆ ♿ PFLAG Montgomery, 8790 Vaughn Rd 334-546-0390 tinyurl.com/md7f76q

Organizations/Resources: Student, Academic, Education

⚥ ★ Spectrum at Auburn University at Montgomery, POB 244023; 36124 334-244-3240 fb.com/groups/aumgsa/

Religious / Spiritual Resources

♀ ☆ &⅘ Immanuel Presbyterian Church, 8790 Vaughn Rd; 36117 334-260-0567 immanuelpcusa.org ⚲ office@immanuelpcusa.org

Selma

AIDS/HIV Services, Education & Support

♂ Selma AIR, 102 Central Park Place; 334-872-6795 www.SelmaAIR.org

Steele

Campgrounds and RV Parks

⚥ ● Bluff Creek Falls, 1125 Loop Rd; 205-515-7882 www.bluffcreekfalls.com **N** ⚲

Tuscaloosa

AIDS/HIV Services, Education & Support

♂ ☆ Five Horizons Health Services, 2720 6th St Ste 100; 35401 205-759-8470 www.fivehorizons.org

---

The Lattice Inn
Award-winning and unique bed and breakfast in the heart of Montgomery's historic Garden District,

**1414 South Hull Street
Montgomery, Alabama 36104-5522
334.263.1414**
www.thelatticeinn.com

Bars, Cafes, Clubs, Restaurants

⚥ Icon, 516 Greensboro Ave fb.com/IconTuscaloosa **D** ▦

Counseling/Psychotherapy/Mental Health

♂ Counseling Center of the University of Alabama, POB 870362; 35487 205-348-3863 counseling.sa.ua.edu

Organizations/Resources: Student, Academic, Education

⚥ ★ University of Alabama Spectrum, 355 Ferguson Center Box 870292; 907-315-4118 tinyurl.com/yypmvfjx

Religious / Spiritual Resources

♂ ☆ &⅘ God's House, POB 2887; 35403 205-242-3162 tinyurl.com/yfwwtda

Alaska
State/County Resources

Information, Media & Publications

⚥ ★ Bent Alaska, tinyurl.com/q2ee2xs

Funding: Endowment, Fundraising

⚥ Imperial Court of All Alaska, POB 212421, Anchorage, AK 99521 www.impcourtak.org

Organizations/Resources: Political/Legislative/Advocacy

⚥ ★ Alaskans Together for Equality, Inc, 336 E 5th Ave, Anchorage, AK 907-929-4528 www.alaskanstogether.org

♀ ☆ &⅘ American Civil Liberties Union of Alaska, 1057 W Fireweed Lane Ste 207, Anchorage, AK 907-258-0044 www.acluak.org

Organizations/Resources: Social, Recreation, Support

⚥ ★ &⅘ Identity, Inc., 801 W Fireweed Ln Ste 103, Anchorage, AK 99503-1893 907-929-4528 identityalaska.org ⚲ info@ identityinc.org

Anchorage

Crisis, Anti-violence, & Helplines

⚥ ★ Anchorage GLBT Helpline, 801 W Fireweed Ln Ste 103; 99503-1893 888-901-9876 907-258-4777 tinyurl.com/y6ufscyf info@identityinc.org

Community Centers and/or Pride Organizations

⚥ ★ Anchorage Pride, 801 W Fireweed Ln Ste 103 99503-1893 907-929-4528 anchoragepride.org info@identityinc.org

♂ ★ ♿ Identity LGBT Community Center, 336 E 5th Ave; 907-929-4528 identityalaska.org info@identityinc.org

Accommodation: Hotels, Inns, Guesthouses, B&B, Resorts

♀ ● City Garden, 1352 W 10th Ave; 99501-3245 907-276-8686 www.citygarden.biz ✂ ⊗ citygarden@acsalaska.net

♀ ● A Wildflower Inn, 1239 I St; 907-274-1239 tinyurl.com/3xm4z7 ⊗

Bars, Cafes, Clubs, Restaurants

♀ ○ Humpy's Great Alaskan Alehouse, 610 W 6th Ave 907-382-4657 www.humpys.com ☕ ✕

♂ ● ♿ Mad Myrna's, 530 E 5th Ave (bet Eagle/Fairbanks) 907-276-9762 fb.com/madmyrnasak **DKV** ☕ ⬗ ✕ ▦ ✂

♂ ♿ Raven, 708 E 4th Ave 907-276-9672 fb.com/TheRavenAK

♀ ○ Snow City Cafe, 1034 W 4th Ave; 907-272-2489 www.snowcitycafe.com ⬗

Bookstores

♀ ● ♿ The Writer's Block Bookstore and Cafe, 3956 Spenard Rd; 907-720-7559 **H?** www.writersblockak.com ⬗ ✂

Counseling/Psychotherapy/Mental Health

♀ ○ ♿ Strisik, Suzanne, PhD, 1500 W 33rd Ave Ste 210 907-868-7843 www.strisik.com

Entertainment-Related Services (see also Performance)

♀ ○ ♿ Cyrano's Theatre Company, 3800 Debarr Rd; 99508 907-274-2599 www.cyranos.org ⬗ info@cyranos.org

Health Care: Physical (see also Counseling/Mental Health)

♀ ○ Polar Pediatrics, 603 W Tudor Rd; 99503 907-522-5437 www.polarpediatrics.com polarpediatrics@gmail.com

Organizations/Resources: Family and Supporters

T ☆ ♿ Anchorage Transgender Community, Identity, Inc. 336 E 5th Ave; 907-929-4528 tinyurl.com/ybm2mofb ✂

♂ ★ ♿ PFLAG Anchorage, POB 210874 99521-0874 907-566-1813 tinyurl.com/gqvj4od ✂ pflag-anchorage@gci.net

T ♿ TransParent, Identity, Inc. 336 E 5th Ave; 907-929-4528 tinyurl.com/ybm2mofb ✂

Organizations/Resources: Senior Resources

♂ ★ ♿ SAGE Alaska, Identity, Inc. 801 W Fireweed Ln Ste 103; 99503-1893 907-929-4528 tinyurl.com/y7hflr9b ✂ info@identityinc.org

Organizations/Resources: Social, Recreation, Support

♂ ★ (♺) The Last Frontier Men's Club, PO Box 202054; 99520 www.tlfmc.com **P**

Organizations/Resources: Student, Academic, Education

♂ ★ University of Alaska Safe Zone, 3700 Sharon Gagnon Lane; 907-751-7396 tinyurl.com/hw2j45s

♂ ★ West Anchorage High School GSA, 1700 Hillcrest Dr; 907-742-2500

Organizations/Resources: Youth (see also Family)

♂ ♿ Q Club Anchorage, Identity, Inc. 336 E 5th Ave; 907-929-4528 tinyurl.com/y9jy5gz7 ✂

T ♿ Translution, Identity, Inc. 336 E 5th Ave; 907-929-4528 tinyurl.com/y9jy5gz7 ✂

Performance: Entertainment, Music, Theater, Space

♂ ★ ♿ Out North Contemporary Art House, 333 W 4th Ave; 907-279-8900 www.outnorth.org

Real Estate (see also Mortgages)

♂ ○ ♿ Florio, Rona, Homes Unlimited, Downtown, 1343 G St Ste 104; 99501 907-748-4500 rona@ak.net

♂ ○ McLane, Mike, Jack White Real Estate, 3801 Centerpoint Dr Ste 200; 99503 907-227-1533 www.mmclane.com mike@mmclane.com

Religious / Spiritual Resources

♂ ☆ ♿ Anchorage Unitarian Universalist Fellowship, 2824 E 18th Ave; 99508-3303 907-248-3737 **HD** www.anchorageuuf.org auuf@gci.net

♂ ☆ ♿ Immanuel Presbyterian Church, 2311 Pembroke St; 99504 907-333-5253 www.ipcanchorage.com ipcanchorage@yahoo.com

♂ ☆ ♿ St Mary's Episcopal Church, 2222 E Tudor Rd; 99507 907-563-3341 **HDS** www.godsview.org ✂

Sports & Outdoor

♂ ★ Anchorage Front Runners, c/o Peter VanDyne, 1230 Pine St; 907-240-2904 tinyurl.com/h6vunbl

Fairbanks

Accommodation: Hotels, Inns, Guesthouses, B&B, Resorts

♂ ● Billie's Backpackers Hostel, 2895 Mack Blvd 99709-4006 907-479-2034 www.AlaskaHostel.com ✂ ⊗ info@alaskahostel.com

AIDS/HIV Services, Education & Support

♂ ☆ Interior AIDS Association, POB 71248; 99707 907-452-4222 www.interioraids.org

Bars, Cafes, Clubs, Restaurants

♂ ○ (♺) Hot Licks Ice Cream, 3453 College Rd (May-Aug) 907-479-7813 www.hotlicks.net ⬗

Organizations/Resources: Family and Supporters

♂ ☆ PFLAG Fairbanks, POB 82290; 99708-2290 907-457-3524 fairbankspflag.org ✂ pflagfairbanks@gmail.com

Organizations/Resources: Transgender/Gender Non-Conforming/Diverse

♂ Gender Pioneers, fb.com/GenderPioneers/

Organizations/Resources: Youth (see also Family)

♂ ☆ Fairbanks Gay Youth, Fairbanks PFLAG, POB 82290; 99708-2290 907-457-3524 www.fairbankspflag.org ✂ pflagfairbanks@gmail.com

Religious / Spiritual Resources

♀ ☆ ♂♂ Unitarian Universalist Fellowship of Fairbanks, 4448 Pike's Landing Rd; 99709 907-451-8838 www.uuff.org info@uuff.org

Homer

Accommodation: Hotels, Inns, Guesthouses, B&B, Resorts

♂ ○ Brigitte's Bavarian Bed & Breakfast, POB 2391; 99603-2391 907-235-6620 brigittesbavarian.com bbbb@xyz.net

♂ ○ (?♂) Sadie Cove Wilderness Lodge, PO Box 2265; 99603-2265 / In Kachemak Bay State Park 907-235-2350 888-283-7234 www.sadiecove.com ⊗ email@sadiecove.com

Juneau

Information, Media & Publications

♀ ★ Southeast Alaska LGBTQ Alliance (SEAGLA), mail to SEAGLA, POB 21542; 99802 www.seagla.org

Accommodation: Hotels, Inns, Guesthouses, B&B, Resorts

♂ ● (?♂) Alaska's Capital Inn B&B, 113 W 5th St; 907-586-6507 www.alaskacapitalinn.com ✔ ⊗

Bookstores

♂ ○ Hearthside Books & Toys, Nugget Mall, 8745 Glacier Hwy; 866-789-2750 www.hearthsidebooks.com

Organizations/Resources: Cultural, Dance, Performance

♀ ★ ♂♂ PFLAG Juneau Pride Chorus, PO Box 32245; 99803 **H?** juneaupridechorus.com

Organizations/Resources: Family and Supporters

♂ ☆ ♂♂ PFLAG Juneau, POB 32245 99803-2245 **H?** pflagjuneau@gmail.com

Ketchikan

Bookstores

♂ ○ Parnassus, 105 Stedman St; 907-225-7690 tinyurl.com/gs75k5q

Kodiak

Organizations/Resources: Social, Recreation, Support

♀ LGBT Kodiak, POB 3267; 99615 fb.com/groups/LGBTKodiak

Mat-Su Valley

Accommodation: Hotels, Inns, Guesthouses, B&B, Resorts
Palmer

♂ ● ♂♂ Alaska Garden Gate B&B, 950 S Trunk Rd, Palmer; 907-746-2333 www.gardengatebnb.com (♣?) ✔

Organizations/Resources: Youth (see also Family)

♀ Q Club Valley, Denali Family Services, 291 E Swanson Ave, Wasilla; 907-929-4528 tinyurl.com/yapvgavg
>> *Palmer: see Mat-Su Valley*

Seward

Accommodation Rental: Furnished / Vacation (& AirBNB)

♂ ● Renfro's Lakeside Retreat, 27177 Seward Hwy 99664 907-288-5059 tinyurl.com/lo9ccms ♣ ✔ ⊗ renfroslakesideretreat@gmail.com

Sitka

Bookstores

♂ ○ ♂♂ Old Harbor Books, 201 Lincoln St 99835 907-747-8808 **H?** www.oldharborbooks.net oldharborbookssitka@gmail.com

Counseling/Psychotherapy/Mental Health

♂ ● ♂♂ Westergaard, Cindy, Neurobehavioral Consultants, 300 Harbor Dr; 99835 907-747-3743 nbc.sitka@live.com

Sterling

Accommodation Rental: Furnished / Vacation (& AirBNB)

♂ ● Alaska Red Fish Lodge, POB 650; 99672 907-262-7080 www.alaskaredfishlodge.com ✔

Talkeetna

Accommodation Rental: Furnished / Vacation (& AirBNB)

♀ ● Hale Kolea Cabin, 21861 S H St 808-237-9651 www.halekoleacabin.com ✔ ⊗ ⊗
>> *Wasilla: see Mat-Su Valley*

Wrangell St. Elias National Park

Accommodation: Hotels, Inns, Guesthouses, B&B, Resorts
McCarthy

♂ ● (?♂) McCarthy Lodge / Ma Johnson's Hotel, POB MXY, McCarthy; 99588 907-554-4402 **H?** www.mccarthylodge.com ✕ (♣?) ✔ ⊗

Arizona
State/County Resources

Information, Media & Publications

♀ ● GayArizona.com, MC Publishing Inc, 5229 N 7th #107B, Phoenix, AZ 85064 602-466-2501 www.GayArizona.com arizona@theprideguides.com

Leather Resources & Groups

♂ Southwest Leather Conference, POB 13531, Tempe, AZ 85284 www.southwestleather.org

Organizations/Resources: Business & Professional Associations, Labor Advocacy

♀ ★ National Lesbian & Gay Journalists Association Arizona, tinyurl.com/yb2symxj

Organizations/Resources: Political/Legislative/Advocacy

♂ ☆ ♂♂ ACLU of Arizona, POB 17148, Phoenix, AZ 85011 602-650-1854 **H?** www.acluaz.org ✔ info@acluaz.org

⚥ ★ Equality Arizona, POB 25044, Phoenix, AZ 85002 602-538-3729 www.equalityarizona.org

⚥ ★ Stonewall Democrats of Arizona, POB 87222, Tucson, AZ 85754 520-481-4118 www.stonewalldemsaz.org

Organizations/Resources: Social, Recreation, Support

⚥ ★ Lambda Car Club, POB 45140, Phoenix, AZ 85064 602-371-8532 www.azgaycar.com

Religious / Spiritual Resources

⚥ ALL: Arizona LDS LGBT, www.allarizona.org

Sports & Outdoor

⚥ Arizona Gay Rodeo Association, POB 40465, Phoenix, AZ 85067 www.agra-phx.com

⚥ ★ ♿ Arizona Gay Volleyball, PO Box 80673, Phoenix, AZ 85060 361-649-0193 **H?** www.azgv.org

Bisbee/Sierra Vista Area

Community Centers and/or Pride Organizations

⚥ ★ (♿) Bisbee Pride, POB 451, Bisbee; 85603 520-261-8415 www.bisbeepride.com

Accommodation: Hotels, Inns, Guesthouses, B&B, Resorts
Bisbee

♀ ○ Canyon Rose Suites, 27 Subway at Shearer 520-432-5098 www.canyonrose.com ✍ ⊗⊗

Hereford

♂ ● ♿ Casa de San Pedro B&B, 8933 S Yell Ln, Hereford; 85615-9250 520-366-1300 www.bedandbirds.com ✍ ⊗ bedandbirds@gmail.com

Accommodation Rental: Furnished / Vacation (& AirBNB)
Bisbee

♂ ● Doublejack Guesthouse, POB 1067, Bisbee 85603 520-559-6708 www.doublejackbisbee.com ✤ ✍ ⊗

Antiques & Collectibles

♂ ● ♿ Finders Keepers Antiques & Collectibles, 81 Main St 520-432-2900 www.fkeepers.com

Bars, Cafes, Clubs, Restaurants
Bisbee

♀ ○ St Elmo's Bar, 36 Brewery Gulch Ave, Bisbee 520-432-5578 tinyurl.com/n3h6mkb

Real Estate (see also Mortgages)

♀ ● Linda Grale Realty, POB 1552, Bisbee; 85603 602-430-7071 www.lindagrale.com linda@lindagrale.com

Religious / Spiritual Resources

♀ ☆ ♿ Sky Island UU Church, 4533A N Commerce Dr, Sierra Vista; 85635 520-378-0197 **H** skyislanduu.org ✍ skyislandchurch@gmail.com

Flagstaff

Community Centers and/or Pride Organizations

⚥ ★ Northern Arizona Pride Association, POB 1604; 86002 928-213-1900 www.flagstaffpride.org

Accommodation: Hotels, Inns, Guesthouses, B&B, Resorts

♂ ● ♿ Inn at 410 Bed & Breakfast, 410 N Leroux St; 86001-4549 928-774-0088 fax 928-774-6354 www.inn410.com ✍ ⊗ info@inn410.com

♂ ● Starlight Pines B&B, 3380 E Lockett Rd 928-527-1912 www.starlightpinesbb.com ✍ ⊗

Bars, Cafes, Clubs, Restaurants

♂ ○ ♿ Charly's Pub & Grill, Weatherford Hotel, 23 N Leroux St; 928-779-1919 www.weatherfordhotel.com **D** ♈ ✕▦ ✍

♂ ○ Macy's European Coffee House, 14 S Beaver St 928-774-2243 www.macyscoffee.net ▷

Organizations/Resources: Social, Recreation, Support

⚥ ★ PEAKS Pride, 3380 E Lockett Rd 928-814-3984 Volunteer services organization www.peakspride.org

Organizations/Resources: Student, Academic, Education

⚥ ★ ♿ Northern Arizona University PRISM, Box 5677; fb.com/prism.nau

Religious / Spiritual Resources

♂ ☆ ♿ First Congregational Church, 740 N Turquoise Dr; 86001 928-774-0890 **H?** www.fccflagstaff.org ✍ fccflagstaff@hotmail.com

>> Glendale: see Phoenix Area
>> Hereford: see Bisbee/Sierra Vista Area

Jerome

Accommodation: Hotels, Inns, Guesthouses, B&B, Resorts

♂ ● Mile High Grill & Inn, 309 Main St 928-634-5094 www.mile-highgrillandinn.com ✕

Lake Havasu City

Recovery

♂ ☆ Lake Havasu City AA, 877-652-9005 www.havasuaa.com

Navajo Nation

Organizations/Resources: Ethnic, Multicultural

♂ Diné Equality, 505-236-4116 www.EqualityNavajo.org

Page/Lake Powell

Accommodation: Hotels, Inns, Guesthouses, B&B, Resorts
Big Water

♂ ● Dreamkatchers Lake Powell, 1055 S American Way, Big Water, UT 84741 435-675-5828 tinyurl.com/bbxks6 ✍ stay@dreamkatcherslakepowell.com

Phoenix Area

Community Centers and/or Pride Organizations

♀ ★ Phoenix Pride, POB 16847, Phx; 85011 602-277-7433
www.phoenixpride.org

Information, Media & Publications

♀ ★ ♿ Lesbian Social Network, Phoenix Pride LGBT Center,
801 N 2nd Ave, Phx; 480-946-5570 tinyurl.com/6glabgq ✓

Accommodation: Hotels, Inns, Guesthouses, B&B, Resorts
Phoenix

♂ ○ (♿) Arizona Royal Villa, 4312 N 12th St, Phx; 602-266-6883
www.royalvilla.com

♂ ● (♿) Arizona Sunburst Inn, 6245 N 12th Pl, Phx; 800-974-
1474 www.azsunburst.com ✓ ⊛

♀ ● Clarendon Hotel & Spa, 401 W Clarendon Ave, Phx; 602-252-
7363 www.goclarendon.com

Accounting, Bookkeeping, Tax Services

♀ ○ Quatrone, Jeffrey J, E.A., 3030 E Cactus Rd Ste 102, Phx;
602-548-0744 www.jjqtaxprep.com

AIDS/HIV Services, Education & Support

♀ ☆ ♿ Aunt Rita's Foundation, 1101 N Central Ave Ste 212, Phx;
602-882-8675 www.auntritasfoundation.org ✓

♂ ♿ For Positive Men, meets Thu 6.30 pm at Casa De Cristo,
1029 E Turney www.forpm.org

♀ ★ ♿ Joshua Tree Feeding Program, Inc., First Congregation
UCC, 214 E Willetta St, Phx; 602-264-0223 www.jtfp.org ✓

♀ ☆ ♿ Phoenix Shanti Group, Inc., 2345 W Glendale Ave, Phx;
602-279-0008 **H** www.shantiaz.org

♀ ☆ Southwest Center for HIV/AIDS, 1101 N Central Ave Ste 200,
Phx; 602-307-5330 www.swcenter.org

Bars, Cafes, Clubs, Restaurants
Phoenix

♂ ● The Anvil, 2424 E Thomas Rd, Phx; 602-334-1462 www.anvil-
baraz.com **DKL** ⬛ ✓

♂ ● Bar 1, 3702 N 16th St, Phx; 602-266-9001 www.bar1bar.com
KV ✓

♀ Boycott, 4301 N 7th Ave, Phx; 602-515-3667 www.boy-
cottbar.com **DK** ⬛

♂ ● Charlie's Phoenix, 727 W Camelback Rd, Phx 602-265-0224
www.charliesphoenix.com **DCW** ⬛

♀ ● ♿ The Coronado PHX, 2201 N 7th St, Phx; 602-252-1322
www.thecoronadophx.com ✕ ✓

♂ ● Cruisin' 7th, 3702 N 7th St, Phx; 602-212-9888
www.cruisin7th.com ⬛ ✓

♂ Dick's Cabaret, 3432 E Illini St, Phx 602-274-3425
dickscabaret.com **D** ⬛

♀ ● ♿ Green: New American Vegetarian, 2022 N 7th St, Phx;
602-258-1870 www.greenvegetarian.com ✕ ✓

♂ Karamba, 1724 E McDowell Rd, Phx; 602-254-0231 www.karam-
banightclub.com **DK** ✦

♂ ● Kobalt Bar at Park Central, 3110 N Central Ave Ste 175, Phx;
602-264-5307 www.kobaltbarphoenix.com **K** ⬛

♂ Los Diablos, 1028 E Indian School Rd, Phx 602-795-7881
tinyurl.com/ycpy39bm ⬦ ✕

♀ ● ♿ Nami Coffee & Vegetarian Sweets, 2014 N 7th St, Phx;
602-258-NAMI www.greenvegetarian.com ☞ ✓

♂ Nutowne Saloon, 5002 E Van Buren St, Phx 602-267-9959
fb.com/NuTowneSaloon ✓

♀ ● (♿) OZ Bar, 1804 W Bethany Home Rd, Phx; 602-242-5114
fb.com/ozbarphx/ **K** ✓

♂ ● ♿ Pat-O's Bunkhouse Saloon, 4428 N 7th Ave, Phx; 602-
200-9154 fb.com/BunkhouseSaloon/ **KLV** ⬛

♀ ● Plazma, 1560 E Osborn Rd, Phx 602-266-0477
fb.com/Plazma-156832864011/ **KV**

♂ ● ♿ The Rock, 4129 N 7th Ave, Phx; 602-248-8559
www.therockdmphoenix.com ⬛

♂ ● ♿ Stacy's at Melrose, 4343 7th Ave, Phx; 602-264-1700
www.stacysatmelrose.com **DK** ✓

Scottsdale

♀ ● ♿ BS West, 7125 E 5th Ave, Scottsdale; 480-945-9028
www.bswest.com **DKV** ⬛ ✓

Tempe

♀ ● ♿ Green: New American Vegetarian, 2240 N Scottsdale Rd
#113, Tempe; 480-941-9003 www.greenvegetarian.com ✕ ✓

Bookstores

♂ ○ ♿ Changing Hands Bookstore, 300 W Camelback Rd, Phx;
602-274-0067 www.changinghands.com ✓

♀ ○ ♿ Changing Hands Bookstore, 6428 S McClintock Dr,
Tempe; 480-730-0205 www.changinghands.com ✓

Counseling/Psychotherapy/Mental Health

♀ ○ House, Sabra, ACSW., The Lighthouse Center, 9929 N 95th
Street Ste 101, Scottsdale; 480-451-0819 www.sabrahouse.com

♀ ♿ Lovejoy, Gary D, PhD, 4500 S Lakeshore Dr #415,
Tempe; 480-756-1669

Funding: Endowment, Fundraising

♀ ★ The Grand Canyon Sisters of Perpetual Indulgence,
fb.com/azsisters/

♀ ★ Imperial Sovereign Empire of Arizona, POB 7608, Phx; 85011
602-999-7601 www.imperialcourtaz.org

Health Care: Physical (see also Counseling/Mental Health)

♂ ○ Boyd, David, MD, 2990 N Litchfield Rd Ste 8, Goodyear; 602-399-0188 Concierge physician www.p3md.com

Leather Resources & Groups

♂ ★ Phoenix Boys of Leather, www.phoenixboysofleather.com

Legal Services

♂ ● ♿ Barber Law Group, PLLC, 2 N Central Ave Ste 1800, Phx; 85004 602-500-2261 criminal defense attorneys tinyurl.com/gp7omsp ✗ bretton@barberlawgroup.com

♀ ● (♿) **Gummere, Kathie, 1215 W Woodland Ave, Phx; 85007 602-952-0293 Estate planning & document preparation: protect your family & your choices. www.kathiegummere.com kathie@ kathiegummere.com**

♂ ○ Rosenstein Law Group, 8010 E McDowell Rd Ste 111, Scottsdale; 85257 480-248-7666 800-666-6DUI fax 480-946-0681 www.scottsdale-duilawyer.com Lesley@Rosen steinLawGroup.com

Men's & Sex Clubs (not primarily Health Clubs)

♂ ● ♿ Chute Health Club, 1440 E Indian School Rd, Phx; 602-234-1654 www.chuteaz.com **PL**

♂ ● (♿) FLEX Phoenix, 1517 S Black Canyon Hwy, Phx; 602-271-9011 www.flexspas.com/phoenix

Organizations/Resources: Business & Professional Associations, Labor Advocacy

♀ ★ (♿) Greater Phoenix Gay & Lesbian Chamber of Commmerce, 1101 N Central Ave Box 108, Phx; 480-748-6681 www.phoenixgaychamber.org

Organizations/Resources: Cultural, Dance, Performance

♀ ★ ♿ Desert Overture Wind Symphony, POB 62391, Phx; 85082 480-818-3871 desertoverture.org

♀ ★ ♿ Desert Valley Squares, 2811 W Pollack St, Phx; 85041 480-818-0846 www.desertvalleysquares.com **D** info@desert valleysquares.com

♀ ★ Desperado LGBT Film Festival, at Paradise Valley Community College, 18401 N 32nd St, Phx; 602-787-7276 tinyurl.com/osz96rx

♂ Phoenix Metropolitan Men's Chorus, Grand Canyon Performing Arts, POB 16462, Phx; 85011 844-688-4272 tinyurl.com/4g9vpo7

♀ ★ Phoenix Women's Chorus, POB 34464, Phx 85067 602-487-1940 www.phoenixwomenschorus.org

Organizations/Resources: Ethnic, Multicultural

♀ Native Out, fb.com/pg/nativeout/

Organizations/Resources: Family and Supporters

♂ ☆ PFLAG Phoenix/Valley of the Sun, 2942 N 24th St Ste 114-310, Phx; 602-843-1404 www.pflagphoenix.org

Organizations/Resources: Naturist/Nudist

♂ ★ (♿) Arizona Nude Dudes, www.aznudedudes.org **N**

Organizations/Resources: Social, Recreation, Support

♂ ★ Bears of the West, POB 33215, Phx; 85067 www.bearsofthewest.org

♀ ★ Lambda Car Club Central Arizona Region, PO Box 45140, Phx; 85064 602-371-8532 www.AzGayCar.com

♂ ★ ♿ Prime Timers of Phoenix, POB 30937, Phx; 85046 602-777-1858 primetimersww.org/phoenix/

♀ Surprise LGBTQ+ & Allies Club, Marley Park Heritage Center, 13243 N Founders Park Blvd, Surprise fb.com/SurpriseLGBTQ

Organizations/Resources: Student, Academic, Education

♀ ★ Arizona State University LGBTQIA Services, POB 871301, Tempe; 85287 480-965-9665 eoss.asu.edu/out

♀ ★ **Arizona State University Ubiquity, c/o Seth Levine, POB 870101, Tempe; 85287 ASU Lesbian, Gay, Bisexual and Transgender Faculty & Staff Organization www.asu.edu/assn/ubiquity/**

♀ ★ ♿ ASU Rainbow Coalition, Student Pavilion, Second Floor, Room 225 301 E Orange Mall, Tempe 480-965-9665 fb.com/AS-URainbowCoalition/

♀ ★ Gamma Rho Lambda Alpha Chapter, Arizona State University, POB 871301, Tempe; 85287 tinyurl.com/y8v67z76

♂ ★ GLSEN Phoenix, POB 2386, Phx; 85002 602-705-9780 www.glsenphoenix.org

♀ ★ ♿ Sandra Day O'Connor College of Law Outlaw, POB 877906, Tempe; 85287 www.law.asu.edu/node/1629

Organizations/Resources: Youth (see also Family)

♀ ♿ Camp OUTdoors!, 602-909-9956 www.outdoorsgay-camp.com ✗

♀ ★ The one n ten youth Services, 602-400-2601 602-279-0894 www.onenten.org ✗

♀ Tumbleweed - Green House Project, 3707 N 7th St Ste 305, Phx; 602-841-5799 www.tumbleweed.org

Real Estate (see also Mortgages)

♂ ○ Hertzog, Shawn, West USA Realty, 7077 E Marilyn Rd Bld 4, Scottsdale; 602-684-2009 www.shawnhertzog.com

Recovery

♀ ★ (♿) Lambda Phoenix Center, 2622 N 16th St 602-635-2090 www.lambdaphx.org

♿ Stonewall Institute, 4020 N 20th St #302, Phx; 602-535-6468 www.stonewallinstitute.com

Religious / Spiritual Resources

♂ ★ ♿ Community Church of Hope, 4121 N 7th Ave, Phx; 602-234-2180 tinyurl.com/3crj3q

♂ ☆ First Congregational Church, 1407 N 2nd St, Phx; 85004 602-258-6891 www.phoenixucc.org office@phoenixucc.org

♂ ☆ KingdomGate Pentecostal Church, 2600 N 59th Ave, Phx; 85035 480-595-6517 www.kingdomgate.church KingdomGPC@ gmail.com

♂ ★ (♿) Metropolitan Community Church Phoenix, 555 W Glendale Rd, Phx; 602-864-6404 www.mccphx.org

♀ ★ ᗷᗷ Solomon's Porch - Phx, 3546 E Thomas Rd, Phx; 623-396-5362 **HS** www.solomonsporchphx.com

♀ ☆ ᗷᗷ Unitarian Universalist Church, 17540 N Ave of the Arts, Surprise; 85378 623-875-2550 **HD** www.uusurprise.org ✔ uucsaz2@gmail.com

Sports & Outdoor

⚥ ★ Cactus Cities Softball League, POB 44342, Phx; 85064 www.cactuscities.com

⚥ ★ Cactus Tennis Alliance, 602-753-7107 fb.com/CactusTennis/

⚥ ★ Desert Adventures, POB 2008, Phx; 85001 www.desertadventures.org

⚥ ★ People & Persons Gay Bowling League, 602-274-3212

⚥ ★ Phoenix Frontrunners, 10015 N 1st Ave, Phx 602-402-3332 phxfr.org

⚥ Phoenix Gay Flag Football League, Inc. (PGFFL), pgffl.com

⚥ ★ Valley of the Sun Pink Pistols of Arizona, fb.com/groups/vsppaz/

Travel & Tourist Services (see also Accommodation)

♀ ○ Dreamweaver Lifestyle Management & Concierge LLC, 20118 N 67th Ave #300-414, Glendale; 85308 623-337-1036 dreamweaverconcierge.com lisa@dreamweaverconcierge.com

Prescott

Accommodation: Hotels, Inns, Guesthouses, B&B, Resorts

♀ ○ The Motor Lodge, 503 S Montezuma St; 86303 928-717-0157 www.themotorlodge.com info@themotorlodge.com

Accommodation Rental: Furnished / Vacation (& AirBNB)

♀ ● ᗷᗷ Log Cabins at Juniper Well Ranch, POB 12407; 86304 / Skull Valley 928-442-3415 juniperwellranch.com ✥ ✔ ⊛

AIDS/HIV Services, Education & Support

♂ ☆ ᗷᗷ Northland Cares, 3112 Clearwater Dr #A; 928-776-4612 **H?** www.northlandcares.org
    » *Scottsdale: see Phoenix Area*

Sedona Area

Community Centers and/or Pride Organizations

⚥ ★ Sedona Pride, POB 3231, Sedona; 86340 480-712-8005 sedonapride.org

Accommodation Rental: Furnished / Vacation (& AirBNB)
Sedona

♀ ● Red Rock Escape, 325 Navahopi, Sedona 602-620-3900 www.redrockescape.com ✥ ⊛

Gifts, Cards, Pride, etc.

♀ ● ᗷ Sedona Wonder, 273 N State Hwy 89A, Sedona; 928-239-5353 www.sedonawonder.com

Organizations/Resources: Family and Supporters

♀ ☆ PFLAG Sedona/Verde Valley, POB 20033, Sedona; 86341 928-351-1076 pflagsedona.org

Antigone Books
411 North 4th Avenue
Tucson, AZ 85705
Tel: 520-792-3715
www.antigonebooks.com

Real Estate (see also Mortgages)

♀ ● ᗷᗷ Stadelman, Audra & Prelle, Carolyn, Coldwell Banker-Mabery Real Estate, 1075 S State Rt 260, Cottonwood 86326 928-649-4634 fax 888-711-4024 www.cottonwoodhometeam.com hometeam2@cwbanker.com
    » *Sierra Vista: see Bisbee/Sierra Vista Area*

Tubac

Accommodation: Hotels, Inns, Guesthouses, B&B, Resorts

♀ ○ Tubac Country Inn, POB 4245; 85646 520-398-3178 www.tubaccountryinn.com ✔

Tucson

Community Centers and/or Pride Organizations

⚥ ★ ᗷ Tucson Lesbian and Gay Alliance/Tucson Pride, POB 18675; 85731 520-329-5047 **H?** www.tucsonpride.org ✔ information@tucsonpride.org

Information, Media & Publications

⚥ ★ Gay Tucson, 520-631-8669 www.gaytucson.com tonyray@gaytucson.com

Accommodation: Hotels, Inns, Guesthouses, B&B, Resorts

♀ ● Catalina Park Inn, 309 E 1st St; 520-792-4541 www.catalinaparkinn.com

♀ ○ (?ᗷ) Desert Trails B&B, 12851 E Speedway Blvd; 520-885-7295 www.deserttrails.com ✔ ⊛

♀ ● Royal Elizabeth B&B Inn, 204 S Scott Ave 520-670-9022 www.royalelizabeth.com

Accommodation Rental: Furnished / Vacation (& AirBNB)

♂ ● (?ᗷ) La Casita Del Sol, 407 N Meyer Ave; 520-623-8882 www.tucsoncasita.com ✔ ⊛

AIDS/HIV Services, Education & Support

♀ ☆ ᗷᗷ Southern Arizona AIDS Foundation, 375 S Euclid Ave; 520-628-7223 saaf.org ✔

♀ ☆ ᗷᗷ Tucson Interfaith HIV/AIDS Network(TIHAN), 2660 N 1st Ave; 520-299-6647 www.tihan.org

Archives/Libraries/Museums/History Projects

♀ ★ Tucson Gay Museum, www.tucsongaymuseum.org

Bars, Cafes, Clubs, Restaurants

♀ ○ Brodie's Tavern, 2449 N Stone St; 520-622-0447 tinyurl.com/lkvnps4

♀ ○ Caruso's Italian Restaurant, 434 N 4th Ave 520-624-5765 www.carusositalian.com ✕

♀ ○ Downtown Kitchen & Cocktails, 135 S 6th Ave 520-615-6100 downtownkitchen.com ¥ ✕

♂ ● IBT's, 616 N 4th Ave; 520-882-3053 www.ibtstucson.com **D** ¥ ✕▥

♀ ○ La Cocina at Old Town Artisans, 201 N Court Ave 520-622-0351 www.lacocinatucson.com ¥ ✕▥

♀ ○ ♿ Revolutionary Grounds Books & Coffee, 606 N 4th Ave; 520-620-1770 tinyurl.com/y2hzk79g ✔

♂ ● ♿ Venture-N, 1239 N 6th Ave 520-882-8224 tinyurl.com/yafljqrt **LW**

Bookstores

♂ ● ♿ **Antigone Books, 411 N 4th Ave; 85705-8444 520-792-3715 www.antigonebooks.com ✔ info@ antigonebooks.com**

♀ ● ♿ Clues Unlimited, 3154 E Fort Lowell Rd; 520-326-8533 www.cluesunlimited.com

♀ ○ ♿ Mostly Books, 6208 E Speedway Blvd; 520-571-0110 www.mostlybooksaz.com

Funding: Endowment, Fundraising

♂ ★ LGBTS Alliance Fund, 6420 E Broadway Blvd Ste A100; 520-770-0800 www.alliancefund.org

Insurance (see also Financial Planning)

♂ ○♿ Cronkhite, Chris, State Farm, 131 S Camino Seco Ste 2; 85710 520-499-3699 www.insuremechris.net chris@ insuremechris.net

Organizations/Resources: Business & Professional Associations, Labor Advocacy

♂ ★ Tucson LGBT Chamber of Commerce, POB 14312; 85732 520-615-6436 tucsonglbtchamber.org

Organizations/Resources: Cultural, Dance, Performance

♂ ● (♪♫) Desert Voices, POB 270 85702-0270 520-791-9662 www.desertvoices.org office@desertvoices.org

♂ ● Reveille Tucson Gay Men's Chorus, POB 43633 85733-3633 520-304-1758 www.reveillemenschorus.org director@reveille menschorus.org

Organizations/Resources: Family and Supporters

♀ ☆ ♿ PFLAG Tucson, POB 36264; 85740 520-360-3795 www.pflagtucson.org

Organizations/Resources: Sexual Focus / Safe Sex

♀ ☆ Desert Dominion, 3843 E 37th St www.desertdominion.org

Organizations/Resources: Social, Recreation, Support

♂ ★ (♪♫) Bears of the Old Pueblo, 520-829-0117 **H?** www.botop.com bop@botop.com

♂ ★ Men's Social Network, 520-398-6826 www.menssocialnetwork.org

♂ ★ Tucson Prime Timers, POB 87822; 85745 512-743-9514 www.tucsonprimetimers.org

Organizations/Resources: Student, Academic, Education

♂ ★ University Of Arizona Institute for LGBT Studies, 1731 E 2nd St #201; 520-626-3431 lgbt.arizona.edu

♂ ★ University of Arizona Office of LGBTQ Affairs, POB 210017; 85721 520-626-1996 tinyurl.com/y8axybt

♂ ★ ♿ University of Arizona OUTreach, POB 210017; 85721 520-626-1996 **H?** lgbtq.arizona.edu/outreach ✔

♂ ★ University of Arizona Pride Alliance, 1303 University Dr; 520-626-1996 fb.com/PrideAlliance

♀ ☆ University of Arizona Women's Resource Center, AZ Student Union, #404, 1303 E University Ave; 520-621-4498 www.rc.arizona.edu

Organizations/Resources: Transgender/Gender Non-Conforming/Diverse

⚧ ☆ ♿ Southern Arizona Gender Alliance, POB 41863; 85717 520-477-7096 www.sagatucson.org ✔

Real Estate (see also Mortgages)

♀ ● Baker, Tony R, Tierra Antigua Realty, 1650 E River Rd Ste 202; 85718 520-631-8669 seetucsonhomes.com TonyRay@See TucsonHomes.com

♂ ● Eggers, Martin G, Totally Tucson Real Estate Services, POB 42443; 85733 520-975-2683 TotallyTucson.com Martin@ TotallyTucson.com

♂ ○ Segal, Sharon, Long Realty, 4051 E Sunrise Dr Ste 101; 520-907-6683 www.sharonsegal.com

Religious / Spiritual Resources

♂ ☆ Borderlands Unitarian Universalist, POB 23, Amado; 85645 520-648-0570 www.uucamado.org uucgv.amado@gmail.com

♀ ☆ ♿ Church of the Painted Hills UCC, 3295 W Speedway Blvd; 85745 520-624-5715 www.cphucc.org office@cphucc.org

♂ ★ ♿ Cornerstone Fellowship, 2902 N Geronimo Ave; 520-622-4626 tinyurl.com/mrlopc

♂ ☆ ♿ Grace-St Paul's Episcopal Church, 2331 E Adams St; 85719 520-327-6857 **H?** www.grace-stpauls.org ✔ Parish Admin@Grace-StPauls.org

♂ ★ JFSA Pride, 3800 E River Rd; 520-299-3000 x168 www.jewishtucson.org/lgbt/ ⚥

♀ ☆ ♿ Kadampa Meditation Center Arizona, 5326 E Pima St; 85712 520-441-1617 **HD** www.meditationintucson.org ✔ info@ meditationintucson.org

♀ ☆ ♿ Saint Philip's in the Hills, 4440 N Campbell Ave 520-229-6421 **H?** www.stphilipstucson.org ✔

♂ ☆ ♿ Shalom Mennonite Fellowship, 6044 E 30th St; 85711 520-748-7082 **H** www.shalommennonite.org ✙ pastor@shalom mennonite.org

♂ ☆ ♿ St Michael's Ecumenical Catholic Church, Chapel at 740 E Speedway 520-575-8486 www.stmichaelsecc.org

⚥ ★ ♿ Water of Life MCC, 3269 N Mountain Ave N; 520-292-9151 tinyurl.com/y92mrohe ✙

Yuma

Organizations/Resources: Family and Supporters

♀ ☆ PFLAG Yuma, 928-362-1551 fb.com/pflagyumaAZ/

Arkansas
State/County Resources

Organizations/Resources: Political/Legislative/Advocacy

♂ ★ (♿) American Civil Liberties Union of Arkansas, 904 W 2nd St #1, Little Rock, AR 501-374-2660 www.acluarkansas.org

⚥ ★ Stonewall Democratic Caucus of Arkansas, PO Box 250253, Little Rock, AR 72225 fb.com/groups/SDCofAR/

Sports & Outdoor

♂ ★ ♿ Diamond State Rodeo Association, POB 190441, Little Rock, AR 72209 501-413-2008 www.dsra.org **CW**
» Bentonville: see Fayetteville Area

Eureka Springs

Information, Media & Publications

⚥ ★ Out in Eureka, www.gayeurekasprings.com

Accommodation: Hotels, Inns, Guesthouses, B&B, Resorts

♂ ○ 11 Singleton House B&B, 11 Singleton St 800-833-3394 www.singletonhouse.com ✙ ⊗

♂ ○ Arsenic & Old Lace, 60 Hillside Ave; 72632 479-253-5454 tinyurl.com/lcvy5em (♣?) ✙ (⊗)

♂ ● The Gardener's Cottage, wooded Historic District 800-833-3394 www.agardenerscottage.com ⊗

♂ ○ Hidden Springs B&B, 23 Hillside Ave; 72632 479-253-8688 www.hiddenspringsbb.com ✙ ⊗ hiddenspringsbb@hotmail.com

⚥ ● Magnetic Valley Resort, 597 Magnetic Rd; 72632 479 363-1143 Also RV sites www.magneticvalleyresort.com

♂ ○ New Orleans Hotel, 63 Spring St; 72632 800-243-8630 **NA** www.theneworleanshotel.com ✙ stay@neworleans hotelandspa.com

♂ (♿) Pond Mountain Lodge & Resort, 1218 Hwy 23 South; 479-253-5877 www.gaypondmountain.com (♣?) ✙ ⊗ ♥

♂ ○ Rose of Sharon Cottage, 11 Cliff St; 72632 479-253-7851 www.roseofsharoncottage.com (♣?) ✙ ⊗ roseofsharoncottage@gmail.com

♂ ● (♿) The Woods Cabins, 50 Wall St 72632-3632 479-253-8281 TheWoodsCabins.com **X** ♣✙ info@TheWoodsCabins.com

Accommodation Rental: Furnished / Vacation (& AirBNB)

♂ ○ Enchanted Cottages, 18 Nut St; 72632-3431 479-253-6790 www.enchantedcottages.com ✙ enchantedcottages@hotmail.com

♀ ● (♿) Little Cabin in the Woods on Beaver Lake, 385 Heritage Dr; 72631-9096 479-253-7344 www.vrbo.com/127741 (♣?) ⊗ rutkin73@aol.com

♂ ● OUT On Main, 269 N Main St; 479-244-5963 fb.com/outon-main/ ✙ ⊗ ♥

♀ ○ Wildflower Cottages, 4 Alexander St; 72632-3404 479-253-9173 www.wildflowercottages.com ♣ ⊗

Art & Craft Galleries/Services, Supplies

♀ ○ Quicksilver Gallery, 73 Spring St; 72632 479-253-7679 www.quicksilvergallery.com info@quicksilvergallery.com

Bars, Cafes, Clubs, Restaurants

♀ ○ Cafe Amore, 2070 E Van Buren (Hwy 62E) 479-253-7192 cafeamoreeureka.com ✕

♀ ○ Chelsea's Corner Cafe & Bar, 10 Mountain St 479-253-8231 (cafe) www.chelseascafeeureka.com ⚋ ✕▥ ✙

♀ ○ DeVito's of Eureka Springs, 5 Center St 479-253-6807 www.devitoseureka.com ⚋ ✕

♀ ○ Ermilio's, 26 White St; 479-253-8806 www.ermilios.com ⚋ ✕

♀ ○ Eureka Live Underground, 35 N Main 479-253-7020 tinyurl.com/buzvu56 **D** ⚋ ▽ ✕ ▥ ✙

♀ ○ Gaskins Cabin Steak House, 2883 Hwy 23 North 479-253-5466 www.gaskinscabin.com ⚋ ✕

♀ ○ Mud Street Cafe, 22G S Main St; 479-253-6732 www.mud-streetcafe.com ▽

♀ ○ Rowdy Beaver Den, 47 Spring St 479-363-6444 www.rowdy-beaver.com **DK** ⚋ ✕

♀ ○ Rowdy Beaver Restaurant, 417 W Van Buren 479-253-8544 www.rowdybeaver.com **DK** ⚋ ✕ ▥

Campgrounds and RV Parks

♀ ○ Kettle Campground, Cabins & RV Park, 4119 E Van Buren (Hwy 62 E); 72632 479-253-9100 www.KettleCampground.net (♣?) ✙ kettleinfo@cox.net

Stained Glass / Fused Glass

♀ ● Fusion Squared, 84 Spring St; 72632 479-253-4999 www.eurekafusion.com info@eurekafusion.com

Weddings and Ceremonies

♀ ○ Eureka Springs Wedding Photography & Video, 479-981-2748 tinyurl.com/lnsw8y9 ♥ eswpv@yahoo.com

Fayetteville Area

Crisis, Anti-violence, & Helplines

♀ Project Arch, NWA Center for Sexual Assault, 2367 N Green Acres Rd #1, Fayetteville; 479-347-2304 tinyurl.com/vmdla3a

Community Centers and/or Pride Organizations

♀ ★ ♿ NWA Equality, Inc, Arthur Beeghly LGBTQ Resource Center, POB 179, Fayetteville; 72702 / 179 N Church Ave Ste 101; 72701 479-966-9014 www.nwaequality.org ✔

Bars, Cafes, Clubs, Restaurants
Fayetteville

♂ ● (♿) Bordinos Restaurant & Wine Bar, 310 W Dickson St, Fayetteville; 479-527-6795 **H?** www.bordinos.com ☿ ✕

Bookstores

♂ ○ ♿ Nightbird Books, 205 W Dickson St, Fayetteville; 72701 479-443-2080 www.nightbirdbooks.com ☛ ✔ nightbird@night birdbooks.com

Organizations/Resources: Family and Supporters

♂ ☆ PFLAG of NW Arkansas/Fayetteville, POB 2897, Fayetteville; 72702 479-310-5205 fb.com/pflagnwa

Organizations/Resources: Student, Academic, Education

♀ ★ ♿ University of Arkansas Pride, A-661 Arkansas Union, Fayetteville; 479-575-7308 fb.com/uarkPRIDE

Fort Smith

Community Centers and/or Pride Organizations

♂ River Valley Equality Center, St. John's Episcopal Church, 215 N 6th St; 479-274-0825 www.rvecark.org

Hot Springs

Information, Media & Publications

♂ ★ Hot Springs LGBT Alliance, POB 4; 71902 www.hslgbta.org info@hslgbta.org

Accommodation: Hotels, Inns, Guesthouses, B&B, Resorts

♂ ● ♿ Hilltop Manor B&B, 2009 Park Ave 501-625-7829 tinyurl.com/2ax42qs ✔ ⊗

AIDS/HIV Services, Education & Support

♂ ☆ Hot Springs AIDS Resource Center & Tuggle Clinic, Consortia-CARE of Arkansas, 1801 Central Ave Ste C; 501-623-5598

Religious / Spiritual Resources

♂ ☆ Unitarian Universalist Church of Hot Springs, PO Box 3125; 71914 501-404-5110 www.uuchurchhotsprings.org

Little Rock

Community Centers and/or Pride Organizations

♂ Center for Artistic Revolution (CAR), 800 Scott St; 501-291-1168 fb.com/CAR4AR/

♂ Central Arkansas Pride, POB 250096; 72225 501-404-8498 centralarkansaspride.com

♂ ★ Conway Pride, 1605 Robinson, Conway 501-697-1651 fb.com/groups/119415671432938

Bars, Cafes, Clubs, Restaurants

♀ ● ♿ Discovery, 1021 Jessie Rd; / Sat 9pm-5am 501-666-6900 Sat only www.latenightdisco.com **DP** ▦
North Little Rock

♂ Chaps, 2695 Pike Ave, North Little Rock 501-313-2836 fb.com/ChapsDiveBar/

♀ ● ♿ Sway, 412 Louisiana St 501-777-5428 clubsway.com **DKP** ▦

♂ Triniti, 1021 Jessie Rd; / Fri 9pm-4am 501-664-2744 www.trinitinightclub.com **D** ▦

Gifts, Cards, Pride, etc.

♂ ○ Domestic Domestic, 5501 Kavanaugh Blvd #C; 72207 501-661-1776 www.domesticdomestic.com hello@domestic domestic.com

♀ ● ♿ A Twisted Gift Shop, 1007 W 7th St; 72201-3901 501-366-3116 tinyurl.com/29qwgsv

Organizations/Resources: Student, Academic, Education

♀ ★ Hendrix College Unity/LGBT, 1600 Washington Ave, Conway; 501-450-1291

♀ ★ University of Central Arkansas PRISM, 210 Harrin Hall, Conway; 501-450-5245 orgsync.com/55897/chapter

Organizations/Resources: Youth (see also Family)

♀ ★ Lucie's Place, POB 751; 72203 501-508-5005 (shelter) www.luciesplace.org

♀ ★ Pridecorps: LGBT Youth Center, 5815 Kavanaugh Blvd; 501-404-8919 www.pridecorps.org

Religious / Spiritual Resources

♀ ☆ Quapaw Quarter UMC, 1601 S Louisiana St; 72206 501-375-1600 www.qqumc.org office@qqumc.org

Texarkana

Bars, Cafes, Clubs, Restaurants

♂ The Chute / Village Station, 714 Laurel St 870-703-3236 fb.com/TheChute/ **DK** ▦

California
State/County Resources

AIDS/HIV Services, Education & Support

♂ AIDS LifeCycle, 1035 Market St Ste 400, San Francisco, CA 415-581-7077 www.aidslifecycle.org

Insurance (see also Financial Planning)

♂ ● (♿) Covered California Agent, POB 2883, Palm Springs, CA 92263 760-323-5157 800-358-5898 fax 888-357-2570 EnrollBy-Mail.com Rick@EnrollByMail.com

Legal Services

♀ ★ ♿ Lambda Legal Defense & Education Fund (LLDEF), Inc: Western Regional Office, 4221 Wilshire Blvd Ste 280, Los Angeles, CA 213-382-7600 www.lambdalegal.org

Organizations/Resources: Business & Professional Associations, Labor Advocacy

⚥ ★ Southern California Lambda Medical Association, 8265 Sunset Blvd Ste 204, West Hollywood, CA 323-465-2322 LGBT Physicians and Health Care Providers www.sclma.org

Organizations/Resources: Cultural, Dance, Performance

⚥ ★ && California LGBT Arts Alliance, #30 AAACC, 1632 N Laurel Ave #238, Los Angeles, CA www.calgbtartsalliance.com

Organizations/Resources: Naturist/Nudist

⚥ ★ California Men Enjoying Naturism (CMEN), 8424-A Santa Monica Blvd #119, West Hollywood, CA 877-683-4781 www.cmen.info **N**

Organizations/Resources: Political/Legislative/Advocacy

⚥ && American Civil Liberties Union Northern California, 39 Drumm St, San Francisco, CA 415-621-2493 www.aclunc.org

⚥ ☆ & American Civil Liberties Union Southern California, 1313 W 8th St, Los Angeles, CA 213-977-9500 www.aclusocal.org

⚥ ★ (?&) Equality California, 3701 Wilshire Blvd Ste 725, Los Angeles, CA 323-848-9801 www.eqca.org

Organizations/Resources: Social, Recreation, Support

⚥ ★ && The Billys, The Billy Foundation, POB 12205, Santa Rosa, CA 95406-2205 707-545-1044 thebillys.org ✗ office@thebillys.org

⚥ ★ California Community of Men, 333 E Molino Rd, Palm Springs, CA 323-314-5420 www.CalComMen.com

⚥ California Men's Gatherings, 1049 Havenhurst Dr #123, Los Angeles, CA 877-984-3264 www.thecmg.org

⚥ California Men's Gatherings, 1049 Havenhurst Dr #123, West Hollywood, CA www.thecmg.org

⚥ Great Autos of Yesteryear, POB 19018, Long Beach, CA 90807 www.greatautos.org

Organizations/Resources: Student, Academic, Education

⚥ ★ Gay-Straight Alliance Network, 1714 Franklin St #100-418, Oakland, CA 415-552-4229 gsanetwork.org

Organizations/Resources: Transgender/Gender Non-Conforming/Diverse

T ★ && Transgender Law center, POB 70976, Oakland, CA 94612 510-587-9696 **H?** www.transgenderlawcenter.org

Organizations/Resources: Youth (see also Family)

♂ ☆ California Youth Crisisline, POB 161448, Sacramento, CA 95816 800-843-5200 916-514-4464 Chat & text 24/7 www.calyouth.org cycl@calyouth.org

Recovery

⚥ ★ && California LGBT Tobacco Education Partnership, 1270 Sanchez St, San Francisco, CA 94114 415-436-9182 www.lgbtpartnership.org

Religious / Spiritual Resources

⚥ ★ Oasis California, c/o St. Cyprian's Church, 2097 Turk St, San Francisco, CA oasisca.org

Sperm Banks

♀ ● && The Sperm Bank of California, 2115 Milvia St, Ste 201, Berkeley, CA 94704-1157 510-841-1858 fax 510-841-0332 www.thespermbankofca.org

» *Amador City: see Gold Country/Sierra*
» *Anaheim: see Orange County*
» *Angels Camp: see Gold Country/Sierra*

Antelope Valley

Community Centers and/or Pride Organizations

⚥ Antelope Valley Pride, OUTreach Center, 44845 Cedar Ave, Lancaster; 661-927-7433 outreachcenterav.org

⚥ ★ && The OUTreach Center, 44845 Cedar Ave, Lancaster; 661-927-7433 www.outreachcenterav.org

AIDS/HIV Services, Education & Support

♂ ☆ && Catalyst Foundation, 44758 Elm Ave, Lancaster; 661-948-8559 www.catalystfdn.org

Sports & Outdoor

⚥ ★ && Get OUT, 44845 Cedar Ave, Lancaster; 661-927-7433 www.outreachcenterav.org

» *Atascadero: see Central Coast*

Bakersfield

Community Centers and/or Pride Organizations

⚥ ★ && Bakersfield LGBTQ+, 2623 F st Ste N; 661-302-4266 **H?** bakersfieldpride.org

⚥ ★ && The Center for Sexuality & Gender Diversity, POB 2712; 93303 / 902 18th St / The Annex 841 Mohawk St ste 661-843-7995 thecenterbak.org ✗ info@thecenterbak.org

Bars, Cafes, Clubs, Restaurants

♂ ♀ Casablanca, 1825 N St; 661-324-0661 tinyurl.com/yafpacoj
D ▥

Counseling/Psychotherapy/Mental Health

♂ ○ && Ritter, Kathleen M, PhD, MFT, 2212 F St; 661-327-7010

Organizations/Resources: Family and Supporters

♂ ☆ PFLAG Bakersfield, POB 42135; 93384 661-527-3524 fb.com/PFLAGBakersfield

Organizations/Resources: Youth (see also Family)

⚥ ★ && Youth Empowerment Pride Project, Bakersfield LGBTQ+ 2623 F st Ste N; 661-302-4266 **H?** fb.com/YEPPBakersfield/

Religious / Spiritual Resources

♂ ☆ First Congregational Church UCC, 5 Real Rd 93309 661-327-1609 www.fccbakersfield-ucc.org firstcongregationalbakersfield@gmail.com

» *Bellflower: see Long Beach*
» *Berkeley: see East Bay Area*
» *Beverly Hills: see Los Angeles Area*

Maisons de Cambria Vacation Rentals
Beautiful Oceanfront or Oceanview Vacation Rentals in Cambria, CA.

www.maisonsdecambria.com   **800-240-2277**

Big Bear/Lake Arrowhead Area

Accommodation Rental: Furnished / Vacation (& AirBNB)
Big Bear Lake
♂ • Shore Acres Lodge, 41693 Big Bear Blvd 877-789-4140 www.shoreacreslodge.com ✣ ⚲ ⊗ ⊗ reservations@bigbear vacations.com

» *Buena Park: see Orange County*
» *Cambria: see Central Coast*
» *Campbell: see San Jose & South Bay Area*
» *Carmel: see Central Coast*
» *Cathedral City: see Palm Springs Area*

Central Coast

Crisis, Anti-violence, & Helplines
Paso Robles
♀ ☆ ⪪ RISE, 1030 Vine St Paso Robles 855-886-7473 805-226-5400 www.RISEslo.org contact@RISEslo.org

San Luis Obispo
♀ ☆ ⪪ RISE, 51 Zaca Ln Ste 100, San Luis Obispo 855-886-7473 805-226-5400 www.RISEslo.org contact@RISEslo.org

Community Centers and/or Pride Organizations
⚢ ★ ⪪ GALA Center, 1060 Palm St, San Luis Obispo; 805-541-4252 galacc.org

⚢ Monterey Peninsula Pride, POB 893, Seaside; 93955 peninsulapride.org

⚢ ★ Pacific Pride Festival, Pacific Pride Foundation, 608 Anacapa St Ste A, Santa Barbara; 805-963-3636 tinyurl.com/q755tzf

⚢ ★ Pacific Pride Foundation - North County, 123 S College Dr, Santa Maria; 805-963-3636 x108 tinyurl.com/ynrw8h

⚢ ★ (♿) Pacific Pride Foundation - South County, Pacific Pride Foundation, 608 Anacapa St Ste A, Santa Barbara 805-963-3636 tinyurl.com/ynrw8h

⚢ Ventura County Pride, Diversity Collective Ventura County, 2471 Portola RdSte 100, Ventura; 805-644-5428 www.vcpride.org

Accommodation: Hotels, Inns, Guesthouses, B&B, Resorts
Carmel
♂ • The Vagabond's House, 4th & Dolores 831-624-7738 800-262-1262 www.vagabondshouseinn.com ⚲ ⊗ ⊗

Monterey
♂ ○ (♿) Monterey Fireside Lodge, 1131 10th St, Monterey; 93940 831-373-4172 www.firesidemonterey.com ✣ ⚲ ⊗ info@firesidemonterey.com

Pacific Grove
♂ ○ Lighthouse Lodge & Suites, 1150 Lighthouse Ave, Pacific Grove; 93950-2360 831-655-2111 lighthouselodgecottages.com frontdesk@lighthouselodgecottages.com

Paso Robles
♂ ○ ⪪ Hotel Cheval, 1021 Pine St, Paso Robles; 93446 805-226-9995 866-522-6999 www.hotelcheval.com ✣ ⚲ ⊗ ⊗ info@hotelcheval.com

♂ • Union Road Guesthouse, 7150 Union Rd, Paso Robles; 310-387-0043 tinyurl.com/hu5sqnm

San Luis Obispo
♂ ○ ⪪ Petit Soleil, 1473 Monterey St, San Luis Obispo; 93401 800-676-1588 www.petitsoleilslo.com ✣ ⚲ ⊗ ⊗ reservations@petitsoleilslo.com

Shell Beach
♂ ○ Palomar Inn, 1601 Shell Beach Road, Shell Bch 93449-1957 805-773-4204 www.thepalomarinn.com thepalomarinn@gmail.com

Solvang
♂ ○ (♿) Meadowlark Inn, 2644 Mission Dr, Solvang; 93463 805-688-4631 www.meadowlarkinnsolvang.com (⚲?) ⚲ ⊗ meadowlarksolvang@gmail.com

Accommodation Rental: Furnished / Vacation (& AirBNB)
Cambria
♂ ○ **Maisons de Cambria Vacation Rentals, 800-240-2277 805-927-0306 Beautiful Oceanfront or Oceanview Vacation Rentals in Cambria, CA. www.maisonsdecambria.com ⚲ ⊗ vacation@maisonsdecambria.com**

AIDS/HIV Services, Education & Support

⚥ Access Support Network, POB 12158, San Luis Obispo; 93406 805-781-3660 www.asn.org

Archives/Libraries/Museums/History Projects

⚥ ★ Hatler Library, GALA, 1060 Palm St, San Luis Obispo; 805-541-4252 tinyurl.com/y2e859pq

Art & Craft Galleries/Services, Supplies

⚥ ○ ♿ Ball & Skein, 4210 Bridge St, Cambria; 805-927-3280 cambriayarn.com

Bars, Cafes, Clubs, Restaurants
Cambria

⚥ ○ Mezzo Italiano, 1622 Main St, Cambria 805-927-1501 www.mezzoitaliano.com ✕

Carmel

⚥ ○ Flaherty's Seafood Grill & Oyster Bar, 6th Ave (btwn Dolores & San Carlos) 831-625-1500 At Flaherty's all of our fish is fresh, most is caught wild and of the highest quality. www.flahertysseafood.com ✕ FlahertySeafood@gmail.com
◆ Advertisement page 82

Castroville

⚥ ● Francos Norma Jean's Nightclub, 10639 Merritt St, Castroville; / Sat 10pm 831-633-2090 Sat only fb.com/Francos831 **D** 🎵 ◆

Cayucos

⚥ ○ Schooners Wharf, 171 N Ocean Ave, Cayucos 805-995-3883 www.schoonerswharf.com ✕

San Luis Obispo

⚥ ○ Big Sky Cafe, 1121 Broad St, San Luis Obispo 805-545-5401 www.bigskycafe.com ✕

⚥ ● ♿ Novo, 726 Higuera St, San Luis Obispo; 805-543-3986 www.novorestaurant.com ♈ ✕

Santa Barbara

⚥ ○ ♿ Opal Restaurant & Bar, 1325 State St, Santa Barbara; 805-966-9676 opalrestaurantandbar.com ♈ ✕

Ventura

⚥ ● ♿ Paddy's, 2 W Main St, Ventura; 805-652-1071 paddysventura.com **DK** 🎵

Bookstores

⚥ ○ Bookworm, 93 Daily Dr, Camarillo; 93010 805-482-1384 fb.com/CamarilloBookworm

⚥ ○ Chaucer's Books, 3321 State St, Santa Barbara 805-682-6787 www.chaucersbooks.com

⚥ ○ Coalesce Bookstore & Garden Wedding Chapel, 845 Main St, Morro Bay; 805-772-2880 www.coalescebookstore.com ♥

⚥ ● ♿ Volumes of Pleasure Bookshop, 1016 Los Osos Valley Rd, Los Osos; 805-528-5565 tinyurl.com/bkrjkn

Erotica / Adult Stores / Safe Sex Supplies

⚥ ● (?♿) The Riv, 4135 State St, Santa Barbara; 93110 805-967-8282 **H?** tinyurl.com/lumzndx info@e-tique.org

Health Care: Physical (see also Counseling/Mental Health)

⚥ ● ♿ Gwen Pillow Chiropractic, Inc., CD, 1502 Spring St Ste B, Paso Robles; 93446 805-237-2654 www.GwenPillowDC.com ⚥ GwenPillowDC@gmail.com

Organizations/Resources: Business & Professional Associations, Labor Advocacy

⚥ ★ Gay & Lesbian Alliance of the Central Coast, 1060 Palm St, San Luis Obispo; 805-541-4252 www.galacc.org

⚥ ♿ Gay & Lesbian Business Association of Santa Barbara (GLBA), POB 90907, Santa Barbara; 93190 805-684-4442 www.glbasb.com

Organizations/Resources: Social, Recreation, Support

⚥ ★ Prime Timers Central Coast, POB 2071, Santa Barbara; 93120 805-260-4415 Santa Barbara, San Luis Obispo

Organizations/Resources: Student, Academic, Education

⚥ ★ ♿ Cal Poly Pride Center, 1 Grand Ave, Bldg 65 Rm 209, San Luis Obispo; 805-756-7733 tinyurl.com/y6knoof9

⚥ ☆ ♿ UCSB Sexual & Gender Diversity Center, Student Resource Building, 3rd Flr, Santa Barbara; 805-893-5847 **H?** rcsgd.sa.ucsb.edu/ ⚥

Organizations/Resources: Transgender/Gender Non-Conforming/Diverse

T ☆ Santa Barbara Transgender Advocacy Network, 2101 State St, Santa Barbara; 93105 www.sbtan.org info@sbtan.org

T ☆ Trans Tuesday, 1060 Palm St, San Luis Obispo 93401 805-541-4252 www.galacc.org email@galacc.org

T ☆ Tranz Central Coast, 1060 Palm St, San Luis Obispo; 93401 805-242-3821 www.tranzcentralcoast.org tranzcentralcoast@gmail.com

Organizations/Resources: Youth (see also Family)

⚥ GALA "Q" Youth Group, 1060 Palm St, San Luis Obispo; 805-541-4252 www.galacc.org

Recovery

⚥ ☆ Alcoholics Anonymous Ventura County Central Service Office, 321 N Aviador St Ste 115, Camarillo; 805-389-1444 www.aaventuracounty.org

Religious / Spiritual Resources

⚥ ★ All Saints Parish, POB 5671, San Buenaventura; 93005 805-648-5636 www.allsaintsv.org

⚥ ☆ Chalice - Unitarian Universalist Fellowship of the Conejo Valley, 3331 Old Conejo Rd, Newbury Park; 91320-2115 805-498-9548 www.chaliceuu.org admin@chaliceuu.org

⚥ ☆ ♿ First Congregational Church of Santa Barbara, UCC, 2101 State St, Santa Barbara; 93105 805-682-7146 **HD** www.santabarbarafirst.org ⚥ fcc-office-805@santabarbarafirst.org

⚥ ☆ ♿ Unitarian Society, 1535 Santa Barbara St, Santa Barbara; 93101-1917 805-965-4583 **H?** www.ussb.org ⚥

⚥ ☆ ♿ United Church of Christ, 11245 Los Osos Valley Rd, San Luis Obispo; 93405 805-544-1373 **HD** www.sloucc.org office@sloucc.org

♀ ☆ Valley of the Flowers UCC, 3346 Constellation Rd, Lompoc; 93436 805-733-3333 ucclompoc.org

Sports & Outdoor

♂ Central Coast Pink Pistols, fb.com/groups/2204691521/

♂ ★ Great Outdoors Santa Barbara/Ventura County, POB 21051, Santa Barbara; 93121 805-588-1142 greatoutdoors.org/SBVC

Travel & Tourist Services (see also Accommodation)

♀ ○ Keep on Traveling, 831-659-4860 Group Travel Services www.keepontraveling.com

Veterinarians

♂ ○ Arroyo Vista Veterinary Hospital, 476 W Los Angeles Ave #B9, Moorpark; 93021 805-529-6833 Y fax 805-529-8573 www.arroyovistavet.com

♀ ○ &⅃ Cat & Bird Clinic, 101 W Mission St, Santa Barbara; 93101 805-569-2287 www.catandbirds.com

Chico

Crisis, Anti-violence, & Helplines

♀ ☆ (?⅃) Catalyst Domestic Violence Services, POB 4184; 95927 800-895-8476 530-343-7711; Oroville Drop-in 530-532-6427 **H?** www.catalystdvservices.org ✗ catalyst@catalystdvservices.org

Community Centers and/or Pride Organizations

♂ ★ &⅃ Stonewall Alliance Center, PO Box 8855; 95927 / 358 E 6th St 530-893-3336 www.stonewallchico.org ✗

Organizations/Resources: Student, Academic, Education

♂ ★ Chico State Pride, CSU Chico, BMU 213, Box 131; 805-509-6256 orgsync.com/73040/chapter

Organizations/Resources: Youth (see also Family)

♂ &⅃ SAY! Youth Services of the Stonewall Alliance Center, POB 8855; 95927 530-893-3336 tinyurl.com/mc8vjro ✗
» *Concord: see East Bay Area*
» *Corte Madera: see Marin County Area*
» *Costa Mesa: see Orange County*
» *Culver City: see Los Angeles Area*
» *Cupertino: see San Jose & South Bay Area*

Davis

Community Centers and/or Pride Organizations

♂ Davis Pride, POB 1902; 95616 www.davispride.org

Bars, Cafes, Clubs, Restaurants

♂ ○ &⅃ Mishka's Cafe, 610 2nd St 530-759-0811 www.mishkascafe.com ☞ ✗

Organizations/Resources: Student, Academic, Education

♂ ★ Asian Pacific Islander Queers at UC Davis, c/o LGBT Resource Center, 1 Shields Ave; 916-370-0555 ✧

♂ ★ Delta Lambda Phi Xi Chapter, UC Davis, SPAC #418 1 Shields Ave; 559-250-2377 www.dlp.org/xi/

♂ ★ &⅃ LGBTQIA Resource Center at University of California, Davis, Student Community Center, 397 Hutchison Dr 95616 530-752-2452 **H?** tinyurl.com/kdr8e6n ✗

♂ ★ UC Davis Lambda Law Students Association, 400 Mark Hall Dr; 530-752-3372 tinyurl.com/d9pbtjw

♀ ☆ Women's Resource Center, UC Davis, 113 North Hall 180 E; 530-752-3372 wrrc.ucdavis.edu

Religious / Spiritual Resources

♀ ☆ &⅃ Cal Aggie Christian Association, 433 Russell Blvd; 95616-3527 530-753-2000 www.cahouse.org ✗ cahouse@cahouse.org

♀ ☆ &⅃ **Davis United Methodist Church, 1620 Anderson Rd; 95616 530-756-2170 H DUMC works for LGBTQ folks' full inclusion in the denomination. www.davisumc.org** ✗

♀ ☆ &⅃ Unitarian Universalist Church, 27074 Patwin Rd; 95616-9720 530-753-2581 **HD** www.uudavis.org office@uudavis.org
» *Dorrington: see Gold Country/Sierra Foothills/Yosemite*

East Bay Area

Crisis, Anti-violence, & Helplines

♀ ☆ Contra Costa Crisis Center, POB 3364, Walnut Creek; 94598 925-939-1916 www.crisis-center.org

♀ ☆ A Safe Place, POB 23006, Oakland; 94623-0006 510-536-7233 www.asafeplacedvs.org

Community Centers and/or Pride Organizations

♂ ☆ La Peña Cultural Center, 3105 Shattuck Ave, Berkeley; 510-849-2568 www.lapena.org ✪

♂ Oakland LGBTQ Community Center Inc, 3207 Lakeshore Ave, Oakland; 510-882-2286 www.oaklandlgbtqcenter.org

♂ ★ Oakland Pride, 2111 Franklin St, Oakland 510-545-6251 www.oaklandpride.org

♂ ★ (&⅃) Pacific Center for Human Growth, 2712 Telegraph Ave, Berkeley; 94705-1117 510-548-8283 pacificcenter.org info@pacificcenter.org

♂ ★ &⅃ Rainbow Community Center of Contra Costa County, 2118 Willow Pass Rd Ste 500, Concord; 925-692-0090 www.rainbowcc.org

Information, Media & Publications

♂ ★ Out on the Island (OOTI), www.outontheisland.or

♂ Queer in Oakland, www.queerinoakland.com ✪

AIDS/HIV Services, Education & Support

♀ ☆ &⅃ AIDS Project East Bay, 8400 Enterprise Way, Oakland; 510-663-7979 **H?** www.apeb.org

♀ ☆ &⅃ Asian Health Services, 416 8th St, Oakland; 94607 510-972-4483 HIV care, Hormone Replacement Treatment, ADAP, Medi-Cal and Covered California enrollment, PrEP, PEP, Education & Support www.hch510.org ✧ testing@ahschc.org

♀ ☆ &⅃ Project Open Hand Grocery Center, 1921 San Pablo Ave, Oakland; 510-622-0221 www.openhand.org

Bars, Cafes, Clubs, Restaurants
Albany
♂ ● ⚥ Ivy Room, 860 San Pablo Ave, Albany; 510-526-5888 **H?** ivyroom.com ▥ info@ivyroom.com

Berkeley
♀ ○ ⚥ Cheese Board Collective, 1504 & 1512 Shattuck Ave, Berkeley; 510-549-3183 cheeseboardcollective.coop ✕

Hayward
♀ ● ⚥ World Famous Turf Club, 22519 Main St, Hayward; 510-881-9877 www.wfturfclub.com **DCLW** ▥ ✕

Oakland
♂ ○ ⚥ The Chocolate Dragon, 5427 College Ave, Oakland; 510-654-7159 1438 Broadway, Oakland; 510-238-8700, 1952 University Ave. Berkeley; 510-883-9850 fb.com/theChocolateDragon/ ☞ ✕

♀ Club 21, 2111 Franklin St, Oakland 510-268-9425 www.club21oakland.com **D** ✦

♀ ○ Equator Coffees, 175 Bay Place, Oakland 510-828-1536 www.equatorcoffees.com ☞ info@equatorcoffees.com

♀ Hella Gay at Uptown, 1928 Telegraph Ave, Oakland; / check site for drtails www.hellagaydanceparty.com

♀ ● The Port Bar, 2023 Broadway, Oakland 510-823-2099 www.portbaroakland.com ▥

♀ Ships in the Night, monthly, check site for details fb.com/shipsin-thanight/z

♀ ● ⚥ White Horse Inn, 6551 Telegraph Ave, Oakland; 510-652-3820 www.whitehorsebar.com **D** whitehorseoakland@gmail.com

Walnut Creek
♀ ● ⚥ Club 1220, 1220 Pine St, Walnut Creek; 925-938-4550 www.club1220.com **DCW** ▥

Bookstores
♂ ○ East Bay Booksellers, 5433 College Ave, Oakland; 510-653-9965 www.ebbooksellers.com

♂ ○ ♿ Pegasus Books, 1855 Solano Ave, Berkeley; 510-525-6888 www.pegasusbookstore.com

♂ ○ ♿ Pegasus Books Downtown, 2349 Shattuck Ave, Berkeley; 510-649-1320 www.pegasusbookstore.com

♂ ○ ♿ Pegasus Books Oakland, 5560 College Ave, Oakland; 510-652-6259 www.pegasusbookstore.com

♂ ○ ⚥ Rakestraw Books, 3 Railroad Ave, Danville; 925-837-7337 www.rakestrawbooks.com

Broadcast Media
♀ ★ outLoud Radio, YR Media, 1701 Broadway, Oakland; 510-251-1101 **H?** yr.media/tag/outloudradio/ ✕

Counseling/Psychotherapy/Mental Health
♂ ● ⚥ **Albert, Guy, PhD, PSY20961, 3036 Regent St, Berkeley; 94705-2551 510-496-3447 Licensed Psychologist, Jungian Analyst, LGBTQ+ activist, teacher, researcher, and consultant. guyalbert.com info@ guyalbert.com**

♂ ○ (?⚥) Bowman, Melissa K, MA, MS, LMFT #78865, 2329 Santa Clara Ave #202, Alameda; 94501 510-263-8476 **H?** (I make house-calls) www.mkbowmanlmft.com melissa@ mkbowmanlmft.com

♀ ● Deaner, Cheryl, LMFT, 1148 Stanford Ave, Oakland; 94608 / 3896 24th St, San Francisco 415-828-2200 www.cheryldeaner.com cdd.mft@gmail.com

♂ ● Felder, Elena, LMFT, MFC 37248, 4281 Piedmont Ave, Oakland; 94611 / 414 Gough St, San Francisco 510-982-1949 www.elenafeldermft.com elenafelder42@gmail.com

♀ ○ (?⚥) Marcus, Lynn Ellen, LMFT, POB 27206, Oakland; 94602 510-632-2244 www.lynnellen.com

♀ ● Odets, Walt, PhD, Berkeley 510-845-4628 fax 510-845-4413 www.waltodets.com waltodets@gmail.com

♀ ● Watson, Courtney, LMFT, CST, Doorway Therapeutic Services, 298 Grand Ave Ste 100, Oakland; 94610 510-463-4471 **H?** www.doorwaytherapeutics.com ❖ Doorwaytherapeutics@ gmail.com

Erotica / Adult Stores / Safe Sex Supplies
♀ ○ Lingerie Etc, 2298 Monument Blvd, Pleasant Hill; 94523 925-676-2962 www.secretsboutiques.com lingerieetc02@gmail.com

♀ ○ ♿ Not Too Naughty #1, 15670 E 14th St, San Leandro; 94578-1950 510-278-4944 www.secretsboutiques.com ntn1@ sbcglobal.net

♂ ○ Not Too Naughty #2, 2121 1st St, Livermore 94550-4543 925-443-2451 www.secretsboutiques.com ntn2@sbcglobal.net

♂ ○ Secrets Boutique, 525 Contra Costa Blvd, Pleasant Hill; 94550 925-681-1400 www.secretsboutiques.com boutique97@ sbcglobal.net

♂ ○ Secrets El Cerrito, 10601 San Pablo Ave, El Cerrito; 94530-2619 510-528-1569 www.secretsboutiques.com secretselcerrito@ gmail.com

♂ ○ Secrets Oakland, 5686 Telegraph Ave, Oakland 94609-1708 510-654-1169 www.secretsboutiques.com secretsoakland@ gmail.com

Funding: Endowment, Fundraising
♀ ★ Imperial Star Empire, Inc, POB 55486, Hayward; 94545 925-292-4367 imperialstarempireinc.org

♂ Out of the Closet Thrift Store, 238 E 18th St, Oakland; 510-251-8671 outofthecloset.org

♀ Royal Grand Ducal Council of Alameda, POB 4561, Hayward; 94540 alameda-ducal.org

Health Care: Physical (see also Counseling/Mental Health)
♀ ☆ ⚥ Berkeley Free Clinic, 2339 Durant Ave, Berkeley; 510-548-2570 www.berkeleyfreeclinic.org

♀ ☆ ⚥ Charlotte Maxwell Clinic Integrative Cancer Care, 411 30th St Ste 508, Oakland; 94609 510-601-7660 www.charlottemaxwell.org mail@charlottemaxwell.org

♂ ● (?⚥) Island Acupuncture, Zollinger, Tracy, L.Ac, 2424 Blanding Ave Ste 102, Alameda; 94501 510-299-0057 tinyurl.com/omdo39z ✕ tracy.zollingerlac@gmail.com

♀ La Clínica de La Raza Inc, POB 22210, Oakland; 94623 510-535-4000 www.laclinica.org ✦

♀ ☆ ♿ Women's Cancer Resource Center, 2908 Ellsworth St, Berkeley; 510-420-7900 www.wcrc.org

Immigration, Citizenship, Political Asylum, Refugees

⚲ OLAS / LGBT Sanctuary Project, 628-888-3854 www.olas-sanctuary.org

Leather Resources & Groups

♂ Alameda County Leather Corps, POB 20759, Castro Valley; 94546 www.acleather.org

Legal Services

♀ ○ ♿ Lee, Richard J, Focus Media Law Group, 11 Embarcadero W Ste 140, Oakland; 94607-4543 510-272-0200 focusmedialaw.com ✗ rjl@focusmedialaw.com

♀ ● ♿ Travelstead, Timothy, Narayan Travelstead P.C., 24301 Southland Dr #607, Hayward; 650-403-0150 **H?** NarayanTravelstead.com ✗

Men's & Sex Clubs (not primarily Health Clubs)

⚲ ● (♺) Steamworks, 2107 4th St, Berkeley; 510-845-8992 www.steamworksbaths.com **P** ✗

Organizations/Resources: Business & Professional Associations, Labor Advocacy

⚲ ★ Kaiser Permanente KP Pride, POB 30573, Oakland; 94604 510-987-4148 tinyurl.com/odentx2

Organizations/Resources: Cultural, Dance, Performance

⚲ Bluegrass Pride, California Bluegrass Association, 29520E 7th St, Oakland; bluegrasspride.net

⚲ ★ Diablo Dancers, POB 4423, Walnut Creek 94596-0423 www.diablodancers.org **D**

⚲ ★ ♿ Oakland East Bay Gay Men's Chorus, 1908 Alcatraz, Berkeley; 800-706-2389 **H** www.oebgmc.org

⚲ ★ Oaktown 8's, www.oaktown8s.org

⚲ Queer Qumbia, tinyurl.com/y36w2ooq

⚲ Trip the Light Fantastic, 200 Grand Ave, Oakland; 510-430-8820

⚲ Voices Lesbian A Cappella For Justice, POB 11054, Oakland; 94611 510-545-3726 voiceslafj.wordpress.com

Organizations/Resources: Ethnic, Multicultural

⚲ ★ Asian & Pacific Islander Family Pride, PO Box 473, Fremont; 94537 510-818-0887 apifamilypride.org ✧

⚲ ★ Asian Pacific Islander Queer Women & Transgender Community (APIQWTC), 708-274-7982 Lesbian, Queer, Transgender www.apiqwtc.org ✧ info@apiqwtc.org

⚲ DeQH - Desi lgbtQ Helpline for South Asians, 908-367-3374 www.deqh.org ✧

Organizations/Resources: Family and Supporters

♀ ☆ PFLAG Oakland/East Bay, POB 21195, Oakland 94620 510-562-7692 pflag-eastbay.org

Organizations/Resources: Political/Legislative/Advocacy

⚲ East Bay Stonewall Democratic Club, POB 386, Berkeley; 94701 tinyurl.com/ncw9ff6

Organizations/Resources: Senior Resources

⚲ Aging Lesbians, Pacific Center, 2712 Telegraph Ave, Berkeley; 510-548-8283 tinyurl.com/y3xs6euo

⚲ ★ ♿ Lavender Seniors of the East Bay, 4123 Broadway Ste #818, Oakland; 94611 510-736-5428 www.lavenderseniors.org ✗ info@lavenderseniors.org

⚲ Queer Femmes Peer Support Group, Pacific Center, 2712 Telegraph Ave, Berkeley; 510-548-8283 tinyurl.com/y5394cqe

⚲ ★ Women Over Fifty & Friends (WOFF), bj_patbond@yahoo.com

Organizations/Resources: Social, Recreation, Support

⚲ Alameda Queer Teen Book Club, Books, Inc 1344 Park St, Alameda; 510-522-2226 tinyurl.com/yxaw5lqj

⚲ ★ (♺) East Bay Network, POB 605, Newark; 94560-0605 510-329-2124 www.eastbaynetwork.org email@eastbaynetwork.org

⚲ The Intimates: East Bay Queer Book Club, Books, Inc 1344 Park St, Alameda; 510-522-2226 tinyurl.com/y4pgbgfq

⚲ ★ Pacific Center Married/Once Married, Pacific Center, 2712 Telegraph Ave, Berkeley; 94705 510-548-8283 tinyurl.com/pnc7d7q marriedmensgroup@pacificcenter.org

Organizations/Resources: Student, Academic, Education

⚲ ★ ♿ Chabot College GSA, 25555 Hesperian Blvd, Hayward; 510-723-6974 **H** fb.com/groups/Chabotgsa ✗

⚲ ★ Gamma Rho Lambda, Lambda Chapter, tinyurl.com/3s8nxpg

⚲ ★ Queer Caucus at UC Berkeley School of Law, 347 Boalt Hall, Berkeley; 94720 queercaucus.wordpress.com

⚲ ★ St Mary's College of California PRIDE, 1928 Saint Mary's Rd, Moraga; 94556 tinyurl.com/yczma7ga pride@stmarys-ca.edu

♀ ☆ ♿ UC Berkeley Gender Equity Center, 202 Cesar Chavez Student Center MC2440, Berkeley; 510-642-4786 **H?** geneq.berkeley.edu

⚲ ★ UC Berkeley Q at Haas, Haas School of Business, 2220 Piedmont Ave, Berkeley; 94720 www.qathaas.org QatHaas@berkeley.edu

Organizations/Resources: Transgender/Gender Non-Conforming/Diverse

♂ Bloom: Transgender Community Healing Project, www.bloomhealing.org

T ● Blumrosen, Daniel, MA, MFT #44056, 2315 Prince St #7, Berkeley; 94705 510-929-1065 tinyurl.com/3x26na ✗

T ★ ♿ Diablo Valley Girls, POB 2377, Pleasant Hill; 94523-0077 925-937-8432 www.diablovalleygirls.org ✗ info@diablovalley girls.org

♂ Intersex & Genderqueer Recognition Project, 40087 Mission Blvd #275, Fremont www.intersexrecognition.org

T Transvision - Tri-City Health Center, 39500 Liberty St, Fremont; 510-252-5822 tinyurl.com/yxjx74lu

T ☆ (♿) Wicked Transcendent Folk (WTF), Pacific Center, 2712 Telegraph Ave, Berkeley; 94705 510-548-8283 **H?** tinyurl.com/t8mq2tq wtfgroup@pacificcenter.org

Organizations/Resources: Youth (see also Family)

👤 ★ ♿ Empowerment Program, Center for Human Development, 301 W 10th St #6, Antioch; 94509 925-753-1004 x102 tinyurl.com/nvh54fz

👤 ★ ♿ Lambda Youth Project, Project Eden, 1866 B St Ste 101, Hayward; 94541 510-247-8200 **H?** www.gayprom.org project.eden@hsimail.org

👤 ★ ♿ LOUD Youth Group, Pacific Center, Jared Fields. Prgram Manager, 2712 Telegraph Ave, Berkeley; 94705 510-548-8283 x221 tinyurl.com/y273ndj2 ✔ jfields@pacificcenter.org

👤 ★ ♿ Our Space / Side By Side, BAYC, 22245 Main St #200, Hayward; 510-566-1226 fb.com/ourspacesidebyside ✔

Religious / Spiritual Resources

♀ ☆ ♿ All Souls Episcopal Parish, 2220 Cedar St, Berkeley; 94709 510-848-1755 **H?** www.allsoulsparish.org allsouls@all soulsparish.org

👤 ★ ♿ Center for LGBTQ and Gender Studies in Religion (CLGS), Pacific School of Religion, 1798 Scenic Ave, Berkeley; 510-849-8206 www.clgs.org

♀ ☆ ♿ Eden United Church of Christ, 21455 Birch St, Hayward; 94541 510-582-9533 **HD** www.edenucc.com ✔

♀ ☆ ♿ First Congregational Church, 2345 Channing Way, Berkeley; 94704-2201 510-848-3696 **HD** firstchurchberkeley.org ✔ info@fccb.org

♀ ☆ ♿ First Congregational Church UCC, 1912 Central Ave, Alameda; 94501-2623 510-522-6012 **H?** www.fccalameda.org ChurchOffice@fccalameda.org

♀ ☆ ♿ First Unitarian Church of Oakland, 685 14th St, Oakland; 94612-1242 510-893-6129 uuoakland.org office@uuoakland.org

♀ ☆ ♿ Lafayette Christian Church, 584 Glenside Dr, Lafayette; 94549 925-283-8304 tinyurl.com/9ohbkn ✔ lcc.disciples@ gmail.com

👤 ♿ Latinx Roundtable, Center for LGBTQ and Gender Studies in Religion (CLGS), Pacific School of Religion, 1798 Scenic Ave, Berkeley; 510-849-8206 www.clgs.org ✚

♀ ☆ ♿ Little Brown Church, 141 Kilkare Rd, Sunol; 94586 925-862-2004 tinyurl.com/psb6n7d contact@thelittlebrown churchofsunol.org

♀ ☆ ♿ Peace Lutheran Church, 3201 Camino Tassajara, Danville; 94506 925-648-7000 **HD** www.peacejourney.org ✔

♀ ☆ Plymouth United Church of Christ, 424 Monte Vista Ave, Oakland; 94611 510-654-5300 www.plymouthoakland.org office@ plymouthoakland.org

♀ ☆ ♿ St John's Presbyterian Church, 2727 College Ave, Berkeley; 94705 510-845-6830 **HD** www.stjohnsberkeley.org ✔ sjoffice@stjohnsberkeley.org

♀ ☆ St Mark's Episcopal Church, 2300 Bancroft Way, Berkeley; 94704 510-848-5107 www.stmarksberkeley.org office@stmarks berkeley.org

♀ ☆ ♿ St Paul Lutheran Church, 1658 Excelsior Ave, Oakland; 94602 510-530-6333 **HD** www.stpaul-lutheran.com info@ stpaul-lutheran.com

♀ ☆ ♿ Temple Israel of Alameda, 3183 Mecartney Rd, Alameda; 94502-6912 510-522-9355 templeisraelalameda.org ⚥

♀ ☆ ♿ Trinity United Methodist Church of Berkeley, 2362 Bancroft Way, Berkeley; 94704 510-548-4716 office@trinity berkeley.org

♀ ☆ ♿ Unitarian Universalist Church, 1893 N Vasco Rd, Livermore; 94551-9793 925-447-8747 www.uucil.org office@uucil.org

♀ ☆ ♿ Unitarian Universalist Church of Berkeley, 1 Lawson Rd, Kensington; 94707-1015 510-525-0302 **HD** uucb.org ✔

Sports & Outdoor

👤 ★ East Bay Frontrunners & Walkers, POB 71722, Oakland; 94612 eastbayfrontrunners.org

Travel & Tourist Services (see also Accommodation)

♀ ● French Escapade, 2389 Blackpool Pl, San Leandro; 94577-6005 510-483-5713 Sightseeing, painting and cooking tours for small groups to Europe. www.frenchescapade.com ✔ contact@french escapade.com

El Centro

Community Centers and/or Pride Organizations

👤 ★ ♿ Imperial Valley LGBT Resource Center, 1073 Ross Ave Ste e; 92243 760-592-4066 **H?** www.ivlgbtcenter.com ✔
» El Cerrito: see East Bay Area

Eureka/Humboldt County

Community Centers and/or Pride Organizations

👤 ★ Redwood Pride, redwoodpride.com redwoodpride@ gmail.com

Information, Media & Publications

👤 ★ The L-Word, POB 272, Bayside; 95524-0272 www.lword.mamajudy.com

Accommodation: Hotels, Inns, Guesthouses, B&B, Resorts
Myers Flat

♀ ○ (♿) Giant Redwoods RV & Camp, POB 83, Myers Flat; 95554 / 400 Myers Ave 707-943-9999 **H?** giantredwoodsrv.com 🐾 ✔

Trinidad

♀ ○ Trinidad Bay Bed & Breakfast Hotel, 560 Edwards St, Trinidad 707-677-0840 **H?** trinidadbaybnb.com ✔ ⊗ innkeeper@ trinidadbaybnb.com

Bars, Cafes, Clubs, Restaurants
Arcata

♀ ● ♿ The Alibi, 744 9th St, Arcata 707-822-3731 thealibi.com ▽ ✗

Eureka

♀ ● ♿ Lost Coast Brewery & Cafe, 617 4th St, Eureka; 707-445-4480 www.lostcoast.com ▽ ✗ ⧉ ✔

Bookstores

♀ ○ ♿ Blake's Books, 2005 Central Ave, McKinleyville; 95519 707-839-8800 tinyurl.com/l9vn9pm ✎ blakesbooks@sbcglobal.net

♂ ● ♿ Northtown Books, 957 H St, Arcata; 707-822-2834 www.northtownbooks.com

Counseling/Psychotherapy/Mental Health

♂ ● ♿ Polesky, Trey, LCSW, 2910 Harris St, Eureka; 95503 707-840-5511 Lic #66343 www.treypolesky.com treypolesky@gmail.com

Erotica / Adult Stores / Safe Sex Supplies

♂ ○ Pleasure Center, 1731 G St Ste D, Arcata 95521-5685 707-840-6135 www.secretsboutiques.com pleasurecenter8@gmail.com

Funding: Endowment, Fundraising

♂ ★ Eureka Sisters of Perpetual Indulgence, Abbey of the Big Red Wood, POB 5625, Eureka; 95502 707-676-3774 fb.com/EurekaSisters

Organizations/Resources: Social, Recreation, Support

♀ ★ Lesbian Single Mingle, 707-822-6470

♀ ★ Queer Humboldt, 707-502-2890 infoline www.queerhumboldt.org info@queerhumboldt.org

Religious / Spiritual Resources

♂ ☆ ♿ Humboldt Unitarian Universalist Fellowship, POB 506, Bayside; 95524-0506 702-822-3793 **H?** huuf.org ✎

Reproductive Medicine & Fertility Services

♂ ☆ ♿ Eureka Health Center, 3225 Timber Fall Court Ste B, Eureka; 707-442-5700 tinyurl.com/ybadtbh4

» *Forestville: see Russian River/Sonoma*
» *Fort Bragg: see Mendocino Area*

Fresno

Community Centers and/or Pride Organizations

♀ Fresno Rainbow Pride / Community Link, PO Box 4959; 93744 559-266-5465 www.fresnorainbowpride.com

Information, Media & Publications

♀ ★ LGBT Fresno, lgbtfresno.com

Bars, Cafes, Clubs, Restaurants

♂ Alibi, 4538 E Belmont Ave; 559-252-2899 fb.com/AlibiFresno/ **D**

♂ Club Legends, 3075 N Maroa Ave; 559-222-2271 www.clublegendsfresno.com **D** ▥

♀ FAB Fresno, 716 E Olive Ave; 559-492-3911 fb.com/FABFresno/ **D**

♂ ● ♿ The Red Lantern, 4618 E Belmont 559-251-5898 fb.com/theredfresno **CW**

Organizations/Resources: Cultural, Dance, Performance

♀ ★ Fresno Reel Pride LGBTQ Film Festival, PO Box 4647; 93744 www.reelpride.com

Organizations/Resources: Family and Supporters

♂ ☆ PFLAG, POB 27382; 93729 559-434-6540 www.pflag-fresno.org

Organizations/Resources: Senior Resources

♀ ★ Gray Alliance, Community Link, POB 4959 93744 559-269-7479 fb.com/grayalliancefresno/

Organizations/Resources: Student, Academic, Education

♀ ★ ♿ Bulldog Pride Scholarship Fund, Fresno State Alumni Association, 2625 E Matoian Way SH 124; 559-278-2586 www.bulldogpride.org ✎

♀ ★ Gay-Straight Alliance Network, 559-268-2780 www.gsanetwork.org

♀ ★ LGBTQ+ Programs and Services, Fresno State Cross Cultural and Gender Center, 5241 N Maple Ave M/S TA35; 559-278-4435 tinyurl.com/n4o28b7

Organizations/Resources: Transgender/Gender Non-Conforming/Diverse

T Trans-E-Motion, POB 16272; 93755 559-464-5806 www.transemotion.com

Organizations/Resources: Youth (see also Family)

♀ Fresno GLBTQ Youth Alliance, Community Link, POB 4959; 93744 559-266-5465 tinyurl.com/y3hytpmo

Religious / Spiritual Resources

♂ ☆ ♿ Unitarian Universalist Church of Fresno, 2672 E Alluvial Ave; 93720 559-322-6146 **HD** www.uufresno.org ✎ office@uufresno.org

♂ ☆ ♿ Unity of Fresno, 723 W Clinton Ave; 93705 559-227-1889 www.unityoffresno.org ✎ info@unityoffresno.org

Sports & Outdoor

♀ ★ Kampout Fresno, kampoutfresno@sbcglobal.net www.kampoutfresno.com

» *Fullerton: see Orange County*
» *Garden Grove: see Orange County*
» *Glendale: see Los Angeles Area*
» *Gold Country: see Gold Country/Sierra*

Gold Country/Sierra Foothills/Yosemite

Crisis, Anti-violence, & Helplines

♂ Center for Violence Free Relationships, 344 Placerville Dr Ste 11, Placerville; 530-626-1131 www.thecenternow.org

Accommodation: Hotels, Inns, Guesthouses, B&B, Resorts

Amador City

♂ ○ (♿?) Imperial Hotel, POB 212, Amador City; 95601-0212 / 14202 Old Highway 49 209-267-9172 www.imperialamador.com ▾ ✕ (♨?) ✎ ⊗

Fish Camp

♀ ○ Yosemite Big Creek Inn, 1221 Highway 41 559-641-2828 www.yosemiteinn.com ✗ ☺ bigcreekinn@gmail.com

Groveland

♀ ○ (?♿) The Groveland Hotel, POB 787, Groveland; 95321 209-962-4000 www.groveland.com (☻?) ✗ ☺☺ guestservices@groveland.com

♀ ○ (?♿) Hotel Charlotte, 18736 Main St, Groveland; 209-962-6455 www.hotelcharlotte.com ✗ (☻?) ✗ ☺ reservations@hotelcharlotte.com

Mariposa

♀ ○ Yosemite Plaisance Bed & Breakfast, POB 639, Mariposa; 95338 209-742-5205 www.YosemitePlaisance.com (☻?) ✗ ☺☺ Ron@YosemitePlaisance.com

Murphys

♀ ○ ♿♿ Courtwood Inn, POB 468, Murphys; 95247 / 2081 Ponderosa Way, Murphys; 209-728-8686 www.CourtwoodInn.com (☻?) ✗ ☺☺ Relax@CourtwoodInn.com

Nevada City

♀ • ♿♿ Harmony Ridge Lodge, 18883 E Highway 20, Nevada City; 530-478-0615 www.harmonyridgelodge.com ☻ ✗ ☺

San Andreas

♀ ○ (?♿) **Robin's Nest, 247 W St Charles St, San Andreas; 209-498-2080 AAA rated Victorian B&B in California Gold Country www.robinest.com** ✗ ☺

Sutter Creek

♀ ○ ♿♿ Grey Gables, 161 Hanford St, Sutter Creek; 209-267-1039 www.greygables.com ✗ ☺☺

AIDS/HIV Services, Education & Support

♀ ☆ Sierra Foothills AIDS Foundation, 12183 Locksley Ln Ste 208, Auburn; 95602-2052 530-889-2437 www.sierrafoothillsaids.org

♀ ☆ Sierra Foothills AIDS Foundation, 550 Main St Ste 1F, Diamond Springs; 95619-9177 530-622-1923 www.sierrafoothillsaids.org

♀ (?♿) Sierra HOPE, POB 159, Angels Camp; 95222 209-736-6792 www.sierrahope.org

Campgrounds and RV Parks

♀ • (?♿) Rancho Cicada Retreat, POB 225, Plymouth; 95669 209-245-4841 www.ranchocicadaretreat.com (☻?) ☺

Organizations/Resources: Family and Supporters

♀ ☆ PFLAG Greater Placer County, 2280 Grass Valley Highway Box #293, Auburn; 95603 916-863-9622 www.pflagplacercounty.org

♀ ☆ PFLAG Nevada County, POB 3236, Grass Valley 95945 530-798-5367 www.pflagnevco.com pflag@pflagnevco.com

♀ ☆ PFLAG Placerville/EDC, 4215 Bonita Vista Court, Placerville; www.pflagplacerville.org

>> *Grass Valley: see Gold Country/Sierra*
>> *Guerneville: see Russian River/Sonoma*
>> *Hayward: see East Bay Area*
>> *Healdsburg: see Russian River/Sonoma*
>> *Hermosa Beach: see Los Angeles Area*
>> *Hollywood: see Los Angeles Area*
>> *Idyllwild: see Inland Empire*
>> *Inglewood: see Los Angeles Area*

Inland Empire

Accommodation: Hotels, Inns, Guesthouses, B&B, Resorts
Idyllwild

♀ • (?♿) Rainbow Inn, POB 3384, Idyllwild; 92549 951-659-0111 www.rainbow-inn.com ☺

AIDS/HIV Services, Education & Support

♀ Bienestar Human Services Pomona Center, 180 E Mission Blvd, Pomona; 909-397-7660 www.bienestar.org ✦

♀ Foothill AIDS Project, 233 W Harrison Ave, Claremont; 800-448-0858 fapinfo.org

♀ Truevolution, 4164 Brockton Ave #A, Riverside 951-888-1346 truevolution.org

Bars, Cafes, Clubs, Restaurants
Pomona

♂ The 340 Restaurant & Nightclub, 340 S Thomas St, Pomona; 909-865-9340 www.340nightclub.com ☡ ✗ 📖

♂ • ♿ Alibi East & Back Alley Bar, 225 S San Antonio Ave, Pomona; 909-623-9422 (Some women) www.alibieast.com **DKLV** 📖 ✗

♂ • (?♿) The Hookup, 1047 E 2nd St, Pomona; 909-620-2844 ☡ ✗ ✗

Riverside

♂ • ♿♿ The Menagerie, 3581 University, Riverside; 951-788-8000 www.menagerieriverside.com **D** 📖 menagerieriverside@gmail.com

♂ • VIP Nightclub, 3673 Merrill Ave, Riverside 951-784-2370 www.vip-nightclub.com ☡ ✗ 📖

Broadcast Media

♂ This Way Out, KUCR 88.3FM Radio, University of California, Riverside; 951-827-3737 tinyurl.com/ocwojp9

Counseling/Psychotherapy/Mental Health

♀ • ♿♿ Hayman, Yisraela, MA. LMFT, 5033 Carriage Rd, Rancho Cucamonga; 91737 310-388-7779 www.yisraelahayman.com ✗ yisraelahayman@gmail.com

Erotica / Adult Stores / Safe Sex Supplies

♀ • (?♿) The Adult Shop, 716 Tennessee St Ste H, Redlands; 92373 909-335-7070 **H?** www.e-tique.org info@e-tique.org

♀ • (?♿) The For Discriminating Adults, 304 S E St, San Bernardino; 92410 909-381-5114 **H?** www.e-tique.org info@e-tique.org

Organizations/Resources: Family and Supporters

♀ ☆ ♿♿ PFLAG, 950 Spruce St, Riverside 951-500-6904 fb.com/pflagriverside/

Organizations/Resources: Student, Academic, Education

♂ ★ Cal Poly Pomona Pride Center, Bldg. 26, Room 107, 3801 W Temple Ave, Pomona; 909-869-2573 www.cpp.edu/oslcc/pride/

♂ ★ ♿♿ Queer Resource Center of the Claremont Colleges, 395 E 6th St, Claremont; 909-607-1817 colleges.claremont.edu/qrc/ ✗

⚥ ★ SMSU Queer and Transgender Resource Center, 5500 University Pkwy, San Bernardino; 909-537-5963 fb.com/SMSUQTRC/

⚥ ★ Sultana High School GSA, 17311 Sultana St, Hesperia; 760-947-6777 tinyurl.com/yyqkpau9

⚥ ★ ♿ University California Riverside LGBT Resource Center, 245 Costo Hall, 900 University Ave, Riverside 951-827-2267 out.ucr.edu

⚥ ★ ♿ University of Redlands Pride Center, 1200 E Colton Ave, Redlands; 909-793-2121 tinyurl.com/3vha4z6 ✗

Organizations/Resources: Transgender/Gender Non-Conforming/Diverse

T NAT ONLY

Religious / Spiritual Resources

♀ ☆ Claremont United Church of Christ, 233 W Harrison Ave, Claremont; 91711 909-626-1201 claremontucc.org

♀ ☆ ♿ Claremont United Methodist Church, 211 W Foothill Blvd, Claremont; 91711 909-624-9021 **HD** www.claremontumc.net ✗

♀ ☆ First Christian Church, 1751 N Park Ave, Pomona; 91768 909-622-1144 fccpomona.org fcc@fccpomona.org

♀ ☆ ♿ Redlands UCC, 168 Bellevue Ave, Redlands; 92373 909-793-3520 **HD** www.uccredlands.org ✗ office@uccredlands.org
>> Irvine: see Orange County

Joshua Tree

Accommodation: Hotels, Inns, Guesthouses, B&B, Resorts

♀ ○ (?♿) Spin & Margies Desert Hideaway, 64491 Twentynine Palms Hwy; 92252 760-459-4959 deserthideaway.com ✗ ⊗ ⊗

Accommodation Rental: Furnished / Vacation (& AirBNB)

♀ ● (?♿) Joshua Tree Highlands Houses, 8229 Fleur Rd; / 8178 Fleur Rd, Joshua Tree; 92252 760-366-3636 tinyurl.com/k9rylp8

Art & Craft Galleries/Services, Supplies

♀ ● Joshua Tree Art Gallery, 61607 29 Palms Hwy Ste B; 92552 760-366-3636 Fine Arts Gallery www.joshuatreeartgallery.com info@Joshuatreeartgallery.com
>> La Jolla: see San Diego Area
>> Laguna Beach: see Orange County
>> Lake Arrowhead: see Big Bear/Lake Arrowhead Area

Lake Tahoe (CA/NV) Area

Crisis, Anti-violence, & Helplines

♀ ☆ Live Violence Free, 2941 Lake Tahoe Blvd, S Lake Tahoe; 530-544-2118 www.liveviolencefree.org

Accommodation: Hotels, Inns, Guesthouses, B&B, Resorts
South Lake Tahoe

⚥ ● Inn the Pines, 2452 Conestoga St, S Lake Tahoe; 96150 530-544-2831 www.TahoeInnThePines.com ✗

Accommodation Rental: Furnished / Vacation (& AirBNB)
South Lake Tahoe

♀ ● (?♿) Holly's Place, 1201 Rufus Allen Blvd, S Lake Tahoe; 800-745-7040 www.hollysplace.com ✗

Bars, Cafes, Clubs, Restaurants
South Lake Tahoe

♀ ○ Driftwood Cafe, 1001 Heavenly Vlg Way #1A, S Lake Tahoe; 530-544-6545 www.driftwoodtahoe.com ✗
>> Lakeport: see Clearlake

Lockeford

Accommodation: Hotels, Inns, Guesthouses, B&B, Resorts

♀ ○ Inn at Locke House, 19960 Elliott Rd; 95237 209-727-5715 www.theinnatlockehouse.com (✿?) ✗ ⊗ ⊗ innkeeper@theinnatlockehouse.com

Long Beach

Community Centers and/or Pride Organizations

⚥ ★ ♿ **The LGBTQ Center of Long Beach, 2017 E 4th St; 90814-1001 562-434-4455 fax 562-433-6428 H?** Counseling/HIV & STI Testing & Treatment/Mental Health/Youth www.centerlb.org info@centerlb.org

⚥ ★ (♿) Long Beach Pride, 1017 Obispo Ave; 592-987-9191 longbeachpride.com

Accommodation: Hotels, Inns, Guesthouses, B&B, Resorts

♀ ● (?♿) The Varden Hotel, 335 Pacific Ave; 562-432-8950 www.thevardenhotel.com ✗ ⊗ ⊗

AIDS/HIV Services, Education & Support

♀ ☆ Bienestar Long Beach, Long Beach Center, 1464 Cherry Ave; 562-438-5800 www.bienestar.org ✦

Bars, Cafes, Clubs, Restaurants
Bellflower

♂ ● Flux, 17817 Lakewood Blvd, Bellflower 562-633-6394 www.fluxbarla.com **DKV** ✗

♂ The Brit, 1744 E Broadway; 562-432-9742 www.thebritbarlb.com

♂ The Broadway Bar, 1100 E Broadway 562-432-3646 www.broadwaycocktails.com

♂ ● ♿ The Crest, 5935 Cherry Ave 562-423-6650 www.thecrestlongbeach.com **L** ✗ thecrestbar@aol.com

♂ Eagle 562, 2020 E Artesia Blvd; 562-269-0313 www.eagle562.com/contact

♂ ● ♿ The Falcon, 1435 E Broadway 562-432-4146 www.falconbar.com

♀ ○ Hamburger Mary's, 330 Pine Ave; 562-436-7900 www.hamburgermaryslb.com ⟁ ✗ ▥

♂ Mineshaft, 1720 E Broadway; 562-436-2433 fb.com/mineshaftLB/

♂ ● Silver Fox, 411 Redondo Ave; 562-439-6343 www.silverfoxlongbeach.com **D**

♂ ● ♿ The Suite, 3428 E Pacific Coast Hwy; 562-597-3884 **H?** www.thesuitelb.com **DKLV** ▥ ✗

♂ Sweetwater Saloon, 1201 E Broadway 562-432-7044 tinyurl.com/2dpjldz

Counseling/Psychotherapy/Mental Health

♂ ○ Kain, Craig, PhD, 3416 E Broadway; 90802 562-987-1766 Licensed Psychologist (Psy14664) www.drcraigkain.com

♀ ○ Pudewa, Pam, 5848 Naples Plaza Dr #204; 90803 562-391-6116 www.pampudewatherapy.com pampudewatherapy@gmail.com

♂ ○ Tessina, Tina B., LMFT, PhD, 562-438-8077 www.tinatessina.com tina@tinatessina.com

Funding: Endowment, Fundraising

♀ ★ International Imperial Court of Long Beach Inc, POB 1835; 90802 iiclb.org

♂ Out of the Closet Thrift Store, 3500 E Pacific Coast Highway; 562-494-0340 outofthecloset.org

Gifts, Cards, Pride, etc.

♀ ● ♿ Hot Stuff, 2121 E Broadway 90803-5704 562-433-0692 hotstufflongbeach.com

Men's & Sex Clubs (not primarily Health Clubs)

♂ ● 1350 Club, 510 W Anaheim, Wilmington 310-830-4784 www.midtowne.com

Organizations/Resources: Business & Professional Associations, Labor Advocacy

♀ Long Beach Gay & Lesbian Chamber of Commerce, 2101 N Lakewood Blvd D #670; 562-225-3198 www.lbglcc.org

Organizations/Resources: Cultural, Dance, Performance

♀ ★ ♿ Long Beach Q Film Festival, The Center, 2017 E 4th St; 90814 562-434-4455 x245 qfilmslongbeach.com ✎ mtaye@centerlb.org

♀ ★ (♖) Shoreline Squares, POB 15394; 90815 323-519-0800 shorelinesquares.com

♀ ★ South Coast Chorale, POB 92524; 90809 562-977-8722 sccsingers.com

Organizations/Resources: Education

♂ ☆ Speak Out! Toastmasters Club, meets at Royal Cup Café, 994 Redondo Ave speakouttoastmasters.org

Organizations/Resources: Ethnic, Multicultural

♀ ★ Black & White Men Together of Southern CA (BWMTSC), 562-366-4573 www.bwmtsc.org ✪ info@bwmtsc.org

Organizations/Resources: Family and Supporters

♂ ★ ♿ PFLAG Long Beach, POB 1132, Los Alamitos, CA 90720 562-773-9801 fb.com/PFLAG-Long-Beach/

Organizations/Resources: Social, Recreation, Support

♀ ★ Gay for Good, 6444 E Spring St Ste 321 90815 562-684-8210 Volunteer organization. www.gayforgood.org info@gayforgood.org

Organizations/Resources: Student, Academic, Education

♀ ★ CSU Dominguez Hills LGBT Faculty & Staff Association, Small College 130, 1000 E Victoria St, Carson 310-243-2519

2017 E 4th St   562-434-4455
www.centerlb.org

Low cost sliding scale mental health counseling program

the center long beach

♂ ★ Delta Lambda Phi Gay Fraternity for Progressive Men, Student Life and Development, USU 206, 1250 Bellflower Blvd; 562-546-2789 fb.com/DLPRHO

♀ ★ ♿ LGBT Resource Center CSU Long Beach, USU 215, 1250 Bellflower Blvd; 562-985-4585 tinyurl.com/y2dpyult

Party/Holiday/Event Services (see also Catering, Weddings)

♂ ● Bravo Productions, 65 Pine Ave #858; 90802 562-435-0065 bravoevents-online.com staff@bravoevents-online.com

Recovery

♂ ☆ Atlantic Alano Club, 600 1/2 Redondo Ave 562-426-6099 www.atlanticalanoclub.org

Religious / Spiritual Resources

♂ ★ Calvary Open Door Worship Center, 16518 Adenmoor Ave, Bellflower; 562-461-7114 www.opendoorcenter.com

♀ First Congregational Church, 241 Cedar Ave 562-436-2256 www.firstchurchlb.org

♀ ★ (♖) The Glory Center, 9812 Walnut St, Bellflower; 562-920-1845 www.gloryctr.org

♀ ★ ♿ Open Door Ministries, 1025 Westminster Mall Unit 1020A, Westminster, CA 714-723-3970 opendooroc.org

♀ ♿ St. Luke's LGBTQ and Friends Ministry, 525 E 7th St; 562-491-3174 www.stlukeslb.org/lgbtq.html

♀ ☆ ♿ Unitarian Universalist Church, 5450 E Atherton St; 90815-4004 562-597-8445 www.uuclb.org office@uuclb.org

Sports & Outdoor

♀ ★ Long Beach Grunions Swim Team, 3350 E 7th St #123; www.lbgrunions.org

♀ Long Beach Pool League, longbeachpl.org

♀ ★ Shoreline Frontrunners, POB 90774 90809-0774 shorelinefrontrunners.org info@sfrlb.com

♀ ★ Surf & Sun Softball League, 5050 E 2nd St #41066; surfandsunsoftball.org

Los Angeles Area

Crisis, Anti-violence, & Helplines

♀ East Los Angeles Women's Center, 1431 S Atlantic Blvd, LA; 323-526-5819 www.elawc.org

Community Centers and/or Pride Organizations

⚨ ★ ♿ Christopher Street West Association, Inc., 8687 Melrose Ave Ste BM48, W Hwd; 323-969-8302 **HS** lapride.org ✒

⚨ ★ ♿ The L.A. Gay & Lesbian Center's Village at Ed Gould Plaza, 1125 N McCadden Pl, LA; 323-993-7400 **HD** lalgbtcenter.org ✒

⚨ ★ ♿ Los Angeles Gay & Lesbian Center, 1625 N Schrader Blvd, Hwd; 323-993-7400 lalgbtcenter.org ✒

⚨ ★ ♿ San Gabriel Valley LGBTQ Center, POB 1395, Monrovia; 91017 / 2607 S Santa Anita Ave, Arcadia 626-578-5772 www.sgvlgbtq.org ✒ info@sgvlgbtq.org

⚨ ★ ♿ South Bay LGBTQ Center, 16610 Crenshaw Blvd, Torrance; 310-328-6550 www.southbaycenter.org ✒

⚨ ★ Venice Pride, 55 N Venice Blvd #502, Venice; 90291 424-330-7788 venicepride.org info@venicepride.org

Information, Media & Publications

⚨ ● Los Angeles Blade, 5455 Wilshire Blvd Flr 21, LA; 90036 310-230-5266 www.losangelesblade.com info@losangelesblade.com

⚨ ★ OutWrite Newsmagazine - UCLA, 149B Kerckhoff Hall 308 Westwood Plz, LA; 310-825-8500 www.outwritenewsmag.org

Accommodation: Hotels, Inns, Guesthouses, B&B, Resorts
Los Angeles

♂ ○ Cinema Suites Bed & Breakfast, 925 S Fairfax Ave, LA; 90036 323-272-3160 www.cinemasuitesbnb.com ✒ ⊗ csreservations@gmail.com

Silverlake

♂ ● Sanborn House, 1005 1/2 Sanborn Ave, LA 90029-3111 323-455-3910 sanbornhouse.com ✒ ⊗

Accommodation: Retirement and/or Assisted Living
Hollywood

⚨ ★ ♿ Triangle Square Affordable Housing, Triangle Square, 1602 N Ivar Ave Aste A, Hwd; 323-860-5830 tinyurl.com/y5bcdy5a

Accounting, Bookkeeping, Tax Services

♀ ● ♿ Wilson, Cathy E, CPA, 11965 Venice Blvd #404, LA; 90066 310-566-7980 fax 310-566-7981 www.cathywilsoncpa.com cathy@cathywilsoncpa.com

AIDS/HIV Services, Education & Support

♀ ☆ ♿ Alliance for Housing and Healing, 825 Colorado Blvd Ste 100, LA; 323-344-4888 **H?** www.alliancehh.org

♀ APAIT Asian Pacific AIDS Intervention Team, 3055 Wilshire Blvd Flr 3, LA; 213-375-3830 www.apaitonline.org ◇

♀ ☆ ♿ APLA Health, 611 S Kingsley Dr, LA; 213-201-1600 www.aplahealth.org

♂ ☆ Being Alive, 7531 Santa Monica Blvd Ste 100, W Hwd; 323-874-4322 www.beingalivela.org

♂ Bienestar Human Services, 3131 Santa Anita Ave Ste 109, El Monte; 626-444-9453 www.bienestar.org ✚

♂ Bienestar Human Services, 5326 E Beverly Blvd, LA; 866-590-6411 www.bienestar.org ✚

♂ Bienestar Human Services Hollywood Center, 4955 Sunset Blvd, LA; 323-660-9680 tinyurl.com/mnawke6 ✚

⚨ ★ Bienestar Human Services San Fernando Valley, 8134 Van Nuys Blvd #200, Panorama City; 818-908-3820 www.bienestar.org

♂ ★ Bienestar Human Services South Los Angeles Center, 130 W Manchester Ave, LA; 323-752-3100 www.bienestar.org ✚

♂ Common Ground, Venice Family Clinic, 622 Rose Ave, Venice; 310-314-5480 commongroundhiv.org

♂ Common Ground Westside, 2401 Lincoln Blvd, Santa Monica; 310-314-5480 www.commongroundhiv.org

♀ ☆ ♿ Hollywood HEART, 301 E Colorado Blvd #430, Pasadena; 626-714-7505 www.hollywoodheart.org ✒

♀ ☆ (?♿) The Life Group LA, 1049 Havenhurst Dr #330, W Hwd; 888-208-8081 **H?** www.thelifegroupla.org

♀ ☆ Project Angel Food, 922 Vine St, LA 323-845-1800 www.angelfood.org

♀ ☆ Project Chicken Soup, POB 480241, LA; 90048 310-836-5402 www.projectchickensoup.org

♀ Project New Hope, 601 E Glenoaks Blvd #100, Glendale; 818-546-8929 www.projectnewhope.org

♂ ★ ♿ Red Circle Project, 2741 S La Brea Ave, LA; 323-329-9905 **H?** Native American HIV/AIDS Prevention & Education Program. redcircleproject.org ✳

♂ ☆ The Wall Las Memorias Project, 5619 Monte Vista St, LA; 323-257-1056 www.thewalllasmemorias.org ✚

Archives/Libraries/Museums/History Projects

⚨ ★ June Mazer Lesbian Archives, POB 691866, W Hwd; 90069 310-659-2478 www.mazerlesbianarchives.org ✒

Bars, Cafes, Clubs, Restaurants
Chino

♂ ● ♿ Riverside Grill, 5258 Riverside Dr, Chino; 909-627-4144 www.riversidegrillchino.com ♈ ✖ ♐✒ roddisum@gmail.com

Hollywood

♀ ○ Avalon, 1735 Vine St, Hwd; 323-462-8900 www.avalonhollywood.com **D** ✚

♂ ○ ♿ Boardner's, 1652 N Cherokee Ave, Hwd; 323-462-9621 www.boardners.com **D** ♈ ✖ ▥ ✒

⚨ Tempo, 5520 Santa Monica Blvd, Hwd 323-466-1094 ✚

♂ ○ TigerHeat, at Avalon, 1735 Vine St, Hwd; / Thu check ahead 323-467-4571 www.clubtigerheat.com **D** ✚

Los Angeles

♂ ● ♿ A.O.C. Wine Bar & Restaurant, 8700 W 3rd St, LA; 323-653-6359 www.aocwinebar.com ♈ ✖ ✒

♀ Booby Trap, check schedule fb.com/BoobyTrapFanClub/

♂ ○ Border Grill Downtown LA, 445 S Figueroa St, LA; 213-486-5171 www.bordergrill.com ♈ ✖

Cafe-Club Fais Do-Do, 5257 W Adams Blvd, LA 323-954-8080 www.faisdodo.com

Cantalini's Express, 11736 Washington Place, LA; 310-572-9157 cantalinisexpress.com

The New Jalisco Bar, 245 S Main St, LA 213-613-1802 tinyurl.com/msn44o3

Precinct, 357 S Broadway, LA; 213-628-3112 www.precinctdtla.com

Redline DTLA, 131 E 6th St, LA; 213-612-0226 www.redlinedtla.com

Rockwell Table & Stage, 1714 N Vermont Ave, LA; 213-669-1550 www.rockwell-la.com

Montebello

Chico, 2915 W Beverly Blvd, Montebello 323-721-3403 www.clubchico.com D

North Hollywood

The Bullet Bar, 10522 Burbank Blvd, N Hwd 818-762-8890 www.BulletBarLA.com L

Cobra, 10937 Burbank Blvd, N Hwd; 818-760-9798 www.clubcobrala.com DCLW

Idle Hour, 4824 Vineland Ave, N Hwd; 818-980-5604 www.idlehourbar.com

The Other Door, 10437 Burbank Blvd, N Hwd; 818-508-7008 www.theotherdoorbar.com DK

Pasadena

The Boulevard, 3199 E Foothill Blvd, Pasadena; 626-356-9304 www.blvdbar.com K

Playa Del Rey

Cantalini's Salerno Beach Restaurant, 193 Culver Blvd, Playa Del Rey; 310-821-0018 salernobeach.com

Redondo Beach

The Artesia Bar, 1995 Artesia Blvd, Redondo Bch; 310-318-3339 www.artesiabar.com

Reseda

C-Frenz Nightclub, 7026 Reseda Blvd, Reseda; 818-996-2976 www.cfrenzbar.com D

Coco Bongo Reseda, 19655 Sherman Way, Reseda; 818-998-8464 fb.com/cocobongoreseda D

Santa Monica

The Birdcage, 2640 Main St, Santa Monica 310-392-4956 www.thebirdcagesm.com

Cora's Coffee Shop, 1802 Ocean Ave, Santa Monica; 310-451-9562 www.corascoffee.com

Golden Bull Bar & Restaurant, 170 W Channel Rd, Santa Monica; 310-230-0402. www.goldenbull.us

Silverlake

Akbar, 4356 W Sunset Blvd, LA 323-665-6810 www.akbarsilverlake.com D

Bigfoot Lodge, 3172 Los Feliz Blvd, LA 323-662-9227 fb.com/bigfootlodge/ D

Bootie LA, n/a, LA; / check schedule for locations 323-666-6669 www.bootiela.com D

Eagle LA, 4219 Santa Monica Blvd, LA; 323-669-9472 www.EagleLA.com L

Faultline, 4216 Melrose Ave, LA 323-660-0889 www.faultlinebar.com L

The Kitchen, 4348 Fountain Ave, LA 323-664-3663 thekitchen.la

Studio City

Aroma Coffee, 4360 Tujunga Ave, Studio City; 818-508-0677 H? www.aromacoffeeandtea.com

Club Shine at Serra's, 12449 Ventura Blvd, Studio City; / unverified, check ahead 818-997-9666 D

Oil Can Harry's, 11502 Ventura Blvd, Studio City; 818-760-9749 www.oilcanharrysla.com CD

Venice

Roosterfish, 1302 Abbot Kinney Blvd, Venice; 310-977-8174 www.roosterfishbar.com

West Hollywood

The Abbey Food & Bar, 692 N Robertson Blvd, W Hwd; 310-590-7440 H? www.theabbeyweho.com DV

Bayou, 8939 Santa Monica Blvd, W Hwd 310-273-3303 thebayouweho.com

Cafe D'Etoile, 8941 1/2 Santa Monica Blvd, W Hwd; 310-278-1011 www.cafedetoile.net

The Chapel at The Abbey, 692 N Robertson Blvd, W Hwd; 310-289-8410 H? tinyurl.com/y4ocmdty DV

Club Papi, at Micky's 8857 Santa Monica Blvd, W Hwd; / check schedule 323-692-9573 www.clubpapi.com clubpapi@aol.com

Fiesta Cantina, 8865 Santa Monica Blvd, W Hwd; 323-652-8865 www.fiestacantina.net

Flaming Saddles, 8811 Santa Monica Blvd, W Hwd 310-855-7501 www.flamingsaddles.com/weho CW

Fubar, 7994 Santa Monica Blvd, W Hwd 323-654-0396 www.fubarla.com D

Girl Bar, check website www.girlbar.com D

Gold Coast, 8228 Santa Monica Blvd, W Hwd 323-656-4879 tinyurl.com/l7stmme

Gym Sportsbar, 8737 Santa Monica Blvd, W Hwd 310-659-2004 www.gymsportsbar.com

Cafe La Boheme, 8400 Santa Monica Blvd, W Hwd; 323-848-2360 www.cafelaboheme.us

Marco's Trattoria, 8200 Santa Monica Blvd, W Hwd; 323-650-1060 www.marcoswesthollywood.com

Micky's, 8857 Santa Monica Blvd, W Hwd 310-657-1176 www.mickys.com D

Mother Lode, 8944 Santa Monica Blvd, W Hwd 310-659-9700 tinyurl.com/6mhx5jr D

Plaza, 739 N La Brea, W Hwd; 323-939-0703 tinyurl.com/y4e78aka D

Rage, 8911 Santa Monica Blvd, W Hwd 310-652-7055 www.ragenightclub.com D

♂ ● (?⚲) Revolver Video Bar, 8851 Santa Monica Blvd, W Hwd; 310-694-0430 **H?** www.revolverweho.com **DKV** 🎞

⚲ Robertson, 665 N Robertson Blvd, W Hwd 310-659-4551 **D**

♀ ○ St Felix, 8945 Santa Monica Blvd, W Hwd 310-275-4428 www.saintfelix.net ⚲ ✕ saintfelix.libertine@gmail.com

♂ ○ Trunks, 8809 Santa Monica Blvd, W Hwd 310-652-1015 trunksbar.com

Body Art

♀ ● ♿ Marginalized Tattoo, 4226 Melrose Ave, LA; 90029 (same lot as Faultline bar) 213-422-4801 www.dogspunk.com

Bookstores

♀ ○ ♿ Book Soup, 8818 Sunset Blvd, LA 310-659-3110 www.booksoup.com

♀ ○ Diesel, A Bookstore, 225 26th St, Santa Monica 310-576-9960 www.dieselbookstore.com

♀ ○ ♿ Skylight Books, 1818 N Vermont Ave, LA; 323-660-1175 www.skylightbooks.com

♀ ○ ♿ Small World Books, 1407 Ocean Front Walk, Venice; 310-399-2360 www.smallworldbooks.com

♀ ○ Stories Books & Cafe, Echo Park, 1716 W Sunset Blvd, LA; 213-413-3733 www.storiesla.com ⌁

Broadcast Media

⚲ (?⚲) IMRU Radio, 3729 Cahunega Blvd W, N Hwd; 818-985-2711 Mon 7pm 90.7 FM. tinyurl.com/y2bj4vd9

Coaching: Career, Life, Relationship etc

♂ ● Bander, Ricki, PhD (CA Psychologist Lic. PSY7652 Board Certified Coach), offices: Los Angeles & Palm Desert 310-470-1435 www.rbanderphd.com

Counseling/Psychotherapy/Mental Health

♂ ● ♿ Chernin, Jeffrey, Ph.D, MFT, 6310 San Vicente Blvd #410, LA; 90048 323-692-7781 www.jeffreychernin.com info@jeffreychernin.com

♂ ● ♿ Cooper, Chris D, PhD, 95 N Marengo Ave Ste 100, Pasadena; 626-744-9472 www.chriscooperphd.com ✎ @ixx=

♂ ● ♿ Hayman, Yisraela, MA. LMFT, 1827 Virginai Rd, LA; 90019 310-388-7779 www.yisraelahayman.com ✎ yisraelahayman@gmail.com

♂ ● ♿ Jordan, Terry, LCSW, DCSW, 2001 S Barrington Ave #202, LA; 90025 310-895-4848 psychotherapyinla.com

♂ ○ ♿ Leviton, Susan J, MA, LMFT, 16055 Ventura Blvd Ste 1110, Encino; 91436 818-788-7101 (experienced with trans people) www.susanlevitonmft.com

♂ ● ♿ Phillips, Stephen, PsyD, JD, 8920 Wilshire Blvd Ste 334, Bev Hills; 90211 310-275-4194 Lic #PSY17868 www.drstephenphillips.com

♂ ☆ Prototypes, 1000 N Alameda St #390, LA 213-542-3838 www.prototypes.org

♂ ○ Quinn, Susan, MA, MFT, 12011 San Vicente Blvd # 402, LA; 310-600-3458 www.susanquinn.net

♂ ● ♿ Schierholz, Neil, PsyD, 11847 Wilshire Blvd Ste 300, LA; 90025 310-866-0440 Lic PSY25154 tinyurl.com/yczkx4ra DrSchierholz@AngelesPsychologyGroup.com

♂ ○ Wright, April, MA. LMFT, 4500 Via Marina, Marina Del Rey; 90292 310-502-4944 aprilwrighttherapy.com april@aprilwright therapy.com

Counseling/Psychiatry

♂ ○ Harris, Stanley, MD, DLFAPA, USC Counseling and Mental Health Services, 1031 W 34th St #304, LA; 90089 213-740-7711 sharris@usc.edu

Dentists

♂ ● ♿♿ Tamura, Daniel H., DDS, 6200 Wilshire Blvd #1209, W Hwd; 90048-5813 323-937-0197 fax 323-937-1257 www.danieltamuradds.com ✎ office@danieltamuradds.com

Erotica / Adult Stores / Safe Sex Supplies

♂ ○ Secrets of Hollywood, 1117 N Western Ave, LA 90029-1016 323-467-1640 www.secretsboutiques.com secretsofhollywood@yahoo.com

Funding: Endowment, Fundraising

⚲ ★ Los Angeles Sisters of Perpetual Indulgence, Inc, 1125 N Fairfax Ave #461160, W Hwd; 323-908-3489 www.lasisters.org

♂ Out of the Closet Thrift Store, 1724 W Sunset Blvd, LA; 213-484-3913 outofthecloset.org

♂ Out of the Closet Thrift Store, 214 Lincoln Blvd, Venice; 310-664-9036 outofthecloset.org

♂ ★ ♿♿ Point Foundation Los Angeles, 5055 Wilshire Blvd, Ste 501, LA; 323-933-1234 National LGBTQ Scholarship Fund pointfoundation.org ✎

Graphic Design/Printing/Type

♂ ● BLK Media Services, POB 83912, LA 90083-0912 213-410-0808 fax 213-410-9250 www.blkmedia.com ✤ ✎

Health Care: Physical (see also Counseling/Mental Health)

♂ ● ♿ Gloin, Matthew, DC, Live Well Chiropractic and Pilates Center, 5553 W Pico Blvd, LA; 90019 323-930-9355 www.livewell-la.com info@livewell-la.com

♂ The Saban Community Clinic, 8405 Beverly Blvd, LA; 323-653-8622 sabancommunityclinic.org

♂ ● Seaton, Jessica, DC, 4212 Overland Ave, Culver City; 424-603-4088 www.drjessicaseaton.com

♂ ☆ ♿♿ Valley Community Healthcare, 6801 Coldwater Canyon Ave, N Hwd; 91605-5162 / HIV/AIDS Services Dept, Room 2A 818-301-6334 tinyurl.com/pzl4sxh kweiler@vchcare.org

♂ ☆ ♿♿ Valley Community Healthcare, 6801 Coldwater Canyon Ave, N Hwd; 91605-5162 818-301-6334 **H?** Hep C, PrEP, & Transgender services tinyurl.com/jvnoc7q ✎ info@valleycommunityhealthcare.org

Hypnotherapy

♂ ○ Holistic Hypnosis & Hypnotherapy - Los Angeles, Brian Green, 7223 Willoughby Ave, LA; 90046 323-851-7208 www.mindmagic123.com mindmagic123@yahoo.com

Immigration, Citizenship, Political Asylum, Refugees

♀ ● ᕫᕫ Fong, J Craig, Fong & Aquino, LLP, 709 E Colorado Blvd #250, Pasadena; 626-577-8020 www.fongaquino.com

Leather Resources & Groups

♂ ★ Avatar Club Los Angeles, 8581 Santa Monica Blvd PMB 481, W Hwd; www.avatarla.org

♀ Los Angeles Leather Coalition, lalc.info

Legal Services

♀ ○ Citywide Law Group, 12424 Wilshire Blvd Ste 705, LA; 90025 424-248-2700 www.citywidelaw.com info@citywidelaw.com

♀ ○ Fisher, Scott D, Esq, 9454 Wilshire Blvd Penthouse Ste, Bev Hills; 90212 323-944-0011 www.scottfisherlaw.com

♀ ● ᕫ Gay Divorce Mediator, 240 N Orange Grove Blvd, Pasadena; 91103 310-598-1970 **H?** www.gaydivorcemediator.com ⚲ bill@gaydivorcemediator.com

♀ ○ Goodman, Diane, 17043 Ventura Blvd, Encino 91316 818-386-2889 www.goodmanmediation.com info@goodmanmediation.com

♀ ● ᕫᕫ Perkowski Legal, PC, 445 S Figueroa St Ste 3100z, LA; 90071 213-426-2137 **H?** www.perkowskilegal.com info@perkowskilegal.com

Men's & Sex Clubs (not primarily Health Clubs)

♂ ● Flex Complex, 4424 Melrose Ave, Hwd 323-663-5858 www.flexspas.com/los-angeles

♂ ● Midtowne Spa, 615 Kohler St, LA; 213-680-1838 www.midtowne.com

♂ ○ (ᕫᕫ) Roman Holiday, 12814 Venice Blvd, LA; 310-391-0200 www.romanholidayclubs.com

♂ ○ ᕫ Roman Holiday, 14435 Victory Blvd, Van Nuys; 818-780-1320 www.romanholidayclubs.com

♂ Slammer, 3688 Beverly Blvd, LA; 213-388-8040 www.slammerclub.com **P**

♂ The Zone, 1037 N Sycamore Ave, Hwd 323-472-6495 www.thezonela.com **P**

Organizations/Resources: Bisexual Focus

♀ ☆ Los Angeles Bi Task Force, c/o The Village, 1125 N McCadden Place, LA; 323-860-5837 fb.com/labitaskforce

Organizations/Resources: Business & Professional Associations, Labor Advocacy

♂ ★ (?ᕫ) LA Gay & Lesbian Chamber of Commerce, 8424 Santa Monica Blvd Ste A508, W Hwd; 323-570-4697 www.laglcc.org

♂ ★ Lesbian & Gay Psychotherapy Association of Southern California, Inc., mail to LAGPA, POB 34142, LA; 90034 310-838-6247 www.lagpa.org

♂ ★ LGBT Bar Association of Los Angeles, 750 W 7th St #811314, LA; 90081 www.lgbtbarla.org lgbtbarla@gmail.com

♂ National Lesbian & Gay Journalists Association Los Angeles, nlgjala.wordpress.com

♂ ★ Pride At Work Los Angeles,

Organizations/Resources: Cultural, Dance, Performance

♂ ★ ᕫᕫ Celebration Theatre, 1049 Havenhurst Dr #101-1, W Hwd; 90046 323-957-1884 www.celebrationtheatre.com info@celebrationtheatre.com

♂ ★ ᕫᕫ The Gay Freedom Band, POB 29628, LA; 90029 626-310-3860 www.gfbla.org

♀ ★ ᕫᕫ Gay Men's Chorus of Los Angeles, 8380 Santa Monica Blvd Ste 206, W Hwd; 424-239-6514 www.gmcla.org

♂ ★ Outfest, 3470 Wilshire Blvd Ste 935, LA 213-480-7088 www.outfest.org

♂ ★ Outfest: Fusion, 3470 Wilshire Blvd Ste 935, LA; 213-480-7088 LGBT People of Color Film Festival www.outfest.org

♀ ☆ POWER UP, 419 N Larchmont Blvd #283, LA 323-463-3154 www.powerupfilms.org

♂ ★ ᕫᕫ Tinseltown Squares, POB 691764, W Hwd; 90069-9764 iagsdc.com/tts/ **D** info@ttsq.org

♀ ☆ Vox Femina, 3341 Caroline Ave, Culver City 310-922-0025 www.voxfemina.org

♂ ★ ᕫᕫ West Coast Singers: the LGBTQ+ Chorus of Los Angeles, POB 46825, W Hwd; 90046-0825 800-439-4927 **HS** www.westcoastsingers.org

Organizations/Resources: Ethnic, Multicultural

♂ ★ Asian/Pacific Gays & Friends, 1049 Havenhurst Dr Box 443, W Hwd; 90046 www.apgf.org ❖ info@apgf.org

♂ Color in Common, LA Gay and Lesbian Center, 1125 N McCadden Place, LA; 323-860-5833 tinyurl.com/y2ymb3o6 ❖

♂ ★ Gay & Lesbian Armenian Society of Los Angeles, 8721 Santa Monica Blvd Box 654, W Hwd; 310-203-1587

♂ In the Meantime Men's Group, 2146 W Adams Blvd, LA; 323-733-4868 inthemeantimemen.org ❖

♂ ★ Long Yang Club of Los Angeles (LYCLA), fb.com/groups/293252197243 ❖

♂ ★ SATRANG, 3055 Wilshire Blvd Ste #300, LA 888-370-9569 www.satrang.org ❖

Organizations/Resources: Family and Supporters

♀ ☆ ᕫᕫ PFLAG Los Angeles, POB 24565, LA; 90024-0565 888-735-2488 www.pflagla.org info@pflagla.org

♀ ★ PFLAG Pasadena, POB 125, Altadena 91003-0125 626-817-3524 www.pflagpasadena.org info@pflagpasadena.org

♀ ☆ PFLAG San Gabriel Valley Asian Pacific Islander, tinyurl.com/avp7d98 ❖

♂ ★ The Pop Luck Club, POB 46760, LA; 90046 323-942-9323 www.popluckclub.org

Organizations/Resources: Naturist/Nudist

♂ ★ CMEN, 8424-A Santa Monica Blvd #119, W Hwd 877-429-6368 www.cmen.org **N**

♂ ★ Los Angeles Nude Guys (LANG), 8424A Santa Monica Blvd PMB 249, W Hwd; www.clublang.com **N**

Organizations/Resources: Political/Legislative/Advocacy

⚲ ★ (?⅃) Stonewall Democratic Club, 1049 Havenhurst Drive #325, W Hwd; 90046 323-650-8190 www.stonewalldems.org info@stonewalldems.org

⚲ Stonewall Young Democrats, 7985 Santa Monica Blvd #325, W Hwd; 310-694-0952 www.stonewallyoungdems.org

Organizations/Resources: Senior Resources

⚲ ★ ♿ Gay Elder Circle, 323-223-7717 **H?** gayeldercircle.net

Organizations/Resources: Social, Recreation, Support

⚲ 100 Gay Men, fb.com/100gaymen

⚲ ★ Gay for Good - Los Angeles, 6444 E Spring St Ste 321, Long Beach, CA 90815 Volunteer organization. gayforgood.org/losangeles/ losangeles@gayforgood.org

⚲ ★ Regiment of the Black & Tans, POB 291157, LA; 90029 310-967-3980 Uniforms fb.com/regiment.bt

⚲ ★ Uptown Gay & Lesbian Alliance, POB 65111, LA; 90065-0111 323-258-8842 www.ugla.org UptownGLA@aol.com

♀ ★ Women on a Roll, POB 4353, Culver City 90231 310-398-1628 womenonaroll.com

Organizations/Resources: Student, Academic, Education

⚲ ★ ♿ Alhambra High School GSA, 101 S 2nd St, Alhambra; 91801 626-308-2342 **H** ⚥

⚲ ★ Citrus College GSA, 1000 W Foothill Blvd, Glendora; 626-914-8603 fb.com/citrusgsa

⚲ ★ El Rancho High School GSA, 6501 Passons Blvd, Pico Rivera; 562-646-7185

⚲ ★ (?⅃) Friends of Project 10 Inc, 115 W California Blvd #116, Pasadena; 91105 **H?** www.project10.org friendofproject10@hotmail.com

♀ ☆ Gamma Rho Lambda Zeta Chapter, Student Activities Center, 220 Westwood Plaza B36, LA fb.com/zeta.uclagrl/

⚲ ★ ♿ Genders & Sexualities Alliance Network, 1145 Wilshire Blvd #100, LA; 213-529-4822 www.gsanetwork.org

⚲ ★ UCLA Anderson GLBA, Box 951481 110 Westwood Plaza Ste F301, LA; 90095-0001 323-739-4522 fb.com/pg/GLBAAlumni/

⚲ ★ ♿ UCLA LGBT Campus Resource Center, 220 Westwood Plz Ste B36, LA; 310-206-3628 **H?** www.lgbt.ucla.edu ⚥

⚲ ★ University of Southern California LGBT Resource Center, STU 202B, 3601 Trousdale Pkwy, LA; 213-740-7619 lgbtrc.usc.edu/

Organizations/Resources: Transgender/Gender Non-Conforming/Diverse

T Center for Transyouth Health and Development, Children's Hospital Los Angeles, 5000 Sunset Blvd Flr 4, LA; 323-361-5372 tinyurl.com/y2wy4n8j ☼

T ☆ Gender Justice LA, 3055 Wilshire Blvd Flr 3, LA; 323-300-8599 www.gjla.org ☼

T ● ♿ Gender Wellness of Los Angeles, 11340 W Olympic Blvd Ste 265, LA; 90064 310-478-0411 www.genwell.org info@genwell.org

T ○ Milrod, Christine, PhD, LMFT, ACS, Southern California Transgender Counseling, 519 N La Cienega Blvd #209, W Hwd 90048-2007 310-281-9658 tinyurl.com/2mys8h info@transgendercounseling.com

Organizations/Resources: Youth (see also Family)

⚲ ★ Camp Lightbulb, POB 845, Hwd; 90078 310-294-4606 Camps for LGBTQ youth www.camplightbulb.org

⚲ ★ LA Youth Center on Highland, 1220 N Highland Ave, LA; 323-860-2280 tinyurl.com/ngt35v6

♂ Reach LA, 1400 E Olympic Blvd #240, LA 213-622-1650 www.reachla.org ❖

♂ Straight But Not Narrow, www.wearesbnn.com

Printing/Mailing & Promotional Items

♂ ● Printing Safari, 9135 Alabama Ave Ste E, Chatsworth; 818-709-3752 www.printingsafari.com

Real Estate (see also Mortgages)

♂ ○ Giardina, John, Realtor, Dilbeck Real Estate. 225 E Colorado Blvd, Pasadena; 213-422-7676 Lic# 01415562 www.johnspasadenahomes.com

♂ ○ Kyle Mathews California Realty, 4348 Van Nuys Blvd 202, Sherman Oaks; 818-470-2435 www.kylemat.com

Recovery

♂ ☆ Alcoholics Anonymous Los Angeles Central Office, 4311 Wilshire Blvd #104, LA; 90010-3714 323-936-434 www.lacoaa.org info@lacoaa.org

⚲ Alcoholics Together Center, 1773 Griffith Park Blvd, LA; 323-663-8882 fb.com/groups/atcenter/

♀ ☆ ♿ Alcoholism Center for Women, 1147 S Alvarado St, LA; 90006-4100 213-381-8500 tinyurl.com/2qtp79 ❖

⚲ Friends Getting Off, 1419 N La Brea Ave, LA 323-463-7001 (methamphetamine) www.friendsgettingoff.org

⚲ ★ Van Ness Recovery House, 1919 N Beachwood Dr, Hwd; 323-463-4266 vannessrecoveryhouse.com

Religious / Spiritual Resources

⚲ ★ ♿ Beth Chayim Chadashim, 6090 W Pico Blvd, LA; 323-931-7023 www.bcc-la.org ✡

♂ ☆ ♿ Christ Chapel of the Valley, 11059 Sherman Way, Sun Valley; 91352 818-985-8977 www.christchapel.com ⚥ pastorjerrell@christchapel.com

♂ ☆ ♿ Congregation Kol Ami, 1200 N LaBrea Ave, W Hwd; 90038-1024 323-606-0996 **H?** www.kol-ami.org ✡⚥ reception@kol-ami.org

♂ ☆ ♿ Congregational Church UCC, 2560 Huntington Dr, San Marino; 91108 626-292-2080 **HD** www.sanmarinoucc.org ⚥

⚲ ★ ♿ Dignity Los Angeles, POB 3886, S Pasadena; 91031 323-344-8064 www.dignitylosangeles.org

⚲ ★ Dignity San Fernando Valley, POB 2715, N Hills; 91343-2715 818-623-7234 www.dignitysfv.org dignitysfv@gmail.com

⚲ ★ ♿ Founders MCC, 4607 Prospect Ave, LA; 90027 323-669-3434 foundersmcc.org info@mccla.org

⚥ ★ Gay & Lesbian Vaishnava Association, www.galva108.org ✧

⚥ ★ &&. MCC United Church of Christ in the Valley, 5730 Cahuenga Blvd, N Hwd; 91601-2105 818-762-1133 mccuccinthevalley.com info@mccuccinthevalley.com

♂ ☆ &&. St Matthew's Lutheran Church, 1920 W Glenoaks Blvd, Glendale; 91201 818-842-3138 www.matthewchurch.com stmatthewspastor@hotmail.com

♂ ☆ &&. St Paul's Lutheran Church, 958 Lincoln Blvd, Santa Monica; 90403-2807 310-451-1346 **HD** www.stpaulssm.org ✗ parish@stpaulsantamonica.org

♂ ☆ Unity of the Westside, 10724 Barman Ave, Culver City; 90230 310-838-4761 unityofthewestside.org office@unityofthe westside.org

♂ ☆ West Hollywood United Church of Christ, 7350 W Sunset Blvd, LA; 90046 323-874-6646. www.wehoucc.org

Sports & Outdoor

⚥ ★ Arriba Ski & Snowboard Club, POB 69611, W Hwd; 90069-0611 www.arribaski.org

⚥ ★ &&. Barnacle Busters Scuba Club, POB 2231, LA; 91393 310-493-9296 www.barnaclebusters.org gaydivers@sbcglobal.net

⚥ Big Gay Frisbee, www.bgfultimate.com

⚥ ★ Cheer LA, 1223 Wilshire Blvd #1580, Santa Monica; www.cheerla.org

⚥ ★ Different Spokes Bicycling Club of Southern California, 4246 Holly Knoll Dr, LA; 323-641-3433 www.differentspokes.com

♂ ★ &&. Funseekers Invitational Bowling League, 818-769-7600 tinyurl.com/au8mtzm

⚥ ★ (♁) Gay & Lesbian Sierrans/Los Angeles, POB 1300z, S Pasadena; 91031 **H?** tinyurl.com/powm5gl

⚥ ★ Great Outdoors - Los Angeles, www.greatoutdoorsla.org

⚥ ★ Greater Los Angeles Softball Association, 1049 Havenhurst Dr Ste 321, LA; www.glasasoftball.org

⚥ ★ LA Flag Football, 458 N Doheny Dr #69544, W Hwd; www.laflagfootball.com

⚥ ★ LA Frontrunners, 2646 Lake View Ave, LA 90039 www.lafrontrunners.com lafrontrunners@gmail.com

⚥ ★ Lambda Basketball League (Los Angeles Gay Basketball), www.lambdabasketball.com

⚥ ★ Los Angeles Blades, 310-571-5423 (ice hockey) www.bladeshockey.com

⚥ ★ Los Angeles Pool League, POB 2227, LA 90078 323-440-6476 www.lapl8ball.org

♂ ☆ Los Angeles Rebellion Rugby Football Club, www.larebellion.org

⚥ ★ (♁) Los Angeles Tennis Association, POB 481226, LA; 90048 www.lataweb.com

⚥ ★ Oedipus Motorcycle Club, POB 65993, LA 90065 www.omcla.org

⚥ Rainbow Skate,

⚥ ★ SAGA Ski & Snowboard Club, POB 931207, LA; 90093 www.sagala.org

⚥ ★ Satyrs Motorcycle Club, POB 1137, LA; 90078 815-439-1720 www.satyrsmc.org

⚥ ★ Southern California Wrestling Club, 1080 S La Cienega Blvd, LA; 90035 818-679-3608 socalwrestlingclub.com

⚥ ★ Studio City Bowling League, 12655 Ventura Blvd, Studio City; 91604 818-769-7600 tinyurl.com/7clf4e9

⚥ ★ Tavern Guild Invitational Bowling League, tavernguild.us

⚥ WeHo Dodgeball, 323-638-4225 www.wehododgeball.com

⚥ West Hollywood Aquatics, POB 691651, W Hwd; 90069 310-288-6555 www.wh2o.org

⚥ West Hollywood Soccer Club, 650-773-1769 www.wehosc.org
» Mammoth Lakes: see Gold Country/Sierra

Marin County Area

Community Centers and/or Pride Organizations

♂ ★ &&. The Spahr Center, 150 Nellen Ave Ste 100, Corte Madera; 94925 415-457-2487 fax 415-457-5687 www.thespahrcenter.org ✗ info@thespahrcenter.org

Bars, Cafes, Clubs, Restaurants
Larkspur

♂ O Equator Coffees, 240 Magnolia Ave, Larkspur 415-720-5701 www.equatorcoffees.com ☞ info@equatorcoffees.com

Mill Valley

♂ O Equator Coffees, 2 Miller Ave, Mill Valley 415-383-1651 www.equatorcoffees.com ☞

♂ O Equator Coffees, Proof Lab, 244 Shoreline Highway, Mill Valley; 415-209-3733 www.equatorcoffees.com ☞ info@equatorcoffees.com

Bookstores

♂ Book Passage & Cafe, 51 Tamal Vista Blvd, Corte Madera; 415-927-0960 www.bookpassage.com ☞

♂ O First Street Books, 850 College Ave, Kentfield 415-456-8770

Counseling/Psychotherapy/Mental Health

♂ O (♁) Tunis, Lawrence, Ed.D, LMFT, 130 Greenfield Ave Ste A, San Anselmo; / 744 Empire St Ste 260, Fairfield 415-847-3677 CA License MFC 47576 Specialist in transgender issues. www.larrytunis.com @ixx=

Organizations/Resources: Social, Recreation, Support

⚥ ★ Out in Suburbia: Gays Living in Marin, fb.com/outinsuburbia

Religious / Spiritual Resources

♂ ☆ &. Community Congregational Church of Belvedere-Tiburon, 145 Rock Hill Dr, Tiburon; 94920 415-435-9108 **HD** www.ccctiburon.org ✗

♂ ☆ Unity in Marin, 600 Palm Dr, Novato; 94949 415-475-5000 unityinmarin.org admin@unityinmarin.org

Mendocino Area

Accommodation: Hotels, Inns, Guesthouses, B&B, Resorts
Mendocino

♀ • (?&) Glendeven Inn, POB 914, Mendocino; 95460 707-937-0083 www.glendeven.com ✗ ⊗

Ukiah

♀ • && Orr Hot Springs Resort, 13201 Orr Springs Rd, Ukiah; 95482 707-462-6277 **H?** www.orrhotsprings.org ⊗ orrreservations@gmail.com

Accommodation Rental: Furnished / Vacation (& AirBNB)
Mendocino

♀ • Sallie & Eileen's Place, POB 409, Mendocino; 95460 707-937-2028 www.seplace.com ❖ ✗ ⊗

AIDS/HIV Services, Education & Support

♀ ☆ (?&) Mendocino County AIDS/Viral Hepatitis Network, POB 1350, Ukiah; 95482 707-462-1932 **H?** www.mcavhn.org ✗

Bars, Cafes, Clubs, Restaurants
Elk

♀ • Queenies Roadhouse Cafe, 6061 S Hwy 1, Elk 707-877-3285 queeniesroadhousecafe.com ⟲

Mendocino

♀ ○ && Cafe Beaujolais, 961 Ukiah St 707-937-5614 www.cafe-beaujolais.com ⟲ ✗

Organizations/Resources: Family and Supporters

♀ ☆ PFLAG Ukiah, POB 449, Philo; 9546S 707-367-8094 www.ukiahpflag.org

Real Estate (see also Mortgages)

♀ • && Priceman, Ann Beth, A.B., Realtor, Garden Ranch Real Estate, 124 E Pine St, Fort Bragg 707-357-1801 **HS** www.ab-sea.com ✗ absea@comcast.net

Merced

Crisis, Anti-violence, & Helplines

♀ ☆ Valley Crisis Center, 1960 P St; 95340 800-799-7233 209-722-4357 www.valleycrisiscenter.org info@alliance4you.org

Organizations/Resources: Social, Recreation, Support

♂ ★ Merced LGBTQ+ Alliance, POB 2104; 95344 209-383-2520 www.mercedlgbtqalliance.org
>> *Middletown: see Napa Valley Area*

Modesto

Community Centers and/or Pride Organizations

♂ Central Valley Pride Center, 400 12th St #2 209-284-0999 centralvalleypridecenter.org

Bars, Cafes, Clubs, Restaurants

♂ • && Brave Bull, 701 S 9th St 209-529-6712 fb.com/TheBrave-Bull **DK** ⬛

♀ ○ (?&) Minnie's Restaurant & Bar, 107 McHenry Ave; 209-524-4621 www.minniesmodesto.com ⏛ ✗ ✗

♀ • Tiki Cocktail Lounge, 932 McHenry Ave 209-577-9969 fb.com/TikiModesto/

Organizations/Resources: Student, Academic, Education

♂ ☆ Central Valley High School GSA, POB 307, Ceres; 95307 209-556-1900 tinyurl.com/c5kh4tx

Organizations/Resources: Youth (see also Family)

♂ • (?&) The PLACE, College Avenue UCC, 1341 College Ave; 209-602-1778 tinyurl.com/y2v53xyr

♂ The Place Youth Group, College Avenue Congregational UCC, 1341 College Ave; 209-522-7244 tinyurl.com/bhar7le
>> *Monte Rio: see Russian River/Sonoma*
>> *Morro Bay: see Central Coast*
>> *Mountain View: see San Jose & South Bay Area*

Napa Valley Area

Accommodation: Hotels, Inns, Guesthouses, B&B, Resorts
Calistoga

♂ ○ (?&) Brannan Cottage Inn, 109 Wappo Ave, Calistoga; 94515 707-942-4200 **H?** www.brannancottageinn.com ✗ ⊗ ⊗ info@ brannancottageinn.com

♂ • Chateau de Vie, 3250 Highway 128, Calistoga 877-558-2513 www.cdvnapavalley.com ❖ ✗

♂ • Meadowlark Country House, 601 Petrified Forest Rd, Calistoga; 707-942-5651 www.meadowlarkinn.com (❖?) ⊗

Middletown

♂ ○ (?&) Backyard Garden Oasis B&B Inn, 24019 Hilderbrand Dr 707-987-0505 www.backyardgardenoasis.com (❖?) ✗ ⊗ greta@ backyardgardenoasis.com

Napa

♂ • && The Inn on First, 1938 1st St, Napa; 707-253-1331 www.theinnonfirst.com (❖?) ✗ ⊗ ⊗

Organizations/Resources: Family and Supporters

♂ ☆ (?&) PFLAG Napa, POB 2661, Napa 94558 707-681-1477 www.pflagnapa.org

Religious / Spiritual Resources

♂ ☆ && First United Methodist Church, 625 Randolph St, Napa; 94559 707-253-1411 **H** napamethodist.org ✗ info@ napamethodist.org
>> *Nevada City: see Gold Country/Sierra*
>> *North Hollywood: see Los Angeles Area*
>> *Oakland: see East Bay Area*
>> *Oceanside: see San Diego Area*

Orange County

Community Centers and/or Pride Organizations

♂ ★ && The LGBT Center OC, 1605 N Spurgeon St, Santa Ana; 714-953-5428 **H?** www.lgbtcenteroc.org ✗

♂ OC Pride, 300 S Harbor Blvd #804, Anaheim 714-869-7392 www.prideoc.com

AIDS/HIV Services, Education & Support

⚥ Asian Pacific AIDS Intervention Team/Turntable, 12900 Garden Grove Blvd #220, Gdn Grv; 714-636-1349 www.apaitonline.org ⟨⟩

⚥ ☆ Radiant Health Centers, 17982-J Sky Park Circle, Irvine; 949-809-5700 radianthealthcenters.org

⚥ ☆ Shanti Orange County, 23461 S Pointe Dr #100, Laguna Hills; 949-452-0888 www.shantioc.org

Art & Craft Galleries/Services, Supplies

⚥ ○ The Vintage Poster, 1492 S Coast Hwy, Laguna Bch; 92651 949-376-7422 www.thevintageposter.com info@thevintageposter.com

Bars, Cafes, Clubs, Restaurants

Anaheim

⚥ ○ Bravo Night Club, 1490 S Anaheim Blvd, Anaheim 714-533-2291 tinyurl.com/j4srxho **D** ⚥ ✕ 🖭 ✦

Costa Mesa

⚦ Tin Lizzie Saloon, 752 St Clair St, Costa Mesa; 714-966-2029 tinlizziesaloon.com

Garden Grove

⚦ ● Frat House, 8112 Garden Grove Blvd, Gdn Grv; 714-373-3728 fb.com/frathouseoc/ **D** 🖭 ✦ ↗

Laguna Beach

⚥ ○ Dizz's As Is, 2794 S Pacific Coast Hwy, Laguna Bch; 949-494-5250 dizzsasis.com ⚥ ✕

⚦ (👥) Main Street Bar & Cabaret, 1460 S Coast Hwy, Laguna Bch; 949-494-0056 www.mainstreet-bar.com **D** 🖭

Santa Ana

⚦ ● 👥 Velvet Lounge, 416 W 4th St, Santa Ana; 714-664-0663 www.velvetoc.com **DKV** ⚥ ✕ 🖭

Bookstores

⚥ ○ 👥 Laguna Beach Books, 1200 S Coast Highway Ste 105, Laguna Bch; 949-494-4779 www.lagunabeachbooks.com

Counseling/Psychotherapy/Mental Health

⚥ ● 👥 Thrasher, Bob, Gay & Lesbian Counseling Services, 610 Pacific Coast Hwy #201, Seal Bch; 90740-6650 562-477-1624 btmfct@aol.com

Funding: Endowment, Fundraising

⚥ ☆ Orange County AIDS Walk, 949-809-5700 www.aidswalk.org/oc/

⚦ ★ Orange County Imperial Court, POB 11332, Westminster; 92685 949-542-6202 tinyurl.com/yyk24kh5

Legal Services

⚥ ○ ♿ Dunbar & Dunbar, 1300 Bristol St N Ste 100, Newport Bch; 92660 949-502-4646 www.DunbarFamilyLaw.com

⚥ ○ McKenzie Legal & Financial, 2631 Copa De Oro Dr, Los Alamitos; 562-594-4200 www.thomasmckenzielaw.com

Organizations/Resources: Cultural, Dance, Performance

⚦ ★ ♿ Golden State Squares, POB 10926, Santa Ana; 92711 www.iagsdc.com/goldenstate/

⚥ ★ 👥 MenAlive, the Orange County Gay Men's Chorus, POB 10754, Santa Ana; 92711 866-636-2548 www.ocgmc.org

Organizations/Resources: Family and Supporters

⚥ ☆ Our Small World Foster Family Agency, 295 N Rampart St Ste A, Orange; 714-704-4545 www.oswffa.org

⚥ ☆ 👥 PFLAG South Orange County/Laguna Hills, POB 2048, Laguna Hills; 92654 949-677-7840 tinyurl.com/lqweonj

⚥ ☆ PFLAG/Orange County, POB 1554, Orange; 92856 714-997-8047 www.lbpflag.org

Organizations/Resources: Naturist/Nudist

⚦ ★ (👥) BA-MEN: Beach Area Men Enjoying Naturism, 714-643-2263 BA-MEN.Org **N**

Organizations/Resources: Political/Legislative/Advocacy

⚦ ★ Orange County Equality Coalition, 5405 Alton Parkway #A250, Irvine; 714-248-6530 www.ocequality.org

Organizations/Resources: Sexual Focus / Safe Sex

⚦ ★ LA/OC Jacks, POB 506, Garden Grove 92842-0506 714-750-0302 www.laocjacks.org ↗ scoutca@hotmail.com

Organizations/Resources: Social, Recreation, Support

⚦ ★ Gay for Good - Orange County / Long Beach, Volunteer organization. gayforgood.org/oclb/

⚦ ★ Laguna Outreach, 3317 S Ross St, Santa Ana 92707 714-313-2069 tinyurl.com/nxz6ezt Cap3317@aol.com

Organizations/Resources: Student, Academic, Education

⚦ ★ (👥) UC Irvine LGBT Resource Center, G301 Student Center, Irvine; 949-824-3277 www.lgbtrc.uci.edu

Organizations/Resources: Transgender/Gender Non-Conforming/Diverse

T ● Cherry, Roxanne, PhD, MFT, 30101 Town Center Dr Ste 210, Laguna Niguel; 949-228-2844 tinyurl.com/nkxhrag ↗

T ☆ Orange County Female to Male (OCFTM), The LGBT Center OC, 1605 N Spurgeon St, Santa Ana; 714-531-2731 www.ocftm.com

Organizations/Resources: Youth (see also Family)

⚥ Christopher Wahl Center, 12401 Slauson Ave Unit G, Whittier; 562-693-2247 www.wrhap.org

Recovery

⚥ ☆ AA: Orange Country Central office, 1526 Brookhollow Dr Ste 75, Santa Ana; 92705-5466 714-556-4555 www.oc-aa.org

⚥ ☆ Alcoholics Anonymous South Orange County Central Office, 30011 Ivy Glenn Drive Ste 104, Laguna Niguel; 92677 949-582-2697 www.oc-aa.org socsoaa@sbcglobal.net

Religious / Spiritual Resources

⚥ ☆ 👥 Community Congregational UCC, 4111 Katella Ave, Los Alamitos; 90720-3406 714-527-2343 **HD** www.ccucclosal.org ↗ office@ccucclosal.org

California: Orange County
Religious

100

GAYELLOW PAGES #42 2020-2021

Palm Springs Area : California
Bars, Cafes, Clubs, Restaurants

♂ ☆ Fairview Community Church, 2525 Fairview Rd, Costa Mesa; 92626 714-545-4610 www.ocfairviewchurch.org office@ocfairviewchurch.org

♥ Good Samaritan MCC, 11931 Washington Blvd, Whittier; 562-696-6213 tinyurl.com/y3y2lqgk

♂ ☆ Irvine United Congregational Church, 4915 Alton Parkway, Irvine; 92604 949-733-0220 www.iucc.org iucc@iucc.org

♥ ★ && Resurrection Beach MCC, 3303 Harbor Blvd #A-104, Costa Mesa; 92626 714-662-6972 rbmcc.org ✐ info@rbmcc.org

♂ ☆ St Anselm of Canterbury Episcopal Church, 13091 Galway St, Gdn Grv; 92843 714-537-0604 saintanselmgg.org saintanselmgg@gmail.com

Sports & Outdoor

♥ ★ Friday Night Trios, 714-794-8273 www.fridaynighttriosoc.com

♥ ★ Great Outdoors/Orange County—Long Beach, greatoutdoors.org/oclb/

Travel & Tourist Services (see also Accommodation)

♥ ● Cruising With Pride Cruises & Tours, 2677 N Main St Ste 550, Santa Ana; 92705 714-321-0700 www.cruisingwithpride.com tom@cruisingwithpride.com

Oroville

Bars, Cafes, Clubs, Restaurants
Oroville

♂ ○ Mug Shots Coffehouse, 2040 Montgomery St, Oroville; 530-538-8342 fb.com/MugShotsOroville/ ⊘ ✐

» Pacific Palisades: see Los Angeles Area
» Palm Desert: see Palm Springs Area

Palm Springs Area

Community Centers and/or Pride Organizations

♥ ★ Greater Palm Springs Pride, Inc., 760-416-8711 www.pspride.org

♥ ★ & The LGBT Community Center of the Desert, 1301 N Palm Canyon Dr 3rd Flr, Palm Sp; 760-416-7790 www.thecenterps.org ✐

Information, Media & Publications

♥ ● Desert Daily Guide, 888-743-3349 fax 760-913-3340 www.desertdailyguide.com

Accommodation: Hotels, Inns, Guesthouses, B&B, Resorts
Cathedral City

♂ ● && CCBC Resort Hotel, 68300 Gay Resort Dr, Cath Cy; 760-324-1350 **H?** www.ccbcresorthotel.com **N** (❀?) ✐ ⑤

Desert Hot Springs

♂ ● El Morocco Inn & Spa, 66810 4th St, Desert Hot Springs; 92240 888-288-9905 760-288-2527 www.elmoroccoinn.com ✐ ⑤ info@elmoroccoinn.com

Morongo Valley

♂ ● (?&) la Maison des Fleurs B&B, 49569 Maccele Rd, Morongo Valley; 92256 760-320-8028 lmdf.us ✐ ⑤

Palm Springs

♂ ● && Ace Hotel & Swim Club, 701 E Palm Canyon Dr, Palm Sp; 92264 760-325-9900 www.acehotel.com/palmsprings ❀ ✐ ⑤ enquire.psp@acehotel.com

♂ ● & All Worlds Resort, 535 Warm Sands Dr, Palm Sp; 760-323-7505 allworlds.com

♂ ● && Bearfoot Inn, 888 N Indian Canyon Dr, Palm Sp; 760-699-7641 **H?** www.bearfootinn.com ❀ ✐ ⑤

♂ ● Caliente Tropics Resort, 411 E Palm Canyon Dr, Palm Sp; 888-277-0999 www.calientetropics.com

♂ ● (?&) Canyon Club Hotel, 960 N Palm Canyon Dr, Palm Sp; 760-778-8042 www.canyonclubhotel.com **N** ❀ ✐

♂ ● (?&) Desert Paradise Resort Hotel, 615 S Warm Sands Drive, Palm Sp; 800-342-7635 desertparadise.com **N** (❀?) ✐ ⑤

♂ ● East Canyon Hotel & Spa, 288 E Camino Monte Vista, Palm Sp; 760-320-1928 www.eastcanyonps.com ✐ ⑤

♂ ● (?&) El Mirasol Villas, 525 Warm Sands Dr, Palm Sp; 800-327-2985 www.elmirasol.com ✐ ⑤

♂ ● (?&) The Hacienda at Warm Sands, 586 Warm Sands Dr, Palm Sp; 800-359-2007 thehacienda.com **N** ⑤

♂ ● INNdulge, 601 Grenfall Rd, Palm Sp 760-327-1408 www.inndulge.com **N**

♂ ● La Dolce Vita, 1491 Via Soledad, Palm Sp 769-325-2686 www.ladolcevitaresort.com **N** ✐

♂ ● Santiago Resort, 650 San Lorenzo Rd, Palm Sp 760-322-1300 www.santiagoresort.com **N** ✐ ♥

♂ ● & Tortuga del Sol, 715 E San Lorenzo Rd, Palm Sp; 760-416-3111 tortugadelsol.com **N** ⑤

♂ ● Triangle Inn Palm Springs, 555 San Lorenzo Rd, Palm Sp; 760-322-7993 www.triangle-inn.com

♂ ● (?&) Vista Grande Resort, 574 Warm Sands Dr, Palm Sp; 800-669-1069 vistagranderesort.com **N** (❀?) ✐

Accommodation Rental: Furnished / Vacation (& AirBNB)
Cathedral City

♥ ● & Villa Mykonos, 67-590 Jones Rd, Cath Cy; 760-321-2898 www.villamykonos.com ✐ (⑤)

Palm Springs

♂ ● & Green Oasis, 2997 E Alta Loma Dr, Palm Sp; 323-655-1069 www.vrbo.com/137550 ✐ ⑤ ⑤

AIDS/HIV Services, Education & Support

♀ ☆ AIDS Assistance Program - Food Samaritans, 1276 N Palm Canyon Dr Ste 108, Palm Sp; 760-325-8481 www.aidsassistance.org

♂ ☆ Desert AIDS Project, 1695 N Sunrise Way, Palm Sp; 760-323-2118 www.desertaidsproject.org

Bars, Cafes, Clubs, Restaurants
Cathedral City

♂ ● && The Barracks, 67625 E Palm Canyon Dr, Cath Cy; 760-321-9688 www.thebarracksbarps.com

♥ The Roost Lounge, 68718 E Palm Canyon Dr #203, Cath Cy; 760-507-8495 www.theroostcc.com

♂ ○ && Runway at CCBC, 68300 Gay Resort Dr, Cath Cy; 760-537-7800 **H?** www.runwayccbc.com ♈ ✖ ▥ ✐ info@runwayccbc.com

California: Palm Springs Area
Bars, Cafes, Clubs, Restaurants

101
GAYELLOW PAGES #42 2020-2021

Palm Springs Area: California
Organizations: Social & Support

♀ • Studio One 11, 67555 E Palm Canyon Dr Ste A103, Cath Cy; 760-328-2900 studio111bar.com **D** ✗ info@studio111bar.com

♂ • ⚲⚲ Trunks Bar, 36737 Cathedral Canyon Dr, Cath Cy; 760-321-0031 **H?** trunkscatcity.com **DKLCWV** ✗ ♈ ▦ ✗

Palm Springs

♀ ⚲⚲ The Alibi Palm Springs, 369 N Palm Canyon Dr, Palm Sp; 760-656-1525 www.thealibipalmsprings.com ♈ ✗

♀ Blackbook, 315 E Arenas Rd, Palm Sp 760-832-8497 blackbookbar.com ♈ ✗

♀ Chill Bar, 217 E Arenas Rd, Palm Sp 760-327-1079 chillbarpalmsprings.com

♀ ○ Copley's, 621 N Palm Canyon Dr, Palm Sp 760-327-9555 www.copleyspalmsprings.com ♈ ✗

♂ • Eagle 501 Bar, 301 E Arenas Rd, Palm Sp 760-327-0753 www.eagle501bar.com

♂ • ⚲⚲ Hunters Palm Springs, 302 E Arenas Rd, Palm Sp; 760-323-0700 hunterspalmsprings.com **DVK** ✗

♀ ○ Jake's, 664 N Palm Canyon Dr, Palm Sp; / check summer schedule 760-327-4400 www.jakespalmsprings.com ✗

♂ • Quadz, 200 S Indian Canyon, Palm Sp 760-778-4326 fb.com/QUADZPalmSpringsCA/ **KV** ▦

♀ RetroRoom Lounge, 125 E Tahquitz Canyon Way #102, Palm Sp; 760-656-8680 www.retroroomlounge.com **K** ▦

♀ Stacy's Palm Springs, 220 E Arenas Rd, Palm Sp; 760-620-5003 stacysbarps.com ▦

♂ • ⚲⚲ Streetbar, 224 E Arenas Rd, Palm Sp; 760-320-1266 www.psstreetbar.com **KV** ▦ ✗

♂ • ⚲⚲ Tool Shed, 600 E Sunny Dunes Rd, Palm Sp; 760-320-3299 www.pstoolshed.com **L** ▦

♀ Toucan's Tiki Lounge, 2100 N Palm Canyon Way; Palm Sp; 760-416-7584 toucanstikilounge.com **D** ▦

♀ ○ Wang's in the Desert, 424 S Indian Canyon, Palm Sp; 760-325-9264 www.wangsinthedesert.com ✗

Rancho Mirage

♀ ○ ⚲⚲ Shame On The Moon, 69950 Frank Sinatra Dr, Rancho Mirage; 760-324-5515 www.shameonthemoon.com ✗

Funding: Endowment, Fundraising

♂ Palm Springs Sisters of Perpetual Indulgence, POB 5192, Palm Sp; 92263 www.pssisters.org

Gifts, Cards, Pride, etc.

♀ • Q Trading Co, 606 E Sunny Dunes, Palm Sp 92264-8192 760-416-7150

Health Clubs, Fitness, Gyms

♀ • ⚲⚲ WorkOUT Gym, 2100 N Palm Canyon Dr Ste C100, Palm Sp; 92262 760-325-4600 www.WorkOUTGymPS.com ✗ info@WorkOUTGymPS.com

Jewelry (see also Gifts)

♀ ○ Hephaestus, 132 La Plaza, Palm Sp; 92262 760-325-5395 fb.com/Hephaestusjewelry/ ♥

Leather Resources & Groups

♀ • ⚲⚲ Off Ramp Leathers, 650 E Sunny Dunes Rd Unit 3, Palm Sp; 760-778-2798 www.offrampleathers.com

♂ ★ ⚲⚲ Palm Springs Leather Order of the Desert, POB 5506, Palm Sp; 92263 760-272-5553 **H?** www.pslod.org

Legal Services

♀ ○ Baker, Elizabeth, 155 W Hermosa Place, Palm Sp 760-320-3556

♀ • Barrett, Barbara, 555 S Sunrise Way #211, Palm Sp; 92264-7869 760-323-2622 www.barbarabarrettlaw.com bbarrett92262@aol.com

♀ ○ Law Office Dale Gribow, 73061 El Paseo Ste 220, Palm Desert; 92260 760-837-7500 www.dalegribowlaw.com dale@dalegribowlaw.com

♀ ○ Rhea, Joseph T, 777 E Tahquitz Canyon #328, Palm Sp; 92262 760-327-3711 tinyurl.com/vz3dcna jtrlawoffice@gmail.com

Organizations/Resources: Business & Professional Associations, Labor Advocacy

♀ ★ ⚲⚲ Desert Business Association, 611 S Palm Canyon Dr #7556, Palm Sp; 760-904-4589 tinyurl.com/ye2yw3s

♂ ★ Desert Gay Tourism Guild, POB 2881, Palm Sp; 92263 www.palmspringsgayinfo.com

Organizations/Resources: Cultural, Dance, Performance

♂ ★ Boots in Squares, POB 5185, Palm Sp 92263 760-914-4907 www.bootsinsquares.com bootsinsquares@gmail.com

♂ ★ Desert Winds Freedom Band, POB 4732, Palm Sp; 92263 760-776-2700 www.desertwindsfb.org

♂ ★ ⚲⚲ Palm Springs Gay Men's Chorus, PO Box 4082, Palm Sp; 92263 760-219-2077 **H** psgmc.com

Organizations/Resources: Family and Supporters

♀ ☆ ⚲ PFLAG Palm Springs/Desert Communities, POB 4326, Palm Sp; 92263 760-202-4430 www.pspflag.org info@pspflag.org

Organizations/Resources: Political/Legislative/Advocacy

♂ ★ Desert Stonewall Democrats, POB 4536, Palm Sp; 92263-4536 www.desert-stonewall.org info@desert-stonewall.org

Organizations/Resources: Senior Resources

♀ ★ Old Lesbians Organizing for Change (OLOC) - Coachella Valley/Palm Springs, 760-318-6794 www.oloc.org

♂ ★ ⚲ The SAGE of the Desert, LGBT Community Center of the Desert, 1301 N Palm Canyon Dr 3rd Flr, Palm Sp 760-416-7790 www.thecenterps.org ✗

Organizations/Resources: Social, Recreation, Support

♀ ★ (♌) Coachella Valley Couples, Bob & Ken, POB 2073, Rancho Mirage; 92270 **H?** tinyurl.com/ms576rg

♂ Gay for Good - Palm Springs, Volunteer organization. gayforgood.org/palmsprings/

♂ Palm Springs Bears, POB 2213, Palm Sp; 92263 www.palmspringsbears.org

California: Palm Springs Area
Organizations: Social & Support

102

GAYELLOW PAGES #42 2020-2021

Russian River/Sonoma: California
AIDS/HIV Support

⚦ ★ Prime Timers of the Desert, 1111 N Palm Canyon Dr #C, Palm Sp; 760-904-5361 www.ptod-ps.org

Real Estate (see also Mortgages)

♀ ● ♿ Lundgren, Melissa, Realtor, Better Homes and Gardens Real Estate Leaskou Partners, 200 N Sunrise Way Ste B, Palm Sp; 92262 760 668-2544 www.melissalundgren.com ✎ melissa@melissalundgren.com

♀ ○ ♿ Russ, Terry, REALTOR (R), Windermere Real Estate, 296 N Palm Canyon Dr, Palm Sp; 92262 760-808-4184 CalDRE #01797261 www.terry-russ.com terry@terry-russ.com

♂ ○ ♿ **Sterling, Harry, Coldwell Banker Residential Brokerage, 1081 N Palm Canyon Dr, Palm Sp; 92262 760-409-7977 Let me help you buy or sell in Palm Springs www.harrysterling.com mail@harrysterling.com**

Recovery

⚥ ★ ♿ Sober in the Sun, POB 4584, Palm Sp; 92263 760-904-8570 Conference soberinthesun.net ✎

♂ ★ ♿ Sunny Dunes 5th Tradition Group, 4711B E Palm Canyon, Palm Sp; / Gay AA Meeting Room **H?** www.gayaainthedesert.org

Religious / Spiritual Resources

♂ ☆ ♿ Bloom in the Desert Ministries UCC, 400 S El Cielo Rd Ste G, Palm Sp; 92262 / Sun worship 3601 E Mesquite Ave 760-327-3802 **H?** www.bloominthedesert.org ✎ revkev@bloominthedesert.org

♂ ● ♿ MCC of the Coachella Valley, PO Box 2949, Cath Cy; 92235 760-512-1700 www.mcccv.net

Sports & Outdoor

♀ ☆ Fun Handicap Bowling League, 760-333-1705 www.funhandicap.org

⚥ ★ ♿ Gay & Lesbian Softball, www.psgsl.org

⚥ ★ Great Outdoors Palm Springs (GOPS), POB 361, Palm Sp; 92263 760-282-4677 www.greatoutdoors.org/ps/

⚥ ★ Greater Palm Springs Rodeo, POB 3262, Palm Sp; 92263 www.psrodeo.org

⚥ ★ Palm Springs Desert Invitational Bowling Tournament, POB 4847, Palm Sp; 92263 760-459-5450 www.psdic.org

⚥ ★ Palm Springs Front Runners & Walkers, POB 2184, Palm Sp; 92263-2184 562-756-2584 www.psfr.org

⚥ ★ Stonewall Golfers, POB 2891, Palm Sp 92263 760-968-0332 stonewallgolfers.com

Travel & Tourist Services (see also Accommodation)

⚥ ● DavidTravel, 949-427-0199 www.DavidTravel.com

♂ ● The Travel Shop, 67665 Garbino Rd, Cath Cy 92234 760-904-4058 800-285-8835 www.travelshopvacations.com mark@travelshopvacations.com

>> *Palmdale: see Antelope Valley*
>> *Pasadena: see Los Angeles Area*
>> *Petaluma: see Russian River/Sonoma*
>> *Placerville: see Gold Country/Sierra*
>> *Rancho Mirage: see Palm Springs Area*

Redding

Community Centers and/or Pride Organizations

⚥ NorCal OUTreach Project, 2553 Victor Ave Ste A; 530-949-6267 www.norcaloutreach.org

Bars, Cafes, Clubs, Restaurants

⚥ Club 501, 1244 California St; 530-243-7869 fb.com/Club501

Erotica / Adult Stores / Safe Sex Supplies

♂ ○ Secrets Redding, 2131 Hilltop Dr; 96002-0522 530-223-2675 secrets30redding@gmail.com

Religious / Spiritual Resources

♂ ☆ Pilgrim Congregational Church, POB 993183 96001 530-243-3121 www.pilgrimchurchredding.org office@pilgrimchurchredding.org

♂ ☆ ♿ Unity in Redding, 2871 Churn Creek Rd; 96002 530-246-9544 **H?** www.unityinredding.org ✎ christnu@sbcglobal.net

>> *Redlands: see Inland Empire*
>> *Redondo Beach: see Los Angeles Area*
>> *Reseda: see Los Angeles Area*

Richmond

Religious / Spiritual Resources

♂ ☆ ♿ Open Door United Methodist Church, 6226 Arlington Blvd; 94805 510-525-3500 **H?** www.opendoorumc.org ✎ office@opendoorumc.org

>> *Riverside: see Inland Empire*

Russian River/Sonoma

Information, Media & Publications

⚥ ● Gay Sonoma, 21003 Broadway, Sonoma; 95476 707-938-0761 www.gaysonoma.com editor@wtppub.com

Accommodation: Hotels, Inns, Guesthouses, B&B, Resorts
Guerneville

⚥ ● ♿ r3 Hotel, POB 450, Guerneville; 95446 / 16390 4th St 707-869-8399 ther3hotel.com ⚲ ✂ (♣?) ✎ ⊛

♂ ● (?♿) Wildwood Retreat Center, POB 78, Guerneville; 95446 707-632-5200 www.wildwoodretreat.com ✎ ⊛

⚥ ● Woods Resort, 16484 4th St, Guerneville 707-869-0600 www.rrwoods.com **N** ⊛ ⊛

Healdsburg

♂ ○ Haydon Street Inn, 321 Haydon St, Healdsburg 95448 707-433-5228 **H** haydon.com ✎ ⊛ innkeeper@haydon.com

Accommodation Rental: Furnished / Vacation (& AirBNB)
Santa Rosa

♂ ● (?♿) Creek House Vacation Rental, 707-539-2825 tinyurl.com/nomqhej ☘ ✎ ⊛

AIDS/HIV Services, Education & Support

♂ ☆ Face to Face/Sonoma County AIDS Network, 873 2nd St, Santa Rosa; 707-544-1581 www.f2f.org

♀ ☆ ♿ Food for Thought, POB 1608, Forestville; 95436-1608 707-887-1647 www.fftfoodbank.org ✔ rekarp@aol.com

Bars, Cafes, Clubs, Restaurants

Glen Ellen

♀ ○ The Fig Cafe & Wine Bar, 13690 Arnold Dr, Glen Ellen; 707-938-2130 www.thefigcafe.com ⴲ ✕

Graton

♀ ○ ♿ Underwood Bar & Bistro, 9113 Graton Rd 707-823-7023 www.underwoodgraton.com ⴲ ✕ info@underwoodgraton.com

♂ ○ Willow Wood Market Cafe, 9020 Graton Rd, Graton; 707-823-0233 www.willowwoodgraton.com ⊐ info@willowwoodgraton.com

Guerneville

♀ ● ♿ boon eat + drink, 16248 Main St, Guerneville; 707-869-0780 eatatboon.com ✕ ⊐ ✔ info@eatatboon.com

♀ ● ♿ Coffee Bazaar, 14045 Armstrong Woods Rd, Guerneville; 707-869-9706 fb.com/CoffeeBazaar ⊐ ✔

♂ ○ ♿ Garden Grill & BBQ, 17132 Highway 116 707-869-3922 tinyurl.com/yxbxmh6h ✕

♀ ○ ♿ Main Street Bistro & Piano Bar, 16280 Main St, Guerneville; 707-869-0501 www.mainststation.com **D** ✔

♂ ○ Mc T's Bull Pen, 16246 1st St, Guerneville 707-869-3377 www.mctsbullpen.com **DKS** ▥ ✔

♀ ● Rainbow Cattle Co, 16220 Main St, Guerneville; 707-869-0206 www.queersteer.com **D**

Monte Rio

♂ ○ Highland Dell Lodge Restaurant & Cocktail Lounge, 21050 River Blvd, Monte Rio; 707-865-2300 www.highlanddell.com ⴲ ✕

Petaluma

♂ ○ Brixx Pizzeria, 16 Kentucky St, Petaluma 707-766-8162 www.brixxpetaluma.com ⴲ ✕

Sebastopol

♂ ○ Coffee Catz, 6761 Sebastopol Ave, Sebastopol 707-829-6600 www.coffeecatz.net ⊐ ▥ ✔

Erotica / Adult Stores / Safe Sex Supplies

♂ ○ Secrets Santa Rosa, 3301 Santa Rosa Ave, Santa Rosa; 95407-7929 707-542-8248 www.secretsboutiques.com secretssantarosa@gmail.com

Funding: Endowment, Fundraising

♀ ★ Russian River Sisters of Perpetual Indulgence, Inc, POB 771, Guerneville; 95446-0771 www.rrsisters.org info@rrsisters.org

Gifts, Cards, Pride, etc.

♂ ● ♿ Milk & Honey, 123 N Main St, Sebastopol; 95472-3448 707-824-1155 www.milk-and-honey.com ⊐ ✔

Organizations/Resources: Cultural, Dance, Performance

♂ ☆ ♿ Pegasus Theater Company, POB 2814, Guerneville; 95446 707-583-2343 Www.pegasustheater.com

♀ ★ ♿ Redwood Rainbows Square Dance Club, 465 Morris St, Sebastopol; 95472 www.redwoodrainbows.org ✔ contact@redwoodrainbows.org

Organizations/Resources: Family and Supporters

♀ ☆ PFLAG Santa Rosa, 1650 W 3rd St, Santa Rosa 707-481-2476 tinyurl.com/ycxl9l5r

Organizations/Resources: Student, Academic, Education

♀ ★ ♿ Center for Culture, Gender & Sexuality, Sonoma State University, 1801 E Cotati Ave, Rohnert Park 707-664-2845 www.sonoma.edu/diversity/ ✔

Organizations/Resources: Youth (see also Family)

♀ ★ Positive Images, 200 Montgomery Dr Ste C, Santa Rosa; 707-568-5830 www.posimages.org

Recovery

♀ Alcoholics Anonymous Sonoma County Intergroup, 750 Mendocino Ave, Santa Rosa; 707-546-2066 www.sonomacountyaa.org

Religious / Spiritual Resources

♀ ☆ ♿ Christ Church United Methodist, 1717 Yulupa Ave, Santa Rosa; 95405 707-542-2569 **HD** fb.com/srchristchurch office@srchristchurch.org

♀ ★ MCC of the Redwood Empire, POB 1055, Guerneville; 95446 214-205-5038 fb.com/groups/404895749628346

♀ ☆ ♿ Unitarian Universalist Congregation, 547 Mendocino Ave, Santa Rosa; 95401-5241 707-568-5381 www.uusantarosa.org ✔

♀ ☆ ♿ United Church of Cloverdale (UCC), 439 N Cloverdale Blvd, Cloverdale; 95425 707-894-2039 www.uccloverdale.org uccoffice@sbcglobal.net

Sports & Outdoor

♀ ☆ ♿ Resurrection Roller Girls, Cal Skate, 6100 Commerce Blvd, Rohnert Park 707-585-0500 fb.com/rrderby/ ✔

Travel & Tourist Services (see also Accommodation)

♂ ● Sharp Tongued Consulting, 9596 Orion Dr, Windsor; 95492-8822 707-481-7692 tinyurl.com/23f5xf sharptongued@mac.com

Wineries & Vineyards

♀ ● ♿ Family Wineries of Dry Creek, 4791 Dry Creek Rd Bldg 11, Healdsburg; 888-433-6555 tinyurl.com/jz64fda ✔

♀ ○ ♿ Korbel Champagne Cellars & Delicatessen, 13250 River Rd, Guerneville; 95446-9538 707-824-7000 707-824-7313 www.korbel.com ✔ info@korbel.com

Sacramento Valley Area

Crisis, Anti-violence, & Helplines

♀ ☆ ♿ WEAVE, 1900 K St, Sacto 916-920-2952 (crisis) **H?** www.weaveinc.org

Community Centers and/or Pride Organizations

♀ ★ ♿ Sacramento LGBT Community Center, 1927 L St, Sacto; 95811 916-442-0185 www.saccenter.org ✔ info@saccenter.org

♀ ★ Sacramento Pride, 1927 L St, Sacto 916-443-3855 sacramentopride.org

California: Sacramento Valley Area
Accommodation
104
GAYELLOW PAGES #42 2020-2021
Sacramento Valley Area: California
Real Estate

Accommodation: Hotels, Inns, Guesthouses, B&B, Resorts
Sacramento

⚥ ● Amber House Inn of Midtown, 1315 22nd St, Sacto; 916-444-8085 www.amberhouse.com (♣?) ⚥ ⊛

AIDS/HIV Services, Education & Support

⚥ ☆ Golden Rule Services, 4433 Florin Rd #820, Sacto; 916-426-4653 tinyurl.com/y2nkkm9p ❖

⚥ ☆ ᏜᏜ One Community Health, 1500 21st St, Sacto; 95814-5216 916-443-3299 **WC** onecommunityhealth.com ✗ info@onecommunityhealth.com

⚥ ☆ Sunburst Projects, 2143 Hurley Way Ste 240, Sacto; 95825 916-440-0889 www.sunburstprojects.org admin@sunburstprojects.org

Archives/Libraries/Museums/History Projects

♂ ★ ᏜᏜ Lavender Library, Archives & Cultural Exchange of Sacramento, 1414 21st St, Sacto; 916-492-0558 www.lavenderlibrary.com ✗

Bars, Cafes, Clubs, Restaurants
Sacramento

♂ Badlands, 2003 K St, Sacto; 916-448-8790 www.badlandssac.com **D**

♂ ● ᏜᏜ The Bolt, 2560 Boxwood St, Sacto; 916-649-8420 www.sacbolt.com **LCW** ✗

♂ ○ ᏜᏜ The Depot, 2001 K St, Sacto 916-441-6823 fb.com/TheDepotSac/ **V** ▥

♂ ● ᏜᏜ Faces, 2000 K St, Sacto 916-448-7798 **H?** www.faces.net **DKCWV** ▥ ✗

♣ ᏜᏜ The Hush at Depot Video Bar, n/a, Sacto; / check schedule 916-441-6823 fb.com/HushLadiesNight **V**

♂ Mercantile Saloon, 1928 L St, Sacto 916-447-0792 fb.com/themercantilesaloon/ ✘

♂ Sidetrax, 2007 K St, Sacto; 916-441-6823 www.sidetraxsac.com **D**

Computer & Software Sales & Services

⚥ ● Fast Break Tech, Inc., 1111 Exposition Blvd Building 100, Sacto; 95815 916-247-2500 www.fastbreaktech.com service@fastbreaktech.com

Counseling/Psychotherapy/Mental Health

⚥ ● ᏜᏜ Arguello, Tyler, PhD, DCSW, LCSW, 4825 J St Ste 100, Sacto; 95816 916-572-7448 **H?** www.drtylerarguello.com drtylerarguello@gmail.com

Erotica / Adult Stores / Safe Sex Supplies

⚥ ○ Goldie's Boutique, 201 N 12th St, Sacto 95814-0616 916-447-5860 www.secretsboutiques.com goldiessacramento@gmail.com

Funding: Endowment, Fundraising

⚥ Capital City AIDS Fund, POB 160636, Sacto 95816 916-448-1110 www.capcityaidsfund.org

♂ ★ Court of the Great Northwest Imperial Empire, POB 161441, Sacto; 95816 www.cgnie.org

Legal Services

⚥ ● The Harned Law Firm, Pete Harned, 900 G St Ste 300, Sacto; 95814-1810 916-441-7383 www.harnedlaw.com

⚥ ● ᏜᏜ Pearce, M Jane, 455 University Ave Ste 370, Sacto; 916-452-3883

Organizations/Resources: Business & Professional Associations, Labor Advocacy

♂ ★ Sacramento Rainbow Chamber of Commerce, PO Box 160126, Sacto; 95816 916-266-9630 www.rainbowchamber.com

Organizations/Resources: Cultural, Dance, Performance

♂ ★ (?Ꮬ) Bent - Sacramento LGBTQ Film Festival, 1017 L St Ste 379, Sacto; 95814 844-474-4553 **H?** bentfilmfest.org

♂ ★ ᏜᏜ Capital City Squares, POB 19986, Sacto; 95819-0986 530-601-6057 www.capitalcitysquares.org **D** capcitysquares@gmail.com

♂ ★ Sacramento Gay Men's Chorus, 2700 L St Ste B, Sacto; 877-283-1567 www.sacgaymenschorus.org

♀ ☆ Ꮬ Sacramento Women's Chorus, PO Box 661705, Sacto; 95866 tinyurl.com/ny93bo

Organizations/Resources: Family and Supporters

⚥ ☆ ᏜᏜ PFLAG Sacramento, POB 661855, Sacto; 95866 916-978-0410 www.pflagsacramento.org

Organizations/Resources: Political/Legislative/Advocacy

♂ ★ Stonewall Democratic Club, POB 161623, Sacto; 95816 www.sacstonewall.org

Organizations/Resources: Social, Recreation, Support

♂ California Men's Gatherings (Sacramento), 5353 Terrace Oak Circle, Fair Oaks; 877-984-3264 x4 www.thecmg.org

♂ ★ Sacramento Valley Bears, POB 13396, Sacto 95813-3396 www.sacbears.org sacsvb@gmail.com

♂ ★ Tri-County Diversity, POB 3702, Yuba City; 95992 530-763-2116 www.tricountydiversity.org

Organizations/Resources: Student, Academic, Education

♂ ★ The CSUS Queer Union, 6000 J St, Sacto fb.com/SacStateQU/

♂ ★ ᏜᏜ Sacramento State PRIDE center, University Union 1st Flr, 6000 J St, Sacto; 916-278-8720 www.csus.edu/pride/

♀ ☆ Women's Resource Center CSU, University Union, 6000 J St, Sacto; 916-278-7388 www.csus.edu/wrc/

Organizations/Resources: Transgender/Gender Non-Conforming/Diverse

T ☆ The Gender Health Center, 2020 29th St Ste 201, Sacto; 916-455-2391 tinyurl.com/23tujhj

♀ ☆ River City Gems, POB 601203, Sacto; 95860 Trans women social group rivercitygems.org info@rivercitygems.org

Real Estate (see also Mortgages)

⚥ ○ Ꮬ Merrill, Randy, Lyon Real Estate, 3360 Coach Ln, Cameron Park; 95682 530-748-5215 530-672-4519 www.RandySells.us rmerrill@golyon.com

Recovery

♂ ☆ ふふ Central California Fellowship of Alcoholics Anonymous, 9960 Business Park Dr #110, Sacto; 916-454-1100 www.aasacramento.org

Religious / Spiritual Resources

♀ ★ Integrity/Northern California, c/o Trinity Cathedral, 2620 Capitol Ave, Sacto; 916-203-5595 trinitycathedral.org

♂ ☆ Spiritual Life Center, 2201 Park Towne Circle, Sacto; 95825 916-448-6508 www.slcworld.org info@slcworld.org

♂ ☆ Trinity Episcopal Cathedral, 2620 Capitol Ave, Sacto; 95816-5991 916-446-2513 trinitycathedral.org trinity@trinitycathedral.org

Sports & Outdoor

♀ ★ Capital City Volleyball League, www.sacvball.com

♀ ★ Capital Crossroads Gay Rodeo Association, PO Box 189305, Sacto; 95818 www.capitalcrossroads.org

♀ ★ Cheer Sacramento, www.cheersacramento.org

♀ ★ FrontRunners Sacramento, POB 22142, Sacto; 95822 fb.com/groups/54997302579/

♀ ★ Gay & Lesbian Sierrans, MotherLode Chapter, POB 160511, Sacto; 95816-0511 tinyurl.com/rzcqqkd

♀ ★ ふふ River City Bowlers, 23 Chief Ct, Sacto; 95823 916-524-4135 **H?** www.rivercitybowlers.com ✓ lezbowl@gmail.com

♀ ★ River City Bowlers, 12771 Casity Lane, Galt; 95632 209-745-1880 Tommy5647@aol.com

♀ ★ Sacramento Valley Pink Pistols, tinyurl.com/p4qur2c

♀ ★ Sisters of Scota Womens Motorcycle Club, 530-635-7797 www.sistersofscotawmc.org soswmc@gmail.com

♀ ★ Team Sacramento, 12771 Casity Lane, Galt 95632 209-745-1880 Tommy5647@aol.com

♀ ★ Valley Knights Motorcycle Club, POB 161636, Sacto; 95816 groups.yahoo.com/group/VKMC/

Travel & Tourist Services (see also Accommodation)

♂ ○ Expo Travel, 4253 Hartlepool Way, Antelope 95843-5101 916-721-1300 www.worldexpotravel.com uwt@worldexpotravel.com

♂ ● Sports Leisure Vacations, 9812 Old Winery Place Ste 1, Sacto; 95827 916-361-2051 800-951-5556 www.sportsleisure.com mark@sportsleisure.com

Websites: Design & Maintenance Services (see also Internet)

♂ ● Mongoose on the Loose Web Design, 916-594-9100 fax 916-933-8516 www.mongooseontheloose.com

» San Andreas: see Gold Country/Sierra

San Diego Area

Crisis, Anti-violence, & Helplines

♂ Center for Community Solutions, 4508 Mission Bay Dr, San Diego; 888-385-4657 www.ccssd.org

♂ Interfaith Shelter Network of San Diego, LGBT Hillcrest Location, 3530 Camino del Rio N Ste 301, San Diego; 619-702-5399 interfaithshelter.org

BED & BREAKFAST
3761 Riviera Dr., San Diego, CA 92109
858-272-6131 beachhutbb@gmail.com
www.beachhutbb.com

♀ ★ ふふ Relationship Violence Treatment & Intervention Program, The Center, POB 3357, San Diego; 92163 619-692-2077 tinyurl.com/kasn2vd

♀ Stonewall Citizens' Patrol, POB 632795, San Diego; 92163 619-320-8219 www.stonewallcitizens.org

Community Centers and/or Pride Organizations

♀ ★ ふふ San Diego LGBT Community Center, POB 3357, San Diego; 92163 / 3909 Centre St 619-692-2077 **H?** www.thecentersd.org ✓

♀ ★ ふふ San Diego Pride, 3620 30th St, San Diego; 619-297-7683 sdpride.org

Information, Media & Publications

♂ ● San Diego Gay & Lesbian News, 16769 Bernardo Center Dr Ste 1-277, San Diego; 92118 619-505-7777 www.sdgln.com

♂ ● San Diego Pix, 16769 Bernardo Center Dr Ste 1-277, San Diego; 92128 619-505-7777 www.sdpix.com cs@sdpix.com

Accommodation: Hotels, Inns, Guesthouses, B&B, Resorts

Encinitas

♂ ○ Inn at Moonlight Beach, 105 N Vulcan Ave, Encinitas; 92024 760-450-5028 innatmoonlightbeach.com info@innatmoonlightbeach.com

San Diego

♂ ○ **Beach Hut Bed and Breakfast, 3761 Riviera Dr, San Diego; 92109-6643 858-272-6131 Amazing and unique private experience in beautiful Mission Bay Park. beachhutbb.com ✓ ⊛ beachhutbb@gmail.com**

♂ ○ Carole's B&B Inn, 3227 Grim Ave, San Diego 92104-4656 619-280-5258 www.carolesbnb.com ✓ ⊛

♂ ○ ふふ Kings Inn, 1333 Hotel Circle S, San Diego; 92108 619-297-2231 www.kingsinnsandiego.com ✓ ⊛

♂ ○ ふふ Lafayette Hotel, Swim Club & Bungalows, 2223 El Cajon Blvd, San Diego; 619-296-2101 www.lafayettehotelsd.com ✓ ⊛ ⊛

AIDS/HIV Services, Education & Support

♂ ☆ AIDS Walk & Run San Diego, POB 3357, San Diego; 92163 619-692-2077 www.aidswalksd.org

♂ ☆ Being Alive, 3940 4th Ave, San Diego 619-291-1400 beingalive.org

♀ ☆ Christie's Place, 2440 3rd Ave, San Diego 619-702-4186 www.christiesplace.org

♂ ☆ Mama's Kitchen, 3960 Home Ave, San Diego 619-233-6262 www.mamaskitchen.org

California: San Diego Area
AIDS/HIV Support

106
GAYELLOW PAGES #42 2020-2021

San Diego Area: California
Men's Clubs

⚦ ★ (♊) POZabilities, POB 34471, San Diego; 92103 619-241-8538 www.pozabilities.org ✏ poz@pozabilities.org

⚥ ☆ 👥 Townspeople, 4080 Centre St, San Diego; 619-295-8802 **H?** Housing www.townspeople.org ✏

Archives/Libraries/Museums/History Projects

⚦ ★ 👥 Lambda Archives of San Diego, 4545 Park Blvd Ste 104, San Diego; 92116 619-260-1522 **H?** www.lambdaarchives.org ✏ info@lambdaarchives.org

Bars, Cafes, Clubs, Restaurants
La Jolla

⚥ ○ Cody's La Jolla, 1025 Prospect St Suite 210, La Jolla; 858-459-0040 www.codyslj.com ✖ 🛏

⚥ ○ 👥 The Cottage, 7702 Fay Ave, La Jolla; 858-454-8409 www.cottagelajolla.com ✖

⚢ Queer Girl Events, www.queergirlevents.com

San Diego

⚦ • ♿ Cheers, 1839 Adams Ave, San Diego; 619-298-3269 cheerssandiego.com

⚦ • 👥 Flicks, 1017 University Ave, San Diego; 619-297-2056 www.sdflicks.com **DV** 🏳️‍🌈

⚢ • 👥 Gossip Grill, 1220 University Ave, San Diego; 619-260-8023 gossipgrill.com **D** ⚲ ✖ ✏

⚢ Hillcrest Brewing Company, 1458 University Ave, San Diego; 619-269-4323 hillcrestbrewingcompany.com ⚲ ✖

⚦ • The Hole in the Wall, 2820 Lytton St, San Diego; 619-996-9000 theholesandiego.com **KLV** 🏳️‍🌈 ✏

⚢ • Loft, 3610 5th Ave, San Diego; 619-296-6407 fb.com/theloftsd/

⚢ • Martinis Above Fourth, 3940 4th Ave Ste 200, San Diego; 619-400-4500 www.martinisabovefourth.com ⚲ ✖ 🏳️‍🌈

⚦ ○ No 1 Fifth Avenue, 3845 5th Ave, San Diego 619-299-1911 fb.com/numberonefifth

⚦ • Pecs, 2046 University Ave, San Diego 619-296-0889 www.pecsbar.com

⚢ • The Rail, 3796 5th Ave, San Diego 619-298-2233 thebrass-railsd.com **D** ✖ 🏳️‍🌈

⚢ • Redwing Bar & Grill, 4012 30th St, San Diego; 619-281-8700 redwingbar.com **K** ⚲ ✖

⚦ • Rich's, 1051 University Ave, San Diego 619-295-2195 richssandiego.com **D**

⚦ ○ 👥 San Diego Eagle, 3040 N Park Way, San Diego; 619-295-8072 www.sandiegoeagle.com **L** ✏ info@sandiegoeagle.com

⚢ • SRO Lounge, 1807 5th Ave, San Diego 619-232-1886 fb.com/srolounge/

⚢ • Urban Mo's Bar & Grill, 308 University, San Diego; 619-491-0400 urbanmos.com **D** ⚲ ✖

Bookstores

⚥ ○ ♿ Bay Books, 1029 Orange Ave, Coronado; 619-435-0070 www.baybookscoronado.com ✏

⚥ ○ Warwick's, 7812 Girard Ave, La Jolla 858-454-0348 www.war-wicks.com

Coaching: Career, Life, Relationship etc

⚥ • Willfully Living, 646-322-7999 wil-fullyliving.com Wil@wil-fullyliving.com

Counseling/Psychotherapy/Mental Health

⚦ • Karmen, Mel D, PhD, 2031 2nd Ave, San Diego; 92101 619-296-9442 namaste-1@cox.net

⚥ • ♿ McNeil, Dana, The Relationship Place, 3232 Fourth Ave, San Diego; 92103 619-535-8890 **H?** www.sdrelationship-place.com ✏ info@sdrelationshipplace.com

⚥ ○ 👥 **Peters, David, MFT, 2525 Camino del Rio S Ste 205, San Diego; 92108 619-491-3492 Lic.# MFC 28846 "With respect and sensitivity to your life and your love." www.davidpeterstherapy.com ✏ davidpetersmft@cox.net**

⚥ ○ (♊) Vernazza, Trish E, MFT, ATR, 2774 Jefferson Street, Carlsbad 760-439-8874 www.trishv.com

⚥ ○ Vernazza, Trish, MA, MFT, 2774 Jefferson St, Carlsbad; 92008 760-439-8874 www.trishv.com info@trishv.com

⚥ • Weissman, Abigail, PsyD, Waves, a Psychological Corporation, 2055 Third Ave #B, San Diego; 92101 619-403-5578 www.wavespsych.com/doctorabi office@wavespsych.com

Funding: Endowment, Fundraising

⚥ ☆ ♿ Auntie Helen's Thrift Shop, 4127 30th St, San Diego; 619-501-0209 www.auntiehelens.org

⚢ ★ Imperial Court de San Diego, POB 34104, San Diego; 92163 619-288-1183 tinyurl.com/2gchly

⚥ ☆ 👥 San Diego Foundation for Change, 3758 30th St, San Diego; 619-692-0527 **H?** www.foundation4change.org ✏

⚦ ★ 👥 San Diego Human Dignity Foundation, 325 Washington St #235, San Diego; 92103 / office 940 Orange Ave, Coronado; 92118 619-291-3383 www.sdhdf.org info@sdhdf.org

Health Care: Physical (see also Counseling/Mental Health)

⚥ Family Health Centers of San Diego, 823 Gateway Center Way, San Diego; 619-515-2300 www.fhcsd.org

⚥ • Farnesi, Darren A, MD, 3911 Normal St, San Diego; 92103 619-795-6700 www.manageyourage.com ✏ info@manageyourage.com

⚥ Progressive Health Services, 4732 Point Loma Ave #D, San Diego; 619-260-0810 www.progressivehealth.org

Home/Building Inspection/Engineering

⚥ • John, Steve, MCI, CNCS, All Pro Home Inspections, 3685 Herbert St, San Diego; 92103-4545 619-283-1123 www.All-ProHI.com 4stevejohn@gmail.com

Legal Services

⚥ ○ The Ahrens Law, APC, 1901 1st Ave 2nd Flr, San Diego; 92101 619-230-0300 fax 619-230-0610 www.ahrenslawoffice.com ka@ahrenslawoffice.com

Men's & Sex Clubs (not primarily Health Clubs)

⚦ Club San Diego, 3955 4th Ave, San Diego 619-295-0850 www.clubsandiego.net

Metaphysical, Occult, Alternative Healing

♀ ● Minerva Wisdom Arts, 541-349-0595 www.minervawisdomarts.com ✗ info@minervawisdomarts.com

Organizations/Resources: Business & Professional Associations, Labor Advocacy

♂ ★ රර Pride At Work San Diego, 3737 Camino del Rio S #403, San Diego; 858-560-0151 fb.com/prideatworksd/

♂ ★ San Diego Equality Business Association, PO Box 33848, San Diego; 92163 619-296-4543 www.sdeba.org

♀ ★ රර Tom Homann LGBT Law Association, 2358 University Ave PMB 137, San Diego; 619-230-0300 Kimberly Ahrens, THLA Co-President thla.org

Organizations/Resources: Cultural, Dance, Performance

♂ ★ රර Finest City Squares, POB 3241, San Diego; 92163 858-435-0243 iagsdc.com/finestcity/

♂ ★ San Diego Gay Men's Chorus, POB 33825, San Diego; 92163 619-432-2244 www.sdgmc.org info@sdgmc.org

♀ ★ රර San Diego Women's Chorus, POB 632794, San Diego; 92163-2794 619-291-3366 **H?** www.sdwc.org info@sdwc.org

♂ ★ Sisters of Perpetual Indulgence - San Diego, 2260 El Cajon Blvd #868, San Diego; 92104 www.sdsisters.org

Organizations/Resources: Ethnic, Multicultural

♂ ★ Long Yang Club San Diego, POB 34102, San Diego; 92163 fb.com/groups/lycsd ✧

Organizations/Resources: Family and Supporters

♀ PFLAG San Diego County, POB 82762, San Diego; 92138 888-398-0006 fb.com/PFLAG.SDCo

Organizations/Resources: Naturist/Nudist

♂ ★ Bare Buns California, POB 17246, San Diego 92177 www.barebunscalifornia.org

Organizations/Resources: Political/Legislative/Advocacy

♀ ACLU San Diego, POB 87131, San Diego; 92138 619-232-2121 www.aclusandiego.org

Organizations/Resources: Senior Resources

♀ ☆ Elder Help of San Diego, 3860 Calle Fortunada Ste 101, San Diego; 619-284-9281 www.elderhelpofsandiego.org

♂ ★ Fellowship of Older Gays (FOG), POB 635062, San Diego; 92163 619-702-4586 fogsd.org

♂ ★ රර Senior Services, The Center, POB 3357, San Diego; 92163 / 3909 Centre St, San Diego 619-692-2077 x205 **H?** www.thecentersd.org ✗

Organizations/Resources: Sexual Focus / Safe Sex

♂ ★ Club X, 1286 University Ave Ste 563, San Diego 619-364-6848 www.clubxsd.org

Organizations/Resources: Social, Recreation, Support

♂ ★ Bears San Diego, POB 3151, San Diego 92163-1151 619-364-6893 www.bearssd.org info@bearssd.org

♂ ★ Butch Voices, POB 635333, San Diego 92163 www.butchvoices.com

♂ ★ California Men's Gatherings (San Diego), www.thecmg.org

♂ ★ Gay for Good - San Diego, Volunteer organization. gayforgood.org/sandiego/ sandiego@gayforgood.org

♂ ★ South Bay Alliance Association, Inc., c/o Law Office of Ariel A. Javier, APC 1901 First Ave Ste 124, San Diego **H?** southbaypride.org

Organizations/Resources: Student, Academic, Education

♂ ★ CSU San Marcos LGBTQA Pride Center, 333 S Twin Oaks Valley Rd, San Marcos; 760-750-3077 tinyurl.com/y4ydbcrl

♂ ★ GLSEN San Diego County, POB 632922, San Diego; 92163 tinyurl.com/koxgkql

♂ ★ LGBTQ+ at USD, Student Life Pavillion 424, 5998 Alcalá Park, San Diego; 92110 619-260-4517 www.sandiego.edu/lgbtq/ lgbtq@sandiego.edu

♂ ★ Pride Law, USD School of Law, 5998 Alcalá Park, San Diego; 92110 tinyurl.com/p4acpfe usdpridelaw@gmail.com

♂ ★ UCSD LGBT Resource Center, 9500 Gilman Dr MC 0023, La Jolla; 858-822-3493 lgbt.ucsd.edu

Organizations/Resources: Youth (see also Family)

♂ ★ Hillcrest Youth Center, 1807 Robinson Ave #106, San Diego; 619-497-2920 fb.com/HYCSD/

Performance: Entertainment, Music, Theater, Space

♂ ★ රර Diversionary Theatre Productions, 4545 Park Blvd #101, San Diego; 619-220-0097 www.diversionary.org

Printing/Mailing & Promotional Items

♀ ○ රර IPM Lithographics Inc, 9040 Carroll Way Ste 4, San Diego; 858-271-0771 www.ipmlitho.com

Real Estate (see also Mortgages)

♀ ○ Hefni-Pyle, Suzanne, Orange & San Diego Counties 760-451-1500 tinyurl.com/yaokufux

♀ ● රර Z (Zyhyli), Tamara, Ascent Real Estate, 410 Kalmia St, San Diego; 92101 619-865-1389 **H?** www.TamaraZhomes.com ✗ Tamara@TamaraZhomes.com

Recovery

♂ ★ Live & Let Live Alano Club, 3847 Park Blvd, San Diego; 619-298-8008 lllac.org

♂ ★ (♺) Stepping Stone of San Diego, 3767 Central Ave, San Diego; 619-278-0777 **H?** www.steppingstonesd.org ✗

Religious / Spiritual Resources

♂ ★ ♿ Dignity/San Diego, POB 33367, San Diego; 92163-3367 619-645-8240 **H?** www.dignitysd.org info@dignitysd.org

♀ ☆ First Lutheran Church, 1420 3rd Ave, San Diego 92101-3193 619-234-6149 www.firstlutheransd.org

♀ ☆ First Unitarian Universalist Church, 4190 Front St, San Diego; 92103 619-298-9978 www.firstuusandiego.org mail@firstuusandiego.org

♂ Integrity San Diego, St Paul's Episcopal Cathedral, 2728 6th Ave, San Diego; 619-298-7261 tinyurl.com/y4ehsy5k

California: San Diego Area
Religious
108
GAYELLOW PAGES #42 2020-2021
San Francisco Bay/Peninsula: California
AIDS/HIV Support

♂ ★ ᕦᕤ Metropolitan Community Church of San Diego, 2633 Denver St; 619-521-2222 **H** www.themetchurch.org ✔

♂ ☆ Palomar Unitarian Universalist Fellowship, 1600 Buena Vista Dr, Vista; 92083 760-941-4319 www.vistauu.org office@vistauu.org

♀ ☆ ᕦᕤ Unitarian Universalist Fellowship of San Dieguito, POB 201, Solana Beach; 92075 858-755-9225 **HD** www.uufsd.org ✔ office@uufsd.org

Sports & Outdoor

♂ ★ 4x4 Pride, fb.com/groups/4x4pride/

♂ America's Finest City Softball League, PO Box 635221, San Diego; 92163 www.afcsl.org

♂ ★ Different Strokes Swim Team, 2358 University Ave PMB 1679, San Diego; 858-863-7781 www.dsst.org

♂ ★ Front Runners & Walkers San Diego, POB 3633, San Diego; 92163 858-413-7973 www.frwsd.org ✔

♂ ★ SAGA Ski Club, POB 3203, San Diego 92163 619-865-1313 sagasd.org

♂ San Diego American Flag Football League, PO Box 33077, San Diego; 92163 www.sdffl.org

♂ ☆ San Diego Armada Rugby Football Club, 619-206-7208 fb.com/SDArmadaRFC/

♂ San Diego Bulldogs Wrestling Club, www.sdwrestling.org

♂ San Diego Great Outdoors, POB 34132, San Diego; 92163 greatoutdoors.org/sd

♂ San Diego Hoops, 2111 Pan American Plaza, San Diego; fb.com/SDHoops/

♂ ★ San Diego Pool League, POB 5692, San Diego; 92165 760-717-9900 www.sdpool.org

♂ ★ San Diego Sparks Soccer Club, sparkssoccer.org

♀ ★ San Diego Tennis Federation, 760-207-7247 www.sdtf.org

♂ ★ San Diego Trail Tramps, www.sandiegotrailtramps.com SanDiegoTrailTramps@gmail.com

Travel & Tourist Services (see also Accommodation)

♂ ● ᕦᕤ Jerry & David's Cruises & Tours, 1901 1st Ave Ste 180, San Diego; 92101-0300 619-233-5199 fax 619-233-3880 www.rsvpcruises.com jerry@rsvpcruises.com

San Francisco Bay/Peninsula

Crisis, Anti-violence, & Helplines

♂ ★ ᕦᕤ Community United Against Violence, 427 S Van Ness Ave, SF; 415-777-5500 www.cuav.org

♀ ☆ SGR - The Sex, Gender, and Relationships Hotline, 415-989-7374 **Z?** sgrhotline.org questions@sgrhotline.org

♀ ☆ W.O.M.A.N., Inc., 26 Boardman Place, SF 877-384-3510 www.womaninc.org

Community Centers and/or Pride Organizations

● ★ ᕦᕤ San Francisco Dyke March, 3543 18th St #2, SF; **HS** www.thedykemarch.org

♂ ★ ᕦᕤ San Francisco Pride, 1841 Market St 4th Flr, SF; 415-864-0831 www.sfpride.org

♂ ★ ᕦᕤ San Mateo County Pride Center, 1021 S El Camino Real, San Mateo; 94402 650-591-0133 sanmateopride.org info@sanmateopride.org

♂ ★ ᕦᕤ SF LGBT Center, 1800 Market St, SF; 415-865-5555 www.sfcenter.org

Information, Media & Publications

♂ ★ OurTownSF, www.ourtownsf.org otsanfran@gmail.com

♂ ★ Queer Things to Do in San Francisco, www.sfqueer.com

♂ ● (?ᕤ) San Francisco Bay Times, 2261 Market St #309, SF; 415-503-1375 www.sfbaytimes.com

Accommodation: Hotels, Inns, Guesthouses, B&B, Resorts
Half Moon Bay

♂ ○ Mill Rose Inn, 615 Mill St, Half Moon Bay 94019-1726 650-726-8750 800-900-7673 www.millroseinn.com ✔ ⊛ info@millroseinn.com

Pescadero

♀ ○ Pescadero Creek Inn, 393 Stage Rd 888-307-1898 www.pescaderocreekinn.com ✔ ⊛ contactus@pescaderocreekinn.com

San Francisco: Castro & Noe Valley

♂ ● The Parker Guest House, 520 Church St, SF 415-621-3222 www.parkerguesthouse.com ✔ ⊛

♀ ● The Willows Inn, 710 14th St, SF; 94114-1106 (Church/Market Sts) 800-431-0277 415-431-4770 www.WillowsSF.com ✔ ⊛ innkeeper@WillowsSF.com

San Francisco: Financial District, Embarcadero

♀ ○ ᕦᕤ Hilton San Francisco Financial District, 750 Kearny St, SF; 94108 415-433-6600 **H?** tinyurl.com/7nqjejz ✿ ✔ ⊛ ⊛ sfofd-salesadm@hilton.com

San Francisco: Haight, Fillmore, Hayes Valley

♀ ○ Chateau Tivoli Bed & Breakfast, 1057 Steiner St, SF; 94115-4620 415-776-5462 800-228-1647 www.chateautivoli.com ✔ ⊛ ⊛

♀ ● The Metro Hotel San Francisco, 319 Divisadero St, SF; 415-861-5364 www.metrohotelsf.com ✔ ⊛

♀ ● ᕦᕤ Queen Anne Hotel, 1590 Sutter St, SF; 94109-5395 415-441-2828 www.queenanne.com ✔ ⊛ stay@queenanne.com

Accommodation Rental: Furnished / Vacation (& AirBNB)
San Francisco: Richmond

♀ ● Anza Studio, sfguesthouse.webs.com ✔ ⊛ ⊛

San Francisco

♀ ● AMSI Real Estate, Housing & Relocation, 2800 Van Ness Ave; SF; 94109-1426 800-747-7784 www.amsires.com

Adoption, Surrogacy, Assisted Fertility Support, see also Reproductive

♀ ☆ ᕦᕤ Family Builders By Adoption, 1900 Embarcadero Ste 303, Oakland, CA 94606 510-536-5437 **H?** Foster-to-Adopt agency www.familybuilders.org ✔ kids@familybuilders.org

AIDS/HIV Services, Education & Support

♀ ☆ ᕦᕤ AIDS Community Research Consortium, 855 Douglas Ave, Redwood City; 650-364-6563 www.acrc.org

♀ ☆ ᕦᕤ AIDS Emergency Fund, Positive Resource Center, 170 9th St, SF; 415-777-0333 **H?** prcsf.org ✔

California: San Francisco Bay/Peninsula
AIDS/HIV Support

109
GAYELLOW PAGES #42 2020-2021

San Francisco Bay/Peninsula: California
Bars, Cafes, Clubs, Restaurants

♀ ☆ Asian & Pacific Islander Wellness Center, 730 Polk St, SF; 415-292-3400 www.apiwellness.org ⟡

♀ Let's Kick ASS, 4111 18th St, Ste 5, SF (AIDS Survivor Syndrome) letskickass.hiv

♂ ☆ Most Holy Redeemer AIDS Support Group, 100 Diamond St, SF; 415-863-6259 www.mhr-asg.com

♀ ☆ 𝄞 Positive Resource Center AIDS Emergency Fund, 170 9th St, SF; 415-777-0333 prcsf.org

♀ ☆ 𝄞 Project Open Hand Kitchen & Grocery Center, 730 Polk St, SF; 415-447-2300 www.openhand.org ✗

♂ ☆ 𝄞 Rafiki Coalition for Health & Wellness, 601 Cesar Chavez St, SF; 415-615-9945 **H?** rafikicoalition.org ♣ ✗

♀ ☆ 𝄞 San Francisco AIDS Foundation /STOP AIDS Project, 1035 Market St #400, SF; 415-487-3000 www.sfaf.org

♀ ★ 𝄞 Shanti, 730 Polk St, SF 415-674-4700 www.shanti.org ✗

Archives/Libraries/Museums/History Projects

♂ AIDS History Project, University of California, 530 Parnassus Ave, SF; 415-476-8112 tinyurl.com/nqfctpg

♀ ☆ Eureka Valley Harvey Milk Memorial Branch Library, 1 Jose Sarria Court, SF; 415-355-5616 tinyurl.com/26hcefm

♥ ★ 𝄞 GLBT History Museum, 4127 18th St, SF; 415-621-1107 **H?** www.glbthistory.org/museum/ ✗

♥ ☆ 𝄞 James C. Hormel LGBT Center, San Francisco Public Library, 100 Larkin St Flr 3, SF; 94102-4705 415-557-4537 **H?** www.sfpl.org/lgbtqia ✗

♥ ★ LGBTQIA Archives, Terry, c/o James Hormel LGBTQIA Ctr SF Library, 100 Larkin St 3rd Flr, SF; 415-557-4400 tinyurl.com/26jyhnz

Art & Craft Galleries/Services, Supplies

♂ ○ 𝄞 Arcadia, 680 8th St Ste 164, SF 94103-4950 415-551-1238 www.arcadiaframing.com mgrover@arcadiaframing.com

Bars, Cafes, Clubs, Restaurants
Half Moon Bay

♂ ○ 𝄞 Sam's Chowder House, 4210 North Cabrillo Hwy, Half Moon Bay 650-712-0245 www.samschowderhouse.com ✗ ✗

San Francisco: Castro & Noe Valley

♂ 440 Castro, 440 Castro St, SF; 415-621-8732 www.the440.com

♂ ● The Academy, 2166 Market St, SF; 415-624-3429 academy-sf.com ✗ info@academy-sf.com

♂ ● Beaux Bar & Dance Club, 2344 Market St, SF www.beauxsf.com **D**

♂ ● 𝄞 Blackbird, 2124 Market St, SF 415-872-5310 www.blackbirdbar.com ✗

♥ ● 𝄞 The Cafe, 2369 Market St, SF; 415-779-3171 **H?** www.CafeSF.com **DV**

♂ ○ 𝄞 The Cafe du Nord, 2174 Market St, SF; 415-471-2969 **H?** www.cafedunord.com ✗ ▥

♥ The Cove on Castro, 434 Castro St, SF 415-626-0462 www.covesf.com ✗ ✗

♂ ● 𝄞 The Edge, 4149 18th St, SF 415-863-4027 www.edgesf.com **LV** ✗

♀ ○ Equator Coffees, 986 Market St, SF 415-614-9129 www.equatorcoffees.com ☞ info@equatorcoffees.com

♥ Harvey's, 500 Castro St, SF; 415-431-4278 www.harveyssf.com Ⴤ ✗ ▥

♥ Hi Tops, 2247 Market St, SF; 415-551-2500 www.hitopsbar.com **S** Ⴤ ✗

♂ ● Last Call Bar, 3988 18th St, SF; 415-861-1310 www.thelastcallbar.com

♂ ● Lookout, 3600 16th St, SF; 415 431-0306 www.lookoutsf.com Ⴤ ✗ ✗ info@lookoutsf.com

♀ ○ Lovejoy's Tea Room, 1351 Church St, SF 415-648-5895 www.lovejoystearoom.com ☞

♀ ● Martuni's, 4 Valencia St, SF; 415-241-0205 tinyurl.com/lg4wma6 ▥

♂ Midnight Sun, 4067 18th St, SF; 415-861-4186 www.midnightsunsf.com **V**

♂ ● 𝄞 The Mint Karaoke Lounge, 1942 Market St, SF; 415-626-4726 themint.net **K** Ⴤ ✗

♂ The Mix, 4086 18th St, SF; 415-431-8616 www.mixbarsf.com

♂ ● 𝄞 Moby Dick, 4049 18th St, SF 415-294-0731 fb.com/Moby-DickBar

♀ ● (?𝄞) Orphan Andy's Restaurant, 3991A 17th St 415-864-9795 ✗ ✗

♥ ● Pilsner Inn, 225 Church St, SF 415-621-7058 www.pilsner-inn.com

♂ Qbar, 456 Castro St, SF; / check for status after fire 415-864-2877 qbarsf.com/QBAR/ **D**

♂ SF Badlands, 4121 18th St, SF; 415-626-9320 www.sfbadlands.com **DV**

♀ ○ Swirl, 572 Castro St, SF; 415-864-2262 www.swirloncastro.com

♀ ○ Toad Hall, 4146 18th St, SF; 415-621-2811 www.toadhallbar.com **D**

♂ ● Twin Peaks Tavern, 401 Castro St, SF 415-864-9470 www.twinpeakstavern.com

San Francisco: Downtown & North Beach

♂ Aunt Charlie's Lounge, 133 Turk St, SF 415-441-2922 www.auntcharlieslounge.com ▥

♀ ○ 𝄞 Caffe Trieste, 601 Vallejo St, SF; 415-392-6739 www.caffetrieste.com ☞ ▥

San Francisco: Financial District, Embarcadero

♂ (?𝄞) Ginger's, 86 Hardie Place, SF 415-862-0545 www.gingers.bar ▥

San Francisco: Haight, Fillmore, Hayes Valley

♀ ○ Garibaldi's, 347 Presidio Ave, SF 415-563-8841 www.garibaldisrestaurant.com

♀ ○ 𝄞 Madrone Art Bar, 500 Divisadero St, SF; 415-241-0202 **H** www.madroneartbar.com ✗

♀ ○ Noc Noc, 557 Haight St, SF; 415-861-5811 www.nocnocs.com

California: San Francisco Bay/Peninsula
Bars, Cafes, Clubs, Restaurants
110
GAYELLOW PAGES #42 2020-2021
San Francisco Bay/Peninsula: California
Counseling

Trax Bar, 1437 Haight St, SF; 415-864-4213 fb.com/SFTrax/

San Francisco: Marina District

Equator Coffees, Fort Mason Center Gatehouse, 2 Marina Blvd, SF; 415-720-1461 www.equatorcoffees.com info@equatorcoffees.com

San Francisco: Mission District

Armory Club, 1799 Mission St, SF; 415-431-5300 www.armoryclub.com

El Rio, 3158 Mission St, SF 415-282-3325 www.elriosf.com **DK**

Jolene's, 2700 16th St, SF; 415-913-7948 jolenessf.com

San Francisco: Polk St Area

The Cinch, 1723 Polk St, SF 415-776-4162 fb.com/thecinchsaloon

San Francisco: South of Market

Bar Basic, 510 Brannan St, SF; 415-227-0449 car-basicbar.business.site/

Bootie SF, at DNA Lounge, 375 11th St, SF; / Sat 415-626-1409 www.bootiesf.com **D**

Cat Club, Cat Club 1190 Folsom St, SF 415-703-8965 www.sfcatclub.com **D**

Club OMG, 43 6th St, SF 415-896-6373 www.clubomgsf.com **D**

Club Papi San Francisco, at Roccapulco Nightclub, 3140 Mission St www.clubpapi.com **D**

Driftwood, 1225 Folsom St, SF www.driftwoodbarsf.com

The Endup, 401 6th St, SF 415-896-1075 theendupsf.com **D**

Equator Coffees, 222 2nd St, SF; 415-872-9482 www.equatorcoffees.com info@equatorcoffees.com

Hole In The Wall Saloon, 1369 Folsom St, SF; 415-431-4695 www.hitws.com **LCW**

Lone Star Saloon, 1354 Harrison, SF 415-863-9999 www.lonestarsf.com **L**

Mezzanine, 444 Jessie St, SF; 415-625-8880 mezzaninesf.com **D**

Oasis, 298 11th St, SF 415-595-3725 www.sfoasis.com **D**

Powerhouse, 1347 Folsom St, SF; 415-552-8689 www.powerhouse-sf.com **L**

SF Eagle, 398 12th St, SF www.sf-eagle.com **L**

The Stud, 399 9th St, SF 415-863-6623 www.studsf.com **D**

UHAUL SF Friday at Oasis, 298 11th St, SF 415-595-3725 fb.com/uhaul.SanFrancis/ **D**

San Francisco

Bearracuda, check schedule www.bearracuda.com **D**

Gus Presents, www.guspresents.com

Mecca 2,00, check schedule fb.com/groups/mecca2.0

Sundance Saloon, Sun & Thu at Space 550, 550 Barneveld Ave (check ahead) 415-820-1403 **H?** www.sundance-saloon.org **DCW** info@sundancesaloon.org

Body Art

Black & Blue Tattoo, 381 Guerrero, SF; 94103 415-626-0770 www.blackandbluetattoo.com

Bookstores

Alley Cat Books, 3036 24th St, SF; 415-824-1761 www.alleycatbookshop.com

Bookshop Benicia, 636 First St, Benicia; 707-747-5155 bookshopbenicia.com

The Booksmith, 1644 Haight St, SF; 94117-2816 415-863-8688 800-493-7323 www.booksmith.com

Borderlands Books, 866 Valencia St, SF; 94110 415-824-8203 www.borderlands-books.com

City Lights Bookstore, 261 Columbus Ave, SF; 415-362-8193 www.citylights.com

Green Apple Books & Music, 506 Clement St, SF; 94118 / and 1231 9th Ave 415-387-2272 www.greenapplebooks.com query@greenapplebooks.com

Kepler's Books, 1010 El Camino Real, Menlo Park; 650-324-4321 www.keplers.com

Broadcast Media

Outlook Video, POB 1650, Palo Alto 94302 408-293-3040 x205 www.outlookvideo.org

Counseling/Psychotherapy/Mental Health

Balderson, Scott, LMFT, MFC 34280, 533A Castro St, SF; 415-255-6181 www.scottbalderson.com

Blum, Adam D, MFT, 538 Hayes St, SF; 94102 415-795-2935 Lic #MFC44892 www.thegaytherapycenter.com adam@thegaytherapycenter.com

Christrup, Jim, LCSW, 4326 18th St, SF 94114-2427 415-242-9866 www.jimchristrup.com jimchristrup@sbcglobal.net

Croner, Barbara, MFT, MFC24761, 1947 Divisadero #1, SF; 94115-2532 415-346-8678

Gaylesta, The Psychotherapist Association for Gender & Sexual Diversity, 584 Castro St #230, SF 510-433-9939 www.gaylesta.org

Grossman, Gary, PhD, 2186 Geary Blvd #211, SF; 415-928-4662 www.garygrossmanphd.com

Martin, John A, PhD, PSY 9128, 220 Montgomery St Ste 400, SF; 94104 415-621-3566 www.jamartin.com johnmphd@gmail.com

Queer LifeSpace, 2275 Market Street #7, SF; 415-358-2000 www.queerlifespace.org

San Francisco Suicide Prevention, POB 191350, SF; 94119 415-781-0500 www.sfsuicide.org

SF Therapy Collective, 2275 Market St #E, SF; 94114 415-659-8282 www.sftherapycollective.org info@sftherapycollective.org

California: San Francisco Bay/Peninsula
Erotica
111
GAYELLOW PAGES #42 2020-2021
San Francisco Bay/Peninsula: California
Organizations: Business

Erotica / Adult Stores / Safe Sex Supplies

♂ ● ♂ Does Your Mother Know, 4141 18th St, SF; 94114 415-864-3160

♂ ○ ♂ Folsom Gulch, 947 Folsom St, SF 94107-1020 415-495-6402 www.folsomgulchsf.com folsomgulchsf@gmail.com

♂ ○ ♂ Mission Secrets, 2086 Mission St, SF; 94110-1218 415-626-0309 www.secretsboutiques.com missionsecrets2086@gmail.com

♂ ○ ♂ Secrets Redwood City, 739 El Camino Real, Redwood City; 94063-1540 650-364-6913 www.secretsboutiques.com gg_3loc13@yahoo.com

♂ ○ Secrets San Mateo, 2297 S El Camino Real, San Mateo; 94403-1808 650-345-4112 www.secretsboutiques.com secretsbbsm93@gmail.com

♂ ○ Secrets SF, 1043 Kearny Street, SF; 94133 415-391-9246 www.secretsboutiques.com kbv@sbcglobal.net

♂ ○ SOMA Secrets, 99 6th St, SF; 94103-1610 415-495-5573 www.secretsboutiques.com somasecrets6@gmail.com

Funding: Endowment, Fundraising

♂ Castro Street Fair, POB 14405, SF; 94114 www.castrostreetfair.org

♂ ★ Horizons Foundation, 550 Montgomery St #700, SF; 94111 415-398-2333 www.horizonsfoundation.org info@horizonsfoundation.org

♂ ★ Imperial Council of San Francisco, 584 Castro St PMB 469, SF; www.imperialcouncilsf.org

♂ Krewe de Kinque, 156 Hancock St #4, SF 415-626-5004 fb.com/KDKinSF

♂ Out of the Closet Thrift Store, 1295 Folsom St, SF; 415-558-7176 outofthecloset.org

♂ Pride Law Fund, POB 2602, SF; 94126 www.pridelawfund.org

♂ ☆ The Richmond/Ermet Aid Foundation, 942 Divisadero St Ste 201, SF; 94115 415-931-2515 www.reaf-sf.org ✗ info@richmondermet.org

♂ ★ (?♿) The Sisters of Perpetual Indulgence, Inc, 584 Castro St #392, SF; 415-820-9697 www.thesisters.org

Gifts, Cards, Pride, etc.

♂ ○ ♂ Cliff's Variety, 479 Castro St, SF; 94114 415-431-5365 www.cliffsvariety.com cliff@cliffsvariety.com

Grooming, Personal Care, Spa Services

♂ ○ Healing Cuts, 3903 18th St, SF; 94114 415-286-2970 healingcutssf.com ismael@healingcutssf.com

Health Care: Physical (see also Counseling/Mental Health)

♀ City Clinic, 356 7th St, SF; 415-487-5500 www.sfcityclinic.org

♀ Clinica Martin-Baro, 3013 24th St, SF 415-933-1198 clinicamb.blogspot.com ✦

♂ ★ ♿ Dimensions, First Floor, Ward 81, 995 Potrero Ave, SF; 628-207-5700 Ages 12-25 www.dimensionsclinic.org

♀ ☆ ♿ Lyon Martin Women's Service, 1735 Mission St, SF; 415-565-7667 All women and transgender people www.lyon-martin.org

♂ ★ ♿ Magnet, 470 Castro St, SF 415-581-1600 www.magnetsf.org ✪

♀ Mission Neighborhood Health Center, 240 Shotwell St, SF; 415-552-1013 www.mnhc.org

♂ ♿ Strut, 470 Castro St, SF 415-437-3400 strutsf.org ✪

♀ Tom Waddell Urban Health Clinic, 230 Golden Gate Ave, SF; 415-355-7400 tinyurl.com/v59chvd

♀ ☆ ♿ Women's Community Clinic, 1735 Mission St, SF; 415-379-7800 tinyurl.com/2kz7wm ✗

Immigration, Citizenship, Political Asylum, Refugees

♀ LGBT Asylum Project, 526 Castro St, SF 415-915-9407 www.lgbtasylumproject.org

Leather Resources & Groups

♂ ★ (?♿) The 15 Association, 584 Castro St PMB 810, SF; www.the15association.org

♂ (?♿) Defenders/San Francisco, PO Box 14564, SF; 94114 tinyurl.com/y4cdyzz3

♀ ★ ♿ The Exiles, POB 14338, SF 94114-0338 415-938-7376 **HS** (women and non males) www.theexiles.org info@theexiles.org

♂ ★ Folsom Street Events, 293 8th St, SF 415-552-3247 www.folsomstreetevents.org

♂ ★ Golden Gate Guards, POB 14478, SF; 94114 www.ggguards.org

♂ ● (♿) Mr S Leather, 385 8th St, SF 415-863-7764 www.mr-s-leather.com

♂ ★ San Francisco Bay Area Leather Alliance, 584 Castro St #660, SF; **H?** www.leatheralliance.org

♀ San Francisco Girls of Leather, fb.com/SFgoL

Legal Services

♂ ☆ ♿ AIDS Legal Referral Panel, 1663 Mission St Ste 500, SF; 415-701-1200 www.alrp.org

♂ ● ♿ Kinney, Deb L, Johnston, Kinney & Zulaica LLP, 101 Montgomery St Ste 1600, SF; 94104 415-693-0550 www.jkzllp.com ✗ office@jkzllp.com

♂ ☆ ♿ San Francisco Human Rights Commission, 25 Van Ness Ave #800, SF; 415-252-2500 **H?** sf-hrc.org

Men's & Sex Clubs (not primarily Health Clubs)

♂ ● ♿ Blow Buddies, 933 Harrison St, SF; 415-777-4323 www.blowbuddies.com **P**

♂ ● (♿) Eros, 2051 Market St, SF 94114-1316 415-255-4921 www.erossf.com **P** info@erossf.com

Organizations/Resources: Business & Professional Associations, Labor Advocacy

♂ ★ Bay Area Lawyers for Individual Freedom (BALiF), POB 193383, SF; 94119 415-874-3045 www.balif.org

♂ ★ (?♿) Bay Area Physicians for Human Rights, POB 14188, SF; 94114 415-937-0204 www.baphr.org

California: San Francisco Bay/Peninsula
Organizations: Business

112

GAYELLOW PAGES #42 2020-2021

San Francisco Bay/Peninsula: California
Organizations: Senior

♀ ★ Charles Schwab & Co. PRIDE, 211 Main St, SF; 866-855-9102 www.aboutschwab.com/diversity

♀ ★ Chevron Pride Employee Network, 6001 Bollinger Canyon Rd, San Ramon; 925-842-1000

♀ ★ ♿ Golden Gate Business Association, 584 Castro St #528, SF; 415-362-4422 ggba.com

♀ Levi Strauss Lesbian & Gay Employee Association, 1155 Battery St, SF; 415-501-6000

♀ ★ PG&E PrideNetwork, POB 191311, SF; 94119 415-973-3902 tinyurl.com/3gu68m2

♀ ★ StartOut, 555 Mission St Ste 2414, SF 415-275-2446 startout.org

♀ Wells Fargo Pride SF Bay Area, MAC A0163-044, 343 Sansome St #450, SF

Organizations/Resources: Cultural, Dance, Performance

♀ ★ Bay Area Rainbow Symphony, 2261 Market St #178A, SF; 415-578-4652 www.bars-sf.org

♀ ☆ Brava! for Women in the Arts, 2781 24th St, SF; 94110 415-641-7657 www.brava.org info@brava.org

♀ ★ CHEER San Francisco, 584 Castro St PMB 307, SF; 94114-2512 415-735-5995 www.cheersf.org

♀ ★ Circle Left Contra Dance, www.lcfd.org/sf/

♀ ★ ♿ Foggy City Dancers, POB 14324, SF; 94114 foggycity.org **D**

♂ ★ Fresh Meat Productions, POB 460670, SF 94146 **HS** www.freshmeatproductions.org

♂ Gay Asian Pacific Men's Chorus (GAPA Chorus), fb.com/GA-PAchorus/ ✧

♂ ★ (⚥) Golden Gate Men's Chorus, 116 Eureka St, SF; 94114-2435 415-668-4462 www.ggmc.org

♀ ★ ♿ Left Coast Theatre Co., EXIT Theater, 156 Eddy St, SF; 415-577-7633 **H?** lctc-sf.org

♀ ★ Lesbian/Gay Chorus of San Francisco, 584 Castro Street #486, SF; 415-779-5428 www.lgcsf.org

♀ ★ ♿ Midnight Squares, POB 14483, SF; 94114 www.midnightsquares.org

♀ ★ National LGBTQ Center for the Arts, 170 Valencia St, SF; 94103 415-865-3650 www.sfgmc.org info@sfgmc.org

♀ ☆ Purple Moon Dance Project, 1385 Mission St Ste 340, SF; 415-552-1105 www.purplemoondance.org ♀

♀ ★ ♿ Queer Cultural Center, c/o African American Art and Culture Complex, 762 Fulton St, SF; 94102 415-933-8722 **H?** qcc2.org info@queerculturalcenter.org

♀ ★ ♿ Queer Women of Color Film Festival, 1014 Torney Ave Ste 111, SF; 94129 415-752-0868 **H** June 14-16, 2019 www.qwocmap.org ❖ ✗ festival@qwocmap.org

♀ ★ (⚥) Queer Women of Color Media Arts Project (QWOCMAP), 1014 Torney Ave Ste 111, SF; 94129 415-752-0868 **H?** Film festival & workshops www.qwocmap.org ✗ festival@qwocmap.org

♀ ★ San Francisco Gay Men's Chorus, Golden Gate Performing Arts, Inc, 170 Valencia St, SF; 94103 415-865-3650 www.sfgmc.org info@sfgmc.org

♀ ★ San Francisco Lesbian/Gay Freedom Band, 584 Castro St PMB 841, SF; 94114-2512 415-255-1355 www.sflgfb.org sflgfb@sflgfb.org

♂ ★ Sundance Association for Country Western Dancing, 2261 Market St PMB 225, SF; 94114-1600 415-820-1403 www.sundance-saloon.org ✪ info@sundancesaloon.org

♀ ★ ♿ Western Star Dancers, c/o 58 Wawona St, SF; 94127 415-863-0990 www.westernstardancers.org **DCW**

Organizations/Resources: Education

♂ Alliant International University Rockway Institute, 1 Beach St #100, SF; 415-955-2115 tinyurl.com/n56dmfb

♀ ★ Rainbow Toastmasters, St Francis Lutheran Parish, 152 Church St www.rainbowtoastmasters.org

Organizations/Resources: Ethnic, Multicultural

♀ ★ Aguilas, 2261 Market St Box 496, SF; / 1800 Market St. 3rd Floor Rm. Q32 415-558-8403 www.sfaguilas.org ✦

♀ ★ Bay Area American Indian Two-Spirits, 77 Van Ness Ave Ste 101-1043, SF; 415-865-5616 www.baaits.org ✳

♂ Bay Area American Indian Two-Spirits (BAAITS), 77 Van Ness Ave #101-1043, SF; 415-865-5616 www.baaits.org

♂ ★ Gay Asian Pacific Alliance, POB 880672, SF 94188 www.gapa.org ✧

♂ ★ United Territories of Polynesian Islanders Alliance (UTOPIA), utopiasf.org ✧

Organizations/Resources: Family and Supporters

♀ ★ ♿ Our Family Coalition, 1385 Mission St #340, SF; 415-981-1960 **H?** LGBTQ-headed families with children www.ourfamily.org ✗

♀ ☆ ♿ PFLAG Danville/San Ramon Valley, POB 40, San Ramon; 94583-0040 925-325-1890 srvpflag.webs.com srvpflag@gmail.com

♀ ☆ ♿ PFLAG San Francisco, 584 Castro St #758, SF; 94114 415-921-8850 www.pflagsf.org ✗ pflagsf@gmail.com

Organizations/Resources: Military/Veterans

♂ ★ ♿ Alexander Hamilton American Legion Post 448, POB 14939, SF; 94114 415-431-1413 www.Post448.org ✗

Organizations/Resources: Naturist/Nudist

♂ ★ LIAHO, POB 31594, SF; 94131 www.liaho.org **N**

Organizations/Resources: Political/Legislative/Advocacy

♀ ★ Alice B Toklas LGBT Democratic Club, 2261 Market St #1800, SF; www.alicebtoklas.org

♀ ★ Harvey Milk LGBT Democratic Club, www.milkclub.org

Organizations/Resources: Senior Resources

♀ ★ Old Lesbians Organizing for Change (OLOC) - San Francisco Bay Area, patcull70@gmail.com

♂ ★ ♿ Openhouse Bob Ross LGBT Senior Center, 65 Laguna St, SF; 94102 415-296-8995 www.openhouse-sf.org ✗ info@openhouse-sf.org

Organizations/Resources: Sexual Focus / Safe Sex

♀ ☆ SF Citadel Club, 181 Eddy St, SF; 94102 415-626-1746 **H?** www.sfcitadel.org

♀ ☆ (♿) Society of Janus, POB 411523, SF; 94141 415-483-2376 BDSM www.soj.org

Organizations/Resources: Social, Recreation, Support

⚥ ★ (♿) adyke (Ain't Dead Yet Kick-Azz Events), For lesbians over 40 www.adyke.org WeAre@adyke.org

♂ ★ Bears of San Francisco, 584 Castro St #266, SF www.bosf.org

♂ ★ Bridgemen, c/o Stop AIDS Project, 2128 15th St, SF; 415-575-0150 x231 Gay Men's Health, Education & Support & Community Service www.bridgemen.org

♂ California Men's Gatherings (Bay Area), 877-984-3264 www.thecmg.org

♂ Comfort & Joy, www.playajoy.org

♂ ★ Discovery Community, 2261 Market St PMB 282A, SF; fb.com/discoverycommunity/

⚥ ★ Freewheelers Car Club, 2060 Cesar Chavez St, SF; www.thefreewheelers.net

⚥ Gay for Good - San Francisco, 415-446-8754 Volunteer organization. gayforgood.org/sanfrancisco/

⚥ ★ Golden Gate Flyers, 584 Castro St PMB #500, SF; www.goldengateflyers.org

⚥ QSF&F Book Club, qsfandf.weebly.com

⚥ ★ ♿ QuickTricks Bridge Club, 415-824-6848 www.quicktricks.org kim4bridge@gmail.com

♂ ★ San Francisco Prime Timers, POB 426741, SF 94142 415-731-7693 www.sfprimetimers.org

⚥ ★ SF Queer Longhair Group, www.sfqueerlonghair.org sfqueerlonghair@willdoherty.org

♀ ☆ ♿ WTF Night at the Bike Kitchen, 650H Florida, SF; 415-506-7433 **H?** tinyurl.com/ms5mqg9

Organizations/Resources: Student, Academic, Education

⚥ ★ CCSF Queer Resource Center, Cloud 203B, 50 Phelan Ave, SF; 415-452-5723 tinyurl.com/2zj38u

⚥ ★ Foothill College Gender and Sexuality Awareness (GSA), 12345 El Monte Road, Los Altos 510-938-9052

⚥ ★ Hastings College Of Law Outlaw, 198 McAllister St, SF

⚥ ★ Stanford Pride, POB 19312, Stanford 94309-9312 www.stanfordpride.org

⚥ ★ UCSF LGBT Resource Center, 500 Parnassus Ave MU108W, SF; 415-476-7700 lgbt.ucsf.edu

⚥ ★ USF Prism, University Center 412, 2130 Fulton St, SF; fb.com/usfqa

Organizations/Resources: Transgender/Gender Non-Conforming/Diverse

T ○ ♿ Bowers, Marci L, MD, POB 1044, Trinidad, CO 81082 / 345 Lorton Ave Ste 101, Burlingame, CA 94010 650-570-2270 www.marcibowers.com ⚕

T El/la Para TransLatinas, 2940 16th St Room 319, SF; 415-864-7278 tinyurl.com/twj5m74 ✦

T San Francisco Transgender Film Festival, Fresh Meat Productions, POB 460670, SF; 94146 sftff.org

T ☆ ♿ Trans Day of Remembrance (TDOR), **HS** Spanish Interpretation provided www.TDoRSF.org ✪ info@TDoRSF.org

T Trans March San Francisco, www.transmarch.org

T ☆ ♿ Trans Thrive, API Wellness Center, 730 Polk St 4th Flr, SF; 415-292-3400 www.transthrive.org ⚕

T TransFamilies of Silicon Valley, - - www.transfamiliessv.org

T ☆ TransGender San Francisco, 3543 18th St #30, SF; 415-839-9448 www.tgsf.org

Organizations/Resources: Youth (see also Family)

⚥ ★ Bay Area Youth Summit, 531 Lasuen Mall, Stanford; 703-655-1041 www.bayareayouthsummit.org

♀ ☆ Huckleberry Youth Programs, 3310 Geary Blvd, SF; 415-621-2929 www.huckleberryyouth.org

♀ ☆ Larkin Street Youth Services, 134 Golden Gate Ave, SF; 94102 415-673-0911 www.larkinstreetyouth.org

⚥ ★ ♿ Lavender Youth Recreation & Information Center (LYRIC), 127 Collingwood St, SF; 415-703-6150 lyric.org ⚕

⚥ ★ ♿ Outlet, program of Adolescent Counseling Services, 643 Bair Island Rd Ste 301, Redwood City; 94063 / LGBTQ+ youth support groups serving Santa Clara and San Mateo Counties. 650-424-0852 x107 www.acs-teens.org ⚕ info@acs-teens.org

Performance: Entertainment, Music, Theater, Space

♂ ● Christopher & Co. Celebrity Impersonations, PO Box 2927, Petaluma, CA 94953 707-762-2596 www.HireAStar.net

⚥ Theatre Rhinoceros, POB 423496, SF 94142 415-552-4100 therhino.org

Real Estate (see also Mortgages)

♀ ● Living Richly Real Estate, Brokered by eXp Realty, 318 Spear St Unit 4A, SF; 94105 877-974-2459 www.livingrichly.net

Recovery

♂ Acceptance Place, Baker Places, 600 Townsend St Ste 200E, SF; 415-864-1515 www.bakerplaces.org

♀ ☆ Castro Country Club, 4058 18th St, SF 415-552-6102 alcohol- & drug-free space www.castrocountryclub.org ⟲ ⚕

♂ ★ Intercounty Fellowship of Alcoholics Anonymous, 1821 Sacramento St, SF; 94109-3528 415-674-1821 415-499-0400 (Marin) aasfmarin.org aa@aasfmarin.org

⚥ ★ Last Drag Smoking Cessation Class, 290 Dolores St, SF; 415-339-7867 fb.com/thelastdragsf

♀ ☆ Narcotics Anonymous SF Area Service Office, 1290 Fillmore St Gallery B, SF; 94115 415-621-8600 www.sfna.org info@sfna.org

⚥ ★ Western Roundup Living Sober, POB 14804, SF; 94114 415-978-2478 livingsober.org

Religious / Spiritual Resources

⚥ ★ Axios - San Francisco, 950 Hotel Ave, Hayward, CA 510-538-1210 saint-seraphim.org

⚣ Black Leather Wings, www.blackleatherwings.org

⚢ ☆ ᏯᏊ College Heights Congregational Church, 1150 W Hillsdale Blvd, San Mateo; 94403 650-341-7311 **HD** www.college-heights.us ✐ office@collegeheights.us

⚢ ☆ Congregation B'nai Emunah, 3595 Taraval St, SF 94116 415-664-7373 www.bnaiemunahsf.org ⚨ office@bnaiemunahsf.org

⚣ ★ ᏯᏊ Congregation Sha'ar Zahav, 290 Dolores St, SF; 415-861-6932 www.shaarzahav.org ⚨ ✐

⚣ ★ (?Ꮬ) Dignity/San Francisco, 1329 7th Ave, SF; 94122-2507 415-681-2491 **H?** GLBT Catholics www.dignitysf.org

⚢ ☆ ᏯᏊ First Congregational Church of San Francisco, 1300 Polk St, SF; 94109 415-441-8901 www.sanfranciscoucc.org office@sanfranciscoucc.org

⚢ ☆ First Evangelical Lutheran Church, 600 Homer Ave, Palo Alto; 94301-2827 650-322-4669 www.flcpa.org office@flcpa.org

⚢ ★ ᏯᏊ Foothills Congregational Church, 461 Orange Ave, Los Altos; 94022 650-282-7718 www.foothills-church.org info@foothills-church.org

⚣ ★ Gay Buddhist Fellowship, 2261 Market St #456-A, SF; 415-974-9878 www.gaybuddhist.org

⚣ ★ Gay Buddhist Sangha, 69 Neptune St, SF 415-822-5224 www.gaybuddhistsangha.org

⚢ ☆ Hartford Street Zen Center, 57 Hartford St, SF 94114-2013 415-863-2507 hszc.org info@hszc.org

⚣ LGBT Alliance of the Jewish Community Federation, 121 Steuart St, SF; 415-777-0411 tinyurl.com/oejbonm ⚨

⚣ ★ Ꭷ Many Journeys MCC, 1150 W Hillsdale Blvd, San Mateo; 94403 650-515-0900 www.manyjourneysmcc.org admin@manyjourneysmcc.org

⚣ ★ (?Ꮬ) Metropolitan Community Church of San Francisco, 1300 Polk St, SF; 415-863-4434 **H** www.mccsf.org ✐ ❤

⚢ ☆ (?Ꮬ) Mission Bay Community Church, 32 Ocean Ave, SF; 94112 415-787-4751 **H?** www.missionbaycc.org ✐ info@missionbaycc.org

⚣ Sacred Space SF, 415-349-0930 sacredspacesf.org

San Francisco

⚣ Keshet SF Bay Office, 2 Embarcadero Center Flr 8, SF; www.keshetonline.org ⚨

⚢ ☆ Seventh Avenue Presbyterian Church, 1329 7th Ave, SF; 94122-2507 415-664-2543 www.seventhavenuechurch.org office@seventhavenuechurch.org

⚣ SF Queer Christians, 415-854-1739 sfqchristians.com

⚢ ☆ ᏯᏊ St Francis Lutheran Church, 152 Church St, SF; 94114-1111 415-621-2635 www.sflcsf.org ✐ stfrancis@sflcsf.org

⚢ ☆ St Paulus Lutheran Church, 1541 Polk St, SF 94109 415-673-8088 saintpaulus.org admin@saintpaulus.org

⚢ ☆ Unitarian Universalists of San Mateo, 300 E Santa Inez Ave, San Mateo; 94401-2506 650-342-5946 uusanmateo.org office@uusanmateo.org

⚢ ☆ Unity Spiritual Center, 2690 Ocean Ave, SF 94132 415-566-4122 www.unitysf.org uscsf@att.net

Reproductive Medicine & Fertility Services

⚢ ☆ LGBTQ Perinatal Wellness Center, 3207 Lakeshore Ave, Oakland, CA 94610 tinyurl.com/y4nwa5bw lgbtqperinatalwellnesscenter@gmail.com

Sports & Outdoor

⚣ ★ BayLands FrontRunners, POB 51456, Palo Alto; 94303 650-681-9002 www.baylands.org frontrunners@baylands.org

⚣ ★ Different Spokes San Francisco Cycling Club, POB 14711, SF; 94114 415-545-8391 www.dssf.org

⚣ ★ (?Ꮬ) Gay & Lesbian Sierrans, Loma Prieta Chapter, 3921 E Bayshore Rd Ste 204, Palo Alto tinyurl.com/2avc2sg

⚣ ★ Gay & Lesbian Tennis Federation of San Francisco, 2261 Market St #109A, SF; www.gltf.org

⚣ ★ Golden Gate Wrestling Club, 63 Whitney St, SF; 94114 / Eureka Valley Rec Center, 100 Collingwood St 415-373-8015 wrestlerswob.com/ggwc

⚣ ★ Golden State Gay Rodeo Association: Bay Area Chapter, POB 14126, SF; 94114 415-484-6494 fb.com/groups/44075527913

⚣ ★ Homoto Motorcycle Club, POB 190683, SF 94119 415-683-1103 www.homoto.us ✐

⚣ Pink Pistols San Francisco, tinyurl.com/yyvxjunt

⚣ ★ Rainbow Sierrans Bay Chapter, 2530 San Pablo Ave #I, Berkeley, CA rainbowsierrans.org

⚣ ★ San Francisco Dykes on Bikes, POB 401166, San Francisco, CA 94140 www.dykesonbikes.com

⚣ ★ ᏯᏊ San Francisco Earthquakes Ice Hockey, www.sfquakes.com

⚤ San Francisco Fog Rugby Football, 2370 Market St #232, SF; www.fogrugby.com

⚣ ★ ᏯᏊ San Francisco FrontRunners, 2261 Market St #484A, SF; 415-846-5494 www.sffr.org

⚣ ★ San Francisco Gay Basketball Association, 584 Castro St Box 451, SF; www.sfgba.com

⚣ San Francisco Gay Flag Football League, PO Box 14463, SF; 94134 www.sfgffl.org

⚣ ★ San Francisco Gay Softball League, 584 Castro St PMB 835, SF; 650-553-0101 www.sfgsl.org

⚣ ★ San Francisco Hiking Club, POB 14065, SF; 94114-0065 640-615-0151 www.sfhiking.com info@sfhiking.com

⚣ San Francisco Pool Association, POB 14258, SF; 94114 916-296-3069 www.sfpapool.org

⚣ ★ San Francisco Spikes (soccer), www.sfspikes.com

⚣ San Francisco Tsunami Water Polo, 415-728-6430 www.tsunamipolo.org

⚣ Team San Francisco, 2215R Market Street PMB 519, SF; teamsf.ning.com

⚣ ★ ᏯᏊ Tsunami Swim Club, sftsunami.org info@sftsunami.org

⚢ ★ ᏯᏊ Wrestlers WithOut Borders, 63 Whitney St, SF; 94131-2742 415-373-8015 **H** www.wrestlerswob.com info@wrestlerswob.com

Transportation: Limo, Taxi, Charter etc.

♀ Homobiles - Queer Car Service, 415-574-5023 Volunteers & designated drivers, optional donation. homobiles.org

Travel & Tourist Services (see also Accommodation)

♀ ● ♿ Cruisin' the Castro LGBTQ Walking Tours, 415-550-8110 www.cruisinthecastro.com kathy@cruisinthecastro.com

Weddings and Ceremonies

♂ ○ (♌) Currier, Kelsey, Coastside Weddings & Events 650-759-8144 tinyurl.com/y3k93was ♥ kelsey@coastsideweddingsand events.com

Women's Centers

♀ ☆ Women's Building, 3543 18th St, SF 415-431-1180 womensbuilding.org ☯

San Jose & South Bay Area

Community Centers and/or Pride Organizations

♂ ★ ♿ Billy DeFrank LGBTQ Community Center, 938 The Alameda, San Jose; 408-293-3040 www.defrankcenter.org

♂ ★ ♿ Silicon Valley Pride, c/o GPCCSJ Inc, 1346 The Alameda Ste 7 PMB 108, San Jose www.svpride.com

AIDS/HIV Services, Education & Support

♂ ☆ ♿ Health Trust Services, 3180 Newberry Dr Ste 200, San Jose; 408-513-8700 **H?** healthtrust.org ✗

Bars, Cafes, Clubs, Restaurants
San Jose

♂ Mac's Club, 39 Post St, San Jose 408-288-8221 fb.com/macsclub/

♂ ♿ Renegades, 501 W Taylor St, San Jose; 408-275-9902 tinyurl.com/ydherxos **L** ▦

♂ Splash, 65 Post St, San Jose; 408-292-2222 www.splashsj.com **DV** ▦

♂ ○ Vin Santo Ristorante, 1346 Lincoln Ave, San Jose; 408-920-2508 www.vin-santo.com ✗

Counseling/Psychotherapy/Mental Health

♂ ☆ (♌) Community Solutions, 9015 Murray #100, Gilroy; 408-842-7138 Also serve survivors of domestic violence, sexual assault and human trafficking. www.communitysolutions.org

Erotica / Adult Stores / Safe Sex Supplies

♂ ○ Secrets San Jose, 1818 W San Carlos Ave, San Jose; 95128 408-291-0441 www.secretsboutiques.com sanjosesecrets78@gmail.com

Health Care: Physical (see also Counseling/Mental Health)

♂ ○ Kamiak, Sandra, MD, 14583 Big Basin Way Ste 3B, Saratoga; 95070-6072 408-741-1332 www.sandrakamiakmd.com skamiak@aol.com

Leather Resources & Groups

♂ ☆ smOdyssey, POB 26372, San Jose; 95159 www.smodyssey.com info@smodyssey.com

Legal Services

♂ Legal Advocates for Children & Youth, Law Foundation Of Silicon Valley, 4 N 2nd St #1300, San Jose; 408-280-2416 tinyurl.com/y8fxphux

Men's & Sex Clubs (not primarily Health Clubs)

♂ ♿ Watergarden, 1010 Alameda, San Jose; 408-275-1215 www.thewatergarden.com **P** ✗

Organizations/Resources: Bisexual Focus

♂ ☆ Bi+ South Bay, c/o Billy DeFrank Center, 938 The Alameda, San Jose; 95126-3134 408-293-3040 tinyurl.com/y47pc42f ✧ fabulous@defrank.org

Organizations/Resources: Business & Professional Associations, Labor Advocacy

♂ ★ Rainbow Chamber Silicon Valley, 1702-L Meridian Ave. #205, San Jose; 408-998-9600 www.rainbowchamber.org

Organizations/Resources: Cultural, Dance, Performance

♂ ★ ♿ El Camino Reelers, POB 391373, Mountain View; 94039-1373 www.reelers.org **D** information@reelers.org

♂ ★ (♌) Rainbow Women's Chorus, 14938 Camden Ave Ste 61, San Jose; 95124 408-603-9367 **H?** www.rainbowwomen.org ✗ contact@rainbowwomen.org

♂ ★ Silicon Valley Gay Men's Chorus, 1100 Shasta Ave, San Jose; www.svgmc.org

Organizations/Resources: Ethnic, Multicultural

♂ ★ South Bay Queer & Asian, 938 The Alameda, San Jose; 408-293-2429 www.sbqa.org ✧

Organizations/Resources: Family and Supporters

♂ ★ ♿ PFLAG San Jose/Peninsula, POB 2718, Sunnyvale; 94087 408-270-8182 **H?** San Mateo County, San Jose & South Bay Area www.pflagsanjose.org

Organizations/Resources: Naturist/Nudist

♂ ★ (♌) Bayside Bare Boys, tinyurl.com/4d7bcfq **N**

Organizations/Resources: Political/Legislative/Advocacy

♂ ★ Bay Area Municipal Elections Committee (BAYMEC), 1855 Hamilton Ave #203, San Jose; 408-622-9632 www.baymec.org

Organizations/Resources: Social, Recreation, Support

♀ ★ Peninsula - Sappho, www.lavenderevents.com/women

♂ ★ Rainbow Recreation, 2040 W Middlefield Rd Apt 4, Mountain View; 94043 www.rainbowrec.org

♀ ★ South Bay Sappho, tinyurl.com/j3mbwd3

♀ ★ Women Over Fifty South Bay, tinyurl.com/dy226x

Organizations/Resources: Student, Academic, Education

♂ ★ ♿ Queer & Asian (Q&A SJSU), Mailbox #53, c/o Student Involvement, 1 Washington Square, 1411 Student Union Building, San Jose; 408-924-5950 **H?** qnasjsu.tumblr.com ✧ ✗

California: San Jose & South Bay Area
Organizations: Student

116

GAYELLOW PAGES #42 2020-2021

Santa Cruz Area: California
Bookstores

♂ ★ ♿ San Jose State University PRIDE Center, Student Union, Room 1600, First Level, 1 Washington Sq, San Jose; 95192-0161 408-924-6157 www.sjsu.edu/pride ✎ sjsupride@gmail.com

♀ ★ Santa Clara University School of Law EQ/SCU, 500 El Camino Real, Santa Clara; law.scu.edu/life/eqscu.cfm

Organizations/Resources: Transgender/Gender Non-Conforming/Diverse

T ☆ ♿ South Bay Transmen, 938 The Alameda, San Jose; 95126-3134 408-293-2429 www.defrank.org ✧ ✎ info@defrank.org

T Transfamily of Santa Clare County, - - tinyurl.com/vbk8h3s

Organizations/Resources: Youth (see also Family)

♀ Bill Wilson Center, 3490 The Alameda, Santa Clara; 408-243-0222 www.billwilsoncenter.org

♀ ★ ♿ LGBTQ Youth Space, 452 S 1st St, San Jose; 95113 408-343-7940 **H?** www.youthspace.org ✧ ✎ YouthSpace@fcservices.org

Recovery

♀ ☆ AA in Santa Clara County, 274 E Hamilton Ave Ste D, Campbell; 408-374-8511 www.aasanjose.org

♀ ★ ♿ Sober & Free, POB 4707, San Jose; 95150 www.soberandfree.org

Religious / Spiritual Resources

♀ ☆ ♿ Campbell UMC, 1675 Winchester Blvd, Campbell; 95008 408-378-3472 **HD** www.campbellunited.org ✎ info@campbellunited.org

♂ ☆ Campbell United Church of Christ, 400 W Campbell Ave, Campbell; 95008 408-378-4418 www.campbellucc.org

♀ ★ (?♿) Celebration of Faith, POB 59330, San Jose; 95159-9330 408-345-2319 www.celebrationoffaith.org ✎ djharvey1955@gmail.com

♂ ☆ Holy Redeemer Lutheran Church, 1948 The Alameda, San Jose; 95126-1427 408-296-4040 www.hrlcsj.org

♂ ☆ ♿ Skyland Community Church, POB 245, Los Gatos; 95033 408-353-1310 www.skylandchurch.com ✎

♂ ☆ Trinity Cathedral, 81 N 2nd St, San Jose; 95113 408-293-7953 www.trinitysj.org trinicat@pacbell.net

Sports & Outdoor

♀ ★ ♿ A League of Our Own (Bowling), Homestead Lanes, Cupertino 408-296-7200 fb.com/groups/45093943781/ dinodapooh@aol.com

♀ San Jose Pink Pistols, tinyurl.com/qb6mo7u

♀ ☆ San Jose Women's Softball League, POB 6112, San Jose; 95150 408-800-2425 www.sjwsoftball.com

♀ ★ Silicon Valley Gay Softball League, POB 28054, San Jose; 95159 612-555-1212 www.svgsl.org

♀ South Bay Volleyball Club, POB 914, Mountain View; 94042 www.sbvbc.org

> *San Luis Obispo: see Central Coast*
> » *San Mateo: see San Francisco Bay/Peninsula*
> » *Santa Barbara: see Central Coast*

» *Santa Clara: see San Jose & South Bay Area*

Santa Clarita Valley Area

AIDS/HIV Services, Education & Support

♂ Project Kindle, POB 800991, Santa Clarita 91355 877-800-2267 www.projectkindle.org

Organizations/Resources: Family and Supporters

♂ ☆ PFLAG Santa Clarita Valley, POB 55776, Valencia; 91385-0776 661-255-9308 www.pflagscv.net info@pflagscv.net

Organizations/Resources: Social, Recreation, Support

♀ ★ Gay & Lesbian Association of Santa Clarita (GLASC), POB 800413, Santa Clarita; 91380 www.glasc.com

Religious / Spiritual Resources

♂ ☆ ♿ St Stephen's Episcopal Church, 24901 Orchard Village Rd, Santa Clarita; 91355 661-259-7307 **H?** www.st-stephens.org ✎ office@st-stephens.org

Santa Cruz Area

Community Centers and/or Pride Organizations

♀ ★ ♿ Diversity Center, POB 8280, Santa Cruz; 95061-8280 1117 Soquel Ave, Santa Cruz 95062 831-425-5422 www.diversitycenter.org ✎ info@diversitycenter.org

♀ ★ Santa Cruz Pride, 404 Woodland Dr, Ben Lomond; 831-234-0259 fb.com/Santa.Cruz.Pride.74

♀ Santa Cruz Pride, fb.com/Santa.Cruz.Pride.74/

Information, Media & Publications

♂ Queer Cruz, www.queercruz.com

AIDS/HIV Services, Education & Support

♂ ☆ ♿ Santa Cruz AIDS Project, 380 Encinal St Ste 200, Santa Cruz; 831-427-3900 tinyurl.com/y6yhxuhz

Bars, Cafes, Clubs, Restaurants
Santa Cruz

♀ ○ ♂ Betty Burgers, 1000 41st Ave, Santa Cruz; 831-475-5901 www.bettyburgers.com ✗ betty@bettyburgers.com

♂ ○ Betty Burgers, 505 Seabright Ave, Santa Cruz 831-423-8190 www.bettyburgers.com ✗ betty@bettyburgers.com

♂ ○ Blue Lagoon, 923 Pacific Ave, Santa Cruz 831-423-7117 www.thebluelagoon.com **D** ▒ ✎

♀ ● ♂ Cafe LimeLight, 1016 Cedar St, Santa Cruz; 831-425-7873 www.cafelimelight.com ✗ ↻ ✎

♀ ○ Saturn Cafe, 145 Laurel St, Santa Cruz 831-429-8505 santacruz.saturncafe.com ↻

Bookstores

♂ ○ ♿ Bookshop Santa Cruz, 1520 Pacific Ave, Santa Cruz; 831-423-0900 www.bookshopsantacruz.com

♂ ○ Crossroads Books, 1935 Main St, Watsonville 831-728-4139 www.watsonvillebooks.com

Funding: Endowment, Fundraising

♂ ☆ ♿ Community Foundation Santa Cruz County, 7807 Soquel Dr, Aptos; 831-662-2000 www.cfscc.org ✔

Legal Services

♂ ○ Law Offices of Moira Leigh, 621 Seabright Ave, Santa Cruz; 831-454-0226 santacruzattorney.com

♀ Watsonville Law Center, 315 Main St Ste 207, Watsonville; 831-722-2845 www.watsonvillelawcenter.org

Organizations/Resources: Family and Supporters

♂ ☆ PFLAG Santa Cruz County, POB 251, Santa Cruz; 95061 831-427-4016 www.pflagscc.org pflagscc@gmail.com

Organizations/Resources: Social, Recreation, Support

⚦ SantaCruzGayMen.com, SantaCruzGayMen.com

Organizations/Resources: Student, Academic, Education

⚦ ★ Harbor High School GSA, 300 La Fonda Ave, Santa Cruz; 831-429-3810 x1320

⚦ ★ ♿ Lionel Cantú Queer Center, Merrill College, University of California Santa Cruz, 1156 High St, Santa Cruz 831-459-2468 **H?** www.queer.ucsc.edu ✔

Organizations/Resources: Transgender/Gender Non-Conforming/Diverse

T Santa Cruz Trans Support Groups and Services, PO Box 8280, Santa Cruz; 95061 831-425-5422 tinyurl.com/yxhrtwyf

Religious / Spiritual Resources

♀ ☆ ♿ Inner Light Ministries, POB 1029, Soquel; 95073-1029 / 5630 Soquel Dr 831-465-9090 www.innerlightministries.com ✔ info@innerlightministries.com

⚦ ★ ♿ Out in Our Faith/Twice Blessed, Temple Beth El, 3055 Porter Gulch Rd, Aptos; 95003 831-479-3444 tinyurl.com/y4mn47gp ⚥ ✔ info@tbeaptos.org

Sports & Outdoor

⚦ ★ Santa Cruz Queer Men's Hikers, fb.com/groups/scqueerhikers/ tmorosco@gmail.com

Women's Centers

♀ ☆ ♿ Walnut Avenue Family & Women's Center, 303 Walnut Ave, Santa Cruz; 95060 831-426-3062 www.wafwc.org
>> *Santa Maria: see Central Coast*
>> *Santa Monica: see Los Angeles Area*
>> *Santa Rosa: see Russian River/Sonoma*

Sequoia National Park Area

Community Centers and/or Pride Organizations

⚦ ★ The Source LGBT Center, POB 188, Visalia; 93279 / 208 W Main St Ste B 559-429-4277 www.thesourcelgbt.org

Accommodation: Hotels, Inns, Guesthouses, B&B, Resorts
Springville

♀ ● Great Energy, 559-539-2382 www.michalreed.com ✔ Ⓢ

Funding: Endowment, Fundraising

⚦ ★ Visalia Pride Lions Club, POB 1384, Visalia; 93279 360-970-3642 tinyurl.com/mv7w5xu visaliapride2009@gmail.com

Organizations/Resources: Family and Supporters

♂ ☆ PFLAG Tulare-Kings Counties, 4125 W Noble Ave #164, Visalia; 559-579-1101 fb.com/pflagtkc/

California: Sequoia National Park Area
Organizations: Social & Support

118

GAYELLOW PAGES #42 2020-2021

Yucca Valley : California
Campgrounds and RV Parks

Organizations/Resources: Social, Recreation, Support

⚥ Tuesday Evening Dining Group (T.E.D.G.), tedg.org

Organizations/Resources: Transgender/Gender Non-Conforming/Diverse

T Transgender Programs, The Source, POB 188, Visalia; 93279 559-372-2889 tinyurl.com/loz4jlk

Religious / Spiritual Resources

♂ ☆ First Congregational Church, 220 W Tulare Ave, Tulare; 93274 559-686-5528 ucctulare.org ucctulare@yahoo.com
» *Sierra Foothills: see Gold Country/Sierra*

Simi Valley

Organizations/Resources: Family and Supporters

♂ ☆ FFLUID, 370 Royal Ave; 805-501-4583 Familes & Friends Living United in Diversity ffluid.org

Solano County

Community Centers and/or Pride Organizations

⚥ ★ ♿ Solano Pride Center, 1234 Empire St Ste 1560, Fairfield; 707-207-3430 **H?** www.solanopride.org ✔

Bars, Cafes, Clubs, Restaurants
Vallejo

♂ ○ Townhouse Cocktail Lounge, 401A Georgia St, Vallejo; 707-553-9109

Erotica / Adult Stores / Safe Sex Supplies

♂ ○ Not Too Naughty #3, 540 Georgia St, Vallejo 94590 707-644-2935 www.secretsboutiques.com ntnvallejo@yahoo.com

♂ ○ Secrets Fairfield, 562 Parker Rd, Fairfield 94533-9000 707-437-9297 www.secretsboutiques.com secrets20@yahoo.com

Organizations/Resources: Social, Recreation, Support

⚥ ★ Vallejo Gay Network (VGN), www.vallejogaynetwork.org info@vallejogaynetwork.org

Organizations/Resources: Student, Academic, Education

⚥ ★ Touro University Rainbow Health Coalition, 1310 Johnson Lane, Vallejo; fb.com/turhc

Religious / Spiritual Resources

♂ ☆ ♿ St Paul's United Methodist Church, 101 West St, Vacaville; 95688 707-448-5154 **H?** www.stpaulsvacaville.com ✔ stpumcvacaville@gmail.com
» *Sonora: see Gold Country/Sierra Foothills/Yosemite*

Stockton

Community Centers and/or Pride Organizations

⚥ San Joaquin Pride Center, 115 N Sutter St Flr 2; 209-466-7572 sjpridecenter.org

Bars, Cafes, Clubs, Restaurants

⚥ ● ♿ Paradise, 10114 Lower Sacramento Rd; 209-477-4724 fb.com/ParadiseNightclub **DVK**

Erotica / Adult Stores / Safe Sex Supplies

♂ ○ Secrets Stockton, 1302 E Harding Way; 95205-3614 209-465-4114 www.secretsboutiques.com

Funding: Endowment, Fundraising

⚥ Imperial San Joaquin Delta Empire, POB 690333; 95269 209-400-8931 tinyurl.com/pc39pt2

Organizations/Resources: Political/Legislative/Advocacy

⚥ Central Valley Stonewall Democrats, POB 4311; 95204 209-227-3115

Religious / Spiritual Resources

⚥ ★ Valley Ministries MCC, 4118 Coronado Ave 209-810-9500 www.vmmcc.org
» *Sunnyvale: see San Jose & South Bay Area*
» *Sutter Creek: see Gold Country/Sierra*

Temecula

Organizations/Resources: Family and Supporters

♂ ☆ PFLAG Temecula Valley, 40335, Winchester Rd E308, Winchester; 951-878-8052 www.pflagtemecula.org
» *Three Rivers: see Sequoia National Park Area*

Tionesta

Campgrounds and RV Parks

♂ ● Eagle's Nest RV Park, 634 County Rd 97A 530-664-2081 www.eaglesnestrvpark.com ✔
» *Upland: see Inland Empire*
» *Vacaville: see Solano County*
» *Vallejo: see Solano County*
» *Van Nuys: see Los Angeles Area*
» *Venice: see Los Angeles Area*
» *Ventura: see Central Coast*

Victorville

Bars, Cafes, Clubs, Restaurants

⚥ ● Ricky's, 13728 Hesperia Rd #12 760-951-5400 fb.com/rickys-bar/ ▦
» *Walnut Creek: see East Bay Area*
» *West Hollywood: see Los Angeles Area*
» *Willits: see Mendocino Area*

Yucca Valley

Campgrounds and RV Parks

⚥ ● Starland Community, 760-364-2069 www.starlandcommunity.org **P** (♣?) ✔ ⊘

Colorado
State/County Resources

Information, Media & Publications

♂ ● ᕫᕫ OUT FRONT, 3535 Walnut St, Denver, CO 80205 303-477-4000 fax 303-325-2642 www.outfrontmagazine.com ⤳ info@outfrontonline.com

AIDS/HIV Services, Education & Support

♀ ☆ Western Colorado AIDS Project, 2352 N 7th St Unit A-1, Grand Junction, CO 970-243-2437 tinyurl.com/hxrntwn

Financial Planning, Investment (see also Insurance)

♀ ● LGBT Financial, 801-613-7119 www.lgbtfinancial.org ryan@lgbtfinancial.org

Funding: Endowment, Fundraising

♂ Alexander Foundation, POB 1995, Denver, CO 80201 303-331-7733 tinyurl.com/4oe9ova

♂ ★ Gill Foundation, 1550 Wewatta St Ste 720, Denver, CO 80202 303-292-4455 www.gillfoundation.org info@gillfoundation.org

Health Care: Physical (see also Counseling/Mental Health)

♀ ● Colorado Mountain Doulas, 719-581-9041 **H?** colorado-mountaindoulas.com comtndoulas@gmail.com

Leather Resources & Groups

♂ ★ Mr. Leather Colorado Foundation, c/o Michael Hobbs, 4886 Joplin St, Denver, CO 720-771-4615 **H?** www.coloradoleather.org

Organizations/Resources: Business & Professional Associations, Labor Advocacy

♂ Colorado GLBT Bar Association, c/o The Center, POB 9798, Denver, CO 80209 303-871-6278 www.coloradoglbtbar.org

Organizations/Resources: Political/Legislative/Advocacy

♂ ★ Log Cabin Republicans Colorado, POB 18137, Denver, CO 80218 tinyurl.com/hwoz5wj

♂ ★ ᕫᕫ ONE Colorado, 1490 Lafayette St Ste 304, Denver, CO 303-396-6170 www.one-colorado.org

Organizations/Resources: Senior Resources

♀ ★ Old Lesbians Organizing for Change (OLOC) - Colorado, OLOCinColorado@comcast.net

Organizations/Resources: Social, Recreation, Support

♂ ★ Sunday Afternoon Car Klub, www.lcci-sack.com

Organizations/Resources: Youth (see also Family)

♂ Colorado GSA Network, 1490 Lafayette St Ste 304, Denver, CO 303-396-6170 fb.com/coloradogsanetwork

Religious / Spiritual Resources

♂ ★ ᕫ Integrity/Colorado, 1515 Bison Ridge Dr, Colorado Springs, CO 80919 719-650-8883 integrity-colorado.org ⤳

Sports & Outdoor

♂ ★ Colorado Frontrunners, www.coloradofrontrunners.org

♂ ★ (?ᕫ) Colorado Gay Rodeo Association, POB 18728, Denver, CO 80218-0728 www.cgrarodeo.com

♂ ★ Colorado Gay Volleyball Association, POB 18576, Denver, CO 80218 www.cgva.org

♂ ★ Team Colorado of the Rockies, Inc., www.teamcolorado-dousa.org

♂ ★ You Can Play, Inc., POB 7460, Denver, CO 80207 720-565-5236 www.youcanplayproject.org

Aspen Area

Organizations/Resources: Social, Recreation, Support

♂ ★ AspenOUT, POB 3143, Aspen; 81612 970-925-4123 www.rfglcf.com

♀ Gay for Good - Rocky Mountains, Volunteer organization. tinyurl.com/tskvrhu

Sports & Outdoor

♂ Aspen Gay Ski Week, POB 3143, Aspen 81612 970-925-4123 gayskiweek.com

---

★ A not-for-profit enterprise (regardless of tax status) primarily operated by lesbian/gay/bisexual/transgender/queer people.
☆ A not-for-profit enterprise (regardless of tax status) not primarily operated by lesbian/gay/ bisexual/ transgender/queer people.
● A business, wishing to be listed as wholly or partly lesbian/ gay/bisexual/transgender/queer owned.
○ A business, not wishing to be listed as wholly or partly lesbian/gay/bisexual/transgender/queer owned.

Any entry which does not have one of the above symbols is believed to welcome gay/lesbian/bisexual/transgender patronage but no direct response received.

☎ **CALL FOR LOCAL INFORMATION**

♂ GLBTQI people ♀ Gay/nongay people ♂ bisexual people
♀ LBTQI women ♀ all women ♀ bisexual women
♂ GBTQI men ♂ all men ♂ bisexual men
T specifically transsexual/transgender/transvestite
ʏ ✕ Bar & Restaurant ✕ Restaurant ⊡ Cafe
▥Entertainment/Shows **D** Dancing **S** Sports bar **V** Video bar
K Karaoke **C** Country **L** Leather/Levi **W** Western
P Private Club (ask about visitor memberships)
N Clothing Optional/Nudist/Naturist
⊗ No indoor smoking (⊗) Some indoor smoking areas
❖ Pets welcome (❖?) Ask about pets
⤳ High speed internet available to visitors
ᕫᕫ Accessible premises and lavatory
(ᕫᕫ) Accessible premises with help; accessible lavatory
ᕫ Accessible premises; lavatory not known to be accessible
(ᕫ) Accessible premises with help
(?ᕫ) Call ahead for details or special arrangements available.
◇Asian ✦Latin/Hispanic ✢African-descent/Black
❖People of Color ⚤Two-Spirit ✪Diverse

Colorado: Boulder Area
Information, Media & Publications

120
GAYELLOW PAGES #42 2020-2021

Colorado Springs Area: Colorado
Accommodation: Rentals

Boulder Area

Information, Media & Publications

⚢ ★ Out Boulder, POB 1018, Boulder; 80306 303-499-5777 www.outboulder.org ✎

Accommodation: Hotels, Inns, Guesthouses, B&B, Resorts

♂ ○ Briar Rose B&B, 2151 Arapahoe Ave, Boulder 80302-6601 303-442-3007 www.briarrosebb.com ✎ ⊛ info@briarrosebb.com

AIDS/HIV Services, Education & Support

♂ ☆ 🦽 Boulder County AIDS Project, 2118 14th St, Boulder; 303-444-6121 www.bcap.org

Bars, Cafes, Clubs, Restaurants

♂ ○ 🦽 Walnut Cafe, 3073 Walnut St, Boulder; 303-447-2315 www.walnutcafe.com ✗ ▷

Bookstores

♂ ○ (?🦽) Boulder Book Store, 1107 Pearl St, Boulder; 303-447-2074 **H?** www.boulderbookstore.net

Counseling/Psychotherapy/Mental Health

♂ ● 🦽 Boulder Emotional Wellness, 3434 47th St Ste 130, Boulder; 80301 303-225-2708 tinyurl.com/b7qogup ✎

Funding: Endowment, Fundraising

⚢ ★ 🦽 Open Door Fund, 1123 Spruce St, Boulder; 303-442-0436 www.opendoorfund.org

Health Care: Physical (see also Counseling/Mental Health)

♂ ☆ Boulder Valley Women's Health Center, 2855 Valmont Rd, Boulder; 80301 303-442-5160 www.boulderwomenshealth.org info@bvwhc.org

♂ ○ 🦽 Lefthand Community Acupuncture, 424 E Simpson St, Lafayette; 80026 720-378-6090 www.lefthandacu.com info@lefthandacu.com

Legal Services

♂ ● 🦽 Lisa A. Polansky, Founding Partner, Polansky Law Firm, 4999 Pearl E Circle Ste 201, Boulder; 80301 303-415-2583 Criminal defense www.polanskylawfirm.com Lisa@polanskylawfirm.com

Organizations/Resources: Cultural, Dance, Performance

♀ ☆ Resonance Women's Chorus of Boulder, 2525 Arapahoe Ave #E4-186, Boulder; 80302 303-473-8337 www.resonancechorus.org resonancechorus@gmail.com

♀ ☆ Sound Circle, 2525 Arapahoe Ave E4-186, Boulder; 80302 303-473-8337 www.soundcirclesings.org soundcircle@ecentral.com

Organizations/Resources: Family and Supporters

♂ ★ 🦽 PFLAG Boulder, POB 19696, Boulder; 80308 303-444-8164 www.pflagboulder.org

Organizations/Resources: Student, Academic, Education

♂ ★ Center for Inclusion & Social Change, Center for Community, room N320, Boulder; 303-492-0272 www.colorado.edu/cisc/ ✎

⚢ ★ 🦽 University of Colorado LGBTQ Studies Certificate Program, Hazel Gates Woodruff Cottage, 246 UCB, Boulder 303-492-8923 **H?** www.colorado.edu/lgbtq/

Religious / Spiritual Resources

♂ ☆ 🦽 Boulder Valley Unitarian Universalist Fellowship, 1241 Ceres Dr, Lafayette; 80026 303-665-4280 **HD** www.bvuuf.org ✎ officemanager@bvuuf.org

♂ ☆ 🦽 First United Methodist Church of Boulder, 1421 Spruce St, Boulder; 80302 303-442-3770 www.fumcboulder.org ✎ office@fumcboulder.org

♂ ☆ 🦽 UCC - Longmont, 1500 9th Ave, Longmont; 80501 303-776-4940 **HD** www.ucclongmont.org

♂ ☆ 🦽 Unitarian Universalist Church, 5001 Pennsylvania Ave, Boulder; 80303-2739 303-494-0195 **HD** www.uuchurchofboulder.org ✎ officeuucb@gmail.com

Travel & Tourist Services (see also Accommodation)

♂ ○ **Adventure Bound Expeditions, 711 Walnut St, Boulder; 80302-5362 303-449-0990 877-440-0990 fax 303-449-9038 Adventure travel for gay men to destinations throughout the world. www.adventureboundmen.com**

Breckenridge

Accommodation: Hotels, Inns, Guesthouses, B&B, Resorts

♂ ○ Fireside Inn, 114 N French St; 970-453-6456 www.fireside-inn.com ✎ ⊛

Organizations/Resources: Social, Recreation, Support

⚢ Snowmos, fb.com/SnowmosCO

Colorado Springs Area

Community Centers and/or Pride Organizations

⚢ ★ Colorado Springs Pride Fest, www.cospridefest.com

Accommodation: Hotels, Inns, Guesthouses, B&B, Resorts
Colorado Springs

♂ ○ 🦽 Old Town GuestHouse, 115 S 26th St, Colorado Springs; 80904-3010 719-632-9194 www.oldtown-guesthouse.com ✎ ⊛ luxury@oldtown-guesthouse.com

Manitou Springs

♂ ○ 🦽 Blue Skies Inn B&B, 402 Manitou Ave, Manitou Springs; 80829-2303 800-398-7949 719-685-3899 www.blueskiesinn.com ✎ ⊛

Woodland Park

♂ ● Pikes Peak Paradise B&B, 236 Pinecrest Rd, Woodland Park; 719-687-6656 www.pikespeakparadise.com ✿ ✎ ⊛

Accommodation Rental: Furnished / Vacation (& AirBNB)
Cascade

♂ ○ Sanctuary of the Rose, 4615 Hagerman Ave, Cascade; 80809 719-433-3072 www.sanctuaryoftherose.com ✎ ⊛ ⊛ thesanctuaryrose@aol.com

AIDS/HIV Services, Education & Support

♀ ☆ Southern Colorado AIDS Project, 1301 S 8th St #200, Colorado Springs; 80905 719-578-9092 fax 719-578-8690 www.scap.org

Bars, Cafes, Clubs, Restaurants
Colorado Springs

♂ ● ♿ Club Q, 3430 N Academy Blvd, Colorado Springs; 719-570-1429 www.clubqonline.com **DKV** ⛾ ✗ ▥ ✈

♀ ○ Odyssey Gastropub, 311 N Tejon St, Colorado Springs; 719-999-5127 www.odysseygastropub.com ⛾ ✗ ▥

Dentists

♀ ○ ♿ Kearney, James W, DDS, Austin Bluffs Dental, 2918 Austin Bluffs Parkway Ste 100, Colorado Springs; 80918 719-593-8488 www.austinbluffsdental.com ✈

Funding: Endowment, Fundraising

♀ ★ United Court of The Pikes Peak Empire, PO Box 6925, Colorado Springs; 80934 www.ucppe.org

Jewelry (see also Gifts)

♀ ○ ♿ Lane Mitchell Jewelers, 102 E Pikes Peak Ave Ste 303, Colorado Springs, 80903 719-632-1170 lanemitchelljewelers.com lanejewelers@gmail.com

Legal Services

♀ ○ ♿ Wolfe, Julie, 10 Boulder Crescent St #201, Colorado Springs; 80903 719-633-7101

Men's & Sex Clubs (not primarily Health Clubs)

♂ ● Buddies, 3430 N Academy Blvd Ste B N, Colorado Springs; 719-591-7660 www.clubbuddies.com **P** ✈

Metaphysical, Occult, Alternative Healing

♀ ○ ♿ Celebration Metaphysical Center, 975 Garden of the Gods Rd Unit C, Colorado Springs; 80907 719-634-1855 www.celebrationstore.com

Organizations/Resources: Cultural, Dance, Performance

♂ ★ (?♫) Out Loud: The Colorado Springs Men's Chorus, 20 E St Vrain st, Colorado Springs, CO 719-314-9183 www.outloudcsmc.com

Organizations/Resources: Family and Supporters

♀ ☆ PFLAG Colorado Springs, POB 49131, Colorado Springs; 80949 719-425-9567 www.cspflag.org

Organizations/Resources: Political/Legislative/Advocacy

♀ ☆ ♿ Citizens Project, 322 N Tejon St Ste 202, Colorado Springs; 719-520-9899 www.citizensproject.org

Organizations/Resources: Transgender/Gender Non-Conforming/Diverse

T ☆ ♿ Peak Area Gender Expressions (PAGE), tinyurl.com/h9h46xg

Organizations/Resources: Youth (see also Family)

♀ ★ ♿ Inside/Out Youth Services, 223 N Wahsatch Ave Ste 101, Colorado Springs; 80903 719-328-1056 www.insideoutys.org ✈ info@insideoutys.org

Religious / Spiritual Resources

♀ ☆ All Souls Unitarian Universalist Church, 730 N Tejon, Colorado Springs; 80903 719-633-7717 www.asuuc.net info@asuuc.net

♀ ★ ♿ Pikes Peak MCC, 1102 S 21st St, Colorado Springs; 80904-3708 719-634-3771 www.ppmcc.org admin@ppmcc.org

Denver Area

Community Centers and/or Pride Organizations

♀ ★ ♿ The Center on Colfax, 1301 E Colfax Ave, Denver; 80218 303-733-7743 lgbtqcolorado.org info@lgbtqcolorado.org

Accommodation Rental: Furnished / Vacation (& AirBNB)
Denver

♂ ● Highland Park Guest House, 3166 N Speer Blvd 303 593-1549 tinyurl.com/olelcuu ✈ ⊗⊗

AIDS/HIV Services, Education & Support

♀ ☆ ♿ Colorado AIDS Project, 6260 E Colfax Ave, Denver; 303-837-0166 www.coloradoaidsproject.org

♀ ☆ ♿ Project Angel Heart, 4950 Washington St, Denver; 80216 303-830-0202 fax 303-830-1840 Meals for those coping with life-threatening illness. www.projectangelheart.org

Archives/Libraries/Museums/History Projects

♀ ★ ♿ Terry Mangan Memorial Library, The Center, 1301 E Colfax Ave, Denver; 303-951-5209 tinyurl.com/gq9jakf

Bars, Cafes, Clubs, Restaurants
Denver

♀ ○ Avenue Grill, 630 E 17th Ave, Denver 303-861-2820 www.avenuegrill.com ⛾ ✗

♀ ● Babes Around Denver, check schedule 303-475-4620 www.babesaroundenver.com

♂ ○ Banzai Sushi, 6655 Leetsdale Dr, Denver 303-329-3366 www.100rolls.com ✗

♀ ○ Bastien's Restaurant, 3503 E Colfax Ave, Denver; 303-322-0363 bastiensrestaurant.com ✗

♀ Blush & Blu, 1526 E Colfax Ave, Denver 303-484-8548 www.blushblubar.com

♂ ● BoyzTown, 117 Broadway, Denver 303-722-7373 strippers www.boyztowndenver.com ▥ ✈

♂ ● (♿) Charlie's Denver, 900 E Colfax Ave, Denver; 303-839-8890 www.charliesdenver.com **DLCW** ⛾ ✗ ▥

♀ ○ The Clocktower Cabaret, 1601 Arapahoe St, Denver; 303-293-0075 www.clocktowercabaret.com ▥

♂ Denver Sweet, 776 N Lincoln St, Denver 720-598-5648 denversweet.com

♀ El Potrero, 4501 E Virginia Ave, Denver 303-388-8889 fb.com/elpotreroclub **D** ⛾ ✗ ▥ ♦

Colorado: Denver Area
Bars, Cafes, Clubs, Restaurants
122
GAYELLOW PAGES #42 2020-2021
Denver Area : Colorado
Organizations: Student

⚥ Gladys: The Nosy Neighbor, 500 Santa Fe Dr, Denver; 303-893-6112 fb.com/gladysdenver/ **D**

⚥ Hip Chicks Out, www.hipchicksout.com

♂ ○ Hooked on Colfax, 3213 E Colfax Ave, Denver 303-398-2665 hookedoncolfax.com ☞ hooked_on_colfax@yahoo.com

⚥ ● ♿ Li'l Devils Lounge, 255 S Broadway, Denver; 303-733-1156 www.lildevilslounge.com ✗

♀ ○ Mercury Cafe, 2199 California St, Denver 303-294-9281 www.mercurycafe.com **D** ✕🎵

⚥ ● Pride and Swagger, 450 E 17th Ave #110, Denver; 720-476-6360 www.prideandswaggerco.com

⚥ ● R&R Denver, 4958 E Colfax, Denver 303-320-9337 fb.com/randrdenver

♂ ○ ♿ To the Wind Bistro, 3333 E Colfax Ave, Denver; 303-316-3333 tothewindbistro.com ✕

♀ ○ Tracks, 3500 Walnut St, Denver; 303-863-7326 www.tracksdenver.com **D** 🎵 ✪

♂ Trade, 475 Santa Fe Dr, Denver; 720-627-5905 fb.com/Tradedenver/home **D**

⚥ Triangle, 2036 N Broadway, Denver 303-658-0914 thetriangledenver.com **D**

⚥ ● ♿ X Bar, 629 E Colfax Ave, Denver; 303-832-2687 www.xbardenver.com **DKV** ⏲ ☞ ✕ 🎵

Bookstores

♂ ○ ♿ Tattered Cover, 1628 16th St, Denver; 303-436-1070 www.tatteredcover.com ✗

♂ ○ ♿ Tattered Cover, 2526 E Colfax Ave; 80206-5626 303-322-7727 www.tatteredcover.com ✗

Counseling/Psychotherapy/Mental Health

♂ ● ♿ Hsieh, Linda, MA, LPC, Open Forest Counseling, 950 S Cherry St #220, Denver; 80246 720-429-3047 lindahsieh.com

♀ ● Solution-Focused Analysis, Psychotherapy for the 21st Century, tinyurl.com/l2sbmdj

♀ ● ♿ Vitaletti, Robert, PhD, 1616 17th St #567, Denver; 303-628-5425

Florists (see also Gifts)

♀ ● (♺) Bouquets, 1525 15th St, Denver 80202-1342 303-333-5500 www.bouquets.org ✗

Funding: Endowment, Fundraising

♂ ★ Krewe of Chaos, 400 S Colorado Blvd Ste 360, Denver; www.KreweofChaos.org

Insurance (see also Financial Planning)

♂ ● ♿ Boynton, Susan, State Farm, 9200 W Cross Dr Ste 122, Littleton; 80123 303-948-2905 www.susanboynton.com sue@sueboynton.com

Leather Resources & Groups

♂ ★ ♿ Denver Boys of Leather, 277 Broadway #314, Denver; www.denverboysofleather.org

Legal Services

⚥ ○ DUI Law Firm Denver, 1890 Gaylord St, Denver 80206 303-404-7492 www.duilawfirmdenver.com

Men's & Sex Clubs (not primarily Health Clubs)

♂ ● Denver Swim Club, 6923 E Colfax, Denver 303-322-4023 www.denverswimclub.com **N** ✗

♂ ● Midtowne Spa, 2935 Zuni St, Denver 303-458-8902 www.midtowne.com

Organizations/Resources: Business & Professional Associations, Labor Advocacy

⚥ ★ Denver Gay & Lesbian Chamber of Commerce (DGLCC), POB 103066, Denver; 80250 720-900-4522 www.colgbtqcc.org

Organizations/Resources: Cultural, Dance, Performance

⚥ ● (♺) Denver Gay Men's Chorus, Rocky Mountain Arts Association, 700 Colorado Blvd #325, Denver; 303-325-3959 www.rmarts.org

♀ ● (♺) Denver Women's Chorus, Rocky Mountain Arts Association, 700 Colorado Blvd #325, Denver; 303-325-3959 www.rmarts.org

⚥ ★ Harmony: A Colorado chorale, POB 13256, Denver; 80201-4656 www.harmonychorale.org support@harmonychorale.org

⚥ ★ Mile High Freedom Bands, 216 S Grant St, Denver; 720-515-6432 www.mhfb.org

⚥ ★ Rocky Mountain Rainbeaus, POB 370813, Denver; 80213 www.rainbeaus.org **D**

Organizations/Resources: Deaf

⚥ ★ Mile High Rainbow Society of the Deaf, 319 Empire St, Aurora; 720-210-5513

Organizations/Resources: Family and Supporters

♂ ● (♺) PFLAG Denver, POB 18901, Denver; 80218 303-573-5861 www.pflagdenver.org ✦

♀ ☆ PFLAG Highlands Ranch, 7522 S Monaco Way, Centennial; www.pflaghighlandsranch.org

Organizations/Resources: Senior Resources

⚥ ♿ SAGE of the Rockies, c/o The Center, 1301 E Colfax Ave, Denver; 970-221-3247 www.glbtcolorado.org/sage/

Organizations/Resources: Social, Recreation, Support

♂ ★ (♺) Colorado Prime Timers, POB 300274, Denver; 80203 303-331-2458 www.coloradoprimetimers.com

♂ ★ Front Range Bears, POB 300534, Denver 80203-0534 www.frontrangebears.com

⚥ Parasol Patrol, 720-298-7244 parasolpatrol.org

Organizations/Resources: Student, Academic, Education

⚥ ★ ♿ LGBTQ Student Resource Center at Auraria, Campus Box 74, POB 173362, Denver; 80217 303-615-0515 www.glbtss.org

♂ ★ oSTEM at Colorado School of Mines, Colorado School of Mines, Arthur Lakes Library, 1400 Illinois St, Golden; 303-273-3022 tinyurl.com/kl9gqbj

Colorado: Denver Area
Organizations: Student
123
GAYELLOW PAGES #42 2020-2021
Fort Collins/Loveland Area: Colorado
Religious

♂ ★ ♿ University of Denver Pride Lounge, 1870 S High St, Denver; 303-871-5428 **H?** www.du.edu/pride/ ⚧

Organizations/Resources: Youth (see also Family)

♂ ★ ♿ Rainbow Alley, 1301 E Colfax Ave, Denver; 303-733-7743 GLBTQI Youth 12-21 tinyurl.com/mreaklm

♀ ☆ Urban Peak Denver, 2100 Stout St, Denver 303-974-2900 www.urbanpeak.org

Real Estate (see also Mortgages)

♀ ● ♿ Mathis, Dawn, Realtor, ABR, GRI, SRES, Coldwell Banker, 141 Union Blvd Ste 200, Lakewood; 80228 970-481-5263 realestatebydawn.com ⚧ Dawn@RealEstateByDawn.com

Religious / Spiritual Resources

♂ ★ Dignity Denver, 1100 Filmore St, Denver 720-515-4528 www.dignitydenver.org

♀ ☆ ♿ Jefferson Unitarian Church, 14350 W 32nd Ave, Golden; 80401 303-279-5282 www.jeffersonunitarian.org ⚧ office@jeffersonunitarian.org

♂ ★ ♿ MCC of the Rockies, 980 Clarkson St, Denver; 720-955-0856 **H?** www.MCCRockies.org ⚧

♀ ☆ ♿ Park Hill Congregational Church UCC, 2600 Leyden St, Denver; 80207 303-322-9122 **HD** www.parkhillucc.org ⚧

♀ ☆ ♿ Parkview United Church of Christ, 12444 E Parkview Dr, Aurora; 80011 303-366-5224 **HD** www.parkviewucc.org ⚧ office@parkviewucc.org

♀ ☆ ♿ Prairie Unitarian Universalist Church, check site for meeting 720-549-0530 www.prairieuu.org

♀ ☆ Saint Paul Lutheran and Roman Catholic Community of Faith, 1600 Grant St, Denver; 80203-1602 303-839-1432 www.stpauldenver.org

Sports & Outdoor

♂ Colorado Squid, POB 7558, Denver; 80207 www.squidswimteam.org

♂ ★ Denver Area Softball League, POB 18958, Denver; 80218 303-377-2781 tinyurl.com/ytwyfq

♂ ★ Denver Gay & Lesbian Flag Football League, POB 18405, Denver; 80218 www.dglffl.com

♂ ★ Denver International Gay & Lesbian Invitational (bowling), POB 18875, Denver; 80002 www.bowldiglit.com

♂ ★ Mile-Hi Bullseye Dart League, 720-939-9088 mhbdl.leaguerepublic.com

♂ ★ OUTspokin', www.outspokin.org

♂ Rocky Mountain Bicycle Boys, www.rmbb.org
   » *Durango: see San Juan National Forest Area*

Estes Park

Accommodation: Hotels, Inns, Guesthouses, B&B, Resorts

♀ ○ Swiftcurrent Lodge on the River, 2512 Hwy 66 80517 970-586-3720 www.swiftcurrentlodge.com ⚧ ❀ info@swiftcurrentlodge.com

Accommodation Rental: Furnished / Vacation (& AirBNB)

♀ ● River Spruce Cabins, 2334 Tunnel Rd 970-586-4543 www.riverspruce.com

Fort Collins/Loveland Area

Crisis, Anti-violence, & Helplines

♀ ☆ ♿ Crossroads Safehouse, POB 993, Fort Collins; 80522 970-482-3502 www.crossroadssafehouse.org

♀ ☆ Sexual Assault Victim Advocate Center, 4812 S College Ave, Fort Collins; 970-472-4204 www.savacenter.org

Accommodation: Hotels, Inns, Guesthouses, B&B, Resorts
Bellvue

♀ ● (?♿) Archer's Poudre River Resort, 33021 Poudre Canyon Highway, Bellvue; 888-822-0588 www.poudreriverresort.com ❀ ⚧

AIDS/HIV Services, Education & Support

♀ ☆ ♿ Northern Colorado AIDS Project, 400 Remington St #100, Fort Collins; 970-484-4469 www.ncaids.org

Counseling/Psychotherapy/Mental Health

♀ ● Blue Spruce Counseling, Judy Underwood, PhD & Pam Gaynor, PhD, 515 S Sherwood St, Fort Collins; 80521-2842 970-221-0581 www.bluesprucecounseling.com judy@bluesprucecounseling.com

Financial Planning, Investment (see also Insurance)

♀ ○ ♿ Contino, Peter, CFP, Wells Fargo Advisors, 1412 Hahns Peak Dr, Loveland; 80538 970-461-6371 tinyurl.com/v6gksy8

Legal Services

♀ ○ ♿ Kling, Celeste Holder, Wallace & Kling, P.C. 425 W Mulberry St Ste 107, Fort Collins; 80521 970-221-5602 www.wallace-kling.com wkpc@frii.com

Organizations/Resources: Family and Supporters

♀ ☆ ♿ PFLAG Fort Collins/Northern Colorado, 305 W Magnolia St PMB 117, Fort Collins; 970-407-0300 pflagftcollins.org

Organizations/Resources: Political/Legislative/Advocacy

♂ ★ Longs Peak Scouts for Equality, 2001 Creekwood Dr, Fort Collins; 80525 970-221-5929 tinyurl.com/rbq2rj6 longspeak@scoutsforequality.com

Organizations/Resources: Social, Recreation, Support

♀ ★ Back Country Bettys, POB 273337, Fort Collins; 80527 970-568-6116 tinyurl.com/lofng9x

Organizations/Resources: Student, Academic, Education

♂ ★ ♿ Colorado State University Pride Resource Center, 8033 Campus Delivery, 174 Lory Student Center, Fort Collins; 970-491-4342 tinyurl.com/j39n5fd

♂ ★ Colorado State University Prism, 8033 Campus Delivery, 113 Lory Student Union, Fort Collins; 505-264-7302 tinyurl.com/ybuwhpjt

Religious / Spiritual Resources

♀ ☆ ♂ MCC Family In Christ, 301 E Drake Rd, Fort Collins; 80525 970-221-0811 www.mccfic.org mccftc@gmail.com

Fraser

Accommodation: Hotels, Inns, Guesthouses, B&B, Resorts

♂ ○ (♿) Wild Horse Inn, 1536 County Road 83; 80442 970-726-0456 www.wildhorseinn.com (❄?) ✗ ⊛ info@wildhorseinn.com

Frisco

Bars, Cafes, Clubs, Restaurants

♂ ○ &♿ Butterhorn Bakery & Cafe, 408 Main St 970-668-3997 www.butterhornbakery.com ♪

Grand Junction

Organizations/Resources: Student, Academic, Education

♀ ★ Colorado Mesa University GSA, 1100 North Ave; 970-248-1205 fb.com/cmugaystraightalliance

Religious / Spiritual Resources

♂ ☆ Koinonia Grand Junction, 730 25th Rd; 81505 970-242-3947 www.koinoniagj.org

Greeley

Crisis, Anti-violence, & Helplines

♂ ☆ Sexual Assault Victim Advocate Center, 929 38th Ave Court #106; 970-506-4059 www.savacenter.org

Insurance (see also Financial Planning)

♂ ● Lozano, Oralia, Farmers, 2122 9th St Ste 3 80631 970-518-7239 www.farmersagent.com/olozano

Organizations/Resources: Student, Academic, Education

♀ ★ &♿ Gender & Sexuality Resource Center, U of Northern Colorado, 2045 10th Ave, Campus Box 78; 970-353-0191 **H?** tinyurl.com/y289cbb4 ✗

Religious / Spiritual Resources

♂ ☆ Lutheran Episcopal Campus Ministry, 1844 11th Ave; 80631 970-451-5811 www.lecmgreeley.org pastor@lecmgreeley.org

» Longmont: see Boulder Area
» Monument: see Colorado Springs Area
» Pagosa Springs: see San Juan National Forest Area

Pueblo

Bars, Cafes, Clubs, Restaurants

♀ G-A-Y Bar At The Cove, Pirates Cove, 105 Central Plz; 719-543-2683 **D**

Organizations/Resources: Education

♀ ★ (&♿) Southern Colorado Equality Alliance, POB 602; 81002 719-685-7900 www.socoequality.org

Organizations/Resources: Family and Supporters

♂ ☆ &♿ PFLAG Pueblo, POB 1184; 81002 719-546-1555 pueblopflag.blogspot.com

Organizations/Resources: Youth (see also Family)

♀ ★ Outfront LGBT Youth Group, c/o SCEA, 304 S Union Ave; 719-685-7900 tinyurl.com/y6aal787

San Juan National Forest Area

Accommodation Rental: Furnished / Vacation (& AirBNB)
Pagosa Springs

♂ ● Redhawk Haven, 970-946-9920 www.redhawkhaven.com ✗ ⊛⊛

Bars, Cafes, Clubs, Restaurants
Durango

♂ ○ Palace Restaurant, 505 Main Ave, Durango 970-247-2018 www.palacedurango.com ♈ ✕

Erotica / Adult Stores / Safe Sex Supplies

♂ ○ Fallen Angel, 801 1/2 B Main Ave, Durango 81301 970-247-0601 www.thefallenangel.com

Funding: Endowment, Fundraising

♀ ☆ Telluride AIDS Benefit, POB 3819, Telluride 81435 970-728-0869 www.aidsbenefit.org

Organizations/Resources: Social, Recreation, Support

♀ ★ Four Corners Alliance for Diversity, POB 1656, Durango; 81302 970-385-7202 4callianceofdiversity.org

♀ ★ Four Corners Lesbian Network, fb.com/groups/fourcornersln/

Organizations/Resources: Student, Academic, Education

♀ ★ Fort Lewis College Gender and Sexuality Resource Center, 1000 Rim Dr, Durango www.fortlewis.edu/gsrc/

Stratton

Accommodation: Hotels, Inns, Guesthouses, B&B, Resorts

♀ ● &♿ Claremont Inn & Winery, 800 Claremont St; 888-291-8910 www.claremontinn.com ✗ ⊛

    » Telluride: see San Juan National Forest Area

Vail

Bars, Cafes, Clubs, Restaurants

♂ ○ Larkspur Restaurant, 458 Vail Valley Dr 970-754-8050 www.larkspurvail.com ✕

Westcliffe

Bars, Cafes, Clubs, Restaurants

♂ ○ &♿ Westcliffe Wine Mine, 109 N 3rd St; 719-783-2490 www.westcliffewinemine.com ♈ ✕✗

Connecticut
State/County Resources

AIDS/HIV Services, Education & Support

♂ ☆ AIDS Connecticut, 110 Bartholomew Ave Ste 3050, Hartford, CT 06106-2251 860-247-AIDS www.aids-ct.org

Computer & Software Sales & Services

♀ ○ ProActive Computer Services, Northeast Connecticut 401-647-7702 860-821-0580 tinyurl.com/yxux3zs6 proactivecs@yahoo.com

Funding: Endowment, Fundraising

♀⚦ ★ The Imperial Sovereign Court of All CT, PO Box 4427, Hartford, CT 06147 www.iscofallct.org

Leather Resources & Groups

⚦ Twilight Guard, www.thetwilightguard.org

Legal Services

♀ ☆ ♿ Connecticut Women's Education & Legal Fund, 75 Charter Oak Ave Ste 1-300, Hartford, CT 860-247-6090 www.cwealf.org

Organizations/Resources: Business & Professional Associations, Labor Advocacy

♀⚦ ★ Greater Connecticut Gay & Lesbian Chamber of Commerce (CTGLC), 141 Weston St #1832, Hartford, CT 06101-1832 860-612-8351 www.ctglc.org Info@ctglc.org

Organizations/Resources: Cultural, Dance, Performance

♀ ☆ (?♿) Another Octave: Connecticut Women's Chorus, POB 185234, Hamden, CT 06518 203-672-1919 www.anotheroctave.org

♀⚦ ★ Connecticut Gay Men's Chorus, POB 8824, New Haven, CT 06532-0824 203-777-2923 www.ctgmc.org info@ctgmc.org

Organizations/Resources: Naturist/Nudist

⚦ ★ (?♿) B&G of Connecticut, POB 380264, East Hartford, CT 06138-0264 www.bandgofct.org **NP** bandgct@gmail.com

Organizations/Resources: Social, Recreation, Support

⚦ ★ (?♿) Northeast Ursamen, 3000 Whitney Ave Ste 346, Hamden, CT ursamen.org

♀⚦ ★ Nutmeg Region chapter - Lambda Car Club, www.lccnutmeg.com lccinutmegpres@gmail.com

⚦ Prime Timers Connecticut, POB 8057, Manchester, CT 06040 860-791-2285 www.ctprimetimers.com

Organizations/Resources: Student, Academic, Education

♀ ★ GLSEN Connecticut, POB 207, New Haven, CT 06501 203-533-9613 www.glsen.org/connecticut connecticut@chapters.glsen.org

Organizations/Resources: Transgender/Gender Non-Conforming/Diverse

T ☆ Connecticut TransAdvocacy Coalition (CTAC), PO Box 575, Hartford, CT 06141 860-255-8812 fb.com/TransAdvocacy

Organizations/Resources: Youth (see also Family)

♀⚦ ★♿ True Colors, Inc, 30 Arbor St Ste 201A, Hartford, CT 06106 860-232-0050 **H?** www.ourtruecolors.org ✎ director@ourtruecolors.org

Recovery

♀⚦ ☆ Al-Anon/Alateen, CT AFG, 277 Main St, Hartford, CT 888-8AL-ANON www.ctalanon.org

♀⚦ ☆ Narcotics Anonymous Connecticut Regional Service Committee, POB 1817, Meriden, CT 06450 800-627-3543 www.ctna.org

Sports & Outdoor

♀⚦ ★ CT Pride Bowlers, c/o Steve Shura, 7 Kenwood Circle, Bloomfield, CT 06002 / Bowlero Wallingford Bowl, 980 N Colony Rd, Wallingford 203-295-0670 tinyurl.com/om8ahan shurshot19@aol.com

Travel & Tourist Services (see also Accommodation)

♀ ● Aldis The Travel Planner, 46 Main St, Danbury, CT 203-778-9399

>> *Branford: see New Haven Area*

Bridgeport

Bookstores

♀ ● ♿ Bloodroot Vegetarian Restaurant & Bookstore, 85 Ferris St; 203-576-9168 www.bloodroot.com ✄ ✎

Health Care: Physical (see also Counseling/Mental Health)

♀ ☆ ♿ Optimus Health Care, Inc, 982 E Main St; 06608-1913 / 471 Barnum Ave; 06008 medical care 203-696-3260 x3435 fax 203-615-0085 www.optimushealthcare.org

Canton

Gifts, Cards, Pride, etc.

♀ ○ ♿ Trading Post Music, 233 Albany Turnpike 860-693-4679 www.tradingpostct.com ✎ tradingpostct@gmail.com

>> *Cos Cob: see Greenwich*
>> *Cromwell: see Hartford Area*

Danbury

AIDS/HIV Services, Education & Support

♀ ☆ (?♿) Interfaith AIDS Ministry of Greater Danbury, 39 Rose St; 203-748-4077 fb.com/interfaithaidsministry

Bars, Cafes, Clubs, Restaurants
Bethel

♀ ○ Molten Java, 213 Greenwood Ave, Bethel 203-739-0313 moltenjava.wordpress.com ⌕ ▥

Organizations/Resources: Student, Academic, Education

♀⚦ ★♿ Western Connecticut State University GSA, Midtown Student Center #202, 181 White St 203-837-9062

Real Estate (see also Mortgages)

♀ ● Fabrizio-Garcia, Don, Realtor, Fab Real Estate, 1 Padanaram Rd Ste 203; 06811 203-947-1107 www.fabrealestate.com

Women's Centers

♀ ☆ (?♿) Women's Center of Greater Danbury, 2 West St; 203-731-5200 www.wcogd.org

>> *East Hartford: see Hartford Area*
>> *East Norwalk: see Stamford*

Connecticut: Fairfield
Bars, Cafes, Clubs, Restaurants

126
GAYELLOW PAGES #42 2020-2021

Hartford Area: Connecticut
Religious

Fairfield

Bars, Cafes, Clubs, Restaurants

⚲ Trevi Lounge, 548 Kings Hwy Cutoff 203-255-0285 www.trevilounge.com **D**

>> *Glastonbury: see Hartford Area*

Greenwich

AIDS/HIV Services, Education & Support

♂ ☆ ♿ Office of Special Clinical Services, c/o Dept of Health, 101 Field Point Rd; 203-622-6496 tinyurl.com/r8z9s2z ✏

>> *Hamden: see New Haven Area*

Hartford Area

Accommodation: Hotels, Inns, Guesthouses, B&B, Resorts
Glastonbury

♀ ● Butternut Farm, 1654 Main St, Glastonbury 860-633-7197 www.butternutfarmbandb.com ⊛

Manchester

♂ ● Seth Cheney House, 139 Hartford Rd, Manchester 06040-5972 508-237-5791 www.sethcheneyhouse.com ✏ ⊛ info@sethcheneyhouse.com

Accounting, Bookkeeping, Tax Services

♀ ○ Rob Matfess & Co, PC, CPA, 7 Hillside Dr, South Windsor; 06074 / Also payroll services 860-648-9870 www.robmatfess.com rob@robmatfess.com

AIDS/HIV Services, Education & Support

♂ Latino Community Services, 184 Wethersfield Ave, Hartford; 860-296-6400 lcs-ct.org ✦

Bars, Cafes, Clubs, Restaurants
Hartford

⚲ ● Chez Est, 458 Wethersfield Ave, Hartford 860-525-3243 www.chezest.com **DK** ⚲ ✕ ▥

⚲ Favela Rooftop, 145C Newfield Ave, Hartford; / Sat 860-571-1339 fb.com/ZodiacNightlife/

West Hartford

♀ ○ ♿ Arugula Bistro, 853 Farmington Ave E, W Hartford; 860-561-4888. www.arugula-bistro.com ✕

♀ ○ Pond House Cafe, 1555 Asylum Ave, W Hartford 860-231-8823 www.pondhousecafe.com ✕

Counseling/Psychotherapy/Mental Health

♂ ● Osadchey, Sherry L, MA, LMFT, SEP, 780 Farmington Ave, Farmington; 06032 860-677-5300 www.sherryosadchey.com Sherry@sherryosadchey.com

♂ ● ♿ Strick, Elliott, MA, LMFT, West Hartford Therapy Center LLC, 10 N Main St Ste 214, W Hartford; 860-231-8459 tinyurl.com/u2q6gcz

♀ ● Women's Center for Psychotherapy, 784 Farmington Ave, W Hartford; 860-523-4450 www.womens-center.com

Health Care: Physical (see also Counseling/Mental Health)

⚲ ★ ♿ Hartford Gay & Lesbian Health Collective, Inc, POB 2094, Hartford; 06145 860-278-4163 www.hglhc.org

Legal Services

♀ ● (♿) Law Office of Thomas R Lindberg, LLC, 11 Vista Way, Bloomfield; 06002 860-656-7476 ✏ lindbergtrlaw@att.net

♀ ○ Serrano Law Firm, LLC, 690 Flatbush Ave, W Hartford; 06110-1308 860-236-9350 www.serranolawyer.com js@serranolawyer.com

Organizations/Resources: Cultural, Dance, Performance

⚲ ★ ♿ Connecticut LGBT Film Festival, Out Film CT, POB 231191, Hartford; 06123 860-586-1136 **H?** www.outfilmct.org

Organizations/Resources: Family and Supporters

♀ PFLAG - Manchester, 63 Linden St, Manchester 860-647-5262

♀ ☆ PFLAG Hartford, POB 260733, Hartford; 06126 860-785-0909 www.pflaghartford.org

Organizations/Resources: Sexual Focus / Safe Sex

♀ ☆ ♿ The Society, 806 Windsor St, Hartford; 860-524-8669 www.thesocietyct.org

Organizations/Resources: Student, Academic, Education

⚲ ★ Lambda Law Society, Uconn Law School, 45 Elizabeth St, Hartford; 860-570-5162 tinyurl.com/swdd9a5

⚲ ★ Manchester Community College Pride, Student Activities Great Path, MS #7 POB 1046, Manchester; 860-512-3384 tinyurl.com/zmhbkqj

⚲ ★ Spectrum, c/o SGA University of Hartford, 200 Bloomfield Ave, W Hartford; 860-560-6864 tinyurl.com/w6bdvgy

⚲ ★ Trinity College EROS, c/o Queer Resource Center, 114 Crescent St, Hartford; 860-987-6273 tinyurl.com/wy4gkzj

⚲ ★ University of CT School of Social Work Pride, 38 Prospect St, Hartford; 06103 959-200-3687

Organizations/Resources: Transgender/Gender Non-Conforming/Diverse

T ☆ Connecticut Outreach Society, POB 163, Farmington; 06034 860-469-2188 www.ctoutreach.org

Religious / Spiritual Resources

♂ ☆ ♿ Center Church, 60 Gold St, Hartford; 06103-2993 860-249-5631 **H** www.centerchurchhartford.org

⚲ First Church of Christ, Congregational, 2183 Main St, Glastonbury; 860-633-4641 www.glastonburyfirst.org

♀ ☆ ♿ St Patrick & St Anthony Church, 285 Church St, Hartford; 06103-1196 860-756-4034 **H** www.spsact.org info@spsact.org

♀ ☆ Unitarian Society, 50 Bloomfield Ave, Hartford 06105-1006 860-233-9897 www.ushartford.com office@ushartford.com

♀ ☆ ♿ Unitarian Universalist Society: East, 153 Vernon St West, Manchester; 06042 860-646-5151 **HD** www.uuse.org ✏

>> *Ledyard: see Mystic Area*

Connecticut: Madison
Accommodation

127
GAYELLOW PAGES #42 2020-2021

New London : Connecticut
Community Centers / Pride

Madison

Accommodation: Hotels, Inns, Guesthouses, B&B, Resorts

♂ ● Scranton Seahorse Inn, 818 Boston Post Rd 203-245-0550 scrantonseahorseinn.com (♣?) ✗ 🚫

Art & Craft Galleries/Services, Supplies

♂ ○ (♂⚧) Wall Street Gallery, 91 Wall St 06443 203-245-2912 fax 203-245-7112 Enjoy expert craftsmanship and explore your individual ideas with us. www.extremeframing.com ✗ wsg@snet.net

Middletown

Organizations/Resources: Student, Academic, Education

⚥ ★ Wesleyan Queer Resource Center, 190 High St Box A; 860-685-2425 www.wesleyan.edu/queer/ ✗

Milford

Religious / Spiritual Resources

♂ ☆ ♿ Mary Taylor Memorial UMC, 168 Broad St; 06460 203-874-1982 **HD** www.mtm-umc.org mtmumc@sbcglobal.net

Mystic Area

Accommodation: Hotels, Inns, Guesthouses, B&B, Resorts
Ledyard

♂ ○ Abbey's Lantern Hill Inn, 780 Lantern Hill Rd, Ledyard; 06339-1459 860-572-0483 www.abbeyslanternhill.com ✗ (♣?) ✗ 🚫 email@abbeyslanternhill.com

♂ ● Mare's Inn B&B, 333 Col Ledyard Hwy, Ledyard 860-572-7556 www.almostinmystic.com (♣?) 🚫
Mystic

♂ ● Mermaid Inn of Mystic, 2 Broadway Ave, Mystic 860-536-6223 mermaidinnofmystic.com ✗ 🚫

Bookstores

♂ ○ (♂⚧) Bank Square Books, 53 W Main St, Mystic; 860-536-3795 **H?** www.banksquarebooks.com ✗

♂ ○ ♿ Breakwater Books, 81 Whitfield St, Guilford; 06437 203-453-4141 www.breakwaterbooks.net

Counseling/Psychotherapy/Mental Health

♂ ● ♿ Korman, Nicki, LMFT, EdD, 2514 Boston Post Rd #8C, Guilford; 06437 203-458-0900

♂ ○ Ziskind, Katie, LMFT, RYT500, 8 W Main St Ste 3-15, Niantic; 06335 860-451-9364KatieZis. fax 860-294-8428 Video and phone sessions available www.WisdomWithinCt.com KatieZiskindMFT@gmail.com

New Britain

Archives/Libraries/Museums/History Projects

♂ ☆ ♿ Burritt Library, Gender Equity Collections (GLBT research collections) Central Connecticut State University 06050 860-832-2085 fax 860-832-2118 tinyurl.com/2cj4ymd vickreyr@ccsu.edu

New Haven Area

Community Centers and/or Pride Organizations

⚥ ★ ♿ New Haven Pride Center, PO Box 8914, New Haven; 06532-0914 / 84 Orange St, New Haven 203-387-2252 www.newhavenpridecenter.org ✗ info@newhavenpridecenter.org

AIDS/HIV Services, Education & Support

♂ ☆ APNH: A Place to Nourish your Health, 1302 Chapel St, New Haven; 06511-4515 203-624-0947 www.apnh.org

Bars, Cafes, Clubs, Restaurants
New Haven

⚥ ● 168 York Street Cafe, 168 York St, New Haven; 203-789-1915 fb.com/168yorkstreetcafe/ ✗ ♈

♂ ○ ♿ The Bar Night Club, 254 Crown St, New Haven; 203-495-8924 www.barnightclub.com **D** ▥ ✗

♂ ○ Claire's Corner Copia, 1000 Chapel St, New Haven; 203-562-3888 www.clairescornercopia.com ✗ ✗ info@clairescornercopia.com

⚥ ● ♿ Partners, 365 Crown St, New Haven; (Park) 203-776-1014 www.partnerscafe.com **D** ▥

♂ ○ Soul de Cuba Cafe, 283 Crown St, New Haven 203-498-2822 www.souldecuba.com ♈ ✗

Bookstores

♂ ○ Atticus Bookstore Cafe, 1082 Chapel St, New Haven; 203-776-4040 www.atticusbookstorecafe.com ☞

Counseling/Psychotherapy/Mental Health

♂ ○ ♿ Altbrandt, Robina, LCSW, MPH, 441 Orange St, New Haven; 203-640-6564 www.robinaaltbrandt.com

Organizations/Resources: Student, Academic, Education

⚥ ★ LGBTQ Student Cooperative at Yale, POB 202031, New Haven; 06520 203-436-4868 tinyurl.com/ycsqre4c

⚥ ★ ♿ Outpatient at Yale School of Medicine, Student Affairs, 333 Cedar St, New Haven; 203-432-4771 **H?** tinyurl.com/ybe93j8v

⚥ ★ Yale University Law School Outlaws, 127 Wall St, New Haven; tinyurl.com/3jw2xp8

♀ ☆ ♿ Yale Women's Center, 198 Elm St, New Haven; 06520 www.yale.edu/wc/ wcboard@mailman.yale.edu

Religious / Spiritual Resources

♂ ☆ ♿ St Thomas's Episcopal Church, 830 Whitney Ave, New Haven; 06511-1398 203-777-7623 www.stthomasnewhaven.org ✗ pastor@stthomasnewhaven.org

♂ ☆ ♿ United Church on the Green, 323 Temple St, New Haven; 06511-6602 203-787-4195 **HD** unitednewhaven.org

New London

Community Centers and/or Pride Organizations

⚥ OutCT, POB 255; 06320 860-339-4060 outct.org

AIDS/HIV Services, Education & Support

♂ Alliance for Living - New London, 860-447-0884 www.allianceforliving.org

Organizations/Resources: Student, Academic, Education

♀ ★ Connecticut College LGBTQIA Center, Box 5292, 270 Mohegan Ave; 860-439-2238 tinyurl.com/ydxshpxc

Organizations/Resources: Youth (see also Family)

♀ OutCT Youth Program, POB 255; 06320 860-339-4060 outct.org/youth-program

Religious / Spiritual Resources

♀ ☆ ♿ All Souls Unitarian Universalist Congregation, 19 Jay St; 06320 860-443-0316 **H** www.allsoulsnewlondon.org ✒
» *New Milford: see Danbury*

Noank

Organizations/Resources: Family and Supporters

♀ ☆ ♿ PFLAG Southeastern CT, c/o Noank Baptist Church, 18 Cathedral Heights; 06340 860-608-1442 www.pflagsect.org pflagsect@snet.net
» *North Stonington: see Mystic Area*

Norwalk

Community Centers and/or Pride Organizations

♀ ★ ♿ **Triangle Community Center, 650 West Ave, Norwalk; 203-853-0600 Serving the greater Fairfield County LGBT community. www.ctpridecenter.org** ✒

AIDS/HIV Services, Education & Support

♂ ☆ Mid-Fairfield AIDS Project, 618 West Ave, Norwalk; 203-855-9535 www.mfap.com

Bars, Cafes, Clubs, Restaurants

♀ ● ♿ **SIREN Party at Troupe429, 3 Wall St, Norwalk; / Every 2nd Sat Troupe429 is Connecticut's best gay bar for the LGBTQ+ community! www.troupe429.com D** 🏳️‍🌈 ✒

♂ ● ♿ **Troupe429: LGBTQ Bar & Performance Space, 3 Wall St, Norwalk; Troupe429 is Connecticut's best gay bar for the LGBTQ+ community! www.troupe429.com D** 🏳️‍🌈 ✒

Health Care: Physical (see also Counseling/Mental Health)

♀ Circle Care Center, 618 West Ave, Norwalk 203-852-9525 www.circlecarecenter.org

Organizations/Resources: Family and Supporters

♂ ☆ ♿ PFLAG Norwalk, World Health Clinicians Building, 618 West Ave, Norwalk; 06851 203-343-3772 www.pflagnorwalk.org ✒ pflagnorwalk@gmail.com

Religious / Spiritual Resources

♂ ☆ ♿ St Paul's On The Green,. 60 East Ave, Norwalk; 06851 203-847-2806 **H** www.stpaulsnorwalk.org ✒ welcome@stpaulsnorwalk.org

Norwich

Organizations/Resources: Student, Academic, Education

♀ ★ ♿ Three Rivers Community College Gender And Sexual Minorities League (GASM), Phil Mayer, 574 New London Tpke 860-215-9453 tinyurl.com/rhyc3qo
» *Pawcatuck: see Mystic Area*

Stamford

AIDS/HIV Services, Education & Support

♂ Stamford CARES, 888 Washington Blvd 8th Flr 203-977-4387 tinyurl.com/yakhosee

Real Estate (see also Mortgages)

♂ ○ Hensley, William, William Raveis, 1022 Long Ridge Rd; 06903 203-273-5806 203-322-0200 williamhensley.raveis.com ✒ william.hensley@raveis.com
» *Storrs: see*

Storrs

Organizations/Resources: Student, Academic, Education

♀ ★ ♿ Rainbow Center at UConn, 2110 Hillside Rd Unit 3096, Storrs; 06269-3096 860-486-5821 fax 860-486-6674 www.rainbowcenter.uconn.edu ✒

Women's Centers

♂ ☆ ♿ Women's Center, SU Room 421, 2110 Hillside Rd Unit 3118, Storrs; 860-486-4738 **H?** www.womenscenter.uconn.edu ✒

» *Stratford: see Bridgeport*

Washington

Bookstores

♂ ○ ♿ The Hickory Stick Bookshop, 2 Green Hill Rd, Washington Depot; 860-868-0525 www.hickorystickbookshop.com
» *West Hartford: see Hartford Area*
» *Westbrook: see Mystic Area*

Westport

Art & Photography (see also Graphic Design)

♂ ● Sheridan Photography, 277A North Ave 203-222-1441 www.suzannesheridan.com

Willimantic

Organizations/Resources: Student, Academic, Education

♀ ★ Eastern Connecticut State University Pride Center, Student Center 108G 83 Windham St; 860-465-0015 tinyurl.com/rk8jt6y

Wilton

Homes & Buildings: Cleaning, Maintenance, Repair, General Contractors

♂ ● Buxton Roofing Services, 39 Danbury Rd 2, Wilton; 06897 203-623-1326 www.ctroofer.com CTRoofer@optonline.net
» *Windsor: see Hartford Area*

Delaware: State/County Resources
Community Centers / Pride

129

GAYELLOW PAGES #42 2020-2021

Rehoboth Area: Delaware
Bars, Cafes, Clubs, Restaurants

Delaware
State/County Resources

Community Centers and/or Pride Organizations

♀ ★ Delaware Pride, POB 9834, Newark, DE 19714 302-265-3020 www.delawarepride.org

AIDS/HIV Services, Education & Support

♀ ★ ♿ AIDS Delaware, 100 W 10th St #315, Wilmington, DE 302-652-6776 www.aidsdelaware.org

♀ Delaware Department of Health & Social Services Ryan White Program, Thomas Collins Building, 540 S DuPont Highway, Dover, DE 302-744-1050 tinyurl.com/mfeqn8s

♀ Delaware HIV Consortium, 100 W 10th St Ste 415, Wilmington, DE 302-654-5471 www.delawarehiv.org

♀ ☆ NAMES Project Delaware, Delaware HIV Consortium, 100 W 10th St Ste 415, Wilmington, DE 302-654-5471 www.delawarehiv.org

Organizations/Resources: Cultural, Dance, Performance

♀ ★ The Rainbow Chorale of Delaware, POB 1467, Wilmington, DE 19899 302-803-4440 www.therainbowchorale.org

Organizations/Resources: Political/Legislative/Advocacy

♀ ☆ ACLU-Delaware, 100 W 10th St Ste 603, Wilmington, DE 302-654-5326 www.aclu-de.org

Organizations/Resources: Social, Recreation, Support

♀ PRIDE Council, United Way of Delaware, 625 N Orange St, Wilmington, DE 302-573-3722 fb.com/groups/uwdpride/

Real Estate (see also Mortgages)

♀ ● ♿ Jeffrey Fowler, Realtor, Keller Williams Realty, 18344 Coastal Highway, Lewes, DE 19958 302-249-6133 **H?** www.jeffreyfowler.com ✔ jeffrey@jeffreyfowler.com

♀ ● Pence, Joe, BHHS Fox & Roach Realtors, 88 Lantana Dr, Hockessin, DE 19707 302-494-0089 joepence.foxroach.com Joe.Pence@foxroach.com

›› Dewey Beach: see Rehoboth Area
›› Lewes: see Rehoboth Area

Milton

Accommodation: Hotels, Inns, Guesthouses, B&B, Resorts

♀ ● Mansion Farm Inn, 26285 Broadkill Rd 302-664-2540 www.mansionfarminn.com ✪ ✔ ⊗ ⊗

Newark

Organizations/Resources: Student, Academic, Education

♀ ★ Office Equity & Inclusion, University of Delaware, 305 Hullihen Hall; 302-831-8063 www.udel.edu/oei

♀ ☆ ♿ University of Delaware Haven, Perkins Student Center Rm 019D, 325 Academy St Rm 019D; 302-831-1514 www.ud-haven.com ✔

Religious / Spiritual Resources

♀ ☆ New Ark UCC, 300 E Main St; 19711 302-737-4711 www.newarkucc.org office@newarkucc.org

Rehoboth Area

Community Centers and/or Pride Organizations

♂ ★ ♿ CAMP Rehoboth Community Center, 37 Baltimore Ave, Rehoboth Bch; 302-227-5620 www.camprehoboth.com ✔

Information, Media & Publications

♂ ★ ♿ Letters from Camp Rehoboth, 37 Baltimore Ave, Rehoboth Bch; 302-227-5620 www.camprehoboth.com ✔

Accommodation: Hotels, Inns, Guesthouses, B&B, Resorts

Lewes

♂ ● Lazy L Bed & Breakfast Resort, 16061 Willow Creek Rd, Lewes; 302-644-7220 www.LazyL.net ✪ ✔ ⊗

Rehoboth Beach

♂ ● Bewitched & BEDazzled B&B, 67 Lake Ave, Rehoboth Bch; 302-226-3900 www.rehobothbandb.com (✪?)

♂ ● (♨) Homestead at Rehoboth B&B, 35060 Warrington Rd, Rehoboth Bch; 302-226-7625 www.homesteadatrehoboth.com ✪ ⊗

♂ ● Rehoboth Guest House, 40 Maryland Ave, Rehoboth Bch; 302-227-4117 www.rehobothguesthouse.com ✔ ⊗

♂ ● The Shore Inn at Rehoboth, 37239 Rehoboth Avenue Ext, Rehoboth Bch; 302-227-8487 www.shoreinn.com **N** ✪ ✔

Bars, Cafes, Clubs, Restaurants

Lewes

♂ ● ♿ Honey's Farm Fresh, 329 Savannah Rd, Lewes; 302-644-8400 fb.com/honeysfarmfresh/ ⊃ ✔ honeysfarmfresh@hotmail.com

Rehoboth Beach

♂ ● ○ Aqua Grill, 57 Baltimore Ave, Rehoboth Bch 302-226-9001 www.aquarehoboth.com ♈ ✕

♂ ● (♨) Back Porch Cafe, 59 Rehoboth Ave, Rehoboth Bch; 302-227-3674 www.backporchcafe.com ⊃ ▦

♂ ● ♿ Blue Moon, 35 Baltimore Ave, Rehoboth Bch; 302-227-6515 www.bluemoonrehoboth.com ♈ ✕▦

♂ ● ♿ Diego's Bar & Nightclub, 37298 Rehoboth Ave Extended, Rehoboth Bch; 302-227-1023 diegosbarnightclub.com **D** Diegosbarnightclub@gmail.com

♂ ● ○ Dogfish Head Brewings & Eats, 320 Rehoboth Ave, Rehoboth Bch; 302-226-2739 www.dogfish.com ♈ ✕

♂ ● ♿ Dos Locos Fajita & Stonegrill, 208 Rehoboth Ave, Rehoboth Bch; 302-227-3353 www.doslocos.com **K** ♈ ✕ ✔

♂ ● ♿ Eden Restaurant, 23 Baltimore Ave, Rehoboth Bch; 302-227-3330 www.edenrestaurant.com ♈ ✕

♂ ● ○ (♨) Iguana Grill, 52 Baltimore Ave, Rehoboth Bch; 302-227-0600 fb.com/IguanaGrillRB/ ♈ ✕

♂ ● Lori's Oy-vey Cafe, 39 Rehoboth Ave, Rehoboth Bch; 302-226-3066 www.lorisoyveycafe.com ⊃

♂ ● The Pond Bar & Grill, 3 S 1st St, Rehoboth Bch 302-227-2234 www.thepondrehoboth.com ▦

♂ ● ⚥ Rigby's Bar & Grill, 404 Rehoboth Ave, Rehoboth Bch; 302-227-6080 rigbysrehoboth.com ⚥ ✕ ▥

Bookstores

♀ ○ Browseabout Books, 133 Rehoboth Ave, Rehoboth Bch; 302-226-2665 browseaboutbooks.com

Food Specialties (see also Catering)

♀ ● Snyders Candy, 60 Rehoboth Ave, Rehoboth Bch 19971 302-226-3994 www.SnydersCandy.com shop@snyderscandy.com

Organizations/Resources: Cultural, Dance, Performance

♀ ☆ ♂♂ Clear Space Theatre Company, 20 Baltimore Ave, Rehoboth Bch; 302-227-2270 www.ClearSpaceTheatre.org

Organizations/Resources: Family and Supporters

♀ ☆ ♂♂ PFLAG Rehoboth Beach, meets 3rd Tue, Lewes Public Library, 111 Adams St 302-841-1339 302-841-1339 www.pflagrehobothbeach.org PFLAGRehobothBeach@gmail.com

Organizations/Resources: Political/Legislative/Advocacy

♂ ★ Delaware Stonewall PAC, POB 1024, Rehoboth Bch; 19971 delawarestonewall.org info@delawarestonewall.org

Organizations/Resources: Social, Recreation, Support

♂ Rehoboth Beach Bears, 302-245-0449 www.rehobothbeachbears.com

Real Estate (see also Mortgages)

♂ ● ♂♂ Giove, Susan, Mann & Sons, 414 Rehoboth Ave, Rehoboth Bch; 19971 302-227-9477 tinyurl.com/y6v6vyhv ✎ sngiove0806@gmail.com

♀ ● Joe Maggio Realty, 37169 Rehoboth Ave Unit #11, Rehoboth Bch; 19971 302-226-3770 302-381-2268 maggiorealty.com joe@maggiorealty.com

♂ ○ Kalvinsky, Shirley, Jack Lingo Realtor, 246 Rehoboth Ave, Rehoboth Bch; 19971 302-236-4254 www.homesofrehoboth.com Shirley@jacklingo.com

Religious / Spiritual Resources

♂ ★ Metropolitan Community Church Rehoboth, PO Box 191, Rehoboth Bch; 19971 / meets at 19369 Plantation Rd 302-645-4945 www.mccrehoboth.org

♀ ☆ ♂♂ Unitarian Universalists of Southern Delaware, 30486 Lewes Georgetown Highway, Lewes; 19958 302-313-5838 uussd.org info@uussd.org

♂ ☆ Unity of Rehoboth Beach, 98 Rudder Rd Ste A-1, Millsboro; 19966 302-945-5253 unityofrehobothbeach.org info@unityofrehobothbeach.org

Wilmington

Bars, Cafes, Clubs, Restaurants

♂ ● (♂♂) Crimson Moon Tavern, 1909 W 6th St; 302-654-9099 www.crimsonmoonde.com **DKV** ▥ ✎

♂ ○ Mrs Robino's, 520 N Union St; 302-652-9223 www.mrsrobinos.com ✕

Counseling/Psychotherapy/Mental Health

♀ ○ ⚥ Alliance Counseling, 3411 Silverside Rd Weldin Building Ste 100; 19810 302-477-0708 fax 302-477-0136 www.getmeaningfulresults.com

Legal Services

♂ ● Minster & Facciolo, LLC, 521 West St, Wilmington, DE 19801 302-777-2201 fax 302-777-2097 www.MinsterandFacciolo.com

Organizations/Resources: Family and Supporters

♀ ☆ ♂♂ PFLAG Wilmington/North Delaware, Inc., POB 26049; 19899-6049 302-654-2995 www.pflagwilmde.org pflagwilmde@att.net

Recovery

♀ ☆ ⚥ AA: Northern Delaware Intergroup, 21 B Trolley Square; 302-655-5113 www.ndiaa.org

Travel & Tourist Services (see also Accommodation)

♀ ○ ⚥ The Travel Company, 302-652-6263 www.travelcompany.ws travelcompany@att.net

District of Columbia
DC Washington Area

Crisis, Anti-violence, & Helplines

⚥ Lesbian, Gay, Bisexual and Transgender Liaison Unit (LGBTLU), Metropolitan Police Department Of DC, 801 Shepherd St NW, DC; 202-727-5427 mpdc.dc.gov/node/139172

Community Centers and/or Pride Organizations

⚥ ★ ♂♂ Capital Pride Alliance, Inc, 2000 14th St NW Ste 105, DC; 202-719-5304 www.capitalpride.org

⚥ ★ ♂♂ The DC Center for the LGBT Community, 2000 14th St NW Ste 105, DC; 202-682-2245 **H?** thedccenter.org ✎ @ixx=

Information, Media & Publications

♀ PhatGirlChic.com, www.phatgirlchic.com ✪

♀ ● Tagg Magazine, 1638 R St NW Ste 210, DC 20009 703-567-7643 www.taggmagazine.com info@taggmagazine.com

♀ Where the Girls Go, fb.com/wherethegirlsgo

Accommodation: Hotels, Inns, Guesthouses, B&B, Resorts
Washington

♂ ● (♂♂) Malolo Bed and Breakfast, 5213 B St SE, DC; 202-670-6332 www.malolobandb.com ✎ ⊛

♀ ● Otis Place B&B, 1003 Otis Pl NW, DC 202-328-3510 tinyurl.com/gv42bm5 ✎ ⊛

AIDS/HIV Services, Education & Support

♀ American Foundation for AIDS Research, 1100 Vermont Ave NW Ste 600, DC; 00-342-2437 www.amfar.org

♀ CAEAR: Communities Advocating Emergency AIDS Relief, POB 21361, DC; 20009 202-789-3565 www.caear.org

♀ ★ && Food & Friends, 219 Riggs Rd Ne, DC; 202-269-2277 www.foodandfriends.org

♂ ★ HOPE DC, 2000 14th Street, NW Ste 105, DC 20009 / (Baltimore/Washington/NOVA) 202-670-1792 (Baltimore/Washington/NOVA) www.hopedc.org

♀ ★ PETS-DC, POB 75125, DC; 20013 202-234-PETS www.petsdc.org

♂ ☆ && Us Helping Us, Inc, 3636 Georgia Ave NW, DC; 202-446-1100 www.uhupil.org ♣

♀ Whitman-Walker Health Youth Services, 651 Pennsylvania Ave SE, DC; 202-543-9355 tinyurl.com/y82oouw9

Archives/Libraries/Museums/History Projects

♂ ★ Latino GLBT History Project, 2000 14th St NW Ste 105, DC; 202-670-5547 www.latinoglbthistory.org ◆

♀ ☆ && National Museum of Women in the Arts, 1250 New York Ave NW, DC; 202-783-5000 **H?** nmwa.org ✗

♀ ★ Rainbow History Project, POB 73176, DC 20056-3176 202-810-5068 www.rainbowhistory.org

Bars, Cafes, Clubs, Restaurants

♂ ● && DC Bear Crue, See web for events 609-232-2327 **HS** www.dcbearcrue.com **KL** ▦ ✗

Washington

♀ ○ Annie's Paramount Steakhouse, 1609 17th St NW, DC; 202-232-0395 tinyurl.com/kktjxty ✗

♀ Avalon Saturdays at Soundcheck, 1420 K St NW, DC; 202-789-5429 tinyurl.com/yastawc8

♂ Bear Nonsense, bearnonsense.com

♀ ○ Busboys & Poets, 2021 14th St NW, DC 202-387-7638 www.busboysandpoets.com ✗ ▦

♂ ● && DC Eagle, 3701 Benning Rd NE, DC; 202-347-6025 www.dceagle.com **L**

♀ ○ DC9, 1940 9th St NW, DC; 202-483-5000 www.dcnine.com **DKV** Y ✗▦ ✗

♀ ● The Dirty Goose, 913 U St, DC www.TheDirtyGooseDC.com Y ✗ info@TheDirtyGooseDC.com

♀ ○ Dupont Italian Kitchen & Bar, 1637 17th St NW, DC; 202-328-3222 www.dupontitaliankitchen.com Y ✗

♂ ● && The Fireplace, 2161 P St NW, DC 202-293-1293 fb.com/thefireplacedc **V** ♻

♀ Floriana Restaurant / Dito's Bar, 1602 17th St NW, DC; 202-667-5937 florianarestaurant.com ✗

♂ ● Green Lantern, 1335 Green Court NW, DC; 202-347-4533 www.greenlanterndc.com **DKL**

♀ ○ Hamilton's Bar & Grill, 233 2nd St NW, DC 202-347-6555 www.hamiltonsdc.com **S** Y ✗

♂ ● JR'S, 1519 17th St NW, DC; 202-328-0090 jrsbar-dc.com

♀ ● && Larry's Lounge, 1840 18th St NW, DC; 202-483-1483 larryslounge-hub.com

♀ A League Of Her Own, 2319 18th St NW, DC 202-733-2568 fb.com/alohodc/ **S**

Robyn S. Zeiger, PhD, LCPC
10300 Sweetbriar Parkway, Silver Spring
301-445-7333
www.drrobynzeiger.com
Licensed Clinical Professional Counselor
Certified Imago Relationship Therapist

♀ ○ Little Miss Whiskey's Golden Dollar, 1104 H St NE, DC; www.littlemisswhiskeys.com **DK**

♀ ○ && Logan Tavern, 1423 P St NW, DC 202-332-3710 www.logantavern.com Y ✗

♀ Lure DC, at Cobalt, 1639 R St NW, DC; / 3rd Sat, check schedule 202-232-4416 fb.com/lurewdc **D**

♀ ○ & Marx Cafe, 3203 Mount Pleasant St NW, DC; 202-518-7600 www.marxcafemtp.com **DV** Y ✗▦ ✗

♂ ● && Nellie's Sports Bar, 900 U St NW, DC; 202-332-6355 www.nelliessportsbar.com **K** Y ✗▦ ✗

♂ ○ Number Nine, 1435 P St NW, DC 202-986-0999 www.NumberNineDC.com

♀ Orchid, 520 8th St SE, DC; 202-544-1168 orchidonthehill.com Y ✗

♀ Pitchers, 2317 18th St NW, DC 202-733-2568 www.pitchersbardc.com **S**

♀ ● && Red Bear Brewing Co, 209 M St NE, DC; 202-849-6130 **HS** www.redbear.beer ✗ info@redbear.beer

♂ Secrets/Ziegfeld's, 1824 Half St SW, DC 202-863-0670 www.secretsdc.com ▦

♀ ○ && Soho Tea & Coffee, 2150 P St NW, DC; 202-463-7646 www.sohoteaandcoffee.com ꙮ ✗

♂ ● Trade, 1410 14th St NW, DC; 202-986-1094 www.tradebardc.com @ixx=

♂ ○ UPROAR Lounge & Restaurant, 639 Florida Ave NW, DC; Bears www.uproarlounge.com Y ✗

♀ ○ Wisdom, 1432 Pennsylvania Ave SE, DC 202-543-2323 www.dcwisdom.com

♀ XX+ Crostino, 1926 9th St NW, DC 202-797-0523 www.xxcrostino.com

Bookstores

♂ ○ G Books, Lower level, 1520 U St NW, DC 202-986-9697 fb.com/gbooksus

♀ Kramer Books & Afterwords Cafe & Grill, 1517 Connecticut Ave NW, DC; 202-387-1400 www.kramers.com ꙮ

Counseling/Psychotherapy/Mental Health

♀ ● Cohen, Larry, LICSW, CGP, 4808 43rd Place NW, DC; 20016 202-244-0903 www.socialanxietyhelp.com larrycohen@socialanxietyhelp.com

District of Columbia: DC Washington Area
Counseling

132

GAYELLOW PAGES #42 2020-2021

DC Washington Area : District of Columbia
Organizations: Multicultural

♀ ● (?⚲) LGBT Counseling, 3000 Connecticut Ave NW Ste 400A; 202-319-8541 www.lgbtc.com information@lgbtc.com

♀ ● ♿ Radkowsky, Michael, Psy.D, Licensed Psychologist, 3000 Connecticut Ave NW Ste 439, DC; 202-234-3278 www.michael-radkowsky.com

♀ ○♿ Riddell, Grace C, LICSW, LCSW-C, MEd, 3000 Connecticut Ave NW Ste 137, DC; 20008-2500 301-942-3237 www.Grace-Riddell.com

♂ ● **Zeiger, Robyn S., PhD, LCPC, 10300 Sweetbriar Parkway, Silver Spring, MD 20903-1523 301-445-7333 Licensed Clinical Professional Counselor and Certified Imago Relationship Therapist www.drrobynzeiger.com drrobynzeiger@aol.com**

Counseling/Psychiatry

♂ ○♿ Perman, Gerald P, MD, PA, 2424 Pennsylvania Ave NW Ste 100, DC; 20037-1793 202-331-8213 Psychiatry www.drperman.com ✗ gpperman@gmail.com

Erotica / Adult Stores / Safe Sex Supplies

♀ ● Bite the Fruit, 1723 Connecticut Ave NW Flr 2, DC; 202-299-0440 www.bitethefruit.com

Financial Planning, Investment (see also Insurance)

♀ ● ♿ Third Eye Associates, Ltd, 1717 K St NW, Ste 900 202-667-2266 www.thirdeyeassociates.com ✗

Funding: Endowment, Fundraising

♂ ★ Brother, Help Thyself Inc., POB 77841, DC; 20013 202-347-2246 www.brotherhelpthyself.org

♂ Cherry Fund, 1930 New Hampshire Ave NW, DC 703-447-333 www.cherryfund.org

♀ ☆♿ Walk & 5K to End HIV, Whitman-Walker Health, 1377 R St NW, DC; 20009 202-332-9255 **H?** walktoendhiv.org walktoendhiv@whitman-walker.org

Health Care: Physical (see also Counseling/Mental Health)

♀ ☆ La Clinica Del Pueblo, 2831 15th St NW, DC 202-462-4788 www.lcdp.org ✦

♀ ★ ♿ Max Robinson Center of Whitman Walker Health, 2301 Martin Luther King Jr Ave SE, DC; 202-745-7000 **H** www.whitman-walker.org

♀ ★ ♿ Whitman-Walker Health, 1701 14th St NW, DC; 202-745-7000 **H** www.whitman-walker.org ✗

Leather Resources & Groups

♂ DC Boys of Leather, c/o The DC Eagle, 639 New York Ave NW, DC; fb.com/DCBOL/

♂ ★ Highwaymen TNT, tinyurl.com/y8csozu9

♂ ★ SigMa, Inc., 1636 R St NW, DC sigmadc.org

Legal Services

♀ ● ♿ Salb, Micah, Lippman, Semsker & Salb, LLC, 7979 Old Georgetown Rd Ste 1100, Bethesda, MD 20814 301-656-6905 **H?** LSSLawyers.com ✗ msalb@lsslawyers.com

Men's & Sex Clubs (not primarily Health Clubs)

♂ ● ♿ Crew Club, 1321 14th St NW, DC 202-319-1333 www.crewclub.net **P** ✗

♂ Glorious Health Club, 2120 W Virginia Ave NE, DC; 202-269-0226 www.ghcdc.com

Organizations/Resources: Business & Professional Associations, Labor Advocacy

♂ ★ (?⚲) Capital Area Gay & Lesbian Chamber of Commerce, POB 73530, DC; 20056 www.caglcc.org

♀ Gay & Lesbian INTernational (GLINT), LGBTI+ working in DC embassies fb.com/glintdc

♂ ★ Gay, Lesbian, & Allies Senate Staff Caucus, www.glasscaucus.org

♂ Lesbian & Gay Congressional Staff Association, Box 2000 Longworth House Office Building, DC www.lgbtcsa.org

♂ ★ (?⚲) LGBT Bar Association of the District of Columbia, POB 34072, DC; 20043 www.lgbtbardc.org

♂ ★ National Lesbian & Gay Journalists Association, 2120 L St NW Ste 850, DC; 20037 202-588-9888 www.nlgja.org info@nlgja.org

♂ Pride At Work Baltimore Washington, 815 16th NW, DC; 202-637-5014 www.prideatwork.org

Organizations/Resources: Cultural, Dance, Performance

♀ ★ (?⚲) DC Lambda Squares, POB 77782, Washington, DC 20013 202-930-1058 www.dclambdasquares.org **D**

♂ ★ DC's Different Drummers, POB 57099, DC 20037 202-403-3669 dcdd.org

♀ ☆♿ Fortissima: DC's Feminist Singers, 728 Fairmont, DC; 20002 202-684-6353 www.fortissima.org goddess@fortissima.org

♂ ★ ♿ Gay Men's Chorus of Washington DC, 1140 3rd St NE Flr2, DC; 202-293-1548 www.gmcw.org

♂ ★ ♿ Lambda DanceSPORT DC, 202-596-4860 www.pleasedancewithme.com

♂ ★ ♿ Reel Affirmations International LGBTQ Film Festival, 2001 14th St NW Ste 105, DC; 202-682-2245 www.reelaffirmations.org

Organizations/Resources: Ethnic, Multicultural

♂ ★ AQUA (Asian/Pacific Islander Queers United for Action), www.aquadc.us ◇

♂ ★ Asians & Friends, POB 18974, DC; 20036 fb.com/groups/AFWashington ◇

♂ ★ DC Black Pride, POB 77313, DC; 20013 202-641-8527 centerforblackequity.org ✤ dcbp@centerforblackequity.org

♂ ★ KhushDC, 571-210-5474 fb.com/khushdc/ ◇

♂ LULAC Lambda DC, z 1204 5th St NW, DC 202-374-9227 lulaclambda.org ✦

♂ ★ Men of All Colors Together of Washington DC, PO Box 77472, DC; 20013 tinyurl.com/y83444dt ✪

Organizations/Resources: Family and Supporters

♂ ☆ ♂ Metro DC PFLAG Chapter, POB 6085, DC; 20005 202-638-3852 www.pflagdc.org

♀ ★ Rainbow Families DC, 5614 Connecticut Ave #309, DC; 202-747-0407 www.rainbowfamiliesdc.org

Organizations/Resources: Military/Veterans

♀ American Military Partner Association, 1725 I St Northwest Ste 300, DC; 202-695-2672 militarypartners.org

Organizations/Resources: Political/Legislative/Advocacy

♀ ★ ♂♂ Gay & Lesbian Activists Alliance of Washington, DC, Inc, POB 75265, DC; 20013 glaa.org

♀ ★ ♂♂ Gertrude Stein Democratic Club, 000 14th St NW POB 9393, DC tinyurl.com/ycwq9lnc

♀ ★ Human Rights Campaign, 1640 Rhode Island Ave NW, DC; 202-628-4160 www.hrc.org

♀ ★ ♂ Log Cabin Republicans, 1090 Vermont Ave NW Ste 850, DC; 202-420-7873 www.dclogcabin.org

♀ ★ ♂♂ National LGBTQ Task Force, 1325 Massachusetts Ave NW Ste 600, DC; 20005-4171 202-393-5177 www.thetaskforce.org

Organizations/Resources: Sexual Focus / Safe Sex

♀ ★ ♂♂ Black Rose, POB 101222, Arlington, VA 22210 202-656-0762 **H?** SM www.br.org

Organizations/Resources: Social, Recreation, Support

♀ Capital Q, - - Capitalqdc.com

♀ ★ Gay District, tinyurl.com/h48plm6 supportdesk@thedccenter.org

♀ GLBT Board Gamers of DC, tinyurl.com/7hgbhx6

♀ ★ ♂♂ GLOE - Kurlander Program for GLBT Outreach & Engagement at the DCJCC, Washington DCJCC, 1529 16th St NW, DC; 202-777-3253 **H?** Jewish LGBT and our friends washingtondcjcc.org/gloe ✡ ✔

♀ Go Gay DC - Metro DC's LGBT Community Club, fb.com/GoGayDC/

♀ ★ Lambda Car Club Straight Eights Region, DC-Baltimore area 240 270-2277 www.straight8s.net

♀ ★ Lambda Sci-Fi: DC Area Gaylaxians, 202-232-3141 www.lambdascifi.org membership@lambdascifi.org

♂ Nice Jewish Boys DC, fb.com/NJB.DC ✡

♀ ★ Nice Jewish Girls DC, fb.com/NJGDC ✡

♂ ★ Prime Timers of DC, 3101 S Manchester St #601, Falls Church, VA 22044 703-671-2454 www.primetimersdc.org dcprimetimers@gmail.com

Organizations/Resources: Student, Academic, Education

♀ ★ ♂♂ American University Center for Diversity & Inclusion, 201/202 Mary Graydon Center, 4400 Massachusetts Ave NW, DC; 202-885-3651 **H** www.american.edu/ocl/cdi/

♀ ★ ♂♂ American University LGBTQA Outreach, 201 Mary Graydon Center, 4400 Massachusetts Ave NW, DC 202-885-3651 tinyurl.com/y9ogc7gd ✔

♀ ★ Association of Queer Women and Allies (AQWA), fb.com/AQWAatGWU/

♀ ★ George Washington University Allied in Pride, Marvin Center #419, 801 21st St NW, DC; 202-242-6678

♀ ★ George Washington University Law School Lambda Law, fb.com/gwlambdalaw

♀ ★ ♂♂ George Washington University LGBTQ Resource Center, 325 Leavey Center, 37 O St NW, DC; 202-994-4568 lgbtq.georgetown.edu/

♀ ★ OutLaw at Georgetown University Law Center, c/o Student Life, 600 New Jersey Ave NW #170, DC; 20001 fb.com/OutlawGulc outlaw@georgetown.edu

♀ ★ Rainbow Society of Gallaudet, 800 Florida Ave, DC; 202-651-5144 fb.com/gurainbowsociety

♀ ★ WCL Lambda Law Society, 4801 Massachusetts Ave NW Ste 533, DC; 202-274-4410 tinyurl.com/82y7ojj

Organizations/Resources: Transgender/Gender Non-Conforming/Diverse

T Metro Area Gender Identity Connection, 703-606-4936 www.magicdc.org

Organizations/Resources: Youth (see also Family)

♂ Advocates for Youth, 1325 G St NW Ste 980, DC 202-419-3420 advocatesforyouth.org

♀ Wanda Alston House, 300 New Jersey NW #900, DC; 202-465-8794 tinyurl.com/l27uveb

Real Estate (see also Mortgages)

♂ ○ Dean, Steven, Realtor, Compass Real Estate, 660 Pennsylvania Ave SE #300, DC; 20003-4306 202-525-6499 202-545-6900 www.mydcagent.com ✔

Recovery

♀ ★ Triangle Club, POB 65458, DC; 20035 202-659-8641 www.triangleclub.org club@triangleclub.org

Religious / Spiritual Resources

♀ ★ Affirmation DC: Gay & Lesbian Mormons, tinyurl.com/jjhaygl

♀ ★ (?♂) Bet Mishpachah, POB 1410, DC; 20013-1410 **H?** www.betmish.org ✡ office@betmish.org

♂ ☆ ♂♂ Christ Lutheran Church, 5101 16th St NW, DC; 20011 202-829-6727 christlutherandc.org ✔ clcoffice@verizon.net

♀ ★ ♂♂ Dignity/Washington, POB 15279, DC; 20003 202-546-2235 www.dignitywashington.org

♂ ☆ First Congregational UCC, 945 G St NW, DC 20001 202-628-4317 www.FirstUCCDC.org churchoffice@FirstUCCDC.org

♀ ★ ♂♂ MCC of Washington, 474 Ridge St NW, DC; 202-638-7373 **H?** www.mccdc.com ✔

♂ ☆ National City Christian Church, 5 Thomas Circle NW, DC; 20005 202-232-0323 NationalCityCC.org connect@nationalcitycc.org

♂ ☆ St Margaret's Episcopal Church, 1830 Connecticut Ave, DC; 20009 202-232-2995 www.stmargaretsdc.org info@stmargaretsdc.org

District of Columbia: DC Washington Area
Religious

134
GAYELLOW PAGES #42 2020-2021

State/County Resources : Florida
Weddings/Unions

♂ ☆ Unitarian Universalists, POB 1632, Sterling, VA 20167 703-406-3068 www.uusterling.org

♂ ☆ && Western Presbyterian Church, 2401 Virginia Ave NW, DC; 20037-2637 202-835-8383 **HD** www.westernpresbyterian.org info@westernpresbyterian.org

♂ ☆ & Westminster Presbyterian Church, 400 I St SW, DC; 20002 202-484-7700 www.westminsterdc.org rwh@westminsterdc.org

Sports & Outdoor

⚲ ★ Adventuring, 202-462-0535 www.adventuring.org craighowell1@verizon.net

⚲ ★ (♨) Atlantic States Gay Rodeo Association, POB 21221, DC; 20009 202-352-2356 www.asgra.org

♂ ● && The Bike Rack Brookland, 716 Monroe St NE, DC; 202-832-2453 www.bikerackdc.com

♂ ● && The Bike Rack Logan Circle, 1412 Q St NW, DC; 202-387-2453 www.bikerackdc.com

⚲ ★ Capital Area Rainbowlers Association, POB 4214, Arlington, VA 22204 www.carabowling.org

♂ ★ (♨) Centaur Motorcycle Club, POB 34061, DC; 20043 202-643-1262 www.centaurmc.org **L**

⚲ ★ Chesapeake & Potomac Softball (CAPS), 1627 Massachusetts Ave SE #202, Washington, DC 20003 www.capssoftball.org capssoftball@gmail.com

⚲ ★ DC Aquatics Club, PO Pox 77125, DC; 20013 410-382-7205 www.swimdcac.org

⚲ ★ DC Front Runners, www.dcfrontrunners.org

⚲ ★ DC Gay Flag Football League, dcgffl.org

⚲ ★ DC Strokes Rowing Club, POB 77643, DC 20013 www.dcstrokes.org

⚲ ★ Federal Triangles Soccer Club, www.federaltriangles.org

⚲ ★ (♨) Lambda Divers, Inc, POB 1621, Annandale, VA 22003 fb.com/groups/LambdaDivers/

♂ ★ Spartan Motorcycle Club, www.spartanmc.com secretary@spartanmc.com

⚲ ★ Team DC, www.teamdc.org

⚲ ★ Washington Renegades Rugby Football Club, Inc., POB 2067, DC; 20013 www.dcrugby.com ✪

♀ ☆ Washington Women Outdoors, POB 9568, Washington, DC 20018 240-720-7819 tinyurl.com/7nwhow9

Transportation: Limo, Taxi, Charter etc.

♂ ○ Kasper's Livery Service, 201 Eye St SW Ste 529, DC; 20024 202-554-2471 www.KasperLivery.com Don@KasperLivery.com

Travel & Tourist Services (see also Accommodation)

♀ ● Howell, Craig, 1825 T St NW, DC; 20009-7135 202-462-0535 craighowell1@verizon.net

Weddings and Ceremonies

♂ ● (&&) The DC Marriage Knot, 4722 Morning Glory Trail, Bowie, MD 202-253-3629 www.thedcmarriageknot.com ♥

Florida
State/County Resources

Information, Media & Publications

⚲ ● GayFlorida.com, POB 796, Gotha, FL 34734 407-896-8431 www.gayflorida.com chris@gayflorida.com

⚲ ● (♨) Hotspots Magazine, 3500 NE 12th Ave, Fort Lauderdale, FL 33334 954-928-1862 fax 954-772-0142 www.hotspotsmagazine.com ✗ info@hotspotsmedia.com

AIDS/HIV Services, Education & Support

♂ ☆ & Florida HIV/AIDS Hotline, 4052 Bald Cypress Way, Tallahassee, FL 850-245-4422 **H?** tinyurl.com/y2vktvgg

Mortgages/Home Ownership (see also Banks, Real Estate)

♂ ● Frey, Carolyn, OH & FL & PA 305-735-2524 www.carolynfrey.com cafrey@mortgagelendingsolutions.com

Organizations/Resources: Cultural, Dance, Performance

♂ ★ && Fort Lauderdale Gay Men's Chorus, POB 9772, Fort Lauderdale, FL 33310 954-832-0060 **H?** theftlgmc.org ✗

Organizations/Resources: Naturist/Nudist

♂ ★ SFMEN, POB 667762, Pompano Beach, FL 33066 www.sfmenclub.com **N**

Organizations/Resources: Political/Legislative/Advocacy

♂ ☆ && American Civil Liberties Union of Florida, 4343 W Flagler St #400, Miami, FL 786-363-2700 www.aclufl.org

⚲ ★ Equality Florida, POB 13184, St Petersburg, FL 33733 813-870-3735 www.eqfl.org

⚲ ★ Florida LGBTQ+ Democratic Caucus, 335 E Linton Blvd Box 2213, Delray Beach, FL 727-469-3367 tinyurl.com/z6fodx9

Organizations/Resources: Social, Recreation, Support

♂ ★ (♨) The Bears of South Florida, www.bosfl.org

⚲ ★ Visuality Florida, POB 9385, Fort Myers, FL 33902 239-898-6124 www.visualityflorida.org

Organizations/Resources: Student, Academic, Education

♂ ☆ Safe Schools South Florida, 1350 E Sunrise Blvd Ste 115, Fort Lauderdale, FL 305-576-2126 tinyurl.com/43nk9e

Organizations/Resources: Transgender/Gender Non-Conforming/Diverse

T Florida Transgender Alliance, 653 W 23rd St #228, Panama City, FL fb.com/FloridatransAlliance/

T ☆ && Phi Epsilon Mu, POB 158, Highland City, FL 33846 Transgender Social & Support Group, transsupportfl.com

Weddings and Ceremonies

♀ ○ Reverend Lyn Daniels, 386-503-6885 www.revlynsweddings.com ♥

Amelia Island

Bookstores

♀ ○ &⅄ Story & Song Bookstore Bistro, 1430 Park Ave, Fernandina Bch; 32034 904-601-2118 storyandsongbookstore.com ✕ ✔
>> *Anna Maria: see Tampa Bay Area*
>> *Auburndale: see Tampa Bay Area*
>> *Boca Raton: see West Palm Beaches Area*
>> *Bradenton: see Sarasota/Bradenton/Venice Area*
>> *Brandon: see Tampa Bay Area*

Brevard County

Accommodation Rental: Furnished / Vacation (& AirBNB)
Indialantic

♀ ○ Beach Bungalow, 312 Wavecrest Ave, Indialantic 32903 321-984-1330 firstbeach.com

AIDS/HIV Services, Education & Support

♀ ☆ &⅄ Project Response AIDS Center, 745 S Apollo Blvd, Melbourne; 32901 321-724-1177 www.projectresponse.org

Bars, Cafes, Clubs, Restaurants
Cape Canaveral

♀ ○ &⅄ Izzy's / Sage Bistro, 6615 N Atlantic Ave, Cape Canaveral; 321-783-4548 www.sagebistroflorida.com ⅄ ✕ ✔

Cocoa Beach

♀ ○ &⅄ Gregory's Steak & Seafood Grille & Comedy Club, 900 N Atlantic Ave, Cocoa Bch; 321-799-2557 gregorysonthebeach.com ⅄ ✕ ▥ ✔

Erotica / Adult Stores / Safe Sex Supplies

♀ ○ &⅄ Fairvilla Boutique, 6103 N Atlantic Ave, Cape Canaveral; 32920 321-799-9961 **H?** www.fairvilla.com

Organizations/Resources: Family and Supporters

♀ ☆ PFLAG Melbourne/Space Coast, POB 2838, Melbourne; 32902 321-750-4141 www.pflagmelbourne.org

Travel & Tourist Services (see also Accommodation)

♀ ○ Beyond & Back, Inc, 401 Ocean Ave, #101, Melbourne Bch; 32951-2567 321-725-9720 www.beyondandback.com info@beyondandback.com

Brooksville

Travel & Tourist Services (see also Accommodation)

♀ ● ⅄ ACBS Travel Agency, 624 Decatur Ave; 34601-3236 352-796-4984 800-449-ACBS **Your ticket to Our World and Beyond since 1970! www.acbstravel.com**
>> *Cape Canaveral: see Brevard County*
>> *Clearwater: see Tampa Bay Area*
>> *Cocoa: see Brevard County*
>> *Cocoa Beach: see Brevard County*
>> *Dade City: see Tampa Bay Area*

Daytona/Flagler/Ormond Beach Area

Community Centers and/or Pride Organizations

⚥ Volusia Pride, Old Fort Park, 115 Julia St, New Smyrna ach; www.volusiapride.com

Accommodation: Hotels, Inns, Guesthouses, B&B, Resorts
Daytona Beach

⚥ ● The Villa B&B, 801 N Peninsula Dr, Daytona Beach; 386-248-2020 www.thevillabb.com ✔ ⊛

AIDS/HIV Services, Education & Support

♂ ☆ Outreach Community Care Network, Volusia/Flagler Counties, 240 N Frederick Ave, Daytona Beach; 386-255-5569 HIV, Hepatitis C, other STDs www.outreachinc.org

♂ ☆ POZ People of Daytona, Our Lady of Lourdes Catholic Church, 1014 N Halifax Ave, Daytona Beach; 386-235-6420 tinyurl.com/zlz5z4v

Bars, Cafes, Clubs, Restaurants
Ormond Beach

♀ ○ FIG Frappes Italian Grille, 123 W Granada Blvd, Ormond Bch; 386-615-4888 frappesnorth.com ⅄ ✕

Organizations/Resources: Social, Recreation, Support

⚥ Over the River, 407-928-8376

Organizations/Resources: Student, Academic, Education

⚥ ★ Stetson University Kaleidoscope, Student Involvement, 421 N Woodland Blvd #8416, Deland; 32723 386-822-7708 orgsync.com/18652/chapter

Organizations/Resources: Youth (see also Family)

⚥ Project Safe Zone, Daytona Beach Universal Ministries Church, 2600 Tulane Ave #10, Daytona Beach; 386-256-8605 projectsafe-zone.webs.com

Recovery

⚥ Lambda Center, 320 Harvey Ave #A, Daytona Beach; 386-255-0280 tinyurl.com/ybuz2q9j

Religious / Spiritual Resources

♀ ☆ Community Unitarian Universalist Church, 403 West St, New Smyrna ach; 32168 386-308-8080 www.dbcuuc.org info@dbcuuc.org

Sports & Outdoor

♀ Operation Blazing Sword, 800 Belle Terre Parkway #200-302, Palm Coast; blazingsword.org

➤➤ *Deerfield Beach: see Fort Lauderdale/Wilton Manors*
➤➤ *Delray Beach: see Fort Lauderdale/Wilton Manors Area*

Fort Lauderdale/Wilton Manors Area

Community Centers and/or Pride Organizations

♀ ★ 춤춤 Pride Center at Equality Park, 2040 N Dixie Hwy, Wilton Manors; 954-463-9005 www.pridecenterflorida.org

♀ ★ 춤춤 Pride Fort Lauderdale, POB 23686, Ft Laud; 33307 754-222-2234 www.pridefortlauderdale.org

Information, Media & Publications

♀ ● GIR(L) Magazine, POB 468, Lake Worth, FL 33460 954-829-1982 www.girlmag.us editor@girlmagazine.us

Accommodation: Hotels, Inns, Guesthouses, B&B, Resorts
Fort Lauderdale

♂ ● Cheston House, 520 N Birch Rd, Ft Laud 954-566-7950 www.chestonhouse.com **N** ⊛

♂ ● Coral Reef Guesthouse, 2609 NE 13th Court, Ft Laud; 33304 954-568-0292 Over 21 only www.coralreefguesthouse.com info@coralreefguesthouse.com

♂ ● The Grand Resort & Spa, 539 North Birch Rd, Ft Laud; 33304-4020 800-818-1211 grandresort.net ✔ ⊛ info@grandresort.net

♂ ● Hotel Lush Royale, 2835 Terramar St, Ft Laud 954-564-6442 tinyurl.com/84hdavt

♂ ● 춤춤 Inn Leather Guest House & Resort, 610 SE 19th St, Ft Laud; 33316-3513 954-467-1444 Clothing optional www.innleather.com **LL** (❄?) ✔ ⊛ ⊛

♂ ● Pineapple Point Guesthouse & Resort, 315 NE 16th Terrace, Ft Laud; 954-527-0094 www.pineapplepoint.com **N** ✔ ⊛

♂ ● The Worthington, 543 N Birch Rd, Ft Laud 954-563-6819 www.theworthington.com **N**

Pompano Beach

♂ ● 춤춤 Sea Horse Motel, 901 N Ocean Blvd, Pompano Bch; 954-786-1359 seahorsepompano.com (❄?) ✔ ⊛

Wilton Manors

♂ ● 춤 The Cabanas Guesthouse & Spa, 2209 NE 26th St, Wilton Manors; 954-564-7764 www.thecabanasguesthouse.com ✔ ⊛

♂ ● Island Sands Inn, 2409 NE 7th Ave, Wilton Manors; 954-990-6499 www.islandsandsinn.com ✔ ⊛

♂ ● Manor Inn, 2408 NE 6th Ave, Wilton Manors 954-566-8223 www.wiltonmanorsinn.com ✔ ⊛

Accounting, Bookkeeping, Tax Services

♂ ● Guzzardo, Paul, CPA, 954-551-0408 paul312@comcast.net

AIDS/HIV Services, Education & Support

♂ ☆ Broward House, Inc., 1726 SE 3rd Ave, Ft Laud 954-522-4749 www.browardhouse.org

Antiques & Collectibles

♀ ● 춤춤 Shades of the Past Antiques, 2360 Wilton Drive, Wilton Manors; 954-829-3726 tinyurl.com/4bfoxr

Archives/Libraries/Museums/History Projects

♀ ★ 춤 Stonewall National Museum & Archives Library, Library, Archives, and Business Office, 1300 E Sunrise Blvd, Ft Laud; 33304 / Stonewall National Museum - Wilton Manors Gallery, 2157 Wilton Dr 954-763-8565 www.stonewall-museum.org info@stonewall-museum.org

Art & Photography (see also Graphic Design)

♀ ★ ArtsUnited, Inc, 1350 E Sunrise Blvd #117, Ft Laud; artsunitedflorida.com

Bars, Cafes, Clubs, Restaurants
Dania Beach

♀ Beach Bettys, 625 E Dania Beach Blvd, Dania Beach; 954-921-9893 tinyurl.com/lgob3hq **KS**

♂ ○ Jimmie's Chocolate Shoppe & Cafe, 148 North Federal Hwy, Dania Beach; 954-921-0688 www.jimmieschocolates.com ☞

Davie

♂ ○ 춤춤 Cloud 9 Lounge, 7126 Stirling Rd, Davie; 954-499-3525 fb.com/cloudninenight/ **CDK** ☲ ✖ ▥

Fort Lauderdale

♂ ● Boardwalk/Beefcake's Grill, 1721 N Andrews Ave, Ft Laud; 954-463-6969 fb.com/boardwalkftl/ ☲ ✖ ▥

♂ ○ J Marks Restaurant, 1245 N Federal Highway, Ft Laud; 954-390-0770 www.jmarksrestaurant.com ☲ ✖

♀ ● J's Bar, 2780 Davie Blvd, Ft Laud 954-581-8400 tinyurl.com/hy8pnnq **D**

♂ ● Le Boy, 1243 NE 11th Ave, Ft Laud 954-368-8786 www.leboy-tonight.com **D** ▥

♂ ● 춤춤 Milk Money Bar & Kitchen, 815 NE 13th St, Ft Laud; 954-990-4189 milkmoneybar.com ☲ ✖ ✔

♂ ● Mona's, 502 E Sunrise Blvd, Ft Laud 954-525-6662 www.monas-bar.com

♂ ● Ramrod, 1508 NE 4th Ave, Ft Laud; 954-763-8219 www.ramrodbar.com **L**

♂ ○ Smarty Pants, 2400 E Oakland Park Blvd, Ft Laud; 954-561-2577 www.smartypantsbar.com **K** ▥ ✔

Pompano Beach

♂ ○ J Marks Restaurant, 1490 NE 23th St, Pompano Bch; 954-782-7000 www.jmarksrestaurant.com ☲ ✖

Wilton Manors

♂ ● 춤춤 The Corner Pub, 1915 N Andrews Ave, Wilton Manors; 954-564-7335 www.cornerpubbar.com ☲ ✖ ✔

♀ ● DrYnk, 2255 Wilton Dr, Wilton Manors 954-530-1800 www.drynkftl.com

♂ ● Georgie's Alibi, 2266 Wilton Dr, Wilton Manors; 954-565-2526 www.alibiwiltonmanors.com ✖ ✔

♂ ● Gym Sportsbar, 2287 Wilton Dr, Wilton Manors 954-368-5318 www.gymsportsbar.com **S**

Florida: Fort Lauderdale/Wilton Manors Area
Bars, Cafes, Clubs, Restaurants

137
GAYELLOW PAGES #42 2020-2021

Fort Lauderdale/Wilton Manors Area: Florida
Organizations: Family

🕯 Hunters, 2232 Wilton Dr, Wilton Manors 954-630-3556 huntersftlauderdale.com **DK** 📖

🕯 Infinity Lounge, 2184 Wilton Dr, Wilton Manors 754-223-3619 infinityloungefl.com

🕯 Johnsons Fort Lauderdale, 2340 Wilton Dr, Wilton Manors; 954-908-1272 johnsonsfl.com 📖 ☯ ✔

♀ The Manor, 2345 Wilton Dr, Wilton Manors 954-626-0082 themanorcomplex.com **D** ⅄ ✕ 📖

🕯 Matty's Wilton Park, 2100 Wilton Dr, Wilton Manors; 954-900-3973 fb.com/Mattyswiltonpark/ ⅄ ✕

🕯 Monkey Business, 2740 N Andrews Ave, Wilton Manors; 954-514-7819 fb.com/MonkeyBusinessBar 📖

♀ ● ♿ The Pub, 2283 Wilton Dr, Wilton Manors; 754-200-5244 www.thepubwm.com **DV** 📖 ✔

♀ ● Rumors, 2426 Wilton Dr, Wilton Manors 954-565-8851 tinyurl.com/c5y2drr ⅄ ✕

🕯 ☯ ♿ Scandals Saloon, 3073 NE 6th Ave, Wilton Manors; 954-567-2432 www.scandalsfla.com **DKLCW** 📖 ✔

♀ ● ♿ Shawn & Nick's Courtyard Cafe, 2211 Wilton Dr, Wilton Manors; 954-563-2499 tinyurl.com/3qxjyx ✕ ↝

Counseling/Psychotherapy/Mental Health

♀ ☯ ♿ Checke, Christopher, MS/MBA, LMHC, CAP, 800 E Broward Blvd #303, Ft Laud; 33301 954-240-6323 www.chris-checke.com ✔

♀ ☯ Fischetto, Julia, MS, LMHC, 218 Commercial Blvd Ste 232, Lauderdale By The Sea; 33308-4457 954-491-9040 fax 954-492-0334 jfpsych218@aol.com

♀ ● ♿ Jamieson, John A, LCSW, CST, Institute for Essential Change, 2630 E Oakland Park Blvd, Ft Laud; 33308 954-463-6563 john jamiesonlcsw@gmail.com

♀ ★ ♿ SunServe Social Services, 2312 Wilton Dr, Wilton Manors; 33305 954-764-5150 Services include individual, couples and family therapy, social support and therapy groups, case management, youth services, senior services & senior day care center www.sunserve.org info@sunserve.org

Erotica / Adult Stores / Safe Sex Supplies

♀ ☯ Bob's News & Books, 1515 S Andrews Ave, Ft Laud; 33316-2507 954-524-4731 www.bobsnewsandbooks.com

Funding: Endowment, Fundraising

♀ Out of the Closet Thrift Store, 1785 E Sunrise Blvd, Ft Laud; 954-462-9442 outofthecloset.org

♀ Out of the Closet Thrift Store, 2097 Wilton Dr, Wilton Manors; 954-358-5580 outofthecloset.org

♀ Sisters of Perpetual Indulgence South Florida, POB 24924, Ft Laud; 33307 754-273-8786 www.southfloridasisters.org

Gifts, Cards, Pride, etc.

♀ ● To The Moon Marketplace, 2205 Wilton Dr, Wilton Manors; 33305-2131 954-564-2987 tothemoonmarketplace.com info@tothemoonmarketplace.com

SAGE of South Florida
Senior Action in a Gay Environment
PO Box 70516 Oakland Park FL 33307-0516
954-634-7219
www.sagewebsite.org

Health Care: Physical (see also Counseling/Mental Health)

♀ ☆ Poverello/Chronic/Critical Illness Food Pantry & Thrift Shop, 2056 N Dixie Highway, Wilton Manors; 954-561-3663 www.poverello.org

Legal Services

♀ ☯ Robert Nichols & Associates, 200 SE 6th St Ste 401, Ft Laud; 954-779-3313 www.bobnicholslaw.com

♀ ● ♿ Sagan, B Adam, 215-985-0366 Practice limited to Social Security Disability saganlaw.net

Massage Therapy (Certified/Licensed only)

♀ ● Cotnoir, Wayne, LMT, Massage Therapist 401-529-1722 www.massagebywayne.net massagebywayneogt@gmail.com

Men's & Sex Clubs (not primarily Health Clubs)

🕯 ● ♿ Club Fort Lauderdale, 110 NW 5th Ave, Ft Laud; 954-525-3344 www.clubftl.com **P** ✔

🕯 ☯ ♿ Clubhouse II, 2650 E Oakland Park Blvd, Ft Laud; 954-566-6750 www.clubhouse2.com **P**

🕯 Slammer, 321 W Sunrise Blvd, Ft Laud 954-524-2625 www.321slammer.com **P**

Organizations/Resources: Business & Professional Associations, Labor Advocacy

🕯 ★ Greater Fort Lauderdale LGBT Chamber of Commerce, 2300 NE 7th Ave, Wilton Manors; 954-523-3500 www.gogayfortlauderdale.com

♀ ★ ♿ Women In Network, POB 9744, Ft Laud; 33310 www.womeninnetwork.com

Organizations/Resources: Cultural, Dance, Performance

🕯 ★ Outshine Film Festival, c/o MGLFF, 6360 NE 4th Ct, Miami, FL 305-751-6305 www.mifofilm.com

🕯 ★ Outshine Film Festival, c/o MGLFF, POB 530280, Miami, FL 33153 877-766-8156 www.mglff.com

🕯 ★ South Florida Mustangs Square Dance Club, PO Box 22792, Ft Laud; 33335 305-899-1710 www.southfloridamustangs.org **D**

🕯 ★ South Florida Pride Wind Ensemble (Flamingo Freedom Band), 1750 E Oakland Park Blvd, Ft Laud; 954-667-9228 www.pridewindensemble.org

Organizations/Resources: Family and Supporters

♀ ☆ ♿ PFLAG Fort Lauderdale, 1480 SW 9th Ave, Ft Laud; 954-665-7002 fb.com/PFLAGFTL/

Organizations/Resources: Military/Veterans

⚣ ★ American Veterans For Equal Rights - Florida Gold Coast Chapter, POB 11247, Ft Laud; 33339-1247 563-508-6492 www.aver-fgc.org Son_oflaw@yahoo.com

Organizations/Resources: Naturist/Nudist

⚣ ★ Gold Coast Bare Skins, POB 5072, Ft Laud 33310 www.gold-coastbareskins.org **N**

⚣ ★ (♿) **WildFyre Society, H? Fun, friendly nude club for vital, active guys. www.WildFyreSociety.org N**

Organizations/Resources: Political/Legislative/Advocacy

⚣ ★ Dolphin Democrats, POB 23194, Ft Laud 33307 954-358-9327 www.dolphindems.org

Organizations/Resources: Senior Resources

⚣ ★ **SAGE of South Florida, POB 70516, Oakland Park; 33307-0516 / 2040 N Dixie Hwy, Bldg A, Ste 225, Wilton Manors 954-634-7219 Senior Action in a Gay Environment www.sagewebsite.org sagesofl@gmail.com**

Organizations/Resources: Social, Recreation, Support

⚣ ★ Flamingo Auto Group South, tinyurl.com/yuuoad

⚣ ★ Fort Lauderdale Prime Gentlemen, POB 100666, Ft Laud; 33310-0666 954-971-6514 ftlprimegentlemen.org ftlprime gentlemen@gmail.com

Organizations/Resources: Student, Academic, Education

⚣ ★ Gay-Straight Student Alliance CPS, Nova Southeastern University, 3301 College Ave, Ft Laud fb.com/gsa.cps

Organizations/Resources: Youth (see also Family)

⚣ Julian's Fountain of Youth, 1400 N Federal Highway, Ft Laud; 754-701-5040 jfoy.org

⚣ ★ ♿ SunServe Broward Youth Groups, 2312 Wilton Dr, Wilton Manors; 33305 954-764-5150 **H?** www.sunserveyouth.org ⚦

⚣ ★ ♿ SunServe Youth Group Coral Springs, St. Mary Magdalene Episcopal Church, 1400 Riverside Dr, Coral Springs; 33071 954-764-5150 **H?** sunserveyouth.wordpress.com/

⚣ ★ (♿) SunServe Youth Group Southwest Ranches, New Horizon United Methodist Church, 5741 S Flamingo Rd, Southwest Ranches; 33330 954-764-5150 **H?** tinyurl.com/ybjnppeu info@sunserve.org

Real Estate (see also Mortgages)

♀ ● ♿ Calhoun, Ken, PA, REMAX Experience, 1103 NE 26 ST, Wilton Manors; 33305 954-567-2222 www.kenhelps.com ⚦ kencanhelp@gmail.com

♂ ● ♿ Weiser, Andy, Better Homes and Gardens Florida 1st, 2700 E Oakland Park Blvd, Ft Laud; 33306 954-560-9667 fax 954-229-0971 www.AndyWeiser.com ⚦ andyweiser@aol.com

♂ ○ Wish, Vickie, GRI, Realtor, Coldwell Banker Residential Real Estate, 5810 Coral Ridge Drive Ste 100, Coral Springs; 33076 954-242-8200 954-688-5406 www.vickiewish.com vickie@vickiewish.com

Recovery

♂ ☆ Alcoholics Anonymous Broward County Intergroup, Inc., 3317 NW 10th Terrace Ste 404, Ft Laud; 33309 954-462-0265 www.aabroward.org help@aabroward.org

⚣ ★ ♿ Lambda South, POB 030339, Ft Laud; 33303 / 1231-A East Las Olas Blvd (access through alley) 954-761-9072 www.lambdasouth.com ⚦

♿ Pride Institute, Fort Lauderdale Hospital, 5757 N Dixie Hwy, Oakland Park; 877-744-3346 tinyurl.com/24q5aou

Religious / Spiritual Resources

♂ ★ (♿) Congregation Etz Chaim, 2038 N Dixie Hwy, Wilton Manors; 954-564-9232 www.EtzChaimFlorida.org ✡

♂ ★ ♿ Sunshine Cathedral MCC, 1480 SW 9th Ave, Ft Laud; 954-462-2004 sunshinecathedral.org

Sports & Outdoor

⚣ ★ (♿) Florida Great Outdoors Association, www.floridagreatoutdoors.org

⚣ ★ Front Runners & Walkers Fort Lauderdale, 2321 Arthur St, Hollywood; 954-247-8642 tinyurl.com/2rvyte

⚣ ★ ♿ Hammerhead Aquatics, 954-588-6371 www.hammerheadaquatics.com swimjohnswim@bellsouth.net

♀ South Florida Amateur Athletic Association, www.sfaaasoftball.com

♀ South Florida Tennis Club, 401 E Las Olas Blvd #130 Box 276, Ft Laud; 754-800-2237 www.sftc.us

Fort Myers

Community Centers and/or Pride Organizations

⚣ ★ Pride-SWFL, Inc, POB 151966, Cape Coral 33915 www.prideswfl.org

AIDS/HIV Services, Education & Support

♂ ☆ Friends-Together, 912 Lee Ave, Lehigh Acres 863-559-8667 www.friendstogether.org

Bars, Cafes, Clubs, Restaurants
Cape Coral

⚣ ● Cruisers Lounge, 1517 SE 47th Terrace, Cape Coral; 239-673-8002 www.cruiserslounge.com

♂ ○ Dixie Roadhouse, 1023 SE 47th Terrace, Cape Coral; 239-541-7900 thedixie.com **D**

♂ ○ ♿ McGregor Grill, 15675 McGregor Blvd Ste 24; 239-437-3499 fb.com/McGregorGrill/ ⚦ ✕ ⚦

♀ Rascals, 3758 Cleveland Ave; 239-931-9976 www.rascalsfortmyers.com

Organizations/Resources: Family and Supporters

♂ PFLAG Fort Myers, 239-898-6124 www.pflagftmyers.com

Organizations/Resources: Naturist/Nudist

♂ ★ TAN, POB 1696, Lehigh Acres; 33970 www.tamiamiareanudist.com **N**

Florida: Fort Myers
Organizations: Political

139

GAYELLOW PAGES #42 2020-2021

Jacksonville : Florida
Organizations: Social & Support

Organizations/Resources: Political/Legislative/Advocacy

♀ ★ Stonewall Democrats of SW Florida, 239-464-5088 tinyurl.com/qfp9erz

Religious / Spiritual Resources

♀ ★ ᕾᕾ St John the Apostle MCC, 3049 McGregor Blvd; 239-344-0012 www.sjamcc.com

Reproductive Medicine & Fertility Services

♀ Planned Parenthood - Fort Myers, 8595 College Parkway #250; 239-481-9999 tinyurl.com/nujn2wf

Travel & Tourist Services (see also Accommodation)

♀ ᕇ ᕾᕾ Frosch Travel, Allen Hill, 8595 College Parkway #150; 33919 239-433-5223 www.frosch.com allen.hill@frosch.com

Gainesville

Community Centers and/or Pride Organizations

♀ ★ ᕾᕾ Pride Community Center of North Central Florida, POB 5383; 32627 / 3131 NW 13th St 352-377-8915 gainesvillepride.org ✚

Bars, Cafes, Clubs, Restaurants

♀ University Club, 18 E University Ave 352-378-6814 fb.com/uc-nightclub/ **D** 🎵

Legal Services

♀ ᕇ ᕾᕾ Pye Law Firm, 3909 W Newberry Rd Bldg C; 352-381-9799 www.pyelaw.com ✚

Organizations/Resources: Family and Supporters

♀ ☆ PFLAG Gainesville, POB 358472; 32635 352-340-3770 www.pflaggainesville.org

Organizations/Resources: General, Umbrella, Pride

♂ ★ Gainesville Community Alliance, POB 357301; 32635 352-284-3881 www.gcaonline.org

Organizations/Resources: Political/Legislative/Advocacy

♂ ★ Human Rights Council of North Central Florida, POB 12912; 32604 352-234-6060 www.hrcncf.org

♂ ★ ᕾᕾ Stonewall Democrats of Alachua County, POB 6208; 32627 www.stonewalldemsac.com

Organizations/Resources: Social, Recreation, Support

♂ ★ GatorBears, fb.com/groups/gatorbears/

Organizations/Resources: Student, Academic, Education

♂ ★ ᕾᕾ Pride Student Union at the University of Florida, 326 J Wayne Rietz Union; fb.com/ufpsu

♂ ★ (⅔) University of Florida LGBTQ Affairs, 655 Reitz Union Dr Ste 2210; 352-294-7851 **H?** lgbtq.multicultural.ufl.edu ✚

Religious / Spiritual Resources

♀ ★ ᕾᕾ Trinity MCC, POB 140535 32614-0535 / 11604 SW Archer Rd 352-495-3378 **HS** www.mccgainesville.org ✚ info@mccgainesville.org

♀ ☆ ᕾᕾ Unitarian Universalist Fellowship, 4225 NW 34th St; 32605-1422 352-377-1669 **H?** www.uufg.org ✚ uuoffice@uufg.org

>> *Holiday: see Tampa Bay Area*
>> *Hollywood: see Fort Lauderdale/Wilton Manors Area*
>> *Homestead: see Miami Area*
>> *Indialantic: see Brevard County*

Inverness

Campgrounds and RV Parks

♂ • ᕇ Camp David, 2000 S Bishop Point 352-344-3445 www.campdavidflorida.com **NP** (💥?) ✚ (🏢)

Organizations/Resources: Family and Supporters

♀ ☆ PFLAG Lecanto, POB 1984, Lecanto; 34460 352-419-2738 tinyurl.com/k9gxg27

Jacksonville

Crisis, Anti-violence, & Helplines

♀ ☆ ᕾᕾ Women's Center of Jacksonville, 5644 Colcord Ave; 904-722-3000 **H?** (Also serve male rape victims) www.womenscenterofjax.org ✚

Community Centers and/or Pride Organizations

♂ River City Pride of Jacksonville, POB 40915; 32203 888-411-6482 www.rivercitypride.org

AIDS/HIV Services, Education & Support

♀ ☆ Boulevard Comprehensive Care Center, Duval County Health Dept, 515 W 6th St; 904-253-1040

♂ Northeast Florida AIDS Network, 2715 Oak St 904-356-1612 www.nfanjax.org

Bars, Cafes, Clubs, Restaurants

♀ ᕇ ᕾᕾ Bistro Aix, 1440 San Marco Blvd 904-398-1949 www.bistrox.com 🍸 ✖ ✚

♂ • Boot Rack Saloon, 4751 Lenox Ave; 904-384-7090 fb.com/boot.rack.5/ ✚

♂ • ᕾᕾ InCahoots Nightclub, 711 Edison Ave; 904-353-6316 www.incahootsnightclub.com **DKLV** ✪ ✚

♂ • ᕾᕾ The Metro, 859 Willow Branch Ave; 904-388-8719 www.metrojax.com **DKLCW** 🎵 ✚

♂ • ᕾᕾ Park Place Lounge, 931 King St; 904-389-6616 tinyurl.com/ycu4kk2r **D** ✪

♂ • The Sappho, Upstairs at Metro, 859 Willow Branch Ave; 904-388-8719 www.metrojax.com **DKLCW** 🎵 ✪ ✚

Organizations/Resources: Family and Supporters

♀ ☆ PFLAG Jacksonville, POB 2971; 32203 904-737-3329 www.pflagjax.org

Organizations/Resources: Social, Recreation, Support

♂ ★ ᕾᕾ Backwoods Bears Club, 11471 Belva Rd; **H?** www.backwoodsbears.com ✚

Florida: Jacksonville
Organizations: Student

140
GAYELLOW PAGES #42 2020-2021

Keys & Key West: Florida
Organizations: Business

Organizations/Resources: Student, Academic, Education

♂ ★ ♿ University of North Florida LGBT Resource Center, Bldg 58E, Rm 1111, 1 UNF Dr; 904-620-4720 www.unf.edu/lgbtrc/

Organizations/Resources: Youth (see also Family)

♂ ★ (♈) Jacksonville Area Sexual Minority Youth Network, POB 380103; 32205 904-389-3857 Ages 13-23 www.jasmyn.org

Religious / Spiritual Resources

♂ ☆ Unitarian Universalist Church, 7405 Arlington Expressway; 32211 904-725-8133 www.uucj.org

Keys & Key West

Community Centers and/or Pride Organizations

♂ ★ ♿ Gay & Lesbian Community Center, 513 Truman Ave, Key West; 305-292-3223 fb.com/keywestglcc

♂ Pride Fest, Key West Business Guild, 808 Duval St, Key West; 305-294-4603 www.keywestpride.org

♂ ★ Space Coast Pride, POB 672, Marathon 32902 321-213-2013 www.spacecoastpride.com

Information, Media & Publications

♂ ● Q Magazine, 305-396-8227 www.QKeyWest.com info@QKeyWest.com

Accommodation: Hotels, Inns, Guesthouses, B&B, Resorts
Key West

♂ ● (♈) Alexander's Guesthouse, 1118 Fleming St, Key West; 305-294-9919 www.alexanderskeywest.com ⊗

♂ ● Equator Resort, 822 Fleming St, Key West 305-294-7775 www.equatorresort.com

♀ ○ ♿ The Gardens Hotel, 526 Angela St, Key West; 33040 305-294-2661 **H?** www.gardenshotel.com ✎ ⊗ reservations@gardenshotel.com

♂ ● ♿ Island House, 1129 Fleming St, Key West; 305-294-6284 www.islandhousekeywest.com **LW** (♣?) ⊗

♀ ● The Knowles House, 1004 Eaton St, Key West 305-296-8132 www.knowleshouse.com

♂ ● ♿ La Te Da Hotel, 1125 Duval St, Key West; 305-296-6706 www.lateda.com ♈ ✕ 🅸 ✎ ⊗

♂ ● ♿ The New Orleans House, 724 Duval St, Key West; 33040-7463 305-293-9800 888-293-9893 www.neworleanshousekw.com ♈ ✕ 🅸⊗ jamesdarby@aol.com

AIDS/HIV Services, Education & Support

♀ ☆ AIDS Help Inc, 1434 Kennedy Dr, Key West 305-296-6196 www.ahmonroe.org

Bars, Cafes, Clubs, Restaurants
Key West

♀ ○ 801 Bourbon Bar, 801 Duval St, Key West 305-294-4737 www.801bourbon.com 🅸

♀ ● (♿) Antonia's Restaurant, 615 Duval St, Key West; 305-294-6565 www.antoniaskeywest.com ♈ ✕

♂ Aqua Nightclub, 711 Duval St, Key West 305-294-0555 www.aquakeywest.com **D** 🅸

♂ Bobby's Monkey Bar, 900 Simonton St, Key West 305-294-2655 tinyurl.com/y8fqyjc2 ✎

♂ ● ♿ Bourbon St Pub, 724 Duval St, Key West; 305-293-9800 www.bourbonStPub.com 🅸

♀ ○ The Courthouse Deli, 600 Whitehead St, Key West; 305-294-2929 courthousedelikw.com ✕ ▷

♀ ○ Croissants de France, 816 Duval St, Key West 305-294-2624 www.croissantsdefrance.com ▷

♀ ○ Deuce's "Off the Hook" Grill, 920 Caroline St, Key West; 305-414-8428 www.offthehookkeywest.com ♈ ✕ othgrillkeywest@gmail.com

♀ ○ DJ's Clam Shack, 629 Duval St, Key West 305-294-0102 djsclamshack.com/keywest/ ✕

♀ ○ ♿ Firefly, 223 Petronia St, Key West; 305-849-0104 www.fireflykeywest.com ♈ ✕ ✎

♀ ○ Hog's Breath Saloon, 400 Front St, Key West 305-292-2032 www.hogsbreath.com/keywest/ 🅸

♂ ● ♿ Island House Café & Bar, 1129 Fleming St, Key West; 305-294-6284 tinyurl.com/z5g2o37 **N** ♈ ✕

♂ ● ♿ La Te Da, 1125 Duval St, Key West; 305-296-6706 lateda.com ♈ ✕ 🅸

♀ ○ ♿ Mangia Mangia, 900 Southard St, Key West; 305-294-2469 www.mangia-mangia.com ✕ mangia-mangia@hotmail.com

♀ ○ Mangoes, 700 Duval St, Key West; 305-294-8002 www.MangoesKeyWest.com ✕

♀ ○ ♿ New York Pasta Garden, 1075 Duval St, Key West; 305-292-1991 www.newyorkpastagarden.com ✕ ✎

♀ ○ Schooner Wharf Bar, 202 William St, Key West 305-292-3302 www.schoonerwharf.com 🅸

♀ ○ Sidebar at Aqua, 504 Angela St, Key West 305-294-0555 www.sidebarkeywest.com **D**

Bookstores

♀ ○ Key West Island Bookstore, 513 Fleming St, Key West; 305-294-2904 www.keywestislandbooks.com

Erotica / Adult Stores / Safe Sex Supplies

♀ ○ (♈) Fairvilla's Sexy Things, 524 Front St, Key West; 33040 305-292-0448 **H?** www.fairvilla.com

Health Care: Physical (see also Counseling/Mental Health)

♀ ☆ Womankind, 1511 Truman Ave, Key West; 33040 305-294-4004 www.womankindkeywest.org info@womankindkeywest.org

Organizations/Resources: Business & Professional Associations, Labor Advocacy

♂ ★ ♿ Key West Business Guild, Inc, 808 Duval St, Key West; 33040 305-294-4603 www.GayKeyWestFL.com

Real Estate (see also Mortgages)

♂ ● Skahen, Daniel, Preferred Properties 520 Southard St, Key West; 33040 305-923-6524 www.danskahen.com DanSkahen@gmail.com

Religious / Spiritual Resources

♀ ★ ర్.ర్. Metropolitan Community Church Key West, 1215 Petronia St, Key West; 305-294-8912 www.mcckeywest.com

Lake Helen

Religious / Spiritual Resources

♂ ☆ (?ర్.) Lake Helen United Church of Christ, 107 N Euclid Ave; 32744 386-218-5976 www.lakehelen-ucc.com ✔ LakeHelenUCC@cfl.rr.com

>> *Lake Worth: see West Palm Beaches Area*
>> *Lakeland: see Tampa Bay Area*
>> *Largo: see Tampa Bay Area*
>> *Madeira Beach: see Tampa Bay Area*
>> *Melbourne: see Brevard County*

Miami Area

Accommodation: Hotels, Inns, Guesthouses, B&B, Resorts
Miami Beach

♂ ● ర్.ర్. Circa 39 Hotel, 3900 Collins Ave, Miami Beach; 305-538-4900 www.circa39.com ♣ ✔ Ⓢ

♂ ● ర్.ర్. Freehand Miami, 2727 Indian Creek Dr, Miami Beach; 305-531-2727 **H** www.thefreehand.com ✔ Ⓢ

♀ ● ర్.ర్. Hôtel Gaythering, 1409 Lincoln Rd, Miami Beach; 786-284-1176 **H** All wecome over 18 www.gaythering.com ♣ ✔ Ⓢ Ⓢ

♀ ● (?ర్.) The Tropics Hotel & Hostel, 1550 Collins Ave, Miami Beach; 305-531-0361 www.tropicshotel.com ✔

Accommodation Rental: Furnished / Vacation (& AirBNB)
Miami Beach

♀ ● (?ర్.) Bresaro Suites at the Mantell Plaza, 255 W 24th St CU-6, Miami Beach; 305-772-5665 www.bresaro.com ✔ (Ⓢ)

AIDS/HIV Services, Education & Support

♀ ☆ Care Resource, 3510 Biscayne Blvd #300, Mi 305-576-1234 www.careresource.org

♀ ☆ ర్.ర్. Food for Life Network, 3400 NE 2nd Ave, Mi; 305-576-3663 **H** www.foodforlifenetwork.org ✔

Bars, Cafes, Clubs, Restaurants
Miami Beach

♀ ● ర్.ర్. Bar Gaythering, 1409 Lincoln Rd, Miami Beach; 786-284-1176 **H** gaythering.com ✔

♀ ○ ర్.ర్. The Cabaret South Beach, at Shelborne South Beach Hotel, 1801 Collins Ave, Miami Beach; 305-504-7500 www.TheCabaretSouthBeach.com ¥ ✕ ▥ ✔

♂ Club Boi, 1216 Washington Ave, Miami Beach; / Sat 10pm 786-617-4746 www.clubboi.com **D** ❖

♂ ● Palace Bar & Grill, 1052 Ocean Dr, Miami Beach; 305-531-7234 www.palacesouthbeach.com **D** ¥ ✕ ▥

♀ ● Pandora Events for Women, Check for current venues 305-975-6933 tinyurl.com/6m3ygku

♂ ● Twist, 1057 Washington Ave, Miami Beach 305-53-TWIST www.twistsobe.com **D**

Miami

♀ Azucar, 2301 SW 32nd Ave, Mi; 786-444-0736 www.Azucar-Miami.net ▥ ✦

♂ Discotekka, 60 NE 11th St, Mi; 305-371-3773 fb.com/discotekka **D**

♂ Jamboree Lounge, 7005 Biscayne Blvd, Mi 305-759-3413 tinyurl.com/gwvgdu5 ▥

♀ ● ర్.ర్. Michael's Genuine Food & Drink, Atlas Plaza, 130 NE 40th St, Mi; 305-573-5550 www.michaelsgenuine.com ¥ ✕ ✔

Bookstores

♀ ○ Books & Books, 265 Aragon Ave, Coral Gables 305-442-4408 www.booksandbooks.com

♀ ○ Books & Books Inc, 927 Lincoln Rd, Miami Beach 305-532-3222 www.booksandbooks.com

Counseling/Psychotherapy/Mental Health

♂ ○ ర్.ర్. Hyman, Stan, PhD, LCSW, Aventura Stress Relief Center, 2999 NE 191st St #703, Mi; 33180 305-933-9779 drstanhyman.com DrStan@DrStanHyman.com

Funding: Endowment, Fundraising

♀ ☆ Aqua Foundation for Women, 1951 NW 7 Ave, Mi 33136 305-576-2782 www.aquafoundation.org info@aquafoundation.org

♀ Out of the Closet Thrift Store, 2900 N Biscayne Blvd, Mi; 305-764-3773 tinyurl.com/ybrtht8q

Legal Services

♀ ○ Angie Angelis Law, 13554 SW 47th Lane Ste 100, Mi; 33175 305-598-2540 fax 305-330-9248 fb.com/AngieAngelisLaw angie@angieangelislaw.com

♀ ○ Law Offices of Barbara Buxton, P.A., 20801 Biscayne Blvd Ste 400, Aventura; 305-932-2293 Elder Law www.buxtonlaw.com

♀ ○ ర్.ర్. Steinberg, Mark S, 6950 N Kendall Dr, Mi; 33156 305-671-0015 www.steinberglawoffices.com mss@steinberg lawoffices.com

Men's & Sex Clubs (not primarily Health Clubs)

♂ ● Club Aqua Miami, 2991 Coral Way, Mi 305-448-2214 www.clubaquamiami.com **P** ✔

Organizations/Resources: Business & Professional Associations, Labor Advocacy

♀ ★ Miami-Dade Gay & Lesbian Chamber of Commerce, 1130 Washington Ave 1st Flr N, Miami Beach; 305-673-4440 www.gay-bizmiami.com

Organizations/Resources: Cultural, Dance, Performance

♂ ★ Miami Gay Men's Chorus, 3010 De Soto Blvd, Coral Gables; 786-671-6599 www.mgmchorus.org

Florida: Miami Area
Organizations: Multicultural

142
GAYELLOW PAGES #42 2020-2021

Orlando Area: Florida
AIDS/HIV Support

Organizations/Resources: Ethnic, Multicultural

Miami Beach Bruthaz, 1850 Collins Ave, Miami Beach; / annual event 866-981-5009 www.miamibeachbruthaz.com ✪

Unity Coalition/Coalicion Unida, 777 Brickell Ave, Mi; 786-271-6982 www.unitycoalition.org ✦

Organizations/Resources: Family and Supporters

★ South Florida Family Pride, tinyurl.com/glcfn5f

Organizations/Resources: Political/Legislative/Advocacy

★ National LGBTQ Task Force, 801 Arthur Godfrey Rd Ste 402, Mi; 305-571-1924 www.thetaskforce.org

SAVE LGBT, 1951 NW 7 Ave Ste 600, Mi 305-751-7283 www.save.lgbt

Organizations/Resources: Social, Recreation, Support

coralGAYbles, www.coralgaybles.com

Rainbow Ladies - Our Space, Inc., fb.com/RainbowLadies ✪

Organizations/Resources: Student, Academic, Education

★ LGBTQA Initiatives at Florida International University, University Park, GC-216, 11200 SW 8th St, Mi; 33199 305-919-5817 lgbt.fiu.edu lgbt@fiu.edu

★ ⚥ SpectrUM, Shalala Student Center, Suite 210-K, 1330 Miller Dr, Coral Gables; 305-284-5520 tinyurl.com/gqrqyxb ✎

Organizations/Resources: Youth (see also Family)

★ Alliance for GLBTQ Youth, 1175 NE 125th St #510, N Miami; 305-899-8087 www.glbtqalliance.com

★ Pridelines, 6360 NE 4th Court, Mi 305-571-9601 www.pridelines.org

☆ YES Institute, 5275 Sunset Dr, Mi 305-663-7195 yesinstitute.org

Religious / Spiritual Resources

☆ St Stephen's Episcopal Church, 2750 McFarlane Rd, Coconut Grove; 33133 305-448-2601 sseccg.org parish@sseds.org

Sports & Outdoor

★ Miami Front Runners, 360 NE 91st St, Mi 305-757-5581 tinyurl.com/7z3pcej

★ Miami Mavericks Tennis Club, 665 NE 25th St Unit 406, Mi; 33137 305-458-1628 www.miamimaverickstennis.com mmtc.10s@gmail.com

Nadadores Swim Team South Florida, POB 190117, Miami Beach; 33119 305-707-8568 www.nadadoresswimteam.org

Naples

Bars, Cafes, Clubs, Restaurants

● Bambusa Bar & Grill, 600 Goodlette Frank Rd N 239-649-5657 www.bambusaonline.com V ⵝ ✕

○ Caffe dell'Amore, 1400 Gulf Shore Blvd N 239-261-1389 www.caffedellamore.com ✕

○ ⚥ Sunburst Cafe, 2340 Pine Ridge Rd; 239-263-3123 www.sunburstnaples.com ☞

Organizations/Resources: Family and Supporters

☆ PFLAG Naples, POB 770294; 34107 239-963-4670 www.pflagnaples.org

Real Estate (see also Mortgages)

○ ⚥ Nardi, Robert L, Lic. Real Estate Broker, Nardi Realty 3400 Tamiami Trail N Ste 103; 34103 239-293-3592 NardiRealty.com

Recovery

☆ Naples Area Intergroup, Inc., 1509 Pine Ridge Rd - Unit B; 239-262-6535 www.naplesintergroup.org
≫ New Port Richey: see Tampa Bay Area

Ocala

Community Centers and/or Pride Organizations

★ Ocala Pride Inc, POB 1064; 34478 352-426-2263 ocalapride.org

Bars, Cafes, Clubs, Restaurants

● Copa Nightclub, 2330 S Pine Ave 352-351-5721 www.thecopaocala.com ⵝ ✕▥

Religious / Spiritual Resources

★ ⚥ God's Acre MCC, POB 770240; 34474 / 700 NW 57th Ave 352-867-5996 godsacremcc.com

Orlando Area

Community Centers and/or Pride Organizations

★ ⚥ Come Out With Pride, 424 E Central Blvd Ste 415, Orl; 32801 **HS** www.comeoutwithpride.com info@comeoutwithpride.org

★ ⚥ LGBT+Center Orlando, 946 N Mills Ave, Orl; 407-228-8272 www.thecenterorlando.org ✎

Information, Media & Publications

● GayOrlando.com, POB 796, Gotha, FL 34734 888-942-9329 www.gayorlando.com

One Orlando Alliance, www.oneorlandoalliance.org

Accommodation: Hotels, Inns, Guesthouses, B&B, Resorts
Mount Dora

○ Adora Inn, 610 N Tremain St, Mount Dora; 32757 352-735-3110 **H?** www.adorainn.com ✎ info@adorainn.com

Accounting, Bookkeeping, Tax Services

● James, Leah, CPA, MSTax, Gecko CPA Firm, POB 5277, Orl; 32793 407-478-4513 www.geckocpa.com

AIDS/HIV Services, Education & Support

☆ ⚥ Hope & Help, 4122 Metric Dr #800, Winter Park; 32792 407-645-2577 **H?** www.hopeandhelp.org ✎ info@hopeandhelp.org

Bars, Cafes, Clubs, Restaurants

Maitland

♀ ○ ♿ Copper Rocket Pub, 106 Lake Ave, Maitland; 407-853-5036 www.copperrocketpub.com **DK** ⅋ ✕ 🏨

Orlando

⚣ Barcodes, 4453 Edgewater Dr, Orl; 407-412-6917 fb.com/barcodesorlando

⚣ ● Bear Den at Parliament House, 410 N Orange Blossom Trail, Orl; 407-425-7571 www.parliamenthouse.com **D** 🏨

♀ ○ ♿ Dandelion Communitea Cafe, 618 N Thornton Ave, Orl; 407-362-1864 www.dandelioncommunitea.com ⟲

♀ ○ The Falcon, 819 E Washington St, Orl 407-423-3060 www.TheFalconBar.com 🏨

⚣ ● ♿ Hank's, 5026 Edgewater Dr, Orl 407-291-2399 www.hanksbarorlando.com **L** info@hanksbarorlando.com

♀ ○ ♿ Nora's Sugar Shack, 636 Virginia Dr, Orl; 407-447-5885 bar package store lounge noraswinecigars.com

⚣ ● Parliament House, 410 N Orange Blossom Trail, Orl; 407-425-7571 www.parliamenthouse.com **D** 🏨

♀ ○ ♿ Pom Pom's Teahouse & Sandwicheria, 67 N Bumby Ave, Orl; 407-894-0865 Art shows pompomsteahouse.com ✕ ⟲ ⚧

⚣ ● Rainbow Cafe at Parliament House, 410 N Orange Blossom Trail, Orl; 407-425-7571 tinyurl.com/zqljdnj **D** 🏨

⚣ ● ♿ Savoy Orlando, 1913 N Orange Ave, Orl; 407-898-6766 www.savoyorlando.com 🏨 ⚧

⚣ (♫) Southern Nights Orlando, 375 S Bumby Ave, Orl; 407-412-5039 **D** 🏨 ⚧

⚣ ● Stonewall Bar / Sky Bar, 741 W Church St, Orl; 407-373-0888 www.stonewallorlando.com ⅋ ✕

♀ ○ White Wolf Cafe, 1829 N Orange Ave, Orl 407-895-9911 www.whitewolfcafe.com ⅋ ✕ ⟲

Clothes (see also Erotica, Leather)

♀ ○ Ritzy Rags, Wigs & More, 928 N Mills Ave, Orl 407-897-2117 www.ritzyrags.com

Erotica / Adult Stores / Safe Sex Supplies

♀ ○ ♿ Fairvilla Megastore, 1740 N Orange Blossom Trl, Orl; 32804-5603 407-425-6005 **H?** www.fairvilla.com

♀ ○ ♿ Fairvilla's Sexy Things, 2145 E Irlo Bronson Memorial Hwy, Kissimmee; 34744 407-782-3473 **H?** www.fairvilla.com

♀ ○ Fairvilla's Sexy Things, 7535 International Dr, Orl; 32819 407-826-1627 www.fairvilla.com

Funding: Endowment, Fundraising

⚣ ★ Sisters of Perpetual Indulgence, POB 3665, Orl; 32790 407-494-6867 www.orlandosisters.org

Legal Services

♂ ○ Law Office of Blaine McChesney, P.A., 390 N Orange Ave Ste 2300, Orl; 32801 407-246-1112 Criminal Defense www.BlaineMcChesneyLaw.com Blaine@BlaineMcChesneyLaw.com

Men's & Sex Clubs (not primarily Health Clubs)

⚣ ● ♿ Club Orlando, 450 E Compton St, Orl; 407-425-5005 www.club-orlando.com **P** ⚧

Organizations/Resources: Business & Professional Associations, Labor Advocacy

⚣ ★ Central Florida Gay & Lesbian Law Association, 280 Wekiva Springs Rd Ste 2030, Longwood; 407-608-6080 fb.com/CFGALLA/

⚣ ★ Pride Chamber / Metropolitan Business Association, 5003 Old Cheney Hwy, Orl; 321-800-3946 **H?** www.mbaorlando.org ⚧

Organizations/Resources: Cultural, Dance, Performance

⚣ Central Florida Sounds of Freedom Band and Color Guard, POB 780343, Orl; 32878 tinyurl.com/whq452x

♀ ★ ♿ Orlando Gay Chorus, POB 3103, Orl; 32802 407-841-7464 **HS** www.orlandogaychorus.org

Organizations/Resources: Family and Supporters

♀ ☆ PFLAG Lady Lake, 352-693-2173 www.pflagladylake.org ✦

♀ ☆ PFLAG Orlando/Central Florida, POB 141312, Orl; 32814 407-236-9177 www.pflagorlando.org

Organizations/Resources: Political/Legislative/Advocacy

♀ ★ ♿ Rainbow Democrats of Orange County, 407-228-8272 rainbowdems.org

Organizations/Resources: Social, Recreation, Support

⚣ ★ ♿ Prime Timers of Central Florida, POB 547003, Orl; 32854 407-325-2694 www.primetimersww.com/cfpt/

Organizations/Resources: Student, Academic, Education

⚣ ★ ♿ Multicultural Student Center Pride Commons, Student Union 207. 4000 Central Florida Blvd, Orl 407-823-0401 sja.sdes.ucf.edu/ ⚧

⚣ ★ Rollins College Spectrum, Office of Career Services, 1000 Holt Ave Box 2587, Orl; 407-646-2195 tinyurl.com/3uurn5zm

⚣ ★ ♿ Seminole Community College Unity GSA, 100 Weldon Blvd UP-2004, Sanford; 407-708-2079 **H?** ⚧

⚣ ★ Valencia College East GSA, 701 N Econlockhatchee Trail, Orl; 407-582-2170 fb.com/ValenciaEastGSA/

Organizations/Resources: Youth (see also Family)

⚣ ★ Orlando Youth Alliance, POB 536944, Orl 32853 407-244-1222 www.orlandoyouthalliance.org

⚣ ★ ♿ Zebra Coalition, 911 N Mills Ave, Orl; 407-228-1446 ages 13-24 www.zebrayouth.org ⚧

Real Estate (see also Mortgages)

♂ ○ Musselman, Kirk, Dave Lowe Realty, 303 N Highland St, Mount Dora; 32757 352-383-7104 www.kirkmusselman.com Kirk@DaveLoweRealty.com

Religious / Spiritual Resources

♀ ☆ ♿ First Unitarian Church, 1901 E Robinson St, Orl; 32803 407-898-3621 www.OrlandoUU.org fuco@cfl.rr.com

⚣ ★ ♿ Joy MCC, 2351 S Ferncreek Ave, Orl; 407-894-1081 www.joymcc.org

Florida: Orlando Area
Religious
144
GAYELLOW PAGES #42 2020-2021
Panama City Area: Florida
AIDS/HIV Support

♂ ★ Open Circle MCC, POB 536, Oxford; 34484 352-753-0260 www.opencirclemcc.org

Sports & Outdoor

♂ Central Florida Softball League, P.O. Box 149692, POB 149692, Orl; 32814 www.cfsleague.org

♀ ★ Gay & Lesbian Bowling League (GLBL), Colonial Lanes, 400 N Primrose Dr, Orl; 407-894-0361 tinyurl.com/yawrpt5j

♀ Orange Blossom Tennis Association, POB 533465, Orl; 32853 407-694-0987 www.theobta.com

♀ ★ Orlando Front Runners & Walkers, POB 11135, Orl; 32803 407-401-7439 fb.com/ORLFrontRunners

♀ ★ Rainbow Paddlers, 407-346-1262 tinyurl.com/4xasz9

Travel & Tourist Services (see also Accommodation)

♀ ● Gay Days, Inc, POB 796, Gotha; 34734 407-896-8431 888-942-9329 www.gaydays.com info@gaydays.com

Palm Beach/West Palm Beaches Area

Crisis, Anti-violence, & Helplines

♂ ☆ 211 Palm Beach/Treasure Coast, POB 3588, Lantana; 33465 561-383-1112 www.211palmbeach.org

Community Centers and/or Pride Organizations

♂ ★ && Compass Gay & Lesbian Community Center of Palm Beach County, 201 N Dixie Hwy, Lake Worth 561-533-9699 **H?** www.compassglcc.com ✔

Accommodation: Hotels, Inns, Guesthouses, B&B, Resorts
West Palm Beach

♂ ● && Grandview Gardens Bed & Breakfast, 1608 Lake Ave, W P Bch; 33401-7006 561-833-9023 www.grandview-gardens.com (❧?) ✔ ⊗

AIDS/HIV Services, Education & Support

♀ ☆ && FoundCare, Inc, 2330 S Congress Ave, Palm Springs; 33406 561-432-5849 **H?** www.FoundCare.org

Bars, Cafes, Clubs, Restaurants
Lake Worth

♂ The Mad Hatter, 1532 N Dixie Hwy, Lake Worth; 561-547-8860 fb.com/MadHatterLounge/ ⵣ ✕

Lantana

♂ Penny's at the Duke, 902B N Dixie Hwy, Lantana; 561-318-7359 fb.com/pennysattheduke/

West Palm Beach

♀ ○ Respectable Street, 518 Clematis St, W P Bch 561-540-8881 tinyurl.com/l53cfdq **D** 🕮

♀ ○ Rhythm Cafe, 3800 S Dixie Hwy #A, W P Bch 561-833-3406 www.rhythmcafe.cc ✕

♂ & Roosters, 823 Belvedere Rd, W P Bch; 561-832-9119 www.roosterswpb.com 🕮

Florists (see also Gifts)

♀ ○ Exceptional Flowers & Gifts, 2800 N Federal Hwy Ste 600-700, Boca Raton; 33431-6838 561-353-4720 exceptionalflowers-gifts.net

Legal Services

♂ ● & Hoch, Rand, Esq, 400 N Flagler Dr #1402, W P Bch; 33401-4315 561-358-0105 ✔ rand-hoch@usa.net

Organizations/Resources: Business & Professional Associations, Labor Advocacy

♂ ★ Pride Business Alliance of the Palm Beaches, Compass, Inc., 201 N Dixie Hwy, Lake Worth; 561-533-9699 tinyurl.com/y5wjkbfj

Organizations/Resources: Cultural, Dance, Performance

♂ Voices of Pride, POB 1313, Lake Worth; 33460 561-247-4554 www.voicesofpride.org

Organizations/Resources: Political/Legislative/Advocacy

♀ ☆ Palm Beach County Human Rights Council, POB 267, W P Bch; 33402 561-346-1263 www.pbchrc.org pbchrc@aol.com

Organizations/Resources: Youth (see also Family)

♀ ★ && Compass Youth Program, 201 N Dixie Hwy, Lake Worth; 33460 561-533-9699 fax 561-586-0635 www.compassglcc.com ✔ youth@compassglcc.com

Pets & Pet Services & Supplies

♀ ○ Village Pet Pals, 8001 W Lake Dr, W P Bch 561-351-7193 www.villagepetpals.com

Recovery

♂ ★ Lambda North, 18 J Street, Lake Worth 561-635-9313 www.lambdanorth.net

Religious / Spiritual Resources

♂ ★ && Church of Our Savior MCC, 2011 S Federal Hwy, Boynton Bch; 561-733-4000 www.churchofoursaviormcc.org

♀ ☆ Church Of The Palms, 1960 N Swinton Ave, Delray Bch; 33444 561-276-6347 www.churchofthepalms.net pastor@church ofthepalms.net

♂ ★ && Dignity/Palm Beach, 561-309-0088 www.dignitypalm-beach.org

♀ ★ & MCC of the Palm Beaches, 4857 Northlake Blvd, Palm Beach Gardens; 561-775-5900 mccpb.org

Panama City Area

Community Centers and/or Pride Organizations

♂ ★ LGBTQ Center of Bay County, 1608 Baker Court, Room 6, Panama City; 850-252-5145 lgbtqcenterofbaycounty.com

Accommodation: Hotels, Inns, Guesthouses, B&B, Resorts
Panama City Beach

♀ ○ (?&) Wisteria Inn, 20404 Front Beach Rd, Panama Cy Bch; 32413-8923 850-234-0557 **H?** Gay-friendly adults only. www.wis-teria-inn.com ❧ ✔ ⊗

AIDS/HIV Services, Education & Support

♀ ☆ && BASIC NWFL, Inc., 432 Magnolia Ave, Panama City; 850-785-1088 fb.com/basicnwfl/

Florida: Panama City Area
Bars, Cafes, Clubs, Restaurants

145
GAYELLOW PAGES #42 2020-2021

Sarasota/Bradenton/Venice Area: Florida
Grooming

Bars, Cafes, Clubs, Restaurants
Panama City Beach

♂ ● ᕳᕲ Splash Bar, 6520 Thomas Dr, Panama Cy Bch; 850-236-3450 www.splashbarflorida.com ▦

Organizations/Resources: Family and Supporters

♀ ☆ PFLAG Panama City, POB 15293, Panama City 32406 850-866-5573 www.pflag-pc.org

» *Pembroke Pines: see Fort Lauderdale/Wilton Manors Area*

Pensacola Area

Community Centers and/or Pride Organizations

♀ ★ ᕳᕲ Gay Grassroots Northwest Florida, 6847 N 9th Ave Ste A Box 317, Pensacola; 850-415-7359 www.ggnwfl.com

AIDS/HIV Services, Education & Support

♀ ☆ OASIS Florida, 1825 Hurlburt Rd Ste 14, Fort Walton Beach; 850-314-0950 www.oasisflorida.org ✔

♀ ☆ OASIS Florida, 25 E Wright St, Pensacola 850-429-7551 www.oasisflorida.org ✔

Bars, Cafes, Clubs, Restaurants
Pensacola

♂ The Cabaret, 101 S Jefferson St, Pensacola 850-607-2020 tinyurl.com/kwjln7s **K** ▦

♀ ○ End of the Line Cafe, 610 E Wright St, Pensacola; 850-429-0336 Vegan www.eotlcafe.com ▷ ✔

♂ ● ᕳᕲ The Roundup, 560 E Heinberg St, Pensacola; 850-433-8482 www.theroundup.net **KLCWV** ✔

Counseling/Psychotherapy/Mental Health

♀ ○ Bright, Regina, MS, LMHC, BCST, Stepping Stones Professional Counseling, 151 Mary Esther Blvd Ste 310 A, Mary Esther 850-226-6430 tinyurl.com/yco2ßo6b

Organizations/Resources: Cultural, Dance, Performance

♀ ★ Stamped: Pensacola LGBT Film Festival, PO Box 12875, Pensacola; 32591 850-696-7348 www.stampedfilmfest.com

Organizations/Resources: Transgender/Gender Non-Conforming/Diverse

T Gulf Coast Transgender Alliance, 850-332-8416 tinyurl.com/jdrmcjr

Recovery

♀ ☆ Pensacola Tri-District Central Office of AA, 600 University Office Blvd Ste 14B, Pensacola; 32504 850-433-4191 www.aapensacola.org info@aapensacola.org

Religious / Spiritual Resources

♀ ★ ᕳᕲ Holy Cross MCC, 3130 W Fairfield Dr, Pensacola; 850-469-9090 fb.com/HolyCrossMCC ✔

♀ ☆ ᕳᕲ Unitarian Universalist Church of Pensacola, 9888 Pensacola Blvd, Pensacola; 32534-1244 850-475-9077 **H** www.uupensacola.org ✔ uucp@bellsouth.net

» *Pinellas Park: see Tampa Bay Area*
» *Pompano Beach: see Fort Lauderdale/Wilton Manors Area*

» *Port Richey: see Tampa Bay Area*

Port Saint Lucie

Pets & Pet Services & Supplies

♀ ● Barmont Cattery, 6124 NW Snook Court; 34983-3342 772-343-1030 www.barmontcat.com barmontcat@aol.com

St Augustine

Accommodation: Hotels, Inns, Guesthouses, B&B, Resorts

♂ ● At Journey's End, 89 Cedar St; 904-829-0076 www.atjourneysend.com (♣?) ✔ ⊕

♀ ○ ᕳᕲ Bayfront Westcott House, 146 Avenida Menendez; 32084-5049 800-513-9814 www.westcotthouse.com ✔ ⊕ OnTheBay@WestcottHouse.com

♀ ● Hemingway House B&B, 54 Charlotte St; 32084 904-829-3819 www.hemingwayhouse.net ✔ ⊕

♀ ● Inn on Charlotte, 52 Charlotte St; 904-829-3819 www.innoncharlotte.com ✔ ⊕

♀ ● Saragossa Inn, 34 Saragossa St; 904-808-7384 www.saragossainn.com (♣?) ✔

Bars, Cafes, Clubs, Restaurants

♀ ○ ᕳᕲ Collage, 60 Hypolita St 904-829-0055 www.collagestaug.com ✕

Organizations/Resources: Family and Supporters

♀ PFLAG St Augustine, POB 573; 32085 904-853-0808 fb.com/pflagstaug

Religious / Spiritual Resources

♀ ★ ᕳᕲ FirstCoast Metropolitan Community Church, 2915 CR 214; 904-824-2802 **H?** www.firstcoastmcc.com

Sarasota/Bradenton/Venice Area

Community Centers and/or Pride Organizations

♀ ★ Sarasota Pride, POB 51032, Sarasota 34232 941-320-9268 www.sarasotapride.org SarasotaPride@gmail.com

Bars, Cafes, Clubs, Restaurants
Sarasota

♂ ● Purple Rhino Lodge, 2920 Beneva Rd, Sarasota; 941-735-6553 fb.com/PurpleRhinoLodge/ **KP** ✕ ⅄ ▦

Counseling/Psychotherapy/Mental Health

♀ ● ᕳᕲ Eslien, Heather D, MA, LHMC, 330 South Pineapple Ave Ste 101, Sarasota; 34236 941-840-0878 www.swfltranssptgp.org heather.d.eslien@gmail.com

♀ ○ Twitchell, Carol, Psy.D., 3205 Southgate Circle Ste 12, Sarasota; 34239 941-954-1506 www.caroltwitchell.com caroltwitchell@comcast.net

Grooming, Personal Care, Spa Services

♀ ● (?♣) Salon Capelli/ Michael Regulbuto, Salon Lofts, Loft #1, 3800 S Tamiami Trail, Sarasota; 941-349-5257 www.saloncapelli.com

Florida: Sarasota/Bradenton/Venice Area
Legal
146
GAYELLOW PAGES #42 2020-2021
Tampa Bay Area: Florida
AIDS/HIV Support

Legal Services

♂ • 👓 Petruff, Patricia, Dye Harrison, 1206 Manatee Ave W, Bradenton; 34205 941-748-4411 dyeharrison.com ✗

Organizations/Resources: Cultural, Dance, Performance

♂ ★ (👫) Diversity: The Voices of Sarasota, POB 2453, Sarasota; 34230-2453 888-550-6279 www.DiversitySarasota.org contact@ DiversitySarasota.org

Organizations/Resources: Social, Recreation, Support

♂ ★ Prime Timers Sarasota, POB 1411, Sarasota 34230 941-556-1344 tinyurl.com/ybtt7dbf

Organizations/Resources: Transgender/Gender Non-Conforming/Diverse

T ☆ Gulf Coast Transgender Group, 330 South Pineapple Ave Ste 101, Sarasota; 34236 941-366-3134 www.swfltranssptgp.org

Organizations/Resources: Youth (see also Family)

♂ ★ 👓 ALSO Youth, 1470 Blvd of the Arts, Sarasota; 941-951-2576 LGBTQ+ youth under 21 and allies www.alsoyouth.org ✗

Recovery

♀ ☆ Central Office of Sara-Mana Inc, Oak Park Business Center, 1748 Independence Blvd Ste B-2, Sarasota; 941-951-6810 www.aasrq.com

Religious / Spiritual Resources

♂ ★ (👫) Church of the Trinity MCC, 7225 N Lockwood Ridge Rd, Sarasota; 941-355-0847 www.trinitymcc.com

♂ ★ Suncoast Cathedral MCC, 3276 E Venice Ave, Venice; 941-484-7068 www.suncoastcathedralmcc.com

Travel & Tourist Services (see also Accommodation)

♂ • A+ Insurance & Travel, 601B N Washington Blvd, Sarasota; 34236-4241 941-951-6866 info@aplusinc.com
>> Satellite Beach: see Brevard County
>> St Petersburg: see Tampa Bay Area

Stuart

Organizations/Resources: Family and Supporters

♀ ☆ PFLAG of Stuart, FL, 954-385-3949 pflagstuartfl.org pflagstuartfl@gmail.com

Tallahassee

AIDS/HIV Services, Education & Support

♀ ☆ 👓 Big Bend Cares, 2201 S Monroe St 850-656-2437 **H?** www.bigbendcares.org

Health Care: Physical (see also Counseling/Mental Health)

♂ ○ 👓 Appelbaum, Jonathan S, MD, FACP, FSU-TMH Internal Medicine Residency Clinic, 1300 Miccosukee Rd; 32308 850-431-7900 www.med.fsu.edu ✗

Organizations/Resources: Cultural, Dance, Performance

♀ Mickee Faust Club, POB 5503; 32314 850-562-7287 www.mickeefaust.com

Organizations/Resources: Social, Recreation, Support

♂ ★ Tallahassee Prime Timers, POB 15065; 32317 850-877-4479 tallahasseeprimetimers.org

Organizations/Resources: Transgender/Gender Non-Conforming/Diverse

T Transgender Tallahassee, Family Tree, 2415 N Monroe St #2064; tinyurl.com/y7hslqgw

Religious / Spiritual Resources

♂ Thrive MCC, 2720 Apalachee Parkway 850-443-1694 www.thrivemcc.com

♀ ☆ 👓 United Church in Tallahassee (UCC), 1834 Mahan Dr; 32308 850-878-7385 www.uctonline.org uctoffice@gmail.com
>> Tampa: see Tampa Bay Area

Tampa Bay Area

Community Centers and/or Pride Organizations

♀ ☆ 👓 Metro Wellness & Community Centers, 3251 3rd Ave N Ste #125, St Pete; 727-321-3854 **H?** www.metrotampabay.org ✪

♀ ☆ Metro Wellness & Community Centers, 4747 US 19 Highway, New Port Richey; 727-494-2625 www.metrotampabay.org

♂ ★ St Pete Pride, POB 12647, St Pete; 33733 727-342-0084 www.stpetepride.com ✗ info@stpetepride.com

♂ ★ Tampa LGBT Metro Center, Metro Wellness & Community Centers, 1315 E 7th Ave, Tampa; 813-232-3808 www.metrotampabay.org **D** ✗

♂ ★ Tampa Pride, 3510 E 8th Ave, Tampa; 33605 813-777-4832 www.tampapride.org c.west@tampapride.org

Information, Media & Publications

♂ ★ 👓 Dishing with Mark and Carrie, 813-777-4832 **H** www.mcfilm.co

♂ ★ ProSuzy: Your LGBT Connection, POB 530544, Gulfport; 33747 727-289-9365 www.prosuzy.com

Accommodation: Hotels, Inns, Guesthouses, B&B, Resorts
St Petersburg

♀ ○ Beach Drive Inn B&B, 532 Beach Dr NE, St Pete 727-822-2244 **HD** www.beachdriveinn.com (✿?) ✗ ⊗

♀ • Dickens House Bed & Breakfast, 335 8th Ave NE, St Pete; 727-822-8622 www.dickenshouse.com ✗ ⊗

♂ • 👓 GayStPete House, 4505 5th Ave N, St Pete; 727-365-0544 www.gaystpetehouse.com **N** ✿ ✗ ⊗

Accounting, Bookkeeping, Tax Services

♀ • ♿ Accounting, Taxes & More, Inc, Bob Ferraro, EA, 1710 N Hercules Ave Ste 104, Clearwater; 33765 727-449-9994 ATMTax-Prep.com

AIDS/HIV Services, Education & Support

♀ ☆ 👓 EPIC - Francis House, 4703 N Florida Ave, Tampa; 813-237-3066 myepic.org ✗

Bars, Cafes, Clubs, Restaurants

Bradley's on 7th, 1510 E 7th Ave, Tampa 813-241-2723 www.bradleyson7th.com **D** 〽

○&& The Bricks of Ybor, 1327 E 7th Ave, Tampa; 813-247-1785 **H?** www.thebricksybor.com ⚨ ✕ ⟲ ∕

Clearwater

● Pro Shop Pub, 840 Cleveland St, Clearwater 727-447-4259 www.proshoppub.us ∕

Dade City

● Woody's Nightclub, Sawmill Campground, 21710 US Hwy 98, Dade City; 352-583-0664 www.flsawmill.com **DP** ∕

Dunedin

○ Blur Nighclub, 325 Main St, Dunedin 727-736-2587 www.blur-dunedin.com **D** 〽 DunedinBlur@gmail.com

Kelly's / Chic A Boom Room, 319 Main St, Dunedin; / Tue, Drag Queen Bingo 727-736-5284 www.kellyschicaboom.com ⚨ ✕

○ Gaspar's Grotto, 1805 E 7th Ave, Tampa 813-248-5900 www.gasparsgrotto.com **DK** ⚨ ✕ ∕

● Honey Pot, 1507 E 7th Ave, Tampa 813-247-4663 tinyurl.com/mjxjszx 〽

Lakeland

Lakeland Pulse, 1030 E Main St, Lakeland 863-370-9146

The Pub/Lakeland, 2523 Broadway St, Lakeland; 863-213-9602 tinyurl.com/y7qpofoq **D**

Largo

● Quench Lounge, 13284 66th St N, Largo 727-754-5900 www.quenchlounge.com info@quenchlounge.com

&& Southern Nights, 1401 E 7th Ave, Tampa; 813-599-8625 fb.com/SouthernNightsTampa/ **DV** 〽∕

St Pete Beach

○ Fetishes Dining & Wine Bar, planned relocation 727-363-3700 www.fetishesrestaurant.com ✕

St Petersburg

○ The Dog Bar, 2300 Central Ave, St Pete 727-317-4968 www.dogbarstpete.com dogbarstpete@gmail.com

○ Enigma, 1110 Central Ave, St Pete 727-235-0867 www.enigmastpete.com **DV** 〽∕

G St Pete, 350 1st Ave, St Pete fb.com/gstpete/

○ The Garage On Central Avenue, 2729 Central Ave, St Pete; 727-235-9086 fb.com/OFCLgaragepage/ **DK**

○ Mad Hatter's Ethnobotanical Tea Bar, 4685 28th St N, St Pete; 727-800-5030 www.madhattersteabar.com ⟲ ∕

○ Punky's Bar and Grill, 3063 Central Ave, St Pete; 727-201-4712 punkysbar.com ⚨ ✕〽

● Steam Fridays at the Honey Pot, 1507 E 7th Ave, Tampa; 813-247-4663 fb.com/SteamFridays/

Tampa

● (♿) City Side, 3703 Henderson Blvd, Tampa; 813-350-0600 **H** citysideloungetampa.com ∕

Cristoph's, 2606 N Armenia Ave, Tampa 813-450-3877 cristophstampa.com **D** 〽

○ Fly Bar & Restaurant, 1202 N Franklin St, Tampa; 813-275-5000 www.flybarandrestaurant.com ⚨ ✕

○ Reservoir Bar, 1518 E 7th Ave, Tampa 813-248-1442 fb.com/reservoirbar/

● Twirl Girl Events & Promotions, fb.com/TwirlGirlPromotions

○&& Ybor City Wine Bar, 1600 E 8th Ave, Tampa; 813-999-4966 www.yborcitywinebar.com ⚨ ✕

Campgrounds and RV Parks

&& Sawmill Campground, 21710 US Hwy 98, Dade City; 352-583-0664 www.flsawmill.com **P** ❀∕

Counseling/Psychotherapy/Mental Health

○ Maguire, Jane, MA, LMHC, MCAP, Integrity Counseling, 1101 Belcher Rd S Ste J, Largo; 727-531-7988 www.janemaguire.com ∕

Funding: Endowment, Fundraising

Tampa Bay Sisters of Perpetual Indulgence, POB 156, Pinellas Park; 33780 tampabaysisters.org

Health Care: Physical (see also Counseling/Mental Health)

○&& Ellquist, Ted, PT, Ekren Physical Therapy Services, Inc, 2349 Sunset Point Rd ste 400, Clearwater; 33765 727-723-8457 ekrenpt.com ∕ Reception1@ekrenpt.com

Legal Services

● Martin Law Office, P.A., POB 130738, Tampa 33681 813-260-1413 fax 888-250-6501 www.martinlawfl.com timm@martinlawfl.com

○ Tripp, Thomas G, 4930 Park Blvd #12, Pinellas Park; 33781-3410 727-544-8819 www.pinellasprobatelaw.com

Massage Therapy (Certified/Licensed only)

● (♿) Brian's Massage & Bodywork, 609 S Himes Ave Ste C-1, Tampa; 33609 813-361-8770 Lic MA28374/MM13274 www.massagebybrian.net contact@massagebybrian.net

Men's & Sex Clubs (not primarily Health Clubs)

● Tampa Men's Club, 4061 W Crest Ave, Tampa 813-876-6367 www.tampamensclub.com

Organizations/Resources: Business & Professional Associations, Labor Advocacy

● ★&& Tampa Bay Diversity Chamber of Commerce, 3251 3rd Ave N Ste 125, St Pete; 727-755-8390 www.diversitytampabay.org

Organizations/Resources: Cultural, Dance, Performance

● ★&& The Gay Men's Chorus of Tampa Bay, Inc, POB 274121, Tampa; 33688-4121 813-389-6313 www.gmctb.org info@gmctb.org

● ★ Suncoast Squares, POB 10952, St Pete 33733 678-656-2523 Square dancing www.suncoastsquares.com suncoastsquares@gmail.com

● ★&& Tampa International Gay & Lesbian Film Festival, POB 17816, Tampa; 33682 813-879-4220 www.tiglff.org

Florida: Tampa Bay Area
Organizations: Family

148
GAYELLOW PAGES #42 2020-2021

State/County Resources : Georgia
Legal

Organizations/Resources: Family and Supporters

♀ PFLAG - Lakeland / Polk County, POB 8978, Lakeland; 33806 www.pflagofpolkcounty.org

♂ ☆ PFLAG Dunedin, 727-279-0449 pflagdunedin.org

♀♂ ☆ &&. PFLAG Tampa, 863-535-5239 www.pflagtampa.org ✗ pflag.tampa@gmail.com

Organizations/Resources: Political/Legislative/Advocacy

♀ ★ Stonewall Democrats of Pinellas County, 2250 1st Ave N, St Pete; 33713-8817 www.stonewallpinellas.org

Organizations/Resources: Sexual Focus / Safe Sex

♂ ★ Tampa Bay Bondage Club, POB 13652, Tampa 33681 tinyurl.com/y9fpwzxg

Organizations/Resources: Social, Recreation, Support

♀ ★ Flamingo Auto Group West, m/a, Tampa tinyurl.com/qn8qa6j

♂ ★ &&. Prime Timers Tampa Bay, POB 15582, St Pete; 33733 727-565-9041 tinyurl.com/7wle8gg

♂ ★ Tampa Bay Bears, www.tampabaybears.org info@tampabaybears.org

Organizations/Resources: Student, Academic, Education

♀ ★ EC Queer Straight Alliance, Eckerd College, 4200 54th Ave S, St Pete; 919-259-0638 fb.com/groups/22016190074/

♀ ★ USF LGBTQ + Alumni, Gibbons Alumni Center, 4202 E Fowler Ave ALC100, Tampa; 727-873-4561 fb.com/US-FALUMLGBTQ

Organizations/Resources: Youth (see also Family)

♀ ★ Lakeland Youth Alliance, POB 8978, Lakeland; 33806 863-661-4502 tinyurl.com/75cms6

♂ Metro Youth Group, 3251 3rd Ave N #125, St Pete; 727-321-3854 x233 www.metrotampabay.org ✪

Pets & Pet Services & Supplies

♂ • Aquarium Illusions, LLC, 813-361-3592 www.kenjifish.com kenjifish@yahoo.com

Real Estate (see also Mortgages)

♂ ○ Markus, Michael K, Realtor, RE/MAX Realty Unlimited, 12965 US Hwy 301, Riverview; 33578 813-494-4702 mkmarkus.mfr.mlsmatrix.com

♂ • McGahan, Pete, Realtor, Keller Williams St Pete Realty, 111 2nd Ave NE Ste 400, St Pete; 727-215-7394 www.peteinstpete.com

♂ • Nabors, Dale, PA, GRI, CRS, Coldwell Banker, 500 N Westshore Blvd Ste 850, Tampa; 33609 813-679-1117 813-289-1712 www.dalenabors.com Dale@DaleNabors.com

Recovery

♀ ★ GALAA Rainbow Club, 720 W Dr MLK Jr Blvd Ste A, Tampa; 813-625-8020 www.rainbowrecoveryclub.com

Religious / Spiritual Resources

♂ ☆ &&. Community of Christ, 1740 N Highland Ave, Clearwater; 33755 **HD** tinyurl.com/3dljy94

♀ ★ &&. King of Peace MCC, 3150 5th Ave N, St Pete; 33713-7610 727-323-5857 **HS** www.churchstpetersburg.org

♀ ★ (&&.) MCC of Tampa, 408 E Cayuga St, Tampa; 813-239-1951 www.MCCTampa.com

♂ ☆ &&. Unitarian Universalist Congregation of Lakeland, 3140 Troy Ave, Lakeland; 33803 863-646-3715 **HD** www.uu-clakeland.org ✗ contact@uuclakeland.org

Sports & Outdoor

♀ ★ Advantage Tampa Bay Tennis, POB 183, Tampa; 33601 813-600-1908 www.atb-tennis.com

♀ Monday Mixed Classic Bowling League, c/o Pin Chasers Bowling Center, 4847 N Armenia Ave, Tampa; 813-699-5670 fb.com/mondaymixedclassic/

♀ ★ Suncoast Softball League, www.suncoastsoftball.org

Weddings and Ceremonies

♂ • (?&.) Ceremonies By Nan, 3402-G S Dale Mabry Hwy, Tampa; 33629 813-839-5564 fax 813-832-8303 www.ceremoniesbynan.com ♥ ceremoniesbynan@aol.com

>> *Tarpon Springs: see Tampa Bay Area*
>> *Venice: see Sarasota/Bradenton/Venice Area*

Venus

Campgrounds and RV Parks

♂ • (?&.) Camp Mars, 326 Goff Rd 863-699-6277 www.campmars.com **N** ✿✗♥

Vero Beach

AIDS/HIV Services, Education & Support

♂ AIDS Research & Treatment Center of the Treasure Coast, 981 37th Place; 772-257-5785 www.artctc.org

>> *West Palm Beach: see West Palm Beaches Area*
>> *Winter Park: see Orlando Area*
>> *Ybor City: see Tampa Bay Area*

Georgia
State/County Resources

Information, Media & Publications

♀ • GA Voice, POB 77401, Atlanta, GA 30357 404-815-6941 www.thegavoice.com

AIDS/HIV Services, Education & Support

♂ ☆ &&. GA AIDS & STD InfoLine, AID Atlanta, 1605 Peachtree Street NE, Atlanta, GA 404-870-7700 **H?** www.aidatlanta.org ✗

Legal Services

♀ ★ &. Lambda Legal Defense & Education Fund (LLDEF), Inc: Southern Regional Office, 730 Peachtree St NE Ste 640, Atlanta, GA 30308-1210 404-897-1880 www.lambdalegal.org @ixx=

♀ ★ Stonewall Bar Association of Georgia, POB 7708, Atlanta, GA 30357-0708 404-936-8545 www.stonewallbar.org

Georgia: State/County Resources
Media Services

149
GAYELLOW PAGES #42 2020-2021

Atlanta Area: Georgia
Bars, Cafes, Clubs, Restaurants

Media Services: Audio, Video, Film, Scanning, CD/DVD etc

♀ ○ Wingers Media Productions, 400 Jamie Dr, Hiram, GA 30141-5604 770-489-3506 tinyurl.com/3aj4wu

Organizations/Resources: Political/Legislative/Advocacy

♀ ★ &&. American Civil Liberties Union of Georgia, POB 77208, Atlanta, GA 30357 770-303-8111 www.acluga.org

♀ ★ Georgia Equality, 1530 DeKalb Ave NE Ste A, Atlanta, GA 404-523-3070 www.georgiaequality.org

♀ ★ Georgia Log Cabin Republicans, POB 78835, Atlanta, GA 30357 www.georgialogcabin.org

♀ ★ Georgia Stonewall Democrats, 4005 Penhurst Dr, Marietta, GA 404-538-4034 www.georgiastonewall.org

Organizations/Resources: Social, Recreation, Support

♀ ★ &&. Fourth Tuesday of Georgia, 404-688-2524 fb.com/FourthTuesdayAtlanta/ ✎

Sports & Outdoor

♂ ★ &&. Wilderness Network of Georgia, PO Box 79131, Atlanta, GA 30357 www.wildnetga.org

Athens

AIDS/HIV Services, Education & Support

♀ ☆ &&. Live Forward, 240 North Ave 30601 706-549-3730 **H?** liveforward.org ✎ info@liveforward.org

Bars, Cafes, Clubs, Restaurants

♀ ○ &&. 40 Watt Club, 285 W Washington St; 706-549-7871 www.40watt.com **D** ▥

♀ ○ &&. The Globe, 199 N Lumpkin St 706-353-4721 fb.com/globe.athens **L** ♈ ✕

♀ ○ The Grit, 199 Prince Ave; 706-543-6592 www.thegrit.com ✕ gogrit@gmail.com

Campgrounds and RV Parks

♂ ● (?&.) The River's Edge, 2311 Pulliam Mill Road, Dewy Rose; 706-213-8081 Clothing optional www.camptheriversedge.com **NP** (✿?) ✎ (◉)

Organizations/Resources: Student, Academic, Education

♂ ★ &&. University of Georgia Lambda Alliance, 222 Memorial Hall; tinyurl.com/yau6cy66 ✎

♂ ★ &&. University of Georgia LGBT Resource Center, 221 Memorial Hall; 706-542-4077 lgbtcenter.uga.edu ✎

♂ ★ University of Georgia School Of Law OutLaw, Student Box 572 Hirsch Hall; www.law.uga.edu/outlaws

Religious / Spiritual Resources

♀ ★ &&. Our Hope Metropolitan Community Church, POB 48713; 30604 706-202-3723 www.ourhopemcc.org Ourhope1999@gmail.com

Atlanta Area

Crisis, Anti-violence, & Helplines

♀ ☆ Women's Resource Center To End Domestic Violence, POB 171, Decatur; 30031 404-688-9436 404-370-7670 www.wrcdv.org info@wrcdv.org

Community Centers and/or Pride Organizations

♂ ★ Atlanta Pride Committee, 1530 Dekalb Ave NE #A, Atl; 404-382-7588 www.atlantapride.org

Information, Media & Publications

♂ ● Peach Atlanta, 925B Peachtree St Ste 168, Atl; 30309 404-814-2014 peachatl.com

Accommodation: Hotels, Inns, Guesthouses, B&B, Resorts
Atlanta

♀ ● (?&.) Stonehurst Place, 923 Piedmont Ave NE, Atl; 404-881-0722 stonehurstplace.com (✿?) ✎

Accommodation Rental: Furnished / Vacation (& AirBNB)
Atlanta

♀ ● BCA Furnished Apartments, 47 25th St, Atl 30309 404-682-2847 www.StayBCA.com ✎ ⊗⊗ Nic@BCAresidential.com

AIDS/HIV Services, Education & Support
Atlanta

♀ ☆ &&. AID Atlanta, 1605 Peachtree Street NE, Atl; 30309-2433 404-870-7700 GA AIDS/STD Infoline 800-551-2728 **H?** www.aidatlanta.org ✎ infoline@aidatlanta.org

♀ ☆ Names Project Foundation AIDS Memorial Quilt, 117 Luckie St, Atl; 404-688-5500 www.aidsquilt.org

♀ ☆ &&. Open Hand Atlanta, 181 Armour Dr NE, Atl; 30324 404-872-8089 Meal & Nutrition Services www.openHandAtlanta.org

Bars, Cafes, Clubs, Restaurants
Atlanta

♀ ○ 10th & Piedmont, 991 Piedmont Ave NE, Atl 404-602-5510 www.10thandpiedmont.com ♈ ✕

♀ ○ Apache Café, 880 Woodrow St SW, Atl 404.594-1170 apache-cafe.info ✕ ▥

♀ ○ Apres Diem, 931 Monroe Dr #C-103, Atl 404-872-3333 www.apresdiem.com ♈ ✕

♂ ● (?&.) The Atlanta Eagle, 306 Ponce de Leon Ave NE, Atl; 404-873-2453 www.atlantaeagle.com **DLL**

♂ ● BJ Roosters, 2043 Cheshire Bridge Rd NE, Atl 404-634-5895 fb.com/bjroostersatlanta

♂ ● Blake's on the Park, 227 10th St NE, Atl 404-892-5786 tinyurl.com/cnmbmz **D** ▥

♂ ● Bulldogs, 893 Peachtree St, Atl; 404-872-3025 fb.com/bulldogsbaratlanta/ ✤ bulldogsbaratl@gmail.com

♂ The Daiquiri Factory, 889 W Peachtree St, Atl; 404-881-8188 thedaiquirifactory.com **K** ♈ ✕

♀ ○ Ecco, 40 7th St NE, Atl; 404-347-9555 midtown.ecco-atlanta.com ✕

♀ ○ Endive Publik House, 1468 Mecaslin St NW, Atl 404-504-9044 endivepublik.com ✕

Georgia: Atlanta Area
Bars, Cafes, Clubs, Restaurants

150
GAYELLOW PAGES #42 2020-2021

Atlanta Area : Georgia
Leather

♂ • Felix's, 1510 Piedmont Rd NE, Atl 404-249-7899 www.felix-satl.com ⚥ ✕

♀ • ♿ Friends on Ponce c, 736 Ponce De Leon Ave, Atl; 404-817-3820 www.friendsonponce.com

♀ ○ ♿ The HALO Lounge, 817 W Peachtree St NW Ste E100, Atl; 404-962-7333 halolounge.com **D** 🎮

♂ • The Heretic, 2069 Cheshire Bridge, Atl 404-325-3061 www.hereticatlanta.com **DLW**

♀ • ♿ Hideaway, Ansley Mall, 1544 Piedmont Ave NE, Atl; 404-874-8247 www.atlantahideaway.com **K** 🎮 ✗

♂ In Da Cut, check site for details 404-839-8230 strippers fb.com/ShowStoppersAtl/

♀ • Mary's, 1287 Glenwood Ave, Atl 404-624-4411 www.marysatlanta.com **DK**

♀ ○ The Masquerade, 695 North Ave, Atl 404-577-8178 www.masq.com 🎮

♂ Mixx, 1492 Piedmont Ave, Atl; 404-228-4372 mixxatlanta.com **DV**

♀ • My Sisters' Room, 66 12th St NE, Atl 678-705-4585 www.mysistersroom.com **S** ⚥ ✕

♂ • Oscar's, 1510 Piedmont Ave Ste C, Atl 404-815-8841 www.oscarsatlanta.com **V** 🎮 ✗

♀ ○ Ria's Bluebird, 421 Memorial Dr SE, Atl 404-521-3737 riasbluebird.com ✕

♂ Sequel Atlanta, 1086 Alco St NE, Atl 404-634-6478 tinyurl.com/tbyspma 🎮

♀ ○ Sutra Lounge, 1136 Crescent Ave NE, Atl 404-607-1160 fb.com/Sutraloungeatl/ **D**

♂ • ♿ Swinging Richards, 1400 Northside Dr NW, Atl; 404-352-0532 strippers www.swingingrichards.com 🎮

♂ • ♿ The T, 465 Boulevard SE, Atl 404-343-2450 modeltatlanta.com 🎮 ✗

♀ • Traxx Atlanta, check schedule 404-740-5122 fb.com/TraxxAtlanta **D** 🎮 ✤

♀ • Traxx Girls, check schedule 888-935-8729 www.traxxgirls.com **D** 🎮 ✤

♂ Tripps Bar, 1931 Piedmont Circle, Atl 404-724-0067 tinyurl.com/jzlcfzk

♂ • Woofs, 494 Plasters Ave NE, Atl; 404-869-9422 woofsatlanta.com **S**

Decatur

♀ ○ Eddie's Attic, 515-B N McDonough St, Decatur 404-377-4976 eddiesattic.com ⚥ ✕ 🎮

Marietta

♀ ○ ♿ The Australian Bakery Cafe, 48 S Park Square, Marietta; 678-797-6222 www.australianbakerycafe.com ✕ ⏏

Stone Mountain

♀ Phaze One, 4933 Memorial Dr, Stone Mountain; 404-296-4895 tinyurl.com/opz6ojq ✤

Bookstores

♀ • ♿ **Charis Books & More, 184 S Candler St, Decatur; 30030 404-524-0304 Best Lesbian Fiction/Erotica/Mystery, LGBTQ Studies, Weekly Author/Social/Political Program Events www.charisbooksandmore.com** ✗ **info@charisbooks andmore.com**

Broadcast Media

♀ Lambda Radio Report, WRFG RADIO, 1083 Austin Ave NE, Atl; 404-523-3471 www.wrfg.org

Counseling/Psychotherapy/Mental Health

♀ • Abbott, Franklin, LCSW, 678-923-6485 www.franklinabbott.com

♀ • (♿) Ballew Consultation Services, 537 Linwood Avenue NE, Atl; 30306-4424 404-874-8536 www.bodymindsoul.org

♀ • Beggs, J Randy, PhD, Atlanta Center for Cognitive Therapy, 62 B Lenox Pointe, Atl; 30324 404-842-0555 x105 404-226-9814 www.midtownpsychotherapy.com drjrbeggs@mindspring.com

♀ ○ Helminiak, Daniel A, PhD, PhD, LPC, 970 Sidney Marcus Blvd NE #2205, Atl; 30324 404-934-8268 www.visionsofdaniel.net

♀ • ♿ Kaufman, Gus Jr, PhD, 317 W Hill St #101, Decatur; 30030 404-371-9171 x2 tinyurl.com/lxjmq5 gkaufmanjr@aol.com

♀ • ♿ Mathis, Stephen, PsyD, Applied Psychology Associates, 555 Sun Valley Dr #M-1, Roswell; 30076 770-645-1800 x3 www.psychdoc.wordpress.com

Funding: Endowment, Fundraising

♂ Joining Hearts, POB 54808, Atl; 30308 678-318-1446 www.joininghearts.org

♀ Sisters of Perpetual Indulgence, POB 244114, Atl; 30324 404-989-0566 atlsisters.org

Gardening/Landscaping Services & Supplies

♂ ○ Appalachian Tree Service, 39 Briar Gate Ln, Marietta; 404-409-9926 tinyurl.com/y8pqpl99

Health Care: Physical (see also Counseling/Mental Health)

♀ ☆ ♿ Feminist Women's Health Center, 1924 Cliff Valley Way NE Flr 2, Atl; 404-728-7900 www.feministcenter.org

♂ ★ The Health Initiative, The Phillip Rush Center. 1530 Dekalb Ave Ste A, Atl; 404-688-2524 www.thehealthinitiative.org

♀ ○ Scoma, Christopher, DC, CNMT, Buckhead Wellness Center, 3575 Piedmont Rd NE Bldg 15 Ste P-130, Atl; 404-477-1589 www.scomahealth.com

♂ Someone Cares Inc, of Atlanta, 1950 Spectrum Circle #145, Marietta; 678-921-2706 www.someonecaresatl.org

Immigration, Citizenship, Political Asylum, Refugees

♀ ○ ♿ **McGrath, Kerry E, 1100 Spring St NW Ste 760, Atl; 30309 404-377-6600 Immigration & Nationality Law www.kerrylaw.com** ✗ **info@kerrylaw.com**

Leather Resources & Groups

♂ ★ ONYX Southeast, www.onyxsoutheast.com ✤

Georgia: Atlanta Area
Leather

151
GAYELLOW PAGES #42 2020-2021

Atlanta Area: Georgia
Real Estate

♀ Panther Leather Levi Club, POB 78813, Atl; 30357 www.PantherLL.org

Legal Services

♂ ☆ &&. AIDS Legal Project, Atlanta Legal Aid Society, 54 Ellis Street NE, Atl; 30303 404-614-3969 404-524-5811 (Atlanta Legal Aid main switchboard) **H?** www.atlantalegalaid.org

♂ ○ &&. DiSalvo, Loraine M, Morgan & DiSalvo, PC, 5755 N Point Parkway Ste 17, Alpharetta; 30022 678-720-0750 www.morgandisalvo.com ✔ info@morgandisalvo.com

♂ ● &&. Katz, Barbara, 3136 Clairmont Road NE; 30329 404-298-5050 www.bekatzlaw.com

♂ ○ &&. **McGrath, Kerry E, 1100 Spring St NW Ste 760, Atl; 30309 404-377-6600 Immigration & Nationality Law www.kerrylaw.com ✔ info@kerrylaw.com**

♀ ○ Scriber Law Group, LLC, 1100 Peachtree St NE Ste 200, Atl; 30309 404-939-7562 www.scriberlaw.com stephen@scriberlaw.com

♀ ● Womack, Kathleen, PC, 750 Hammond Dr Bldg 9 Ste 300, Atl; 404-303-0130 www.kwomacklaw.com

Men's & Sex Clubs (not primarily Health Clubs)

♂ ● &&. The Den, 2135 Liddell Dr, Atl 404-292-7746 thedenatlanta.com **P** ❖

♂ ● &&. Flex, 76 4th St NW, Atl 404-815-0456 www.flexspas.com

♂ ● &&. Manifest4U, 2103 Faulkner Rd NE, Atl; 404-549-2815 www.manifest4u.org **P** ✔

♂ Qi Clay Sauna, 7130 Buford Hwy #A-107, Doraville; 770-733-0988 www.qiclaysauna.com **P**

Organizations/Resources: Business & Professional Associations, Labor Advocacy

♂ ★ &&. Atlanta Gay & Lesbian Chamber of Commerce (AGLCC), The Phillip Rush Center, 1530 Dekalb Ave #A, Atl 404-267-1854 www.atlantagaychamber.org

♂ ★ Metro Atlanta Association of Professionals (MAAP), POB 78302, Atl; 30357 www.maapatl.org

Organizations/Resources: Cultural, Dance, Performance

♂ ★ &&. Atlanta Freedom Bands, 1579F Monroe Dr #173, Atl; 404-941-0250 www.atlantafreedombands.com

♂ ★ & Atlanta Gay Men's Chorus, 781 Peachtree St NE, Atl; 404-320-1030 www.voicesofnote.org/agmc/

♂ ★ &&. Hotlanta Squares, POB 15533, Atl; 30333 www.hotlantasquares.org hotlanta.squares@gmail.com

♂ ★ OurSong Atlanta, POB 53405, Atl; 30355 404-487-8717 www.OurSongAtlanta.org

♂ ★ &&. Out on Film, 9075 Cobbler Ct, Roswell; 404-296-3807 GLBTQ Film Festival www.outonfilm.org ✔

Organizations/Resources: Ethnic, Multicultural

♂ In The Life Atlanta, 1530 Dekalb Ave NE, Atl; 678-964-4852 www.inthelifeatlanta.org ❖

♂ ★ People of All Colors Together Atlanta, PO Box 14858, Atl; 30324 www.bwmtatlanta.org ❸

Organizations/Resources: Family and Supporters

♂ ☆ &&. PFLAG Atlanta, 2484 Briarcliff Rd NE Ste 22-252 (mail only), Atl; 678-561-7354 www.pflagatl.org

♀ ☆ PFLAG Marietta, c/o Pilgrimage UCC, 3755 Sandy Plains Rd, Marietta; 678-318-1887 tinyurl.com/mx49jyh

Organizations/Resources: Naturist/Nudist

♂ ★ Rainbow Naturist Brotherhood, POB 44, Decatur; 30031 678-723-5762 www.RNBatlanta.com **N**

Organizations/Resources: Political/Legislative/Advocacy

♀ ☆ 9to5 Atlanta, 501 Pulliam St SW #344, Atl 404-222-0001 9to5.org/chapters/georgia/ ✔

♂ ★ &&. Southerners on New Ground (SONG), 561 W Whitehall St, Atl; 404-549-8628 tinyurl.com/6nqa9p ❸ ✔

Organizations/Resources: Social, Recreation, Support

♀ Atlanta Outworlders Inc., 375 Highland Ave #201, Atl; SF fans outworlders.org

♂ ★ &&. Atlanta Prime Timers, POB 13285, Atl; 30324-3285 770-284-0513 www.atlantaprimetimers.com

♀ Decatur Rainbow Pride Flag Corps, tinyurl.com/spj3m6f

♂ ★ Lambda Car Club/Dogwood Region, POB 660743, Atl; 30366 www.LCC-Dogwood.org

Organizations/Resources: Student, Academic, Education

♂ ★ (?&) Emory University Office of LGBT Life, 605 Asbury Circle, Atl; 404-727-0272 **H?** www.lgbt.emory.edu ✔

♂ ★ Georgia Tech Pride Alliance, 2217 Student Center Commons, 350 Ferst Dr NW, Atl; 404-385-6554 pride.gatech.edu

♂ ★ Oglethorpe University Outlet, 4484 Peachtree Road, NE, Atl; 404-364-8892 tinyurl.com/y8m8ngoz

Organizations/Resources: Transgender/Gender Non-Conforming/Diverse

T ☆ &&. Atlanta Gender Explorations, 404-429-0509 tinyurl.com/yablcg3o

T ☆ Sigma Epsilon Tri Ess, POB 930516, Norcross 30003 770-552-4415 www.sigmaepsilonatlanta.org

Organizations/Resources: Youth (see also Family)

♀ ☆ &&. CHRIS 180, 1030 Fayetteville Rd SE; 30316 404-486-9034 **H?** www.chris180.org ✔

♀ Lost N Found (shelter), 2585 Chantilly Dr, Atl; 678-856-7825 lnfy.org

Publishers/Publishing-related Services

♂ ● (?&) McWit Creative Works, 770-385-0007 **H?** www.mcwit.net ♥ info@mcwit.net

Real Estate (see also Mortgages)

♂ ● &&. Carroll, Chris, Atlanta Intown Real Estate Servicesm 181 10th St NE, Atl; 30309 404-388-0023 404-881-1810 www.AtlantaEcoBroker.com ✔

♀ ○ Mike Russell Realtor, 1874 Piedmont Ave Ste300-C, Atl; 404-892-8111 www.appraiserassociates.com

Georgia: Atlanta Area
Recovery

152

GAYELLOW PAGES #42 2020-2021

Duluth : Georgia
Grooming

Recovery

♂ ★ Galano Club, 585 Dutch Valley Rd NE, Atl galano.org

Religious / Spiritual Resources

♂ ★ ♿ Congregation Bet Haverim, PO Box 29548, Atl; 30359 404-315-6446 tinyurl.com/36q9m8 ✡

♀ ★ ♿ First Existentialist Congregation, 470 Candler Park Dr NE, Atl; 404-378-5570 www.firstexistentialist.org ✗

♂ ★ ♿ NAT ONLY

♀ ☆ Gentle Spirit Christian Church, 601 W Ponce de Leon Ave Flr 2, Decatur; 30030 / Meets as The Church Without Walls, Sundays at 10:30am Candler Park, Picnic Pavilion 2 404-604-8124 gentlespirit.org ✗

♂ ★ Integrity/Atlanta, fb.com/IntegrityAtlanta

♀ ☆ ♿ New Covenant Church, 1600 Eastland Rd SE, Atl; 30016 404-929-1400 **H?** www.newcovenantatlanta.com ✗ contact@newcovenantatlanta.com

♀ ☆ ♿ Oakhurst Baptist Church, 222 E Lake Dr, Decatur; 30030-3526 404-378-3677 **HD** www.Oakhurstbaptist.org ✗ info@Oakhurstbaptist.org

♂ ★ ♿ Unitarian Universalist Congregation of Atlanta, 1190 W Druid Hills Dr NE Ste 150, Atl; 404-634-5134 www.uuca.org

Sports & Outdoor

♂ ★ Atlanta Bucks, 400 W Peachtree St NW Ste #4 - 678, Atl; 404-713-1465 www.atlantabucksrugby.org

♀ Atlanta Rainbow Trout, 750 Ferst Drive NW, Atl www.atlantarainbowtrout.com

♀ ☆ Atlanta Rollergirls, POB 8629, Atl; 31106 www.atlantarollergirls.com

♂ ★ Atlanta Team Tennis Association, 2107 N Decatur Rd #354, Decatur; www.atta.org

♂ ★ Front Runners Atlanta, POB 8141, Atl 31106 423-304-3435 www.frontrunnersatlanta.org

♂ ★ Hotlanta Softball League, POB 14582, Atl; 30324 404-915-8136 www.hotlantasoftball.org

♂ ★ Hotlanta Volleyball Association, www.hotlantavolleyball.org

♀ ☆ National Flag Football League of Atlanta, 404-307-5793 www.nffla.com

♀ ☆ Women's Outdoor Network, www.wonatlanta.com

Augusta GA/North Augusta (SC)

Community Centers and/or Pride Organizations

♂ ★ Augusta Pride, Inc., POB 3281, Augusta 30914 762-233-5313 www.prideaugusta.org

Information, Media & Publications

♂ ★ GAYAugusta.com, GayAugusta.com

Accommodation: Hotels, Inns, Guesthouses, B&B, Resorts
Augusta

♂ ● (♿) Parliament Resort, Metropolis Complex, 1250 Gordon Hwy, Augusta; 706-722-1155 www.p-house.com (♣?) ✗

Bars, Cafes, Clubs, Restaurants
Augusta

♂ Edge Nightclub, Metropolis Complex, 1258 Gordon Hwy, Augusta; 706-722-1155 tinyurl.com/zdvnyod **D**

Religious / Spiritual Resources

♂ ★ ♿ MCC of Our Redeemer, POB 1412, Augusta; 30903 706-722-6454 www.mccoor.com

♀ ☆ ♿ Unitarian Universalist Church, 3501 Walton Way Extension, Augusta; 30909-1821 706-733-7939 **H?** www.uuaugusta.org ✗ info@uuaugusta.org

Blairsville

Organizations/Resources: Family and Supporters

♀ ☆ PFLAG Blairsville, POB 1051; 30514 706-389-5269 www.pflagblairsville.org info@pflagblairsville.org

Brunswick

Organizations/Resources: Family and Supporters

♀ PFLAG Brunswick, 912-275-0890 fb.com/PFLAGBrunswick
» Byron: see Macon Area

Canon

Campgrounds and RV Parks

♂ ● In the Woods Campground, 142 Casey Ct 706-246-0152 **HS** inthewoodscampground.com (♣?) Ⓢ

Cherry Log

Campgrounds and RV Parks

♀ ● Fox Mountain Camp & Artist Retreat, 350 Black Ankle Way; 30522 404-502-3538 Women's campground, men welcome as guests of women www.foxmtncamp.com ♣ foxmountaincamp@gmail.com

Collins

Campgrounds and RV Parks

♂ ● Roy's Hideaway, 268 Catfish Lane; 912-225-3900 royshideaway.com **P**

Columbus

Religious / Spiritual Resources

♂ ★ ♿ Forgiving Heart Christian Community Church, 2946 Grant Rd; 706-681-5246 forgivingheartchurch.com

Duluth

AIDS/HIV Services, Education & Support

♂ Positive Impact Health Centers, 3350 Breckinridge Ste 200; 770-962-8396 tinyurl.com/zp4u824 ✗

Grooming, Personal Care, Spa Services

♂ ○ ♿ Johnson, Shawn, Master Barber / Instructor, Gwinnett Barber Institute, 3500 Gwinnett Place Dr; 404-915-6815 tinyurl.com/jfqwguh

Georgia: Kennesaw
Organizations: Student
153
GAYELLOW PAGES #42 2020-2021
Savannah Area: Georgia
Religious

Kennesaw

Organizations/Resources: Student, Academic, Education

♀ ★ Kennesaw State University LGBTQ Resource Center, Student Center #164, 1000 Chastain Rd NW; 770-794-7557 lgbtq.kennesaw.edu/

♀ ★ Kennesaw State University Pride Alliance, RSO Center, Cubicle #12, 1000 Chastain Rd; 770-423-6280 fb.com/kennesawpridealliance

Lavonia

Health Care: Physical (see also Counseling/Mental Health)

♀ ● (?♂) Payne, Patty, Reiki Master, PO Box 280; 30553 678-696-1787 706-356-1776 www.georgiahealing.com

Macon Area

Organizations/Resources: Student, Academic, Education

♀ ★ Wesleyan College GLBAL, 4760 Forsyth Rd, Macon; 478-757-5120 fb.com/WesleyanGLBAL

Milledgeville

Organizations/Resources: Student, Academic, Education

♀ ★ Pride Alliance at Georgia College, POB 100 CPOB #54; 31061 478-445-2962 pridegc.webs.com

Morganton

Accommodation Rental: Furnished / Vacation (& AirBNB)

♂ ● (?♂) 6 Ponds Farm, 3155 Squirrel Hunting Rd; 423-505-2227 www.6pondsfarm.com ❖ ✔ ⊗ ♿

Ringgold

Pets & Pet Services & Supplies

♂ ○ Classie Dawg Grooming, 6709 Hwy 41; 30736 706-937-2121 classiedawggrooming.com classiedawggrooming@gmail.com

Religious / Spiritual Resources

♂ ☆ Kingdom Seekers, 6735 Hwy 41; 30736 706-618-4732 tinyurl.com/ycw6exgb

Savannah Area

Community Centers and/or Pride Organizations

♀ Savannah LGBT Center, 1515 Bull St, Savannah; 912-304-5428 www.savannahlgbtcenter.org

♀ ★ Savannah Pride, POB 6044, Savannah 31414 www.savannahpride.com

Information, Media & Publications

♀ First City Network (FCN), POB 2442, Savannah; 31402 912-236-2489 firstcitynetwork.org

Accommodation: Hotels, Inns, Guesthouses, B&B, Resorts
Savannah

♂ ○ Catherine Ward House, 118 E Waldburg St, Savannah; 31401 912-234-8564 tinyurl.com/6c95uw (❖?) ✔ ⊗ contact@catherinewardhouseinn.com

♂ ○ Green Palm Inn, 548 E President St, Savannah 31401-3546 912-447-8901 www.greenpalminn.com ✔ ⊗ info@greenpalminn.com

♂ ○ Roussell's Garden B&B, 208 E Henry St, Savannah; 31401 912-239-1415 www.RoussellsGarden.com ✔ ⊗ info@RoussellsGarden.com

AIDS/HIV Services, Education & Support

♂ Chatham County Health Department HIV Program, 2 Roberts St, Savannah; 912-527-1100 tinyurl.com/y9jqe7d9

Bars, Cafes, Clubs, Restaurants
Savannah

♂ ● Bar Food, 4523 Habersham St, Savannah 912-355-5956 www.savannahbarfood.com ☥ ✕

♂ ○ Churchill's Pub, 13 W Bay St, Savannah 912-232-8501 www.thebritishpub.com ☥ ✕

♀ ● ♿ Club One Jefferson, 1 Jefferson St; 31401 912-232-0200 www.clubone-online.com **DK** ☥ ✕ ♿

♂ ○ Driftaway Cafe, 7400-D Skidaway Rd, Savannah 912-303-0999 tinyurl.com/hnafmem ✕

♂ ○ Elan, 301 Williamson St, Savannah 912-662-3526 www.elansavannah.com ♿

♂ ○ Sentient Bean, 13 E Park Ave, Savannah 912-232-4447 www.sentientbean.com ♿ ♿

♂ ● Wright Square Cafe, 21 W York St, Savannah 912-238-1150 www.WrightSquareCafe.com ✕ ♿ ✔

Tybee Island

♂ ● Fannie's on the Beach, 1613 Strand, Tybee Island; 912-786-6109 fanniesonthebeach.com **D** ☥ ✕

♂ ○ North Beach Bar and Grill, 33 Meddin Dr 912-786-4442 northbeachbarandgrill.net ☥ ✕

Counseling/Psychotherapy/Mental Health

♀ Union Mission, Inc., 120 Fahm St, Savannah 912-236-7423 www.unionmission.org

Dentists

♂ ○ Dye, Mark N, DMD, 310 Eisenhower Dr Bldg 14, Savannah; 31406 912-355-2424 www.thesavannahdentist.com

Organizations/Resources: Student, Academic, Education

♀ ★ ♿ Georgia Southern University GSA, GSU Box 8068, Statesboro; 478-308-2156 tinyurl.com/y9f2z4j8 ✔

Real Estate (see also Mortgages)

♂ ○ Callahan, Don, Keller Williams Realty, 912-441-4416 www.DonCallahan.com don@doncallahan.com

Religious / Spiritual Resources

♂ ☆ Unity of Savannah, 2320 Sunset Blvd, Savannah 31404-4944 912-355-4704 unitysavannah.org office@unitysavannah.org

» *Statesboro: see Savannah Area*

Suwanee

Organizations/Resources: Student, Academic, Education

♀ ★ North Gwinnett High School GSA, 20 Level Creek Rd; 770-945-9558

>> *Tybee Island: see Savannah Area*

Valdosta

Community Centers and/or Pride Organizations

♀ ★ South Georgia Pride, POB 132; 31603 229-444-3090 www.southgapride.com

Organizations/Resources: Family and Supporters

♂ ☆ PFLAG Valdosta, 709 W Alden Ave; 229-375-9094 pflagvaldosta.wordpress.com

Organizations/Resources: Student, Academic, Education

♀ ★ Valdosta State University Genders and Sexualities Alliance (GSA), 1500 N Patterson St; 229-333-5674 fb.com/vsugsa/

Religious / Spiritual Resources

♂ ☆ && Unitarian Universalist Church of Valdosta, POB 2342; 31602 / 1951 E. Park Ave 229-242-3714 www.uuvaldosta.net uuvaldosta@yahoo.com

>> *Warner Robins: see Macon Area*

Watkinsville

Accommodation: Hotels, Inns, Guesthouses, B&B, Resorts

♂ ● (?&) Ashford Manor, 5 Harden Hill Rd 706-769-2633 www.ambedandbreakfast.com (✿?) ⚥ ⊛

Hawaii
Statewide/County Resources

Crisis, Anti-violence, & Helplines

♀ Sexual Assault Services, YWCA, 145 Ululani St, Hilo, HI 808-935-0677 tinyurl.com/l2qqxut

Information, Media & Publications

♀ ● GoGayHawaii.com / Hawaii Pride Guide, MC Publishing Inc, POB 45243, Phoenix, AZ 85013 888-830-3022 GoGayHawaii.com Hawaii@ThePrideGuides.com

AIDS/HIV Services, Education & Support

♂ ☆ && Gregory House Programs, 200 N Vineyard Blvd #A310, Honolulu, HI 808-592-9022 **H?** www.gregoryhouse.org

Funding: Endowment, Fundraising

♀ ★ Imperial Court of the Rocky Mountain Empire, POB 46275, Denver, CO 80201 www.icrmedenver.org

Recovery

♂ ☆ NA Hawaii, POB 7669, Hilo, HI 96720 www.na-hawaii.org

Hawaii (Big Island) before eruption

Accommodation: Hotels, Inns, Guesthouses, B&B, Resorts
Captain Cook

♂ ○ (?&) Dragonfly Ranch, 84-5146 Keala O Keawe Rd, Captain Cook; 96704 808-328-2159 www.dragonflyranch.com ✿⊛ info@dragonflyranch.com

♂ ● && Horizon Guest House, POB 957, Honaunau; 96726 808-938-7822 www.horizonguesthouse.com ⚥ ⊛

♂ ○ Rainbow Plantation, 81-6327 B Mamalahoa Hwy, Captain Cook; 96704 808-323-2393 www.rainbowplantation.com ⚥ ⊛ info@rainbowplantation.com

♂ ● (?&) South Kona Hideaway, 83-5399 Middle Keei Rd, Captain Cook; 96704 808-339-7265 southkonahideaway.com ⚥ ⊛ Reefhab@gmail.com

Kailua-Kona

♂ ● KonaLani Hawaiian Inn & Coffee Plantation, 76-5917 Hookahi St, Holualoa; 96725-9717 808-324-0793 www.konalani.com (✿?) ⚥ ⊛

Kalapana

♀ ● Sapphire Moon's Mermaid Palace, 12-7825 Kalapana Kapoho Beach Rd 808-965-1733 Sacred Space for Spiritual Women and Ho'omana Initiations www.greenfireproductions.com ⚥ ⊛⊛ ♥

Na'alehu

♂ ● Kalaekilohana Inn & Retreat, POB 1125, Na'alehu; 96772 808-939-8052 www.kau-hawaii.com ⊛

Pahoa

♂ ● Isle of You, POB 587, Pahoa; 96778-0587 808-965-1639 www.isleofyounaturally.com ⚥ ⊛

Pepeekeo

♂ ● Hamakua House, 28-1435 Old Mamalahoa Hwy, Pepeekeo HI 96783 330-590-0646 www.hamakuahouse.com ⊛ mat@hamakuahouse.com

Volcano

♂ ● && Hale Ohia Cottages, POB 758, Volcano; 96785-0758 808-967-7986 800-455-3803 fax 808-985-8887 www.haleohia.com ⚥ reservations@haleohia.com

♂ ○ The Kilauea Hospitality Group, POB 998, Volcano; 96785 800-937-7786 www.volcano-hawaii.com

♀ ● Kulana Goddess Sanctuary, POB 783, Volcano 96785 creative/spiritual retreat; mostly women but check ahead tinyurl.com/jojo573 ❂ (✿?) ⚥ ⊛⊛ discoverkulana@yahoo.com

Accommodation Rental: Furnished / Vacation (& AirBNB)
Captain Cook

♂ ● Makalani OceanView Cottage, 87-3011 Mamalahoa Hwy, Captain Cook; 808-328-9730 www.vrbo.com/199288 ⚥ ⊛

♂ ● (?&) Tara Cottage, POB 211, Kealakekua; 96750 808-328-9607 www.taracottagehawaii.com ⚥ ⊛

Kealakekua

♀ ● (?&) Hale Lana at Kealakekua Bay, 82-6277 Kahauloa St, Captain Cook; 808-328-7338 www.vrbo.com/95119 ⚥ ⊛

Opihikao

♂ ● Rainbow Dreams Cottage, 13-6412 Kalapana Kapoho Beach Road, Pahoa, HI 96778 808-936-9883 www.rainbowdreamscottage.com ⊛

Pahoa

⚥ ● Hale 'Ohai, 415-509-3120 www.punatreehouse.com ✄ ⊛

⚥ ● Jungle Farmhouse, 15-3001 Mako Way, Pahoa 808-640-1113 www.pahoa.info ♣ ✄ ⊛

♂ ● Rainbow Dreams Cottage, 13-6296 Kapoho-Kalapana Rd, Pahoa; 808-936-9883 tinyurl.com/aunn4o9 ✄ ⊛

Volcano

⚥ ○ Maile Tree House, Maile Ave, Volcano Village 808-987-0417 www.mailetreehouse.com ✄ ⊛

AIDS/HIV Services, Education & Support

♂ ☆ ♿ Hawaii Island HIV/AIDS Foundation East, 16-204 Melekahiwa Pl, Kea'au; 808-982-8800 www.hihaf.org

♀ ☆ ♿ Hawaii Island HIV/AIDS Foundation West, West Side, 74-5620 Palani Rd Ste 101, Kailua Kona; 808-331-8177 www.hihaf.org

Bars, Cafes, Clubs, Restaurants
Kailua Kona

⚥ ○ ♿ Huggo's, 75-5828 Kahakai Rd, Kailua Kona; 808-329-1493 www.huggos.com **D** ⊻ ✕ ✄

♂ ● The Mask-Querade Bar, 75-5660 Kopiko St, Kailua Kona; 808-329-8558 www.themask-queradebar.com

♀ ○ My Bar, 75-5606 Luhia St, Kailua Kona 808-331-8789 www.mybarkona.com

Volcano

♂ ○ Cafe Ono, Volcano Garden Arts, 19-3834 Old Volcano Rd, Volcano; 808-985-8979 www.cafeono.net ☞

Bookstores

♂ ○ ♿ Basically Books, 1672 Kamehameha Ave, Hilo; 96720 808-961-0144 basicallybooks.com bbinfo@hawaiiantel.net

♀ ○ Kona Stories, 78-6831 Ali'i Dr #142, Kailua Kona; 808-324-0350 www.konastories.com

Organizations/Resources: Student, Academic, Education

♂ ★ ♿ University of Hawaii Hilo Pride, 200 W Kawili St, Hilo; fb.com/groups/71153530715/ ✄

♀ ☆ University of Hawaii Women's Center, 2600 Campus Rd. QLCSS #211, Hilo; 808-956-8059 **WC** tinyurl.com/yc88o7hn ✄

Religious / Spiritual Resources

♂ ★ ♿ Open Arms MCC, POB 1292, Pahoa; 96778 808-937-0422 fb.com/OpenArmsPuna/

Kauai

Accommodation: Hotels, Inns, Guesthouses, B&B, Resorts
Poipu Beach

♂ ● (?♿) Poipu Plantation Resort, 1792 Pe'e Rd, Koloa; 96756-9535 808-742-6757 800-634-0263 www.poipubeach.com ✄ ⊛

Accommodation Rental: Furnished / Vacation (& AirBNB)
Kapaa

⚥ ● (?♿) 17 Palms Kauai, 414 Wailua Kai St, Kapaa 888-725-6799 www.17palmskauai.com ✄ ⊛

AIDS/HIV Services, Education & Support

♂ ☆ ♿ Malama Pono Health Services, 4370 Kukui Grove St Ste 115, Lihue; 96766 808-246-9577 mphskauai.org info@ mphskauai.org

Bars, Cafes, Clubs, Restaurants
Hanalei

♀ ○ Tahiti Nui, 5-5134 Kuhio Hwy, Hanalei 808-826-6277 www.thenui.com **D** ⊻ ✕ 🎵

Organizations/Resources: Family and Supporters

♀ ☆ PFLAG Kauai, POB 1832, Lihue; 96766 808-634-0127 fb.com/groups/PFLAGKauai/

Maui

Community Centers and/or Pride Organizations

♂ ★ Maui Pride, POB 1259, Puunene; 96784 808-463-4636 www.mauipride.org

Accommodation: Hotels, Inns, Guesthouses, B&B, Resorts
Kihei

♂ ● Dreams Come True on Maui B&B, 3259 Akala Dr, Kihei; 808-879-7099 www.mauibednbreakfast.com (♣?) ✄ ⊛ ⊛

Accommodation Rental: Furnished / Vacation (& AirBNB)
Haiku

♂ ○ Ho'okipa Bayview Cottage, 1250 Kauhikoa Rd, Haiku; 96708 808-575-7888 www.hookipabayview.com ✄ ⊛ ⊛

Hana

♂ ● (?♿) The Guest Houses at Malanai, 808-248-8706 www.hanaguesthouses.com ✄ ⊛

Kihei

♀ ○ Dolphins Point Maui, 2274 S Kihei Rd, Kihei 808-283-2614 www.dreambeachmaui.com ✄ ⊛

Lahaina

♀ ○ ♿ Maui Kai 807, 832 14th Avenue, Menlo Park, CA 94025 650-325-2441 www.mauikai.biz ♣ ✄ (⊛)

♀ ○ Maui Rainbow Guest Condo, 106 Kaanapali Shores Pl 807, Lahaina; 96761 650-325-2441 tinyurl.com/47h9t3n ✄ ⊛ ⊛ dgbender@aol.com

♀ ○ MauiCalls.com, Donna Bender, 832 14th Ave, Menlo Park, CA 94025-1912 650-325-2441 www.mauicalls.com ✄ DGBender@ aol.com

AIDS/HIV Services, Education & Support

♂ ☆ ♿ Maui AIDS Foundation, POB 858, Wailuku; 96793 808-242-4900 www.mauiaids.org

Bars, Cafes, Clubs, Restaurants
Kihei

♀ ○ ♿ Diamonds Ice Bar & Grill, 1279 S Kihei Rd, Kihei; 808-874-9299 www.diamondsicebar.com **DP** ⊻ ✕ ✄

♀ ○ JAWZ Fish Tacos, 41 E Lipoa St, Kihei 808-874-8226 jawztacosmaui.com ✄

♀ ○ ♿ Vibe Bar Nightclub, 1913-H S Kihei Rd, Kihei; 808-891-1011 www.vibenightclubmaui.com **D** ✄

Hawaii: Maui
Bars, Cafes, Clubs, Restaurants
156
GAYELLOW PAGES #42 2020-2021
Oahu: Hawaii
Weddings/Unions

Lahaina

♀ ○ Lahaina Coolers, 180 Dickenson St, Lahaina 808-661-7082 www.lahainacoolers.com ⚥ ✂

Makawao

♀ ○ & Casanova Restaurant & Deli, 1188 Makawao Ave, Makawao; 808-572-0220 www.casanovamaui.com ⚥ ▯✂ ▦ ✎

Health Care: Physical (see also Counseling/Mental Health)

♀ ● (?&) Maya, Lucia, Reiki Master, 808-866-8246 www.luminousadventures.com lucia@luminousadventures.com

Real Estate (see also Mortgages)

♀ ● Burton, Sylvia, 808-446-0256 MauiPropertiesBySylvia.com ✎

Oahu

Community Centers and/or Pride Organizations

♂ Hawai'i LGBT Center-Waikiki, POB 23300, Honolulu; 96822 / 310 Paoakalani Avenue, Ste 206E 808-369-2000 tinyurl.com/ybznj4qu

Information, Media & Publications

♂ Hawaii LGBT Legacy Foundation, POB 23300, Honolulu; 96822 808-369-2000 tinyurl.com/j4fbgrn

Accommodation Rental: Furnished / Vacation (& AirBNB)

Honolulu

♀ ● & Waikiki Place, 364 Seaside Ave 808-271-4800 www.WaikikiPlace.com ✎ ⊗ⓢ

AIDS/HIV Services, Education & Support

♀ ☆ Hawaii AIDS Education & Training Center & AIDS Education Project, c/o Cyril Goshima, MD, 3221 Waialae Ave Ste 362, Honolulu 808-356-0313

♀ ☆ Hawai'i Health & Harm Reduction Center (HHHRC), 677 Ala Moana Blvd Ste 226, Honolulu; 808-521-2437 Free HIV testing www.hhhrc.org

Bars, Cafes, Clubs, Restaurants

Honolulu

♂ ● Bacchus Waikiki, 408 Lewers St, Honolulu 808-926-4167 www.bacchus-waikiki.com Bacchuswaikiki@gmail.com

♂ Chiko's Tavern, 930 McCully St, Honolulu 808-949-5440 chikostavern.com ⚥ ✂ ▦

♂ ● && Hula's Bar & Lei Stand, Waikiki Grand, 134 Kapahulu Ave, 2nd flr, Honolulu; 808-923-0669 **H?** www.hulas.com **D** ⚥ ✂▦ ✎

♂ ● (?&) In-Between, 2155 Lau'ula St, Honolulu; 808-926-7060 www.inbetweenwaikiki.com **K**

♀ ○ Rock Island Cafe, 1911 Kalakaua Ave, Honolulu 808-923-8033 www.rockislandcafe.com ▯ rockislandcafe@aol.com

♂ Scarlet, 80 S Pauahi St, Honolulu 808-555-5555 scarlethonolulu.com **D** ▦

♀ ○ && Tiki's Grill & Bar, 2570 Kalakaua Ave, Honolulu; 808-923-8454 www.tikisgrill.com ⚥ ✂♥

♂ Wang Chung's Karaoke Bar, Stay Hotel, 2424 Koa Ave, Honolulu; 808-921-9176 wangchungs.com **K**

Legal Services

♀ ● (?&) Yarbrough, Lee M, Attorney at Law/CPA, POB 4157, Honolulu; 96812 808-735-9103

Liquor & Wine Stores

♀ ● Speakeasy Productions, 1154 Fort St Mall Ste 206, Honolulu; 96813 808-721-1688 Bar Catering and Gifts tinyurl.com/y2c4s4lu

Organizations/Resources: Cultural, Dance, Performance

♂ ★ && Blazing Saddles Hawaii, LGBT Country Western Dance www.blazingsaddleshi.org **CW** BlazingSaddlesHI@yahoo.com

♂ ★ Gay Men's Chorus of Honolulu, 2700 S King St #11707 (mail only), Honolulu; 96828 / contact for location www.gmcofh.org GMCofH@gmail.com

♂ ★ Honolulu Rainbow Film Festival, 1670 Makaloa St #204 PMB #370, Honolulu; 808-675-8428 www.hglcf.org

Organizations/Resources: Naturist/Nudist

♂ ★ Males Au Natural of Hawaii (MANOH), www.hawaiimanohman.com **N**

Organizations/Resources: Political/Legislative/Advocacy

♂ ★ && LGBT Caucus Hawaii Democratic Party, 1050 Ala Moana Blvd, Honolulu; 808-596-2980 www.glbtcaucushawaii.org ✎

Organizations/Resources: Social, Recreation, Support

♂ ★ (?&) Aloha Bears, **H?** www.thealohabears.com ✎

Real Estate (see also Mortgages)

♀ ● & Walt Flood Realty, 2092 Kuhio Ave #1903, Honolulu; 808-922-1659 www.waltfloodrealty.com

Religious / Spiritual Resources

♀ ☆ && The Church of the Crossroads, 1212 University Ave, Honolulu; 96826 808-949-2220 **H** tinyurl.com/a4gt37m ✎ ccrhi@hawaiintel.com

♀ ☆ First Christian Church Disciples of Christ, 1516 Kewalo St, Honolulu; 96822 808-521-3500 tinyurl.com/dxsv9a fccoffice@hawaii.rr.com

♀ ☆ && First Unitarian Church of Honolulu, 2500 Pali Hwy, Honolulu; 96817-1487 808-595-4047 uuhonolulu.org/

♀ ☆ && Lutheran Church of Honolulu, 1730 Punahou St, Honolulu; 96822-3337 808-941-2566 www.lchwelcome.org ✎ lch@lchwelcome.org

Sports & Outdoor

♂ ★ && Honolu Frontrunners/Frontwalkers, 702-546-6937 www.honolulufrontrunners.org contact@honolulufrontrunners.org

♂ ● Rainbow Sailing Charters, Kewalo Basin, 1125 Ala Moana Blvd, Honolulu; 96814 808-347-0235 tinyurl.com/32eblj

Weddings and Ceremonies

♀ ● A Rainbow in Paradise Weddings/Gay Wedding Planner, POB 64, Kailua; 96734-0064 808-372-0343 www.arainbowinparadise.com ♥ info@arainbowinparadise.com

Idaho
State/County Resources

Crisis, Anti-violence, & Helplines

♂ ☆ Idaho Coalition Against Sexual & Domestic Violence, 1402 W Grove St, Boise, ID 208-384-0419 idvsa.org

AIDS/HIV Services, Education & Support

♂ ☆ Idaho Department of Health & Welfare Family Planning, STD & HIV Programs, POB 83720, Boise, ID 83720 208-334-5612 www.safesex.idaho.gov

Counseling/Psychotherapy/Mental Health

♂ The Idaho Association of Lesbian, Gay, Bisexual, and Transgender Issues in Counseling, 2184 Channing Way #438, Idaho Falls, ID tinyurl.com/y9ntrk8r

Organizations/Resources: Political/Legislative/Advocacy

♀ ☆ (?♋) American Civil Liberties Union of Idaho, POB 1897, Boise, ID 83701-1897 208-344-9750 **H?** www.acluidaho.org

♀ ☆ Idaho Commission on Human Rights, 317 W Main St, Boise, ID 208-334-2873 www.humanrights.idaho.gov

Religious / Spiritual Resources

♂ Integrity Idaho, c/o St. Michael's Cathedral, 1858 W Judith Lane, Boise, ID 208-860-8024 integrity.episcopalidaho.org

Boise

Community Centers and/or Pride Organizations

♂ ★ Boise Pridefest, POB 1924; 83701 **H** fb.com/BoisePrideFest/

♂ ★ The Community Center, 1088 N Orchard St 208-336-3870 www.tccidaho.org ✗

Accommodation: Hotels, Inns, Guesthouses, B&B, Resorts

♂ ● Bed & Buns, 10325 W Victory Rd; 208-362-1802 www.bedandbuns.com

AIDS/HIV Services, Education & Support

♀ ☆ Allies Linked for the Prevention of HIV & AIDS (ALPHA), 575 N 8th St; 208-424-7799 www.alphaidaho.org

Bars, Cafes, Clubs, Restaurants

♂ ● The Balcony Club, 150 N 8th St 208-336-1313 www.thebalconyclub.com **D** ▦

♂ ○ ♿ The Flicks & Rick's Café Americain, 646 Fulton St; 208-342-4222 **HD** Cafe and Movie Theater www.theflicksboise.com ✗ ↻

Nampa

♀ ○ ♿ Flying M Coffeegarage, 1314 2nd St S, Nampa; 208-467-5533 www.flyingmcoffee.com ↻ ▦ ✗ nampa@flyingmcoffee.com

♀ ○ Neurolux, 111 N 11th St; 208-343-0886 www.neurolux.com **K** ✗

Counseling/Psychotherapy/Mental Health

♀ ○ ♿ Stewart, Jill, MA, LCPC, NCC, 1674 Hill Rd #12; 83702 208-890-8366 **H?** tinyurl.com/y8lnt4qw ✗

Funding: Endowment, Fundraising

♂ ★ Imperial Sovereign Gem Court of Idaho, PO Box 6338; 83707 208-794-0161 www.idahogemcourt.org

Health Care: Physical (see also Counseling/Mental Health)

♀ ○ ♿ Weyhrich, Darin, MD, 222 N 2nd St Ste 206; 208-342-2516 weyhrichobgyn.com

Organizations/Resources: Cultural, Dance, Performance

♀ ☆ ♿ Common Ground Community Chorus, POB 7174; 83707 www.commongroundboise.org

Organizations/Resources: Family and Supporters

♂ PFLAG Boise/Treasure Valley, 208-863-5831 tccidaho.org/we-are-family/

Organizations/Resources: Student, Academic, Education

♂ ★ Boise State University Pride Alliance, Student Activities, 1910 University; tinyurl.com/he58287

Organizations/Resources: Transgender/Gender Non-Conforming/Diverse

T ☆ ♿ Tri-State Transgender Support Group, c/o The Community Center, POB 9078; 83707 / 1088 N Orchard St 208-336-3870 www.tccidaho.org ✗

Organizations/Resources: Youth (see also Family)

♂ ★ ♿ Youth Alliance For Diversity, The Community Center, 1088 N Orchard; 208-841-3220 tccidaho.org ✗

Recovery

♀ ☆ Alcoholics Anonymous Idaho Area 18, POB 696 83701 208-344-6611 www.idahoarea18aa.org

♀ ☆ Treasure Valley Intergroup & Central Office AA, 1111 S Orchard #180; 208-344-6611 www.tvico.net

Religious / Spiritual Resources

♀ ☆ ♿ First Congregational UCC, 2201 Woodlawn Ave; 83702-3848 208-344-5731 **H?** www.boisefirstucc.org church@boisefirstucc.org

♂ ★ ♿ Liberating Spirit MCC, POB 1959; 83701 208-401-8442 **H?** fb.com/liberatingspiritmcc/ ✗

Coeur d'Alene

AIDS/HIV Services, Education & Support

♂ ☆ ♿ North Idaho AIDS Coalition, 2201 Government Way Ste E; 208-665-1448 **H?** northidahoaidscoalition.org

Counseling/Psychotherapy/Mental Health

♀ ○ ♿ Asbell, Laura, 17080 W Laura Ln, Post Falls 509-534-1731 www.asbellhealth.com ✗ ahs@asbellhealth.com

Idaho: Coeur d'Alene
Organizations: Business

158
GAYELLOW PAGES #42 2020-2021

Bloomington/Normal: Illinois
Organizations: Political

Organizations/Resources: Business & Professional Associations, Labor Advocacy

♀ ★ Inland Northwest Business Alliance, 9 S Washington Ste 201; 509-455-3699 inbachamber.org

Organizations/Resources: Family and Supporters

♂ ☆ ♿ PFLAG Coeur d'Alene, POB 2471 83816 208-907-1078 **H?** pflagcda.wordpress.com

Organizations/Resources: Student, Academic, Education

♀ ★ ♿ North Idaho College Gender and Sexuality Alliance, Associated Students of NIC, 1000 W Garden Ave 208-769-7706 fb.com/nicgsa

Idaho Falls

Counseling/Psychotherapy/Mental Health

♀ ● Barret, Bob, 609 Bainbridge Lane; 83402 704-342-0808 bob@docbb.com

Organizations/Resources: Family and Supporters

♀ ☆ IFPFLAG, POB 52242; 83405 208-538-9217 www.ifpflag.com

Moscow

Community Centers and/or Pride Organizations

♀ ★ (♿) Inland Oasis, POB 8205, Moscow; 83843 208-596-4449 www.inlandoasis.org ⚢

Bookstores

♂ ○ BookPeople, 521 S Main St, Moscow 208-882-2669 www.bookpeopleofmoscow.com

Organizations/Resources: Social, Recreation, Support

♂ ★ North Idaho Gay Men's Association, tinyurl.com/2n8kyl

Organizations/Resources: Student, Academic, Education

♀ ★ Gender and Sexuality Alliance at the University of Idaho, ASUI Office, Idaho Commons, Room 302, Moscow orgsync.com/41817/chapter

♀ ★ ♿ University of Idaho LGBTQA Office, 875 Perimeter Dr MS 2431, Moscow; 208-885-6583 www.uidaho.edu/lgbtqa ⚢

♀ ☆ ♿ Women's Center, University of Idaho, MS 1064, 875 Perimeter Dr, Moscow; 208-885-2777 www.uidaho.edu/womenscenter ⚢

Organizations/Resources: Youth (see also Family)

♀ ★ (♿) Inland Oasis, Inc. Youth Program, POB 8205, Moscow; 83843 208-596-4449 www.inlandoasis.org ⚢

Religious / Spiritual Resources

♀ ☆ ♿ Unitarian Universalist Church of the Palouse, POB 9342, Moscow; 83843 / 420 E 2nd St 208-882-4328 palouseuu.org uuchurch@moscow.com

Pocatello

Community Centers and/or Pride Organizations

♀ ★ All Under One Roof LGBT Advocates of Southeastern Idaho, 234 N Main St; 208-251-1661 www.allunderoneroof.org

Bars, Cafes, Clubs, Restaurants

♀ ● Club Charley's, 331 E Center; 208-239-0885 charleys.club **D**

Sandpoint

Accommodation Rental: Furnished / Vacation (& AirBNB)
Clark Fork

♂ ○ ♿ Last Resort Vacation Cabin, PO Box 644, Clark Fork; 83811 / 58 East River Dr, Clark Fork 208-266-0525 www.lastresortvacation.com ♣ ⚢ ⊗ info@lastresortvacation.com

Illinois
State/County Resources

Crisis, Anti-violence, & Helplines

♀ ☆ Illinois Coalition Against Sexual Assault, 100 N 16th St, Springfield, IL 217-753-4117 www.icasa.org

Legal Services

♀ ★ ♿ Lambda Legal Defense & Education Fund (LLDEF), Inc, Midwest Regional Office, 105 W Adams 26th Flr, Chicago, IL 312-663-4413 www.lambdalegal.org/mro

Organizations/Resources: Family and Supporters

♀ ☆ PFLAG Northern Illinois Council, POB 734, Elmhurst, IL 60626 630-415-0622 www.pflagillinois.org

Organizations/Resources: Political/Legislative/Advocacy

♀ ☆ ♿ American Civil Liberties Union of Illinois, 180 N Michigan Ave #2300, Chicago, IL 312-201-9740 www.aclu-il.org

♀ ★ Equality Illinois, 17 N State St, Chicago, IL 773-477-7173 www.eqil.org

Sports & Outdoor

♀ ★ Illinois Gay Rodeo Association, POB 14878, Chicago, IL 60614 630-776-4426 www.ilgra.com
» Alton: see St Louis Area (MO & IL)

Bloomington/Normal

Gifts, Cards, Pride, etc.

♂ ○ ♿ Garlic Press, 108 North St, Normal; 309-452-8841 www.thegarlicpress.com ⚢

Organizations/Resources: Family and Supporters

♀ PFLAG Bloomington/Normal, 321 Emerson St, Bloomington; 309-828-5554 fb.com/PFLAGBN

Organizations/Resources: Political/Legislative/Advocacy

♀ ★ Prairie Pride Coalition, POB 5048, Bloomington; 61702 www.ppc-il.org

Illinois: Bloomington/Normal
Organizations: Student

159
GAYELLOW PAGES #42 2020-2021

Chicago Area: Illinois
Community Centers / Pride

Organizations/Resources: Student, Academic, Education

♂ ★ ♿ Illinois State University Pride, Professional Development Annex, 205 S Main St, Normal; 309-438-8969 **H?** www.iwu.edu/lgbt/Pride.html

♂ ★ ♿ Triangle Association, Illinois State University, LGBT/Queer Studies and Services Institute, 205 S Main St/Campus Box 1969, Normal; 61790-1969 309-438-8540 **H?** triangle.illinois-state.edu ✎ triangle@illinoisstate.edu

Religious / Spiritual Resources

♀ ♿ New Covenant Community Church, 210 W Mulberry St, Normal; 61761-2530 309-454-7362 www.nccnormal.org ✎
  » Brookfield: see Chicago Area
  » Calumet City: see Chicago Area

Carbondale

Organizations/Resources: Student, Academic, Education

♂ ★ ♿ Southern Illinois University LGBTQ Resource Center, Student Center 318, Mail Code 4724, 275 E Park St 618-453-3740 **H?** smrc.siu.edu/lgbtq/ ✎

Organizations/Resources: Youth (see also Family)

♀ ★ ♿ Rainbow Cafe, POB 2; 62903 815-408-6963 www.rainbowcafe.org ✎

Religious / Spiritual Resources

♀ ☆ ♿ First Christian Church (DOC), 306 W Monroe St; 62901 618-457-6817 **HD** www.cdalefcc.org ✎ office@cdalefcc.org

Champaign/Urbana Area

Community Centers and/or Pride Organizations

♀ UP Center of Champaign County, 217-992-0095 www.uniting-pride.org

AIDS/HIV Services, Education & Support

♀ ☆ ♿ Greater Community AIDS Project, POB 713, Champaign; 61824-0713 217-351-2437 www.gcapnow.com info@gcapnow.com

Architectural Services

♀ ○ Fell Architecture & Design, 515 N Hickory Ste 101, Champaign; 217-363-2890

Bars, Cafes, Clubs, Restaurants
Champaign

♀ ○ ♿ Cafe Kopi, 109 N Walnut St, Champaign; 217-359-4266 www.cafe-kopi.com ✎

♂ ● ♿ Fiesta Cafe, 216 S 1st St, Champaign; 217-352-5902 www.fiestacafe.com ☞

♀ ○ Pekara Bakery & Bistro, 116 N Neil, Champaign 217-359-4500 www.pekarabakery.com ✘

Bookstores: Used

♂ ○ Priceless Books, 112 W Main, Urbana; 61801 217-344-4037 tinyurl.com/n65gdbx priceles@advancenet.net

Bookstores

♀ ○ (?♿) Jane Addams Book Shop, 208 N Neil St, Champaign; 61820-4013 217-356-2555 www.janeaddamsbooks.com ✎ info@janeaddamsbooks.com

Counseling/Psychotherapy/Mental Health

♂ ● ♿ Shea, Tim, LCSW, 507 W Springfield Ave, Urbana; 61801 217-649-9076 www.timshealcsw.com tim_shea@comcast.net

Organizations/Resources: Cultural, Dance, Performance

♀ ★ Amasong, c/o McKinley Foundation, 809 S 5th St, Champaign; 61820 www.amasong.org office@amasong.org

Organizations/Resources: Student, Academic, Education

♀ ★ Parkland College PRIDE, 2400 W Bradley Ave, Champaign; 217-351-2492 tinyurl.com/z2wxabc

♀ ★ ♿ University of Illinois LGBT Resource Center, Rm 323 Illini Union, MC-384, 1401 W Green St, Urbana 217-244-8863 tinyurl.com/z7zd95f ✎

♀ ★ ♿ University of Illinois Urbana-Champaign Pride, c/o LGBT Resource Center, 1401 W Green St, Urbana 217-244-8863 fb.com/illinoispride ✎

Organizations/Resources: Transgender/Gender Non-Conforming/Diverse

T ☆ Chi Upsilon Iota, 209 N Randolph St M102, Champaign; www.cui-triess.org

Religious / Spiritual Resources

♀ ☆ ♿ Community United Church of Christ, 805 S 6th St, Champaign; 61820 217-344-5091 www.community-ucc.org ✎ info@community-ucc.org

♂ ☆ ♿ McKinley Presbyterian Church & Foundation, 809 S 5th St, Champaign; 61820-6215 217-344-0297 www.mckinley-church.org ✎

♂ ☆ ♿ Unitarian Universalist Church, 309 W Green St, Urbana; 61801 217-244-8862 www.uucuc.org ✎

Charleston

Organizations/Resources: Student, Academic, Education

♂ ★ ♿ EIU Pride, Gender & Sexual Diversity Center, 1525 7th St Room 203; 217-581-7117 fb.com/groups/EIUPride/

Chicago Area

Crisis, Anti-violence, & Helplines

♂ ☆ ♿ Anti-Violence Project, Center on Halsted, 3656 N Halsted, Chi; 773-472-6469 tinyurl.com/hlcejq2 ✎

♂ ☆ ♿ South Suburban Family Shelter, PO Box 937, Homewood; 60430 708-335-3028 (hotline) www.ssfs1.org

Community Centers and/or Pride Organizations

♀ ★ ♿ Center on Halsted, 3656 N Halsted St, Chi; 60613 773-472-6469 **H?** www.centeronhalsted.org ✎

♀ ★ Oak Park Area Lesbian & Gay Association, PO Box 1460, Oak Park; 60304 www.opalga.org info@opalga.org

⚥ ★ PRIDEChicago, 3712 N Broadway PMB 544, Chi 60613-4235 773-348-8243 Organizers of the Chicago Annual LGBTQ Pride Parade. www.chicagopridecalendar.org Pridechgo@aol.com

Information, Media & Publications

⚥ ● Windy City Times, 5315 N Clark St #192, Chi; 773-871-7610 www.windycitymediagroup.com

Accommodation: Hotels, Inns, Guesthouses, B&B, Resorts
Chicago

♀ ★ Athena's House: a women's residence, Chicago Urban Art Retreat Center, 1957 S Spaulding Ave, Chi; 60623-2616 773-542-9126 www.urbanartretreat.com ✎ ☺ contact@urbanart retreat.com

♂ ○ Chicago Getaway Hostel, 616 W Arlington Pl, Chi; 60614 773-929-5380 www.getawayhostel.com ☺ info@getawayhostel.com

♂ ○ Lang House Chicago, 7421 N Sheridan Rd, Chi 60626 773-764-9851 www.langhousechicago.com ✎ ☺ ☺ Info@langhouse chicago.com

♂ ● (♿) Publishing House Bed and Breakfast, 108 N May St, Chi; 60607 312-554-5857 **H?** www.publishinghousebnb.com ✎ ☺ ☺ info@publishinghousebnb.com

♂ ● The Villa Toscana Chicago, 3447 N Halsted St, Chi; 60657-2414 773-404-2416 All welcome www.thevillatoscana.com ✎ ☺ ☺ info@thevillatoscana.com

Oakbrook Terrace

♂ ● (♿) Comfort Suites Oakbrook Terrace, 17W445 Roosevelt Rd, Oakbrook Terrace; 60181 630-916-1000 www.csobtc.com ☺ ☺ gm@csobtc.com

Ottawa

♂ ● ♿ Fox River Bed & Breakfast Inn, 3367 E 2072nd Rd, Ottawa; 815-431-9257 www.foxriverbnb.com ✎ ☺

Accommodation Rental: Furnished / Vacation (& AirBNB)
Chicago

♂ ○ Aster House Apts, 1020 W Altgeld St, Chi; 60614 773-552-5275 **H?** AsterHouseChicago.com ✎ ☺ AsterHouseApts@ aol.com

AIDS/HIV Services, Education & Support

♂ ☆ (♿) AIDS Foundation of Chicago, 200 W Jackson Blvd #2100, Chi; 312-922-2322 www.aidschicago.org

♂ ☆ Alexian Brothers Housing and Health Alliance, 825 W Wellington Ave, Chi; 773-327-9921 alexianbrothershousing.org

♂ ☆ ♿ Chicago House Social Services Agency, 1925 N Clybourn Ave Ste 401, Chi; 773-248-5200 www.chicagohouse.org

♀ ☆ ♿ Chicago Women's AIDS Project, 1815 E 71st St, Chi; 773-329-3941 cwapchicago.org

♂ ○ Christoff, Eric, MD, AAHIVS, Howard Brown Health, 6500 N Clark St, Chi; 60626 773.388.1600 www.howardbrown.org

⚥ ★ ♿ Howard Brown Health, 4025 N Sheridan Rd, Chi; 773-388-1600 howardbrown.org

♂ ☆ Legal Council for Health Justice, 17 N State St Ste 900, Chi; 312-427-8990 www.legalcouncil.org

♂ ☆ ♿ NAMES Project Chicago, Center on Halsted, 3656 N Halsted St, Chi; 773-472-6469 x294 **H?** ✎

♂ ☆ Project Vida, 2659 S Kedvale Ave, Chi 773-277-2291 www.projectvida.org ☺

♂ ☆ ♿ TPAN, 5537 N Broadway, Chi 773-989-9400 www.tpan.com ✎

Archives/Libraries/Museums/History Projects

⚥ Chicago Gay & Lesbian Hall of Fame, 3712 North Broadway Ste 637, Chi; 773-281-5095 www.glhalloffame.org

⚥ ★ ♿ Gerber/Hart Library and Archives, 6500 N Clark St, Chi; 60626 773-381-8030 www.gerberhart.org ✎ info@gerberhart.org

⚥ ★ Leather Archives & Museum, 6418 N Greenview Ave, Chi; 773-761-9200 **H?** www.LeatherArchives.org ✎

⚥ ★ Legacy Project Outdoor Museum Walk (Chicago), 312-608-1198 **H?** www.legacyprojectchicago.org ☺

Bars, Cafes, Clubs, Restaurants
Blue Island

⚥ ● (♿) Club Krave, 13126 S Western Ave, Blue Island; 708-597-8379 www.clubkrave.com **DKCWV** ✎

Chicago

⚥ ● ♿ Atmosphere, 5355 N Clark St, Chi; 773-784-1100 www.atmospherebar.com **D** 🏳️‍🌈

♂ ● ♿ Baton Show Lounge, 4713 N Broadway, Chi; 312-644-5269 **H?** www.thebatonshowlounge.com ✎ thebaton1969@ yahoo.com

⚥ ● ♿ Berlin, 954 W Belmont, Chi 773-348-4975 www.berlinchicago.com **D** 🏳️‍🌈

♂ ● ♿ Big Chicks, 5024 N Sheridan Rd, Chi; 773-728-5511 www.bigchicks.com **D** ✕ 🟡 ✎

⚥ ● Bobby Love's, 3729 N Halsted, Chi 773-525-1200 www.bobbyloves.com

⚥ ● ♿ The Call, 1547 W Bryn Mawr Ave, Chi; 773-334-2525 www.callbarchicago.com **DV** 🏳️‍🌈

⚥ ● ♿ Cell Block, 3702 N Halsted St, Chi; 773-665-8064 cellblockchi.com **D** ✎

⚥ Chances Dances, n/a, Chi; / check schedule www.chancesdances.org

⚥ ● Charlie's Chicago, 3726 N Broadway St, Chi 773-871-8887 www.charlieschicago.com **DC**

♂ ○ Chicago Diner, 3411 N Halsted, Chi 773-935-6696 www.veggiediner.com ✕

⚥ Closet, 3325 N Broadway, Chi; 773-477-8533 www.theclosetchicago.com

⚥ Club Escape, 1530 E 75th St, Chi 773-599-9372 tinyurl.com/y82uloyp **D** 🏳️‍🌈 ✚

⚥ ● (♿) Dinotto Pizza e Vino, 1551 N Wells St, Chi; 312-202-0302 www.dinotto.com 🟡 ✕ ☐ ✎

♂ ○ Drew's on Halsted, 3201 N Halsted, Chi 773-244-9191 www.drewsonhalsted.com ✕

⚥ Elixir Lounge, 3452 N Halsted St, Chi 773-975-9244 www.elixirchicago.com

⚥ Granville Anvil, 1137 W Granville Ave, Chi 773-973-0006 www.theanvilbar.com **L**

⚥ ○ Hamburger Mary's/Mary's Attic, 5400 N Clark St, Chi; 773-784-6969 tinyurl.com/m7bsvct ✕

⚦ • ♿ Hydrate, 3458 N Halsted St, Chi; 773-975-9244 www.hydratechicago.com **D** ▦

⚦ • InnExile, 5758 W 65th St, Chi 773-582-3510 **V** ↗

⚦ Jackhammer, 6406 N Clark, Chi; 773-743-5772 tinyurl.com/jym8avq **DL**

⚦ • Jeffery Pub, 7041 S Jeffery Blvd, Chi 773-363-8555 fb.com/thejefferypub/ **DS** ▦ ✚

⚥ ○ Joie de Vine, 1744 W Balmoral Ave, Chi 773-989-6846 tinyurl.com/y8x3oyte

⚥ • Kit Kat Lounge & Supper Club, 3700 N Halsted St, Chi; 773-525-1111 www.kitkatchicago.com ✕ ▦

⚥ ○ ♿ KOPI: A Travelers Cafe, 5317 N Clark St, Chi; 773-989-5674 www.kopicafechicago.com ⟲

⚦ • ♿ Little Jim's, 3501 N Halsted, Chi; 773-871-6116 fb.com/littlejims

⚦ • ♿ Lucky Horseshoe, 3169 N Halsted St, Chi; 773-404-3169 Strippers luckyhorseshoelounge.com ▦ info@luckyhorseshoelounge.com

⚦ Manhandler Saloon, 1948 N Halsted St, Chi 773-871-3339 fb.com/manhandlersaloon/

⚦ Meeting House Tavern, 5025 N Clark St, Chi 773-696-4211 meeting housetavern.com

⚦ • ♿ The North End, 3733 N Halsted St, Chi 773-477-7999 www.northendchicago.com **S** ▦

⚦ • Progress Bar, 3359 N Halsted St, Chi 773-697-9268 www.progressbarchicago.com **D** ⟍ ✕ ▦

⚦ Replay Beer & Bourbon, 3439 N Halsted, Chi 773-661-9632 www.replaylakeview.com

⚦ • Roscoe's Tavern & Cafe, 3356 N Halsted St, Chi; 773-281-3355 www.roscoes.com **D** ⟍ ✕ ▦

⚦ • ♿ Scarlet, 3320 N Halsted St, Chi 773-348-1053 www.scarletchicago.com ▦

⚦ • (?♿) Second Story Bar, 157 E. Ohio St 312-923-9536 fb.com/secondstorybar/ ⟍ ✕

⚥ ○ Shakers on Clark, 3160 N Clark, Chi 773-327-5969 fb.com/shakersonclark ▦ shakersonclark@gmail.com

⚦ Sidetrack, 3349 N Halsted, Chi 773-477-9189 www.sidetrackchicago.com

⚦ • ♿ The SoFo Tap, 4923 N Clark, Chi 773-784-7636 www.TheSoFoTap.com **V** ↗

⚦ • Touché, 6412 N Clark, Chi; 773-465-7400 www.touchechicago.com **L**

⚥ • Tweet, 5020 N Sheridan Rd, Chi; 773-728-5576 www.tweet.biz ✕ ↗

⚦ • Urbano, at Fantasy Nightclub, 3641 N Halsted St, Chi; / check schedule 773-957-4021 www.facebook.com/SXChicagoNet ✪

⚥ • ♿ Wilde Bar & Restaurant, 3130 N Broadway, Chi; 773-244-0404 **H?** wildechicago.com ⟍ ✕ ↗

Hammond

⚥ • Dick's RU Crazee, 1221 E 150th St, Hammond, IN 219-852-0222 www.dicksrucrazee.com **D**

Bookstores

⚥ ○ (?♿) 57th St Books, 1301 E. 57th St, Chi; 773-684-1300 www.semcoop.com

⚥ ○ After-Words Bookstore, 23 E Illinois St, Chi 60611 312-464-1110 www.after-wordschicago.com

⚥ ○ ♿ Quimby's, 1854 W North Ave, Chi 773-342-0910 www.quimbys.com

⚥ ○ ♿ Seminary Co-op Bookstore, 5751 S Woodlawn Ave, Chi; 773-752-4381 www.semcoop.com

⚥ • Unabridged Books, 3251 N Broadway, Chi 60657-3571 773-883-9119 fax 773-883-9559 www.unabridgedbookstore.com

⚥ • ♿ Women & Children First, 5233 N Clark St, Chi 773-769-9299 tinyurl.com/2rmskv

Counseling/Psychotherapy/Mental Health

⚥ • ♿ Cole, Jon, PhD, Center For Positive Change, 205 Commerce Dr Ste C, Grayslake; 60030 847-529-0558 www.poschange.com

⚥ ☆ Community Counseling Centers of Chicago, 4740 N Clark St, Chi; 773-769-0205 www.c4chicago.org

⚥ ○ Ettner, Randi, PhD, 1214 Lake St, Evanston 60201 847-328-3433 rettner@aol.com

⚥ • ♿ Hoffman, Andrew, Center For Positive Change, 205 Commerce Dr Ste C, Grayslake; 60030 847-409-6932 www.poschange.com

⚥ ○ Hoffman, Andrew, PsyD, Center For Positive Change, 128 Newberry Ave, Libertyville; 60048 847-409-6932 www.poschange.com

⚥ • Ritzman, Elizabeth, LCPC, 6832 W North Ave, Chi; 60707 312-815-9607 www.elizabethritzman.com elizabeth@elizabethritzman.com

⚥ • Sholl, Starla R, LCSW, PC, 5349 N Winthrop Ave #2, Chi; 60640-2309 773-878-5809 www.starlasholl.com

⚥ Thrive Counseling Center, 120 S Marion St, Oak Park; 708-383-7500 www.thrivecc.org

Funding: Endowment, Fundraising

⚦ ★ Chicago Spirit Brigade, 4119 N Maplewood Ave #1, Chi; www.chicagospiritbrigade.org

⚦ ★ Imperial Windy City Court of the Prairie State Empire, INC NFP, POB 804545, Chi; 60680 224-434-4923 windycityempire.org

⚥ ☆ Ride for AIDS Chicago, 5050 N Broadway Ste 300, Chi; 773-898-9400 www.rideforaids.org

⚥ ☆ Season of Concern, 8 S Michigan #601, Chi 312-332-0518 www.seasonofconcern.org

Health Care: Physical (see also Counseling/Mental Health)

⚥ ☆ ♿ Chicago Women's Health Center, 1025 W Sunnyside Ave, Chi; 773-935-6126 Transgender welcome tinyurl.com/yufmrd

Illinois: Chicago Area
Home & Building

162
GAYELLOW PAGES #42 2020-2021

Chicago Area: Illinois
Organizations: Naturist/Nudist

Homes & Buildings: Cleaning, Maintenance, Repair, General Contractors

♂ ○ A Better Plumber & Sewer Company Inc, 112 Sydenham, Spring Grove; 60081 847-223-8837 773-847-2400 www.abetter-plumberonline.com

Leather Resources & Groups

♂ ★ Chicago Hellfire Club, POB 577618, Chi 60657 www.hellfire13.org

♂ Chicago Leather Club, POB 60214, Chi; 60660 tinyurl.com/ycbe5ovq

♂ ★ ONYX/Midwest, 3712 N Broadway PMB #271, Chi www.onyxmidwest.com ✤

Legal Services

♂ AIDS/HIV Housing Law Project, Legal Assistance Foundation, 120 S LaSalle St #900, Chi; 312-341-1070 www.lafchicago.org

♂ ○ Ankin Law Office LLC, 10 N Dearborn Ste 500, Chi; 60602 312-600-0000 www.ankinlaw.com

♂ ○ Lyster Firm Law Offices, 221 N LaSalle St Ste 1550, Chi; 60601 312-855-0875 www.lysterfirm.com office@lysterfirm.com

♀ ● Metz + Jones LLC, 5443 N Broadway #2-North, Chi; 60640-1703 773-878-4480 www.metzandjoneslaw.com ✔

♂ ● ♿ Schuman, Joseph, 4753 N Broadway #821, Chi; 60640-4991 773-784-1899 www.schumaniselt.com joe@schumaniselt.com

♂ ● (?♿) Sullivan, Mario, Johnson and Sullivan Ltd 11 E Hubbard St Ste 702, Chi; 60611 312-396-8000 fax 312-396-8001 www.johnsonsullivan.com mario@johnsonsullivan.com

♀ ● (?♿) Yearwood & Associates, 636 S River Rd Ste 104, Des Plaines; 60016 847-824-0358 www.ellenyearwoodlaw.com

Men's & Sex Clubs (not primarily Health Clubs)

♂ ● Steamworks Chicago, 3246 N Halsted St, Chi 773-929-6080 www.steamworksbaths.com ✔

Organizations/Resources: Business & Professional Associations, Labor Advocacy

♂ ★ ♿ Chicago Area Gay & Lesbian Chamber of Commerce, 3179 N Clark St, Chi; 773-303-0167 www.lgbtcc.com

♀ ☆ Chicago Women In Trades, 2444 W 16th St Ste 3E, Chi; 312-942-1444 www.chicagowomenintrades.org

♂ ★ Lesbian & Gay Bar Association of Chicago (LAGBAC), POB 64933, Chi; 60664 lagbac.org

♀ LGPA/GOAL Chicago, POB 597468, Chi 60659 www.goalchicago.info

♀ Pride at Work Chicago, fb.com/PrideatWorkChicago

Organizations/Resources: Cultural, Dance, Performance

♀ ★ (?♿) Artemis Singers, POB 578296, Chi; 60657-8296 773-764-4465 **H?** www.artemissingers.org info@artemissingers.org

♂ ★ Chi-Town Squares, dances at Ebenezer Lutheran Church, 1640 W. Foster, 773-339-6743 www.chitownsquares.org **DCW** info.chitownsquares@gmail.com

♀ ★ (?♿) Chicago Gay Men's Chorus, 5756 N Ridge Ave Ste 1, Chi; 773-296-0541 www.cgmc.org

♀ GayCo Productions, 5353 N Magnolia, Chi 312-451-9630 www.gayco.com

♀ ★ Lakeside Pride Music Ensembles, Inc, 3656 N Halsted St, Chi; 60613 773-381-6693 lakesidepride.org info@lakesidepride.org

♂ ☆ (♿) Reeling: Chicago Lesbian & Gay International Film Festival, c/o Chicago Filmmakers, 5243 N Clark St, Chi 773-293-1447 www.reelingfilmfestival.org

♂ ★ (?♿) Windy City Gay Chorus, Windy City Performing Arts, 3656 N Halsted St, Chi; 773-661-0928 Www.windycitysings.org

Organizations/Resources: Ethnic, Multicultural

♀ ★ (?♿) Affinity, 2850 S Wabash Ste 108, Chi; 773-324-0377 **H?** www.affinity95.org ✤

♂ ★ Asians & Friends Chicago, POB A3916, Chi 60690 312-409-1573 www.afchicago.org ◇

♂ ★ (?♿) **Association of Latino Men for Action, 3656 N Halsted St, Chi; 773-234-5591 ALMA is an educational, social, advocacy, and support group. www.almachicago.org ✦♥**

♂ ★ ♿ Chicago Black Gay Men's Caucus, Public Health Institute of Metropolitan Chicago, 180 N Michigan Ave #1200, Chi 312-629-2988 x12 www.chiblackgaycaucus.org ✤

♂ ★ (?♿) I2I: Invisible to Invincible, **H?** www.invisible2invincible.org ◇

Organizations/Resources: Family and Supporters

♂ ☆ (?♿) PFLAG Aurora/Fox Valley, 5700 Hillcrest Lane #2A, Aurora; 815-886-6951 tinyurl.com/gqhdgbz

♂ ☆ PFLAG Chicago Metro, Center on Halsted, Senior Room location, 3656 N Halsted, Chi; 630-415-0622 www.pflagillinois.org

♂ ☆ PFLAG Chicago Metro, POB 734, Elmhurst 60626 773-472-6469 tinyurl.com/y8shtb7b

♂ ☆ ♿ PFLAG Deerfield / N. Suburban Chicago, Congregation BJBE, 1201 Lake Cook Rd, Deerfield; 630-415-0622 tinyurl.com/glajjdb

♂ ☆ ♿ PFLAG DuPage, POB 1333, Wheaton; 60189 630-415-0622 www.pflagdupage.org

♂ ☆ ♿ PFLAG Hinsdale/West Suburban, UU Church, 11 W Maple Ave, Hinsdale; 630-415-0622 www.pflagchicago.com

♂ ☆ ♿ PFLAG Oak Park Area, 708-386-3016 tinyurl.com/yrcqu8

Organizations/Resources: Military/Veterans

♂ ★ ♿ American Veterans for Equal Rights - Chicago, POB 29317, Chi; 60629-0317 773-752-0058 www.averchicago.org info@averchicago.org

Organizations/Resources: Naturist/Nudist

♂ ★ BNC (Bear Naked Chicago), POB 268142, Chi 60626 www.bearnaked.org **N**

♂ ★ Chicago Area Naturist Sons (C.A.N.S), www.cansguys.org **N** ✪

Organizations/Resources: Political/Legislative/Advocacy

♂ ★ ♂♂ Gay Liberation Network, PO Box 409204, Chi; 60640 Formerly known as Chicago Anti-Bashing Network tinyurl.com/2r4qbx

Organizations/Resources: Senior Resources

♀ SAGE West Suburban Senior Services, 439 Bohland Ave, Bellwood; 708-547-5600 wsseniors.org/lgbt-program/

Organizations/Resources: Sexual Focus / Safe Sex

♂ ★ MAFIA, POB 25107, Chi; 60625 312-401-8893 www.mafiaff.org ✍

Organizations/Resources: Social, Recreation, Support

♀ ★ BUNGALO (Berwyn United Neighborhood Gay & Lesbian Organization), www.bungalo.org bungalo_org@yahoo.com

♀ ★ Lambda Car Club Lake Michigan Region, 773-636-0303 ' www.lcclmr.org/ mcwasil@gmail.com

♀ ★ ♂♂ NewTown Writers, 773-528-3637 fb.com/workshopandpublishing/

♂ ★ Prime Timers Chicago, POB 146681, Chi; 60614 872-588-1624 www.chicagoprimetimers.org

♀ Suburban Adventures, tinyurl.com/yax4hxa

♂ ★ West Suburban Gay Association (WSGA), POB 161, Glen Ellyn; 60138 630-861-9742 www.wsga.com

Organizations/Resources: Student, Academic, Education

♂ ★ Chicago Kent College of Law Lambdas, 565 W Adams St, Chi; tinyurl.com/ycrtxbe4

♀ ★ Columbia College LGBTQ Office of Culture & Community, 618 S Michigan 4th Flr, Chi; 312-369-8594 tinyurl.com/nmyhvml

♂ ★ ♂♂ Elgin Community College SWANS, 1700 Spartan Dr, Elgin; 847-697-1000 **H** fb.com/eccswans ✍

♂ ★ Elmhurst College Queer Straight Alliance, 190 Prospect Ave, Elmhurst; 630-617-3071 tinyurl.com/v9m6hhg

♂ ★ Illinois Institute of Technology PRISM, c/o Student Activities, 3201 S State St Room 206-208, Chi; 312-567-3720 tinyurl.com/yc58jdwm

♀ ★ Illinois Valley Community College GSA, 815 N Orlando Smith Rd, Oglesby; 815-224-0366 fb.com/ivccgsa/

♂ ★ ♂♂ LGBTQIA Resource Center, Northwestern University, Norris University Center, Office 3L, 1999 Campus Dr, Evanston; 847-467-6200 tinyurl.com/y7q2ce99

♂ ★ Northeastern Illinois University LGBTQA Resource Center, 5500 N St Louis Ave, Chi tinyurl.com/jk64g66

♂ ★ ♂♂ Northwestern University Rainbow Alliance, 1999 S Campus Dr Office O, Evanston tinyurl.com/yxt4a9c5

♂ ★ ♂♂ Northwestern University School of Law OUTLaw, 357 E Chicago Ave, Chi; 312-503-3100

♂ ★ ♂♂ Office of LGBTQA Student Services, DePaul University, 2250 N Sheffield Ave S#307, Chi; 773-325-7759 **H?** go.depaul.edu/lgbtqa ✍

♂ ★ OneWheaton, www.onewheaton.com/untold

♂ ★ PRIDE at Lake Forest College, Gates Center, 555 N Sheridan Blvd, Lake Forest; 847-735-6294 fb.com/groups/258976150808039

♂ ★ Spectrum DePaul, 2250 N Sheffield Ave #307A, Chi; fb.com/SpectrumDePaul

♂ ★ UIC John Marshall Law School OUTlaw, 315 S Plymouth Court, Chi; 60604-3968 312-427-2737 org-outlaw@jmls.edu

♂ ★ University of Chicago LGBTQ Student Life, 5710 S Woodlawn Ave, Chi; 773-702-5710 lgbtq.uchicago.edu

♂ ★ (?♂) University of Illinois Gender & Sexuality Center, 1007 W Harrison St (M/C 369), Chi; 312-413-8619 genderandsexuality.uic.edu

♂ ★ University of Illinois Pride, 1007 W Harrison St Room 183, Chi; 312-413-8619 fb.com/groups/27494512761/

Organizations/Resources: Transgender/Gender Non-Conforming/Diverse

T ☆ ♂♂ Chi Chapter, POB 303, Wood Dale; 60191 708-383-1677 chi-chapter.org ✍ chi.chapterchicago@yahoo.com

T ★ Chicago Gender Society, POB 66595, Chi 60666-0595 www.chicagogender.com

T ☆ ♂♂ Transgender & Intersex Support Groups, Howard Brown Health, 4025 N Sheridan Rd, Chi; 773-388-1600 **H?** tinyurl.com/za4f5qv

T ☆ (?♂) Transgender Youth Resource and Advocacy Group, 4025 N Broadway, Chi; 773-388-1600 **H?** howardbrown.org/byc/ ✍

Organizations/Resources: Youth (see also Family)

♂ ★ Broadway Youth Center, 4009 N Broadway, Chi; 773-935-3151 **H?** howardbrown.org/byc/

♂ ★ Pride Youth Program, Youth Services of Glenview/Northbrook, 3080 W Lake Ave, Glenview; 60026 847-724-2620 www.ysgn.org/pride info@ysgn.org

♀ ☆ Youth Outlook, 1828 Old Naperville Rd, Naperville; 815-754-5331 **H?** www.youth-outlook.org

Performance: Entertainment, Music, Theater, Space

♀ ☆ About Face Theatre, 5252 N Broadway St Flr 2, Chi; 773-784-8565 www.aboutfacetheatre.com ✍

Recovery

♀ ☆ Alcoholics Anonymous, 180 N Wabash Ave Ste 305, Chi; 800-371-1475 www.chicagoaa.org

♀ ☆ (?♂) Chicago Recovery Alliance, 312-953-3797 **H?** www.anypositivechange.org

♀ ☆ Newtown Alano Club, 909 W Belmont Ave 2nd flr, Chi; 773-529-0321 www.newtownalanoclub.com

Religious / Spiritual Resources

♂ ★ ♂♂ A Church 4 Me MCC, 7366 N Clark St, Chi; 60626 773-951-4268 **H?** www.achurch4me.org questions@achurch4me.com

♂ ★ ♂♂ Archdiocesan Gay & Lesbian Outreach, c/o OLMC, 708 W Belmont Ave, Chi; 60657 773-525-3872 **HD** www.aglochicago.org aglo@aglochicago.org

♀ ☆ ♂♂ Augustana Lutheran Church of Hyde Park and Lutheran Campus Ministry, 5500 S Woodlawn Ave, Chi; 60637-1683 773-493-6451 **HD** www.augustanahydepark.org ✍ office@augustanahydepark.org

Illinois: Chicago Area
Religious

164

GAYELLOW PAGES #42 2020-2021

Galena : Illinois
Accommodation

♂ ★ ♿ Congregation Or Chadash, Temple Sholom of Chicago, 3480 N Lake Shore Dr, Chi; 773-271-2148 fb.com/orchadashchicago/ ⚥

♀ ☆ ♿ Countryside Church UU, 1025 N Smith Rd, Palatine; 60067 847-359-8440 **HD** www.ccuu.org ✎ ccuu@ccuu.org

♂ ★ ♿ Dignity/Chicago, 3023 N Clark St Box 237, Chi; 312-458-9438 www.dignity-chicago.org

♂ ★ Fellowship of The Phoenix, POB 13352, Chi 60613-0352 773-789-8582 fellowshipofthephoenix.org info@fellowshipofthephoenix.org

♀ ☆ First United Church, 848 Lake St, Oak Park 60301 708-386-5215 www.firstunitedoakpark.com office@firstunitedoakpark.com

♀ ☆ Highland Avenue Church of the Brethren, 783 W Highland Ave, Elgin; 60123 847-741-5124 **HD** www.hacob.org ✎

♂ ★ ♿ Holy Covenant MCC, 9145 Grant Ave, Brookfield; 708-387-1611 www.holycovenantmcc.org

♀ ☆ ♿ Holy Covenant UMC, 925 W Diversey Pkwy, Chi; 60614-1415 773-528-6462 www.holycovenantumc.org

♀ ★ Holy Trinity Lutheran Church, 1218 Addison St, Chi; 773-248-1233 www.holytrinitychicago.org

♀ ☆ ♿ Our Saviour's Lutheran Church, 1234 N Arlington Rd, Arlington Hts; 60004-4741 847-255-8700 www.oursaviours.org ✎

♀ ☆ St Michael's UCC, 400 W Washington, West Chicago; 60185 630-231-0687 www.stmichaelsucc.org churchoffice@stmichaelsucc.org

♀ ☆ St Paul Lutheran Church, 515 S Wheaton Ave, Wheaton; 60187-5270 630-668-5953 www.stpaulwheaton.org office@stpaulwheaton.org

♀ ☆ United Church of Rogers Park, 1545 W Morse Ave, Chi; 60626 773-761-2500 www.ucrogerspark.org

♀ ☆ ♿ United in Faith Lutheran Church, 6525 W Irving Park Rd, Chi; 60634 773-283-2326 www.unitedinfaith.org revctp@unitedinfaith.org

♀ ☆ University Church, 5655 S University Ave, Chi 60637 773-363-8142 tinyurl.com/pp9krm uchurch@universitychurchchicago.org

♀ ☆ ♿ Wellington Ave United Church of Christ, 615 W Wellington Ave, Chi; 60657 773-935-0642 www.waucc.org office@waucc.org

♀ ☆ Wicker Park Lutheran Church, 1500 N Hoyne Ave 773-276-0263 www.wickerparklutheran.org office@wickerparklutheran.org

Sports & Outdoor

♂ ★ 9 to 12 Bowling Leagues, c/o River Rand Bowl, 191 S River Rd, Des Plaines

♂ ★ Athletic Alliance of Chicago, 4837 N Claremont #1, Chi; 773-492-1222 www.sportsaac.com

♀ ☆ Chicago Dragons Rugby Football Team, www.chicagodragons.org

♂ ★ Chicago Gay Hockey Association, chicagogayhockey.org

♂ ★ Chicago Metropolitan Sports Association (CMSA), 3023 N Clark St #806, Chi; www.chicagomsa.org

♂ ★ ♿ Chicago Smelts Masters Swim Team, www.chicagosmelts.org info@chicagosmelts.org

♂ ★ ♿ Frontrunners/Frontwalkers Chicago, POB 13232, Chi; 60613 www.frfwchicago.org

♂ ★ Second City Tennis, 773-609-4604 www.secondcitytennis.com

♂ ★ Windy City Cycling Club, 1658 N Milwaukee #171, Chi; www.windycitycyclingclub.com

Thrift/Consignment Stores

♂ The Brown Elephant, 217 Harrison St, Oak Park 708-445-0612 tinyurl.com/zxrsqjf

♂ The Brown Elephant, 3020 N Lincoln Ave, Chi 773-549-5943 tinyurl.com/zxrsqjf

♂ The Brown Elephant, 5404 N Clark St, Chi 773-271-9382 tinyurl.com/zxrsqjf

Weddings and Ceremonies

♂ ○ Pine Manor, 401 S Pine St, Chi; 60602 847-873-7463 773-307-2128 samesexweddingvenue.com ✎ ♥ info@gaywedding chicagosite.com

Clinton

Florists (see also Gifts)

♀ ○ Grimsley's Flowers, SW Corner Square, 102 Jones Ct; 61727-1948 217-935-2197 800-437-1918 www.grimsleysflowers.com info@grimsleysflowers.com

DeKalb

Organizations/Resources: Student, Academic, Education

♂ ★ ♿ Gender & Sexuality Resource Center, Northern Illinois University, 105 Normal Rd; 815-753-4772 **H** www.niu.edu/lgbt/ ✎

♂ ★ (♿) Northern Illinois University PRISM, Holmes Student Center Room 705; 815-753-0584 fb.com/niuprism

Religious / Spiritual Resources

♀ ☆ Unitarian Universalist Fellowship of DeKalb, 158 N 4th St; 60115-3304 815-756-7089 www.uufdekalb.org office@uufdekalb.org

Dixon

Organizations/Resources: Family and Supporters

♀ ☆ PFLAG Sauk Valley, POB 261; 61021 815-440-2672 tinyurl.com/7esfwsx

»» East St Louis: see St Louis Area (MO & IL)
»» Elgin: see Chicago Area
»» Elk Grove Village: see Chicago Area
»» Evanston: see Chicago Area
»» Forest Park: see Chicago Area
»» Franklin Park: see Chicago Area

Galena

Accommodation: Hotels, Inns, Guesthouses, B&B, Resorts

♂ ● Aldrich Guest House, 900 3rd St; 815-777-3323 www.aldrich-guesthouse.com ⊛⊛

♀ ● (♿) Inn at Irish Hollow, 2800 S Irish Hollow Rd; 815-777-6000 www.irishhollow.com ✎ ⊛

♀ ○ Steamboat House B&B, 605 S Prospect St 61036-2519 815-777-2317 www.thesteamboathouse.com ✎

Illinois: Galesburg
Men's Clubs

165
GAYELLOW PAGES #42 2020-2021

Rockford: Illinois
Counseling

Galesburg

Men's & Sex Clubs (not primarily Health Clubs)

♂ ● 👬 Hole in the Wall Men's Club, 1438 Knox Highway 9; (I-74 & Exit 51) 309-289-2375 tinyurl.com/dy9rnq **P** ✂

Organizations/Resources: Student, Academic, Education

♂ ★ Knox College Common Ground, 2 East South St tinyurl.com/j8e5smd
>> Glen Ellyn: see Chicago Area

Great Lakes

Organizations/Resources: Military/Veterans

♂ Gay, Lesbian and Supportive Sailors (GLASS), tinyurl.com/y6wrgllk

Joliet

Community Centers and/or Pride Organizations

♂ ★ (?👬) Community Alliance & Action Network, 2405 Essington Rd Ste 103, Joliet; 815-726-7906 **H?** www.caanmidwest.org ✂

AIDS/HIV Services, Education & Support

♀ ☆ 👬 Agape Missions, 840 Plainfield Rd, Joliet; 60435 815-723-1548 fax 815-740-5910 Housingvention/Care/ Medical Case Management/ Health Clinic onsite/HOPWA www.agapemissionsnfp.org ✂

Bars, Cafes, Clubs, Restaurants

♂ ● Maneuvers, 118 E Jefferson St, Joliet 815-727-7069 fb.com/maneuversjoliet/ ▦

Religious / Spiritual Resources

♂ ☆ Universalist Unitarian Church, 3401 W Jefferson St, Joliet; 60432 815-744-9020 www.uujoliet.org uucjoffice@att.net

Kankakee

Organizations/Resources: Family and Supporters

♂ ☆ 👬 PFLAG Kankakee, 815-932-2845 tinyurl.com/y7sgl4q9 pflagkankakee@pflagillinois.org
>> Lincoln: see Springfield/Lincoln Area

Macomb

Organizations/Resources: Student, Academic, Education

♂ ● 👬 Western Illinois University Unity, 1 University Circle; 309-298-3232 **H?** fb.com/UNITYatWIU

Mattoon

Organizations/Resources: Student, Academic, Education

♂ ★ Lake Land College Pride, 5001 Lake Land Blvd; 61938 217-234-5359 tinyurl.com/ylrdpol msatterw@lakeland.cc.il.us

McHenry

Organizations/Resources: Family and Supporters

♀☆ 👃 PFLAG McHenry, Tree of Life UUC, 5603 W Bull Valley Rd, McHenry; 815-385-9068 tinyurl.com/ydacemqe

Organizations/Resources: Social, Recreation, Support

♂ ★ (?👬) McHenry County Pride, Congregational Unitarian Church, 5603 Bull Valley Rd, McHenry www.mchenrycountypride.org

Religious / Spiritual Resources

♀ ☆ Tree of Life Unitarian Universalist Congregation, 5603 West Bull Valley Road, McHenry; 60050 815-322-2464 www.treeoflifeuu.org office@treeoflifeuu.org
>> Oak Park: see Chicago Area

Peoria

AIDS/HIV Services, Education & Support

♀ ☆ 👬 Friends of Central Illinois, 120 NE Glen Oak Ave #201; 309-671-2144 tinyurl.com/zl957po ☯

♀ ☆ 👬 Positive Health Solutions, University of Illinois College of Medicine, 1 Illini Dr; 309-671-8457 **H** tinyurl.com/j5eskg7

Counseling/Psychotherapy/Mental Health

♂ ○ 👬 Joy Miller & Associates, 7617 N Villa Wood Lane; 61614-1588 309-693-8200 www.joymiller.com ✂

Funding: Endowment, Fundraising

♂ ★ Acorn Equality Fund, POB 6286; 61601 www.acornequalityfund.org

Grooming, Personal Care, Spa Services

♀ (?👬) Shear Pzazz Salon & Day Spa, 1311 E Duryea Ave; 309-685-5253 www.shearpzazz.com

Metaphysical, Occult, Alternative Healing

♀ ○ 👬 Temple of the Phoenix, aka Illinois Institute of Metephysics, 817 SW Adams; 309-282-6768 www.mysticartsltd.com ✂

Real Estate (see also Mortgages)

♀ ○ (?👬) McDonald, John, Broker, Kallister Realty, 512 W Main St; 61606-1449 309-253-3073 www.kallister-realty.com ✂

Quincy

Erotica / Adult Stores / Safe Sex Supplies

♀ ○ 👬 Chelsea Adult Superstore, 4804 Gardner Expwy; 62305 217-224-7000 **H?** chelseaadultsuperstore.com chelseaadultsuperstore@gmail.com
>> Rock Island: see Davenport/Quad Cities Area (IA & IL)

Rockford

Bars, Cafes, Clubs, Restaurants

♂ Office Niteclub, 513 E State St, Rockford 815-965-0344 fb.com/officeniteclub ▦

Counseling/Psychotherapy/Mental Health

♂ ★ 👃 Spectrum of Rockford LGBT Counseling, Harmony Center for Holistic Psychotherapy, 6625 N 2nd St, Loves Park; 815-639-0300 **H?** tinyurl.com/ndgu7hf ✂

Religious / Spiritual Resources

♂ ☆ Spring Creek UCC, 4500 Spring Creek Rd, Rockford; 61114 815-877-2576 www.springcreekucc.com office@springcreekucc.com

Sheffield

Accommodation: Hotels, Inns, Guesthouses, B&B, Resorts

♂ ○ Chestnut Street Inn, 301 E Chestnut St; 61361 815-454-2419 www.chestnut-inn.com ✔ Ⓢ monikaandjeff@chestnut-inn.com

Springfield/Lincoln Area

Community Centers and/or Pride Organizations

⚥ ★ Phoenix Center, 109 E Lawrence Ave, Springfield; 217-528-5253 tinyurl.com/2oqsq4

AIDS/HIV Services, Education & Support

♀ Fifth Street Renaissance/SARA Center, POB 5181, Springfield; 62705 217-544-5040 www.fsr-sara.org

Bars, Cafes, Clubs, Restaurants
Springfield

⚥ ● The Club Station House, 306 E Washington St, Springfield; 217-525-0438 tinyurl.com/ybus6cvp **D**

Gifts, Cards, Pride, etc.

♂ ○ The Cardologist Card (& Sock!) Store, 627 E Adams, Springfield; 217-525-4121 tinyurl.com/ycubebd6

Organizations/Resources: Student, Academic, Education

⚥ ★ Lincoln Land Community College Gay-Straight Alliance, 5250 Shepherd Rd, Springfield; 217-786-2394 tinyurl.com/hfr7tgu

♀ ☆ University of Illinois Springfield Gender & Sexuality Student Services, Student Life Building SLB 22, 1 University Plaza, Springfield; 217-206-8316 tinyurl.com/y7slzylf

Religious / Spiritual Resources

♂ ★ ♿ Heartland Community MCC, 402 N Dawson St, Springfield; 217-726-8411 www.2guysdesign.com/mcc/

Taylorville

Accommodation: Hotels, Inns, Guesthouses, B&B, Resorts

♂ ○ (♿) Market Street Inn, 220 E Market St; 62568 217-824-7220 www.marketstreetinn.com ✔ ⊗Ⓢ innkeeper@marketstreetinn.com

Tiskilwa

Accommodation: Hotels, Inns, Guesthouses, B&B, Resorts

♂ ● Tiskilwa Inn, 155 High St; 61368 815-646-1300 www.thetiskilwainn.com ✔ Ⓢ info@thetiskilwainn.com

>> *Urbana: see Champaign/Urbana Area*
>> *Wilmette: see Chicago Area*

Indiana
State/County Resources

Information, Media & Publications

⚥ ★ (♿) Tri-State Alliance, POB 2901, Evansville, IN 47728 812-480-0204 www.tsagl.org

AIDS/HIV Services, Education & Support

♀ ☆ ♿ Indiana AIDS Fund, 429 E Vermont St Ste 300, Indianapolis, IN 46202 317-630-1805 www.indianaaidsfund.org ✔ info@thfgi.org

♀ ☆ ♿ NAMES Project Indiana Chapter, 429 E Vermont St #300, Indianapolis, IN 317-630-1805 tinyurl.com/ybrcalzg

Organizations/Resources: Naturist/Nudist

♂ ★ Bare Indy Boys, POB 421, Brazil, IN 47834 tinyurl.com/65zgfn bareindyboys-owner@yahoogroups.com

Organizations/Resources: Political/Legislative/Advocacy

♀ ☆ (♿) American Civil Liberties Union of Indiana, 1031 E Washington St, Indianapolis, IN 317-635-4059 www.aclu-in.org

⚥ Indiana Stonewall Democrats, POB 132, Indianapolis, IN 46206 www.instonewalldems.org

Organizations/Resources: Social, Recreation, Support

⚥ ★ Michiana Dunes Lambda Car Club, 19155 Beaver Dam Rd, Galien, MI 49113 / W Michigan & NW Indiana www.michianadunes.com michianadunes@gmail.com

⚥ ★ (♿) Sappho's Network, sandlisa@sbcglobal.net

Organizations/Resources: Youth (see also Family)

⚥ ★ ♿ Indiana Youth Group, POB 20716, Indianapolis, IN 46220 317-541-8726 ages 12-21 www.indianayouthgroup.org ✔

⚥ ★ (♿) TSA Youth Group, POB 2901, Evansville, IN 47728 812-480-0204 www.tsagl.org

Bloomington

Community Centers and/or Pride Organizations

⚥ ★ ♿ Spencer Pride commUnity center, POB 585, Spencer; 47460 / 17 E Franklin St 812-652-5000 spencerpride.org/unity

⚥ ★ ♿ Spencer Pride commUnity center, POB 585, Spencer; 47460 / 17 E. Franklin St 812-652-5000 spencerpride.org/unity

AIDS/HIV Services, Education & Support

♂ ☆ Positive Link, Bloomington Hospital, 333 E Miller Dr; 812-353-9150 tinyurl.com/8g3l53d

Bars, Cafes, Clubs, Restaurants

⚥ ● ♿ The Back Door, 207 S College Ave; 812-333-3123 fb.com/backdoorbloomington **DK** 🎱✔ thebackdoor bloomington@gmail.com

Bookstores

♂ ● ♿ Boxcar Books & Community Center, Inc, 408 E 6th St; 812-339-8710 www.boxcarbooks.org ✔

Indiana: Bloomington
Broadcast Media
167
GAYELLOW PAGES #42 2020-2021
Hanover : Indiana
Organizations: Youth

Broadcast Media

⚥ ★ bloomingOUT, WFHB Bloomington Community Radio, 108 W 4th St; 812-323-1200 **H?** tinyurl.com/shvxwqg

Legal Services

♀ ○ Bauer, Jawn J, Bauer & Densford, Attorneys at Law, POB 1332; 47402-1332 812-334-0600 www.jawnbauer.com jawnlaw@jawnbauer.com

♀ ○ **Graham, Roy, 3330 N Russell Rd; 47408 812-269-2923 fax 812-339-3633 Practicing family and criminal law in Monroe and surrounding counties since 1991. Flexible fees. www.roygrahamlaw.com grahamatty@aol.com**

Organizations/Resources: Cultural, Dance, Performance

⚥ ★ && PRIDE Film Festival, POB 554; 47402 812-323-3022 **HD** tinyurl.com/hgexdrm

♂ ★ Quarryland Men's Chorus, POB 3345; 47402 812-727-8149 www.quarryland.org

Organizations/Resources: Prisoner Resources

♀ ★ && The Midwest Pages to Prisoners Project, 408 E 6th St; 812-339-8710 www.boxcarbooks.org ✎

Organizations/Resources: Student, Academic, Education

⚥ ★ Indiana University GLBT Alumni, Virgil T. DeVault Alumni Center, 1000 E 17th St; 812-855-4822 alumni.indiana.edu/glbtaa/

⚥ ★ && LGBTQ+ Culture Center, Indiana University, 705 E 7th St; 812-855-4252 **H?** lgbtq.indiana.edu/ ✎

⚥ ★ Outlaw, Indiana University School of Law, 211 S Indiana Ave

Religious / Spiritual Resources

♀ ☆ && St Thomas Lutheran Church, 3800 E 3rd St; 47401-5510 812-332-5252 **H** www.stlconline.org officestaff@stlconline.org

♀ ☆ && Unity of Bloomington, 4001 S Rogers St; 47403-4823 812-333-2484 www.unityofbloomington.org ✎ ministry@unityof bloomington.org

Columbus

Organizations/Resources: Political/Legislative/Advocacy

⚥ Pride Alliance Columbus, IN, POB 966 47202 fb.com/groups/102771544255/

Crown Point

Community Centers and/or Pride Organizations

⚥ Northwest Indiana Pride, 10769 Broadway #188; 219-216-1356 www.lgbtq-nwi.org

Organizations/Resources: Family and Supporters

♀ ☆ Pride Initiative, an LGBTQAI+ affirming support group, Crown Counseling, 1308 N Main St; 46307 219-663-6353 tinyurl.com/y7n5pz6d nataliel@crowncounseling.org

Evansville

AIDS/HIV Services, Education & Support

♂ ☆ AIDS Resource Group of Evansville, Inc, 101 NW 1st St Ste 213; 812-421-0059 www.argevansville.org

Bars, Cafes, Clubs, Restaurants

⚥ Someplace Else, 930 Main St; 812-424-3202 tinyurl.com/pjt8mmd **D** 🏳️‍🌈

Fort Wayne

Community Centers and/or Pride Organizations

⚥ ★ && Fort Wayne Pride, c/o Nikki Fultz, 7829 Noble Ridge Place; 260-602-6860 www.fwpride.org

Archives/Libraries/Museums/History Projects

⚥ ★ && Northeast Indiana Diversity Library, POB 5537; 46895 / Transitioning to a New Location 260-241-7719 www.nidl.info ✎ thelibrary@nidl.info

Bars, Cafes, Clubs, Restaurants

⚥ After Dark/Babylon, 112 Masterson Ave 260-456-6235 fb.com/babylonftwayne **D** 🏳️‍🌈

♀ ○ && Mad Anthony Brewing Company, 2002 Broadway; 260-426-2537 www.madbrew.com Ⓨ ✕

Organizations/Resources: Family and Supporters

♀ ☆ & PFLAG Fort Wayne, 260-577-3524 tinyurl.com/yxdmvmlc pflagfortwayne@gmail.com

Religious / Spiritual Resources

♀ ☆ && Unitarian Universalist Congregation, 5310 Old Mill Rd; 46807-3017 260-744-1867 www.uufortwayne.org ✎

Gary Area

Crisis, Anti-violence, & Helplines

♀ ☆ Crisis Center, Inc, 101 N Montgomery, Gary 219-938-7070 www.crisiscenterysb.org

AIDS/HIV Services, Education & Support

♀ Aliveness Project NWI, 5490 Broadway #L3, Merrillville; 219-985-6170 tinyurl.com/zqetcxc
» **Hammond: see Chicago Area**

Hanover

Organizations/Resources: Family and Supporters

♀ ☆ && PFLAG Hanover, Inc, POB 276 47243 812-624-5244 tinyurl.com/yaubwsxz

Organizations/Resources: Youth (see also Family)

♀ ☆ && PFLAG Teen Youth Group, PFLAG Hanover, Inc POB 276; 47243 812-624-5244 tinyurl.com/yaubwsxz

Indianapolis Area

Community Centers and/or Pride Organizations

⚥ ★ Circle City In Pride, POB 44403, Indpls 46244 www.circlecityin-pride.org

Information, Media & Publications

⚥ ● Pride Journeys - LGBT Travel News, 407-496-8751 www.pridejourneys.com joey@pridejourneys.com

Accommodation: Hotels, Inns, Guesthouses, B&B, Resorts
Franklin

♂ ● The Flying Frog Bed & Breakfast, 396 N Main St, Franklin; 46131 317-697-3212 tinyurl.com/ya9afn48 ⚕ ☺

Morgantown

♂ ○ (?&) 4 Seasons Lodge, 8670 Spearsville Rd, Morgantown; 812-597-2450 www.campbuckwood.com **P** (♣?) ☺

AIDS/HIV Services, Education & Support

♂ ★ Brothers United, 3737 N Meridian St Ste 401, Indpls; 317-931-0292 www.brothersunitedinc.org ✚

♀ ★ && The Damien Center, 26 N Arsenal Ave, Indpls; 317-632-0123 www.damien.org

♀ ☆ Step-Up, Inc, 850 N Meridian St Flr 1, Indpls 317-259-7013 www.stepupin.org

Bars, Cafes, Clubs, Restaurants
Indianapolis

⚥ Downtown Olly's, 822 N Illinois St, Indpls 317-636-5597 downtownollys.net **S** ⚲ ✕ ⚕

⚥ ● & Greg's, 231 E 16th St, Indpls 317-638-8138 www.gregsourplace.com **DLW**

⚥ ● (&&) Metro Nightclub & Restaurant, 707 Massachusetts Ave, Indpls; 317-639-6022 www.metro-indy.com ⚲ ✕ ▥

⚥ Tini, 717 Massachusetts Ave, Indpls 317-986-6603 tiniontheave.com

♀ ○ && White Rabbit Cabaret, 1116 E Prospect St, Indpls; 317-686-9550 www.whiterabbitcabaret.com ▥

Campgrounds and RV Parks

♂ ○ (?&) CampBuckwood, 8670 Spearsville Rd, Morgantown; 812-597-2450 www.campbuckwood.com **NP** (♣?) ⚕ ☺

Counseling/Psychotherapy/Mental Health

♀ ● & O'Mara, Michele, LCSW, 2680 E Main St #121, Plainfield; 46168 317-517-0065 www.micheleomara.com ⚕

Legal Services

⚥ ● && Baird, Barbara J, 445 N Pennsylvania #401, Indpls; 317-637-2345 www.bjbairdlaw.com

♀ ● && Duvall, Lesa, Duvall & Fall, PC, 4911 E 56th St, Indpls; 46220 317-634-9100 www.duvallfall.com. ⚕ lduvall@duvallfall.com

Massage Therapy (Certified/Licensed only)

♀ ● Gentle Kneads Massage, 1060 N Capitol Ave E290, Indpls; 46204 317-797-9799 www.gentlekneads.com

Men's & Sex Clubs (not primarily Health Clubs)

♂ ● && Club Indianapolis, 620 N Capitol, Indpls; 317-635-5796 www.theclubs.com **P** ⚕

♂ The Works, 4120 N Keystone Ave, Indpls 317-547-9210 www.worksindy.com **P**

Organizations/Resources: Business & Professional Associations, Labor Advocacy

⚥ ★ Indy Rainbow Chamber of Commerce, POB 441491, Indpls; 46244 www.gayindynow.com

Organizations/Resources: Cultural, Dance, Performance

⚥ ★ Indianapolis LGBT Film Festival, 4033 N Central Ave, Indpls; 317-966-6039 www.indylgbtfilmfest.com

♂ ★ && Indianapolis Men's Chorus, POB 414, Indpls; 46206 317-855-8706 tinyurl.com/zy9lvwt

♀ ★ && Indianapolis Women's Chorus, 4550 Central Ave, Indpls; 46205 317-682-4946 indianapoliswomenschorus.org info@indianapoliswomenschorus.org

⚥ ★ (?&) Pride of Indy Bands, Inc, 609 E 29th St, Indpls; www.prideofindy.org

Organizations/Resources: Family and Supporters

♀ ☆ & PFLAG Greenwood, Meets at Yeager Office Building, 3209 W Smith Valley Rd, Greenwood; 317-440-1745 PFLAGGreenwoodinfo@gmail.com

♀ ☆ && PFLAG Indianapolis, POB 502033, Indpls; 46250 317-759-3397 www.indypflag.org

Organizations/Resources: Social, Recreation, Support

♂ ● Fellowship Indy, POB 2331, Indpls 46206-2331 317-563-1760 **WC** www.FellowshipIndy.org
@ixx=

♂ ★ Midwest Bearpack, www.bearpack.org

♂ ★ Prime Timers Indianapolis, 812-661-488 tinyurl.com/y69tuwrw

Organizations/Resources: Student, Academic, Education

⚥ ★ Butler University Alliance, 4600 Sunset Ave, Indpls; 317-940-8404 tinyurl.com/js5tmt9

⚥ ★ Franklin College Pride Alliance, 101 Branigin Blvd, Franklin; 317-738-8119 tinyurl.com/yckrntjd

⚥ ★ && LGBTQ Student Alliance at IUPUI, Multicultural Success Center, 815 W Michigan St, Indpls **H** fb.com/lgbtqstudentalliance ⚕

Organizations/Resources: Transgender/Gender Non-Conforming/Diverse

T ☆ Trans Indy, www.transindy.org

Real Estate (see also Mortgages)

♀ ○ Baiz, Eric, F.C. Tucker, 3405 E 86th St, Indpls; 46240 317-626-6364 www.ericbaiz.com ebaiz@talktotucker.com

♀ ○ Doug Dilling Team, United Real Estate Indianapolis, 1425 E 86th St Ste 200, Indpls; 317-965-1001 www.dougdilling.com

Lafayette

Community Centers and/or Pride Organizations

♂ ★ 占占 Pride Lafayette, POB 4221 47903 / 640 Main St 765-423-7579 www.pridelafayette.org ✔

Bookstores

♀ ○ Von's Book Shop, 319 W State St, W Lafayette 765-743-1915 vonsshops.com/Book_Shop.html

Organizations/Resources: Family and Supporters

♀ ☆ 占占 PFLAG Lafayette/Tippecanoe County, POB 59, Battle Ground; 47920-0059 765-567-2478 765-491-6357

Organizations/Resources: Political/Legislative/Advocacy

♀ ☆ Citizens for Civil Rights, c/o Pride Lafayette, Inc, 640 Main St; fb.com/citizensforcivilrights

Organizations/Resources: Student, Academic, Education

♂ ★ Delta Lambda Phi Alpha Beta Chapter, dlp.org/alphabeta/ alphabeta.chapter@dlp.org

♂ ★ 占占 The Purdue LGBTQ Center, SCHL Rm 230, 475 Stadium Mall Dr, W Lafayette; 765-496-6231 **H?** www.purdue.edu/lgbtq/

Mauckport

Accommodation: Hotels, Inns, Guesthouses, B&B, Resorts

♂ ● Stag Run Club, Overlook Farm, 2150 Overlook Dr 12-844-5838 Also abins, tent & RV sites stagrunclub.com **P**

Muncie

Bars, Cafes, Clubs, Restaurants

♀ Mark III Tap Room, 306 S Walnut St 765-216-1327 www.markiii-taproom.com ⬛

Organizations/Resources: Student, Academic, Education

♀ ★ 占占 Ball State University Spectrum, Student Center 134, Box 16; 47306-0001 www.bsu.edu/spectrum/ bsuspectrum@gmail.com

Organizations/Resources: Youth (see also Family)

♀ ★ Muncie OUTreach, 310 E Charles St; 47305 765-744-7436 muncieoutreach.org muncieoutreach@gmail.com

>> New Albany: see Louisville
>> Nineveh: see Columbus

North Manchester

Organizations/Resources: Student, Academic, Education

♂ ★ Manchester University United Sexualities, Student Activities Office, 604 E College Ave; 260-982-5365 tinyurl.com/y6vq6ama

Religious / Spiritual Resources

♂ ☆ Manchester Church of the Brethren, POB 349 46962 260-982-7523 manchestercob@gmail.com

Notre Dame

Organizations/Resources: Student, Academic, Education

♂ ★ 占占 St Mary's College Straight & Gay Alliance, College Student Center

Portage

Religious / Spiritual Resources

♀ ★ MCC Illiana, 5579 Clem Rd; 219-764-7100 www.mccilliana.org

South Bend/Michiana

Community Centers and/or Pride Organizations

♂ ★ The LGBTQ Center, 1522 Mishawaka Ave, South Bend; 574-234-1411 www.thelgbtqcenter.org ✔

Accommodation: Hotels, Inns, Guesthouses, B&B, Resorts

Michigan City

♀ ○ Duneland Beach Inn, 3311 Pottawattomie Trl, Michigan City; 46360 219-874-7729 www.dunelandbeachinn.com ♈ ✗ ✔ ⊛ info@dunelandbeachinn.com

Mishawaka

♀ ● Beiger Mansion Inn, 317 Lincolnway E, Mishawaka; 800-437-0131 www.beigermansion.com ✔ ⊛

South Bend

♀ ○ Innisfree B&B, 702 W Colfax Ave, South Bend 46601-1404 574-318-4838 www.innisfreebnb.com ✔ innisfreebnb@gmail.com

AIDS/HIV Services, Education & Support

♀ AIDS Ministries, POB 11582, South Bend 46634 574-287-8888 www.aidsministries.org

Bars, Cafes, Clubs, Restaurants

South Bend

♀ Jeannie's Tavern, 621 S Bendix Dr, South Bend; 574-288-2826

♀ ○ Vickie's Bar & Grill, 112 W Monroe St, South Bend; 574-232-4090 tinyurl.com/hu695qg ♈ ✗

Counseling/Psychotherapy/Mental Health

♀ ☆ 占占 Oaklawn, POB 809, Goshen 46527 574-533-1234 **H?** www.oaklawn.org

Grooming, Personal Care, Spa Services

♀ ○ Cheveux Hair Salon, 1315 Mishawaka Ave, South Bend; 46615 574-234-1455 www.itsallaboutthecut.com ✔

Religious / Spiritual Resources

♀ ☆ Unitarian Universalist Fellowship of Elkhart, 1732 Garden St, Elkhart; 46514-3429 574-264-6525 www.uufe.org uuelkhart@gmail.com

Terre Haute

Bars, Cafes, Clubs, Restaurants

♀ ● (♚) ZimMarss Show Bar, 1500 Locust St; 812-232-3026 fb.com/ZimMarss.Night.Club/ **DL** ✔

Iowa
State/County Resources

Funding: Endowment, Fundraising

♂ ★ Eychaner Foundation, POB 1797, Des Moines, IA 50305 515-218-1549 www.eychanerfoundation.org

Organizations/Resources: Political/Legislative/Advocacy

♂ ☆ Iowa NOW, 3635 E 43rd Crt, Des Moines, IA 515-265-3193 www.iowanow.org

♀ University of Iowa Center for Human Rights (UICHR), 1120 University Capitol Centre, Iowa City, IA 319-335-3900 uichr.uiowa.edu

Organizations/Resources: Youth (see also Family)

♥ GLBT Youth in Iowa Schools Task Force, PO Box 704, Des Moines, IA 50303 515-381-0588 www.iowasafeschools.org

Reproductive Medicine & Fertility Services

♀ ☆ Planned Parenthood of the Heartland, POB 4557, Des Moines, IA 50305 515-280-7000 www.ppheartland.org

Ames

Organizations/Resources: Family and Supporters

♀ ☆ PFLAG Ames, 25218 580th Ave, Nevada 515-708-1582

Organizations/Resources: Student, Academic, Education

♂ ★ ♿ Center for LGBTQIA+ Student Success, Iowa State University, 3224 Memorial Union, 2229 Lincoln Way 515-294-5433 center.dso.iastate.edu

♂ ★ Delta Lambda Phi Beta Lambda Chapter, Office of Greek Affairs, 0355 Memorial Un; 515-294-5931 www.dlp.org/betalambda/

♀ ☆ Margaret Sloss Center for Women and Gender Equity, Iowa State University, 203 Sloss House, 501 Farm House Lane 515-294-1020 sloss.dso.iastate.edu

Organizations/Resources: Youth (see also Family)

♀ ☆ ♿ YsS (Youth Standing Strong), PO Box 1628; 50010 515-233-3141 **HS** yss.org ✔

Recovery

♀ ☆ Ames Intergroup, POB 1772; 50010 515-232-8642 www.amesaa.org

Burlington

Community Centers and/or Pride Organizations

♥ Burlington Pride, - - fb.com/burlingtonpride

Accommodation: Hotels, Inns, Guesthouses, B&B, Resorts

♂ ● Arrowhead Motel, 2520 Mt Pleasant St 319-752-6353 www.arrowheadia.com ✔

» *Cedar Falls: see*

Cedar Falls

Religious / Spiritual Resources
Cedar Falls

♀ ☆ ♿ Cedar Valley Unitarian Universalists, 3912 Cedar Heights Dr, Cedar Falls; 50613 319-266-5640 www.cedarvalleyuu.org ✔ administrator@cedarvalleyuu.org

Cedar Rapids

Community Centers and/or Pride Organizations

♥ ★ CRPrideFest, POB 1643, Cedar Rapids 52406 crpridefest.com

Bars, Cafes, Clubs, Restaurants
Cedar Rapids

♂ ● Belle's Basix, 3916 1st Ave NE, Cedar Rapids; 319-363-3194 fb.com/bellesbasix **D** ▦ ✪

Organizations/Resources: Family and Supporters

♀ ☆ PFLAG Cedar Rapids, 319-560-0776 www.pflagcr.com pflagcr@gmail.com

Organizations/Resources: Student, Academic, Education

♥ ★ Coe College Queer Resource Center, 1220 1st Ave NE, Cedar Rapids; 319-399-6025 tinyurl.com/y2nmvnp7

Religious / Spiritual Resources

♀ ☆ ♿ Lovely Lane United Methodist Church, 2424 42nd St NE, Cedar Rapids; 52402 319-393-6674 **HD** www.lovelylane.org ✔

Davenport/Quad Cities Area (IA & IL)

Community Centers and/or Pride Organizations
Davenport

♥ ★ QC Pride, c/o 2930 W Locust, Davenport 52804 www.qcpride.org

AIDS/HIV Services, Education & Support

♀ ☆ The Project of the Quad Cities, 1701 River Dr #110, Moline, IL 309-762-5433 tinyurl.com/y5aumaox
Rock Island

♀ DeLaCerda House, Inc., 2827 7th Ave #11, Rock Island, IL 309-786-7386 www.delacerdahouseinc.org

Bars, Cafes, Clubs, Restaurants
Davenport

♥ Mary's on 2nd, 832 W 2nd St, Davenport 563-884-8014 fb.com/maryson2ndst/ ▦

Recovery
Davenport

♀ ☆ ♿ Alcoholics Anonymous - Quad Cities, 1706 Brady St Ste 201, Davenport; 52803 309-764-1016 **H?** www.aaquadcities.org ✔

Religious / Spiritual Resources
Davenport

♥ ★ MCC Quad Cities, 2930 W Locust, Davenport 563-324-8281 www.mccqc.com

Rock Island

♀ ☆ St John's Lutheran Church, 4501 7th Ave, Rock Island, IL 61201 309-786-6333 www.stjohnsri.org welcome@stjohnsri.org

Decorah

Bookstores

♀ ○ ⅋ Dragonfly Books, 112 W Water St 563-382-4275 www.dragonflybooks.com

Organizations/Resources: Student, Academic, Education

♀ ★ ⅋⅋ Luther College Pride, SPO #97, 700 College Dr; 563-223-8830 www.luther.edu/pride/ ✎

Des Moines

Community Centers and/or Pride Organizations

♀ ★ Capital City Pride, POB 73; 50301 www.capitalcitypride.org marketing@capitalcitypride.org

♀ Des Moines Pride Center, 1620 Pleasant St Ste 244; 515-277-7884 www.dsmpridecenter.org

AIDS/HIV Services, Education & Support

♂ The Project of Primary HealthCare, 1200 University Ave #120; 515-248-1595 phctheproject.org

Bars, Cafes, Clubs, Restaurants

♂ ● ⅋⅋ Blazing Saddle, 416 E 5th St 515-246-1299 www.theblazingsaddle.com **CLD** ▦ ✎

♂ ● ⅋⅋ The Garden Nightclub, 112 SE 4th St; 515-243-3965 www.grdn.com **DK** ▦

♀ ● ⅋⅋ Ritual Cafe, 1301 Locust St Ste D; 515-288-4872 www.ritualcafedsmiowa.net ✎

♂ ○ ⅋⅋ Zanzibar's Coffee Adventure, 2723 Ingersoll Ave; 515-244-7694 www.zanzibarscoffee.com ✕ ▱

Computer & Software Sales & Services

♂ ● Crisp Solutions, LLC, 515-423-0160 Macintosh based networks etc www.crispsolutions.net info@crispsolutions.net

Counseling/Psychotherapy/Mental Health

♂ ○ (⅋⅋) Stewart-Sandusky, Shelly, 4725 Merle Hay Rd #205; 50322 515-528-8135 **H?** tinyurl.com/yxdwyl99 sandusky@sstherapyandconsulting.com

Funding: Endowment, Fundraising

♂ ★ ⅋⅋ **First Friday Breakfast Club, 515-288-2500** Educational, non-profit corporation for gay men; raises money for a scholarship fund. www.ffbciowa.org

♂ Imperial Court of Iowa, POB 1491; 50305 515-979-9157 www.imperialcourtofiowa.org

Immigration, Citizenship, Political Asylum, Refugees

♂ ● ⅋⅋ Mike Keller Immigration Law, PLLC, 6611 University Ave Ste 200, Windsor Heights; 50324 515-255-5616 **H?** www.kellerimmigrationlaw.com ✎ mike@mikekellerlaw.com

Leather Resources & Groups

♂ ★ Corn Haulers L&L Club, POB 632; 50303 fb.com/groups/433717655570/ **L**

Organizations/Resources: Cultural, Dance, Performance

♂ ★ Des Moines Gay Men's Chorus, POB 12269; 50312 515-999-5636 www.dmgmc.org

Organizations/Resources: Family and Supporters

♀ ☆ PFLAG Des Moines, 515-650-9042 preview.tinyurl.com/y6hblkaw

Organizations/Resources: Political/Legislative/Advocacy

♂ ★ ⅋ One Iowa, 950 Office Park Road, # 240z, W Des Moines; 515-288-4019 **H?** www.oneiowa.org

Organizations/Resources: Social, Recreation, Support

♀ ☆ (⅋⅋) Women's Cultural Collective, www.iowawcc.com iowawcc@gmail.com

Religious / Spiritual Resources

♂ ☆ (⅋⅋) Trinity Las Americas United Methodist Church., POB 41005; 50311 515-288-4056 trinitylasamericas.org ✦ ✎ Office@TrinityLasAmericas.org

Sports & Outdoor

♂ Pride Sports League of Central Iowa, - - www.pridesportsleague.org

Women's Centers

♀ ☆ Young Women's Resource Center, 818 5th Ave 515-244-4901 www.ywrc.org

Dubuque

Accommodation: Hotels, Inns, Guesthouses, B&B, Resorts

♂ ○ ⅋⅋ Mandolin Inn, 199 Loras Blvd 52001-4857 563-556-0069 mandolininn.com ✎ ⊛

Organizations/Resources: Youth (see also Family)

♂ ★ ⅋⅋ LGBTQ Youth Network, Multicultural Family Center Dubuque, 1157 Central Ave; 563-589-4191 **H** www.mfcdbq.org ✎

Greenfield

Community Centers and/or Pride Organizations

♂ ★ Adair County GLBT Resource Center, 604 SE 6th St; 50849 641-278-6972 fb.com/AdaircoGLBT adaircoglbtcenter@outlook.com

Grinnell

Organizations/Resources: Student, Academic, Education

♂ ★ Grinnell College Stonewall Resource Center, 1015 8th Ave; 641-269-4000 tinyurl.com/mxnkyd5

Iowa: Indianola
Organizations: Student
172
GAYELLOW PAGES #42 2020-2021
Waverly : Iowa
Organizations: Student

Indianola

Organizations/Resources: Student, Academic, Education

♂ ★ Simpson College Pride, 701 N C St 515-961-1746 fb.com/SimpsonPride

Iowa City/Cedar Rapids/Marion Area

Crisis, Anti-violence, & Helplines

♂ ☆ ♿ The CommUnity Crisis Services and Food Bank, 1121 Gilbert Ct, Iowa City; 52240-4528 855-325-4296 319-351-0140 builtbycommunity.org

Community Centers and/or Pride Organizations

♀ ★ Iowa City Pride, POB 2910, Iowa City 52244. www.iowacitypride.org ⚥

Information, Media & Publications

♀ ● GoGUIDE, 402 21st Av Pl, Coralville; 52241 319-800-3223 www.GoGuideMagazine.com

Accommodation: Hotels, Inns, Guesthouses, B&B, Resorts
Iowa City

♂ ○ A Bella Vista B&B, 2 Bella Vista Pl, Iowa City 52245-5840 319-338-4129 abellavista.net ⊗

♂ ● The Brown Street Inn, 430 Brown St, Iowa City 319-338-0435 brownstreetinn.com ⚥ ⊗

Bars, Cafes, Clubs, Restaurants
Iowa City

♂ ○ ♿ The Mill, 120 E Burlington St, Iowa City; 319-351-9529 icmill.com **D** ⍩ ✕ ▦

♀ Queer Guerrilla Brunch, fb.com/groups/icqgb/

♀ ● ♿ Studio 13, 13 S Linn St, Iowa City; (alley) 267-713-2697 www.sthirteen.com **D** ✪

Bookstores

♂ ○ ♿ Prairie Lights Bookstore, 15 S Dubuque St, Iowa City; 319-337-2681 www.prairielightsbooks.com

Health Care: Physical (see also Counseling/Mental Health)

♂ Free Medical Clinic, 2440 Towncrest Dr, Iowa City; 319-337-4459 www.freemedicalclinic.org

Organizations/Resources: Cultural, Dance, Performance

♀ ★ The Quire: Eastern Iowa's GLBT Chorus, PO Box 1101, Iowa City; 52244 319-214-0450 www.thequire.org

Organizations/Resources: Student, Academic, Education

♀ ★ University of Iowa LGBT Staff & Faculty Association, 202 Jessip Hall, Iowa City; 319-335-0750 lgbtqsf.org.uiowa.edu

♀ ★ University of Iowa Pride Alliance Center, 125 Grand Ave Court, Iowa City; / open to the public 319-335-7123 tinyurl.com/y487btxq ⚥

Organizations/Resources: Youth (see also Family)

♀ ♿ United Action for Youth, PO Box 892, Iowa City; 52244 319-338-7518 **H?** www.unitedactionforyouth.org ⚥

Religious / Spiritual Resources

♂ ☆ ♿ Unitarian Universalist Society, 2355 Oakdale Rd, Coralville; 52241 319-337-3443 **H** www.uusic.org ⚥

Women's Centers

♀ ☆ ♿ Women's Resource & Action Center, 230 N Clinton St, Iowa City; 319-335-1486 wrac.uiowa.edu

Lamoni

Accommodation: Hotels, Inns, Guesthouses, B&B, Resorts

♂ ○ Maple Street Bed and Breakfast LLC, 108 N Maple St; 50140 641-223-2575 www.maplestbnb.com maplestbnb2009@gmail.com

Lansing

Accommodation: Hotels, Inns, Guesthouses, B&B, Resorts

♂ ● Thornton House B&B, 371 Diagonal St; 52151 563-538-3373 www.thethorntonhouse.com (♣?) ⚥ ⊗ ⊛

Mount Vernon

Organizations/Resources: Student, Academic, Education

♀ ★ Cornell College Alliance, 810 Commons Cir Sw #2035; fb.com/groups/ccalliance

Oskaloosa

Organizations/Resources: Family and Supporters

♂ PFLAG Oskaloosa, www.pflagoskaloosa.com

Sioux City

Health Care: Physical (see also Counseling/Mental Health)

♂ ☆ ♿ Siouxland Community Health Center, 1021 Nebraska St; 712-252-2477 **H** www.slandchc.com ⚥

Organizations/Resources: Family and Supporters

♂ ☆ (?♿) PFLAG Siouxland, First Unitarian Church, 2508 Jackson St; 712-258-3116 fb.com/pflagofsiouxland/

Organizations/Resources: Student, Academic, Education

♀ ★ (?♿) Morningside College GSA, Student Services, 1501 Morningside Ave; 800-831-0806

Waterloo/Cedar Falls Area

AIDS/HIV Services, Education & Support

♂ Cedar AIDS Support System (CASS), POB 2880, Waterloo; 50704 800-617-1972 www.cvhospice.org

Waverly

Organizations/Resources: Student, Academic, Education

♀ ★ Wartburg College Alliance, Diers House 101, 100 Wartburg Blvd; 319-352-8580 tinyurl.com/25c4tk

Kansas: State/County Resources
Crisis, Anti-violence, & Helplines
173
GAYELLOW PAGES #42 2020-2021
Lawrence : Kansas
Counseling

Kansas
State/County Resources

Crisis, Anti-violence, & Helplines

♂ ★ Kansas City Anti-Violence Project, 4050 Pennsylvania Ave Ste 135, Kansas City, MO 816-561-0550 www.kcavp.org

Organizations/Resources: Education

♀ ☆ Equality Kansas, 800 N Market St, Wichita, KS 316-683-1706 www.eqks.org

♀ Equality Kansas - Hutchinson, POB 3117, Hutchinson, KS 67504 :620-712-9873 www.eqks.org

Reproductive Medicine & Fertility Services

♀ Planned Parenthood of Kansas & Mid-Missouri, 4401 W 109th St, Overland Park, KS 913-312-5100 www.ppkm.org

Dodge City

Organizations/Resources: Political/Legislative/Advocacy

♂ Kansas Equality Coalition of Southwest Kansas, POB 1261; 67801 620-910-1230 www.eqks.org

Emporia

Organizations/Resources: Political/Legislative/Advocacy

♂ Kansas Equality Coalition of the Central Plains, 413 Union St; 785-367-1624 www.eqks.org

Organizations/Resources: Student, Academic, Education

♂ ★ Emporia State University PRIDE, 1 Kellogg Circle Box 22y; 620-341-5723 www.emporia.edu/mps/

Hays

Organizations/Resources: Political/Legislative/Advocacy

♂ Kansas Equality Coalition of Northwest Kansas, POB 214; 67601 785-261-1606 www.eqks.org

Organizations/Resources: Student, Academic, Education

♂ ★ Fort Hays State University Gay/Straight Alliance, 600 Park St; tinyurl.com/ychlwmhe

Hutchinson

Organizations/Resources: Family and Supporters

♂ PFLAG Hutchinson, 620-842-8272 pflaghutchinson.com
» Kansas City: see Kansas City Metro Area (MO & KS)

Lawrence

Crisis, Anti-violence, & Helplines

♂ ☆ ๒๒ Sexual Trauma & Abuse Care Center, 708 W 9th St Ste 105; 785-843-8985 **H?** www.stacarecenter.org ✍

♀ ☆ The Willow Domestic Violence Center, POB 633 66044 800-770-3030 **H** www.willowdvcenter.org

Information, Media & Publications

♂ ★ NetworQ, POB 1954; 66044 www.kansasnetworq.org

Bars, Cafes, Clubs, Restaurants

♂ ○ Bourgeois Pig, 6 E 9th St; 785-843-1001 fb.com/TheBourgeoisPig

♂ ○ ๒๒ Granada, 1020 Massachusetts St 785-842-1390 www.the-granada.com **D** ✍

♂ ○ Java Break, 17 E 7th St; 785-749-5282 www.thejavabreak.com ☞

♂ ○ The Jazzhaus, 926 1/2 Massachusetts St 785-749-3320 www.jazzhaus.com ▥ ✍

Bookstores

♂ ○ ๖ Raven Bookstore, 6 E 7th St 785-749-3300 **H?** www.ravenbookstore.com ✍

Counseling/Psychotherapy/Mental Health

♂ ☆ ๒๒ Headquarters Counseling Center, POB 999; 66044-0999 785-841-2345 tinyurl.com/6mz6xs2

♂ GLBTQI ♀ Gay/nongay ♂ bisexual
♀ LBTQI women ♀ all women ♀ bisexual women
♂ GBTQI men ♂ all men ♂ bisexual men
т specifically transsexual/transgender/transvestite

Υ ✖ Bar and Restaurant ✖ Restaurant ☞ Cafe
▥ Entertainment/Cabaret/Showbar
D Dancing **V** Video bar **K** Karaoke **S** Sports bar
C Country **L** Leather/Levi **W** Western
P Private Club (ask about visitor memberships)

♥ Wedding-related services or marriage equality
H Assistance available for the deaf and hearing-impaired
HD devices **HS** sign **HDS** devices and sign
H? Check for assistance available for the deaf and. hearing-impaired
⊛ ⊛ smoke-free property ⊛ smoke-free indoors
(⊛) indoor smoking areas
❖ Pets welcome (❖?) Ask about pets
✍ High speed internet available to visitors
Wheelchair Accessibility of premises or meeting place:
๒๒ Accessible premises and lavatory
(๒๒) Accessible premises with help; accessible lavatory
๖ Accessible premises; lavatory not known to be accessible
(๖) Accessible premises with help
(?๒) Call ahead for details: places of meetings or activities vary, or special arrangements available.
◇ Asian ✦ Latin/Hispanic
✤ African-descent/Black
❖ People of Color ✚ Two-Spirit ✱ Diverse

Kansas: Lawrence
Jewelry (see also Gifts)
174
GAYELLOW PAGES #42 2020-2021
Wichita : Kansas
Art & Photography

Jewelry (see also Gifts)

♀ ○ Etc. Shop, 928 Massachusetts St; 785-843-0611 www.theetc-shop.com

Legal Services

♂ ● ♿ The Law Offices of David J. Brown, LC, 1040 New Hampshire; 66044-3044 785-842-0777 www.davidbrownlaw.com ✎

Organizations/Resources: Student, Academic, Education

♂ ★ KU Center for Sexuality and Gender Diversity, Kansas Union, Room 400, 1301 Jayhawk Blvd; 785-864-4256 sgd.ku.edu

♂ ★ ♿ Spectrum KU, 1301 Jayhawk Blvd Rm 423; 785-864-3091 tinyurl.com/zkjq835

Real Estate (see also Mortgages)

♂ ○ Hess, Mark, Keller Williams Integrity, 545 Columbia Dr; 66049 785-979-4663 fax 785-856-0928 LawrenceHomeBuyers.com markhess@realtor.com

Religious / Spiritual Resources

♀ ☆ Ecumenical Campus Ministries, 1204 Oread Ave 66044 785-843-4933 www.ecmku.org ✎ ecmatku@gmail.com

Manhattan/Flint Hills

Community Centers and/or Pride Organizations

♂ ★ Flint Hills Pride, 913-202-3005 fb.com/fhpride/

Organizations/Resources: Education

♀ ☆ Flint Hills Human Rights Project, POB 906, Manhattan; 66505 www.fhhrp.com

Organizations/Resources: Social, Recreation, Support

♂ ★ Junction City Teddy Bears, c/o Kevin Stilley, 2 Oak Valley Dr, Manhattan, KS

Organizations/Resources: Student, Academic, Education

♀ ☆ ♿ Kansas State University Center for Advocacy, Response and Education (CARE), 207A/B Holton Hall, Manhattan 785-532-6444 www.k-state.edu/care/ ✎

♂ ★ LGBT Resource Center, Kansas State University, 207 Holton Hall, Manhattan; 66506 785-532-5352 www.k-state.edu/lgbt/ lgbt@k-state.edu

Salina

Bookstores

♀ Ad Astra Books & Coffee House, 141 N Santa Fe Ave; 785-833-2235 adastrabooksandcoffee.com ▽

Organizations/Resources: Political/Legislative/Advocacy

♀ ☆ Kansas Equality Coalition of North Central Kansas, POB 3020; 67402 785-655-0011 www.eqks.org

» Shawnee Mission: see Kansas City Metro Area (MO & KS)

Topeka

Community Centers and/or Pride Organizations

♀ ☆ Equality House, Planting Peace, 1200 SW Orleans St; tinyurl.com/y8pcvcsj

♂ Topeka Pride, www.topekapride.org

AIDS/HIV Services, Education & Support

♀ ☆ ♿ Positive Connections, 2044 SW Fillmore St; 66608 785-232-3100 fax 785-232-3186 www.pcneks.org ✎ pcadmin@pcneks.org

Organizations/Resources: Family and Supporters

♀ ☆ (♂) PFLAG Lawrence-Topeka, 1910 SW Sieben Ct; 66611 785-235-3831 www.pflagnekansas.org sffeist@msn.com

Organizations/Resources: Political/Legislative/Advocacy

♀ Kansas Equality Coalition of Topeka, Inc., PO Box 3824; 66604 785-409-1408 www.eqks.org

♀ ☆ ♿ Topeka Center for Peace & Justice, 2914 SW MacVicar; 785-232-4388 www.topekacpj.org

Organizations/Resources: Youth (see also Family)

♂ Beacon Youth Group, fb.com/beaconks

Religious / Spiritual Resources

♀ ☆ Central Congregational Church UCC, POB 4521 66604 785-235-2376 fb.com/centraltopeka/ info@centraltopekachurch.org

♀ ★ ♿ Metropolitan Community Church of Topeka, POB 4776; 66604 785-272-1442 www.MCCTopeka.org ✎

Wichita

Crisis, Anti-violence, & Helplines

♀ Wichita Area Sexual Assault Center, 355 N Waco #100; 316-263-3002 www.wichitasac.com

♀ Wichita Family Crisis Center, 1111 N St Francis; 316-263-7501 tinyurl.com/y6usdt3q

Community Centers and/or Pride Organizations

♂ ★ The Center of Wichita, 800 N Market St 67214 316-285-0007 www.thecenterofwichita.org TheCenterOfWichita@gmail.com

♂ Wichita Pride, 800 N Market St 316-530-LGBT www.wichitapride.org

Information, Media & Publications

♂ ★ The Land of Awes, POB 16782; 67216 www.awes.com/egcm/

AIDS/HIV Services, Education & Support

♀ ☆ Positive Directions Inc, 416 S Commerce #108 316-263-2214 www.pdiks.com

Art & Photography (see also Graphic Design)

♂ ○ Images by Kelsy Gossett, 316-263-8500 www.images-bykelsy.com kelsy@imagesbykelsy.com

Kansas: Wichita
Bars, Cafes, Clubs, Restaurants

175

GAYELLOW PAGES #42 2020-2021

Brownsville : Kentucky
Accommodation

Bars, Cafes, Clubs, Restaurants

♂ ○ && Beautiful Day Cafe, 2516 E Central; 316-977-9333 beautifuldaycafe.com ✕ ☐ ↗ beautifuldaycafe@gmail.com

♀ ● && Club Boomerang, 1400 E 1st 316-247-0350 clubboomerang.com **DKV** ⅄ ✕ ▥ ↗

♀ ● ♿ J's Lounge, 513 E Central 316-262-1363 www.jsloungewichita.com ▥

♀ Kirby's Beer Store, 3210 E Osie St 316-683-9781 kirbysbeerstore.com

♀ Rocky's Bar, 604 S Topeka St; 316-440-4979 fb.com/pg/Rockys-BarWichita/

♀ XY Bar, 235 N Mosley; 316-201-4670 fb.com/xybarict/ **D**

Bookstores

♂ ○ Watermark Books & Cafe, 4701 E Douglas 316-682-1181 www.watermarkbooks.com ☐

Health Care: Physical (see also Counseling/Mental Health)

♀ ☆ && Hunter Health Clinic, 2318 E Central Ave; 316-262-2415 www.hunterhealthclinic.org ✳

Leather Resources & Groups

♂ ☆ WOOLF Inc, 800 N Market st www.woolfks.com

Organizations/Resources: Cultural, Dance, Performance

♂ ☆ Heart of America Men's Chorus, Newman University DeMattias, 3100 W McCormick; 316-708-4837 www.hoamc.org

Organizations/Resources: Social, Recreation, Support

♀ ★ Prime Timers Wichita, POB 2375; 67201 316-737-2694 wichitaprimetimers.org ICTPrimeTimers@aol.com

Organizations/Resources: Student, Academic, Education

♀ ★ Spectrum LGBTQ & Allies, Wichita State University, 1845 Fairmont, Campus Box 56; 316-978-7010 tinyurl.com/y69hb6qq

Recovery

♀ ☆ ♿ AA Wichita Central Office, 2812 E English; 67211 316-684-3661 www.aawichita.org info@aawichita.org

Religious / Spiritual Resources

♂ ☆ && First Unitarian Universalist Church of Wichita, 7202 E 21st St N; 67206 316-684-3481 **HD** www.firstuu.net ↗ office@firstuu.net

♀ ★ Table of Hope MCC, 156 S Kansas Ave 67211-1922 316-267-1852 www.mccwichita.com info@mccwichita.com

Reproductive Medicine & Fertility Services

♂ Planned Parenthood, 2226 E Central 316-263-7575 www.ppkm.org

Kentucky
State/County Resources

Information, Media & Publications

♀ Queer Kentucky, queerkentucky.com

AIDS/HIV Services, Education & Support

♂ ☆ AIDS Volunteers, Inc., 365 Waller Ave Ste 100, Lexington, KY 859-225-3000 www.avolky.org

Archives/Libraries/Museums/History Projects

♀ ★ (?&) Williams-Nichols Collection, Archives and Special Collections, Ekstrom LL 17, University of Louisville, 2301 S 3rd St, Louisville, KY 40292 502-852-6752 **H?** tinyurl.com/r6h376c ↗

Legal Services

♀ ★ Kentucky Youth Law Project, Inc, 820 Tremont Ave, Lexington, KY 40502 844-220-0226 859-255-0711 www.kylp.org kylplegal@kylpinc.org

Organizations/Resources: Political/Legislative/Advocacy

♀ ☆ && American Civil Liberties Union of Kentucky, 325 W Main St Ste 2210, Louisville, KY 502-581-1181 www.aclu-ky.org

♀ ★ Kentucky Equality Federation, 2008 Merchant Dr Ste 2 #200, Richmond, KY 502-219-2533 www.kyequality.org

♀ ★ Kentucky Fairness Campaign, 2263 Frankfort Ave, Louisville, KY 502-893-0788 www.Fairness.org

Recovery

♀ ☆ Al-Anon Information Services, 4400 Bishop Ln Ste 104, Louisville, KY 502-458-1234 www.kyal-anon.org

Sports & Outdoor

♀ Bluegrass Classic Bowling League, POB 39493, Louisville, KY 40233 502-551-8637 bluegrassclassic.org

Bardstown
Accommodation: Hotels, Inns, Guesthouses, B&B, Resorts

♀ ● Bourbon Manor Bed & Breakfast Inn, 714 N 3rd St 40004 502-350-1010 www.bourbonmanor.com ❣ ⊛ stay@bourbonmanor.com

Bowling Green
Counseling/Psychotherapy/Mental Health

♂ ○ Jones, Jessica, M.Ed. LPCC-S, NCC, Mapletree Mental Wellness, 1183 Kentucky St; 42101 270-282-2202 tinyurl.com/ryl6lhh jessicaj@mapletreemw.com

Brownsville
Accommodation: Hotels, Inns, Guesthouses, B&B, Resorts

♂ ○ Serenity Hill B&B, 3600 Mammoth Cave Rd; 42210 270-597-9647 tinyurl.com/d8xdczp ↗

» *Covington: see Cincinnati Area*

Kentucky: Elizabethtown
Organizations: Social & Support

176

GAYELLOW PAGES #42 2020-2021

Louisville : Kentucky
Bars, Cafes, Clubs, Restaurants

CARMICHAEL'S BOOKSTORE
1295 Bardstown Road · 456-6950
2720 Frankfort Avenue · 896-6950
Louisville's Oldest Independent Bookstore

Elizabethtown

Organizations/Resources: Social, Recreation, Support

⚥ LGBT Elizabethtown, fb.com/LGBTElizabethtown

Frankfort

Organizations/Resources: Family and Supporters

♀ ☆ PFLAG Central Kentucky, POB 415; 40602 859-338-4393 www.pflagcentralky.org

Organizations/Resources: Student, Academic, Education

⚥ ★ ♿ The OUTlet Center, Kentucky State University, Student Center Room 404, 400 E Main St; 502-597-6000 fb.com/ksutheoutletcenter/ ✎

Henderson

AIDS/HIV Services, Education & Support

♀ Matthew 25 AIDS Services, 452 Old Corydon Rd 270-826-0200 www.matthew25clinic.org

Lexington

Community Centers and/or Pride Organizations

⚥ Kentucky Black Pride Inc, 859-285-3091 tinyurl.com/r7stdhl ♣

⚥ ★ ♿ Pride Community Services Organization, 389 Waller Ave Ste 100; 859-253-3233. www.pcsoky.org ✎

Information, Media & Publications

⚥ ★ ♿ Linq, Pride Community Services Organization, 389 Waller Ave Ste 100; 859-253-3233. www.pcsoky.org ✎

Accommodation: Hotels, Inns, Guesthouses, B&B, Resorts
Versailles

♂ ○ (♿) Montgomery Inn B&B, 270 Montgomery Ave, Versailles; 40383 859-251-4103 **H?** www.montgomeryinnbnb.com ✎ ☺ ☺ innkeeper@montgomeryinnbnb.com

AIDS/HIV Services, Education & Support

♂ ☆ ♿ Moveable Feast, POB 367; 40588 859-252-2867 www.feastlex.org

Bars, Cafes, Clubs, Restaurants

♂ ○ ♿ Alfalfa Restaurant, 141 E Main St; 859-253-0014 www.alfalfarestaurant.com ✕

⚥ ● (♿) The Bar Complex, 224 E Main St; 859-255-1551 www.thebarcomplex.com **D** ▦ ✎

♂ ● ♿ Crossings Lexington, 117 N Limestone; 859-303-5005 www.crossingslexington.com **LW**

♂ ○ (♿) HIGH on Art & Coffee, 523 E High St; 859-396-4366 130469 **H** highonartandcoffee.com **K** ✕ ⊃ ✎ highonart andcoffee@gmail.com

Bookstores

♂ ○ Sqecial Media, 371 S Limestone St; 859-255-4316 www.sqecial.com

Funding: Endowment, Fundraising

⚥ ★ Imperial Court of Kentucky, POB 265 40588 tinyurl.com/qlsk79

Legal Services

♂ ● Elston Law Office, PLLC, Keith Doniphan Elston, Esq. 820 Tremont Ave; 40502 859-225-2348 www.eloplic.com elstonlaw@gmail.com

Organizations/Resources: Political/Legislative/Advocacy

⚥ ★ ♿ Lexington Fairness, POB 417; 40588 859-951-8565 www.lexfair.org

Organizations/Resources: Social, Recreation, Support

⚥ Lexington Lesbian Coffee House, fb.com/groups/LexLCH

Pets & Pet Services & Supplies

♂ ● Rainbow Watchers LLC - Professional Pet Care, 859-951-6391 www.rainbow-watchers.com petcare@rainbow-watchers.com

Real Estate (see also Mortgages)

♂ ○ Combs, Teresa, ABR, GRI, QSC, 859-489-1150 859-276-4811 teresacombs.rhr.com teresasellsky@gmail.com

Louisville

Community Centers and/or Pride Organizations

⚥ ★ Kentuckiana Pride Foundation, POB 32216 40232 502-649-4851 kypride.com

Accommodation: Hotels, Inns, Guesthouses, B&B, Resorts

♂ ● Columbine B&B, 1707 S 3rd St; 502-635-5000 www.thecolumbine.com ☺

AIDS/HIV Services, Education & Support

♀ House of Ruth, St. Mathews Campus, 607 E St Catherine St; 502-587-5080 www.houseofruth.net

Bars, Cafes, Clubs, Restaurants

⚥ ● Big Bar, 1202 Bardstown Rd; 502-618-2237 fb.com/BigBar-Louisville

♂ ○ Chill Bar Highlands, 1117 Bardstown Rd 859-913-8679 www.chillbarlouisville.com

♂ ○ Day's Espresso & Coffee Bar, 1420 Bardstown Rd 502-456-1170 dayscoffee.com ⊃

⚥ ○ El Mundo, 2345 Frankfort Ave; 502-899-9930 www.502elmundo.com ✕ @ixx=

Kentucky: Louisville
Bars, Cafes, Clubs, Restaurants

177

GAYELLOW PAGES #42 2020-2021

Paducah : Kentucky
AIDS/HIV Support

♂ ○ Magnolia Bar & Grill, 1398 S 2nd St 502-637-9052 www.magbarlouisville.com ⚤ ✕▥

♂ ○ ♿ Mayan Cafe, 813 E Market St 502-566-0651 www.themayancafe.com ✕

New Albany

⚲ PRIDE Bar & Lounge, 504 State St, New Albany, IN 812-200-9546 fb.com/NewAlbanyPride/

♂ ○ Nowhere Bar, 1133 Bardstown Rd; 502-451-0466 fb.com/NowhereLouisville/ **D**

⚲ Play Louisville, 1101 E Washington St 502-882-3615 www.playdancebar.com **D** ▥

♂ ● Teddy Bears Bar & Grill, 1148 Garvin Pl 502-589-2619 fb.com/myteddybearsbar/

♂ ● Tryangles, 209 S Preston St; 502-583-6395 fb.com/tryangleslouisville/

Bookstores

♀ ○ (?♿) **Carmichael's Bookstore, 1295 Bardstown Rd; 40204-1303 502-456-6950 Louisville's oldest independent bookstore. www.carmichaelsbookstore.com info@carmichaelsbookstore.com**

♀ ○ **Carmichael's Bookstore, 2720 Frankfort Ave 40206-2769 502-896-6950 Louisville's oldest independent bookstore. www.carmichaelsbookstore.com info@carmichaelsbookstore.com**

Clothes (see also Erotica, Leather)

♀ ○ Dirty Tease, 1551 Bardtown Rd; 40205 502-637-4601 www.dirtytease.net info@dirtytease.net

Counseling/Psychotherapy/Mental Health

♀ ○ Heitzman, Judy C, PhD, LCSW, 1711 Bardstown Rd #102; 40205 502-608-2472 www.drjudyheitzman.com drjudyheitzman@gmail.com

Funding: Endowment, Fundraising

♀ ☆ Louisville AIDS Walk, 326 E Main St 502-938-9255 www.kyaids.org/walk

Furniture

♀ ○ Red Tree, Inc, 701 E Market St; 502-582-2555 www.redtreefurniture.com

Legal Services

♀ ● (?♿) Diane Haag Law, 2241 State St Ste A PMB 240, New Albany, IN 47150 812-301-2155 fax 812-610-8259 **H?** Small business law dianehaaglaw.com admin@dianehaaglaw.com

Men's & Sex Clubs (not primarily Health Clubs)

♂ ● Vapor, 227 E Breckinridge St; 502-785-0818 www.vapor-spa.com

Organizations/Resources: Cultural, Dance, Performance

♂ Louisville Gay Men's Chorus, tinyurl.com/v379zse

⚲ Louisville LGBT Film Festival, 502-544-1975 tinyurl.com/meuwpmv

♀ ★ ♿ Pandora Productions, POB 4185; 40204 502-216-5502 (ticketing) 502-592-6009 (business) **H?** pandoraprods.org info@pandoraprods.org

♂ ★ ♿♿ Voices of Kentuckiana, POB 2904; 40201 502-583-1013 www.voicesky.org

Organizations/Resources: Family and Supporters

♀ ☆ (?♿) PFLAG Louisville, POB 5002 40255 502-233-1323 www.pflaglouisville.org

Organizations/Resources: Student, Academic, Education

♀ ★ Indiana University Southeast Spectrum, 4201 Grant Line Rd, New Albany, IN 47150-6405 812-941-2090 tinyurl.com/y9owf4xr sespectr@ius.edu

♀ ★ ♿♿ LGBT Center at University of Louisville, 502-852-0696 www.louisville.edu/lgbt ⚲

Organizations/Resources: Youth (see also Family)

♀ ★ Louisville Youth Group, 417 E Broadway 502-430-2016 louisvilleyouthgroup.org

Party/Holiday/Event Services (see also Catering, Weddings)

♂ ● ♿♿ Stephon & Friends, 502-551- 5021 fb.com/StephonLLC Stephoncamp@gmail.com

Real Estate (see also Mortgages)

♂ ● ♿♿ Ali, Ton A, Broker/Owner, Cornerstone Group Realtors, 2948 Yorkshire Blvd; 502-386-6244 cgr-ky.com ⚲

♀ ● McGill, Todd, Realtor, Forman, Jones & Associates Realtors, c02-418-5397 tinyurl.com/yb2qdj7d

Recovery

♂ ☆ Alcoholics Anonymous Kentucky Area 26, 332 W Broadway #620; 502-582-1849 www.area26.net/wp/

Religious / Spiritual Resources

♂ ☆ ♿♿ First Unitarian Church, 809 S 4th St; 40203 502-585-5110 www.firstulou.org ⚲ office@firstulou.org

♀ ★ ♿♿ MCC Louisville, St Andrew UCC, 2608 Browns Lane; 40220 502-587-6225 www.louisvillemcc.org louisvillemcc@gmail.com

♂ ☆ ♿♿ Thomas Jefferson Unitarian Church, 4936 Brownsboro Rd; 40222 502-425-6943 **H** www.tjuc.org ⚲ ❤ office@tjuc.org

Veterinarians

♂ ○ ♿ Downtown Animal Hospital, 120 N Clay St; 40202 502-585-1010 tinyurl.com/zshp55j

Owensboro

Religious / Spiritual Resources

♂ ☆ Unitarian Universalist Congregation, 1221 Cedar St; 42301 270-684-1548 www.uucowensboro.org hermitstuff@bellsouth.net

Paducah

AIDS/HIV Services, Education & Support

♀ Heartland Cares, POB 2875; 42002 270-444-8183 www.hca-res.org

Kentucky: Paducah
Religious
178
GAYELLOW PAGES #42 2020-2021
Lafayette : Louisiana
Community Centers / Pride

Religious / Spiritual Resources

⚥ ★ ♿ River of Hope MCC Of Paducah, 728 Tennessee St; 270-933-1673 fb.com/riverofhopepaducah

Somerset

Accommodation Rental: Furnished / Vacation (& AirBNB)

♂ ○ Lost Lodge Resort, 265 Lost Lodge Rd; 42501-6040 606-561-4451 lostlodge.com ⚓ ⊗ info@lostlodge.com

Organizations/Resources: Family and Supporters

♂ PFLAG Somerset, 606-425-7387 tinyurl.com/vuxf2xx

Springfield

Accommodation: Hotels, Inns, Guesthouses, B&B, Resorts

♂ ● Maple Hill Manor, 2941 Perryville Rd (US 150 E) 859-336-3075 www.maplehillmanor.com ⚓ ⊗

Louisiana
State/County Resources

Archives/Libraries/Museums/History Projects

⚥ ★ LGBT+ Archives Project, Inc., lgbtarchiveslouisiana.org

Health Care: Physical (see also Counseling/Mental Health)

♂ ☆ CrescentCare, 1631 Elysian Fields Ave, New Orleans, LA 504-821-2601 www.crescentcarehealth.com

Organizations/Resources: Political/Legislative/Advocacy

⚥ ★ Forum For Equality, 4519 S Claiborne Ave, New Orleans, LA 504-569-9156 www.forumforequality.com

⚥ ★ Louisiana Human Rights Campaign, 5721 Magazine St PMB #214, New Orleans, LA hrc.org/neworleans

ᴛ Louisiana Trans Advocates, 4500 Government St #66193, Baton Rouge, LA 504-450-7496 www.latransadvocates.org

⚥ ★ People Acting for Change & Equality, POB 52256, Shreveport, LA 71115 www.pacelouisiana.org pacelouisiana@gmail.com

Organizations/Resources: Youth (see also Family)

⚥ ★ PACE People Acting for Change & Equality, 1as, POB 52256, Shreveport, LA 71115 tinyurl.com/y55l288w PACEYoungAdult@gmail.com

Abbeville

Religious / Spiritual Resources

♂ ☆ ♿ St Pelagius of the Celts Chapel, 101 E Vermilion St, Abbeville; 70510 337-240-7773 fb.com/stpelagiuschapel/ stpelagiuschapel@gmail.com

Alexandria

Community Centers and/or Pride Organizations

⚥ CENLA PRIDE, 318-442-1010 fb.comm/CENLACLASSPRIDE/

AIDS/HIV Services, Education & Support

♀ ☆ Central Louisiana AIDS Support Services, 1785 Jackson St; 318-442-1010 class.life

♂ ☆ CLASS Gay Men's Wellness Center, 1785 Jackson St; 318-442-1010 class.life

Baton Rouge

AIDS/HIV Services, Education & Support

♀ ☆ Baton Rouge AIDS Society (BRASS), 4560 North Blvd Ste 1001; 225-923-2437 tinyurl.com/2kav8u

Bars, Cafes, Clubs, Restaurants

⚥ ● ♿ George's Place, 860 St Louis St; 225-387-9798 www.georgesplacebr.com **KV** ▥

⚥ ● Splash, 2183 Highland Rd; 225-242-9491 www.splashbr.com **D** ▥

Counseling/Psychotherapy/Mental Health

♀ ○ ♿ Cuneo, Carlo, LCSW, 3080 Teddy Dr Ste A; 70809-1925 225-923-8255 (923-TALK) www.redstickmh.com carlo@redstickmh.com

Grooming, Personal Care, Spa Services

♀ ● ♿ Shear Illusions Hair Salon, 7942 Picardy Ave Ste A; 70809 225-757-9118 tinyurl.com/292ghc ✗ shear illusions_salon@yahoo.com

Locksmiths

♀ ○ Automotive Locksmith, 225-907-1231 Mobile State licensed locksmith www.locksmithsbatonrouge.com

Organizations/Resources: Social, Recreation, Support

⚥ ★ Capital City Alliance (CCA), POB 1583 70821 225-366-7487 www.ccabatonrouge.org

⚥ ★ Mystic Krewe of Apollo Baton Rouge, POB 3591 70821 www.apollobatonrouge.com

Religious / Spiritual Resources

⚥ ★ MCC Baton Rouge, 7747 Tom Dr; 225-248-0404 www.mccbr.org

♀ ☆ ♿ University Presbyterian Church, 3240 Dalrymple Dr; 70802 225-383-0345 **HD** www.upcbr.org ✗

Hammond

Organizations/Resources: Student, Academic, Education

⚥ ★ ♿ Southeastern Louisiana University standOUT, Dept. of Sociology/Criminal Justice, Box 10686 985-549-2108 ✗

» Harvey: see New Orleans Area
» Kenner: see New Orleans Area

Lafayette

Community Centers and/or Pride Organizations

⚥ Acadiana Pride, - - www.acadianapride.org

Louisiana: Lafayette
Accommodation
179
GAYELLOW PAGES #42 2020-2021
New Orleans Area: Louisiana
Accommodation

Accommodation: Hotels, Inns, Guesthouses, B&B, Resorts
Breaux Bridge

♂ ○ Maison Des Amis, 111 Washington St, Breaux Bridge; 70517-5141 337-507-3399 www.maisondesamis.com ⚲ ⊛ seeyou@maisondesamis.com

AIDS/HIV Services, Education & Support

♀ Acadiana CARES, 809 Martin Luther King Jr Dr 337-233-2437 www.acadianacares.org

Bars, Cafes, Clubs, Restaurants

♀ Bolt Bar and Patio, 114 McKinley St 337-534-4913 fb.comm/Bolt-laffy **D**

Counseling/Psychotherapy/Mental Health

♀ ○ Huval, James, LCSW, 143 Ridgeway Dr 337-356-1343 www.huvalmsw.com

Health Care: Physical (see also Counseling/Mental Health)

♂ ★ Acadiana Gay Mens Wellness Center, 811 Martin Luther King Jr Dr; 337-233-2437 x150 fb.com/agmwc/

Organizations/Resources: Social, Recreation, Support

♂ ★ ♿ Mystic Krewe of Apollo de Lafayette, POB 53251; 70505 337-443-0669 kreweofapollo.com

♀ Royal Order of Unicorn, royalorderofunicorn.com

Lake Charles

Accommodation: Hotels, Inns, Guesthouses, B&B, Resorts

♀ ● Aunt Ruby's B&B, 504 Pujo St; 337-430-0603 auntrubys.com ⚲

AIDS/HIV Services, Education & Support

♀ ☆ Southwest Louisiana AIDS Council, 425 Kingsley St; 337-439-5861 www.slac.org

Bars, Cafes, Clubs, Restaurants

♀ Crystal's Downtown, 112 W Broad St 337-433-5457 fb.com/crystaldowntown/ **D** 🎵

♀ ● Pujo St Cafe, 901 Ryan St; 337-439-2054 www.pujostreet.com ⛃

>> Metairie: see New Orleans Area

Monroe

AIDS/HIV Services, Education & Support

♀ GO CARE (Greater Ouachita Coalition), 1801 N 7th St Ste A, West Monroe; 800-286-1092 www.go-care.org

Bars, Cafes, Clubs, Restaurants

♀ Club Pink, 1914 Roselawn Ave; 318-654-7030 fb.com/CLUB-PINKMONROE **D** 🎵

New Orleans Area

Community Centers and/or Pride Organizations

♀ ★ LGBT Community Center of New Orleans, Administrative Office, 2727 S Broad St Ste 101, NO; 70125 **H?** lgbtccneworleans.org ⚲ support@lgbtccneworleans.org

♀ ★ New Orleans Pride, POB 52343, NO 70152-2343 togetherwenola.com/pride/ info@neworleanspridefestival.com

Information, Media & Publications

♀ Dykeadence, fb.com/dykeadence/

Accommodation: Communities, Intentional

♀ ☆ ♿ Hagar's House, First Grace Community Alliance, 3401 Canal St, NO; 504-210-5064 Trans-inclusive www.HagarsHouseNOLA.org ⚲

Accommodation: Hotels, Inns, Guesthouses, B&B, Resorts
New Orleans

♀ ● Aaron Ingram Haus, 504-949-3110 www.ingramhaus.com ⚲ ⊛ ingramhaus@yahoo.com

♂ ● (?♿) Antebellum Guest House, 1333 Esplanade Ave, NO; 504-943-1900 www.antebellumguesthouse.com ⚲ ⊛

♀ ○ B&W Courtyard B&B, 2425 Chartres St, NO 70117-8606 800-585-5731 www.bandwcourtyards.com **X** ⚲

♀ ● Bon Maison Guest House, 835 Bourbon St, NO 504-561-8498 www.bonmaison.com

♂ ● The Burgundy Bed & Breakfast, 2513 Burgundy St, NO; 70117-7831 504-261-9477 www.theburgundy.com ⚲ ⊛ joe@theburgundy.com

♀ ● Bywater Bed & Breakfast, 1026 Clouet St, NO 504-944-8438 www.bywaterbnb.com ⊛

♂ ○ (?♿) Creole Gardens B&B Hotel, 1415 Prytania St, NO; 70130-4413 504-569-8700 creolegardens.com ☪ ⚲ ⊛

♂ ● Crescent City Guest House, 612 Marigny St, NO 504-944-8722 www.crescentcitygh.com ⚲ ⊛

♂ ○ ♿ The Frenchmen Hotel, 417 Frenchmen St, NO; 70116-2000 504-945-5453 www.frenchmenhotel.com info@frenchmenhotel.com

Louisiana: New Orleans Area
Accommodation

180

GAYELLOW PAGES #42 2020-2021

New Orleans Area: Louisiana
Organizations: Family

♀ ● Garden District B&B, 2418 Magazine St, NO 70130-5604 504-895-4302 tinyurl.com/ywffkr ✄ ⊕ ⊕

♂ ● The Green House Inn, 1212 Magazine St, NO 70130-4220 504-525-1333 www.thegreenhouseinn.com **N** (☀?) ✄ ⊕ thegreenhouseinn@gmail.com

♀ ● HH Whitney House, 1923 Esplanade Ave, NO 70116-1706 504-948-9448 800-924-9448 www.hhwhitneyhouse.com ✄ ⊕ stay@hhwhitneyhouse.com

♂ ● La Dauphine, 2316 Dauphine St, NO 70117-8506 504-948-2217 fax 504-948-3420 www.ladauphine.com ✄ ⊕

♀ ● La Maison Marigny Bed & Breakfast, 1421 Bourbon St, NO; 504-948-3638 www.lamaisonmarigny.com ✄ ⊕

♀ ○ ♿ Maison Dupuy Hotel, 1001 Rue Toulouse, NO; 70112 504-586-8000 **H** ● www.maisondupuy.com ✄ ⊕ ⊕

♀ ○ Nine-O-Five Royal Hotel, 905 Royal St, NO 70116-2701 504-523-0210 www.905royalHotel.com info@905royalHotel.com

♀ ● Pierre Coulon Guest House, 714 Spain St, NO 504-943-6692 tinyurl.com/yxmlbrt3 ✄ ⊕

♀ ○ ♿ **Royal Frenchmen Hotel and Bar, 700 Frenchmen St, NO; 70116 504-619-9660 Mention Gayellow Pages and book direct by calling for 10 percent discount. www.royalfrenchmenhotel.com** ✄ ⊕ ⊕ ♥ info@royalfrenchmenhotel

♀ ○ St Philip Hotel, 612 Rue St Philip, NO 504-523-2197 www.thestphiliphotel.com (☀?) ✄ ⊕ @ixx=

♀ ● Sunburst Inn, 819 Mandeville St, NO 504-947-1799 www.sunburstinn.net ✄ ⊕

AIDS/HIV Services, Education & Support

♂ ☆ ♿ New Orleans Regional AIDS Planning Council (NO-RAPC), 2601 Tulane Ave Ste 400, NO; 504-821-7334 **H?** no-rapc.org

♂ ☆ Project Lazarus, POB 3906, NO; 70177 504-949-3609 www.projectlazarus.net

Archives/Libraries/Museums/History Projects

♀ Last Call: New Orleans Dyke Bar History Project, 504-358-8654 www.lastcallnola.org

Bars, Cafes, Clubs, Restaurants
Metairie

♂ ● (?♿) The Four Seasons & Patio Stage Bar, 3229 N Causeway Blvd, Metairie; 504-832-0659 www.fourseasonsbar.com **DCW** ▥

New Orleans

♂ ● 700 Club, 700 Burgundy St, NO 504-561-1095 www.700club-neworleans.com

♀ ● ♿ All Ways Lounge & Theater, 2240 St Claude, NO; 504-218-5778 theallwayslounge.com **D** ▥ ✄

♂ (?♿) Big Daddy's, 2513 Royal St, NO; 504-948-6288 **D**

♂ ● Bourbon Pub & Parade Disco, 801 Bourbon St, NO; 504-529-2107 fax 504-524-2864 www.bourbonpub.com **D** ✄ info@bourbonpub.com

♀ ○ ♿ Cafe Amelie, 912 Royal St, NO 504-412-8965 www.cafeamelie.com ⚲ ✖ ♂

♂ ● Cafe Lafitte in Exile, 901 Bourbon St, NO 504-522-8397 www.lafittes.com **DK** ✖ ⚲

♀ ● Clover Grill, 900 Bourbon St, NO; 504-523-0904 www.clover-grill.com ✖

♂ ● Corner Pocket, 940 St Louis, NO; 504-568-9829 fb.com/cornerpocketnola/ **D** ▥

♂ Crossing NOLA, 439 Dauphine St, NO 504-523-4517 www.cross-ingnola.com

♂ Cutter's, 706 Franklin Ave, NO; 504-948-4200 fb.com/CuttersNOLA/

♂ Friendly Bar, 2301 Chartres St, NO 504-943-8929 tinyurl.com/nz5abpt

♀ Golden Lantern Bar, 1239 Royal St, NO 504-529-2860 fb.com/GoldenLanternBar/ ⚲ ✖

♂ Good Friends Bar & Queens Head Pub, 740 Dauphine St, NO; 504-566-7191 www.goodfriendsbar.com **S**

♂ GrandPre's, 834 N Rampart St, NO 504-267-3615 fb.com/grandpres/ ▥

♂ ○ Kajun's Pub, 2256 St Claude Ave, NO 504-947-3735 www.kajunpub.com

♀ Mag's 940, 940 Elysian Fields, NO 504-948-1888 tinyurl.com/y343gjpb **D** ▥

♀ ○ Meauxbar Bistro, 942 N Rampart St, NO 504-569-9979 www.meauxbar.com ✖

♂ ● Napoleon's Itch, 734 Bourbon St, NO 504-237-4144 fb.com/Napoleonsitch/

♂ ● Oz, 800 Bourbon St, NO; 504-593-9491 www.oznew-orleans.com **D** ▥

♀ ○ ♿ Pal's Lounge, 949 N Rendon St, NO; 504-488-PALS www.PalsLounge.com ✄ info@PalsLounge.com

♀ ● (?♿) Phillips, 733 Cherokee St, NO 504-865-1155 www.phillipsbar.com **D** ⚲ ✖ ♂ ✄

♂ ● The Phoenix/Eagle, 941 Elysian Fields Ave, NO 504-945-9264 phoenixbarnola.com **L**

♂ ● Rawhide 2010, 740 Burgundy St, NO 504-525-8106 www.rawhide2010.com **LW**

♂ ○ Spotted Cat Music Club, 623 Frenchmen St, NO www.spottedcatmusicclub.com ▥

Conferences/Events/Festivals/Workshops

♂ Saints and Sinners Literary Festival, 938 Lafayette St #514, NO; 504.581.1144 sasfest.org

Organizations/Resources: Cultural, Dance, Performance

♂ ★ (?♿) New Orleans Gay Men's Chorus, mail to NOGMC, POB 19365, NO; 70179 504-322-7007 www.nogmc.com

Organizations/Resources: Family and Supporters

♀ ☆ (♿) PFLAG New Orleans, POB 15515, NO; 70175 504-862-5912 www.pflagno.org

Louisiana: New Orleans Area
Organizations: Political

181

GAYELLOW PAGES #42 2020-2021

State/County Resources : Maine
Health Care

Organizations/Resources: Political/Legislative/Advocacy

♂ ☆ (♀♂) American Civil Liberties Union: Louisiana Affiliate, POB 56157, NO; 70156 504-522-0617 www.laaclu.org

Organizations/Resources: Senior Resources

♀ NOAGE:New Orleans Advocates for GLBT Elders, 504-517-2345 www.noagenola.org

Organizations/Resources: Social, Recreation, Support

♀ Girl Crush, www.xxcrush.com

♂ ★ Greater New Orleans Prime Timers, 504-681-5728 tinyurl.com/omen4ya

♀ Krewe of Amon-Ra, POB 7033, Metairie 70010 kreweofamon-ra.com

♂ ★ Krewe of Armeinius, 435 N Broad St, NO 920-306-1969 Armeinius.org

♂ ★ Lords of Leather Mardi Gras Krewe, 1000 Bourbon St #B415, NO; 985-687-7380 www.lordsofleather.org **L**

♀ Renegade Bears of Louisiana, POB 10497, NO 70119 www.renegadebearsofla.com

Organizations/Resources: Student, Academic, Education

♂ ★ Loyola PLUS+, Student Activities Office, Box 214 6363 St Charles Ave, NO; 504-865-2835 orgsync.com/67502/chapter

♂ ★ Tulane Law School Lambda Law Alliance, Weinmann Hall Room 349, 6329 Freret St, NO; 801-376-8620 tinyurl.com/y6o6vcnb

♂ ★ Tulane University Office of Gender & Sexual Diversity (OGSD), Lavin-Bernick Center (LBC), 29 McAlister Dr, NO; 70118 504-314-2183 tinyurl.com/y2bjj3j8 ogsd@tulane.edu

♂ ★ University of New Orleans Unity, Office of Student Involvement and Leadership, 2000 Lakeshore Dr, NO; 504-616-2625 tinyurl.com/y6zu3d83

Organizations/Resources: Youth (see also Family)

♀ Break OUT, 4327 Canal St, NO; 504-252-9025 www.youthbreakout.org

♀ LOUD: New Orleans Queer Youth Theater, neworleansqyt.wix.com/loud

Pets & Pet Services & Supplies

♂ ● Chi-wa-wa Ga-ga, 511 Dumaine St, NO 504-581-4242 **Pet costumes, clothing, and accessories for your petite pampered pooch. www.chiwawagaga.com**

Pharmacies (see also Health Care Supplies)

♀ ○ Mumfrey's Pharmacy, 1021 W Judge Perez Dr, Chalmette; 70043-4703 504-279-6312 fax 504-279-6314 mumfreyspharmacy.com Mumfreyspharmacy@bellsouth.net

Recovery

♂ ☆ AA New Orleans Central Office, 638 Papworth Ave Ste A, Metairie; 70005-3123 504-838-3399 www.aaneworleans.org office@aaneworleans.org

Religious / Spiritual Resources

♂ ★ ♿ The Metropolitan Community Church of New Orleans, 5401 S Claiborne Ave, NO; 504-270-1622 mccneworleans.com

♀ ☆ St Anna's Episcopal Church, 1313 Esplanade Ave, NO; 70116 504-947-2121 www.stannanola.org

Sports & Outdoor

♀ ☆ Big Easy Rollergirls, www.bigeasyrollergirls.com

♂ Crescent City Rougaroux Rugby, www.rougarouxrugby.org

♀ NOLA's Softball League, nolasoftball.org

♀ Stonewall Sports - New Orleans, tinyurl.com/y3wv2535

Shreveport

AIDS/HIV Services, Education & Support

♀ ☆ The Philadelphia Center, 2020 Centenary Blvd 318-222-6633 www.philadelphiacenter.org

Bars, Cafes, Clubs, Restaurants

♀ ● ♿ Central Station, 1025 Marshall St; 318-222-2216 fb.com/centralstation **D** 🍽

♀ Korner Lounge II, 800 Louisiana Ave 318-222-9796 fb.com/KornerLounge

Organizations/Resources: Cultural, Dance, Performance

♀ ★ North Louisiana Gay & Lesbian Film Festival (NLGLFF), c/o PACE, POB 52256; 71135 nlglff.org

Organizations/Resources: Family and Supporters

♂ ☆ ♿ PFLAG of Shreveport & Bossier City, 318-638-8609 tinyurl.com/84tcpmq

Organizations/Resources: Student, Academic, Education

♀ ★ Centenary College of Louisiana Outreach, 2911 Centenary Blvd; 318-294-2207 fb.com/groups/178691860755

Maine
State/County Resources

AIDS/HIV Services, Education & Support

♂ ☆ ♿ AIDS Response Seacoast, 7 Junkins Ave, Portsmouth, NH 603-433-5377 www.aidsresponse.org

♀ ♿ Maine General Horizon HIV Program, 35 Medical Center Parkway, Augusta, ME 855-464-4463 tinyurl.com/pysk4cy

Campgrounds and RV Parks

♂ ● 'Camp' Camp, 347-453-5257 www.campcamp.com ⊛ info@campcamp.com

Health Care: Physical (see also Counseling/Mental Health)

♀ ☆ Maine Center For Disease Control & Prevention, 11 State House Station, 286 Water St, Augusta, ME 207-287-8016 www.maine.gov/dhhs/boh/

Maine: State/County Resources
Insurance

182

GAYELLOW PAGES #42 2020-2021

Blue Hill Peninsula: Maine
Religious

Insurance (see also Financial Planning)

♂ ○ Web Insurance Agency, POB 9, Rollinsford, NH 03869-0009 603-740-4353 fax 603-740-2953

Organizations/Resources: Political/Legislative/Advocacy

♀ ☆ ACLU of Maine, 121 Middle St Ste 301, Portland, ME 207-774-5444 www.aclumaine.org

⚥ ★ EqualityMaine, 207-761-3732 www.equalitymaine.org

♀ ☆ Religious Coalition Against Discrimination, 68 Pleasant St, Brunswick, ME 207-370-7382 www.rcadmaine.org

Organizations/Resources: Transgender/Gender Non-Conforming/Diverse

т ☆ MaineTransNet, Equality Community Center, 511 Congress St, Portland, ME 04101 207-370-0359 www.mainetransnet.org info@mainetransnet.org

т ☆ Trans Youth Equality Foundation, c/o SMFA, PO Box 7441, Portland, ME 04112 207-478-4087 www.transyouthequality.org

Organizations/Resources: Youth (see also Family)

⚥ ★ OUT Maine, POB 1723, Rockland, ME 04841 800-530-6997 OUTMaine.org info@outmaine.org

Recovery

♀ ☆ Alcoholics Anonymous Central Service Office, 47 Portland St, Portland, ME 800-737-6237 www.csoaamaine.org

Albion

Accommodation: Hotels, Inns, Guesthouses, B&B, Resorts
China Village

♂ ● 🐾 Twin Ponds Lodge, POB 6288, China Village, ME 04926 207-437-2200 www.TwinPondsLodge.com **NP** ✔ 🚭
>> Auburn: see Lewiston

Augusta

Accommodation: Hotels, Inns, Guesthouses, B&B, Resorts
Hallowell

♀ ● 🐾 Maple Hill Farm B&B Inn, 11 Inn Rd, Hallowell; 04347-3241 207-622-2708 800-622-2708 fax 207-622-0655 www.MapleBB.com ✔ 🚭 stay@MapleBB.com

Accommodation: Residential/Sharing/Roommates

⚥ ★ (?⚥) EGR Writers House, Winthrop Smith, program manager, 28 Blaine Ave; 04330 Subsidised housing for writers from the LGBTQ community. See blog for details. egrwritershouse.blogspot.com ✔ mainepoet@gmail.com

Bars, Cafes, Clubs, Restaurants
Hallowell

♂ ○ 🐾 Slate's Restaurant & Bakery, 163 Water St, Hallowell; 207-622-9575 www.slatesrestaurant.com 🍴 ✖ ✔

Legal Services

♂ ● (?⚥) Farnsworth, Susan, Esq, Farnsworth Law Office, 2 Beech St, Hallowell; / 100 2nd St 207-626-3312 www.susan-farnsworth.com

Bangor

AIDS/HIV Services, Education & Support

♂ ☆ 🐾 Health Equity Alliance, 304 Hancock St Ste 3B; 207-990-3626 www.mainehealthequity.org

Bookstores

♂ ○ ♿ Pro Libris Bookshop, 10 3rd St 207-942-3019 tinyurl.com/5vr5oor

Health Care: Physical (see also Counseling/Mental Health)

♀ ☆ Mabel Wadsworth Women's Health Center, 700 Mount Hope Ave #420; 800-948-5337 www.mabelwadsworth.org

Religious / Spiritual Resources

♂ ☆ (?⚥) Hammond Street Congregational Church, 28 High Street; 04401 207-942-4381 **H** hammondstreetchurch.org hscc@midmaine.com

♂ ☆ Unitarian Universalist Society of Bangor, 120 Park St; 04401 207-947-7009 www.uubangor.org uubangor@gmail.com
>> Bar Harbor: see Down East, Acadia, Mt Desert Isle

Bath

Accommodation: Hotels, Inns, Guesthouses, B&B, Resorts

♂ ● Benjamin F. Packard House, 45 Pearl St 866-361-6004 benjaminfpackardhouse.com ✔ 🚭

Religious / Spiritual Resources

♂ ☆ 🐾 The Neighborhood, United Church of Christ, 798 Washington St; 04530 207-443-2187 www.faithinbath.org ✔ neighborhooducc@gmail.com

Bethel

Accommodation: Hotels, Inns, Guesthouses, B&B, Resorts

♂ ● Chapman Inn, POB 1067; 04217 207-824-2657 877-359-1498 www.chapmaninn.com (⚥?) 🚭
Rumford Point

♂ ● Perennial Inn, 141 Jed Martin Rd, Rumford Point; 207-369-0309 www.perennialinn.com (⚥?) 🚭

Blaine

Accommodation: Hotels, Inns, Guesthouses, B&B, Resorts

♂ ● Magic Pond Wildlife Sanctuary & Guest House, PO Box 174; 04734 215-287-4174 Magicpondmaine.com (⚥?)

Blue Hill Peninsula

Accommodation: Hotels, Inns, Guesthouses, B&B, Resorts
Blue Hill

♂ ● (?⚥) Blue Hill Inn, 40 Union St, Blue Hill; 207-374-2844 **HC** www.bluehillinn.com (⚥?) ✔ 🚭 🚭

Religious / Spiritual Resources

♂ ☆ 🐾 Unitarian Universalist Congregation, POB 520, Castine; 04421 / 86 Court St 207-326-9083 **H?** www.uucastine.org ✔

Maine: Brunswick
Bookstores

183

GAYELLOW PAGES #42 2020-2021

Ogunquit Area: Maine
Information, Media & Publications

Brunswick

Bookstores

♂ ○ (♿) Gulf of Maine Books, 134 Maine St; 207-729-5083 tinyurl.com/kvhf3d

Organizations/Resources: Student, Academic, Education

⚥ ★ (♿) Bowdoin Queer-Straight Alliance, 24 College St; 207-798-4223 tinyurl.com/y7tedbpo

Camden

Accommodation: Hotels, Inns, Guesthouses, B&B, Resorts

♂ ○ Blue Harbor House Inn, 67 Elm St; 04843-1904 800-248-3196 **H?** www.blueharborhouse.com (♣?) ✔ ⊛ info@blueharborhouse.com

♀ ● (♿) The Towne Motel, 68 Elm St 207-236-3377 www.camdenmotel.com (♣?) ✔ ⊛

Bookstores

♂ ○ Owl & Turtle Bookshop Cafe, 33 Bayview St; 04843 207-230-7335 www.owlandturtle.com ☞ info@owlandturtle.com

Caratunk

Accommodation: Hotels, Inns, Guesthouses, B&B, Resorts

♀ ● The Sterling Inn, 1041 US Rte 201; 04925 207-672-3333 www.mainesterlinginn.com ♣ ✔ ⊛⊛ maineskeptsecret@yahoo.com

» Castine: see Blue Hill Peninsula

Corea

Accommodation: Hotels, Inns, Guesthouses, B&B, Resorts

♂ ○ Black Duck Inn, POB 157; 04624 207-963-2689 blackduckme.com (♣?) ✔ ⊛⊛ info@blackduckme.com

Cumberland

Religious / Spiritual Resources

♀ ☆ ♿ Cumberland Congregational UCC, 282 Main St 207-829-3419 **HD** www.cumberlanducc.org ✔

Denmark

Accommodation Rental: Furnished / Vacation (& AirBNB)

♂ ○ Red Shed Cottage, Pickett Hill Farm, 133 Pickett Hill Rd; 207-452-2239 www.picketthillfarm.com ✔ ⊛

Down East, Acadia, Mt Desert Isle

AIDS/HIV Services, Education & Support

♂ ☆ ♿ Health Equity Alliance, 25A Pine St, Ellsworth; 207-667-3506 www.mainehealthequity.org

♂ ☆ ♿ Health Equity Alliance, 7 VIP Road, Machias; 207-255-5849 www.mainehealthequity.org

Bars, Cafes, Clubs, Restaurants
Bar Harbor

♂ ○ ♿ Cafe This Way, 14 1/2 Mt Desert St, Bar Harbor; 207-288-4483 www.cafethisway.com ⚧ ✂☞

♂ ● Mama DiMatteo's, 34 Kennebec Pl, Bar Harbor 207-288-3666 www.mamadimatteos.com ⚧ ✂ ✔

Organizations/Resources: Student, Academic, Education

⚥ ★ ♿ Omicron Delta Pi, University of Maine Machias, 116 O'Brien Ave, Machias tinyurl.com/z9hd5wt

♂ ☆ ♿ University of Maine Machias 100% Society, 116 O'Brien Ave, Machias; 04654 207-255-1200. **H?** tinyurl.com/z9hd5wt ✔

» Ellsworth: see Down East, Acadia, Mt Desert Isle

Falmouth

Accommodation: Hotels, Inns, Guesthouses, B&B, Resorts

♂ ○ Quaker Tavern B&B Inn, 377 Gray Rd; 04105-2520 207-797-5540 quakertavern.com (♣?) ✔ ⊛⊛ quakerbb@aol.com

Farmington

Bookstores

♀ ○ ♿ Devany Doak & Garrett Booksellers, 193 Broadway; 04938-5909 207-778-3454 www.ddgbooks.com kenny@ddgbooks.com

Organizations/Resources: Student, Academic, Education

⚥ ★ ♿ University of Maine at Farmington Rainbow League, 117 South St; 04938 207-778-7335 fb.com/TRLUMF/ umf.rainbowleague@gmail.com

Georgetown

Accommodation: Hotels, Inns, Guesthouses, B&B, Resorts

♂ ○ ♿ Grey Havens Inn, 96 Seguinland Rd; 207-371-2616 www.greyhavens.com ✔ ⊛⊛

Kittery

Organizations/Resources: Social, Recreation, Support

⚥ ★ Seacoast Gay Men, 33 Government St seacoastgaymen.org

Lewiston

Organizations/Resources: Youth (see also Family)

⚥ ★ Outright Lewiston/Auburn, POB 433; 04243 207-795-4077 LGBTQ youth age 21 & under www.outrightla.org

Religious / Spiritual Resources

♂ ☆ ♿ First Universalist Church, 207-783-0461 www.auburnuu.org office@auburnuu.org

Ogunquit Area

Information, Media & Publications

⚥ ★ Gay Ogunquit, 954-816-5286 www.gayogunquit.com

Maine: Ogunquit Area
Accommodation

184

GAYELLOW PAGES #42 2020-2021

Portland Area: Maine
Community Centers / Pride

Accommodation: Hotels, Inns, Guesthouses, B&B, Resorts
Kennebunk

♂ ○ Waldo Emerson Inn, 108 Summer St, Kennebunk 207-985-4250 www.waldoemerson.com

Ogunquit

♀ ● 2 Village Square Inn, 14 Village Square Lane, Ogunquit; 207-646-5779 www.2vsquare.com ✔

♂ ● Beauport Inn, POB 811, Ogunquit; 03907 / 339 Clay Hill/Agamenticus Rd 207-361-2400 www.beauportinn.com ✔ ⊛ ⊛ info@beauportinn.com

♂ ● Black Boar Inn, POB 854, Ogunquit; 03907 207-646-2112 www.blackboarinn.com

♂ ● The Dolphin Den - Ogunquit, POB 1496, Ogunquit; 03907 / 69 Cottage St 207-646-5639 www.thedolphinden.com (♣?) (⊛)

♂ ● Gazebo Inn, 572 Main St, Ogunquit 207-646-3733 www.gazeboguesthouse.com

♀ ● Leisure Inn, POB 2113, Ogunquit; 03907 / 73 School St 207-646-2737 www.Theleisureinn.com ✔

♂ ● Moon Over Maine, 22 Berwick Rd, Ogunquit 207-646-6666 www.moonovermaine.com ✔ ⊛

♀ ● (?♧) Ogunquit Beach Inn, 67 School St, Ogunquit; 207-646-1112 www.ogunquitbeachinn.com ✔

♀ ● The Ogunquit Inn, 17 Glen Ave, Ogunquit 207-646-3633 www.theogunquitinn.com ✔ ⊛

♂ ● Rockmere Lodge B&B, POB 278, Ogunquit; 03907 207-646-2985 www.rockmere.com ⊛

♂ ● Yellow Monkey Guest Houses & Motel, POB 478, Ogunquit; 03907 / 280 Main St 207-646-9056 Seven Guest homes consisting of deluxe rooms, apartments & cottages. tinyurl.com/ydxgj5u8

Wells

♂ ● Holiday Guest House, 68 Post Rd, Wells 207-646-5400 www.holidayguesthousebnb.com ✔

Bars, Cafes, Clubs, Restaurants
Cape Neddick

♂ ○ Clay Hill Farm, 220 Clay Hill Road, Cape Neddick 207-361-2272 www.clayhillfarm.com ♈ ✖

Ogunquit

♀ ● (?♧) Amore Breakfast, 87 Main St, Ogunquit; 207-646-6667 www.amorebreakfast.com ☞ ✔

♀ ○ Angelina's Ristorante, 655 Main St, Ogunquit 207-646-0445 www.angelinasogunquit.com ♈ ✖

♂ ○ Backyard Coffeehouse & Eatery, Rte 1, Ogunquit 207-251-4554 www.backyardogunquit.com ✖

♀ ○ BeachFire Bar & Grille, 658 Main St (Rte 1, Footbridge Village) 207-646-8998 www.beachfiremaine.com ♈ ✖

♀ ● Bessie's, 8 Shore Rd 207-646-0888 eatatbessies.com ♈ ✖

♀ ○ Bintliff's Ogunquit, 335 Main St, Ogunquit 207-646-3111 bintliffsogunquit.com ✖

♂ ○ Bread & Roses Bakery, 246 Main Stt 207-646-4227 www.breadandrosesbakery.com ☞

♂ ○ Caffé Prego, 44 Shore Rd, Ogunquit 207-646-7734 www.caffepregoogt.com ☞

♀ ○ Five-O, 50 Shore Road, Ogunquit; 207-646-5001 five-oshoreroad.com ♈ ✖

♀ ● The Front Porch Piano Bar & Restaurant, 9 Shore Rd, Ogunquit; 207-646-4005 www.thefrontporch.com ♈ ✖ ▥

♂ ○ Jonathan's, 92 Bourne Ln 207-646-4777 www.jonathansogunquit.com ✖▥ info@jonathansogunquit.com

♀ ● ᴕᴕ Maine Street, 195 Main St (Rte 1) 207-646-5101 www.mainestreetogunquit.com **DKV** ▥ ✔

♀ ○ ᴕᴕ MC Perkins Cove, 111 Perkins Cove Rd 207-646-6263 fb.com/MCPerkinsCove ♈ ✖

♀ ○ Old Village Inn, 250 Main St, Ogunquit 207-646-7088 www.theoldvillageinn.net ♈ ✖

♀ ○ Pizza Napoli, 667 Main St, Ogunquit 207-646-0303 www.pizzanapoliogunquit.com ✖

♀ ○ Robertos Italian Restaurant, 200 Shore Rd, Ogunquit; 207-646-8130 robertos.com ✖ info@robertos.com

♀ ● ᴕᴕ Roost Cafe & Bistro, 262 Shore Rd, Ogunquit; 207-646-9898 www.RoostCafeandBistro.com ♈ ✖ ☞ ✔

♀ ● ᴕᴕ Women's T Dance at Maine Street, check schedule 207-646-5101 tinyurl.com/h62b8mp **DV**

Massage Therapy (Certified/Licensed only)

♀ ● Cotnoir, Wayne, LMT, Massage Therapist, Yellow Monkey Guest House, Main St 401-529-1722 www.massagebywayne.net massagebywayneogt@gmail.com

Religious / Spiritual Resources

♀ ☆ ᴕᴕ United Methodist Church, POB 521, York; 03909 / 1026 US RT 1, York 207-363-2749 **H?** www.youmc.org ✔ pastor.youmc@gmail.com

Orland

Accommodation Rental: Furnished / Vacation (& AirBNB)

♀ ○ Riverhouse, 1175 Castine Rd, Orland; 04472-3714 207-469-2533 www.riverhouse.me ✔ ⊛

Orono

Organizations/Resources: Student, Academic, Education

♀ ★ ᴕᴕ University of Maine Wilde Stein Alliance / Rainbow Resource Center, Room 162, 5748 Memorial Union 207-581-1439 tinyurl.com/hx5aexd ✔

» Penobscot: see Blue Hill Peninsula

Portland Area

Crisis, Anti-violence, & Helplines

♀ ☆ ᴕᴕ Family Crisis Services, POB 704, Portland; 04104 800-537-5066 **H** www.familycrisis.org

♀ ☆ Sexual Assault Response Services of Southern Maine, POB 1371, Portland; 04104 800-871-7741 www.sarssm.org

Community Centers and/or Pride Organizations

♀ ★ Pride Portland, POB 11141, Portland 04104 prideportland.org

Maine: Portland Area
Accommodation

185

GAYELLOW PAGES #42 2020-2021

Waldoboro : Maine
Accommodation

Accommodation: Hotels, Inns, Guesthouses, B&B, Resorts

Portland

♂ • The Chadwick Bed & Breakfast, 140 Chadwick St, Portland; 207-774-5141 www.thechadwick.com ✗ ⊛⊛

♀ • (?⚥) The Inn at St John, 939 Congress St, Portland; 800-636-9127 www.innatstjohn.com

♀ • West End Inn, 146 Pine St, Portland; 04102-3541 800-338-1377 www.westendbb.com ✗ ⊛ innkeeper@westendbb.com

AIDS/HIV Services, Education & Support

♀ ★ ♿ Frannie Peabody Center, 30 Danforth St #311, Portland; 207-774-6877 www.peabodycenter.org ✗

Bars, Cafes, Clubs, Restaurants

Portland

♂ • (?⚥) Blackstones, 6 Pine St, Portland; 207-775-2885 www.blackstones.com

♀ ○ David's, 22 Monument Sq, Portland 207-773-4340 www.davidsrestaurant.com ✗

♀ ○ Walter's, 2 Portland Sq, Portland 207-871-9258 www.walter-sportland.com ✗

Bookstores

♀ ○ ♿ Longfellow Books, 1 Monument Way, Portland; 207-772-4045 www.longfellowbooks.com

♀ ○ ♿ Nonesuch Books & Cards, 50 Market St, S Portland; 207-799-2659 www.nonesuchbooks.com

Counseling/Psychotherapy/Mental Health

♀ ○ (?⚥) Kingsbury, Josh, PhD, 251 Woodford St, Portland; 04103-5617 207-370-2823 **H?** www.kingsburycounseling.com josh@kingsburycounseling.com

Leather Resources & Groups

♂ ★ Harbor Masters of Maine, Inc, POB 4044, Portland; 04101 www.harbormastersofmaine.com

Legal Services

♀ ○ Buchanan, Brenda M., 57 Exchange St #201, Portland; 04101-5000 207-772-1262 fax 207-772-1279 www.wacubu.com

♀ • Dubois, Matthew R, Esq, Vogel and Dubois, POB 3649, Portland; 04104 207-761-7796 fax 207-761-6946 maine-elderlaw.com

Organizations/Resources: Cultural, Dance, Performance

♂ Maine Gay Men's Chorus, 1310 Congress St, Portland; 207-712-0629 www.mainegaymenschorus.com

♀ ☆ Women In Harmony, POB 8042, Portland; 04104 www.wihmaine.org

Organizations/Resources: Family and Supporters

♀ ☆ PFLAG Portland, POB 8742, Portland; 04104 207-831-3015 www.pflagportlandmaine.org

Organizations/Resources: Student, Academic, Education

♂ ★ ♿ Center for Sexualities & Gender Diversity, University of Southern Maine, 43A Woodbury Campus Center, Portland; 207-228-8200 usm.maine.edu/diversity

♂ ☆ GLSEN Southern Maine, POB 10334, Portland 04104-0334 207-619-1417 www.glsen.org/southernme glsensomaine@gmail.com

Religious / Spiritual Resources

♂ ☆ ♿ Congregation Bet Ha'am, 81 Westbrook St, S Portland; 04106-5232 207-879-0028 **H?** www.bethaam.org ⚥✗ karen@bethaam.org

♂ ☆ Williston-Immanuel United Church, 156 High St, Portland; 04101-2825 207-775-2301 www.williston-immanuel.org office@williston-immanuel.org

Presque Isle

AIDS/HIV Services, Education & Support

♂ Aroostook County Action Program, POB 1116 04769 207-764-3721 www.acap-me.org

Rockland

Accommodation: Hotels, Inns, Guesthouses, B&B, Resorts

♂ • LimeRock Inn, 96 Limerock St; 800-546-3762 www.limerock-inn.com

Bars, Cafes, Clubs, Restaurants

♂ ○ ♿ Rock City Cafe, 316 Main St 207-594-4123 www.rockcity-coffee.com ➦ ✗

Saco / Biddeford

Conferences/Events/Festivals/Workshops

♂ ★ Gayla At Ferry Beach, 5 Morris Ave, Saco; 04072 207-282-4489 www.ferrybeach.org/GAYLA gayla.at.ferry.beach@gmail.com

Organizations/Resources: Student, Academic, Education

♂ ★ University of New England LGBTQ Services, Biddeford Campus, 11 Hills Beach Rd, Biddeford; 207-602-2826 tinyurl.com/shpmw5d

Religious / Spiritual Resources

♂ ☆ First Parish Congregational Church, 12 Beach St, Saco; 04072 207-283-3771 www.firstparishsaco.org office@firstparishsaco.org

Stockton Springs

Accommodation Rental: Furnished / Vacation (& AirBNB)

♂ • (?⚥) Cabin on the Ocean Cove, 2 W Eagle Way; 04981 330-414-0695 **H?** www.cabinontheoceancove.com ✗ ⊛⊛ cabinontheoceancove@gmail.com

Waldoboro

Accommodation: Hotels, Inns, Guesthouses, B&B, Resorts

♂ • Le Vatout, 218 Kaler's Corner 207-832-5150 www.leva-tout.com ✗ ⊛

Waterville

Organizations/Resources: Student, Academic, Education

⚥ ★ The Bridge, Colby College, Office of Campus Life, 4000 Mayflower Hill; 207-872-3000 tinyurl.com/27zxdvd

Winthrop

Accommodation: Hotels, Inns, Guesthouses, B&B, Resorts

♂ ● ♿ Annabessacook Farm B&B, 192 Annabessacook Rd; 207-377-3276 www.annabessacookfarm.com ⊗ ⊗

Yarmouth

Bookstores

♀ ○ ♿ Royal River Books, 355 Main St 207-846-8006 www.royalriverbooks.com

>> York: see Ogunquit Area

Maryland

State/County Resources

Crisis, Anti-violence, & Helplines

♀ ☆ ♿ House of Ruth Maryland, 2201 Argonne Dr, Baltimore, MD 410-889-RUTH (7884) **H?** www.hruth.org

Legal Services

⚥ ★ (?♿) Free State Justice, 2526 Saint Paul St, Baltimore, MD 410-625-5428 freestate-justice.org

Organizations/Resources: Political/Legislative/Advocacy

♀ ☆ ACLU of Maryland, 3600 Clipper Mill Rd #350, Baltimore, MD 443-524-2558 www.aclu-md.org

Recovery

♀ ☆ Alcoholics Anonymous Maryland General Service, POB 8043, Elkridge, MD 21075 www.marylandaa.org

Annapolis/Solomons Area

Community Centers and/or Pride Organizations

⚥ Annapolis Pride, annapolispride.org

Organizations/Resources: Student, Academic, Education

⚥ ★ ♿ Anne Arundel Community College Gay-Straight Alliance, Office of Student Life, Student Union, Room 202, Arnold; **H** tinyurl.com/yyycou2r ✓

⚥ ★ US Naval Academy Alumni Out, POB 3571, Annapolis; 21403 www.usnaout.org

Baltimore Area

Crisis, Anti-violence, & Helplines

♀ ☆ ♿ Turnaround, 8503 LaSalle Rd flr 2, Towson; 21286 410-377-8111 443-279-0379 (helpline 24/7) **H?** Domestic violence, sexual assault and sex trafficking www.turnaroundinc.org info@turnaroundinc.org

Community Centers and/or Pride Organizations

⚥ ★ Baltimore Pride, GLCCB, 2530 N Charles St Flr 3, Balt; 410-777-8145 baltimorepride.org

⚥ ★ Pride Center of Maryland, GLCCB, 2530 N Charles St Flr 3, Balt; 410-777-8145 www.pridecentermd.org ✓

AIDS/HIV Services, Education & Support

♂ ★ (?♿) AIDS Action Baltimore, Inc, 14 East Eager Street, 1-A, Balt; 21202 410 837-2437 www.aidsactionbaltimore.org ✓ baltoaids@aol.com

♂ HopeSprings, 5400 Loch Raven Blvd Flr 3, Balt 410-323-0005 www.hopesprings.org

♂ ☆ ♿ Moveable Feast, 901 N Milton Ave, Balt; 21205 410-327-3420 fax 410-327-3426 **H?** www.mfeast.org ✓

Bars, Cafes, Clubs, Restaurants
Baltimore

♂ ○ ♿ Aldo's Ristorante Italiano, 306 S High St, Balt; 410-727-0700 www.aldositaly.com ✕ ✓

⚥ ● ♿ Baltimore Eagle, 2022 N Charles St, Balt; 443-759-8228 baltimoreeagle.com **DLV** ♈ ✕ 🎱 ✓

♂ ○ The Brewer's Art, 1106 N Charles St, Balt 410-547-6925 www.thebrewersart.com ♈ ✕

♂ ○ Cafe Hon, 1002 W 36th St, Balt; 410-243-1230 cafehon.com ◻

⚥ ● The Drinkery, 205 W Read St, Balt 410-225-3100 tinyurl.com/n6vt7ew

⚥ Gallery Bar & Restaurant, 1735 Maryland Ave, Balt; 410-539-6965 **DL** ♈ ✕ ◯

⚥ ● Grand Central Nightclub, 1001 N Charles St, Balt; / planned move to 15 E. Centre St 410-752-7133 www.grandcentralclub.com **DK** ♈ ✕

⚥ ○ ♿ Helmand Restaurant, 806 N Charles St, Balt; 410-752-0311 Braille menu available www.helmand.com ✕

⚥ ● Leon's, 870 Park Ave, Balt; 410-539-4993 leonsbaltimore.tripod.com/ ♈ ✕

⚥ Mixers, 6037 Bel Air Rd, Balt 443-885-9799 mixersbaltimore.com

⚥ ● The Rowan Tree Tavern, 1633 S Charles St, Balt; 410-468-0550 tinyurl.com/y95b7mfs

Body Art

♂ ● Jacki Randall's Charm City Tattoo, 300 S Monroe St, Balt; 21223 410-566-7528 charmcitytattoo.com ta2jac@verizon.net

Counseling/Psychotherapy/Mental Health

⚥ ● Barb Elgin, LGBTQIA affirmative therapy and life coaching., 410-967-3848 www.barbelgin.com

♂ ● (?♿) Brinkerhoff, Sara, MA, LCPC, LCDP, MAC, 4 North Ave, Ste 303B, Bel Air; 21014 410-457-7767 Substance abuse

♂ ○ ♿ Broadbent, Janan, PhD, 2 Hamill Rd Ste 120, Balt; 21210 410-825-5577 **H?** drjanan.com drjanan@hush.com

♀ ● ♿ Lehne, Gregory, PhD, 4419 Falls Rd, Balt; 410-366-0642

Maryland: Baltimore Area
Counseling

187
GAYELLOW PAGES #42 2020-2021

Chestertown : Maryland
Organizations: Family

♂ ☆ ♿ Women's Growth Center, 5209 York Rd #B12, Balt; 410-532-2476 womensgrowthcenter.com

Financial Planning, Investment (see also Insurance)

♂ ○ (♿) Partnership Wealth Management, LLC, 2809 Boston St Ste 509, Balt; 21224 410-732-2633 877-807-2633 fax 410-732-2634 CA Insurance Lic# 0C40217 www.partnershippwm.com woody@partnershipwm.com

Health Care: Physical (see also Counseling/Mental Health)

⚥ ★ ♿ Chase Brexton Health Care, 1111 N Charles St flr 5, Balt; 410-837-2050 www.chasebrexton.org

Leather Resources & Groups

⚥ ★ COMMAND, MC, mail to C.O.M.M.A.N.D., M.C., POB 22415, Balt; 21203 443-296-2198 www.commandmc.org

Legal Services

♂ ○ Law Office of David M Lutz, 1901 Fleet St, Balt; 21231 410-558-3700 410-299-2898 (español) www.lawlutz.com LawLutz@aol.com

Organizations/Resources: Cultural, Dance, Performance

⚥ Charm City Kitty Club, Baltimore Theater Project, 45 W Preston St, Balt; 443-468-0102 charmcitykittyclub.org

⚥ ★ ♿ Chesapeake Squares, POB 1633, Balt; 21203 www.chesapeakesquares.org **D**

♀ ★ ♿ New Wave Singers, POB 2012, Balt; 21203 410-558-4692 newwavesingers.org

Organizations/Resources: Ethnic, Multicultural

⚥ ★ The Center for Black Equity-Baltimore, 2530 N Charles St 3rd Flr, Balt; 443-218-2478 www.cbebaltimore.org ✥ ✎

♀ Sistahs of Pride, GLCCB, 2530 N Charles St Flr 3, Balt; 410-777-8145 tinyurl.com/zqx35qp

Organizations/Resources: Social, Recreation, Support

⚥ ★ Hearts & Ears, 611 Park Ave, Balt 410-523-1694 www.heartsandears.org

⚥ ★ Prime Timers of Baltimore, POB 22122, Balt 21203 410-252-7239 tinyurl.com/ycocmduu info@ptbalto.org

Organizations/Resources: Student, Academic, Education

⚥ ★ Goucher College TALQ BIG, 1021 Dulaney Valley Rd, Balt; 410-337-6000 tinyurl.com/hfuynhx

⚥ ★ ♿ LGBTQ Life at Johns Hopkins University, 3003 N Charles St Ste 102, Balt; 21202 410-516-2359 **H?** studentaffairs.jhu.edu/lgbtq ✎ lgbtq@jhu.edu

⚥ ★ ♿ Loyola University in Maryland Spectrum LGBTQ Resource Centre, MS 2170, 4501 N Charles St, Balt 410-617-2805 **H** tinyurl.com/avqulkt ✎

⚥ ★ ♿ Maryland Institute College of Art LGBTQ Resources, Office of Diversity & Intercultural Development, 1300 W Mount Royal Ave, Balt; 443-552-1659 tinyurl.com/y5njhzd2 ✎

⚥ ★ ♿ OutLaw at the University of Maryland Carey School of Law, 500 W Baltimore St, Balt **H?** tinyurl.com/y55qrpub

♂ ☆ University of Maryland Baltimore County Women's Center, The Commons, Room 004, 1000 Hilltop Circle, Balt; 410-455-2714 womenscenter.umbc.edu/

Organizations/Resources: Transgender/Gender Non-Conforming/Diverse

T ☆ Baltimore Trans-Masculine Alliance, GLCCB, 2530 N Charles St Flr 3, Balt; 21218 410-777-8145 ✎ baltimoretransmasculine@gmail.com

Real Estate (see also Mortgages)

♂ ● ♿ Curtis, Wayne, ABR, RE/MAX Advantage Realty, 100 International Dr Ste 2309, Balt; 21202 410-779-2000 410-467-8950 **H?** www.charmcityrealestate.com ✎ info@charmcityrealestate.com

Religious / Spiritual Resources

⚥ ★ ♿ Metropolitan Community Church of Baltimore, 401 W Monument St, Balt; 410-669-6222 **H?** mccbaltimore.org ✎

♂ ☆ ♿ St John's of Baltimore City UMC, 2640 St Paul St, Balt; 21818 410-366-7733 **H?** www.stjohnsbaltimore.org ✎ info@stjohnsbaltimore.org

♂ ☆ ♿ St Mark Lutheran Church, 1900 St Paul St, Balt; 21218 410-752-5804 www.stmarksbaltimore.org ✎

Sports & Outdoor

⚥ ★ Baltimore FrontRunners/Walkers, baltimorefrontrunners.com

♀ Charm City Roller Girls, LLC, POB 19939, Balt; 21211 443-475-0088 www.charmcityrollergirls.com

Bethesda/Rockville Area

Accounting, Bookkeeping, Tax Services

♂ ● ♿ **CPA Connie, LLC, 15811 Crabbs Branch Way, Rockville; 20855 301-987-0048 www.cpaconnie.com ✎ connie@cpaconnie.com**

Counseling/Psychotherapy/Mental Health

♂ ● ♿ **Lebolt, Jonathan, PhD, LCSW-C, CGP, 4401 East-West Hwy Ste 304, Bethesda; 20814 240-507-7696 Individuals, couples, groups. LGBTQIA+. Recovery from depression, bipolar, anxiety, trauma, addictive behaviors; career/vocation; cultural issues; spirituality. www.doctor-jon.com ✎**

Organizations/Resources: Youth (see also Family)

⚥ ★ Rainbow Youth Alliance, c/o Unitarian Universalist Church, 100 Welsh Park Dr, Rockville; 240-324-7823 tinyurl.com/kommb6y

Chestertown

Organizations/Resources: Family and Supporters

♂ ☆ PFLAG Mid-Shore / Chestertown, 914 Gateway Dr 443-480-3138 pflagchestertown.com

Maryland: Churchville
Religious

188

GAYELLOW PAGES #42 2020-2021

Potomac : Maryland
Legal

Churchville

Religious / Spiritual Resources

♂ ☆ ♿ Unitarian Universalist Fellowship of Harford County, 2515 Churchville Rd; 21028 410-734-7122 www.uufhc.net office@uufhc.net

College Park

Organizations/Resources: Student, Academic, Education

⚥ ★ ♿ LGBT Equity Center, University of Maryland, 2218 Marie Mount Hall; 20742 301-405-8720 www.lgbt.umd.edu ✎ lgbt@umd.edu

Religious / Spiritual Resources

⚥ ★ Holy Redeemer MCC, 4907 Niagara Rd Ste 101 301-982-5775 hrmcc.org

Columbia

Organizations/Resources: Family and Supporters

♂ ☆ PFLAG Columbia-Howard County, POB 1479; 21044 443-518-6998 www.pflaghoco.org

Organizations/Resources: Youth (see also Family)

⚥ ★ Rainbow Youth & Allies - Howard County, PO Box 1479; 21044 443-518-6998 tinyurl.com/y3mow9ep

Religious / Spiritual Resources

♂ ☆ ♿ Columbia United Christian Church, 5885 Robert Oliver Place; 21045 410-730-1770 **H?** www.cucc-md.org ✎ admin@cucc-md.org

♂ ☆ ♿ St John United Church, Wilde Lake Interfaith Center, 10431 Twin Rivers Rd; 21044-2331 410-730-9137 www.sjunited.org ✪ ✎ SJUColumbia@gmail.com

♂ ☆ ♿ Unitarian Universalist Congregation of Columbia, Owen Brown Interfaith Center, 7246 Cradlerock Way 21045 410-381-0097 **HD** uucolumbia.net

Elkton

Accommodation: Hotels, Inns, Guesthouses, B&B, Resorts

♂ ○ Elk Forge B&B Inn, Spa and Events, 807 Elk Mills Rd; 410-392-9007 www.elkforge.com ❖

Frederick Area

Crisis, Anti-violence, & Helplines

♂ ☆ Heartly House, POB 857, Frederick; 21705 301-662-8800 www.heartlyhouse.org

Community Centers and/or Pride Organizations

⚥ ★ The Frederick Center, POB 3231, Frederick; 21705 www.thefrederickcenter.org

Bars, Cafes, Clubs, Restaurants
Brunswick

♂ ○ Beans in the Belfry, 122 W Potomac St, Brunswick; 301-834-7178 www.beansinthebelfry.com ✎

Frederick

♂ ○ Firestone's Culinary Tavern, 105 N Market St, Frederick; 301-663-0330 firestonesrestaurant.com ♀ ✗

♂ ○ JoJo's Restaurant & Tap House, 16 E Patrick St, Frederick; 301-732-5197 tinyurl.com/zfwgcrf ♀ ✗ info@jojosrestauranttaphouse.com

Religious / Spiritual Resources

♂ ☆ ♿ Grace Episcopal Church, 114 E A St, Brunswick; 21766 301-834-8540 www.gracebrunswick.org ✎ info@gracebrunswick.org

⚥ ★ ♿ Open Door MCC, POB 127, Boyds; 20841 / 15817 Barnesville Rd 301-916-5777 www.opendoormcc.org

Hagerstown

Community Centers and/or Pride Organizations

⚥ ★ Hagerstown Hopes, 22 N Mulberry St Ste 016 240-347-1321 www.hagerstownhopesmd.org

Bars, Cafes, Clubs, Restaurants

♂ ○ 28 South, 28 S Potomac St; 240-347-4932 www.28south.net ♀ ✗

Boonsboro

⚥ ● ♿ The Lodge, 21614 National Pike, Boonsboro; 301-591-4434 www.thelodgemd.com **DC** ▥ ✎

♂ ● ♿ Gourmet Goat, 41 N Potomac St 301-790-2343 www.thegourmetgoat-ggs.com ♀ ▱ ✗▥ ✎

Religious / Spiritual Resources

⚥ ★ ♿ New Light MCC, 40 W Church St; 21740-4808 717-682-1873 newlightmcc.com ✎ newlightmcc@gmail.com

Havre de Grace

Accommodation: Hotels, Inns, Guesthouses, B&B, Resorts

⚥ ● La Cle D'or Guesthouse, 226 N Union Ave 888-HUG-GUEST www.lacledorguesthouse.com ☺

Laurel

Metaphysical, Occult, Alternative Healing

♂ ● (?♿) The Crystal Fox, 311 Main St 20707-4129 301-317-1980 thecrystalfox.com

Marion

Accommodation: Hotels, Inns, Guesthouses, B&B, Resorts

♂ ● Kingsbay Mansion Executive B&B, 27999 Coulbourn Creek Rd; 301-346-8411 www.kingsbaymansion.com ❖ ✎ ☺

Potomac

Legal Services

♂ ● ♿ Jacobs, Lawrence S, McMillan Metro, PC, 7811 Montrose Rd #400; 20854 240-778-2330 www.partnerplanning.com ✎
≫ Rockville: see Bethesda/Rockville Area

Maryland: Silver Spring
Counseling

189

GAYELLOW PAGES #42 2020-2021

: Massachusetts
Organizations: Political

Silver Spring

Counseling/Psychotherapy/Mental Health

♂ ○ (?⚧) Riley, E. Anne, PhD, 3144 Gracefield Rd Apt T-19, Silver Spring; 301-273-2424 thetherapist.homestead.com

⚢ ● Zeiger, Robyn S., PhD, LCPC, 10300 Sweetbriar Parkway, Silver Spring; 20903-1523 301-445-7333 Licensed Clinical Professional Counselor and Certified Imago Relationship Therapist www.drrobynzeiger.com drrobynzeiger@aol.com

Legal Services

♂ ● ♿ Zavos Juncker Law Group PLLC, 8455 Colesville Rd Ste 1500, Silver Spring; 301-562-8220 **H?** www.zavosjunckerlaw-group.com ✗

Religious / Spiritual Resources

♂ ☆ ♿ Unitarian Universalist Church of Silver Spring, 10309 New Hampshire Ave, Silver Spring; 20903 301-273-9745 **H?** www.uucss.org

Snow Hill

Accommodation: Hotels, Inns, Guesthouses, B&B, Resorts

♂ ● River House Inn, 201 E Market St; 410-632-2722 www.river-houseinn.com ✤✗ ⊗ ⊛
@ixx=

Tilghman Island

Accommodation: Hotels, Inns, Guesthouses, B&B, Resorts

♂ ● ♿ Black Walnut Point Inn, 4417 Black Walnut Point Rd 410-886-2452 www.blackwalnutpointinn.com ✗ ⊗

Westminster

Community Centers and/or Pride Organizations

⚢ ★ Westminster Pride, westminsterpride.org

Organizations/Resources: Family and Supporters

♂ ☆ ♿ PFLAG Westminster/Carroll County Representative, POB 474; 21158 410-861-0488 **H?** www.pflagwcc.org

Massachusetts

Crisis, Anti-violence, & Helplines

⚢ ★ ♿ The Network/La Red, POB 6011, Boston, MA 02114 617-742-4911 **H** www.tnlr.org ⊙

Information, Media & Publications

⚢ ● Bay Windows, POB E14, Boston, MA 02127-0004 617-464-7280 www.baywindows.com

⚢ ● ♿ The Rainbow Times, 617-444-9618 www.therainbowtimes-mass.com

---

Robyn S. Zeiger, PhD, LCPC
10300 Sweetbriar Parkway, Silver Spring
301-445-7333
www.drrobynzeiger.com
Licensed Clinical Professional Counselor
Certified Imago Relationship Therapist

AIDS/HIV Services, Education & Support

♂ ☆ ♿ AIDS Action Committee of Massachusetts, Inc., 75 Amory St, Boston, MA 617-437-6200 **H?** www.aac.org ✗

♂ ☆ ♿ Community Research Initiative of New England, The Schrafft's City Center, 529 Main St Ste 301, Boston, MA 02129 617-502-1700 888-253-2712 www.crine.org info@crine.org

♂ ☆ ♿ Multicultural AIDS Coalition, Inc, 566 Columbus Ave, Boston, MA 617-442-1622 www.mac-boston.org ⊙ ✗

Archives/Libraries/Museums/History Projects

⚢ ★ (?⚧) Sexual Minorities Archives, POB 6579, Holyoke, MA 01041 413-538-4750 **H** tinyurl.com/luo5zja ✗ sexual minorities.archives@yahoo.com

Funding: Endowment, Fundraising

⚢ ★ Imperial Court of Massachusetts, POB 52271, Boston, MA 02205 www.imperialcourtofma.org

Health Care: Physical (see also Counseling/Mental Health)

♂ ☆ TapestryHealth, 296 Nonotuck St, Florence, MA 413-586-2016 www.tapestryhealth.org

Leather Resources & Groups

♂ ☆ New England Leather Alliance, POB 51361, Boston, MA 02205 857-293-9502 www.nelaonline.org

Legal Services

⚢ ★ ♿ GLBTQ Legal Advocates & Defenders - GLAD, 18 Tremont St Ste 950, Boston, MA 02108 617-426-1350 800-455-GLAD hotline (New England) fax 617-426-3594 www.glad.org gladlaw@glad.org

⚢ (?⚧) Massachusetts LGBTQ Bar Association, c/o Boston Bar Association, 16 Beacon St, Boston, MA www.masslgbtqbar.org

Organizations/Resources: Business & Professional Associations, Labor Advocacy

⚢ Gay Officers Action League of New England, POB 171587, Boston, MA 02117 781-983-5816 fb.com/NewEnglandGOAL/

Organizations/Resources: Cultural, Dance, Performance

⚢ ★ ♿ Lavender Country & Folk Dancers, 617-876-5461 www.lcfd.org **D** ✗

Organizations/Resources: Political/Legislative/Advocacy

♀ ☆ ACLU of Massachusetts, 211 Congress St Third Flr, Boston, MA 02110 617-482-3170 www.aclum.org info@aclum.org

♀ ☆ ♿ American Civil Liberties Union, 39 Main St Ste 8, Northampton, MA 413-586-9115 www.aclum.org

Massachusetts:
Organizations: Political

190

GAYELLOW PAGES #42 2020-2021

Boston Area: Massachusetts
Accommodation

♀ ★ Bay State Stonewall Democrats, POB 837, Pepperell, MA 01463 tinyurl.com/62jb7p

♀ Massachusetts Gay & Lesbian Political Caucus, 11 Beacon St Ste 430, Boston, MA 617-248-0776 fb.com/MGLPCaucus/

т ☆ ♿ Massachusetts Transgender Political Coalition, POB 960784, Boston, MA 02196 617-778-0519 www.masstpc.org

♀ ★ ♂ MassEquality, 128A Tremont St Ste 4R, Boston, MA 02108 617-878-2300 www.MassEquality.org ✗ info@MassEquality.org

Organizations/Resources: Senior Resources

♀ ★ LGBT Aging Project, Fenway Institute, 1340 Boylston St, Boston, MA 02215 857-313-6590 www.lgbtagingproject.org

Organizations/Resources: Social, Recreation, Support

♀ ★ Yankee Lambda Car Club, POB 3296, Wakefield, MA 01880 / New England Area New England Area www.yankeelcc.com

Organizations/Resources: Student, Academic, Education

♂ ★ GLSEN Massachusetts, POB 2563, Amherst, MA 01004 617-684-5736 tinyurl.com/yfgg4ume

Organizations/Resources: Transgender/Gender Non-Conforming/Diverse

т ☆ ♿ Compass (FTM), compassftm.org info@compassftm.org

т ☆ Trans Club of New England, POB 540071, Waltham, MA 02454-0071 781-891-9325 www.tcne.org info@tcne.org

Organizations/Resources: Youth (see also Family)

♀ ☆ Massachusetts Commission on LGBTQ Youth, MA Department of Public Health, 250 Washington St Flr 4, Boston, MA 617-624-5495 www.mass.gov/cgly

Recovery

♂ ☆ Al-Anon/Alateen Al-Anon Family Groups of Massachusetts, 57 E Main St Ste 109, Westborough, MA 508-366-0556 www.ma-al-anon-alateen.org

♂ ☆ Sex & Love Addicts Anonymous New England Intergroup, POB 1375, Brookline, MA 02446 617-625-7961 www.slaanei.org

Reproductive Medicine & Fertility Services

♂ Planned Parenthood League of Massachusetts, 1055 Commonwealth Ave, Boston, MA 617-284-8092 www.pplm.org

Sports & Outdoor

♀ ★ Chiltern Mountain Club, POB 850711, Braintree, MA 02185 617-306-3840 www.chiltern.org

Acton/Stow

Religious / Spiritual Resources

♂ ☆ ♿ St Matthew's UMC, 435 Central St, Acton; 01720 978-263-2822 **HD** www.saint-matthews.org office@saint-matthews.org

   ›› *Arlington: see Boston Area*

Attleboro

Organizations/Resources: Student, Academic, Education

♀ ★ Wheaton College Alliance, 26 E Main St, Norton; 508-286-8222 tinyurl.com/yxmaodo8

Religious / Spiritual Resources

♂ ☆ ♿ Immanuel Lutheran Church Attleboro, 647 N Main St, Attleboro; 02703-1518 508-222-2898 **H** www.immanuellc.org ✗ office@immanuellc.org

Barre

Accommodation: Hotels, Inns, Guesthouses, B&B, Resorts

♂ ● ♿ The Jenkins Inn, POB 779 01005-0779 / 7 West St, Barre Common/Rt 122 978-355-6444 www.jenkinsinn.com (♣?) ✗ ☺ jenkinsinnbarre@gmail.com

   ›› *Bedford: see Boston Area*
   ›› *Belmont: see Boston Area*
   ›› *Beverly: see North Shore Area*

Boston Area

Crisis, Anti-violence, & Helplines

♂ ☆ ♿ Boston Area Rape Crisis Center, 99 Bishop Allen Dr, Cambridge; 800-841-8371 **H** www.barcc.org ✗

♀ ★ ♿ Fenway Health Peer Listening Line, 1340 Boylston St, Boston; 617-267-2535 fenwayhealth.org

♀ ★ ♿ LGBT Helpline and Peer Listening Line, Fenway Health, 1340 Boylston St, Boston; 617-267-9001 www.fenwayhealth.org ✗

Community Centers and/or Pride Organizations

♀ ★ ♿ Boston Pride, 398 Columbus Ave #285, Boston; 02116-6008 617-262-9405 **H?** www.bostonpride.org parade@bostonpride.org

♀ Latino Pride, 398 Columbus Ave #285, Boston; 617-262-9405 tinyurl.com/oxbn5jo ✦

Information, Media & Publications

♀ ● New England's Community Pink Pages, KP Media, 333 Washington St Ste 714, Boston; 02108 617-423-1515 www.linkpink.com kpmedia@aol.com

♀ ● SavoirFlair Magazine, KP Media, 333 Washington St #714, Boston; 02108 617-423-1515 tinyurl.com/5r34y3j kpmedia@aol.com

Accommodation: Hotels, Inns, Guesthouses, B&B, Resorts
Boston

♂ ● 14 Union Park, 14 Union Park, Boston; 02118 617-236-6961 www.14unionpark.com ✗ ☺ info@14unionpark.com

♂ ● Clarendon Square Inn, 198 West Brookline St, Boston; 617-536-2229 www.clarendonsquare.com ✗ ☺

♂ ● Encore Bed & Breakfast, 116 W Newton St, Boston; 617-247-3425 www.encorebandb.com ✗ ☺

♂ ● Gryphon House, 9 Bay State Rd, Boston 617-375-9003 www.innboston.com ✗ ☺

Massachusetts: Boston Area
Accommodation
191
GAYELLOW PAGES #42 2020-2021
Boston Area: Massachusetts
Leather

♀ ● Oasis Guest House, 22 Edgerly Rd, Boston 617-267-2262 www.oasisgh.com ⚧ ♿

Jamaica Plain

♀ ● Taylor House B&B, 50 Burroughs St, Jamaica Plain; 617-983-9334 www.TaylorHouse.com ⚧ ⚧ ♿ ♿

AIDS/HIV Services, Education & Support

♀ ☆ ♿ Boston Living Center, Inc., Victory Programs, Inc, 29 Stanhope St, Boston; 617-236-1012 **H?** www.vpi.org/boston

ᴛ ☆ ♿ TransCend, 75 Amory St, Boston 02119 857-313-6513 www.aac.org/transcend/ ⚧

Archives/Libraries/Museums/History Projects

⚧ ★ The History Project, 29 Stanhope St, Boston; 617-266-7733 www.historyproject.org

Bars, Cafes, Clubs, Restaurants

Boston

⚧ ● The Alley, (at 275 Washington St) 14 Pi Alley, Boston; (274 Washington St) 617-263-1449 www.TheAlleyBar.com **D**

⚧ ● Boston Eagle, 520 Tremont, Boston 617-542-4494

⚧ ● ♿ Cathedral Station, 1222 Washington St, Boston; 617-338-6060 **H?** www.cathedralstation.com **S** ⚲ ✗ ↻ ⚧

♀ ● ♿ Club Cafe / Napoleon Cabaret, 209 Columbus Ave, Boston; 617-536-0966 www.clubcafe.com **V** ⚲ ✗ ▦ ⚧

⚧ ● (?♿) Dyke Night, check event schedule www.kristenporterpresents.com **D** ✪

⚧ ● Jacques, 79 Broadway, Boston; 617-426-8902 www.jacquescabaret.com ▦

⚧ ● ♿ Machine, 1254 Boylston St, Boston; 617-536-1950 www.machineboston.club

♀ ● South End Buttery, 314 Shawmut Ave, Boston 617-482-1015 www.SouthEndButtery.com ⚲ ✗ ↻

♀ ● Sweet Cheeks Q, 1381 Boylston St, Boston 617-266-1300 www.sweetcheeksq.com ✗

♀ ● ♿ Trophy Room, 28 Chandler St, Boston; 617-482-3450 www.trophyboston.com **S** ⚲ ✗ ▦ ⚧

Cambridge

♀ ● Veggie Galaxy, 450 Massachusetts Ave, Cambridge; 617-497-1513 www.veggiegalaxy.com ✗

Dorchester

♀ ● Ashmont Grill, 555 Talbot Ave, Dorchester 617-825-4300 www.ashmontgrill.com ✗ ⚧

Jamaica Plain

♀ ● ♿ Bella Luna Restaurant & Milky Way Lounge, 284 Amory St, Jamaica Plain; 617-524-3740 www.milkywayjp.com **D** ⚲ ✗ ▦ ✪

Somerville

♀ ● ♿ Diesel Cafe, 257 Elm St, Somerville; 617-629-8717 **H?** www.diesel-cafe.com ✗ ↻ ⚧

Body Art

⚧ ● ♿ Body Xtremes, 417 Hancock St, N Quincy; 02171-2408 617-471-5836 www.bodyxtremes.com ⚧

Bookstores

♀ ● ♿ Brookline Booksmith, 279 Harvard St, Brookline; 617-566-6660 www.brooklinebooksmith.com

♀ ● ♿ Harvard Book Store, 1256 Massachusetts Ave, Cambridge; 617-661-1515 www.harvard.com ⚧

♀ ● ♿ MIT Press Bookstore, 301 Massachusetts Ave, Cambridge; 617-253-5249 mitpressbookstore.mit.edu/ ⚧

♀ ● ♿ Porter Square Books, 25 White St, Cambridge; 617-491-2220 www.portersquarebooks.com

♀ ● ♿ Trident Booksellers & Cafe, 338 Newbury St, Boston; 617-267-8688 www.tridentbookscafe.com ✗ ⚧

♀ ● ♿ Whitelam Books, 610 Main St, Reading; 01867 781-779-1833 www.whitelambooks.com ⚧

Counseling/Psychotherapy/Mental Health

♀ ● Zoldan, Judi, 67 Leonard St #3, Belmont; 02478 617-484-5522 judizoldan@gmail.com

Dentists

♀ ● ♿ Moody Street Dental on Elm, 52 Elm St, Waltham; 02453 781-894-0889 www.moodystreetdental.Com ⚧ info@moodystreet dental.Com

Entertainment-Related Services (see also Performance)

⚧ ☆ (?♿) Femme Show, **H** www.thefemmeshow.com

Funding: Endowment, Fundraising

⚧ ☆ Harbor to the Bay Ride, POB 990243, Boston 02199 www.harbortothebay.org info@harbortothebay.org

⚧ Sisters of Perpetual Indulgence, www.thebostonsisters.org

Health Care: Physical (see also Counseling/Mental Health)

♀ ● ♿ Buckle, David, MD, Beth Israel Deaconess Family Medicine-Dedham/Westwood, 333 Elm St #220, Dedham; 02026 781-329-7311 dbuckle@caregroup.harvard.edu

⚧ ★ ♿ Fenway Health, 1340 Boylston St, Boston; 617-267-0900 **H** Also offers behavioral health services. fenwayhealth.org ⚧

⚧ ★ ♿ Fenway: South End, 142 Berkeley St, Boston; 617-247-7555 **H?** Also offers behavioral health services. fenwayhealth.org ⚧

⚧ Geiger Gibson Community Health Center, 250 Mt Vernon St, Dorchester; 617-288-1140 www.hhsi.us/geigergibson.php

♀ ● Hill, Peter, DC, 687 Wellesley St, Weston 02493 781-772-2500 www.chirohill.com chirohill@aol.com

♀ ● Taylor, Robert, MD, 1101 Beacon St #8 W, Brookline; 02446 617-232-1459 www.drroberttaylormd.com bobtaylor1755@gmail.com

♀ ● ♿ Turnock, Elizabeth, MD, North End Waterfront Health, 332 Hanover St, Boston; 617-643-8000 northendwaterfront-health.org

Leather Resources & Groups

⚧ ★ Bay State Marauders, POB 35411, Brighton 02135-0003 www.baystatemarauders.org info@baystatemarauders.org

Massachusetts: Boston Area
Legal
192
GAYELLOW PAGES #42 2020-2021
Boston Area: Massachusetts
Organizations: Student

Legal Services

♀ ● (?♿) Kauffman, Joyce, Kauffman Law & Mediation, 4238 Washington St Ste 313, Roslindale; 02131 617-577-1505 fax 617-469-8440 www.kauffmanlaw.net ✎ joyce@kauffmanlaw.net

♂ ● Koffman & Dreyer, 324 Common St, Belmont 617-965-9525 **H?** www.koffmandreyer.com ✎

♀ ○ **Macy, Barbara J, 65A Atlantic Ave, Boston 02110 617-720-4005 Thoughtfully serving the GLBTQ community since 1985 www.barbarajmacy.com bjm@macwein.com**

Organizations/Resources: Bisexual Focus

♀ ★ ♿ Bisexual Resource Center, POB 170796, Boston; 02117 617-424-9595 www.biresource.org ✎

♀ ★ Boston Bisexual Women's Network, POB 301727, Jamaica Plain; 02130 www.biwomenboston.org biwomeneditor@gmail.com

Organizations/Resources: Business & Professional Associations, Labor Advocacy

♀ National Lesbian & Gay Journalists Association, tinyurl.com/yd3x2283

Organizations/Resources: Cultural, Dance, Performance

♂ ★ Boston Gay Men's Chorus, 539 Tremont St, Boston; 617-542-7464 www.bgmc.org

♀ ★ ♿ Boston Gender-Free Contra Dance, 617-852-4042 www.lcfd.org/jp

♀ ★ (?♿) Coro Allegro, 67 Newbury St, Boston; 617-236-4011 **H?** www.coroallegro.org ✎

♀ ★ Freedom Trail Band, POB 1759, Somerville; 02144 617-970-4930 www.freedomtrailband.org

♀ ★ Gays for Patsy, POB 302147, Jamaica Plain; 02130 gaysforpatsy.org

♀ ★ OUT to Dance, 617-363-0029 www.outtodance.com

♀ ★ Swingtime Boston, www.swingtimeboston.com swingtimeboston@gmail.com

♀ ☆ (?♿) The Theater Offensive, 565 Boylston St, Boston; 02116 617-661-1600 **H?** www.thetheateroffensive.org office@thetheateroffensive.org

♀ ☆ ♿ True Colors: Out Youth Theater, c/o Theater Offensive, 565 Boylston St, Boston; 02116 617-661-1600 **H?** www.thetheateroffensive.org ✎ truecolors@thetheateroffensive.org

♀ ★ ♿ Voices Rising, POB 300476, Jamaica Plain; 02130 617-396-7086 www.voicesrising.org

♀ ★ Wicked Queer: Boston LGBT Film Festival, 955 Massachusetts Ave #361, Cambridge; www.wickedqueer.org

Organizations/Resources: Education

♀ ★ SpeakOUT, POB 301223, Boston; 02130 877-223-9390 www.SpeakOutBoston.org

Organizations/Resources: Ethnic, Multicultural

♀ ★ Boston MASALA - Massachusetts Area South Asian Lambda Association, South Asian tinyurl.com/y95hn5qa ✧

♀ ★ Queer Asian Pacific Alliance, **H?** www.qapa.org ✧

♀ Somos Latinos LGBT Coalition/ Latino Pride of New England, 398 Columbus Ave #285, Boston; 617-262-9405 tinyurl.com/oxbn5jo ✦

Organizations/Resources: Family and Supporters

♂ ★ ♿ Gay Fathers of Greater Boston, 738 Main St #323, Waltham; 781-333-8429 www.gayfathersboston.org

♀ ☆ Greater Boston PFLAG, POB 541619, Waltham 02454 781-891-5966 www.gbpflag.org

Organizations/Resources: Naturist/Nudist

♂ ★ BANG: Boston Area Naturist Group, POB 180036, Boston; 02118-0001 www.bangma.org bang@bangma.org

Organizations/Resources: Political/Legislative/Advocacy

♀ ★ National LGBTQ Task Force, 1151 Massachusetts Ave, Cambridge; 617-492-6393 www.thetaskforce.org

Organizations/Resources: Social, Recreation, Support

♂ ★ Boston Gay & Bisexual Married Men's Support Group, c/o The Living Center, 29 Stanhope St, Boston; 617-549-4043 (Jim) www.bmmg.org

♂ ★ ♿ Boston Prime Timers, Inc, 566 Columbus Ave, Boston; 617-447-2344 bostonpt.org

♀ ★ DotOUT, 42 Plympton St, Boston www.dotout.org

♀ ☆ Family Tree, POB 441275, Somerville; 02144 603-437-1337 www.polyfamilytree.org

♀ ★ Gay for Good - Boston, Volunteer organization. gayforgood.org/boston/ boston@gayforgood.org

Organizations/Resources: Student, Academic, Education

♀ ★ Berklee College Of Music LGBT+ United, 7 Haviland #123, Boston; 02115 617-747-2560 www.berklee.edu/clubs/bugle lgbtunited@berklee.edu

♀ ★ Boston Architectural College Studio Q, 320 Newbury St Flr 2, Boston; 508-851-0317 tinyurl.com/3cp8z5o

♀ ★ Boston College LGBT at BC, 140 Commonwealth Ave, Chestnut Hill; 617-552-6346 **H?** tinyurl.com/zupgb4j

♀ ★ Brandeis University Queer Resource Center, Winer Lobby in Usdan 415 South St, Waltham; 781-736-3749 qrcbrandeis.weebly.com

♀ ☆ (?♿) Center for Student Diversity & Inclusion, Suffolk University, 8 Ashburton Pl, Sawyer 828, Boston 617-573-8613 www.suffolk.edu/diversity

♀ ★ Emerson's Alliance of Gays, Lesbians, & Everyone (EAGLE), 120 Boylston St #L133A, Boston; 617-824-8620 tinyurl.com/y84536sd

♀ ★ (?♿) Harvard Gender and Sexuality Caucus, POB 381809, Cambridge; 02238 hgsc.sigs.harvard.edu

♀ ★ Harvard Law School Lambda, 1585 Massachusetts Ave, Cambridge; harvardlambda.org

♀ ★ Harvard QSA, Thayer Basement, North Harvard Yard, Cambridge; fb.com/HarvardQSA/

♀ ★ LBGT at tMIT, Walker Memorial 50-005, Cambridge; 617-253-0684 web.mit.edu/lbgt/

Massachusetts: Boston Area
Organizations: Student
193
GAYELLOW PAGES #42 2020-2021
Bridgewater : Massachusetts
Organizations: Student

⚥ ★ && Lexington High School GSA, 251 Waltham St, Lexington; 781-861-2320 x3071 **H** ✗

⚥ ★ MIT SloanLGBT, Sloan School of Management, 50 Memorial Dr, Cambridge; web.mit.edu/sloan-lgbt/

⚥ ★ New England School of Law OUTLaws, 154 Stuart St, Boston; tinyurl.com/26pvzlw

⚥ ★ && Noble & Greenough School LGBTQS, 10 Campus Dr, Dedham; 02026 781-326-3700 **H?** ✗

⚥ ★ && Northeastern University NU PRIDE, 328 Curry Student Center, 360 Huntington Ave, Boston nupride.wordpress.com

⚥ ★ Tufts University LGBT Center, Bolles House, 226 College Ave, Medford; 617-627-3770 www.ase.tufts.edu/lgbt

⚥ ★ University of Massachusetts Queer Student Center, 100 Morrissey Blvd, Boston; 617-894-7535 tinyurl.com/3jkxz29

⚥ ★ Wellesley College LGBTQ Programs and Services, Billings Hall 106 Central St, Wellesley; 781-283-2682 tinyurl.com/ka9vb9q

Organizations/Resources: Youth (see also Family)

⚥ ★ && Boston Alliance of GLBT Youth (BAGLY, Inc), POB 960814, Boston; 02196 617-227-4313 **H** www.bagly.org ☯

⚥ ★ && Boston GLASS Community Center, 75 Amory St Garden Level, Boston; 857-399-1920 tinyurl.com/moy7mxj ❖

⚥ ★ && Boston GLASS Community Center for GLBTQ Youth & Young Adults, 75 Amory St, Roxbury; 857-399-1920 Ages 13-25 tinyurl.com/moy7mxj ❖

т Camp Aranu'tiq, POB 920251, Needham; 02192 781-400-1617 www.camparanutiq.org

⚥ Waltham House - LGBTQ Group Home, The Home for Little Wanderers, 10 Guest St, Boston; 617-267-3700 tinyurl.com/lh6xmjv

Recovery

♀ ☆ CASPAR. Inc, POB 45538, Somerville; 02145 617-628-3850 www.casparinc.org

♀ ☆ Overeaters Anonymous Mass Bay Intergroup, POB 74, Arlington; 02476 781-641-2303 www.oambi.org info@oambi.org

Religious / Spiritual Resources

♀ ☆ Church of the Covenant, 67 Newbury St, Boston 02116 617-266-7480 www.cotcbos.org info@cotcbos.org

⚥ ★ Congregation Am Tikva, POB 990441, Boston; 02199 617-383-9539 www.amtikva.org ✡

♀ ☆ The Congregational Church of Needham, 1154 Great Plain Ave, Needham; 02492 781-444-2510 www.needhamucc.org office@needhamucc.org

⚥ ★ Dignity Boston, POB 170428, Boston 02117 617-421-1915 www.dignityboston.org

♀ ☆ && First Baptist JP, 633 Centre St, Jamaica Plain; 02130-2526 617-524-3992 www.firstbaptistjp.org

♀ ☆ && First Church Somerville UCC, 89 College Ave, Somerville; 02144 617-625-6485 **H?** firstchurchsomerville.org fcs@firstchurchsomerville.org

♀ ☆ && First Parish of Watertown, 35 Church St, Watertown; 02472 617-924-6143 www.fpwatertown.org ✗ office@fpwatertown.org

♀ ☆ && First Parish UU, POB 397, Wayland; 01778 / 50 Cochituate Rd 508-358-6133 **H** www.uuwayland.org ✗ office@uuwayland.org

⚥ ★ Keshet, 284 Amory St, Boston; 617-524-9227 www.keshetonline.org ✡

⚥ ★ & MCC Boston, POB 15590, Boston; 02215 617-973-0404 www.mccboston.org

♀ ☆ && The United Parish in Brookline, 210 Harvard St, Brookline; 02446-5066 617-277-6860 **HD** tinyurl.com/yf9njnq office@upbrookline.org

♀ ☆ Unity Church, 9 Main St, North Easton; 02356 508-238-6373 tinyurl.com/u4s8uf3 welcome2ucne@gmail.com

♀ ☆ && Winchester Unitarian Society, 478 Main St, Winchester; 01890 781-729-0949 **HD** www.winchesteruu.org ✗ office@winchesteruu.org

Sports & Outdoor

⚥ ★ Beantown Soft-Tip Dart League, www.bsdl.org

⚥ ★ Beantown Softball League, POB 230734, Boston; 02123 617-297-7490 www.beantownsoftball.com

⚥ Boston Gay Basketball League, 5 Northampton St, Boston; bgbl.com

⚥ Boston Ironsides Rugby Team, www.bostonironsides.org

⚥ ★ Boston Pride Hockey, www.bostonpridehockey.org

⚥ Boston Strikers Soccer Club, POB 170569, Boston; 02117 www.bostonstrikers.com

♀ Boston Women's Flag Football League, www.bwffl.com

⚥ ★ CBVA Inc, POB 425734, Cambridge; 02142 www.cbvolleyball.net

⚥ ★ Greater Boston Flag Football League, PO Box 180559, Boston; 02118 www.flagflagfootball.com

⚥ ★ LANES: Liquid Assets New England Swim Team, POB 990537, Boston; 02199 www.swim-lanes.org

⚥ Monday Night Bowling League, 1666 Washington St #2, Boston; www.mnbl.net

♀ ☆ Moving Violations Motorcycle Club, 16 Cummins Highway #14, Roslindale; 02131 www.movingviolationsmc.com info@movingviolationsmc.com

⚥ ★ OutRiders, www.outriders.org

⚥ ★ Tennis 4 All, www.tennis4all.org

Travel & Tourist Services (see also Accommodation)

♂ ● 5 Star Travel Tzell, One Appleton St, Boston 02116 617-536-1999 www.5star-travel.com startrvl@aol.com

Women's Centers

♀ ★ (?&) Women's Center, 46 Pleasant St, Cambridge; 617-354-8807 tinyurl.com/2jdbw5 ✗

Bridgewater

Organizations/Resources: Student, Academic, Education

⚥ ★ && Bridgewater State University GLBTA Pride Center, Rondileau Campus Center, Room 109; 02325 508-531-1408 **H?** www.bridgew.edu/pride-center ✗

» *Brookline: see Boston Area*
» *Cambridge: see Boston Area*

Cape Cod & Islands

Accommodation: Hotels, Inns, Guesthouses, B&B, Resorts

Barnstable

⚥ ○ Lamb and Lion Inn, POB 511, Barnstable 02630 800-909-6923 www.lambandlion.com 🐾 ⚡ ⊗ info@lambandlion.com

Brewster

⚥ ● Candleberry Inn on Cape Cod, 1882 Main St, Brewster; 508-896-3300 candleberryinn.com ⚡ ⊗⊗

Eastham

⚥ ○ Fort Hill B&B, 75 Fort Hill Rd, Eastham; 02642 508-240-2870 tinyurl.com/yh8h8wm ⚡ ⊗⊗

Falmouth

⚥ ○ Captain Lawrence Inn, 75 Locust St, Falmouth 02540-2658 508-548-9178 www.captainlawrenceinn.com (🐾?) ⚡ frontdesk@captainlawrenceinn.com

AIDS/HIV Services, Education & Support

⚥ AIDS Support Group of Cape Cod, 96 Bradford St, Provincetown, MA 800-905-1170 www.asgcc.org

Bookstores

Martha's Vineyard

⚥ ○ Bunch of Grapes, 23 Main St 508-693-2291 www.bunchofgrapes.com

Organizations/Resources: Family and Supporters

⚥ ☆ PFLAG Cape Cod, POB 262, Marston Mills 02648 www.pflag-capecod.org

Organizations/Resources: Social, Recreation, Support

♂ ★ Gay Men's Social Group of Falmouth, 508-801-7375 www.falmouthmensgroup.org

Organizations/Resources: Youth (see also Family)

⚥ ★ ♿♿ Thrive! at CIGSYA, Cape & Islands Gay & Straight Youth Alliance, 56 Barnstable Rd, Hyannis; 508-778-7744 tinyurl.com/y2hmx36n ⚡

Weddings and Ceremonies

⚥ ○ Weddings By Design, 142 Brier Lane, Brewster 02631 508-896-8121 www.weddingsbydesign.info ♥ brwstr@verizon.net

» *Conway: see Western MA/Berkshires*

Dartmouth

Organizations/Resources: Student, Academic, Education

⚥ ★ Pride Alliance, UMASS Dartmouth, Campus Center Room 208, 285 Old Westport Rd, N Dartmouth; 508-999-8163 fb.com/umassdpridealliance/

» *Dorchester: see Boston Area*
» *Edgartown: see Cape Cod & Islands*

Fall River

AIDS/HIV Services, Education & Support

♂ TWIST: The Men's Health Project, 314 S Main St 508-672-0378 tinyurl.com/35sq9rb

Health Care: Physical (see also Counseling/Mental Health)

⚥ Stanley Street Treatment & Resources (SSTAR), 386 Stanley St; 508-324-3500 www.sstar.org

Fitchburg

Organizations/Resources: Student, Academic, Education

⚥ ★ ♿♿ Fitchburg State University GSA, Office of Student Development, 160 Pearl St; 978-665-3164 **H?** tinyurl.com/o4uy249 ⚡

Framingham

Counseling/Psychotherapy/Mental Health

⚥ Tempo Young Adult Resource Center, 68 Henry St, Framingham; 508-879-1424 tempoyoungadults.org

Religious / Spiritual Resources

⚥ ☆ ♿♿ Edwards Church UCC, 39 Edwards St, Framingham; 01701 508-877-2050 **HD** www.edwardschurch.org ⚡ office@edwardschurch.org

» *Gloucester: see North Shore Area*
» *Great Barrington: see Western MA/Berkshires*
» *Greenfield: see Western MA/Berkshires*
» *Haverhill: see Merrimack Valley*
» *Hull: see South Shore Area*
» *Hyannis: see Cape Cod & Islands*
» *Jamaica Plain: see Boston Area*
» *Lawrence: see Merrimack Valley*
» *Lenox: see Western MA/Berkshires*
» *Lexington: see Boston Area*
» *Lowell: see Merrimack Valley*
» *Lynn: see North Shore Area*
» *Marblehead: see North Shore Area*
» *Martha's Vineyard: see Cape Cod & Islands*
» *Medford: see Boston Area*

Merrimack Valley

Bars, Cafes, Clubs, Restaurants

Haverhill

⚥ ○ Wicked Big Cafe, 19 Essex St, Haverhill 978-556-5656 wickedbigcafe.biz ☕

Counseling/Psychotherapy/Mental Health

⚥ ● ♿♿ Counts, Holly, PsyD, Life Transformations, LLC, POB 15, Newburyport; 01950 / 21 Pleasant St Ste 235 802-359-9139 tinyurl.com/y3zotwn4 ⚡

Funding: Endowment, Fundraising

⚥ ★ ♿♿ The Miracle Providers NorthEast, 122 Western Ave Box 121, Lowell; 978-616-6991 www.miracleprovidersne.org ⚡

Massachusetts: Merrimack Valley
Organizations: Student

195

GAYELLOW PAGES #42 2020-2021

Provincetown Area: Massachusetts
Accommodation

Organizations/Resources: Student, Academic, Education

♀ ★ Merrimack College GSA, Student Involvement Office, Sakowich Campus Center Room 370, N Andover 978-837-5508

Organizations/Resources: Youth (see also Family)

♀ ★ ♂♂ Merrimack Valley Alliance of GLBT Youth (McVAGLY), 190 Academy Rd, N Andover; Youth ages 14-22 fb.com/McVagly ✔
>> *Methuen: see Merrimack Valley*

Middleboro

Religious / Spiritual Resources

♂ ☆ First Unitarian Universalist Society of Middleborough, 25 S Main St; 02346 508-947-1935 www.uumiddleboro.org office@uumiddleboro.org
>> *Newburyport: see Merrimack Valley*

North Shore Area

Community Centers and/or Pride Organizations

♀ ★ North Shore Pride, POB 355, Manchester 01944 978-808-5451 www.northshorepride.org

Accommodation: Hotels, Inns, Guesthouses, B&B, Resorts
Gloucester

♂ ● Inn At Babson Court, 55 Western Ave, Gloucester; 01930-3647 978-281-4469 www.babsoncourt.com ✔ ⊛ ⊛ inn@babsoncourt.com

Rockport

♂ ♡ (?♂) Sally Webster Inn, 34 Mount Pleasant St, Rockport; 01966 978-546-9251 sallywebster.com ✔ ⊛ ⊛ info@sallywebster.com

Counseling/Psychotherapy/Mental Health

♂ ★ ♂♂ Amico, Joseph, M.Div, CAS, LADC-I, 50 Washington St, Salem; 01970 603-852-3168 www.joeamico.com joe@joeamico.com

Organizations/Resources: Family and Supporters

♂ PFLAG - Essex/Cape Ann, POB 156, Essex 01929 978-745-9019 gbpflag.org

Organizations/Resources: Social, Recreation, Support

♂ ★ North Shore Men, POB 4444, Peabody; 01961 Gay/bi men www.northshoremen.org

Organizations/Resources: Student, Academic, Education

♀ ★ Endicott College EC Alliance, 376 Hale St, Beverly; 978-232-2146

♀ ★ Salem State College Alliance, 352 Lafayette St, Salem; 978-542-7541 tinyurl.com/y9fj9uol

♀ ☆ Salem State College Florence Luscomb Women's Center, Women Center Office, ECC211, 352 Lafayette St, Salem; 978-542-6555 tinyurl.com/y82zyhmr

Organizations/Resources: Youth (see also Family)

♀ ★ ♂♂ North Shore Alliance of GLBT Youth (NAGLY), Museum Place Mall, 2 E India Square Ste #121, Salem; 01970 978-224-2101 www.nagly.org ✔ naglyleaders@gmail.com

Sports & Outdoor

♀ ☆ Boston Roller Derby, www.bostonrollerderby.com
>> *North Truro: see Provincetown Area*
>> *Northampton: see Western MA/Berkshires*
>> *Peabody: see North Shore Area*
>> *Pittsfield: see Western MA/Berkshires*

Provincetown Area

Accommodation: Hotels, Inns, Guesthouses, B&B, Resorts
Provincetown

♂ ● 8 Dyer Hotel, 8 Dyer St, Provincetown 508-487-0880 www.8dyer.com

♀ ● Admiral's Landing, 158 Bradford St, Provincetown; 508-487-9665 www.admiralslanding.com ✔ ⊛

♂ ● Aerie House, 184 Bradford St, Provincetown 02657-2427 508-487-1197 www.aeriehouse.com (♿?) ✔

♀ ● Beaconlight Guesthouse, 12 Winthrop St, Provincetown; 508-487-9603 tinyurl.com/38vdde ✔ ⊛

♀ ● Benchmark Inn, 6 Dyer St, Provincetown 508-487-7440 www.benchmarkinn.com

♂ ● (?♂) The Boatslip, 161 Commercial St, Provincetown; 508-487-1669 www.boatslipresort.com ⚥ ✗ ✔ (⊛)

♂ ● (?♂) The Bradford, 41 Bradford St, Provincetown; 02657-1357 508-487-0173 **H?** www.thebradfordptown.com ✔ ⊛ info@thebradfordptown.com

♀ ● Bradford-Carver House, 70 Bradford St, Provincetown; 02657-1363 508-487-0728 800-826-9083 bradfordcarver.com ✔ info@bradfordcarver.com

♂ ● ♂♂ The Brass Key Guesthouse, 67 Bradford St, Provincetown; 508-487-9005 www.brasskey.com ⊛

♂ ● The Captain's House, 350A Commercial St, Provincetown; 508-487-9353 www.captainshousetown.com ✔ ⊛ ⊛

♂ ● Carl's Guest House, 68 Bradford St, Provincetown; 02657-1363 508-487-1650 www.CarlsGuestHouse.com ✔ ⊛

♀ ● Carpe Diem Guesthouse & Namasté Spa, 12 Johnson St, Provincetown; 02657-2312 508-487-4242 800-487-0132 www.carpediemguesthouse.com ✔ ⊛ info@carpediemguesthouse.com

♀ ● Chicago House, 6 Winslow St, Provincetown 508-487-9353 www.chicagohouseptown.com ✔ ⊛

♂ ● Christopher's by the Bay, 8 Johnson St, Provincetown; 508-487-9263 www.christophersbythebay.com (♿?) ✔ ⊛ ⊛

♀ ● The Crew's Quarters, 198 Commercial St, Provincetown; 508-487-5900 www.CrewsQuartersPtown.com ✔ ⊛

♀ ● ♂♂ Crown & Anchor Inn, 247 Commercial St, Provincetown; 508-487-1430 www.onlyatthecrown.com **D** ▦ ✔

♀ ● ♂♂ Crowne Pointe Historic Inn, 82 Bradford St, Provincetown; 508-487-6767 www.crownepointe.com

♂ ● Eben House, 90 Bradford St, Provincetown 508-487-0386 www.ebenhouse.com ✔ ⊛

♂ ● (?♂) Gifford House Inn, 9 Carver St, Provincetown; 508-487-0688 www.giffordhouse.com **D** ▦ ✔ (⊛)

Massachusetts: Provincetown Area
Accommodation

196

GAYELLOW PAGES #42 2020-2021

Provincetown Area: Massachusetts
Funding: Endowment Fundraising

⚥ ● John Randall House, 140 Bradford St, Provincetown; 508-487-3533 www.johnrandallhouse.com

♂ ● Land's End Inn, 22 Commercial St, Provincetown 508-487-0706 www.landsendinn.com (♣?) ⚲ ⊗

⚥ ● Moffett House, 296A Commercial St, Provincetown; 508-487-6615 www.moffetthouse.com ⚲

♂ ● Prince Albert Guest House, 164 Commercial St, Provincetown; 508-487-1850 www.pagh.us (♣?) ⚲ ⊗

♂ ● (?⅊) The Provincetown Hotel at Gabriel's, 102 Bradford St, Provincetown; 508-487-3232 www.provincetownhotel.com ♣ ⚲ ⊗

♀ ○ The Red Inn, 15 Commercial St, Provincetown 02657-1909 508-487-7334 theredinn.com ⚒ ✂ info@theredinn.com

⚥ ● Revere Guest House, 14 Court St, Provincetown; 800-487-2292 reverehouse.com

♂ ● ♿ Rose & Crown Guest House, 158 Commercial st, Provincetown; 508-487-3332 www.roseandcrownptown.com ♣ ⊗

♀ ● Rose Acre, 5 Center St, Provincetown 508-487-2347 www.RoseAcreGuests.com ⚲ ⊗

♂ ● Salt House Inn, 6 Conwell St, Provincetown 508-487-1911 www.salthouseinn.com ⚲ ⊗

♂ ● Sandcastle Resort & Club, 929 Commercial St 508-487-9300 www.sandcastlecapecod.com ⚲

♂ ● A Secret Garden Inn, 300A Commercial St, Provincetown; 508-487-9027 www.secretgardenptown.com ♣ ⚲ ⊗ ⊗

♂ ● Somerset House, 378 Commercial St, Provincetown; 800-575-1850 www.somersethouseinn.com ⚲ ⊗

♀ ○ (?⅊) Surfside Hotel & Suites, 543 Commercial St, Provincetown; 02657-1724 508-487-1726 fax 508-487-6556 www.surfside-inn.cc ♣ ⚲ ⊗ surfsidehotelandsuites.elaine@gmail.com

♂ ● Tucker Inn, 12 Center St, Provincetown 508-487-0381 thetuck-erinn.com (♣?) ⚲ ⊗

⚥ ● Watership Inn, 7 Winthrop St, Provincetown 02657-2116 800-330-9413 508-487-0094 www.watershipinn.com ⚲ ⊗ info@watershipinn.com

♂ ● West End Inn, 44 Commercial St, Provincetown 02657-1912 508-487-9555 800-559-1220 www.westendinn.com warren@westendinn.com

♂ ● White Wind Inn, 174 Commercial St, Provincetown; 508-487-1526 www.whitewindinn.com

♀ ● Women Innkeepers of Provincetown, POB 573, Provincetown; 02657 www.womeninnkeepers.com

Accommodation Rental: Furnished / Vacation (& AirBNB)
Provincetown

⚥ ● Bayshore, 493 Commercial St, Provincetown 508-487-9133 www.bayshorechandler.com

Art & Photography (see also Graphic Design)

♂ ○ Song of Myself Photography, 349 Commercial St, Provincetown; 02657 508-487-5736 www.songofmyself.com ♥ info@songofmyself.com

Bars, Cafes, Clubs, Restaurants
North Truro

♂ ● ♿ Top Mast Cafe, 209 Shore Rd, North Truro; 508-487-2099 (seasonal) fb.com/topmastcafe ⊳

Provincetown

⚥ ● ♿ The A-House, 4 Masonic Pl, Provincetown; 508-487-3169 www.ahouse.com **DKL** ⚲ theahouse1@verizon.net

♂ ○ ♿ **Bayside Betsy's, 177 Commercial St, Provincetown; 508-487-6566 fax 508-487-5537 "The People you know and the Place you Love." Year round casual Waterfront dining in the heart of Provincetown. Bar open till 1am. www.baysidebetsys.com** ⚒ ✂ **BaysideBetsys@aol.com**

♂ ○ Big Daddy's Burritos, 205 Commercial St, Provincetown; 508-487-4432 www.bigdaddysburritos.com ⊳

♂ ○ Bubala's by the Bay Restaurant, 185 Commercial St, Provincetown; 508-487-0773 www.bubalas.com ✂

⚥ ● ♿ Central House, Crown & Anchor, 247 Commercial St, Provincetown; 508-487-1430 www.onlyatthecrown.com ⚒ ✂ ▦ ⚲

⚥ ● ♿ Central House, Crown & Anchor, 247 Commercial St, Provincetown; 508-487-1430 onlyatthecrown.com/dining **D** ✂ ⚲

⚥ ● Club Purgatory, c/o Gifford House Inn, 11 Carver St, Provincetown; 508-487-8442 tinyurl.com/ptz95cz **L**

⚥ ● Girl Power Events, www.provincetownforwomen.com ✪

♂ ● ♿ Mews Restaurant & Cafe, 429 Commercial St, Provincetown; 508-487-1500 mewsptown.com ⚒ ⊳ ✂ ▦ ⚲

♀ ○ Napi's Restaurant, 7 Freeman St, Provincetown 508-487-1145 www.napisptown.com ✂

⚥ ● ♿ Paramount, Crown & Anchor, 247 Commercial St, Provincetown; 508-487-1430 onlyatthecrown.com/venue/5 **D** ⚲

♀ ○ Patio American Grill & Blue Bar, 328 Commercial St, Provincetown; 508-487-4003 ptownpatio.com ⚒ ✂

⚥ ● (?⅊) The Porchside Lounge, Gifford House Inn, 11 Carver St, Provincetown; 508-487-0688 tinyurl.com/y8q6rx **D** ⚲

♂ ○ Spiritus Pizza, 190 Commercial St, Provincetown; 508-487-2808 spirituspizza.com ✂

⚥ ● ♿ Vault, Crown & Anchor, 247 Commercial St, Provincetown; 508-487-1430 tinyurl.com/lcyds **L**

⚥ ● ♿ Wave Video Bar, Crown & Anchor, 247 Commercial St, Provincetown; 508-487-1430 onlyatthecrown.com/venue/7 **DKV**

Bookstores

♂ East End Books Ptown, 389 Commercial St, Provincetown; 508-413-9059 www.eastendbooksptown.com

♂ ● Provincetown Bookshop, 246 Commercial St, Provincetown; 508-487-0964 tinyurl.com/p7rkyag

Funding: Endowment, Fundraising

♂ ★ ♿ Provincetown Harbor Swim for Life & Paddler Flotilla, POB 819, Provincetown; 02657-0819 508-487-1930 www.swim4life.org ⚲ thecompact@comcast.net

Health Care: Physical (see also Counseling/Mental Health)

♀ ☆ Helping Our Women, 34 Conwell St, Provincetown; 508-487-4357 All women living with chronic, life threatening, or disabling illness on outer Cape Cod www.helpingourwomen.org ⚥

Organizations/Resources: Business & Professional Associations, Labor Advocacy

⚥ ★ ♿ Provincetown Business Guild, 3 Freeman St Unit #2, Provincetown; 508-487-2313 www.ptown.org

Organizations/Resources: Social, Recreation, Support

♂ ★ Provincetown Bears, POB 1724, Provincetown 02657 www.ptownbears.org

Sports & Outdoor

♀ ● Ptown Bikes, 42 Bradford St, Provincetown 02657-1338 508-487-8735 www.ptownbikes.com ptownbikes@gmail.com
>> *Randolph: see South Shore Area*
>> *Revere: see North Shore Area*
>> *Rockport: see North Shore Area*
>> *Salem: see North Shore Area*
>> *Salisbury: see Merrimack Valley*
>> *Saugus: see North Shore Area*
>> *Somerville: see Boston Area*

South Shore Area

Information, Media & Publications

⚥ ★ South Coast LGBTQ Network, POB 8473, New Bedford; 02740 774-775-2656 www.sclgbtqnetwork.org

Bars, Cafes, Clubs, Restaurants
New Bedford

⚥ Le Place, 20 Kenyon St, New Bedford 508-990-1248 fb.com/Le-PlaceNB/ **D** ▦ ⚥

Taunton

⚥ ● Bobby's Place Nightclub, 60 Weir St, Taunton; 508-824-9997 www.BobbysPlaceMA.com **DK** ▦

Health Care: Physical (see also Counseling/Mental Health)

♀ ☆ Health Imperatives, 942 W Chestnut St, Brockton; 508-583-3003 healthimperatives.org

Legal Services

♀ ○ Gaughen, Gaughen, Lane & Hernando, 528 Broad St, East Weymouth; 02189 781-335-0374 www.gaughenlane.com

♀ ○ Gaughen, Gaughen, Lane & Hernando, 528 Broad St, East Weymouth; 781-335-0374 www.gaughenlane.com

Organizations/Resources: Family and Supporters

♀ ○ PFLAG - South Shore-Duxbury, First Parish Church, 842 Tremont St (Rt 3A), Duxbury; 02332 781-891-5966 gbpflag.org duxburypflag@gmail.com

Organizations/Resources: Social, Recreation, Support

♂ ★ Plymouth Men's Group, 508-747-6324 tinyurl.com/jylju5m

Organizations/Resources: Youth (see also Family)

⚥ ★ Brockton Alliance of GLBT Youth (BrAGLY), Health Imperatives, 942 W Chestnut St, Brockton; 508-583-3005 tinyurl.com/w86ht8q

⚥ New Bedford Alliance of GLBT Youth (NB-AGLY), A Perfect Place, 484 Pleasant St, New Bedford; 508-977-8040 aperfectplace.org

Religious / Spiritual Resources

♂ ☆ First Parish Church Plymouth, 12 Church St, Plymouth; 02360 508-747-1606 firstparishplymouthuu.org office@firstparish plymouthuu.org

♂ ☆ ♿ Foxborough Universalist Church, 6 Bird St, Foxborough; 02035-2301 508-543-4002 www.uufoxborough.org

♂ ☆ ♿♿ Hingham Congregational Church UCC, 378 Main St 781-749-1276 **HD** www.hccucc.com ⚥ churchoffice@hccucc.com

♂ ☆ Old Ship Church UU, 107 Main St, Hingham; 02043 781-749-1679 www.oldshipchurch.org office@oldshipchurch.org
>> *Southbridge: see Sturbridge*
>> *Springfield: see Western MA/Berkshires*
>> *Stow: see Acton/Stow*
>> *Taunton: see South Shore Area*
>> *Vineyard Haven: see Cape Cod & Islands*
>> *Waltham: see Boston Area*
>> *Wayland: see Boston Area*

Webster

Bookstores

♂ ○ Booklovers' Gourmet, 55 E Main St; 508-949-6232 www.bookloversgourmet.com ⚥ ⚥

Western MA/Berkshires

Crisis, Anti-violence, & Helplines

⚥ ☆ ♿♿ Elizabeth Freeman Center LGBQT Services, 43 Francis Ave, Pittsfield; 01201 866-401-2425 413-499-2425 **H** tinyurl.com/o39bcsz info@elizabethfreemancenter.org

⚥ ☆ ♿♿ Safe Passage,. Carlon Drive, Northampton; 888-345-5282 **H?** www.safepass.org ⚥

Community Centers and/or Pride Organizations

⚥ ★ NoHo Pride, POB 866, Northampton; 01061 413-341-0122 www.nohopride.org

Information, Media & Publications

⚥ GLBT Springfield, www.glbtspringfield.com

Accommodation: Hotels, Inns, Guesthouses, B&B, Resorts
Adams

♂ ● ♿♿ Topia Inn, 10 Pleasant St, Adams; 413-743-9600 **H?** www.topiainn.com ⚥ ⊗ ⊗

Great Barrington

♂ ● ♿♿ The Barrington, 281 Main St Level 3, Great Barrington; 413-528-6159 thebarringtongb.com ⚥ ⊗ ⊗

♀ ○ ♿♿ Windflower Inn, 684 S Egremont Rd, Great Barrington; 01230-8804 413-528-2720 www.windflowerinn.com ⚥ ⊗

Massachusetts: Western MA/Berkshires
Accommodation
198
GAYELLOW PAGES #42 2020-2021
Western MA/Berkshires: Massachusetts
Religious

Lenox

♀ ● ♿ Kemble Inn, 2 Kemble St, Lenox 413-637-4113 www.kembleinn.com ✎ ♥

♀ ○ Rookwood Inn, 11 Old Stockbridge Rd, Lenox 01240-1717 800-223-9750 413-637-9750 www.rookwoodinn.com (☺?) ✎ ☺ ♥ innkeeper@rookwoodinn.com

Shelburne Falls

♀ ○ **Bird's Nest Bed & Breakfast, 2 Charlemont Rd, Buckland; 413-625-9523 Winner of the TripAdvisor Certificate of Excellence 2013-2018. All are welcome! www.birdsnestbnb.com** ✎ ☺

Williamstown

♀ ○ Guest House at Field Farm, 554 Sloan Rd, Williamstown; 01267-3059 413-458-3135 tinyurl.com/k9a5tfz ✎ ☺☺ fieldfarm@ thetrustees.org

♀ ○ River Bend Farm B&B, 643 Simonds Rd, Williamstown; 01267 413-458-3121 www.riverbendfarmbb.com ✎ ☺ riverbendfarmbb@gmail.com

AIDS/HIV Services, Education & Support

♀ ☆♿ A Positive Place, POB 1299, Northampton; 01061 413-586-8288 **H** Bilingual/bicultural staff in Spanish and interpretation available for other languages tinyurl.com/ybgdth27 ◑ ✎

Bars, Cafes, Clubs, Restaurants

Northampton

♀ ○ Haymarket Cafe, 185 Main St, Northampton 413-586-9969 www.haymarketcafe.com ✕

♀ ○ Pearl Street Nightclub, 10 Pearl St, Northampton; 413-586-8686 tinyurl.com/8h2hb **D** ▥

Springfield

● ● ♿ X Room at Mardi Gras & 350 Grill, 87 Taylor St, Springfield; 413-732-4562 **H?** Strip club www.clubxroom.com **K** ♈ ✕▥ ✎

Williamstown

♀ ○♿ Mezze Bistro + Bar, 777 Cold Spring Rd (Rt 7), Williamstown; 413-458-0123 www.mezzerestaurant.com ♈ ✕

Bookstores

♀ ○ ♿ World Eye Bookshop, 134 Main St, Greenfield; 413-772-2186 tinyurl.com/yc9s932s

Food Specialties (see also Catering)

♀ ● Indigo Coffee Roasters, Inc., 660 Riverside Dr, Northampton; 01062-2753 800-447-5450 www.indigocoffee.com info@ indigocoffee.com

Legal Services

♀ ○ ♿ Law Office of David W Sanborn, 185 Belmont Ave, Springfield; 01108 413-734-2156 www.bsmllplaw.com ✎ david@ bsmllplaw.com

Organizations/Resources: Family and Supporters

♀ ☆♿ PFLAG Franklin-Hampshire Chapter, meets 2nd Tue 6-8 pm at 325 King St, Northampton MA 413-625-6636 fhcpflag.weebly.com ✎

Organizations/Resources: Senior Resources

♀ ● Barton's Angels, Inc., POB 343, Northampton 01061 413-582-0220 **HD** Home Health Care www.bartonsangels.com

Organizations/Resources: Social, Recreation, Support

● ★ MONOHO: Men of Western Mass, tinyurl.com/yc4oggl2

Organizations/Resources: Student, Academic, Education

● ★ ♿ Amherst College Queer Resource Center, 213 Keefe Campus Center, 16 Barrett Hill Dr, Amherst; 413-542-5964 **H?** tinyurl.com/ycqryj28 ✎

● ★ Hampshire College Queer Community Alliance, 893 West Street, Amherst; 413-559-5320 tinyurl.com/o8dc6ay

● ★ ♿ Holyoke Community College Rainbow Club, c/o Student Activities, 303 Homestead Ave, Holyoke 413-552-2515 tinyurl.com/y7sv7p7m ✎

● ★ ♿ LGBTQ Community at Williams College, Jenness House, 10 Morley Dr, Williamstown; 413-597-4573 lgbt.williams.edu ✎

● ★ Mount Holyoke College Jeannette Marks House, 47 Morgan St, S Hadley; 01075 413-538-2012 tinyurl.com/3fu2n7n

● ★ Mount Holyoke Lyon's Pride, www.mhlp.org

● ★ ♿ Smith College Resource Center for Sexuality & Gender, Wesley Basement, Northampton; 413-585-6014 smith.edu/ose/rcsg.php

● ★ ♿ The Stonewall Center, University Of Massachusetts 256 Sunset Ave Ofc, Amherst; 413-545-4824 www.umass.edu/stonewall ✎

Organizations/Resources: Transgender/Gender Non-Conforming/Diverse

⊤ ☆♿ UniTy of the Pioneer Valley, 860-604-6343 tinyurl.com/5cvgxe dejavudeja@sbcglobal.net

Organizations/Resources: Youth (see also Family)

● ★ ♿ Generation Q - Greenfield, Community Action, 154 Federal St, Greenfield; 413-774-7028 x5 tinyurl.com/y5ple6v3 ✎

● ★ ♿ Generation Q - Northampton, 17 New S St Ste 116, Northampton, MA 413-475-1798 tinyurl.com/y5ple6v3 ✎

● ★ ♿ Out Now, POB 5321, Springfield; 01103 413-736-4610 **H?** www.outnowyouth.org ✎

Real Estate (see also Mortgages)

♀ ● Berkshire Property Agents, 12 Railroad St, Great Barrington; 01230 413-528-6800 **H** tinyurl.com/d2gds2v ✎ info@ bpagents.com

Recovery

♀ ☆ Alcoholics Anonymous Western Mass Intergroup, 474 Pleasant St, Holyoke; 413-532-2111 www.westernmassaa.org

Religious / Spiritual Resources

♀ ☆ Edwards Church, 297 Main St, Northampton; 01060 413-584-5500 tinyurl.com/9cjfp2n info@edwardschurchnorthampton.org

♀ ☆♿ First Churches ABC/UCC, 129 Main St, Northampton; 01060 413-584-9392 www.firstchurches.org

♀ ☆ & & First Congregational Church, 906 Main St, Williamstown; 01267 413-458-4273 **HD** tinyurl.com/9xoncgl ✔

♂ ☆ South Congregational Church, 45 Maple St, Springfield; 01105 413-732-0117 www.sococh.org secretary@sococh.org

♀ ☆ Unitarian Society of Northampton & Florence, 220 Main St, Northampton; 01060 413-584-1390 www.uunorthampton.org office@uunorthampton.org

♂ ☆ Unitarian Universalist Society, POB 502, Amherst; 01004 413-253-2848 www.uusocietyamherst.org office@uusociety amherst.org

Women's Centers

♀ ☆ (?&) Center for Women & Community, New Africa House, 180 Infirmary Way, Amherst; 01003-9315 413-545-0883 www.umass.edu/cwc/ ✪ cwc@umass.edu
» Williamstown: see Western MA/Berkshires

Worcester Area

Automobile Services

♂ ● Mackoul's Cars Inc, 220 Worcester St #122, N Grafton; 01536-1258 508-839-2324 www.mackoulscars.net ✔ mackoulscars@verizon.net

Organizations/Resources: Student, Academic, Education

♀ ★ Algonquin Regional High School GSA, 79 Bartlett St, Northborough; 508-351-7010 tinyurl.com/y8a7myvg

Worcester

Community Centers and/or Pride Organizations
Worcester

♀ ★ Worcester Pride, POB 1126; 01613 www.worcesterpride.org

AIDS/HIV Services, Education & Support
Worcester

♂ ☆ & & AIDS Project Worcester, 85 Green St; 508-755-3773 www.aidsprojectworcester.org

Bars, Cafes, Clubs, Restaurants
Worcester

♀ ● MB Lounge, 40 Grafton St; 508-799-4521 www.mblounge.com **DKL** ✔

Immigration, Citizenship, Political Asylum, Refugees

♀ ☆ & & LGBT Asylum Task Force, Hadwen Park Congregational Church, 6 Clover St; www.lgbtasylum.org ✪

Organizations/Resources: Family and Supporters

♂ ☆ & & Greater Worcester PFLAG, The Bridge of Central MA, 4 Mann St; 508-631-2699 www.worcesterpflag.org

Organizations/Resources: Student, Academic, Education
Worcester

♀ ★ & & Becker Pride, 61 Sever St ✔

♀ (?&) Clark University Prism, 950 Main St, Box B-5; 508-793-7549 fb.com/clarkuniversityprism

♀ ★ Worcester State College Pride Alliance, Student Center #319, 486 Chandler St; 508-929-8625

Organizations/Resources: Youth (see also Family)
Worcester

♂ ☆ Safe Homes, The Bridge of Central MA, Inc, 4 Mann St; 508-755-0333 www.safehomesma.org

♀ ★ Supporters of Worcester Area GLBT Youth (SWAGLY), AIDS Project Worcester, 85 Green St; 508-755-3773 tinyurl.com/y6lorf2m

Religious / Spiritual Resources
Worcester

♂ ☆ & & First Unitarian Church, 90 Main St; 01608 508-757-2708 www.firstunitarian.com office@firstunitarian.com
» Yarmouth Port: see Cape Cod & Islands

Michigan
State/County Resources

Community Centers and/or Pride Organizations

♀ ★ & & Michigan Pride, POB 11171, Lansing, MI 48901 www.michiganpride.org

Information, Media & Publications

♀ ● Metra Magazine, POB 71844, Madison Heights, MI 48071 248-543-3500 www.metramagazine.com

♀ ★ What Helen Heard, Ambitious Amazons, POB 811, East Lansing, MI 48826-0811 517-371-5257 fax 517-371-5200 What's Happening For Michigan Lesbians www.lconline.org LC@LConline.org

AIDS/HIV Services, Education & Support

♂ Matrix Human Services Central Office, 120 Parsons St, Detroit, MI 313-831-1000 www.matrixhumanservices.org ✔

Organizations/Resources: Cultural, Dance, Performance

♀ ★ Equality Band of Michigan, fb.com/groups/104491206256867

Organizations/Resources: Political/Legislative/Advocacy

♂ ☆ ACLU of Michigan, 2966 Woodward Ave, Detroit, MI 48201 313-578-6800 www.aclumich.org

♂ ☆ Equality Michigan, 19641 W Seven Mile Rd, Detroit, MI 313-537-7000 www.equalitymi.org

♀ Michigan Coalition for Human Rights, 9200 Gratiot, Detroit, MI 313-579-9071 www.mchr.org

Organizations/Resources: Social, Recreation, Support

♀ ★ Michiana Dunes Lambda Car Club, 19155 Beaver Dam Rd, Galien, MI 49113 / W Michigan & NW Indiana www.michianadunes.com michianadunes@gmail.com

Organizations/Resources: Transgender/Gender Non-Conforming/Diverse

T ☆ TransGender Michigan, 23211 Woodward Ave #309, Ferndale, MI 48220 855-345-TGMI www.transgendermichigan.org info@transgendermichigan.org

Sports & Outdoor

♀ ★ Michigan International Gay Rodeo Association, POB 7559, Dearborn, MI 48121 248-562-2560 fb.com/migra.michigan/

Michigan: Adrian
Organizations: Student

200
GAYELLOW PAGES #42 2020-2021

Ann Arbor/Ypsilanti Area: Michigan
Organizations: Student

317 Braun Court
Ann Arbor
734-663-0036

book BAR™

Common Language™

www.glbtbooks.com

Adrian

Organizations/Resources: Student, Academic, Education

♀ ★ ♿ Adrian College Safe Place, 1325 Williams St; 517-265-5161 tinyurl.com/jk3z5yl ✔

Allendale

Organizations/Resources: Student, Academic, Education

♀ ★ Grand Valley State University Faculty & Staff Association, 240 Library, GVSU, 1 Campus Dr; 49401 616-331-2633 www.gvsu.edu/lgbtfacstaff lgbtfsa@gvsu.edu

♀ ★ Milton E. Ford LGBT Resource Center, GVSU, 1161 Kirkhof Student Center; 616-331-2530 www.gvsu.edu/lgbtrc/

Ann Arbor/Ypsilanti Area

Community Centers and/or Pride Organizations

♀ ★ (♿) Jim Toy Community Center, 319 Braun Court, Ann Arbor; 734-274-9551 www.jimtoycenter.org

AIDS/HIV Services, Education & Support

♂ ☆ ♿ Unified HIV Health and Beyond, 2287 Ellsworth Rd Ste B, Ypsilanti; 48197 734-572-9355 **H?** miunified.org ✔ info@miunified.org

Bars, Cafes, Clubs, Restaurants
Ann Arbor

♀ ● ♿ Aut Bar, 315 Braun Court, Ann Arbor; 734-994-3677 fb.com/a2autbar/ ♈ ✖

♂ ○ Cafe Verde, 214 N 4th Ave, Ann Arbor 734-994-9174 www.peoplesfood.coop ↻ ✔

♂ ○ ♿ The Earle Restaurant, 121 W Washington St, Ann Arbor; 734-994-0211 www.theearle.com ♈ ✖ ✔

♂ ○ (♿) The Necto, 516 E Liberty St, Ann Arbor; / Pride Fridays 734-994-5436 www.necto.com **D** 🎵 ✔

♂ ○ Seva, 2541 Jackson Ave, Ann Arbor 734-662-1111 www.sevarestaurant.com ✖

♂ ○ ♿ Zingerman's Delicatessen & Next Door Coffeehouse, 422 Detroit St, Ann Arbor; 734-663-3354 **H?** www.zingermansdeli.com ↻ ✔

Bookstores

♀ ● ♿ Common Language Bookstore, 317 Braun Court, Ann Arbor; 734-663-0036 fax 734-994-1396 www.glbtbooks.com

♂ ○ (♿) Crazy Wisdom Bookstore & Tea Room, 114 S Main St, Ann Arbor; 734-665-2757 www.crazywisdom.net ↻

♂ ○ ♿ Nicola's Books, Westgate Shopping Center, 2513 Jackson Rd, Ann Arbor; 734-662-0600 www.nicolasbooks.com ✔

Counseling/Psychotherapy/Mental Health

♂ ○ Greene, Marge, LMSW LMFT, 2311 Shelby Ave Ste 106, Ann Arbor; 48103 734-668-8667

♂ ○ ♿ Keith, Ralph P, PhD, 424 Little Lake Dr, Ann Arbor; 48103 734-516-5470 www.ralphkeithphd.com ✔ ralphkeith@gmail.com

♂ ○ ♿ Krauth, Laurie, MA, 2002 Hogback Rd #15, Ann Arbor; 48105 734-973-3100 www.lauriekrauth.com LKrauth@comcast.net

♂ ○ ♿ Samuel, Michelle, LLP, LCSW, ACSW, 1817 W Stadium BLVD Ste G, Ann Arbor; 734-926-9169 tinyurl.com/4ggk7to ✔

Jewelry (see also Gifts)

♂ ○ Lewis Jewelers, 2000 W Stadium Blvd, Ann Arbor 48103 734-994-5111 www.LewisJewelers.com LewisA2@LewisJewelers.com

Legal Services

♂ ● ♿ Bassett, Jane, Bassett & Associates, PLLC, 2045 Hogback Rd, Ann Arbor; 734-930-9200 www.bassettlaw.com

♂ ○ Mullkoff, Douglas, PLCC, 402 W Liberty, Ann Arbor; 734-761-8585 Criminal law douglasmullkoff.com

Massage Therapy (Certified/Licensed only)

♂ ● Rosenberg, David, 209 W Kingsley St, Ann Arbor 48103-3313 734-662-6282 www.trymassage.com massage4@aol.com

Organizations/Resources: Cultural, Dance, Performance

♀ ★ ♿ Out Loud Chorus, POB 7107, Ann Arbor; 48107-7107 734-265-0740 olconline.org outloudchorus@gmail.com

Organizations/Resources: Family and Supporters

♂ ☆ PFLAG/Ann Arbor, POB 7471, Ann Arbor 48107-7471 734-741-0659 www.pflagaa.org info@pflagaa.org

Organizations/Resources: Political/Legislative/Advocacy

♀ University of Michigan Stonewall Democrats, 500 S State St, Ann Arbor; fb.com/UMStonewallDems

Organizations/Resources: Sexual Focus / Safe Sex

♂ ★ (♿) Group Massage for Gay & Bisexual Men, 209 W Kingsley St, Ann Arbor; 48103-3313 734-662-6282 fax 734-662-0710 www.trymassage.com Massage4@aol.com

Organizations/Resources: Student, Academic, Education

♀ ★ Eastern Michigan University LGBT Resource Center, 354 EMU Student Center, Ypsilanti; 48197-2239 734-487-4149 www.emich.edu/lgbtrc/ lgbtrc@emich.edu

♀ ★ ♿ GLSEN Liaison Ann Arbor/Ypsilanti Area, 734-913-4541 **H?**

Michigan: Ann Arbor/Ypsilanti Area
Organizations: Student

201
GAYELLOW PAGES #42 2020-2021

Big Rapids : Michigan
Organizations: Student

♀ ★ Huron High School Rainbow Rats, 2727 Fuller Road, Ann Arbor; 48105-2499 734-994-2040

♀ ★ Jim Toy Library, University of Michigan Spectrum Center, 1443 Washtenaw Ave, Ann Arbor; 734-763-4186 tinyurl.com/nvbp4bo ✗

♀ ★ Outlaws, University of Michigan Law School, 625 S State St, Ann Arbor; www.mlawoutlaws.org/

♀ ★ &&. Spectrum Center, Michigan Union, 3020 Spectrum Center, 530 S State St, Ann Arbor; 48109 734-763-4186 www.spectrumcenter.umich.edu ✗ spectrumcenter@umich.edu

Organizations/Resources: Transgender/Gender Non-Conforming/Diverse

♂ ☆ &&. Comprehensive Gender Services Program, University of Michigan Health System, 2025 Traverwood Dr Ste A-1, Ann Arbor; 734-998-2150 tinyurl.com/2earwkk

Organizations/Resources: Youth (see also Family)

♀ ★ Pride Zone, c/o Ozone House Drop-In, 102 N Hamilton St, Ypsilanti; 734-662-2265 tinyurl.com/yxg3bm3q

♀ ★ (?&) Riot Youth Program, Neutral Zone, 310 E Washington St, Ann Arbor; 48104 734-214-9995 **H?** neutral-zone.org ✗ info@neutral-zone.org

Real Estate (see also Mortgages)

♂ ☆ & Greg Johnson Realtor, 555 Briarwood Circle Ste 200, Ann Arbor; 48108 734-929-3984 fax 734-239-8384 tinyurl.com/28jveh ✗ GLJRealtor@aol.com

♀ ● &&. Lombardini, Linda, Trillium Real Estate, 323 Braun Court, Ann Arbor; 48104 734-216-6415 **H** www.LindaLom.com Linda@TrilliumRealtors.com

Religious / Spiritual Resources

♂ ☆ Journey of Faith Christian Church, 1900 Manchester Rd, Ann Arbor; 48104 734-971-4245 www.journeyoffaitha2.org jofdisciples@gmail.com

♀ ☆ (?&) Lord of Light Lutheran Church, 801 S Forest Ave, Ann Arbor; 48104-3540 734-668-7622 www.lcm-um.org ✗ lol-lcm@comcast.net

♀ ☆ &&. Northside Presbyterian Church, 1679 Broadway St, Ann Arbor; 48105-1811 734-663-5503 www.northsidepres.org info@northsidepres.org

♂ ☆ St Clare's Episcopal Church, 2309 Packard Rd, Ann Arbor; 48104 734-662-2449 www.saintclareschurch.org welcome@saintclareschurch.org

♀ ☆ Trinity Lutheran Church, 1400 W Stadium Blvd, Ann Arbor; 48103 734-662-4419 trinityaa.org

Sports & Outdoor

♀ ★ Rainbow Bowling League, Lodge Lanes, 46255 S Interstate 94 Service Dr, Belleville; 48111 734-697-9178 www.rainbowbowlingleague.com info@a2bowling.com

Veterinarians

♀ ○ &&. Brookeside Veterinary Hospital, 3010 Warren Rd, Ann Arbor; 48105 734-761-7523 brookesidevet.net ✗ brookesidevet@sbcglobal.net

Battle Creek

Community Centers and/or Pride Organizations

♀ ★ &&. Battle Creek Pride, POB 715; 49017 / 145 Capital Ave NE. upstairs at end of hall to the left www.battlecreekpride.org ✗ info@battlecreekpride.org

Bars, Cafes, Clubs, Restaurants

♀ ● 910 The Underground, 910 North Ave 269-964-7276 fb.com/910TheUnderground/ **D** ▥ ✗

Organizations/Resources: Transgender/Gender Non-Conforming/Diverse

T ☆ &&. Transgender Support Group, Battle Creek Pride, POB 715; 49017 / 145 Capital Ave NE. upstairs at end of hall to the left www.battlecreekpride.org ✗ deanaspencer@battlecreekpride.org

Bay City/Midland/Saginaw Area

AIDS/HIV Services, Education & Support

♀ Hearth Home, 732 Hoyt St, Saginaw 989-753-9011 tinyurl.com/hkrswn4

Organizations/Resources: Family and Supporters

♀ ☆ PFLAG Tri-Cities, POB 362, Bay City; 48707 989-971-7085 fb.com/PFLAGTriCities

Organizations/Resources: Social, Recreation, Support

♀ ★ (?&) Perceptions, POB 1525, Midland; 48641 989-891-1429 www.perceptionsmi.org

Organizations/Resources: Transgender/Gender Non-Conforming/Diverse

T ☆ Transgender Michigan Mid-Michigan/Tri-Cities Chapter, 842-2954 x108 www.transgendermichigan.org info@transgendermichigan.org

Religious / Spiritual Resources

♀ ☆ Midland UCC, 4100 Chestnut Hill Dr, Midland 48642-6206 989-631-1136 www.uccmidland.org

Bellaire

Accommodation: Hotels, Inns, Guesthouses, B&B, Resorts

♀ ○ Applesauce Inn Bed & Breakfast, 7296 S M-88 Highway; 49615 231-533-6448 www.applesauceinn.com ✗ ⊛ info@applesauceinn.com

♀ ○ Bellaire B&B, 212 Park St; 49615-9595 231-533-6077 bellaire-bandb.com

» Benton Harbor: see Saint Joseph
» Berkley: see Detroit Area

Big Rapids

Organizations/Resources: Student, Academic, Education

♀ ★ Diverse Sexuality & Gender Alliance, Ferris State University, 805 Campus Dr, Rankin 175, Box 084 fb.com/ferrisdsaga

» Birmingham: see Detroit Area

Michigan: Central Lake
Accommodation: Rentals

202
GAYELLOW PAGES #42 2020-2021

Detroit Area: Michigan
Legal

Central Lake

Accommodation Rental: Furnished / Vacation (& AirBNB)

♂ ● (?⚥) Hanley Lake Hideaway, Rushton Rd 49622 734-649-8357 airbnb.com/rooms/6966585 ❀ ⚲ ⊗ ⊕ hanleylake@gmail.com

>> *Chelsea: see Ann Arbor/Ypsilanti Area*

Clarklake

Religious / Spiritual Resources

♂ ☆ ⚥⚥ Universalist Unitarian Church of East Liberty, 2231 Jefferson Rd; 49234 517-529-4221 **HD** www.libertyuu.org uucel_bellnote@yahoo.com

>> *Dearborn: see Detroit Area*

Detroit Area

Community Centers and/or Pride Organizations

♀ ★ ⚥⚥ Affirmations, 290 W 9 Mile Rd, Ferndale; 48220 248-398-7105 www.goaffirmations.org ⚲ info@goaffirmations.org

♀ ★ Ferndale Pride, www.ferndalepride.com

♀ ★ (?⚥) Motor City Pride, 440 Burroughs St Ste 650, Det; motorcitypride.org

Accommodation: Hotels, Inns, Guesthouses, B&B, Resorts
Detroit

♀ ○ ⚥⚥ Atheneum Suite Hotel, 1000 Brush St, Det; 800-772-2323 www.atheneumsuites.com ⚲ ⊗

AIDS/HIV Services, Education & Support

♀ ⚥⚥ Community Health Awareness Group, 1300 W Fort St, Det; 313-963-3434 **H?** www.chagdetroit.org

♂ Health Emergency Lifeline Programs, 1726 Howard St, Det; 888-435-5655 www.helpoffice.org

♀ ★ (?⚥) Unified HIV Health and Beyond, 3011 W Grand Blvd Ste 230, Det; 313-446-9800 www.miunified.org

Bars, Cafes, Clubs, Restaurants
Detroit

♀ ● Adam's Apple, 18931 W Warren Ave, Det 313-240-8482 fb.com/adamsapple.mi/ � ✂

♂ Backstreet at Large Multiplex, 14925 Livernois Ave, Det; tinyurl.com/yxq9cnjo

♂ Briggs Sports Bar, 519 E Jefferson, Det 313-656-4820 www.briggsdetroit.com **DS** ⚲ ✂

♀ ○ (?⚥) Cass Cafe, 4620 Cass Ave, Det 313-1400 **H?** www.casscafe.com ⚲ ✂ ▦ ⚲

♂ ● Detroit Vegan Soul, 8029 Agnes St, Det 313-649-2759 www.DetroitVeganSoul.com ✂

♂ ⚲ Escape Lounge, 19404 Sheerwood St, Det; / after hours 313-892-1765 fb.com/EscapeLounge.gaybar/ ⚲ ✂ ▦

♂ ● (?⚥) Gigi's Gay Bar, 16920 W Warren, Det; 313-584-6525 fb.com/gigisgaybar **D** ▦

♂ ● Hayloft Saloon, 8070 Greenfield Rd, Det 313-581-8913 fb.com/HayloftSaloonDetroit/ **L**

♂ ● ⚲ Menjo's, 928 W McNichols, Det; 313-863-3934 www.new-menjoscomplex.com **D**

♀ ○ Temple, 2906 Cass Ave, Det; 313-832-2822 tinyurl.com/yyu56hca **D**

♀ ○ Traffic Jam & Snug, 511 W Canfield St, Det 313-831-9470 www.traffic-jam.com ⚲ ✂ tjsnug@traffic-jam.com

♂ Woodward Bar & Grill, 6426 Woodward, Det 313-872-0166 tinyurl.com/otxnln9 **DV** ⚲ ✂ ▦ ♣

Ferndale

♂ Soho Ferndale, 205 W 9 Mile Rd, Ferndale 248-542-7646 www.ferndalesoho.com

Pontiac

♂ Liberty Bar, 85 N Saginaw, Pontiac 248-758-0771 www.thelibertybar.com **DV** ⚲ ✂

Royal Oak

♀ ○ Five15, 600 S Washington Ave, Royal Oak 248-515-2551 www.five15.net ⟐▦ ⚲

♀ ● ⚥⚥ Pronto!, 608 S Washington, Royal Oak; 248-544-7900 fb.com/prontovideobar/ ⚲ ✂

Counseling/Psychotherapy/Mental Health

♀ ● ⚥⚥ Caretto, Antonia, PhD, PLLC, 25882 Orchard Lake Rd Ste 201, Farmington Hills; 48336 248-553-9053 www.betreatedwell.com drcaretto@aol.com

♀ ○ ⚥⚥ Counseling Associates, Inc, 6960 Orchard Lake Rd Ste 100, West Bloomfield; 48322 248-626-1500 www.counselingassociates.com ⚲

♀ ○ ⚥⚥ Eisenshtadt, James, PhD, 5600 W Maple Rd Ste B-208, West Bloomfield; 48322 248-851-7181 jephd@aol.com

♀ ● ⚥⚥ Sweet, Matt, MSW, PC, 25600 Woodward Ave Ste 100, Royal Oak; 48067 248-930-2137 www.mattsweet.com

Florists (see also Gifts)

♀ ○ Blossoms, 33866 Woodward Ave, Birmingham 48009-0914 248-644-4411 888-820-6597 www.blossomsbirmingham.com

Funding: Endowment, Fundraising

♂ ★ The HOPE Fund, The Community Foundation For SE MI, 333 W Fort St #2010, Det; 313-961-6675 cfsem.org/hope-fund

Health Care: Physical (see also Counseling/Mental Health)

♀ ○ Benson, Paul, DO, 1964 W 11 Mile, Berkley 48072 248-544-9300 www.doctorbewell.com drpaulbenson@doctorbewell.com

♂ Corktown Health Center, 1726 Howard St, Det; 888-435-5655 corktownhealth.org

♀ ☆ ⚥⚥ Gilda's Club Metro Detroit, 3517 Rochester Rd, Royal Oak; 248-577-0800 Cancer support www.gildasclubdetroit.org

Legal Services

♀ ● ⚥⚥ Buckstad & Associates, 1755 W Big Beaver Rd, Troy; 48084 248-822-4800 **H?** Bankruptcy www.buckstadbankruptcy.com ⚲ ebuckstad248@aol.com

♀ ○ (?⚥) Serra, Rudy, Serra Services PLLC, 1705 Wordsworth St, Ferndale; 48220 313-331-7839 fax 248-548-7839 www.rudyserra.net rudy.serra@sbcglobal.net

Michigan: Detroit Area
Men's Clubs
203
GAYELLOW PAGES #42 2020-2021
Grand Rapids : Michigan
Community Centers / Pride

Men's & Sex Clubs (not primarily Health Clubs)

Body Zone, 1617 E McNichols Rd, Det 313-366-9663 fb.com/bodyzonedetroit/ **P**

Organizations/Resources: Business & Professional Associations, Labor Advocacy

Detroit Regional LGBT Chamber of Commerce, POB 32446, Det; 48232 detroitlgbtchamber.com

Organizations/Resources: Cultural, Dance, Performance

♂ ★ ᕼᕼ Detroit Together Men's Chorus, 2441 Pinecrest Dr, Ferndale; 248-544-3872 www.dtmc.org

♀ ★ Sing Out Detroit, POB 2031, Royal Oak 48068 248-943-2411 singoutdetroit.org

Organizations/Resources: Ethnic, Multicultural

♀ ★ Al Gamea, POB 471, Hazel Park; 48030 313-427-3771 LGBT Middle Eastern www.algamea.org

Organizations/Resources: Family and Supporters

♀ ☆ PFLAG Clinton Township, Hope UCC, 35127 Garfield Rd, Clinton Township; www.PFLAGCT.org

♀ ☆ ᕼᕼ PFLAG/Detroit, POB 1169, Royal Oak; 48068 248-656-2875 www.pflagdetroit.org

Organizations/Resources: Social, Recreation, Support

♀ ★ Lambda Car Club Detroit Region, POB 446, Royal Oak; 48068-0446 www.LCCDetroit.org info@LCCDetroit.org

♂ ★ (?ᕼ) Motor City Bears, POB 1894, Royal Oak; 48068 www.motorcitybears.com

Organizations/Resources: Student, Academic, Education

♀ ★ Wayne State University JIGSAW, 5221 Gullen Mall room 309, Det; fb.com/groups/2202047607/

Organizations/Resources: Transgender/Gender Non-Conforming/Diverse

T ⚬ ᕼ Janet's Closet, 2317 Fort St, Wyandotte; 48192 734-285-2609 www.janetscloset.com janetscloset@aol.com

Organizations/Resources: Youth (see also Family)

♀ ★ ᕼᕼ Affirmations Youth Empowerment Programs (YEP), 290 W 9 Mile Rd, Ferndale; 248-398-7105 tinyurl.com/y5spg7n9 ✗

♀ ★ Ruth Ellis Center, 77 Victor St, Highland Park; 313-252-1950 www.ruthelliscenter.org

Religious / Spiritual Resources

♀ ★ Dignity/Detroit, POB 558, Royal Oak 48068 313-278-4786 www.dignitydetroit.org

♀ ★ ᕼᕼ Divine Peace Metropolitan Community Church, 6650 Elizabeth Lake Rd, Waterford; 248-332-1186 www.dpmcc.net

♀ ★ ᕼᕼ Gay Spiritual Support Group, 248-349-6143 tinyurl.com/y4yaxdzn rainbowcross@comcast.net

♀ ★ ᕼᕼ Metropolitan Community Church of Detroit, POB 836, Royal Oak; 48068-0836 248-399-7741 fax 248-399-7693 www.mccdetroit.org MCCDetroit@gmail.com

♀ ☆ ᕼᕼ Northwest Unitarian Universalist Congregation, 23925 Northwestern Highway, Southfield; 48075-2528 248-354-4488 **HD** www.northwestuu.org

Sports & Outdoor

♀ ☆ ᕼᕼ Detroit Derby Girls, Masonic Temple, 500 Temple St, Detroit www.detroitderbygirls.com

♀ ★ Metro Detroit Softball League (MDSL), POB 20215, Ferndale; 48220 586-945-4029 www.mdsl.org

♀ ★ Motown Frontrunners, 1718 W Twelve Mile Rd, Royal Oak; 48073-3920 248-542-3829 tinyurl.com/y3vflt redforddave@ameritech.net

» *Douglas: see Saugatuck/Douglas Area*
» *East Lansing: see Lansing Area*

Empire

Accommodation: Hotels, Inns, Guesthouses, B&B, Resorts

♀ ⚬ (?ᕼ) Duneswood, 7194 S Dune Hwy 231-668-6789 www.duneswood.com (⚙?) ✗ ⊖

» *Fennville: see Saugatuck/Douglas Area*
» *Ferndale: see Detroit Area*

Flint

AIDS/HIV Services, Education & Support

♀ ☆ Wellness AIDS Services, 311 E Court St 810-232-0888 www.wellnessaids.org

Bars, Cafes, Clubs, Restaurants

Burton

♀ ⚬ ᕼᕼ Pachyderm Pub, 1408 Hemphill Rd, Burton; 810-744-4960 tinyurl.com/znfo4gj **V** ♈ ✕ ✗

♀ ⚬ ᕼᕼ The Good Beans Cafe, 328 N Grand Traverse St; 810-237-4663 www.thegoodbeanscafe.com ☞ 🏠 ✗ kengoodbeans@yahoo.com

Counseling/Psychotherapy/Mental Health

♀ ⚬ ᕼᕼ Wedda, Sue, MSW, LMSW, BCD, DCSW, 3549 S Dort Highway Ste 114; 810-742-7052

Organizations/Resources: Family and Supporters

♀ ☆ ᕼᕼ PFLAG Genesee County, c/o UU Church of Flint, 2474 S Ballenger Highway; 810-496-8302 tinyurl.com/y7yo9u7d

Organizations/Resources: Student, Academic, Education

♀ ★ ᕼᕼ Ellen Bommarito LGBTQ Center, University of Michigan-Flint, 303 E Kearsley St; 810-237-6648 www.umflint.edu/lgbt

Organizations/Resources: Youth (see also Family)

♀ ★ ᕼᕼ Our Safe Space, Wellness Inc, 311 E Court St; 810-232-0888 **H?** wellnessaids.org

Grand Rapids

Community Centers and/or Pride Organizations

♀ ★ ᕼᕼ Grand Rapids Pride Center, 345 Atlas Ave SE; 616-458-3511 www.grpride.org ✗

Michigan: Grand Rapids
Community Centers / Pride

204

GAYELLOW PAGES #42 2020-2021

Kalamazoo : Michigan
Community Centers / Pride

♥ ★ Grand Rapids Pride Festival, 343 Atlas Ave SE; 49506 616-458-3511 www.grpride.org/festival info@grpride.org

Accommodation: Hotels, Inns, Guesthouses, B&B, Resorts
Grandville

♂ ○ Prairieside Suites Luxury B&B, 3180 Washington Ave SW, Grandville; 49418 616-538-9442 www.prairieside.com (♣?) ✍ ⊗ reservations@prairieside.com

AIDS/HIV Services, Education & Support

♀ ☆ &♿ The Grand Rapids Red Project, 401 Hall St SE; 616-456-9063 redprojectgr.org ❖

Bars, Cafes, Clubs, Restaurants

♥ ● &♿ Apartment Lounge, 33 Sheldon Ave NE; 616-451-0815 www.apartmentloungegr.com **L** ✍

♥ ● &♿ Rumors Night Club, 69 S Division Ave; 616-454-8720 www.rumorsnightclub.net **DKLC** ▦ ✍

Bookstores

♂ ○ ♿ Books & Mortar, 955 Cherry Street SE; 49506 616-214-8233 www.booksandmortar.com

♂ ○ &♿ Schuler Books & Music, 2660 28th St SE; 616-942-2561 www.schulerbooks.com ✍

Leather Resources & Groups

♂ Grand Rapids Rivermen, POB 3497; 49501 www.grrivermen.net **L**

Men's & Sex Clubs (not primarily Health Clubs)

♂ (?♿) Diplomat Health Club, 2324 S Division Ave; 616-452-3754 www.thediplomatclub.com **P**

Organizations/Resources: Cultural, Dance, Performance

♀ ☆ Grand Rapids Women's Chorus, POB 68486 49516 grwc.org info@grwc.org

♥ ★ Grand River Renegades, fb.com/GRRDance

♥ ★ Grand River Squares, 2453 Michigan St NE 49506-1234 grsquares.org info@grsquares.org

♂ ★ West Michigan Gay Men's Chorus, POB 150194 49515 fb.com/WMGMC.ORG/

Organizations/Resources: Youth (see also Family)

♥ ★ &♿ Youth Group (13-17), Grand Rapids Pride Center, 343 Atlas Ave SE; 616-458-3511 tinyurl.com/y673648f ✍

Religious / Spiritual Resources

♥ ★ &♿ GIFT (Gays In Faith Together), 207 E Fulton St E; 616-774-0446 www.giftgr.org ✍

Sports & Outdoor

♀ Grand Raggidy Roller Girls, 616-752-8475 grandraggidy.com
>> *Grosse Pointe: see Detroit Area*
>> *Highland Park: see Detroit Area*

Holland

Organizations/Resources: Family and Supporters

♀ ☆ (?♿) **Holland/Lakeshore PFLAG, POB 1246, Holland; 49422-1246 616-399-2161 616-494-0765 www.pflag.org**

Organizations/Resources: Transgender/Gender Non-Conforming/Diverse

T ☆ Transgender Michigan Lakeshore Chapter, 842-2954 x110 www.transgendermichigan.org info@transgendermichigan.org

Honor

Accommodation Rental: Furnished / Vacation (& AirBNB)

♀ ● Labrys Wilderness Resort, 231-882-5994 www.labrys-woods.com (♣?) ⊗

♂ ● Ursa Minor Cottage, www.ursaminorcottage.com ⊗

Houghton

Organizations/Resources: Family and Supporters

♂ ☆ &♿ PFLAG Keweenaw, POB 276; 49931 906-482-4357 tinyurl.com/p2meg4e ✍ keweenawpflag@gmail.com

Religious / Spiritual Resources

♂ ☆ &♿ Good Shepherd Lutheran Church, 1100 College Ave; 49931 906-482-5410 gs-luth.org gslc_lcm@att.net

♂ ☆ &♿ Keweenaw Unitarian Universalist Fellowship, BHK Center, POB 276; 49931 906-482-5586 www.kuuf.net office@keweenawuu.org

Howell

Organizations/Resources: Family and Supporters

♂ ☆ PFLAG Livingston County, POB 2116; 48844 517-548-0839 www.pflaglivingston.org

Interlochen

Accommodation: Hotels, Inns, Guesthouses, B&B, Resorts

♂ ○ Lake 'N Pines Lodge, 10354 Mud Lake Rd; 49643 231-275-6671 www.lakenpineslodge.com ✍ ⊗⊗ olsen@lakenpineslodge.com

Jackson

Organizations/Resources: Family and Supporters

♂ ☆ &♿ PFLAG, fb.com/pflagjacksonmich/

Organizations/Resources: Social, Recreation, Support

♂ The Dandelion Project, 601-283-8090 fb.com/projectdandelion/

Kalamazoo

Community Centers and/or Pride Organizations

♥ ★ &♿ OutFront Kalamazoo, 340 S Rose St; 269-349-4234 outfrontkzoo.org ✍ @ixx=

Michigan: Kalamazoo
Accommodation

205

GAYELLOW PAGES #42 2020-2021

Olivet : Michigan
Organizations: Student

Accommodation: Hotels, Inns, Guesthouses, B&B, Resorts

♀ ○ Kalamazoo House B&B, 447 W South St 269-382-0880 www.thekalamazoohouse.com ✔ (◉)

Organizations/Resources: Business & Professional Associations, Labor Advocacy

♂ ★ First Thursdays - LGBTQ Networking Group, tinyurl.com/y4luslbu Office@outfrontkzoo.org

Organizations/Resources: Student, Academic, Education

♂ ★ (?♿) Western Michigan University LGBT Student Services, 1903 W Michigan Ave; 269-387-2133 www.wmich.edu/lbgt/

Organizations/Resources: Transgender/Gender Non-Conforming/Diverse

т ☆ ♿ Transcend, c/o OutFront Kalamazoo, 340 S Rose St; 49007 269-349-4234 **H?** tinyurl.com/6ltftyy ✔ Office@outfrontkzoo.org

Religious / Spiritual Resources

♂ ★ ♿ Phoenix Community Church UCC, 2208 Winchell Avenue; 49008 269-383-3222 www.phoenixchurch.org office@phoenixchurch.org

♀ ☆ Skyridge Church of the Brethren, 394 S Drake Rd 49009-1112 269-375-3939 www.skyridge.org office@skyridge.org

Lansing Area

Community Centers and/or Pride Organizations

♂ ★ Salus Center, 408 S Washington Square, Lansing; 48933 517-580-4593 www.saluscenter.org info@saluscenter.org

AIDS/HIV Services, Education & Support

♀ ★ ♿ Lansing Area AIDS Network, 913 W Holmes Rd Ste 115, Lansing; 517-394-3560 www.laanonline.org

Bars, Cafes, Clubs, Restaurants
Lansing

♂ ○ Club Tabu, Fantasies Unlimited 3208 S MLK Blvd, Lansing; 517-393-1159 clubtabu.info

♀ ● Esquire Club, 1250 Turner St, Lansing 517-487-5338 tinyurl.com/y39mx2mb **CLW** ▦ ✔

♀ ● ♿ Spiral Dance Bar, 1247 Center St, Lansing; 517-371-3221 **H?** spiraldancebar.com **D** ▦

Bookstores

♀ ○ ♿ Everybody Reads, 2019 E Michigan Ave, Lansing; 517-346-9900 **H?** fb.com/EverybodyReads ✔

♀ ○ ♿ Schuler Books & Music, 1982 Grand River Ave, Okemos; 517-349-8840 **H** www.schulerbooks.com ✔

Organizations/Resources: Cultural, Dance, Performance

♂ ★ LanSINGout Gay Men's Chorus, POB 11146, Lansing; 48901 www.lansingout.org info@lansingout.org

♀ ☆ Sistrum, POB 4191, E Lansing; 48826 www.sistrum.org

Organizations/Resources: Family and Supporters

♀ ☆ PFLAG Manistee, 313-670-2613 pflagmanistee.org pflagmanistee@gmail.com

Organizations/Resources: Political/Legislative/Advocacy

♂ ★ (?♿) Lansing Association for Human Rights, POB 14009, Lansing; 48901 www.lahronline.org

Organizations/Resources: Social, Recreation, Support

♂ ★ Suits & the City, POB 16201, Lansing 48901 517-402-2314 www.suitsandthecity.org

Organizations/Resources: Student, Academic, Education

♂ ★ Lansing Community College GSA, MC 1130, PO Box 40010, Lansing; 48901 517-483-1209 fb.com/groups/lccgsa/

♂ ★ LBGT Resource Center, Michigan State University, 302 Student Services, E Lansing; 517-353-9520 www.lbgtc.msu.edu

Real Estate (see also Mortgages)

♀ ● ♿ O'Connell, Rayce, Licensed Real Estate Agent, RE/MAX Real Estate Professionals, 300 Lake Lansing Rd, E Lansing; 248-563-4234 fb.com/TheAdrianeLauTeam/

Religious / Spiritual Resources

♀ ☆ ♿ Red Cedar Friends Meeting, 1400 Turner St, Lansing; 48906 517-371-1047 **HD** redcedarfriends.org ✔

♀ ☆ ♿ Unitarian Universalist Church of Greater Lansing, 5509 S Pennsylvania Ave, Lansing; 48911 517-351-4081 www.uu-lansing.org office@uulansing.org

» Livonia: see Detroit Area

Macomb

Health Care: Physical (see also Counseling/Mental Health)

♀ ● ♿ Partridge Creek Obstetrics and Gynecology, 19991 Hall Rd Ste 105; 586-247-8609 www.partridgecreekobgyn.com

Marquette

Accommodation: Hotels, Inns, Guesthouses, B&B, Resorts

♂ ● Birchmont Motel, 2090 US 41 South; 877-458-7805 www.Birchmontmotel.com ✤ ✔ ◉

Religious / Spiritual Resources

♀ ☆ ♿ Marquette UU Congregation, POB 687; 49855 906-249-9450 **H?** www.mqtuu.org ✔ mqtuuadassist@gmail.com

Mount Pleasant

Organizations/Resources: Student, Academic, Education

♂ ★ Office of LGBTQ Services, Central Michigan University, Bovee University Center 108B; 989-774-3637 fb.com/cmulgbtq/

» Muskegon: see Grand Rapids

Olivet

Organizations/Resources: Student, Academic, Education

♂ ★ ♿ Olivet College Gay-Straight Alliance, 320 S Main; 269-749-7607 fb.com/ocgsa ✔

Michigan: Owosso
Organizations: Family

206

GAYELLOW PAGES #42 2020-2021

Williamston : Michigan
Religious

Owosso

Organizations/Resources: Family and Supporters

♀ ☆ PFLAG Owosso, POB 23; 48867 pflagowossoarea.org

Port Huron

Organizations/Resources: Transgender/Gender Non-Conforming/Diverse

т ☆ Transgender Michigan - Port Huron Chapter, 800-842-2954 x132 tinyurl.com/yb7v28np info@transgendermichigan.org
➤➤ *Redford: see Detroit Area*

Rochester

Organizations/Resources: Student, Academic, Education

♂ ★ ♿ Oakland University Gender & Sexuality Center, Oakland Center Room 47, 312 Meadow Brook Rd; 48309-4454 248-370-4336 **H?** www.oakland.edu/gsc/ GSC@oakland.edu
➤➤ *Royal Oak: see Detroit Area*

Saint Joseph

Community Centers and/or Pride Organizations

♂ ★ ♿ OutCenter, 132 Water St, Benton Harbor; 269-925-8330 outcenter.org ✔

Saugatuck/Douglas Area

Accommodation: Hotels, Inns, Guesthouses, B&B, Resorts
Douglas

♂ ● Blue Star Motel, 167 Blue Star Hwy, Douglas 49406 269-348-0199 www.bluestardouglas.com (🐾?) ✔ 😊 info@bluestardouglas.com

♂ ● Bunkhouse Bed & Breakfast, at Campit Outdoor Resort, POB 339, Douglas; 49406 269-543-4335 tinyurl.com/oknxj7k ✔

♂ ● Pines Motor Lodge/Maple Ridge Cottages, 56 Blue Star Hwy, Douglas; 49406 269-857-5211 www.thepinesmotorlodge.com ✔ 😊 info@thepinesmotorlodge.com

♀ ● Sherwood Forest B&B, 938 Center St, Douglas 269-857-1246 www.sherwoodforestbandb.com (🐾?) ✔ 😊

Saugatuck

♀ ● Beechwood Manor Inn & Cottage, 736 Pleasant St, Saugatuck; 877-857-1587 beechwoodmanorinn.com (🐾?) ✔

♂ ● ♿ Dunes Resort, 333 Blue Star Hwy, Douglas; 49406 269-857-1401 www.dunesresort.com **D** ♀ ✗🏨 🐾

♀ ● ♿ The Kirby, 294 W Center St, Saugatuck; 269-857-5472 thekirbyhotel.com ♀ ✗ ✔ ♥

♀ ● The Saugatuck Retro Resort Motel., 6190 Blue Star Hwy, Saugatuck; 269-857-8888 thesaugatuck.com ✔ 😊 @ixx=

♀ ● Twin Oaks Inn, POB 579, Saugatuck; 49453 269-857-1600 twinoaksbb.com ✔ 😊

Accommodation Rental: Furnished / Vacation (& AirBNB)
Saugatuck

♀ ● Lake Street Commons Lodging, John Porzondek / Bryan Serman, 790 Lake St, Saugatuck; 269-414-9444 www.lakestreetcommons.com ✔ 😊

Bars, Cafes, Clubs, Restaurants
Douglas

♂ ○ Back Alley Pizza Joint, 22 Main St, Douglas 269-857-7277 www.backalleypizzajoint.com ✗

Saugatuck

♀ ○ Phil's Bar & Grille, 215 Butler St, Saugatuck, MI 269-857-1555 www.philsbarandgrille.com ♀ ✗ philsbarandgrille@gmail.com

♂ ● ♿ Uncommon Coffee Roasters, 127 Hoffman St 269-857-3333 uncommoncoffeeroasters.com ↻ ✔

Campgrounds and RV Parks

♂ ● (🐾) Campit Outdoor Resort & Cabins, POB 339, Douglas; 49406 877-226-7481 www.campitresort.com ✔ 😊

Funding: Endowment, Fundraising

♂ ★ West Shore Aware, POB 33, Douglas; 49406 269-206-3061 www.westshoreaware.org

Traverse City

Accommodation: Hotels, Inns, Guesthouses, B&B, Resorts

♂ ○ ♿ Innisfaire Bed and Breakfast, 7930 S W Bay Shore Dr; 49684 231-846-3031 www.innisfaire.com Innisfaire@InnisfaireLLC.com

♀ ○ ♿ The Neahtawanta Inn, 1308 Neahtawanta Rd; 49686-9716 800-220-1415 neahtawantainn.com ✔ 😊

Bars, Cafes, Clubs, Restaurants

♂ ● Side Traxx Nite Club, 520 Franklin St 231-935-1666 www.sidetraxxtc.com **DV** 🏨

Organizations/Resources: Student, Academic, Education

♂ ★ (🐾) Northwestern Michigan College PRIDE, 1701 E Front St; 231-995-1118 **H?** fb.com/nmcpride/ ✔

Organizations/Resources: Transgender/Gender Non-Conforming/Diverse

т ☆ Transgender Michigan Traverse City Chapter, 842-2954 x107 www.transgendermichigan.org info@transgendermichigan.org

Real Estate (see also Mortgages)

♂ ○ Cummings, Mike, Realtor, Grand Traverse Real Estate, 620 Second St Ste B; 49684 231-570-1111 www.tcarea.com

Religious / Spiritual Resources

♀ ☆ Unitarian Universalist Congregation of Grand Traverse, 6726 Center Rd; 49686-1802 231-947-3117 www.uucgt.org office@uucgt.org

Williamston

Religious / Spiritual Resources

♂ ☆ Williamston UMC, 211 S Putnam St; 48895 517-655-2430 **HD** www.williamstonumc.org
➤➤ *Ypsilanti: see Ann Arbor/Ypsilanti Area*

Minnesota: State/County Resources
AIDS/HIV Support

207
GAYELLOW PAGES #42 2020-2021

Duluth/Superior Area: Minnesota
Organizations: Student

Minnesota
State/County Resources

AIDS/HIV Services, Education & Support

♂ ☆ ⚭ Minnesota AIDS Project, 2577 W. Territorial Rd, Saint Paul, MN 612-341-2060 **H?** www.mnaidsproject.org ✔

♀ ☆ Positive Link, 2577 Territorial Rd, Saint Paul, MN 612-373-2464 tinyurl.com/y8kh8om4

♀ ☆ Rural AIDS Action Network, 300 E St Germain St Ste 220, St Cloud, MN 800-966-9735 **IAS** www.raan.org

♀ ☆ ♿ Youth & AIDS Projects, Infectious Disease & International Medicine, Department of Medicine, UM, 2929 4th Ave S Ste 203, Minneapolis, MN 651-627-6820 **H?** www.yapmn.com ✔

Legal Services

♀ ★ Minnesota Lavender Bar Association, 2751 Hennepin Ave S #703, Minneapolis, MN www.mnlavbar.org

Organizations/Resources: Bisexual Focus

⚥ ☆ Bisexual Organizing Project, 310 E 38th St Ste 209, Minneapolis, MN tinyurl.com/yhho2mw

Organizations/Resources: Business & Professional Associations, Labor Advocacy

♀ ★ MN LGBT+ Therapists Network, www.lgbttherapists.org

♀ ★ National Lesbian & Gay Journalists Association, Minnesota, tinyurl.com/9hqwojm

♀ ★ Workplace Alliance, Twin Cities Quorum, 18 N 12th St, Minneapolis, MN 612-460-8153 www.twincitiesquorum.com/wpa

Organizations/Resources: Political/Legislative/Advocacy

♀ ☆ ACLU of Minnesota, POB 14720, Saint Paul, MN 55114 651-645-4097 www.aclu-mn.org

♀ ★ OutFront Minnesota, 310 E 38th St #209, Minneapolis, MN 800-800-0350 www.outfront.org ✔

♀ ★ ⚭ Stonewall DFL, 255 Plato Blvd E, Saint Paul, MN 612-229-3355 www.dfl.org

Organizations/Resources: Social, Recreation, Support

♀ ★ Prairie Equality Initiative, Sexual Orientation And Human Rights fb.com/groups/466398613394533

Organizations/Resources: Student, Academic, Education

♀ ★ Minnesota GLBTA Campus Alliance, 2136 Ford Parkway #131, Saint Paul, MN www.mncampusalliance.org

♀ ★ Out4Good, 425 5th St NE, Minneapolis, MN 612-668-0191 tinyurl.com/9c8qo9t

Organizations/Resources: Transgender/Gender Non-Conforming/Diverse

T ☆ ⚭ Minnesota Transgender Health Coalition, 730 E 38th Street Ste 108, Minneapolis, MN 55407 612-823-1152 **H?** www.mntransgenderhealth.org ✔ director@mntransgenderhealth.org

Recovery

♀ ★ Out & Sober Minnesota, www.outandsoberminnesota.org

⚭ PRIDE Institute, 14400 Martin Dr, Eden Prairie, MN 800-547-7433 www.pride-institute.com

Sports & Outdoor

♀ ★ North Star Gay Rodeo Association, POB 581157, Minneapolis, MN 55458 www.nsgra.org

Austin

Religious / Spiritual Resources

♀ ☆ ⚭ Christ Church, 301 3rd Ave NW 55912 507-433-3782 www.christchurchaustin.com office@christchurchaustin.org
>> *Bloomington: see Minneapolis/St Paul Area*
>> *Burnsville: see Minneapolis/St Paul Area*

Duluth/Superior Area

Community Centers and/or Pride Organizations

♀ ★ Duluth-Superior Pride, POB 3198, Duluth 55803 218-461-0726 www.dspride.com

♂ ★ Northland Gay Men's Group, tinyurl.com/y9hohgs8

AIDS/HIV Services, Education & Support

♂ AIDS Resource Center of Wisconsin, 1507 Tower Ave Ste 230, Superior, WI 715-394-4009 www.arcw.org

Bars, Cafes, Clubs, Restaurants
Duluth

♀ ● ⚭ At Sara's Table: Chester Creek Cafe, 1902 E 8th St, Duluth; 218-724-6811 www.astccc.net ⚥ ✂ ⊂⊃ ✔

♀ Duluth Flame, 28 N 1st Ave W, Duluth 218-727-2344 www.duluthflame.com **DK** ▥

♀ ○ Zeitgeist Arts Cafe, 222 E Superior St, Duluth 218-722-9100 www.zeitgeistarts.com ⊃

Superior

♀ Flame, 1612 Tower Ave, Superior, WI 715-395-0101 www.theflamenightclub.com **K** ▥ ✔

♂ ● Main Club, 1217 Tower Ave, Superior, WI 715-392-3335 mainclubwi.com **D**

Bookstores

♀ ○ ⚭ Zenith Bookstore, 318 N Central Ave, Duluth; 218-606-1777 www.zenithbookstore.com

Health Care: Physical (see also Counseling/Mental Health)

♀ Lake Superior Community Health Center, 4325 Grand Ave Ste 1, Duluth; 218-722-1497 www.lschc.org

Men's & Sex Clubs (not primarily Health Clubs)

♂ ● Duluth Family Sauna, Bullpen downstairs, 18 N 1st Ave E, Duluth; 218-726-1388 www.duluthsauna.com ✔

Organizations/Resources: Student, Academic, Education

♀ ★ College of Saint Scholastica SAGA (Sexuality and Gender Advocates), 1200 Kenwood Ave, Duluth; 800-447-5444

Minnesota: Duluth/Superior Area
Organizations: Student

208
GAYELLOW PAGES #42 2020-2021

Minneapolis/St Paul Area: Minnesota
Bars, Cafes, Clubs, Restaurants

⚥ ★ Sexuality & Gender Equity Initiatives, University of Minnesota Duluth, Kirby 245 1120 Kirby Dr, Duluth; 218-726-7300 www.d.umn.edu/sgei/

⚥ ★ University of Wisconsin Superior Alliance, POB 2000, Superior, WI 54880 715-394-8312 tinyurl.com/zdp7sl7

Recovery

♂ ☆ Alanon/Al-Ateen Minnesota North Area Information Services Center, 3005 Restormel St, Duluth; 218-624-2764 tinyurl.com/444nxm8

Geenwood

Organizations/Resources: Family and Supporters

♂ PFLAG - Greenwood, 2309 Smith Valley Rd fb.com/PFLAG-Greenwood

Lakeville

Erotica / Adult Stores / Safe Sex Supplies

♂ O Fantasy Gifts, 11276 210th St #108; 55044 952-469-1008 www.fantasygifts.com

Lanesboro

Accommodation: Hotels, Inns, Guesthouses, B&B, Resorts

♂ O Mrs. B's Historic Lanesboro Inn, POB 315 55949 507-467-2154 www.mrsbsinn.com ✔ ⊗ ⊗ Mrsbsinn@Gmail.com

Mankato

Crisis, Anti-violence, & Helplines

♂ ☆ 🔊 Committee Against Domestic Abuse (CADA), POB 466; 56002 800-477-0466 507-625-8688 www.cadamn.org

Community Centers and/or Pride Organizations

⚥ ★ 🔊 South Central Minnesota Pride, POB 3012; 56002 507-339-4740 www.scmnpride.org

Bars, Cafes, Clubs, Restaurants

♂ ● 🔊 Coffee Hag, 329 N Riverfront Dr 507-387-5533 fb.com/thecoffeehag/

Organizations/Resources: Student, Academic, Education

⚥ ★ 🔊 Minnesota State University LGBT Center, 194 Centennial Student Union; 507-389-5131 www.mnsu.edu/lgbtc/

♀ ★ 🔊 Women's Center at Minnesota State University, Mankato, 218 Centennial Student Union; 507-389-6146 www.mnsu.edu/wcenter/

Religious / Spiritual Resources

♂ ☆ 🔊 Unitarian Universalist Fellowship, 937 Charles Ave; 56001 507-388-5022 www.uumankato.org uufm@hickorytech.net

Marshall

Organizations/Resources: Family and Supporters

♂ PFLAG Marshall-Buffalo Ridge, POB 324; 56258 507-476-8335 tinyurl.com/d68f3kg

Minneapolis/St Paul Area

Crisis, Anti-violence, & Helplines

♀ ☆ 🔊 Sexual Violence Center, 2021 E Hennepin Ave Ste 418, Mpls; 55413 612-871-5111 **H?** www.sexualviolencecenter.org ✔ info@sexualviolencecenter.org

Community Centers and/or Pride Organizations

⚥ ★ 🔊 Twin Cities Pride, 2021 E Hennepin Ave Ste 402-7, Mpls; 55413 612-255-3260 **HS** www.tcpride.org ✔ info@tcpride.org

Information, Media & Publications

⚥ 🔊 Twin Cities Pride Magazine, 2021 E Hennepin Ave Ste 402-7, Mpls; 651-528-8752 **HS** www.tcpride.org ✔

Accommodation: Hotels, Inns, Guesthouses, B&B, Resorts
Stillwater

♂ ● (🔊) Rivertown Inn, 306 W Olive St, Stillwater; 651-430-2955 www.rivertowninn.com ✔ ⊗ ⊗

Accounting, Bookkeeping, Tax Services

♂ O 🔊 Palm, Karen R, CPA, CFP, CMA, 940 E Hennepin Ave, Mpls; 612-379-1393 www.palmkcpa.com ✔

♀ ● 🔊 ROR Tax Professionals, 4500 Park Glen Road Ste 100, St Louis Park; 55416 612-822-7177 **H?** www.rortax.com ✔

AIDS/HIV Services, Education & Support

♀ ☆ Aliveness Project, 3808 Nicollet Ave, Mpls 612-824-5433 www.aliveness.org

♀ ☆ Clare Housing, 929 Central Ave NE, Mpls 612-236-9515 www.clarehousing.org

♀ ★ 🔊 Indigenous People's Task Force, 1335 E 23rd St, Mpls; 612-870-1723 indigenouspeoplestf.org ✳

♀ ☆ Open Arms of Minnesota, Inc, 2500 Bloomington Avenue S, Mpls; 612-872-1152 www.openarmsmn.org

⚥ ★ PrideAlive, 2577 Territorial Rd, St Paul 612-373-2475 fb.com/pridealive

Archives/Libraries/Museums/History Projects

⚥ ★ 🔊 Quatrefoil Library, 1220 E Lake St, Mpls; 55407-2787 612-729-2543 www.qlibrary.org ✔ info@qlibrary.org

⚥ ★ 🔊 **Tretter Collection in GLBT Studies, 111 Elmer L Andersen Library, U of Minnesota, 222 21st Ave S, Mpls 55455-4400 612-624-7526 The Collection is dedicated to preserving GLBT history and culture.** tinyurl.com/m9mr9lk ✔

Bars, Cafes, Clubs, Restaurants
Minneapolis

⚥ ● 🔊 19 Bar, 19 W 15th St, Mpls 612-871-5553 fb.com/the19bar

♀ O 🔊 Barbette, 1600 W Lake St, Mpls 612-827-5710 www.barbette.com ⅄ ✕ ⊅ ✔

⚥ ● (🔊) The Brass Rail, 422 Hennepin Ave, Mpls; 612-332-7245 www.thebrassraillounge.com **D** 🎵

Minnesota: Minneapolis/St Paul Area
Bars, Cafes, Clubs, Restaurants
209
GAYELLOW PAGES #42 2020-2021
Minneapolis/St Paul Area: Minnesota
Leather

♀ ○ ♿ Bryant Lake Bowl, 810 W Lake St, Mpls; 612-825-3737 www.bryantlakebowl.com ♈ ✗ ▦ ✓

♀ ○ ♿ Butter Bakery Cafe, 3700 Nicollet Ave S, Mpls; 612-521-7401 www.butterbakerycafe.com ✓ info@butterbakerycafe.com

♂ ● ♿ eagleBOLTbar, 515 Washington Ave S, Mpls; 612-338-4214 www.eagleboltbar.com **DL** ♈ ✗

♂ ● Gay 90s, 408 Hennepin Ave, Mpls 612-333-7755 www.gay90s.com **D** ♈ ✗ ▦

♀ ○ Herkimer Pub & Brewery, 2922 Lyndale Ave S, Mpls; 612-821-0101 www.theherkimer.com ♈ ✗

♀ ○ ♿ Keegan's Pub, 16 University Ave NE, Mpls; 612-252-0880 www.keeganspub.com ♈ ✗ ✓

♂ Lush Food Bar, 990 Central Ave NE, Mpls 612-208-0358 lushmpls.com **DV** ♈ ✗ ▦

♀ ○ ♿ Midori's Floating World Cafe, 2629 E Lake St, Mpls; 612-721-3011 www.floatingworldcafe.com ✗

♀ ○ ♿ Red Stag Supperclub, 509 1st Ave NE, Mpls; 612-767-7766 www.redstagsupperclub.com ♈ ✗ ▦ ✓

♂ ● ♿ The Saloon, 830 Hennepin Ave, Mpls; 612-332-0835 www.saloonmn.com **D**

♀ ● ♿ Wilde Cafe, 65 Main St SE Ste 143, Mpls; 612-331-4544 www.wildecafe.com ♈ ✗ ▷ ✓

Saint Paul

♀ ○ ♿ The Black Dog, Lowertown, 308 Prince St, St Paul; 651-228-9274 www.blackdogstpaul.com ♈ ✗ ▷ ✓ blackdogcafe2@comcast.net

♂ ● The Black Hart, 1415 University Ave W, St Paul; 651-646-7087 www.blackhartstp.com **S** ▦

♂ ● Camp Bar and Cabaret, 490 N Robert St, St Paul; 800-838-3006 www.camp-bar.net ▦

Bookstores

♀ ○ (♿) Birchbark Books & Native Arts, 2115 W 21st St, Mpls; 612-374-4023 www.birchbarkbooks.com ✓

♀ ○ DreamHaven Books, Comics & Art, 2301 E 38th St, Mpls; 612-823-6161 www.dreamhavenbooks.com

♀ ○ Mayday Books, 301 Cedar Ave S, Mpls 612-333-4719 www.maydaybookstore.org

Broadcast Media

♂ ★ Fresh Fruit, KFAI FM, 1808 Riverside Ave, Mpls; 612-341-3144 Thu 7pm 90.3 FM Mpls, 106.7 St Paul www.kfai.org/freshfruit

Counseling/Psychotherapy/Mental Health

♂ ● ♿ The Family Partnership LGBTQ Counseling Services, 4123 E Lake St, Mpls; 612-728-2061 www.thefamilypartnership.org

♀ ☆ ♿ Headway Emotional Health Services, 6425 Nicollet Ave S, Richfield; 55423 612-861-1675 **H?** www.headway.org ✓ information@headway.org

♀ ● ♿ Northland Therapy Center, 2324 University Ave W Ste 100, St Paul; 55114-1854 651-641-1009 fax 651-789-5677 **H?** tinyurl.com/qdr6rj3 info@northlandtherapycenter.com

♀ ○ Twin Cities Psychological Services, Ltd, 825 Nicollet Mall Ste 1455, Mpls; 612-345-5194 www.twincitiespsych.com

♀ ● ♿ Ulbee, Maureen, MS, MSW, LICSW, 2446 University Ave W Ste 108, Mpls; 55414 651-209-2767 moulbee@hotmail.com

Erotica / Adult Stores / Safe Sex Supplies

♀ ○ Fantasy Gifts, 1031 E. Moore Lake Dr, Fridley 55432 763-572-1075 www.fantasygifts.com

♀ ○ Fantasy Gifts, 11055 Crooked Lake Blvd, Coon Rapids; 55433 763-433-2690 www.fantasygifts.com

♀ ○ Fantasy Gifts, 2125 W Hwy 13 #100, Burnsville 55433 952-882-0313 www.fantasygifts.com

♀ ○ Fantasy Gifts, 375 7th St E, St Paul; 55102 651-665-0622 www.fantasygifts.com

♀ ○ Fantasy Gifts, 5805 Excelsior Blvd, St Louis Park; 55416 952-922-0838 www.fantasygifts.com

♀ ○ Fantasy Gifts, 6522 Bass Lake Rd, Crystal 55428 763-504-0428 www.fantasygifts.com

Financial Planning, Investment (see also Insurance)

♂ ● ♿ Cassidy, Michael D, CFP, ChFC, Ameriprise Financial, 4500 Park Glen Road Ste 100, St Louis Park; 55416 952-767-5547 **H?** tinyurl.com/9behx6x ✓

Funding: Endowment, Fundraising

♂ ★ Imperial Court of Minnesota, POB 582601, Mpls; 55458 651-270-4693 www.impcourtmn.com

♂ ★ ♿ PFund (Philanthrofund) Foundation, 2801 21st Ave S Ste 132B, Mpls; 612-870-1806 www.pfundfoundation.org

♀ ☆ Red Ribbon Ride, 2101 Hennepin Ave Ste 200, Mpls; 612-822-2110 www.redribbonride.org

Gardening/Landscaping Services & Supplies

♀ ○ Tangletown Gardens, 5353 Nicollet Ave, Mpls 55419 612-822-4769 www.tangletowngardens.com info@tangletowngardens.com

Health Care: Physical (see also Counseling/Mental Health)

♀ ☆ ♿ Red Door Services, 525 Portland Ave Flr 4, Mpls; 612-543-5555 **H?** www.reddoorclinic.com

♀ ○ ♿ Thorp, Deborah, MD, OB/GYN Care, Women's Center, 6500 Excelsior Blvd, Flr 5 HVC, St Louis Park; 55426 952-993-3282 **H?** www.parknicollet.com ✓

♂ ★ Wilder Pride Employee Resource Group, Amherst H. Wilder Foundation, 451 Lexington Parkway N, St Paul; 55104 651-280-2420 www.wilder.org GLBTEmployeeResourceNetwork@wilder.org

Leather Resources & Groups

♂ ★ ATONS of Minneapolis, POB 580517, Mpls 55458 612-562-8667 www.atons.net **L**

♂ ★ Black Guard of Minneapolis, c/o Mike Delorme 1343 75th Ave NE, Fridley; 763-780-5559 blackguardmpls@comcast.net

♀ ★ Knights of Leather, POB 7684, Mpls; 55407 www.knightsofleather.com **L**

Minnesota: Minneapolis/St Paul Area
Legal

210

GAYELLOW PAGES #42 2020-2021

Minneapolis/St Paul Area: Minnesota
Real Estate

Legal Services

⚥ ● Gaborsky, Kelli A, Gaborsky Law Office, LLC, 10 S 5th St Ste 1005, Mpls; 612-275-0169 Criminal defense www.gaborskylaw.com

♀ Gender Justice, 200 W University Ave #200, St Paul; 651-789-2090 www.genderjustice.us

Organizations/Resources: Business & Professional Associations, Labor Advocacy

♂ ★ Faegre Baker Daniels Diversity and Inclusion, 612-766-8818 tinyurl.com/yd836avg

♂ ★ ♿ Quorum, The Twin Cities GLBTA Chamber of Commerce, 18 N 12th St Ste 3606, Mpls; 612-460-8153 www.twinciti-esquorum.com

♂ ★ ♿ University of Minnesota Pride at Work, 128 Pleasent St SE, Mpls; 612-625-0537 **H?** tinyurl.com/y4ksbrcv ✎

Organizations/Resources: Cultural, Dance, Performance

♀ ★ Calliope Women's Chorus, POB 4474, St Paul 55104 www.Calliopewomenschorus.org

♂ ★ ♿ Minnesota Freedom Band, PO Box 3689, Mpls; 55403 612-564-0632 www.mnfreedomband.org

♂ ★ ♿ Minnesota Philharmonic Orchestra, 4101 Harriet Ave, Mpls; 612-656-5676 **HD** www.mnphil.org

♂ ★ ♿ One Voice Mixed Chorus, 732 Holly Ave Ste Q, St Paul; 55104-7125 651-298-1954 www.OneVoiceMN.org

♂ Out Twin Cities Film Festival, St. Anthony Main Theater, 115 Main St SE, Mpls

♂ ★ Twin Cities Country Dancers, 3712 46th Ave S, Mpls; 612-669-1922 TwinCitiesCountryDancers.org

♂ ★ ♿ Twin Cities Gay Men's Chorus, 528 Hennepin Ave #307, Mpls; 612-339-7664 **H** www.tcgmc.org

Organizations/Resources: Family and Supporters

♂ ★ (♺) GAMMA, 612-822-5002

♀ PFLAG Anoka/North Metro, c/o UCC of Anoka, 1923 3rd Ave S, Anoka; www.anokanorthmetropflag.com

Organizations/Resources: Political/Legislative/Advocacy

♂ ★ National LGBTQ Task Force, 122 W Franklin Ave Ste 210, Mpls; 612-821-4397. www.thetaskforce.org

Organizations/Resources: Social, Recreation, Support

♂ Minneapolis Movie Bears, fb.com/groups/MMBears/

♂ ★ North Country Bears, www.ncbears.com

♂ North Country Gaylaxians, www.ncgaylaxians.org

♀ ★ Out To Brunch, POB 582682, Mpls 55458-2682 763-391-3449 www.outtobrunch.org outtobrunch1@gmail.com

♂ ★ Prime Timers MSP, PMB 198 2136 Ford Parkway, Mpls; 55416 612-371-9537 www.primetimersww.org/ptmsp info@primetimersmsp.com

♀ ☆ (♺) The Twin Cities Men's Center, 3249 Hennepin Ave S #55, Mpls; 612-822-5892 www.tcmc.org ✪

Organizations/Resources: Student, Academic, Education

♂ ★ Anoka Ramsey Community College GSA, 11200 Mississippi Blvd NW, Coon Rapids; 763-433-6156 tinyurl.com/y94nxkdz

♂ ★ Anoka Ramsey Community College Queer-Trans Union Club, 11200 Mississippi Blvd NW, Coon Rapids; 763-433-1225 tinyurl.com/y94nxkdz

♂ ★ ♿ Augsburg College LGBTQIA Student Service, 2211 River-side Ave, Mpls; 612-330-1499 tinyurl.com/zmawt2z ✎

♂ ★ (♺) Delta Lambda Phi - Delta Chapter, University of Minne-sota, www.dlp.org/delta/

♂ ★ ♿ The Gender and Sexuality Center for Queer and Trans Life, University of Minnesota, 128 Pleasant St SE, 46 Appleby Hall, Mpls; 55455 612-625-0537 **H?** diversity.umn.edu/gsc/ ✎ gsc@umn.edu

♂ ★ ♿ Metropolitan State University Women's and LGBTQ Student Resource Center, 700 E 7th St, St Paul 651-793-1544 **H?** tinyurl.com/yyqkrcfx ✎

♂ ★ Out For Equity St Paul Public Schools, 345 Plato Blvd E, St Paul; 651-744-6095 www.spps.org/outforequity

♂ ★ Queer Student Cultural Center, University of Minnesota, 300 Washington Ave SE Rm 217, Mpls; 55455-0396 www.qscc.org ✎ qscc@umn.edu

♂ ★ (♺) University of St Thomas School of Law Outlaw, 1000 LaSalle Ave, Mpls tinyurl.com/ycogk3s8

Organizations/Resources: Transgender/Gender Non-Conforming/Diverse

т ○ ♿ Thorp, Deborah, MD, Gender Services Clinic, 2001 Blais-dell Ave S, Mpls; 55401 952-993-8052 www.parknicollet.com ✎

т Transforming Families, 612-321-8416 tffmn.org

Organizations/Resources: Youth (see also Family)

♂ ☆ Avenues for Homeless Youth, GLBT Host Home Program. 1708 Oak Park Ave N, Mpls; 612-968-1672 avenuesforyouth.org ✎

♀ ☆ ♿ The Bridge for Youth, 1111 W 22nd St, Mpls; 612-377-8800 **H?** Youth ages 10-17, needing shelter or crisis counseling. www.bridgeforyouth.org

♂ Camp True Colors, MN, One Heartland, 2101 Hennepin Ave #200, Mpls; 888-216-2028 www.oneheartland.org

♀ ☆ Face to Face Health & Counseling Services, 1165 Arcade St, St Paul; 651-772-5555 www.face2face.org

♂ ★ Family Partnership GLBT Counseling Services, 4123 E Lake St, Mpls; 877-452-8543 www.thefamilypartnership.org

♂ Reclaim, 771 Raymond Ave, St Paul 612-235-6743 reclaim.care

Real Estate (see also Mortgages)

♂ ● ♿ Coldwell Banker Burnet Realty, Michael McGee, 3033 Excelsior Blvd Ste 100, Mpls; 55416-4678 612-924-4389 888-372-9832 fax 612-920-4706 www.msp-properties.com ✎ mmcgee@cbburnet.com

♂ ○ (♺) RE/MAX Results, Shannon Lindstrom, REALTOR(R), AHWD, CRS, GREEN 748 Grand Ave, St Paul; 55105 612-616-9714 **H?** ShannonLindstromRealtor.com ✎ Shannon@ShannonLindstromRealtor.com

Minnesota: Minneapolis/St Paul Area
Recovery

211
GAYELLOW PAGES #42 2020-2021

Rushford : Minnesota
Accommodation

Recovery

♀ ☆ (?⚥) AA Saint Paul & Suburban Area Intergroup, 608 W 7th St, St Paul; 651-227-5502 www.aastpaul.org

♀ ☆ Al-Anon/Alateen Information Services of Minneapolis, 7204 W 27th St Ste 101, Mpls; 952-920-3961 www.al-anon-alateen-msp.org

Religious / Spiritual Resources

♂ ★ ⚥⚥ All God's Children MCC, 3100 Park Ave, Mpls; 612-824-2673 www.agcmcc.org

♀ ☆ ⚥⚥ Bethany Lutheran Church, 2511 E Franklin Ave, Mpls; 55406 612-332-2397 www.bethanyinseward.org bethanyinseward@gmail.com

♂ ★ ⚥⚥ Dignity/Twin Cities, POB 583402, Mpls; 55458 612-721-6341 www.dignitytwincities.org

♂ ☆ Edina Community Lutheran Church, 4113 W 54th St, Edina; 55424-1432 952-926-3808 www.eclc.org

♀ ☆ Episcopal Church of the Nativity, 15601 Maple Island Rd, Burnsville; 55306 952-435-8687 nativitymn.org nativity@nativitymn.org

♀ ☆ ♿ Good Samaritan UMC, 5730 Grove St, Edina; 55436- 952-929-0049 www.good.org office@good.org

♀ ☆ (?⚥) Lutheran Church of the Resurrection, 3115 Victoria St N, Roseville; 55113 651-484-1292 www.lcrelca.org ✎ office@lcrelca.org

♀ ☆ ⚥⚥ Pilgrim House UU, 1212 W Highway 96, Arden Hills; 55112 651-631-2582 www.pilgrimhouseuua.org ✎ pilgrimhouse@pilgrimhouseuua.org

♀ ☆ ⚥⚥ Plymouth Congregational Church, 1900 Nicollet Ave S, Mpls; 55403-3789 612-871-7400 **HD** www.plymouth.org ✎ churchinfo@plymouth.org

♀ ☆ ⚥⚥ Spirit of Hope UMC, 7600 Harold Ave, Golden Valley; 55427 763-545-0239 **HD** www.spiritofhopeumc.org

♀ ☆ St Anthony Park UCC, 2129 Commonwealth Ave, St Paul; 55108 651-646-7173 www.sapucc.org

♀ ☆ ⚥⚥ St Christopher's Episcopal Church, 2300 N Hamline Ave, Roseville; 55113 651-633-4589 www.stchristophers-mn.org ✎ office@stchristophers-mn.org

♀ ☆ (?⚥) Unity Minneapolis, 4000 Golden Valley Rd, Golden Valley; 55422 763-521-4793 **H** www.unityminneapolis.org ✎

♀ ☆ University Baptist Church, 1219 University Ave SE, Mpls; 55414-2087 612-331-1768 www.ubcmn.org info@ubcmn.org

♀ ☆ ⚥⚥ University Lutheran Church of Hope, 601 13th Ave SE, Mpls; 55414-1437 612-331-5988 **HD** . www.ulch.org ulch@ulch.org

Sports & Outdoor

♂ ★ Gay & Lesbian Amateur Sport Society, www.glassports.org

♂ ★ (?⚥) Hump Day Bowlers League, Concord Lanes, 365 N Concord Exchange S, St Paul; 55075 www.humpdaybowlers.com ✎ info@humpdaybowlers.com

♂ Minneapolis Mayhem Rugby, POB 50681, Mpls 55405 mayhemrugby.org

♂ ★ (?⚥) Outwoods, 3905 Bloomington Ave S, Mpls; www.outwoods.org

---

♂ ★ TC Jacks MN LGBT Soccer, 612-927-2257 **H?** www.tcjacks.org

♂ ★ Twin Cities Goodtime Softball League, POB 580264, Mpls; 55458 tcgsl.leagueapps.com

♂ Twin City Riders, www.twincityriders.com

Travel & Tourist Services (see also Accommodation)

♀ ● ♿ New Departures, 625 2nd Ave S, #408, Mpls; 55402-1909 612-305-0025 fb.com/NewDepartures/

Women's Centers

♀ ☆ ⚥⚥ Harriet Tubman Center, 3111 1st Ave S, Mpls; 612-825-0000 www.tubman.org
>> *Moorhead: see Fargo/Moorhead Area*

Morris

Organizations/Resources: Student, Academic, Education

♂ ★ Morris Queer Student Initiative for Equality, POB #45SC 600 E 4th St; tinyurl.com/wfbamnt not responding
>> *New Hope: see Minneapolis/St Paul Area*

New Prague

Organizations/Resources: Family and Supporters

♀ ☆ PFLAG New Prague Area,

Northfield

Organizations/Resources: Student, Academic, Education

♂ ☆ Carleton College Gender & Sexuality Center, Clader House, 209 E 2nd St; 55057 507-222-5222 tinyurl.com/ybdxroyr gsc@carleton.edu

Pine City / East Central Minnesota

Community Centers and/or Pride Organizations

♂ ★ East Central Minnesota Pride, 1030 Southview Ave, Braham; 320-396-3726 eastcentralminnesotapride.com

Organizations/Resources: Family and Supporters

♂ ☆ East Central Minnesota PFLAG, 320-272-0069 www.ecmnpflag.org pschroeder54@gmail.com

Organizations/Resources: Social, Recreation, Support

♀ East Central Purple Circle, ecpurplecircle.blogspot.com

Rochester

Organizations/Resources: Student, Academic, Education

♂ ★ Full Spectrum: WSU Gender and Sexuality Alliance, Kryzsko Commons, Student Clubs, POB 5838, Winona; 55987 507-547-5314 tinyurl.com/6rgaw8

Rushford

Accommodation: Hotels, Inns, Guesthouses, B&B, Resorts

♀ ○ Windswept Inn, POB 21; 55971 507-864-2545 www.windsweptinn.net ✤ ✎

Minnesota: St Cloud
Community Centers / Pride

212
GAYELLOW PAGES #42 2020-2021

Jackson : Mississippi
Bars, Cafes, Clubs, Restaurants

St Cloud

Community Centers and/or Pride Organizations

St Cloud Pride, POB 5114, St Cloud 56302 320-428-0020 www.stcloudpride.org

Organizations/Resources: Family and Supporters

Central MN PFLAG, POB 7597, St Cloud; 56302 www.centralmnpflag.com

Organizations/Resources: Student, Academic, Education

St. Cloud State University LGBT Resource Center, 142 Atwood Memorial Center, 720 4th Ave S, St Cloud 320-308-5166 www.stcloudstate.edu/lgbt/

Religious / Spiritual Resources

LuMin in St. Cloud., POB 1001, St Cloud; 56302 320-252-6183 www.luminstcloud.com ✗ Pastor@lcminsc.com

St Cloud Unitarian Universalist Fellowship, 3226 Maine Prairie Rd, St Cloud; 56301 320-252-0020 www.uufstcloud.org info@uufstcloud.org

» *Saint Paul: see Minneapolis/St Paul Area*
» *Wolverton: see Fargo/Moorhead Area*

Mississippi
State/County Resources

Community Centers and/or Pride Organizations

Mississippi Rainbow Center, POB 66, Biloxi, MS 39533 601-336-0162 www.msrainbowcenter.org

Organizations/Resources: Political/Legislative/Advocacy

American Civil Liberties Union of Mississippi, POB 2242, Jackson, MS 39225 601-354-3408 www.aclu-ms.org

Organizations/Resources: Student, Academic, Education

Mississippi Safe Schools Coalition, 510 George Street, Suite 306, Jackson, MS 39202 662-205-6772 www.mssafeschools.org info@mssafeschools.org

Religious / Spiritual Resources

Episcopal Diocese of Mississippi Gay & Lesbian Ministries, POB 23107, Jackson, MS 39225 601-948-5954 tinyurl.com/htealus

Reproductive Medicine & Fertility Services

Planned Parenthood of Tennessee and North Mississippi (PPTNM), 2430 Poplar Ave #100, Memphis, TN 38112 866-711-1717 tinyurl.com/y3qaqgf5 info@pptnm.org

Biloxi

Bars, Cafes, Clubs, Restaurants

• Just Us Lounge, 906 Division St 228-374-1007 fb.com/JustUs-Lounge **D**

Columbus

Counseling/Psychotherapy/Mental Health

• ♿ Hawkins, John, LPC, NCC, 413 4th Ave S Ste 16; 39701 662-435-0050 www.johnhawkinslpc.com johnhawkinslpc@gmail.com

Hattiesburg

Crisis, Anti-violence, & Helplines

The Shafer Center for Crisis Intervention, PO Box 1525; 39401 / 3605 Azalea 601-264-7777 www.theshafercenter.info theshafercenter@aol.com

Community Centers and/or Pride Organizations

Pine Belt Pride, Spectrum Center, POB 17679; 39404 601-909-5338 /tinyurl.com/y6yz5v44

Spectrum Center, POB 17679; 39404 601-909-5338 /tinyurl.com/y6yz5v44

AIDS/HIV Services, Education & Support

AIDS Services Coalition, POB 169; 39403 601-450-4286 www.ascms.net

Bars, Cafes, Clubs, Restaurants

Xclusive, 5729 US Highway 49; 601-270-7953 fb.com/TeamXclusiv/ **D**

Organizations/Resources: Student, Academic, Education

★ ♿ Southern Miss Prism LGBTQ+ Resource Office, The Hub, Room 114A, 118 College Dr. #5002; 601-266-4453 tinyurl.com/y4kma4mj

Religious / Spiritual Resources

★ Joshua Generation MCC, POB 18483; 39404 / 4906 Old Highway 11 #5B 601-329-0774 www.joshuageneration.rocks ✗

Hernando

Florists (see also Gifts)

• (♿) Hernando Flower Shop, 141 W Commerce St; 662-429-5281 **H?** www.hernandoflowershop.com ♥

Jackson

AIDS/HIV Services, Education & Support

Grace House, 2219 Lamar St; 601-353-1038 www.gracehousems.org

Bars, Cafes, Clubs, Restaurants

Bar 3911, 3911 Northview Dr; 601-586-1468 tinyurl.com/uxc8cwg **D**

Metro 2001, 4670 Hwy 80 West; / Fri (ladies night) & Sat 601-259-0661 fb.com/MetroFridayNights/ **D** 🎵

♿ Soul Wired Cafe, 4147 Northview Dr Ste D; 601-790-0864 www.soulwiredcafe.com **DK** ✕⊡ ✗

Mississippi: Jackson
Counseling
213
GAYELLOW PAGES #42 2020-2021
Bourbon : Missouri
Accommodation: Rentals

Counseling/Psychotherapy/Mental Health

♂ ○ ᵫ Weems, Julia L, LCSW, 200 Park Circle Dr, Flowood; 39232 601-933-1136 juliakweemslcsw@gmail.com

Erotica / Adult Stores / Safe Sex Supplies

♀ ○ Romantic Adventures, 175 Hwy 80 E, Pearl; 39208 601-932-2811 www.romanticadventures.com

Health Care: Physical (see also Counseling/Mental Health)

♀ Leandro, Mena, MD, MPH, GLMA member, Open Arms Health Care Center, 805 E River Place; 601-500-7660 www.oahcc.org

Jewelry (see also Gifts)

♀ ● ᵫ Beckham Custom Jewelry, The District at Eastover, 120 District Blvd Ste D110; 39211 601-665-4642 beckhamcustomjewelry.com ⚥ ♥ info@beckhamjewelry.com

Organizations/Resources: Family and Supporters

♂ PFLAG of Jackson, 4623 Maurey Rd; / meets Fondren Presbyterian Church 601-842-2274 tinyurl.com/zwkx3ko

Natchez

Accommodation: Hotels, Inns, Guesthouses, B&B, Resorts

♀ ● Historic Oak Hill Inn B&B, 409 S Rankin St 601-446-2500 www.historicoakhill.com

Ocean Springs

Legal Services

♀ ○ Silin Law Firm PLLC, 1016 Robinson St; 39564 228-244-9987 www.silinlaw.com ⚥ rita@silinlaw.com

Oxford

Organizations/Resources: Family and Supporters

♀ PFLAG Oxford / North Mississippi, POB 2142 38655 662-801-2820 fb.com/PFLAGOxfordMS

Organizations/Resources: Student, Academic, Education

♥ ★ ᵫ University of Mississippi Pride Network, 203 Johnson Commons E; tinyurl.com/y779mr6y ⚥

Religious / Spiritual Resources

♀ ☆ ᵫ Unitarian Universalist Congregation of Oxford, 31 County Road 198; 38655 662-513-0970 www.uuoxford.com ⚥

Starkville

Community Centers and/or Pride Organizations

♥ Starkville Pride, 662-523-6834 fb.com/Starkville-Pride/

Bookstores

♂ SAGE coffee & books, 19 Page Ave; 662-883-1870 fb.com/sage-goods/ ☞

Tupelo

Community Centers and/or Pride Organizations

♥ Pride Resource Center of North MS, 1800 W Main St Ste 134; 662-372-0091 prideresourcecenter.org

Organizations/Resources: Family and Supporters

♀ ☆ PFLAG Tupelo, 783 CR 1253, Saltillo; Amanda Daniels fb.com/pflagtupelo

Water Valley

Bookstores

♥ Violet Valley Bookstore, 303 N Main St; / open Saturday 662-506-2750 fb.com/violetvalleybooks/

Missouri
State/County Resources

Crisis, Anti-violence, & Helplines

♥ ★ Kansas City Anti-Violence Project, 4050 Pennsylvania Ave Ste 135, Kansas City, MO 816-561-0550 www.kcavp.org

AIDS/HIV Services, Education & Support

♀ ☆ ᵫ AIDS Project of the Ozarks, 1636 S Glenstone Ave Ste 100, Springfield, MO 417-881-1900 apo-ozarks.org

Organizations/Resources: Political/Legislative/Advocacy

♀ ☆ PROMO, 2200 Gravois Ave Ste 201, St Louis, MO 314-862-4900 www.promoonline.org

Sports & Outdoor

♥ ★ ᵫ Missouri Gay Rodeo Association, Inc., POB 45073, Kansas City, MO 64171 816-237-8420 www.mgra.us info@mgra.us

Ava

Campgrounds and RV Parks

♂ ● ᵫ Cactus Canyon Campground, POB 266; 65608 417-683-9199 tinyurl.com/ahup2 N (♣?) ⊗

Boonville

Men's & Sex Clubs (not primarily Health Clubs)

♥ The Megaplex, 11674 Old Hwy 40; 660-882-0008 www.megaplexgym.com P

Bourbon

Accommodation Rental: Furnished / Vacation (& AirBNB)

♀ ○ (?ᵫ) Meramec Farm Cabins & Horseback Riding Vacations, 208 Thickety Ford Rd; 65441-9141 573-732-4765 573-205-9395 www.meramecfarm.com ⚥ ⊗

>> *Bridgeton: see St Louis Area (MO & IL)*

Missouri: Cape Girardeau
Bars, Cafes, Clubs, Restaurants

214

GAYELLOW PAGES #42 2020-2021

Kansas City Metro Area (MO & KS): Missouri
Bars, Cafes, Clubs, Restaurants

Cape Girardeau

Bars, Cafes, Clubs, Restaurants

⚥ ● Independence Place, Holiday Happenings, 5 S Henderson; 573-334-2939 fb.com/IndpendencePlace **D**

Columbia

Community Centers and/or Pride Organizations

⚥ ★ ⚤⚤ The Center Project, POB 521; 65205 / 515 Hickman Ave 573-449-1188 www.thecenterproject.org ✓

⚥ ★ MidMO PrideFest, POB 10216; 65205 www.midmopride.org

Bars, Cafes, Clubs, Restaurants

⚥ Arch & Column Pub, 1301 Business Loop 70E 573-441-8088 fb.com/ArchandColumnPub

♂ ○ ⚤⚤ Main Squeeze Natural Foods Cafe, 28 S 9th St; 573-817-5616 www.main-squeeze.com ⬮ ✓

Bookstores

♂ ○ ⚤ The Peace Nook, 804 E Broadway Ste C; 65201-4828 573-875-0539 www.midmopeaceworks.org mail@midmopeaceworks.org

Organizations/Resources: Cultural, Dance, Performance

♂ ☆ Ragtag Cinema, 10 Hitt St; 573-441-8504 www.ragtag-cinema.org ⬮

Organizations/Resources: Student, Academic, Education

⚥ ★ ⚤⚤ LGBTQ Resource Center, University of Missouri, G225 MU Student Center; 573-884-7750 **H?** lgbtq.missouri.edu ✓

⚥ ★ ⚤⚤ Rockbridge High School GSA, 4303 S Providence Rd; 573-214-3100 www.cpsk12.org/Page/6552

♀ ☆ University of Missouri Women's Center, G108 MU Student Center; 573-882-6621 womenscenter.missouri.edu

Dixon

Accommodation Rental: Furnished / Vacation (& AirBNB)

♂ ○ Rock Eddy Bluff Farm Cabins, 10245 Maries Road 511; 65459-7446 573-759-6081 Cottages & cabins www.rockeddy.com ⚘✓ ⊛

Hannibal

Accommodation: Hotels, Inns, Guesthouses, B&B, Resorts

♂ ● Garden House B&B, 301 N 5th St; 573-221-7800 tinyurl.com/3ay8a8 (⚘?) ✓ ⊛

♂ ● Rockcliffe Mansion, 1000 Bird St; 63401 573-221-4140 www.rockcliffemansion.com ✓ ⊛⊛ info@rockcliffe mansion.com

Bars, Cafes, Clubs, Restaurants

♀ ● LaBinnah Bistro, 207 N 5th St; 573-221-8207 www.Labin-nahBistro.com ✕ ✓ LaBinnahBistro@gmail.com

Hermann

Accommodation: Hotels, Inns, Guesthouses, B&B, Resorts

♂ ○ The Rafters Bed & Breakfast, 301 Schiller St 65041 573-486-2035 www.theraftersbb.com ✓ ⊛⊛ TheRaftersBB@gmail.com

Jefferson City

Religious / Spiritual Resources

♂ ☆ Unitarian Universalist Fellowship, 1021 Northeast Dr; 65109 573-636-0684 www.uufjc.org uufjc1@gmail.com

Joplin

Community Centers and/or Pride Organizations

⚥ Joplin Pride Community, 417-317-3659 tinyurl.com/y8s87zmc

Kansas City Metro Area (MO & KS)

Crisis, Anti-violence, & Helplines

⚥ ★ Kansas City Anti-Violence Project, 4050 Pennsylvania Ave Ste 135, KC; 816-561-0550 www.kcavp.org

♂ ☆ Safe Home, 913-262-2868 www.safehome-ks.org

Community Centers and/or Pride Organizations

⚥ ★ Kansas City Center for Inclusion, 3911 Main St, KC; 64111 816-753-7770 www.inclusivekc.org info@inclusivekc.org

⚥ ★ Kansas City PrideFest, 315 Lawrence St, KC 64111 816-960-3400 www.kcpridefest.org info@kcpridefest.org

Information, Media & Publications

⚥ ● Camp Magazine, POB 22601, KC; 64113 816-221-0199 camp.lgbt

⚥ ● K.C. Exposures, 122 N Clinton Pl Ste 1, KC 64123-1702 816-753-4500 kcexposures@aol.com

Accommodation: Hotels, Inns, Guesthouses, B&B, Resorts
Kansas City, Missouri

♂ ● Hydes KC Guesthouse, POB 414297, KC; 64141 816-561-1010 www.hydeskc.com (⚘?) ✓ (⊛)

AIDS/HIV Services, Education & Support

♀ ☆ Good Samaritan Project, 3030 Walnut St, KC 816-561-8784 www.gsp-kc.org

♀ ☆ Good Samaritan Project, 3030 Walnut, Kansas City, KS 816-561-8784 www.gsp-kc.org

♀ ☆ Hope Care Center, 115 E 83rd St, KC 816-523-3988 Skilled nursing facility www.hopecarecenter.org

♀ ☆ SAVE (AIDS Housing), 911 E 31st St, KC 816-531-8340 www.saveinckc.org

Bars, Cafes, Clubs, Restaurants
Kansas City, Missouri

♀ ○ Broadway Cafe, 4106 Broadway, KC; 816-531-2432 broad-wayroasting.com ⬮ broadwayroasting@yahoo.com

♀ ○ Cafe Trio & Starlet Lounge, 4558 Main St, KC 816-756-3227 www.cafetriokc.com ⍩ ✕ ▥

♀ ● Missie B's, 805 W 39th St, KC 816-561-0625 www.missiebs.com ▥

♀ ● Sidekicks Saloon, 3707 Main St, KC 816-931-1430 fb.com/sidekickssaloonkc/ **DCW** ▥

♀ ● Sidestreet Bar & Grill, 413 E 33rd St, KC 816-531-1775 fb.com/SidestreetbarKC/ ⚲ ✂ ✗

♀ Woody's KC, 3740 Broadway Blvd, KC 816-888-3340 woodyskc.com **S**

Counseling/Psychotherapy/Mental Health

♀ ● ♿ Carrigan, Jason, Diversity Counseling, LLC, 4010 Washington St #405, KC; 64111 816-756-3858 **H?** www.diversitycounselingkc.com ✗ kcmolpc@aol.com

♀ ● ♿ Monroe, Megan, MSW, LSCSW, Country Club Plaza area 816-435-2829 www.meganmonroemsw.com mmonroemsw@gmail.com

Funding: Endowment, Fundraising

♀ ★ AIDS Walk Kansas City, POB 32192, KC; 64171 816-931-0959 www.aidswalkkansascity.org

Health Care: Physical (see also Counseling/Mental Health)

♀ ♿ KC Free Health Clinic, 3515 Broadway St, KC; 816-753-5144 www.kccareclinic.org

Legal Services

♀ ○ Foley, Rachel Lynn, 4016 S Lynn Court #B, Independence; 64055 816-472-4357 www.kcbankruptcy.com clients@kcbankruptcy.com

Organizations/Resources: Cultural, Dance, Performance

♀ ★ Heartland Men's Chorus, POB 32374, KC 64171-5374 816-931-3338 **HDS** www.hmckc.org

♀ ★ The Kansas City LGBT Film Festival, 4050 Pennsylvania, KC; 816-200-2059 www.outherenow.com

Organizations/Resources: Family and Supporters

♀ ☆ ♿ PFLAG KC, POB 414101, KC 64141 816-765-9818 www.pflagkc.org ✗

Organizations/Resources: Political/Legislative/Advocacy

♀ (♲) American Civil Liberties Union of Missouri KC office, 406 W 34th St Ste 420, KC; 816-470-9933 www.aclu-mo.org ✗

♀ Kansas Equality Coalition of Metropolitan Kansas City, Inc., 9218 Metcalf Ave PMB 180, Overland Park, KS 913-735-4629 www.eqks.org

Organizations/Resources: Social, Recreation, Support

♂ ★ Prime Timers of Kansas City, David Shubkagel, 6422 Rockhill Rd, KC; 64131 816-830-7439 primetimersww.com/kc/ ptkansascity@yahoo.com

Organizations/Resources: Student, Academic, Education

♀ ☆ GLSEN Greater Kansas City, 4741 Central St Ste 220, KC; 64112 913-608-4528 tinyurl.com/spmh6e6 chapter@gkc.glsen.org

♀ ★ University Of Missouri Kansas City LGBTQIA Programs and Services, Student Union #320, 5100 Cherry St, KC; 816-235-1639 www.umkc.edu/lgbt

Organizations/Resources: Youth (see also Family)

♀ ★ ♿ Passages Youth Center, POB 10083, KC; 64171 816-348-3665 fb.com/kcpassages ✗

Real Estate (see also Mortgages)

♀ ○ Jones, Matthew, Keller Williams, 6850 College Blvd, Overland Park, KS 66211 913-558-2296 www.yourheartlandrealtor.com your heartlandrealtor@gmail.com

Recovery

♀ ★ (♲) Live & Let Live AA, 3901 Walnut Ste 211, KC; 816-531-9668

Religious / Spiritual Resources

♀ ☆ All Souls UU Church, 4501 Walnut St, KC; 64111 816-531-2131 www.allsoulskc.org

♀ ☆ Broadway Church, 1017 W 29th St, KC; 64108 816-213-4225 www.broadwaychurchkc.org office@broadwaychurchkc.org

♀ ★ Grace Episcopal Church, 520 S 291 Highway, Liberty; 816-781-6262 tinyurl.com/5oyndp

♀ Integrity of Greater Kansas City, c/o Scott Schaefer Salon, 8833 Roe Ave, Prairie Village, KS 913-484-2084 fb.com/integritykc

♀ ★ ♿ Spirit of Hope MCC, 3801 Wyandotte, KC; 816-931-0750 **HS** www.spiritofhopemcc.org ✗

♀ ☆ (♲) St Mark Hope & Peace Lutheran Church, 3800 Troost Ave, KC; 64109 816-561-9677 www.stmarkhopeandpeacekc.org ✗

♀ ☆ Trinity UMC, 620 E Armour Blvd, KC; 64151 816-931-1100 www.trinitykc.org info@trinitykc.org

Sports & Outdoor

♀ ★ Heart of America Softball League, POB 30342, KC; 64112 www.haslkc.com

♀ ☆ Kansas City Roller Warriors, POB 901383, KC; 64190 816-809-8496 www.kcrollerwarriors.com

Veterinarians

♀ ○ ♿ Rainbow Pet Hospital, 4468 Rainbow Blvd, Kansas City, KS 66103-3447 913-831-2034 www.rainbowpethospital.com info@rainbowpethospital.com

Kirksville

Organizations/Resources: Student, Academic, Education

♀ ★ Kirksville High School GSA, 1300 S Cottage Grove Ave; 660-234-5178 kirksvillegsa.weebly.com

♀ ★ Truman State University Prism, Center for Student Involvement, 100 E Normal St; 816-689-8034 fb.com/TrumanGSA/
» Osage Beach: see Lake of Ozarks

St Joseph

Organizations/Resources: Family and Supporters

♀ ☆ PFLAG St Joseph, tinyurl.com/y3768ufw

Missouri: St Joseph
Organizations: Student
216
GAYELLOW PAGES #42 2020-2021
St Louis Area (MO & IL): Missouri
Leather

Organizations/Resources: Student, Academic, Education

⚥ ★ Missouri Western State University Pride Alliance, 816-646-7088 fb.com/MWSUPrideAlliance

St Louis Area (MO & IL)

Crisis, Anti-violence, & Helplines

⚥ ☆ ALIVE (Alternatives To Living In Violent Environments), POB 28733, St Louis; 63146 800-941-9144 **H?** www.alivestl.org

⚥ ● ♿ Call for Help, 9400 Lebanon Rd, East St Louis, IL 62203 618-397-0968 **H** www.callforhelpinc.org info@callforhelpinc.org

♀ ☆ Safe Connections, 2165 Hampton Ave, St Louis 63139 314-531-2003 314-646-7500 www.safeconnections.org info@safeconnections.org

Community Centers and/or Pride Organizations

⚥ ★ ♿ Pride St Louis, 3738 Chouteau Ave Ste 200, St Louis; 314-500-1260 www.pridestl.org ✏

Accommodation: Hotels, Inns, Guesthouses, B&B, Resorts
St Louis

♂ ● ♿ Moonrise Hotel, 6177 Delmar, St Louis; 314-721-1111 **H** www.MoonriseHotel.com (♣?) ✏ ⊛ ⊛

Accommodation Rental: Furnished / Vacation (& AirBNB)
Festus

♂ ● The Cabin Collinwood, 314-375-6565 www.cabincollinwood.com ✏ ⊛ ⊛ cabincollinwood@gmail.com

Accounting, Bookkeeping, Tax Services

♂ ○ ♿ Rosenthal, Packman & Co, PC, 222 S Central Ave Ste 801, Clayton; 63105-3509 314-726-0020 www.rosenthalpackman.com support@rosenthalpackman.com

AIDS/HIV Services, Education & Support

♂ Bethany Place, 821 W A St, Belleville, IL 618-234-0291 fb.com/bethanyplace

♂ ☆ (♿) Doorways, 4385 Maryland Ave, St Louis; 314-535-1919 www.doorwayshousing.org

♂ ☆ ♿ Food Outreach, Inc., 3117 Olive St, St Louis; 63103 314-652-3663 **H?** www.foodoutreach.org ✏ info@foodoutreach.org

♀ Project ARK, 4169 Laclede Ave, St Louis 314-535-7275 projectark.wustl.edu

♂ ☆ Saint Louis Effort for AIDS, 1027 S Vandeventer Ave Ste 700, St Louis; 314-645-6451 www.stlefa.org

Archives/Libraries/Museums/History Projects

⚥ St Louis LGBT History Project, 314-740-0298 www.stlouislgbthistory.com

Bars, Cafes, Clubs, Restaurants
Alton

⚥ Bubby & Sissy's, 602 Belle St, Alton, IL 618-465-4773 tinyurl.com/ybho28d8 **D** ▦

Belleville

⚥ ● Club Escapade, 133 W Main St, Belleville, IL 618-222-9597 fb.com/clubescapade133/ ✏

Centreville

♂ (♿) Boxers-n-Briefs, 55 Four Corners Ln, Centreville, IL 618-332-6141 Strippers fb.com/BoxersNBriefs/ **D** ⚲ ✂ ▦

St Louis

♀ ● Atomic Cowboy, 4140 Manchester Ave, St Louis 314-775-0775 www.atomiccowboystl.com **D** ⚲ ▷ ✂ ▦ ✏

⚥ Attitudes Nightclub, 4100 Manchester Ave, St Louis; 314-534-0044 fb.com/AttitudesNightclubSTL

⚥ Bar: PM, 7109 S Broadway, St Louis 314-312-6682 fb.com/BarPMSTL **K** ⚲ ✂ ▦

♂ ○ (♿) Bissell Mansion Restaurant & Dinner Theatre, 4426 Randall Place, St Louis; 314-533-9830 800-690-9838 tinyurl.com/3xo5u7 **D** ⚲ ✂ ▦

♂ ● ♿ Crafted, 3200 Shenandoah, St Louis; 314-865-3345 craftedstl.com **K** ⚲ ✂ ✏

⚥ The Grey Fox Pub, 3503 S Spring, St Louis 314-772-2150 www.greyfoxstl.com ▦

⚥ Hummel's Pub, 7101 S Broadway, St Louis 314-353-5080 tinyurl.com/zxgaavq ⚲ ✂

♂ ● ♿ JJ's Clubhouse & Bar, 3858 Market, St Louis; 314-535-4100 www.jjsclubhouse.com **L** ✏

⚥ ● Just John, 4112 Manchester Ave, St Louis 314-371-1333 justjohnclub.com **D**

⚥ Keypers Piano Bar, 2280 S Jefferson, St Louis 314-664-6496 keypersstl.com

⚥ ● The Monocle, 4510 Manchester Rd, St Louis 314-932-7003 www.themonoclestl.com ▦

♀ ○ Soulard Bastille, 1027 Russell Blvd, St Louis; 314-664-4408 ⚲ ✂

♂ ○ ♂ Wild Flower, 4590 Laclede Ave, St Louis; 314-279-5746 www.wildflowerstl.com ⚲ ✂

Bookstores

♂ ● ♿ Left Bank Books, 399 N Euclid Ave, St Louis; 314-367-6731 www.left-bank.com ✏

Counseling/Psychotherapy/Mental Health

⚥ ● Betz, Cindy, MSW, LCSW, LGBT Counseling STL, 3115 Hampton Ave, St Louis; 63139 314-602-5534 www.lgbtcounselingstl.com cbetzcounseling@gmail.com

♂ ○ Marshall, Michele, MSW., 1606 S Big Bend Blvd, St Louis; 314-645-1075

⚥ ● (♿) Murrell, Pat, NA, MSW, St Louis metro area 314-973-1890 618-462-4051 tinyurl.com/2kv7pg ✏ mothersource@gmail.com

♂ ○ ♿ Pevnick, Linda, MSW, LCSW, 655 Craig Rd Ste 320, Creve Coeur; 314-567-5360 www.lindapevnickmsw.com

Leather Resources & Groups

♂ ★ Blue Max Cycle Club, 3852 A Market St, St Louis; www.bluemaxcc.org

Legal Services

♀ ● (?&) Wysack-Rood, Kathryn J., 3203A S Grand Blvd Ste A, St Louis; 63118 314-771-4494 618-791-8091 www.kathywysack.com kathy@kathywysack.com

♀ ● (?&) Zarembka, Arlene, 9378 Olive Blvd #206, St Louis; 63132 / Missouri clients only 314-567-6355 Probate www.zarembkalaw.justia.net arlenezarembkalaw@sbcglobal.net

Men's & Sex Clubs (not primarily Health Clubs)

♂ ● && Club St Louis, 2625 Samuel Shepherd Dr, St Louis; 314-533-3666 theclubs.com/club_st_louis **P** ✗

Organizations/Resources: Bisexual Focus

⚥ ☆ (?&) Bisexual Alliance of St Louis, fb.com/BIALLIANCESTL/ ✗

Organizations/Resources: Cultural, Dance, Performance

⚥ ★ && BandTogether, 4579 Laclede Ave #259, St Louis; www.bandtogetherstl.com

♀ ☆ CHARIS: St Louis Women's Chorus, POB 21624, St Louis; 63104 314-664-9340 www.charischorus.org

♂ ★ (?&) Gateway Men's Chorus, Centene Center for The Arts, 3547 Olive St Ste 300, St Louis; 314-287-5669 **H** www.gmcstl.org

⚥ QFest, Cinema St. Louis, 3547 Olive St, St Louis; 314-289-4150 www.cinemastlouis.org/qfest

Organizations/Resources: Family and Supporters

♀ && PFLAG - Ferguson, St. Peter's UCC, 1425 Stein Road, St Louis; 63146 314-666-0197 **H?** pflagferguson.wordpress.com ✗ pflagferguson@gmail.com

♀ ☆ && PFLAG Belleville, POB 65, Belleville, IL 62222 618-977-5078 www.pflagbelleville.org ✗

♀ PFLAG St Louis, 314-872-0288 tinyurl.com/ydxpazdo

♀ ☆ && St Charles PFLAG, 3805 Chardonnay Court, St Charles; 63304 636-928-5639 www.stcharlespflag.org StCharlesPFLAG@gmail.com

Organizations/Resources: Political/Legislative/Advocacy

♀ ☆ American Civil Liberties Union of Missouri St Louis office, 906 Olive Street Ste 1130, St Louis; 314-652-3111 www.aclu-mo.org

Organizations/Resources: Senior Resources

⚥ ★ SAGE of PROMO Fund, 2200 Gravois Ave Ste 201, St Louis; 314-862-4900 www.PROMOonline.org

Organizations/Resources: Social, Recreation, Support

♂ ★ && GAMMA: Gay Married Men's Association of St Louis, 314-567-2076 www.stl-gamma.com ✗

♂ ★ && Show Me Bears, 3858A Market St, St Louis; **H?** www.showmebears.org ✗

Organizations/Resources: Student, Academic, Education

⚥ ★ St Louis Community College Florissant Valley Friendly Colors, 3400 Pershall Rd, St Louis; 314-513-4510 tinyurl.com/ybmv2fou

⚥ ★ (?&) Washington University Pride Alliance, 1 Brookings Dr, St Louis; **H?** ✗ @ixx=

Organizations/Resources: Transgender/Gender Non-Conforming/Diverse

τ ☆ && St Louis Gender Foundation, PO Box 179103, St Louis; 63117-9103 314-607-4163 tinyurl.com/79j74m6 info@stlgf.org

Organizations/Resources: Youth (see also Family)

⚥ Growing American Youth, c/o Trinity Church, 600 N Euclid, St Louis; 314-669-5428 www.growingamericanyouth.org

♂ ☆ Youth Emergency Service Hotline, Epworth Children & Family Service, 110 N Elm Ave, St Louis; 63119 800-899-5437 314-727-6294 Call 24/7 Helpline tinyurl.com/jt4uzhe

♀ Youth in Need, 1815 Boone's Lick Rd, St Charles; 636-946-3771 www.youthinneed.org

Religious / Spiritual Resources

♀ ☆ && Bethel Lutheran Church, 7001 Forsyth Blvd, St Louis; 63105 314-863-3112 www.bethelstl.org ✗ office@bethelstl.org

♀ ☆ & Bethel United Church of Christ, 2200 Camp Jackson Rd, Cahokia, IL 62206 618-939-4835 tinyurl.com/z7cwyp8 bethelucc ministries@gmail.com

♀ ☆ First Congregational UCC, 6501 Wydown Blvd, St Louis; 63105 314-721-5060 www.firstcongregational.org office@firstcon gregational.org

♀ ☆ First Presbyterian Church, 7200 Delmar Blvd, St Louis; 63130 314-726-6677 www.firstpres-stl.org

⚥ ★ & MCC of Greater St Louis, 7423 Michigan Ave, St Louis; 63111 314-361-3221 www.mccgsl.org ✆ info@mccgsl.org

♀ ☆ && Unity of St. Louis - South, 3701 Bayless Ave, St Louis; 63125 314-631-2466 www.unitystlouis.org unitystlouis@sb cglobal.net

Sports & Outdoor

⚥ Big Crank Cycling Club, 4152 Oleatha Ave, St Louis; fb.com/Big-Crank

♂ ★ Saint Louis Frontrunners, POB 775553, St Louis; 63177 314-881-8292 www.stlouisfrontrunners.org

♂ ★ (?&) TEAM St Louis, 4455 Ridgewood Ave #2742, St Louis; 314-492-6503 www.teamsaintlouis.org

Travel & Tourist Services (see also Accommodation)

♀ ○ Patrik Travel, 22 N Euclid Ave #101, St Louis 63108 314-367-1468 rskinnercci@hotmail.com

Springfield

Community Centers and/or Pride Organizations

⚥ ★ && Gay & Lesbian Community Center of the Ozarks, POB 225; 65801 417-869-3978 www.glocenter.org ✗

Bars, Cafes, Clubs, Restaurants

⚥ ● && Martha's Vineyard, 219 W Olive St; 417-864-4572 tinyurl.com/r7gya2v **D** 🏳️‍🌈

Missouri: Springfield
Bars, Cafes, Clubs, Restaurants

218
GAYELLOW PAGES #42 2020-2021

Great Falls : Montana
Organizations: Military/Veterans

♂ Mix UltraLounge, 1221 E Saint Louis St 417-866-7166
www.springfieldmix.com **D**

Organizations/Resources: Family and Supporters

♀ ☆ PFLAG of the Ozarks, POB 1752; 65801 417-350-5300
www.pflagoftheozarks.org

Organizations/Resources: Student, Academic, Education

♂ ★ Drury University Allies, 900 N Benton Ave 417-873-7416
tinyurl.com/h4cxut7

Religious / Spiritual Resources

♀ ☆ ♿ First Unitarian Universalist Church, 2434 E Battlefield;
65804 417-883-3922 www.springfielduu.org admin@
springfielduu.org

Montana
State/County Resources

Community Centers and/or Pride Organizations

♂ Big Sky Pride, www.bigskypride.com

AIDS/HIV Services, Education & Support

♂ ★ Gay Health Task Force, POB 7984, Missoula, MT 59807 406-
829-8075 gayhealthtaskforce.org

Funding: Endowment, Fundraising

♂ ★ Imperial Sovereign Court of the State of Montana, POB 4681,
Missoula, MT 59806 www.iscsm.org

Organizations/Resources: Political/Legislative/Advocacy

♀ ☆ ACLU of Montana, POB 9138, Missoula, MT 59807 406-443-
8590 www.aclumontana.org

♀ ☆ (?♿) Montana Human Rights Network, PO Box 1509, Helena,
MT 59624 406-442-5506 mhrn.org

Recovery

♀ ☆ Al-Anon/Al-Ateen Information Services, 11853 Bench Rd, Missoula, MT 406-721-5818 www.mt.al-anon.alateen.org

♀ ☆ Montana Region Narcotics Anonymous, POB 1085, Helena,
MT 59624 800-990-6262 www.namontana.com

Billings

Bars, Cafes, Clubs, Restaurants

♂ ● ♿ The Loft Dance Club, 1123 1st Ave N; 406-259-9074
fb.com/theloftbillings/

Bookstores

♂ ● ♿ Barjon's Books, Music & Gifts, 223 N 29th St; 406-252-
4398 www.barjonsbooks.com

Erotica / Adult Stores / Safe Sex Supplies

♀ ○ ♿ Adam & Eve, 1211 Mullowney Lane 59101 406-259-4688
www.adamevestores.com

Religious / Spiritual Resources

♀ ☆ ♿ Billings UU Fellowship, POB 20615; 59104 406-652-1893
H? www.billingsuuf.org ✈ Uubillings@gmail.com

Bozeman

Accommodation: Hotels, Inns, Guesthouses, B&B, Resorts
Belgrade

♂ ● Artful Lodger Bed & Breakfast, 8160 Springhill Community Rd,
Belgrade; 406-587-2015 www.artfullodgermontana.com ✈ ⊗ ⊗

♂ ● Lehrkind Mansion B&B, 719 N Wallace Ave 406-585-6932
tinyurl.com/32j262 (☻?) ✈ ⊗

AIDS/HIV Services, Education & Support

♂ ☆ Bridgercare, 300 N Willson Ave # 2001 406-587-0681
www.bridgercare.org

Bars, Cafes, Clubs, Restaurants

♂ ○ ♿ Nova Cafe, 312 E Main 406-587-3973 www.thenova-
cafe.com ✂ ↧ ✈

♀ ○ ♿ Plonk, 29 E Main St 406-587-2170 **H?** www.plonk-
wine.com ☂ ✂ ▥ ✈

Organizations/Resources: Family and Supporters

♀ PFLAG Bozeman/Gallatin Valley, 406-579-9102 www.pflagboze-
man.org

Organizations/Resources: Student, Academic, Education

♂ ★ ♿ Montana State QSA, SUB POB 51; 59717-0001 **H?**
www.montana.edu/qsa/ ✈ qsamsubozeman@gmail.com

♀ ○ ♿ Montana State University Women's Center, 372 Strand
Union Building; 59717 406-994-3836 www.mon-
tana.edu/wwwwomen

Religious / Spiritual Resources

♂ ☆ ♿ Unitarian Universalist Fellowship of Bozeman, 325 N 25th
Ave; 59718 406-586-1368 www.uufbozeman.org

Butte

Bars, Cafes, Clubs, Restaurants

♂ ○ ♿ Uptown Cafe, 47 E Broadway St 406-723-4735 www.up-
towncafe.com ✂ ↧ ✈

Great Falls

Community Centers and/or Pride Organizations

♂ ★ Great Falls LGBTQ Center, 600 Central Ave Ste 323; 59401
406-290-7338 greatfallslgbtqcenter.org center@greatfalls
lgbtqcenter.org

Erotica / Adult Stores / Safe Sex Supplies

♀ ○ ♿ Adam & Eve Great Falls, 416 Central Ave; 59401 406-
727-4688 www.adamevestores.com

Organizations/Resources: Military/Veterans

♂ Proud Airmen and Allies, Malmstrom Air Force Base;
tinyurl.com/ojkwca9

Montana: Livingston
Accommodation
219
GAYELLOW PAGES #42 2020-2021
Lincoln : Nebraska
Crisis, Anti-violence, & Helplines

Livingston

Accommodation: Hotels, Inns, Guesthouses, B&B, Resorts

♂ ○ A Stone's Throw Bed and Breakfast, 105 S 5th St 59047 406-222-5221 www.astonesthrowbandb.com ✗ Ⓢ Ⓢ info@astonesthrowbandb.com

Missoula

Community Centers and/or Pride Organizations

♂ ★ (♿) Western Montana LGBTQ+ Community Center., 127 N Higgins Ave Ste 202; 59802-4457 406-543-2224 www.gaymontana.org info@gaymontana.org

AIDS/HIV Services, Education & Support

♀ ○ ♿ Open Aid Alliance, 1500 W Broadway Suite A, 1500 W Broadway Ste A; 406-543-4770 www.openaidalliance.org

Bars, Cafes, Clubs, Restaurants

♀ ○ ♿ The Catalyst Cafe & Espresso Bar, 111 N Higgins Ave; 406-542-1337 www.thecatalystcafe.com ☞

Bookstores

♂ ○ Fact & Fiction, 220 N Higgins; 406-721-2881 www.factandfictionbooks.com

♂ ○ University Center Bookstore, 5 Campus Dr 406-243-1234 www.montanabookstore.com

Erotica / Adult Stores / Safe Sex Supplies

♀ ○ ♿ Adam & Eve Missoula, 3209 Brooks St; 59801 406-549-4688 www.adamevestores.com

Organizations/Resources: Cultural, Dance, Performance

♂ ★ Missoula Gay Men's Chorus, 406-370-9876 tinyurl.com/oqxk92d

Organizations/Resources: Political/Legislative/Advocacy

♀ ☆ ♿ Jeannette Rankin Peace Center, 519 S Higgins Ave; 59801-2735 406-543-3955 www.jrpc.org ✗

Organizations/Resources: Student, Academic, Education

♂ ★ ♿ University of Montana Lambda Alliance, 32 Campus Dr Ste 209; 59812 406-243-5922 fb.com/umtlambda ✗ umlambda@gmail.com

♀ ☆ Women's Resource Center, University Of Montana, UC 210; 406-243-4153 tinyurl.com/y4v8fdq8

Organizations/Resources: Youth (see also Family)

♂ MpowerMT, POB 7984; 59807 406-829-8075 tinyurl.com/n4acd8e

Real Estate (see also Mortgages)

♂ ○ ♿ Portico Real Estate, K D, 445 W Alder; 59802 406-240-5227 www.porticorealestate.com ✗ kd@porticorealestate.com

Swan Valley

Accommodation: Hotels, Inns, Guesthouses, B&B, Resorts

♀ ○ Holland Lake Lodge, 1947 Holland Lake Rd; 59826 406-754-2282 www.hollandlakelodge.com info@hollandlakelodge.com

Three Forks

Erotica / Adult Stores / Safe Sex Supplies

♂ ○ ♿ Adam & Eve Three Forks, 10771 US Hwy 287; 59752 406-285-4688 www.adamevestores.com

Nebraska
State/County Resources

Community Centers and/or Pride Organizations

♂ Heartland Pride, POB 8273, Omaha, NE 68108 www.heartland-pride.org

Information, Media & Publications

♂ ★ OutNebraska, POB 84253, Lincoln, NE 68501 402-488-1130 outnebraska.org

Funding: Endowment, Fundraising

♂ ★ Imperial Court of Nebraska (ICON), POB 3772, Omaha, NE 68103 tinyurl.com/2lerks

Organizations/Resources: Political/Legislative/Advocacy

♀ (♿) ACLU Nebraska, 134 S 13th St #1010, Lincoln, NE 855-557-2258 www.aclunebraska.org

Recovery

♀ ☆ Al-Anon/Alateen, POB 30082, Lincoln, NE 68503 402-477-9662 nebr-al-anon-alateen.org

♀ ☆ Narcotics Anonymous, POB 80091, Lincoln, NE 68501 www.nebraskana.org

Hastings

Organizations/Resources: Family and Supporters

♀ ☆ ♿ PFLAG South Central (Hastings) Nebraska, POB 83, Sutton; 68979 402-460-8696 tinyurl.com/yd6dgtyd

Organizations/Resources: Student, Academic, Education

♂ ★ Hastings College Gay/Straight Alliance, 710 N Turner Ave; 402-461-7351 ✗

Kearney

Organizations/Resources: Family and Supporters

♂ PFLAG Kearney, 34 Riverside Trailer Court 720-684-8097 tinyurl.com/pz5qodb

Lincoln

Crisis, Anti-violence, & Helplines

♀ ☆ Friendship Home, POB 85358; 68501 402-437-9302 www.friendshiphome.org

Nebraska: Lincoln
Crisis, Anti-violence, & Helplines

220
GAYELLOW PAGES #42 2020-2021

Omaha : Nebraska
Sports & Outdoor

♀ ☆ Voices of Hope, 2545 N St; 402-475-7273 www.voicesofhope-lincoln.org

Community Centers and/or Pride Organizations

⚥ Star City Pride, POB 81703; 68501 402-540-1099 starcitypride.org

Information, Media & Publications

♀ ☆ Common Root - Mutual Aid Center, 211 N 14th St #323; 68503 www.commonroot.net contact@commonroot.net

AIDS/HIV Services, Education & Support

♀ ☆ Nebraska AIDS Project - STD Testing Lincoln, 1919 S 40th St #320; 402-476-7000 www.nap.org

Bars, Cafes, Clubs, Restaurants

⚥ • ♿ Panic, 200 S 18th St 402-435-8764 fb.com/panic.bar

Counseling/Psychotherapy/Mental Health

♀ ○♿ Furr, Gina, PhD, 1919 S 40th St Ste 111; 402-617-7237 www.drginafurr.com

♀ ○ Wellman, Carrie Ann, 1701 S 17th St Ste #1C 402-560-4683

Counseling/Psychiatry

♀ ○♿ Dohrman, Heather, MA, LIMHP, 3701 Union Dr Ste 100; 68516 402-875-9270 www.cheneypsych.com hdohrman@cheneypsych.com

Legal Services

♀ ○♿ Mary Kay Hansen Law and Mediation, PC LLO, 1101 Cornhusker Hwy Ste 201; 68521 402-477-0230 **H?** mkhansenlaw.com ✐ marykay@mkhansenlaw.com

Organizations/Resources: Family and Supporters

♀ ☆♿ PFLAG Lincoln, POB 82034 68501 402-466-4599 www.pflaglincoln.org

Organizations/Resources: Student, Academic, Education

⚥ ★ (?♿) University of Nebraska LGBTQA+ Center, 346 Nebraska Union; 68588-0446 402-472-1652 lgbtqa.unl.edu/welcome ✐ lgbtqa.ga@unl.edu

Real Estate (see also Mortgages)

♀ ○ Keck, Victoria, Realtor, Team Victory at Nebraska Realty, 6301 S 58th St; 68516 402-730-4878 victoriamkeck@gmail.com

Recovery

♀ ☆ CenterPointe, 2633 P St; 68503 402-475-8717 www.centerpointe.org info@centerpointe.org

Religious / Spiritual Resources

⚥ ★ Plymouth Pride Fellowship, 2000 D St 402-476-7565 www.firstplymouth.org

Norfolk

AIDS/HIV Services, Education & Support

♀ ☆ Nebraska AIDS Project - Norfolk Office, POB 423; 68702 402-649-3584 www.nap.org

Omaha

AIDS/HIV Services, Education & Support

♂ ☆ Nebraska AIDS Project Main Office, 250 S 77th St; 402-552-9260 www.nap.org

Bars, Cafes, Clubs, Restaurants

⚥ • Flixx Cabaret & Show Bar, 1019 S 10th St 402-408-1020 www.flixxomaha.com ▥ ✐

⚥ • ♿ The Max, 1417 Jackson St 402-346-4110 www.themaxomaha.com **DV** ▥

⚥ The RUN / Omaha Mining Co, 1715 Leavenworth St 402-449-8703 tinyurl.com/6jfx2m4 **D**

Body Art

♀ ○ Villains Inc, 3629 Q St; 68107 402-731-0202 villainstattoo.com villainstattoo@gmail.com

Counseling/Psychotherapy/Mental Health

♀ ○ Dross, Jack D, MS, LMHP, 8031 West Center Road Ste 302; 68124-3134 402-334-6869 fax 402-504-1092

Entertainment-Related Services (see also Performance)

♀ ☆♿ SNAP! Productions, POB 8464 68108 **H** www.snapproductions.com ✐

Organizations/Resources: Cultural, Dance, Performance

♀ ★♿ River City Mixed Chorus, POB 3267; 68103 402-341-7464 www.rcmc.org

Organizations/Resources: Family and Supporters

♀ ★♿ PFLAG Omaha, POB 390064; 68139 402-291-6781 www.pflag-omaha.org

Organizations/Resources: Student, Academic, Education

⚥ ★ GLSEN, POB 540413; 68154 glsen.org/chapters/omaha

Organizations/Resources: Youth (see also Family)

♀ ♿ Proud Horizons, c/o Heartland Pride, POB 8273; 68108 402-291-6781 proudhorizons.com

Religious / Spiritual Resources

♀ ☆♿ First Central UCC, 421 S 36th St 68131 402-345-1533 **HD** www.firstcentral.org ✐

⚥ ★ (?♿) Metropolitan Community Church of Omaha, 819 S 22nd St; 68108 402-345-2563 www.mccomaha.org mccomaha@mccomaha.org

Sports & Outdoor

⚥ ★ Omaha Front Runners/Walkers, tinyurl.com/jva9y2v

⚥ Omaha Metro GLBT Sports League, POB 460991, Papillion; 68046 www.oglbtsports.com

Nebraska: Scottsbluff
AIDS/HIV Support

221

GAYELLOW PAGES #42 2020-2021

Las Vegas Area: Nevada
Bookstores

Scottsbluff

AIDS/HIV Services, Education & Support

♂ ☆ Nebraska AIDS Project - Scottsbluff Office, PO Box 1626; 69363 308-635-3807 www.nap.org

Wayne

Organizations/Resources: Student, Academic, Education

⚥ ★ ♿ Wayne State College PRIDE, Student Activities, 1111 Main St; 402-375-7322 **H?** tinyurl.com/hyc2vkg ✏

Nevada
State/County Resources

AIDS/HIV Services, Education & Support

♀ ☆ Aid for AIDS of Nevada, 1120 Almond Tree Lane, Las Vegas, NV 702-382-2326 www.afanlv.org ✏

Organizations/Resources: Business & Professional Associations, Labor Advocacy

⚥ ★ Gay & Lesbian Chamber of Commerce of Nevada, 2610 S Jones Blvd #3, Las Vegas, NV 702-625-3882 www.glccnv.com ✏

Organizations/Resources: Political/Legislative/Advocacy

⚥ ★ Nevada Impact, Political endorsements by the LGBTQ community Nevadalmpact.com

♀ ☆ Nevada Women's Lobby, POB 5565, Reno, NV 89513 www.nevadawomenslobby.org

Organizations/Resources: Transgender/Gender Non-Conforming/Diverse

⚧ ☆ Gender Justice Nevada, 2441 Tech Center Ct #113, Las Vegas, NV 702-425-7288 www.genderjusticenv.com

Carson City

Organizations/Resources: Family and Supporters

♀ PFLAG Carson Region, 312 Tahoe Dr; 775-600-2905 pflagcarson.org

» Henderson: see Las Vegas Area
» Lake Tahoe: see Lake Tahoe (CA/NV) Area

Las Vegas Area

Crisis, Anti-violence, & Helplines

♀ ☆ Rape Crisis Center, 801 S Rancho Ste B-2, LV 888-366-1640 www.rcclv.org

Community Centers and/or Pride Organizations

⚥ ★ ♿ Gay & Lesbian Community Center of Southern Nevada, 401 S Maryland Pkwy, LV; 702-733-9800 www.thecenterlv.org ✏

⚥ ★ Southern Nevada Association of Pride, Inc., 4001 S Decatur Blvd #37-540, LV; 866-930-3336 www.lasvegaspride.org

Information, Media & Publications

♀ ★ ♿ The Lambda Smart Pages, c/o The Center, 401 S Maryland Pkwy, LV; 702-813-6214 www.lambdalv.com

⚥ ● Las Vegas Spectrum, 2550 E Desert Inn Rd #242, LV; 89121 702-813-6214 LGBTQ & Progressive News Magazine. The first publication to use marriage license lists for direct mail. www.LasVegasSpectrum.com Rob@LasVegasSpectrum.com

♀ Lesbians in Vegas, fb.com/lezinvegas/

Accounting, Bookkeeping, Tax Services

♂ ● ♿ Stout, Brenda, CPA, 5836 S Pecos Rd Ste 104, LV; 89120 702-736-0992 Tax debt resolution, IRS Nonprofit compliance www.brendastoutcpa.com ✏ brenda@brendastoutcpa.com

AIDS/HIV Services, Education & Support

♂ ☆ Golden Rainbow, 714 E Sahara Ste 101, LV 702-384-2899 www.goldenrainbow.org

Bars, Cafes, Clubs, Restaurants
Las Vegas

♂ ● (?♿) Badlands, 953 E Sahara #22-B, LV; 702-792-9262 www.badlandsbarlv.com **DCW** ▦

⚥ ● Charlie's Las Vegas, 5012 S Arville St #4, LV; 702-876-1844 www.charlieslasvegas.com **BCWD**

♂ ○ ♿ Flex Cocktail Lounge, 4371 W Charleston Blvd, LV; 702-878-3355 flexlasvegas.com **D** ▦

⚥ ● ♿ Freezone, 610 E Naples Dr, LV; 702-794-2300 www.freezonelv.com **D** ⚥ ✂ ▦

♂ Fun Hog Ranch, 495 E Twain Ave, LV 702-791-7001 www.funhogranchlv.com **L** ⚥ ✂

⚥ ● ♿ The Garage, 1487 E Flamingo RD Ste C, LV; 702-440-6333 www.thegaragelv.com ✏ info@thegaragelv.com

⚥ Hamburger Mary's Las Vegas, 1700 E Flamingo Rd, LV; 702-733-8787 tinyurl.com/uluyjhw **D** ⚥ ✂

♂ ● Las Vegas Eagle, 3430 E Tropicana, LV 702-458-8662 fb.com/thelasvegaseagle **L**

⚧ Las Vegas Lounge, 900 E Karen Ave, LV 702-737-9350 thelasvegaslounge.com ▦

♀ ● ♿ Mingo Kitchen & Lounge, 1017 S First St #180, LV; 702-685-0328 www.eatmixmingo.com ⚥ ✂ ↻ ✏

♂ ○ Paymon's Mediterranean Cafe & Hookah Lounge, 4147 S Maryland Pkwy, LV; / and 8380 W Sahara Ave 702-731-6030 www.paymons.com ⚥ ✂

⚥ The Phoenix Bar & Lounge, 4213 W Sahara Ave, LV; 702-826-2422 fb.com/thephoenixlv/ ▦

⚥ ● Piranha, 4633 Paradise Rd, LV 702-791-0100 www.piranhavegas.com **D** ▦

⚥ The QuadZ, 4640 Paradise Rd, LV 702-733-0383 www.quadzbar.com **V** ▦

Bookstores

⚥ ● ♿ Get Booked, 4640 Paradise Rd #15, LV; 702-737-7780 getbooked.com

Nevada: Las Vegas Area
Counseling

222

GAYELLOW PAGES #42 2020-2021

Las Vegas Area: Nevada
Weddings/Unions

Counseling/Psychotherapy/Mental Health

♂ ☆ && Community Counseling Center, 714 E Sahara Ave, LV; 702-369-8700 www.cccofsn.org

Erotica / Adult Stores / Safe Sex Supplies

♀ ● && Adam & Eve, 3231 North Decatur Blvd #137, LV; 702-478-6969 www.adamevestores.com

Funding: Endowment, Fundraising

♀ ★ Imperial Royal Sovereign Court, POB 46481, LV; 89114 702-806-8212 fb.com/irscde/

♀ ★ Sisters of Perpetual Indulgence, 702-591-6969 www.sinsitysisters.org

Health Care: Physical (see also Counseling/Mental Health)

♂ ○ (?&) AAA Wuxin Healing Arts, Fiona Kelley, OMD 2920 N Green Valley Pkwy Ste 723, Henderson; 89014 702-369-3406 www.acupuncturelasvegas.com ✎ drkelley@acupuncturelasvegas.com

♂ ○ (?&) Kelley, Fiona, OMD, 2920 N Green Valley Parkway Ste 723, Henderson; 89014 702-369-3406 www.acupuncturelasvegas.com drkelley@acupuncturelasvegas.com

Leather Resources & Groups

♂ ☆ (?&) Leather Uniform Club of Las Vegas, 3003 Wrangler St, LV; 702-204-8632 **H?** www.lucoflv.com

Legal Services

♂ ○ Craig P Kenny & Associates, 501 S 8th St, LV 89101-6907 702-380-2800 www.cpklaw.com

♂ ○ Kunin Law Group, 10845 Griffith Peak Dr Ste 200, LV; 89135 702-438-8060 www.kuninlawgroup.com info@kuninlawgroup.com

♂ ○ LV Criminal Defense, 400 S 7th St, LV; 89101 702-623-6362 lvcriminaldefense.com info@lvcriminaldefense.com

♂ ○ && Smith, James, 7251 W Lake Mead Blvd #300, LV; 89128 702-460-3765 www.james-smith.com jamessmith@aol.com

Men's & Sex Clubs (not primarily Health Clubs)

♂ ● && Entourage Vegas, 953 E Sahara #A19, LV; 702-650-9191 www.entouragevegas.com

♂ ● Hawks Gym & Spa, 953 E Sahara Ave #35B, LV 702-731-4295 hawksgym.com **P**

Organizations/Resources: Business & Professional Associations, Labor Advocacy

♂ ★ && **Lambda Chamber of Commerce, c/o The Center, 401 S Maryland Pkwy, LV; 89101 702-813-6214 Lambda Business Association since 1991 www.lambdalv.com Directory@LambdaLV.com**

Organizations/Resources: Family and Supporters

♂ ☆ PFLAG Las Vegas Chapter, POB 20145, LV 89112 702-438-7838 tinyurl.com/cx9llxs

Organizations/Resources: Naturist/Nudist

♂ Sunrunners, POB 750213, LV; 89136 702-363-6862 tinyurl.com/64qkqnr **N**

Organizations/Resources: Political/Legislative/Advocacy

♂ ☆ && ACLU of Nevada Las Vegas Office, 601 S Rancho Dr Ste 11, LV; 702-366-1226 www.aclunv.org

♂ ★ Stonewall Democrats of Southern Nevada, The Center, 401 S Maryland Pkwy, LV; fb.com/StonewallSNV/

Organizations/Resources: Social, Recreation, Support

♂ ★ Betty's Outrageous Adventures, 702-636-8552 www.bettysout.com

♂ ★ Las Vegas Prime Timers, POB 42424, LV; 89116 702-527-2360 primetimersww.net/lasvegas/

Organizations/Resources: Student, Academic, Education

♀ ☆ University of Nevada Jean Nidetch Women's Center, Box 452025, 4505 Maryland Parkway, LV; 702-895-4475 tinyurl.com/oqd237r

Real Estate (see also Mortgages)

♂ ● && Hiatt, Bruce, Luxury Realty Group Inc 10161 Park Run Dr Ste 150, LV; 89145 702-456-7080 www.LuxuryRealtyGroup.com

♂ ○ **Liz Thompson, Desert Realty, 3160 W Sahara Ave #A22; 89102 702-876-0098 Email: liz@realtysales.estate For all your residential & commercial needs. Your family Realtor, since 1985. www.desert-realty.com liz@realtysales.estate**

♂ ● && Margolin, Sandy, Urban Nest Realty, 10220 W Charleston Blvd #3, LV; 89135 702-683-3362 **HS** SandyMargolin.com Realtrchik@gmail.com

♂ ● && **Schlegel, Rob, Realtor, Elite Realty 702-813-6214 Also publisher/journalist at Las Vegas Spectrum, LGBTQIA+ & progressive news www.RobLasVegas.com Rob@RobLasVegas.com**

Recovery

♂ ☆ Las Vegas AA Central Office, 1431 E Charleston Blvd #15, LV; 89108 702-598-1888 www.lvcentraloffice.org lvaa@lvcoxmail.com

Religious / Spiritual Resources

♂ ★ Imago Dei: Gay/Lesbian Catholic Ministries of Southern Nevada, St Thomas Aquinas Catholic Newman Center, 4765 Brussels St, LV; 702-354-2294 www.imagodeilv.com

♂ ★ && Love MCC Vegas, 1140 Almond Tree Ln Ste 302, LV; 702-369-4380 www.lovemcclv.org

Travel & Tourist Services (see also Accommodation)

♂ ○ (?&) Adventure Photo Tours, 3111 S Valley View Blvd #X-106, LV; 89102 702-889-8687 888-363-8687 www.adventurephototours.com

Weddings and Ceremonies

♂ ○ (&&) Sweethearts Wedding Chapel, 1735 S Las Vegas Blvd, LV; 89104 800-444-2932 www.sweetheartschapel.com ♥ eren@sweetheartschapel.com

Nevada: Reno
Community Centers / Pride
223
GAYELLOW PAGES #42 2020-2021
State/County Resources : New Hampshire
Recovery

Reno

Community Centers and/or Pride Organizations

⚥ ★ Northern Nevada Pride, POB 54; 89504 775-624-3720 www.northernnevadapride.org info@northernnevadapride.org

⚥ ★ ර්ර් Our Center, POB 54; 89504 / 1745 S Wells Ave 775-624-3720 **H?** www.ourcenterreno.org ✔ center@ourcenterreno.org

Information, Media & Publications

⚥ ★ The Reno Gay Page, POB 6316; 89513 775-453-4058 tinyurl.com/y9m45o2y

Bars, Cafes, Clubs, Restaurants

⚥ ○ ර්ර් 5 Star Saloon, 132 West St 775-499-5655 5starsaloon.com **D** 🍴 ✔

⚥ Cadillac Lounge, 1114 E 4th St 775-324-7827 fb.com/Cadillaclounge

⚥ ර්ර් Carl's The Saloon, 3310 S Virginia St; 775-829-0099 www.carlsthesaloon.com **LCW** ✔

⚥ FacesNV, 239 W 2nd St; 775-470-8590 www.facesnv.net

⚥ Splash Reno, 340 Kietzke Lane; 775-686-6681 fb.com/Splashrno/

Counseling/Psychotherapy/Mental Health

♂ ○ Jackson, Karen, LCSW, 1325 Airmotive Way Ste 175; 89502 775-786-1179 www.karenjacksontherapy.com karen@karenjacksontherapy.com

Funding: Endowment, Fundraising

⚥ Biggest Little Sisters, Inc, 805 S Virginia St #69; fb.com/RenoSisters

⚥ ★ Silver Dollar Court, POB 6581; 89513 renosdc.org

Health Care: Physical (see also Counseling/Mental Health)

♂ ☆ ර්ර් Northern Nevada HOPES, 580 W 5th St; 775-997-7503 **H?** www.nnhopes.org

Leather Resources & Groups

♂ ☆ National Leather Association - Northern Nevada, POB 6752; 89513 fb.com/nlannevada

Men's & Sex Clubs (not primarily Health Clubs)

♂ Steve's Bathhouse, 1030 W 2nd St; 775-323-8770 www.stevesreno.com **P**

Organizations/Resources: Political/Legislative/Advocacy

♂ ☆ ACLU of Nevada Reno Office, 1325 Airmotive Way Ste 202; 775-786-6757 www.aclunv.org

Organizations/Resources: Social, Recreation, Support

♂ ★ Comstock Grizzlies, POB 60535; 89506 775-359-4538 fb.com/ComstockGrizzlies

♂ (?ර) High Sierra Prime Timers, POB 5103; 89513 www.hsptreno.com

⚥ ★ Spectrum Northern Nevada, ! POB 336 89504 www.SpectrumNV.org

Organizations/Resources: Transgender/Gender Non-Conforming/Diverse

т Transgender Social Group TINN, POB 336; 89504 www.spectrumnv.org

Religious / Spiritual Resources

♂ ☆ ර්ර් Religious Society of Friends (Quakers), 497 Highland Ave; 89512-2219 775-329-9400 www.renofriends.org ✔

♂ ☆ ර්ර් Temple Sinai, 3405 Gulling Rd 89503-2043 775-747-5508 **HD** www.sinaireno.org ⚥✔ admin@sinaireno.org

New Hampshire
State/County Resources

Community Centers and/or Pride Organizations

♀ Rural Outright, TLC Family Resource Center, PO Box 1098, Claremont, NH 03743 603-542-1848 tinyurl.com/uc9ssvc

AIDS/HIV Services, Education & Support

♀ ☆ ර්ර් AIDS Response Seacoast, 7 Junkins Ave, Portsmouth, NH 603-433-5377 www.aidsresponse.org

♀ ☆ ර්ර් HIV/HCV Resource Center, 2 Blacksmith St, Lebanon, NH 03766 603-448-8887 800-816-2220 fax 603-448-8885 www.h2rc.org laura@h2rc.org

♀ NAMES Project Northern New England Chapter, 215 S Broadway #247, Salem, NH 603-425-4802 newenglandaidsquilt.org

♀ ☆ ර්ර් Southern NH HIV/AIDS Task Force, 45 High St, Nashua, NH 603-595-8464 www.aidstaskforcenh.org

Insurance (see also Financial Planning)

♀ ○ Web Insurance Agency, POB 9, Rollinsford, NH 03869-0009 603-740-4353 fax 603-740-2953

Organizations/Resources: Family and Supporters

♀ ☆ (?ර) PFLAG:NH, POB 957, Concord, NH 03302-0957 603-536-3823 www.pflagnh.org

Organizations/Resources: Political/Legislative/Advocacy

♀ ACLU of New Hampshire, 18 Low Ave, Concord, NH 603-225-3080 aclu-nh.org

Organizations/Resources: Social, Recreation, Support

♀ ☆ Family Tree, POB 441275, Somerville, MA 02144 / Southern NH/MA 603-437-1337 www.polyfamilytree.org

♂ ★ Granite State Gay Men, 40 Joshua Dr, Manchester, NH 603-203-3444 fb.com/GraniteStateGayMen/

Organizations/Resources: Transgender/Gender Non-Conforming/Diverse

т ☆ TransGender New Hampshire (TG-NH), fb.com/groups/TGNH.Support/

Recovery

♀ ☆ Alcoholics Anonymous, 1330 Hooksett Rd, Hooksett, NH 800-593-3330 www.nhaa.net

Weddings and Ceremonies

⚥ ○ Siebert, Carol, JP, 603-494-7586 ♥ jotp2008@yahoo.com

›› *Albany: see White Mountains Area*
›› *Antrim: see Monadnock Area*
›› *Bethlehem: see White Mountains Area*
›› *Chocorua: see White Mountains Area*

Concord

Counseling/Psychotherapy/Mental Health

⚥ ★ (?♿) Womankind Counseling Center, 21 Green St; 603-225-2985 womankindcounseling.webs.com

Health Care: Physical (see also Counseling/Mental Health)

⚥ ☆ (?♿) Equality Health Center, 38 S Main St; 603-225-2739 equalityhc.org

Organizations/Resources: Social, Recreation, Support

⚥ ★ ♿♿ Capital Gay Men, POB 985 03302 603-229-1381 www.cgminc.org

Organizations/Resources: Student, Academic, Education

⚥ ★ NHTI Alliance, 31 College Dr; 603-271-6484 x4206

›› *Conway: see White Mountains Area*

Durham

Organizations/Resources: Student, Academic, Education

⚥ ★ ♿♿ The UNH Alliance, University of New Hampshire, 83 Main St, MUB Rm 7; tinyurl.com/yx3mnqpz

Exeter

Organizations/Resources: Student, Academic, Education

⚥ ★ Phillips Exeter Academy Gender Sexuality Alliance - GSA, 20 Main St; 603-772-4311 fb.com/lgbtq.PEA/

›› *Franconia: see White Mountains Area*

Hanover

Organizations/Resources: Student, Academic, Education

⚥ ☆ ♿♿ Sexuality, Women, and Gender Advising in the Office of Pluralism and Leadership, Hinman Box 3217, 2 N Main St, Collis 211; 603-646-0987 **H?** www.dartmouth.edu/~cgse/ ⚡

›› *Hart's Location: see White Mountains Area*
›› *Keene: see Monadnock Area*

Kensington

Bakeries

⚥ ○ (?♿) Hippie Chick Bakery, 118 South Rd; 03833 / appointment only 603-347-1487 **H?** www.hippiechickbakery.com

Lebanon

Crisis, Anti-violence, & Helplines

⚥ ☆ ♿♿ Women's Information Service (WISE), 38 Bank St; 03766 866-348-9473 **H** www.wiseuv.org

Manchester

Bars, Cafes, Clubs, Restaurants

⚥ ● Breezeway Pub, 14 Pearl St; 603-621-9111 fb.com/BreezewayPub **DK** 🍸 ✕

⚥ ● Doogie's Bar & Grill, 37 Manchester St 603-232-0732 www.doogies.net 🍸 ✕
@ixx=

⚥ ○ Element Lounge, 1055 Elm St; 603-627-2922 www.elementlounge.net **D**

Organizations/Resources: Cultural, Dance, Performance

⚥ ★ New Hampshire Gay Men's Chorus, POB 6251 03108 603-263-4333 www.nhgmc.com

T TransPosition Vocal Ensemble, tinyurl.com/uljs5on

Organizations/Resources: Student, Academic, Education

⚥ ★ ♿♿ University of New Hampshire, Manchester Common Ground (GLBTA), 400 Commercial St **H?** tinyurl.com/psaedxb ⚡

Monadnock Area

Accommodation: Hotels, Inns, Guesthouses, B&B, Resorts

Fitzwilliam

⚥ ○ (?♿) Fitzwilliam Inn, 62 NH 119 W, Fitzwilliam; 03447 603-585-9000 fitzwilliaminn.com ✕ (🐾?) ⚡ 🚭 info@fitzwilliaminn.com

Bookstores

⚥ ○ ♿♿ Toadstool Bookshop, 12 Emerald St, Keene; (Colony Mill Marketplace) 603-352-8815 www.toadbooks.com ⚡

⚥ ○ Toadstool Bookshop, 12 Depot Sq, Peterborough 603-924-3543 www.toadbooks.com

Organizations/Resources: Family and Supporters

⚥ ☆ ♿ PFLAG NH Keene Chapter, Monadnock Area Peer Support (MPS) Location, 64 Beaver St (no mail), Keene; 03431 fb.com/PFLAGKeene pflagkeene@gmail.com

Organizations/Resources: Student, Academic, Education

⚥ ★ (♿♿) Keene State College Pride, 229 Main St, Keene; 03435-3003 603-358-2099 fb.com/KSCPride kscpride@gmail.com

Religious / Spiritual Resources

⚥ ☆ ♿♿ Peterborough Unitarian Universalist Church, 25 Main St, Peterborough; 03458 603-924-6245 **HD** www.uupeterborough.org

Nashua

Bookstores

⚥ ○ Toadstool Bookshop, Somerset Plaza, 375 Amherst St, Rte 101 A; 603-673-1734 www.toadbooks.com

Counseling/Psychotherapy/Mental Health

⚥ ○ Hindy, Carl G, PhD, 120 Main St Ste 103; 03060 603-880-8773 www.hindyassociates.com

Religious / Spiritual Resources

♂ ☆ ᏥᏥ Unitarian Universalist Church, 58 Lowell St; 03064 603-882-1091 www.uunashua.org ✔ uucnoffice@uunashua.org

Newfound Lake Area

Accommodation: Hotels, Inns, Guesthouses, B&B, Resorts
Bridgewater

♂ ● The Inn on Newfound Lake, 1030 Mayhew Tpk, Bridgewater; (Rte 3A) 603-744-9111 www.newfoundlake.com Ⴤ ✕
 » North Conway: see White Mountains Area
 » North Woodstock: see White Mountains Area

Pelham

Religious / Spiritual Resources

♀ ☆ ᏥᏥ First Congregational UCC, 3 Main St; 03076 603-635-7025 **HD** www.uccpelham.org ✔ uccpelham@gmail.com
 » Peterborough: see Monadnock Area

Plymouth

Accommodation: Hotels, Inns, Guesthouses, B&B, Resorts

♀ ○ Federal House Inn, 27 Route 25; 03264-3141 603-536-4644 www.federalhouseinnnh.com FederalHouseNH@gmail.com

Portsmouth

Accommodation: Hotels, Inns, Guesthouses, B&B, Resorts

♂ ● Ale House Inn, 121 Bow St; 603-431-7760 www.alehouse-inn.com ⊛

Bars, Cafes, Clubs, Restaurants

♂ ○ ᏥᏥ Mombo, 66 Marcy St; 603-433-2340 **H?** www.momborestaurant.com ✕

Bookstores

♂ ○ (?Ꮵ) RiverRun Bookstore, 142 Fleet St 603-431-2100 www.riverrunbookstore.com

Health Care: Physical (see also Counseling/Mental Health)

♀ ☆ (?Ꮵ) The Joan G Lovering Health Center, POB 456, Greenland; 03840 / 559 Portsmouth Ave 603-436-7588 **H?** www.jglhc.org

Organizations/Resources: Cultural, Dance, Performance

♥ ᏥᏥ Women Singing Out!, POB 1553; 03802 tinyurl.com/t69cqoc

Organizations/Resources: Youth (see also Family)

♂ ★ ᏥᏥ Seacoast Outright, POB 842; 03802 603-552-5824 www.seacoastoutright.org

Religious / Spiritual Resources

♂ ☆ Christ Episcopal Church, 1035 Lafayette Rd 03801 603-436-8842 www.christepiscopalchurch.us christportsnh@comcast.net

♀ ☆ ᏥᏥ South Church UU, 73 Court St 03801 / church at 292 State St 603-436-4762 **HD** www.southchurch-uu.org ✔ info@southchurch-uu.org
 » Sugar Hill: see White Mountains Area

 » Surry: see Monadnock Area
 » Temple: see Monadnock Area
 » Westmoreland: see Monadnock Area

White Mountains Area

Accommodation: Hotels, Inns, Guesthouses, B&B, Resorts
Bethlehem

♥ ● (?Ꮵ) The Highlands Inn, POB 118GP, Bethlehem; 03574 603-869-3978 www.highlandsinn-nh.com (♣?) ✔ ⊛ ♥
Eaton Center

♀ ● Inn at Crystal Lake & Palmer House Pub, 2356 Eaton Rd, Eaton Center; 603-447-2120 www.innatcrystallake.com ✕
Franconia

♀ ● (?Ꮵ) The Horse & Hound Inn, 205 Wells Rd, Franconia; 603-823-5501 www.horseandhoundnh.com ✕ ✔
Hart's Location

♀ ● (?Ꮵ) The Notchland Inn, 2 Morey Rd, Hart's Location; 03812 603-374-6131 800-866-6131 www.notchland.com ✕♣✔ ⊛ innkeepers@Notchland.com
Hebron

♀ ○ (?Ꮵ) Coppertoppe, 8 Range Rd, Hebron; 03241 603-744-3636 866-846-3636 www.coppertoppe.com ♣✔ ⊛ ⊛ info@coppertoppe.com
North Conway

♀ ● (?Ꮵ) Cranmore Inn, 80 Kearsarge Rd, North Conway 03860 603-356-5502 www.cranmoreinn.com (♣?) ✔ ⊛
Randolph

♀ ● (?Ꮵ) Inn at Bowman, 1174 US Route 2, Randolph; 603-466-5006 www.innatbowman.com ✔ ⊛ ⊛
Wilmot

♂ ● New Hampshire Mountain Inn, 318 New Canada Rd, Wilmot; 03267 888-797-2899 603-735-6900 www.nhmountaininn.com ✔ ⊛ ⊛ info@nhmountaininn.com

Bookstores

♀ ○ (?Ꮵ) White Birch Books, 2568 Main St 603-356-3200 www.whitebirchbooks.com

New Hampshire: White Mountains Area
Religious

226

GAYELLOW PAGES #42 2020-2021

State/County Resources : New Jersey
Security Services

Religious / Spiritual Resources

♀ ☆ All Saints' Episcopal Church, 35 School St, Littleton; 03561 603-444-3414 www.allsts.org allstslittleton@allsts.org
>> *Whitefield: see White Mountains Area*
>> *Woodstock: see White Mountains Area*

New Jersey
State/County Resources

Crisis, Anti-violence, & Helplines

♀ ☆ (?⚥) 180 Turning Lives Around Inc., 1 Bethany Rd Bldg 3 #42, Hazlet, NJ 888-843-4262 **HD** 180nj.org

♀ New Jersey Coalition to End Domestic Violence, 1670 White-horse-Hamilton Square Rd, Trenton, NJ 800-572-7233 www.njcedv.org

Information, Media & Publications

♂ ★ NJGayLife.com, POB 224, Metuchen, NJ 08840-0224 732-549-9054 fax 732-549-9056 www.njgaylife.com bonnie@njgaylife.com

♀ ● Out in Jersey Magazine, 737 Hamilton Ave, Trenton, NJ 08629 609-213-9310 www.outinjersey.net contactus@outinjersey.net
◆ *Advertisement page 225*

♂ ★ Pride Guide: A Guide to Gay New Jersey, GAAMC, POB 137, Convent Station, NJ 07961 973-285-1595 www.gaamc.org

AIDS/HIV Services, Education & Support

♂ ☆ ♂♂ Buddies of New Jersey, Franklin A. Smith Resource Center, 149 Hudson St, Hackensack, NJ 800-508-7577 www.njbuddies.org

♀ ☆ (?⚥) Hyacinth AIDS Foundation, 317 George St, New Brunswick, NJ 800-433-0254 www.hyacinth.org

♀ ☆ Names Project Foundation Northern New Jersey Chapter, POB 222, Port Reading, NJ 07064 201-265-0600 www.namesnnj.org

♀ ☆ ♂♂ New Jersey AIDS Services, 3 Executive Dr, Morris Plains, NJ 973-285-0006 www.njas-inc.org ⚕

♂ North Jersey Community Research Initiative, 393 Central Ave FL 3, Newark, NJ 973-483-3444 www.njcri.org ◐

♀ ☆ ♂♂ South Jersey AIDS Alliance, 19 Gordon's Alley, Atlantic City, NJ 08401-7406 609-347-1085 800-281-AIDS www.sjaids.org info@sjaids.org

Counseling/Psychotherapy/Mental Health

♂ ♂♂ Carrier Foundation, 252 Rte 601, Belle Mead, NJ 800-933-3579 www.carrierclinic.org

Editing/Writing/Proofreading Services

♂ ○ (?⚥) EditAmerica, Paula Plantier, 115 Jacobs Creek Rd, Ewing, NJ 08628-1014 609-882-5852 fax 609-882-5851 www.edi-tamerica.com ⚕ paula@editamerica.com

Insurance (see also Financial Planning)

♀ ● **Shrem, Eileen, RHU, CLTC, LUTCF, 215 McCabe Ave #C1, Bradley Beach, NJ 732-988-7256 fax 732-988-3009 tinyurl.com/y83w7w78**

Organizations/Resources: Business & Professional Associations, Labor Advocacy

⚥ Greater New Jersey Pride At Work, fb.com/njprideatwork

⚥ ★ New Jersey LGBT Chamber, 155 Willowbrook Blvd Ste 350, Wayne, NJ 07470 973-869-9567 www.njlgbtchamber.org info@njlgbtchamber.org

Organizations/Resources: Cultural, Dance, Performance

♂ ★ New Jersey Gay Men's Chorus, POB 21, Princeton, NJ 08542-0021 732-579-8449 www.njgmc.org

Organizations/Resources: Ethnic, Multicultural

♂ ★ Long Yang Club New Jersey, 85 Raritan Ave Ste 100, New Brunswick, NJ 732-247-0515 Ray or Bob www.lycnj.com ⟡

Organizations/Resources: Family and Supporters

♀ ♂♂ PFLAG Bergen County, 201-503-4470 www.bergenpflag.com

Organizations/Resources: Political/Legislative/Advocacy

♀ ☆ ♂♂ American Civil Liberties Union of New Jersey, POB 32159, Newark, NJ 07102 973-642-2084 www.aclu-nj.org

⚥ ★ Garden State Equality, 40 S Fullerton Ave, Montclair, NJ 973-473-5428 www.GardenStateEquality.org

Organizations/Resources: Student, Academic, Education

♀ ☆ GLSEN Central New Jersey, POB 261, Hightstown, NJ 08520 609-448-5215 www.glsen.org/centralnj

Organizations/Resources: Transgender/Gender Non-Conforming/Diverse

⚦ ☆ ♂♂ Pathways - A Transgender Support Group, 61 Church St, Teaneck, NJ www.pathwaystg.org

Organizations/Resources: Youth (see also Family)

♂ Project WOW, NJCRI, 393 Central Ave FL 3, Newark, NJ 866-448-5812 tinyurl.com/c5bw263 ◐

Recovery

♀ ☆ Alcoholics Anonymous Southern New Jersey, POB 3724, Cherry Hill, NJ 08034 www.snjaa.org

♀ ☆ Narcotics Anonymous New Jersey Regional Service Area, POB 4257, Trenton, NJ 08610 800-992-0401 732-933-0462 www.nanj.org recovery@nanj.org

Religious / Spiritual Resources

⚥ ★ (?⚥) The Oasis - Diocese of Newark, 31 Mulberry St, Newark, NJ 07102-5284 www.oasisnewark.org chair@oasisnewark.org

Security & Investigation Services

♂ ● Martinez Security & Investigations, LLC, POB 2286, Trenton, NJ 08629 609-924-7949
>> *Asbury Park: see Jersey Shore*

New Jersey: Belle Mead
Legal

227
GAYELLOW PAGES #42 2020-2021

Fort Lee : New Jersey
Health Care

>> Atlantic City: see Jersey Shore
>> Barnegat: see Jersey Shore

Belle Mead

Legal Services

⚥ ● (♁⚲) Singer & Fedun LLC, POB 134 08502-0134 / 2230 Route 206 908-359-7873 fax 908-359-0128 www.singerfedun.com
>> Belleville: see Newark/Montclair Area
>> Belmar: see Jersey Shore

Berlin

Legal Services

⚥ ● (♁⚲) Law Offices of Kristine W. Holt, 339 Rte 73 N; 08009 856-599-5555 Bankruptcy; transgender issues www.HoltEsq.com
>> Bloomfield: see Newark/Montclair Area
>> Brick: see Jersey Shore
>> Cape May: see Southern Shore of NJ

Cherry Hill

Community Centers and/or Pride Organizations

⚥ ★ Southern New Jersey LGBTQA Pride, 190 S Warwick Rd #113, Stratford; 08084 856-248-0332 www.jerseygaypride.com snjgaypride@gmail.com

Legal Services

⚥ ○ ♿ Borger Matez, P.A., 1415 Marlton Pike (Rte 70) E Ste 305; 08034-2210 856-424-3444 www.njfamilylaw.net gborger@njfamilylaw.net

Clifton

Weddings and Ceremonies

⚥ ● ♿ The Wedding Man, Rev Gregg Kits, DD, 37 Frederick Ave; 07013 973-220-9400 **H** www.theweddingman.net ✎ ♥ gregg@theweddingman.net

Clinton

Organizations/Resources: Youth (see also Family)

⚥ ★ LGBTQ Support Group of Hunterdon County, Library, 65 Halsted St; 08809 908-788-1444 tinyurl.com/3ukvmxt

Collingswood

Bars, Cafes, Clubs, Restaurants

⚥ ● (♁⚲) Grooveground, 647 Haddon Ave 856-869-9800 www.grooveground.com ✕ ⚥ ✎

Organizations/Resources: Family and Supporters

⚥ ☆ ♿ PFLAG Collingswood, POB 8941 08108 856-834-6355 fb.com/collingswood.pflag ✎ pflagcollingswood@gmail.com

Religious / Spiritual Resources

⚥ ☆ Holy Trinity Episcopal Church, 839 Haddon Ave 08108 856-858-0491 www.holytrinity.us holytrinity1@verizon.net

Cresskill

Organizations/Resources: Youth (see also Family)

⚥ ★ ♿ Rainbow Cafe of Northern New Jersey, Cresskill Congregational Church, 85 Union Ave; 07626 201-568-0608 www.rainbowcafennj.org rainbowcafecresskill@gmail.com

Dover

Health Care: Physical (see also Counseling/Mental Health)

⚥ Zufall Heath Center, 18 W Blackwell St 973-328-9100 www.zufallhealth.org

Organizations/Resources: Student, Academic, Education

⚥ ★ County College of Morris LGBT+ Student Union, Student Community Center, Room 226, 214 Center Grove Rd 973-328-5000

Eatontown

Legal Services

⚥ ○ ♿ Posnock, Leslie B, Schwartz and Posnock, 99 Corbett Way Ste 203, Eatontown; 07724 / offices Livingston, East Brunswick and Linden 732-544-1460 www.schwartzposnock.com ✎
>> Edison: see New Brunswick Area

Flemington

Organizations/Resources: Family and Supporters

⚥ ☆ PFLAG Hunterdon County, c/o Flemington Presbyterian Church, 10 East Main St; 908-507-9328 tinyurl.com/u93aws6 @ixx=

Fort Lee

Health Care: Physical (see also Counseling/Mental Health)

⚥ ○ ♿ Brauner, Gary J., MD, 1625 Anderson Ave #201; 201-461-5522
>> Freehold: see Jersey Shore

New Jersey: Frenchtown
Accommodation

228

GAYELLOW PAGES #42 2020-2021

Jersey Shore: New Jersey
Bars, Cafes, Clubs, Restaurants

Frenchtown

Accommodation: Hotels, Inns, Guesthouses, B&B, Resorts

⚥ ○ ♿ Widow McCrea House, 53 Kingwood Ave; 08825 908-996-4999 www.widowmccrea.com (☹?) ⚘ ⊗

Glassboro

Organizations/Resources: Student, Academic, Education

⚥ ★ Rowan University Prism, Student Affairs, Savitz Hall, 201 Mullica Hill Rd; 856-256-4540 tinyurl.com/plo4qky

Hackensack

Crisis, Anti-violence, & Helplines

♀ Healing Space, YWCA Northern New Jersey, 214 State St; 201-881-1750 tinyurl.com/y5fo6pag

Hazlet

Legal Services

⚥ ● ♿ Wernik & Salvatore, Robin T, Esq., 34 Village Ct; 07730-1534 732-888-3338 For caring, committed and comprehensive guidance on any family law matter. www.robinwernik.com

» Highland Park: see New Brunswick Area

Hoboken

Bookstores

⚥ ○ Little City Books, 100 Bloomfield St 201-626-READ www.littlecitybooks.com

Real Estate (see also Mortgages)

⚥ ○ Bistany, David J, Keller Williams City Life Realty, 100 Washington Street; 07030 201-852-3291 tinyurl.com/y5bdhcut @ixx=

Religious / Spiritual Resources

⚥ ☆ All Saints Episcopal Parish, 701 Washington St 07030 201-792 3563 www.allsaintshoboken.com office@allsaints hoboken.com.

Jersey City

Community Centers and/or Pride Organizations

⚥ ★ Hudson Pride Center, 176 Palisade Ave, 3 East, Jersey City; 201-963-4779 www.hudsonpride.org ⚘

Bars, Cafes, Clubs, Restaurants

⚥ ○ LITM, 140 Newark Ave, Jersey City 201-536-5557 www.litm.com ☿ ✗

⚥ ○ ♿ Six 26, The Ashford, 128 Christopher Columbus Dr, Jersey City; 201-706-2273 six26.co ☿ ✗ ▦

Bookstores

⚥ ● WORD, 123 Newark Ave, Jersey City 201-763-6611 www.wordbookstores.com ☞

Counseling/Psychotherapy/Mental Health

⚥ ● ♿ Institute for Personal Growth, Offices in High-land Park, Freehold and Jersey City 800-379-9220 **ℍ?** Providing psychotherapy, relationship counseling and sex therapy to our community. www.ipgcounseling.com

Organizations/Resources: Student, Academic, Education

⚥ ★ Hudson County Community College LGBTQIA Club, 70 Sip Ave, Jersey City; 201-360-4195

Organizations/Resources: Youth (see also Family)

⚥ ★ Youth Connect at Hudson Pride Center, 176 Palisade Ave, 3 East, Jersey City; 201-963-4779 Fri 6-8pm tinyurl.com/yytdadbo ⚘

Jersey Shore

Community Centers and/or Pride Organizations

⚥ Jersey Pride, POB 7973, Princeton, NJ 08543 jerseypride.org

⚥ ★ QSpot LGBT Community Center, 66 S Main St, Ocean Grove; 732-455-3373 qspot.org

Information, Media & Publications

⚥ Greater Atlantic City GLBT Alliance, POB 7941, Atlantic City; 08404 609-226-5430 www.acglbt.org

Accommodation: Hotels, Inns, Guesthouses, B&B, Resorts

Asbury Park

⚥ ● ♿ Paradise, 101 Asbury Ave, Asbury Park (Ocean Ave) 732-988-6663 fax 732-988-7910 NJ's ultimate club complex and dance party all year 'round. www.paradisenj.com ⚘ ⊗

Atlantic City

⚥ ● Ocean House, 127 S Ocean Ave, Atlantic City 08401-7202 609-345-8203 tinyurl.com/2c7t9g ⚘

Ocean Grove

⚥ ○ Inn at Ocean Grove, 27 Webb Ave, Ocean Grove 07756 732-775-8847 theinnatoceangrove.com (☹?) ⚘ ⊗ ⊗ info@theinna toceangrove.com

⚥ ● The Melrose B&B, 34 Seaview Ave, Ocean Grove 732-774-5404 www.melroseog.com (☹?) ⊗

AIDS/HIV Services, Education & Support

♀ ♿ The Center in Asbury Park, 806 3rd Ave, Asbury Park; 732-774-3416 www.thecenterinap.org

♀ HIV & AIDS Ambulatory Care Clinic (A Team), Jersey City Medical Center, 1828 W Lake Ave #203, Neptune; 732-776-4700 tinyurl.com/bmcgh5g

Bars, Cafes, Clubs, Restaurants

Asbury Park

⚥ ● Georgie's Bar, 810 5th Ave, Asbury Park 732-988-1220 georgiesbarap.com **K** ☿ ✗ ▦

⚥ ● ♿ Moonstruck, 517 Lake Ave, Asbury Park; 732-988-0123 moonstrucknj.com ☿ ✗

New Jersey: Jersey Shore
Bars, Cafes, Clubs, Restaurants

229

GAYELLOW PAGES #42 2020-2021

Morristown Area: New Jersey
Community Centers / Pride

⚲ ● ♿ **Paradise, 101 Asbury Ave, Asbury Park**
(Ocean Ave) 732-988-6663 fax 732-988-7910 NJ's ulti-
mate club complex and dance party all year 'round.
www.paradisenj.com ✔ c

Atlantic City

⚲ OUT at Borgata, 1 Borgata Way, Atlantic City; 609-317-1000
www.theborgata.com/out 🖼

♂ ○♿ Palm Restaurant, Tropicana Resort, 2801 Pacific Ave Ste
102, Atlantic City; 609-344-7256 www.thepalm.com ✖ ✔

⚲ Rainbow Room, 55 S Bellevue Ave, Atlantic City; 609-317-4593
rainbowroomacnj.com 🖼

Long Branch

♂ ● Mix Lounge & Food Bar, 71 Brighton Ave, Long Branch; 732-
923-9100 www.mixloungefoodbar.com ⅄ ✖

Ocean Grove

⚲ ● Library Lounge, QSpot LGBT Community Center, 66 S Main
St, Ocean Grove; 732-455-3373 qspot.org ▷

Counseling/Psychotherapy/Mental Health

⚲ ● ♿ **Institute for Personal Growth, Offices in High-**
land Park, Freehold and Jersey City 800-379-9220 H?
Providing psychotherapy, relationship counseling
and sex therapy to our community. www.ipgcounsel-
ing.com

Florists (see also Gifts)

♂ ○ PeterJames Floral Couture, 732-455-3959 www.peterjames-
floral.com peterjamesfloral@gmail.com

Leather Resources & Groups

♂ ★ Promethean Guard, POB 1144, Asbury Park 07712
www.prometheanguard.org

Legal Services

♀ ● Alba, David L, 8 Broad St, Freehold; 07728 732-866-9797

Massage Therapy (Certified/Licensed only)

⚲ ● Sprick, Dennis M., 973-901-2306 www.heartfultouch.com

Organizations/Resources: Family and Supporters

♂ ☆ PFLAG Jersey Shore, POB 677, Howell; 07731 908-814-2155
www.pflagjerseyshore.org info@pflagjerseyshore.org

Organizations/Resources: Student, Academic, Education

⚲ ★ Ocean County College Ocean Pride, POB 2001, Toms River;
08754

Sports & Outdoor

⚲ ★ Asbury Park Volleyball, 917-727-5670 www.apvolleyball.org

⚲ ★ Central Jersey Rainbows Bowling League, Sun 5:30pm, Sept
to April, The Lanes at Sea Girt, 2106 Hwy 35 N, Sea Girt, NJ 08750
(bowling) fb.com/groups/CJRBowling/
» *Lambertville: see New Hope PA/Lambertville NJ Area*

Lawrenceville

Organizations/Resources: Student, Academic, Education

⚲ ★ ♿ Rider University Spectrum Pride Alliance, Office of Campus Life, 2083 Lawrenceville Rd; 609-896-5057 fb.com/groups/rider-
spectrum ✔

Lincroft

Religious / Spiritual Resources

♂ ☆ ♿ UU Congregation of Monmouth County, 1475 W Front St;
07738 732-747-0707 **HD** www.uucmc.org ✔ uucmc@
uucmc.org
» *Long Branch: see Jersey Shore*

Long Valley

Accommodation: Hotels, Inns, Guesthouses, B&B, Resorts

♂ ○ The Neighbour House, 143 W Mill Rd; 07853 908-876-3519
www.neighbourhouse.com ✔ ⊗ neighbourhouse@comcast.net

Madison

Religious / Spiritual Resources

♂ ☆ ♿ Grace Episcopal Church, 4 Madison Ave; 07940 973-377-
0106 **HD** www.gracemadison.org GraceMadisonNJ@gmail.com

Mahwah

Organizations/Resources: Student, Academic, Education

♀ ☆ Ramapo College of New Jersey Women's Center, 505
Ramapo Valley Rd #C-Wing 220; 201-684-7468
www.ramapo.edu/womenscenter/
» *Maplewood: see Newark/Montclair Area*

Maywood

Health Care: Physical (see also Counseling/Mental Health)

♂ ● ♿ Eustace, Timothy J., DC, Family Chiropractic Center, 106
W Pleasant Ave; 201-843-3111

Metuchen

Websites: Design & Maintenance Services (see also Internet)

♂ ● Pressing Issues, Inc., POB 224; 08840-0224 732-549-9054
www.pressingissues.com info@pressingissues.com

Milltown

Legal Services

♂ ● Lozito Law LLC, 187-189 N Main St; 08850 848-202-1650 lozi-
tolaw.com ✔ lozito@lozitolaw.com
» *Montclair: see Newark/Montclair Area*

Morristown Area

Community Centers and/or Pride Organizations

⚲ Edge Pride Center, 3 Executive Dr, Morris Plains; 973-285-0006
www.edgepridecenter.org

New Jersey: Morristown Area
Information, Media & Publications

230
GAYELLOW PAGES #42 2020-2021

Newark/Montclair Area : New Jersey
Catering

We meet each Monday evening, in Morristown, NJ, to provide discussion groups and social, educational, entertainment, and activism programs to NJ's GLBTIQ community...since 1972.

www.GAAMC.org

Information, Media & Publications

♂ (♿) Gay Activist Alliance in Morris County (GAAMC), POB 137, Convent Station; 07961-0137 / Meets Mon 7pm at Morristown Unitarian Fellowship, Normandy Hts Rd, Morristown. 973-285-1595 www.gaamc.org info@gaamc.org

AIDS/HIV Services, Education & Support

♀ ☆ ♿ Morristown Medical Center, 200 South St 3rd flr, Morristown; 973-889-6810 tinyurl.com/yyldxv2h ✦ ✗

Counseling/Psychotherapy/Mental Health

♀ ○ ♿ Vlazny, Maggie, MSW, LCSW, GAT. LLC, 973-236-0020 www.florhamparkcounsleing.com maggievlazny@gmail.com

Religious / Spiritual Resources

♀ ☆ (♿) St Paul's Episcopal Church, 29 Hillview Ave, Morris Plains; 07950 973-285-0884 www.stpaulsmp.org stpaulsmp@optonline.net

Mount Holly

Legal Services

♂ ● (♿) Shreter, Stephanie, 105 High St #1; 08060 609-265-9600 Bankruptcy thebankruptcycounselor.com sshreter@comcast.net

» Neptune: see Jersey Shore

New Brunswick Area

Community Centers and/or Pride Organizations

♀ ★ ♿ **The Pride Center of New Jersey, 85 Raritan Ave Ste 100, Highland Park; 732-846-2232 H? www.pridecenter.org** ✗

Bars, Cafes, Clubs, Restaurants
Jamesburg

♀ ● Fiddleheads Restaurant, 27 E Railroad Ave, Jamesburg; 732-521-0878 www.fiddleheadsjamesburg.com ✗ ✗
New Brunswick

♀ ○ ♿ The Frog and the Peach, 29 Dennis St, NB; 732-846-3216 www.frogandpeach.com ♈ ✗↻✗

♀ ○ ♿ Stage Left Steak, 5 Livingston Ave, NB; 732-828-4444 www.stageleft.com ♈ ✗ info411@stageleft.com
Somerset

♀ ○ ♿ Sophie's Bistro, 700 Hamilton St, Somerset; 732-545-7778 www.sophiesbistro.net ♈ ✗✗

Counseling/Psychotherapy/Mental Health

♂ ● ♿ **Institute for Personal Growth, Offices in Highland Park, Freehold and Jersey City 800-379-9220 H?** Providing psychotherapy, relationship counseling and sex therapy to our community. www.ipgcounseling.com

Organizations/Resources: Social, Recreation, Support

♂ ★ Gay Men's Social Group, Pride Center of NJ, 85 Raritan Ave Ste 100, Highland Park; 08904-2701 / 4th Tue 8pm 732-846-2232

Organizations/Resources: Transgender/Gender Non-Conforming/Diverse

т ☆ ♿ TrueSelves, c/o The Pride Center, 85 Raritan Ave #100, Highland Park; 08904 732-846-2232 www.pridecenter.org/groups ✗ patti@pridecenter.org

Religious / Spiritual Resources

♀ ☆ ♿ Christ Episcopal Church, 5 Paterson St, NB; 08901 732-545-6262 tinyurl.com/bo6dv9w

♂ ★ ♿ Dignity/New Brunswick, POB 10781, NB; 08906 732-968-9263 tinyurl.com/26pmmt

Transportation: Limo, Taxi, Charter etc.

♀ ○ Signature Limousine Services, LLC, 1835 Rte 130 Ste 1A, North Brunswick 877-336-0900 www.signature-limo.net

Newark/Montclair Area

Community Centers and/or Pride Organizations

♂ ★ Newark LGBTQ Community Center, POB 200434, Newark; 07102 973-424-9555 www.newarklgbtqcenter.org ✪ ✗

AIDS/HIV Services, Education & Support

♂ ★ African American Office of Gay Concerns, 877 Broad St Ste 211, Newark; 973-639-0700 www.aaogc.org ✤

♀ Broadway House for Continuing Care, 298 Broadway, Newark; 973-268-9797 www.broadwayhouse.org ✪

Bookstores

♀ ○ ♿ Montclair Book Center, 221 Glenridge Ave, Montclair; 973-783-3630 www.montclairbookcenter.com

♀ ○ Watchung Booksellers, 54 Fairfield St, Montclair; 973-744-7177 www.watchungbooksellers.com

Catering (see also Party/Holiday/Event Services)

♀ ● New World Catering, 1753 Springfield Ave, Maplewood; 973-378-9445 www.newworldcateringco.com

Counseling/Psychotherapy/Mental Health

♀ ● (⚧) Boyer, Carol A, MA, LPC, NCC, 50 Church St Ste L3, Montclair; 07042 973-493-8006 www.carolboyerlpc.com carolboyerlpc@gmail.com

♀ ● ♂♂ Center for Identity Development, 31 Trinity Place, Montclair; 07042-2773 973-744-6386 Psychotherapy & counseling (individual, couple, group, family) serving gay/lesbian community since 1980. www.centeridentity.qpg.com

♂ ○ Chan, Joseph A, MSW, LCSW, 94 Valley Rd, Montclair; 07042 973-202-1421 ✪

♀ ● ♂♂ Koempel, Stephanie, MA, LPC, LCADC, 2115 Millburn Ave 908-581-5681 tinyurl.com/yd8vnmgu

♀ ● ♂♂ **Mahon, James V, LCSW, BCD, 31 Trinity Place, Montclair; 07042-2773 973-744-6386 Psychotherapy & counseling (individual, couple, group, family) serving gay/lesbian community since 1980. Moderate fees, sliding scale. www.centeridentity.qpg.com**

♀ ● Maplewood Counseling Services, 973-902-8700 MaplewoodCounseling.com

♀ ● Martinez, Israel, LCSW, 973-866-5120 www.lgbttherapynj.com Israel@MartinezLCSW.com

♀ ● Perez, Jose M, MA, LMFT, 311 Claremont Ave, Montclair; 07042 973-900-0005 www.jperezmamft.com jperezmamft@gmail.com

♀ ● Rosen, Laurence, CSW, LCSW, BCD, 170 N Mountain Ave, Upper Montclair; 973-783-8673 www.psychotherapisttoday.com

♀ ● Sherman, Eric, LCSW, 12 Garfield Place, Montclair; 07043-1512 973-655-1534

Health Care: Physical (see also Counseling/Mental Health)

♂ Newark Community Health Centers, Inc., 741 Broadway, Newark; 973-483-1300 www.nchcfqhc.org

Organizations/Resources: Family and Supporters

♀ ☆ ♂ **PFLAG North Jersey, c/o Christ Episcopal Church, 74 Park Ave, Glen Ridge, NJ 07028 908-300-4227 Provides support, education, advocacy to lgbt people, & their families. www.pflagnorthjersey.org pflagwaver@aol.com**

Organizations/Resources: Student, Academic, Education

♂ ★ ♂♂ Montclair State University LGBTQ Center, One Normal Ave SC 113, Montclair; 07043 973-655-7916 tinyurl.com/yylbssry ✎ lgbtq@mail.montclair.edu

Organizations/Resources: Youth (see also Family)

♂ Essex County LGBT RAIN Foundation, 168 Park St, E Orange; 973-675-6780 essexlgbthousing.org

Religious / Spiritual Resources

♀ ☆ ♂♂ First Congregational Church, 40 S Fullerton Ave, Montclair; 07042 973-744-4856 fccmontclair.org ✎

♀ ☆ (⚧) Grace Church in Newark (Episcopal), 950 Broad St, Newark; 07102 973-623-1733 www.gracechurchinnewark.org office@gracechurchinnewark.org

♀ ☆ St Stephen's, 119 Main St, Millburn; 07041-1115 973-376-0688 www.ststephensmillburn.org church@ststephensmillburn.org

♂ ☆ UFC NewArk, POB 9891, Newark; 07104 973-565-9340 www.ufcnewark.org ✪ info@ufcnewark.org

Sports & Outdoor

♂ North Jersey Gay & Lesbian Bowlers League, 973-634-6507 ww.njglb.net

Nutley

Legal Services

♀ ○ Fine, James F, 596 Franklin Ave; 07110-1253 973-667-1414 973-432-5993 fax 973-667-1953 jamesfine.justia.com JamesFineLaw@gmail.com

Oaklyn

Religious / Spiritual Resources

♀ ☆ ♂♂ St Mark's Lutheran Church, 409 White Horse Pike; 08107 856-854-7959 www.stmarksoaklyn.com

» Ocean City: see Southern Shore of NJ

Oceanport

Counseling/Psychotherapy/Mental Health

♀ ● ♂♂ Bradley, Carolyn A, PhD, LCSW, LCADC, 108 Main St Ste 5; 07757 732-768-5781

Paramus

Organizations/Resources: Student, Academic, Education

♂ ★ ♂♂ Bergen Community College PRIDE, Student Leadership Commons - SC-110 400 Paramus Rd Room 110E; 07652 201-447-7215 **HS** tinyurl.com/y35rf6qj ✎

Park Ridge

Sports & Outdoor

♀ ○ Cyclesport, 1 Hawthorne Ave; 07656 201-391-5269 www.cyclesportonline.com

Piscataway

Legal Services

♀ ○ ♂ Law Office of Jennifer Marshall. LLC, 200 Centennial Ave Ste 101; 732-412-3737 www.jlmarshallesq.com @ixx=

Plainfield Area

Real Estate (see also Mortgages)

♀ ○ John Nash, Joe Burris, eXp Realty-The Sleepy Hollow Team. 1030 Central Ave Ste E, Plainfield; 07062-1937 908-305-1583 www.njhomesales.com SellAHom@aol.com

Religious / Spiritual Resources

♀ ☆ First Unitarian New Jersey, 2560 NJ Highway 22 #324, Scotch Plains; 07076 / Sun 3.30pm Fanwood Presbyterian Church, 74 S Martine Ave, Fanwood 908-312-1815 www.fusp.org info@fusp.org

» Plainsboro: see Princeton Area

New Jersey: Princeton Area
Organizations: Family

232

GAYELLOW PAGES #42 2020-2021

Summit : New Jersey
Organizations: Youth

Princeton Area

Organizations/Resources: Family and Supporters

♀ ☆ ♿ PFLAG, 609-791-9740 www.pflagprinceton.org

Organizations/Resources: Student, Academic, Education

⚲ ★ ♿ LGBT Center, Princeton University, 246 Frist Campus Center, Princeton; 609-258-1353 www.princeton.edu/lgbt ✔

⚲ ★ Princeton University Queer Graduate Caucus, 609-258-1353 www.princeton.edu/~qgc

Organizations/Resources: Youth (see also Family)

⚲ ☆ ♿♿ First & Third, LGBTQ adolescent support, HiTOPS 21 Wiggins St, Princeton; 609-683-5155 www.hitops.org/lgbtq/

Women's Centers

♀ Princeton University Women's Center, 33 Frist Campus Center Room 243, Princeton; 609-258-5565 www.princeton.edu/~womenctr/

Ramsey

Religious / Spiritual Resources

♂ ☆ ♿♿ St John's Memorial Church, 299 E Main St; 07446 201-327-0703 www.stjohnsramsey.org ✔
>> Red Bank: see Jersey Shore

Ridgewood

Counseling/Psychotherapy/Mental Health

♂ O Sileo, Frank J, PhD, Center for Psychological Enhancement LLC 550 N Maple Ave Flr 2; 07450 201-447-0705 Licensed Psychologist (NJ #3678) www.drfranksileo.com

Religious / Spiritual Resources

♂ ☆ Heart Circle Sangha Zen Community, 451 Hillcrest Rd; 07450-1520 877-442-7936 www.heartcirclesangha.org

♂ ☆ ♿♿ Reconstructionist Congregation Beth Israel, c/o Temple Israel & JCC, 475 Grove St; 07450 201-444-9320 www.synagogue.org ✡ ✔ rcbi@synagogue.org

Ringoes

Religious / Spiritual Resources

♂ ☆ ♿♿ Living Waters Lutheran Church, 11 Old York Rd; 08551 908-284-9455 www.lwlcnj.org ✔

River Edge

Bars, Cafes, Clubs, Restaurants

⚲ ● Feathers, 77 Kinderkamack Rd; 201-342-6410 www.clubfeathers.com D ▥

Roseland

Counseling/Psychotherapy/Mental Health

♂ O Demarest, Mark, LPC, 101 Eisenhower Parkway Ste 300; 07068 973-986-3998

Seabrook

Recovery

♂ ☆ (♿♿) Seabrook, POB 5055; 08302 800-761-7575 856-455-7575 www.seabrook.org ✔ info@seabrook.org
>> Sergeantsville: see New Hope PA/Lambertville NJ Area
>> Short Hills: see Newark/Montclair Area
>> Shrewsbury: see Jersey Shore

Somerville

Legal Services

♂ O (♿) Gargano, Francine A., Esq, 34 E Main St; 08876 908-753-2079 fax 908-755-3586 A General Practice for the Gay, Lesbian and Transgender Community and Their Families. garganof@msn.com

Southern Shore of NJ

Accommodation: Hotels, Inns, Guesthouses, B&B, Resorts
Cape May

♀ ● Bacchus Inn Bed & Breakfast, 719 Columbia Ave, Cape May; 609-884-2302 **H?** www.bacchusinn.com ✔ ⊛ ⊛

♂ O Highland House, 131 N Broadway, Cape May; 08204 609-898-1198 www.highlandhousecapemay.com ❖ ✔ highlandhousecapemay@mail.com

♀ ● (♿) The Virginia Hotel, 25 Jackson St, Cape May; 800-732-4236 www.virginiahotel.com ✕

Accommodation Rental: Furnished / Vacation (& AirBNB)
Cape May

♂ ● Antoinette's Apartments & Suites, 717 Washington St, Cape May; 08204-2330 609-898-0502 www.antoinettescapemay.com ✔ ⊛

Organizations/Resources: Social, Recreation, Support

⚲ ★ ♿♿ Gays, Bisexuals & Lesbians (GABLES) of Cape May County, POB 641, Cape May Court House; 08210 www.gablescapemay.com

Religious / Spiritual Resources

♂ ☆ ♿♿ Unitarian Universalist Congregation of the South Jersey Shore, POB 853, Pomona; 08240 609-965-9400 www.uucsjs.org ✔ uucsjsadmin@gmail.com
>> Spring Lake: see Jersey Shore
>> Stockton: see New Hope PA/Lambertville NJ Area
>> Stone Harbor: see Jersey Shore

Summit

Organizations/Resources: Youth (see also Family)

⚲ Cafe Q, Congregation Beth Hatikvah, 36 Chatham Rd; / LGBT youth meets 3rd Sun 3-5pm 908-277-0200 www.bethhatikvah.org ✡

>> Toms River: see Jersey Shore

New Jersey: Trenton Area
Counseling
233
GAYELLOW PAGES #42 2020-2021
Albuquerque : New Mexico
Bars, Cafes, Clubs, Restaurants

Trenton Area

Counseling/Psychotherapy/Mental Health

♀ ● Heid, Richard J, PhD, Licensed Psychologist, 2620 White-horse-Hamilton Square Rd Flr 2, Hamilton Square; 08690 609-933-5572 tinyurl.com/2u4k37d

Trenton

Bars, Cafes, Clubs, Restaurants

♀ ○ Mill Hill Saloon, 300 S Broad St; 609-989-1600 www.themill-hill.com ⅋ ✕ ▥

Organizations/Resources: Student, Academic, Education

♂ ★ College of New Jersey Prism, 2000 Pennington Rd; 609-771-2390 www.tcnj.edu/~prism/

Organizations/Resources: Youth (see also Family)

♀ ☆ Lifeties, Inc., John S Watson Sr Building, 2205 Pennington Rd; 609-771-1600 www.lifeties.org

Turnersville

Erotica / Adult Stores / Safe Sex Supplies

♀ ○ Fantasy Gifts, 5101 Black Horse Pike 856-228-7002 fantasygiftsnj.com

» *Wall Township: see Jersey Shore*
» *West Orange: see Newark/Montclair Area*

Westfield

Real Estate (see also Mortgages)

♀ ○ Smythe, Duncan, Coldwell Banker, 209 Central Ave; 07090-2151 908-244-9621 908-233-5555 www.duncansmythe.net
» *Wildwood: see Southern Shore of NJ*

Woodcliff Lake

Counseling/Psychotherapy/Mental Health

♀ ● Panozzo, Dwight, PhD, LCSW, 60 Werimus Ln 07677-8240 201-476-1816 www.dwightpanozzophd.com info@dwightpanozzophd.com

New Mexico
State/County Resources

Information, Media & Publications

♂ ★ Common Bond New Mexico Foundation, POB 26836, Albuquerque, NM 87125 505-636-0845 www.commonbondnm.org

♂ ● Pride Guide New Mexico, POB 45243, Phoenix, AZ 85013 888-830-3022 www.GoGayNewMexico.com NewMexico@ThePrideGuides.com

AIDS/HIV Services, Education & Support

♀ ⚤ New Mexico AIDS Services, 3900 Osuna Rd NE, Albuquerque, NM 505-938-7100 www.nmas.net

Organizations/Resources: Military/Veterans

♂ American Veterans for Equal Rights Bataan Chapter, Dorothy Seaton, POB 288, Cedar Crest, NM 512-618-3600 www.avernm.org

Organizations/Resources: Political/Legislative/Advocacy

♀ ☆ American Civil Liberties Union of New Mexico, PO Box 566, Albuquerque, NM 87103 505-266-5915 www.aclu-nm.org

♂ ★ Equality New Mexico, POB 27070, Albuquerque, NM 87125 505-244-2766 855-542-8766 www.eqnm.org info@eqnm.org

Organizations/Resources: Student, Academic, Education

♂ ★ (?⚤) New Mexico Genders and Sexualities Alliance Network, Santa Fe Mountain Center, POB 449, Tesuque, NM 87574 505-983-6158 **H?** tinyurl.com/yd2olleo ✗

Religious / Spiritual Resources

♂ ★ ♿ Dignity/New Mexico, POB 67818, Albuquerque, NM 87193 GLBT Catholics pages.swcp.com/~dignity/

Sports & Outdoor

♂ ★ ⚤ New Mexico Gay Rodeo Association, POB 35381, Albuquerque, NM 87176 505-883-7519 www.nmgra.org

♂ ★ New Mexico Outdoors, 505-822-1093 tinyurl.com/zwtvky8

Abiquiu

Accommodation Rental: Furnished / Vacation (& AirBNB)

♀ ● ♿ Casita de Chuparosa, 505-685-0823 www.casitadechuparosa.com ✗ ⊗

Albuquerque

Crisis, Anti-violence, & Helplines

♀ ☆ Agora Crisis Center, UNM 1; MSC 02 1675 505-277-3013 www.agoracares.com

♀ ☆ Rape Crisis Center of Central New Mexico, 9741 Candelaria NE; 505-266-7711 www.rapecrisiscnm.org

Community Centers and/or Pride Organizations

♂ ★ ⚤ Albuquerque Pride, 2610 San Mateo Blvd NE Ste E; 505-873-8084 abqpride.com

Accommodation Rental: Furnished / Vacation (& AirBNB)

♀ ● Golden Guesthouses, 2645 Decker NW; 87107-2917 505-344-9205 Short term rentals ❀ ✗ ⊗

Architectural Services

♀ ○ JAF Concepts LLC, POB 9252; 87119 505-315-9644 Architectural Design and Working Drawings www.jafconcepts.com

Bars, Cafes, Clubs, Restaurants

♂ ● (⚤) Albuquerque Social Club, 4021 Central Ave NE 505-255-0887 **DP** ▥

♂ ● ⚤ EFFEX Night Club, 420 Central Ave SW; 505-842-8870 www.effexabq.com **D** ▥ ✗

♂ Sidewinders, 8900 Central AVE SE; 505-554-2078 fb.com/sidewindersabq **D**

New Mexico: Albuquerque
Bars, Cafes, Clubs, Restaurants

234

GAYELLOW PAGES #42 2020-2021

Las Cruces Area : New Mexico
Organizations: Family

♂ ○ ♿ Zinc Wine Bar & Bistro, 3009 Central Ave NE; 505-254-9462 www.zincabq.com ⚲ ▭ ✕ ▥ ∥

Counseling/Psychotherapy/Mental Health

♂ ○ (?♿) Johnson, Lisa, PhD, LMFT, 505-288-2162 lisa-johnsonlmft.com

Erotica / Adult Stores / Safe Sex Supplies

♂ ● Self Serve Toys, 112 Morningside Dr NE; 87108 505-265-5815 www.selfservetoys.com ∥ info@selfservetoys.com

Funding: Endowment, Fundraising

⚢ ★ United Court of the Sandias, POB 80343 87198 www.ucsnm.org

Insurance (see also Financial Planning)

♂ ● ♿ Sweda, John, Edward Jones, 4583 Corrales Rd, Corrales; 505-639-5407 **H?** tinyurl.com/yamwryvo @ixx=

Organizations/Resources: Business & Professional Associations, Labor Advocacy

⚢ Albuquerque GLBT Chamber of Commerce, POB 37115; 87176 505-917-8308 abqgaychamber.org

Organizations/Resources: Cultural, Dance, Performance

⚢ ★ (?♿) New Mexico Gay Men's Chorus, POB 3822; 87190 505-569-0139 **H?** www.nmgmc.org

♀ ○ New Mexico Women's Chorus, 215 Locust St NE 505-750-3038 www.nmwomenschorus.org

⚢ ★ Way OUT West Film Fest, 3405 Central Ave NE 505-255-1848 www.wayoutwestfilmfest.com

⚢ ★ ♿ Wilde Bunch, POB 40393 87196-0393 505-034-5979 www.wildebunch.org **D**

Organizations/Resources: Family and Supporters

♀ ☆ PFLAG Albuquerque, POB 30771; 87190-0771 505-873-7373 www.pflagabq.org contact@pflagabq.org

Organizations/Resources: Military/Veterans

⚢ Gay-Straight Alliance of Military At Kirtland/Albuquerque, fb.com/KirtlandGSA/

Organizations/Resources: Political/Legislative/Advocacy

♂ ☆ ♿ Albuquerque Center for Peace & Justice, 202 Harvard Dr SE; 505-268-9557 **H?** www.abqPeaceAndJustice.org ∥

♂ ☆ Office of Equity & Inclusion, POB 1293; 87103 505-768-4712 www.cabq.gov/humanrights/

Organizations/Resources: Social, Recreation, Support

⚢ Sandia Bears, tinyurl.com/y7gq7bwg

Organizations/Resources: Student, Academic, Education

⚢ ★ ♿ University of New Mexico Queer Straight Alliance, Student Union Building Room 1036; 505-277-6739 fb.com/UNMQSA

♀ ☆ ♿ UNM Women's Resource Center, MSC06 3910, #1 UNM; / Mesa Vista Hall Room 1160 505-277-3716 **H?** women.unm.edu ∥

Organizations/Resources: Transgender/Gender Non-Conforming/Diverse

⚲ ★ ♿ Transgender Resource Center of New Mexico, 149 Jackson St NE; 505-200-9086 **H?** www.tgrcnm.org ∥

Organizations/Resources: Youth (see also Family)

⚢ ★ U-21 Youth Program, Common Bond New Mexico, 1103 Texas St NE; 505-636-0845 commonbondnm.org/u21

Public Relations/Advertising/Marketing

♂ ● ♿ Graphicbliss Branding Agency, 4200 Silver Ave SE Ste C; 87108 505-299-0713 Branding agenyc www.gblissdesigns.com ∥ graphicblissgd@gmail.com

Real Estate (see also Mortgages)

♂ ● Talia Freedman and Co, 4116 Lomas Blvd NE 505-263-7892 **H?** www.abq-realty.com

Religious / Spiritual Resources

⚢ ★ ♿ MCC Albuquerque, 1103 Texas St NE; 505-268-5252 www.mccabq.com

♂ ☆ ♿ Unitarian Universalist Westside Congregation, POB 15146, Rio Rancho; 87174 505-896-8192 www.uuwestside.org office@uuwestside.org

Sports & Outdoor

♂ Sunday Night Out Bowling, www.abq-sno.org
» Chimayo: see Taos

Farmington

Community Centers and/or Pride Organizations

⚢ ★ ♿ Identity Inc! Community Center, 204 W Main St, Farmington; 505-427-3383 www.identity-inc.org ∥

Health Care: Physical (see also Counseling/Mental Health)

♀ Southwest CARE Center, 626 E Main St#2, Farmington; 505-327-7043 southwestcare.org

Gallup

Community Centers and/or Pride Organizations

⚢ The Rainbow / Naatsiilid Center, fb.com/RainbowCenterGallup

Las Cruces Area

Bars, Cafes, Clubs, Restaurants
Las Cruces

♂ ○ Boba Cafe & Cabaret, 1900 S Espina St #8, Las Cruces; 575-647-5900 tinyurl.com/mhm6cwn ✕ ▥

♂ ○ ♿ Spirit Wind Gift Source & Coffee Bar, 2260 S Locust St, Las Cruces; 575-521-0222 tinyurl.com/q4atn73 ▭

Organizations/Resources: Family and Supporters

♂ ☆ ♿ PFLAG Las Cruces, POB 2495, Las Cruces; 88004 575-323-9375 www.pflaglascruces.org

Organizations/Resources: Student, Academic, Education

♂ ★ LGBT+ Programs, New Mexico State University, 3024 Locust Ave, Garcia Annex Room 146, Las Cruces; 575-646-7031 lgbt.nmsu.edu ✔

Organizations/Resources: Transgender/Gender Non-Conforming/Diverse

⊤ ☆ (?⚧) Las Cruces Trans People, 575-201-3241 www.lascrucestrans.org

Religious / Spiritual Resources

♀ ☆ ♿ Peace Lutheran Church, 1701 E Missouri, Las Cruces; 88001 575-522-7119 **HD** www.peacelutheranlc.com ✔ office@peacelutheranlc.com

Madrid

Bars, Cafes, Clubs, Restaurants

♀ ○ ♿ Mine Shaft Tavern, 2846 State Hwy 14; 505-473-0743 www.themineshafttavern.com ⚥ ✕
>> *Mesilla: see Las Cruces Area*
>> *Pecos: see Santa Fe/Pecos/Tesuque Area*

Pinehill

Organizations/Resources: Social, Recreation, Support

♂ ★ Zuni Mountain Sanctuary, 96 Zuni Mountain Sanctuary Rd; 505-717-7365 Radical Faeries www.zms.org ✔
>> *Placitas: see Albuquerque*

Ramah

Bars, Cafes, Clubs, Restaurants

♂ ● ♿ Ancient Way Cafe, 4018 Hwy 53 East 505-783-4612 www.elmorro-nm.com ☞ ✔

Campgrounds and RV Parks

♂ ● (?⚧) El Morro RV Park & Cabins, Sharron, HC 61 Box 44; 87321-9603 505-783-4612 www.elmorro-nm.com ✣ ✔ Ⓢ elmorrorv@gmail.com

Santa Fe/Pecos/Tesuque Area

Crisis, Anti-violence, & Helplines

♀ ☆ ♿ Solace Crisis Treatment Center, 6601 Valentine Way, SFe; 505-988-1951 **H?** www.findsolace.org

Information, Media & Publications

♂ ★ Santa Fe Gay, 505-670-1783 www.SantaFeGay.com

Accommodation: Hotels, Inns, Guesthouses, B&B, Resorts
Santa Fe

♂ ● El Farolito B&B Inn, 514 Galisteo St, SFe 505-988-1631 www.farolito.com ✔ Ⓢ

♂ ● ♿ Inn of the Turquoise Bear, 342 E Buena Vista St, SFe; 505-983-0798 www.turquoisebear.com (✣?) ✔ Ⓢ

♂ ○ (?⚧) Inn on the Paseo, 630 Paseo de Peralta, SFe; 87501 855-984-8200 505-984-8200 www.innonthepaseo.com ✣ ✔ Ⓢ Ⓢ iotpsantafe@gmail.com

Serafina

♀ ● (?⚧) New Mexico Women's Guest House Retreat & Healing Center, POB 130, Serafina; 87569 575-421-2533 www.NMWomensRetreat.org ✔ Ⓢ

Accommodation Rental: Furnished / Vacation (& AirBNB)
Santa Fe

♂ ● ♿ Artist's Hacienda, 10 B Tano Rd, SFe; 505-983-1751 www.artistshacienda.com ✣ ✔ Ⓢ

AIDS/HIV Services, Education & Support

♂ ☆ Kitchen Angels, 1222 Siler Rd, SFe; 87507 505-471-7780 Free, nutritious meals to our homebound neighbors facing life-challenging conditions. www.kitchenangels.org

Bars, Cafes, Clubs, Restaurants
Santa Fe

♂ ○ 315 Restaurant & Wine Bar, 315 Old Santa Fe Trail, SFe; 505-986-9190 315santafe.com ⚥ ✕

♂ ○ Cafe Pasqual's, 121 Don Gaspar, SFe 505-983-9340 www.pasquals.com ☞

♂ ○ ♿ Cowgirl BBQ, 319 S Guadalupe, SFe; 505-982-2565 www.cowgirlsantafe.com **DK** ⚥ ☞ ✕ ▥ ✔

♂ ○ Coyote Cafe, 132 W Water St, SFe; 505-983-1615 www.coyotecafe.com ✕

♂ ○ Geronimo's, 724 Canyon Rd, SFe; 505-982-1500 www.geronimorestaurant.com ✕

♂ ○ The Pink Adobe, 406 Old Santa Fe Trail, SFe 505-983-7712 www.thepinkadobe.com ⚥ ✕

♂ ○ Santacafe, 231 Washington Ave, SFe 505-984-1788 www.santacafe.com ☞

♂ ○ Vanessie's, 434 W San Francisco St, SFe 505-982-9966 www.vanessiesantafe.com ⚥ ✕ ▥

Bookstores

♂ ○ Collected Works Bookstore & Coffeehouse, 202 Galisteo St, SFe; 505-988-4226 tinyurl.com/2w75g4 ☞

♂ ○ Downtown Subscription Coffeehouse & News, 376 Garcia St, SFe; 505-983-3085 tinyurl.com/hf86rek ☞

♂ ○ (?⚧) Garcia Street Books, 376 Garcia St, SFe; 505-986-0151 www.garciastreetbooks.com

Counseling/Psychotherapy/Mental Health

♂ ○ Giudici, Paolo, Santa Fe Psychotherapy, 1660 Old Pecos Trail Ste C, SFe; 87505 505-424-3119 www.santafepsychotherapy.org santafepsychotherapy@gmail.com

Health Care: Physical (see also Counseling/Mental Health)

♂ ☆ ♿ Southwest CARE Center, 649 Harkle Rd Ste E, SFe; 505-989-8200 southwestcare.org

Organizations/Resources: Family and Supporters

♂ ☆ PFLAG Santa Fe, POB 32053, SFe; 87594 www.pflagsantafe.org

New Mexico: Santa Fe/Pecos/Tesuque Area
Organizations: Political
236
GAYELLOW PAGES #42 2020-2021
Truth or Consequences : New Mexico
Accommodation

GLBT National Help Center
Serving the Gay, Lesbian, Bisexual & Transgender Community

GLBT National Hotline
Toll-free 1-888-THE-GLNH
(1-888-843-4564)

GLBT National Youth Talkline
Toll-free 1-800-246-PRIDE
(1-800-246-7743)

GLBT National Help Center
2261 Market Street, PMB #296
San Francisco, CA 94114

www.GLBTNationalHelpCenter.org

Organizations/Resources: Political/Legislative/Advocacy

♂ ● ★ Santa Fe Human Rights Alliance / Santa Fe Pride, POB 8640, SFe; 87504 505-428-9167 www.santafepride.org

Organizations/Resources: Student, Academic, Education

♂ ● ★ Monte del Sol Gay Straight Alliance, 4157 Walking Rain Rd, SFe; 505-982-5225

Real Estate (see also Mortgages)

♀ ● ♐♐ Orth, Susan, Realtor, City Different Realty 518 Old Santa Fe Trail #190, SFe; 87505 505-216-6688 www.susaninsantafe.com ✐ SantaFe@SusanOrth.com
>> *Serafina: see Santa Fe/Pecos/Tesuque Area*

Silver City

Information, Media & Publications

♂ ● ★ LGBTQ Grant County, 505 N Hudson 575-313-3845 gaysilver.org ✐

Accommodation: Hotels, Inns, Guesthouses, B&B, Resorts

♀ ● (♿) Bear Mountain Lodge, POB 1163 88062 575-538-2538 www.bearmountainlodge.com (♣?) ✐ ⊗ info@bearmountainlodge.com

Organizations/Resources: Family and Supporters

♂ ☆ PFLAG Silver City, POB 813; 88062-0813 575-590-8797 pflag-silver.org

Taos

Crisis, Anti-violence, & Helplines

♂ ☆ Community Against Violence, POB 169; 87571 575-758-8082 www.taoscav.org

Accommodation: Hotels, Inns, Guesthouses, B&B, Resorts

♂ ○ Touchstone Inn, 110 Mabel Dodge Ln; 87571 575-758-0192 575-770-3246 www.touchstoneinn.com touchstoneinn@gmail.com

Accommodation Rental: Furnished / Vacation (& AirBNB)

♂ ○ Burch Street Casitas, 310 Burch St; 87571 575-737-9038 www.casitasintaos.com ✐ ⊗ reservations@casitasintaos.com

♂ ● (♿) Casa Gallina, POB 63 87571-0063 575-758-2306 www.casagallina.net (♣?) ✐ ⊗ richard@casagallina.net
>> *Tesuque: see Santa Fe/Pecos/Tesuque Area*

Truth or Consequences

Accommodation: Hotels, Inns, Guesthouses, B&B, Resorts

♂ ● (♿) Blackstone Hotsprings, 410 Austin St; 87901 575-894-0894 www.blackstonehotsprings.com (♣?) ✐ ⊗ ⊗ stay@blackstonehotsprings.com

New York: State/County Resources
AIDS/HIV Support

237
GAYELLOW PAGES #42 2020-2021

Albany & Capital Area: New York
Information, Media & Publications

New York
State/County Resources

AIDS/HIV Services, Education & Support

♂ ☆ ᏰᏰ ACR Health, 627 W Genessee St, Syracuse, NY 315-475-2430 GRADS (Guys Responding and Demanding Safety) www.acr-health.org ✪ ✎

♀ ☆ HIV Uninsured Care Programs, POB 2052 Empire Stn, Albany, NY 12220 518-459-1641 tinyurl.com/m2d47y9

♀ ☆ ᏰᏰ Southern Tier AIDS Program, Inc, 22 Riverside Dr, Binghamton, NY 607-798-1706 **H?** www.stapinc.org

Organizations/Resources: Family and Supporters

♀ ★ Lesbian & Gay Family Building Project / Pride and Joy Families, c/o Binghamton University, POB 6000, Binghamton, NY 13902 607-777-3717 www.PrideAndJoyFamilies.org

Organizations/Resources: Senior Resources

♀ ★ ᏰᏰ Sage Rochester, 100 College Ave, Rochester, NY 585-244-8640 **H?** tinyurl.com/nl3cb2y ✎

Organizations/Resources: Transgender/Gender Non-Conforming/Diverse

T ☆ New York Association for Gender Rights Advocacy (NYA-GRA), 24 W 25th St Fl 9, New York, NY 10010-2725 212-675-3288 www.transgenderrights.org

Organizations/Resources: Youth (see also Family)

♀ ★ ᏰᏰ Gay & Lesbian Youth Services of Western New York, 393 Delaware Ave, Buffalo, NY 14202 716-855-0221 glyswny.org ✎ executive@glyswny.org

♀ A Thousand Moms, 2367 Curry Rd, Schenectady, NY 518-322-0607 www.athousandmoms.org

Recovery

♂ ☆ Alcoholics Anonymous AA for New York State, www.ny-aa.org

Sports & Outdoor

♀ ★ Ski Bums, 347-542-8670 www.ski-bums.org

Adirondacks Area

Accommodation: Hotels, Inns, Guesthouses, B&B, Resorts
Keene Valley

♂ O Trail's End Inn, 62 Trail's End Way, Keene Valley; 12943-9701 518-576-9860 800-281-9860 trailsendinn.com (❤?) ✎ 🚭

Lake Placid

♂ O The Reiss House Bed & Breakfast, 92 Stevens Rd. Lake Placid 518-380-6002 www.reisshouse.com ✎ 🚭🚭 contact@reisshouse.com

Rock City Falls

♂ ● (?Ᏸ) The Mansion, 801 Rte 29, Rock City Falls; 518-885-1607 www.themansionsaratoga.com

Saranac Lake

♂ O Kiwassa Lake B&B, 1150 Kiwassa Lake Rd, Saranac Lake; 12983 518-891-5721 tinyurl.com/j4lxpr3 ✎ 🚭🚭

Bookstores

♀ O ᏰᏰ Battenkill Books, 15 E Main St, Cambridge; 12816 518-677-2515 www.battenkillbooks.com ✎ info@battenkillbooks.com

Organizations/Resources: Student, Academic, Education

♀ ★ ᏰᏰ SUNY Adirondack Pride, 640 Bay Rd, Queensbury; 518-743-2200 **H?** ✎

Albany & Capital Area

Community Centers and/or Pride Organizations

♀ ★ ᏰᏰ Pride Center of the Capital Region, 332 Hudson Ave, Albany; 518-462-6138 www.capitalpridecenter.org

♀ ★ Saratoga Pride, www.saratogapride.com

Information, Media & Publications

♀ ★ ᏰᏰ CommUNITY Newsletter, Pride Center of the Capital Region, 332 Hudson Ave, Albany; 518-462-6138 www.capitalpridecenter.org

---

♀ GLBTQI ♀ Gay/nongay 🏳️ bisexual
● LBTQI women ♀ all women ? bisexual women
♂ GBTQI men ♂ all men ♂ bisexual men
T specifically transsexual/transgender/transvestite

Ψ ✗ Bar and Restaurant ✗ Restaurant ▷ Cafe
▥Entertainment/Cabaret/Showbar
D Dancing **V** Video bar **K** Karaoke **S** Sports bar
C Country **L** Leather/Levi **W** Western
P Private Club (ask about visitor memberships)

♥ Wedding-related services or marriage equality
H Assistance available for the deaf and hearing-impaired
HS devices **HDS** devices and sign
H? Check for assistance available for the deaf and. hearing-impaired
🚭 🚭 smoke-free property 🚭smoke-free indoors
(🚭) indoor smoking areas
❤ Pets welcome (❤?) Ask about pets
✎ High speed internet available to visitors
Wheelchair Accessibility of premises or meeting place:
ᏰᏰ Accessible premises and lavatory
(ᏰᏰ) Accessible premises with help; accessible lavatory
Ᏸ Accessible premises; lavatory not known to be accessible
(Ᏸ) Accessible premises with help
(?Ᏸ) Call ahead for details: places of meetings or activities vary, or special arrangements available.
◈ Asian ✦ Latin/Hispanic
♣ African-descent/Black
♦ People of Color ✳ Two-Spirit ✪ Diverse

RiverStone Consulting

1448 Dalton Drive, Schenectady, NY 12308

Gender identity specialist: practice is open to all LBGTIQ clients and their allies.

518-506-1261

www.riverstoneconsult.com

Accommodation: Hotels, Inns, Guesthouses, B&B, Resorts
Saratoga Springs

♂ ● Saratoga Farmstead B&B, 41 Locust Grove Rd, Saratoga Springs; 12866-9108 518-587-2074 www.saratogafarmstead.com ✂ ☺ saratogafarmstead@gmail.com

AIDS/HIV Services, Education & Support

♂ Albany Damien Center, 728 Madison Ave #100, Albany; 518-449-7119 www.AlbanyDamienCenter.org

♂ ☆ Albany Medical Center AIDS Program, Mailcode: 158, 43 New Scotland Ave, Albany; 518-262-4043 www.amc.edu/hiv

♂ ☆ ♿ Alliance for Positive Health, 927 Broadway, Albany; 12207-1306 518-434-4686 tinyurl.com/y7un8ttp info@alliancefph.org

Bars, Cafes, Clubs, Restaurants
Albany

♂ ● ♿ Athos Restaurant, 1814 Western Ave, Albany; 518-608-6400 www.athosrestaurant.com ☂ ✂ ✂ athosrestaurant@yahoo.com

♂ ○ (♿) El Loco Mexican Cafe, 465 Madison Ave, Albany; 518-436-1855 www.ElLocoMexicanCafe.com ✂

♂ ○ Fuze Box, 12 Central Ave, Albany; 518-703-8937 fb.com/Albany.FuzeBox/ **D** ▥

♂ ○ ♿ New World Bistro Bar, 300 Delaware Ave, Albany; 518-694-0520 www.newworldbistrobar.com ☂ ✂

♀ ● Oh Bar, 304 Lark St, Albany; 518-463-9004 www.ohonlark.com

♀ ● ♿ Rocks, 77 Central Ave, Albany; 518-472-3588 www.rocks77.com **DLKV** ▥ ✂

♀ ● ♿ WaterWorks Pub, 76 Central Ave, Albany; 518-465-9079 www.waterworkspub.com **DKV** ▥ ✂
Schenectady

♂ Clinton Street Pub, 159 Clinton St, Schenectady; 518-377-8555 ▥
Troy

♀ OUT in Troy, 518-618-2751 fb.com/OUTinTroy/

Bookstores

♂ ○ I Love Books, 380 Delaware Ave, Delmar 518-478-0715 fb.com/pg/ILOVEBOOKSDELMAR/

Broadcast Media

♀ HomoRadio LGBT News & Public Affairs, WRPI 91.5 FM, 1 WRPI Plaza, Troy; 518-276-6248 Sun 11am-2pm. www.wrpi.org

Counseling/Psychotherapy/Mental Health

♂ ● ♿ RiverStone Consulting, 1448 Dalton Drive, Schenectady, NY 12308 518-506-1261 Gender identity specialist: practice is open to all LBGTIQ clients and their allies. www.riverstoneconsult.com

Entertainment-Related Services (see also Performance)

♂ Team A-Man Karaoke, POB 2400, Albany; 12220 518-221-3723 www.amankaraoke.com amanalbany@yahoo.com

Health Care: Physical (see also Counseling/Mental Health)

♂ ☆ ♿ Whitney M. Young, Jr. Health Center, 920 Lark Dr, Albany; 518-465-4771 www.wmyhealth.org

Legal Services

♂ ○ ♿ Copps DiPaola, Kathleen ("Casey"), Copps DiPaola Silverman, PLLC, 126 State St, Albany; 518-436-4170 **H?** www.thecdslawfirm.com ✂

Men's & Sex Clubs (not primarily Health Clubs)

♂ ● ♿ River Street Club, 540 River St, Troy; (Hoosick St) 518-272-0340 www.riverstreetclub.com **P** ✂

Organizations/Resources: Cultural, Dance, Performance

♀ Capital Pride Singers, POB 5261, Albany 12205 www.capitalpridesingers.org

Organizations/Resources: Ethnic, Multicultural

♀ ★ In Our Own Voices, Inc, 245 Lark St Ste 1, Albany; 518-432-4188 www.inourownvoices.org ❖

Organizations/Resources: Social, Recreation, Support

♂ ★ ♿ Bear Albany, c/o ROCKS, 77 Central Ave, Albany; www.bearalbany.com

♂ ★ (♿) The Alternate Universe (TAU) LGBTA Science Fiction Fantasy Club, 518-767-9722 **H?** tinyurl.com/zhvvkug

Organizations/Resources: Student, Academic, Education

♂ ☆ GLSEN New York Capital Region, POB 5392, Albany; 12205 518-635-0552 www.glsennycr.org

♀ ★ Rensselaer LGBTQ Task Force, Student Union, 110 8th St, Troy; 518-276-6000 info.rpi.edu/diversity/lgbtq

♀ ★ Skidmore Pride Alliance, Office of Campus Life, 815 N Broadway, Saratoga Springs; 518-580-8210 tinyurl.com/ja4yvd5

♀ ★ ♿ SUNY Albany Gender and Sexuality Resource Center, 1400 Washington Ave, Campus Center W 0190, Albany www.albany.edu/lgbt/

Organizations/Resources: Youth (see also Family)

♀ ★ (♿) Pride Center of the Capital Region - Youth Group, 332 Hudson Ave, Albany; 518-462-6138 tinyurl.com/zlkftp3 ✂

Recovery

♀ ★ LGBT Alcoholics Anonymous, 332 Hudson Ave, Albany; 518-462-6138 www.capitalpridecenter.org

Religious / Spiritual Resources

♂ ☆ Emmanuel Baptist Church, 275 State St, Albany 12210-2197 518-465-5161 www.emmanuelalbany.net emmanuelalbany@juno.com

♀ ☆ ♿ First Lutheran Church, 646 State St, Albany; 12203 / Sanctuary at 181 Western Ave 518-463-1326 **HD** www.firstlutheranalbany.org flc.office@albany.twcbc.com

♀ ☆ First United Methodist Church, 603 State St, Schenectady; 12305 518-374-4403 www.fumcschenectady.org fumcschenectady@yahoo.com

♀ ☆ ♿ Presbyterian New England Congregational Church, 24 Circular St 518-584-6091 **HD** www.pnecchurch.org
>> *Amherst: see Buffalo/Niagara Falls Area*

Batavia

Organizations/Resources: Student, Academic, Education

♀ ★ SUNY Genesee Community College SAGA (Sexuality and Gender Alliancee), 1 College Rd; 14020 585-343-0055 ✔
>> *Bellmore: see New York City & Long Island Area*
Long Island

Binghamton

Crisis, Anti-violence, & Helplines

♀ ☆ ♿ A New Hope Center, 20 Church Street, Owego; 800-696-7600 **H?** www.anewhopecenter.org ✔

Community Centers and/or Pride Organizations

♀ ★ Binghamton Pride Coalition, www.binghamtonpride.org

Bars, Cafes, Clubs, Restaurants

♀ ○ ♿ Lost Dog Cafe & Lounge, 222 Water St; 607-771-6063 www.lostdogcafe.net ☕ ✖ 🎵 ✔

♀ (♿) Squiggy's, 34 Chenango St (back of Mid-Town Antiques) 607-722-2299 fb.com/squiggys.bar/ **D** 🎵

♀ ○ ♿ Whole in the Wall Restaurant, 43 S Washington St; 607-722-5138 www.wholeinthewall.com ✖ ✔

Organizations/Resources: Student, Academic, Education

♀ ★ ♿ SUNY Binghamton Rainbow Pride Union, SA Box 2000; 13902-2000 607-777-2202 www.binghamtonrpu.com director@binghamtonrpu.com

Organizations/Resources: Youth (see also Family)

♀ ★ ♿ Identity Youth Center, 206 State St; 607-651-9120 **H?** www.idyouth.org ✔
>> *Bovina: see Hudson Valley & Catskills Area*

Brockport

Organizations/Resources: Student, Academic, Education

♀ ★ ♿ The Brockport Pride Association, c/o Brockport Student Government, 350 New Campus Dr; 585-395-5269 **H** tinyurl.com/y7fw4bnb ✔
>> *Bronx: see New York City & Long Island Area*
>> *Brooklyn: see New York City & Long Island Area*

Buffalo/Niagara Falls Area

Community Centers and/or Pride Organizations

♀ ★ Pride Center of Western New York, 200 S Elmwood Ave, Buffalo; 716-852-7743 www.pridecenterwny.org

Information, Media & Publications

♀ ★ Buffalogaybars.com, buffalogaybars.com

AIDS/HIV Services, Education & Support

♀ AIDS Network of Western New York, 16 Linwood Ave, Buffalo; 716-882-7840 www.aidsnetwork.net

Bars, Cafes, Clubs, Restaurants
Buffalo

♀ ● ♿ Cathode Ray, 26 Allen St, Buffalo; 716-884-3615 fb.com/cathoderaybar

♀ ● ♿ Club Marcella, 439 Pearl St, Buffalo; 716-847-6850 www.clubmarcella.com **D** 🎵

♀ ○ Fugazi, 503 Franklin St, Buffalo; (Near Allen) 716-881-3588 fb.com/fugazi.buffalo/

♀ Funky Monkey Nite Club, 26 Allen St, Buffalo; 716-248-1991 www.funkymonkeyniteclub.com **D** 🎵

♀ ● Q Buffalo, 44 Allen St, Buffalo 716-332-2223 tinyurl.com/y72ulj26 🎵

♂ ○ The Underground Niteclub, 274 Delaware Ave, Buffalo; 716-853-0092 tinyurl.com/5su8ty7

Bookstores

♀ ○ (♿) Talking Leaves..Elmwood, 951 Elmwood Ave, Buffalo; 716-884-9524 www.tleavesbooks.com

Counseling/Psychotherapy/Mental Health

♀ ○ Urdang, Nicole, MS, NCC, DHM, 650 Lafayette Ave, Buffalo; 14222-1436 716-882-0848 tinyurl.com/9gyu84y info@nicoleurdang.com

Funding: Endowment, Fundraising

♀ ★ (♿) Imperial Court of Buffalo, dba The Community Services Foundation, Inc, 266 Elmwood Ave #187, Buffalo **H?** tinyurl.com/9uttjk

Health Care: Physical (see also Counseling/Mental Health)

♀ ☆ ♿ Evergreen Health Services, 206 S Elmwood Ave, Buffalo; 716-847-2441 evergreenhs.org

♀ ★ MOCHA Center, 1092 Main St, Buffalo 716-852-1142 www.mochacenter.org ❖

Jewelry (see also Gifts)

♂ ● Aurum Jewelers, 487 Elmwood Ave, Buffalo 716-886-1300 www.aurumonelmwood.com

Organizations/Resources: Cultural, Dance, Performance

♂ ★ Buffalo Gay Men's Chorus, 51 Colonial Circle, Buffalo; 716-883-1277 buffalogaymenschorus.com

♀ ☆ ᕦᕤ Buffalo United Artists, POB 687, Buffalo; 14205 716-886-9239 buffalobua.org

Organizations/Resources: Family and Supporters

⚦ ☆ (ᕦᕤ) PFLAG Buffalo/Niagara, POB 617, Buffalo; 14207-0617 716-883-0384 www.pflagbuffalo.org info@pflagbuffalo.org

Organizations/Resources: Political/Legislative/Advocacy

⚦ ★ Stonewall Democrats of WNY, POB 857, Buffalo; 14205 716-541-5557 www.SDWNY.org

Organizations/Resources: Social, Recreation, Support

⚦ ★ Buffalo Bears, POB 622, Buffalo; 14205 www.buffalobears.org

Organizations/Resources: Student, Academic, Education

⚦ ★ SUNY Fredonia Pride Alliance, E125 Thompson Hall, Fredonia; tinyurl.com/pevc8vy

Organizations/Resources: Transgender/Gender Non-Conforming/Diverse

T ☆ Buffalo Belles, Buffalo / Western New York Support Group for Crossdressers and emerging Transgendered

T ☆ ᕦᕤ Spectrum Transgender Support of Western New York, c/o Pride Center, 206 S Elmwood Ave, Buffalo; 716-541-7003 www.spectrumwny.org

Religious / Spiritual Resources

⚦ ☆ ♂ Riverside-Salem UCC, POB 207, Grand Island; 14072 / 3449 W River Rd 716-773-1426 www.riversidesalem.org ✔

⚦ ☆ ♂ Unitarian Universalist Church, 695 Elmwood Ave, Buffalo; 14222-1697 716-885-2136 www.uubuffalo.org Office@Buffalouu.org

Reproductive Medicine & Fertility Services

⚦ ☆ ᕦᕤ Planned Parenthood of Central and Western New York, 2697 Main St, Buffalo; 716-831-2200 tinyurl.com/guvvhx6

Sports & Outdoor

⚦ ★ Buffalo Alternative Volleyball, tinyurl.com/4vkz5q4

⚦ ★ Buffalo Front Runners/Front Walkers, fb.com/BuffaloFRW/ engelbwe@gmail.com

⚦ ★ Buffalo Historic Bowling League, 716-876-6020 tinyurl.com/ydx7lwa4

♀ ☆ Queen City Roller Girls, POB 225, Buffalo 14205 888-740-7274 www.qcrg.net

⚦ ★ Queen City Softball League, POB 322, Buffalo; 14201 716-514-9995 www.queencitysoftball.com

Canton/Massena/Potsdam Area

Bars, Cafes, Clubs, Restaurants
Potsdam

⚦ O ᕦᕤ 1844 House, 6885 SR 11, Potsdam 315-268-1844 www.1844house.com ⚥ ♡ ✕▦ ✔

Organizations/Resources: Social, Recreation, Support

⚦ ★ ᕦᕤ North Country PRISM, POB 634, Canton; 13617 315-347-2178 www.prismny.org

Organizations/Resources: Student, Academic, Education

⚦ ★ Clarkson University GSA, Student Affairs Office, POB 8715, Potsdam; 13699 315-268-7146 gaystr8@clarkson.edu

⚦ ★ SUNY Canton Spectrum GSA, Office of Diversity Affairs, 34 Cornell Dr, Canton fb.com/groups/SUNYCantonGSA

⚦ ★ ᕦᕤ SUNY Potsdam Gender and Sexuality Alliance, 9029 Barrington Dr, Potsdam tinyurl.com/yy8ka59g

Religious / Spiritual Resources

⚦ ☆ First Presbyterian Church of Ogdensburg, 423 Ford St, Ogdensburg; 13669 315-393-2510 www.fpcogdensburg.com ogdfpc@slic.com

⚦ ☆ Unitarian Universalist Church of Canton, 3 1/2 E Main St, Canton; 13617-1416 315-386-2498 www.uucantonny.org office@uucantonny.org

>> *Catskill: see Hudson Valley & Catskills Area*
>> *Catskills: see Hudson Valley & Catskills Area*

Chautauqua Lake

Accommodation: Hotels, Inns, Guesthouses, B&B, Resorts
Chautauqua

⚦ O The Spencer Hotel & Spa, 25 Palestine Ave, Chautauqua; 14722 716-357-3785 800-398-1306 thespencer.com spencerhotel@gmail.com

Organizations/Resources: Family and Supporters

⚦ ☆ PFLAG - Chautauqua, POB 658, Chautauqua 14722 716-753-7254 tinyurl.com/ycsdcqj9

>> *Cherry Grove: see New York City & Long Island Area*

De Kalb Junction

Organizations/Resources: Social, Recreation, Support

⚦ ★ Blue Heron Farm, 68 Streeter Rd; 13630 315-347-2178 blueheronfae.net thompsbs@tds.net

>> *Delmar: see Albany & Capital Area*
>> *East Hampton: see New York City & Long Island Area*
>> *Elmira: see Rochester & Finger Lakes Area*
>> *Endicott: see Binghamton*
>> *Finger Lakes Area: see*
>> *Fire Island Pines: see New York City & Long Island*
>> *Long Island*
>> *Fleischmanns: see Hudson Valley & Catskills Area*
>> *Fredonia: see Buffalo/Niagara Falls Area*

Geneseo

Organizations/Resources: Student, Academic, Education

⚦ ★ SUNY Geneseo Pride Alliance, Multicultural Programs, College Union Room 308; 585-245-5620 www.geneseo.edu/lgbtq

Hamilton

Organizations/Resources: Student, Academic, Education

⚦ ★ ᕦᕤ Colgate University Office of LGBTQ Initiatives, Cutten Complex, 12 Oak Dr; 315-228-6840 **H?** tinyurl.com/yy8butxm ✔

New York: Hudson Valley & Catskills Area
Crisis, Anti-violence, & Helplines

241
GAYELLOW PAGES #42 2020-2021

Hudson Valley & Catskills Area: New York
Accommodation: Rentals

Hudson Valley & Catskills Area

Crisis, Anti-violence, & Helplines

♂ My Sisters' Place, 1 Water St 3rd Flr, White Plains; 800-298-7233 www.mspny.org

♀ ☆ Putnam/Northern Westchester Women's Resource Center, 935 South Lake Blvd Ste 2, Mahopac; 845-628-2166 Northern Westchester, Putnam & lower Dutchess counties www.pnwwrc.org

♀ Women's Justice Center, Pace Law School, 27 Crane Ave, White Plains; 914-287-0739 www.law.pace.edu/wjc

Community Centers and/or Pride Organizations

⚥ ★ Catskills Pride, POB 154, Barryville 12719 www.catskillspride.com

⚥ ★ ♿ Hudson Valley LGBTQ Community Center, POB 3994, Kingston; 12402 300 Wall St 845-331-5300 **H?** www.lgbtqcenter.org ✎

⚥ ★ ♿ The LOFT: LGBT Community Services Center, 252 Bryant Ave, White Plains; 10605 914-948-2932 **H?** E-News Alerts, Advocacy, Education, Celebration for LGBT/supportive communities, lower Hudson Valley. loftgaycenter.org ✎ info@gaycenter.org

⚥ ★ ♿ Rockland County Pride Center, POB 505, Nyack; 10960 845-353-6300 www.rocklandpridecenter.org

Information, Media & Publications

⚥ ★ Big Gay Hudson Valley, POB 2623, Poughkeepsie; 12603 www.biggayhudsonvalley.com

Accommodation: Hotels, Inns, Guesthouses, B&B, Resorts

Barryville

♂ ● Stickett Inn, 3380 Route 97, Barryville 845-557-0913 www.stickettinn.com ♣ ✎ ☻

Bovina

♂ ● Mountain Brook Inn, 5333 County Hwy 6, Bovina 13740-6510 877-692-7665 607-832-4662 fax 607-832-4246-Private www.themountainbrookinn.com ♣ ✎ ☻

Callicoon Center

♂ ○ Apple Pond Farm & Renewable Energy Education Center, Box 371 80 Hahn Rd, Callicoon Center; 12724 845-482-4764 www.applepondfarm.com ♣ ✎ ☻☻ info@applepondfarm.com

Catskill

♂ ○ The Post Cottage, 174 Spring St, Catskill 12414 518-719-0747 www.ThePostCottage.com ✎ ☻☻ Contact@ThePostCottage.com

Claryville

♂ ● Blue Horizon B&B, 60 Coons Rd, Claryville 845-985-0351 tinyurl.com/4986afx ✎ ☻

Cochecton

♂ ○ Fosterdale Motor Lodge, 1166 County Rd 114, Cochecton; 12726 845-932-8538 www.fmlodge.com fmlodge@yahoo.com

Hunter

♂ ● (?♿) The Fairlawn Inn, 7872 Main St 518-263-5025 www.fairlawninn.com (♣?) ✎ ☻ info@fairlawninn.com

Marlboro

♂ ○ Saint Hubert's Lodge & Club, 626 Lattintown Rd, Marlboro; 12542 845-795-0037 www.sainthubertslodge.com info@sainthubertslodge.com

Mt Tremper

♀ ○ (?♿) Catskill Rose Dining & Lodging, 5355 Route 212, Mt Tremper; 12457-5404 845-688-7100 www.catskillrose.com ♈ ✖ ✎ ☻ chefs@catskillrose.com

Rock Hill

♀ ○ Ramada at The Sullivan Event Center, 283 Rock Hill Dr, Rock Hill; 12775 845-796-3100 ✎

Roxbury

♂ ● (?♿) The Roxbury, 2258 County Hwy 41, Roxbury; 607-326-7200 www.theroxburymotel.com ✎ ☻

Saugerties

♂ ● (?♿) Bluestone Bed & Basecamp, 4170 RT 9W, Saugerties 845-247-7446 www.bluestonebasecamp.com (♣?) ✎ ☻ info@bluestonebasecamp.com

♀ ○ Grouse House, 21 Adrienne Ln, Saugerties; 12477 845-246-1852 www.grousehouse.net ✎ ☻

Sharon Springs

♀ ● American Hotel, 192 Main St 518-284-2105 www.americanhotelny.com ♈ ✖ (♣?) ✎ ☻

♀ ● Edgefield, POB 152, Sharon Springs; 13459 518-284-3339 www.edgefieldbb.com (♣?) ✎ ☻

♀ ○ The New York House, 110 Center St, Sharon Springs; 13459 518-284-6027 www.TheNewYorkHouse.com thenewyorkhouse@gmail.com

Stone Ridge

♀ ○ Elmrock Inn / Harvest Real Food Catering, 4496 Rte 209, Stone Ridge; 12484 845-687-4492 www.elmrockinn.com (♣?) ✎ ☻ ☻ ♥ info@elmrockinn.com

Wallkill

♀ ○ ♿ Bernetta's Place, 12 Calderone Dr, Wallkill; 12589 845-464-5106 www.bernettasplace.com ♣ ✎ ☻ ☻ bbrusq@hvc.rr.com

Warwick

♀ ● Inn at Stony Creek, 34 Spanktown Road, Warwick 845-986-3660 www.innstonycreek.com ☻

White Lake

♀ ● (?♿) Bradstan Country Hotel, POB 312, White Lake; 12786 845-583-4114 www.bradstancountryhotel.com ▥

Windham

♀ ● ♿ Beds on Clouds Bed and Breakfast Inn, 5320 Main St, Windham; 518-734-4692 www.bedsonclouds.com (♣?) ✎ ☻ ☻

♀ ○ (?♿) Cuomo's Cove, 33 Cuomo's Cove Rd, Windham; 12496 800-734-5903 www.cuomoscove.com (♣?) ✎ ☻ landinthesky@aol.com

Accommodation Rental: Furnished / Vacation (& AirBNB)

Denver

♀ ○ Catskill Mountain View House, Charles Morse Rd 917-848-7074 tinyurl.com/3otbcvn ✎ ☻ ☻ Jencole88@yahoo.com

Narrowsburg

♀ ○ ♿ Beaverbrook Cottage, 1256 Crystal lake Rd, Narrowsburg; 12764 845-252-7506 www.beaverbrookcottage.com ♣ ✎ ☻ beaverbrookcottage@gmail.com

Woodstock

♀ ○ (?♿) Dreamcatcher Cottage, 131 Ohayo Mountain Rd, Woodstock; 12498 646-831-3808 www.dreamcatcherwoodstock.com ✎ ☻ ☻ idreamofwoodstock@gmail.com

AIDS/HIV Services, Education & Support

♂ ☆ Angel Food East Inc, POB 3813, Kingston 12402 845-331-6538 www.angelfoodeast.org

♀ ☆ NETWORTH/Positive Action Inc, POB 1374, Pleasant Valley; 12569-1374 518-339-2437 networthpa.blogspot.com

♀ ☆ Together Our Unity Can Heal (TOUCH), 209 Rt 9W, Congers; 845-268-8023 www.touch-ny.org

Antiques & Collectibles

♀ ○ The Country Bum'kin, 1100 Rte 17B, Mongaup Valley; 845-583-7937 www.thecountrybumkin.net

Art & Craft Galleries/Services, Supplies

♀ ○ The Corner Frame Shop, 40 S Franklin St, Nyack 10960 845-727-1240 thecornerframeshop.com hal@thecornerframeshop.com

♀ ○ John Davis Gallery, 362 1/2 Warren St, Hudson 15234 518-828-5907 www.johndavisgallery.com

♀ ○ Knitting Nation, 30 N Broadway, Nyack 845-348-0100 www.knittingnation.com

Bakeries

♀ ○ &&. The Alternative Baker, 407 Main St, Rosendale; 12472-0022 845-658-3355 www.lemoncakes.com ✔

Bars, Cafes, Clubs, Restaurants

Beacon
♀ ● Chill Wine Bar, 173 Main St, Beacon 845-765-0885 Www.chillwinebarbeacon.com chillwinebar@gmail.com

Bethel
♀ ○ Dancing Cat Saloon, 2037 Rte 17B, Bethel 845-583-3141 www.dancingcatsaloon.com ⌖ ✕

Highland
♀ ○ The Would Restaurant, 120 North Road, Highland 845-691-9883 www.thewould.com ⌖ ✕

Hudson
♀ ○ Georgia Ray's Kitchen, 9 Ginsberg Lane, Hudson 518-828-3245 georgiarays.com ✕ georgiarays@verizon.net

♀ ● Home/Made Hudson, 119 Warren St, Hudson Homemadehudson.com ✕ ✔

Kingston
♀ ○ Armadillo Bar & Grill, 97 Abeel St, Kingston 845-339-1550 www.armadillos.net ⌖ ✕

Marlboro
♀ ○ &&. The Falcon, 1348 Route 9W, Marlboro; 845-236-7970 www.liveatthefalcon.com D ⌖ ⊡ ✕ ▦ ✔ info@liveatthefalcon.com

Narrowsburg
♀ ○ The Heron, 40 Main St, Narrowsburg 845-252-3333 www.theheronrestaurant.com ✕

Nyack
♀ ○ Maureen's Jazz Cellar, 2 N Broadway, Nyack 845-535-3143 www.maureensjazzcellar.com ▦

♀ ○ &&. Murasaki Japanese Restaurant, 138 Main St, Nyack; 845-358-3222 H www.murasakinyack.com ✕

♀ ○ Sour Kraut, 118 Main St, Nyack; 845-358-3122 fb.com/sourkrautnyack ✕

♀ ○ Wasabi, 110 Main St, Nyack; 845-358-7977 www.wasabiny.com ✕ @ixx=

Rhinebeck
♀ ○ &&. Terrapin Restaurant, 6426 Montgomery St, Rhinebeck; 845-876-3330 www.terrapinrestaurant.com K ⌖ ✕ ⊡ ✔

Rock Hill
♀ ○ &&. Bernie's Holiday Restaurant, 277 Rock Hill Dr 845-796-3333 bhr-sullivan.com ✕ ✔ info@bhr-sullivan.com

♀ ○ Crust Italian Eatery, 277 Rock Hill Dr, Rock Hill; 845-796-4444 ✕ ✔

Roxbury
♀ ○ &&. Public Restaurant & Lounge, 2318 County Highway 41 (Bridge St), Roxbury; 607-326-4026 tinyurl.com/qyuq4qo ⌖ ✕ ✔

Sparkill
♀ ○ D'Vine Bar, 4 Depot Square, Sparkill 915-359-2141 x1 www.dvinebar.com @ixx=

Stone Ridge
♀ ○ &&. Lydia's, 7 Old US Highway 209, Stone Ridge; 845-687-6373 lydias-cafe.com ⊡ ▦ ✔

Tivoli
♀ ○ &&. The Corner, 53 Broadway, Tivoli 845-757-2100 hoteltivoli.org/the-corner/ ✕ ✔

Bookstores

♀ ○ & Golden Notebook, 29 Tinker St, Woodstock; 845-679-8000 www.goldennotebook.com

♀ ○ &&. Oblong Books & Music, 6422 Montgomery St Ste 6, Rhinebeck; 845-876-0500 www.oblongbooks.com ✔

♀ ○ Oblong Books & Music, 26 Main St, Millerton 518-789-3797 www.oblongbooks.com ✔

♀ ○ &&. Rough Draft Bar & Books, 82 John St, Kingston; 12401 917-620-0939 www.roughdraftny.com ✔ roughdraftbar@gmail.com

♀ ○ &&. The Spotty Dog Books & Ale, 440 Warren St, Hudson; 12534 518-671-6006 www.thespottydog.com ✔ spottydogbooks@aol.com

♀ ○ Village Bookstore, 10 Washington Ave, Pleasantville; 914-769-8322

Catering (see also Party/Holiday/Event Services)

♀ ○ BHR Caterers, 277 Rock Hill Dr, Rock Hill 12775 845-796-3333 ✔

Counseling/Psychotherapy/Mental Health

♀ ● Greenman, Janet, LCSW-R POB 602, Hopewell Junction; 12533 845-227-0161 jvgreenman@aol.com

♀ ☆ &&. The Guidance Center, 256 Washington Street, Mount Vernon; 914-613-0700 H? Serving Westchester County www.theguidancecenter.org

♀ ○ Kuhn, Andrew E, PhD Psychologist, 275 Main St, Mount Kisco; 10549 914-261-2657 andrewekuhn@gmail.com

♀ ○ Shuman, Randee, LCSWR, 55 Old Turnpike Rd Ste 206, Nanuet; 10954 845-708-0143 www.randeeshuman.com rlynne345@aol.com

Counseling/Psychiatry

⚲ ○ Lovrin, Mellen, DNP, Psychiatric Nurse Practitioner, 50 Piermont Ave, Nyack; 845-353-6780

Financial Planning, Investment (see also Insurance)

⚲ ● Third Eye Associates, Ltd, 38 Spring Lake Rd, Red Hook; 12571 845-752-2216 www.thirdeyeassociates.com bjones@thirdeyeassociates.com

Furniture

⚲ ○ Romancing the Woods, POB 130, Saugerties 12477 845-246-6976 Rustic garden structures www.romancingthewoods.com davis@romancingthewoods.com

Gifts, Cards, Pride, etc.

⚲ ○ ♿ Dreaming Goddess, 44 Raymond Ave, Poughkeepsie; 12603 845-473-2206 **H?** DreamingGoddess.com ✔ info@DreamingGoddess.com

Insurance (see also Financial Planning)

⚲ ○ ♿ McGuinness, Debbie, State Farm Insurance, 75 Lake Rd Ste C & D, Congers; 10920-2323 845-267-2900 www.debbiemcguinness.com ✔ debbie@debbiemcguinness.com

Jewelry (see also Gifts)

⚲ ○ Hudson Babylon, 315 Warren St, Hudson 518-828-1047 ✔ linda@hudsonbabylon.com

Legal Services

⚲ ○ ♿ Fellows Hymowitz, PC, 254 S Main St Ste 500, New City; 10956 845-639-9300 www.PILaw.com ✔ Lawyers@PILaw.com

⚲ ○ Gary Levine & Susan Htoo, PC, Attorneys at Law, 290 Hooker Ave, Poughkeepsie; 12603-3103 845-452-2366 levineandhtoolaw.com LevineandHtooLaw@aol.com

⚲ ○ (♿) Law & Mediation Offices of Carolyn M. Laredo, PLLC, 28 New Hempstead Rd Ste A, New City; 10956 845-639-1836 **H?** Divorce services www.lawmediationny.com ✔

Organizations/Resources: Business & Professional Associations, Labor Advocacy

⚥ ★ Mid Hudson Valley Gay & Lesbian Professional Alliance, 845-226-8107 tinyurl.com/6gc7kgk

Organizations/Resources: Family and Supporters

⚲ ☆ ♿ PFLAG, GLBTQ Center, Kingston, NY 845-853-5798 ✔

⚲ ☆ PFLAG Rockland, POB 653, Palisades; 10964 845-202-1620 RocklandPFLAG.org info@rocklandpflag.org

⚲ ☆ PFLAG Westchester, c/o The Loft, 252 Bryant Ave, White Plains; 10605 914-468-4636 www.pflagwestchester.org ✦ info@pflagwestchester.org

Organizations/Resources: Senior Resources

⚥ ★ Old Lesbians Organizing for Change (OLOC-HV) - Hudson Valley, meets at Hudson Valley LGBTQ Community Center 845-679-7586 www.oloc.org

⚥ ★ Senior Silver Connections, c/o The LOFT, 252 Bryant Ave, White Plains; 914-948-2932 **H?** tinyurl.com/y28h6juj ✔

Organizations/Resources: Social, Recreation, Support

⚥ ★ (♿) The Link, POB 505, Nyack 10960 / Hudson Valley & Northern NJ linkmembers@gmail.com

Organizations/Resources: Student, Academic, Education

⚥ ★ (♿) Clarkstown High School North GSA, 151 Congers Rd, New City; **H?** ✔

⚲ ★ GLSEN Hudson Valley, POB 604, Yorktown Hts 10598 914-962-7888 www.glsen.org/hudsonvalley

⚲ ★ GLSEN Hudson Valley (Ulster), POB 14, Milton; 12547-0014 845-554-5733 www.glsen.org/hudsonvalley ulsterny@chapters.glsen.org

⚥ ★ SUNY New Paltz Pride, Women's Studies Program, 1 Hawk Drive, New Paltz fb.com/groups/483729481760008

⚥ ★ ♿ SUNY Oneonta Gender and Sexuality Resource Center, 219 Hunt Union, 108 Ravine Parkway, Oneonta 607-436-2190 **H?** tinyurl.com/yk8cte4 ✔

⚥ ★ SUNY Purchase LGBTQU, 1012 Campus Center N, 735 Anderson Hill Rd, Purchase; 914-251-6000 fb.com/groups/2202128889

⚥ ★ Vassar College Campus Life LGBTQ Center, College Center 213, 124 Raymond Ave Box 555, Poughkeepsie; 845-451-3521 lgbtq.vassar.edu

Organizations/Resources: Transgender/Gender Non-Conforming/Diverse

T ☆ Transgender Support Group, c/o The Loft, 252 Bryant Ave, White Plains; 10605 914-948-2932 **H?** www.loftgaycenter.org ✔ info@loftgaycenter.org

Organizations/Resources: Youth (see also Family)

⚥ ★ Center Lane, Westchester Jewish Community Services, 30 S Broadway Flr 6 Rm 7, Yonkers; 10701 914-423-0610 www.centerlaneny.org centerlane@wjcs.com

⚥ ★ Center Lane LGBTQ Youth and Community Education Center, 30 South Broadway Rm 7, Yonkers; 914-423-0610 www.centerlaneny.org

⚲ ☆ TRUST, c/o CANDLE, 120 N Main St #301, New City; 845-634-6677 x20 tinyurl.com/zqvnlrh

Party/Holiday/Event Services (see also Catering, Weddings)

⚲ ☆ Hudson Hall at the historic Hudson Opera House, 327 Warren St, Hudson; 518-822-1438 www.hudsonhall.org

Real Estate (see also Mortgages)

⚲ ● CENTURY 21 Country Realty, 540 Broadway, Monticello; 12701 845-791-5280 tinyurl.com/jdlvya6 ✔ info@century21countryrealty.com

⚲ ● Mordica, Kristi, Gay Broker, Welch Realty, PO Box 833, Kerhonkson; 12446 661-607-6559 welchrealtyny.com

⚲ ○ ♿ Silverberg, Diane B., Lic Assoc RE Broker, CRS, ABR, Westwood Metes & Bounds Realty, Main St. (Rte 209) 845-750-0744 845-687-0232 x109 www.buyfromdi.com ✔ dsilverberg@bhhshudsonvalley.com

Recovery

♿ Lanzone, Joseph, LCSWR, CASAC, 20 N Broadway Ste 4, Nyack; 845-358-0925

New York: Hudson Valley & Catskills Area
Recovery

244

GAYELLOW PAGES #42 2020-2021

New York City & Long Island Area : New York
Crisis, Anti-violence, & Helplines

♂ ☆ (♌) Rockland Al-Anon Information Service, POB 127, Thiells; 10984 845-727-2050 www.rockland-al-anon.org

Religious / Spiritual Resources

♂ ★ ♿ Dignity-Integrity/Mid-Hudson, PO Box 864, Poughquag; 12570 845-724-3209 Catholics, Episcopalians and their friends

♂ ☆ Holy Trinity Episcopal Church, 22 Coulter Ave, Pawling; 12564 845-855-5276 www.holytrinitypawling.org info@holytrinity pawling.org

♂ ☆ Nauraushaun Presbyterian Church, 51 Sickletown Rd, Pearl River; 10965-2855 845-735-4565 fb.com/nauraushaunchurch npcpearl@verizon.net

♂ ☆ St John's Memorial Episcopal Church, Rev. Canon Jeff Golliher, Ph.D., TSSF, Missioner, POB 262, Ellenville; 12428 845-626-2605 www.stjohnsellenville.org

♂ ☆ Unitarian Universalist Congregation of Rockland, 130 Concklin Rd, Pomona; 10970-3606 845-354-1789 www.uurocklandny.org administrator@uurocklandny.org

♂ ☆ Unitarian Universalist Congregation of the Hudson Valley, 2021 Albany Post Rd, Croton On Hudson; 10520 914-271-4283 www.uuchudsonvalley.org office@uuchudsonvalley.org

♂ ☆ Unitarian Universalist Fellowship of Poughkeepsie, 67 S Randolph Ave, Poughkeepsie; 12601-5127 845-471-6580 www.uupok.org office@uupok.org

Travel & Tourist Services (see also Accommodation)

♂ ● ♿ Hollow Brook Travel, 17 Old Main St, Fishkill; 12524 845-896-0227 www.hollowbrooktravel.biz ✈ info@hollow brooktravel.biz

Veterinarians

♂ ○ Nanuet Animal Hospital, 4 Ave C, Nanuet; 10954 845-623-4469 www.NanuetAnimalHospital.com info@NanuetAnimal Hospital.com

Weddings and Ceremonies

💕 ● Hudson Valley Officiants & LGBTQ Ceremonies, 102 Lucas Ave, Kingston; 12401 845-248-2903 tinyurl.com/rl9cw89 ❤ hvofficiants@gmail.com

>> *Hyde Park: see Hudson Valley & Catskills Area*

Ithaca

Community Centers and/or Pride Organizations

💕 ★ Cortland LGBTQ Center, 165 Main St #B, Cortland; 13045 607-756-8970 www.cortlandlgbtcenter.org lbarbin@fcscortland.org

Accommodation: Hotels, Inns, Guesthouses, B&B, Resorts

♂ ○ Rogues Harbor Inn, POB 347; 14882 607-533-3535 www.roguesharbor.com ♣ ✈ reservations@roguesharbor.com

Trumansburg

♂ ● Juniper Hill B&B, 16 Elm St, Trumansburg 607-387-3044 juniperhillbnb.com ✈ 🚭

♂ ○ ♿ William Henry Miller Inn, 303 N Aurora St; 14850-4201 607-256-4553 www.millerinn.com (♣?) ✈ 🚭🚭 millerinn@ aol.com

Bookstores

♂ ○ ♿ Buffalo Street Books, 215 N Cayuga St; 607-273-8246 www.buffalostreetbooks.com ✈

Organizations/Resources: Family and Supporters

♀ ☆ PFLAG Ithaca/Cortland, 73 Main St, Cortland 607-423-1078 www.pflagithacacortland.com

Organizations/Resources: Student, Academic, Education

💕 ★ Center for LGBT Education, Outreach & Services, Ithaca College, 953 Danby Rd; 607-274-7394 www.ithaca.edu/lgbt

♀ ☆ Cornell University Women's Resource Center, 209 Willard Straight Hall Mailbox 71; 607-255-0015 tinyurl.com/ybxxbpx8

💕 ★ ♿ LGBT Resource Center, Cornell University, 626 Thurston Ave 3rd Flr; 607-254-4987 www.lgbtrc.cornell.edu ✈

Religious / Spiritual Resources

♀ ☆ ♿ Christ Community Church ABC/UCC/PCUSA, 292 Tompkins St, Cortland; 13045 607-756-1710 tinyurl.com/y4rg63lo ✈ christcommunitychurchcortland@gmail.com

Jamestown

Bars, Cafes, Clubs, Restaurants

💕 ● ♿ Sneakers, 100 Harrison St, Jamestown; 716-484-8816 fb.com/sneakersjamestown/ **D**

Counseling/Psychotherapy/Mental Health

♀ ☆ ♿ Mental Health Association, 31 Water St Ste 7, Jamestown; 14701 716-661-9044 **H?** www.mhachautauqua.org ✈ info@mhachautauqua.org

Health Care: Physical (see also Counseling/Mental Health)

♀ ♿ Evergreen Health Services Southern Tier, 408 W 5th St, Jamestown; 716-664-7855 www.evergreenhs.org

Religious / Spiritual Resources

💕 Unitarian Universalist Congregation of Jamestown, 1255 Prendergast Ave, Jamestown; 716-488-1902 fb.com/jamestownuu

>> *Kingston: see Hudson Valley & Catskills Area*
>> *Lake George: see Adirondacks Area*
>> *Middletown: see Hudson Valley & Catskills Area*

Morrisville

Organizations/Resources: Student, Academic, Education

💕 ★ SUNY Morrisville State College Mo'Pride, PO Box 901; 13408 315-684-6554 tinyurl.com/hnlmwhf ⊙

>> *New Paltz: see Hudson Valley & Catskills Area*

New York City & Long Island Area

Crisis, Anti-violence, & Helplines

♂ ☆ The Center for Anti-Violence Education, 327 7th St Flr 2, Bklyn; 718-788-1775 All women, girls, trans-adults and trans-youth www.caeny.org

♀ Connect, 127 W 127th St Ste 431; 212-683-0015 www.connect-nyc.org

♀ Joyful Heart Foundation, 212-475-2026 tinyurl.com/d7qmpu

Long Island

♀ ☆ (?⚲) Long Island Crisis Center, 2740 Martin Ave, Bellmore; 11710-3200 516-679-1111 24 hrs longislandcrisiscenter.org

♀ ☆ Response Crisis Center, POB 300, Stony Brook; 11790-0300 631-751-7500 www.responsecrisiscenter.org info@responsehotline.org

Manhattan & Citywide

♂ ★ **Gay & Lesbian Switchboard of New York, 212-989-0999 www.GLBTNationalHelpCenter.org**
◆ *Advertisement page 2*

♂ ★ ♿ New York City Anti-Violence Project, 116 Nassau St 3rd Flr; 212-714-1141 www.avp.org

♂ ★ ♿ New York City Anti-Violence Project, 116 Nassau St 3rd Flr; 212-714-1141 www.avp.org

♀ ☆ Safe Horizon, Victim Services Agency, 2 Lafayette St 3rd Flr; 800-621-4673 www.safehorizon.org

♀ The Samaritans, POB 1259; 10159 212-673-3000 www.samaritansnyc.org

♀ ☆ Sanctuary for Families, POB 1406 Wall St Stn; 10268 212-349-6009 www.sanctuaryforfamilies.org

---

Community Centers and/or Pride Organizations

Bronx

♂ Latino Pride Center, 975 Kelly St #402, Bronx; 718-328-4188 www.latinopridecenter.org ◆

Brooklyn

♀ ★ (?⚲) Audre Lorde Project, 147 W 24th St 3rd Flr; 212-463-0342 alp.org ❖

♀ ★ (?⚲) Audre Lorde Project, 85 S Oxford St Flr 3, Bklyn; 718-596-0342 alp.org ❖

♂ ★ ♿ Brooklyn Community Pride Center, 1360 Fulton St Ground Flr, Bklyn; 347-889-7719 www.lgbtbrooklyn.org ✗

♂ ★ Brooklyn Pride, POB 150508, Bklyn; 11215 718-928-3320 www.BrooklynPride.org

Long Island: Sag Harbor

♂ ★ ♿ The LGBT Network Hamptons LGBT Center, 44 Union St, Sag Harbor; 631-899-4950 lgbtnetwork.org/the-center ✗

Long Island: Woodbury

♂ ★ ♿ The LGBT Network Center at Woodbury, 20 Crossways Dr N Ste 110, Woodbury; 516-323-0011 lgbtnetwork.org/the-center ✗

Long Island

♂ ★ LGBT Network Hauppauge Center, 125 Kennedy Dr Ste 100, Hauppauge; 631-665-2300 lgbtnetwork.org/the-center

♂ ★ Long Island Pride, 516-323-0011 prideonthebeach.org

Manhattan

♂ ★ Harlem Pride, 42 Macombs Place 347-846-0362 www.harlempride.org ☺

♂ ★ The Harlem SGL/LGBTQ Center, 42 Macombs Place; 212-634-7895 fb.com/HarlemCenterNYC/ ☺

♂ ★ (?⚲) The LGBT Community Center, 208 W 13th St; 10011-7702 212-620-7310 fax 212-924-2657 **H?** www.gaycenter.org ✗

♀ ★ New York City Dyke March, www.nycdykemarch.com

♂ ★ (?⚲) New York City Pride, Heritage Of Pride, Inc 154 Christopher St #1D; 212-807-7433 www.nycpride.org

Queens

♂ ★ Queens Community House, 108-25 62nd Dr, Forest Hills; 718-592-5757 www.qchnyc.org

♂ ★ Queens LGBT Center (Q Center), 37-18 Northern Blvd Ste 107, Long Island City; 718-514-2155 lgbtnetwork.org/q-center

♂ ★ Queens Pride, POB 720464, Jackson Hts 11372 347-494-1899 www.queenspride.org

♂ ★ **Queens Pride House, 76-11 37th Ave Ste 206, Jackson Hts; 718-429-5309 www.queenspridehouse.org** ✗

New York: New York City & Long Island Area
Community Centers / Pride
246
GAYELLOW PAGES #42 2020-2021
New York City & Long Island Area : New York
AIDS/HIV Support

Staten Island

♀ ★ ♿ Pride Center of Staten Island, 25 Victory Blvd 3rd Flr, Staten Island; 718-808-1360 www.pridecentersi.org ✎

Information, Media & Publications

♀ ● Gayellow Pages, POB 533 Village Stn 10014-0533 646-213-0263 v/f **Classified directory of services, businesses, resources, etc in USA & Canada. Mailing lists available.** www.gayellowpages.com gypages@gmail.com

♀ ★ Gayletter, 195 Chrystie St Ste 600A www.gayletter.com

♀ ● **Get Out Magazine, 646-761-3325 Featuring content from the hottest gay and gay-friendly spots in NYC, LI & NJ.** www.getoutmag.com mike@getoutmag.com

♂ ★ LGBT Network, 125 Kennedy Dr Ste 100, Hauppauge; 631-665-2300 www.lgbtnetwork.org

♂ ★ Living Out, 125 Kennedy Dr, Hauppauge 11788 516-323-0011 www.livingoutli.org info@livingoutli.org

♀ ● (♿) Metrosource, 213 W 35th St 12W; 212-315-0800 www.metrosource.com ✎

♀ ★ NYC Up & Out, POB 242, Calverton; 11933 646-598-9920 Events guide www.nycupandout.com

Accommodation: Hotels, Inns, Guesthouses, B&B, Resorts
Brooklyn

♂ ● The Loralei B&B, 667 Argyle Rd, Bklyn 646-228-4656 www.loraleinyc.com ✎

Long Island: Fire Island: Cherry Grove

♂ ● ♿ Belvedere Guest House for Men, PO Box Box 4026, Cherry Grove; 11782 631-597-6448 www.belvederefireisland.com ✎ (☹)

Long Island: Fire Island: Fire Island Pines

♂ ● Fire Island Pines Resort, 631-597-6500 www.pinesfi.com

♂ ● The Hotel by ShareGurl, Botel, Harbor Walk, FI Pines; 917-336-9299 hotel.sharegurl.com (♣?) ✎ ☹ ☹

♂ ● The Madison Fire Island Pines, 22 Atlantic Walk 631-597-6061 www.themadisonfi.com ✎ ☹

♀ ● Pines Bluff Overlook, POB 5330, FI Pines 11782 631-597-3064 www.pinesbluffoverlook.com pinesbluffoverlook@gmail.com

Long Island: Greenport

♀ ● Stirling House B&B, 104 Bay Ave, Greenport 631-477-0654 www.stirlinghousebandb.com ✎ ☹

♀ ○ Wells House B&B, 530 Main St, Greenport; 11944 631-477-0674 wellshouse.com ✎ ☹ ☹ Info@wellshouse.com

Long Island: Jamesport

♀ ● (♿) The Duncan Inn, 1399 Main Rd, Jamesport; 631-722-4024 www.duncaninn.com ♣ ✎ ☹ ☹

Manhattan

♂ ● Chelsea Mews Guest House, 344 W 15th St 212-255-9174 tinyurl.com/7rxlf4x ☹

♂ ● Colonial House Inn, 318 W 22nd St 800-689-3779 www.colonialhouseinn.com

Accommodation Rental: Furnished / Vacation (& AirBNB)
Long Island: Fire Island: Cherry Grove

♂ ● Dune Point, 134 Lewis Walk, Cherry Grove 631-597-6261 www.dunepoint.com ♣ ✎ ☹

Manhattan

♀ ● Bubba & Bean Lodges, 1598 Lexington Ave (102/103 St) 917-345-7914 www.bblodges.com ✎

♂ ○ A Garden In Chelsea, 439 W 22nd St; 10011-2512 212-243-8621 www.agardeninchelsea.com ✎ ☹

Accommodation: Residential/Sharing/Roommates

♀ ● ♿ Rainbow Roommates, Douglass M. Leavy, 75 W End Ave; 10023 212-757-2865 www.rainbowroommates.com info@rainbowroommates.com

Accounting, Bookkeeping, Tax Services
Long Island

♂ ● Corsentino, Robert A, CPA, PC, 105 Maxess Rd Ste 124, Melville; 11747 631-574-4500 www.corsentinocpa.com bob@corsentinocpa.com

Queens

♂ ● BGS Services, Inc., 718-459-3690 www.bgsservices.com

AIDS/HIV Services, Education & Support
Bronx

♂ Boom! Health Bronx AIDS Services, 540 E Fordham Rd #2, Bronx; 718-295-5605 www.boomhealth.org

Brooklyn

♂ ☆ Bridging Access To Care Inc, 260 Broadway, Bklyn; (Crown Heights) 347-505-5120 www.bac-ny.org ✎

♂ ☆ ♿ Housing Works, 57 Willoughby St, Bklyn; 347-473-7400 **H?** www.housingworks.org

♂ ☆ ♿ God's Love We Deliver, 166 Ave of the Americas; / Five boroughs & Hudson County, NJ 212-294-8100 www.godslovewedeliver.org

Long Island

♂ ☆ ♿ Long Island Association for AIDS Care, Inc., 60 Adams Ave, Hauppauge; 877-865-4222 www.liaac.org

♂ ☆ ♂ Suffolk Project for AIDS Resource Coordination (SPARC), 30 W Main St, Riverhead; 631-369-8696

♂ ★ ♿ Thursday's Child of LI, 475 E Main St Ste 209, Patchogue; 631-447-5044 www.thursdayschildofli.org ✎

Manhattan & Citywide

♂ Aaron Diamond AIDS Research Center, 455 1st Ave Flor 7; 212-448-5000 www.adarc.org

♂ ☆ ♿ ACT UP / NY, 511 Ave of the Americas Mailbox G5; 212-966-4873 actupny.com

♂ ☆ The Alliance for Positive Change, 64 W 35th St 3rd Flr; 212-645-0875 alliance.nyc ●

♂ American Run for the End of AIDS, 2350 Broadway #1016; 212-580-7668 www.americanrunendaids.org

♀ amFAR - American Foundation for AIDS Research, 120 Wall St FI 13; 212-806-1600 www.amfar.org

♂ ☆ (♿) Bailey House, 1751 Park Ave 212-633-2500 www.baileyhouse.org

♂ ☆ Chinese-American Planning Council, Community Health Services - HIV/AIDS Services, 150 Elizabeth St; 212-941-0920 www.cpc-nyc.org ✧

♀ ☆ (?⚥) FACES, 123 W 115th St; 10026 212-283-9180 fax 212-283-9195 www.facesny.org ☯

♀ ☆ Fortune Society Health Services Unit, 625 W 140th St; 10031 212-690-6202 www.fortunesociety.org info@fortunesociety.org

♀ Gay Health Advocacy Project, Columbia University Health Clinic, 519 W 114th St Mail Code 3601; 212-854-2284 tinyurl.com/y4h9orgo

♂ ★ ⚥⚥ Gay Men's Health Crisis, 307 W 38th St; 212-367-1000 **H?** www.gmhc.org ↗

♀ ☆ ⚥⚥ Harlem United Community AIDS Center, Inc., 306 Malcolm X Blvd 3rd Fl; 10027 212-803-2850 www.harlemunited.org ☯ intake@harlemunited.org

♂ Hispanic AIDS Forum, 1767 Park Ave 5th Flr 212-563-4500 ✦

♂ HIV Law Project, 57 Willoughby St Flr 5, Bklyn 212-577-3001 www.hivlawproject.org

♀ Latino Commission on AIDS, 24 W 25th St Fl 9 212-675-3288 www.latinoaids.org ✦

♂ NYC AIDS Memorial, 76 Greenwich Ave nycaidsmemorial.org

♀ ☆ S.H.I.N.E. Project, Community Healthcare Network, 150 Essex St; 646-276-3383 www.chnnyc.org

♀ ☆ SMART/Smart University, East Harlem Neighborhood Health Action Center, 158 E 115th St; 10029 212-289-3900 www.smartuniversity.org info@smartuniversity.org

♀ Village Care of New York AIDS Treament Program, 121B W 20th St; 212-337-9220 tinyurl.com/h6pomv6

Queens

♀ ☆ AIDS Center of Queens County, 161-21 Jamaica Ave, Jamaica; 718-896-2500 www.acqc.org

♂ ☆ AIDS Center of Queens County Far Rockaway, 1600 Central Ave, Far Rockaway; 718-868-8645 www.acqc.org

♂ ☆ AIDS Center of Queens County LIC I, 62-07 Woodside Ave 3rd Flr, Woodside; 718-472-9400 www.acqc.org

Staten Island

♂ ★ ⚥⚥ Community Health Action of Staten Island, 56 Bay St 4th Flr, Staten Island; 718-808-1300 www.chasiny.org ↗

Archives/Libraries/Museums/History Projects

♥ ☆ ⚥⚥ Black Gay & Lesbian Archive, Schomburg Center for Research in Black Culture, New York Public Library, 515 Malcolm X Blvd; 212-491-2200 www.nypl.org/archives/4117 ✦↗

♥ ★ **Lesbian Herstory Archives/Lesbian Herstory Educational Foundation, Inc, 484 14th St, Bklyn 718-768-3953 Lesbian history and cultural resource center. Please check on line for info on how to contact or visit. www.lesbianherstoryarchives.org** ↗

♥ ★ Leslie-Lohman Museum of Art, 26 Wooster St 10013-2227 212-431-2609 www.leslielohman.org info@leslielohman.org

♥ ★ ⚥⚥ LGBT Community Center National History Archive, 208 W 13th St; 10011-7702 212-620-7310 x205 **H?** tinyurl.com/9eeye4 ✦ ↗ archive@gaycenter.org

♂ ☆ Museum of Sex, 233 5th Ave; (27th St) 212-689-6337 Www.museumofsex.com

♥ ★ Queery Librarians, www.queeryparty.org

Art & Photography (see also Graphic Design)

♂ ● David J. Martin Photography, 66 W 38th St 7K 10018 917-309-8638 www.davidjmartin.com photo@davidjmartin.com

---

Bars, Cafes, Clubs, Restaurants
Brooklyn: Bushwick

♥ Happyfun Hideaway, 1211 Myrtle Ave, Bklyn 917-999-9982 fb.com/HappyfunHideaway/

Brooklyn: Ditmas Park

♀ ○ Sycamore, 1118 Cortelyou Rd, Bklyn 347-240-5850 www.sycamorebrooklyn.com

Brooklyn: DUMBO

♀ ○ Superfine, 126 Front St, Bklyn; 718-243-9005 www.superfine.nyc ♈ ✕ iheartsuperfine@gmail.com

Brooklyn: Park Slope

♀ ○ ⚥⚥ The Bell House, 149 7th St, Bklyn; (Gowanus) 718-643-6510 **H?** www.thebellhouseny.com **KP** ♈ ✕ ▦ ↗

♀ ● Bogota Latin Bistro, 141 5th Ave, Bklyn 718-230-3805 www.BogotaBistro.com ♈ ✕

♥ ● Ginger's Bar, 363 5th Ave, Bklyn 718-788-0924 fb.com/Gingersbar/ **DK** ↗

Brooklyn: Prospect Hts

♀ ● ⚥⚥ Branded Saloon, 603 Vanderbilt Ave, Bklyn; 718-484-8704 www.brandedsaloon.com **KCWL** ♈ ✕ ▦ ↗

Brooklyn: Sunset Park

♥ Xstasy, 758 5th Ave, Bklyn; 718-499-2348 fb.com/clubxstasybk/ **D** ▦ ✦

Brooklyn: Williamsburg

♥ 3 Dollar Bill (3DB), 260 Meserole St, Bklyn; 718-366-3031 3dollarbillbk.com ▦

♥ Macri Park, 462 Union Ave, Bklyn 718-599-4999 www.macripark.com **D**

♥ ● Metropolitan, 559 Lorimer St, Bklyn 718-599-4444 www.metropolitanbarny.com ↗

♀ ○ Spectrum, at 3 Dollar Bill, 260 Meserole St, Bklyn; fb.com/TheSpectrumBk/ thespectrum6@gmail.com

Long Island: Bay Shore

♥ ● Long Island Eagle, 94 N Clinton Ave, Bay Shore; 631-968-2750 tinyurl.com/y5paa3eu **DKLV** ▦ ↗

♀ ○ Tula Kitchen, 41 E Main St, Bay Shore 631-539-7183 www.tulakitchen.com ✕

Long Island: Bohemia

♀ ○ Lizard Lounge, 4589 Sunrise Hwy, Bohemia 631-244-7300 fb.com/lizardloungeli/ **D**

Long Island: Fire Island: Cherry Grove

♀ ● (?⚥) Cherry Lane Restaurant, 158 Bayview Walk 631-597-7859 www.cherrysonthebay.com **D** ✕

♀ ● (?⚥) Cherry's on the Bay, 158 Bayview Walk 631-597-7859 www.cherrysonthebay.com **D** ▦

• Ice Palace, POB 4199, Sayville; 11782 631-597-6600 www.icepalacefi.com **D** ▦ ✕

○ Sandcastle, 106 Lewis Walk, Cherry Grove 631-597-4174 fireislandsandcastle.com ⅄ ✕

Long Island: Fire Island: Fire Island Pines

• Blue Whale Restaurant & Bar, Harbor Walk, Fl Pines; 631-597-6500 pinesfi.com/BlueWhale/ ⅄ ✕

• Pavilion Nightclub, 37 Fire Island Blvd, Fl Pines; 631-597-6500 pinesfi.com/Pavilion/

○ Sip-n-Twirl / Pines Bistro / Pines Pizza, 36 Fire Island Blvd, Fl Pines; 631-597-3599 pinesfi.com/SipnTwirl/

Long Island: Hauppauge

M Lounge, check schedule 631-436-7330 tinyurl.com/ay8y6o9

Long Island: Sayville

○ La Tavola Trattoria, 183 W Main St, Sayville; 631-750-6900 www.latavolasayville.com ⅄ ✕ ✕

Long Island: South Farmingdale

• NuBar: Booze & Bites, 47 Boundary Ave, S Farmingdale; 516-694-6906 www.nubarli.com **D** ▦

Manhattan & Citywide

• Alegria, www.alegriaevents.com

A Different Kind of Ladies' Night, tinyurl.com/j58dhs9

• girlNATIONnyc, check for details www.girlnation-nyc.com ⅄ ✕ girlnationnyc1@aol.com

• Habibi, Monthly party for gay Middle Eastern Men 646-431-5369 www.habibinyc.com ✎

• Lovergirl, Sat, check details 212-252-3397 www.lover-girlnyc.com **D** ✪

Sholay Productions, 212-713-5111 www.sholayevents.com ✎

Manhattan: Chelsea

• Barracuda, 275 W 22nd St; (8th Ave) 212-645-8613 fb.com/BarracudaLounge/ ▦

• Boxers Chelsea, 37 W 20th St 212-255-5082 www.boxersnyc.com **S** ✕

• The Eagle, 554 W 28th St; 646-473-1866 www.eaglenyc.com **LW**

• The Gym Sportsbar, 167 8th Ave; 212-337-2439 www.gymsportsbar.com **S**

Rebar, 225 W 19th St; 646-863-2914 www.rebarchelsea.com

○ Restivo Ristorante, 209 7th Ave; (22nd St) 212-366-4133 www.restivorestaurant.com

Manhattan: East Side

• Adonis Lounge, Evolve. 221 E 58th St; / Wed & Sat 845-536-3323 Strippers theadonislounge.com/nyc/ ▦

• Boxers UES, 1664 3rd Ave 212-255-5082 www.boxersnyc.com **S** ✕

• Brandy's Piano Bar, 235 E 84th St; (2nd/3rd Ave) 212-744-4949 www.brandyspianobar.com ▦

Evolve, 221 E 58th St; 212-355-3395 evolvebarandloungenyc.com ▦

○ Lips Restaurant, 227 E 56th St 212-675-7710 Drag dining www.lipsnyc.com ⅄ ✕▦

• The Tool Box, 1742 2nd Ave; (91st St) 212-348-1288 www.thetoolboxnyc.com

The Townhouse, 236 E 58th; 212-754-4649 www.townhouseny.com ⅄ ✕ ▦

• Uncle Charlie's Piano Bar & Lounge, 139 E 45th St Flr 2; 646-476-9532 www.unclecharliesnyc.com ▦

Manhattan: East Village & Lower East Side

○ Bedlam, 40 Ave C; 646-870-0150 www.bedlamnyc.com

• Big Gay Ice Cream, 125 E 7th St www.biggayicecream.com ⭧

• The Boiler Room, 86 E 4th St 212-254-7536 fb.com/boilerroomnyc/ ✕

(♿) Club Cumming, 505 E 6th St; (Ave A) 917-265-8006 **H?** clubcummingnyc.com **D** ▦

• The Cock, 93 2nd Ave www.thecockbar.com **D**

• Nowhere, 322 E 14th St; (1st Ave) 212-477-4744 www.nowherebarnyc.com

Phoenix, 447 E 13th St; (Ave A) 212-477-9979 www.phoenixbarnyc.com

Manhattan: Harlem

• Alibi, 2376 Adam Clayton Powell 917-472-7789 fb.com/alibi-harlem ✚

• Bsquared Harlem, 271 W 119th St; 212-280-2248 www.b2harlem.com **KP** ⅄ ✕▦ info@b2harlem.com

Manhattan: Hell's Kitchen

• 44 & X Hell's Kitchen, 622 10th Ave; (44th) 212-977-1170 www.44andX.com ✕

• 9th Avenue Saloon, 656 9th Ave; (46th St) 212-307-1503 fb.com/9thAveSaloon

Atlas Social Club, 753 9th Ave; 212-262-8527 www.atlassocialclub.Com

• Barrage, 401 W 47th St; (9th Ave) 212-586-9390 fb.com/barrage.bar/

Bottoms Up & Vodka Soda, 315 W 46th St 212-969-0460 fb.com/vodkasodabottomsuphk/ ⅄ ✕▦

• Boxers HK, 742 9th Ave 212-951-1518 www.boxersnyc.com **S** ✕

Flaming Saddles, 793 9th Ave; 212-713-0481 www.flamingsaddles.com **CW**

Hardware, 697 10th Ave; 212-924-9885 www.hardware-bar.com

• Industry, 355 W 52nd St 646-476-2747 www.industrybar.com **V** ▦

○ Lucky Cheng's, 605 W 48th St 212-995-5500 Drag cabaret Shows www.luckychengs.com **D** ⅄ ✕▦ ✧✕ info@luckychengs.com

• Posh, 405 W 51st St; (9th Ave) 212-957-2222 www.poshbarnyc.com **D** ▦ ✕

Rise Bar, 859 9th Ave; 646-892-3313 fb.com/risebarnyc/ ▦

New York: New York City & Long Island Area
Bars, Cafes, Clubs, Restaurants
249
GAYELLOW PAGES #42 2020-2021
New York City & Long Island Area : New York
Bookstores

● The Ritz, 369 W 46th St; 212-333-4177 ritzbarandlounge.com
D

Manhattan: Midtown

○ Bann, 350 W 50th St; 212-582-4446 Korean www.bannrestaurant.com ✕

○ (♂♀) Don't Tell Mama, 343 W 46th St (8th/9th Ave) 212-757-0788 donttellmamanyc.com ♈ ✕ info@donttellmamanyc.com

● ♿ Therapy, 348 W 52nd St; (8th/9th Aves) 212-397-1700 www.therapy-nyc.com **D** ♈ ♐ ✕ ✎

Manhattan: Tribeca

Gentlemen's Club Haus, 285 W Broadway; / Sun 7pm-1am 212-625-4287 fb.com/Gentlemensclubhaus

Manhattan: West Side

○ Suite, 992 Amsterdam Ave; (109th St) 212-222-4600 www.suitenyc.com

Manhattan: West Village

● Big Gay Ice Cream, 61 Grove St www.biggayicecream.com ☞

● Cubby Hole, 281 W 12th St (at 4th St) 212-243-9041 www.cubbyholebar.com

○ The Duplex, 61 Christopher St; (7th Ave) 212-255-5438 www.theduplex.com **V** ✕ ♈ ✎

The Hangar, 115 Christopher St; (Bleecker St) 212-627-2044 fb.com/TheHangarBarNYC/

● ♿ Henrietta Hudson, 438 Hudson St; (Morton St) 212-924-3347 www.henriettahudson.com ✎

● Julius, 159 W 10th St; (Waverly) 877-746-0528 www.juliusbarnyc.com

○ ♿ Marie's Crisis, 59 Grove St (7th Ave) 212-243-9323 tinyurl.com/y4j2nrka

● The Monster, 80 Grove St; (Sheridan Sq) 212-924-3558 monsterbarnyc.com **D**

○ (♂♀) Philip Marie, 569 Hudson St; (W 11th) 212-242-6200 philipmarie.com ✕ ♢

● ♿ Pieces, 8 Christopher St 212-929-9291 www.piecesbar.com **K** ♈ ✕

Playhouse Bar, 100 7th Ave; 212-427-2567 www.playhousebar.com **D**

● Rockbar NYC, 185 Christopher St; 212-675-1864 rockbarnyc.com **L**

● The Stonewall Inn, 53 Christopher St 212-488-2705 www.thestonewallinnnyc.com

● Ty's, 114 Christopher St; (Bleecker/Hudson Sts) 212-741-9641 www.tys.nyc @ixx=

● Pure Silk Productions, 516-474-1707 tinyurl.com/yybnvdk2 puresilkproductions@gmail.com

Queens: Astoria

Albatross, 3619 24th Ave, Astoria 718-204-9707 www.albatrossastoria.com **K**

Icon, 31-84 33rd St, Astoria; 917-832-6364 www.iconastoria.com **D**

Queens: Elmhurst

Music Box, 4008 74th St, Elmhurst (Broadway) 718-424-8612 ✦

Queens: Jackson Heights

● Friends Tavern, 7811 Roosevelt Ave, Jackson Hts; (78th St) 718-397-7256 fb.com/friendstavern ✦

Hombres Lounge, 8525 37th Ave, Jackson Hts 718-930-0886 www.hombreslounge.com

True Colors, 79-15 Roosevelt Ave, Jackson Hts; 718-672-7505 fb.com/truecolorsbarNY/ **DK** ✦

Queens: Ridgewood

● The Deep End, 1080 Wyckoff Ave, Ridgewood 347-689-4996 www.thedeepend.nyc ♈ ✕ @ixx=

Queens

Kings Tapas Bar, 7004 Roosevelt Ave, Woodside; 917-745-0040 www.kingsnewyork.com ♈ ✕

Staten Island

○ ♿ Every Thing Goes Book Cafe and Neighborhood Stage, 208 Bay St, Staten Island; 718-447-8256 www.etgstores.com/bookcafe/ ✎

○ Flagship Brewing Co., 40 Minthorne St, Staten Island; 718-448-5284 www.theflagshipbrewery.com

---

Bookstores
Brooklyn

○ ♿ Books Are Magic, 225 Smith St, Bklyn; 11231 718-246-2665 **H?** www.booksaremagic.net hello@booksaremagic.net

○ ♿ Community Bookstore, 143 7th Ave, Bklyn; (Park Slope) 718-783-3075 www.communitybookstore.net

● ♿ Quimby's Bookstore NYC, 536 Metropolitan Ave, Bklyn; 11211 347-889-5569 fb.com/quimbysnyc ✎

○ ♿ Spoonbill & Sugartown, Booksellers, 218 Bedford Ave, Bklyn; 718-387-7322 www.spoonbillbooks.com

● WORD, 126 Franklin St, Bklyn; 718-383-0096 www.wordbookstores.com

Manhattan

● ♿ Bluestockings Bookstore & Activist Center, 172 Allen St; (Rivington & Stanton St) 212-777-6028 bluestockings.com ☞

○ Bookbook, 266 Bleecker St; 212-807-8655 www.bookbooknyc.com

● ♿ **Bureau of General Services-Queer Division, LGBT Community Center, 208 W 13th St Rm 210 10011-7702 646-457-0859 H? Tue-Sun 1-7pm www.bgsqd.com contact@bgsqd.com**

○ (♂♀) McNally Jackson Booksellers, 52 Prince St; 212-274-1160 www.mcnallyjackson.com ☞ ✎

○ Three Lives & Company, 154 W 10th St 212-741-2069 www.threelives.com

Queens

● ♿ Astoria Bookshop, 31-29 31st Street, Astoria; 718-278-2665 www.astoriabookshop.com

Broadcast Media

♂ ★ Out FM Collective, c/o WBAI 99.5 FM, 388 Atlantic Ave 3th Flr, Bklyn; 917-653-7267 www.outfm.org ✪

Coaching: Career, Life, Relationship etc
Manhattan

♂ ● (♂♀) Schall, Mark, MA, PCC, ELI-MP, Life Coaching 646-201-5318 www.markschall.com mark@markschall.com

Counseling/Psychotherapy/Mental Health
Brooklyn

♀ ○ Ben-Israel, Ady, PhD, 44 Court St, Bklyn; 11201 347-788-1636 www.adybenisrael.com AdyBenIsrael@gmail.com

♀ ● Geier, Patti, LCSW, Park Slope 347-262-0905 www.pattigeier.com

♀ ○ ㅿㅿ Gottlieb, Andrew R, PhD, 26 Court St Ste 2207, Bklyn; 11242 718-624-0263 347-451-5715 www.andrewrgottlieb.com agott116@aol.com

T ○ **Juran, Shelley, PhD, 163 Clinton St, Brooklyn Heights 718-625-6526 Specialist in sexual orientation & gender-identity. Non-sexist. Gay & transgender individuals & couples welcome. www.brooklyntherapist.org**

♀ ● ㅿㅿ Ortega Psychology PLLC, 16 Court St Ste 2405, Bklyn; 11241 347-689-9914 347-450-4356 www.drtonyortega.com drorteganyc@gmail.com

♀ ○ ㅿㅿ Pech, Sidney, CSW, 2626 E 14th St, Bklyn; 11235 718-715-6666

♀ ★ ㅿㅿ Rainbow Heights Club, 25 Flatbush Ave Flr 3, Bklyn; 718-852-2584 **H?** www.rainbowheights.org

♀ ★ ㅿㅿ Rainbow Heights Club, Community Advisory Board, 25 Flatbush Ave 3rd Flr, Bklyn; 718-852-2584 LGBT people living with mental illness www.rainbowheights.org

♂ ● Goldstein, Nancy R, LCSW, 12 Deering St, E Setauket; 11733 631-941-4704 www.nancygoldstein.net ✉ nancygoldstein1@gmail.com

Long Island

♂ ● Dyer, Theresa M, LCSW-R, 137 Bay Ave, Patchogue; 11772 631 553-5212 tmdlcsw@gmail.com

♀ ● ㅿㅿ Heart & Soul Counseling, 17 Fordham Rd, W Babylon; 11704-5803 / 1400 Wantagh Ave Wantagh NY 631-321-7011 fax 631-669-8532 www.heartandsoulcenter.com heartsoul@att.net

♂ ○ ㅿㅿ Kranenberg, Laura Ann, LCSW, 2175 Wantagh Ave, Wantagh; 11793 516-319-7896 Laurakranenberglcsw.com laura@laurakranenberglcsw.com

♂ ○ Shapiro, Joan E, LCSW, BCD, 177 Main St #207, Huntington; / 153 Main St, Roslyn 631-271-4037 www.talkpsychotherapy.com

♂ ○ ㅿㅿ Sunrise Counseling Center, 107 W Main St, E Islip; 11730 631-666-1615 fax 631-666-1709 tinyurl.com/23aarr info@sunrisecounselingcenter.com

Manhattan

♀ ● ㅿㅿ Cipriani, Maria, LCSW, 19 W 34th St, PH and in Kings Park, LI 212-594-4659 www.mariacipriani.com maria.cipriani@gmail.com

♀ ● (♂♀) Davies, Ann C., LCSW, 740 West End Ave Ste 1 (96 & WEA) 917-923-2257

♀ ● ㅿㅿ Evans, Mark J, PhD, 1430 Broadway #304; 917-747-6591 www.drmjevans.com ✉

♂ ○ Frank, Michele, LCSW-R, 19 W 34th St #PH; 10001 212-947-7111 x255 www.MicheleFrank.com helper50@gmail.com

♀ ○ Frankel, Susan, LCSW, BCD, CGP, 365 West End Ave 11J; 10024 212-866-5756 tinyurl.com/ydmzkav susanif@verizon.net

♀ ● ㅿ Friedrich, Robert A, LCSW, SEP, 245 W 29th St Ste 304; 10001 917-940-1007 ✉

♀ GLBTQ Counseling Unit, Jewish Board of Family & Children's Services, 135 W 50th St; 212-632-4482 tinyurl.com/y86jw2pr

♂ ● (♂♀) **Gringorten, Judith, LCSW, ACSW, CGP, Psychotherapy and Training Collective of New York, 853 Broadway Ste 1608 10003 845-709-1939 Individual, Couples, Family, Group (short & long-term) www.psychotherapistsnyc.com judithgringorten@gmail.com**

♀ ● ㅿㅿ Horowitz, Richard, CSW, CAC, 31 Washington Square W PH-E; 10011 212-780-9400 www.richardthetherapist.com

♀ ★ ㅿㅿ Identity House, POB 829 10156 212-243-8181 www.identityhouse.org

♀ ★ ㅿㅿ The IHI Therapy Center, 322 8th Ave Ste 802 212-243-2830 www.ihitherapy.org

♀ ○ Jarratt, Kent D., LCSW, 928 Broadway Ste 1200 10010 917-686-6179 Hypnotherapy www.kentjarratt.com kentjar@aol.com

♀ ● ㅿㅿ Kaplan, Ami B, LCSW, 113 University Place Ste #1008; 10003 212-358-1884 www.amikaplan.net info@amikaplan.net

♀ ○ ㅿㅿ Kassan, Lee D., MA, 240 Madison Ave Ste 10J; 10016 212-687-2059 www.leekassan.com

♀ ○ (♂♀) Kuhn, Andrew E, PhD Psychologist, 5 E 94th St; 10128 212-480-2426 andrewkuhnphd.com ✉ aek@andrewkuhnphd.com

♀ ● Manhattan Psychotherapy, Upper West Side 212-724-8767 call 10am-noon tinyurl.com/y5sydack

♀ ● Mayer, Eliezer R, PsyD, 26 W 9th St; 10011 212-242-2219 www.drelimayer.com ✉ elimayerpsyd@gmail.com

♀ ☆ Mitteldorf, Darryl, LCSW, The LGBT Cancer Project, Inc, 85 Delancey St #39; 212-673-4920 www.lgbtcancer.com

♀ ○ ㅿㅿ **Nelke, Carl, MA, LCSW, LLC, 200 W 60th St #32C; 10023 212-989-7303 Convenient midtown west location. www.carlnelkelcsw.com**

♂ ○ New York Psychotherapy Network, 113 University Place #1008; 10003-4527 347-708-6972 www.ny-psychotherapy.com contact@ny-psychotherapy.com

♀ ● ㅿㅿ Ortman, Jeremy, LMHC, 49 W 24th St; 10010 646-707-2224 www.jeremyortman.com ✉ jeremyportman@gmail.com

♀ ★ The Paul Rosenfels Community, 151 1st Ave #200; www.rosenfels.org

♀ ★ ㅿㅿ The PCGS (Psychotherapy Center for Gender and Sexuality), 33 W 60th St Flr 4; 10023 212-333-3444 **H?** icp-nyc.org/pcgs ✉ pcgs@icpnyc.org

♀ ● ㅿㅿ Prottas, Gary M, LCSW-R, LP, 20 W 20 St Room 239; 10011-3649 212-645-1152 www.garymprottas.com ✉ gmprottas@nyc.rr.com

♀ ● Saint-Laurent, Roger, PsyD, CGP, SEP, 917-716-1057 via video in tri-state area www.drsaintlaurent.com RstIpsyd@aol.com

⚥ ● Sherman, Eric, LCSW, 30 Greenwich Ave #GFB 10011 973-797-9244 tinyurl.com/yahm8ag4

♀ ● Singer, Michael C, PhD, 365 W End Ave Ste 1B 10024 917-689-1746 tinyurl.com/ljnmfx8 drmichaelsinger@gmail.com

♀ ○ Tallent, Marc A, PhD, 51 Fifth Ave Ste B; 10003 212-645-5795 tinyurl.com/2cnel34 mat1@pipeline.com

⚥ ● Voorhees, Ken, LCSW, Chelsea location 347-831-1799 www.kenvoorhees.com

♀ ● Wind, Mark N., PhD, MSC, CASAC, MAC, CH, 10 W 15th St #609; 10011-6821 212-929-4390 alcohol & other addictions. wind@nyct.net

♀ ● ⚕ Yonkin, David, LCSW-R WPATH GEI Certified, 211 W 56th St Ste 30-G; 10019 917-842-2655 www.davidyonkin.com davidyonkin@aol.com

Counseling/Psychiatry
Long Island

♀ ● ⚕⚕ Rubinstein, Joan, MD, 60 N Country Rd Ste 104, Port Jefferson; 11777-2188 631-331-0974 joan.rubinstein27@gmail.com

Manhattan

♂ ○ Merlino, Joseph P, MD, 205 E 78th St; 10075 Drjoseph merlino@gmail.com

⚥ ● ⚕ Pearl, Alan, MD, 135 W 70th St; 212-724-5188 @ixx=

Dentists
Manhattan

♂ ○ Cauntiz, Beth, DDS, 30 E 40th St Ste 406; 10016 212-206-9002 www.bethcaunitzdds.com caunitzdds@gmail.com

⚥ ● ⚕⚕ DeBonis, William B, DDS, World Wide Plaza Dental Associates, 370 W 50th St; 212-333-2650 www.wwpdental.com ↗

♀ ● ⚕⚕ Krochak, Michael, DMD, 30 E 60th St #1201; 10022 212-838-2900 www.nycsmilespa.com ↗ drk@nycsmilespa.com

Erotica / Adult Stores / Safe Sex Supplies
Manhattan

⚥ ● **Les Hommes, 217B W 80th St Flr 2; 10024-7002 212-580-2445 fb.com/LesHommesPrime/**

Financial Planning, Investment (see also Insurance)

♂ ● Third Eye Associates, Ltd, 745 Fifth Ave Ste 500; 10151 212-787-4292 www.thirdeyeassociates.com

Funding: Endowment, Fundraising

⚥ ● ⚕⚕ ASTRAEA Lesbian Foundation for Justice, 116 E 16th St 7th flr; 212-529-8021 www.astraeafoundation.org ✤

⚥ ★ ⚕ Bee's Fund, Stonewall Community Foundation, 1270 Broadway Ste 501; 212-457-1341 **H?** Small grants for LBT women discarded by their families. tinyurl.com/yxcnccom ↗

♂ Broadway Cares/Equity Fights AIDS, 165 W 46th St #1300; 212-840-0770 www.broadwaycares.org

⚥ ★ Broadway Sings for Pride, tinyurl.com/ntob9j3

⚥ ★ Cheer New York, www.cheernewyork.org

⚥ Colin Higgins Foundation, c/o Tides, 55 Exchange Place Ste #402; 212-509-1052 www.colinhiggins.org

♂ ☆ (?⚕) Cycle for the Cause, LGBT Community Center, 208 W 13th St; 212-620-7310 **H?** www.cycleforthecause.org ↗

♀ ☆ DIFFA (Design Industries Foundation Fighting AIDS), 16 W 32nd St Ste 402; 212-727-3100 www.diffa.org

⚥ Folsom Street East, POB 1695; 10113 www.folsomstreeteast.org

⚥ ★ The Imperial Court of NY, Inc, 208 W 13th St; 212-533-4797 www.icny.org

Long Island

♂ ☆ 5K AIDS / Cancer Run Walk, Richard M. Brodsky Foundation, 1247 Mara Court, Atlantic Bch; 11509-1635 516-770-7724 www.5kaidscancer.com RichardM.Brodsky@gmail.com

⚥ ★ Auntie M's Helping Hands, POB 332, Massapequa Park; 11762 631-610-5620 tinyurl.com/yc2f777f

⚥ ★ New York Gay Pool League, 554 W 28th St 212-496-4585 www.nygpl.org

⚥ ★ **North Fork Women For Women Fund, Inc., POB 804, Greenport; 11944-0924 631-477-8464 Helping lesbians on the North Fork for over 25 years. www.nfwfwf.org**

⚥ ★ ⚕⚕ Stonewall Community Foundation, 1270 Broadway Ste 501; 212-457-1341 **H?** www.stonewallfoundation.org

Gardening/Landscaping Services & Supplies

♂ ● Gardens by Robert, 134 W 95th St Apt #1 10025-6600 917-499-2413 gardensby.roberturban.com themusenyc@aol.com

♂ ● Gardens by Robert, 917-499-2413 www.gardensby.roberturban.com themusenyc@aol.com

Health Care: Physical (see also Counseling/Mental Health)
Brooklyn

♀ Caribbean Women's Health Association, 3512 Church Ave, Bklyn; 718-826-2942 www.cwha.org ✤

Manhattan

⚥ ★ APICHA Community Health Center, 400 Broadway; 866-274-2429 www.apicha.org ◈

♂ ○ ⚕⚕ Brauner, Gary J., MD, 1317 3rd Ave; 212-421-5080

⚥ ★ ⚕⚕ Callen-Lorde Community Health Center, 356 W 18th St; (8th/9th Aves) 212-271-7200 www.callen-lorde.org

♂ ○ ⚕⚕ Cole, Curtis L, MD, Weill Cornell Internal Medicine Associates, 505 E 70th St HT4; 10021 212-746-0483 tinyurl.com/4522gx2

♀ Greenberg, Elizabeth, DC, 89 5th Ave #604; 10003 212-627-2660

♂ ○ Physical Exam NYC, 1550 York Ave; 212-960-8643 www.physicalexamnyc.com

♂ ● Repetto, Vittoria, DC, 230 W 13th St; 10011 212-431-3724 www.drvittoriarepetto.com DrVittoriaRepett@aol.com

Queens

⚥ ★ APICHA Community Health Center, 400 Broadway; 866-274-2429 www.apicha.org ◈

Homes & Buildings: Cleaning, Maintenance, Repair, General Contractors

♂ ● Paul's Apt Cleaning, 475 W 57th St #9A2; 10019 / NYC & NJ 212-967-8240 www.paulscleaningnyc.com Redcleaningguy@gmail.com

New York: New York City & Long Island Area
252
New York City & Long Island Area : New York
Insurance
GAYELLOW PAGES #42 2020-2021
Organizations: Bisexual

Insurance (see also Financial Planning)

♀ ○ Swicker, Bruce R, Frenkel & Company, 350 Hudson St 4th Flr; 212-764-6740

Interior Design/Home Decor, Furnishings, Accessories

♀ ● Delphinium Home, 353 W 47th St; 10036 212-333-7732 Gifts for the home. www.delphiniumhome.com Delphiniumhome@gmail.com

Leather Resources & Groups
Long Island

♀ ○ ♂ Adam & Gillian's Sensual Whips & Toys, 40 Grant Ave, Copiague; 11726-3817 631-842-1711 www.aswgt.com siradam@ix.netcom.com

♂ ★ Long Island Ravens M.C., POB 220, Brightwaters; 11718 www.liravensmc.org **L**

Legal Services
Brooklyn

♀ ○ Silver, Jacob, 26 Court St Ste 1201, Bklyn 718-855-3434 Bankruptcy www.silverbankruptcy.com

Huntington

♀ ○ ♿ Law Office of Louis L Sternberg, Esq., 775 Park Ave Ste 356, Huntington; 631-600-3295 www.SuffolkDivorceLawyer.com

♂ ★ ♿ Lambda Legal Defense & Education Fund (LLDEF), Inc, 120 Wall St #1500, New York, NY 212-809-8585 www.lambdalegal.org

Long Island

♀ ○ ♿ Law Offices of Alan J Schwartz, PC, 1050 Franklin AveSte 404, Garden City; 516-248-6311 www.ajslaw.com

♀ ○ ♿ Margiotta, Paul J, Esq, The Margiotta Law Firm, P.C. 85 E Main St; Ste R, Bay Shore; 11706 631-968-9494 www.margiottalaw.com

♀ ● ♿ Milizio, Joseph G, Vishnick McGovern Milizio LLP, 3000 Marcus Ave Ste 1E9, Lake Success; 11042 516-437-4385 www.vmmlegal.com ✎ jmilizio@vmmlegal.com

Manhattan & Citywide

♂ ★ LGBTQ Law Project at NYLAG, 7 Hanover Pl Flr 18; 212-613-5000 www.nylag.org/lgbtq-law

Manhattan

♀ ● ♿ Antollino, Gregory, 275 Seventh Ave Ste 705; 10001 212-334-7398 **HC** Discrimination & civil rights cases www.antollino.com ✎

♀ ○ ♿ Bukh Law Firm P.C., 14 Wall St 212-729-1632 www.nyccriminallawyer.com

♀ ○ DeLaurentis, Brian M., 36 W 44th St #911 10036-8105 212-354-6300 www.DeLaurentisLaw.com

♀ ☆ ♿ Legal Action Center, 225 Varick St; 212-243-1313 www.lac.org

♀ ★ LeGaL: LGBT Bar Association of Greater New York, 212-353-9118 www.lgbtbarny.org info@le-gal.org

♀ ○ Ross, Maurice, Partner, Barton LLP, 711 Third Ave 14 Flr; 10017 212-885-8845 212-687-6262 www.bartonesq.com mross@bartonesq.com

♀ ● ♿ Sommer, Kenneth A., Esq, 100 W 31st St #45L; 10001 212-967-5383

T ☆ ♿ Sylvia Rivera Law Project, 147 W 24th St 5th Flr; 10001 212-337-8550 **H?** www.srlp.org 212-337-8550

⚥ ● ♿ Tesler, Richard E., Esq., 41 W 72nd St Lobby Ste F; 10023-3413 212-362-6961 Real Estate, Wills, Medical Malpractice. "At-home or off-hour appointments easily made."

Queens

♀ ○ ♿ Srulowitz, Marvin, Esq, 107-19 70th Ave #505, Forest Hills; 11375 917-783-1891 ✎ marvinlaw@aol.com

Mailing Lists

⚥ ● **Gayellow Pages Mailing Lists, POB 533 Village Stn; 10014-0533 646-213-0263 v/f Contents of Gayellow Pages on mailing lists, constantly updated. (NOT a list of individual buyers!) gayellowpages.com/mailing.htm** ✎ ♥ **gypages@gmail.com**

Massage Therapy (Certified/Licensed only)

♀ ● Elchert, Kenn Maxwell, LMT, 208 W 23rd St; 10011 917-449-8859 www.deepmassagenyc.com ✎ kenn@deepmassagenyc.com

Meeting/Dating/Introduction/Relationships

♂ ● ManMate & ManMate Dinners for 8, 1501 Broadway 12th Flr; 10023 212-564-4025 www.manmate.com grant@manmate.com

Men's & Sex Clubs (not primarily Health Clubs)
Manhattan

♂ ● East Side Club, 227 E 56th St; 212-753-2222 www.eastsideclubnyc.com **P**

♂ ● West Side Club, 27 W 20th St, 2nd floor 212-691-2700 www.westsideclubnyc.com

Queens

♂ ● ♿ Northern Men's Sauna & Health Club, 33-61 Farrington St, Flushing; 718-445-9775

Moving/Transportation/Storage

♀ ○ **All Star Moving & Storage, 2525 Tilden Ave c, Bklyn; 11226 718-643-4705 NY DOT #12364, US DOT #515137 Serving the 5 Boroughs and surrounding areas for over 25 years! www.allstarnewyork.com**

Music Lessons

♀ ● Robert Urban/Urban Productions, 134 W 95th St Apt #1; 10025-6600 917-499-2413 www.roberturban.com themusenyc@aol.com

Optometrists, Opticians
Long Island

♀ ○ Singer, Arthur, Optic Masters, 8025 Jericho Tpk, Woodbury; 11797 516-364-7474 www.opticmasters.com opticmasters@aol.com

Organizations/Resources: Bisexual Focus

⚥ ★ (?⚢) Bi-Perspective, LGBT Community Center, 208 W 13th St; 908-469-0966 **H?** www.nyabn.org/BiPerspective/ ✎

⚥ ☆ (?⚢) BiRequest, LGBT Community Center, 208 W 13th St; 212-620-7310 **H?** www.birequest.org ✎

♀ ☆ New York Area Bisexual Network, POB 497 Times Square Stn; 10108 212-459-4784 www.nyabn.org

Organizations/Resources: Business & Professional Associations, Labor Advocacy

♀ ★ Brookhaven National Laboratory LGBT Employees Club, POB 5000, Upton; 11973-5000 tinyurl.com/7vx7el

♀ ★ Citibank Pride Network - NYC, 111 Wall St 6th Flr; 800-285-3000 tinyurl.com/y8nbg4h8

♀ Citibank Pride Network - NYC, 111 Wall St 6th Flr

♀ ★ (?⚲) FireFLAG/EMS, LGBT Community Center, 208 W 13th St; 917-885-0127 **H?** fb.com/fireflag.ems ✎

♀ ★ ᕫᕫ Gay Officers Action League (GOAL), POB 1774 Old Chelsea Stn; 10113 212-691-4625 www.goalny.org

♀ GLBT at McKinsey (GLAM), 55 E 52nd St

♀ ★ National Association of Social Workers - NY LGBT Committee, 305 Seventh Ave #13A; 212-668-0050 naswnyc.org

♀ ★ National Lesbian & Gay Journalists Association/New York Area, fb.com/groups/NLGJA.NY/

♀ New York LGBT & Allied Business Network - nglccNY, 340 E 42nd St #841; 646-964-5027 www.nglccny.org

♀ ★ ᕫᕫ Out Professionals, 332 Bleecker St PMB #G16; www.outprofessionals.org

♀ ★ Publishing Triangle, 511 Ave of the Americas #D36; 10011 www.publishingtriangle.org

♀ ★ ᕫᕫ Village Playwrights, 614-285-2515 tinyurl.com/a9rgxe villageplaywrights@gmail.com

Organizations/Resources: Cultural, Dance, Performance

♂ ☆ Arthur Aviles Typical Theatre, c/o BAAD, 2474 Westchester Ave, Bronx; 718-918-2110

♀ ★ ♂ Big Apple Ranch, check for location Dancing 2nd & 4th Sats www.bigappleranch.com ranch@bigappleranch.com

♂ ☆ Cinekink, 1092 St Georges Ave #190, Rahway, NJ 07065 www.cinekink.com

♀ ★ ᕫᕫ Empire City Men's Chorus, POB 1017; 10185 212-545-4110 **H?** www.empirecitymenschorus.org

♀ ★ ᕫᕫ Fresh Fruit Festival of LGBTQ Arts & Culture, various venues www.freshfruitfestival.com ✎

♀ ★ ᕫᕫ Lavender Light Gospel Choir, 70-A Greenwich Ave #315; 212-714-7072 www.lavenderlight.com ✪

♀ ★ Lesbian & Gay Big Apple Corps Marching & Symphonic Band, 511 6th Ave, #K48; 10011 212-591-2886 www.lgbac.org info@lgbac.org

Long Island

♀ ★ The Long Island Gay & Lesbian Film Festival, POB 360, E Northport; 11731 516-316-2266 www.liglff.org

♂ ★ Long Island Gay Men's Chorus, POB 6, Selden 11784 www.ligmc.org

♀ ★ (?⚲) Long Island Pride Chorus, Rehearsals: Huntington 516-804-8766 www.lipridechorus.org info@lipridechorus.org

♀ ★ (?⚲) MIX: New York Queer Experimental Film Festival, 1022 Wyckoff Ave, Ridgewood; 212-742-8880 www.mixnyc.org

♂ ★ ᕫᕫ New York City Gay Men's Chorus, 561 7th Ave #803; 212-344-1777 **HS** www.nycgmc.org

♀ ★ (?⚲) NewFest, 601 W 26th St Ste 325-95; www.newfest.org

♀ ★ ᕫᕫ Queer Urban Orchestra (QUO), POB 438 Radio City Stn; 10101 646-233-4113 www.queerurbanorchestra.org

♂ ● Robert Urban/Urban Productions, 134 W 95th St Apt #1; 10025-6600 917-499-2413 www.roberturban.com themusenyc@aol.com

♀ ★ ᕫᕫ **The Stonewall Chorale, POB 920; 10113 The nation's first Lesbian and Gay chorus. www.stonewall-chorale.org**

♀ ★ (?⚲) The Times Squares Square Dance Club, POB 1229 Ansonia Stn; 10023 212-749-4291 fb.com/timessquaresclub **DCW**

♀ ★ (?⚲) Village Contra Gender-Free Dance, LGBT Community Center, 208 W 13th St; 718-972-3191 **H?** www.lcfd.org/nyc ✎

♀ ★ (?⚲) WOW Cafe Theatre, 59 E 4th St #4W; 917-725-1482 **H?** www.wowcafe.org ✎

Organizations/Resources: Differently Abled (see also Blind, Deaf)

♂ ☆ ᕫᕫ DIA: Disabled In Action of Metropolitan New York, POB 30954; 10011 917-733-3794 www.disabledinaction.org

Organizations/Resources: Education

♀ ★ ♂ GLAAD, 104 W 29th St 4th Flr 800-429-6334 www.glaad.org

Organizations/Resources: Ethnic, Multicultural

♀ ★ (?⚲) African Ancestral Lesbians United for Societal Change, Inc., LGBT Community Center, 208 W 13th St 475-422-5872 **H?** fb.com/AALUSC1974 ✤ ✎

♀ ★ (?⚲) Armenian Gay & Lesbian Association, **H?** www.aglany.org ✎

♀ ★ ᕫᕫ The Barbershop, c/o GMHC, 307 W 38th St; 10018-9502 212-367-1388 **H?** tinyurl.com/wdg6tly ✤ ✎ durellk@gmhc.org

♀ ★ Black & Latino LGBTQ Coalition, 55 W 116th St Ste 236; 10026 212-457-8954 bllgbtqc.org info@bllgbtqc.org

♀ ★ Caribbean American PRIDE, fb.com/caribameripride ✤

♀ Caribbean Equality Project, 347-709-3179 tinyurl.com/ya4y42ka ✤

♀ ★ Chutney Pride (Caribbean), 347-869-2601 fb.com/chutneypridelgbt ✤

♀ ★ ᕫᕫ Gay Asian/Pacific Islander Men of NY (GAPIMNY), POB 1608; 10113 www.gapimny.org ✦

♀ ★ ᕫᕫ Gay Men of African Descent, Inc., 540 Atlantic Ave - Lower Level, Bklyn; 718-222-5555 www.gmad.org ✤

♀ (?⚲) Irish Queers, 212-289-1101 **H?** irishqueers.blogspot.com ✎

♀ ★ (?⚲) Italian Conversation Group, LGBT Community Center, 208 W 13th St; 10011-7702 212-772-3511 **H?** ✎

♂ ★ **Jacks of Color, 212-222-9794 NYC's Pre-Eminent Safer Sex Club for Gay Men Of Color 'And Their Friends'. www.JacksOfColor.com** ✤

♀ ★ Puerto Rican Initiative to Develop Empowerment (PRIDE), 24 W 25th St Flr 9; 212-675-3288 x469 www.prideny.org ◆

♀ ★ Q-Wave, POB 1896; 10013 fb.com/groups/qwave/ ✧

♂ ★ (?♿) South Asian Lesbian & Gay Association, LGBT Community Center, 208 W 13th St; 212-358-5132 **H?** Serving the Desi Queer Community of New York www.salganyc.org ✧ ✐

♀ Tarab NYC, Arab, Middle Eastern, and/or North African www.tarabnyc.org

Organizations/Resources: Family and Supporters

♀ ☆ (?♿) Center Families, LGBT Community Center, 208 W 13th St; 636-556-9300 **H?** tinyurl.com/hzgw7fa ✐

♀ Desi Rainbow Parents and Allies, PFLAG NYC, 130 E 25th St #M1; 646-397-4032 www.pflagnyc.org/support/api ✧

Long Island

♀ ☆ ♿ PFLAG Long Island, POB 364, Jericho; 11753 www.pflagli.org info@pflagli.org

♀ ☆ ♿ **PFLAG New York City, 130 E 25th St #M1; 212-463-0629 646-240-4288 www.pflagnyc.org**

♀ ☆ PFLAG Queens, POB 751043, Forest Hills 11375 www.pflag-queens.org pflag@pflag-queens.org

♀ (?♿) PFLAG Staten Island, c/o Pride Center, 25 Victory Blvd 3rd fl, Staten Island; 718-808-1397 fb.com/pflag.statenisland

Organizations/Resources: Military/Veterans

♀ ★ ♿ American Veterans for Equal Rights New York (AVERNY), POB 150160, Kew Gardens; 11415 718-849-5665 averny.tripod.com

Organizations/Resources: Naturist/Nudist

♂ ★ (?♿) Males Au Naturel, 347-704-0704 **H?** www.males.org **PN**

Organizations/Resources: Political/Legislative/Advocacy

♀ ☆ ♿ American Civil Liberties Union, 125 Broad St, 18th fl; 212-549-2600 www.aclu.org

♀ ★ Jim Owles Liberal Democratic Club, Allen Roskoff 450 W 17th St #2405; 10011 212-741-3677 jimowles.org jimowles@gmail.com

♀ ★ Lambda Independent Democrats of Brooklyn, PO Box 150614, Bklyn; 11215 917-696-1781 www.lidbrooklyn.org

Long Island

♀ ★ Gay & Lesbian Democrats of Long Island, PO Box 270, Brookhaven; 11719 tinyurl.com/nvbt9bc

♀ ★ National LGBTQ Task Force, 116 Nassau St Fl 3; 212-604-9830 www.thetaskforce.org

♀ ★ ♿ Stonewall Democratic Club of NYC, POB 514 Old Chelsea Stn; 10113 212-330-6572 www.sdnyc.org

♀ ★ ♿ STONEWALL Rebellion Veterans' Association, Willson Henderson, Founder, 70-A Greenwich Ave #120; 10011-8300 212-627-1969 fax 718-294-1969 S.V.A. meets monthly the last Saturday at NYC Gay Center at 3:15 p.m.until 6 p.m. www.STONEWALLvets.org ✐ SVA@STONEWALLvets.org ✐

Organizations/Resources: Senior Resources

Brooklyn

♂ ★ ♿ GRIOT Circle, Inc, 25 Flatbush Ave. F5, Bklyn; 718-246-2775 www.griotcircle.org ❖

Hauppauge

♂ ★ ♿ Services & Advocacy for LGBT Elders, Long Island (SAGE-LI), LGBT Network, 125 Kennedy Dr Ste 100, Hauppauge; 11788 516-323-0011 lgbtnetwork.org/sage-li ✐ info@lgbtnetwork.org

Long Island

♂ ★ ♿ Services & Advocacy for GLBT Elders, Long Island (SAGE-LI)., The Center at Bay Shore, 34 Park Ave, Bay Shore; 631-665-2300 lgbtnetwork.org/sage-li ✐

Manhattan & Citywide

♂ ★ (?♿) **SAGE (Services & Advocacy for GLBT Elders), 305 7th Ave Fl 15; 212-741-2247 www.sageusa.org**

♀ ★ SAGE Center Harlem, 220 W 143rd St; 10027 646-660-8951 tinyurl.com/y3zcamhj ✖ sageharlem@sageusa.org

Queens

♂ ★ Queens Center for Gay Seniors, Jewish Center, 37-06 77th St, Jackson Hts; 718-533-6459 www.qchnyc.org

Organizations/Resources: Sexual Focus / Safe Sex

Manhattan & Citywide

♂ ☆ ♂ The Eulenspiegel Society (TES), Box 2783; www.tes.org

♀ ★ (?♿) Lesbian Sex Mafia, LGBT Community Center, 208 W 13th St; 10011 646-450-0576 **H?** www.lesbiansexmafia.org ✐ lesbiansexmafia@gmail.com

Manhattan

♂ ★ Footmen NYC, www.footmennyc.com

♂ Masters and Slaves Together, The Center, 208 W 13th St; - - tinyurl.com/umhgwfa

♂ ★ New York Bondage Club, POB 20064; 10014 212-620-7673 www.nybondageclub.com

Organizations/Resources: Social, Recreation, Support

Bronx

♀ Destination Tomorrow, 2825 Third Ave Ste 301, Bronx; 646-723-3325 www.destinationtomorrow.org

Brooklyn

♂ ★ **Brooklyn Gay Network of Friends, Free e-group for socializing in and around Brooklyn and NYC. tinyurl.com/yca2fs**

Long Island

♀ First Presbyterian Church, 7 North Lane, Glen Cove; 516-671-0258 tinyurl.com/hfm8e52

Manhattan & Citywide

♂ ★ (?♿) 20SomethingNYC, LGBT Community Center, 208 W 13th St; 10011-7702 212-620-7310 **H?** www.20somethingnyc.com ✐

♀ ★ ♿ Butch/Femme Society, POB 750652, Forest Hills; 11375 347-709-0561 tinyurl.com/24r7pb

♀ ★ Lambda Car Club Empire Region, www.empirelambda.com

♀ ★ (?♿) The LGBTQ Opera Club of New York City, LGBT Community Center, 208 W 13th St **H?** tinyurl.com/y9kzr2lm ✐

⚥ ★ (♿) **Natural History Group of NY, 646-469-4149 H? Lesbian & Gay Naturalists of NYC. Meets at LGBT Center, 208 W 13th St. www.lgnhg.org** ✎

⚥ ★ ♿ New York Prime Timers, POB 20418; 10001 **H** NYPrime69.com NYPrime69@gmail.com

⚥ ★ Out at the J, Jewish Community Center in Manhattan, 334 Amsterdam Ave; 646-505-5472 x727 tinyurl.com/y848u6uy ⚨

⚥ ★ Zappalorti Society: GLBT Psychiatric Survivors, c/o Bert Coffman, 14 E 28th St #10-14; 10016-7464 212-889-4262 917-286-0616 bertcoffman1949@gmail.com

Manhattan

⚥ Gay for Good - New York City, Volunteer organization. gayfor-good.org/nyc

⚥ HEBRO, www.myhebro.com ⚨

♀ Lezervations New York, - - lezervations.com

⚥ ★ (♿) LGBT Reading Group, **H?** tinyurl.com/6l88tz7 ✎

⚥ ★ (♿) Photography Club, LGBT Community Center, 208 W 13th St; **H?** fb.com/groups/183594658375670 ✎

⚥ ★ (♿) Scrabblers, LGBT Community Center, 208 W 13th St; 10011-7702 212-362-5889 **H?** ✎

Queens

⚥ Queens Pride Lions Club, www.queenspridelionsclub.org

⚥ Queens Pride Lions Club, Queens Pride House, 76-11 37th Ave #206, Jackson Hts www.queenspridelionsclub.org

Organizations/Resources: Student, Academic, Education

Bronx

⚥ ★ Albert Einstein College of Medicine EAGLBT, 1300 Morris Park Ave, Forch G-35, Bronx

⚥ ★ Fordham University Pride Alliance, Rose Hill Campus, #B-62, 441 E Fordham Rd, Bronx; 718-817-4387 orgsync.com/39677/chapter

Brooklyn

⚥ ★ Brooklyn Law School Outlaws, 250 Joralemon St, Bklyn

⚥ ★ ♿ CUNY Brooklyn College LGBT Alliance, 1433 Ingersoll, Bklyn; 718-951-5712 fb.com/groups/2216537858/

♀ ☆ CUNY Brooklyn College Women's Center, 227 New Ingersoll Hall, 2900 Bedford Ave, Bklyn; 718-951-5777 tinyurl.com/tnzvrqk

⚥ ★ Queer Pratt, OSA, Chapel Hall, Pratt Institute, 200 Willoughby Ave, Bklyn; 718-230-6855 tinyurl.com/v7qo4f3

Long Island

⚥ ★ LGBTQ Services, Stony Brook University, 222 Student Activities Center, Stony Brook; 631-632-2941 stonybrook.edu/lgbtq

⚥ ★ SUNY Suffolk Community College GRANT Campus GSA, Caumsett Hall#20, 1000 Crooked Hill Rd, Brentwood; 631-851-6552 tinyurl.com/3mgkrtz

Manhattan

⚥ ★ ♿ City University of New York Center for LGBTQ Studies, 365 5th Ave #7115; 212-817-1955 www.clags.org

⚥ ★ Columbia University Pride, 622 W 113th St 212-851-7484 tinyurl.com/27t8ad8 ✎

⚥ ★ ♿ Columbia University School of Law Outlaws, Box E27, 435 W 116th St; tinyurl.com/yga6vz6 ✎

⚥ ★ CUNY Baruch College GLASS, VC-239 1 Bernard Baruch Way Box 2-210; 212-312-4550 fb.com/baruch.glass

⚥ ★ Delta Lambda Phi Beta Xi at NYU, 80 Lafayette St; www.dlp.org/betaxi/

⚥ ★ Fordham OUTLaws, Office of Student Affairs, 150 W 62nd St; 212-636-6968 fb.com/fordhamoutlaws

⚲ ★ (♿) GLSEN, 110 William St 212-727-0135 www.glsen.org

⚥ ★ (♿) Harvey Milk High School, 2 Astor Place 3rd Flr; 212-477-1555 tinyurl.com/4zgbgbx

⚥ ★ ♿ New York University LGBTQ Student Center, Kimmel Center, 60 Washington Sq S Ste 602; 212-998-4424 **H** www.nyu.edu/lgbt ✎

⚥ ★ New York University School of Law Outlaw, 40 Washington Square S Room 11; 212-998-6575 tinyurl.com/yfelyco

⚥ ★ New York University Stern School of Business OutClass, 44 W 4th St; fb.com/groups/161772110533021

⚥ ★ NYU LGBTQ Alumni Council, 25 W 4th St Rm 404A; 212-992-6892 tinyurl.com/ybczcnxb

Queens

⚥ ★ ♿ Queens College Prism, SU LL 7, 65-30 Kissena Blvd #LL32C, Flushing; **H?** ✎

Riverdale

⚥ ★ Manhattan College LGBT Friends and Allies, 4513 Manhattan College Parkway, Riverdale; 718-862-7137

Organizations/Resources: Transgender/Gender Non-Conforming/Diverse

Bronx

T ☆ Community Kinship Life, POB 6060, Bronx 10451 347-866-9002 www.cklife.org

Long Island

T ☆ Trans-Affirmations Group, 2233 Nesconset Hwy Ste 104, Lake Grove; 631-737-5559 tinyurl.com/yd6bvny2

Manhattan & Citywide

T ★ CDI-NYC's CrossGender Community, 212-564-4847 (Wed 6-9pm EST) www.cdinyc.org

T (♿) Gender Identity Project, LGBT Community Center, 208 W 13th St; 646-556-9300 **H?** gaycenter.org/tgnc ✎

T • Kaufman, Randi, PsyD, 113 University Pl; 10003 212-979-1110 tinyurl.com/ycyft8tt randi.kaufman2@verizon.net

T ○ ♿ Metamorphosis, POB 5622, Long Island City; 11105 718-728-4615 Member WPATH/HBIGDA therapist1@aol.com

T ☆ (♉) Trans Families & Friends Support, LGBT Comm. Ctr-Gender Identity Project, 208 W 13th St; 646-556-9300 **H?** gaycenter.org/tgnc ⚥

T ☆ ♿ Transgender Legal Defense & Education Fund, Inc., 20 W 20th St #705; 646-862-9396 www.transgenderlegal.org

Organizations/Resources: Youth (see also Family)
Long Island

⚥ ★ ⚸⚸ Long Island Gay & Lesbian Youth (LIGALY), The Center at Bay Shore, 34 Park Ave, Bay Shore; 631-665-2300 lgbtnetwork.org/ligaly ⚥

⚥ ★ ⚸⚸ Long Island Gay & Lesbian Youth (LIGALY), The Center at Woodbury, 20 Crossways Park Dr N Ste 110, Woodbury; 516-323-0011 lgbtnetwork.org/ligaly ⚥

⚥ ★ Pride For Youth, (A Division of Long Island Crisis Center) 2050 Bellmore Ave, Bellmore; 516-679-9000 www.prideforyouth.org

♂ ☆ Youth Enrichment Services, POB 105, W Islip 11795 631-587-5172 www.yesnews.org

Manhattan & Citywide

⚥ ★ Ali Forney Center, 224 W 35th St #1500 212-222-3427 www.aliforneycenter.org

♂ ☆ ⚸⚸ The Door, 555 Broome St 212-941-9090 www.door.org ✪

⚥ ★ FIERCE!, 2427 Morris Ave, Bronx; 10468 929-246-5473 www.fiercenyc.org ❖ info@fiercenyc.org

⚥ Forty to None Network, 311 W 43rd St 12th Flr; 212-461-4401 tinyurl.com/y7locbqz

⚥ Health Outreach To Teens (HOTT), Callen-Lorde Community Health Center, 356 W 18th St; 212-271-7200 tinyurl.com/bwyjcv9

⚥ ★ (♉) Hetrick-Martin Institute, 2 Astor Place 3rd Flr; 212-674-2400 www.hmi.org

⚥ ★ Live Out Loud, 25 Broadway 12th Flr 212-378-4095 www.liveoutloud.info

♂ ☆ (♉) MCCNY Homeless Youth Services/Sylvia's Place, 446 W 36th St; 212-629-7440 **H?** www.mccnycharities.org ⚥

⚥ ★ Peter Cicchino Youth Project, Urban Justice Center, 40 Rector St 9th Fl; 10006 877-542-8529 fax 212-533-4598 pcyp.urbanjustice.org pcyp@urbanjustice.org

⚥ ★ (♉) Project Speak Out Loud, Grand St. Settlement, 80 Pitt St; 10002 646-201-4255 www.grandsettlement.org ❖ ⚥ psol@grandsettlement.org

⚥ ☆ Trinity Place, 164 W 100th St; 646-580-7045 shelter for homeless LGBTQ youth 18-24 www.trinityplaceshelter.org ⚥

Queens

⚥ ★ Generation Q, Queens Community House, 108-25 62nd Dr, Forest Hills; 718-592-5757 www.qchnyc.org

⚥ ☆ LGBT Homeless Youth Drop in Center, 62-07 Woodside Ave 3rd Flr, Woodside; 718-472-9400 tinyurl.com/yao4cefk

Staten Island

⚥ ★ (♉) Youth Services at the Pride Center of Staten Island, 25 Victory Blvd 3rd fl, Staten Island; 718-808-1378 13-24 year olds www.pridecentersi.org/youth ⚥

Organizers & Life Management

♂ ☆ U Name It Organizers, Eleni O, 629 E 11 St Ste 4C; 917-880-8031 www.masterorganizers.com ♥

Performance: Entertainment, Music, Theater, Space

⚥ • Music By Sandy Rapp, 66 Hildreth Place, E Hampton; 11937 631-329-5193 www.SandyRapp.com sandyrapp@aol.com

Pets & Pet Services & Supplies
Queens

♂ ○ ♿ Rainbow Pet Supplies & Grooming, 3940 58th St, Woodside; 11377-3352 718-426-0222 www.rainbowpetsupplies.com rainbowpetsupplies@yahoo.com

Real Estate (see also Mortgages)
Long Island: Fire Island: Cherry Grove

♂ • **A Summer Place Realty, POB 4062, Cherry Grove; 11782-0997 / Bay & Main Walks 631-597-6140 summer; 212-752-8074 winter The most exclusives in Cherry Grove - Fire Island Rentals & Sales www.asummerplacerealty.com asprcg@aol.com**

Long Island

♂ • Leatherman, Kevin, Real Estate Broker/Owner, Leatherman Homes, 25 S Village Ave, Rockville Centre; 11570 516-362-1828 www.leathermanhomes.com kevin@leathermanhomes.com

Manhattan

♂ • (♉) Bank Neary Real Estate, 57 W 16th St; 10011-6564 646-431-7330 www.bankneary.com ⚥ Gil@BankNeary.com

Recovery
Manhattan

♂ ☆ Alcoholics Anonymous Inter-Group of New York, 307 7th Ave #201; 212-647-1680 www.nyintergroup.org

⚥ ★ (♉) Center Recovery Substance Use Program, LGBT Community Center, 208 W 13th St; 10011-7702 646-556-9300 **H?** tinyurl.com/y8ye2rcn ⚥ recovery@gaycenter.org

♂ ☆ Crystal Meth Anonymous Intergroup, POB 1517 10113 212-642-5029 www.nycma.org

♂ ☆ Greater New York Al-Anon Family Intergroup, 4 W 43rd St #308; 212-941-0094 www.nycalanon.org

♂ ☆ Services for the UnderServed, 463 7th Ave 17th Flr; 212-633-6900 www.sus.org

♂ ☆ Sexual Compulsives Anonymous, 70A Greenwich Ave #337; 10113 917-722-6912 www.scany.org info@scany.org

♀ ☆ Win (Women in Need), 115 W 31st St Fl 7 212-695-4758 www.winnyc.org

Religious / Spiritual Resources
Brooklyn

♀ ☆ Park Slope United Methodist Church, 410 6th Ave, Bklyn; 11215 718-768-3093 www.parkslopeumc.net

Long Island

♀ ☆ First Congregational Church of Riverhead, 103 1st St, Riverhead; 11901 631-727-2621 www.fccr.us firstccr@optimum.net

♂ ★ Gay & Lesbian Inclusion Committee (GLIC), Temple Beth-El of Great Neck, 5 Old Mill Rd, Great Neck; 516-487-0900 tinyurl.com/l6ldx34 ✡

♂ ★ Long Island Community Fellowship of West Babylon, 411A Lexington Ave, W Babylon; 631-647-8701 www.licf.net

♀ ☆ ₺₺ Old South Haven Presbyterian Church, South Country & Beaverdam Rds 631-286-0542 www.oldsouthhavenchurch.org

♂ ★ Unitarian Universalist Fellowship, 109 Browns Rd, Huntington; 11743-1898 631-427-9547 www.uufh.org info@uufh.org

Manhattan & Citywide

♀ ☆ ₺₺ B'nai Jeshurun, 270 W 89th St 10024 Community House & offices / Synagogue at 257 W 88th St 212-787-7600 **HD** www.bj.org ✡ ✐

♂ ★ ₺₺ Catholic Lesbians, Church of St. Francis Xavier, 55 W 15th St; 10011 929) 333-5011 www.sfxavier.org SFXWomen@aol.com

♀ ☆ Church of St Paul & St Andrew UMC, 263 W 86th St; 10024 212-362-3179 www.stpaulandstandrew.org info@stpaulandstandrew.org

♀ ☆ The Church of the Village, 201 W 13th St; 10011 212-243-5470 www.churchofthevillage.org office@churchofthevillage.org

♂ ★ ₺ Congregation Beit Simchat Torah, 130 W 30th St; 212-929-9498 **H?** www.cbst.org ✡ ✐

♂ ★ ₺₺ Dignity/New York, POB 1554 FDR Stn; 10150 646-418-7039 www.dignityny.org

♂ ★ Eshel, c/o Makom Hadash, 125 Maiden Lane Ste 8B; 724-374-3501 www.eshelonline.org ✡

♂ ★ Evangelicals Concerned, 311 E 72nd St #1G 212-517-3171 www.ecinc.org

♀ ☆ Fourth Universalist Society in New York City, 160 Central Park W; 10023-1502 212-595-1658 www.4thu.org office@4thu.org

♂ ★ ₺₺ Gay & Lesbian Yeshiva Day School Alumni Association, 212-780-4656 orthogays.org/glydsa.html ✡

♂ ★ ₺₺ Gay Catholics Group, Church of St. Francis Xavier, 55 W 15th St; 10011 212-627-2100 www.sfxavier.org sfxgcgroup@gmail.com

♂ ★ GIFTS: An LGBTQ Fellowship at Marble Collegiate Church, 1 W 29th St; 212-686-2770 x260 tinyurl.com/n8rs3mb

♂ Jewish Queer Youth, 551-579-4673 www.jqyouth.org ✡

♂ ★ ₺₺ Maranatha, Riverside Church, 490 Riverside Dr; 212-870-6700 **HDS** tinyurl.com/yc3gwowx ✐

♂ ★ Metropolitan Community Church of New York, 446 W 36th St; 212-629-7440 www.MCCNY.org

♀ ☆ ₺₺ Middle Collegiate Church, 50 E 7th St; 10003 212-477-0666 **HD** www.middlechurch.org ✐ middleinfo@middlechurch.org

♀ ☆ ₺₺ Morningside Monthly Meeting of the Religious Society of Friends (Quakers), Riverside Church, 91 Claremont Ave 10003 212-787-3903 **H?** www.morningsidemeeting.org

♂ ★ ₺₺ New York Christian Science Group, LGBT Community Center, 208 W 13th St; 10016-6043 212-532-8379 www.nycsgroup.com

♀ ☆ Our Saviour's Atonement Lutheran Church, 178 Bennett Ave; 10019 212-923-5757 www.osanyc.org office@osanyc.org

♂ ★ Wind, Rev. Mark N, MSC, 10 W 15th St #609 10011-6821 212-929-4390 ♥

Manhattan

♂ JQYouth, 1460 Broadway; 551-579-4673 Social support group for Orthodox Jewish youth. www.jqyouth.org ✡

♂ Keshet NY Office, 60 1 W 26th St Ste 325 www.keshetonline.org ✡

Queens

♀ ☆ First Congregational Church, UCC, 320 Beach 94th St, Rockaway Beach; 11693 718-634-4701 tinyurl.com/y7vf2umc first94th@gmail.com

♀ ☆ ₺ Unitarian Universalist Society of South Suffolk, 28 Brentwood Rd, Bay Shore; 11706-8011 631-968-0667 www.uusouthsuffolk.org uusssbayshore@gmail.com

Spiritual Counseling
Manhattan

♂ ● Dr Chaplain Eléni, 629 E 11 St Ste 4C 917-880-8031 www.masterorganizers.com ♥

Sports & Outdoor

♂ ★ Big Apple Recreational Sports, POB 218 10101 www.bigapplerecsports.com

♂ ★ (?₺) Big Apple Softball League, LGBT Community Center, 208 W 13th St; 212-696-7327 **H?** www.bigapplesoftball.com ✐

♂ ★ (?₺) City Cruisers Motorcycle Club NYC, LGBT Community Center, 208 W 13th St; 10011-7702 212-620-7310 **H?** www.citycruisers.com ✐ clubinfo@citycruisers.com

♂ ★ Empire City Motorcycle Club, 10 W 15th St Ste 609; 10011-6821 www.empirecitymc.com **LL** ecmc@empirecitymc.com

♂ ★ Excelsior M.C., 415 W 55th St #4D www.ExcelsiorMC.com

♂ ★ Front Runners New York, 236 W 73rd St www.frny.org

♂ ★ Gotham Knights Rugby Football Club, POB 30353; 10011 www.gothamrfc.org

♂ ★ Gotham Volleyball, POB 961; 10113 www.gothamvolleyball.org

♂ ★ Knickerbocker Sailing Association, POB 1608; 10113 **HC** www.ksasailing.org

Long Island

♂ Gotham Open Bowling Tournament, POB 333, East Islip, NY 11730 www.gothambowling.com

♂ ★ (?₺) Long Island Pride Sports Association (LIPSA), POB 126, Selden; 11784 fb.com/LIPSASports/

♂ ★ Monday Night Fourplay Bowling, Farmingdale 516-249-4300 tinyurl.com/zdh9n8b

♂ ★ (?₺) Metropolitan Tennis Group, PO Box 1021; 10113 646-417-0910 www.metrotennisgroup.com ✐

♂ New York Gay Football League, 260 Madison Ave 8th Flr; www.nygayfootball.org

♀ ★ New York Ramblers Soccer, Inc., nyramblers.com

♂ ★ NYC Gay Hockey Association, POB 2158 Grand Central Stn; 10163 www.nycgha.org

♂ ★ Out of Bounds, POB 372 Times Sq Stn 10108 www.oob-nyc.org

♂ ★ Pride Basketball League NYC Men's Division, PO Box 1244; 10163 508-364-2860 www.nycgaybasketball.org

♀ ★ Pride Basketball League NYC Women's+ Division (PBLNYC), POB 1244; 10163-1244 www.pblnyc.org women@pride basketballnyc.org

♀ ★ (♿) Sirens Women's Motorcycle Club, LGBT Community Center, 208 W 13th St; 10011-7702 212-620-7310 **H?** www.sirensnyc.com ↗

♂ ★ (♿) Sundance Outdoor Adventure Society, LGBT Community Center, 208 W 13th St; 212-663-9198 **H?** www.sundanceoutdoor.org ↗

♂ ★ (♿) Sunday Bowling League, check location and schedule www.nycsbl.com ↗

♂ ★ ♿ Team New York Aquatics, **H?** www.tnya.org ↗

♂ Village Dive Club, 241 West 23rd St #4B fb.com/groups/307150844463/

Travel & Tourist Services (see also Accommodation)
Manhattan

♂ • Kennedy Travel, 130 W 42nd St Ste 401 10036-7802 212-398-0999 800-237-7433 fax 212-730-2269 Full-service agency serving the community for over 40 years. www.kennedytravel.com

Queens

♂ • Pied Piper Travel & Cruises, 70-50 Austin St Ste 112UL, Forest Hills; 11375 718-261-4596 800-874-7312 www.gaygroupcruises.com info@piedpiInter.com

Weddings and Ceremonies

♂ • Dr Chaplain Eléni, 629 E 11 St Ste 4C 917-880-8031 www.masterorganizers.com ♥

>> *Niagara Falls: see Buffalo/Niagara Falls Area*

North Salem

Bars, Cafes, Clubs, Restaurants

♀ ○ Vox, 721 Titicus Rd; 914-669-5450 www.voxnorthsalem.com ♈ ✕

Olean

Organizations/Resources: Social, Recreation, Support

♂ Colors Unity, www.colorsunity.com

Oswego

Organizations/Resources: Student, Academic, Education

♂ ★ ♿ SUNY Oswego Pride Alliance, The Point, Campus Center 131, 7060 State Route 104; 13126 315-312-2955 alliance@oswego.edu

>> *Poughkeepsie: see Hudson Valley & Catskills Area*

Rochester & Finger Lakes Area

Community Centers and/or Pride Organizations

♂ ★ ♿ Out Alliance, 100 College Ave, Roch; 585-244-8640 **H?** outalliance.org ↗

♂ ★ ♿ Roc Pride, 100 College Ave, Roch; 585-244-8640 **HS** tinyurl.com/wasfb5h ↗

Information, Media & Publications

♂ ★ ♿ Empty Closet, 100 College Ave, Roch; 585-244-8640 **HS** tinyurl.com/4am9a3z ↗

Accommodation: Hotels, Inns, Guesthouses, B&B, Resorts
Canandaigua

♂ ○ 1840 Inn on the Main Bed and Breakfast, 176 N Main St, Canandaigua; 14424 585-394-0139 877-659-1643 www.innonthemain.com ↗ ⊗ questions@innonthemain.com

♂ ○ Bed & Breakfast at Oliver Phelps, 252 N Main St, Canandaigua; 14424 585-396-1650 www.oliverphelps.com ↗ ⊗ innkeeper@oliverphelps.com

♀ ○ Bella Rose B&B, 290 N Main St, Canandaigua 14424 585-393-9937 www.bellarosebb.com ✗ ⊗ innkeeper@bellarosebb.com

♂ ● The Chalet of Canandaigua, 3770 State Route 21, Canandaigua; 14424 585-394-9080 chaletbandb.com ✗ ⊗ staychalet@chaletbandb.com

Groton

♂ ● Benn Conger Inn, 206 W Cortland St, Groton 607-898-5817 www.benncongerinn.com

Hammondsport

♀ ○ The Black Sheep Inn, 8329 Pleasant Valley Rd, Hammondsport; 14840 607-569-3767 www.stayblacksheepinn.com ✗ ⊗ mirandagjones3@gmail.com

Penn Yan

♀ ○ Los Gatos Bed & Breakfast, 1491 Route 14A, Penn Yan; 14527 315-536-0686 866-289-7381 www.losgatosbandb.com ✗ info@losgatosbandb.com

Sodus Point

♂ ● Silver Waters B&B, 8420 Bay St, Sodus Point 14555 315-483-8098 www.silver-waters.com ✗ ⊗ innkeeper@silver-waters.com

Adoption, Surrogacy, Assisted Fertility Support, see also Reproductive

♀ ○ ♿ Franklin, Gregory A, Esq, Ashcraft Franklin & Young, LLP, 150 Allens Creek Rd, Roch; 14618 585-442-0540 x307 **HS** www.afylaw.com GFranklin@afylaw.com

AIDS/HIV Services, Education & Support

♀ ☆ ♿ Trillium Health, 259 Monroe Ave, Roch; 585-545-7200 **HDS** www.trilliumhealth.org ◆✗

Archives/Libraries/Museums/History Projects

● ★ ♿ Out Alliance Library & Archives, 100 College Ave, Roch; 585-244-8640 **H?** tinyurl.com/y6vad4nx ✗

Bars, Cafes, Clubs, Restaurants

Rochester

● Avenue Pub, 522 Monroe Ave, Roch 585-244-4960 tinyurl.com/yd4y9yrx

● ● Bachelor Forum, 670 University Ave, Roch 585-271-6930 www.bachelor4m.com **L** ✗

● ● ♿ Equal=Grounds Coffee House & Gift Shoppe, 750 South Ave, Roch; 585-256-2362 www.equalgrounds.com ✗

♂ ○ ♿ The Little Theatre Cafe, 240 East Ave, Roch; 585-258-0400 (business office) **H?** www.thelittle.org ⟳📶 ✗

♀ ○ Starry Nites Cafe, 696 University Ave, Roch 585-271-2630 www.StarryNitesCafe.com ♆ ✗⟳ ✗

Campgrounds and RV Parks

● ● (♿) Jones Pond Campground, 9835 Old State Rd, Angelica; 585-567-8100 www.jonespond.com **CLWD** (♣?) ✗

Counseling/Psychotherapy/Mental Health

♀ ○ ♿ Russow, Tara, PhD, 120 Allens Creek Rd, Roch; 14618 585-442-4447 www.RussowConsulting.com

Dentists

♀ ● ♿ Raetz, Randy G., DDS, 2273 Clinton Ave S, Roch; 14618-2623 585-473-1550 www.drrandydds.com ✗

Leather Resources & Groups

● ★ Rochester Rams, POB 31727, Roch; 14603 fb.com/RochesterRams/ **LL**

Legal Services

♀ ○ (?♿) Krieger Family Law, 75 S Clinton Ave, Clinton Sq, Ste 510, Roch; 14604 585-773-1991 **H?** fb.com/kriegerfamilylaw ✗ legalteam@kriegerfamilylaw.com

♀ ● ♿ Law Offices of Todd Gustafson, Esq, 340 Packett's Landing, Fairport; 14450 585-230-6298 **H?** www.guslawfirm.com todd@guslawfirm.com

Men's & Sex Clubs (not primarily Health Clubs)

♂ ● Rochester Spa & Body Club, 109 Liberty Pole Way, Roch; 585-454-1074 **H?** www.rochesterspa.com ✗

Organizations/Resources: Business & Professional Associations, Labor Advocacy

● Pride at Work Rochester - Finger Lakes, PO Box 18562, Roch; 14618

● ★ Spectra at Corning, 1 W Market St, Corning tinyurl.com/ybqrsny3

Organizations/Resources: Cultural, Dance, Performance

● ★ Flower City Pride Band, 585-420-8621 www.flowercitypride.com

● ★ ♿ ImageOut, 274 N Goodman St #A203, Roch; 585-271-2640 **H** www.imageout.org ✗

● ★ ♿ Rochester Gay Men's Chorus, 121 N Fitzhugh St #325, Roch; 585-423-0650 www.thergmc.org

♀ ☆ ♿ Rochester Women's Community Chorus, Inc, 121 N Fitzhugh St Ste 314, Roch; 14614 585-376-7464 www.therwcc.org therwcc@gmail.com

Organizations/Resources: Family and Supporters

♀ ☆ ♿ PFLAG/Rochester, 585-993-3297 **H?** fb.com/PFLAGRochester ✗ rochesterpflag@gmail.com

Organizations/Resources: Political/Legislative/Advocacy

♀ ☆ New York Civil Liberties Union- Genesee Valley Chapter, 121 N Fitzhugh St, Roch; 585-454-4334 tinyurl.com/ydcsaobl

Organizations/Resources: Student, Academic, Education

● ★ Keuka College LGBTQA+ Resource Center, 141 Central Ave, Keuka Park; 315-279-5000 tinyurl.com/glbqkar

● ★ ♿ Nazareth College Lambda Association, 4245 E Ave, Roch; 14618 fb.com/pg/nazarethlambda/ ✗ lambda@mail.naz.edu

● ★ ♿ Pride Network, University of Rochester, Wilson Commons Box #101K, Roch; 585-275-3068 tinyurl.com/y8so8vwk

● ★ ♿ Rochester Institute of Technology Q Ceenter, Student Alumni Union 4-A530, 34 Lomb Memorial Dr, Roch 585-475-6355 www.rit.edu/qcenter ✗

New York: Rochester & Finger Lakes Area
Organizations: Youth

260
GAYELLOW PAGES #42 2020-2021

Watertown : New York
Organizations: Youth

Organizations/Resources: Youth (see also Family)

♂ ★ ⚥ Out Alliance Youth Program, 100 College Ave, Roch; 585-244-8640 x13 **H?** tinyurl.com/y9zqtagb ✁

Recovery

♀ ☆ AA: Rochester Area Intergroup, 1000 Elmwood Ave, Roch; 585-232-6720 www.rochester-ny-aa.org

Religious / Spiritual Resources

♀ ☆ Christ Episcopal Church, 33 E 1st St, Corning 14830 607-937-5449 tinyurl.com/3jpohta cepiscopal@stny.rr.com

♂ ★ ⚤ Dignity/Integrity Rochester, 17 S Fitzhugh St, Roch; 585-234-5092 **H?** www.di-rochester.org

♀ ☆ First Unitarian Church, 220 Winton Rd, Roch 14610 585-271-9070 www.rochesterunitarian.org office@rochesterunitarian.org

♀ ☆ ⚥ First Universalist Church, 150 Clinton Ave S, Roch; 14604 585-546-2826 **HD** www.uuroc.org office@rochesterunivesalist.org

♂ ★ ⚤ Open Arms MCC, 707 E Main St, Roch; 585-271-8478 www.openarmsmcc.org

♂ ★ ⚥ Ray of Hope Church of Our Lord Jesus Christ, 380 W 1st St, Elmira; 14901 607-280-0374 www.rayofhopechurch.com ◐ ✁

♀ ☆ St Luke & St Simon Cyrene Episcopal Church, 17 S Fitzhugh St, Roch; 14614 585-546-7730 **H?** www.twosaints.org ✁ office@twosaints.org

♀ ☆ ⚥ Unitarian Universalist Church, 3024 Cooley Rd, Canandaigua; 14224 585-396-1370 www.canandaiguauu.org ✁ uucc@rochester.rr.com

Sports & Outdoor

♂ Rochester Historical Bowling Society, 585-755-7159 www.rhbs.org

Travel & Tourist Services (see also Accommodation)

♀ ● (?⚬) The Skalny Travel Group, Van Zile Travel, 3540 Winton Pl, Roch; 14623-2829 585-244-8430 888-244-8430 fax 585-697-0677 www.vanzile.com
>> *Saratoga Springs: see Albany & Capital Area*
>> *Schenectady: see Albany & Capital Area*
>> *Sharon Springs: see Hudson Valley & Catskills Area*
>> *Staten Island: see New York City & Long Island Area*
>> *Stony Brook: see New York City & Long Island Area*

Long Island

Syracuse

Community Centers and/or Pride Organizations

♂ ★ CNY Pride, POB 6608; 13217 315-254-2386 www.cnypride.org

AIDS/HIV Services, Education & Support

♀ ☆ AIDS Community Resources, 627 W Genesee St 800-475-2430 www.acrhealth.org ◐

Bars, Cafes, Clubs, Restaurants

♂ Rain Lounge, 103 N Geddes St; 315-218-5951 fb.com/Rain-LoungeSyracuse/ ▦ ◐

♂ Syracuse Guerrilla Gay Bar, syrguerrillagaybar.com

♂ ● ⚥ Trexx, 319 N Clinton St Thu-Sat (Harold Pl) 315-474-6408 www.trexxonline.com **D** ▦

♂ Wolf's Den, 617-619 Wolf St; 315-560-5637 www.wolfsden-syracuse.com **D**

Counseling/Psychotherapy/Mental Health

♂ ● Stein, Linda J., LCSW, PC, 132 Albany St, Cazenovia; 13035 315-655-0699 www.lindajsteintherapy.com

Health Care: Physical (see also Counseling/Mental Health)

♀ ● ⚤ Harrington, Laura E, DC, Liverpool Chiropractic & Wellness, PLLC, 403 Tulip St, Liverpool; 13088-4966 315-461-4510 tinyurl.com/494t4d

Men's & Sex Clubs (not primarily Health Clubs)

♂ ● Red Gym Men's Club, 448 E Brighton Ave; 13210 315-472-0380 www.redgymmensclub.com **P** redgymmensclub@gmail.com

Organizations/Resources: Cultural, Dance, Performance

♂ Syracuse Gay & Lesbian Chorus, Inc, POB 6796; 13217 www.syrglc.org

Organizations/Resources: Senior Resources

♂ ★ ⚥ SAGE/Upstate, SAGE Upstate Center, 431 E Fayette St #050; 315-478-1923 fb.com/Sageupstate1/ ✁

Organizations/Resources: Student, Academic, Education

♂ ★ Syracuse University LGBT Resource Center, 750 Ostrom Ave; 315-443-3983 lgbt.syr.edu

Religious / Spiritual Resources

♀ ☆ ⚥ First UU Society, 109 Waring Rd 13224 315-446-5940 **HD** www.firstuusyr.org ✁ office@firstuusyr.org

♀ ☆ ⚥ Plymouth Congregational Church, 232 E Onondaga St; 13202 315-474-4836 **HD** www.plymouthsyr.org ✁ office@plymouthsyr.org
>> *Troy: see Albany & Capital Area*

Utica Area

Accommodation: Hotels, Inns, Guesthouses, B&B, Resorts

♀ ● ⚥ The Inn at Stone Mill, 410 Canal Pl, Little Falls; 315-823-0208 www.theinnatstonemill.com ✁ ⊘

Organizations/Resources: Student, Academic, Education

♀ ☆ Hamilton College Womyn's Center, Days-Massolo Center 2nd Flr, 198 College Hill Rd, Clinton; 315-859-4398 fb.com/HCWomxnsCenter

Watertown

Organizations/Resources: Youth (see also Family)

♂ ★ Q Center Northern New York, ACR Health, 120 Washington St 3rd Flr; 315-898-2515 tinyurl.com/y6uym3cd
>> *White Plains: see Hudson Valley & Catskills Area*
>> *Woodstock: see Hudson Valley & Catskills Area*

North Carolina: State/County Resources
Crisis, Anti-violence, & Helplines
261
GAYELLOW PAGES #42 2020-2021
Asheville/Smoky Mtns Area: North Carolina
Accommodation

North Carolina
State/County Resources

Crisis, Anti-violence, & Helplines

♂ Coastal Horizons, 615 Shipyard Blvd, Wilmington, NC 800-672-2903 www.coastalhorizons.org

♂ ☆ North Carolina Coalition Against Domestic Violence, NCCADV, 3710 University Dr Ste 140, Durham, NC 27707 888-232-9124 nccadv.org

Information, Media & Publications

♂ ★ Carolina Rainbow News, NC & SC carolinarainbownews.org hello@carolinarainbownews.org

♂ ● QNotes, POB 221841, Charlotte, NC 28222-1841 704-531-9988 fax 704-531-1361 www.goqnotes.com editor@goqnotes.com

AIDS/HIV Services, Education & Support

♀ ☆ && AIDS Leadership Foothills Area, 1120 Fairgrove Church Rd SE Ste 28, Hickory, NC 828-322-1447 www.alfainfo.org ✗

♂ ☆ Alliance of AIDS Services Carolina, Tillery Place, 1637 Old Louisburg Rd, Raleigh, NC 919-834-2437 www.aas-c.org

♂ Carolinas CARE Partnership, 5855 Executive Center Drive Ste 101, Charlotte, NC 704-531-2467 www.carolinascare.org

♀ ☆ && Western North Carolina AIDS Project, POB 2411, Asheville, NC 28801 828-252-7489 **H?** www.wncap.org ✗ wncap@wncap.org

Funding: Endowment, Fundraising

♀ Southern Equality Fund, POB 364, Asheville, NC 28802 828-242-1559 southernequality.org

Health Care: Physical (see also Counseling/Mental Health)

♂ North Carolina Community Health Services, 4917 Waters Edge Drive Ste 165, Raleigh, NC 919-469-5701 www.ncchca.org

Organizations/Resources: Military/Veterans

T ☆ Sparta - A Transgender Military Advocacy Organization, spartapride.org inquiries@spartapride.org

Organizations/Resources: Political/Legislative/Advocacy

♀ ☆ & American Civil Liberties Union of North Carolina, POB 28004, Raleigh, NC 27611 919-834-3466 www.acluofnorth-carolina.org

♀ Equality NC, POB 28768, Raleigh, NC 27611 919-829-0423 www.equalitync.org

Organizations/Resources: Transgender/Gender Non-Conforming/Diverse

T ☆ Carolina Transgender Society, tinyurl.com/23865au

Asheville/Smoky Mtns Area

Crisis, Anti-violence, & Helplines

♂ ☆ && Helpmate, POB 2263, Asheville; 28802 828-254-0516 **H?** www.helpmateonline.org

Community Centers and/or Pride Organizations

♀ Blue Ridge Pride, 917-822-9085 blueridgepride.org

Information, Media & Publications

♂ ★ Gay Asheville NC, www.gayashevillenc.com

♂ ● RomanticAsheville.com Travel Guide, tinyurl.com/7erxx4d

♀ ★ Sheville of Western Carolina, 23 A Trillium Court, Asheville; 828-215-2915 www.sheville.org

Accommodation: Hotels, Inns, Guesthouses, B&B, Resorts
Asheville

♂ ● (?&) 1889 WhiteGate Inn & Cottage, 173 E Chestnut St, Asheville; 828-253-2553 www.WhiteGate.net ❤ ✗ ⊛ ⊛

♂ ● 27 Blake St, 27 Blake St, Asheville; 28801-2203 828-252-7390 www.sheville.org/27blake ✗ ⊛ 27blake@charter.net

♂ ● Applewood Manor Inn B&B, 62 Cumberland Cir, Asheville; 828-254-2244 www.applewoodmanor.com (❤?) ✗ ⊛

♀ ○ A Bed of Roses Bed & Breakfast, 135 Cumberland Ave, Asheville; 28801-1737 828-258-8700 888-290-2770 abedofroses.com ✗ ⊛ ⊛ stay@abedofroses.com

---

♂ GLBTQI ♀ Gay/nongay ♂ bisexual

♀ LBTQI women ♀ all women ♂ bisexual women

♂ GBTQI men ♂ all men ♂ bisexual men

T specifically transsexual/transgender/transvestite

♀ ✕ Bar and Restaurant ✕ Restaurant ⊽ Cafe
▥ Entertainment/Cabaret/Showbar
D Dancing **V** Video bar **K** Karaoke **S** Sports bar
C Country **L** Leather/Levi **W** Western
P Private Club (ask about visitor memberships)

♥ Wedding-related services or marriage equality
H Assistance available for the deaf and hearing-impaired
HD devices **HS** sign **HDS** devices and sign
H? Check for assistance available for the deaf and. hearing-impaired
⊛ ⊛ smoke-free property ⊛ smoke-free indoors
(⊛) indoor smoking areas
❤ Pets welcome (❤?) Ask about pets
✗ High speed internet available to visitors
Wheelchair Accessibility of premises or meeting place:
&& Accessible premises and lavatory
(&&) Accessible premises with help; accessible lavatory
& Accessible premises; lavatory not known to be accessible
(&) Accessible premises with help
(?&) Call ahead for details: places of meetings or activities vary, or special arrangements available.
✧ Asian ✦ Latin/Hispanic
✚ African-descent/Black
✦ People of Color ✳ Two-Spirit ❍ Diverse

♀ O Hill House Bed & Breakfast Inn, 120 Hillside St, Asheville; 28801 828-232-0345 855-447-0002 www.hillhousebb.com info@hillhousebb.com

♂ O The Lion and the Rose, 276 Montford Ave, Asheville; 28801 828-255-7673 **H?** www.lion-rose.com ✔ ⊗ info@lion-rose.com

♂ ● (?⚥) Mountain Light Sanctuary, POB 18909, Asheville; 28814 828-626-3966 mountainlightsanctuary.com ✔ ⊗

♂ ● (?⚥) North Lodge on Oakland, 84 Oakland Rd, Asheville; 828-252-6433 www.northlodge.com ✔ ⊗

Brevard

♀ O (?⚥) Ash Grove Mountain Cabins & Camping, 749 E Fork Rd, Brevard; 28712-8803 828-885-7216 www.ash-grove.com (♣?) ✔ ⊗ info@ash-grove.com

Leicester

♂ ● (?⚥) Compassionate Expressions Mountain Inn & Healing Sanctuary, 828-683-6633 tinyurl.com/lo453 ⊗

Mills River

♂ ● Acorn B&B, 5136 Old Haywood Road, Mills River 828-891-4652 www.acornbedbreakfast.com ♣ ✔ ⊗

Waynesville

♀ ● Brookside Mountain Mist Inn, 142 Country Club Dr, Waynesville; 828-452-6880 tinyurl.com/254uttn ✔ ⊗

Accommodation Rental: Furnished / Vacation (& AirBNB)
Asheville

♂ ● **Asheville's Downtown Loft, 828-713-0141 828-337-3362 (Sarah Nie) Live in the heart of downtown Asheville. Free parking. Walk to all galleries, bookstores, restaurants. www.vrbo.com/218070** ✔ ⊗ **ashevillesdowntownloft@gmail.com**

♂ ● Wolf Branch Cabin, Near Asheville, NC 828-231-2152 www.wolfbranchcabin.com ♣ ⊗

Hendersonville

♂ ● Brightwaters Vacation Rentals, Tioga Trl, Hendersonville NC 828-513-0528 fb.com/bwcabins ✔ ⊗ ⊗

AIDS/HIV Services, Education & Support

♂ Loving Food Resources, POB 25142, Asheville 28813 828-255-9282 www.lovingfood.org

Astrology/Numerology/Tarot/Psychic Readings

♂ O ♿ Gunther, Christy, MA, 3 Woodfin Ave, Asheville; 28804 828-258-3229 astrocounseling.byregion.net ✔

Bars, Cafes, Clubs, Restaurants
Asheville

♂ ● ♿ 67 Biltmore Downtown Eatery & Catering, 67 Biltmore Ave, Asheville; 828-252-1500 **H?** www.67biltmore.com ✗ ⊡ ✔ hello@67biltmore.com

♂ O Avenue M, 791 Merrimon Ave, Asheville 828-350-8181 www.avenuemavl.com ✗ ✔

♂ O ♿ The Cantina Fresh Mex and Tequila Bar, 10 Biltmore Plaza, Asheville; 828-505-7682 **H?** www.cantinabiltmore.com ⵝ ✗ ✔

♂ O ♿ Laughing Seed Cafe, 40 Wall St, Asheville; 828-252-3445 www.laughingseed.com ⵝ ✗ ⊡ ✔

♀ O Limones, 13 Eagle St, Asheville; 828-252-2327 www.limones-restaurant.com ✗

♂ O ♿ The Lobster Trap Seafood Oyster Bar, 35 Patton Ave, Asheville; 828-350-0505 www.thelobstertrap.biz ✗

♂ O The Market Place, 20 Wall St, Asheville 828-252-4162 tinyurl.com/yavnqlz ✗

♀ ● ♿ O'Henry's / Underground, 237 Haywood St, Asheville; 828-254-1891 www.ohenrysofasheville.com **DP** ▦

♂ ● ♿ Scandals Nightclub, 11 Grove St, Asheville; 828-505-1612 scandalsnightclub.com **DVP** ▦ ✔

♂ O The Southern Kitchen & Bar, 41 N Lexington Ave, Asheville; 828-251-1777 tinyurl.com/6uoprnl ⵝ ✗

♂ O Tupelo Honey Cafe, 12 College St, Asheville 828-255-4863 tupelohoneycafe.com ⵝ ✗

♂ O Zambra, 85 W Walnut St, Asheville 828-232-1060 www.zambratapas.com ✗

Brevard

♂ ● ♿ The Square Root, 33 Times Arcade Alley, Brevard; 828-884-6171 www.squarerootrestaurant.com ⵝ ✗ ✔

Weaverville

♂ O Blue Mountain Pizza & Brew Pub, 55 N Main St, Weaverville; 828-658-8778 www.bluemountainpizza.com ⵝ ✗ ▦ owner@bluemountainpizza.com

Bookstores

♂ ★ ♿ Firestorm Books & Coffee, 610 Haywood Rd, Asheville; 28801 828-255-8115 www.firestorm.coop ⊡ ✔ info@firestorm.coop

♂ O ♿ Malaprop's Bookstore/Cafe, 55 Haywood St, Asheville; 828-254-6734 www.malaprops.com ⊡ ✔

Legal Services

♂ O ♿ The Law Office of Leah Broker, P.A., One Oak Plaza Ste 201, Asheville; 28801 828-253-0336 Social Security disability, workers' compensation www.leahbrokerlaw.com ✔

♂ ● (?⚥) Rockey, Arlaine, POB 656, Marshall; 28753 828-279-6735 **H?** www.arlainerockey.com ✔ AttorneyRockey@gmail.com

♀ O Sluder, Curt, POB 4, Asheville; 28802 / 260 New Leicester Hwy 828-254-9505 www.sluderlaw.com

Metaphysical, Occult, Alternative Healing

♂ ● ♿ Crystal Visions, 5426 Asheville Hwy, Hendersonville 828-687-1193 crystalvisionsbooks.com

Organizations/Resources: Cultural, Dance, Performance

♂ ★ Asheville Gay Men's Chorus, www.avlgmc.org info@avlgmc.org

♀ ☆ Different Strokes Performing Arts Collective, PO Box 1131, Asheville; 28801 828-484-2014 www.differentstrokespac.org info@differentstrokespac.org

♀ Womansong Asheville, POB 61, Asheville 28802 www.womansong.org

Organizations/Resources: Family and Supporters

♂ PFLAG Asheville, 828-365-8814 tinyurl.com/wdb37b9

♀ ☆ && PFLAG Flat Rock/Hendersonville, POB 6063, Hendersonville; 28793 828-697-0690 tinyurl.com/235u442 pflaghendersonville@gmail.com

Organizations/Resources: Senior Resources

♂ LGBTQ Elder Advocates of Western North Carolina, 828-251-6622 tinyurl.com/wchvl6v

Organizations/Resources: Social, Recreation, Support

♂ ★ Asheville Supper Club, tinyurl.com/thfdhul ashevillegaysupperclub@gmail.com

♂ Men's Garden Club of Asheville, POB 633, Asheville; 28802 828-350-1897

♀ ★ Mitchell County Gay Straight Alliance, fb.com/mitchellcounty-gsa

Organizations/Resources: Transgender/Gender Non-Conforming/Diverse

T Tranzmission, 70 Woodfin Place #419, Asheville 828-771-6995 tranzmission.org

Organizations/Resources: Youth (see also Family)

♀ ★ Youth OUTright, POB 1893, Asheville 28802 866-881-3721 www.youthoutright.org

Pets & Pet Services & Supplies

♀ ○ Canine Shear Heaven, 422 McDowell St, Asheville; 828-254-3386 www.canineshearheaven.com

Real Estate (see also Mortgages)

♀ ● && Armstrong, Ron E, Realtor, eXp Realty, 28 Schenck Pkwy Ste 200, Asheville; 28803-5088 828-338-9662 **H?** www.AshevilleAndBeyond.com ✐

Recovery

♀ ☆ && Alcoholics Anonymous - Western NC, North Carolina Mountain Central Office, North Carolina Mountain Central Office, 70 Woodfin Place Ste 206, Asheville; 28801 828-254-8539 **H?** www.aaNCMCO.org info@ncmco.net

Religious / Spiritual Resources

♀ ☆ Jubilee! Community Church, 46 Wall St, Asheville; 28801 828-252-5335 www.jubileecommunity.org jubilee@jubileecommunity.org

♀ ☆ Kenilworth Presbyterian Church, 123 Kenilworth Rd, Asheville; 28803 828-252-8872 kenilworthchurch.org kenilworthpresbyterianchurch@gmail.com

♀ ☆ MCC Sacred Journey, 1735 5th Ave W, Hendersonville; 28793 828-693-9110 www.mccsacredjourney.org mccsacredjourney@yahoo.com

Sports & Outdoor

♂ Pink Pistols - Asheville, tinyurl.com/qsxr3fj

♂ Walk it out!, www.walkitout.net

Travel & Tourist Services (see also Accommodation)

♀ ● && Great Expeditions Travel and Weddings, 65 Westover Dr, Asheville; 828-255-0249 www.greatexpeditions.net ♥

Weddings and Ceremonies

♀ ○ Marlan, Susan, Interfaith Officiant, Asheville & Western North Carolina 828-891-6323 828-505-5220 www.belovedceremony.com ♥

Yoga

♂ Men's Nude Yoga, 90 Biltmore Ave, Asheville 828-255-7650 tinyurl.com/tjsg7jx
>> *Black Mountain: see Asheville/Smoky Mtns Area*

Blowing Rock/Boone Area

Accommodation Rental: Furnished / Vacation (& AirBNB)
Boone

♂ ● Hill Crest Cabin, Downtown Boone 828-719-6034 Dog friendly airbnb.com/rooms/5112234 ❄ ✐ ⊗ ⊛

vilas

♀ ● Mountain Song Cabin, 139 Mountain St., vilas 828-572-3257 www.mountainsongcabin.com ❄ ✐ ⊗ ⊛

Organizations/Resources: Transgender/Gender Non-Conforming/Diverse

T Appalachian State University TRANSaction, 221 College St, Boone; 828-262-8566 fb.com/transactionappstate/
>> *Boone: see Blowing Rock/Boone Area*
>> *Brevard: see Asheville/Smoky Mtns Area*
>> *Burlington: see Triad Area*
>> *Chapel Hill: see Triangle Area*

Charlotte Area

Community Centers and/or Pride Organizations

♂ ★ && Charlotte Pride, POB 32362, Charlotte; 28233 charlottepride.org

AIDS/HIV Services, Education & Support

♀ ☆ House of Mercy, Inc., POB 808, Belmont 28012 704-825-4711 www.thehouseofmercy.org houseofmercync@gmail.com

♀ ☆ && RAIN, 601 E 5th St Ste 470, Charlotte; 704-372-7246 www.carolinarain.org ✐

Bars, Cafes, Clubs, Restaurants
Charlotte

♀ ○ 300 East, 300 East Blvd, Charlotte 704-332-6507 www.300east.net ✖
@ixx=

♀ ○ && Amelie's French Bakery & Cafe, 2424 N Davidson St, Charlotte; 704-376-1781 www.ameliesfrenchbakery.com ✖ ⫿

♂ Bar Argon, 4544 S Blvd Ste H, Charlotte 704-525-7787 www.BarArgon.com **DV**

♀ ● && Bar at 316, 316 Rensselaer Ave, Charlotte; 704-910-1478 www.thebarat316.com **K** ▦ ▥

♂ && Chasers, 3217 The Plaza, Charlotte; 704-339-0500 tinyurl.com/y6vqndtb **P** ▦

North Carolina: Charlotte Area
Bars, Cafes, Clubs, Restaurants

264
GAYELLOW PAGES #42 2020-2021

Charlotte Area: North Carolina
Sports & Outdoor

♀ ○ The Diamond Restaurant, 1901 Commonwealth Ave, Charlotte; 704-375-8959 www.diamondcharlotte.com ✕

♂ ● Dish, 1220 Thomas Ave, Charlotte; 704-344-0343 www.eatatdish.com ✕ ▷

♂ ● Petra's, 1919 Commonwealth Ave, Charlotte 704-332-6608 petrasbar.com **K** ▥

⚥ ● (♿) The Scorpio, 2301 Freedom Dr 704-373-9124 www.thescorpio.com **D** ▥

⚥ ● ♿ Sidelines Sports & Billiards, 4544 South Blvd, Charlotte; 704-525-2608 thesidelinesbar.com **PS** ✓

♂ ○ Smelly Cat Coffeehouse, 514 E 36th St, Charlotte; 704-374-9656 www.Smellycatcoffee.com ▷

♀ ○ Soul Gastrolounge, 1500-B Central Ave, Charlotte; 704-348-1848 www.soulgastrolounge.com ⚲ ✕

⚥ ● The Woodshed Bar, 4000 Queen City Dr, Charlotte; 704-394-1712 www.woodshedlounge.com **L** ▥

Bookstores

♀ ○ Paper Skyscraper, 330 East Blvd, Charlotte 704-333-7130 www.paperskyscraper.com

♂ ○ ♿ Park Road Books, 4139 Park Rd, Charlotte; 704-525-9239 www.parkroadbooks.com

⚥ ● ♿ **White Rabbit, 920 Central Ave, Charlotte; 704-377-4067 www.WhiteRabbitBooks.com**

Counseling/Psychotherapy/Mental Health

♀ ● ♿ Green, Jim, M.Div, 2434 Commonwealth Ave, Charlotte; 28204 980-307-1131 www.jamesmatthewgreen.com JimGreenMDiv@gmail.com

♂ ○ Winokuer Center for Counseling & Healing, 715 Providence Rd, Charlotte; 704-333-5598 www.thewinokuercenter.com

Leather Resources & Groups

⚥ ★ ♿ Tradesmen Levi/Leather Club, PO Box 31654, Charlotte; 28231 **H?** www.charlottetradesmen.org **LW** ○ ✓

Men's & Sex Clubs (not primarily Health Clubs)

♂ Eros Men's Spa, 5101-D Nations Ford Rd, Charlotte; 704-605-5849 erosmensspa.com **P**

Organizations/Resources: Business & Professional Associations, Labor Advocacy

⚥ ★ Charlotte LGBT Chamber of Commerce, POB 33371, Charlotte; 28233 704-750-5224 www.clgbtcc.org

Organizations/Resources: Cultural, Dance, Performance

⚥ ★ Gay Men's Chorus of Charlotte, POB 560661, Charlotte; 28256 704-549-9202 www.gmccharlotte.org

⚥ ● (♿) One Voice Chorus, POB 9241, Charlotte; 28299 336-794-6831 onevoicechorus.com

⚥ Southern Country Charlotte, POB 668690, Charlotte; 28266 980-277-0330 tinyurl.com/3twdlr9 **DCW**

Organizations/Resources: Ethnic, Multicultural

⚥ ★ Charlotte Black Pride, 5009 Beatties Ford Rd Ste 107-347, Charlotte; charlotteblackpride.org ✤

Organizations/Resources: Family and Supporters

⚥ ☆ PFLAG Charlotte, POB 472532, Charlotte 28247 704-942-6857 www.pflagcharlotte.org

Organizations/Resources: Social, Recreation, Support

⚥ ★ (♿) Prime Timers of Charlotte, POB 49275, Charlotte; 28277 704-236-3775 tinyurl.com/w2whsta primetimersclt@gmail.com

Organizations/Resources: Student, Academic, Education

⚥ ★ ♿ UNCC PRIDE, Student Org. Box 209, 9201 University City Blvd, Charlotte; 704-687-7127 tinyurl.com/y26jt4xd

Organizations/Resources: Youth (see also Family)

⚥ ★ ♿ Time Out Youth Center, 3800 Monroe Rd, Charlotte; 704-344-8335 www.timeoutyouth.org ✓

Printing/Mailing & Promotional Items

♂ ○ ♿ Sir Speedy Printing, 301 N Caswell Rd, Charlotte; 28204-2403 704-375-8349 www.sirspeedy.com/midtown

Real Estate (see also Mortgages)

♂ ○ ♿ Brown, Tim, eXp Realty LLC, 18505 Statesville Rd, Cornelius; 28031 704-619-1008 www.carolinahomes4sale.com ✓ me@realtortimbrown.com

Recovery

♂ ☆ AA: Metrolina Intergroup Association, 1427 Elizabeth Ave, Charlotte; 704-332-4387 charlotteaa.org

♂ ☆ Al-Anon/Alateen Information Services of Metrolina, 2810 Providence Rd #A4, Charlotte; 877-523-1159 www.charlottealanon.org

Religious / Spiritual Resources

♂ ☆ ♿ Caldwell Presbyterian Church, 1609 E 5th St, Charlotte; 28204 704-334-0825 www.caldwellpresby.org ✓

♂ ☆ (♿) Havurat Tikvah, POB 12684, Charlotte; 28220 980-225-5330 www.HavuratTikvah.org ✡ havurattikvah@gmail.com

♂ ☆ ♿ Holy Covenant UCC, 3501 WT Harris Blvd 704-599-9810 **H?** www.holycovenantucc.org office@holycovenantucc.org

⚥ ★ ♿ MCC Charlotte, 7121 Orr Rd, Charlotte; 704-563-5810 www.mymcccharlotte.org

⚥ ★ Myers Park Baptist Church LGBT Fellowship, 1900 Queens Rd, Charlotte; 704-334-7232 tinyurl.com/s3hhro2

⚥ ☆ Temple Beth El Keshet Committee, 5101 Providence Rd, Charlotte; 704-366-1948 Welcoming, pro-LGBT rights Reform Jewish community. tinyurl.com/yac43grn ✡

Sports & Outdoor

♂ Charlotte Royals Rugby Football Club, 4820 Tuckaseegee Rd, Charlotte; www.charlotteroyals.org

Concord/Kannapolis Area

Organizations/Resources: Family and Supporters

♂ PFLAG - Concord/Kannapolis, 38 Church St N, Concord; tinyurl.com/w2fvxpd

Organizations/Resources: Social, Recreation, Support

♀ ★ Queers United in Concord/Kannapolis, 704-425-3341 tinyurl.com/ysf4r2
>> *Fairview: see Asheville/Smoky Mtns Area*

Fayetteville Area

Community Centers and/or Pride Organizations

♀ ★ Fayetteville PRIDE, 100 Hay St 6th Flr, Fayetteville; 28301 910-302-3878 **HS** www.FayettevillePride.org Contact@ FayettevillePride.org

Gastonia

Community Centers and/or Pride Organizations

♀ Gaston Pride, 704-842-0597 gastonpride.com

Organizations/Resources: Family and Supporters

♂ PFLAG Gaston, tinyurl.com/wysqkgr

Religious / Spiritual Resources

♀ ★ &&. New Life MCC, 1201 S New Hope Rd 28054 704-334-0350 **H?** www.newlifemccnc.org ✎ ♥ newlifemccgastonia@ gmail.com

Greenville

AIDS/HIV Services, Education & Support

♂ ☆ (?&) Pitt County AIDS Services Organization, 3219 Landmark St Ste 1B; 252-830-1660 picaso.org

Organizations/Resources: Student, Academic, Education

♀ ★ &&. East Carolina University LGBT Resource Office, Brewster B-103, Campus Mailstop 567. 501 E 10th St 252-737-2514 lgbtq.ecu.edu
>> *Hendersonville: see Asheville/Smoky Mtns Area*

Hickory

Community Centers and/or Pride Organizations

♀ Catawba Valley Pride, POB 3551; 28603 828-475-5559 www.catawbavalleypride.org

Bars, Cafes, Clubs, Restaurants

♀ ● &&. Club Cabaret, 101 N Center St 828-322-8103 www.clubcabarethickory.net **D** ▥ ✎

Counseling/Psychotherapy/Mental Health

♂ ● Brand New Day Counseling, POB 242, Conover 28613 828-310-2959 tinyurl.com/yewgw3e ✎ brandnewdaycounseling@ gmail.com

Legal Services

♂ ● (?&) Johnson, Larry, POB 2222 28603-2222 828-304-0600 fax 866-609-5669 ljohnson@ljohnsonlawoffice.com

Organizations/Resources: Youth (see also Family)

♀ ★ &&. OUTright Youth of Catawba Valley, POB 2222; 28603 828-320-1937 LGBT youth and allies ages 13-18 www.outrightyouthcv.org

Religious / Spiritual Resources

♀ ⅋ Christ's Church of the Foothills, POB 877; 28603 828-261-5647 tinyurl.com/vs24f33
>> *High Point: see Triad Area*
>> *Kannapolis: see Concord/Kannapolis Area*
>> *Kure Beach: see Wilmington*

Lake Norman

Bars, Cafes, Clubs, Restaurants
Denver

♂ ● &&. Pomodoro's Italian American Cafe, 7925 Natalie Commons Dr, Denver; 980-222-7474 www.pomodoros.com ✕ ✎

Mooresville

♂ ● &&. Pomodoro's Italian American Cafe, 168 Norman Station Blvd, Mooresville; 704-663-6686 www.pomodoros.com ✕ ✎

Lexington

AIDS/HIV Services, Education & Support

♂ ☆ &&. Positive Wellness Alliance, PO Box 703; 27293 336-248-4646 **H?** tinyurl.com/crvmpet ✎

New Bern

Accommodation: Hotels, Inns, Guesthouses, B&B, Resorts

♂ ○ Benjamin Ellis House Bed & Breakfast, 215 Pollock St; 28560-4942 252-259-2311 benjaminellishouse.com ✎ benjaminellis house@gmail.com

Organizations/Resources: Family and Supporters

♂ ☆ PFLAG Carteret-Craven, POB 245; 28563 252-515-1058 tinyurl.com/yygbj7c7

Outer Banks Area

Community Centers and/or Pride Organizations

♀ ★ &&. OBX Pride, Inc, POB 1241, Manteo; 27954 **H?** www.obxpridefest.com ✎

Bars, Cafes, Clubs, Restaurants
Kill Devil Hills

♂ ○ &&. Outer Banks Brewing Station, 600 S Croatan Hwy, Kill Devil Hills; 252-449-2739 www.obbrewing.com ✎ thecrew@ obbrewing.com

Nags Head

♂ ○ New York Pizza Pub, 2217 S Croatan Hwy, Nags Head; 252-441-2660 www.nypizzapub.com ⅋ ✕ ▥
>> *Raleigh: see Triangle Area*

North Carolina: Spring Lake
Religious
266
GAYELLOW PAGES #42 2020-2021
Triangle Area: North Carolina
Crisis, Anti-violence, & Helplines

Spring Lake

Religious / Spiritual Resources

♀ ☆ United Ministries in Christ Church, 751 Lillington Highway; 28390 910-302-6683 tinyurl.com/r8heh47 umic.nc@gmail.com
» *Spruce Pine: see Asheville/Smoky Mtns Area*

Triad Area

Community Centers and/or Pride Organizations

♀ Greensboro Pride, POB 29272, Greensboro 27429 336-505-9020 greensboropride.org

♀ ♿ LGBTQ Youth Programs, North Star LGBTQ Community Center, 930 Burke St, Winston-Salem; 336-893-9053 **H?** www.northstarlgbtcc.com ✎

♀ ★ (♿) LGBTQIA Community Center, Guilford Green Foundation, 1205 W Bessemer Ave Ste 226, Greensboro 336-790-8419 **H?** guilfordgreenfoundation.org ✎

♀ ★ ♿ North Star LGBTQ Community Center, 930 Burke St, Winston-Salem; 336-893-9053 **H?** www.northstarlgbtcc.com ✎

♀ PRIDE Winston-Salem, POB 20732, Winston-Salem; 27120 336-365-8453 pridews.org

AIDS/HIV Services, Education & Support

♀ ☆ ♿ Alamance Cares, POB 205, Burlington; 27216 / 3025 S Church St 336-538-8111 **H?** www.alamancecares.com

♀ ☆ ♿ Central Carolina Health Network, 1 Centerview Dr Ste 202, Greensboro; 27407 336-292-0665 **H?** cchnetwork.org ✎ info@cchn4.org

♀ ★ ♿ Triad Health Project, 801 Summit Ave, Greensboro; 336-275-1654 www.triadhealthproject.com

♀ ★ ♿ Triad Health Project,. 620 W English Rd, High Point; 336-884-4116 www.triadhealthproject.com

Bars, Cafes, Clubs, Restaurants
Greensboro

♂ ● Chemistry Nightclub, 2901 Spring Garden St, Greensboro; 336-617-8571 chemistrynightclub.com ▦

Funding: Endowment, Fundraising

♀ Guilford Green Foundation, 121 N Greene St, Greensboro; 336-790-8419 guilfordgreenfoundation.org

Health Care: Physical (see also Counseling/Mental Health)

♂ Wellness and Education Community Action Health Network, 2966 S Church St #261, Burlington; 919-742-3762 fb.com/we-cahnorg

Leather Resources & Groups

♀ ★ (♿) Tarheel Leather Club, 336-312-8832 tarheelleather-club.org

Legal Services

♀ ○ ♿ David, Cheryl K, 528 College Rd, Greensboro; 27410 336-547-9999 Estate & Elder Law www.cheryldavid.com ✎

♂ ● ♿ Ervin, III, Justin R, Johnson Peddrick & McDonald, 440 W Market St #300, Greensboro; 27401 336-574-9720 **H?** www.jplegal.net ✎ jrervin@jplegal.net

♀ ● ♿ Johnson, Ronald P, Johnson Peddrick & McDonald, 440 W Market St #300, Greensboro; 336-574-9720 **H?** www.jplegal.net ✎

♀ ○ ♿ Overfield, John C, Coltrane & Overfield, PLLC, 106 N Elm St Ste 300, Greensboro; 27401 336-279-8707 www.caolaw.com ✎ overfield@caolaw.com

♀ ● ♿ Weidemann, Bradley J, Weidemann Law Firm, PC, 102 W 3rd St Ste 485, Winston-Salem; 27101 336-725-8557

Organizations/Resources: Cultural, Dance, Performance

♀ Out at the Movies, 336-918-0902 outatthemovieswinston.org

♂ ★ Triad Pride Men's Chorus, 200 N Davie St Box 20, Greensboro; 336-589-6267 triadprideperformingarts.org

♀ ★ Triad Pride Women's Chorus, 200 N Davie St Box 20, Greensboro; 336-589-6267 triadprideperformingarts.org

Organizations/Resources: Family and Supporters

♀ ☆ ♿ PFLAG Alamance County, POB 623, Elon; 27244 336-584-8722 www.pflagalamance.org

♀ ☆ ♿ PFLAG Greensboro, POB 4153, Greensboro; 27404 336-541-6754 www.pflaggreensboro.org

♀ PFLAG High Point, 303 Eastchester Dr, High Point; 336-880-6945 fb.com/pflag.highpoint

♀ PFLAG Winston-Salem, POB 24334, Winston-Salem; 27114 336-448-4250 www.pflagws.org

Organizations/Resources: Student, Academic, Education

♀ ☆ Elon University Gender & LGBTQIA Center, Campus Box #2984, Elon; 27244 336-278-6228 www.elon.edu/glc lgaray@elon.edu

♀ ★ ♿ Wake Forest University LGBTQ Center, Campus Box 7203, Winston-Salem; 27109 / 311 Benson University Center 336-758-4665 **H?** lgbtq.wfu.edu ✎ lgbtq@wfu.edu

Recovery

♀ ☆ (♿) Al-Anon/Alateen Information Services, POB 10274, Greensboro; 27404 800-449-1287 greensboroalanon.org

Religious / Spiritual Resources

♀ ★ ♿ New Faith Metropolitan Community Church, 4105 Patsy Dr, Winston-Salem; 336-784-8009 www.newfaithmcc.org

Sports & Outdoor

♀ Stonewall Sports - Greensboro, n/a., Greensboro; stonewall-greensboro.org

♀ ★ Triad Softball League, Inc., 336-287-2451 www.triadsoftball.com

Triangle Area

Crisis, Anti-violence, & Helplines

♀ ☆ Hopeline, 919-231-4525 Crisis Intervention www.hopeline-nc.org

♂ ☆ Orange County Rape Crisis Center, POB 4722, Chapel Hill; 27514 866-935-4783 www.ocrcc.org

Community Centers and/or Pride Organizations
Durham
♀ LGBTQ Center of Durham, 114 Hunt St, Durham; 919-827-1436 www.lgbtqcenterofdurham.org

♂ Pride: Durham, NC, 114 Hunt St, Durham 919-827-1436 www.pridedurhamnc.org

Raleigh
♀ ★ The LGBT Center of Raleigh, 119 E Hargett St B 010, Raleigh; 27601-1579 919-832-4484 www.lgbtcenterofraleigh.com info@lgbtcenterofraleigh.com

Information, Media & Publications
♀ ★ Visit Raleigh, www.visitraleigh.com/lgbt/ visit@ visitRaleigh.com

Accommodation: Hotels, Inns, Guesthouses, B&B, Resorts
Durham
♀ ○ TheLRoom, 919-638-0050 www.thelroombnb.com ✂ ⊗ ⊗ TheLRoomNC@gmail.com

Efland
♂ ● Farm Stay at Fickle Creek Farm, 919-304-6287 www.fickle-creekfarm.com (♣?) ✂ ⊗

AIDS/HIV Services, Education & Support
Durham
♂ CAARE, Inc., 214 Broadway St, Durham 919-683-5300 www.caare-inc.org

Archives/Libraries/Museums/History Projects
♀ ★ The LGBT Center of Raleigh Library, 119 E Hargett St B 010, Raleigh; 27601 919-832-4484 www.lgbtcenterofraleigh.com info@ lgbtcenterofraleigh.com

Bars, Cafes, Clubs, Restaurants
Carrboro
♂ ○ Cat's Cradle, 300 E Main St, Carrboro 919-967-9053 www.cat-scradle.com ▥

♀ ○ ♿ Spotted Dog Restaurant & Bar, 111 E Main St, Carrboro; 919-933-1117 thespotteddogrestaurant.com 🍸 ✕ ✂

Chapel Hill
♀ ○ Caffe Driade, 1215-A E Franklin St, Chapel Hill; 919-942-2333 www.caffedriade.com 🗗 ▥

♀ ○ ♿ Crook's Corner, 610 W Franklin St, Chapel Hill; 919-929-7643 crookscorner.com 🍸 ✕

Durham
♂ ♿ The Bar, 711 Rigsbee Ave, Durham; 984-244-7117 www.the-bardurham.com **PD** ▥

♀ ○ ♿ Fullsteam Brewery, 726 Rigsbee Ave, Durham; 919-682-2337 **H?** www.fullsteam.ag ✂ office@fullsteam.ag

♀ ○ Mad Hatter's Bakeshop & Cafe, 1802 W Main St, Durham; 919-286-1987 www.madhatterbakeshop.com 🗗

♀ ● ♿ The Pinhook, 117 W Main St, Durham; 919-677-1100 www.thepinhook.com **DK** ▥ ✂

♀ ○ Rue Cler, 401 E Chapel Hill St, Durham 919-682-8844 www.ruecler-durham.com ✕

♀ ○ Social Games & Brews, 1007 W Main St, Durham 919-687-6969 www.socialdurham.com

Raleigh
♂ ● Flex, 2 S West St, Raleigh; 919-832-8855 www.flex-club.com ▥

♀ ● The Green Monkey, LLC, 1217 Hillsborough St, Raleigh; 984-200-5682 www.peacelovemonkey.com rusty@ peacelovemonkey.com

♀ ○ ♿ Irregardless Cafe, 901 W Morgan St, Raleigh; 919-833-8898 www.irregardless.com ✕ ▥ ✂

♀ ● ♿ Legends/View, 330 W Hargett St, Raleigh; 919-831-8888 legends-club.com **DV** ▥

♀ ○ ♿ The Pit, 328 W Davie St, Raleigh; 919-890-4500 www.thepit-raleigh.com 🍸 ✕

♂ ○ Third Place Coffee, 1811 Glenwood Ave, Raleigh 919-834-6566 fb.com/thirdplacecoffee 🗗 thethirdplacecoffeeshop@ gmail.com

Bookstores: Used
Durham
♀ ○ Books Do Furnish A Room, 1809 W Markham Ave, Durham; 27705-4806 919-286-1076 www.booksdofurnisharoom.com

Bookstores
Durham
♀ ○ ♿ Regulator Bookshop, 720 9th St, Durham; 919-286-2700 www.regulatorbookshop.com ✂

Raleigh
♀ ○ ♿ Quail Ridge Books, 4209-100 Lassiter Mill Rd, Raleigh; 919-828-1588 www.quailridgebooks.com ✂

Conferences/Events/Festivals/Workshops
♀ ★ Pride Life Expo, POB 18844, Raleigh 27619 / April 2020 www.pridelifeexpo.org info@raleighlgbtchamber.org

Counseling/Psychotherapy/Mental Health
Cary
♀ ● ♿ Powell, Judith C, PhD, 1135 Kildaire Farm Rd Ste 200, Cary; 27511 / 301 W Weaver St, Carrboro 919-467-4782 fax 919-420-0199 tinyurl.com/2wqcenr

Durham
♀ ● ♿ Androgyny Center, POB 51997, Durham; 27717 919-489-8753

♀ ○ Grigsby, Mary K, 6208 Fayetteville Rd Ste 106, Durham; 27713 919-286-9659 www.counselingdurhamnc.com mkgrigsby03@gmail.com

♀ ● ♿ Levine, Kenny, LCSW, 1502 Hwy 54 West Ste 505, Durham; 919-475-3068 www.kennylevine.com

Fuquay Varina
♀ ○ Maltbie, Alice, RN, MS, LMHC, 206 Raleigh St, Fuquay Varina; 27526 518-463-6582 www.alicemaltbie.com alicemaltbie@ gmail.com

Raleigh
♀ ● ♿ Katz, Michael, PhD, 280 W Millbrook Rd, Raleigh; 27609 919-559-6380 www.drmichaelkatznc.com katzpsych@gmail.com

North Carolina: Triangle Area
Counseling
268
GAYELLOW PAGES #42 2020-2021
Triangle Area: North Carolina
Sports & Outdoor

♂ ○ (♿) Luper, Suzanne W., Triangle Pastoral Counseling, Inc., 312 W Millbrook Rd #109, Raleigh; 27609 919-845-9977 x206 tpccounseling.org SWLuper59@gmail.com

Dentists
Durham

♂ ● ♿ Conner, Deb, DDS, MS, Endodontist, 922 Broad St Ste B, Durham; 27705 919-416-4200 Practice limited to endodontics www.debconnerdds.com ✔

Funding: Endowment, Fundraising

♂ ★ Crape Myrtle Festival, Inc., POB 12201, Raleigh; 27605 www.crapemyrtlefestival.org

Legal Services
Durham

♂ ○ (♿) Ellison, Daniel M, POB 25005, Durham; 27702 919-491-4625 fax 888-596-0919 **H?** artandmuseumlaw@aol.com

♂ ● (♿) The Law Office of Cheri Patrick, 3500 Westgate Dr Ste 701, Durham; 919-956-7171 **H?** cheripatricklaw.com ✔

♂ ● ♿ Thompson, Sharon, 113 Broadway St, Durham; 919-688-9646 **H** www.nicholsonpham.com ✔

♂ ○ ♿ Whisnant, Judy, 123 W Main St Ste 612, Durham; 919-688-6860 www.judywhisnantlaw.com
Raleigh

♂ ○ ♿ Edelstein & Payne, Attorneys, PO Box 28186, Raleigh; 27611-8186 / 315 E Jones St 919-828-1456 **H?** www.edelstein-payne.com ✔

♂ ● (♿) Haas, Angela L, Haas Tharrington, PA, 5100 Oak Park Rd Ste 200, Raleigh; 27612 919-783-9669 **H?** www.carolinafamilylaw.com ✔

Organizations/Resources: Business & Professional Associations, Labor Advocacy

♀ ★ Raleigh Business & Professional Network, PO Box 18844, Raleigh; 27619 www.raleighlgbtchamber.org info@raleighlgbtchamber.com

♀ ★ Triangle Area Gay Scientists, POB 1137, Chapel Hill; 27514 www.meetup.com/gaypros-328

Organizations/Resources: Cultural, Dance, Performance

♀ ☆ Common Woman Chorus, POB 51631, Durham 27717 www.commonwomanchorus.net

♀ ★ North Carolina Gay & Lesbian Film Festival, The Carolina Theatre, 309 W Morgan St, Durham; 919-560-3030 ncglff.org

♂ ★ ♿ Triangle Gay Men's Chorus, 514 Daniels St # 251, Raleigh; 919-696-6366 www.tgmchorus.org ✔

Organizations/Resources: Family and Supporters

♂ ☆ ♿ PFLAG Raleigh-Durham/Triangle, PO Box 51776, Durham; 27717 www.pflagtriangle.org

Organizations/Resources: Social, Recreation, Support
Durham

♂ Carolina Bear Lodge, POB 61794, Durham 27715 carolinabearlodge.club

♂ ★ RDU Prime Timers, POB 33306, Raleigh; 27633 919-229-4482 www.meetup.com/rdu-pt

Organizations/Resources: Student, Academic, Education
Chapel Hill

♀ ★ ♿ LGBTQ Center UNC Chapel Hill, SASB CB #5100, 385 Manning Dr Ste 3308, Chapel Hill; Student Academic Services Building (North), Ste 32266 919-843-5376 lgbtq.unc.edu ✔
Durham

♀ ★ ♿ Duke OUTlaw, Science Dr and Towerview Rd, Durham; sites.duke.edu/outlaw/

♀ ★ ♿ Duke University Center for Sexual and Gender Diversity, 100 Bryan Center, Box 90958, 125 Science Drive, Durham; 919-684-6607 tinyurl.com/p7qngwh

♀ ☆ (♿) Duke University Women's Center, POB 90920, Durham; 27708 / 001 Crowell Building 919-684-3897 tinyurl.com/y8lno9j ✔
Raleigh

♀ ★ ♿ NC State GLBT Center, 5230 Talley Student Union, Campus Box 7285, Raleigh; 919-513-9742 **H?** ncsu.edu/glbt ✔

Real Estate (see also Mortgages)
Chapel Hill

♀ ○ Tanson, Wendy, Realtor, RE/MAX United, 1526 E Franklin St Ste 101, Chapel Hill; 27514 919-971-7180 www.wendytanson.com wendy@tanson.com
Raleigh

♀ ○ ♿ Menges, Tom, ABR, CRS, GRI, SRES, Coldwell Banker Howard Perry & Walston, 5000 Falls of Neuse Ste 100, Raleigh 27609 919-274-5645 www.tommenges.hpw.com ✔ thmenges@gmail.com

Religious / Spiritual Resources
Chapel Hill

♀ ☆ Amity UMC, 825 N Estes Dr, Chapel Hill; 27514 919-967-7546 amityumc.org amityumc@ncrrbiz.com

♀ ☆ Community Church, 106 Purefoy Rd, Chapel Hill 27514-4853 919-942-2050 www.c3huu.org c3hoffice@gmail.com
Durham

♀ ☆ ♿ Durham Friends Meeting (Quakers), 404 Alexander Ave, Durham; 27705 984-377-4492 **HD** www.durhamfriends.org ✔ ♥ nc.durhamfriendsmeeting@gmail.com

♀ ☆ Eno River Unitarian Universalist Fellowship, 4907 Garrett Rd, Durham; 27707 919-489-2575 www.eruuf.org office@eruuf.org

♀ ★ ♿ Imani MCC of Durham, POB 13172, Durham; 27709 / 3602 C-View St 919-251-6275 www.imanimcc.org ✔
Raleigh

♀ ☆ ♿ Holy Trinity Evangelical Lutheran Church, 2723 Clark Ave, Raleigh; 27607-7101 919-828-1687 **HD** www.htelc.org

♀ ★ ♿ St Francis of Assisi GLBT Ministry, 11401 Leesville Rd, Raleigh; 919-467-6135 www.stfrancisglbt.org

♀ ★ ♿ St John's MCC, 622 Maywood Ave, Raleigh; 919-834-2611 www.stjohnsmcc.org

♀ ☆ ♿ Umstead Park UCC, 8208 Brownleigh Dr, Raleigh; 27617 919-844-6661 www.upucc.org office@upucc.org

Sports & Outdoor

♂ Triangle Rainbow Bowling League, trianglerainbowbowling.org

Women's Centers
Chapel Hill

♀ ☆ (?⚧) The Compass Center for Women and Families, POB 1057, Chapel Hill; 27514 / 210 Henderson St 919-968-4610 compassctr.org

Raleigh

♀ Women's Center of Wake County, 112 Cox Ave, Raleigh; 919-829-3711 www.wcwc.org

» Waynesville: see Asheville/Smoky Mtns Area

West Jefferson

Food Specialties (see also Catering)

♂ ● West Jefferson Specialty Foods, 11 E 2nd St 28694 704-641-6605 tinyurl.com/y4ot6fwn

Wilmington

Crisis, Anti-violence, & Helplines

♂ Domestic Violence Shelter, POB 1555; 28402 910-343-0703 tinyurl.com/7zns9sl

Accommodation: Hotels, Inns, Guesthouses, B&B, Resorts

♂ ○ C.W. Worth House Bed and Breakfast, 412 S 3rd St; 28401-5102 910-762-8562 www.worthhouse.com ✗ ⊛ relax@worthhouse.com

Accommodation Rental: Furnished / Vacation (& AirBNB)
Kure Beach

♂ ● (?⚧) Palm Air Vacation Rentals & Sales, 133 N Fort Fisher Blvd, Kure Beach; 28449 910-458-5269 www.palmairrealtync.com ✗ ⊛ rentals@palmairrealtync.com

Bars, Cafes, Clubs, Restaurants

♀ ○ Front Street Brewery, 9 N Front St 910-251-1935 www.frontstreetbrewery.com ⵙ ✗

♂ ● Ibiza, 118 Market St; 910-251-1301 fb.com/ibizawilmington/
D

Counseling/Psychotherapy/Mental Health

♂ ○ ᕦᕤ Insight Wellness Services, 720 N 3rd St Ste 101; 28401 910-251-2106 tinyurl.com/3l9d6w

♀ ● Tilley, Ed, LCSW, 313 Walnut St #103; 28401 910-508-7400 www.tilleycounseling.com tgeorge187@outlook.com

Organizations/Resources: Family and Supporters

♂ ᕦᕤ PFLAG Wilmington/Cape Fear, PO Box 16287; 28408 910-228-2052 inyurl.com/rc9oumz

Organizations/Resources: Senior Resources

♂ SAGE, Frank Harr Foundation, 1624 Princess St; 910-538-1393 frankharrfoundation.org

Organizations/Resources: Social, Recreation, Support

♂ ★ ᕦᕤ Frank Harr Foundation, 1624 Princess St; 28401 910-538-1393 frankharrfoundation.org ✗ info@frankharrfoundation.org

Organizations/Resources: Transgender/Gender Non-Conforming/Diverse

T ☆ Wilmington Transgender Support Services, 910-343-6890 fb.com/ctcwilmington trleonunley@gmail.com

Religious / Spiritual Resources

♂ ★ ᕦᕤ St Jude's MCC, 19 N 26th St 910-762-5833 www.stjudesmcc.org

Sports & Outdoor

♂ Stonewall Sports - Wilmington, tinyurl.com/y79u99r6

» Winston-Salem: see Triad Area
» Wrightsville Beach: see Wilmington

North Dakota
State/County Resources

Crisis, Anti-violence, & Helplines

♂ ☆ FirstLink, POB 447, Fargo, ND 58107-0447 / ND & Clay County MN 701-235-7335 www.myfirstlink.org info@myfirstlink.org

AIDS/HIV Services, Education & Support

♂ ☆ North Dakota Department of Health HIV/AIDS Program, 2635 E Main Ave, Bismarck, ND 701-328-2378 www.ndhealth.gov/hiv

Organizations/Resources: Political/Legislative/Advocacy

♂ ☆ American Civil Liberties Union of North Dakota, 112 N University Dr #301, Fargo, ND 651-917-3880 www.aclund.org

♀ North Dakota Human Rights Coalition, POB 1961, Fargo, ND 58107 701-239-9323 www.ndhrc.org

Recovery

♂ ☆ Narcotics Anonymous Upper Midewest Region, PO Box 5393, Fargo, ND 58105 www.umrna.org

Fargo/Moorhead Area

Community Centers and/or Pride Organizations

♂ ★ Pride Collective & Community Center, POB 941, Fargo; 58107 / 1105 1st Ave S, Fargo; 218-287-8034 fmpride.com

♂ Pride Fargo-Moorhead, 1105 1st Ave S, Fargo; 218-287-8034 www.fmpride.com

Organizations/Resources: Cultural, Dance, Performance

♂ Fargo-Moorhead Gay men's Chorus, 1104 2nd Ave S #319, Fargo; 701-566-0289 www.fmgaymenschorus.org

Organizations/Resources: Transgender/Gender Non-Conforming/Diverse

T TriState Transgender Meeting, Pride Collective, POB 941, Fargo; 58107 701-404-9955 fb.com/TristateTrans

Organizations/Resources: Youth (see also Family)

♂ Kaleidoscope, Pride Center, 1105 1st Ave S, Fargo; 320-204-6786 tinyurl.com/yae8mx7q

Religious / Spiritual Resources

♂ ☆ St Mark's Lutheran Church, 417 Main Ave #401, Fargo; 58103 701-235-5591 www.stmarkslutheranfargo.com admin@stmarkslutheranfargo.com

♂ ☆ ♿ Unitarian Universalist Church of Fargo-Moorhead, 121 S 9th St, Fargo; 58103 701-235-0394 **H?** www.fmuu.org ✎ fmuu@fmuu.org

Grand Forks

Organizations/Resources: Student, Academic, Education

♀ ★ UND Ten Percent Society, POB 8385; 58202 701-777-3269 tinyurl.com/yyzf4tzk

Ohio
State/County Resources

Information, Media & Publications

♀ ★ Prizm, 7575 Huntington Park Dr Ste 200, Columbus, OH 43235 www.prizmnews.com

AIDS/HIV Services, Education & Support

♂ ★ ♿ Equitas Health, 4400 N High St Ste 300, Columbus, OH / and 750 E Long St Ste 3000; 43203 614-340-6700 614-299-2437 **H?** www.equitashealth.com

Archives/Libraries/Museums/History Projects

♀ ★ ♂ Ohio Lesbian Archives, POB 20075, Cincinnati, OH 45220-0075 513-256-7695 tinyurl.com/97r3dbf ✎ OLArchives@gmail.com

Mortgages/Home Ownership (see also Banks, Real Estate)

♂ ● Frey, Carolyn, OH & FL & PA 614-891-9625 www.carolynfrey.com cafrey@mortgagelendingsolutions.com

Organizations/Resources: Political/Legislative/Advocacy

♂ ☆ ♿ American Civil Liberties Union of Ohio, 4506 Chester Ave, Cleveland, OH 216-472-2200 www.acluohio.org

♀ ★ ♿ Equality Ohio, 118 E Main Ste 200, Columbus, OH 43215 614-224-0400 www.equalityohio.org info@equalityohio.org

Organizations/Resources: Social, Recreation, Support

♂ ★ ♿ Tri-State Prime Timers, POB 141205, Cincinnati, OH 45250 513-956-4398 **H?** www.tristateprimetimers.com

Organizations/Resources: Student, Academic, Education

♂ ☆ GLSEN Northeast Ohio, POB 93513, Cleveland, OH 44101 216-556-0960 www.glsen.org/northeastoh

Organizations/Resources: Transgender/Gender Non-Conforming/Diverse

T ☆ Heartland Trans Wellness Group, 103 William Howard Taft Rd, Cincinnati, OH 513-549-4447 **H?** transwellness.org

T ☆ TransOhio, POB 14481, Columbus, OH 43214 614-441-8167 www.transohio.org

Recovery

♂ ☆ ♿ Al-Anon Family Groups of Ohio, Inc, POB 610, Cortland, OH 44410 888-425-2666 **H?** www.ohioal-anon.org chairman@ohioal-anon.org

» Akron: see Akron/Canton/Kent Area

Akron/Canton/Kent Area

AIDS/HIV Services, Education & Support

♂ ☆ ♿ Community AIDS Network / Akron Pride Initiative (CA-NAPI), 759 W Market St Flr 1, Akron; 330-252-1559 www.canapi.org

♀ ♿ Teen Pride Network, CANAPI, 759 W Market St Flr 1, Akron; 330-252-1559 tinyurl.com/yahmnwbk

Bars, Cafes, Clubs, Restaurants
Akron

♂ ● ♿ Angel Falls Coffee Company, 792 W Market St, Akron; 330-376-5282 tinyurl.com/283c88k ⟳

♂ ○ Bricco Restaurant, 1 W Exchange St, Akron 330-475-1600 www.briccoakron.com ✗

♂ Cocktails, 33 Mapledale Ave, Akron 330-376-2625 fb.com/CocktailsAkron **D** 🍸

♀ Interbelt Nite Club, 70 N Howard St, Akron 330-253-5700 www.interbelt.com **D** 🍸

♂ ● Square Nightclub, 820 W Market St, Akron 330-374-9661 www.squarenight.club **D** 🍸

♂ ● ♂ Tear-Ez Lounge, 360 S Main St, Akron; 330-376-0011 fb.com/tearezlounge/ 🍸 ✎

Canton

♂ ● Crew Night Club, 304 Cherry Ave NE, Canton 330-575-5748 fb.com/CrewNightClub/ **D**

Kent

♂ ○ Bricco Restaurant, 210 S Depeyster St, Kent 330-677-1335 www.briccokent.com ✗

Leather Resources & Groups

♂ ★ The Iron Eagles, POB 9772, Canton; 44711 www.ironeagles.com

Men's & Sex Clubs (not primarily Health Clubs)

♂ Akron Steam & Sauna, 41 S Case Ave, Akron; / check ahead, may be moving 330-252-2791

Organizations/Resources: Family and Supporters

♂ ☆ ♿ PFLAG Akron, POB 5471, Akron 44334 330-342-5825 www.pflagakron.org

Organizations/Resources: Social, Recreation, Support

♂ ★ Arktos Bears of NE Ohio, POB 2577, Akron 44309 www.arktosbears.org

Organizations/Resources: Student, Academic, Education

♀ ★ ♿ Kent State University LGBTQ Center, POB 5190, Kent; 44242 330-672-8580 **H?** www.kent.edu/lgbtq ✎ lgbtqsc@kent.edu

♀ ★ ♿ PRIDE! Kent, Box 17, Office of Campus Life, Kent; fb.com/pridekent/ ⟳

Ohio: Akron/Canton/Kent Area
Organizations: Student

271
GAYELLOW PAGES #42 2020-2021

Cincinnati Area : Ohio
Bars, Cafes, Clubs, Restaurants

♂ ★ University of Akron LGBT Union (LGBTUA), The Hub-Student Union, Akron; 330-826-1429 orgsync.com/36333/chapter

Organizations/Resources: Transgender/Gender Non-Conforming/Diverse

T ☆ 👫 TransAlive - Akron Transgender Support Group, Fairlawn-West United Church of Christ, 2095 W Market St, Akron 330-240-1600 **H?** tinyurl.com/h5xs7gk ✒

Recovery

♀ ☆ (?👫) Alcoholics Anonymous Canton Area Intergroup Council, 4125 Hills and Dales Rd NW Ste 400B, Canton; 44708-1676 330-491-1989 www.aaincantonohio.org ✒

Religious / Spiritual Resources

♀ ☆ 👫 Unitarian Universalist Church of Kent, 228 Gougler Ave, Kent; 44240 330-673-4247 **HD** www.kentuu.org ✒ churchoffice@kentuu.org

♀ ☆ UU Congregation of Greater Canton, 2585 Easton St NE 330-492-4004 www.uucantonoh.org ✒ carerespectgrow@gmail.com

Sports & Outdoor

♂ ★ Summit Bowling Association, 580 E Cuyahoga Falls Ave, Akron; 330-928-2161 www.summitbowling.com

Alliance

Organizations/Resources: Student, Academic, Education

♂ ★ Mount Union College GSA/Pride, 1972 Clark Ave; 330-823-6051 tinyurl.com/y2benaav

Athens

Accommodation: Communities, Intentional

♂ ★ SuBAMUH, POB 5853; 45701 740-448-6424 Susan B. Anthony Memorial Unrest Home Womyn's Land Trust. All women, LGBTQ people, and allies welcome. www.subamuh.com SuBAMUH@gmail.com

Organizations/Resources: Student, Academic, Education

♂ ★ 👫 Ohio University LGBT Center, 354 Baker University Center; 740-593-0239 www.ohio.edu/lgbt ✒

♂ ★ 👫 Ohio University LGBTA Society of Alumni, LGBT Center, 354 Baker University Center; 740-593-0239 tinyurl.com/ydyakljj ✒

Bellevue

Accommodation: Hotels, Inns, Guesthouses, B&B, Resorts

♀ ● (?👫) Victorian Tudor Inn, 408 W Main St; 419-483-1949 www.victoriantudor.com (♣?) ✒ (☺)

Bowling Green

Organizations/Resources: Social, Recreation, Support

♀ ★ 👫 Bowling Green Lavender Women, fb.com/BGLavender-Women/

Organizations/Resources: Student, Academic, Education

♂ ★ 👫 Bowling Green State University LGBTQ+ Resource Center, 427 Bowen Thompson Student Union; 419-372-2642 tinyurl.com/y9n7r42v ✒

♀ ☆ 👫 Center for Women and Gender Equity, BGSU, 280 Hayes Hall; 43403 419-372-7227 tinyurl.com/zxosz8t cwge@bgsu.edu

» Canton: see Akron/Canton/Kent Area

Cincinnati Area

Community Centers and/or Pride Organizations

♂ ★ 👫 Cincinnati Pride, c/o Andrew Morano, POB 14246, Cinci; 45250 **HS** www.cincinnatipride.org

Information, Media & Publications

♂ ★ Gay & Lesbian Community Center of Greater Cincinnati, POB 23159, Cinci; 45223 / resources only www.cincyglbt.com

Accommodation: Hotels, Inns, Guesthouses, B&B, Resorts
Bellevue

♀ ○ (?👫) **Christopher's B&B**, 604 Poplar St, Bellevue, KY 41073-1204 859-491-9354 888-585-7085 **Celebrate your special occasion getaway in this B&B (renovated church)! www.christophersbb.com** ✒ ☺ christophers@twc.com

♀ ○ Weller Haus Bed, Breakfast & Event Center, 319 Poplar St, Bellevue, KY 41073-1108 859-391-8315 800-431-4287 www.weller-haus.com ♣ ✒ ☺

Cincinnati

♀ ○ (?👫) Six Acres B&B, 5350 Hamilton Ave, Cinci; 45224 513-541-0873 www.sixacresbb.com ♣ ✒ ☺ ☺ kristin@sixacresbb.com

Petersburg

♀ ○ (?👫) First Farm Inn, 2510 Stevens Rd, Petersburg, KY 41080 859-586-0199 (8am-8pm please) www.firstfarminn.com (♣?) ✒ ☺ jen@firstfarminn.com

AIDS/HIV Services, Education & Support

♀ ☆ 👫 Caracole, Inc, 4138 Hamilton Ave, Cinci; 45223 513-761-1480 **H?** www.caracole.org ✒

Bars, Cafes, Clubs, Restaurants
Cincinnati

♂ Bar 901 at the Brittany, 901 Race St, Cinci; 513-421-1663 fb.com/newbar901/

♂ ● 👫 Below Zero Lounge, 1122 Walnut St, Cinci; 513-421-9376 belowzerolounge.com **DKV** ▥ ✒

♀ The Birdcage, 927 Race St, Cinci thebirdcagecincinnati.com

♀ ○ 👫 Boca Restaurant, 114 E 6th St, Cinci; 513-542-2022 www.bocacincinnati.com ✂ ✒

♂ The Cabaret, 1122 Walnut St Flr 2, Cinci 513-202-4052 www.cabaretcincinnati.com **D** ▤

Ohio: Cincinnati Area
Bars, Cafes, Clubs, Restaurants

272
GAYELLOW PAGES #42 2020-2021

Cleveland Area: Ohio
Community Centers / Pride

♀ ● 👬 College Hill Coffee Co. & Casual Gourmet, 6128 Hamilton Ave, Cinci; 513-542-2739 www.collegehillcoffeeco.com ✎

♀ ● 👬 Home Base Tavern, 2401 Vine St, Cinci; 513-721-1212 tinyurl.com/wktusfs **DK** ▥ ✎

♂ ○ 👬 Northside Tavern, 4163 Hamilton Ave, Cinci; 513-542-3603 www.northsidetav.com/cincy/ ▥ ✎

Covington

♂ ○ Rosie's Tavern, 643 Bakewell St, Covington, KY 859-291-9707 www.rosiestavernnky.com rosiestav@aol.com

Monroe

🔴 Old Street Saloon, 13 Old St, Monroe 513-539-9183 www.old-streetbar.com ▥

Newport

♂ ○ Crazy Fox Saloon, 901 Washington Ave, Newport, KY 859-261-2143 tinyurl.com/y8ty5bdc

Counseling/Psychotherapy/Mental Health

♀ ● 👤 Herriford, Whayne, MS, LPCC, 902 Monmouth St, Newport, KY 859-951-6162 www.whayneherriford.com whayneherriford@gmail.com

♀ ● (♺) Mysonhimer, Jill, MSW, LISW-S, 10979 Reed Hartman Highway #331D, Cinci; 45242 513-900-1223 tinyurl.com/yyyln5nv ✎ jmysonhimer@gmail.com

Legal Services

♂ ○ (♺) **Bouldin, Michael William, 618 Washington St, Covington, KY 41011 859-581-6453 Proudly providing service in Kentucky and Ohio for 25 years. fb.com/bouldinlawfirm1/**

♀ ● (♺) Cook, Cathy R, 114 E 8th St, Cinci; 45202-2102 513-241-4029 www.cathycooklaw.com info@cathycooklaw.com

♀ ● 👤 Knox, Scott E, 13 E Court St Ste 300, Cinci; 45202-1143 513-241-3800 www.scottknox.com ✎ scott@scottknox.com

Organizations/Resources: Business & Professional Associations, Labor Advocacy

🔴 ★ Gay Chamber of Commerce of Greater Cincinnati, POB 141461, Cinci; 45250 www.gaychambercincinnati.com

Organizations/Resources: Cultural, Dance, Performance

♂ Cincinnati Men's Chorus, POB 3061, Cinci 45201 513-542-2626 www.cincinnatimenschorus.org

♀ ☆ 👬 MUSE, Cincinnati's Women's Choir, POB 23292, Cinci; 45223 513-221-1118 **HS** www.musechoir.org

🔴 OutReels Cincinatti, 108 E 24th St, Covington, KY 859-379-2193 www.outreelscincy.org

Organizations/Resources: Family and Supporters

♀ ☆ 👬 PFLAG/Greater Cincinnati, POB 19634, Cinci; 45219-0634 513-721-7900 www.pflagcinci.org info@pflagcinci.org

Organizations/Resources: Naturist/Nudist

♂ ★ (♺) Southern Ohio Naturists Society (SONS), POB 9151, Cinci; 45209 www.cincinnatisons.org secretary@cincinnatisons.org

Organizations/Resources: Student, Academic, Education

♀ ★ GLSEN Cincinnati, POB 19856, Cinci 45219-0856 866-934-9119 tinyurl.com/rzojy8d

🔴 ★ 👬 University of Cincinnati LGBTQ Center, POB 210173, Cinci; 45220 513-556-4329 www.uc.edu/lgbtq.html

♀ ☆ 👬 University of Cincinnati Women's Center, POB 210179, Cinci; 45221 513-556-4401 www.uc.edu/ucwc/

🔴 ★ 👬 Xavier LGBTQ+ Alliance, GSC 210 3800 Victory Parkway, Cinci; 45207 513-745-3598 **H?** ✎ xualliance@xavier.edu

Organizations/Resources: Transgender/Gender Non-Conforming/Diverse

🔴 ★ (♺) CrossPort, POB 19936, Cinci; 45219 513-344-0116 www.crossport.org crossportcincy@yahoo.com

Organizations/Resources: Youth (see also Family)

🔴 ★ Greater Cincinnati GLBTQ Youth Summit, 866-934-9119 tinyurl.com/j3bok4c

Real Estate (see also Mortgages)

♂ ● Fletcher Realty, Inc, 1624 Bruce Ave, Cinci 45223-2002 513-542-5877 fax 513-542-3877 www.fletcherrealtyinc.com

Recovery

♂ ☆ Alcoholics Anonymous, 2245 Gilbert Ave Ste 304, Cinci; 513-351-0422 www.aacincinnati.org

♂ ☆ Sex & Love Addicts Anonymous, www.slaacincinnati.org

Religious / Spiritual Resources

🔴 ★ 👬 New Spirit Oasis Community - MCC, 4033 Hamilton Ave, Cinci; 45223 513-570-0983 fb.com/newspiritoasismcc/ ✎ newspiritoasismcc@gmail.com

♂ ☆ St John's UU Church, 320 Resor Ave, Cinci 45220-1698 513-961-1938 www.stjohnsuu.org

Sports & Outdoor

🔴 ★ Frontrunners Cincinnati, 513-315-8772 fb.com/groups/131439685434

🔴 ★ River City Softball, 513-231-2100 www.myrivercitysoftball.com

Travel & Tourist Services (see also Accommodation)

♂ ● Dan Howell Travel, 1749 Chase Ave, Cinci 45223-2090 513-541-2187 866-541-2187 www.vacationgay.com

Cleveland Area

Crisis, Anti-violence, & Helplines

♂ Domestic Violence & Child Advocacy Center, PO Box 5466, Cleveland; 44101 216-391-4357 www.dvcac.org

Community Centers and/or Pride Organizations

🔴 Cleveland Pride, 6600 Detroit Ave, Cleveland; 216-651-5428 tinyurl.com/ybzf53dw

🔴 ★ 👬 LGBT Community Center of Greater Cleveland, 6705 Detroit Ave, Cleveland; 44102 216-651-5428 lgbtcleveland.org ✎ info@lgbtcleveland.org

Ohio: Cleveland Area
Accommodation
273
GAYELLOW PAGES #42 2020-2021
Cleveland Area : Ohio
Organizations: Student

Accommodation: Hotels, Inns, Guesthouses, B&B, Resorts
Cleveland

♂ • Clifford House B&B, 1810 W 28th, Cleveland 216-589-0121 www.cliffordhouse.com (♣?) ⚥ ☹

♂ • Wallace Manor B&B, 4724 Franklin Blvd, Cleveland; 44102 216-961-6298 wallacemanor.com ⚥ ☹ wallacemanor@gmail.com

AIDS/HIV Services, Education & Support

♀ AIDS Taskforce of Greater Cleveland, 2829 Euclid Ave, Cleveland; 216-621-0766 www.aidstaskforce.org

Archives/Libraries/Museums/History Projects

⚥ ★ && Northeast Ohio LGBT Archives, Western Reserve Historical Society, 10825 E Blvd, Cleveland; 216-721-5722 **H?** tinyurl.com/gvheu7a

Bars, Cafes, Clubs, Restaurants
Cleveland

♂ Cocktails Cleveland, 9208 Detroit Ave, Cleveland; 216-961-3115 fb.com/CocktailsCleveland **VDLW** ▥

♂ • The Hawk, 11217 Detroit Ave, Cleveland 216-521-5443 thehawkbar.com **LW**

♂ ○ Hecks Cafe, 2927 Bridge Ave, Cleveland 216-861-5464 www.heckscafe.com ✗

♀ ○ Johnny Mango World Cafe & Bar, 3120 Bridge Ave, Cleveland; 216-575-1919 www.jmango.com ⊻ ✗

♀ ○ && Jukebox, 1404 W 29th ST, Cleveland; 216-206-7699 www.jukeboxcle.com ⊻ ✗ ⚥ jukeboxcle@gmail.com

♂ • Leather Stallion Saloon, 2205 St Clair Ave, Cleveland; 216-589-8588 tinyurl.com/ujo8wp4 **LW**

♀ ○ Lucky's Cafe, 777 Starkweather Ave, Cleveland 216-622-7773 www.luckyscafe.com ⊡

♀ ○ Now That's Class, 11213 Detroit Ave, Cleveland 216-221-8576 www.nowthatsclass.net ⊻ ✗ info@nowthatsclass.net

♂ Twist, 11633 Clifton Blvd, Cleveland 216-221-2333 www.twistsocialclub.com

♂ • Vibe, 11633 Lorain Ave, Cleveland 216-476-1970 vibecleveland.com

Bookstores

♀ ○ && Loganberry Books, 13015 Larchmere Boulevard, Shaker Heights; 216-795-9800 www.loganberrybooks.com

Business Services

♀ ○ Moyer Paralegal Services, Ltd, 8440 Edge Lake Oval, Sagamore Hills; 44067 877-460-0478 www.moyerparalegal.com dmoyer@moyerparalegal.com

Funding: Endowment, Fundraising

♂ Northern Ohio Coalition, Inc, POB 110343, Cleveland; 44111 216-556-0129 www.mynoci.org

Gifts, Cards, Pride, etc.

♂ ○ ♿ Sweetie's Big Fun, Orange Village, 10 Park Ave #108, Beachwood; 216-371-4386 fb.com/sweetiesbigfunstore/

Health Care: Physical (see also Counseling/Mental Health)

♀ ☆ && Circle Health Services, 12201 Euclid Ave, Cleveland; 216-721-4010 **H?** thecentersohio.org

Leather Resources & Groups

♀ ☆ CLAW: Cleveland Leather Awareness Weekend, PO Box 111282, Cleveland; 44111 **H?** www.clawinfo.org

Men's & Sex Clubs (not primarily Health Clubs)

♂ • Flex Cleveland, 2600 Hamilton Ave, Cleveland 216-812-3304 www.flexspas.com/cleveland ☢

Organizations/Resources: Bisexual Focus

⚥ ☆ && BIGC: Bisexual Initiative of Greater Cleveland, mail to BIGC, 216-203-4166 Primarily bisexual & pansexual women & men bigcleveland.wordpress.com ⚥ bngcohio@gmail.com

Organizations/Resources: Business & Professional Associations, Labor Advocacy

⚥ ★ Plexus LGBT & Allied Chamber of Commerce, PO Box 91697, Cleveland; 44101 888-753-9879 www.thinkplexus.org

Organizations/Resources: Cultural, Dance, Performance

⚥ Good Company, 440-847-9889 www.good-co.org

♂ ★ North Coast Men's Chorus, POB 770664, Cleveland; 44107 216-556-0590 **H** www.ncmchorus.org

♀ Windsong, Cleveland's Feminist Chorus, POB 771212, Lakewood; 44107 216-521-5434 www.windsongcleveland.com

Organizations/Resources: Ethnic, Multicultural

⚥ ★ (♿) Asians & Friends Cleveland, POB 25095, Cleveland; 44125 www.afcleveland.org ✦

Organizations/Resources: Family and Supporters

♀ PFLAG Cleveland, 216-556-1701 www.pflagcleveland.org

Organizations/Resources: Political/Legislative/Advocacy

⚥ ★ Cleveland Stonewall Democrats, POB 91453, Cleveland; 44101 clevelandstonewalldems.org

Organizations/Resources: Social, Recreation, Support

♂ ★ Cleveland Bears, POB 14756, Cleveland; 44114 www.clevelandbears.org

♂ ★ Prime Timers Cleveland, POB 91683, Cleveland; 44101 216-233-9146 primetimersww.com/cleveland/

Organizations/Resources: Student, Academic, Education

⚥ ★ Baldwin Wallace University Allies and LGBT Contact Resource, 275 Eastland Rd, Berea; 440-826-2404 www.bw.edu/stulife/glbt/

⚥ ★ Case Western Reserve School of Law Lambda Law Students Association, 11075 East Blvd, Cleveland tinyurl.com/y9bffdsc

⚥ ★ && Case Western Reserve University LGBT Center, 11038 Bellflower Rd, Cleveland; 216-368-5428 www.case.edu/lgbt/

⚥ ★ && John Carroll Allies, Center forDiversity and Inclusion #126, 1 John Carroll Blvd, University Hts; 44118 ⚥

Ohio: Cleveland Area
Organizations: Transgender

274

GAYELLOW PAGES #42 2020-2021

Columbus Area: Ohio
Counseling

Organizations/Resources: Transgender/Gender Non-Conforming/Diverse

T ★ Alpha Omega Society, www.aosoc.org

T ○ && Medalie, Daniel A, MD, 25700 Science Park Dr Ste 190, Beachwood; 44122 216-393-9924 **H?** tinyurl.com/y99lb2ul ⚲ valerie@clevelandplasticsurgery.com

T ☆ TransFamily, 216-691-4357 Age 18-30 www.transfamily.org

Recovery

♀ Women's Recovery Center, 6209 Storer Ave, Cleveland; 216-651-1450 www.womensctr.org

Religious / Spiritual Resources

⚥ ★ Catholic Gay and Lesbian Family Ministry of Cleveland, 795 Russell Ave, Akron, OH 44307 tinyurl.com/y784ek7b glfm@dioceseofcleveland.org

⚥ ★ && Chevrei Tikva Chavurah, Anshe Chesed Fairmount Temple, 23737 Fairmount Blvd, Beachwood; 44122-2296 216-464-1330 x126 tinyurl.com/ohjkou4 ✡ mail@fairmounttemple.org

♂ ☆ Community Church of Chesterland UCC, 11984 Caves Rd, Chesterland; 44026 440-729-7898 chesterlanducc.org chesterlanducc@gmail.com

♂ ☆ (♨) Peace Lutheran Church, 3740 Mayfield Rd, Cleveland Hts; 44121 216-382-4545 peacelutheran-clehts.org peaceclehts@gmail.com

Sports & Outdoor

⚥ ★ Cleveland Out & About, www.clevelandoutandabout.org mail@clevelandoutandabout.org

♂ ★ North Coast Softball, www.northcoastsoftball.org commissioner@northcoastsoftball.org

Clifton

Accommodation: Hotels, Inns, Guesthouses, B&B, Resorts

♂ ○ Clifton Garden Cabin, 8 Clinton St; 45316 937-769-5040 www.cliftongardencabin.com CliftonGardenCabin@gmail.com

Columbus Area

Crisis, Anti-violence, & Helplines

⚥ ★ && Buckeye Region Anti-Violence Organization, POB 82068, Col; 43202 614-294-7867 (STOP) www.bravo-ohio.org

♀ Center for New Beginnings, POB 786, Newark 43058 800-686-2760 tinyurl.com/y9pzmwaj

Community Centers and/or Pride Organizations

⚥ ★ && The Center on High, Stonewall Columbus, 1160 N High St, Col; 614-299-7764 stonewallcolumbus.org

Information, Media & Publications

⚥ ● Lavender Listings, Stonewall Columbus, 1160 N High St, Col; 614-299-7764 www.lavenderlistings.com

Accommodation: Hotels, Inns, Guesthouses, B&B, Resorts
Columbus

♂ ● Wayfaring Buckeye Hostel, 2407 Indiana Ave, Col; 614-754-0945 www.wayfaringbuckeye.com (♣?) ⚲ ⊘

AIDS/HIV Services, Education & Support

⚥ ☆ Greater Columbus Mpowerment Center, Equitas Health, 889 E Long St, Col; 614-359-2033 **H?** Gay/bi men of color, ages 13-29 www.columbusmpowerment.org ❖ ⚲

♀ LifeCare Alliance, 1699 W Mound St, Col 614-278-3130 www.lifecarealliance.org

♀ ☆ Ohio State University Hospital AIDS Clinical Trials Unit, N 1149 Doan Hall, 410 W 10th Ave, Col; 614-293-5667 tinyurl.com/lbk8r85

Automobile Services

♂ ● ♂ Alternative Auto Care, 136 W 5th St, Col; 43201-3221 614-294-0580 www.alternativeautocare.com chris@alternativeautocare.com

Bars, Cafes, Clubs, Restaurants
Columbus

⚥ ● ♂ A.W.O.L., 49 Parsons Ave, Col 614-621-8779 www.awol-bar.com **K** ▥

⚥ ● && Axis, 775 N High St, Col 614-291-4008 axisonhigh.com **D** ▥

⚥ Boscoe's, 1224 S High St, Col 614-826-3758 www.boscoes-bar.com ▥

⚥ ● && Cavan Irish Pub, 1409 S High St, Col; 614-725-5502 www.cavanirishpub.com **K** ▥

⚥ ● (♨) Club Diversity, 863 S High St, Col; 614-224-4050 www.clubdiversity.biz **K** ▥ ⚲

⚥ O'Connors Club 20, 20 E Duncan, Col 614-447-9173 www.oconnorsclub20.com

⚥ ● ♂ South Bend Tavern, 126 E Moler St, Col; 614-444-3386 southbendtavern.com **DK** ▥ ⚲

⚥ Toolbox Saloon, 744 Frebis Ave, Col 614-670-8113 fb.com/ToolboxSaloon/ ▥

⚥ ● (♨) Tremont, 708 S High St, Col 614-444-2041 fb.com/TremontColumbus **D**

⚥ Union Cafe, 782 N High St, Col 614-421-2233 fb.com/UnionCafe/ **V** ▽ ✕ ⚲

Bookstores

♂ ● Book Loft, 631 S 3rd St, Col; 614-464-1774 www.bookloft.com

Counseling/Psychotherapy/Mental Health

⚥ ● (♨) Affirmations: A Center for Psychotherapy & Growth, 620 E Broad St Ste 301, Col; 43215 614-914-6690 www.affirmationstherapy.com affirmationstherapy2@gmail.com

♂ ● (♨) Shannon, Joseph W, PhD, 1155 W 3rd Ave, Col; 43212-3043 614-297-0422 JShannon@insight.rr.com

♂ ☆ Southeast, Inc, POB 1809, Col; 43216-1809 614-225-0990 www.southeastinc.com info@southeastinc.com

♂ ☆ Syntero Counseling, 299 Cramer Creek Court, Dublin; 43019 614-889-5722 www.syntero.org info@syntero.org

♂ ☆ Syntero Counseling, 3433 Agler Rd Ste 2000, Col; 43026 614-600-2708 www.syntero.org info@syntero.org

♀ ☆ Syntero Counseling, 3645 Ridge Mill Dr, Hilliard; 43026 614-457-7876 www.syntero.org info@syntero.org

♀ ☆ Syntero Counseling, 7100 Graphics Way Ste 3100, Lewis Center; 43035 740-428-0428 www.syntero.org info@syntero.org

Dentists

♀ ● ᏜᏜ Ford, James B, DDS, 118 N High St, Col; 43215 614-228-1113 www.drjamesbford.com drjamesbford@gmail.com

Funding: Endowment, Fundraising

♀ ● ᏜᏜ Legacy Fund of the Columbus Foundation, 1234 E Broad St, Col; 614-251-4000 www.thelegacyfund.org ↗

Health Care: Physical (see also Counseling/Mental Health)

♂ ☆ ᏜᏜ Equitas Health Medical Center & Pharmacy, 1033 N High St, Col; 614-340-6777 **H?** www.equitashealth.com

Legal Services

♂ ● Ꮬ Ball, Karen, POB 2815, Col 43216 614-743-2315 KBLawOhio@gMail.com

♀ ○ Golden & Meizlish Co, LPA, 923 E Broad St, Col; 43205-1101 614-258-1983 www.golmeizlaw.com info@golmeiz.com

♀ ○ Luftman, Heck & Associates, LLP, 601 S High St, Col; 43215 614-500-3836 tinyurl.com/cpr32g6 advice@columbus criminalattorney.com

♀ ○ ᏜᏜ Pamela N Maggied Co, LPA, 85 E Gay St Ste 600, Col; 43215 614-464-2236 **H?** Bankruptcy www.pamelamaggied.com maggiedlaw@pamelamaggied.com

Men's & Sex Clubs (not primarily Health Clubs)

♂ ● ᏜᏜ Club Columbus, 795 W 5th Ave, Col; 614-291-0049 tinyurl.com/y5am4bky **P** ↗

Organizations/Resources: Business & Professional Associations, Labor Advocacy

♀ Dames Bond, 1188 N High St, Col; 614-209-3556 www.damesbond.com

Organizations/Resources: Cultural, Dance, Performance

♀ ● ★ Ꮬ The Capital Pride Band of Columbus, POB 8147, Col; 43201 www.CapPride.org ↗

♂ ★ Columbus Gay Men's Chorus, 51 Jefferson Ave, Col; 614-228-2462 www.cgmc.com

♀ ★ Columbus Stompers, POB 163131, Col 43216 fb.com/Columbus.Stompers

♀ ☆ (♲) Columbus Women's Chorus, POB 141542, Col; 43214-1542 614-636-3541 www.colswomenschorus.org info@colswomenschorus.org

Organizations/Resources: Deaf

♀ Buckeye Rainbow Alliance of the Deaf, www.bradohio.com

Organizations/Resources: Family and Supporters

♀ ☆ PFLAG Columbus, 614-313-9956 www.columbuspflag.org

Organizations/Resources: Naturist/Nudist

♂ ★ CONGA (Central Ohio Naturist Guy Alliance), www.congaline.org **N**

Organizations/Resources: Political/Legislative/Advocacy

♀ ★ Stonewall Democrats of Central Ohio, 929 Harrison Ave #100, Col

Organizations/Resources: Social, Recreation, Support

♂ ★ Columbus Ohio Prime Timers, 1928 Dandridge Dr, Col; 614-885-0846 www.primetimersww.org/copt/

Organizations/Resources: Student, Academic, Education

♀ ★ Denison University Outlook, Slayter Box 18904, Granville; fb.com/duoutlook/

♀ ★ (♲) FreeZone Alliance, Box 13304, 1 Otterbein College, Westerville

♀ ★ Ohio State University Moritz College of Law Outlaws, Law Building #42, 55 W 12th Ave, Col tinyurl.com/ycwz6o47

♀ ★ ᏜᏜ Ohio Wesleyan Spectrum Resource Center, Avenue, HWCC 205 40 Rowland Ave, Delaware; 43015 740-368-3196 tinyurl.com/j2hhnjs ↗ spectrumrc@owu.edu

♀ ★ Ohio Wesleyan University PRIDE, 61 S Sandusky St, Delaware; tinyurl.com/zghlctc

♀ ★ Scarlet & Gay OSU LGBTQ Alumni Society, PO Box 2012, Col; 43216-2012 614-292-5130 scarletandgay.alumni.osu.edu

Organizations/Resources: Youth (see also Family)

♀ Huckleberry House, 1421 Hamlet St, Col 614-294-5553 www.huckhouse.org

♀ ★ (♲) Kaleidoscope Youth Center, 603 E Town St, Col; 614-294-5437 **H?** www.kycohio.org ↗

Recovery

♀ ☆ ᏜᏜ AA Central Ohio, 651 W Broad St, Col; 43215 614-253-8501 **H?** www.aacentralohio.org

♀ ☆ Amethyst, 455 E Mound St, Col; 614-242-1284 www.amethyst-inc.org

Religious / Spiritual Resources

♀ ★ ᏜᏜ B'nai Keshet at OSU, OSU Hillel, Wexner Jewish Student Center, 46 E 16th St, Col; 614-294-4797 **H?** www.osuhillel.org ✡ ↗

♀ ☆ Broad Street UMC, 501 E Broad St, Col 43215-3822 614-221-4571 www.broadstreetumc.net

♀ Dignity/Columbus, www.dignitycolumbus.org

♀ ☆ First Unitarian Universalist Church, 93 W Weisheimer Rd, Col; 43214-2544 614-267-4946 www.firstuucolumbus.org

♀ ★ ᏜᏜ Integrity/Central Ohio, c/o St. Stephen's Episcopal Church, 30 W Woodruff Ave, Col; 614-294-3749 www.ststephens-columbus.org

♀ ☆ ᏜᏜ Just North Congregational UCC, 2040 W Henderson Rd, Col; 43220 614-451-1835 www.northchurchucc.org ↗

♀ ☆ (♲) Maynard Avenue UMC, 2350 Indianola Ave, Col; 43202-3055 614-263-5145 www.maynardaveumc.org ↗

Ohio: Columbus Area
Religious
276
GAYELLOW PAGES #42 2020-2021
Lima: Ohio
Organizations: Student

⚥ ★ New Creation MCC, 116 E Williams Rd, Col 43207 614-409-9610 newcreationmcc.org

♀ ☆ The Oasis, see website for meetings in Reynoldsburg/Pickerington area www.theoasisucc.com theoasisucc@yahoo.com

♀ ☆ &&. Summit on 16th (UMC), 82 E 16th Ave, Col; 43201 614-291-3324 **H?** www.summitumc.org ✎ sumc@summitumc.org

Sports & Outdoor

⚥ ★ Capital City Volleyball, c/o Stonewall Columbus, POB 10814, Col; 43201 614-270-1274 inyurl.com/yjftbsu

⚥ Columbus Lesbian & Gay Softball, 605 N High St #203, Col; www.clgsa.net

⚥ ★ Flaggots Ohio LLC, 1790 Kenview Rd, Col 614-562-6288 www.flaggotsohio.org

⚥ Ohio Splash, ohiosplash.com

Coshocton

Accommodation: Hotels, Inns, Guesthouses, B&B, Resorts

♂ ○ Apple Butter Inn, 455 Hill St; 43812 740-622-1329 www.apple-butterinn.net applebutterinn@yahoo.com
>> *Creola: see Hocking Hills*
>> *Danville: see Columbus Area*

Dayton/Springfield Area

Community Centers and/or Pride Organizations

⚥ ★ &&. Greater Dayton LGBT Center, 24 N Jefferson St Ste 200, Dayton; 45402 937-274-1776 www.daytonlgbtcenter.org info@daytonlgbtcenter.org

Information, Media & Publications

⚥ Lesbian Dayton, tinyurl.com/ycnj8pyf

Bars, Cafes, Clubs, Restaurants
Dayton

♂ ● Argos, 301 Mable Ave, Dayton; 937-301-9043 argosleatherbar.com **L**

⚥ Club Evolution, 130 N Patterson Blvd, Dayton; 937-203-2582 www.evolutionnightclub.net

♂ ● &&. Masque, 34 N Jefferson St, Dayton; 937-228-2582 clubmasque.com ▥

⚥ ● &&. Mj's on Jefferson, 20 N Jefferson St, Dayton; 937-223-3259 www.mjsonjefferson.com **DKLV** ⚥ ✕ ▥ ✎

⚥ ● &&. The Right Corner, 105 E 3rd St, Dayton; 937-228-2033 fb.com/RightCornerBar ⚥ ✕

♂ Stage Door, 44 N Jefferson, Dayton 937-223-7418 fb.com/thestagedoor **L** ▥

Springfield

⚥ ● (?&.) Diesel, 1914 Edwards Ave, Springfield; 937-324-0383 fb.com/Dieselspringfield/ **DKV** ▥ ✎

Yellow Springs

♂ ○ &&. Winds Cafe, 215 Xenia Ave, Yellow Springs; 937-767-1144 www.windscafe.com ⚥ ✕

Organizations/Resources: Cultural, Dance, Performance

♂ ★ Dayton Gay Men's Chorus, POB 642, Dayton 45401-0642 937-530-0642 www.daytongaymenschorus.org info@daytongaymenschorus.org

⚥ Dayton Lesbian & Gay Film Festival, The New Neon Movies, 130 E 5th St, Dayton; 937-222-7469 www.daytonlgbt.com

Organizations/Resources: Family and Supporters

♀ ☆ &&. PFLAG Dayton, POB 3721, Dayton; 45401-3721 937-640-3333 www.pflagdayton.org daytonpflag@yahoo.com

Organizations/Resources: Social, Recreation, Support

♂ ★ Miami Valley Ohio Prime Timers, POB 750831, Dayton; 45475 937-520-6413 mvopt.com

♂ ★ Mu Crew, c/o AIDS Resource Center Ohio, 15 W 4th St #200, Dayton; 937-461-2437 x2015 www.themucrew.com

Organizations/Resources: Student, Academic, Education

⚥ ★ &. Wittenburg University Gender and Sexual Diversity Alliance, 641 Faculty Court, W Ward St, Springfield 937-327-9210 fb.com/wittlbgqt ✎

Religious / Spiritual Resources

⚥ ★ &&. Eternal Joy MCC, 20 W First St, Dayton; 937-254-2087 fb.com/groups/EJMCC/ ✎ ♥

⚥ &&. Living Beatitudes/Dignity Dayton, Christ Episcopal Church, 20 W First St, Dayton; 937-223-2239 www.livingbeatitudes.org

Sports & Outdoor

♂ Dayton Gay Volleyball, tinyurl.com/me8oww
>> *Glouster: see Athens*

Hocking Hills

Accommodation Rental: Furnished / Vacation (& AirBNB)

♂ ○ (?&.) Lazy Lane Cabins, POB 907, Logan; 43138 877-225-6572 www.lazylanecabins.com ⚘ ✎ ⊛ info@lazylanecabins.com
>> *Kent: see Akron/Canton/Kent Area*
>> *Lakewood: see Cleveland Area*

Lima

Bars, Cafes, Clubs, Restaurants

⚥ ● & Somewhere In Time, 804 W North St; 419-227-7288 www.somewherelima.com **D** ▥

Organizations/Resources: Family and Supporters

♀ ☆ PFLAG Lima, 309 W High St; 419-979-9353 pflag.org/chapter/pflag-lima

Organizations/Resources: Student, Academic, Education

⚥ ★ (?&.) Ohio Northern University Open Doors, 402 W College Ave Unit 1053, Ada; webstu.onu.edu/od/node/6 ✎
>> *Logan: see Hocking Hills*

Ohio: Mansfield
Bars, Cafes, Clubs, Restaurants

277
GAYELLOW PAGES #42 2020-2021

Toledo : Ohio
Organizations: Student

Mansfield

Bars, Cafes, Clubs, Restaurants

Sami's Bar, 178 Wayne St; 419-522-1500 fb.com/samis419 **D**

Medina

Organizations/Resources: Social, Recreation, Support

Out Support, 330-461-5545 outsupport.org
>> *Monroe: see Cincinnati Area*

New Concord

Organizations/Resources: Student, Academic, Education

★ Muskingum University Equality Alliance, 163 Stormont St; 740-826-8080 tinyurl.com/zmsf3fo

New London

Campgrounds and RV Parks

● Freedom Valley, 1875 US 250 S; 44851 419-929-8100 www.FreedomValleyCamping.com ✿ ✔ ⊛ info@FreedomValley Camping.com

Oberlin

Archives/Libraries/Museums/History Projects

Oberlin College LGBT Community History Project, Wilder 208-105, 135 W Lorain St, Oberlin; 440-775-8802 www.oberlin.edu/mrc

Bookstores

○ (♲) Ben Franklin/MindFair Books, 13 W College St, Oberlin; 440-774-6463 www.benfranklinoberlin.com

Counseling/Psychotherapy/Mental Health

○ Miller, Jane, LISW, CDBC, 5 S Main St #205, Oberlin; 44074 800-457-0345 www.healing-companions.org jmiller@oberlin.net

Organizations/Resources: Student, Academic, Education

★ Oberlin College LGBTQ Community Multicultural Resource Center, 135 W Lorain St Wilder 208-105, Oberlin; 440-775-8802 fb.com/oberlin.mrc

Religious / Spiritual Resources

☆ ♿ Oberlin Unitarian Universalist Fellowship, 355 E Lorain St, Oberlin; 44074 440-775-0355 www.ouuf.org

☆ Peace Community Church, 44 E Lorain St, Oberlin; 44074-1128 440-774-3031 www.pccoberlin.org

Oxford

Organizations/Resources: Student, Academic, Education

★ ♿ LGBTQ Services, Armstrong Student Center Ste 3012, 550 E Spring St; 513-529-6510 www.muohio.edu/glbt ✔

★ Miami University 1809 LGBT Alumni, 725 E Chestnut; 513-529-3587

★ ♿ Miami University Spectrum, 3037 Armstrong Student Center; 513-529-0831 spectrummiami.wordpress.com ✔

☆ Miami University Women's and LGBTQ Center, Armstrong Student Center 3012; 513-529-1510 tinyurl.com/249dyun

Sandusky

Bars, Cafes, Clubs, Restaurants

○ Mona Pizza Gourmet, 135 Columbus Ave 419-626-8166 www.sanduskyslice.com ⟨P

● Sandusky Crowbar, 206 W Market St fb.com/sandusky.crow-bar/ **D** ✔

Scio

Accommodation: Hotels, Inns, Guesthouses, B&B, Resorts

● ♿ Circle JJ Ranch, 1104 Amsterdam Rd SE; 330-627-3101 www.circlejjranch.com **P** ✿ ✔
>> *Springfield: see Dayton/Springfield Area*

Toledo

AIDS/HIV Services, Education & Support

★ ♿ Toledo Mpowerment, c/o AIDS Resource Center Ohio, 3450 W Central Ave Ste #210; 419-241-9444 x413 toledompowerment.arcohio.org

Bars, Cafes, Clubs, Restaurants

Legends Showclub, 117 N Erie St 567-315-8333 **D**

○ McCune's Other Side Bistro Bar, 5038 Lewis Ave 419-476-1577 fb.com/OtherSideBistro5038/ **DK** ♈ ✕

Mojo's, 115 N Erie St; 567-315-8333 fb.com/mojostoledo/ ▥

R House, 5534 Secor Rd; 419-984-5011 toledorhouse.com **D**

Counseling/Psychotherapy/Mental Health

● ♿ Meiring, Thomas, PhD, LPCC, Innerview Behavioral Care, 27475 Holiday Lane #2, Perrysburg; 43551-3350 419-872-0619 fax 419-872-2466 www.mbhcinnerview.com tommeiring phd@gmail.com

Legal Services

○ ● ♿ Kirby, Cindy M., Atty at Law, Kirby & Kirby, Ltd. 316 N Michigan St Ste 818; 43604 419-693-4433 KirbyFamilyLaw.com Cindy@KirbyFamilyLaw.com

Organizations/Resources: Education

★ EqualityToledo, POB 2659; 43606 419-407-6225 www.equalitytoledo.org

Organizations/Resources: Family and Supporters

☆ PFLAG Toledo, 4623 Ottawa Trail; 419-386-7830 www.pflagtoledo.org

Organizations/Resources: Student, Academic, Education

★ Delta Lambda Phi Beta Omicron Chapter, University of Toledo/Bowling Green State University www.dlp.org/betaomicron

Ohio: Toledo
Organizations: Youth

278

GAYELLOW PAGES #42 2020-2021

Grand Lake : Oklahoma
Bars, Cafes, Clubs, Restaurants

Organizations/Resources: Youth (see also Family)

♂ Harvey House, 1415 W Sylvania Ave 419-356-1256 www.harvey-housenwo.org

>> *Warren: see Youngstown Area*

West Lafayette

Bars, Cafes, Clubs, Restaurants

♀ ● 点点 Lava Rock Grill at Unusual Junction, 56310 US 36 W; 740-545-9772 www.theunusualjunction.com ✖ ⇖ ✗

Wooster

Accommodation: Hotels, Inns, Guesthouses, B&B, Resorts

♀ ○ Black Squirrel Inn, 636 College Ave; 44691 330-317-6627 www.blacksquirrelinn.com (✿?) ✗ ⊗ ⊗ black.squirrel.inn@gmail.com

Religious / Spiritual Resources

♀ ☆ 点点 UU Fellowship of Wayne County, 3186 Burbank Rd; 44691 330-262-9194 **HD** www.uufwc.org fellowship@uufwc.org
>> *Yellow Springs: see Dayton/Springfield Area*

Youngstown Area

Community Centers and/or Pride Organizations

♂ Pride Youngstown, POB 2891, Ytn; 44511 330-518-4718 tinyurl.com/y9dkfdwy

Bars, Cafes, Clubs, Restaurants
Warren

♂ The Funky Skunk, 143 E Market St, Warren tinyurl.com/9ecmvzb
D ▮▮▮

Youngstown

♂ Mineshaft, 1105 Poland Ave, Ytn; / check ahead 330-207-6437 youngstownmineshaft.com **LL**

♂ Switch, 221 Belmont Ave, Ytn; 234-228-9261 fb.com/ytown-switch/

Organizations/Resources: Family and Supporters

♀♂ ☆ Youngstown Area PFLAG, 330-747-2696 www.young-stownpflag.org

Organizations/Resources: Political/Legislative/Advocacy

♀♂ ★ Mahoning Valley Stonewall Democrats, www.mvstonewall.com

Organizations/Resources: Student, Academic, Education

♀♂ ★ 点点 Youngstown State University YSUnity: LGBTQIA, Student Government, 1 University Plaza, Kilcawley Center, Ytn; 330-892-8318 www.ysunity.ysu.edu ✗

Recovery

♀♂ ☆ Alcoholics Anonymous, 3373 Youngstown - Canfield Rd, Ytn; 330-270-3000 www.aayaig.org

Travel & Tourist Services (see also Accommodation)

♀♂ ○ (♿) Burger Travel Service, 2324 Coronado Ave, Ytn; 330-744-5035 www.burgertravel.com

Oklahoma
State/County Resources

Crisis, Anti-violence, & Helplines

♀♂ ☆ Oklahoma Coalition Against Domestic Violence & Sexual Assault, 3815 N Santa Fe Ave #124, Oklahoma City, OK 405-524-0700 www.ocadvsa.org

Community Centers and/or Pride Organizations

♀♂ ★ Diversity Center of Oklahoma, 2242 NW 39th, Oklahoma City, OK 73112 405-604-5217 diversitycenterofoklahoma.org info@diversitycenterofoklahoma.org

AIDS/HIV Services, Education & Support

♀♂ ☆ 点点 RAIN OK (Regional AIDS Intercommunity Network), 3800 N Classen Blvd Ste 200, Oklahoma City, OK 73118 405-232-2437 800-285-2273 www.rainoklahoma.org info@rainoklahoma.org

Funding: Endowment, Fundraising

♀♂ ★ Imperial Court of All Oklahoma Inc, POB 14533, Tulsa, OK 74159 www.impcourtok.org impcourtok@gmail.com

Legal Services

♀♂ ☆ 点点 AIDS Legal Resource Project, Legal Aid Services of Oklahoma Inc, 2915 N Classen Blvd Ste 500, Oklahoma City, OK 800-421-1641 www.legalaidok.org

Organizations/Resources: Political/Legislative/Advocacy

♀♂ ☆ & American Civil Liberties Union of Oklahoma, POB 1626, Oklahoma City, OK 73102 405-524-8511 www.acluok.org

♀♂ ★ Oklahomans for Equality, 621 E 4th St, Tulsa, OK 918-743-4297 www.okeq.org

Recovery

♀♂ ☆ Alcoholics Anonymous, POB 18415, Oklahoma City, OK 73154 405-524-1100 www.aaoklahoma.org

Sports & Outdoor

♀♂ ★ Sooner State Softball Alliance, www.soonerstatesoftball.org
>> *Broken Arrow: see Tulsa*
>> *Edmond: see Oklahoma City Area*

Enid

Organizations/Resources: Social, Recreation, Support

♀♂ ★ Enid LGBT Coalition, POB 775; 73702 800-878-5298 www.enidlgbtcoalition.org

Grand Lake

Bars, Cafes, Clubs, Restaurants
Langley

♀♂ ○ Artichoke Restaurant & Bar, 35878 S Hwy 82, Langley; 918-782-9855 theartichokeatgrand.com ⚲ ✖

Oklahoma: Lawton
Organizations: Student

279
GAYELLOW PAGES #42 2020-2021

Oklahoma City Area: Oklahoma
Reproductive Medical Services

Lawton

Organizations/Resources: Student, Academic, Education

♂ ★ Cameron University Pride, c/o Student Activities, 2800 W Gore Blvd; 580-581-2236 fb.com/CAMERONUNIVPRIDE
>> *Muskogee: see Muskoka Region*
>> *Norman: see Oklahoma City Area*

Oklahoma City Area

Crisis, Anti-violence, & Helplines

♀ ☆ ♂♂ Women's Resource Center, Inc., PO Box 5089, Norman; 73070 405-701-5540 **H** WRCNormanOK.org

Community Centers and/or Pride Organizations

♀ ★ ♂♂ OKC Pride, Inc, POB 12240, OKC; 73157 405-466-5428 www.okcpride.org

Accommodation: Hotels, Inns, Guesthouses, B&B, Resorts
Oklahoma City

♀ ● ♂♂ Habana Inn, 2200 NW 39th Expressway, OKC; 405-528-2221 www.habanainn.com **DLCW** ✕

AIDS/HIV Services, Education & Support

♂ Expressions Community Center, 2245 NW 39th St 405-528-2210 www.eccokc.org

Bars, Cafes, Clubs, Restaurants
Oklahoma City

♀ Alibis Club, 1200 N Pennsylvania Ave, OKC 405-604-3684 fb.com/alibisclubokc

♂ The Apothecary 39 OKC, 2125 Nw 39th St, OKC; 405-605-4100 www.apothecary39.com **D** 🏳️‍🌈

♂ The Boom, 2218 NW 36th St, OKC 405-601-7200 www.theboomokc.com 🏳️‍🌈

♀ ● ♂ Copa, Habana Inn, 2200 NW 39th Expressway, OKC; 405-525-0730 fb.com/thecopaokc/ **DW**

♀ ○ Edna's, 5137 N Classen Blvd, OKC; 405-840-3339 www.ednasokc.com ⚥ ✕ tammy@ednasokc.com

♀ ● ♂ Finishline, Habana Inn, 2200 NW 39th Expressway, OKC; 405-525-2900 fb.com/finishline.okc/ **DW**

♂ ● ♂ Gushers - Ledo, Habana Inn, 2200 NW 39th Expressway, OKC; 405-525-0730 www.habanainn.com **DW** ⚥ ✕

♂ ● Hi-Lo Club, 1221 NW 50th St, OKC 405-843-1722 fb.com/Hilo-clubokc/ **D** 🏳️‍🌈

♂ ● ♂♂ Partners, 2805 NW 36th St, OKC; 405-942-2199 www.partnersokc.com **DK** 🏳️‍🌈

♂ Phoenix Rising, 2120 NW 39th Ave, OKC 405-601-3711 www.phoenixrisingokc.com **D**

♂ Tramps, 2201 NW 39th St, OKC 405-528-9888

♀ ○ Vito's Ristorante, 7628 N May Ave, OKC 405-848-4867 www.vitosokc.com ✕

♀ Wreck Room, 2127 NW 39th St - check schedule 405-525-7610 **D** 🏳️‍🌈

Counseling/Psychotherapy/Mental Health

♂ ☆ ♂♂ Red Rock Behavioral Health Services (BHS), 4400 N Lincoln Blvd, OKC; 405-424-7711 www.red-rock.com

Funding: Endowment, Fundraising

♀ ☆ AIDS Walk of Oklahoma City, POB 60778, OKC 73146 405-673-3786 aidswalkokc.org

Organizations/Resources: Business & Professional Associations, Labor Advocacy

♂ Diversity Business Association, 4001 N Classen #116, OKC; 405-802-8229 fb.com/dbaokc

Organizations/Resources: Family and Supporters

♂ ☆ ♂♂ PFLAG Norman, POB 721692, Norman; 73070-8298 405-360-4497 **H?** fb.com/PFLAGNorman/ normanpflag@gmail.com

♂ ☆ ♂♂ PFLAG Oklahoma City, 4001 N Classen Blvd Ste 116, OKC; 405-456-9975 www.pflagoklahomacity.org ✔

Organizations/Resources: Political/Legislative/Advocacy

♂ ★ Freedom Oklahoma, POB 18711, OKC; 73154 405-446-8836 freedomoklahoma.org info@freedomoklahoma.org

Organizations/Resources: Social, Recreation, Support

♂ ★ (?♂) Central Oklahoma Prime Timers, 5030 N May Ave #134, OKC; 405-771-6578 www.centralokpt.com

♀ ★ ♂♂ Herland Sisters, 2312 NW 39th St, OKC; Feminist bookstore & women's resource center; of various events, concerts, retreats, etc. www.herlandsisters.org ⚲ ✔

♀ ☆ The Welcoming Project, www.thewelcomingproject.org

Organizations/Resources: Student, Academic, Education

♀ ★ ♂♂ Student Alliance for Equality (SAFE), University of Central Oklahoma, 100 N University Dr Box 184, Edmond 73034-5209 405-974-5605 www.uco.edu/safe ✔

♂ ★ (?♂) University of Oklahoma GLBTF, c/o Center for Student Life, 900 Asp Ave, OMU, Room 247, Norman; 405-325-4929 www.glbtf.org ✔

Recovery

♂ ☆ Al-Anon/Alateen Al-Anon Info Service, 3801 NW 63rd St Bldg 3, #129, OKC; 405-767-9071 www.okcalanon.org

Religious / Spiritual Resources

♀ ★ (♂♂) Cathedral of Hope OKC, 3131 N Pennsylvania Ave, OKC; 73112-7931 405-232-HOPE **H?** www.cohokc.com ♥

♀ ☆ Expressions Church, 3209 N May Ave, OKC; 73112 405-525-2903 www.expressionsokc.com contactus@expressionsokc.com

♀ ☆ ♂♂ First Unitarian Church, 600 NW 13th St, OKC; 73103-2296 405-232-9224 **HD** www.1UC.org ✔

Reproductive Medicine & Fertility Services

♂ Planned Parenthood of Central Oklahoma, 619 NW 23rd St, OKC; 405-528-2157 www.ppcok.org

Oklahoma: Stillwater
Organizations: Family

280

GAYELLOW PAGES #42 2020-2021

State/County Resources : Oregon
Counseling

Stillwater

Organizations/Resources: Family and Supporters

♀ ☆ && Stillwater PFLAG, 405-714-0064 www.pflagstillwater.org

Tulsa

Community Centers and/or Pride Organizations

♂ ★ && Dennis R. Neill Equality Center, 621 E 4th St; 918-743-4297 www.okeq.org ✔

♂ ★ && Tulsa Pride, 621 E 4th St 918-743-4297 www.tulsapride.org ✔

Accounting, Bookkeeping, Tax Services

♀ ● && Kirby, Kelly, CPA, PC, 4815 S Harvard Ste 205; 74135-3066 918-747-5466 www.KKirby.com ✔ Kelly@KKirby.com

AIDS/HIV Services, Education & Support

♀ ☆ && Tulsa CARES, 3712 E 11th St 74112-3952 918-834-4194 www.tulsacares.org tulsacares@tulsacares.org

Archives/Libraries/Museums/History Projects

♂ ★ && Nancy & Joe McDonald Rainbow Library, Dennis R. Neill Equality Center, 621 E 4th St; 918-743-4297 tinyurl.com/m8edq8r ✔

♂ ★ Tulsa LGBT History Project, c/o OKEQ, POB 2687; 74101 918-743-4297 tinyurl.com/kgda46h

Art & Photography (see also Graphic Design)

♂ ● Steven Michael's Photography, 3171 E 26th St 74114 918-759-3333 www.StevenMichaels.com ✔ Steven@StevenMichaels.com

Bars, Cafes, Clubs, Restaurants

♂ ● && Club Majestic, 124 N Boston Ave; 918-584-9494 www.clubmajestictulsa.com D 🍺 ✔

♀ ○ Juniper Restaurant & Martini Lounge, 324 E 3rd St; 918-794-1090 www.JuniperTulsa.com ⛾ ✗

♀ ○ Mixed Company, 3rd & Denver 918-932-8571 www.mixco-tulsa.com

♂ The Revue, Thelma's Bar, 2008 E Admiral Blvd; / check schedule 918-836-5272 www.therevuetulsa.com 🍺

♂ Tulsa Eagle, 1338 E 3rd St; 918-592-1188 tinyurl.com/y5qheqvq

♂ Yellow Brick Road Pub, 2630 E 15th St 918-293-0304 fb.com/YBRTulsa

Health Care: Physical (see also Counseling/Mental Health)

♀ ○ Acupuncture Associates of NE OK, 302 N McKinley Ave, Sand Springs; 918-261-1126

♀ ○ && LaButti, Ronald, DO, FAOAO, 6585 S Yale Ste 200; 74136 918-514-3009 **H?** www.hipandkneedoc.com ✔ ronlabutti@cox.net

Leather Resources & Groups

♂ ☆ T.U.L.S.A., POB 470612; 74147 www.tulsaleather.com

Legal Services

♀ ○ (♿) Wilkins, Karen Keith, 1515 S Denver Ave; 74119 918-599-8118 www.wilkinslawtulsa.com Karen@WilkinsLawTulsa.com

Organizations/Resources: Cultural, Dance, Performance

♀ ☆ Council Oak Men's Chorale, POB 1062; 74101 www.counciloak.org

Organizations/Resources: Family and Supporters

♀ ☆ && PFLAG Tulsa, POB 52800; 74152 918-928-7818 www.pflagtulsa.org

Organizations/Resources: Naturist/Nudist

♂ ★ North East Oklahoma Nudists, 1303 E 9th St, Okmulgee, OK 74447-5209 918-857-3366 neonmen@gmail.com

Organizations/Resources: Social, Recreation, Support

♂ ★ Tulsa Area Prime Timers (TAPT), POB 9224 74157 405-603-8997 www.tulsaareaprimetimers.com

Organizations/Resources: Youth (see also Family)

♀ ☆ Youth Services of Tulsa, 311 S Madison Ave 918-582-0061 www.yst.org

Recovery

♀ ☆ AA: Central Services, 4853 S Sheridan Rd Ste 600; 918-627-2224 www.aaneok.org

♀ ☆ Al-Anon/Alateen Al-anon Family Groups Intergroup, 4867 S Sheridan Ste 705; 866-210-3426 www.tulsaiso.org

Religious / Spiritual Resources

♀ ☆ All Souls Unitarian Church, 2952 S Peoria Ave 74114 918-743-2363 www.allsoulschurch.org info@allsoulschurch.org

♀ ☆ (♿) Fellowship Congregational Church UCC, 2900 S Harvard Ave; 74114 918-747-7777 www.ucctulsa.org ucctulsa@swbell.net

Sports & Outdoor

♂ ★ Tulsa Lambda Bowling League, POB 4147 00741 fb.com/tulsalambdaleague

♂ ★ Tulsa Metro Softball League, c/o OKEQ, PO Box 2687; 74101 www.tulsametrosoftball.com

Oregon
State/County Resources

Campgrounds and RV Parks

● ● (♿) Oregon Women's Land Trust-OWL Farm, 541-844-5038 Welcomes women-born-women visitors to our forests & meadows. tinyurl.com/z52cohd ✤ ☻

Counseling/Psychotherapy/Mental Health

♀ Cascadia Behavioral Healthcare, POB 8459, Portland, OR 97207 503-238-0769 www.cascadiabhc.org

Oregon: State/County Resources
Organizations: Business

281
GAYELLOW PAGES #42 2020-2021

Corvallis/Albany: Oregon
AIDS/HIV Support

Organizations/Resources: Business & Professional Associations, Labor Advocacy

♂ ★ OGALLA: The LGBT Bar Association of Oregon, POB 40171, Portland, OR 97240 www.ogalla.org

Organizations/Resources: Political/Legislative/Advocacy

♂ ☆ ACLU of Oregon, POB 40585, Portland, OR 97240 503-227-3186 www.aclu-or.org

♀♂ ☆ && Basic Rights Oregon (BRO), 620 SW 5th Ave Ste 1210, Portland, OR 503-222-6151 **H?** www.basicrights.org ✔

♂ ☆ Rural Organizing Project, POB 664, Cottage Grove, OR 77424 503-543-8417 www.rop.org office@rop.org

Organizations/Resources: Social, Recreation, Support

♀ ★ Lavender Womyn, Lesbian, bi, & trans women tinyurl.com/lb2c38

Organizations/Resources: Student, Academic, Education

♂ ☆ && GLSEN Oregon, POB 2945, Portland, OR 97208 503-683-1748 **H?** www.glsen.org/oregon ✔ oregon@chapters.glsen.org

♂ ★ Oregon Safe Schools and Communities Coalition, POB 14896, Portland, OR 97293 www.oregonsafeschools.org

Religious / Spiritual Resources

♂ ★ (?&) Integrity Oregon, c/o St. Stephen's Episcopal Church, 1432 SW 13th Ave, Portland, OR 503-991-9510

Arch Cape

Accommodation: Hotels, Inns, Guesthouses, B&B, Resorts
Cannon Beach

♂ ● Ocean Point Inn & Spa, POB 832, Cannon Beach; 97110 / 79819 Ocean Point Rd, Arch Cape 503-436-1833 www.oceanpoint-inn.com ✔ ◈ info@ocean-point.com

Ashland/Medford/Rogue River Valley

Crisis, Anti-violence, & Helplines

♂ ☆ && Community Works, 2594 E Barnett Rd - Ste C, Medford; 541-779-2393 **H?** www.community-works.org

♀ ☆ Women's Crisis Support Team, 560 NE F St #A430, Grants Pass; 800-750-9278 www.wcstjoco.org

Accommodation: Hotels, Inns, Guesthouses, B&B, Resorts
Ashland

♂ ● (?&) Arden Forest Inn, 261 W Hersey St, Ashland; 541-488-1496 www.afinn.com ✔ ◈

AIDS/HIV Services, Education & Support

♂ Josephine County HIV Prevention Programs, 715 NW Dimmick, Grants Pass; 541-474-5325 tinyurl.com/ydaxdnoo

♂ OnTrack / the Allan Collins AIDS Project, 221 W Main St, Medford; 541-772-1777 ontrackroguevalley.org

Bars, Cafes, Clubs, Restaurants
Ashland

♂ ○ (?&) The Black Sheep Pub & Restaurant, 51 N Main St, Ashland; 541-482-6414 www.theblacksheep.com ⚑ ✕▥ ✔

♂ ○ & Greenleaf Restaurant, 49 N Main St, Ashland; 541-482-2808 www.greenleafrestaurant.com ✕ ☞ ✔

Grants Pass

♂ ○ && Sunshine Natural Foods Cafe, 128 SW H St, Grants Pass; 541-474-5044 tinyurl.com/qzg9xe3 ☞ ✔

Bookstores

♂ ○ Bloomsbury Books, 290 E Main St, Ashland 541-488-0029 ☞

Erotica / Adult Stores / Safe Sex Supplies

♂ ● & As You Like It - A Love Revolution, 383 E Main St, Ashland; 97520 541-201-2060 Awareness - Love - Pleasure. Serving all people with love & care since 2011. www.asyoulikeitshop.com

Organizations/Resources: Bisexual Focus

⚥ amBI, www.ambi.org/ashland/

Organizations/Resources: Cultural, Dance, Performance

♂ The Heather and the Rose Country Dancers, 645 Glenwood Drive, Ashland; 541-482-9586 heatherandrose.org

Organizations/Resources: Student, Academic, Education

♂ ★ && Queer Resource Center, Southern Oregon University, 1250 Siskiyou Blvd SU308, Ashland; 97520-5001 541-552-8329 **H?** www.sou.edu/qrc ✔ qrc@sou.edu

Religious / Spiritual Resources

♂ ☆ && UCC Ashland First Congregational, 717 Siskiyou Blvd, Ashland; 97520 541-482-1981 AshlandPeaceChurchon.org ✔ ucc@opendoor.biz

Bend

Organizations/Resources: Education

♂ ☆ Human Dignity Coalition, 155 NW Irving Ave 541-385-3320 fb.com/HumanDignityCo/

Organizations/Resources: Family and Supporters

♂ ☆ && PFLAG Central Oregon, POB 1165, Redmond; 97756 541-728-3843 www.pflagcentraloregon.org

Religious / Spiritual Resources

♂ ☆ && Unitarian Universalist Fellowship of Central Oregon, 61980 Skyline Ranch Rd; 97703-9400 541-385-3908 **HD** www.uufco.org ✔

Corvallis/Albany

Community Centers and/or Pride Organizations

♂ ★ && Pride Center, Oregon State University, 1553 SW 'A' Ave, 149 MU East, Corvallis; 541-737-9161 dce.oregonstate.edu/pc ✔

AIDS/HIV Services, Education & Support

♂ ☆ (?&) Valley AIDS Information Network Inc. (VAIN), POB 971, Corvallis; 97339 541-752-6322 Linn & Benton Counties www.valleyaidsinfo.org

Oregon: Corvallis/Albany
Bookstores
282
GAYELLOW PAGES #42 2020-2021
Eugene/Springfield Area: Oregon
Recovery

Bookstores

♂ ○ ♿ Grass Roots Books & Music, 227 SW 2nd St, Corvallis; 541-754-7668 www.grassrootsbookstore.com

Organizations/Resources: Family and Supporters

♂☆ (♿) PFLAG Corvallis/Albany, POB 544, Corvallis; 97339-0544 541-782-8829 www.jam-assoc.com/PFLAG pflagcorvallisalbany@gmail.com

Organizations/Resources: Student, Academic, Education

♂ ★ ♿ Oregon State University Rainbow Continuum, Benton Annex / Women's Center, 1700 SW Pioneer Place, Corvallis; 541-737-6360 tinyurl.com/ly375a7

♀ ☆ ♿ OSU Women's Center, Benton Annex, 1700 SW Pioneer Place, Corvallis; 541-737-3186 dce.oregonstate.edu/wc

Religious / Spiritual Resources

♂ ☆ First UMC, 1165 NW Monroe, Corvallis; 97330 541-752-2491 www.corvallisfumc.org fumc@corvallisfumc.org

Crater Lake/Klamath Falls Area

Accommodation: Hotels, Inns, Guesthouses, B&B, Resorts
Fort Klamath

♂ ● (♿) Aspen Inn, 52250 Highway 62 541-381-2321 April-Oct www.theaspeninn.com ♣ ✂ ⊗

Klamath Falls

♂ ● CrystalWood Lodge, POB 1117, Klamath Falls 97601 866-381-2322 www.crystalwoodlodge.com ♣ ✂ ⊗
» Dillard: see Roseburg

Eugene/Springfield Area

Crisis, Anti-violence, & Helplines

♂ Looking Glass Community Services, 1790 W 11th Ave Ste 200, Eugene; 541-689-3111 www.lookingglass.us

♂ ☆ Womenspace, POB 50127, Eugene; 97405 / 1577 Pearl St #200 800-281-2800 (crisis) www.womenspaceinc.org

Community Centers and/or Pride Organizations

♂ ★ ♿ Eugene/Springfield Pride, PO Box 1321, Eugene; 97440 541-321-0356 fb.com/EugPRIDE

AIDS/HIV Services, Education & Support

♂ ☆ ♿ HIV Alliance, 1195A City View St, Eugene; 97402 541-342-5088 hivalliance.org

Bars, Cafes, Clubs, Restaurants
Eugene

♂ ● Spectrum, 150 W Broadway, Eugene 541-654-4424 www.spectrumeugene.com ✕ ☲ ▥ info@spectrumeugene.com

Campgrounds and RV Parks

♂ ● (♿) Umpqua's Last Resort, 115 Elk Ridge Lane, Idleyld Park; 541-498-2500 www.umpquaslastresort.com ♣ ✂ ⊗

Counseling/Psychotherapy/Mental Health

♂ ○ ♿ Fletcher, Grace, MA, ATR, LPC, 390 Lincoln St #240, Eugene; 97401 541-954-6494 tinyurl.com/yams99tw ✂ grace@artwithgracecounseling.com

♂ ● Norberg, Patricia L, MS, NCC, 541-345-9409

Funding: Endowment, Fundraising

♂ ★ ♿ Imperial Sovereign Court of the Emerald Empire, POB 3243, Eugene; 97403 541-912-5899 www.iscee.org

Insurance (see also Financial Planning)

♂ ● ♿ Dambach, Christine, Farmers' Insurance, 313 E 8th Ave, Eugene; 97401 541-743-4388 fax 800-346-1853 tinyurl.com/y5lw5uhr cdambach@farmersagent.com

Legal Services

♂ ○ ♿ Livermore, Megan, Hutchinson Cox, POB 10886, Eugene; 97440 541-686-9160 **H?** www.eugenelaw.com ✂ mlivermore@eugenelaw.com

Organizations/Resources: Cultural, Dance, Performance

♀ ★ (♿) Soromundi Lesbian Chorus, POB 40934, Eugene; 97404-0169 541-520-0753 www.soromundi.org

♂ ★ Spin Cycle Squares, 1029 N St, Springfield 541-998-1683 www.spincyclesquares.org

Organizations/Resources: Political/Legislative/Advocacy

♂ ☆ ♿ Community Alliance of Lane County, 458 Blair Blvd, Eugene; 541-485-1755 www.calclane.org

Organizations/Resources: Student, Academic, Education

♂ ★ ♿ University of Oregon LGBTQA, Room 16G, EMU Basement, Eugene; 541-346-3360 dos.uoregon.edu/lgbt#lgbtqa

♀ ☆ UO Women's Center, 1228 Emu University Ste 3, Eugene; 541-346-4095 blogs.uoregon.edu/women/ ✂

Organizations/Resources: Transgender/Gender Non-Conforming/Diverse

T ★ (♿) Trans*Ponder, 541 Willamette St #310, Eugene; 97401 508-443-6337 **H?** www.Transponder.community info@Transponder.community

Organizations/Resources: Youth (see also Family)

♂ GLBTQ Youth Group, c/o Amazon Community Center, 2700 Hilyard St, Eugene; 541-302-4422

Real Estate (see also Mortgages)

♂ ○ ♿ Swing, Rebecca, Windermere Real Estate/Lane County, 1600 Oak St, Eugene; 97401 541-465-8177 **H?** www.swingonhome.com ✂ swingonhome@windermere.com

Recovery

♂ ☆ AA Emerald Valley Intergroup, 1259 Willamette St, Eugene; 541-342-4113 www.eviaa.org

Oregon: Florence
Organizations: Family
283
GAYELLOW PAGES #42 2020-2021
Portland/Vancouver Area: Oregon
Accounting/Tax

Florence

Organizations/Resources: Family and Supporters

♂ ☆ PFLAG Florence Oregon, POB 1074, Florence 97439 541-991-8550 www.pflagflorenceoregon.org

Forest Grove

Organizations/Resources: Education

♂ ☆ ♿ Center for Gender Equity, Pacific University, 2043 College Way, Forest Grove; 503-352-2044 tinyurl.com/yfz9oy

Gearhart

Accommodation: Hotels, Inns, Guesthouses, B&B, Resorts

♀ ○ Gearhart Ocean Inn, POB 2161, Gearhart 97138 / 67 N Cottage Ave 503-738-7373 www.gearhartoceaninn.com ✿ ✗ ⊗ @ixx=

Gold Beach

Organizations/Resources: Family and Supporters

♂ ☆ ♿ PFLAG Gold Beach/Curry County, PO Box 131; 97444 541-933-5412 tinyurl.com/kfvbrtf ✗

» Gresham: see Portland/Vancouver Area
» Klamath Falls: see Crater Lake/Klamath Falls Area

La Grande

Organizations/Resources: Family and Supporters

♂ ☆ PFLAG Union County, POB 173; 97850 tinyurl.com/kfsq4gn

La Pine

Accommodation: Hotels, Inns, Guesthouses, B&B, Resorts

♂ ○ DiamondStone Guest Lodges, 16693 Sprague Loop 541-536-6263 www.diamondstone.com (✿?) ✗ ⊗ @ixx=

Sports & Outdoor

♂ ○ Motofantasy, 16693 Sprague Loop; 541-536-6263 Motorcycle Rentals www.motofantasy.net (✿?) ✗ @ixx=

Lincoln City

Accommodation: Hotels, Inns, Guesthouses, B&B, Resorts

♀ ● (?♿) Ashley Inn and Suites, 3430 NE Hwy 101; 541-996-7500 **H** www.ashleyinnlincolncity.com (✿?) ✗ ⊗

» Medford: see Ashland/Medford/Rogue River Valley

Monmouth

Organizations/Resources: Student, Academic, Education

♀ ★ Safe Zone, Western Oregon University, 345 N Monmouth Ave; tinyurl.com/2kzmz3

Newport

Organizations/Resources: Family and Supporters

♂ ☆ ♿ PFLAG Oregon Central Coast, PO Box 2172; 97365 541-265-1904 www.occpflag.org pflagocc@gmail.com

Pendleton

Accommodation: Hotels, Inns, Guesthouses, B&B, Resorts

♂ ● ♿ Pendleton House B&B, 311 N Main St; 541-276-8581 www.pendletonhousebnb.com (✿?) ✗ ⊗ ⊗

Organizations/Resources: Family and Supporters

♂ PFLAG Pendleton, POB 1819; 97801 541-966-8414 fb.com/PFLAG.Pendleton

Portland/Vancouver Area

Crisis, Anti-violence, & Helplines

♂ ☆ ♿ Bradley Angle, 5432 N Albina Ave, Portland; 503-232-1528 www.bradleyangle.org ✗

♀ ☆ Call to Safety, POB 42610, Portland; 97242 503-235-5333 calltosafety.org

♀ ☆ ♿ Clackamas Women's Services, 256 Warner Milne Rd, Oregon City; 97045 503-654-2288 888-654-2288 **H?** www.cwsor.org ✗ info@cwsor.org

♀ ☆ Domestic Violence Resource Center, 735 SW 158th Ave Ste 100, Beaverton; 97006 503-640-5352 www.dvrc-or.org dvrc@dvrc-or.org

Community Centers and/or Pride Organizations

♥ ★ Pride Northwest, Inc/Portland Pride Festival and Parade., POB 6611, Portland; 97228 / 4115 N Mississippi Ave 503-295-9788 www.pridenw.org

♥ ★ ♿ Q Center, 4115 N Mississippi Ave, Portland; 503-234-7837 **H?** www.pdxQcenter.org ✗

Accommodation: Hotels, Inns, Guesthouses, B&B, Resorts
Portland

♀ ○ Bluebird Guesthouse, 3517 SE Division St, Portland; 97202-1567 503-235-3089 866-717-4333 www.bluebirdguesthouse.com ✗ ⊗

♀ ● The Lion & The Rose B&B, 1810 NE 15th Ave; 97212 503-287-9245 www.lionrose.com ⊗

♂ ● Portland International Guesthouse, 2185 NW Flanders St, Portland; 503-224-0500 www.pdxguesthouse.com

♂ ● Portland's White House, 1914 NE 22nd Ave, Portland; 503-287-7131 portlandswhitehouse.com ✗ ⊗ ⊗ @ixx=

Accounting, Bookkeeping, Tax Services

♂ ○ ♿ Kennedy, Amy, CPA, LTC, Clarity Tax Service, 1730 SW Skyline Blvd Ste 201, Portland; 97221 503-236-1040 (WA #31861/OR #28250) www.claritytax.net ✗

AIDS/HIV Services, Education & Support

♂ ☆ ⚧ Cascade AIDS Project, 520 NW Davis St Ste 215, Portland; 97209 503-223-5907 www.cascadeaids.org info@cascadeaids.org

♂ ⚥ ⚧⚧ Ecumenical Ministries of Oregon HIV Day Center, 2941 NE Ainsworth, Portland; 503-460-3822 emoregon.org/hiv-services/ ✔

♂ ☆ Our House, 2727 SE Alder St, Portland 503-234-0175 www.ourhouseofportland.org

Archives/Libraries/Museums/History Projects

♀ ★ (⚧⚧) Gay & Lesbian Archives of the Pacific Northwest, POB 3646, Portland; 97208-3646 www.glapn.org ✔ info@glapn.org

Bars, Cafes, Clubs, Restaurants
Beaverton

♂ ● ⚧⚧ MiNGO, 12600 SW Crescent St, Beaverton; 503-646-6464 www.mingowest.com ⚥ ✕ ✔

Portland

♂ ○ ⚧⚧ Besaws, 1545 NW 21st Ave, Portland; 503-228-2619 www.besaws.com ✕ ✔

♂ ● ⚧⚧ Bijou Cafe, 132 SW 3rd Ave, Portland; 503-222-3187 bijoucafepdx.com ✕ @ixx=

♂ ● ⚧⚧ Bluehour, 250 NW 13th Ave, Portland; 503-226-3394 **H?** www.bluehouronline.com ⚥ ✕ ⊅ ✔

⚲ Bridge Club, check event schedule bridgeclubpdx.com

⚹ ● ⚧⚧ CC Slaughters, 219 NW Davis, Portland; 503-248-9135 ccslaughterspdx.com **LL** ▥ ✔

♂ ○ Chopsticks, 3390 NE Sandy Blvd, Portland 503-234-6171 chopstickskaraoke.com **K** ⚥ ✕ ✔

♂ ● ⚧⚧ Crush Bar, 1400 SE Morrison St, Portland; 503-235-8150 www.crushbar.com ⚥ ✕▥

♂ ● ⚧⚧ Darcelle XV Showplace, 208 NW 3rd Ave, Portland; 503-222-5338 www.darcellexv.com ▥

♂ ○ Doug Fir, 830 E Burnside St, Portland 503-231-9663 www.dougfirlounge.com ⚥ ✕▥

⚹ Eagle Portland, 835 N Lombard St, Portland 503-283-9734 www.eagleportland.com

♂ ○ Hobo's, 120 NW 3rd St, Portland; 503-224-3285 www.hobospdx.com ✕

♂ ● Holocene, 1001 SE Morrison, Portland 503-239-7639 www.holocene.org **D** ✕▥✔

⚥ ● ⚧⚧ Hot Flash Women's Dances, www.hotflashdances.com **P**

♂ ○ ⚧⚧ Le Bistro Montage, 301 Se Morrison St, Portland; 503-234-1324 www.montageportland.com ⚥ ✕

♂ ● ⚧⚧ Local Lounge, 3536 NE MLK, Portland; 503-282-1833 pdxlocallounge.com **D** ✔

♂ ○ ⚧⚧ Mama Mia Trattoria, 439 W 2nd Ave, Portland; 503-295-6464 www.mamamiatrattoria.com ⚥ ✕ ✔

♂ ○ ⚧⚧ Mother's Bistro & Bar, 212 SW Stark St, Portland; 503-464-1122 www.mothersbistro.com ⚥ ✕⊅ ✔

♀ ○ Noho's Hawaiian Cafe, 4627 NE Fremont St, Portland; 503-445-6646 www.nohos.com ✕ ✔

♀ ○ Nostrana, 1401 Se Morrison St, Portland 503-234-2427 www.nostrana.com ✕ info@nostrana.com

♂ ○ Original Dinerant, 300 SW 6th Ave, Portland 503-546-2666 www.originaldinerant.com ✕

⚥ ● ⚧⚧ Scandals, 1125 SW Stark St, Portland; 503-227-5887 www.scandalspdx.com ⚥ ✕

⚹ ● ⚧ Silverado, 610 NW Couch St, Portland; 503-224-4493 Strippers www.silveradopdx.com **D** ▥

♂ ● Sloan's Tavern, 36 N Russell St, Portland 503-287-2262 www.sloanstavern.com

⚹ Stag PDX, 317 NW Broadway, Portland 971-407-3132 Strippers fb.com/stagpdx/

♂ ○ Tasty n Daughters, 4537 SE Division St, Portland; 503-621-1400 www.tastyndaughters.com ⚥ ✕ inquiries@tastyndaughters.com

Vancouver

♂ ○ La Bottega, 1905 Main St, Vancouver, WA 360-571-5010 www.labottegafoods.com ✕ ⊅

Bookstores

♂ ○ Annie Bloom's Books, 7834 SW Capitol Hwy, Portland; 97219-2498 503-246-0053 www.annieblooms.com books@annieblooms.com

♂ ○ ⚧ Broadway Books, 1714 Northeast Broadway St, Portland; 503-284-1726 www.broadwaybooks.net

♂ ○ ⚧⚧ Powell's Books, 1005 W Burnside, Portland; 503-228-4651 www.powells.com

Clothes (see also Erotica, Leather)

♂ ● ⚧ underU4men, 800 SW Washington, Portland; 503-274-2555 www.underu4men.com

Counseling/Psychotherapy/Mental Health

♂ ● ⚧⚧ Alexander, Gary, MS, MFT, 15110 Boones Ferry Rd, Lake Oswego; 97035 503-862-8050 tinyurl.com/ydhmacg9 ✔

♂ ● (⚧⚧) Faver, Lee M, PhD PLLC, 303 E 16th St; Ste 302, Vancouver, WA 98663 360-524-3616 www.leemfaver.com

♀ ○ Hort, Barbara, PhD, Jungian Consultant, 3485 NW Thurman St, Portland; 97210 503-285-4212 ✔

♂ ● ⚧⚧ Kibel, Laney, LCSW, 1020 SW Taylor #820, Portland; 97205 503-781-3900 www.laneykibel.com ✔ laneykibel@hotmail.com

⚥ ● O'Dell, Steven (Bo), MSW, LCSW, 1732 SE Ash St, Portland; 97214-1526 503-249-7844 **HS** www.thelighterheart.com

⚹ ● O'Dell, Susan, PhD, LCSW, 1732 SE Ash St, Portland; 97214 503-232-5640 susan@susanodellphd.com

♂ ☆ Sexual Assault Resource Center, 4900 SW Griffith Dr #100, Beaverton; 97005 888-640-5311 503-640-5311 www.sarcoregon.org sarc@sarcoregon.org

♂ ○ Steinbrecher, Diane, LCSW, A Safe Place for Growth and Healing, 2700 SE 26th Ave #C, Portland; 97202-1288 503-235-2005 archetypalassociates.com

Oregon: Portland/Vancouver Area
Dentists

285

GAYELLOW PAGES #42 2020-2021

Portland/Vancouver Area : Oregon
Organizations: Multicultural

Dentists

♂ ○ Powell Dental, 3435 SE 75th Ave, Portland 97206 503-777-5544 www.PowellDental.com

Erotica / Adult Stores / Safe Sex Supplies

♀ ○ ♿ She Bop, 3213 SE Division St, Portland; 97202 503-688-1196 **HS** www.shebeoptheshop.com

♀ ○ ♿ She Bop, 909 N Beech St, Portland; 97227 503-473-8018 **HS** www.shebeoptheshop.com

Florists (see also Gifts)

♀ ● ♿ Botanica Floral Design, 503-358-4687 www.botanicafloralpdx.com

Funding: Endowment, Fundraising

♀ ★ Imperial Sovereign Court of the Raintree Empire, POB 966, Vancouver, WA 98666 www.raintreeempire.org

♀ ★ Imperial Sovereign Rose Court, POB 4864, Portland; 97208-4864 www.rosecourt.org

♀ ★ Portland Sisters of Perpetual Indulgence, 5331 SW Macadam Ave Ste 258-420, Portland portlandsisters.org

Gardening/Landscaping Services & Supplies

♀ ○ Rejuvenation Artisans Landscapes, 5010 SE 44th Ave, Portland; 97206 503-459-9541 www.rejuve.net rejuve@rejuve.net

Gifts, Cards, Pride, etc.

♀ ○ ♿ Presents of Mind, 3633 SE Hawthorne Blvd, Portland; 97214 503-230-7740 www.presentsofmind.tv presentsofmind.tv@hotmail.com

Health Care: Physical (see also Counseling/Mental Health)

♀ ★ (♿) Common Ground Wellness Cooperative, 5010 NE 33rd Ave, Portland; 503-238-1065 Spa, Wellness, Massage, Health, Hot tub etc cgwc.org

♀ ☆ ♿ Quest Center for Integrative Health, 2901 E Burnside Ave, Portland; 503-238-5203 www.quest-center.org

Immigration, Citizenship, Political Asylum, Refugees

♂ ○ ♿ Riggs Immigration Law, 405 W 13th St, Vancouver, WA 98660 360-553-7210 www.riggsimmigrationlaw.com mercedes@riggsimmigrationlaw.com

Leather Resources & Groups

♀ ☆ Portland Leather Alliance, 4110 SE Hawthorne #611, Portland; 503-358-0927 www.portlandleather.org

Legal Services

♀ ● ♿ **Edgel Law Group, Michael Edgel and Bryan Hedlind, 1800 Blankenship Rd #370, West Linn; 97068 503-765-8400 Estate Planning & Elder Law firm, advice tailored to each client's unique needs. edgellawgroup.com**

♀ ● ♿ Findling, Marlene E, Findling Law Office, PC 2105 NE Cesar Chavez Blvd Ste 250, Portland; 97212 503-288-3133 www.findlinglawoffice.com marlene@findlinglawoffice.com

♀ ○ (♿) Hamalian, Alexander, 5220 NE Sandy Blvd, Portland; 97213 503-222-3641 **HC** www.rosecitylaw.com

♀ ○ ♿ **Kramer & Associates, 520 SW 6th Ave Ste 1010, Portland; 97204-1595 503-243-2733 fax 503-274-4774 Over 30 years of Civil & Family law trial experience including contested custody, personal injury, domestic partnership, civil rights matters. Free parking. www.kramer-associates.com mark@kramer-associates.com**

♀ ○ Matthews, Scott K, 710 W Evergreen Blvd, Vancouver, WA 98660 360-606-9302 www.scottmatthewslaw.com scott@scottmatthewslaw.com

♀ ● ♿ Paulson, Jane, Paulson Coletti Trial Attorneys PC, 1022 NW Marshall #450, Portland; 97209 503-433-3524 Www.paulsoncoletti.com ✎ jane@paulsoncoletti.com

♀ ○ ♿ Schneider Rasche LLC, 2455 NW Marshall St Ste 11, Portland; 97210-2949 503-241-1215 Estate planning www.rbsllc.com information@rbsllc.com

♀ ○ Sherwood Family Law, 16103 SW 1st St, Sherwood 97140 503-655-7199 fax 503-655-7169 www.sherwoodfamilylaw.com

♀ ● ♿ Wolfsong Law PC, 9900 SW Wilshire St Ste 100, Portland; 97225 503-616-8880 www.wolfsonglaw.com

Men's & Sex Clubs (not primarily Health Clubs)

♂ ● ♿ Hawks PDX, 234 SE Grand Ave, Portland; 503-946-8659 www.hawkspdx.club ✎

♂ ● ♿ Steam Portland, 2885 NE Sandy Blvd, Portland; 503-736-9999 **H?** www.steamportland.com ✎

Organizations/Resources: Bisexual Focus

♀ amBi, www.ambi.org/ashland/

Organizations/Resources: Cultural, Dance, Performance

♂ ★ ♿ Out Dancing, 503-318-1031 www.outdancing.info

♂ ★ ♿ Portland Gay Men's Chorus, POB 3223, Portland; 97208-3223 503-226-2588 www.pdxgmc.org pgmc@pdxgmc.org

♀ Portland Lesbian & Gay Film Festival, Cinema 21, 616 NW 21st Ave, Portland; www.pdxqueerfilm.com

♀ ★ (♿) Portland Lesbian Choir, POB 12693, Portland; 97212 www.plchoir.org

♀ ★ QDoc Film Festival, POB 19905, Portland 97280 qdocfilmfest.org

♀ ★ Rose City Gay Freedom Bands, POB 8615, Portland; 97207 www.rcgfb.org

♀ (♿) Rosetown Ramblers, POB 5352, Portland; 97228 503-610-8154 www.rosetownramblers.org **D**

Organizations/Resources: Deaf

♀ Prism of Portland, POB 86938, Portland 97286 **HS** Deaf and hearing gatherings fb.com/prismofportland/

Organizations/Resources: Ethnic, Multicultural

♀ ★ ♿ Portland Black Pride, POB 6743, Portland; 97228 503-232-7676 fb.com/PortlandBlackPride ♣

Oregon: Portland/Vancouver Area
Organizations: Multicultural

286

GAYELLOW PAGES #42 2020-2021

Portland/Vancouver Area : Oregon
Sports & Outdoor

⚲ Portland Two Spirit Society, 971-231-4999 fb.com/Portland2Spir-its/

⚲ ★ ♿ Sankofa Collective Northwest, 4115 N Mississippi Ave, Portland; 503-234-7837 **H?** (previously PFLAG Portland Black Chapter) sankofanw.org ✤ ⚯

Organizations/Resources: Family and Supporters

⚦ ☆ ♿ PFLAG Clackamas County, POB 291, Clackamas; 97015 503-887-4556 tinyurl.com/mhf6qjd

⚦ ☆ ♿ PFLAG Portland, POB 6743, Portland; 97228 503-232-7676 www.pflagpdx.org

⚦ ☆ ♿ PFLAG Southwest Washington, PO Box 605, Vancouver, WA 98660 360-562-0491 pflagswwa.org pflagswwa@gmail.com

Organizations/Resources: Senior Resources

⚦ ☆ ♿ SAGE Metro Portland, Friendly House, 1737 NW 26th Ave 503-224-2640 **H?** tinyurl.com/y8fhxnza ⚯

Organizations/Resources: Sexual Focus / Safe Sex

♀ ★ Bad Girls, POB 14113, Portland; 97293 www.pdxbadgirls.net

⚦ ☆ ♿ MAsT: Portland, 503-880-5282 www.mastpnw.org

Organizations/Resources: Social, Recreation, Support

⚲ Dykes on Bikes - Portland Oregon Chapter, - - www.dykeson-bikespdx.org

⚦ ★ Oregon Bears, 8630 SW Schools Ferry Rd, #112, Beaverton; www.oregonbears.org

⚦ ★ (♿) Portland Metro Prime Timers, PO Box 5884, Portland; 97228-5884 portlandprimetimers.org info@portland primetimers.org

Organizations/Resources: Student, Academic, Education

⚲ ★ Audria M. Edwards Scholarship Fund, POB 16337, Portland; 97292 www.peacockinthepark.org

⚲ ★ Lewis & Clark Law School Outlaw, 10015 SW Terwilliger Blvd, Portland; 503-768-6955 tinyurl.com/nyl778t

⚲ ★ ♿ Portland Community College Sylvania Queer Campus Coalition, 12000 SW 49th Ave, Portland; 971-722-8525 www.pcc.edu/queer/ ⚯

⚲ ★ ♿ Portland State University Queer Resource Center, Smith Memorial Student Union, 1825 SW Broadway Ste 458, Portland; 503-725-9742 **H?** www.pdx.edu/queer ⚯ @ixx=

⚲ ★ ♿ Reed College Office for Inclusive Community, Student Center 110, 3203 SE Woodstock Blvd, Portland 503-777-7518 tinyurl.com/yb2kr4z9

Organizations/Resources: Youth (see also Family)

⚲ Living Room, The, POB 332, Gladstone 97027 503-901-5971 www.thelivingroomyouth.org

⚦ ☆ Outside In, 1132 SW 13th Ave, Portland 503-535-3800 Counseling/Medical Care/Mental Health/Youth Services under age 24 www.outsidein.org

⚲ (♿) Queer Youth Resource Center, POB 605, Vancouver, WA 98666 **H?** www.qyrcvancouverwa.org

Real Estate (see also Mortgages)

⚦ ● Betron, Deborah, Principal Broker, Bridgetown Realty, 3300 NW 185th #232, Portland; 97229 503-679-9741 www.bridgetownrealty.com ⚯ deborah@bridgetownrealty.com

⚦ O Casteel, Shelly, Oregon Realty Co, 8552 SW Apple Way, Portland; 97225 503-957-7705 503-297-2523 oregonrealty.com/shellyc

Recovery

⚦ ☆ Al-Anon/Alateen Information Service, 1750 SW Skyline Blvd #133, Portland; 97221 503-292-1333 tinyurl.com/7j5c9d

⚦ ☆ Alano Club, 909 NW 24th Ave, Portland 503-222-5756 www.portlandalano.org

⚦ ☆ ♿ Narcotics Anonymous Portland Area, POB 42453, Portland; 97242 503-345-9839 **H?** www.portlandna.com

Religious / Spiritual Resources

⚦ ☆ ♿ Bethel Congregational UCC, 5150 SW Watson Ave, Beaverton; 97005 503-646-1191 **H** www.bethelbeaverton.org office@bethelbeaverton.org

⚦ ☆ Central Lutheran Church, 1820 NE 21st Ave, Portland; 97212 503-284-2331 www.centralportland.org office@centralportland.org

⚦ ☆ Congregation Neveh Shalom, 2900 SW Peaceful Lane, Portland; 97239 503-246-8831 www.nevehshalom.org ✡

⚦ ★ ♿ MCC of The Gentle Shepherd, 1220 NE 68th St, Vancouver, WA 360-695-1480 tinyurl.com/q6263t

⚦ ★ ♿ MCC Portland, 2828 SE Stephens St, Portland; 97214 503-281-8868 **H?** www.mccportland.com ⚯

⚦ ☆ ♿ SisterSpirit, POB 9246, Portland; 97207-9246 503-736-3297 tinyurl.com/y93w9nl6 ⚯ sisterspirit.portland@gmail.com

⚦ ☆ ♿ Unitarian Universalist Church of Vancouver, 4505 E 18th St, Vancouver, WA 98661 360-695-1891 **HD** www.uucvan.org ⚯ office@uucvan.org

⚦ ☆ ♿ UU Community Church of Washington County, 22785 NW Birch St, Hillsboro; 97124 503-648-1720 **HD** www.uuccwc.org ⚯

⚦ ☆ ♿ Wy'east Unitarian Universalist Congregation, 3439 NE Sandy Blvd #368, Portland; 97232-1959 / Sun 10.30am at Hollywood Senior Center, 1820 NE 40th Ave 503-777-3704 www.wyeastuu.org office@wyeastuu.org

Sports & Outdoor

⚦ ★ Adventure Group, tinyurl.com/ju5vao4

⚲ Amazon Dragons Paddling Club, POB 13111, Portland; 97213 www.amazondragons.org

⚦ ★ Border Riders Motorcycle Club, 1122 E Pike St #550, Seattle, WA Pacific Northwest www.borderriders.com

⚲ Gay Skate, tinyurl.com/y7tgrx9j

⚦ ★ Outkayaking, www.outkayaking.org

⚲ ★ ♿ Portland Community Bowling League, POB 2941, Oregon City; 97045 503-475-5203 www.pdxbowl.com

⚲ ★ Portland Frontrunners, POB 8651, Portland; 97207 www.portlandfrontrunners.org

♀ Portland Shockwave, Women's Full Contact Football tinyurl.com/ybb5dy2g

♀ Rose City Rollers, POB 86885, Portland 97286 www.rosecityrollers.com

♂ ★ Rose City Softball Association, POB 12522, Portland; 97212 503-552-4769 www.rosecitysoftball.org

♂ ★ Team Portland Tennis Association, POB 28489, Portland; 97228 teamportlandtennis.com teamportlandtennis@gmail.com

Travel & Tourist Services (see also Accommodation)

♂ ● ♿ Travel Gay Portland, 800 SW Washington St Ste M1, Portland; 97206 **H?** www.travelgayportland.com ✎ info@travelgayportland.com

Salem

Crisis, Anti-violence, & Helplines

♀ ☆ The Center for Hope & Safety, 605 Center St NE 97301 503-399-7722 hopeandsafety.org ☯

Community Centers and/or Pride Organizations

♂ ★ Capitol Pride, POB 243; 97308 www.capitolpride.org

Bars, Cafes, Clubs, Restaurants

♀ ○ Davinci Restaurant, 180 High St SE 504-399-1413 www.davincisofsalem.com ♈ ✗

♂ ● ♿ Southside Speakeasy & Dance Pub, 3529 Fairview Industrial Dr SE; 503-362-1139 www.southsidespeakeasy.com **D** ♈ ✗▥ ✎

Funding: Endowment, Fundraising

♂ ★ Imperial Sovereign Court of the Willamette Empire, POB 2263; 97308 www.iscwe.org

Legal Services

♂ ● ♿ Pacheco, Monica D, Douglas, Conroyd, Gibb & Pacheco, P.C., POB 469; 97308 503-364-7000 Planning dcm-law.com monica@dcm-law.com

Organizations/Resources: Cultural, Dance, Performance

♂ ★ Confluence: The Willamette Valley LGBT Chorus, POB 2772; 97308 www.confluencechorus.org

Organizations/Resources: Social, Recreation, Support

♂ ★ **The Capitol Forum, 1808 Berry St S; A GLBT social service orgaization that raises funds for charity. www.capitolforum.org**

♀ ★ Salem Lavender Womyn, tinyurl.com/oxq2tx5

Organizations/Resources: Youth (see also Family)

♂ Home Youth & Resource Center, 625 Union St NE 503-391-6428 tinyurl.com/yaluyoen

♂ ● ♿ Rainbow Youth, POB 13002 97309 rainbowyouth.org info@rainbowyouth.org

Recovery

♀ ☆ AA Willamette Valley Intergroup, 687 Cottage St NE; 503-399-0599 www.aa-salem.com

Religious / Spiritual Resources

♂ ☆ ♿ Freedom Friends (Quaker) Worship Group, meet at Ike Box Cafe, Salem tinyurl.com/uxf454k ✎ freedomfriendschurch@gmail.com

♂ ☆ Salem Spirit of Life Church, 420 Pine St NE 97301 503-689-1436 www.salemspiritoflife.org spiritoflife76@gmail.com

Seaside

Accommodation: Hotels, Inns, Guesthouses, B&B, Resorts

♂ ○ ♿ Hillcrest Inn, 118 N Columbia 97138 503-738-6273 www.seasidehillcrest.com (♿?) ✎ ⊗ ⊗ hillcrestinn@mail.com
》 Veneta: see Eugene

Wolf Creek

Organizations/Resources: Social, Recreation, Support

♂ ★ (♿) Nomenus/Wolf Creek Sanctuary, POB 312; 97497 541-866-2678 **H?** nomenus.org

Yachats

Accommodation Rental: Furnished / Vacation (& AirBNB)

♂ ● Ocean Odyssey Vacation Rentals, POB 491 97498 541-547-3637 www.ocean-odyssey.com

Pennsylvania
State/County Resources

AIDS/HIV Services, Education & Support

♂ AIDS Law Project of Pennsylvania, 1211 Chestnut St #600, Philadelphia, PA 215-587-9377 www.aidslawpa.org

Legal Services

♂ ● ♿ McClain, John L, POB 123, Narberth, PA 19072 215-893-9357 www.attorneymcclain.com

Mortgages/Home Ownership (see also Banks, Real Estate)

♂ ● Frey, Carolyn, OH & FL & PA 614-891-9625 www.carolynfrey.com cafrey@mortgagelendingsolutions.com

Organizations/Resources: Business & Professional Associations, Labor Advocacy

♂ Pride at Work - Pennsylvania, fb.com/prideatworkPA

Organizations/Resources: Political/Legislative/Advocacy

♂ ☆ ♿ American Civil Liberties Union of Pennsylvania, POB 60173, Philadelphia, PA 19102 215-592-1513 www.aclupa.org

♂ Equality Pennsylvania, 1211 Chestnut St #605, Philadelphia, PA 570-238-4356 fb.com/equalitypa

♂ Pennsylvania Equality Project, POB 976, Edinboro, PA 16412 814-245-1375 www.paequality.org

Religious / Spiritual Resources

♂ ★ United Church of Christ Open and Affirming Coalition, c/o N. Krody, 801 Crum Creek Rd, Springfield, PA 19064-1002 215-429-8216 www.ucccoalition.org nkrody@temple.edu

Pennsylvania: State/County Resources
Reproductive Medical Services

288

GAYELLOW PAGES #42 2020-2021

Erie : Pennsylvania
Body Art

Reproductive Medicine & Fertility Services

♂ Planned Parenthood Keystone (PPKey), POB 813, Trexlertown, PA 18087 610-481-0481 tinyurl.com/n3nnojh

➤➤ *Allentown: see Lehigh Valley Area*

Altoona

Bars, Cafes, Clubs, Restaurants

♀ ● Escapade, 2523 Union Ave Rte 36 814-946-8195 escapadepa.weebly.com ✔

Organizations/Resources: Student, Academic, Education

♀ ★ Pride Club - PSUA, 101 Boucke Bldg, 3000 Ivyside Dr; 814-949-5105 fb.com/groups/psuapride/

➤➤ *Bethlehem: see Lehigh Valley Area*

Bloomsburg

Accommodation: Hotels, Inns, Guesthouses, B&B, Resorts

♂ ● ♿ Pump House Bed and Breakfast, 623C State Rd; 570-784-6730 www.pumphousebandb.com (✿?) ✔ ⊘

Organizations/Resources: Student, Academic, Education

♀ ★ ♿ Bloomsburg University LGBTQA Resource Center, SSC 265, 400 E 2nd St; 570-389-2819 www.bloomu.edu/LGBTQA

Boyers

Campgrounds and RV Parks

♂ ● (♿) Camp Davis, 311 Redbrush Rd 724-637-2402 campdavispa.com **P** ✿ ✔

➤➤ *Bryn Mawr: see Philadelphia Area*

Clarion

Organizations/Resources: Student, Academic, Education

♀ ★ Clarion University Allies, 840 Wood St 814-393-2484 tinyurl.com/nggjabv

Collegeville

Organizations/Resources: Student, Academic, Education

♀ ★ Ursinus College Gender and Sexuality Alliance, Student Activities Office, 601 Main St; 412-268-2142 tinyurl.com/qb93jk6

Connellsville

Accommodation: Hotels, Inns, Guesthouses, B&B, Resorts

♂ ○ Fox Castle Bed and Breakfast, 1131 S Pittsburgh St; 15425 724-603-3699 www.foxcastle.com ✔ ⊘ innkeeper@foxcastle.com

➤➤ *Downingtown: see Philadelphia Area*
➤➤ *Doylestown: see New Hope PA/Lambertville NJ Area*
➤➤ *Duncannon: see Harrisburg Area*
➤➤ *East Stroudsburg: see Poconos Area*
➤➤ *Easton: see Lehigh Valley Area*
➤➤ *Edinboro: see Erie*

Elizabethtown

Organizations/Resources: Student, Academic, Education

♀ ★ Elizabethtown College Allies, 1 Alpha Dr groups.etown.edu/allies/

Ephrata

Accommodation: Hotels, Inns, Guesthouses, B&B, Resorts

♂ ○ (♿) Tree Top B&B, 326 Ridge Ave 17522 717-733-9578 treetopbandb.com (✿?) ✔ ⊘ bonpaul@ptd.net

Erie

Crisis, Anti-violence, & Helplines

♂ ☆ ♿ Crime Victim Center of Erie County, 125 W 18th St; 814-455-9414 www.cvcerie.org

♂ ☆ ♿ SafeNet, POB 1436; 16512 814-454-8161 www.safeneterie.org ✔

Community Centers and/or Pride Organizations

♀ ★ **NW PA Pride Alliance, Inc, POB 11448 16514 814-314-9075 Improving visibility of the LGBTQIA community and facilitating communication & collaboration. www.nwpapride.org president@nwpapride.org**

Information, Media & Publications

♀ ★ **Erie Gay News, 1115 W 7th St; 16502-1105 814-456-9833 Mike; fax 530-451-9833 Covering news & events in the Erie PA, Cleveland, Pittsburgh, Buffalo & Chautauqua County NY region. www.eriegaynews.com info@eriegaynews.com**
◆ *Advertisement page 289*

AIDS/HIV Services, Education & Support

♂ ☆ ♿ NW PA Rural AIDS Alliance - Erie Office, 1001 State St Ste 606; 800-400-2437 ✔

Art & Craft Galleries/Services, Supplies

♂ ○ Glass Growers Gallery, 10 E 5th St; 16507-1510 814-453-3758 www.glassgrowersgallery.com glassgrowersgallery@Yahoo.com

Bars, Cafes, Clubs, Restaurants

♂ ○ Jr's Last Laugh, 1402 State St; 814-461-0911 www.jrslastlaugh.com ⊻ ✕ ▥

♀ ○ The Zone Dance Club, 133 W 18th St 814-452-0125 www.thezonedanceclub.com

Body Art

♂ ○ Buddha's Body Art, 2761 W 12th St; 814-833-0439 www.buddhas.com

♂ ○ Karma Tattoo Studio, 5006 Iroquois Ave 814-384-7861 fb.com/karmatattoostudio/
@ixx=

Pennsylvania: Erie
Organizations: Political

289
GAYELLOW PAGES #42 2020-2021

Harrisburg Area: Pennsylvania
Health Care

Organizations/Resources: Political/Legislative/Advocacy

♀ ★ Greater Erie Alliance for Equality, 301 W 10th St; 866-229-1974 greatereriealliance.com

Organizations/Resources: Social, Recreation, Support

♂ ★ Drenched Fur, Gary Snyder, 3502 Plum St; 16508 814-384-0463 www.drenchedfur.com info@drenchedfur.com

♀ ★ LBT Women of Erie, 814-490-3994 Fb.Com/Lbtwomenoferie

Organizations/Resources: Student, Academic, Education

★ Edinboro University LGBTQIA Commission, Office of Social Equity, 219 Meadville St, Reeder Hall Flr 3, Edinboro; 814-732-2167 tinyurl.com/nznhpb9

♀ ★ ♿ Gender and Sexuality Equality Club - Penn State Behrend, Multi-Cultural Council, 5091 Station; 814-898-7162 fb.com/PSBTrigon

Organizations/Resources: Transgender/Gender Non-Conforming/Diverse

T Erie Sisters, POB 395, Conneaut, OH 44030 440-265-8191 eriesisters.ning.com

T Erie Sisters and Brothers Transgender Support Group, tinyurl.com/y9zzfgqt

T TransFamily of NWPA Transgender Support Group, 814-823-1969 fb.com/TransfamilyOfNWPA

Real Estate (see also Mortgages)

♂ ○ ♿ NeCastro, Tom, Realtor, Coldwell Banker Select Realtors, 4664 W 12th St; 16505 814-881-1186 814-452-2100 tomnecastro.com ✎ necastro@peoplepc.com

Religious / Spiritual Resources

♀ ☆ Temple Anshe Hesed, 5401 Old Zuck Rd; 16506 814-454-2426 www.anshehesederie.org ✡ office@taherie.org
>> Etters: see Harrisburg Area
>> Fayetteville: see Gettysburg

Gettysburg

Accommodation: Hotels, Inns, Guesthouses, B&B, Resorts

♂ ● ♿ Battlefield Bed & Breakfast Inn, 2264 Emmitsburg Rd; 717-334-8804 gettysburgbattlefield.com ✻ ✎

Organizations/Resources: Student, Academic, Education

♂ ★ ♿ Office of LGBTQA Advocacy & Education, Campus Box 430, 300 N Washington St; 717-337-7577 tinyurl.com/yxksgqvo

Gibson

Campgrounds and RV Parks

♂ ● Hillside Campgrounds, 948 Creek Rd, New Milford, PA 18834 570-756-2007 Men only www.hillside.camp ✻ ✎ ⊗ info@hillside.camp

Glen Mills

Accommodation: Hotels, Inns, Guesthouses, B&B, Resorts

♂ ○ (?♿) The Inn at Grace Winery, 50 Sweetwater Rd; 19342-1709 610-459-4711 800-SWEETWATER gracewinery.com ✻ ⊗ info@gracewinery.com
>> Greensburg: see Pittsburgh Area

Harrisburg Area

Community Centers and/or Pride Organizations

♂ ★ ♿ LGBT Community Center of Central PA, 1306 N 3rd St, Harrisburg; 17102 717-920-9534 **H?** www.centralpalgbtcenter.org ✎ info@centralpalgbtcenter.org

♂ ★ Pride Festival of Central Pennsylvania, PO Box 4213, Harrisburg; 17111 717-801-1830 tinyurl.com/ouob5z8

Accounting, Bookkeeping, Tax Services

♂ ● Miller Dixon Drake, CPA, 701 N 2nd St, Harrisburg; 17102-3211 717-234-2250 www.millerdixondrake.com ✎ dmiller@millerdixondrake.com

Bars, Cafes, Clubs, Restaurants
Harrisburg

♂ Brownstone Lounge, 412 Foster St, Harrisburg; 717-234-7009 fb.com/BrownstoneLounge ⚥ ✕

♂ ● Stallions Entertainment Complex, 706 N 3rd St, Harrisburg; 717-232-3060 www.stallionsclub.com **D** ▥

Funding: Endowment, Fundraising

♂ ☆ ♿ The LGBT Fund, Foundation for Enhancing Communities (TFEC). 200 N 3rd St 8th Fl, Harrisburg; 717-236-5040 **H?** tinyurl.com/jancpq8 ✎

Health Care: Physical (see also Counseling/Mental Health)

♀ ☆ ♿ Alder Health Services, 100 N Cameron St Ste 201, Harrisburg; 17101 717-233-7190 fax 717-509-6351 **HD** www.alderhealth.org ✎ info@alderhealth.org

♀ ☆ Alder Health Services, 100 N Cameron St #201-East, Harrisburg; 717-233-7190 www.alderhealth.org

Pennsylvania: Harrisburg Area
Leather

290

GAYELLOW PAGES #42 2020-2021

Lehigh Valley Area: Pennsylvania
Community Centers / Pride

Leather Resources & Groups

♂ The Pennsmen, POB 401, Harrisburg; 17108 www.pennsmen.com

Legal Services

♀ ○ ♂♂ Miner, Steven P, Esq, Daley Zucker Meilton & Miner, LLC, 635 N 12th St Ste 101, Lemoyne; 717-890-1768 www.daleyzucker.com ✔

Organizations/Resources: Business & Professional Associations, Labor Advocacy

♀ ★ ♂♂ Keystone Business Alliance, POB 135, Harrisburg; 17108 www.cpglcc.org ✔

Organizations/Resources: Cultural, Dance, Performance

♀ ☆ ♂♂ Central Pennsylvania Womyn's Chorus, POB 60426, Harrisburg; 17106-0426 717-564-0112 www.cpwchorus.org cpwc@lucytv.net

♂ ★ Harrisburg Gay Men's Chorus, POB 62201, Harrisburg; 17106 tinyurl.com/kw68rc9

Organizations/Resources: Family and Supporters

♀ ☆ ♂♂ Central Pennsylvania PFLAG, PO Box 812, Mechanicsburg; 17055 717-728-8800 www.pflagcentralpa.org

Organizations/Resources: Political/Legislative/Advocacy

♀ American Civil Liberties Union (ACLU), NWPA Chapter, POB 11761, Harrisburg; 17108 717-238-2258 tinyurl.com/pa5xpbx

♀ ☆ American Civil Liberties Union Central PA Office, zask? POB 11761, Harrisburg; 17108 717-238-2258 tinyurl.com/6yrrda

♀ ★ Capital Region Stonewall Democrats, POB 11938, Harrisburg; 17108 www.capitalstonewall.org

Organizations/Resources: Transgender/Gender Non-Conforming/Diverse

T ☆ TransCentralPA, c/o MCC of the Spirit, 2973 Jefferson St, Harrisburg; 717-831-8142 www.transcentralpa.org

Organizations/Resources: Youth (see also Family)

♀ ★ ♂♂ Common Roads Youth and Young Adult groups, 1306 N 3rd St, Harrisburg; 17102 717-920-9534 H? tinyurl.com/y43jozxy ✔ info@centralpalgbtcenter.org

Religious / Spiritual Resources

♀ Dignity/Central Pennsylvania, 717-652-7683 GLBT Catholics

♀ ★ (♂♂) MCC of the Spirit, 2973 Jefferson St, Harrisburg; 17110-2119 717-236-7387 www.mccofthespirit.org info@mccofthespirit.org

Hershey

Accommodation: Hotels, Inns, Guesthouses, B&B, Resorts
Palmyra

♀ ○ 1825 Inn, 409 S Lingle Ave, Palmyra 717-838-8282 www.1825inn.com

Huntingdon

Organizations/Resources: Student, Academic, Education

♀ ★ Juniata College PRISM, 1700 Moore St 814-641-3467 fb.com/prism.juniata/

Indiana

Organizations/Resources: Student, Academic, Education

♀ ★ Indiana University of Pennsylvania Pride Alliance, c/o Student Co-op Assn, 319 Pratt Drive Rm 213, Indiana 724-357-1264 pridealliance.wordpress.com

Johnstown

Bars, Cafes, Clubs, Restaurants

♀ ● (♂♂) Lucy's Place, 520 Washington St, Johnstown; 814-539-4448 fb.com/lucillesjohnstown DK ▥ ✪

Kutztown

Organizations/Resources: Student, Academic, Education

♀ ★ Kutztown University GLBTQ Resource Center, 15200 Kutztown Rd; 484-646-4111 www.kutztown.edu/glbtqcenter

Lancaster

Accommodation: Hotels, Inns, Guesthouses, B&B, Resorts

♀ ○ The Australian Walkabout Inn, 837 Village Rd 717-464-0707 www.walkaboutinn.com ✔ ⊗ ⊗

♀ ● E.J. Bowman House, 2672 Lititz Pike 17-519-0808 www.ejbowmanhouse.com ✔

Bars, Cafes, Clubs, Restaurants

♀ ○ The Loft, 201 W Orange St; 717-299-0661 www.theloftlancaster.com ✕

♂ ● Tally Ho Tavern, 201 W Orange St 717-299-0661 fb.com/TallyHoLancaster D ▥

Religious / Spiritual Resources

♀ LGBTAmish.com, www.lgbtamish.com

♀ ★ Vision of Hope MCC, 130 E Main St, Mountville; 717-285-9070 www.visionofhopemcc.com

Lebanon

Organizations/Resources: Student, Academic, Education

♀ ★ Lebanon Valley College Freedom Rings, Multicultural Office, 101 N College Ave, Annville; 717-867-6165 tinyurl.com/5yzmfv

Lehigh Valley Area

Crisis, Anti-violence, & Helplines

♀ ☆ ♂♂ Turning Point of Lehigh Valley, (Administrative Office) 444 E Susquehanna St, Allentown; 18103 610-437-3369 (24/7 helpline) H? www.turningpointlv.org ✔

Community Centers and/or Pride Organizations

♀ ★ (♂♂) Bradbury-Sullivan LGBT Community Center, 522 W Maple St, Allentown; 18101 610-347-9988 tinyurl.com/o8pdz8u

Pennsylvania: Lehigh Valley Area
Community Centers / Pride

291

GAYELLOW PAGES #42 2020-2021

New Hope PA/Lambertville NJ Area: Pennsylvania
Bars, Cafes, Clubs, Restaurants

⚥ ★ The LGBT Center of Greater Reading, 1501 N 13th St, Reading; 19604 610-864-5800 www.lgbtcenterofreading.com mdech@lgbtcenterofreading.com

⚥ ★ Pride of the Greater Lehigh Valley, Bradbury-Sullivan LGBT Community Center, 522 W Maple St, Allentown 610-347-9988 tinyurl.com/y27qvt8a

⚥ ★ Reading Pride Celebration, POB 15242, Reading; 19612 484-240-9660 tinyurl.com/oofbbs5

Information, Media & Publications

⚥ ● Gay Journal, Gaugler-Libby, LLC, POB 421, Stockertown; 18083 www.thegayjournal.net lvgayjournal@gmail.com

AIDS/HIV Services, Education & Support

♂ ☆ ♿ AIDSNET, 31 S Commerce Way #400, Bethlehem; 18017 610-882-1119 www.aidsnetpa.org info@aidsnetpa.org

♂ ☆ (♿) Fighting AIDS Continuously Together, POB 1028, Allentown; 18105 610-820-5519 www.factlv.org

Bars, Cafes, Clubs, Restaurants
Allentown

♂ O Allentown Brew Works, 812 Hamilton St, Allentown; 610-433-7777 www.thebrewworks.com ⚚ ✖

⚥ ● Stonewall Lehigh Valley, 28 N 10th St, Allentown; 610-432-0215 fb.com/stonewall.lehighvalley **D**

Bethlehem

♂ O Bethlehem Brew Works, 569 Main St, Bethlehem 610-882-1300 www.thebrewworks.com ⚚ ✖

Catasauqua

♂ O ♿ Cathy's Creative Catering & Cafe, 752 Front St, Catasauqua; 610-443-0670 tinyurl.com/y3msrfu8 ▷

Easton

⚥ La Pazza, 1251 Ferry St, Easton 610-515-0888

Reading

♂ O Judy's on Cherry, 332 Cherry St, Reading 610-374-8511 judysoncherry.com ✖

Clothes (see also Erotica, Leather)

⚥ ● Drop Me A Line Costume Shop, 1050 Lehigh St, Allentown; 610-435-7481 www.dropmealinecostumes.com

Food Specialties (see also Catering)

♂ O Sweet Girlz Bakery, 40 N Third St, Easton 610-829-1030 www.sweetgirlzpa.com

Funding: Endowment, Fundraising

⚥ ★ Diversity Alliance Fund, Berks County Community Foundation, 237 Court St, Reading; 19601 610-685-2223 www.bccf.org info@bccf.org

Massage Therapy (Certified/Licensed only)

♂ O ♿ Body Central, Inc., 32 S Main St, Coopersburg; 18036 610-282-3122 license #MSG000268 www.bodycentral.abmp.com bodycentral@massagetherapy.com

Organizations/Resources: Cultural, Dance, Performance

♂ ★ Lehigh Valley Gay Men's Chorus, POB 20712, Lehigh Valley; 18002 484-862-5050 www.lvgmc.org

Organizations/Resources: Student, Academic, Education

⚥ ★ Cedar Crest College Out There, 100 College Dr, Allentown; 610-437-4471

⚥ ★ Muhlenberg College Students for Queer Advocacy, Multicultural Center, 2251 Chew St, Allentown; 484-664-3228 tinyurl.com/y2zdostv

⚥ ★ ♿ The Pride Center for Sexual Orientation and Gender Diversity, Lehigh University, 29 Trembley Dr UC #C212, Bethlehem; 610-758-4574 **H?** tinyurl.com/otab9qh ✔

⚥ ★ Rainbow Alliance, Penn State Berks, POB 7009, Reading; 19610 610-396-6080 berks.psu.edu/diversity

Organizations/Resources: Youth (see also Family)

♂ ★ HAVEN Youth Group, c/o UUCLV, 424 Center St, Bethlehem; 610-868-1013 www.uuclvpa.org/haven.php

⚥ ★ The SPECTRUM, Planned Parenthood Keystone, 48 S 4th St, Reading; 610-376-0137 fb.com/theSPECTRUM.Berks

⚥ Valley Youth House, 1500 Sansom St #300A, Bethlehem; 215-925-3180 tinyurl.com/tmeg72k

Religious / Spiritual Resources

♂ ★ ♿ All Souls Ecumenical Catholic Church, 640 Centre Ave, Reading; 19601 610-621-1738 allsoulsecumenical.org allsoulsecc@gmail.com

⚥ ★ ♿ MCC of the Lehigh Valley, 1401 Greenview Ave, Bethlehem; 18018 ! 610-866-8223 www.mcclv.org ✔ info@mcclv.info
» *Manheim: see Lancaster*
» *Marshalls Creek: see Poconos Area*

Meadville

Organizations/Resources: Student, Academic, Education

⚥ ★ ♿ The Allegheny College Gender and Sexuality Alliance, Henderson Campus Center, 520 N Main St; 814-332-2301 tinyurl.com/h5lmecs ✔
» *Milford: see Poconos Area*

New Hope PA/Lambertville NJ Area

Community Centers and/or Pride Organizations
New Hope

⚥ ★ New Hope Celebrates, POB 266, New Hope 18938 newhopecelebrates.com

Accommodation: Hotels, Inns, Guesthouses, B&B, Resorts
New Hope

♂ ● Pineapple Hill Inn, 1324 River Rd, New Hope 888-866-8404 www.pineapplehill.com ✔ ⊗

♂ ● Raven, 385 W Bridge St, New Hope; 215-862-2081 www.theravennewhope.com ⚚ ✖

♂ ● Wishing Well B&B, 144 Old York Road, New Hope 215-736-6743 www.wishingwellbnb.com

Bars, Cafes, Clubs, Restaurants
New Hope

♂ O Greenhouse, 90 S Main St, New Hope 215-693-1657 www.greenhousenewhope.com ⚚ ✖ greenhouse@greenhousenewhope.com

♂ • Raven, 385 W Bridge St, New Hope; 215-862-2081 www.theravennewhope.com ⚤ ✕ 🎵

♂ • ♿ The RRazz Room, at The Clarion, 6426 Lower York Rd, New Hope; 888-596-1027 **H?** www.TheRrazzRoom.com 🎵 ✎

Bookstores
New Hope

♀ ○ Farley's Bookshop, 44 S Main St, New Hope 215-862-2452 www.farleysbookshop.com

Grooming, Personal Care, Spa Services
New Hope

♂ ○ Bangz Salon, 3 Market Pl, New Hope; 18938 215-862-9877 www.bangznewhope.com bangznewhope@gmail.com

Organizations/Resources: Family and Supporters

♀ ☆ PFLAG Bucks County, BucksCountyPFLAG@gmail.com

Organizations/Resources: Youth (see also Family)

♀ ★ ♿ The Rainbow Room, Planned Parenthood Keystone, 186 E Court St, Doylestown; 18901 267-282-4117 tinyurl.com/zanwbgn ✎ rainbowroom@ppkeystone.org
» New Kensington: see Pittsburgh Area

New Milford

Accommodation Rental: Furnished / Vacation (& AirBNB)

♂ • Table Rock Refuge, 1756 Sutton Rd www.tablerockrefuge.com ⊛

Campgrounds and RV Parks

♀ • (♿) Oneida Campground & Lodge, PO Box 537; 18834 570-465-7011 **H?** www.Oneidaresort.com **PDL** 🎵 (⚤?) ✎

Philadelphia Area

Crisis, Anti-violence, & Helplines

♂ Menergy, Rodin Place, 2000 Hamilton St Ste 304, Phila; 215-242-2235 www.menergy.org

♀ (♿) Women In Transition, 718 Arch St Ste 401N, Phila; 19106 215-751-1111 www.helpwomen.org witinfo@helpwomen.org

♀ ☆ (♿) Women Organized Against Rape, 1617 JFK Blvd #1100, Phila; 215-985-3333 www.woar.org

Community Centers and/or Pride Organizations

♀ ★ Philly Pride, 252 S 12th St Basement, Phila; 19107 215-875-9288 www.phillygaypride.org phillygaypride@aol.com

♀ ★ ♿ William Way Community Center, 1315 Spruce St, Phila; 215-732-2220 www.waygay.org ✎

Information, Media & Publications

♀ • **Philadelphia Gay News, 505 S 4th St, Phila 19147-1506 215-625-8501 www.epgn.com pgn@epgn.com**
◆ *Advertisement page 293*

♀ ★ Philly Gay Calendar, www.phillygaycalendar.com

Accommodation: Hotels, Inns, Guesthouses, B&B, Resorts
Chadds Ford

♀ ○ The Pennsbury Inn by Wild Wisteria BnB, 883 Baltimore Pike, Chadds Ford; 19317-9305 610-388-1435 **H?** www.pennsbury-inn.com (⚤?) ✎ ⊛ info@pennsburyinn.com

Philadelphia

♀ • Alexander Inn, 301 S 12th St, Phila 215-923-3535 www.alexanderinn.com ✎

♀ • Gables B&B, 4520 Chester Ave, Phila 215-662-1918 www.gablesbb.com ⊛

AIDS/HIV Services, Education & Support

♀ ☆ ♿ Action Wellness, 1216 Arch St 6th Flr, Phila; 19107-2835 215-981-0088 **HDS** www.ActionWellness.org

♀ AIDS Care Group of Chester, 2304 Edgemont Ave, Chester; 610-872-9101 aidscaregroup.org

♀ ☆ AIDS Fund, 2628 Orthodox St, Phila 215-731-9255 aidsfundphilly.org

♀ Community AIDS Hotline, 1101 Market St, Phila 215-985-2437

♀ ☆ ♿ Critical Path Learning Center, The AIDS Library. 1233 Locust St Flr 2, Phila; 215-985-4448 x143 www.critpath.org ✎

♀ ★ GALAEI: Gay & Lesbian Latino AIDS Education Initiative, 149 W Susquehanna Ave, Phila; 267-457-3912 www.galaei.org ◆

♀ ☆ ♿ MANNA (Metropolitan Area Neighborhood Nutrition Alliance), 420 N 20th St, Phila; 215-496-2662 www.mannapa.org

♀ ☆ Philadelphia AIDS Consortium, 112 N Broad St Flr 5, Phila; 215-988-9970 www.tpaconline.org

♀ ☆ ♿ Philadelphia FIGHT - AIDS Library, 1233 Locust St 2nd Flr, Phila; 215-985-4851 tinyurl.com/yyn4do97 ✎

♀ ☆ Siloam, 850 N 11th St, Phila; 19123 215-765-6633 www.siloamwellness.org sdibianca@siloamwellness.org

Archives/Libraries/Museums/History Projects

♀ ★ ♿ John J. Wilcox Jr. Archives of Philadelphia, William Way LGBT Community Center, 1315 Spruce St, Phila 215-732-2220 www.waygay.org/archives ✎

Bars, Cafes, Clubs, Restaurants
Conshohocken

♀ ○ Guppys Good Times, 2 Maple St, Conshohocken 610-828-0300 www.guppysgoodtimes.com ⚤ ✕ 🎵

Philadelphia

♀ ○ The Adobe Café Bar & Grill, 4550 Mitchell St, Phila; 215-483-3947 adobecafephiladelphia.com ⚤ ✕

♀ • (♿) Bike Stop, 204-206 S Quince St, Phila; 215-627-1662 www.thebikestop.com **DL**

♀ ○ Bob & Barbara's, 1509 South St, Phila 215-545-4511 www.bobandbarbaras.com 🎵

Pennsylvania: Philadelphia Area
Bars, Cafes, Clubs, Restaurants
293
GAYELLOW PAGES #42 2020-2021
Philadelphia Area : Pennsylvania
Counseling

The Boxers PHL, 1330 Walnut St, Phila 215-735-2977 www.boxersphl.com **S** ♈ ✕ 🏨

♀ ● ♿ Knock Restaurant & Bar, 225 S 12th St, Phila; 215-925-1166 www.knockphilly.com **K** ♈ ✕ ⦿

♀ ○ L'Etage / Beau Monde, 624 S 6th St, Phila 215-592-0656 www.creperie-beaumonde.com **D** ✕🏨

♀ ○ North Third, 801 N 3rd St, Phila; 215-413-3666 www.norththird.com ♈ ✕

♀ ○ Raven Lounge, 1718 Sansom St, Phila 215-840-3577 fb.com/theravenlounge/🏨

The Rosewood, 1302 Walnut St, Phila; / sat night 215-545-1893 tinyurl.com/yyun4ab2

♀ ○ (♿) Silk City, 435 Spring Garden St, Phila; 215-592-8838 www.silkcityphilly.com **D** ♈ ✕🏨 ✗

♀ Stimulus, Check monthly party fb.com/TheStimulus ✪

♀ ○ Stir Lounge, 1705 Chancellor St, Phila 215-732-2700 www.stirphilly.com 🏨

♀ ● (♿) Tabu Lounge & Sports Bar, 200 S 12th St, Phila; 215-964-9675 www.tabuphilly.com **DK** ♈ ✕ 🏨

♀ ○ Tattooed Mom, 530 South St, Phila 215-238-9880 www.tattooedmomphilly.com ♈ ✕ tattooedmomphilly@gmail.com

♀ ● Tavern on Camac, 243 S Camac St, Phila 215-545-0900 www.tavernoncamac.com **DKV** ♈ ✕ 🏨

♀ Toasted Walnut Bar & Kitchen, 1316 Walnut St, Phila; 215-546-8888 www.toastedwalnut.com

The UBar, 1220 Locust St, Phila; 215-546-6660 www.ubarphilly.com

♀ ● ♿ Valanni, 1229 Spruce St, Phila 215-790-9494 valanni.com ✕

The Voyeur Nightclub, 1221 St James St, Phila 215-735-5772 www.voyeurnightclub.com **D** 🏨

The ● ♿ Woody's, 202 S 13th St, Phila 215-545-1893 www.woodysbar.com **D** ♈ ✕

Bookstores

♀ ● Big Blue Marble Bookstore, 551 Carpenter Lane, Phila; 215-844-1870 www.bigbluemarblebooks.com ⦿ ✗

♀ ● (♿) **Philly AIDS Thrift at Giovanni's Room, 345 S 12th St, Phila; 215-923-2960 www.queerbooks.com** ✗

Counseling/Psychotherapy/Mental Health

♀ ○ Alternative Choices, 319 Vine St #110, Phila 19106 215-592-1333 www.alternativechoices.com cariel@alternativechoices.com

♀ ○ (♿) Carter, Bonnie Frank, PhD, 640 Crestwood Rd, Wayne; 19087-2315 610-213-6695 www.bfcnetworks.net bonnie.frank.carter@bfcnetworks.net

♀ ● Jeanette, Doris, PsyD, Center for New Psychology, 503 S 21st St, Phila; 215-732-6197 www.drjeanette.com

♀ ● Lambda Counseling Center, Parkway House, 2201 Pennsylvania Ave #101, Phila; 19130-3521 215-751-9087 fax 215-546-4759 lambdadoctor@aol.com

Pennsylvania: Philadelphia Area
Counseling
294
GAYELLOW PAGES #42 2020-2021
Philadelphia Area : Pennsylvania
Organizations: Naturist/Nudist

♀ ● Lavender Visions, 215-242-6334 Counseling, phone consultation, workshops: for lesbian, bisexual & questioning women. www.lavendervisions.com

♂ ★ (♿) LGBT Peer Counseling Services, William Way Community Center, 1315 Spruce St, Phila; 19107-5601 215-732-TALK www.lgbtpeercounseling.com ✎ lgbtpeercounseling@yahoo.com

♀ ☆ ♿ Therapy Center of Philadelphia, 1315 Walnut St Ste 1004, Phila; 215-567-1111 Women & Transgender Communities www.therapycenterofphila.org ✎

Erotica / Adult Stores / Safe Sex Supplies

♀ ○ Pleasure Chest, 2039 Walnut St, Phila; 19103 215-561-7480 pleasurechestphilly.com papleasurechest@verizon.net

Funding: Endowment, Fundraising

♀ ☆ Bread & Roses Community Fund, 1315 Walnut St Ste 1300, Phila; 215-731-1107 breadrosesfund.org

♂ ★ ♿ Delaware Valley Legacy Fund, 1835 Market St Ste 2410, Phila; 215-863-8110 www.dvlf.org

Health Care: Physical (see also Counseling/Mental Health)

♀ ○ ♿ Bettiker, Robert, MD, Temple University Hospital, 3322 N Broad St Ste 203, Phila; 215-707-3807 **HS** tinyurl.com/y4t4cqdd ✎

♂ Einstein Healthcare Network, 5501 Old York Rd, Phila; 215-456-7045 tinyurl.com/sfwjjv6

♀ ☆ ♿ Mazzoni Center LGBT Health & Well-Being, 1348 Bainbridge St, Phila; 215-563-0652 www.mazzonicenter.org

♂ ○ ♿ Myers, Allison, MD, MPH, Penn Family Care, 3737 Market St Flr 9, Phila; 19104 215-662-8777 tinyurl.com/jxdtagw

♀ ☆ ♿ Philadelphia FIGHT, 1233 Locust St Flr 3, Phila; 19107-5453 215-985-4448 fax 215-985-4952 www.fight.org

♀ ☆ Prevention Point Philadelphia, 2913 Kensington Ave, Phila; 215-634-5272 **H?** ppponline.org ✎

♀ ☆ Rainbow Circle of the Linda Creed Breast Cancer Org, 614 S 8th St #277, Phila; 19147 877-992-7333 215-564-3700 www.lindacreed.org contact@lindacreed.org

Immigration, Citizenship, Political Asylum, Refugees

♀ ○ Hykel Law, 1500 JFK Blvd #1040, Phila; 19102 215-246-9400 www.hykellaw.com info@hykellaw.com

Legal Services

♀ ○ Dimmerman, Harper J, Dimmerman PC, POB 2134, Phila; 19103-9997 / 2037 Chestnut St, Flr 1 215-545-0600 fax 215-240-1673 Real estate law dimmermanlaw.com hdimmerman@dimmermanlaw.com

♀ ○ Giampolo Law Group, 319 S 12th St #1F, Phila 215-645-2415 Business, family, estate, LGBT law www.giampololaw.com

♀ ● (♿) Law Offices of Kristine W. Holt, 525 S 4th St Ste240A, Phila; 215-545-7789 Bankruptcy; transgender issues www.HoltEsq.com ✎

♀ ● Minster & Facciolo, LLC, 521 S 2nd St, Phila 19147-2417 215-627-8200 fax 215-928-0015 www.MinsterandFacciolo.com

♀ ○ Robinette, Justin F, 2 Penn Ctr, Ste 1240, Phila; 19102 610-212-6649 www.1800cantwork.com justinr@ericshore.com

♀ ● Steerman, Amy F, 1900 Spruce St, Phila; 19103 215-735-1006 www.amysteerman.com ✎

Men's & Sex Clubs (not primarily Health Clubs)

♂ ○ Club Philly, 1220 Chancellor St, Phila 215-735-7671 www.clubphilly.com

♂ Philly Jacks, check schedule 215-618-1519 www.philadelphiajacks.com

♂ ● Sansom Street Gym, 2020 Sansom St, Phila 267-330-0151 www.sansomstreetgym.com

Moving/Transportation/Storage

♀ ○ Mambo Movers, 1205 S 15th St, Phila 215-670-9535 PUC # A-00115371 DOT # 958067 www.mambomovers.com

Organizations/Resources: Cultural, Dance, Performance

♀ ☆ (♿) Anna Crusis Women's Choir, POB 42277, Phila; 19101-2277 267-825-7464 **H** www.annacrusis.org info@annacrusis.org

♂ ★ (♿) Independence Squares, POB 42126, Phila; 19101 267-270-5103 www.independencesquares.org **D**

♂ ★ (♿) Philadelphia Gay Men's Chorus, PO Box 30185, Phila; 19103 215-731-9230 www.pgmc.org

♀ ★ ♿ Philadelphia Voices of Pride, 1315 Spruce St, Phila; pvop.org

♀ qFLIXphiladelphia, www.qflixphilly.com

Organizations/Resources: Education

♂ ★ Equality Forum, 1420 Locust St Ste 300, Phila; 215-732-3378 equalityforum.com

Organizations/Resources: Ethnic, Multicultural

♂ ★ The COLOURS Organization, Inc, 1211 Chestnut St Ste 910, Phila; 215-832-0100 coloursorganization.org ✚ ✎

♂ ★ (♿) Men of All Colors Together/MACT Philadelphia, POB 42257, Phila; 19101 215-397-3669 tinyurl.com/p8e4l7f ✪

♂ ★ Philadelphia Black Pride, POB 22515, Phila; 19110 www.phillyblackpride.org ✚

Organizations/Resources: Family and Supporters

♀ ☆ PFLAG Media, POB 69, Broomall; 19008-0069 610-368-2021 jcbort@comcast.net

♀ ☆ PFLAG Philadelphia Area, POB 15711, Phila 19103 215-572-1833 www.pflagphila.org

♀ ☆ PFLAG West Chester / Chester County, POB 2527, West Chester; 19380 484-354-2448

♀ ★ Philadelphia Family Pride, POB 31848, Phila 19104 215-888-0722 www.phillyfamilypride.org ✪

Organizations/Resources: Naturist/Nudist

♂ ★ (♿) Bare Bucks Club, 215-331-4564 x7

♂ ★ Philadelphia Area Naturist Guys (PANG), POB 578, Rising Sun, MD 21911 pang.memberclicks.net **N**

Pennsylvania: Philadelphia Area
Organizations: Political
295
GAYELLOW PAGES #42 2020-2021
Philadelphia Area: Pennsylvania
Weddings/Unions

Organizations/Resources: Political/Legislative/Advocacy

♀ ☆ Act Up Philadelphia, POB 36697, Phila; 19110 215-360-3086 www.actupphilly.org

⚥ Liberty City LGBT Democratic Club, POB 58385, Phila; 19102 www.libertycity.org

Organizations/Resources: Social, Recreation, Support

♀ ★ (?⚦) Ladies 2000, POB 1, Oaklyn, NJ 08107 856-869-0193 www.ladies2000.com

♀ ★ Sisterspace of the Delaware Valley, POB 22476, Phila; 19110 888-294-1110 www.sisterspace.org

Organizations/Resources: Student, Academic, Education

⚥ ★ LGBT Center at Penn, 3907 Spruce St, Phila 215-898-5044 www.vpul.upenn.edu/lgbtc/

⚥ ★ ♿ PSU Brandywine Rainbow Alliance, 25 Yearsley Mill Rd, Media; 610-892-1270 **H?** fb.com/Brandywine.LGBTQIA/

⚥ ★ Swarthmore College Intercultural Center, 500 College Avenue, Swarthmore; 610-328-7353 tinyurl.com/y5vtndcx

⚥ ★ ♿ West Chester University Center for Trans and Queer Advocacy, 250 Sykes Student Union, West Chester 610-436-3147 **H?** tinyurl.com/y3nw2pwg ✍

Organizations/Resources: Transgender/Gender Non-Conforming/Diverse

T ☆ Evolutions - Transgender Support Group, Mazzoni Center, 1348 Bainbridge St, Phila; 215-563-0652 x568 tinyurl.com/z7khk7u

T ★ Transequity Project, GALAEI, 149 W Susquehanna Ave, Phila; 267-457-3912 www.galaei.org/programs#tip

Organizations/Resources: Youth (see also Family)

⚥ The Attic Youth Center, 255 S 16th St, Phila; 215-545-4331 www.atticyouthcenter.org

⚥ ★ The Bryson Institute, 255 S 16th St, Phila; 215-545-4331 tinyurl.com/y2wuzaab

⚥ ★ Main Line Youth Alliance, POB 442, Wayne; 19087 www.myaonline.org

Real Estate (see also Mortgages)

♀ ● Fontaine, Paul, Realtor, Keller Williams Realty, Society Hill, 604 S Washington Square, Phila; 19106 215-917-2276 215-600-0123 www.bestphillyhomes.com Paul@BestPhillyHomes.com

Recovery

♂ ☆ AA: Southeastern Pennsylvania Intergroup Association, 444 N 3rd St Ste 3E, Phila; 19123 877-934-2522 215-923-7900 www.aasepia.org info@aasepia.org

♂ ☆ Livengrin Foundation, 4833 Hulmeville Rd, Bensalem; 215-638-5200 www.livengrin.org

Religious / Spiritual Resources

♂ ☆ ♿ Central Baptist Church, POB 309, Wayne; 19087-0309 610-688-0664 www.cbcwayne.org ✍

♂ ☆ ♿ Collenbrook United Church, 5290 Township Line Rd, Drexel Hill; 19026-4797 610-789-9590 www.collenbrook.org ✍ CollenbrookUnited@Gmail.com

⚥ ★ ♿ Dignity/Philadelphia, POB 53348, Phila; 19105 215-546-2093 **H?** www.dignityphila.org

♂ ☆ ♿ Main Line Unitarian Church, 816 S Valley Forge Rd, Devon; 19333-1825 610-688-8332 **HD** www.mluc.org ✍ info@mluc.org

♂ ☆ ♿ Old First Reformed Church UCC, 151 N 4th St, Phila; 19106 215-922-4566 oldfirstucc.org

♂ ☆ ♿ Resurrection Lutheran Church, 620 E Welsh Rd, Horsham; 19044 215-646-2597 www.rlchorsham.org ✍ rlcoffice@verizon.net

♂ ☆ ♿ St Mary of Grace Parish, 145 W Rose Tree Rd, Media; 19063 267-909-3333 Independent Catholic Christian Church www.inclusivecatholics.org @ixx=

♂ ☆ ♿ Tabernacle UCC, 3700 Chestnut St, Phila; 19104 215-386-4100 www.tabunited.org tabernacleunited@gmail.com

♂ ☆ ♿ University Lutheran Church of the Incarnation, 3637 Chestnut St, Phila; 19104-2670 215-387-2885 www.uniluphila.org ✍ administrator@uniluphila.org

⚥ ★ Whosoever Metropolitan Community Church, 3637 Chestnut St, Phila; 215-873-5719 whosoevermccp.com

Sports & Outdoor

⚥ ★ Bucks M.C., POB L-543, Langhorne; 19047 609-266-2634 www.bucksmc.org

⚥ ★ City of Brotherly Love Softball League, PO Box 53836, Phila; 19105 www.cblsl.org

♀ Fairmont Park Women's Softball League, 267-225-4848 www.fpwsl.com

⚥ Fins Aquatics Club, www.philadelphiafins.org

⚥ ★ Greater Philadelphia Flag Football League, POB 21, Phila; 19105 www.phillyflagfootball.com

⚥ LezRun Philadelphia, fb.com/LezRun

⚥ ★ Philadelphia Falcons Soccer Club, 744 South St #755, Phila; 19147 www.phillyfalcons.org

♀ ☆ Philadelphia Flames Soccer Club, 107 Alison Road #F-24, Horsham; 19044 267-784-5663 www.flamessc.us

⚥ ★ (?⚦) Philadelphia Frontrunners, www.phillyfr.org

⚥ ★ Philadelphia Gay Bowling League, fb.com/PhilaGayBowling/ @ixx=

⚥ ★ Philadelphia Gryphons Rugby Football Club, 1229 Chestnut St #180, Phila; 19107 www.phillygryphons.org play@philadelphiagryphons.org

⚥ ★ Philadelphia Liberty Tennis Association, PO Box 1794, Phila; 19105 tinyurl.com/44xx35d

⚥ ★ Philadelphians Motorcycle Club, 1315 Spruce St, Phila; www.philadelphiansmc.org

⚥ ★ Spartans Wrestling Club of Philadelphia, www.phillyspartans.com

Weddings and Ceremonies

♂ ○ Journeys of The Heart, 215-633-8980 www.journeysoftheheart.org ♥

≫ Pipersville: see New Hope PA/Lambertville NJ Area

Pennsylvania: Pittsburgh Area
Community Centers / Pride
296
GAYELLOW PAGES #42 2020-2021
Pittsburgh Area: Pennsylvania
Organizations: Family

Pittsburgh Area

Community Centers and/or Pride Organizations

♂ ★ (♿) Delta Foundation of Pittsburgh/Pittsburgh Pride, 911 Galveston Ave, Pgh; 412-322-2800 www.pittsburghpride.org ⚲

♀ ★ ♿ PGH Equality Center, 5840 Ellsworth Ave Ste 100, Pgh; 15232 412-422-0114 www.pghequalitycenter.org ⚲ info@pghequalitycenter.org

Accommodation: Hotels, Inns, Guesthouses, B&B, Resorts
Addison

♀ ○ ♿ Hartzell House Bed & Breakfast, 728 Main St, Addison; 814-395-5248 **H** www.hartzellhouse.com ⚲ ⊗ ⊗ @ixx=

Pittsburgh

♀ ● The Parador of Pittsburgh, 939 Western Ave, Pgh; 15233 412-231-4800 877-340-1443 theparadorinn.com ⚲ ⊗

Accounting, Bookkeeping, Tax Services

♂ ● **Schneider, Kathleen, Atty/CPA, 1227 S Braddock Ave, Pgh; 15218-1239 412-371-8831 Tax preparation & planning: individuals. estates, businesses. Convenient location, free parking. www.kdschneiderlawoffice.com office@kdschneider.law**

AIDS/HIV Services, Education & Support

♀ ☆ ♿ Allies Pittsburgh for Health and Wellbeing, 5913 Penn Ave Flr 2, Pgh; 412-345-7456 alliespgh.org

♂ ★ ♿ Pitt Men's Study, University of Pittsburgh, POB 7319, Pgh; 15213 412-624-2008 www.pittmensstudy.com

♀ Shepherd Wellness Community, 4800 Sciota St, Pgh; 412-683-4477 www.swconline.com

Bars, Cafes, Clubs, Restaurants
Butler

♀ ● M&J's Lounge, 124 Mercer St, Butler 724-602-8447 fb.com/MandJsLounge **DP** 🎵

Pittsburgh

♂ ● ♿ 5801 Video Lounge & Cafe, 5801 Ellsworth Ave, Pgh; 412-661-5600 www.5801videolounge.com **SV** ☂ ✕ ⚲

♀ ● 941 Saloon, 941 Liberty Ave Flr 2, Pgh 412-281-5222 fb.com/941saloon/ **DP**

♀ Blue Moon, 5115 Butler St, Pgh 412-781-1119 https://www.facebook.com/pages/The-Blue-Moon/196366240379852 tinyurl.com/zeaxwtw

♂ ● Cattivo, 146 44th St, Pgh; 412-687-2157 www.cattivopgh.com ☂ ✕ 🎵

♂ ● G2H2/ Gay Guy Happy Hour, www.g2h2pittsburgh.com

♂ ● ♿ Images, 965 Liberty Ave, Pgh 412-391-9990 fb.com/imagespgh/ **KV** ☂ ✕ 🎵 ⚲

♂ ● PTown, 4740 Baum Blvd, Pgh; 412-621-0111 ptownbar.com **D** 🎵 ⚲

♀ ● ♿ Real Luck Cafe, 1519 Penn Ave, Pgh; 412-471-7832 tinyurl.com/yc3gfcnu **D** ☂ ✕ 🎵

♂ ○ Square Cafe, 1137 S Braddock Ave, Pgh 412-244-8002 www.square-cafe.com ☐⚲

♀ There Ultra Lounge, 931 Liberty Ave, Pgh 412-642-4435 fb.com/THEREUltra/ **V**

♂ Tilden, 941 Liberty Ave, Pgh; / upstairs Fri & Sat afterhours 412-391-0804 fb.com/tildenclub/ **DP**

♂ ○ ♿ Zeke's Coffee, 6015 Penn Ave, Pgh; / coffee drive-thru 6314 Broad St 412-737-0862 **H?** www.zekescoffeepgh.com ✕ ☐⚲ zekespgh@gmail.com

Bookstores

♂ The Big Idea Bookstore, 4812 Liberty Ave, Pgh 412-687-4323 thebigideapgh.org ☐⚲ ❸

♂ ○ City Books, 908 Galveston Ave, Pgh; 15233 412-321-7323 **H?** www.citybookspgh.com ⚲ citybookspgh@gmail.com

Clothes (see also Erotica, Leather)

♂ ○ ♿ Spotlight Costumes, LLC, 22 Wabash St, Pgh; 15220 412-381-7733 www.spotlightcostumes.com

Counseling/Psychotherapy/Mental Health

♂ ○ ♿ Bertini, Michele, PhD, MEd, NCC, 5850 Ellsworth Ave, Pgh; 412-365-2020 www.michelebertini.com

♀ ● (♿) Huggins, James, PhD, 401 Shady Ave Ste A106, Pgh; 15206-4457 412-362-9388

♀ ★ ♿ Persad Center, Inc, 5301 Butler St Ste 100, Pgh; 888-873-7723 persadcenter.org

Leather Resources & Groups

♂ ★ Three Rivers Leather Club, POB 5298, Pgh 15206 www.trlc.net

Legal Services

♂ ● **Schneider, Kathleen, Atty/CPA, 1227 S Braddock Ave, Pgh; 15218-1239 412-371-8831 Tax preparation & planning: individuals. estates, businesses. Convenient location, free parking. www.kdschneiderlawoffice.com office@kdschneider.law**

Men's & Sex Clubs (not primarily Health Clubs)

♂ ○ Club Pittsburgh, 1139 Penn Ave 4th flr, Pgh 412-471-6790 www.clubpittsburgh.com **P** ⚲

Organizations/Resources: Cultural, Dance, Performance

♂ ☆ Dreams of Hope, Queer Youth Arts, POB 4912, Pgh; 15206 412-361-2065 www.dreamsofhope.org

♂ ★ Iron City Squares, 6 Miller Dr, Blairsville; 15717 412-372-1450 724-464-4324 beknupp@iup.edu

♂ ★ ♿ Pittsburgh Lesbian & Gay Film Society, POB 81237, Pgh; 15217-4237 412-422-6776 www.reelq.org

♂ ★ ♿ Renaissance City Choir, 116 S Highland Ave, Pgh; 412-345-1722 www.rccpittsburgh.com

Organizations/Resources: Family and Supporters

♂ ☆ PFLAG Greensburg, 139 N Main St, Greensburg 724-610-9388 fb.com/PFLAGGreensburg/

Pennsylvania: Pittsburgh Area
Organizations: Family
297
GAYELLOW PAGES #42 2020-2021
Scranton/Wilkes-Barre Area: Pennsylvania
AIDS/HIV Support

♂ ☆ (&&) PFLAG Pittsburgh, POB 5406, Pgh; 15206 412-833-4556 www.pflagpgh.org

Organizations/Resources: Political/Legislative/Advocacy

♂ ☆ && American Civil Liberties Union of Pennsylvania, POB 23058, Pgh; 15222 412-681-7736 To request assistance with a legal complaint, use online intake form at www.aclupa.org/complaint www.aclupa.org

♀ ★ Gertrude Stein Political Club of Greater Pittsburgh, POB 8108, Pgh; 15217-0108 www.gertrudesteinclub.org gspcgp@gmail.com

♀ ★ Steel City Stonewall Democrats, SMC 1015, PO Box 99382, Pgh; 15233 www.steel-city.org

Organizations/Resources: Social, Recreation, Support

♂ ★ (?&) Burgh Bears, POB 6426, Pgh 15212 www.burghbears.org

♂ ★ (?&) Pittsburgh Prime Timers, POB 99292, Pgh; 15233 412-519-4320 tinyurl.com/2d52mb

Organizations/Resources: Student, Academic, Education

♀ ★ Community College of Allegheny County GSA, 115 SSC, 808 Ridge Ave, Pgh; 412-237-2545

♀ ★ Penn State Beaver LGBTQ Alliance, 100 University Dr, Monaca; 724-773-3959

♀ ★ && Rainbow Alliance, University of Pittsburgh, 611 William Pitt Union, Pgh; 412-648-2105 pittrainbow.tumblr.com

Real Estate (see also Mortgages)

♂ ● Myers, Mark, Realtor, Berkshire Hathaway, 1376 Freeport Rd, Pgh; 412-952-2581

Religious / Spiritual Resources

♀ ☆ Allegheny Unitarian Universalist Church, 416 W North Ave, Pgh; 15212 412-322-4261 **H?** alleghenyuu.org ✔

♀ ★ && Bet Tikvah, POB 10140, Pgh; 15232-0140 412-256-8317 www.bettikvah.org ⚥✔ info@bettikvah.org

♀ Butler LGBTQ Interfaith Network, 412-518-1515 tinyurl.com/nqqeao3

♀ ★ && Dignity Pittsburgh, POB 362, Pgh; 15230 412-362-4334 www.dignitypgh.org

♀ ☆ ♂ East Suburban UU Church, 4326 Sardis Rd, Murrysville; 15668 724-739-3788 www.esuuc.org

♀ ☆ && First Presbyterian Church, 100 E Wheeling St, Washington; 724-225-5415 www.fpc1793.org

♀ ★ && MCC Pittsburgh, 4503 Old William Penn Highway, Monroeville; 412-683-2994

Sports & Outdoor

♀ Pittsburgh Frontrunners, 412-926-9866 tinyurl.com/3b8ssav

♀ ★ Steel City Bowling League, tinyurl.com/y6cur8p5

♀ ★ Steel City Softball League, POB 9118, Pgh; 15224 steelcitysoftball.com

♀ ★ Steel City Sports, www.steelcitysports.org

♀ ★ Steel City Volleyball League (SCVL), POB 16406, Pgh; 15242 412-506-3187 www.steelcityvolleyball.org

♀ Stonewall Sports Pittsburgh, 901 Western Ave Courtyard, Pgh; stonewallsportspgh.org

Poconos Area

Information, Media & Publications

♀ ★ TriVersity (Upper Delaware GLBT Center), PO Box 1295, Milford; 18337 PA Poconos Area including Sussex County, NJ, Pike County PA, and Orange and Sullivan Counties, NY www.udglbt.org

Accommodation: Hotels, Inns, Guesthouses, B&B, Resorts
East Stroudsburg

♀ ● && Rainbow Mountain Resort, 210 Mt Nebo Rd, E Stroudsburg; 570-223-8484 www.rainbowmountain.com **D** Y ✗ ▥ (⚘?) ✔ ⊗

Jim Thorpe

♀ ● The Parsonage B&B, 61 W Broadway, Jim Thorpe 570-325-4462 **H?** www.theparsonagebandb.com (⚘?) ✔ ⊗

Milford

♂ ● && Hotel Fauchere, 401 Broad St, Milford; 18337-1532 570-409-1212 www.hotelfauchere.com ⚘✔ ⊗ info@hotelfauchere.com

Bars, Cafes, Clubs, Restaurants
Milford

♂ ● && Bar Louis, Hotel Fauchere, 401 Broad St, Milford; 570-409-1212 www.hotelfauchere.com Y ✗✔ info@hotelfauchere.com

♂ ● && The Delmonico Room, Hotel Fauchere, 401 Broad St, Milford; 570-409-1212 **H?** www.hotelfauchere.com Y ✗✔

Campgrounds and RV Parks

♀ ● (?&) The Woods Campground, 3500 Forest St, Lehighton; 610-377-9577 www.thewoodscampground.com **N** ⚘✔ ⊗ @ixx=

Organizations/Resources: Student, Academic, Education

♀ ★ (?&) Gender and Sexuality Center, East Stroudsburg University LGBTQA Program Center, 200 Prospect St, E Stroudsburg; 570-422-3614 **H?** tinyurl.com/y5h9bqdx ✔

Railroad

Accommodation: Hotels, Inns, Guesthouses, B&B, Resorts

♀ ○ Jackson House B&B, POB 123; 17355 / 6 E Main St 717-227-2022 www.jacksonhousebandb.com ⚘ ✔

>> *Reading: see Lehigh Valley Area*
>> *Scotrun: see Poconos Area*

Scranton/Wilkes-Barre Area

AIDS/HIV Services, Education & Support

♀ ☆ Wyoming Valley AIDS Council, 330 Bowman St #1, Wilkes Barre; 18702 570-823-5808 www.wvacinc.org info@wvacinc.org

Bars, Cafes, Clubs, Restaurants
Moosic
⚲ ● Twelve Penny Saloon, 3501 Birney Ave, Moosic; 570-941-0444 12pennysaloon.com **L** ⵎ ✕▦ ⋈

Wilkes Barre
⚲ Heat, 71 N Main St, Wilkes Barre 570-266-8952 www.heat-nepa.com

Gifts, Cards, Pride, etc.
♀ ○ Magikal Garden, 1174 Wyoming Ave, Exeter 570-655-0924 www.magikalgarden.com

Leather Resources & Groups
♂ ★ (🐾) Northeast PA Leatherman, POB 1492, Scranton; 18501 tinyurl.com/jp75vr3

Organizations/Resources: General, Umbrella, Pride
⚲ Northeast Pennsylvania Rainbow Alliance, c/o DCS, POB 1044, Wilkes Barre; 18703 neparainbowalliance.org

Slippery Rock

Organizations/Resources: Student, Academic, Education
⚲ ★ ♿ Slippery Rock University Pride Center, 1 Morrow Way; 724-738-4378 tinyurl.com/zjs8opt
>> *Smithton: see Pittsburgh Area*
>> *Spring Grove: see York*

Starlight

Accommodation: Hotels, Inns, Guesthouses, B&B, Resorts
♂ ● ♿ Starlight Lodge, 169 Starlight Lake Rd 570-798-2350 www.starlightlodge.com (🐾?) ⋈ ⊗ @ixx=

State College

Crisis, Anti-violence, & Helplines
♂ ☆ ♿ Centre Safe, 140 W Nittany Ave 814-234-5050 **H** ccwrc.org

Bars, Cafes, Clubs, Restaurants
⚲ ● Chumley's, 108 W College St; 814-238-4446 fb.com/Chumleys

Organizations/Resources: Student, Academic, Education
⚲ ★ ♿ Bucknell University Office of LGBTQ Resources, Elaine Langone Center, Room 302, Lewisburg; 570-577-1609 www.bucknell.edu/LGBTQ ⋈

⚲ ★ ♿ LBGTA Student Resource Center, Pennsylvania State University, 101 Boucke Building, University Park 814-863-1248 tinyurl.com/gm9e9gy
>> *University Park: see State College*
>> *Wilkes Barre: see Scranton/Wilkes-Barre Area*

Williamsport

AIDS/HIV Services, Education & Support
♀ ☆ AIDS Resource Alliance, Inc., 500 W 3rd St 570-322-8448 aidsresource.com

Organizations/Resources: Student, Academic, Education
⚲ ★ (?♿) Lycoming College Gender and Sexuality Alliance, 700 College Place; tinyurl.com/qbpo8x3 ⋈

⚲ ★ ♿ Penn College Alliance, 1 College Ave; **H?** tinyurl.com/knxacq4 ⋈

York

Community Centers and/or Pride Organizations
⚲ The Equality Fest, 15 N Cherry Ln www.equalityfestyork.com

⚲ ★ The Rainbow Rose Center, 15 N Cherry Ln 17401 **H?** rainbowrosecenter.org ⋈ rainbowrosecenter@gmail.com

Bars, Cafes, Clubs, Restaurants
⚲ Guerrilla Gay Bar, check schedule fb.com/GGBYorkPA/

Health Care: Physical (see also Counseling/Mental Health)
♀ ☆ Family First Health Caring Together, 116 S George St; 717-846-6776 www.familyfirsthealth.org

Organizations/Resources: Family and Supporters
♀ ☆ ♿ PFLAG/York, UU Congregation of York, 925 S George St; 17403-3706 pflagyork.org ⋈ pflagyork@gmail.com

Organizations/Resources: Political/Legislative/Advocacy
⚲ New Birth of Freedom Scouts for Equality, tinyurl.com/tpxafxv

Organizations/Resources: Student, Academic, Education
⚲ ★ ♿ York College of Pennsylvania Lambda, Student Activities, Main Level Student Union Room 205; 717-815-1239 yorklambda.weebly.com/

Puerto Rico
State/County Resources

Information, Media & Publications
⚲ ★ Orgullo Boricua LGBT, fb.com/groups/19481998232 ◆

AIDS/HIV Services, Education & Support
♀ ★ PR CoNCRA, Urb. García Ubarri, Calle Brumbaugh # 1162, Rio Piedras, PR 787-753-9443 www.prconcra.net

Organizations/Resources: Social, Recreation, Support
⚲ Puerto Rico Para Todos, PMB 231 52 Ave. Esmeralda Ste 2, Guaynabo, PR 787-602-5954 www.prparatodos.org

Organizations/Resources: Youth (see also Family)
♀ ★ PR CoNCRA Centro de Jóvenes, Urb. García Ubarri, Calle Brumbaugh # 1162, Rio Piedras, PR 787-753-9443 www.centrode-jovenespr.com

Bayamon

Bars, Cafes, Clubs, Restaurants
⚲ Start Night Private Club, Calle Ongay #31 Santa Cruz; 787-536-3579 tinyurl.com/hpdh2wh **P** ▦

Puerto Rico: Ponce
Bars, Cafes, Clubs, Restaurants

299

GAYELLOW PAGES #42 2020-2021

State/County Resources : Rhode Island
AIDS/HIV Support

Ponce

Bars, Cafes, Clubs, Restaurants

Ashé Bar, 2313 Ave Eduardo Ruberte 787-603-8095 tinyurl.com/zud77lr

Punta Santiago

Accommodation: Hotels, Inns, Guesthouses, B&B, Resorts

Barefoot Travelers Rooms, Keishya Salko, POB 868; 00741 787-850-0508 tinyurl.com/7hnerm4 (♣?) ✗ ⊗⊗

San Juan Area

Community Centers and/or Pride Organizations

★ Centro Comunitario LGBTT de Puerto Rico, PO Box 9501, San Juan; 00908 / Calle Mayaguez #37, Urb Perez Morris, San Juan 00917 787-294-9850 www.centrolgbttpr.org ✦ centrolgbttpr@gmail.com

Information, Media & Publications

★ **Gay Guide to San Juan, PR, sanjuangay-guide.com rholm@caribbeanconsulting.com**

Accommodation: Hotels, Inns, Guesthouses, B&B, Resorts
San Juan

Andalucia Guesthouse, 2011 McLeary St, San Juan; 787-309-3373 www.andalucia-puertorico.com

Coqui del Mar, 2218 Calle General del Valle, San Juan; 00913 787-220-4204 www.coquidelmar.com ✗ ⊗ CoquiDelMar@gmail.com

⚷ ⚲ The Dreamcatcher, 2009 Calle Espana, San Juan; 00911 787-455-8259 www.dreamcatcherpr.com ✗ info@dreamcatcherpr.com

AIDS/HIV Services, Education & Support

Coai, Inc, POB 8634, San Juan; 00910-0634 787-793-7550 fax 787-793-7530 www.coaipr.org ✗ coai09@gmail.com

Bars, Cafes, Clubs, Restaurants
San Juan

Aguaviva, 364 Calle De La Fortaleza, San Juan; 787-722-0665 violeta@oofrestaurants.com ✗ ✗

Babylon, Ponce de Leon Avenue and Calle Bolivar, San Juan; **D**

Bear Tavern, Calle Loiza 101 Esq Degetau 4, San Juan; fb.com/beartavernpr/ **D** ✗ ✗

Circo Bar, 650 Calle Condado, San Juan 787-725-9676 **DK**

Dragonfly, 364 Calle de la Fortaleza, San Juan 787-977-3886 www.dragonflysanjuan.com ✗

El Chinchorro de W, calle del carmen esq.condado 1199, San Juan; 787-532-4772 unverified ✗ ✗

M - The Club, 1501 Ave. Ponce De León, San Juan; fb.com/moreno.mclub

Mujer-es Bar, 151 Calle O'Neill, San Juan; / Fri/Sat

Oasis, 6 Ave Condado, San Juan; 787-781-5172 fb.com/oasis-condado/ ✗ ✗

Tia Maria Liquor Store, 326 Av De Diego, San Juan; 787-724-4011 fb.com/TiaMariaSanturce/

• Toxic Night Club, 613 Calle Condado, San Juan (Santurce) 787-302-2777 www.toxicnightclub.com hello@toxicnightclub.com

VIP Bar, 613 Calle Condado, San Juan (Santurce) 787-722-5509 **L** ✪

Santurce

SX, 1204 Ponce de Leon, Santurce fb.com/Sxtheclub/ ✦

Broadcast Media

★ Saliendo del Closet, POB 9501 Santurce Stn, San Juan; 00908 787-607-3939 fb.com/SaliendoDelCloset/ ✦

Men's & Sex Clubs (not primarily Health Clubs)

Xteamworks, 1752 Av Fernández Juncos, Santurce 787-800-0004 www.xteamworksstudios.com **P**

Organizations/Resources: Cultural, Dance, Performance

★ Puerto Rico Queer FilmFest, POB 9021099, San Juan; 00902 tinyurl.com/kjmptvm pr.queer.filmfest@gmail.com

Real Estate (see also Mortgages)

⚷ • **Holm, Richard, 456 Calle Saldaña, San Juan 00909 787-455-4216 puertoricopropertysales.com rholm@caribbeanconsulting.com**

Vieques Island

Accommodation Rental: Furnished / Vacation (& AirBNB)
Vieques

⚷ • (?⚷) Rainbow Realty & Vacation Rentals, HC-01 Box 6307, Vieques; 00765-9019 / 278 Calle Flamboyan Esperanza 787-741-4312 787-435-2063 www.viequesrainbowrealty.com rainbowrealtylin@gmail.com

⚷ ⚲ (?⚷) Villa Vista Linda, POB 1409, Vieques; 00765 315-706-9494 www.vistalinda-vieques.com ✗ ⊗ megan.granata@gmail.com

⚷ • Vista dos Mares, www.vistadosmares.com ✗ ⊗

Rhode Island
State/County Resources

Community Centers and/or Pride Organizations

★ ⚲ Rhode Island Pride, POB 1082, Providence, RI 02901 401-467-2130 www.prideri.com ✗

Information, Media & Publications

★ (?⚷) Options Magazine, POB 6406, Providence, RI 02940 401-217-3939 **H?** www.optionsri.org ✗

AIDS/HIV Services, Education & Support

⚷ ⚲ AIDS Care Ocean State, 18 Parkis Ave, Providence, RI 401-521-3603 www.aidscareos.org

Rhode Island: State/County Resources
AIDS/HIV Support

300
GAYELLOW PAGES #42 2020-2021

Providence Area: Rhode Island
Bars, Cafes, Clubs, Restaurants

♂ ☆ &ᴗ AIDS Project Rhode Island, POB 6688, Providence, RI 02940 401-831-5522 www.aidsprojectri.org
@ixx=

♂ ☆ AIDS Quilt Rhode Island, POB 2591, Newport, RI 02840 401-847-7637 **Z?** www.aidsquiltri.org

Counseling/Psychotherapy/Mental Health

♂ ☆ Comprehensive Community Action Program, 311 Doric Ave, Cranston, RI 401-467-9610 www.comcap.org

Legal Services

♀ Rhode Island Commission for Human Rights, 180 Westminster St 3rd Flr, Providence, RI 401-222-2661 www.richr.ri.gov

Organizations/Resources: Political/Legislative/Advocacy

♀ ☆ American Civil Liberties Union, 128 Dorrance St #220, Providence, RI 401-831-7171 www.riaclu.org

Organizations/Resources: Social, Recreation, Support

● ★ RIWA (RI Women's Association), POB 3586, Cranston, RI 02910-0586 www.riwa.net

Recovery

♂ ☆ AA Rhode Island Central Service Committee, 1005 Waterman Ave E, East Providence, RI 800-439-8860 www.RhodeIsland-AA.org

♂ ☆ Al-Anon/Alateen, 106 Rolfe St #200, Cranston, RI 401-781-0044 www.riafg.org

Sports & Outdoor

● ★ Frontrunners Rhode Island, 401-751-7643 www.frontrunnersri.com

Block Island

Accommodation: Hotels, Inns, Guesthouses, B&B, Resorts
New Shoreham

♀ ○ Old Town Inn, 508 Old Town Rd, New Shoreham 02807 401-466-5958 www.oldtowninnbi.com oldtowninnblockisland@yahoo.com

East Greenwich

Religious / Spiritual Resources

♂ ☆ Westminster Unitarian Church, 119 Kenyon Ave 02818 401-884-5933 www.westminsteruu.org info@westminsteruu.org
  » *Jamestown: see Newport*
  » *Kingston: see Wakefield*
  » *Lincoln: see Providence Area*

Narragansett

Bars, Cafes, Clubs, Restaurants

♂ ○ Crazy Burger Cafe & Juice Bar, 144 Boon St 401-783-1810 www.crazyburger.com ✖

♂ ○ Iggy's, 1157 Point Judith Rd; 401-783-5608 www.iggysri.com ✖

Newport

Accommodation: Hotels, Inns, Guesthouses, B&B, Resorts

♀ ● Architect's Inn & Inn Bliss, 2 Sunnyside Place 877-466-2547 www.architectsinn.com ✔ ⊛

♂ ● Hydrangea House Inn, 16 Bellevue Ave 401-846-4435 www.hydrangeahouse.com

♂ ● Inn on Bellevue, 30 Bellevue Ave; 401-848-6242 www.innsonbellevue.com ♣ ✔ ⊛ ⊛

Women's Centers

♀ ☆ &ᴗ Women's Resource Center, 114 Touro St; 02840 401-846-5263 **H?** www.wrcnbc.org ✔ info@wrcnbc.org

Pawtucket

Counseling/Psychotherapy/Mental Health

● ● Johnson, Ros, LICSW, 100 Lafayette St 02860-6008 401-727-4749 www.mindingtherapy.com

Religious / Spiritual Resources

♂ ☆ Park Place Church, 71 Park Place; 02860 401-726-2800 www.parkplaceucc.com office@ppucc.necoxmail.com

Providence Area

Accommodation: Hotels, Inns, Guesthouses, B&B, Resorts
Providence

♂ ● (?&) Hotel Dolce Villa, 63 De Pasquale Ave, Providence; 401-383-7031 **H?** www.dolcevillari.com ✔ ⊛ ⊛

AIDS/HIV Services, Education & Support

♂ ☆ &ᴗ Brown University AIDS program at The Miriam Hospital, The RISE Building, 14 Third St, Providence; 401-793-4787 **H?** www.brown.edu/brunap ✔

Art & Craft Galleries/Services, Supplies

♂ ● &ᴗ Get The Picture Custom Framing Gallery, 893 Smithfield Ave, Lincoln; 02865 401-725-3400 www.getthepictureframing.com

Bars, Cafes, Clubs, Restaurants
Providence

♀ Alley Cat, 19 Snow St, Providence 401-272-6369 tinyurl.com/yd9ehm4s **D**

♂ ● Brooklyn Coffee Tea House / Guest House, 209 Douglas Ave, Providence; 401-345-9099 tinyurl.com/2lwp4n ⊡▥ ✔

♂ ○ Camille's, 71 Bradford St, Providence 401-751-4812 www.camillesonthehill.com ✖
@ixx=

♂ ○ Coffee Exchange, 207 Wickenden St, Providence 401-273-1198 www.thecoffeeexchange.com ⊡

● Dark Lady, 19 Snow St, Providence 401-272-6369 tinyurl.com/bqhmo58 **D** ▥

● ● &ᴗ EGO, 73 Richmond St, Providence / check schedule 401-383-1208 www.egopvd.com **D**

Rhode Island: Providence Area
Bars, Cafes, Clubs, Restaurants

301
GAYELLOW PAGES #42 2020-2021

State/County Resources : South Carolina
AIDS/HIV Support

♂ ○ Mill's Tavern, 101 N Main St, Providence 401-272-3331 millstavernrestaurant.com ✖
@ixx=

♂ ● Mirabar, 15 Elbow St, Providence; 401-331-6761 www.mirabar.com **DK** ✗

♂ The Providence Eagle, 124 Snow St, Providence 401-421-1447 www.providenceeagle.com

♂ ● ♿ The Stable, 125 Washington St, Providence; 401-272-6950 fb.com/TheStableProvidence **V** ▦ ✗

Bookstores

♂ ○ ♿ Books on the Square, 471 Angell St, Providence; 401-331-9097 www.booksq.com

Funding: Endowment, Fundraising

♂ Imperial Court of RI at Providence, POB 6583, Providence; 02940 401-952-4778 www.icriprov.org

Men's & Sex Clubs (not primarily Health Clubs)

♂ The Mega-Plex, 257 Allens Ave, Providence 401-441-0072

Organizations/Resources: Cultural, Dance, Performance

♂ ★ Providence Gay Men's Chorus, POB 41482, Providence; 02940 www.provgmc.org

Organizations/Resources: Family and Supporters

♀ ☆ ♿ PFLAG Greater Providence, POB 41344, Providence; 02940 401-307-1802 **H?** www.pflagprovidence.org

Organizations/Resources: Student, Academic, Education

♂ ★ ♿ Brown University LGBTQ Center, Box 1915, Providence; 02912 401-863-3062 **H?** www.brown.edu/lgbtq ✗ lgbtq@brown.edu

♂ ★ ♿ Brown University Queer Alliance, 69 Brown Street, Box 1915, Providence; 401-863-3062 fb.com/BrownQueerAlliance

♂ ★ Brown University TBGALA (Alumni), Brown Alumni Association, POB 1859, Providence; 02912 fb.com/BrownTBGALA

♂ ★ ♿ CCRI Triangle Alliance, Community College of Rhode Island, 400 East Ave, Warwick; 401-455-6104 www.ccri.edu/triangle/

♂ ★ Johnson & Wales University Pride Alliance, Student Activities Center, 8 Abbott Park Place, Providence; 401-598-1195 fb.com/JWUPRIDEAlliance/

♂ ★ Rhode Island College Pride Alliance, Student Union Bldg #425, 600 Mt Pleasant Ave, Providence; 401-456-8121 tinyurl.com/yalgsns9

♂ ★ Rhode Island School Of Design Queer Student Association, RISD Office Of Student Life, 2 College St, Providence 401-709-8459 fb.com/qsa.risd/

♀ ☆ (?⚧) Sarah Doyle Center for Women and Gender, POB 1829, Providence; 02912-1829 401-863-2189 **H?** tinyurl.com/cn37cx ✗ sdwc@brown.edu

Organizations/Resources: Youth (see also Family)

♂ ★ ♿ Youth Pride, Inc., 743 Westminster St, Providence; 02903 401-421-5626 www.youthprideri.org ✗

Religious / Spiritual Resources

♂ ☆ (?♿) Providence Presbyterian Church, 500 Hope St, Providence; 02906 401-861-1136 www.provpresri.org provpresri@verizon.net

♂ ☆ ♿ St Peter's & St Andrew's Episcopal Church, 25 Pomona Ave, Providence; 02908 401-272-9649 **HS** www.stpeters-standrews.org ✗ stpanda25@verizon.net

Sports & Outdoor

♀ ☆ ♿ Providence Roller Derby, POB 2516, Providence; 02096 tinyurl.com/44oeoq

Wakefield

Organizations/Resources: Student, Academic, Education

♂ ★ University of Rhode Island Gender and Sexuality Center, 19 Upper College Rd, Kingston; 401-874-2894 www.uri.edu/glbt
>> *Warwick: see Providence Area*

Westerly

Bookstores

♂ ● ♿ Savoy Bookshop & Café, 10 Canal St; 401-213-3901 **H?** www.banksquarebooks.com ☞ ✗
@ixx=

Woonsocket

Florists (see also Gifts)

♂ ● Park Square Florist, Inc, 1300 Park Ave 02895-6546 401-766-2232 www.parksquarefloristinc.com

Organizations/Resources: Social, Recreation, Support

♂ ★ ♿ Rhode Island Prime Timers, POB 491; 02895 401-996-3010 **H?**

Wyoming

Accommodation: Hotels, Inns, Guesthouses, B&B, Resorts

♂ ○ Stagecoach House Inn, POB 828; 02898 401-539-9600 888-814-9600 www.stagecoachhouse.com stagecoachhouse@gmail.com

South Carolina
State/County Resources

Information, Media & Publications

♂ ★ Carolina Rainbow News, NC & SC carolinarainbownews.org hello@carolinarainbownews.org

AIDS/HIV Services, Education & Support

♀ ☆ Palmetto AIDS Life Support Services (PALSS), 2638 Two Notch Road Ste 108, Columbia, SC 803-779-7257 www.palss.org

♂ South Carolina HIV/AIDS Council, 1813 Laurel St, Columbia, SC 803-254-6644

South Carolina: State/County Resources
Organizations: Business

302

GAYELLOW PAGES #42 2020-2021

Greenville Area: South Carolina
Community Centers / Pride

Organizations/Resources: Business & Professional Associations, Labor Advocacy

⚥ ★ South Carolina Gay & Lesbian Business Guild, POB 7913, Columbia, SC 29202 www.scglbg.org

Organizations/Resources: Ethnic, Multicultural

⚥ ★ South Carolina Black Pride, POB 8191, Columbia, SC 29202 410-207-3822 scblackpride.weebly.com ♣

Organizations/Resources: Political/Legislative/Advocacy

⚥ ☆ &♿ Alliance for Full Acceptance, PO Box 22088, Charleston, SC 29413 843-883-0343 www.affa-sc.org ✎

♂ ☆ American Civil Liberties Union of South Carolina (ACLU), POB 20998, Charleston, SC 29413 843-720-1423 www.aclusc.org

⚥ ★ South Carolina Equality Coalition, POB 544, Columbia, SC 29202 803-256-6500 www.scequality.org

Aiken

Organizations/Resources: Family and Supporters

♀ PFLAG Aiken, POB 5951; 29804 803-341-3675 www.pflagaiken.org

Organizations/Resources: Student, Academic, Education

⚥ ★ University of South Carolina Unity Alliance, Box 39 471 University Parkway; 803-641-3774

Religious / Spiritual Resources

♂ ☆ ♿ Aiken Unitarian Universalists, PO Box 2231; 29802 803-502-0404 www.aikenuu.org

» Cayce: see Columbia

Charleston Area

Community Centers and/or Pride Organizations

⚥ ★ Charleston Pride, POB 61558, N Charleston; 29419 843-410-9924 www.charlestonpride.org

AIDS/HIV Services, Education & Support

♂ ☆ Palmetto Community Care, 3547 Meeting Street Rd, N Charleston; 843-747-2273 palmettocommunitycare.org

Bars, Cafes, Clubs, Restaurants
Charleston

♀ ● Dudley's on Ann, 42 Ann St, Charleston 843-577-6779 www.dudleysonann.com

Organizations/Resources: Social, Recreation, Support

⚥ ★ Charleston Social Club, www.charlestonsocialclub.com

Organizations/Resources: Student, Academic, Education

⚥ ★ Medical University of South Carolina Alliance for Equality, 45 Courtenay Dr SW 213, Charleston; 843-792-2146 tinyurl.com/y3gcwxcq

Organizations/Resources: Youth (see also Family)

⚥ ★ We Are Family, POB 21806, Charleston 29413 843-637-9379 www.waf.org

Real Estate (see also Mortgages)

♂ ● Smith, Charlie, CSA Real Estate Services 333 Wappoo Rd, Charleston; 29407 843-813-0352 www.csarealestate.com

Religious / Spiritual Resources

♂ ★ &♿ MCC Charleston, 7860 Dorchester Rd, N Charleston; 843-760-6114 www.mcccharleston.com

Columbia

Crisis, Anti-violence, & Helplines

♀ ☆ Sistercare, Inc., POB 1029; 29202 803-765-9428 www.sistercare.org

Community Centers and/or Pride Organizations

⚥ ★ Famously Hot South Carolina Pride, 931-D Senate St; 29201 www.scpride.org info@scpride.org

⚥ ★ The Harriet Hancock LGBT Center, 1108 Woodrow St; 803-771-7713 harriethancockcenter.org

Bars, Cafes, Clubs, Restaurants

♂ ○ &♿ Art Bar, 1211 Park St 803-929-0198 www.artbarsc.com ▥

♂ ● &♿ Capital Club, 1002 Gervais St 803-256-6464 www.capitalclubsc.com **P**

♂ ● PT's 1109, 1109 Assembly St; 803-253-8900 fb.com/Pts1109 **KP** ▥

Music Sales: Recordings etc

♂ ○ ♿ PapaJazz Record Shoppe, 2014 Greene St; 29205-1639 803-256-0095 www.papajazz.com info@papajazz.com

Organizations/Resources: Family and Supporters

♀ PFLAG Columbia, Reformation Lutheran Church, 118 Union St; 803-665-4445 www.pflagcolasc.org

Organizations/Resources: Youth (see also Family)

⚥ Youth Out Loud, c/o Harriet Hancock Center, 1108 Woodrow St; 803-445-3114 tinyurl.com/yc2cmato

Pets & Pet Services & Supplies

♂ ● Watchful Owl PetSitters, 803-606-0403 fb.com/TheWatchfulOwls WatchfulOwl@aol.com

Florence

Health Care: Physical (see also Counseling/Mental Health)

♂ Hope Health, 600 E Palmetto St; 888-841-5855 www.hopehealth.org

Greenville Area

Community Centers and/or Pride Organizations

⚥ ★ Upstate Pride SC, POB 9128, Greenville 29604 www.upstatepridesc.org

South Carolina: Greenville Area
AIDS/HIV Support

303

GAYELLOW PAGES #42 2020-2021

Vermillion : South Dakota
Organizations: Student

AIDS/HIV Services, Education & Support

♂ ☆ ♿ AID Upstate, 13 S Calhound St, Greenville; 864-250-0607 www.aidupstate.org

Legal Services

♀ ○ Chamberlain, Margaret A., Chamberlain Law Firm, LLC 600 Pettigru St, Greenville; 29601 864-250-0505 www.chamberlainlaw-firmllc.com info@chamberlainlawfirmllc.com

Organizations/Resources: Family and Supporters

♀ ☆ PFLAG, POB 7056, Spartanburg; 29304 864-381-8187 pflag-spartanburg.org

♀ ☆ ♿ PFLAG Greenville, www.pflagupstatesc.org

Organizations/Resources: Student, Academic, Education

⚥ ★ BJUnity, 4768 Broadway #911, New York, NY 864-735-7598 Bob Jones University Students & Alumni bjunity.org

⚥ ★ Furman University Pride Alliance, Office of Diversity and Inclusion, 3300 Poinsett Highway, Greenville; 864-294-2202 www.us-fpridealliance.org

Religious / Spiritual Resources

♀ ☆ Greenville Unitarian Universalist Fellowship, 1135 State Park Rd, Greenville; 29609 864-271-4883 www.greenvilleuu.org office@greenvilleuu.org

Greenwood

AIDS/HIV Services, Education & Support

♂ Upper Savannah Care Consortium, POB 3203 29648 864-229-9029 www.usccgleams.org

Myrtle Beach

AIDS/HIV Services, Education & Support

♀ ☆ ♿ Careteam Plus, Inc., 100 Professional Park Dr, Conway; 843-234-0005 **H?** services include PrEP www.careteamplus.org ⚥

Bars, Cafes, Clubs, Restaurants

⚥ ● Pulse Ultra Club, 2701 S Kings Hwy 843-315-0019 fb.com/PulseUltraClub **D**

⚥ St. George, 503 8th Ave N; 843-712-1964 fb.com/stgeorgre/

Organizations/Resources: Social, Recreation, Support

⚥ ★ Prime Timers Myrtle Beach, 704-450-0775 tinyurl.com/z24aj6a
» North Augusta: see Augusta GA/North Augusta (SC)

Rock Hill

Bars, Cafes, Clubs, Restaurants

⚥ The Hideaway, 405 E Baskins Rd 803-328-6630 fb.com/the-hideawaysc/ **DP**

Health Care: Physical (see also Counseling/Mental Health)

♀ ☆ ♿ Affinity Health Center, 455 Lakeshore Parkway; 29730 877-647-6363 803-909-6363 tinyurl.com/oagay9j

Walterboro

Accommodation: Hotels, Inns, Guesthouses, B&B, Resorts

♀ ● Hampton House B&B, 500 Hampton St; 843-542-9498 www.hamptonhousebandb.com (☆?) ⚥ (♿)

South Dakota
State/County Resources

AIDS/HIV Services, Education & Support

♀ ☆ South Dakota Department of Health HIV/AIDS Prevention, 615 E 4th St, Pierre, SD 605-773-3737 tinyurl.com/gv8bmhe

Organizations/Resources: Political/Legislative/Advocacy

♀ ☆ American Civil Liberties Union of South Dakota, POB 1170, Sioux Falls, SD 57101 605-332-2508 www.aclusd.org

⚥ ★ Equality South Dakota, 928 8th St, Brookings, SD www.eqsd.org

Rapid City

Community Centers and/or Pride Organizations

⚥ ★ Black Hills Center for Equality, POB 1558; 57709 605-348-3244 www.bhcfe.org ⚥

Accommodation: Hotels, Inns, Guesthouses, B&B, Resorts
Piedmont

⚥ ● (?♿) Camp Michael, 21683 Piedmont Meadows Rd, Piedmont; 57769 605-209-3503 ☆ ⚥ ♿ tablemannerllc@gmail.com

Counseling/Psychotherapy/Mental Health

♀ ○ ♿ Summers Temple, Irene, PhD LLC, 2218 Jackson Blvd Ste 13; 57702 605-519-8744 www.irenestphd.com ⚥ irene@irenestphd.com

Health Care: Physical (see also Counseling/Mental Health)

♀ ○ ♿ Big Sun Acupuncture, 2050 W Main St #8; 57702 605-389-1639 **H?** www.bigsunacupuncture.com ⚥

Sioux Falls

Community Centers and/or Pride Organizations

♀ ☆ ♿ Sioux Falls Pride, POB 2403 57101 605-610-9206 sioux-fallspride.org ⚥

Spearfish

Organizations/Resources: Family and Supporters

♀ PFLAG Spearfish, 605-269-1054 fb.com/PFLAGBlackHills/

Vermillion

Organizations/Resources: Student, Academic, Education

⚥ ★ Spectrum, University of South Dakota Coyote Student Center, 414 E Clark St; usd.edu/diversity

Tennessee: State/County Resources
Information, Media & Publications
304
GAYELLOW PAGES #42 2020-2021
Knoxville : Tennessee
AIDS/HIV Support

Tennessee
State/County Resources

Information, Media & Publications

⚥ • Out & About Nashville, 3951 Moss Rose Dr, Nashville; 37216 615-596-6210 Monthly publication: Nashville, Knoxville, Chattanooga, Tennessee; Atlanta, Georgia outandaboutnashville.com jjones@outandaboutnashville.com

AIDS/HIV Services, Education & Support

♂ Team Friendly Tennessee, teamfriendlytennessee.org

Organizations/Resources: Business & Professional Associations, Labor Advocacy

⚥ ★ Stonewall Bar Association of Tennessee, 615-726-5558 www.tnstonewallbar.org

Organizations/Resources: Political/Legislative/Advocacy

♂ ☆ American Civil Liberties Union of Tennessee, PO Box 120160, Nashville, TN 37212 615-320-7142 www.aclu-tn.org

♀ ☆ National Organization For Women, POB 120523, Nashville, TN 37212 615-269-7141 tinyurl.com/ycdvbl9u

⚥ Tennessee Equality Project, POB 330895, Nashville, TN 37203 615-390-5252 www.tnep.org

Reproductive Medicine & Fertility Services

♂ O Planned Parenthood of Tennessee and North Mississippi (PPTNM), 2430 Poplar Ave #100, Memphis, TN 38112 866-711-1717 tinyurl.com/y3qaqgf5 info@pptnm.org

Butler

Accommodation: Hotels, Inns, Guesthouses, B&B, Resorts

♀ O Iron Mountain Inn, POB 30; 37640-7235 / 286 Moreland Dr 423-768-2446 www.ironmountaininn.com ✗ ⊛ⓢ ironmountaininn@gmail.com

Accommodation Rental: Furnished / Vacation (& AirBNB)

♂ O 👀 House on Watauga Lake, POB 30 37640 423-768-2446 www.houseonwataugalake.com ❖ ✗ ⊛ⓢ

Chattanooga Area

Community Centers and/or Pride Organizations

⚥ ★ Tennessee Valley PRIDE, Inc., POB 8116, Chattanooga; 37414 423-402-0408 www.tennesseevalleypride.com

AIDS/HIV Services, Education & Support

♂ ☆ 👀 Cempa Community Care, 1000 E 3rd St #300, Chattanooga; 37403 423-265-2273 **H?** www.cempa.org ✗

Bars, Cafes, Clubs, Restaurants
Chattanooga

⚥ • ♿ Alan Gold's, 1100 McCallie Ave, Chattanooga; 423-629-8080 www.alangolds.com **D**

Organizations/Resources: Family and Supporters

♀ ☆ 👀 PFLAG Chattanooga, POB 17252, Chattanooga; 37415 423-802-0449 tinyurl.com/h6mcfq5

Organizations/Resources: Social, Recreation, Support

⚥ ★ Lookout Bears, 99 Tuxedo Circle, Chattanooga tinyurl.com/j7kc38x

Organizations/Resources: Student, Academic, Education

⚥ ★ University of Tennessee Spectrum, 615 McCallie Ave, Chattanooga; fb.com/UTCSpectrum

Religious / Spiritual Resources

♀ ☆ Pilgrim Church, 400 Glenwood Dr, Chattanooga 37404 423-698-5682 www.pilgrim-church.com mail@pilgrim-church.com

⚥ ★ ♿ The Rock Metropolitan Community Church, 1601 Foust St, Chattanooga; 423-629-2737 **H?** fb.com/TheRockMCC/ ✗

Columbia

AIDS/HIV Services, Education & Support

♂ Columbia Cares, 1202 S James Campbell Blvd 931-381-0114 www.columbiacares.org

Gatlinburg

Accommodation Rental: Furnished / Vacation (& AirBNB)
Seymour

♂ O Moonshine Cabin, Pigeon Forge 865-446-0182 www.moonshinecabin.com ken@moonshinecabin.com

⚥ • Stonecreek Cabins, 865-429-0400 www.stonecreekcabins.com (❖?) ⊛ stonecreekcabins@gmail.com

Greeneville

Accommodation: Hotels, Inns, Guesthouses, B&B, Resorts

⚥ • Timberfell Lodge, 1416 Baileyton Main St PMB #110; 800-437-0118 www.timberfell.com

Johnson City/Kingsport/Bristol

Bars, Cafes, Clubs, Restaurants
Johnson City

⚥ • (👀) New Beginnings Restaurant & Nightclub, 2910 N Bristol Highway, Johnson City; 423-282-4446 fb.com/newbsjc **D** ♈ ✖🎰

Organizations/Resources: Family and Supporters

♂ ☆ PFLAG Tri-Cities, POB 1782, Johnson City 37605 / Johnson City, Kingsport, Bristol 423-218-9790 www.pflagtricities.org

Knoxville

Community Centers and/or Pride Organizations

⚥ ★ Knox Pride, POB 30315; 37930 865-300-5274 knoxpride.com

AIDS/HIV Services, Education & Support

♂ Positively Living, 1501 E 5th Ave; 865-525-1540 positively-living.org

Tennessee: Knoxville
AIDS/HIV Support

305
GAYELLOW PAGES #42 2020-2021

Memphis : Tennessee
Organizations: Youth

♂ ☆ && Samaritan Ministry, 6300 Deane Hill Dr; 37919-4901 865-450-1000 x827 HIV & Hepatitis C testing, referral, support www.samaritancentral.org ✎ info@samaritancentral.org

Bars, Cafes, Clubs, Restaurants

♥ ● Club XYZ, 1215 N Central St; 865-637-4999 fax 865-523-3336 fb.com/Club-XYZ-499364900273/ **DV** ⊻ ✕▦ clubxyz@comcast.net

♥ The Edge Knox, 7211 Kingston Pike 865-602-2094 edgeknox.webs.com **DK** ✕▦

Counseling/Psychotherapy/Mental Health

♂ ● (?&) Mott, Nancy, MS, Ed.S, 3117 E 5th Ave; 37914-4427 865-637-8801 Licensed in Psychology fb.com/nancymottcounseling ✎ nancymott16@gmail.com

Organizations/Resources: Social, Recreation, Support

♂ ★ Gay Men's Discussion Group, Tennessee Valley Unitarian Church, 2931 Kingston Pike; 37919 865-567-6953 www.gaygroup-knoxville.org rfsawyer@bellsouth.net

♂ ★ Knoxville Monday Gay Men's Group, meets at Unitarian Church, 2931 Kingston Pike 865-567-6953 www.gaygroup-knoxville.org

♥ ★ && Lesbian Social Group (LSG), www.lesbiansocial-group.com

Organizations/Resources: Transgender/Gender Non-Conforming/Diverse

T ☆ && Knox Boyz of East Tennessee FTM Support Group, POB 27746; 37927 865-226-9411 tinyurl.com/gwabyyw

Religious / Spiritual Resources

♂ ★ Community of Saint Ninian, www.saintninianswell.org

♂ ★ (?&) Integrity East Tennessee, c/o St Luke's Episcopal Church, 600 S Chestnut St; 37914-5829 865-637-8801 Ask for Nancy. fb.com/integrityeasttn

♂ ★ && MCC Knoxville, 7820 Redeemer Lane; 865-531-2539 **H?** www.mccknoxville.org

Sports & Outdoor

♂ K-Town Softball league, tinyurl.com/y56otdz6

Lancaster

Accommodation Rental: Furnished / Vacation (& AirBNB)

♂ ● Bear Lodge at Cove Hollow Bay, 830 Harbor Dr 38569 303-884-3534 fb.com/bearlodgecovehollow/ admin@bearlodgetn.com

Liberty

Organizations/Resources: Social, Recreation, Support

♂ Short Mountain Sanctuary, 247 Sanctuary Lane 615-563-4397 www.radfae.org/sms.htm

Memphis

Crisis, Anti-violence, & Helplines

♂ ☆ Memphis Crisis Center, 901-274-7477 www.memphiscrisis-center.org

Community Centers and/or Pride Organizations

♂ ★ && Mid-South Pride, 111 S Highland St Ste 322; 901-210-9092 www.midsouthpride.org

♂ ★ && OUTMemphis, 892 S Cooper St 38104-5603 901-278-6422 www.outmemphis.org ✎ info@outmemphis.org

AIDS/HIV Services, Education & Support

♂ ☆ && Friends For Life HIV Resources, 43 N Cleveland; 901-272-0855 www.fflmemphis.org ✪

Bars, Cafes, Clubs, Restaurants

♂ ○ Cafe Society, 212 N Evergreen St; 901-722-2177 www.cafeso-cietymemphis.com ✕

♂ ○ P&H Cafe, 1532 Madison Ave; 901-726-0906 www.pandhcafe.com ▭▦

♂ ● & Pumping Station, 1382 Poplar Ave 901-272-7600 tinyurl.com/2ofoxa **L**

♂ ○ RP Tracks, 3547 Walker Ave; 901-327-1471 rptracks.com ✕ rptracks@gmail.com

Entertainment-Related Services (see also Performance)

♂ ★ Emerald Theatre Company, 2085 Monroe Ave 38104 www.etcmemphistheater.com hharmon299@aol.com

Health Care: Physical (see also Counseling/Mental Health)

♂ ★ && CHOICES: Memphis Center for Reproductive Health, 1726 Poplar Ave; 901-274-3550 **H?** tinyurl.com/y2cfk4mq ✎

Leather Resources & Groups

♂ ★ Tennessee Leather Tribe, 1568 Rolling Hills Dr; 901-357-1921 fb.com/TNLeatherTribe

Legal Services

♂ ○ & Mackenzie, Susan, 2157 Madison Ave Ste 104; 901-272-2729 www.susanmackenzielaw.com

♂ ○ && Wurzburg, Jocelyn D., JD, 5159 Wheelis Ste 101; 38117-4519 901-684-1332 Mediation services. www.wurzburgmedia-tion.com ✎ wurzburg@mediate.com

Organizations/Resources: Cultural, Dance, Performance

♂ ★ Outflix LGBT Film Festival, 892 S Cooper St 901-278-6422 www.outflixfestival.org

Organizations/Resources: Senior Resources

♂ ★ && Seniors OUT for Coffee, 892 S Cooper St; 38104-5603 / 2nd Sun check schedule 901-278-6422 tinyurl.com/ycaouh3v ✎ seniors@outmemphis.org

Organizations/Resources: Student, Academic, Education

♂ ★ Rhodes College LGBTQ Resources, 2000 N Parkway; tinyurl.com/y5zo85va

♂ ★ && University of Memphis Stonewall Tigers, UCC 241; 901-678-8679 tinyurl.com/y6lng5m8

Organizations/Resources: Youth (see also Family)

♂ ★ & Memphis Area Gay Youth, 1000 S Cooper St; 901-335-6249 fb.com/memphisareagayyouth

Tennessee: Memphis
Organizations: Youth

306

GAYELLOW PAGES #42 2020-2021

Nashville Area: Tennessee
Legal

♀ Youth Services at OUTMemphis, 892 S Cooper St; 901-278-6422 outmemphis.org

Real Estate (see also Mortgages)

♂ ○ Solomon, Steve, Sowell & Company, 54 S Cooper 38104-4211 901-278-4380 901-454-1931

Recovery

♂ ☆ AA Intergroup, 3540 Summer Ave #104 901-454-1414 www.memphis-aa.org

Religious / Spiritual Resources

♂ ★ (♿) Holy Trinity UCC, 685 S Highland St; 901-320-9376 www.holytrinitymemphis.org

Sports & Outdoor

♂ ★ Bluff City Sports Association, tinyurl.com/y9maupwv

♂ ★ Brothers & Sisters Bowling League, Winchester Lanes, 3703 S Mendenhall Rd fb.com/groups/81046699566/

♂ St Patrick's Invitational Tournament, www.spitmemphis.com

Murfreesboro

Organizations/Resources: Student, Academic, Education

♂ ★ ♿ MTSU Lambda Association, MTSU Box X-174, 1301 E Main St; 615-898-5489 MTSU Gay Straight Alliance fb.com/mtlambda ⚧

Nashville Area

Community Centers and/or Pride Organizations

♂ ★ Nashville Pride, POB 330931, Nashville 37203 615-844-4159 www.nashvillepride.org

Information, Media & Publications

♂ ● Out & About Nashville, 3951 Moss Rose Dr, Nashville; 37216 615-596-6210 Monthly publication: Nashville, Knoxville, Chattanooga, Tennessee; Atlanta, Georgia outandaboutnashville.com jjones@outandaboutnashville.com

Accommodation: Hotels, Inns, Guesthouses, B&B, Resorts
Hampshire

♂ ● Whispering Oaks Retreat, 926 Walker Rd, Portland; 931-446-1171 mywhisperingoaks.org **N**

AIDS/HIV Services, Education & Support

♂ ☆ Metropolitan Interdenominational Church First Response Center, LLC, 1219 9th Ave N, Nashville; 37208 615-321-9791 metropolitanfrc.com ♣

♂ ☆ Nashville Cares, 633 Thompson Lane, Nashville 615-259-4866 www.nashvillecares.org ♣

♂ ☆ Street Works, 1215 9th Ave Ste 202, Nashville 615-259-7676 www.street-works.org

♂ ☆ Vanderbilt AIDS Clinical Trials Center, 1211 Medical Center Dr, Nashville; 615-322-5000 tinyurl.com/y2ml3aml

Art & Photography (see also Graphic Design)

♂ ● Photo Captures by Jeffery, 615-579-4471 photocapturesbyjeffery.com JefferyJohnson@photocapturesbyjeffery.com

Bars, Cafes, Clubs, Restaurants
Nashville

♂ ○ The Bluebird Cafe, 4104 Hillsboro Pike, Nashville; 615-383-1461 bluebirdcafe.com ▦

♂ ○ (♿) Cafe Coco, 210 Louise Ave, Nashville; 615-321-2626 cafecoco.com ▾ ✕ ▦

● Canvas Lounge, 1707 Church St, Nashville 615-320-8656 fb.com/canvasnashville/ **D** ▦

♂ ● ♿ The Lipstick Lounge, 1400 Woodland St, Nashville; 615-226-6343 www.thelipsticklounge.com **DK** ▾ ✕ ▦ ⚧

● ● ♿ Pecker's Bar & Grill, 237 Hermitage Ave, Nashville; 615-678-1042 Art shows www.peckersnashville.com **K** ✕ ▾ ▦ ⚧

♂ ○ The Pharmacy Burger Parlor & Beer Garden, 731 Mcferrin Ave, Nashville; 615-712-9517 thepharmacynashville.com ▾ ✕

● Play Dance Bar, 1519 Church St, Nashville 615-322-9627 www.playdancebar.com **D**

● ● ♿ Suzy Wong's House of Yum, 1515 Church St, Nashville; 615-329-2913 www.suzywongsnashville.com **D** ✕ ▦ ⚧

● Trax, 1501 2nd Ave S (Ensley Blvd), Nashville 615-742-8856 trax-gay-bar.business.site/

● ● ♿ Tribe, 1517 Church St, Nashville; 615-329-2912 www.tribenashville.com **V** ▦

♂ ○ ♿ The Wild Cow Vegetarian Restaurant, 1100 Fatherland St Ste 104, Nashville; 615-262-2717 thewildcow.com ✕ ⚧

Bookstores

♂ ○ ♿ Parnassus Books, 3900 Hillsboro Pike Ste 14, Nashville; 615-953-2243 www.parnassusbooks.net

Counseling/Psychotherapy/Mental Health

♂ ○ ♿ Ingram, Jeannie, LPC, 4525 Harding Pike Ste 200, Nashville; 37205 404-444-1058 www.jeannieingram.com Ingram.jeannie@gmail.com

♂ ○ ♿ Sanders, Barbara, LCSW, 1710 Stokes Lane, Nashville; 37215 615-414-2553 dignitytherapynashville.com Barbara SandersLCSW@gmail.com

Funding: Endowment, Fundraising

♀ Music City Sisters, 626 Shelby Ave, Nashville; www.musiccitysisters.org

Health Care: Physical (see also Counseling/Mental Health)

♂ ● (♫) May, Christopher, DC, 2933 Berry Hill Dr, Nashville; 37204 615-220-0777 www.doctormay.net c@doctormay.net

♀ Vanderbilt Health LGBTQ Programs, 7069-B H ighway 70 S, Nashville; 615-538-3668 www.vumc.org/lgbtq/

Leather Resources & Groups

♂ ★ ♿ Conductors LL Club, POB 40261, Nashville; 37204 www.conductors.net

Legal Services

♂ ● Rubenfeld, Abby R, Rubenfeld Law Office, PC 202 S 11th St, Nashville; 615-386-9077 www.rubenfeldlaw.com

Tennessee: Nashville Area
Organizations: Business

307
GAYELLOW PAGES #42 2020-2021

State/County Resources : Texas
Leather

Organizations/Resources: Business & Professional Associations, Labor Advocacy

⚥ Nashville LGBT Chamber of Commerce, 41 Peabody St, Nashville; 615-507-5185 www.nashvillelgbtchamber.org

Organizations/Resources: Cultural, Dance, Performance

⚥ ★ Nashville in Harmony, POB 159156, Nashville; 37215 www.nashvilleinharmony.org

Organizations/Resources: Ethnic, Multicultural

⚥ ★ ♿ Brothers United, Nashville Cares, POB 68335, Nashville; 37206 615-921-0340 fb.com/BrothersUnitedTN ✤

⚥ ★ Nashville Black Pride, POB 68335, Nashville; 37206 615-974-2832 www.nashvilleblackpride.org ✤

Organizations/Resources: Family and Supporters

♀ ☆ ♿ PFLAG Franklin, POB 832, Franklin; 37065 615-591-5324 **H?** fb.com/PFLAGFranklinTN

♀ ☆ ♿ PFLAG Nashville, POB 331562, Nashville; 37203-1562 615-208-4528 www.pflagnashville.org info@pflagnashville.org

Organizations/Resources: Social, Recreation, Support

⚥ Lambda Car Club - Cumberland Region, POB 330397, Nashville; 37203 www.lccumberland.com

♂ Nashfae, the Nashville Radical Faerie Circle, tinyurl.com/mxpum4d

Organizations/Resources: Student, Academic, Education

⚥ ★ Vanderbilt University School of Law OUTlaw, 131 21st Ave S, Nashville; 37203 615-322-2615 tinyurl.com/gl9kx6d vls.outlaw@vanderbilt.edu

Organizations/Resources: Transgender/Gender Non-Conforming/Diverse

T ★ ♿ Tennessee Vals, POB 331006, Nashville; 37203 615-664-6883 **H?** www.tvals.org

Organizations/Resources: Youth (see also Family)

♂ Oasis Center, 1704 Charlotte Ave #200, Nashville; 615-327-4455 www.oasiscenter.org

⚥ ☆ ♿ Young Brothers United, Nashville Cares, 442 Metroplex Dr Bldg D STE 100, Nashville; 615-974-2832 tinyurl.com/ya8nmldu ✤

Real Estate (see also Mortgages)

♀ ○ Sheila D Barnard, Realtor, 3 Yrs FAV GLBTQ Realtor 615-424-6924 tinyurl.com/yxadrjyv Barnard@realtracs.com

Recovery

♀ ☆ Al-Anon/Alateen Al-Anon Family Servs of Middle Tennesee, 176 Thompson Lane Ste G-3, Nashville; 615-333-6066 www.middletnalanon.org

Religious / Spiritual Resources

♀ ☆ Brookmeade Congregational Church UCC, 700 Bresslyn Rd, Nashville; 37205 615-352-4702 www.brookmeadeucc.org brookmeade@comcast.net

♀ ☆ Church of the Living Water, 731 S Dickerson Pike, Goodlettsville; 37072 615-948-2679 tinyurl.com/jrnjvb5 revtonyand ronnie@comcast.net

♀ ☆ Edgehill UMC, POB 128258, Nashville 37212-8258 615-254-7628 www.edgehill.org

♀ ☆ ♿ Glendale Baptist Church, 1021 Glendale Ln, Nashville; 37204-4110 615-269-0926 **HD** www.glendalebaptist.org

♀ ☆ ♿ Metropolitan Interdenominational Church, POB 280779, Nashville; 37228 / 2128 11th Ave N; 37208 615-726-3876 www.micwhosoever.org mic4cynthia@aol.com

⚥ ★ More Light Presbyterians in Middle Tennessee, POB 158478, Nashville; 37215 615-403-2587 tinyurl.com/jnygbno

⚥ ★ Stonewall Mission Church, 612 Shelby Ave, Nashville; 37206 615-242-2534 tinyurl.com/bpttb4j rev.james.hawk@gmail.com

Sports & Outdoor

⚥ ★ Nashville Grizzlies Rugby Football Club, POB 330568, Nashville; 37203 www.grizzliesrugby.org

Oak Ridge

Organizations/Resources: Family and Supporters

♀ PFLAG Oak Ridge, 130 Windham Rd; 865-556-3099 tinyurl.com/y2gzkvyd

» Pigeon Forge: see Gatlinburg

Pleasant Hill

Organizations/Resources: Family and Supporters

♀ ☆ PFLAG Crossville/Cumberland County, POB 272 38578-0272 931-277-5853 tinyurl.com/y62o7r5u

Texas
State/County Resources

Crisis, Anti-violence, & Helplines

♀ ☆ ♿ Texas Advocacy Project, 800-374-4673 **H?** www.texasadvocacyproject.org info@texasadvocacyproject.org

Information, Media & Publications

⚥ ● This Week in Texas, SLP Enterprises, LLC, 6537 Wanda Ln, Houston, TX 77074-6821 713-779-4366 thisweekintexas.com

Archives/Libraries/Museums/History Projects

⚥ ★ ♿ Gulf Coast Archive & Museum of GLBT History, Inc., 822 W 14th St, Houston, TX 77008 832-722-5785 www.gcam.org ✗ info@gcam.org

Leather Resources & Groups

♀ ☆ South Plains Leatherfest, SPL Enterprises, 22136 Westheimer Parkway #202, Katy, TX 713-299-9696 tinyurl.com/m3kuqe3

⚥ ★ (♿) Texas Conference of Clubs, Inc, 254-605-0801 tinyurl.com/nkse4p8

Texas: State/County Resources
Legal
308
GAYELLOW PAGES #42 2020-2021
Austin Area: Texas
Bars, Cafes, Clubs, Restaurants

Legal Services

♂ ★ ♿ Lambda Legal Defense & Education Fund (LLDEF), Inc: South Central Regional Office, 3500 Oak Lawn Ave Ste 500, Dallas, TX 214-219-8585 www.lambdalegal.org @ixx=

♀ Lone Star Legal Aid, POB 398, Houston, TX 77001 800-733-8394 www.lonestarlegal.org

Organizations/Resources: Ethnic, Multicultural

♂ ★ ♿ ALLGO, 701 Tillery St Box 4, Austin, TX 512-472-2001 www.allgo.org ❖

♂ ★ Texas Two Spirit Society, POB 141361, Dallas, TX 75214 www.texastwospirits.org

Organizations/Resources: Political/Legislative/Advocacy

♀ ☆ ♿♿ American Civil Liberties Union of Texas, POB 8306, Houston, TX 77288 713-942-8146 www.aclutx.org ✔

♂ ★ (♿) Equality Texas, POB 2340, Austin, TX 78768 512-474-5475 www.equalitytexas.org ✔

♀ ★ Log Cabin Republicans of Texas, POB 66162, Houston, TX 77006 832-782-7394 www.logcabintexas.us

Organizations/Resources: Transgender/Gender Non-Conforming/Diverse

T ☆ Transgender Education Network of Texas (TENT), POB 41363, Austin, TX 78704 877-532-6789 www.transtexas.org

Sports & Outdoor

♂ ★ Texas Gay Rodeo Association, 214-346-2107 www.tgra.org

Abilene

Organizations/Resources: Family and Supporters

♀ ☆ ♿ PFLAG of the Big Country, POB 6981; 79608 325-232-4726 www.pflagbc.weebly.com

Religious / Spiritual Resources

♂ ★ (♿) Exodus MCC, POB 7547 79608 / 1933 S 27th 325-795-8384 **H?** www.exodusmcc.org @ixx=

Amarillo

Community Centers and/or Pride Organizations

♂ ★ Panhandle Pride, POB 19984; 79114 806-414-5704 panhandle-pride.org

AIDS/HIV Services, Education & Support

♀ ☆ ♿♿ Panhandle AIDS Support Organization, 1501 SW 10th Ave; 79101 806-372-1050 www.panhandleaso.org ✔

Bars, Cafes, Clubs, Restaurants

♂ ○ The 212 Club, 212 SW 6th St; 79101 806-372-7997 tinyurl.com/gusweqp **D** ▦

♀ ○ Furrbie's, 210 W 6th Ave; 806-220-0841 tinyurl.com/3d9aqnh ✖

♂ ○ R&R Bar, 701 S Georgia St; 806-341-5141 fb.com/RRBarAmarilloTX/ ▦

Organizations/Resources: Transgender/Gender Non-Conforming/Diverse

T ☆ Transgender Support Group of Amarillo, 1503 SW 10th; 79101 806-373-9966 **H?** bmclpc@gmail.com

Religious / Spiritual Resources

♂ ★ ♿♿ MCC Amarillo, 2123 S Polk St 79109-2651 806-418-6856 **H?** www.mccamarillo.com mccamarillo2@gmail.com
>> *Arlington: see Dallas/Fort Worth Area*

Austin Area

Crisis, Anti-violence, & Helplines

♀ ☆ ♿♿ The SAFE Alliance, POB 19454, Austin; 78760 512-267-7233 **H** www.safeaustin.org ✔

Community Centers and/or Pride Organizations

♂ ★ Austin Pride, POB 162924, Austin; 78716 512-468-8113 www.austinpride.org

♂ ★ ♿♿ The Q Austin, 2906 Medical Arts St, Austin; 512-420-8557 **H?** www.theqaustin.org ✔

Information, Media & Publications

♂ Gay in Austin, 210-501-5435 www.gayinaustintexas.com

♂ ● therepubliq, POB 11619, Austin; 78711 512-200-3040 www.therepubliq.com

Accommodation: Hotels, Inns, Guesthouses, B&B, Resorts
Austin

♂ ● Kimber Modern, 110 The Circle, Austin; 78704 512-985-9990 www.kimbermodern.com ✔ ⊛ ⊛ info@kimbermodern.com

♂ ● Park Lane Guest House, 221 Park Lane, Austin 512-447-7460 parklaneguesthouse.com (❖?) ✔ ⊛ ⊛

Kingsbury

♂ ● River Barn Suites, Fentress Area 512-488-2175 www.riverbarnsuites.com ⊛ ⊛

AIDS/HIV Services, Education & Support

♀ ☆ ♿♿ AIDS Services of Austin, 7215 Cameron Rd, Austin; 512-458-2437 **H?** www.asaustin.org

♀ ☆ ♿♿ The ASHwell Austin Sexual Health & Wellness, 8101 Cameron Rd Ste 105, Austin; 512-467-0088 **H?** ashwellatx.org

♀ ☆ Project Transitions, 7101-B Woodrow Ln, Austin 512-454-8646 www.projecttransitions.org

Bars, Cafes, Clubs, Restaurants
Austin

♂ ○ ♿♿ Bennu Coffee, 2001 E MLK Blvd, Austin; 512-478-4700 www.bennucoffee.com ⊓ ✔

♂ ○ ♿♿ Bouldin Creek Cafe, 1900 S 1st St, Austin; 512-416-1601 www.bouldincreek.com ⊓ info@bouldincreek.com

♂ ● Bout Time II / BT2, 6607 N Interstate 35, Austin; 512-419-9192 fb.com/bt2.atx **D** ✔

♂ ● Cheer Up Charlie's, 900 Red River St, Austin; 512-431-2133 www.cheerupcharlies.com **D** ♈ ✖ ▦ ✔

Texas: Austin Area
Bars, Cafes, Clubs, Restaurants

309
GAYELLOW PAGES #42 2020-2021

Austin Area : Texas
Organizations: Business

♀ ○ Cherrywood Coffeehouse, 1400 E 38th 1/2 St, Austin; 512-538-1991 cherrywoodcoffeehouse.com ☞

♂ ○ Clay Pit, 1601 Guadalupe, Austin; 512-322-5131 claypit.com ☿ ✗

♂ ○ (?⅄) Elysium, 705 Red River St, Austin; 512-478-2979 Alternative/Retro/Goth/Dance, drag and queer events. www.elysiumonline.net **D** ⏚ ✁ elysiumaustin@aol.com

♀ ○ Genuine Joe Coffeehouse, 2001 W Anderson Lane, Austin; 512-220-1576 www.genuinejoecoffee.com ☞ ⏚

⚥ ● ♿ Highland Lounge, 404 Colorado St, Austin; 512-649-1212 www.highlandlounge.com **DK** ⏚

♂ ○ ♿ House Wine, 408 Josephine St, Austin; 512-322-5210 www.housewineaustin.com ⏚ ✁ @ixx=

⚥ ● The Iron Bear, 121 W 8th St, Austin 512-482-8993 www.theironbear.com

♂ ○ Mother's Cafe & Garden, 4215 Duval St, Austin 512-451-3994 motherscafeaustin.com ✗

⚥ ● OilCan Harry's, 211 W 4th, Austin 512-320-8823 www.oilcanharrys.com **D** ⏚

♂ ○ ♿ Péché, 208 W 4th St, Austin 512-494-4011 www.pecheaustin.com ✗ ✁

⚥ ● Rain on 4th, 217B W 4th St, Austin 512-494-1150 www.rainon4th.com **DK** ⏚

⚥ Sellers Underground, 213 W 4th St, Austin 512-215-9491 www.sellersunderground.com

Bookstores

♂ ○ ♿ BookPeople, 603 N Lamar Blvd, Austin; 512-472-5050 www.bookpeople.com ✁

♂ ● ♿ **BookWoman, 5501 N Lamar Blvd # A-105, Austin; 78751 512-472-2785 Support your feminist bookstore, she supports you! www.ebookwoman.com** ✁ **bookwomanaustin@gmail.com**

♂ ○ MonkeyWrench Books, 110 E North Loop, Austin 512-407-6925 www.monkeywrenchbooks.org

♂ ○ Red Salmon Arts (casa de Resistencia Books), 4926 E Cesar Chavez St Unit C1, Austin; / check schedule 512-389-9881 www.resistenciabooks.com ✪

Broadcast Media

⚥ OutCast, KOOP 91.7 FM POB 2116, Austin 78768 512 472-KOOP www.OutCastAustin.com

Clothes (see also Erotica, Leather)

♂ ○ (?⅄) Charm School Vintage, 1111 E. 11th St Ste 150, Austin; 78702 512-524-0166 www.charmschoolvintage.com ✁ charmschoolvintage@gmail.com

Counseling/Psychotherapy/Mental Health

♂ ● ♿ Leighton, Derek, LMFT, LPC, CGP, Raintree Office Park, 3534 Bee Caves Rd Ste 114, Austin; 78746 512-658-2960 www.LeightonTherapy.com Derek@LeightonTherapy.com

♀ ☆ ♿ Waterloo Counseling Center, 314 Highland Mall Blvd Ste 301, Austin; 512-444-9922 **H?** www.waterloocounseling.org

Erotica / Adult Stores / Safe Sex Supplies

♂ ● ♿ Dreamers - 3401, 3401 N I-35, Austin; 512-469-0539 **H?** dreamerstexas.com

♂ ○ ♿ Dreamers North Austin, 11218 N Lamar Blvd, Austin; 512-837-5534 **H?** dreamerstexas.com

⚥ ● ♿ Forbidden Fruit, 108 E North Loop Blvd, Austin; 78751-1227 512-453-8090 **HS** www.forbiddenfruit.com **L** info@forbiddenfruit.com

Funding: Endowment, Fundraising

♂ ☆ Austin Babtist Women, c/o Garry Holley, 2501 Crownspoint Dr, Austin; 78748 512-484-3398 fb.com/babtistwomen/ spiderpower2@yahoo.com

♂ ☆ Hill Country Ride for AIDS, POB 49097, Austin; 78765 512-371-7433 www.hillcountryride.org

♂ ★ United Court of Austin Inc., POB 2567, Austin; 78768 www.unitedcourtofaustin.org

Gardening/Landscaping Services & Supplies

♂ ● Red Sun Landscape Design, POB 2575, Austin 78630-2575 512-844-6493 redsunlandscapedesign.com michelle.austen07@gmail.com

Health Care: Physical (see also Counseling/Mental Health)

♂ ☆ ♿ David Powell Health Center, 4614 N IH 35, Austin; 512-978-9100 tinyurl.com/n448qky ✁

Legal Services

♂ ○ ♿ Andresen, Christine Henry, 4103 Manchaca Rd 512-394-4230 www.chalaw.com/lgbt ✁ @ixx=

♂ ● ♿ The Shefman Law Group, 4131 Spicewood Springs Rd Ste A-6, Austin; 78759 512-975-1005 Personal Injury www.shefmanlawgroup.com

Organizations/Resources: Business & Professional Associations, Labor Advocacy

⚥ Austin LGBT Bar Association, tinyurl.com/y7b3vjaq

Texas: Austin Area
Organizations: Business
310
GAYELLOW PAGES #42 2020-2021
Austin Area : Texas
Travel

♀ ★ Austin LGBT Chamber of Commerce, 600 Congress Ave Flr 14, Austin; 78701 512-761-5428 www.austinlgbtchamber.com info@austinlgbtchamber.com

Organizations/Resources: Cultural, Dance, Performance

♀ ★ All Genders, Lifestyles and Identities Film Festival, 1107 S 8th St, Austin; 512-275-6227 www.agliff.org

♂ ★ && Austin Gay Men's Chorus, POB 50082, Austin; 78763-0082 512-477-7464 austingaymenschorus.org contactus@austin gaymenschorus.org

♀ ★ Lone Star Lambdas Square Dance Club, 1430 Yaupon Valley Rd, Austin; www.lonestarlambdas.org

Organizations/Resources: Family and Supporters

♂ ☆ PFLAG Austin, POB 49881, Austin; 78765 512-302-3524 www.pflagaustin.org
@ixx=

Organizations/Resources: Naturist/Nudist

♂ ★ Austin Gay Nudists, mail to AGN, POB 256, Dripping Springs; 78620 www.agntx.org membership@agntx.org

Organizations/Resources: Political/Legislative/Advocacy

♂ ☆ Atticus Circle, 2901 Via Fortuna Ste 450, Austin; 512-275-7880 www.atticuscircle.org

♀ ★ Human Rights Campaign - Austin, 800-777-4723 tinyurl.com/kedbasw

♀ ★ && Stonewall Democrats of Austin, POB 40898, Austin; 78704 512-771-3538 www.stonewallaustin.org

Organizations/Resources: Social, Recreation, Support

♀ Austin Lesbian CoffeehouseAustin, tinyurl.com/btj858v

♂ ★ && Austin Prime Timers, POB 142303, Austin; 78714 www.austinptww.org

♀ ★ Classic Chassis Car Club Austin, www.cccc-austin.org

♂ ★ Heart of Texas Bears, POB 200673, Austin 78720 www.hear-toftexasbears.org

Organizations/Resources: Student, Academic, Education

♀ ★ Gender & Sexuality Center, Student Activity Center, University of Texas at Austin, 2201 Speedway, Austin; 512-232-1907 www.utgsc.org

♀ ★ PRIDE at St Edward's University, 3001 S Congress Ave CM 38, Austin; 414-807-1571 tinyurl.com/7upwf9m

♀ ★ Southwestern University Pirates for Pride, 1001 E University, Georgetown; 512-863-6511

♀ ★ University of Texas Law School OUTlaw, 727 E Dean Keeton St, Austin; sites.utexas.edu/outlaw ✐

Organizations/Resources: Youth (see also Family)

♂ ★ && Out Youth, 909 E 49 1/2 St, Austin; 78751-2714 512-419-1233 **H?** Drop-in center for LGBTQ youth ages 12-23 www.outy-outh.org ✐ hello@outyouth.org

Pets & Pet Services & Supplies

♂ ○ DogBoy's Dog Ranch, 2615 Crystal Bend Dr, Pflugerville; 78660 512-251-7600 www.dogboys.com

Real Estate (see also Mortgages)

♀ ● Hunter, Janie, Broker/Owner, Austin Homes Realty, 512-507-8252 www.austinhomesrealty.com janie@austinhomesrealty.com

♂ ● Jacobs, Doug, Broker, 512-462-1866 www.jacobsand-mikeska.com ✐ AusTXrltrs@aol.com

♂ ● && Midtown Independence Title, 3009 N Lamar Blvd, Austin; 78705 512-459-1110 **H** www.midtowntitle.com ✐ douglas.plum mer@ilawpc.com

Recovery

♀ Austin Galano Club, 6809 Guadalupe St, Austin; www.austin-galano.org

♂ ☆ Hill Country Intergroup AA, 1825 Fortview Rd Ste 102, Austin; 512-444-0071 www.austinaa.org

Religious / Spiritual Resources

♂ ☆ (♿) Central Presbyterian Church, 200 E 8th St, Austin; 78701 512-472-2445 **HD** www.cpcaustin.org ✐

♂ ☆ && Live Oak Unitarian Universalist Church, 3315 El Salido Parkway, Cedar Park; 78613 512-219-9008 **HD** Smoke-free property www.liveoakuu.org ❤ administrator@liveoakuu.org

♂ ☆ && Living Word Lutheran Church, PO Box 412, Buda; 78610 / 2315 FM 967, Buda 512-295-9996 www.livingwordbuda.org

♂ ★ && MCC Austin at Freedom Oaks, 8601 S 1st St, Austin; 512-291-8601 www.mccaustin.com

♂ ☆ && Saint Andrew's Presbyterian Church, 14311 Wells Port Dr, Austin; 78728 512-251-0698 **H** www.staopen.org ✐ admin@ staopen.org

♂ ☆ && Trinity Church of Austin, 4001 Speedway, Austin; 78751 512-459-5835 www.trinitychurchofaustin.org office@trinitychurch ofaustin.org

♂ ☆ University Baptist Church, 2130 Guadalupe St, Austin; 78705-5516 512-478-8559 www.ubcaustin.org

Sports & Outdoor

♀ ★ Adventuring Outdoors, www.main.org/adventuring

♀ ★ Austin Front Runners, 1811 Santa Clara St, Austin; www.austinfrontrunners.org

♀ ★ Austin Gay Basketball League, 512-814-6495 www.agbl.org

♀ Austin Tennis Club, POB 2621, Austin 78768 www.austintennis-club.com

♀ ☆ Austin Valkyries (Rugby), www.austinvalkyries.com

♀ Softball Austin, www.softballaustin.org

♀ ★ Texas Gay Rodeo Association - Austin, www.tgra.org

♀ ★ Volleyball Austin, www.volleyballaustin.com

Thrift/Consignment Stores

♂ ☆ Top Drawer Thrift, 4902 Burnet Rd, Austin 512-454-5161 www.topdrawerthrift.org

Travel & Tourist Services (see also Accommodation)

♂ ○ Amazon Adventures, 2711 Market Garden, Austin 78745 512-443-5393 800-232-5658 www.amazonadventures.com ✐ jmc12@ amazonadventures.com

Texas: Austin Area
Travel

311
GAYELLOW PAGES #42 2020-2021

Dallas/Fort Worth Area: Texas
AIDS/HIV Support

♂ • ♿ Century Travel, 2714 Bee Cave Rd #101, Austin; 512-327-8760 www.centurytravelaustin.com ✎
>> *Bandera: see San Antonio Area*

Beaumont

Bars, Cafes, Clubs, Restaurants

♂ • Rumors Beaumont, 650 Orleans St 713-539-5183 www.rumorsbeaumont.com **D** ▥

Health Care: Physical (see also Counseling/Mental Health)

♀ Triangle Area Network, 1495 N 7th St 409-832-8338 www.tanhealthcare.org

Organizations/Resources: Family and Supporters

♀ ☆ PFLAG Beaumont, fb.com/pflagbeaumont/

Recovery

♂ ☆ AA Ninth District Intergroup Association, Inc., 4224 College St; 77707 409-832-1107 aabeaumont.org intergroup9@att.net
>> *Boerne: see San Antonio Area*
>> *Canutillo: see El Paso*

College Station

Bars, Cafes, Clubs, Restaurants
Bryan

♂ • Halo Bar, 121 N Main St, Bryan / check for planned reopening after fire 979-823-6174 All welcome fb.com/HALOBCS **DV** ▥

♀ ○ Revolution Cafe & Bar, 211 B S Main St (in Carnegie Alley), Bryan; 979-823-4044 fb.com/revolutionbcs ✕ ♈ ▥ ✎

Organizations/Resources: Student, Academic, Education

♂ ★ Texas A&M University GLBT Resource Center, Student Life 3, Student Services at White Creek; 979-862-8920 studentlife.tamu.edu/glbt/

Corpus Christi

Community Centers and/or Pride Organizations

♂ ★ Coastal Bend PRIDE Center, 2882 Holly Rd 78415 361-814-2001 www.cbpridecenter.org info@cbpridecenter.org

Information, Media & Publications

♂ Corpus Christi LGBTQIA, 6430 Beechwood Dr 361-587-6364 www.cclgbt.com

♂ • Hard Candy Magazine, 2882 Holly Rd; 78415 361-814-2001 www.cbpridecenter.org info@cbpridecenter.org

Accommodation: Hotels, Inns, Guesthouses, B&B, Resorts
Rockport

♀ • (?♿) Anthony's By The Sea, 732 S Pearl St, Rockport; 78382-2420 361-729-6100 800-460-2557 www.anthonysbythesea.com (✿?) ✎ ⊛ anthonysbandb@att.net

Bars, Cafes, Clubs, Restaurants

♂ Club Iconic, 4223 S Alameda; 361-425-8374 fb.com/ClubIconicCC/ **D**

Corpus Christi

♀ Connect Patio Bar & Ultra Lounge, 512 S Staples; 361-299-0080 fb.com/connectincorpus/ ▥

♂ • ♿ Hidden Door, 802 S Staples; 78404 361-882-5002 www.thehiddendoorcc.com ▥

Funding: Endowment, Fundraising

♂ ★ (?♿) Royal Sovereign Imperial Court of the Texas Riviera Empire, POB 3882; 78463-3882 www.texasrivieraempire.org

Health Care: Physical (see also Counseling/Mental Health)

♀ ☆ ♿ Coastal Bend Wellness Foundation, 2882 Holly Rd; 78415 361-814-2001 www.cbwellness.org info@cbpridecenter.org

Recovery

♀ ☆ AA: Coastal Bend Intergroup Association, 3833 S Staples Ste S-212; 361-992-8911 www.cbiaa.org

Travel & Tourist Services (see also Accommodation)

♀ • (?♿) 3rd Coast Captains, Capt James Cook, POB 181173; 78480 361-563-8277 www.3rdCoastCaptains.com

Dallas/Fort Worth Area

Community Centers and/or Pride Organizations

♂ ★ Dallas Pride, POB 192608, Dallas; 75219 dallaspride.org ✎

♂ North Texas Pride Foundation, www.northtexaspride.com

♂ ★ ♿ Resource Center, 5750 Cedar Springs Rd, Dallas; 75235 214-521-5124 www.myresourcecenter.org ✎ info@myresourcecenter.org

♂ ★ Tarrant County Gay Pride Association, Inc, POB 3459, FW; 76113 www.tcgpwa.org

Accommodation: Hotels, Inns, Guesthouses, B&B, Resorts
Ben Wheeler

♀ • Cross Timber Ranch B&B, 6271 Farm to Market Rd 858, Ben Wheeler; 903-833-9000 www.crosstimberranch.com ✎ ⊛

Dallas

♀ ○ ♿ Warwick Melrose Hotel, 3015 Oak Lawn Ave, Dallas; 75219-4135 214-521-5151 www.warwickmelrosedallas.com ✿ ✎ ⊛

Accounting, Bookkeeping, Tax Services

♀ • Fisher Tax Services LLC, 7962 Southbrook Circle, FW; 76134 817-720-6600 www.fishertaxfirm.com hfisher@fishertaxfirm.com

AIDS/HIV Services, Education & Support

♀ ☆ ♿ Access and Information Network (AIN), 2600 N Stemmons Fwy Ste 151, Dallas; 214-943-4444 **H?** www.AINDallas.org ✦ @ixx=

♀ ☆ ♿ AIDS Outreach Center, 400 North Beach St, FW; 76111 817-335-1994 www.aoc.org info@aoc.org

♀ ☆ Legacy Counseling, 4054 McKinney Ave #102, Dallas; 214-520-6308 www.legacycares.org

♀ ☆ ♿ Prism Health North Texas, 351 W Jefferson Blvd #300, Dallas; 214-521-5191 www.prismhealthntx.org

Texas: Dallas/Fort Worth Area

AIDS/HIV Support

312

GAYELLOW PAGES #42 2020-2021

Dallas/Fort Worth Area: Texas

Erotica

♀ ☆ ᏰᏰ Resource Center Health Campus, 2701 Reagan St, Dallas; 75219 214-528-0144 All welcome www.myresourcecenter.org ✎ info@myresourcecenter.org

AIDS/HIV Housing

♂ ☆ ᏰᏰ AIDS Services of Dallas, POB 4338, Dallas; 75208 214-941-0523 www.aidsdallas.org

Archives/Libraries/Museums/History Projects

♂ Resource Center Dallas LGBT Collection of the UNT Libraries, 1155 Union Circle #305190, Denton; 940-565-2411 tinyurl.com/lkq4w3c

Bars, Cafes, Clubs, Restaurants
Addison

♂ ○ ᏰᏰ Blue Mesa Grill, 14866 Montfort Dr, Addison 972-934-0165 www.bluemesagrill.com ✕

Arlington

♀ ● 1851 Club, 931 W Division St, Arl 817-642-5554 www.1851club.com **D** ▥

Dallas

♀ Alexandre's, 4026 Cedar Springs Rd, Dallas 214-559-0720 fb.com/AlexandresBar/ ▥

♂ ○ Barbara's Pavillion, 325 Centre St, Dallas 214-941-2145

♀ Cedar Springs Tap House, 4123 Cedar Springs Rd Ste 100, Dallas; 214-377-7446 cedarspringstaphouse.com **S** ♈ ✕

♂ Club Los Rieles, 4930 Military Pkwy, Dallas 214-546-1109 fb.com/clublosrielesdallas/ ✕

♂ Club Stallions, 11311 Harry Hines Blvd #203, Dallas; 214-791-3585 fb.com/clubstallions.dallas **P**

♀ ● ᏰᏰ Dallas Eagle, 5740 Maple Ave, Dallas; 214-357-4375 www.dallaseagle.com **L**

♀ ○ **The Grapevine, 3902 Maple Ave, Dallas 214-522-8466 Neighborhood bar voted best ally of the LGBTQ+ community 10 years running. www.thegrapevine-bar.com**

♀ Havana Bar & Grill, 4006 Cedar Springs Rd, Dallas; 214-886-6804 fb.com/HavanaDallas/ **D** ♈ ✕ ▥ ◆

♀ ● ᏸ Hidden Door, 5025 Bowser Ave, Dallas; 214-526-0620 www.hiddendoor.com **L** ✎

♂ ● Hunky's Hamburgers, 3930 Cedar Springs Rd, Dallas; 214-522-1212 www.hunkys.com ✕

♂ ᏰᏰ JR's Bar & Grill, 3923 Cedar Springs Rd, Dallas; 214-528-1004 www.jrsdallas.com ♈ ✕

♀ ● Kaliente, 4350 Maple Ave, Dallas 469-556-1395 fb.com/kalienteclub ◆

♂ Magnum Dallas, 1820 W. Mockingbird Lane, Dallas; 469-525-3445 magnumdallas.com

♀ Marty's Live, 4207 Maple Ave, Dallas; / Tue Lesbian night 214-599-2151 tinyurl.com/q8vysae **D** ▥ ◆

♀ ● Pekers, 2615 Oak Lawn Rd, Dallas 214-528-3333 www.pekersbar.com

♂ Rose Room, 3911 Cedar Springs Rd, Dallas 214-526-7171 www.theroseroomdallas.com **D** ▥

♂ ● The Round-Up Saloon and Dance Hall, 3912 Cedar Springs Rd, Dallas; 214-522-9611 www.roundupsaloon.com **CDW**

♂ Station 4, 3911 Cedar Springs Rd, Dallas 214-526-7171 station4dallas.com **D** ▥

♀ Sue Ellen's, 3014 Throckmorton St, Dallas 214-559-0707 sueellensdallas.com **D**

♂ ● Tin Room, 2514 Hudnall St, Dallas 214-526-6365 fb.com/tinroom/

♂ ᏸ The TMC, 3903 Cedar Springs, Dallas; 214-521-4205 fb.com/TMCDallas/

♂ ● ᏰᏰ Union Coffee, 3705 Cedar Springs Rd, Dallas; 469-501-5440 www.uniondallas.org ☞ coffee@uniondallas.org

♀ Woody's, 4011 Cedar Springs Rd, Dallas 214-520-6629 www.dallaswoodys.com **SV**

♂ Zippers, 3333 N Fitzhugh Ave, Dallas 214-526-9519 fb.com/dallas.zippers/ **D**

Fort Worth

♂ ○ ᏰᏰ Blue Mesa Grill, 612 Carroll St, Ft Worth 817-332-6372 www.bluemesagrill.com ✕

♂ Club Changes, 2637 E Lancaster Ave, FW 817-413-2332 fb.com/ChangesFW **D**

♂ Club Reflection, 604 S Jennings Ave, FW 817-870-8867 tinyurl.com/y7y2r2nd **CWD**

♀ The Urban Cowboy Saloon, 2620 E Lancaster Ave, FW; 682-707-5663 fb.com/TheUrbanCowboySaloon/ **D** ▥

Plano

♀ ○ ᏰᏰ Blue Mesa Grill, 8200 Dallas Parkway, Plano 214-387-4407 www.bluemesagrill.com ✕

♂ ○ Roy's, 2840 Dallas Pkwy, Plano; 972-473-6263 www.roysrestaurant.com ✕

Bookstores

♀ ★ (ᏰᏰ) Sources of Hope Gifts & Books, 5910 Cedar Springs Rd, Dallas; 800-501-4673 ✎

Broadcast Media

♀ ★ Lambda Weekly, Sun 1pm, KNON 89.3-FM www.lambdaweekly.com

Counseling/Psychotherapy/Mental Health

♂ ○ Inclusive Counseling, 2121 W Spring Creek Pkwy Ste 110, Plano; 75023 214-504-4420 www.inclusivecounseling.com therapy@inclusivecounseling.com

♂ ● ᏰᏰ New Perspective Counseling Services, 9555 Lebanon Rd Ste 602, Frisco; 75035 469-362-8004 www.npcs.com info@npcs.com

♂ ● Spillman, Craig W., PhD, PC, LPC, LMFT,NCC, Counseling Institute of Irving, 1300 Walnut Hill Lane #200, Irving; 75038-3074 972-550-8369 fax 972-550-8531 www.DrSpillman.com

Erotica / Adult Stores / Safe Sex Supplies

♂ ○ ᏰᏰ Dreamers Hillsboro, 2705 N. IH 35 Exit 364A, Hillsboro; 254-582-9305 **H?** dreamerstexas.com

Funding: Endowment, Fundraising

⚥ ★ Black Tie Dinner, Inc., 3824 Cedar Springs #335, Dallas; 469-224-0436 www.blacktie.org

♀ ☆ DIFFA Dallas, 2050 Stemmons Fwy Mail Unit 262, Dallas; 214-748-8580 www.diffadallas.org

⚥ ★ Gay & Lesbian Fund for Dallas, 3824 Cedar Springs Rd #101 Box 371, Dallas; www.glfd.org

♀ Greg Dollgener Memorial AIDS Fund, Inc., 901 Mossvine Dr, Plano; 972-743-6323 www.gdmaf.org

⚥ ★ Imperial Court de Fort Worth/Arlington, PO Box 365, FW; 76101 www.icfwa.org

⚥ ★ United Court of the Lone Star Empire, POB 190865, Dallas; 75219 www.dallascourt.org

Health Care: Physical (see also Counseling/Mental Health)

♀ ☆ Health Services of North Texas, 4401 N I-35 Ste 312, Denton; 940-381-1501 www.healthntx.org

♀ ☆ 🖧 Nelson-Tebedo Community Clinic, Resource Center Dallas, 4012 Cedar Springs, Dallas; 214-528-2336 **H?** www.rcdallas.org

Immigration, Citizenship, Political Asylum, Refugees

♀ ○ 🖧 Kinser, Kimberly J, 2425 N Central Expressway Ste 200, Richardson; 75080 972-491-1145 www.kinserlaw.com ✔

Insurance (see also Financial Planning)

♀ ○ 🖧 Dirk Hilkmann State Farm Agency, ., 9330 LBJ Fwy Ste 1188, Dallas; 75243 214-343-2500 www.dirk4u.com

Leather Resources & Groups

⚥ ★ Cowtown Leathermen, POB 3494, FW; 76113 www.cowtownleathermen.com

♀ ☆ Firedancers Dallas, POB 190223, Dallas 75219 firedancersdallas.org

♀ National Leather Association- NLA-Dallas, POB 190432, Dallas; 75219 nladallas.org

Legal Services

♀ ● 🖧 English, Jay, English Law Group, P.L.L.C., 12222 Merit Dr Ste 1200, Dallas; 75251 214-528-4300 www.englishpllc.com jenglish@englishpllc.com

♀ ● Herrera, Roger, 1005 W Jefferson Blvd Ste 403 214-943-6062 tinyurl.com/ksjgz5 ✦ law_rogelioherrera@sbcglobal.net

♀ ○ 🖧 Law Office of Jodi McShan, PLLC, 4144 N Central Expy Ste 1000, Dallas; 75204 214-800-2091 www.jodimcshanlaw.com ✔ jodi@jodimcshanlaw.com

♀ ● 🖧 Rob Wiley, PC, 2613 Thomas Ave, Dallas; 75204 214-528-6500 fax 214-528-6511 Employment law. www.robwiley.com rwiley@robwiley.com

Men's & Sex Clubs (not primarily Health Clubs)

⚥ ● 🖧 Club Dallas, 2616 Swiss Ave, Dallas; 214-821-1990 tinyurl.com/y76y8p3p **P** ✔

Organizations/Resources: Business & Professional Associations, Labor Advocacy

⚥ Business Network Collin County, 214-232-6252 www.meetup.com/BNCC-plano/

⚥ ★ 🖧 Dallas LGBT Bar Association, 2101 Ross Ave, Dallas; www.DLGBTBA.org ✔

⚥ ★ Dallas Tavern Guild, POB 192608, Dallas 75219 dallaspride.org ✔

⚥ ★ League at AT&T, 208 S Akard St, Dallas 75201 www.league-att.org

⚥ ★ North Texas GLBT Chamber of Commerce, 4123 Cedar Springs Rd Ste 1206, Dallas; 214-821-4528 www.glbtchamber.org

Organizations/Resources: Cultural, Dance, Performance

⚥ ★ Fears for Queers, c/o DOA Blood Bath Entertainment, POB 643, Farmersville; 75442 fb.com/bloodbathfilmfests/

⚥ ★ Oak Lawn Band, POB 191677, Dallas; 75219 469-616-0138 www.oaklawnband.org

⚥ ★ Pegasus Squares, LGBTQ Square Dance Club, 214-444-9696 www.pegasus-squares.com

⚥ ★ 🖧 QCinema, Fort Worth's Gay & Lesbian International Film Festival, 1300 Gendy #217, FW; 76107 www.qcinema.org ✔ kathryn@qcinema.org

♀ ★ 🖧 Turtle Creek Chorale, 3630 Harry Hines Blvd #306, Dallas; 75219 214-526-3214 www.turtlecreekchorale.com info@turtlecreek.org

♀ ☆ Women's Chorus of Dallas, 3630 Harry Hines Blvd #210, Dallas; 75219-3201 214-520-7828 www.twcd.org TWCDoffice@twcd.org

Organizations/Resources: Ethnic, Multicultural

⚥ ★ Dallas Southern Pride, 1075 W Griffin St Ste 204, Dallas; 214-405-5475 www.dallassouthernpride.com ❖

♀ ☆ LULAC 4871 - Dallas Rainbow Council, POB 192336, Dallas; 75219 www.lulac4871.org ✦ LULAC4871@gmail.com

Organizations/Resources: Family and Supporters

♀ ☆ 🖧 PFLAG Dallas, POB 190193, Dallas; 75219 972-849-0383 tinyurl.com/uldvf8o

♀ ☆ PFLAG Denton, tinyurl.com/y972fuby

♀ ☆ PFLAG Fort Worth, POB 8279, FW; 76124-0279 817-382-7353 pflagfortworth.org Info@pflagfortworth.org

Organizations/Resources: Naturist/Nudist

♂ D.A.M.N of North Texas, POB 190869, Dallas 75219 214-521-5342 x1739 damnmen.weebly.com **N**

Organizations/Resources: Political/Legislative/Advocacy

⚥ ★ (♻) Stonewall Democrats of Dallas, POB 192305, Dallas; 75219 214-506-3367 tinyurl.com/2sr3gw

⚥ ★ Stonewall Democrats of Denton County, c/o DCDP, 1710 W University #110, Denton tinyurl.com/yb5ryz72

Organizations/Resources: Social, Recreation, Support

⚥ ★ Classic Chassis Car Club Dallas, POB 225463, Dallas; 75222 214-446-0606 www.classicchassis.com

Texas: Dallas/Fort Worth Area
Organizations: Social & Support

314

GAYELLOW PAGES #42 2020-2021

Dallas/Fort Worth Area: Texas
Reproductive Medical Services

♂ ★ Cross-Timbers Prime Timers, 832-326-2080 tinyurl.com/da2n2g

♂ ★ Dallas Bears, POB 191223, Dallas; 75219 www.dallas-bears.org

♀ ★ Gay and Lesbian Alliance of North Texas, www.galanorthtexas.org

♀ ★ ⚥ Gaybingo, c/o Resource Center Dallas, POB 190869, Dallas; 75219 / check schedule online 214-540-4495 tinyurl.com/nnwkypq ✔

♀ OUTreach Denton - Adult Social Group, tinyurl.com/y9n2x9u2

♂ ★ ⚥ Prime Timers-Dallas/Fort Worth, POB 191101, Dallas; 75219-8101 214-218-0912 tinyurl.com/y4takrfs primetimersdfw@gmail.com

♀ ★ Rainbow Garden Club, POB 226811, Dallas 75222 www.rainbowgardenclub.com

♀ ★ Tarrant County Lesbian Gay Alliance, Inc, PO Box 471637, FW; 76147 817-877-5544 www.tclga.org

♂ ★ Trinity River Bears, www.trinityriverbears.com

♀ ★ Women with Pride, 2701 Reagan St, Dallas; 214-528-0144 tinyurl.com/y8tabqov

♀ Words of Women, POB 180777, Dallas; 75218 347-933-1256 www.wordsofwomen.org

Organizations/Resources: Student, Academic, Education

♀ ★ ⚥ Collin College Prism, 2200 W University Dr, McKinney; **H** tinyurl.com/y6osxtvf ✔

♀ ★ ⚥ Southern Methodist University SPECTRUM, POB 750172, Dallas; 75275 / Hughes-Trigg Student Center #313, 3140 Dyer St 214-768-4412 **H?** people.smu.edu/spectrum/ ✔

♀ ⚥ Southern Methodist University Women & LGBT Center, POB 750172, Dallas; 75275 / 3140 Dyer Street, Ste. 313 214-768-4792 **H?** www.smu.edu/womenscenter ✔

♀ ★ ⚥ TCU Spectrum, 2800 S University Dr, FW; 512-619-0649 **H?** fb.com/TCUSpectrum/

♀ ★ ⚥ Texas Christian University Allies, POB 298750, FW; 76129 817-257-7855 **H?** www.allies.tcu.edu

♀ ★ Texas Women's University LGBTQIA Resources, Jones Hall Ste 200, Denton; 940-898-3679 tinyurl.com/y7m99bju

♀ ★ University of North Texas GLAD, 1155 Union Circle #310937, Denton; 76203 tinyurl.com/wyrp75l gladatunt@gmail.com

♀ ★ ⚥ University Of Texas Arlington GSA, POB 19348, Arl; 76019 tinyurl.com/y75m2vv9

Organizations/Resources: Transgender/Gender Non-Conforming/Diverse

T ☆ Black Trans Advocacy, 3530 Forest Lane Ste 290, Dallas; 855-255-8636 www.blacktrans.org ✤

T ☆ Black Transmen, 3530 Forest Lane Ste 290, Dallas; 855-255-8636 www.blacktransmen.org ✤

T ☆ Black Transwomen, 3530 Forest Lane Ste 290, Dallas; 855-255-8636 BlackTranswomen.org ✤

T ☆ GenderBrave, Resource Center, 5750 Cedar Springs Rd, Dallas; 214-540-4415 tinyurl.com/y9atqaov

T Trans Kids & Families of Texas, 11450 US Hwy 380 Ste 130 #121, Crossroads; 972-850-8405 dfwtkf.com

T Transgender Support Group, St Stephen's Episcopal Church, 463 W Harwood Rd, Hurst; 817-680-9084 www.ssechurst.org/out-reach/

Organizations/Resources: Youth (see also Family)

♂ ★ ⚥ DFW Fuse, 3918 Harry Hines Blvd, Dallas; 214-540-4435 www.dfwfuse.com ✔

♀ GALA Youth, Horizon UCC, 1641 W Hebron Pkwy, Carrollton 972-855-8456 tinyurl.com/y9tq3g8g

♂ Promise House, Inc., 224 W Page Ave, Dallas 214-941-8578 www.promisehouse.org

♀ ★ ⚥ Youth First Drop-In Center, 5750 Cedar Springs Rd, Dallas; 214-540-4471 **H?** LGBTQ & Allies 12-18 and families. tinyurl.com/zrh56m6 ✔

Real Estate (see also Mortgages)

♀ ● Hewitt Habgood Realty Group, Dave Perry-Miller InTown, 2828 Routh St #100, Dallas; 75201 214-752-7070 214-684-1233 www.hewitthabgood.com ✔

Recovery

♂ ☆ Dallas AA, 6162 E Mockingbird Lane Ste 213, Dallas; 214-887-6699 www.aadallas.org

♂ ★ Lambda AA, 1575 W Mockingbird Lane Ste 625, Dallas; 214-267-0222 tinyurl.com/p6qx5k4

Religious / Spiritual Resources

♀ ★ ⚥ Agapé MCC of Fort Worth, 4615 E California Pkwy, FW; 817-535-5002 www.agapemcc.com

♂ ☆ ⚥ Cathedral of Hope UCC, 5910 Cedar Springs Rd, Dallas; 75235 214-351-1901 800-501-HOPE (4673) **H?** www.cathedralofhope.com ✔ cathedralofhope@cathedralofhope.com

♂ ☆ Cathedral of Light, 2570 Valley View Lane, Farmers Branch; 75234 972-245-6520 www.colight.org info@colight.org

♂ ★ Congregation Beth El Binah, 11211 Preston Road www.bethelbinah.org ✡

♂ ☆ Crossroads Community Church, POB 191576, Dallas; 75219 214-529-9090 tinyurl.com/2f9qe6g info@crossroadscommunitychurch.us

♂ ☆ ⚥ Denton UU Fellowship, 1111 Cordell St, Denton; 76201-2676 940-566-1286 www.dentonuuf.org info@dentonuuf.org

♂ ★ ⚥ Harvest MCC, 2281 N Masch Branch Rd Ste 100, Denton; 940-484-6159 www.harvestmcc.com

♀ ★ Seventh Day Adventist Kinship International - Region 5, 972-416-1358 www.sdakinship.org

♂ ☆ ⚥ St Stephen UMC, 2520 Oates Dr, Mesquite; 75150 972-279-3112 www.ststephenumctx.org office@ststephenumctx.org

♀ ★ ⚥ Trinity Metropolitan Community Church, 933 E Ave J, Grand Prairie; 817-265-5454 www.trinitymcc.org ✔

Reproductive Medicine & Fertility Services

♂ ○ Berkson, Mindy, Newborn Advantage, 3131 McKinney Ave Ste 600, Dallas; 75204 847-989-8628 www.NewbornAdvantage.com mindy@NewbornAdvantage.com

Texas: Dallas/Fort Worth Area
Sports & Outdoor
315
GAYELLOW PAGES #42 2020-2021
Gun Barrel City: Texas
Campgrounds and RV Parks

Sports & Outdoor

♂ ★ Dallas Diablos Rugby Club, POB 190862, Dallas; 75219 469-693-1942 fb.com/DallasDiablosRugby/

♀ ★ Dallas Independent Volleyball Association (DIVA), POB 191869, Dallas; 75219 972-757-2740 www.divadallas.org

♀ ★ Different Strokes Golf Association, www.dsgadallas.org ✪

♀ ★ Different Strokes Golf Association, www.dsgadallas.org

♀ ★ Oak Lawn Tennis Association, 807 Allen St # 385, Dallas; 701-335-6582 www.oltadallas.org

♀ ★ Pegasus Slowpitch Softball Association, PO Box 191075, Dallas; 75219 972-879-7900 www.dallaspssa.org

♀ ★ Texas Gay Rodeo Assoc. - Dallas, POB 191168, Dallas; 75219 214-832-8236 tinyurl.com/jg5s4s7

El Paso

Community Centers and/or Pride Organizations

♂ El Paso Sun City Pride, 510 N Stanton St www.suncitypride.org

AIDS/HIV Services, Education & Support

♀ ☆ La Fe Care Center, 1314 E Yandell Dr 915-209-2667 www.lafe-ep.org ◆

Bars, Cafes, Clubs, Restaurants

♂ 8 1/2, 506 N Stanton St; 915-351-0262 fb.com/8-12-105161009523930/ ▥

♀ ○ Black Orchid Lounge, 6127 N Mesa St Ste A 915-235-9145 www.theblackorchidlounge.com info@theblackorchidlounge.com

♂ The Briar Patch/Hyde Patio Bar, 508 N Stanton St; 915-577-9555 fb.com/BriaratHyde/ **D**

Canutillo

♀ ○ Little Diner, 7209 7th St, Canutillo 915-877-2176 fb.com/little-dinercorp/ ✕

♂ ● Chiquitas Bar, 310 E Missouri Ave 915-351-0095 tinyurl.com/yc874cww ◆

♂ Epic, 510 N Stanton St; 915-525-0984 tinyurl.com/pxckw32 **D** ▥

♂ Old Plantation, 301 S Ochoa St 915-303-9211 theopnight.club

♀ ○ Tanya's Gridiron, 4620-A Dyer; 915-566-8188 fb.com/Tanyas-Gridiron/ **S** ♈ ✕▥

♂ Tool Box, 506 N Stanton St; 915-351-1896 fb.com/tool.box.507/ **D**

♂ Touch Bar & Nightclub, 11395 James Watt Dr fb.com/touchbarelpaso **D** ▥

Organizations/Resources: Family and Supporters

♀ ☆ ♿ PFLAG El Paso, POB 23086 79923 915-209-2667 www.pflagelpaso.org

Organizations/Resources: Social, Recreation, Support

♂ The M Factor, 701 Montana Ave; 915-212-0242 fb.com/MFactor915

Religious / Spiritual Resources

♀ ★ ♿ MCC El Paso, POB 3121 79923 915-533-0111 www.mccelpaso.com ✎

Forest Hill

Erotica / Adult Stores / Safe Sex Supplies

♀ ● ♿ Dreamers North Austin, 6616 Oak Crest Dr; 817-516-7708 **H?** dreamerstexas.com
» Fort Worth: see Dallas/Fort Worth Area

Galveston

Accommodation: Hotels, Inns, Guesthouses, B&B, Resorts

♀ ○ Lost Bayou Guesthouse B&B, 1607 Ave L 409-770-0688 www.lostbayou.com ✎ ⊗ @ixx=

AIDS/HIV Services, Education & Support

♀ ☆ (♿) Access Care of Coastal Texas, 707 23rd St; 409-763-2437 **H?** www.supportacct.org ✎

Bars, Cafes, Clubs, Restaurants

♀ ● 23rd Street Station Piano Bar, 1706 23rd St 409-443-5678 www.23rdstreetstation.com **K** ▥ ✎

♀ ○ Eat Cetera, 408 25th St; 409-762-0803 www.eatcetera.net ✕

♀ ○ ♿ Mod Coffeehouse, 2126 Post Office St; 409-765-5659 www.modcoffeehouse.com ⏦ ✎ info@modcoffeehouse.com

♀ ○ Mosquito Cafe, 628 14th St; 409-763-1010 www.mosquito-cafe.com ✕

♀ ● ♿ Robert's Lafitte, 2501 Ave Q 409-765-9092 **D** ▥

♀ ● Rumors Beach Bar, 3102 Seawall Blvd 409-974-4617 galveston.rumorsbars.com **D** ▥

Groesbeck

Campgrounds and RV Parks

♀ ● (♿) Rainbow Ranch Campground, 1662 LCR 800; 76642-2275 888-875-7596 254-729-8484 www.rainbowranch.net (♣?) ✎ (⊗) info@rainbowranch.net

Gun Barrel City

Bars, Cafes, Clubs, Restaurants

♂ ● Garlow's, 308 E Main St; 903-887-0853 www.garlows.club ✎

Campgrounds and RV Parks

♂ ● (♿) Circle J Ranch & Cattle Company, 903-479-4189 www.campcirclej.com ♣ ✎
» Harlingen: see Rio Grande Valley

Texas: Houston Area
Crisis, Anti-violence, & Helplines
316
GAYELLOW PAGES #42 2020-2021
Houston Area: Texas
Health Care

Houston Area

Crisis, Anti-violence, & Helplines

♂ ★ Gay & Lesbian Switchboard Houston, 713-529-3211 tinyurl.com/2smrol

♀ ☆ ♿ Houston Area Women's Center, 1010 Waugh Dr, Houston; 800-256-0551 www.hawc.org

Community Centers and/or Pride Organizations

♂ ★ ♿ Montrose Center, 401 Branard St Flr 2, Houston; 713-529-0037 **H?** www.montrosecenter.org ✎

♂ ★ ♿ Pride Houston, POB 541713, Houston; 77254 713-529-6979 www.pridehouston.org

AIDS/HIV Services, Education & Support

♀ ☆ ♿ AIDS Foundation Houston, Inc., 6260 Westpark Dr Ste 100, Houston; 713-623-6796 www.aidshelp.org

♂ ♿ Houston Regional HIV/AIDS Resource Group, 500 Lovett Blvd #100, Houston; 713-526-1016 www.hivtrg.org

Archives/Libraries/Museums/History Projects

♂ ★ Houston Area Rainbow Collective History (Houston ARCH., houstonarch.pbworks.com

Bars, Cafes, Clubs, Restaurants
Houston

♀ ○ Baba Yega's, 2607 Grant St, Houston 713-522-0042 www.babayega.com ♈ ✖

♂ ● ♿ Beaver's, 6025 Westheimer Rd, Houston; 713-714-4111 www.beavershtx.com ✖ ✎

♀ Blur, 710 Pacific, Houston; 713-529-3447 www.blurbar.com **D**

♂ ● Crocker Bar, 2312 Crocker St, Houston 713-529-3355 fb.com/crocker.bar

♂ Crystal, 6680 Southwest Freeway, Houston 713-532-2582 fb.com/LatinClub/ **D** ▦ ◆

♂ ● Eagle Houston, 611 Hyde Park Blvd, Houston 713-523-2473 www.houstoneagle.com **DL**

♂ George Country Sports Bar, 617 Fairview St, Houston; 713-528-8102 tinyurl.com/c8kdup3 **S**

♂ ● Guava Lamp, 570 Waugh Dr, Houston 713-524-3359 www.guavalamphouston.com **KV** ▦

♂ ● Hamburger Mary's Houston, 2409 Grant St, Houston; 713-677-0674 tinyurl.com/jjuzelm

♂ ● ♿ JR's Bar & Grill, 808 Pacific St, Houston; 713-521-2519 www.jrsbarandgrill.com ♈ ✖ ▦

♀ ● Mary's Alibi, 2409 Grant St, Houston 713-522-2867 fb.com/marysalibihtx/ **D**

♂ ● Michael's Outpost, 1419 Richmond Ave, Houston 713-520-8446 www.michaelsoutpost.com ▦

♀ ● ♿ Neon Boots Dancehall and Saloon., 11410 Hempstead Highway, Houston; 713-677-0828 www.neonbootsclub.com **CWDK** ▦ ✎

♀ ○ Numbers, 300 Westheimer Rd, Houston 713-521-1121 www.numbersnightclub.com ▦

♀ ○ The Path of Tea, 2340 W Alabama St, Houston 713-252-4473 www.thepathoftea.com ☞

♀ Pearl, 4216 Washington Ave, Houston 832-740-4933 www.pearlhouston.com **D** ♈ ✖ ▦

♂ ● ♿ RIPCORD, 715 Fairview St, Houston; 713-521-2792 fb.com/ripcordbar/ **L**

♀ ● ♿ Sparrow Bar & Cook Shop, 3701 Travis St, Houston; 713-524-6922 www.sparrowhouston.com ✖

♂ ● Tony's Corner Pocket, 817 W Dallas St, Houston y3-571-7870 ▦

♂ Viviana's, 4624 Dacoma St, Houston 713-681-4101 fb.com/7132690493vnc/ **D** ▦ ◆

Spring

♂ ● Ranch Hill Saloon, 24704 I-45 N, Spring 281-298-9035 www.ranchhill.com **DK**

♂ The Room Bar & Lounge, 4915 FM 2920 #148, Spring; 281-907-6866 fb.com/theroombar **D**

Bookstores

♀ ○ Brazos Bookstore, 2421 Bissonnet St, Houston 713-523-0701 www.brazosbookstore.com

Broadcast Media

♂ ★ Queer Voices, queervoices.org

Counseling/Psychotherapy/Mental Health

♀ ☆ Bering Connect, 713-526-1017 x206 beringconnect.org

♀ ● ♿ Gray, Enod, LCSW, CSAT-S, CGP, Trueself Transitions, 3100 Edloe #290, Houston; 281-788-9436 www.trueselftransitions.com @ixx=

♂ ★ ♿ The Montrose Center, 401 Branard St Flr 2, Houston; 77006-5015 713-529-0037 videophone on request **H?** www.montrosecenter.org ✎

Financial Planning, Investment (see also Insurance)

♀ ○ Devine, Patrick, CFP(R), Fleetwood Financial Solutions, 718 Trademark Pl, Houston; 77079-2413 281-293-7779 www.fleetwoodfs.com pat@fleetwoodfs.com

Funding: Endowment, Fundraising

♀ ☆ Bunnies on the Bayou, POB 66832, Houston 77226 www.bunniesonthebayou.org

♂ ★ The Empire of the Royal Sovereign & Imperial Court of the Single Star, Inc., POB 980444, Houston; 77098-0444 www.ersicss.org

Health Care: Physical (see also Counseling/Mental Health)

♀ ★ ♿ AssistHers, 401 Branard St 2nd Flr, Houston; 713-521-4628 **H?** Disabled or chronically ill Lesbian Women www.assisthers.org ✎

♀ ● ♿ Franco Chiropractic Clinic, 415 Westheimer Ste 211, Houston; 77006 713-526-5959 francochiropractic.com

♀ ☆ ♿ Legacy Community Health Services, POB 66308, Houston; 77266 832-548-5000 **H?** tinyurl.com/yt9ets

Leather Resources & Groups

♂ ★ Misfits, 713-261-8689 misfitshouston.com

Legal Services

♀ ☆ Houston Volunteer Lawyers, 1111 Bagby Ste FLB300, Houston; 713-228-0732 www.hvlp.org

♀ ○ ♿ Kalish Law Texas, 3 Grogan's Park Dr Ste 200, The Woodlands; 77380 281-363-3700 fax 281-367-7340 www.kalishlawtexas.com laura@kalishlawtexas.com

Men's & Sex Clubs (not primarily Health Clubs)

♂ ● ♿ Club Houston, 2205 Fannin, Houston; 713-659-4998 www.club-houston.com **P** ✗

Organizations/Resources: Business & Professional Associations, Labor Advocacy

♂ ★ Executive & Professional Association of Houston, POB 130227, Houston; 77219 www.epah.org

♂ ★ Greater Houston LGBT Chamber of Commerce, 5340 Weslayan St #25011, Houston; 832-510-3002 www.houstonlgbtchamber.com

Organizations/Resources: Cultural, Dance, Performance

♂ Art League of Houston, 1953 Montrose Blvd, Houston; 713-523-9530 www.artleaguehouston.org

♀ ★ ♿ Bayou City Women's Chorus, Bayou City Performing Arts, POB 541004, Houston; 77254 832-835-1643 www.bcpahouston.org/

♀ ☆ ♿ DiverseWorks, 3400 Main St #292, Houston; 77002 713-223-8346 www.diverseworks.org ✗

♀ ★ ♿ Gay Men's Chorus of Houston, Bayou City Performing Arts, POB 541004, Houston; 77254 832-835-1643 www.bcpahouston.org

♀ ★ ♿ Houston Pride Band, POB 7124, Houston; 77248 832-356-7476 www.houstonprideband.org

♂ ★ QFest, c/o Aurora Picture Show, 2442 Bartlett St, Houston; www.q-fest.com

Organizations/Resources: Education

● ★ ♿ Lesbian Health Initiative of Houston, Inc (LHI), 401 Branard St, Houston; 77006 713-426-3356 www.lhihouston.org info@lhihouston.org

Organizations/Resources: Ethnic, Multicultural

♂ ★ (?♿) Asians & Friends Houston, PO Box 667100, Houston; 77266 tinyurl.com/yo3od7 ✧

♂ Houston Splash, 6017 Ardmore St, Houston www.houstonsplash.com ❖

Organizations/Resources: Family and Supporters

♂ ★ Houston Gay & Lesbian Parents, Inc., www.hglp.org

♀ ☆ PFLAG Houston, POB 667665, Houston; 77266 713-467-3524 www.pflaghouston.org

Houston GLBT COMMUNITY CENTER
"Your Queer Home in Houston"
www.houstonglbtcenter.org
713-524-3818

Organizations/Resources: Political/Legislative/Advocacy

♂ ★ ♿ Houston GLBT Political Caucus (HGLBTPC), POB 66664, Houston; 77266 713-521-1000 www.thecaucus.org

Organizations/Resources: Social, Recreation, Support

♂ ★ Houston Area Bears, houstonbears.org

♀ ★ Krewe of Olympus, POB 920794, Houston; 77292 www.kreweofolympus.org

♂ ★ Prime Timers Houston, POB 980612, Houston 77098-0612 713-867-3903 primetimershouston.com primetimer_houston@yahoo.com

Organizations/Resources: Student, Academic, Education

♀ ☆ Center for the Study of Women, Gender, & Sexuality, POB 1892, Houston; 77251 713-348-5784 cswgs.rice.edu

♂ ★ Gamma Rho Lambda Colonies - Kappa Chapter, 832-429-8475 fb.com/GammaRhoLambdaUH/

♂ ★ ♿ GLOBAL, Campus Activities Box 211, 4800 Calhoun, Houston; 713-743-7539 fb.com/uhoustonglobal/ ✗

♂ ★ Rice Alumni Pride (RAP), POB 1892, Houston; 77251 713-348-4057 alumni.rice.edu/rap

♂ ★ ♿ Rice University Queers & Allies / Pride, MS 530, POB 1892, Houston; 77251 **H?** pride.rice.edu ✗

♂ ★ University of Houston Law Center Outlaws, 100 Law Center, Houston

Organizations/Resources: Transgender/Gender Non-Conforming/Diverse

T ☆ Tau Chi Tri Ess, POB 20785, Houston; 77225 (heterosexual crossdressers) www.tau-chi.org

Organizations/Resources: Youth (see also Family)

♂ ★ ♿ HATCH Youth, c/o The Montrose Center, 401 Branard St 1st Flr Room 101, Houston; 713-529-3590 www.hatchyouth.org ✗

Real Estate (see also Mortgages)

♀ ● ♿ Copenhaver, Mike, CRS, ABR, RE/MAX Metro, 2626 Richmond Ave, Houston; 77098-5504 713-528-4963 800-519-1800 www.mikecopenhaver.com ✗ mikecopenhaver@remax.net

Recovery

⚥ Lambda Center, 1201 W Clay St, Houston 713-521-1243 www.lambdahouston.org

Religious / Spiritual Resources

⚥ ☆ Bay Area Unitarian Universalist Church/Interweave, 17503 El Camino Real, Houston; 77058 281-488-2001 www.bauuc.org office@bauuc.org

⚥ ☆ Church of the Epiphany, 9600 S Gessner Dr, Houston; 77071-1099 713-774-9619 www.epiphany-hou.org welcome@epiphany-hou.org

⚥ ★ ♿ Dignity Houston, POB 66821, Houston; 77266-6821 www.dignityhouston.org dignityhouston@gmail.com

⚥ ☆ ♿ First Unitarian Universalist Church, 5200 Fannin St, Houston; 77004-5808 713-526-5200 **H?** www.firstuu.org ✗ office@firstuu.org

⚥ ★ Keshet Houston, POB 920552, Houston 77292-0552 832-429-5392 www.keshethouston.org ✡ info@keshethouston.org

⚥ ★ (♿) Resurrection MCC, 2025 W 11th St, Houston; 713-861-9149 **H** www.resurrectionmcc.org ✗

⚥ ☆ St Stephen's Episcopal Church, 1805 W Alabama St, Houston; 77098 713-528-6665 www.ststephenshouston.org info@ssesh.org

⚥ ☆ Unitarian Fellowship of Houston, 1504 Wirt Rd, Houston; 77055-4919 713-686-5876 www.ufoh.org ufhouston@comcast.net

Sports & Outdoor

⚥ ★ Different Spokes Houston, POB 10496, Houston; 77007 fb.com/groups/209985735792357

⚥ ★ FrontRunners Houston, 713-303-1429 frontrunnershouston.org

⚥ ★ Houston Hurricanes (Flag Football), tinyurl.com/zbrmdfy

⚥ ★ Houston Invitational Tournament, 615 Texas St, Houston; www.houstoninvite.com

⚥ ★ Houston Mixers, 2517 Julian, Houston; 77009 713-851-3265 Bowling Mon or Tue at Delmar Lanes www.houstoninvite.com wiccado@sbcglobal.net

⚥ ★ Houston Tennis Club, POB 130705, Houston; 77219 281-463-8794 www.houstontennisclub.org

⚥ ★ Inner Loop Alternatives, 2517 Julian, Houston 77009 713-851-3265 Bowling www.houstoninvite.com wiccado@sbcglobal.net

⚥ ★ Lone Star Volleyball Association, www.lonestarvolleyball.org

♀ ★ Monday Night Women, 2517 Julian, Houston 77009 281-437-6218 Bowling www.houstoninvite.com wiccado@sbcglobal.net

⚥ ★ Montrose Softball League, 1302 Waugh Dr PMB 744, Houston; 281-849-7675 www.houstonmsla.org

Kerrville

Recovery

⚥ Lambda Group (Kerrville), 720 Club 980 Barnett; www.aasanantonio.org/LGBT

» Longview: see Tyler/Longview Area

Lubbock

Bars, Cafes, Clubs, Restaurants

♂ ● Club Luxor, 2211 Marsha Sharp Freeway 806-744-3744 www.clubluxor.com **DK** 🎵

Organizations/Resources: Family and Supporters

♂ ♿ PFLAG Lubbock, POB 94493 79493 806-795-4502 www.pflaglubbock.org

Recovery

⚥ ★ ♿ Lambda AA, MCC Lubbock, 4501 University Ave; 806-792-5562 www.mcclubbock.org

Religious / Spiritual Resources

⚥ ★ ♿ MCC Lubbock, 4501 University Ave; 806-792-5562 www.mcclubbock.org

» McAllen: see Rio Grande Valley

Nacogdoches

Organizations/Resources: Student, Academic, Education

⚥ ★ Stephen F. Austin State University Pride NAC, 1936 North St; 936-468-3401 pridenac.tumblr.com

Navasota

Campgrounds and RV Parks

♂ ● Grizzly Pines, 16930 Whippoorwill Rd; 77868-8301 936-894-2030 www.grizzlypines.com grizzlypinespark@gmail.com

New Braunfels

Religious / Spiritual Resources

♀ ☆ ♿ Unitarian Universalists of New Braunfels, POB 311414; 78131-1414 / 135 Alves Lane 830-632-5461 **HD** www.uunb.org ✗ uunb135@gmail.com

» Plano: see Dallas/Fort Worth Area
» Port Aransas: see Corpus Christi

Rio Grande Valley

Bars, Cafes, Clubs, Restaurants
McAllen

♂ ● ♿ PBD's, 2908 N Ware Rd, McAllen 956-682-8019 www.pbds-mcallentx.com **DV** 🎵

Organizations/Resources: Family and Supporters

♂ PFLAG Harlingen, 1327 E Washington St PMB 300, Harlingen; 956-507-0570 fb.com/pflag.harlingen

Organizations/Resources: Political/Legislative/Advocacy

⚥ ★ STEP South Texas Equality Project, 2306 Camelot Circle, Harlingen; 956-244-5798 www.our-step.org

Organizations/Resources: Social, Recreation, Support

♂ Rio Grande Valley Prime Timers, POB 5566, McAllen; 78502 www.primetimersww.com/rgv/

Texas: Rio Grande Valley
Real Estate
319
GAYELLOW PAGES #42 2020-2021
San Antonio Area: Texas
Organizations: Political

Real Estate (see also Mortgages)

♂ • (?⚧) Hewey, Joseph, Grove Realty, 2027 E Price Rd #E, Brownsville; 78523 956-622-7395 www.brownsvillerelo.com Joseph@brownsvillerelo.com

» Rockport: see Corpus Christi

San Antonio Area

Crisis, Anti-violence, & Helplines

♂ Rape Crisis Center, 4606 Centerview Ste 200, San Antonio; 210-349-7273 rapecrisis.com

Community Centers and/or Pride Organizations

⚥ ★ The Pride Center San Antonio, 1303 McCullough Ave Ste 160, San Antonio; 210-370-7743 www.pridecentersa.org

⚥ ★ Pride San Antonio Inc, POB 120185, San Antonio; 78212 210-287-3970 www.pridesanantonio.org

Accommodation: Hotels, Inns, Guesthouses, B&B, Resorts
Boerne

♂ ○ Paniolo Ranch B & B Spa, 1510 Ranch Rd 473, Boerne; 78006 830-324-6666 www.panioloranch.com ✂ ⊗⊗ paniolo@panioloranch.com

San Antonio

♀ • Arbor House Suites B&B, 109 Arciniega, San Antonio; 210-472-2005 www.arborhouse.com ✢ ✂ ⊗

Accommodation Rental: Furnished / Vacation (& AirBNB)
Bandera

♀ • (?⚧) Desert Hearts Cowgirl Club, 10101 Hwy 173 N, Bandera; 830-796-7001 tinyurl.com/huv4tws (✢?) ⊗

AIDS/HIV Services, Education & Support

♂ ☆ ♿ Alamo Area Resource Center, PO Box 830048, San Antonio; 78283-0048 210-625-7200 www.aarcsa.com aarc@aarcsa.com

♀ ☆ ♿ Beat AIDS Coalition Trust, 1017 N Main Ste 200, San Antonio; 210-212-2266 beataids.org ✂

♀ ☆ ♿ San Antonio AIDS Foundation, 818 E Grayson St, San Antonio; 210-225-4715 sanantonioaids.org

Bars, Cafes, Clubs, Restaurants
San Antonio

⚥ • (?⚧) 2015 Place, 2015 San Pedro Ave, San Antonio; 210-733-3365 tinyurl.com/yadkarf8 **K** ▦

⚥ • (?⚧) The Annex, 330 San Pedro Ave, San Antonio; 210-223-6957 fb.com/ANNEXSA/ **L** ✂

⚥ • Bonham Exchange, 411 Bonham, San Antonio 210-224-9219 www.bonhamexchange.com **D** ▦

♂ • (?⚧) The Candlelight Coffee House & Wine Bar, 3011 N St Mary's, San Antonio; 210-738-0099 www.candlelightsatx.com ✕ ✂ candlelightsa@gmail.com

⚥ • ♿ Heat Nightclub, 1500 N Main Ave, San Antonio; 210-227-2600 www.heatsa.com **DKV** ▦ ✂

♀ ○ Ivory Lounge, 5152 Fredericksburg Rd, San Antonio; 210-340-4879 www.ivoryloungesa.com

♂ • ♿ Luther's Cafe, 1503 N Main Ave, San Antonio; 210-223-7727 www.lutherscafe.com **K** ☂ ✕ ☐ ✂

♂ ○ Madhatters Tea House & Cafe, 320 Beauregard St, San Antonio; 210-212-4832 www.madhatterstea.com ☐

⚥ • Pegasus, 1402 N Main Ave, San Antonio 210-299-4222 www.pegasussanantonio.com

♂ ○ The SA Country Saloon, 10127 Coachlight St, San Antonio; 210-525-0915 fb.com/SaCountrySaloon **D**

⚥ • Silver Dollar Saloon, 1812 N Main Ave, San Antonio; 210-227-2623 www.tejanotalk/ **DW** ◆

⚥ Sparks, 8011 Webbles Dr, San Antonio 210-257-0712 fb.com/SparksClubSATX/

⚥ • ♿ Sparkys Pub, 1416 N Main Ave, San Antonio; 210-320-5111 www.sparkyspub.com **DV** ✕ ☐

Erotica / Adult Stores / Safe Sex Supplies

♂ • ♂ Dreamers San Antonio, 2376 Austin Hwy, San Antonio; 210-653-3538 **H?** dreamerstexas.com

Funding: Endowment, Fundraising

⚥ ★ Royal, Sovereign & Imperial Court of the Alamo Empire, Inc, POB 120111, San Antonio; 78278 www.alamoempire.org

Gifts, Cards, Pride, etc.

⚥ • ♂ ZEBRAZ.com, 1608 N Main Ave, San Antonio; 78212-4311 210-472-2800 800-788-4729 orders only www.zebraz.com zebraz@zebraz.com

Health Care: Physical (see also Counseling/Mental Health)

♂ El Centro del Barrio/CentroMed, 3750 Commercial Ave, San Antonio; 210-922-7000 centromedsa.com

Men's & Sex Clubs (not primarily Health Clubs)

⚥ Alternative Club Inc, 827 E Elmira St, San Antonio; 210-223-2177

Organizations/Resources: Business & Professional Associations, Labor Advocacy

⚥ San Antonio LGBT Chamber of Commerce, POB 15120, San Antonio; 78212 210-504-9429 www.salgbtchamber.org

Organizations/Resources: Cultural, Dance, Performance

⚥ San Antonio Q Fest, fb.com/sa.Q.fest

Organizations/Resources: Family and Supporters

♂ ☆ ♿ PFLAG, POB 761475, San Antonio; 78245 210-848-7407 pflagsanantonio.org ◆

♂ ☆ PFLAG Seguin, 512-426-7599 fb.com/PFLAGSeguinTX/ pflagseguin@gmail.com

Organizations/Resources: Political/Legislative/Advocacy

♂ ☆ ♿ Esperanza Peace & Justice Center, 922 San Pedro Ave, San Antonio; 78212-4642 210-228-0201 Also cultural arts center. www.esperanzacenter.org ◆ esperanza@esperanzacenter.org

⚥ ★ (?⚧) Stonewall Democrats of San Antonio, POB 12814, San Antonio; 78212-0814 210-843-5766 www.stonewallsa.org admin@stonewallsa.org

Texas: San Antonio Area
Organizations: Social & Support

320
GAYELLOW PAGES #42 2020-2021

Winnsboro : Texas
Accommodation

Organizations/Resources: Social, Recreation, Support

♂ ★ Classic Chassis Car Club San Antonio, POB 15544, San Antonio; 78212 210-422-5313 www.cccc-sanantonio.com

♂● ★ San Antonio Prime Timers, POB 6421, San Antonio; 78209 301-257-7308 www.primetimersww.com/sapt/

Pets & Pet Services & Supplies

⚥ ● Four Paws Pet Sitting, 210-446-7387 4pawspetsittingsa.com

Recovery

♀ Lambda Group, Madison Square Presbyterian Church, 319 Camden, San Antonio; www.aasanantonio.org/LGBT

Religious / Spiritual Resources

♀ ★ ఉఉ Dignity/San Antonio, POB 12544, San Antonio; 78212 210-340-2230 www.dignitysanantonio.com

♂ ★ (♈) MCC of San Antonio, 611 E Myrtle St, San Antonio; 210-472-3597 www.mccsanantonio.com

Sports & Outdoor

♀ ★ Jans RainbowLeague, 3607 Grissom Mist, San Antonio; 210-609-2348 fb.com/jans.rainbowleague.5

San Marcos

Crisis, Anti-violence, & Helplines

♂ ☆ (♈) Hays-Caldwell Women's Center, PO Box 234, San Marcos; 78667 800-700-4292 **H** www.hcwc.org

AIDS/HIV Services, Education & Support

♀ Community Action, Inc, POB 748, San Marcos 78667 512-392-1161 www.communityaction.com

Bars, Cafes, Clubs, Restaurants

♀ Stonewall Warehouse, 141 E Hopkins St, San Marcos; fb.com/stonewallwarehouse/ **DE**

Terrel

Erotica / Adult Stores / Safe Sex Supplies

♂ ● ఉ Dreamers, 6086 W Us Highway 80 972-524-1449 **H?** dreamerstexas.com

Tyler/Longview Area

Information, Media & Publications

♀ ★ (♈) Tyler Area Gays, POB 6331, Tyler; 75711 903-526-9692 East Texas resource for LGBT community with news, forums, more. tylerareagays.com info@tylerareagays.com

Bars, Cafes, Clubs, Restaurants
Longview

♀ ● Rainbow Members Club (RMC), 203 S High S, Longview; 903-753-9393 fb.com/longviewrmc/ **DP** 🎱

Health Care: Physical (see also Counseling/Mental Health)

♂ Jim Meyer Comprehensive Health Center, 410 N 4th St, Longview; 903-234-8808 www.specialhealth.org

Organizations/Resources: Family and Supporters

♀ PFLAG Longview, POB 5703, Longview; 75608 fb.com/PFLAGLongviewTexas/

Religious / Spiritual Resources

♂ ☆ Congregation Beth El, 1010 Charleston Dr, Tyler; 75703 903-581-3764 www.jewishtyler.com ✡

Waco Area

Information, Media & Publications

♀ Gay Central Texas, www.gaycentraltexas.com

Accommodation: Hotels, Inns, Guesthouses, B&B, Resorts
Crawford

♂● ● ఉఉ The Homestead at 3218, 3218 Canaan Church Rd, Crawford; 76638-3334 254-486-0032 www.thehomesteadat3218.com **N** (♣?) 🚲 🚭

Funding: Endowment, Fundraising

♀ ★ Royal, Sovereign, Imperial Court of the Central Texas Empire, POB 20761, Waco; 76702 centraltexasempire.com

Leather Resources & Groups

♂ ☆ Touch of Leather, POB 1453, Temple; 76503 713-876-3930 www.touchofleather.org

Religious / Spiritual Resources

♀ Central Texas MCC, POB 1722, Waco; 76703 254-752-5331 www.centexmcc.com

Wichita Falls

Bars, Cafes, Clubs, Restaurants

♂ ○ Krank It Karaoke Kafe, 1400 N Scott Ave 940-761-9099 fb.com/krankitkaraokekafe **K**

Religious / Spiritual Resources

♀ ★ ఉ Wichita Falls MCC, 1401 Travis St; 940-322-4100 www.wichitafallsmcc.org

Wimberley

Accommodation Rental: Furnished / Vacation (& AirBNB)

♀ ● (♈) Abundance: A Hill Country River Retreat, 330 Mill Race Lane, Wimberley, TX 713-819-9339 www.abundanceretreat.com 🚲🐾🚭

♂ ○ ఉ Cypress Creek Cottages, 104 Scudder Ln, Wimberley; 78676 512-847-5950 www.cypresscreekcottages.com 🐾 🚲🚭

Winnsboro

Accommodation: Hotels, Inns, Guesthouses, B&B, Resorts

♂ ● (♈) Thee Hubbell House B&B, 307 W Elm St; 903-342-5629 **H?** www.theehubbellhouse.com 🍴 (♣?) 🚲 🚭

Utah: State/County Resources
Information, Media & Publications

321

GAYELLOW PAGES #42 2020-2021

Park City : Utah
Bars, Cafes, Clubs, Restaurants

Utah
State/County Resources

Information, Media & Publications

♂ ● ♿ The Q Pages, Salt Lick Publishing, 222 S Main St Ste 500, Salt Lake City, UT 801-997-9763 qpages.com ✎

♂ ● ♿ QSaltLake, Salt Lick Publishing, 222 S Main St Ste 500, Salt Lake City, UT 801-997-9763 www.qsaltlake.com

AIDS/HIV Services, Education & Support

♀ ☆ Utah AIDS Foundation, 1408 S 1100 E, Salt Lake City, UT 801-487-2323 www.utahaids.org

Counseling/Psychotherapy/Mental Health

♀ ★ LGBTQ-Affirmative Psychotherapist Guild of Utah, POB 651464, Salt Lake City, UT 84105 www.lgbtqtherapists.com robin@lgbtqtherapists.com

Financial Planning, Investment (see also Insurance)

♀ ● **LGBT Financial, 801-613-7119 Your premier LGBTQIA+ partner for insurance, investments, and financial planning. www.lgbtfinancial.org ryan@lgbtfinancial.org**

Organizations/Resources: Business & Professional Associations, Labor Advocacy

♀ ☆ LGBTQ-Affirmative Psychotherapist Guild of Utah, POB 651464, Salt Lake City, UT 84165 www.lgbtqtherapists.com

Organizations/Resources: Family and Supporters

♀ LDS Family Fellowship, 879 E 400 S, Orem, UT 801-226-5322 www.ldsfamilyfellowship.org

Organizations/Resources: Naturist/Nudist

♂ ☆ Utah Male Naturists, www.umen.org

Organizations/Resources: Political/Legislative/Advocacy

♀ ☆ American Civil Liberties Union, 355 N 300 W, Salt Lake City, UT 801-521-9862 www.acluutah.org

♀ ☆ ♿ Equality Utah, 175 W 200 S Ste 1004, Salt Lake City, UT 801-355-3479 www.equalityutah.org ✎

Organizations/Resources: Senior Resources

♀ ★ ♿ SAGE Utah, Utah Pride Center, 1380 Main St, Salt Lake City, UT 801-539-8800 Service and Advocacy for GLBT Elders fb.com/sageutah ✎ SAGE@utahpridecenter.org

Organizations/Resources: Youth (see also Family)

♀ ☆ Youth Futures, POB 160301, Clearfield, UT 84016 / shelter 2760 S Adams Ave, Ogden 801-528-1214 www.yfut.org

Recovery

♀ ☆ Narcotics Anonymous Utah Region (State-wide), PO Box 1409, Salt Lake City, UT 84110 877-479-6262 www.nautah.org

Religious / Spiritual Resources

♂ ☆ Mormons Building Bridges, 978-394-4947 mormonsbuildingbridges.org info@mormonsbuildingbridges.org

Cedar City

Organizations/Resources: Student, Academic, Education

♀ ★ ♿ Pride and Equality Club at SUU, 351 W University Blvd; tinyurl.com/ybj2zz9m

Escalante

Accommodation: Hotels, Inns, Guesthouses, B&B, Resorts

♂ ○ Rainbow Country Bed & Breakfast, POB 333 84726 435-826-4567 www.bnbescalante.com ✛ ⊛

Logan

Community Centers and/or Pride Organizations

♀ ★ ♿ Logan Pride, POB 3589 84323 / 69 E 100 N 435-227-5824 **H?** www.loganpride.org ✎ info@loganpride.org

Organizations/Resources: Family and Supporters

♂ PFLAG Logan/Cache Valley, POB 1271; 84322 208-315-0117 tinyurl.com/vxh7vqu

Organizations/Resources: Student, Academic, Education

♀ ★ ♿ Inclusion Center LGBTQIA+ Programs, Utah State University, 0185 Old Main Hall; 435-797-1924 tinyurl.com/rgcvfer ✎

Moab

Community Centers and/or Pride Organizations

♀ ★ Moab Pride, 375 S Main St; 970-639-0285 www.moab-pride.com

Ogden

AIDS/HIV Services, Education & Support

♂ Northern Utah Coalition, 536 24th St Ste 2B 801-393-4153

Funding: Endowment, Fundraising

♀ ★ Imperial Rainbow Court, POB 3131; 84409 www.irconu.org

Organizations/Resources: Family and Supporters

♂ Mama Dragons, Support for mothers of LGBTQIA children. mamadragons.org

Religious / Spiritual Resources

♂ ★ ♿ Glory to God Old Catholic Church, 375 Harrison Blvd; 801-394-0204 www.glory2god.org

♀ ☆ ♿ Unitarian Universalist Church of Ogden, 705 23rd St; 84401 801-394-3338 **HD** www.uuco.org office.uuco@gmail.com

Park City

Bars, Cafes, Clubs, Restaurants

♂ ○ ♿ Squatters Roadhouse Grill and Pub., 1900 Park Ave; 435-649-9868 www.squatters.com ⍩ ✗ ✎

Utah: Park City
Bars, Cafes, Clubs, Restaurants

322

GAYELLOW PAGES #42 2020-2021

Salt Lake City Area: Utah
Organizations: Student

♀ ⚲ ♿ Wasatch Brew Pub, 250 Main St 435-649-0900
www.wasatchbeers.com ⚥ ✗ ∥

Provo

Community Centers and/or Pride Organizations

⚦ ★ (♿) Provo Pride, POB 50423 84606 www.provopride.org
@ixx=

Counseling/Psychotherapy/Mental Health

⚦ Encircle: LGBT+ Family & Youth Resource Center, 91 W 200 S;
encircletogether.org

Religious / Spiritual Resources

♂ ☆ Provo Community Congregational United Church of Christ,
175 N University Ave; 84601 801-375-9115 www.provocommu-
nityucc.org

St George

Community Centers and/or Pride Organizations

⚦ Pride of Southern Utah, 307 N Main St, St George; www.prideof-
southernutah.org

Organizations/Resources: Family and Supporters

♂ ☆ PFLAG St George, 823 Harrison, St George 435-673-3356
fb.com/PflagStGeorgeUtah

Salt Lake City Area

Crisis, Anti-violence, & Helplines

♂ ☆ ♿ Rape Recovery Center, 2035 E 1300 E, Salt Lake City;
84105 801-467-7273 801-467-7282 www.raperecoverycenter.org
∥

Community Centers and/or Pride Organizations

⚦ ★ ♿ Utah Pride, 1380 Main St, Salt Lake City; 801-539-8800
www.utahpridefestival.org ∥

⚦ ★ ♿ Utah Pride Center, 1380 Main St, Salt Lake City; 84115
801-539-8800 www.utahpridecenter.org ∥

Bars, Cafes, Clubs, Restaurants
Salt Lake City

⚦ ● ⚲ Club Try-Angles, 251 W Harvey Milk Blvd W 900 S, Salt
Lake City; 801-364-3203 clubtryangles.com **DK** ∥

♂ ⚲ ♿ Squatters Pub Brewery, 147 W Broadway, Salt Lake City;
801-363-2739 www.squatters.com ∥

⚦ ● ⚲ Sun Trapp, 102 W 600 S, Salt Lake City; 385-235-6786
fb.com/thesuntrapp/ **CWP**

♂ ⚲ Tavernacle Social Club, 201 E Broadway, Salt Lake City; 801-
519-8900 www.tavernacle.com **P** ▦

♂ ⚲ Zest Kitchen & Bar, 275 S 200 W, Salt Lake City; 801-433-
0589 www.ZestSlc.com ⚥ ✗

Bookstores

♂ ⚲ Golden Braid Books, 151 S 500 E, Salt Lake City; 801-322-
1162 www.goldenbraidbooks.com

♀ ⚲ (♿) The King's English Bookshop, 1511 S 1500 E, Salt Lake
City; 84105-2896 801-484-9100 www.kingsenglish.com

♀ ⚲ Weller Book Works, 607 Trolley Square, Salt Lake City; 801-
328-2586 www.wellerbookworks.com ∥

Counseling/Psychotherapy/Mental Health

♂ ⚲ McQuade, Shannon, LCSW, LMT, 2290 E 4500 S #210, Holladay; 84117 801-712-6140 www.realcaring.org shannon@
realcaring.org

Funding: Endowment, Fundraising

⚦ ★ Royal Court of the Golden Spike Empire, PO Box 521126,
Salt Lake City; 84152 rcgse.org

Homes & Buildings: Cleaning, Maintenance, Repair,
General Contractors

♂ ⚲ Capitol Hill Construction, 814 E 100 S, Salt Lake City; 84102
801-533-0204 www.caphillcon.com dsr@caphillcon.com

Insurance (see also Financial Planning)

♂ ● Heath, Hans, LGBT Financial, 280 S Navajo St, Salt Lake
City; 84104 801-410-0739 www.lgbtfinancial.org ∥ Hans@
LGBTFinancial.org

Legal Services

♂ ● ♿ Wharton O'Brien, PLLC, 165 S Main St Ste 200, Salt
Lake City; 84111 801-649-3529 **H?** www.wolawutah.com ∥
chris@wolawutah.com

Organizations/Resources: Cultural, Dance, Performance

⚦ Damn These Heels LGBT Film Festival, Utah Film Center, 50 W
Broadway Ste 1125, Salt Lake City; 801-746-7000
tinyurl.com/msauvqv

♂ ☆ Salt Lake Men's Choir, 825 N 300 W #NE111, Salt Lake City;
www.saltlakemenschoir.org

⚦ ★ Temple Squares, POB 22447, Salt Lake City; 84122 801-449-
1293

Organizations/Resources: Family and Supporters

♂ ☆ PFLAG Salt Lake City, POB 520434, Salt Lake City; 84106
801-688-2281 pflag-saltlakecity.org

Organizations/Resources: Social, Recreation, Support

⚦ Queer Friends, POB 712483, Salt Lake City; 84171 801-810-
5773 www.queerfriends.org

⚦ ★ ⚲ Utah Bears, POB 2158, Salt Lake City; 84110
fb.com/utahbears/ ∥

Organizations/Resources: Student, Academic, Education

⚦ ★ GLBT Alliance in Social & Personality Psychology, University
of Utah Psych Department, 380 S 1530 E Room 502, Salt Lake
City; www.psych.utah.edu/gasp/

⚦ ★ Salt Lake Community College Rainbow Pride, 4600 S Redwood Rd, Salt Lake City; 84123 orgsync.com/38129/chapter
slcc.gsa@gmail.com

♀ ☆ ♿ U of U Women's Resource Center, 200 S Central Campus Dr Rm 411, Salt Lake City; 84112 801-581-8030 **H?** women-
scenter.utah.edu ∥ wrc@sa.utah.edu

Utah: Salt Lake City Area
Organizations: Student

323

GAYELLOW PAGES #42 2020-2021

State/County Resources : Vermont
Organizations: Youth

♀ ★ & University of Utah LGBT Resource Center, 200 S Central Campus Dr Room 409, Salt Lake City 801-587-7973 **HD** lgbt.utah.edu ✐

Organizations/Resources: Transgender/Gender Non-Conforming/Diverse

T ☆ Trans Adult Support Group, Utah Pride Center, 1380 Main St, Salt Lake City; 801-539-8800 utahpridecenter.org

Organizations/Resources: Youth (see also Family)

♀ ★ (?&) Utah Pride's Youth Activity Center, 1380 Main St, Salt Lake City; 801-539-8800 tinyurl.com/uhasls8 ✐

Real Estate (see also Mortgages)

♀ ● &♂ Lindsay, Dwight, Realtor, Imagine Real Estate, 5058 Three Fountains Circle, Salt Lake City; 84107 801-205-3166 fax 801-303-6901 www.dwightlindsay.com ✐ dwight@dwightlindsay.com

Religious / Spiritual Resources

♀ ☆ (?&) Holladay United Church of Christ, 2631 E Murray-Holladay Rd, Holladay; 84117 801-277-2631 www.holladayucc.org office@holladayucc.org

♂ ★ (?&) Sacred Light of Christ Community Church, 823 S 600 E, Salt Lake City; 801-595-0052 www.slccchurch.org

♀ ☆ &♂ Salt Lake Center for Spiritual Living, 193 W 2100 S, N Salt Lake; 84115 385-424-0126 **H?** www.spirituallyfree.org ✐

♀ ☆ &♂ St James Episcopal Church, 7486 S Union Park Ave, Midvale; 84047 801-566-1311 **HD** www.stjamesutah.com ✐ office@stjamesutah.com

Sports & Outdoor

♂ ★ Mountain West Flag Football League, fb.com/UtahGayFootballLeague/

♂ ★ Queer Utah Aquatic Club, POB 522263, Salt Lake City; 84152 www.quacquac.org

Zion & Bryce Canyon National Parks Area

Accommodation: Hotels, Inns, Guesthouses, B&B, Resorts

Rockville

♂ ● (?&) 2 Cranes Inn Zion, 125 E Main St (Hwy 9), Rockville; 84763 435-216-7700 2craneszion.com (☺?) ✐ ☺☺

Springdale

♂ ○ (?&) Red Rock Inn B&B Cottages, 998 Zion Park Blvd, Springdale; 84767 435-772-3139 www.redrockinn.com ✐ ☺☺ info@redrockinn.com

♂ ● Under The Eaves Inn, POB 29, Springdale 84767 435-772-3457 www.undertheeaves.com ✐ ☺☺

Vermont
State/County Resources

Crisis, Anti-violence, & Helplines

♂ ☆ &♂ Vermont Network Against Domestic & Sexual Violence, POB 405, Montpelier, VT 05601 802-223-1302 **H?** www.vtnetwork.org ✐ vtnetwork@vtnetwork.org

Community Centers and/or Pride Organizations

♂ ★ Pride Vermont, 255 S Champlain St Ste 12, Burlington, VT 05401 802-860-7812 www.pridevt.org

AIDS/HIV Services, Education & Support

♀ AIDS Project of Southern Vermont - Bennington, POB 1486, Brattleboro, VT 05302 802-254-4444 tinyurl.com/298slo9

♀ ☆ & Vermont CARES, POB 5248, Burlington, VT 05402-5248 802-863-2437 800-649-2437 **H?** www.vtcares.org ✐

♀ Vermont Department of Health Aids Services, Drawer 41 - H.A.S.H. POB 70, Burlington, VT 05402 802-863-7200 tinyurl.com/y9vu99y6

♀ ☆ Vermont People With AIDS Coalition, POB 11, Montpelier, VT 05601 802-229-5754 www.vtpwac.org

Financial Planning, Investment (see also Insurance)

♀ ● Lescoe, Donna, Choice Financial Services, POB 42, Starksboro, VT 05487 802-453-6677 www.donnalescoe.com

Funding: Endowment, Fundraising

♂ ★ Gay & Lesbian Fund of Vermont, POB 42, Randolph, VT 05060 www.glfundvt.org

♂ ★ &♂ Samara Fund at the Vermont Community Foundation, 3 Court St, Middlebury, VT 802-388-3355 **H?** www.vermontcf.org/samara

Health Care: Physical (see also Counseling/Mental Health)

♂ ★ &♂ Vermont Diversity Health Project, 255 S Champlain St Ste 12, Burlington, VT 802-860-7812 **H?** www.vdhp.org ✐

Leather Resources & Groups

♂ Green Mountain Leather Club, www.greenmountainleather.com

Organizations/Resources: Cultural, Dance, Performance

♀ CineSLAM: Vermont's LGBT Short Film Festival, 158 Kopkind Rd, Guilford, VT www.cineslam.com

Organizations/Resources: Political/Legislative/Advocacy

♂ ☆ &♂ American Civil Liberties Union of Vermont, POB 277, Montpelier, VT 05601 802-223-6304 www.acluvt.org

♂ ☆ Vermont Human Rights Commission, 14-16 Baldwin St, Montpelier, VT 802-828-1625 (members of protected categories) www.hrc.vermont.gov

Organizations/Resources: Social, Recreation, Support

♂ ★ (?&) Faerie Camp Destiny, POB 517, Chester, VT 05143 www.faeriecampdestiny.org

♂ ★ Green Mountain Growlers, groups.yahoo.com/group/GMGB/

♂ ★ Vermont Gay Social Alternatives, POB 237, Burlington, VT 05402 fb.com/groups/49624922906/

Organizations/Resources: Youth (see also Family)

♂ ★ &♂ Outright Vermont, POB 5235, Burlington, VT 05402 802-865-9677 www.outrightvt.org

Recovery

♂ ☆ Vermont Area Al-Anon and Alateen, POB 916, Barre, VT 05641 866-972-5266 www.vermontalanonalateen.org

Sports & Outdoor

♀ ☆ (?♿) Vermont Outdoors Woman, POB 10, North Ferrisburg, VT 05473 800-425-8747 www.voga.org
» Arlington: see Green Mountains Area

Barre

Crisis, Anti-violence, & Helplines

♂ ☆ ♿ Circle, POB 652; 05641 877-543-9498 **H** Services to abused women & men, but only women in our shelter. www.circlevt.org

Bellows Falls

Bookstores

♂ ○ ♿ Village Square Booksellers, 32 The Square; 802-463-9404 www.villagesquarebooks.com ∕
» Bolton Valley: see Burlington/Lake Champlain Area
» Brandon: see Green Mountains Area

Brattleboro

Crisis, Anti-violence, & Helplines

♀ Women's Freedom Center, POB 933; 05302 802-257-7364 www.womensfreedomcenter.net

Accommodation: Hotels, Inns, Guesthouses, B&B, Resorts
Newfane

♂ ● Frog Meadow, POB 332, Newfane; 05345 802-365-7242 877-365-7242 www.frogmeadow.com **N** ∕ ☺

♂ ○ The One Cat, 43 Clark St; 05301 802-579-1905 Guest rooms on 2nd floor www.theonecatvermont.com ∕ ☺☺ stay@ theonecatvermont.com

Bars, Cafes, Clubs, Restaurants

♂ ○ Metropolis Wine Bar, 55 Elliot St; 802-490-2255 fb.com/The-Metropolisbar/

Bookstores

♀ ○ ♿ Everyone's Books, 25 Elliot St 05301-3376 802-254-8160 **H?** www.everyonesbks.com ∕ everyonesbks@gmail.com

Campgrounds and RV Parks

♂ ● (?♿) MountainSide, 603-398-7871 www.mountainsidenh.com ☀∕ ☺

Recovery

● Brattleboro Retreat, POB 803; 05302 802-257-7785 www.brattlebororetreat.org

♂ ☆ Narcotics Anonymous Green Mountain Area Services, POB 6414; 05302 802-773-5575 www.gmana.org

Religious / Spiritual Resources

♂ ☆ ♿ All Souls Church UU, POB 2297 05303-2297 802-254-9377 www.ascvt.org ∕

Burlington/Lake Champlain Area

Crisis, Anti-violence, & Helplines

♂ ☆ ♿ HOPE Works, POB 92, Burlington; 05402 802-864-0555 Rape Crisis www.hopeworksvt.org ∕

● ★ ♿ SafeSpace Anti-Violence Program, Pride Center of Vermont, 255 S Champlain St Ste 12, Burlington; 05401 802-863-0003 866-869-7341 **H?** www.pridecentervt.org ∕

♂ ☆ ♿ Steps to End Domestic Violence, POB 1535, Burlington; 05402 802-658-1996 www.stepsvt.org

Community Centers and/or Pride Organizations

● ★ ♿ Pride Center of Vermont, 255 S Champlain St Ste 12, Burlington; 05401 802-860-7812 **H?** www.pridecentervt.org ∕ info@pridecentervt.org

Bars, Cafes, Clubs, Restaurants
Burlington

♂ ○ Club Metronome, 188 Main St, Burlington 802-658-4771 www.clubmetronome.com **D** ▦ ∕

♂ ○ The Daily Planet, 15 Center St, Burlington 802-862-9647 dailyplanetvt.com ✕

♂ ○ Leunig's Bistro & Lounge, 115 Church St, Burlington; 802-863-3759 www.leunigsbistro.com ⌕ ✕ @ixx=

♂ ○ ♿ Nectar's, 188 Main St, Burlington; 802-658-4771 www.liveatnectars.com **D** ▦ ∕

♂ ○ Red Square, 136 Church St, Burlington 802-859-8909 fb.com/redsquarevt/ **D** ⌕ ✕ ▦ ∕
Shelburne

♂ ○ Barkeaters, 97 Falls Rd, Shelburne 802-985-2830 www.barkeatersrestaurant.com ✕

Bookstores

♂ ● The Flying Pig Bookstore, 5247 Shelburne Rd, Shelburne; 802-985-3999 www.flyingpigbooks.com

♂ ○ ♿ Phoenix Books, 2 Carmichael St, Essex; 802-872-7111 www.phoenixbooks.biz ▯ ∕

♂ ○ ♿ Phoenix Books, 191 Bank St, Burlington; 05401 802-448-3350 www.phoenixbooks.biz info@phoenixbooks.biz

Counseling/Psychotherapy/Mental Health

♂ ● ♿ Barnett, Autumn, MSW, 270 Battery St, Burlington; 05401 802-622-1131 www.autumnbarnett.net autumn@ autumnbarnett.net

Erotica / Adult Stores / Safe Sex Supplies

♂ ○ ♿ Imago, 257 Jasper Mine Rd Ste 100, Colchester; 05446 802-893-2977 www.imagoxxx.com

Gifts, Cards, Pride, etc.

♂ ○ ♿ Peace & Justice Store, 60 Lake St, Burlington; 05401 802-863-2345 x2 A fair trade, socially responsible marketplace carrying a wide assortment of products. www.pjcvt.org info@pjcvt.org

Grooming, Personal Care, Spa Services

♀ ○ ♿ Bare Medical Spa + Laser Center, 95 St Paul St Ste 110, Burlington; 05401 802-861-2273 www.barevt.com ✗ info@barevt.com

Health Care: Physical (see also Counseling/Mental Health)

♀ ● ♿ Boyman, Kym, MD, FACOG, Vermont Gynecology, 1775 Williston Rd #110, S Burlington; 05403 802-735-1252 877-698-8496 (transmen & transwomen welcome) www.vtgyn.com ✗ kboyman@vtgyn.com

Legal Services

♂ ● Keller, Mark J, 8 Essex Way Ste 104 B, Essex Jct; 05452 802-879-7211 www.mkellerlaw.com lawofficemjkeller@gmail.com

♂ ● ♿ Lashman, Deborah, PC, 47 Maple St Ste 318, Burlington; 05401 802-861-7800 **H?** dlashman@lashmanlaw.com

Organizations/Resources: Cultural, Dance, Performance

♀ ★ House of LeMay, tinyurl.com/ycodx5an

Organizations/Resources: Social, Recreation, Support

♂ Glam Vermont, Pride Center of Vermont, 255 S Champlain St #12, Burlington; 802-860-7812 glamvt.org

♀ Pop-Up! A Queer Dance Party, fb.com/PopUpQDP

Organizations/Resources: Student, Academic, Education

♀ ★ ♿ Include: LGBTQQIAA, Champlain College, POB 670, Burlington; 05402 802-865-5487 tinyurl.com/c544e8

♀ ★ ♿ Prism Center at UVM, 100 Allen House, 461 Main St, Burlington; 802-656-8637 **H?** www.uvm.edu/prism ✗

♀ ★ St Michaels College Common Ground, LIGHT Office, Room 223A in Alliot Hall, Colchester; 802-654-2235

♀ ★ ♿ University of Vermont Free To Be, SGA Galaxy Space 311-L, Burlington www.uvm.edu/~free2b

Recovery

♂ ☆ Narcotics Anonymous Champlain Valley Area, PO Box 64714, Burlington; 05406 802-862-4516 www.cvana.org

Religious / Spiritual Resources

♂ ☆ ♿ College Street Congregational Church, 265 College St, Burlington; 05401 802-864-7704 www.collegestreetchurch.org info@collegestreetchurch.org
>> *Cambridge: see Smugglers' Notch Area*
>> *Chester: see Green Mountains Area*
>> *Colchester: see Burlington/Lake Champlain Area*

Dorset

Organizations/Resources: Family and Supporters

♂ PFLAG Dorset, POB 263; 05251 802-768-1585 tinyurl.com/kufjsxo
>> *Essex: see Burlington/Lake Champlain Area*
>> *Goshen: see Green Mountains Area*

Green Mountains Area

Accommodation: Hotels, Inns, Guesthouses, B&B, Resorts
Hyde Park

♂ ○ Fitch Hill Inn B&B, 258 Fitch Hill Rd, Hyde Park; 05655-9363 802-888-3834 800-639-2903 www.fitchhillinn.com ✗ ⊛ innkeeper@fitchhillinn.com

Killington

♂ ○ ♿ North Star Lodge, 78 Weathervane Dr, Killington; 05751 802-422-4040 **H?** www.northstarinn.com ✗ ⊛ ⊛

Marshfield

♂ ● (?♿) Marshfield Inn & Motel, 5630 US Rte 2, Marshfield; 05658 802-426-3383 www.marshfieldinn.com (♣?) ✗ ⊛

Stowe

♂ ● Northern Lights Lodge, 4441 Mountain Road, Stowe; 802-253-8541 www.stowelodge.com

Sunderland

♂ ● The Ira Allen House, 6311 Vermont Route 7A, Sunderland; 05250 802-362-2284 www.IraAllenHouse.com (♣?) ✗ ⊛ iraallenhouse@gmail.com

Waitsfield

♂ ● Farm On Mad River, 240 Kingsbury Rd, Waitsfield; 802-496-7133 www.madriverfarm.com

♂ ● White Horse Inn, 999 German Flats Rd, Waitsfield; 05673 802-496-9448 tinyurl.com/mn2ejao (♣?) ✗ ⊛ ⊛ bob@whitehorse inn-vermont.com

Waterbury

♂ ● Grunberg Haus B&B & Cabins, 94 Pine St, Waterbury; 802-244-7726 www.grunberghaus.com (♣?) ✗ ⊛

♂ ● (?♿) **Moose Meadow Lodge & Treehouse, 607 Crossett Hill Rd, Waterbury; 05676 802-244-5378 fax 802-244-1713 Luxury log home B&B, 86 acres, weddings, serenity. www.moosemeadowlodge.net** ✗ ♥

♂ ○ The Old Stagecoach Inn, 18 N Main St, Waterbury; 05676-1810 802-244-5056 www.oldstagecoach.com ✗ ⊛ ⊛ lodging@oldstagecoach.com

Woodstock

♂ ○ Ardmore Inn, 23 Pleasant St, Woodstock; 05091 802-457-3887 www.ardmoreinn.com ✗ ⊛ Innkeeper@Ardmoreinn.com

♂ ● Deer Brook Inn, 4548 W Woodstock Rd, Woodstock 802-672-3713 www.deerbrookinn.com (♣?) ✗ ⊛

♂ ● (?♿) The Lincoln Inn & Restaurant At The Covered Bridge, 2709 W Woodstock Rd, Woodstock; 05091 802-457-7052 www.lincolninn.com ✗ ✗ ⊛ info@lincolninn.com

♂ ○ (?♿) The Village Inn of Woodstock, 41 Pleasant St, Woodstock; 05091-1146 802-457-1255 tinyurl.com/39n6od ✗ ⊛ stay@villageinnofwoodstock.com

♂ ○ The Woodstocker B&B, 61 River St, Woodstock 05091 802-457-3896 www.thewoodstockerbnb.com ✗ ⊛ stay@thewoodstockerbnb.com

Accommodation Rental: Furnished / Vacation (& AirBNB)
Northfield

♂ ○ (?♿) The Woods Lodge, 900 Bull Run Rd, Northfield; 05663 802-778-0205 www.thewoodsvt.com ✗ ⊛ info@thewoodsvt.com

Vermont: Green Mountains Area
Accommodation: Rentals

326

GAYELLOW PAGES #42 2020-2021

S Barre: Vermont
Campgrounds and RV Parks

Stowe

♂ • (⅔) Stowe Cabins in the Woods, Route 100 Box 128, Waterbury Center; 802-244-8533 www.stowecabins.com ♣ ✗ ☺

Bars, Cafes, Clubs, Restaurants
Ludlow

♂ ○ ♿ Downtown Grocery, 41 Depot St, Ludlow; 802-228-7566 www.thedowntowngrocery.com ✗

Waterbury Center

♂ ○ ♿ Michael's on the Hill, 4182 Waterbury-Stowe Rd, Route 100 N, Waterbury Center; 802-244-7476 www.michaelsonthehill.com ☂ ✗ ✗ mail@michaelsonthehill.com

Bookstores

♂ ○ ♿ Northshire Bookstore, 4869 Main St, Manchester Center; 802-362-2200 www.northshire.com

♂ ○ ♿ Phoenix Books, 2 Center St, Rutland; 05701 802-855-8078 www.phoenixbooks.biz info@phoenixbooks.biz

Sports & Outdoor

♂ ★ Winter Rendezvous Gay Ski Week, 50 Victory Rd, Boston, MA 617-504-3131 www.winterrendezvous.com

Hardwick

Bookstores

♂ ○ ♿ Galaxy Bookstore, Box 1219; / 41 S Main St 802-472-5533 www.galaxybookshop.com

Huntington

Accommodation: Communities, Intentional

♀ ☆ (⅔) Huntington Open Women's Land (HOWL), POB 53; 05462 802-434-3953 www.howlvt.org ✗ howlvt@gmail.com

Jay

Accommodation: Hotels, Inns, Guesthouses, B&B, Resorts
Montgomery Center

♂ • (⅔) The INN, 241 Main St / POB 420, Montgomery Center 05471 802-326-4391 www.theinn.us (♣?) ✗ ☺ ☺

» *Jeffersonville: see Smugglers' Notch Area*
» *Jerusalem: see Green Mountains Area*
» *Killington: see Green Mountains Area*
» *Lincoln: see Green Mountains Area*

Londonderry

Accommodation Rental: Furnished / Vacation (& AirBNB)

♂ • ♿ Justin Lake Lodge, 2232 Little Pond Rd; 802-558-7661 www.justinlake.com ✗ ☺

» *Ludlow: see Green Mountains Area*
» *Manchester: see Green Mountains Area*
» *Manchester Center: see Green Mountains Area*
» *Manchester Village: see Green Mountains Area*
» *Marshfield: see Green Mountains Area*

Middlebury

Crisis, Anti-violence, & Helplines

♀ ☆ (⅔) WomenSafe, Inc, POB 67; 05753 802-388-4205 www.womensafe.net ✗

Organizations/Resources: Student, Academic, Education

♂ ★ ♿ Middlebury College Queers and Allies, 452 College St; fb.com/MiddQandA

Montpelier

Bookstores

♂ ○ ♿ Bear Pond Books, 77 Main St 802-229-0774 www.bearpondbooks.com

» *Moretown: see Green Mountains Area*

Mount Snow

Accommodation: Hotels, Inns, Guesthouses, B&B, Resorts
West Dover

♂ • Inn at Mount Snow, 401 Route 100, West Dover 802-464-8388 www.theinnatmountsnow.com (♣?) ✗ ☺

» *Newfane: see Brattleboro*

Norwich

Financial Planning, Investment (see also Insurance)

♂ ○ (⅔) Clean Yield Asset Management, Elizabeth Glenshaw, POB 874; 05055 802-526-2525 800-809-6439 www.cleanyield.com elizabeth@cleanyield.com

» *Plainfield: see Green Mountains Area*

Quechee

Accommodation: Hotels, Inns, Guesthouses, B&B, Resorts

♂ ○ (⅔) Inn at Clearwater Pond, 984 Quechee-Hartland Rd; 05059 802-295-0606 www.innatclearwaterpond.com (♣?) ✗ ☺ innatclearwaterpond@gmail.com

Richmond

Bars, Cafes, Clubs, Restaurants

♂ ○ (⅔) The Kitchen Table Bistro, 1840 Main St; 802-434-8686 kitchentablebistro.com ✗

Rochester

Accommodation: Hotels, Inns, Guesthouses, B&B, Resorts

♂ • (⅔) Huntington House Inn, 19 Huntington Place; 802-767-9140 www.huntingtonhouseinn.com ♣ ✗ ☺

S Barre

Campgrounds and RV Parks

♂ • ♿ Lazy Lions Campground, POB 269, S Barre; 05670 802-479-2823 www.lazylions.com ♣ ✗

Vermont: St Johnsbury
Crisis, Anti-violence, & Helplines
327
GAYELLOW PAGES #42 2020-2021
State/County Resources : Virginia
Organizations: Student

St Johnsbury

Crisis, Anti-violence, & Helplines

♀ ☆ 👬 Umbrella, 1216 Railroad St Ste C 802-748-1992 **H?** www.umbrellanek.org

Saxtons River

Accommodation Rental: Furnished / Vacation (& AirBNB)

♂ • Saxtons River Getaway, POB 69; 05154 802-869-1236 www.saxtonsgetaway.com ⚦ ⊛

Springfield

Campgrounds and RV Parks

♂ ○ Tree Farm Campground, 53 Skitchewaug Trail 05156 802-885-2889 www.treefarmcampground.com ⚤ ⚦ treefarm campground@gmail.com

>> *Stowe: see Green Mountains Area*
>> *Waitsfield: see Green Mountains Area*
>> *Warren: see Green Mountains Area*
>> *Waterbury: see Green Mountains Area*

Wells River

Accommodation: Hotels, Inns, Guesthouses, B&B, Resorts

♂ • The Gargoyle House, 3351 Wallace Hill Rd 802-429-2341 www.gargoylehouse.com **N** (⚤?) ⚦ ⊛
>> *Woodstock: see Green Mountains Area*

Virgin Islands
State/County Resources

Accommodation Rental: Furnished / Vacation (& AirBNB)

♂ ○ Rent A Villa, 800-533-6863 www.stcroixrentavilla.com ⚦ ⊛ vivillas@aol.com

St Croix

Accommodation: Hotels, Inns, Guesthouses, B&B, Resorts
Frederiksted

♂ • (⚤) Sand Castle on the Beach Hotel & Resort, 127 Smithfield / Veterans Shore Dr, Frederiksted; 00840-3677 340-772-1205 www.sandcastleonthebeach.com � ✕ (⚤?) ⚦ ⊛ info@sand castleonthebeach.com

Accommodation Rental: Furnished / Vacation (& AirBNB)
Christiansted

♂ ○ Longford Hideaway, POB 895, Christiansted 00821-0895 340-277-9851 www.longfordhideaway.com ⚦ ⊛ ⊛ valeria@longford hideaway.com

St John

Accommodation Rental: Furnished / Vacation (& AirBNB)

♂ ○ Great Expectations, 165 Chocolate Hole, St John; 00831 617-314-6836 greatexpectationsstj.com ⚦ ⊛ relax@great expectationsstj.com

♀ ○ The Hillcrest Guest House, 157 Enighed, Cruz Bay, St John; 00830 340-776-6774 340-998-8388 www.HillcrestStJohn.com ⚦ ⊛ ♥ hillcrestguesthouse@yahoo.com

♀ ○ (⚤) Private Homes for Private Vacations, Inc., 7605 Mamey Peak, St John; 00830-9512 340-776-6876 www.private-homesvi.com ⚦ ⊛

St Thomas

Bars, Cafes, Clubs, Restaurants
Charlotte Amalie

♀ ○ Oceana Restaurant & Wine Bar, 8 Honduras - Villa Olga, Charlotte Amalie; 340-774-4262 www.oceanavi.com � ✕

♀ ○ Mafolie Hotel & Restaurant, 7091 Estate Mafolie, St Thomas; 340-774-2790 www.mafolie.com � ✕ ⊓ ⚦

♀ ○ Virgilio's, 5150 Dronnigens Gade Ste 7, St Thomas; 340-776-4920 www.virgiliosvi.com ✕

Virginia
State/County Resources

Crisis, Anti-violence, & Helplines

♂ The James House, 6610 Commons Dr Suite C, Prince George, VA 804-458-2840 thejameshouse.org

⚥ ★ 👬 Virginia Anti-violence Project, POB 7445, Richmond, VA 23221 804-925-9242 virginiaavp.org

Community Centers and/or Pride Organizations

⚥ ★ Virginia Pride, 1407 Sherwood Ave, Richmond, VA 804-592-1093 www.vapride.org

Mortgages/Home Ownership (see also Banks, Real Estate)

♂ ○ 👬 Wilt, Tammy L., NMLS #195702, Movement Mortgage, 3510 Remson Cr Ste 301, Charlottesville, VA 434-242-0046 movement.com/lo/tammy-wilt/

Organizations/Resources: Political/Legislative/Advocacy

♀ American Civil Liberties Union, 701 E Franklin St #1412, Richmond, VA 804-644-8022 www.acluva.org

⚥ ★ Equality Virginia, POB 17860, Richmond, VA 23226 804-643-4816 www.equalityvirginia.org

⚥ ★ LGBT Democrats of Virginia, POB 25037, Richmond, VA 23260 www.lgbtvadem.org

♀ Virginia Organizing, 703 Concord Ave, Charlottesville, VA 434-984-4655 virginia-organizing.org

Organizations/Resources: Sexual Focus / Safe Sex

♂ (⚤) Teddy Bear Leather Club of Virginia, www.tblcofvirginia.com

Organizations/Resources: Student, Academic, Education

♀ ☆ (⚤) GLSEN Northern Virginia, 7105 Sudley Rd, Manassas, VA 571-208-2424 **H?** www.glsen.org/nova ⚦

Organizations/Resources: Transgender/Gender Non-Conforming/Diverse

T ☆ Virginia Transgender Resource and Referral List, Virginia Department of Health, 109 Governor Street, Room 326, Richmond, VA 23219 804-864-8012 tinyurl.com/yachln7l Ted.Heck@vdh.virginia.gov

Organizations/Resources: Youth (see also Family)

♂ ★ ♂♂ Side by Side, POB 5542, Richmond, VA 23220 888-644-4390 www.sidebysideva.org ✗

Religious / Spiritual Resources

♂ ★ Dignity/Northern Virginia, POB 100566, Arlington, VA 22210-3566 www.dignitynova.org DignityNova@gmail.com

Sports & Outdoor

♂ Mid-Atlantic Amateur Softball Association, www.mid-atlanticsoftball.org

♂ Rainbow Spinnakers Sailing Club, fb.com/groups/78486506950/

Afton

Accommodation: Hotels, Inns, Guesthouses, B&B, Resorts

♂ ○ WildManDan Beercentric B&B and Brewery, 279 Avon Rd; 22920 434-270-0404 www.wmdb3.com ✗ ⊗ terri@tatarka.me

Alexandria

Antiques & Collectibles

♀ ● Spurgeon Lewis Antiques, 112 N Columbus St 703-548-4917 www.spurgeonlewis.com

Organizations/Resources: Political/Legislative/Advocacy

♀ Equality Prince William, POB 6983, Woodbridge; 22195 703-791-3479 tinyurl.com/khkwwha

Religious / Spiritual Resources

♀ ☆ Fairlington Presbyterian Church, 3846 King St 22302 703-931-7344 www.fpcusa.org office@fpcusa.org

Annandale

Accounting, Bookkeeping, Tax Services

♀ ● Kresslein, George Jr, CPA, 5155 Piedmont Place 22003 703-354-1750 www.kressleincpa.com ✗ gkresslein@kressleincpa.com

Religious / Spiritual Resources

♀ ☆ ♂♂ Little River United Church of Christ, 8410 Little River Turnpike (Route 236); 22003-3798 703-978-3060 www.lrucc.org office@lrucc.org

♀ ☆ ♂♂ Ravensworth Baptist Church, 5100 Ravensworth Rd; 22003 703-941-4113 **HD** www.ravensworthbaptist.org rbc@ravensworthbaptist.org

Appomattox

Accommodation: Hotels, Inns, Guesthouses, B&B, Resorts

♂ ○ ♂♂ The Babcock House, 250 Oakleigh Ave; 24522 434-352-7532 babcockhouse.com ✗ ⊗ babcockhousebnb@aol.com

» *Arlington: see also Washington Area*

Arlington

Information, Media & Publications

♂ ★ (?♂) Arlington Gay & Lesbian Alliance, POB 100324, Arlington; 22210 571-969-4370 www.agla.org

Bars, Cafes, Clubs, Restaurants

♂ ● Federico Ristorante Italiano, 519 23rd St S, Arlington; 703-486-0519 tinyurl.com/y42lnq9s ✗

♀ ● Freddie's Beach Bar & Restaurant, 555 S 23rd St, Arlington; 703-685-0555 www.freddiesbeachbar.com ♉ ✗ ▥

Health Care: Physical (see also Counseling/Mental Health)

♀ ○ Advanced Health Center, 46 S Glebe Rd Ste 100, Arlington; 22204 703-521-0644 www.advhealthctr.com

♂ ● ♂ Sansfaute, Jean-Luc, DC, Skyline Wellness Center, 1600 Wilson Blvd Ste 22209, Arlington; 22209 703-879-5144 www.skylinewellness.com drjls@skylinewellness.com

Organizations/Resources: Social, Recreation, Support

♀ NOVA GLBTQ Professionals, www.meetup.com/novaglp/

Organizations/Resources: Transgender/Gender Non-Conforming/Diverse

T ☆ ♂♂ TransGender Education Association, 5765 F Burke Centre Parkway Ste 167, Burke www.tgeagw.org

Printing/Mailing & Promotional Items

♀ ● ♂♂ DKG Promotions, 1608 S Taylor St, Arlington; 22204 202-639-8570 www.dkgpromotions.com

Real Estate (see also Mortgages)

♀ ○ ♂♂ Mentis, John, Realtor, Long & Foster Real Estate, 4600 Lee Highway, Arlington; 22207 703-522-0500 202-549-0081 www.johnmentis.com ✗ john.mentis@longandfoster.com

Blacksburg

Religious / Spiritual Resources

♀ ☆ ♂♂ UU Congregation of Blacksburg, PO Box 10116; 24062-0116 540-552-9716 **HD** uucnrv.org ✗ administrator@uucnrv.org

Brookneal

Bars, Cafes, Clubs, Restaurants

♀ ● ♂♂ Staunton River Brewing Co. at Sans Soucy Vineyards, 1571 Mount Calvary Rd; 434-376-9463 www.stauntonriverbrewing.com

Charlottesville Area

Community Centers and/or Pride Organizations

♀ Charlottesville Pride Community Network, PO Box 1512, Charlottesville; 22902 cvillepride.org

Accommodation: Hotels, Inns, Guesthouses, B&B, Resorts
Charlottesville

♂ ● Inn at Court Square, 410 Jefferson St, Charlottesville; 434-295-2800 www.innatcourtsquare.com ✔ ⊗

♀ ○ Inn at the Crossroads, POB 6519, Charlottesville; 22906 / 5010 Plank Rd at Pippin Hill Farm & Vineyard 434-979-6452 www.crossroadsinn.com ✔ ⊗ ⊗ innkeeper@crossroadsinn.com

Accommodation Rental: Furnished / Vacation (& AirBNB)
Crozet

♀ ○ (?⬥) Montfair Resort Farm, 2500 Bezaleel Dr, Crozet; 22932 434-823-5202 www.montfairresortfarm.com ❖ ✔ ⊗ montfair@montfairresortfarm.com

Bars, Cafes, Clubs, Restaurants
Charlottesville

♂ ★ (?⬥) Impulse Gay Social Club, 1417 N Emmet St, Charlottesville; / Fri, Sat, 1st Sun check schedule 434-973-1821 **H?** impulse-gsc.com **DKP** ▦

Lovingston

♀ ○ Rapunzels Coffee & Books, 924 Front St, Lovingston; 434-263-6660 www.rapunzelscoffee.com ⫟

Campgrounds and RV Parks

♀ ● (?⬥) CampOut, 9505 Minna Dr, Henrico, VA 804-301-3553 www.campoutva.com **P** (❖?) ⊗

Counseling/Psychotherapy/Mental Health

♀ ○ Albemarle Counseling Associates, PLLC, 106 Caty Lane, Charlottesville; 22901 434-978-3900 acamentalhealth.com johnpenn@acamentalhealth.com

♀ ○ McKinley-Oakes, Jim, LCSW, 1020 E Jefferson St, Charlottesville; 434-760-1057 www.jimmckinley-oakes.com ✔

♀ ● Turner, John Penn, LPC, LSATP, Albemarle Counseling Associates, PLLC, 106 Caty Lane, Charlottesville; 22901 434-978-3900 www.acamentalhealth.com johnpenn@acamentalhealth.com

Legal Services

♀ ○ Tiller, Jessica A, Estate Planning of Charlottesville, PLLC, POB 6094, Charlottesville; 22906 434-219-9896 tinyurl.com/zvyjulj

Organizations/Resources: Family and Supporters

♀ ☆ PFLAG Blue Ridge, POB 5057, Charlottesville 22905 www.pflagblueridge.org

Organizations/Resources: Student, Academic, Education

♂ ★ ⬥⬥ LGBTQ Center, University of VIrginia, POB 400701, Charlottesville; 22904 434-982-2843 tinyurl.com/nt7wzpk ✔

♀ ☆ University of Virginia Women's Center, 1400 University Ave, Charlottesville; 434-982-2361 tinyurl.com/y9dvope

Real Estate (see also Mortgages)

♂ ○ Hitt, Kevin W, Realtor, Keller Williams Alliance 434-529-7948

Religious / Spiritual Resources

♀ ☆ Thomas Jefferson Memorial Church UU, 717 Rugby Rd, Charlottesville; 22903 434-293-8179 www.uucharlottesville.org info@uucharlottesville.org

---

» Chesapeake: see Hampton Roads Area

Danville

Organizations/Resources: Family and Supporters

♀ ☆ PFLAG Danville, POB 3569; 24541 434-429-1078 tinyurl.com/y9grennb

Fairfax

Legal Services

♀ ● ⬥⬥ Abrams, Sheri R., 10467 White Granite Dr Ste 306, Oakton; 22124 571-328-5795 www.sheriabrams.com sheri@sheriabrams.com

Organizations/Resources: Student, Academic, Education

♂ ★ George Mason University Office of LGBTQ Resources, SUB I, Room 2200 MSN 2F6 4400 University Drive, MSN 2F6, Fairfax 703-993-2702 lgbtq.gmu.edu

♂ ★ ⬥⬥ George Mason University Pride Alliance, Student Union Building 1 Room 225, Mailstop 2D6, 4400 University Dr, Fairfax; tinyurl.com/yyr7yv7n ✔

Religious / Spiritual Resources

♂ ★ ⬥⬥ MCC of Northern Virginia, 10383 Democracy Ln, Fairfax; 703-691-0930 www.mccnova.org

Ferrum

Organizations/Resources: Student, Academic, Education

♂ ★ Ferrum College Spectrum - LGBT Club, POB 1000; 24088 540-365-4494

Floyd

Organizations/Resources: Family and Supporters

♀ ☆ PFLAG Floyd, 276-734-5544 floydpflag.org

Fredericksburg

AIDS/HIV Services, Education & Support

♀ ☆ FAHASS, 4701 Market St Ste B; 22408 540-907-4555 fax 540-907-4318 www.fahass.org

Organizations/Resources: Family and Supporters

♀ ☆ PFLAG Fredericksburg, Christ Lutheran Church, 1300 Augustine St, Spotsylvania; 540-369-6002 fb.com/PFLAG-Fredericksburg

Organizations/Resources: Student, Academic, Education

♂ ★ University of Mary Washington Prism, 1301 College Ave; fb.com/umwprism

» Goshen: see Shenandoah Valley
» Hampton: see Hampton Roads Area

Hampton Roads Area

Community Centers and/or Pride Organizations

♂ ★ Hampton Roads Pride, POB 41082, Norfolk 23541 757-889-9101 www.hamptonroadspride.org

Virginia: Hampton Roads Area
Community Centers / Pride

330

GAYELLOW PAGES #42 2020-2021

Marion : Virginia
Accommodation

♂ ★ && The LGBT Life Center, 248 W 24th St, Norfolk 757-640-0929 www.lgbtlifecenter.org ✒

Accommodation: Hotels, Inns, Guesthouses, B&B, Resorts
Virginia Beach

♂ ● (♿) The Capes Hotel, 2001 Atlantic Ave, Va Bch; 757-428-5421 www.capeshotel.com ✒ Ⓢ

Accounting, Bookkeeping, Tax Services

♂ ● Hartman, Gary D, CPA, 2545 Bombay Landing, Va Bch; 23456 757-301-1040 hartmancpa.com ✒ garyd@hartmancpa.com

Bars, Cafes, Clubs, Restaurants
Norfolk

♀ 37th and Zen, 1083 W 37th St, Norfolk 757-533-5151 fb.com/37thandzen/ 🍸 ✕ 🍽

♀ Hershee Bar at 37th and Zen, 1083 W 37th St, Norfolk; 757-533-5151 tinyurl.com/ybk38qmy 🍸 ✕🍽

♂ ○ MJ's Tavern, 4019 Granby St, Norfolk 757-648-8942 www.mjtavern.com 🍸 ✕

♀ ● The Wave, 4107 Colley Ave, Norfolk 757-440-5911 tinyurl.com/46dyg35 D 🍸 ✕ 🍽

Virginia Beach

♀ Rainbow Cactus, 3472 Holland Rd, Va Bch 757-368-0441 www.therainbowcactus.com

Counseling/Psychotherapy/Mental Health

♂ ○ Hansen, Cynthia A, LCSW, 1878 E Ocean View Ave, Norfolk; 23503-2564 757-583-1878 lcswhansen@cox.net

♂ ● && Hooper, Kathleen, LCSW, Associates At York, Inc 909 Glenrock Rd Ste A, Norfolk; 23502 757-828-4893 **H?** www.therapistnorfolkva.com

Legal Services

♂ ○ ⚢ Kistler, K Page, PC, Family Law, 909 First Colonial Rd Ste 101, Va Bch; 757-271-3279 www.kpagekistler.com

Organizations/Resources: Business & Professional Associations, Labor Advocacy

♀ ★ (♿) Hampton Roads Business Outreach (HRBOR), POB 11650, Norfolk; 23517 757-324-3782 **H?** www.hrbor.org

Organizations/Resources: Cultural, Dance, Performance

♀ ★ Reel it Out, 248 W 24th St, Norfolk 757-640-0929 www.reelitout.com

Organizations/Resources: Family and Supporters

♂ ☆ PFLAG Norfolk/S Hampton Roads, LGBT Center, 247 W 25th St, Norfolk; 23517 757-640-0929 www.pflaghr.com pflagnorfolk@gmail.com

Organizations/Resources: Social, Recreation, Support

♀ ★ && Tidewater Prime Timers of SE Va, POB 11647, Norfolk; 23517-0647 757-623-6943 **H?** primetimersww.com/tidewater/tidewaterpters@gmail.com

Organizations/Resources: Student, Academic, Education

♀ ★ Christopher Newport University Spectrum, David Student Union 357, 1000 University Place, Newport News; 757-594-7260 fb.com/groups/2201142654

♀ ★ && ODU Sexuality and Gender Alliance, 1075 Webb Center #1059, Norfolk; 757-683-4328 sites.wp.odu.edu/odusaga

♀ ★ William & Mary Lambda Alliance, Organization 104, 110 Sadler Center, Williamsburg; tinyurl.com/y85t2ez3

Organizations/Resources: Transgender/Gender Non-Conforming/Diverse

T Trans Masculine Peer Group, LGBT Life Center 247 W 25th St, Norfolk; 757-640-0929 tinyurl.com/yxmoc8r4

Real Estate (see also Mortgages)

♂ ○ && Judy Boone Realty, 809 E Ocean View Ave, Norfolk; 23503 757-587-2800 www.judyboonerealty.com ✒ jbr@judyboonerealty.com

♂ ○ Kovach, Colleen, Howard Hanna/WEW, 2204 Hampton Blvd, Norfolk; 23517 757-575-9005 757-625-2580 tinyurl.com/yamxdz88 ColleenKovach@howardhanna.com

Religious / Spiritual Resources

♀ ★ && New Life MCC of Hampton Roads, 1000 Sunset Dr, Norfolk; 757-434-2892 www.newlifemcc.net ✒

♂ ☆ (♿) Warwick United Church of Christ, POB 120491, Newport News; 23612 / 10 Matoaka Lane 757-599-5164 www.warwickucc.com welcome@warwickucc.com

Sports & Outdoor

♀ ★ Friday Night Out Bowling League, 757-754-9665 tinyurl.com/64nump

♀ ☆ Womens United Softball Association, www.norfolkwusa.com

Independence

Accommodation: Hotels, Inns, Guesthouses, B&B, Resorts

♂ ● (♿) Ward Manor At Buck Mountain, 1298 Saddle Creek Rd; 276-773-3390 www.wardmanor.com (🐾?) (Ⓢ)
>> Lexington: see Shenandoah Valley
>> Luray: see Shenandoah Valley

Manassas

Organizations/Resources: Family and Supporters

♀ PFLAG - Prince William, Bull Run Unitarian Universalists, 9350 Main St

Marion

Accommodation: Hotels, Inns, Guesthouses, B&B, Resorts

♂ ○ Collins House Inn, 204 W Main St; 24354 276-781-0250 www.collinshouseinn.com ✒ Ⓢ Ⓢ stay@collinshouseinn.com
>> McLean: see DC Washington Area

Virginia: Meadowview
Religious

331
GAYELLOW PAGES #42 2020-2021

Richmond Area: Virginia
Organizations: Student

Meadowview

Religious / Spiritual Resources

♀ ☆ ♿ Unitarian Universalist Church of the Highlands, POB 238; 24361 **HD** www.myuuch.org contactus@myuuch.org
» *Newport News: see Hampton Roads Area*

Onancock

Accommodation: Hotels, Inns, Guesthouses, B&B, Resorts

♀ ○ Inn at Onancock, 30 North St; 757-789-7711 Dog friendly www.innatonancock.com ⚘ ✗ ⊛
» *Portsmouth: see Hampton Roads Area*

Radford

Organizations/Resources: Student, Academic, Education

⚢ ★ Radford University Spectrum, 801 E Main St fb.com/spectrum-radford/

Reston

Bars, Cafes, Clubs, Restaurants

♀ ○ Lake Anne Coffee House & Wine Bar, 1612 Washington Plaza N; 703-481-9766 lakeannecoffeehouse.com

Organizations/Resources: Social, Recreation, Support

⚢ ★ ♿ Dulles Triangles, POB 3411; 20195 www.dullestriangles.com

Richmond Area

Community Centers and/or Pride Organizations

⚢ ★ Diversity Richmond, 1407 Sherwood Ave, Richmond; 804-622-4646 diversityrichmond.org

Accommodation: Hotels, Inns, Guesthouses, B&B, Resorts
King William

♂ ○ Zebulon's Grotto, Charles, 281 Roane Oak Trail, King William; / Clothing Optional Bed & Breakfast for Men; Recreation Area and Tent Camping Sites Available 804-240-7823 www.zebulonsgrotto.com **N** (⚘?) ✗ ⊛

Bars, Cafes, Clubs, Restaurants
Petersburg

♀ ● ♿ Wabi-Sabi, 29 Bollingbrook St, Petersburg; 804-862-1365 www.eatwabisabi.com **D** ⚥ ✗ wabisabi708@gmail.com
Richmond

⚢ ● Babe's of Carytown, 3166 W Cary St, Richmond; 804-355-9330 fb.com/babesofcarytown ⚥ ✗

⚢ ● Barcode, 6 E Grace St, Richmond 804-648-2040 www.barcoderva.com ▥

♀ ○ Bistro Bobette, 1209 E Cary St, Richmond 804-225-9116 www.bistrobobette.com ✗

⚢ Club Colours, After 7 Lounge, 5737 Hull Street Rd, Richmond; / check schedule 804-353-9776 tinyurl.com/3pm35gn **D** ❖

♀ ○ Fallout, 117 N 18th St, Richmond; 804-343-3688 Goth, fetish falloutrva.com **P**

⚢ ● Godfrey's, 308 E Grace St, Richmond 804-648-3957 www.godfreysva.com ⚥ ✗ ▥

♀ ○ New York Deli, 2920 W Cary St, Richmond 804-358-3354 www.ny-d.com ☞

⚢ ○ Strange Matter, 929 W Grace St, Richmond 804-447-4763 www.strangematterrva.com ✗ ▥ ✗

Counseling/Psychotherapy/Mental Health

♀ ○ ♿ Cypress Counseling, LLC, 1312-A W Main St, Richmond; 23220 804-651-3941 www.cypresscounseling.com ✗ chris@cypresscounseling.com

♀ ● Jean, Paula J., PhD, 907 Westwood Ave, Richmond; 23222-2533 804-329-3940 fax 804-329-3945 tinyurl.com/oqer5eg drpjjean3@gmail.com

Funding: Endowment, Fundraising

⚢ ★ Diversity Thrift, 1407 Sherwood Ave, Richmond; 23220-1004 804-353-8890 www.diversitythrift.org divthrift@gmail.com

Health Care: Physical (see also Counseling/Mental Health)

♀ ☆ ♿ Health Brigade, 1010 N Thompson St, Richmond; 804-358-6343 **H?** www.healthbrigade.org ✗

Legal Services

♀ ● (?♿) Bary Law, POB 13890, Richmond; 23225 804-482-1649 **H?** www.barylaw.com ✗

♀ ○ ♿ North, Pia J, 5913 Harbour Park Dr, Midlothian; 23112 804-739-3700 Bankruptcy www.pianorth.com ✗ help@pianorth.com

Organizations/Resources: Business & Professional Associations, Labor Advocacy

⚢ ★ Richmond Business Alliance, 1407 Sherwood Ave, Richmond; 804-464-8826 richmondbusinessalliance.com

Organizations/Resources: Cultural, Dance, Performance

⚢ ★ ♿ Richmond Triangle Players, PO Box 6905, Richmond; 23230 / 1300 Altamont Ave 804-346-8113 www.rtriangle.org ✗ crosby@rtriangle.com

Organizations/Resources: Family and Supporters

⚢ ★ Gay Fathers Coalition Richmond, POB 75, Richmond; 23173 804-347-9760 www.GFCRVA.org

♀ ☆ PFLAG Richmond, POB 36392, Richmond 23235-8008 www.pflagofrichmond.org pflagrichmondva@gmail.com

Organizations/Resources: Naturist/Nudist

⚢ ★ Richmond Area Nude Guys, 804-240-7823 (ask for Charles) www.zebulonsgrotto.com **N**

Organizations/Resources: Social, Recreation, Support

⚢ ★ Prime Timers - Central Virginia, POB 7054, Richmond; 23221-0054 804-905-8483 ptcva.org

Organizations/Resources: Student, Academic, Education

♀ ☆ ♿ GLSEN Richmond, C/O Diversity Richmond, 1407 Sherwood Ave, Richmond www.glsen.org/richmond

Virginia: Richmond Area
Organizations: Transgender

332
GAYELLOW PAGES #42 2020-2021

South Boston : Virginia
Accommodation

Organizations/Resources: Transgender/Gender Non-Conforming/Diverse

T James River Transgender Society, University Of Richmond, Richmond; www.jrts.org

T ♿ Richmond Transformers FTM/Transmasculine Support Group, Health Brigade, 1010 N Thompson St, Richmond; 804-864-8012

Real Estate (see also Mortgages)

⚥ ● (♿) Fears, Wanda, ABR GRI CRS Realtor, Treehouse Realty VA, 1100 Jefferson Green Cir, Midlothian; 804-909-2777 **H?** www.bestRVAhomes.com ⚥

⚥ ○ Moss, Robb, Long & Foster Christies International Real Estate. 8411 Patterson Ave, Richmond; 23226 804-402-3504 www.robbmoss.com robb.moss@LNF.com

Recovery

⚥ ☆ ♿ AA: Richmond Intergroup, 5310 Markel Rd #108, Richmond; 804-355-1212 www.aarichmond.org

Religious / Spiritual Resources

⚥ ☆ Beth Ahabah, 1121 W Franklin St, Richmond 23220-3700 804-358-6757 www.bethahabah.org ✡

⚥ ● MCC of Richmond, 2501 Park Ave, Richmond 804-353-9477 www.mccrichmond.org

⚥ ☆ ♿ St Stephen's Episcopal Church, 6000 Grove Ave, Richmond; 23226 804-288-2867 **HD** www.ststephensrva.org ⚥

Roanoke

Crisis, Anti-violence, & Helplines

⚥ ☆ ♿ Arch, 404 Elm Ave SW 540-344-8060 www.archservices.org ⚥

Community Centers and/or Pride Organizations

⚥ ★ (♿) Roanoke Diversity Center (RDC), 806 Jamison Ave SE; 540-491-4165 tinyurl.com/m58kqx7 ⚥

⚥ ★ Roanoke Pride, POB 18121; 24014 www.roanokepride.org

Bookstores

⚥ ○ Book No Further, 16 Church Ave SW; 540-206-2505 www.booknofurther.com

Organizations/Resources: Student, Academic, Education

⚥ ★ Hollins University OUTloud, POB 9632 24020 tinyurl.com/y8ug974

Religious / Spiritual Resources

⚥ ★ (♿) MCC of the Blue Ridge, 806 Jamison Avenue SE; 540-344-4444 **H?** www.mccroanoke.org

Shenandoah Valley

Community Centers and/or Pride Organizations

⚥ ★ Shenandoah LGBTQ Center, 13 W Beverley St 5th Flr, Staunton; 24401 540-466-3320 www.shenlgbtqcenter.org hello@shenlgbtqcenter.org

⚥ Staunton Pride, www.stauntonpride.org

Information, Media & Publications

⚥ LGBT Technology Partnership & Institute, 202-888-7109 www.lgbttech.org

⚥ ★ Shenandoah Valley Equality, POB 1023, Harrisonburg; 22803-1023 www.svgla.org ShenandoahValleyEquality@gmail.com

Accommodation: Hotels, Inns, Guesthouses, B&B, Resorts
Lexington

⚥ ● Frog Hollow Bed & Breakfast, 492 Greenhouse Rd, Lexington; 540-463-5444 www.froghollowbnb.com ⊛

Luray

⚥ ○ MayneView B&B, 439 Mechanic St, Luray 540-669-5105. www.mayneview.com (♚?) ⚥ ⊛

⚥ ● Piney Hill Bed & Breakfast and Cottages, 1048 Piney Hill Rd, Luray; 22835 540-860-8470 www.pineyhillbb.com ⚥ ⊛

AIDS/HIV Services, Education & Support

⚥ ☆ AIDS Response Effort, 124 W Piccadilly St, Winchester; 540-536-5291 aidsresponseeffort.org

Bars, Cafes, Clubs, Restaurants
Luray

⚥ ○ (♿) Rainbow Hill Restaurant & Shops, 2547 US Hwy 211 W, Luray; 540-743-6009 www.rainbow-hill.com ✕

Organizations/Resources: Student, Academic, Education

⚥ ★ ♿ James Madison University LGBT & Ally Education Program, Student Success Center Room 1313, 738 S Mason St, Harrisonburg; 540-568-5428 www.jmu.edu/lgbta/ ⚥

⚥ ★ James Madison University Safe Zone, www.jmu.edu/safezone

Real Estate (see also Mortgages)

⚥ ○ Aguilar, Betty, Nest Realty, 105 Baldwin St, Staunton; 24401 434-996-9699 tinyurl.com/ycxtyar4 Betty.aguilar@NestRealty.com

Religious / Spiritual Resources

⚥ Shenandoah Valley MCC, Friends Centre Meeting House. 203 N Washington St, Winchester; 540-315-3574 fb.com/svmccwinc/

Smith Mountain Lake

Accommodation: Hotels, Inns, Guesthouses, B&B, Resorts
Moneta

⚥ ● Bedford Landings, 1995 Buccaneer Rd, Moneta 540-488-4600 www.bedfordlandings.com ⚥ (⊛)
@ixx=

South Boston

Accommodation: Hotels, Inns, Guesthouses, B&B, Resorts

⚥ ● Charles Bass House B&B, 1505 N Main St 434-575-6291 www.CharlesBassHouse.com ⚥ ⊛

» *Stanardsville: see Charlottesville Area*
» *Staunton: see Shenandoah Valley*
» *Suffolk: see Hampton Roads Area*
» *Virginia Beach: see Hampton Roads Area*

Virginia: Waynesboro
Religious

333
GAYELLOW PAGES #42 2020-2021

Bellingham : Washington
Organizations: Youth

Waynesboro

Religious / Spiritual Resources

♂ ☆ && Unitarian Universalist Fellowship, 565 Pine Ave; 22980 540-942-5507 www.uufw.org
>> *Williamsburg: see Hampton Roads Area*

Wintergreen

Accommodation Rental: Furnished / Vacation (& AirBNB)
Afton

♂ ○ Resort Reservations - Wintergreen, POB 25, Afton, VA 22920 540-456-8300 www.rentalsatwintergreen.com ✎ ⊛

Washington
State/County Resources

Information, Media & Publications

♀ • GLBT Yellow Pages, 1122 E Pike St #936, Seattle, WA 206-322-6600 www.glbtyp.com
@ixx=

Archives/Libraries/Museums/History Projects

♀ ★ Northwest Lesbian & Gay History Museum Project, 1122 E Pike St PMB #797, Seattle, WA 98122 www.lgbthistorynw.org info@lgbthistorynw.org

Counseling/Psychotherapy/Mental Health

♀ ★ && NW Network of BTLG Survivors of Abuse, POB 18436, Seattle, WA 98118 206-568-7777 www.nwnetwork.org

Funding: Endowment, Fundraising

♀ ★ && Pride Foundation, 2014 E Madison St Ste 300, Seattle, WA 800-735-7287 www.pridefoundation.org

♂ ☆ Sisters of the Mother House of Washington, Attn: Aaron McCartney, 6303 21st Ave SW, Seattle, WA fb.com/groups/134535475872/

Leather Resources & Groups

♂ ☆ Washington State Mr. & Ms. Leather Organization, 1122 E Pike St #1032, Seattle, WA 98122 www.wsmlo.org wsmlo@aol.com

Organizations/Resources: Political/Legislative/Advocacy

♂ ☆ && American Civil Liberties Union of Washington, 901 5th Ave Ste 630, Seattle, WA 206-624-2184 www.aclu-wa.org

♀ ★ && Equal Rights Washington, PO Box 2388, Seattle, WA 98111 206-324-2570 tinyurl.com/46e3z4

Organizations/Resources: Social, Recreation, Support

♀ ★ && Mpowerment Washington, POB 2692, Olympia, WA 98507 360-352-2375 mpowerwa.org info@mpowerwa.org

Organizations/Resources: Student, Academic, Education

♀ ★ && GLSEN Washington State, 1605 12th Ave Ste 35, Seattle, WA 206-330-2099 www.glsenwa.org

Organizations/Resources: Transgender/Gender Non-Conforming/Diverse

T ☆ Washington Gender Alliance, 360-445-2411 tinyurl.com/38oeev

Travel & Tourist Services (see also Accommodation)

♀ ○ Adventure Associates of WA, Inc, POB 16304, Seattle, WA 98116-0304 206-932-8352 www.adventureassociates.net info@adventureassociates.net
>> *Bellevue: see Seattle & Tacoma Area*

Bellingham

Community Centers and/or Pride Organizations

♀ ★ Bellingham Pride, POB 903; 98227 360-305-5009 www.bhampride.org

Information, Media & Publications

♀ ★ **Bellingham Area GLBTQ Guide, POB 2161 98227-2161 360-325-1507 Web page of links to Bellingham area things and information. www.gaybellingham.org**

AIDS/HIV Services, Education & Support

♂ ☆ && Sean Humphrey House, 1630 H St 360-733-0176 www.seanhumphreyhouse.org
@ixx=

Bars, Cafes, Clubs, Restaurants

♀ • & Rumors Cabaret, 1119 Railroad Ave; 360-671-1849 www.rumorscabaret.com D ▥

♂ ○ && Skylark's Hidden Cafe, 1308 11th St; 360-715-3642 www.skylarkshiddencafe.com ⵗ ✕▥

Bookstores

♂ ○ && Village Books, 1200 11th St 98225-7015 360-671-2626 800-392-BOOK fax 360-734-2573 www.villagebooks.com ✎

Funding: Endowment, Fundraising

♀ ★ Imperial Sovereign Court of the Evergreen Empire, c/o POB 5809; 98227 360-319-2815 www.courtofbellingham.org

Organizations/Resources: Family and Supporters

♀ ☆ PFLAG Bellingham/Whatcom County, POB 28704 98228-0704 360-255-3408 www.whatcompflag.org whatcompflag@gmail.com

Organizations/Resources: Student, Academic, Education

♀ ★ && Queer Resource Center, Western Washington University. Viking Union Box 515; 360-650-6120 as.wwu.edu/qrc/ ✎

♀ ☆ && Western Washington University Womxn's Identity Resource Center, Viking Union #514; 360-650-6114 as.wwu.edu/womxn/

Organizations/Resources: Youth (see also Family)

♀ Queer Youth Project, Northwest Youth Services, 1020 N State St; 360-734-9862 tinyurl.com/ybkdcuhk
>> *Bremerton: see Olympic Peninsula*

Washington: Carnation
Religious
334
GAYELLOW PAGES #42 2020-2021
Olympic Peninsula : Washington
Organizations: Youth

Carnation

Religious / Spiritual Resources

♂ ☆ ♿ Tolt Congregational UCC, POB 447, Carnation; 98014 425-333-4254 www.toltucc.org tolt@toltucc.org

Everett

AIDS/HIV Services, Education & Support

♂ Snohomish Country Health District, HIV/AIDS Prevention, 3020 Ruckner Ave #208; 425-339-5261 www.snohd.org/160/HIV-AIDS

Health Care: Physical (see also Counseling/Mental Health)

♀ ☆ Citrine Health, 2940 W Marine View Dr 425-259-9899 www.citrinehealth.org

Organizations/Resources: Family and Supporters

♂ ☆ PFLAG Everett, POB 12884; 98206 425-405-5407 www.pflageverett.org

Organizations/Resources: Social, Recreation, Support

♂ ★ Gay Men's Quilting Club, 360-202-3978 tinyurl.com/lr7jv5x

♂ ★ ♿ Snohomish County Gay Men's Task Force, www.gaysnohomish.org johndmarsh@mac.com

Organizations/Resources: Youth (see also Family)

♂ ☆ ♿ Cocoon House, 2929 Pine St 425-259-5802 **H?** 14-24 years www.cocoonhouse.org ✎

♂ ★ ♿ GLOBE, POB 12884; 98206 425-242-6188 www.globeyouth.com

» *Kennewick: see Tri-Cities Area*
» *Kent: see Seattle & Tacoma Area*

Longview

Organizations/Resources: Family and Supporters

♂ ☆ ♿ PFLAG Lower Columbia, Longview UMC, POB 368, Cathlamet; 98612 Longview and Cathlamet meetings 360-431-7603 tinyurl.com/pl3wlfy

» *Lopez Island: see San Juan Islands*
» *Mercer Island: see Seattle & Tacoma Area*

Mt Baker/Glacier Area

Accommodation Rental: Furnished / Vacation (& AirBNB)
Maple Falls

♂ ● (♿) Mt. Baker Lodging, Inc., POB 2002, Maple Falls; 98266 / 7463 Mt Baker Hwy 800-709-7669 360-599-2453 fax 360-599-1000 (limited wifi) www.mtbakerlodging.com ✎ Ⓢ reservations@ mtbakerlodging.com

Campgrounds and RV Parks

♀ ● Triangle Recreation Camp, POB 1226, Granite Falls; 98252 www.camptrc.org (♿?)

Olympia Area

Crisis, Anti-violence, & Helplines

♂ ☆ Crisis Clinic of Thurston & Mason Counties, PO Box 13453, Olympia; 98508 360-586-2800 www.crisis-clinic.org

♀ ☆ Human Response Network, POB 337, Chehalis 98532 800-244-7414 www.hrnlc.org

♀ ☆ ♿ SafePlace, 360-754-6300 **H?** www.safeplaceolympia.org ✎ safeplace@safeplaceolympia.org

Community Centers and/or Pride Organizations

♀ ★ Capital City Pride, POB 7221, Olympia 98507 www.capitalcitypride.net

AIDS/HIV Services, Education & Support

♀ ☆ ♿ PCAF (Pierce County AIDS Foundation), (Olympia office) 2101 4th Ave E, #103, Olympia; 98506 360-352-2375 **H?** www.pcaf-wa.org ✎

Bars, Cafes, Clubs, Restaurants
Olympia

♀ Jake's on 4th, 311 4th Ave W, Olympia 360-956-3247 fb.com/Olympiagaybar/ **DK** ▥

Organizations/Resources: Family and Supporters

♀ ★ ♿ PFLAG Olympia, POB 12732, Olympia; 98508 360-207-1608 www.pflag-olympia.org

Organizations/Resources: Youth (see also Family)

♀ ★ ♿ Pizza Klatch, 312 4th Ave E, Olympia; 98506 360-339-7574 **H?** pizzaklatch.org ✎ info@pizzaklatch.org

♀ ★ ♿ Stonewall Youth, POB 7383, Olympia; 98507-7383 360-888-4273 **H?** www.stonewallyouth.org ✎ info@ stonewallyouth.org

Religious / Spiritual Resources

♀ ☆ ♿ Olympia Unitarian Universalist Congregation, 2315 Division St NW, Olympia; 98502 360-786-6383 **H?** www.ouuc.org ✎

Olympic Peninsula

Accommodation: Hotels, Inns, Guesthouses, B&B, Resorts
Port Angeles

♀ ● (♿) Domaine Madeleine, 146 Wildflower Lane, Port Angeles; 360-457-4174 domainemadeleine.com ✎ Ⓢ Ⓢ

Organizations/Resources: Family and Supporters

♀ ☆ PFLAG Kitsap County, POB 2552, Bremerton 98310 888-636-0652 www.kitsappflag.org

Organizations/Resources: Student, Academic, Education

♀ ☆ Kitsap Safe Schools Network, c/o KUUF, POB 2015, Bremerton; 98310 800-503-7615 www.kitsapsafeschools.org

Organizations/Resources: Youth (see also Family)

♀ Q Youth Resources, POB 2169, Silverdale 98383 360-515-2220 qyouthresources.org

Washington: Olympic Peninsula
Religious

335
GAYELLOW PAGES #42 2020-2021

Seattle & Tacoma Area: Washington
Bars, Cafes, Clubs, Restaurants

Religious / Spiritual Resources

♀ ☆ &⅄ Olympic Unitarian Universalist Fellowship, POB 576, Carlsborg; 98324 / 1033 N Barr Rd 360-417-2665 **H** olympicuuf.com ✎ Admin@OlympicUUF.com
>> *Orcas Island: see San Juan Islands*
>> *Port Townsend: see Olympic Peninsula*

Pullman

Organizations/Resources: Student, Academic, Education

⚥ ★ Gender Identity/Expression & Sexual Orientation Resource Center, Washington State University, POB 647204; 99163 509-335-8841 www.thecenter.wsu.edu

♀ ☆ &⅄ Washington State University Women's Center, POB 644005; 99164 509-335-6849 **H?** www.women.wsu.edu ✎

San Juan Islands

Accommodation: Hotels, Inns, Guesthouses, B&B, Resorts
Eastsound

♀ ○ Kangaroo House B&B, POB 334, Eastsound 98245-0334 360-376-2175 www.kangaroohouse.com ✎ ⊛⊗ innkeeper@kangaroohouse.com

Seattle & Tacoma Area

Crisis, Anti-violence, & Helplines

♀ ☆ Crisis Connections, 866-427-4747 **H** www.crisisconnections.org

♀ New Beginnings, POB 75125, Seattle; 98175 206-522-9472 www.newbegin.org

Community Centers and/or Pride Organizations

⚥ ★ &⅄ Gay City: Seattle's LGBTQ Center, 517 E Pike St, Seattle; 98122 206-860-6969 fax 206-860-0195 **H** www.gaycity.org ✎ info@gaycity.org

⚥ ★ &⅄ Peer Seattle, 1520 Bellevue Ave Ste 100, Seattle; 98122 206-322-2437 www.peerseattle.org ✎ info@peerseattle.org

⚥ ★ &⅄ Rainbow Center, 2215 Pacific Ave, Tacoma; 253-383-2318 **H?** www.rainbowcntr.org ✎

⚲ ★ Seattle Dyke March, www.seattledykemarch.com

⚥ ★ &⅄ Seattle Pride, 1605 12th Ave Ste 2, Seattle; 98122-2480 206-322-9561 www.seattlepride.org hello@seattlepride.org

⚥ Seattle Pridefest, 1122 E Pike St #940, Seattle; 206-701-0272 www.seattlepridefest.org

Information, Media & Publications

⚥ Seattle Gay Scene, 1122 East Pike #985, Seattle; 206-457-2432 www.seattlegayscene.com

⚲ ● The Seattle Lesbian, 206-714-2277 www.theseattlelesbian.com info@theseattlelesbian.com

⚥ ● UNITE Seattle, 1820 Minor Ave, Seattle 98101 206-306-4599 uniteseattlemag.com Unitesea@gmail.com

Accommodation: Hotels, Inns, Guesthouses, B&B, Resorts
Seattle

♂ ● Ace Hotel, 2423 1st Ave, Seattle; 206-448-4721 www.acehotel.com/seattle ✿ ✎

♂ ● (?&⅄) Bacon Mansion, 959 Broadway E, Seattle; 98102-4528 206-329-1864 www.baconmansion.com (✿?) ✎ ⊗ info@baconmansion.com

♂ ● Gaslight Inn, 1727 15th Ave, Seattle 206-325-3654 www.gaslight-inn.com ✎ ⊗

♂ ○ & Hotel Andra, 2000 Fourth Ave, Seattle; 98121 877-448-8600 206-448-8600 **H** www.hotelandra.com ✿ ✎ ⊛⊗

♂ ○ &⅄ Silver Cloud Hotel - Seattle Broadway, 1100 Broadway, Seattle; 98122 206-325-1400 **H** tinyurl.com/y7cmowzg ✎ ⊛⊗ webcontact@broadway.silvercloud.com

♂ ○ &⅄ Warwick Seattle, 401 Leonora St, Seattle; 98121-2515 206-443-4300 **H** tinyurl.com/y6txnwvw ✎ ⊛⊗ info.seattle@warwickhotels.com

Accommodation Rental: Furnished / Vacation (& AirBNB)
Seattle

♂ ● Moore Mansion, 811 14th Ave E, Seattle 206-325-2245 ✎ ⊗

Adoption, Surrogacy, Assisted Fertility Support, see also Reproductive

♂ ☆ &⅄ Open Adoption & Family Services, 2815 Eastlake Ave E Ste 160, Seattle; 206-782-0442 www.openadopt.org

AIDS/HIV Services, Education & Support

♀ ☆ Babes Network, 1118 5th Ave, Seattle; 98101 888-292-1912 206-720-5566 www.babesnetwork.org the_staff@babesnetwork.org

♂ Bailey Boushay House, 2720 E Madison St, Seattle; 206-322-5300 www.baileyboushay.org

♂ ☆ &⅄ Lifelong, 210 S Lucile St, Seattle; 206-957-1600 www.lifelong.org

♂ ☆ &⅄ PCAF (Pierce County AIDS Foundation), (Main office) 3009 S 40th St, Tacoma; 98409 253-383-2565 **H?** www.pcafwa.org ✎

♂ ★ &⅄ People of Color Against AIDS Network, 4437 Rainier Ave S, Seattle; 206-322-7061 www.pocaan.org ❖

♂ ☆ Pet Partners, 345 118th Ave SE Ste 200, Bellevue; 425-679-5500 www.petpartners.org

Bars, Cafes, Clubs, Restaurants
Seattle

♂ ● &⅄ AzuQar! Queer latinx Dance Night, Re-bar, 1114 Howell St, Seattle; 206-233-9873 Theater and Nightclub fb.com/azuqar.dance/ **D** ✪ ✎

♂ ● &⅄ The Bottleneck Lounge, 2328 E Madison St, Seattle; 206-323-1098 www.bottlenecklounge.com ✎

♂ ○ Cafe Flora, 2901 E Madison St, Seattle 206-322-3626 www.cafeflora.com ✕ info@cafeflora.com

♂ CC Attle's, 1701 E Olive Way, Seattle 206-323-4017 www.ccattles.net ⅄ ✕

♂ Changes In Wallingford, 2103 N 45th St, Seattle; 206-545-8363 fb.com/ChangesInWallingford **K** ⅄ ✕

♂ ● &⅄ The Cuff, 1533 13th Ave, Seattle; 206-323-1525 www.cuffcomplex.com **D**

Washington: Seattle & Tacoma Area
Bars, Cafes, Clubs, Restaurants

336

GAYELLOW PAGES #42 2020-2021

Seattle & Tacoma Area: Washington
Counseling

♂ Diesel, 1413 14th Ave, Seattle; 206-322-1080 www.dieselseattle.com

♀ ● ⚥⚥ Dimitriou's Jazz Alley, 2033 6th Ave, Seattle; 206-441-9729 **H?** www.jazzalley.com ☿ ✕ ▦ jazzalley@jazzalley.com

♀ ● ⚥⚥ Flying Fish, 300 Westlake Ave N, Seattle; 206-728-8595 www.flyingfishseattle.com ☿ ✕ info@flyingfishseattle.com

⚢ ● ⚥⚥ Hot Flash Women's Dances, www.hotflashdances.com **P**

♀ ○ Hula Hula, 1501 E Olive Way, Seattle 206-284-5003 www.hulahula.org

♂ ● ⚥⚥ Julia's, 300 Broadway E, Seattle; 206-860-1818 tinyurl.com/4jyo6oq ☿ ✕ ✗

⚢ ● Kremwerk, 1809 Minor Ave # 10, Seattle 206-682-2935 www.kremwerk.com **DKL** ▦ ✗

⚢ ● Lumber Yard Bar, 9619 16th Ave SW, Seattle 206-695-2007 www.thelumberyardbar.com badbearllc@gmail.com

⚢ ● ⚥⚥ Madison Pub, 1315 E Madison St, Seattle; 206-325-6537 www.madisonpub.com **S** ✗

⚢ ● (⚥⚥) Neighbours Nightclub and Lounge, 1509 Broadway Ave, Seattle; 206-324-5358 www.neighboursnightclub.com **D**

⚢ ● ⚥⚥ OutWest Bar, 5401 California Ave SW, Seattle; 206-937-1540 www.outwestbar.com

⚢ Palace Theatre & Bar, 5813 Airport Way S, Seattle; 206-420-3037 www.palaceartbar.com ▦

♀ ● ⚥⚥ Poco Wine + Spirits, 1408 E Pine St, Seattle; 206-322-9463 www.pocowineandspirits.com ☿ ✕ ✗

⚢ ● ⚥⚥ Pony, 1221 E Madison St, Seattle; 206-324-2854 www.ponyseattle.com **K** ▦ ✗

♂ ● ⚥⚥ Poppy, 622 Broadway E, Seattle 206-324-1108 www.poppyseattle.com ☿ ✕

⚢ ● Q Nightclub, 1426 Broadway, Seattle 206-432-9306 www.qnightclub.com **D**

⚢ ● Queer/Bar, 1518 11th Ave, Seattle 206-687-7491 thequeerbar.com

⚢ ● ⚥⚥ R Place, 619 E Pine St, Seattle 206-322-8828 www.rplaceseattle.com **DKV** ☿ ✕ ▦ ✗

♂ ● ⚥⚥ Re-bar, 1114 Howell St, Seattle 206-233-9873 Theater and Nightclub www.rebarseattle.com **D** ▦ ✗ info@rebarseattle.com

♂ ○ (⚥⚥) Rendezvous, 2322 2nd Ave, Seattle; 206-441-5823 www.seattlerendezvous.com **BR** ✕ ▦

⚢ ● Seattle Eagle, 314 E Pike St, Seattle 206-621-7591 www.seattleeagle.com **LL**

⚢ The Swallow, 9608 16th Ave SW, Seattle 206-257-0217 theswallowbar.com

♂ ○ Temple Billiards, 126 S Jackson, Seattle 206-682-3242 www.templebilliards.com

♂ ○ Unicorn, 1118 E Pike St, Seattle; 206-325-6492 www.unicornseattle.com ☿ ✕

⚢ Union Seattle, 1318 E Union St, Seattle 206-328-1318 www.unionseattle.com

♀ ● (⚥⚥) WildRose, 1021 E Pike St, Seattle; 206-324-9210 www.thewildrosebar.com **DK** ☿ ✕ ▦

Tacoma

⚢ ○ Club Silverstone, 739 1/2 St Helens Ave, Tacoma; 253-404-0273 www.clubsilverstone.com **D** ☿ ✕

⚢ ● The Mix, 635 St Helens Ave, Tacoma 253-383-4327 www.themixtacoma.com **K** ✗

Bookstores

♂ ○ Elliott Bay Book Company, 1521 10th Ave, Seattle; 206-624-6600 www.elliottbaybook.com

♂ ● ⚥⚥ King's Books, 218 St Helen's Ave, Tacoma; 98402-2522 253-272-8801 www.kingsbookstore.com ✗

♂ ☆ (⚥) Left Bank Books, 92 Pike St, Seattle; 206-622-0195 www.leftbankbooks.com

Coaching: Career, Life, Relationship etc

♂ ● ⚥⚥ SharonSanborn, 206-283-9767 www.SharonSanborn.com ✗ Sharon@SharonSanborn.com

Counseling/Psychotherapy/Mental Health

♂ ● Hencken, Joel, PhD, Rainier Behavioral Health, 5909 Orchard St W, Tacoma; 98467 617-864-7711 rainierassociates.com

♂ ☆ ⚥⚥ Jewish Family Service, 1601 16th Ave, Seattle; 206-461-3240 **H?** www.jfsseattle.org

⚢ ● Lathrop, Jarred, LMHCA, LGBTQ Counseling, 1812 E Madison St Ste 101, Seattle; 98122 253-906-8738 tinyurl.com/dyygltf

♂ ● ⚥⚥ MacQuivey, Karen, LICSW, 6527 21 Ave NE #4, Seattle; 98115-6947 206-285-9168

♂ ● ⚥⚥ McCarthy, Dennis, MA LMHC, 1904 3rd Ave Ste 915, Seattle; 98101 206-595-2659 www.unstuckseattle.com dennis@unstuckseattle.com

♂ ● ⚥⚥ Mending Connections, PllC, 4141 6th Ave STE C, Tacoma; 98406 253-303-2074 www.annemauro.com ✗ contact@mendingmyconnections.com

♂ ● ⚥⚥ Partlow, Mac, MA, ABS, 901 Boren Ave #1300, Seattle; 98104 206-276-0325 seattle-gay-counseling.com mac@seattle-gay-counseling.com

♂ ● ⚥⚥ Salewske, Cassie, LMHC, Healing Tree Counseling & Wellness, LLC, 1812 E Madison St Ste 106, Seattle; 98122 206-595-8621 www.healingtreeseattle.com ✗ cassie.salewske@gmail.com

♂ ● ⚥⚥ Scherer, Taen M, MA, LMFT, Abanian Counseling, 19550 International Blvd Ste 105, SeaTac; 98188 / and 4218 S Chicago St 206-303-7584 www.abaniancounseling.com

⚢ ★ ⚥⚥ Seattle Counseling Service, 1216 Pine St Ste 300, Seattle; 206-323-1768 www.seattlecounseling.org

♂ ☆ Seattle Institute for Sex Therapy, Education & Research, 102 NE 56th St, Seattle; 98105-3738 206-522-8588 **H?** www.sextx.com therapy@sextx.com

♂ ● ♂ SharonSanborn.com, 18 W Mercer St Ste 360, Seattle; 98119 206-283-9767 www.SharonSanborn.com ✗ Sharon@SharonSanborn.com

♀ O ♿ Skoorsmith, Christian, MA, CH, IWLC, WholeHealth Hypnosis, 9421 35th Ave SW, Seattle; 98126 206-457-9275 www.wholehealth.today ✂ christian@wholehealth.today

♀ ● (♿) transMISSION wellness, 650 S Orcas St Ste 218, Seattle; 98108 www.transmissionwellness.com transmissionwellness@gmail.com

Dentists

♂ ● ♿ Veigl, Mark, DDS, 509 Olive Way #1329, Seattle; 206-382-0461 www.markveigldds.com ✂ @ixx=

Food Specialties (see also Catering)

♂ ● ♿ Cupcake Royale: Madrona, 1101 34th Ave, Seattle; 98122-5138 206-701-6240 www.cupcakeroyale.com ✂ Madrona@cupcakeroyale.com

Funding: Endowment, Fundraising

⚥ ★ Imperial Sovereign Court of Seattle & the Olympic & Rainier Empire, 1122 E Pike St #1300, Seattle tinyurl.com/mg62rk

⚥ ★ ♿ Imperial Sovereign Court of Tacoma - Diamond Empire of the Cascades, POB 488, Tacoma; 98401 fb.com/CourtOfTacoma ✂

⚥ ★ Sisters of Perpetual Indulgence, The Abbey of Saint Joan, The Abbey of St Joan, 1122 E Pike St #486, Seattle; 98122-3916 theabbey.org sisters@theabbey.org

Funeral Directors/Cemeteries/Mausoleums

♂ O ♿ The Co-op Funeral Home of People's Memorial, 1801 12th Ave Ste A, Seattle; 98122 206-529-3800 **H?** www.funerals.coop info@funerals.coop

Graphic Design/Printing/Type

♀ ● Henry Waymack Design, www.henrywaymack.com

Health Care: Physical (see also Counseling/Mental Health)

♂ Cedar River Clinics LGBTQ Wellness Services, 1401-A Martin Luther King Way, Tacoma; 800-572-4223 tinyurl.com/ydazh8eb

♂ ☆ Country Doctor Community Clinic, 500 19th Ave E, Seattle; 206-299-1600 countrydoctor.org

♂ O Jyringi, Mark, DC, Roosevelt Chiropractic, 5029 Roosevelt Way NE #101A, Seattle; 98105 206-547-4427 rooseveltchiropractic.com ✂ Mark_Jyringi@MSN.Com

♂ ● ♿ McIntosh, Bryan, MD, Puget Sound Plastic Surgical Group, PLLC, 12301 NE 10th Pl Ste 101, Bellevue; 98005 425-420-2663 www.drbryanmcintosh.com office@drbryanmcintosh.com

♂ ● ♿ Shalit, Peter, MD, 901 Boren Ave Ste 850, Seattle; 98104 206-624-0688 **H?** www.doctorshalit.com ✂ peter@tribalmed.com

♂ ● ♿ Yarnell, Eric, ND, Northwest Naturopathic Urology, 1207 N 200th St Ste 210, Shoreline; 98133 206-542-4325 **H?** www.urologynd.com ✂ urologynd@gmail.com

Homes & Buildings: Cleaning, Maintenance, Repair, General Contractors

♂ O Sound View Window & Door, Inc., 2626 15th Ave W, Seattle; 98119 206-402-4229 tinyurl.com/2aqcqm3 contact@soundviewseattle.com

Insurance (see also Financial Planning)

♂ ● ♿ Hallman, Jerry, Ste 200 1712 6th Ave, Tacoma; 98405 253-272-1843 tinyurl.com/z7ymecy jhallman@farmersagent.com

Leather Resources & Groups

⚣ ★ (♿) Seattle Men In Leather, 1122 E Pike St PMB 1199, Seattle; 98122-3934 www.seattlemeninleather.org **L** info@seattlemeninleather.org

Legal Services

♂ O ♿ A. Alene Anderson Law Offices, 1455 NW Leary Way Ste 400, Seattle; 206-781-2570 www.aleneandersonlaw.com @ixx=

♀ ● ♿ Buhr, Cynthia F, Law Offices of Cynthia F. Buhr PLLC, 1700 7th Ave Ste 2100, Seattle; 98101 206-357-8565 fax 206-357-8565 www.cbuhrlaw.com cynthia@cbuhrlaw.com

♂ O ♿ Hall, Keith, Newton & Hall, Attorneys at Law, PLLC, 610 Central Ave S, Kent; 98032 253-852-6600 www.NewtonandHall.com keith@NewtonandHall.com

♂ O (♿) Hiscock, David K, 2208 NW Market St #315, Seattle; 98107 206-789-9551 stratman@scn.org

♀ Legal Voice, 907 Pine St #500, Seattle 206-682-9552 www.legalvoice.org

♂ O (♿) Longley, Sara D, Ivy Law Group PLLC, 1734 NW Market St, Seattle; 98107 206-706-2909 www.ivylawgroup.com sara@ivylawgroup.com

⚣ ★ ♿ QLaw Foundation, 101 Yesler Way #300, Seattle; 98104 206-235-7235 **H?** www.qlawfoundation.org info@qlawfoundation.org

♂ ● Smith, Mona, PLLC, 500 Union St Ste 505, Seattle; 98101 206-285-1687 425-246-3191 fax 425-246-3191 www.smith-law.net mona@smith-law.net

♂ O ♿ Spencer, James W, Brothers & Henderson PS, 2722 Eastlake Ave E Ste 200, Seattle; 98102 206-324-4300 x106 fax 206-324-3106 **H?** www.brothershenderson.com ✂ jamess@brothershenderson.com

♂ O (♿) Teller, Stephen, Teller & Associates, PLLC, 1139 34th Ave Ste B, Seattle; 98122 206-324-8969 **H?** www.stellerlaw.com ✂ steve@stellerlaw.com

♂ O ♿ Trombold, Kevin J, 720 Third Ave #2015, Seattle; 98104 206-382-9200 www.tromboldlaw.com kevin@tromboldlaw.com

Men's & Sex Clubs (not primarily Health Clubs)

⚣ ● Club Z, 1117 Pike St, Seattle; 98101-1923 206-622-9958 fax 206-622-6651 www.thezclub.com **LLP** ✂ info@thezclub.com

⚣ ● Steamworks, 1520 Summit Ave, Seattle 206-388-4818 www.steamworksbaths.com ✂

Organizations/Resources: Business & Professional Associations, Labor Advocacy

⚥ ★ Boeing Employees Association of Gays, Lesbians & Friends - Puget Sound, POB 3707 MC OL-AJ, Seattle; 98124 206-930-0416 tinyurl.com/jqm5f3y

⚥ ★ GLAmazon, c/o Amazon.com, POB 81226, Seattle; 98108 206-266-1000

♂ ★ ♂♂ Greater Seattle Business Association, 400 E Pine St Ste 322, Seattle; 98122 206-363-9188 fax 206-568-3123 www.thegsba.org office@thegsba.org

♂ ★ Microsoft GLEAM, One Microsoft Way, Redmond; tinyurl.com/lmf3op8

♂ ★ QLaw Association of Washington, POB 1991, Seattle; 98111 www.q-law.org

♂ Starbucks Pride Alliance Network, 2401 Utah Ave S, Seattle; fb.com/StarbucksPride

Organizations/Resources: Cultural, Dance, Performance

♂ ☆ Diverse Harmony, 1111 Harvard Ave, Seattle 206-389-5858 Youth chorus www.diverseharmony.org

♂ ★ (?♂) Puddletown Squares, POB 20671, Seattle; 98102-1671 www.puddletownsquares.org D

♀ ☆ Rain Country Dance Association, 1122 E Pike St PMB 1155, Seattle; 206-852-3326 www.raincountrydance.com

♂ ★ Rainbow City Band, POB 51006, Seattle 98115 866-841-9139 x2126 www.rainbowcityband.com

♂ ★ ♂♂ Seattle Men's Chorus, 319 12th Ave, Seattle; 206-323-0750 www.seattlechoruses.org

♀ ★ ♂♂ Seattle Women's Chorus, 319 12th Ave, Seattle; 206-323-0750 www.seattlechoruses.org

♂ Three Dollar Bill Cinema, 122 E Pike St #1313, Seattle; 206-323-4274 tinyurl.com/nlydkoa

T ☆ Translations: The Seattle Transgender Film Festival, Three Dollar Bill Cinema, 1122 E Pike St #1313, Seattle 206-323-4274 translationsfilmfest.org

Organizations/Resources: Deaf

♀ ★ Northwest Rainbow Alliance of the Deaf, PO Box 94116, Seattle; 98124 503-388-5132 www.nwrad.org

Organizations/Resources: Education

♂ Freely Speaking Toastmasters, Gay City, 517 E Pike St, Seattle; www.freelyspeaking.org

Organizations/Resources: Ethnic, Multicultural

♂ ★ Entre Hermanos, 1105 23rd Ave, Seattle 206-322-7700 www.entrehermanos.org ◆

♂ ★ Trikone Northwest, 1122 E Pike St #1174, Seattle; LGBT South Asians www.trikonenw.org ◇

♂ UTOPIA - United Territories of Pacific Islanders Alliance - Seattle, POB 68206, Seattle; 98168 253-478-3941 www.utopiaseattle.org ◇

Organizations/Resources: Family and Supporters

♂ ★ Gay Fathers Association of Seattle, 1122 E Pike #1270, Seattle; 98122-3916 www.gfas.org info@gfas.org

♀ ☆ ♂♂ PFLAG Bellevue/Eastside, POB 52863, Bellevue; 98015 425-310-5390 H? pflagbellevue.org

♂ ☆ (♂♂) PFLAG Seattle, 1122 E Pike St PMB 620, Seattle; 98122-3916 206-325-7724 www.pflagseattle.org info@pflagseattle.org

♀ ☆ ♂♂ PFLAG Tacoma, 3800A Bridgeport Way #124, Tacoma; 98466-4416 253-234-9790 www.pflagtacoma.org mail@pflagtacoma.org

♂ ☆ Rainbow Families of Puget Sound, fb.com/groups/rfops/

Organizations/Resources: Naturist/Nudist

♂ ★ (?♂) The OLYMPIANS, 641-715-3900 x591098 www.theolympians.net N olynewsletter@aol.com

Organizations/Resources: Political/Legislative/Advocacy

♀ ☆ ♂♂ Radical Women, 5018 Rainier Ave S, Seattle; 206-722-6057 H? www.radicalwomen.org ✔

♂ ☆ SEAMEC: Seattle Metropolitan Elections Committee, 1122 E Pike #901, Seattle; www.voteseamec.org

♂ ★ (?♂) Seattle LGBTQ Commission, 810 Third Ave #750, Seattle; 206-684-4500 H? www.seattle.gov/lgbt ✔

Organizations/Resources: Senior Resources

♂ ★ Mature Friends, POB 21203, Seattle 98111 Over 40 www.maturefriends.org

♂ ★ Puget Sound Old Lesbians Organizing for Change (PS OLOC), 253-777-3357 www.psoloc.org

Organizations/Resources: Social, Recreation, Support

♂ BentCarGuys, POB 2284, Lynnwood; 98036 fb.com/groups/33585876049/

♂ ★ Northwest Bears, 1122 E Pike PMB #802, Seattle www.nwbears.com

♂ ★ Seattle Gay Couples, www.seattlegaycouples.org

♂ ★ Seattle Prime Timers, POB 75651, Seattle 98175-0651 www.seattleprimetimers.org

♂ ★ (?♂) Tacoma Lesbian Connection, PO Box 64487, Tacoma; 98464 253-777-3357 www.tacomalesbianconcern.org tacomalesbianconcern@gmail.com

Organizations/Resources: Student, Academic, Education

♂ ★ Delta Lambda Phi Psi, 1410 NE Campus Parkway, Seattle; 949-330-0741 dlp.org/psi/

♂ ★ ♂♂ Queer Seattle University, The Student Center #320, 901 12th Ave, Seattle; 206-296-6070 fb.com/groups/25472354398/ ✔

♂ ★ (?♂) Safe Schools Coalition, c/o Equal Rights Washington, POB 2388, Seattle; 98111 206-451-7233 www.safeschoolscoalition.org

♂ ★ ♂♂ Seattle Office of Multicultural Affairs, 901 12th Ave, Seattle; 206-296-6070 tinyurl.com/ybzf6rp5 ✔

♂ ★ ♂♂ University of Washington Q Center, HUB 315, Box 352235, Seattle; 206-897-1430 H? www.qcenter.washington.edu ✔

♂ ★ University Of Washington Queer Student Commission, POB 352238, Seattle; 98195 206-685-4252 qsc.asuw.org

Organizations/Resources: Transgender/Gender Non-Conforming/Diverse

T ☆ Emerald City Social Club, POB 59893, Renton 98058 425-827-9494 www.theemeraldcity.org

Washington: Seattle & Tacoma Area
Organizations: Transgender

339
GAYELLOW PAGES #42 2020-2021

Seattle & Tacoma Area: Washington
Sports & Outdoor

T ☆ ⚢ Gender Alliance of the South Sound, Oasis Rainbow Center, 2215 Pacific Ave, Tacoma; 253-383-2318 www.southsoundgender.com

T ★ ⚢⚢ Gender Odyssey Conference, 6523 California Ave SW #360, Seattle; 855-443-6337 **H?** www.genderodyssey.org ✔

T ★ ⚢⚢ Ingersoll Gender Center, 911 E Pike St Ste #221, Seattle; 98122 / 911 E Pike St #221 206-849-7859 ingersollgendercenter.org ✔ info@ingersollgendercenter.org

T ☆ ⚢ Tacoma T-Men, Rainbow Center, 2215 Pacific Ave, Tacoma; 253-383-2318 tacomatmen.com

Organizations/Resources: Youth (see also Family)

♂ ★ (?⚢) Lambert House, POB 23111, Seattle; 98102 206-322-2515 LGBTQI youth ages 11 through 22 www.lamberthouse.org

♂ ★ ⚢⚢ Oasis Youth Center, 2215 Pacific Ave, Tacoma; 253-671-2838 **H?** www.oasisyouthcenter.org

♂ Queer Youth Space, 205-395-5501 fb.com/qysseattle/

♀ ☆ ⚢⚢ Youth Eastside Services, 999 164th Ave NE, Bellevue; 425-747-4937 tinyurl.com/c9btq8r

♂ ★ ⚢⚢ YouthCare, Isis at Ravenna House, 2500 NE 54th St, Seattle; 206-694-4500 **H?** www.youthcare.org/40percent

♀ ☆ ⚢⚢ YouthCare, 2500 NE 54th St, Seattle; 206-694-4500 **H?** www.youthcare.org ✔

Real Estate (see also Mortgages)

♀ ○ Grassley, Teresa J, Windermere Real Estate, 4526 California Ave SW, Burien; 98166 206-650-3141 tinyurl.com/bfqlzln real estate@teresagrassley.com

♀ ○ Hinckley, Brad, Compass Washington, 500 E Pike St #200A, Seattle; 98122 206-330-1388 www.bradhinckley.com brad.hinckley@compass.com

♀ ● ⚢⚢ Robison, Eric, Keller Williams, 2033 6th Ave Ste 600, Seattle; 98121 206-499-9103 **H?** www.uniongrouprealty.com ✔ eric@uniongrouprealty.com

Recovery

♀ ☆ Puget Sound Central Service Office, 3640 S Cedar Ste S, Tacoma; 98409-5700 253-474-8897 pugetsoundaa.org

♂ ★ ⚢⚢ Seattle Counseling Service, 1216 Pine St Ste 300, Seattle; 206-323-1768 www.seattlecounseling.org

Religious / Spiritual Resources

♀ ☆ ⚢⚢ Bellevue First UMC, 1934 108th Ave NE, Bellevue; 98004-2828 425-454-2059 **HD** www.fumcbellevue.org office@fumcbellevue.org

♀ ☆ (?⚢) Center for Spiritual Living, 206 N J St, Tacoma; 98403-1928 253-383-3151 www.csltacoma.org

♂ ★ (?⚢) Congregation Tikvah Chadashah, 1122 E Pike St PMB 734, Seattle; 206-355-1414 www.tikvahchadashah.org ⚨

♂ ★ ⚢⚢ Dharma Buddies, c/o Cal Anderson House, 400 Broadway, Seattle; 98122 **H?** tinyurl.com/hb63ako

♂ ★ Dignity/Seattle, Box 20325, Seattle 98102-1325 206-659-5519 www.dignityseattle.org dignity.seattle@gmail.com

♀ ★ ⚢⚢ Emerald City Metropolitan Community Church (MCC) Seattle, meets Chapel of University Temple UMC, 1415 43rd St NE 206-325-2421 **HD** www.mccseattle.org info@mccseattle.org

♀ ☆ ⚢⚢ First Congregational Church, 11061 NE 2nd St, Bellevue; 98004 425-454-5001 **HD** www.fccbellevue.org welcome@fccbellevue.org

♀ ☆ Gift of Grace Lutheran Church, 2102 N 40th St, Seattle; 98103-8312 206-632-2662 www.giftofgrace.org gofgchurch@gmail.com

♀ ☆ ⚢⚢ Holy Spirit Lutheran Church, 10021 NE 124th St, Kirkland; 98034-6798 425-823-2727 **HD** www.hslckirkland.org ✔ office@hslckirkland.org

♀ ★ Lotus Sister LBQT Women's Insight Meditation Sangha, 206-329-5908 www.lotussisters.org @ixx=

♀ ☆ ⚢⚢ Normandy Park United Church of Christ, 19247 1st Ave S, Seattle; 98148 206-824-1770 **H?** www.npucc.org ✔ info@npucc.org

♀ ☆ ⚢⚢ Prospect Congregational UCC, 1919 E Prospect St, Seattle; 98112 206-322-6030 **HD** www.prospectseattle.org prospectucc@yahoo.com

♀ ☆ ⚢⚢ St Paul's United Church of Christ, 6512 12th Ave NW, Seattle; 98117 206-783-6733 www.stpucc.org info@stpucc.org

♀ ☆ (?⚢) Woodinville Unitarian Universalist Church, POB 111, Woodinville; 98072 425-788-6044 www.wuuc.org office@wuuc.org

♀ ☆ ⚢⚢ Woodland Park United Methodist Church, 302 N 78th St, Seattle; 98103 206-784-6969 www.woodlandparkumc.org ✔ woodlandparkumc@gmail.com

Reproductive Medicine & Fertility Services

♀ Cedar River Clinics LGBTQ Wellness Services, 264 Rainier Ave S #200, Renton; 800-572-4223 tinyurl.com/ydazh8eb

♀ Cedar River Clinics LGBTQ Wellness Services, 509 Olive Way Suite 1454, Seattle; 800-572-4223 tinyurl.com/ydazh8eb

Sports & Outdoor

♂ ★ Bottom Dwellers Scuba Club, www.bottomdwellers.org

♀ ☆ Emerald City Mudhens, Rugby mudhenrugby.com

♀ ★ ⚢⚢ Emerald City Softball Association Open Division, **H?** emeraldcitysoftball.org info@emeraldcitysoftball.org

♂ ★ Olympic Yacht Club, 1122 E Pike St #1025, Seattle; www.oycnw.org

♂ ★ Orca Swim Team, www.orcaswimteam.org

♂ ★ OutVentures, www.outventures.org

♂ ★ Rain City Soccer Club, www.raincitysoccer.org

♂ ★ Seattle Frontrunners, POB 23292 212 Broadway E, Seattle; 98102 www.seattlefrontrunners.org

♂ Seattle Otters, POB 95396, Seattle 98145 www.otterpolo.com

♂ Seattle Quake Rugby, 1122 E Pike St #1124, Seattle; www.quakerugby.org

♂ Seattle Tennis Alliance, POB 23004, Seattle; 98102 tinyurl.com/lzd843

♂ Seattle Volleyball Club, tinyurl.com/lv6dq2

Washington: Seattle & Tacoma Area
Sports & Outdoor

340
GAYELLOW PAGES #42 2020-2021

Tri-Cities Area: Washington
Organizations: Social & Support

⚲ Ski Buddies, POB 20003, Seattle; 98102 www.skibuddies.org

⚲ ★ (♺) Team Seattle, 1122 E Pike St PMB 515, Seattle; 206-367-4064 www.teamseattle.org

♀ Tilted Thunder Rail Birds, www.tiltedthunder.com

» *Silverdale: see Olympic Peninsula*

Skagit Valley Area

Community Centers and/or Pride Organizations

⚲ Cascades Rainbow Community Center, 24733 Minkler Rd, Mount Vernon; 360-840-8499 tinyurl.com/spnfl24

Grooming, Personal Care, Spa Services

⚲ ● ⚹ Hair and Body Mechanix, 412 S 1 st St, Mount Vernon; 98273 360-399- 7045 www.hairandbodymechanix.com ⚸ HairAndBodyMechanix@gmail.com

Organizations/Resources: Family and Supporters

♂ ☆ PFLAG Skagit/Sedro-Woolley/Stanwood, 23262 Meadow View Lane, Sedro-Woolley; 360-856-4676 www.pflagskagit.org

Organizations/Resources: Student, Academic, Education

⚲ ★ ⚹⚹ Skagit Valley College Rainbow Alliance, 2405 E College Way, Mount Vernon; 360-679-5297 fb.com/svc.rainbowalliance ⚸

Travel & Tourist Services (see also Accommodation)

♂ ○ ⚹⚹ Plumeria Breezes Travel, 810 Metcalf St, Sedro-Woolley; 98284 360-391-6001 Destination Wedding Planning tinyurl.com/zkaolka ❤ monique@plumeriabreezestravel.com

Spokane

Bars, Cafes, Clubs, Restaurants

⚲ The Blind Buck, 204 N Division St 509-443-4014 theblindbuck.com

♂ ○ Mizuna, 214 N Howard St; 509-747-2004 www.mizuna.com ⚥ ✕

♂ ○ Wild Sage American Bistro, 916 W 2nd Ave 509-456-7575 www.wildsagebistro.com ⚥ ✕

Funding: Endowment, Fundraising

⚲ Imperial Sovereign Court of Spokane, POB 65; 99210 509-251-1242 tinyurl.com/zk8esle

Health Care: Physical (see also Counseling/Mental Health)

♂ ☆ Community Health Association of Spokane (CHAS), 203 N Washington Ste 300; 99201 / check for clinic locations 509-444-8888 866-840-2427 communications@chas.org

Legal Services

♂ Center for Justice, 35 W Main Ste 300 509-835-5211 www.CForJustice.org

♂ ○ ⚹⚹ Kuznetz, Larry J, 316 W Boone Ste 380; 99201-2346 509-455-4151 tinyurl.com/282kx2 larry@pkp-law.com

♀ ○ ⚹⚹ **Sayre, Sayre & Fossum, PS, 201 W North River Dr Ste 460; 99201-2262 509-325-7330 H?** Employment law; estate, disability & long term care planning for special needs of G/L Partners & their families. www.sayrelaw.com ⚸ info@sayrelaw.com

Organizations/Resources: Business & Professional Associations, Labor Advocacy

⚲ ★ Inland Northwest Business Alliance, 9 S Washington Ste 201; 509-455-3699 inbachamber.org

Organizations/Resources: Family and Supporters

♂ ☆ Spokane PFLAG, POB 10292; 99209 509-593-0191 fb.com/SpokanePFLAG/

Organizations/Resources: Social, Recreation, Support

⚲ ★ OutSpokane, POB 883; 99210 509-720-7609 **H?** www.outspokane.org

Organizations/Resources: Student, Academic, Education

⚲ ★ ⚹ Eastern Washington University Pride Center/Eagle Pride, 336 Pence Union Building, Cheney; 99004 509-359-7870 **H?** sites.ewu.edu/pridecenter/ ⚸ pride@ewu.edu

⚲ ★ Gonzaga University Lincoln LGBTQ+ Resource Center, 730 E Boone Ave; 509-313-5760 tinyurl.com/yboga36l

⚲ ★ Spokane Falls Community College Alliance, 3410 W Fort George Wright Dr; 99224-5288 509-533-3599 tinyurl.com/ybye7wga

Organizations/Resources: Youth (see also Family)

⚲ ★ (♺) Odyssey Youth Center, 1121 S Perry St; 509-325-3637 **H?** www.odysseyyouth.org ⚸

Religious / Spiritual Resources

⚲ ★ Spokane Integrity, 245 E 13th Ave 509-939-2344

⚲ ★ ⚹⚹ Unitarian Universalist Church PRIDE Committee, 4340 W Fort George Wright Dr; 509-325-6383 www.UUSpokane.org ⚸

Suquamish

Religious / Spiritual Resources

♂ ☆ ⚹⚹ Suquamish Community Congregational UCC, 18732 Division Ave NE; 98392 360-598-4434 **H?** www.suquamishucc.org ⚸ office@suquamishucc.org

Tri-Cities Area

Community Centers and/or Pride Organizations

⚲ ★ Mid-Columbia Pride, POB 2412, Richland 99352 fb.com/MidColumbiaPRIDE

Bars, Cafes, Clubs, Restaurants
Pasco

⚲ Out & About, 327 W Lewis St, Pasco 509-543-3796 www.cloboutandabout.com ⚥ ✕ ▥

Organizations/Resources: Social, Recreation, Support

♂ ☆ (♺) Tri-City Freethinkers, POB 4387, Pasco; 99302 509-539-7064 www.tricityfreethinkers.org

Washington: Tri-Cities Area
Religious
341
GAYELLOW PAGES #42 2020-2021
Huntington : West Virginia
Bars, Cafes, Clubs, Restaurants

Religious / Spiritual Resources

♂ ★ ♿ River of Life MCC Church, 2625 W Bruneau Pl #148, Kennewick; 509-628-4047 ✎

Walla Walla

AIDS/HIV Services, Education & Support

♀ Blue Mountain Heart to Heart, 520 Kelly Place Ste 120; 509-529-4744 www.bluemountainheart.org

Bookstores

♂ ○ Earthlight Books, 321 E Main St; 99362-4801 509-525-4983 www.earthlightbooks.com

Organizations/Resources: Student, Academic, Education

⚢ ★ ♿ Whitman College PRISM, 345 Boyer Ave; 509-526-3021 **H** tinyurl.com/y7ewhsys ✎

Organizations/Resources: Youth (see also Family)

⚢ ★ ♿ Triple Point Youth Group Walla Walla, Children's Home Society of WA, 1612 Penny Lane; 99362 509-529-2130 Ages 13-18 tinyurl.com/jujf8ck ✎ triplepoint@chs-wa.org

Whidbey Island

Accommodation: Hotels, Inns, Guesthouses, B&B, Resorts
Coupeville

♂ ● Whidwood Inn, 360-720-6228 Discover a log house b&b hideaway near historic Coupeville. www.whidwood.com ✎

Greenbank

♂ ● A Lagoon Point Bed and Breakfast, 3617 Marine View Dr, Greenbank; 818-895-7464 www.lagoonpoint-bandb.com 🐾😺

Organizations/Resources: Family and Supporters

♂ ☆ PFLAG Whidbey, 5074 Mutiny Bay Rd, Freeland 360-331-1950 fb.com/WhidbeyPflag

Yakima

Religious / Spiritual Resources

⚢ ★ ♿ Rainbow Cathedral MCC/UCC, 225 N 2nd St; 253-678-5098 tinyurl.com/ys6z9k ✎

West Virginia
State/County Resources

Crisis, Anti-violence, & Helplines

♂ ☆ West Virginia Coalition Against Domestic Violence, 5004 Elk River Rd S, Elkview, WV 304-965-3552 www.wvcadv.org

Community Centers and/or Pride Organizations

⚢ ★ ♿ Rainbow Pride Of West Virginia, 501 Elizabeth St, Charleston, WV **H?** www.wvpride.org ✎

AIDS/HIV Services, Education & Support

♂ ★ (♿) AIDS Task Force of the Upper Ohio Valley, POB 6360, Wheeling, WV 26003-0805 304-232-6822 **H?** www.atfuov.org ✎ wvhivcare@yahoo.com

♀ ★ (♿) NAMES Project Upper Ohio Valley, AIDS Task Force, POB 6360, Wheeling, WV 26003-0805 304-232-6822 **H?** www.atfuov.org jayadams3@sbcglobal.net

Organizations/Resources: Political/Legislative/Advocacy

♂ ☆ American Civil Liberties Union of West Virginia Foundation, POB 3952, Charleston, WV 25339 304-345-9246 www.acluwv.org

⚢ ★ ♿ Fairness West Virginia, 405 Capitol St Ste 405, Charleston, WV 681-265-9062 www.fairnesswv.org

Charleston

Crisis, Anti-violence, & Helplines

♂ Covenant House, 600 Shrewsbury St #3 304-344-8053 www.wvcovenanthouse.org

Information, Media & Publications

⚢ Queer Appalachia / Electric Dirt, www.queerappalachia.com

AIDS/HIV Services, Education & Support

♂ ☆ ♿ The Living AIDS Memorial Garden, POB 11704; 25339 304-346-0246 tinyurl.com/l39oen4 ✎ mail@livingaidsmemorialgarden.org

Bars, Cafes, Clubs, Restaurants

⚢ Atmosphere Ultra Lounge, 706 Lee St 304-343-3737 **D** 🍸

♂ ○ Bluegrass Kitchen, 1600 Washington St E 304-346-2871 www.bluegrasswv.com ✗ contact@bluegrasswv.com

♂ ● (♿) Broadway, 210 Leon Sullivan Way 304-343-2162 www.BroadwayWV.Com **DP** 🍸

♂ ○ Ellen's Homemade Ice Cream, 225 Capitol St 304-343-6488 www.ellensicecream.com ↻ ellensicecream@gmail.com

♂ ○ Starlings Coffee & Provisions, 1599-A Washington St E; 304-205-5920 www.starlingswv.com ↻ contact@starlingswv.com

♂ ○ ♿ Tricky Fish, 1611 Washington St E; 304-344-FISH www.trickyfish.net ✗ ✎ contact@trickyfish.net

Bookstores

♂ ○ ♿ Taylor Books, 226 Capitol St 304-342-1461 www.taylorbooks.com ↻ ✎

Organizations/Resources: Family and Supporters

♂ ☆ PFLAG Charleston/Huntington, 304-541-5470 fb.com/pflagswv lesbak44@gmail.com

Davis

Accommodation: Hotels, Inns, Guesthouses, B&B, Resorts

♂ ● Bright Morning Inn, 454 William Ave; 26260 304-259-5119 www.brightmorninginn.com ✗ 🐾 ✎ 😺 info@brightmorninginn.com

Huntington

Bars, Cafes, Clubs, Restaurants

⚢ The Stonewall, (alley entrance) 820 7th Ave 304-523-2242 www.stonewallclub.com **D**

Lost River

Accommodation: Hotels, Inns, Guesthouses, B&B, Resorts

♀ ● The Guesthouse at Lost River, 288 Settlers Valley Way; 304-897-5707 www.guesthouselostriver.com ⚥ ✕

♀ ● Lost River Grill, Motel & B&B, 8079 State Road 259; 304-897-6482 lostrivergrill.com ⚥ ✕ ✗ Ⓢ

Martinsburg

AIDS/HIV Services, Education & Support

♂ Community Networks, Inc., POB 3064; 25402 304-263-3510

Morgantown

AIDS/HIV Services, Education & Support

♀ ☆ ♿ Caritas House, 391 Scott Ave 304-985-0021 www.caritashouse.com

Bars, Cafes, Clubs, Restaurants

⚥ ● Vice Versa, 335 High St; 304-292-2010 Thu-Sun www.viceversaclub.com **PD**

Organizations/Resources: Student, Academic, Education

⚥ ★ ♿ WVU LGBTQ+ Center, POB 6701; 26506 / Maple House, 742 College Ave 304-293-9593 lgbtq.wvu.edu lgbtq@mail.wvu.edu

Proctor

Accommodation: Hotels, Inns, Guesthouses, B&B, Resorts

⚥ ● Roseland Resort & Campground, 925 Nolte Lane 304-455-3838 www.roselandwv.com (♣?) Ⓢ

Purgitsville

Accommodation: Hotels, Inns, Guesthouses, B&B, Resorts

♂ ● (?♿) Man Place Bed & Breakfast, 444 Man Pl US-220; 304-289-5491 www.manplacegbb.com (♣?) ✗ Ⓢ

Shepherdstown

Information, Media & Publications

⚥ Eastern Panhandle LGBTQ Alliance, 304-728-0247 tinyurl.com/sa4777n

Accommodation: Hotels, Inns, Guesthouses, B&B, Resorts

♀ ○ Thomas Shepherd Inn, POB 3634; 25443-3634 / 300 W German St 304-876-3715 888-889-8952 www.thomasshepherdinn.com ✗ Ⓢ

Organizations/Resources: Student, Academic, Education

⚥ ★ Shepherd University Gender-Sexuality Alliance (GSA), 301 N King St; 304-676-6768 tinyurl.com/vx7a3q9

Slatyfork

Accommodation: Hotels, Inns, Guesthouses, B&B, Resorts

♀ ○ (?♿) Morning Glory Inn, POB 116 26291-0116 304-572-5000 866-572-5700 www.morninggloryinn.com (♣?) ✗ Ⓢ mgi@citlink.net

---

» Walton: see Charleston

Wisconsin
State/County Resources

Funding: Endowment, Fundraising

♂ ☆ AIDS Walk Wisconsin & 5K Run, 820 N Plankinton Ave, Milwaukee, WI 800-348-9255 www.aidswalkwis.org

⚥ ★ Rainbow Over Wisconsin, POB 2211, Appleton, WI 54912 www.rainbowoverwisconsin.org

Leather Resources & Groups

⚥ ★ Argonauts of Wisconsin, argonautsofwi.com

Organizations/Resources: Business & Professional Associations, Labor Advocacy

⚥ Wisconsin LGBT Chamber, 5027 W North Ave, Milwaukee, WI 414-678-9275 wislgbtchamber.com

Organizations/Resources: Political/Legislative/Advocacy

♂ ☆ American Civil Liberties Union of Wisconsin, 207 E Buffalo St #325, Milwaukee, WI 414-272-4032 www.aclu-wi.org

⚥ ★ ♿ Diverse & Resilient, 2439 N Holton St, Milwaukee, WI 53212 414-390-0444 **H?** www.diverseandresilient.org ✗ info@diverseandresilient.org

⚥ ★ ♿ Fair Wisconsin, 122 E Olin Ave Ste 100, Madison, WI 53713 608-441-0143 www.fairwisconsin.com info@fairwisconsin.com

Organizations/Resources: Senior Resources

T Transgender Aging Network (TAN), POB 1272, Milwaukee, WI 53201 414-559-2123 forge-forward.org/aging

Organizations/Resources: Student, Academic, Education

♀ ☆ GSAFE: Gay Straight Alliance for Safe Schools, 122 E Olin Ave Ste 100, Madison, WI 53713 608-661-4141 www.gsafewi.org info@gsafewi.org

Organizations/Resources: Youth (see also Family)

⚥ ★ (?♿) Rainbow Alliance for Youth (RAY), 2439 N Holton St, Milwaukee, WI 414-390-0444 tinyurl.com/y2tme96v

» Algoma: see Door County Area
» Appleton: see Fox Valley

Chippewa Valley Area

Community Centers and/or Pride Organizations

⚥ ★ ♿ LGBT Community Center of the Chippewa Valley, 505 Dewey St S, Eau Claire; 715-552-5428 cvlgbt.info ✗

Bars, Cafes, Clubs, Restaurants
Eau Claire

⚥ ● ♿ Scooters, 411 Galloway, Eau Claire; 715-835-9959 fb.com/ScootersEC **D**

Health Care: Physical (see also Counseling/Mental Health)

♂ ○ ♿ Radiant Health Chiropractic, 115 9th Ave, Eau Claire; 54703 715-838-9432 www.radianthealthchiro.com

Wisconsin: Chippewa Valley Area
Organizations: Student

343
GAYELLOW PAGES #42 2020-2021

La Crosse : Wisconsin
Community Centers / Pride

Organizations/Resources: Student, Academic, Education

♂♀ ★ (?&) University Of Wisconsin - Stout The Qube, 141 Price Commons, 1110 S Broadway, Menomonie; 715-232-5471 **H?** tinyurl.com/jxlvptq ✒

♂♀ ★ (?&) UW-Stout Gender & Sexuality Alliance, 141 Price Commons, POB 790, Menomonie; 54751 715-232-1122 **H?** fb.com/uwstoutgsa/ ✒

Religious / Spiritual Resources

♀ ☆ && Unitarian Universalist Congregation, 421 S Farwell St, Eau Claire; 54701 715-834-0690 **HD** tinyurl.com/y3nq6hbr ✒ uuoffice@uueauclaire.com

Door County Area

Accommodation: Hotels, Inns, Guesthouses, B&B, Resorts
Baileys Harbor

♀ ○ (?&) Beachfront Inn, POB 460, Baileys Harbor; 54202 920-839-2345 855-350-1200 beachfrontinn.net ✣ ✒ ⊗ stay@ beachfrontinn.net

Sturgeon Bay

♀ ● (?&) Chanticleer Guest House, 4072 Cherry Rd, Sturgeon Bay; (Hwy H.H.) 920-746-0334 www.chanticleerguesthouse.com

♀ ● Cliff Dwellers Resort, 3540 N Duluth Ave, Sturgeon Bay; 54235 920-333-1551 www.CliffDwellersResort.com ✒ ⊗ ⊗ Stay@CliffDwellersResort.com

Organizations/Resources: Family and Supporters

♂♀ ☆ && PFLAG Sturgeon Bay/Door County, POB 213, Sturgeon Bay; 54235-0213 920-421-8814 www.pflagdoorcounty.org pflagsturgeonbay@gmail.com

»» Eau Claire: see Chippewa Valley Area

Elkhorn

Accommodation: Hotels, Inns, Guesthouses, B&B, Resorts

♀ ○ Ye Olde Manor House B&B, N7622 US 12; 53121 262-742-2450 fax 262-742-2425 www.yeoldemanorhouse.com ✣ ✒ ⊗ ⊗ innkeeper@yeoldemanorhouse.com

Fox Valley

Community Centers and/or Pride Organizations

♀ Pride Alive, POB 2211, Appleton; 54915 920-418-4185 www.newpridealive.org

Information, Media & Publications

♂♀ ★ (?&) Positive Voice, Inc, POB 1381, Green Bay; 54305 920-435-4404 **H?** www.pvinc.org

AIDS/HIV Services, Education & Support

♀ AIDS Resource Center of Wisconsin, 633 C W Wisconsin Ave, Appleton; 920-733-2068 www.arcw.org

♀ ☆ && AIDS Resource Center of Wisconsin, Inc., 445 S Adams St, Green Bay; 920-437-7400 www.arcw.org

Bars, Cafes, Clubs, Restaurants
Appleton

♂♀ ● (?&) Rascals Bar & Grill, 702 E Wisconsin Ave, Appleton; 920-954-9262 www.rascalsbar.com �Y ✗

Green Bay

♂♀ ● && Napalese Lounge & Grille, 1351 Cedar St, Green Bay; 920-432-9646 tinyurl.com/y9hqoljv **DCWLV** Y ↧ ✗▥

♀ No Limits Bar, 500 N Baird St, Green Bay 920-544-4963 tinyurl.com/htphly9 ▥

♀ The Roundabout, 1264 Main St, Green Bay 920-544-9544 fb.com/TheRoundabout

♂ ● XS Nightclub, 1106 Main St, Green Bay 920-430-1301 fb.com/XSnightclub **D**

Neenah

♀ ReMixx, 8386 State Rd 76, Neenah 920-725-6483 fb.com/Re-MixxNeenah **D** Y ✗▥

Organizations/Resources: Social, Recreation, Support

♂ && N.E.W Bears, tinyurl.com/jlmvky5

Organizations/Resources: Student, Academic, Education

♂♀ ★ Rainbow Alliance for Hope, Reeve 105N, 748 Algoma Blvd, Oshkosh; 920-424-3182 tinyurl.com/pzxqwbh

♂♀ ★&& Ripon College: Queer Straight Alliance, POB 248, Ripon; 54971 920-748-8112 fb.com/groups/TheNetworkRipon ✒

♂♀ ★ UW Oshkosh LGBTQ+ Resource Center, 717 W Irving Ave, Oshkosh; 54901 920-424-3465 **H?** www.uwosh.edu/lgbtqcenter lgbtqcenter@uwosh.edu

Organizations/Resources: Youth (see also Family)

♂♀ ☆ && LGBT Partnership - Fox Valley, 1800 Appleton Rd, Menasha; 920-968-6863 tinyurl.com/hlvl4nz ↧ ✒

Religious / Spiritual Resources

♂♀ ★ ♿ Angels of Hope Metropolitan Community Church, POB 672, Green Bay; 54305 / The Heritage Mall, 139 E 2nd St Ste L-4, Kaukauna; www.angelsofhopemcc.org

»» Green Bay: see Fox Valley

Hudson

Accommodation: Hotels, Inns, Guesthouses, B&B, Resorts

♂ ○ Phipps Inn, 1005 3rd St; 54016 715-386-0800 www.phippsinn.com ✒ ⊗ ⊗ info@phippsinn.com

Bookstores

♂ ○ Chapter 2 Books, 226 Locust St; 715-220-8818 www.chapter2books.com

Janesville

Financial Planning, Investment (see also Insurance)

♂ ○ && Kamler, Jason G, MBA, CFP(R), Wells Fargo Advisors, 400 Midland Court #103; 53546 608-758-5312 **H?** tinyurl.com/yx-poprdv jason.kamler@wellsfargoadvisors.com

»» Kenosha: see Racine/Kenosha Area

La Crosse

Community Centers and/or Pride Organizations

♂♀ ★ The Center: 7 Rivers LGBTQ Connection, PO Box 3313; 54602 608-784-0452 7riverslgbt.org ✒

Wisconsin: La Crosse
Community Centers / Pride

344
GAYELLOW PAGES #42 2020-2021

Madison Area: Wisconsin
Organizations: Social & Support

♀ ★ La Crosse Pride, POB 3313; 54602 608-784-0452 tinyurl.com/y2o8f7eb ✎

AIDS/HIV Services, Education & Support

♀ ☆ ♿ AIDS Resource Center of Wisconsin, 811 Rose St; 608-785-9866 www.arcw.org

Bars, Cafes, Clubs, Restaurants

♀ ● Chances R, 417 Jay St; 608-782-5105 fb.com/karlachancesr/

♀ ● My Place, 3201 South Ave; 608-788-9073 fb.com/Myplacelacrosse/

♀ ♿ Players, 300 S 4th St 608-784-4200 www.playersbar-lacrosse.com **DK** ▦ ✎

Bookstores

♂ ○ Pearl Street Books, 323 Pearl St; 608-782-3424 fb.com/PSBooks

Erotica / Adult Stores / Safe Sex Supplies

♂ ○ Pleasures, 405 3rd St S; 608-784-6350 www.pleasuresoflacrosse.com

Organizations/Resources: Student, Academic, Education

♀ ★ ♿ Pride Center, University of Wisconsin, 42 Cartwright Center, 1725 State St, 2214 Student Union 608-785-8887 www.uwlax.edu/pride-center/ ✎

Organizations/Resources: Youth (see also Family)

♀ ★ ♿ GALAXY, LGBT Resource Center Seven Rivers Region, POB 3313; 54601 608-784-0452 tinyurl.com/o8og2tq

Lake Mills

Accommodation: Hotels, Inns, Guesthouses, B&B, Resorts

♀ ● Fargo Mansion Inn, 406 Mulberry St 920-648-3654 www.fargomansion.com (♣?) ✎ ⊗

Madison Area

Crisis, Anti-violence, & Helplines

♀ ☆ ♿ Rape Crisis Center, 2801 Coho St #301, Madison; 53713 608-251-7273 608-251-5126 **H?** www.thercc.org info@thercc.org

Community Centers and/or Pride Organizations

♀ ★ ♿ OutReach LGBT Community Center, 2701 International Lane #101, Madison; 608-255-8582 www.lgbtoutreach.org ✎

♀ ★ OutReach Pride Parade, OutReach LGBT Community Center, 2701 International Lane #101, Madison; 608-255-8582 www.outreachprideparade.org ✎

AIDS/HIV Services, Education & Support

♂ ☆ ♿ Public Health Madison & Dane County, 2705 E Washington Ave, Madison; 53704 608-243-0411 fax 608-266-4858 **H?** www.publichealthmdc.com ✎ health@publichealthmdc.com

Bars, Cafes, Clubs, Restaurants
Madison

♀ ● ♿ Five Nightclub, 5 Applegate Ct, Madison; 608-271-1768 www.fivenightclub.com **D** ▦ ✎

♀ ○ Java Cat, 3918 Monona Dr, Madison 608-223-5553 www.javacatmadison.com ⊃

♂ ○ Monty's Blue Plate Diner, 2089 Atwood Ave, Madison; 608-244-8505 montysblueplatediner.com ✖

♀ ● ♿ Prism, 924 Williamson St, Madison; 608-692-1900 www.prismmadison.com **D** ✎

♀ Shamrock Bar & Grille, 117 W Main St, Madison; 608-259-8480 fb.com/ShamrockBG ⚣ ✖

♀ Sotto, 303 N Henry St, Madison 920-251-2753 fb.com/sottomadison **D**

♀ ● Woof's, 114 King St, Madison; 608-204-6222 www.mad-woofs.com **S**

Bookstores

♂ ● ♿ **A Room of One's Own Books & Gifts, 315 W Gorham St, Madison; 53703 608-257-7888 H?** Feminist/LGBT/Used Books www.roomofonesown.com room.bookstore@gmail.com

♂ ○ ♿ University Bookstore, 711 State St, Madison; 608-257-3784 www.uwbookstore.com

Broadcast Media

♀ ★ Queery, WORT-FM 89.9, 118 S Bedford St, Madison; 608-256-2001 tinyurl.com/j84cuf3

Erotica / Adult Stores / Safe Sex Supplies

♂ ● ♿ A Woman's Touch Sexuality Resource Center, 302 S Livingston St, Madison; 53703 608-250-1928 888-621-8880 **H?** www.a-womans-touch.com

Funding: Endowment, Fundraising

♀ ★ New Harvest Foundation, POB 1786, Madison; 53701 608-467-4445 www.newharvestfoundation.org

Health Care: Physical (see also Counseling/Mental Health)

♂ ☆ ♿ Sexual Health Clinic at University Health Services, 333 E Campus Mall 6th Flr, Madison; 608-265-5600 **H?** UW-Madison students only. tinyurl.com/2aesduz ✎

Organizations/Resources: Cultural, Dance, Performance

♀ ★ ♿ Dairyland Cowboys & Cowgirls, 621 Emerson St, Madison; 608-255-9131 tinyurl.com/y5v3lsqv

♂ ★ Perfect Harmony Men's Chorus, POB 14706, Madison; 53708 608-571-7462 www.perfectharmonychorus.org

Organizations/Resources: Family and Supporters

♂ ☆ ♿ PFLAG Madison, 608-848-2333 pflag-madison.org ✎

Organizations/Resources: Senior Resources

♀ (?♿) LGBTQ 50Plus Alliance, c/o OutReach, 2701 International Lane Ste 101, Madison; 53704 608-255-8582 **H?** Lgbtq50plusalliance.org ✎ lgbtq50plus@gmail.com

Organizations/Resources: Social, Recreation, Support

♂ ★ (?♿) Madison Gay Video Club, c/o Outreach, 2701 International Lane #101, Madison; 608-244-8690 www.mgvc.org

Wisconsin: Madison Area
Organizations: Social & Support

345
GAYELLOW PAGES #42 2020-2021

Milwaukee Area: Wisconsin
Bars, Cafes, Clubs, Restaurants

♀ Madison Gaymers, OutReach LGBT Community Center, 2701 International Lane #101, Madison fb.com/madisongaymers

Organizations/Resources: Student, Academic, Education

♂ ☆ && Campus Women's Center, 333 East Campus Mall Room 4416, Madison; 608-262-8093 www.campuswomenscenter.org

♂ ★ && LGBT Campus Center, 716 Langdon St Room 123, Madison; 608-265-3344 **H?** lgbt.wisc.edu ✒

♂ ☆ && Malcolm Shabazz City High School, 1601 N Sherman Ave, Madison; 53704 608-204-2440 (Alternative) shabazz.madison.k12.wi.us ✒

♂ ★ UW-Madison GLBT Alumni Council, 650 N Lake St, Madison; 608-262-2551 tinyurl.com/qalpnm2

♂ ★ && UW-Madison Pride Society, 123 Red Gym, 716 Langdon St, Madison; 608-265-3344 tinyurl.com/qaqz7px ✒

Organizations/Resources: Youth (see also Family)

♀ Teens Like Us, Briarpatch Youth Services, 2720 Rimrock Rd, Madison; 608-245-2550 www.youthsos.org

Performance: Entertainment, Music, Theater, Space

♂ ★ && StageQ, Inc, 113 E Mifflin St, Madison; **H?** www.stageq.com

Religious / Spiritual Resources

♂ ☆ First Baptist Church, 518 N Franklin Ave, Madison; 53705-3699 608-233-1880 firstbaptistmadison.org fbcoffice@firstbaptistmadison.org

♂ ★ (&&) Integrity/Dignity of Madison, 6767 Frank Lloyd Wright Ave Apt 220, Middleton; 53562-1795 608-437-7776 www.id-madison.org ✒ info@idmadison.org

♂ ☆ James Reeb UU Congregation, 2146 E Johnson St, Madison; 53704 608-242-8887 www.jruuc.org

♂ ☆ && Middleton Community Church UCC, 645 Schewe Rd, Middleton; 53562 608-831-4694 **HD** www.middletonucc.org ✒ MCCUCC@middletonucc.org

♀ ☆ Re-formed Congregation of the Goddess, POB 6677, Madison; 53716 608-226-9998 www.rcgi.org

Sports & Outdoor

♂ ★ Madison Gay Hockey Association, www.madisongayhockey.org

Manitowoc

Organizations/Resources: Family and Supporters

♂ ☆ PFLAG of Manitowoc County, POB 2122; 54221 920-374-3524 tinyurl.com/btje6fw

>> *Mazomanie: see Madison Area*

Milwaukee Area

Crisis, Anti-violence, & Helplines

♀ Milwaukee Women's Center, 728 N James Lovell St, Milwaukee; 414-449-4777 tinyurl.com/cvlt5gd

315 W Gorham St
Madison, WI 53703
Tel: 608-257-7888
Fax: 608-257-7457
room@chorus.net

A Room of One's Own Feminist Bookstore

www.roomofonesown.com

Community Centers and/or Pride Organizations

♂ ★ && Milwaukee LGBT Community Center, 1110 N Market St, Milwaukee; 414-271-2656 **H?** www.mkelgbt.org ✒

♂ ★ Milwaukee Pride Parade Inc, POB 0091, Milwaukee; 53201 414-607-3793 www.prideparademke.org

AIDS/HIV Services, Education & Support

♀ AIDS Resource Center of Wisconsin, 820 N Plankinton Ave, Milwaukee; 414-273-1991 www.arcw.org

Archives/Libraries/Museums/History Projects

♂ ★ && Milwaukee LGBT History Project, Inc., Milwaukee Pride, 1110 N Market St Ste 204M, Milwaukee 414-272-3378 www.mkelgbthist.org

♀ ★ University of Wisconsin-Milwaukee Archives, PO Box 604, Milwaukee; 53201 414-229-5402 tinyurl.com/yzmxdrs

Bars, Cafes, Clubs, Restaurants
Mequon

♀ ○ Harvey's Central Grille, 1340 W Towne Square Rd, Mequon; 262-241-9589 www.harveyscentralgrille.com ✗ ▦

Milwaukee

♀ ● Art Bar, 722 E Burleigh St, Milwaukee 414-372-7880 fb.com/artbarmke/ ▦ ✒

♂ D.I.X., 739 S 1st St, Milwaukee; 414-231-9085 dixmke.com **V**

♂ ● Fluid, 819 S 2nd St, Milwaukee 414-643-5843 fluid.gaymke.com

♂ ● Harbor Room, 117 E Greenfield Ave, Milwaukee 414-672-7988 tinyurl.com/zpmo5g9 **L**

♂ Kruz, 354 E National Ave, Milwaukee 414-272-5789

♂ ● (&&) LVL Dance/LVL Complex, 801 S 2nd St, Milwaukee; 414-383-8330 fb.com/LVLDanceMKE/ **D** ▼ ✗ ▦

♂ ○ Riverwest Public House Cooperative, 815 E Locust St, Milwaukee; 414-562-9472 rwph.org ▦

♂ This Is It, 418 E Wells St, Milwaukee 414-278-9192 www.thisisitbar.com

♂ ○ Two, 718 E Burleigh, Milwaukee; 414-372-7553 fb.com/twobar/

Wisconsin: Milwaukee Area
Bars, Cafes, Clubs, Restaurants

346

GAYELLOW PAGES #42 2020-2021

Milwaukee Area : Wisconsin
Religious

♀ • Walker's Pint, 828 S 2nd St, Milwaukee 414-643-7468 www.walkerspint.com **D** ✓

♂ • (♂♀) Woody's, 1579 S 2nd St, Milwaukee; 414-672-0806 fb.com/woodys.mke **S** ✓

Bookstores

♂ ○ Boswell Book Company, 2559 N Downer Ave, Milwaukee; 414-332-1181 www.boswellbooks.com

♀ • ♿ Outwords Books, Gifts & Coffee, 2710 N Murray Ave, Milwaukee; 53211-3645 414-963-9089 www.outwordsbooks.com ☞ ✓ outwordsbooks@msn.com

Erotica / Adult Stores / Safe Sex Supplies

♂ • ♿ Tool Shed: An Erotic Boutique, 2427 N Murray Ave, Milwaukee; 53211 414-906-5304 www.toolshedtoys.com info@toolshedtoys.com

Funding: Endowment, Fundraising

♀ Courage MkE, 270 E Highland Ave Ste I, Milwaukee; 414-704-3856

♀ ★ ♿ Cream City Foundation, 759 N Milwaukee St Ste 522, Milwaukee; 414-225-0244 www.creamcityfoundation.org

♀ Lesbian Fund, c/o Women's Fund Greater Milwaukee, 316 N Milwaukee St #215, Milwaukee; 414-290-7350 tinyurl.com/ctlk5lj

Health Care: Physical (see also Counseling/Mental Health)

♀ ★ ♿ BESTD Clinic, 1240 E Brady St, Milwaukee; 414-272-2144 (Brady East STD Clinic) www.bestd.org

Leather Resources & Groups

♂ ★ Castaways MC, 1035 W Ravine Lane, Bayside www.castawaysmc.org

Legal Services

♂ ○ ♿ Andriusis Law Firm LLC, 985 W Oklahoma Ave, Milwaukee; 53215 414-831-7929 **H** www.andriusislaw.com ✓ andriusis@andriusislaw.com

♀ • ♿ Lewison, Brenda, Law Offices of Arthur Heitzer, 633 W Wisconsin Ave #1410, Milwaukee; 53203 414-273-1040 **H?** www.equalrightswi.com ✓ lewisonlaw@yahoo.com

Organizations/Resources: Cultural, Dance, Performance

♀ ★ ♿ Cream City Squares, 414-445-8080 iagsdc.com/creamcity **D** creamcitysquares@gmail.com

♀ ★ ♿ Miltown Kings, **H?** fb.com/miltownkings/

♀ Milwaukee LGBT Film Festival, University of Wisconsin, Mitchell Hall B70 3203 N Downer Ave, Milwaukee; 414-229-4758 uwm.edu/lgbtfilmfestival/

♀ ☆ Women's Voices Milwaukee, fb.com/womensvoicesmilwaukee

Organizations/Resources: Family and Supporters

♂ ☆ PFLAG, 1110 N Market St 2nd Flr, Milwaukee 414-299-9198 www.milwaukee-pflag.org

Organizations/Resources: Senior Resources

♀ ★ ♿ Older Adults Program/SAGE Milwaukee, Milwaukee LGBT Community Center. 1110 N Market St 2nd Flr, Milwaukee; 414-276-2656 **H?** tinyurl.com/hqqzed5 ✓

Organizations/Resources: Social, Recreation, Support

♀ ★ (♂♀) GAMMA, POB 1900, Milwaukee; 53201 414-418-9198 milwaukeegamma.org

♀ ★ Lesbian Alliance Metro Milwaukee, 315 W Court St, Milwaukee; 414-272-9442 fb.com/groups/16093277822

Organizations/Resources: Student, Academic, Education

♂ ☆ Alliance School of Milwaukee, 850 W Walnut, Milwaukee; 414-267-5400 www.allianceschool.net ✪

♀ ★ ♿ UWM LGBT Resource Center, UWM Student Union WG89, 2200 E Kenwood Blvd, Milwaukee; 414-229-4116 **H?** www.lgbt.uwm.edu ✓

Organizations/Resources: Transgender/Gender Non-Conforming/Diverse

T ☆ FORGE, POB 1272, Milwaukee; 53201 414-559-2123 www.forge-forward.org

T ★ ♿ Milwaukee Transgender Program, Pathways Counseling Center, 13105 W Bluemound Rd #100, Brookfield 262-641-9790 tinyurl.com/ny2j4gj

T ☆ SHEBA (Sisters Helping Each Other Battle AIDS), Diverse and Resilient, 2439 N Holton St, Milwaukee; 414-390-0444 African American MTF tinyurl.com/bpmndzf

Organizations/Resources: Youth (see also Family)

♀ ★ Milwaukee LGBT Community Center's youth services: Project Q, 1110 N Market St Flr 2, Milwaukee; 414-223-3220 www.mkelgbt.org/youth/

♂ Pathfinders, 4200 N Holton St Ste 400, Milwaukee; 414-964-2565 www.pathfindersmke.org

Recovery

♀ ★ Galano Recovery Club, 7210 W Greenfield Ave, Milwaukee; 414-276-6936 LGBT and All in Recovery www.galanoclub.org ✓

Religious / Spiritual Resources

♂ ☆ ♿ Congregation Shir Hadash, POB 170632, Milwaukee; 53217 414-297-9159 shirmke.org ⚥ ✓ info@shirmke.org

♂ ☆ ♿ Cross Lutheran Church, 1821 N 16th St, Milwaukee; 53205 414-344-1746 crosslutheranmke.org office@crosslutheranmke.org

♀ Good Shepherd Catholic Church, N88 W17658 Christman Road, Menomonee Falls; 262-255-2035 mygoodshepherd.org

♂ ☆ ♿ Lake Park Lutheran Church, 2647 N Stowell Ave, Milwaukee; 53211 414-962-9190 lakeparklutheran.com ✓ office@lakeparklutheran.com

♀ ★ (♂♀) Milwaukee Metropolitan Community Church, 1239 W Mineral St, Milwaukee; 53217 414-383-1100 **H** www.milmcc.org ✓ info@queerchurch.org

♂ ☆ ♿ Plymouth United Church of Christ, 2717 E Hampshire St, Milwaukee; 53211-3184 414-964-1513 **H?** www.plymouth-church.org plymouthchurchmke@gmail.com

♀ ☆ ᚛᚛ Unitarian Church North, 13800 N Port Washington Rd, Mequon; 53097 262-375-3890 **HD** www.ucnorth.org ✎ info@ucnorth.org

Sports & Outdoor

♂ ★ Holiday Invitational Bowling Tournament, PO Box 899, Milwaukee; 53201 www.hitmilwaukee.com

♂ Milwaukee Gay Volleyball, 2555 S Bay St, Milwaukee; tinyurl.com/bujyohp

♂ ★ ᚛ Saturday Softball Beer League, ssblmilwaukee.com

Mineral Point

Accommodation Rental: Furnished / Vacation (& AirBNB)

♀ ● Maple Wood Lodge, 2950 State Highway 39; 53565 608-987-2324 www.maplewoodlodge.com ✎ ✉ coleman@maplewoodlodge.com

Mount Horeb

Organizations/Resources: Family and Supporters

♀ PFLAG Mt. Horeb, 102 S 3rd St; 608-658-5246 www.pflagmoho.org

» New Lisbon: see Wisconsin Dells

Norwalk

Campgrounds and RV Parks

♀ ● (?᚛) Daughters of the Earth, 18134 Index Ave; 54648-7028 608-269-5301 Bio female born, and still bio female women only (♣?) ✎ ✉ doejo777@yahoo.com

Oconomowoc

Organizations/Resources: Family and Supporters

♂ PFLAG Oconomowoc, tinyurl.com/y3ywyyay

» Oshkosh: see Fox Valley
» Poynette: see Madison Area

Racine/Kenosha Area

Community Centers and/or Pride Organizations

♂ ★ ᚛᚛ LGBT Center of SE Wisconsin, 1456 Junction Ave, Racine; 262-664-4100 lgbtsewi.org ✎

AIDS/HIV Services, Education & Support

♂ AIDS Resource Center of Wisconsin, POB 0173, Kenosha; 53140 262-657-6644 www.arcw.org

Bars, Cafes, Clubs, Restaurants
Kenosha

♂ ● Club Icon, 6305 120th Ave, Kenosha 262-857-3240 clubiconkenosha.com **D** ✗

Funding: Endowment, Fundraising

♂ ★ Sisters of Perpetual Indulgence - Brew City Sisters, fb.com/brewcitysisters/

Organizations/Resources: Student, Academic, Education

♂ ★ University of Wisconsin - Parkside LGBTQ Resource Center, Wyllie Hall D171, 900 Wood Rd, Kenosha; 262-595-2456 tinyurl.com/yxchp9g2

♂ ★ University of Wisconsin Whitewater Impact, University Center 145, 800 W Main St, Whitewater; 262-472-1961 tinyurl.com/vn5dn2l

Richland Center

Organizations/Resources: Student, Academic, Education

♂ ★ SAGA (Sexuality and Gender Alliance) at UW-Richland, 1200 Highland 14 W; 53581 608-647-6186

River Falls

Organizations/Resources: Family and Supporters

♀ ☆ PFLAG River Falls, 612-817-9742 fb.com/PFLAGRiverFalls

Organizations/Resources: Student, Academic, Education

♂ ★ UW River Falls Gender & Sexuality Alliance, 410 S 3rd St; tinyurl.com/jx7o38q

Sheboygan

Bars, Cafes, Clubs, Restaurants

♂ ● ᚛᚛ Blue Lite, 1029 N 8th St 920-457-1636 www.thebluelite.com **D** ▦

Stevens Point

Organizations/Resources: Student, Academic, Education

♂ ★ UW-Stevens Point Gender & Sexuality Alliance, 1015 Reserve St Rm 206; 715-346-4366 tinyurl.com/hgfmu3g

» Stoughton: see Madison Area
» Sturgeon Bay: see Door County Area
» Superior: see Duluth/Superior Area

Wascott

Campgrounds and RV Parks

♂ ● (?᚛) Wilderness Way Resort/Campground, 16139 S Chipmunk Hollow Rd, Gordon; 715-466-2635 tinyurl.com/j39tn5v (♣?) ✉

Washburn

Organizations/Resources: Family and Supporters

♀ PFLAG Wasburn, 715-209-1100 www.pflagwashburn.org

Wausau

Bars, Cafes, Clubs, Restaurants

♂ ● ᚛ Oz Night Club Llc, 320 Washington St; 715-842-3225 tinyurl.com/z46hjup **D** ▦

Wyoming: State/County Resources
Community Centers / Pride
348
GAYELLOW PAGES #42 2020-2021
Sheridan : Wyoming
Organizations: Political

GLBT National Help Center
Serving the Gay, Lesbian, Bisexual & Transgender Community

GLBT National Hotline
Toll-free 1-888-THE-GLNH
(1-888-843-4564)

GLBT National Youth Talkline
Toll-free 1-800-246-PRIDE
(1-800-246-7743)

GLBT National Help Center
2261 Market Street, PMB #296
San Francisco, CA 94114

www.GLBTNationalHelpCenter.org

Wyoming
State/County Resources

Community Centers and/or Pride Organizations

♀ ★ Wyoming Equality, POB 2531, Cheyenne, WY 82003 307-778-7645 www.wyomingequality.org

Information, Media & Publications

♀ ★ Out in Wyoming, outinwyo.org

AIDS/HIV Services, Education & Support

♂ ☆ Wyoming Department of Health HIV/AIDS/Hepatitis Program, 6101 Yellowstone Rd #510, Cheyenne, WY 307-777-8939 www.knowyo.org

Organizations/Resources: Political/Legislative/Advocacy

♂ ACLU Wyoming, POB 20706, Cheyenne, WY 82003 307-637-4565 www.aclu-wy.org

Recovery

♂ ☆ Al-Anon/Alateen Wyoming Al-Anon Intergroup, www.wyomingal-anon.org

Casper

Community Centers and/or Pride Organizations

♀ Casper Pride, POB 335; 82602 www.casperpride.com

AIDS/HIV Services, Education & Support

♀ ☆ Wyoming AIDS Education & Training, 111 W 2nd St Ste 514; 307-265-0413 www.wyaetc.org

Organizations/Resources: Family and Supporters

♀ ☆ PFLAG Casper, 307-439-4302 www.casperpflag.com casperpflag@gmail.com

Religious / Spiritual Resources

♂ ☆ St Mark's Episcopal Church, 701 S Wolcott St 82601 307-234-0831 stmarks.diowy.org stmarkscasper5@gmail.com

Cheyenne

Accounting, Bookkeeping, Tax Services

♀ ○ 㧴 Richey, Mary, CPA, MER Tax, Accounting, and Consulting, 4104 Laramie St; 82001 307-632-0841 www.mer-tax.com merichey@mer-tax.com

Gillette

Organizations/Resources: Family and Supporters

♀ PFLAG - Gillette, 307-228-4528 tinyurl.com/ybzwprnb

Jackson

Organizations/Resources: Family and Supporters

♂ PFLAG Jackson, POB 2683; 83001 307-733-8349 www.jacksonpflag.com

Laramie

Community Centers and/or Pride Organizations

♀ Laramie PrideFest, fb.com/LaramiePrideFest

Accommodation: Hotels, Inns, Guesthouses, B&B, Resorts

♂ ● Cowgirls Horse Hotel, 6822 Black Elk Trail 307-745-8794 www.cowgirlshorsehotel.com ❀ ✔ ♿

Organizations/Resources: Student, Academic, Education

♀ ★ 㧴 University of Wyoming Rainbow Resource Center, Wyoming Union 106, Dept 3135 1000 E University Ave 307-766-3478 www.uwyo.edu/rrc ✔

Powell

Organizations/Resources: Student, Academic, Education

♀ ★ 㧴 Northwest College GSA, 231 W 6th St; 307-754-6159 tinyurl.com/wxby3hu ✔

Riverton

Bars, Cafes, Clubs, Restaurants

♂ ● 㧴 Country Cove, 301 E Main St 307-856-9813 ✕

Sheridan

Organizations/Resources: Political/Legislative/Advocacy

♀ Sheridan Supports LGBTQ, 866-881-2742 x705 A Wyoming Equality Satellite Group www.lgbtqsheridanwy.net

INDEX

Bayside WI   **Bisexual Resource Center**

Claremont United Methodist Church   **Community Against Violence**

Gamma Mu Foundation   **Gender Identity Project**

Whosoever Metropolitan Community Church   Wrestlers WithOut Borders

CPSIA information can be obtained
at www.ICGtesting.com
Printed in the USA
LVHW080815010520
654553LV00012BA/255